2 for 1

Terms: This voucher is valid at any venue specified as accepting vouchers within the AA 'The Days Out Guide 2004'. This voucher admits one adult or child free when presented at the time of purchase of one fully priced adult ticket. Valid until 31 Oct 2004. Subject to availability at the venue when presented. Photocopies will <u>not</u> be accepted.

AA Lifestyle Guides

 2 for

Terms: This voucher is valid at ... when presented at the time of purchase of one fully priced adult ticket. Valid until 31 Oct 2004. Subject to availability at the venue when presented. Photocopies will <u>not</u> be accepted.

AA Lifestyle Guides

 KU-413-223

 2 for 1

Terms: This voucher is valid at any venue specified as accepting vouchers within the AA 'The Days Out Guide 2004'. This voucher admits one adult or child free when presented at the time of purchase of one fully priced adult ticket. Valid until 31 Oct 2004. Subject to availability at the venue when presented. Photocopies will <u>not</u> be accepted.

AA Lifestyle Guides

 2 for 1

Terms: This voucher is valid at any venue specified as accepting vouchers within the AA 'The Days Out Guide 2004'. This voucher admits one adult or child free when presented at the time of purchase of one fully priced adult ticket. Valid until 31 Oct 2004. Subject to availability at the venue when presented. Photocopies will <u>not</u> be accepted.

AA Lifestyle Guides

 2 for 1

Terms: This voucher is valid at any venue specified as accepting vouchers within the AA 'The Days Out Guide 2004'. This voucher admits one adult or child free when presented at the time of purchase of one fully priced adult ticket. Valid until 31 Oct 2004. Subject to availability at the venue when presented. Photocopies will <u>not</u> be accepted.

AA Lifestyle Guides

 2 for 1

Terms: This voucher is valid at any venue specified as accepting vouchers within the AA 'The Days Out Guide 2004'. This voucher admits one adult or child free when presented at the time of purchase of one fully priced adult ticket. Valid until 31 Oct 2004. Subject to availability at the venue when presented. Photocopies will <u>not</u> be accepted.

AA Lifestyle Guides

 2 for 1

Terms: This voucher is valid at any venue specified as accepting vouchers within the AA 'The Days Out Guide 2004'. This voucher admits one adult or child free when presented at the time of purchase of one fully priced adult ticket. Valid until 31 Oct 2004. Subject to availability at the venue when presented. Photocopies will <u>not</u> be accepted.

AA Lifestyle Guides

 2 for 1

Terms: This voucher is valid at any venue specified as accepting vouchers within the AA 'The Days Out Guide 2004'. This voucher admits one adult or child free when presented at the time of purchase of one fully priced adult ticket. Valid until 31 Oct 2004. Subject to availability at the venue when presented. Photocopies will <u>not</u> be accepted.

AA Lifestyle Guides

 2 for 1

Terms: This voucher is valid at any venue specified as accepting vouchers within the AA 'The Days Out Guide 2004'. This voucher admits one adult or child free when presented at the time of purchase of one fully priced adult ticket. Valid until 31 Oct 2004. Subject to availability at the venue when presented. Photocopies will <u>not</u> be accepted.

AA Lifestyle Guides

 2 for 1

Terms: This voucher is valid at any venue specified as accepting vouchers within the AA 'The Days Out Guide 2004'. This voucher admits one adult or child free when presented at the time of purchase of one fully priced adult ticket. Valid until 31 Oct 2004. Subject to availability at the venue when presented. Photocopies will <u>not</u> be accepted.

AA Lifestyle Guides

The
Days Out
Guide

The AA Days Out Guide provides useful information about a large number of museums, art galleries, theme parks, national parks, visitor centres and stately homes across Britain and Ireland. Entries include contact details for each attraction, along with a short description and details of opening times, prices and special facilities. Each county has a list of events and festivals.

We hope that this guide will help you and your family get the most out of your time.

Happy Visiting!

Produced by AA Publishing

© Automobile Association Developments Limited 2003

A CIP catalogue record for this book is available from the British Library

Directory generated by the AA Establishment Database, Information Research, AA Hotel Services

Design by Kingswood Graphics, Reading, Berkshire

Cover pictures: AA Picture Library

Advertisement Sales: advertisingsales@theAA.com

Lifestyle Guides: lifestyleguides@theAA.com

Typeset/Repro by Microset Graphics Ltd, Basingstoke, England

Printed in Italy by Graficas Estella, S.A., Navarra, Spain

The contents of this book are believed correct at the time of printing. Nevertheless, the Publisher cannot be held responsible for any errors or omissions, or for changes in the details given in this guide or for the consequences of any reliance on the information provided in the same. This does not affect your statutory rights. We have tried to ensure accuracy in this guide but things do change and we would be grateful if readers would advise us of any inaccuracies they may encounter.

This product includes mapping data licensed from Ordnance Survey® with the permission of the Controller of Her Majesty's Stationery Office ©Crown copyright 2002. All rights reserved. Licence number 399221

Northern Ireland mapping reproduced by permission of the Director and Chief Executive, Ordnance Survey of Northern Ireland, acting on behalf of the Controller of Her Majesty's Stationery Office ©Crown copyright 2002. Permit No. 1674

Republic of Ireland mapping based on Ordnance Survey Ireland by permission of the Government .
Permit No. MP004202 ©Government of Ireland.

Maps prepared by the Cartographic Department of The Automobile Association Maps © The Automobile Association 2002

Published by AA Publishing, which is a trading name of Automobile Association Developments Limited whose registered office is Millstream, Maidenhead Road, Windsor, Berkshire, SL4 5GD Registered number 1878835.

ISBN 0749537981

A1702

Contents

How to Use This Guide

THE DIRECTORY
The directory is arranged in countries, counties, then in alphabetical location order within each county. Each county has an introductory panel that gives general information on selected events and festivals.

① MAP REFERENCES AND ATLAS
Map references for attractions are based on the National Grid, and can be used with the Atlas at the back of this book.

First comes the map page number, followed by the National Grid reference. To find the location, read the first figure horizontally and the second figure vertically within the lettered square.

② DIRECTIONS may be given after the address of each attraction and where shown have been provided by the places of interest themselves.

③ TELEPHONE NUMBERS have the STD code shown before the telephone number. (If dialling Northern Ireland from England use the STD code, but for the Republic you need to prefix the number with 00353, and drop the first zero from the Irish area code).

④ 2-FOR-1 **2 for 1** **VOUCHER SCHEME**
This symbol indicates which attractions have chosen to participate in our new 2-for-1 voucher scheme. Visitors using one of the vouchers from the front of this guide will be able to buy 2 tickets for the price of one, with certain restrictions that are detailed on the voucher itself.

⑤ OPENING TIMES quoted in the guide are inclusive - for instance, where you see Apr-Oct, that place will be open from the beginning of April to the end of October.

⑥ FEES quoted for the majority of entries are current. If no price is quoted, you should check with the attraction concerned before you visit. Places which are open 'at all reasonable times' are usually free, and many places which do not charge admission at all may ask for a voluntary donation. Remember that prices can go up, and those provided to us by the attractions are provisional.

FREE **FREE ENTRY** These attractions do not charge a fee for entry, although they may charge for use of audio equipment, for example. We have not included attractions that expect a donation in this category.

⑦ FACILITIES
This section includes parking, dogs allowed, refreshments etc. See page 6 for a key to Symbols and Abbreviations used in this guide.

⑧ VISITORS WITH MOBILITY DISABILITIES should look for the wheelchair symbol showing where all or most of the establishment is accessible to the wheelchair-bound visitor. We strongly recommend that you telephone in advance of your visit to check the exact details, particularly regarding access to toilets and refreshment facilities. Assistance dogs are usually accepted where the attractions show the 'No Dogs' symbol ✖ unless stated otherwise. For the hard of hearing induction loops are indicated by a symbol at the attraction itself.

⑨ CREDIT & CHARGE CARDS are taken by a number of attractions for admission charges. To indicate which accept credit cards we have used this symbol at the end of the entry. ◥

PHOTOGRAPHY is restricted in some places and there are many where it is only allowed in specific areas. Visitors are advised to check with places of interest on the

Sample Entry

BEDFORD	**Map 04 TL04** ——①

BEDFORD MUSEUM
Castle Ln MK40 3XD   **2 for 1** ——④
② —— ◐ (close to town bridge and Embankment)
③ —— ☎ 01234 353323   🖳 01234 273401
e-mail: bmuseum@bedford.gov.uk
Embark on a fascinating journey through the human and natural history of north Bedfordshire, pausing briefly to glimpse at wonders from more distant lands. The courtyard and galleries provide an excellent setting for the varied collections.
⑤ —— **Times:** Open all year, Tue-Sat 11-5, Sun 2-5. (Closed Mon ex BH Mon afternoon, Good Fri & Xmas). **Fee:** ✱ £2.20 (ch, pen & con free). Fri —— ⑥ free for everyone. Annual ticket £8.80. **Facilities:** Ⓟ (50mtrs) ◥ —— ⑦
⑧ —— ♿ (lift available on request, subject to staff availability) toilets for disabled shop ✖ (ex guide dogs) ◥ —— ⑨

rules for taking photographs and the use of video cameras.

SPECIAL EVENTS are held at many of these attractions, and although we have listed a few of the more important ones on the county introduction pages, we cannot hope to give details of them all, so please ring the places of interest for details of exhibitions, themed days, talks, guided walks and more.

ATTRACTIONS WITH ITALIC HEADINGS.
These are entries that were unable to provide the relevant information in time for publication.

...AND FINALLY
Opening times and admission prices can be subject to change. Please check with the attraction before making your journey.

Public Holidays

New Year's Day	1 January	Battle of the Boyne *(Orangemen's Day)* *(N.I. only)*	12 July
Bank Holiday *(Scotland only)*	2 January		
St Patrick's Day *(N.I. & R.O.I. only)*	17 March	Summer Bank Holiday *(Scotland & R.O.I. only)*	2 August
Good Friday	9 April	Summer Bank Holiday *(excluding R.O.I.)*	30 August
Easter Monday	12 April		
May Day Bank Holiday	3 May	Bank Holiday *(R.O.I. only)*	25 October
Spring Bank Holiday *(excluding R.O.I.)*	31 May		
		Christmas Day	25 December
June Bank Holiday *(R.O.I. only)*	7 June	Boxing Day *(St Stephen's Day in R.O.I.)*	26 December

Key to Symbols and Abbreviations

SYMBOLS

In order to give you as much information as possible in the space available, we have used the following symbols in the guide:

	ENGLISH	FRANÇAIS	DEUTSCH	ITALIANO	ESPAÑOL
☎	Telephone number	Numéro de téléphone	Telefonnummer	Numero telefonico	Número telefónico
🖷	Fax number				
♿	Suitable for visitors in wheelchairs	Les invalidens fauteuils roulants pourrant y accéder	Für Rollstuhltahrer zugänglich	Accessibile agli handicappeti	Acondicionado para visitantes en silla de reudas
🅿	Parking at Establishment	Stationnement à l'établissement	Parken an Ort und Stelle	Parcheggio in loco	Aparcamiento en el establecimiento
🅿	Parking nearby	Stationnement tout près	Parken in der Nähe	Parcheggio nelle vicinanze	Aparcamiento cerca del
☕	Refreshments	Rafraîchissements	Erfrischungen	Snack-bar	Refrescos
✗	Restaurant	Restaurant	Restaurant	Ristorante	Restaurante
🐕	No dogs	Chiens non permis	Hundeverbot	Cani non accettati	Se prohiben los perros
🚌	No coaches	Les groupes en cars pas admis	Keine Reisebusgesellschaften	Non si accettano comitive in pullman	Non se admiten los grupos de viajeros en autobús
★	Admission prices relate to 2003. It should be noted that in some entries the opening dates and times may also have been supplied as 2003. Please check with the establshment before making your journey.				
⊕	Cadw (Welsh Historic Monuments)	Cadw Monument ancien (Pays de Galles)	Cadw Historiches Gebaude (Walisland)	Cadw Monumento storico (Galles)	Cadw Monumento histórico (Gales)
⧉	English Heritage (opening times: see advert on opposite page)	English Heritage	English Heritage	English Heritage	English Heritage
❄	National Trust	National Trust	National Trust	National Trust	The National Trust
♛	National Trust for Scotland	National Trust en Ecosse	National Trust in Schottland	National Trust per la Scozia	The National Trust de Escocia
▮	Historic Scotland				

ABBREVIATIONS

In the same way, we have abbreviated certain pieces of information:

	ENGLISH	FRANÇAIS	DEUTSCH	ITALIAN	ESPAÑOL
BH	Bank Holidays	Jours fériés	Bankfeiertage	Festività nazionale	Días festivos (bancos y comercio)
PH	Public Holidays	Jours fériés	Feiertage	Festività nazionale	Días festivos
Etr	Easter	Pâques	Ostern	Pasqua	Semana Santa
ex	except	sauf	ausser	eccetto	excepto
Free	Admission free	Entrée gratuit	Freier eintritt	Ingresso gratuito	Entrada gratuita
£1	Admission £1	Entrée £1	Eintritt £1	Ingresso £1	Entrada £1
ch 50p	Children 50p	Enfants 50p	Kinder 50p	Bambini 50p	Niños 50p
ch 15 50p	Children under 15 50p	Enfants de moins de 15 ans 50p	Kinder unter 15 Jahren 50p	Bambini sotto i 15 anni 50p	Los niños de menores de 15 años 50p
Pen	Senior Citizens	Retraites	Rentner	Pensionati	Jubilados
Party	Special or reduced rates for parties booked in advance	Tarifs spéciaux ou réduits pour groupes réservés d'advance	Sondertarife oder Ermässigungen für im voraus bestellte Gesellschaften	Tariffe speciali o ridotte per comitive che prenotano in anticipo	Tarifas especiales o reducidas para los grupos de viajeros que reserven de anternano
Party 30+	Special or reduced rates for parties of 30 or more booked in advance	Tarifs spéciaux ou réduits pour groupes de 30 ou plus réservés d'advance	Sondertarife oder Ermässigungen für im voraus bestellte Gesellschaften von wenigstens 30 Personen	Tariffe speciali o ridotte per comitive di 30 o più persone che prenotano in anticipo	Tarifas especiales o reducidas para grupos de 30 viajeros, o más, que reserven de anternano

6

How do I find the perfect place?

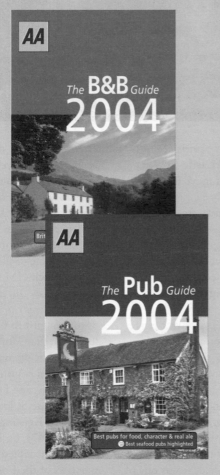
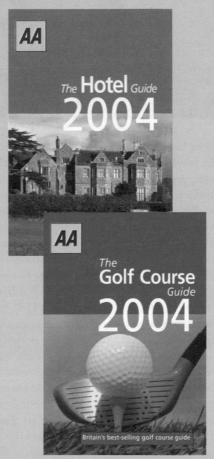

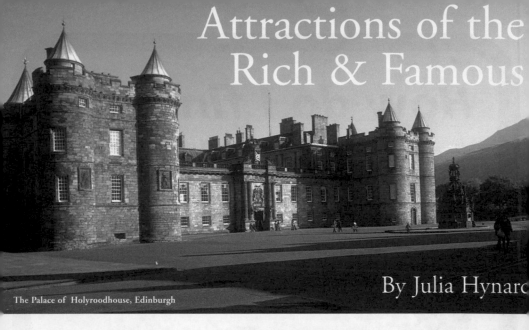

Attractions of the Rich & Famous

The Palace of Holyroodhouse, Edinburgh

By Julia Hynard

If you're fascinated by the lives of the fabulously rich and famous, you'll find a peek around a palace impossible to resist. Royal residences are astonishingly accessible these days, so you can make your own royal progress from Aberdeenshire to the Isle of Wight.

In these egalitarian times the hoi polloi may visit both of the Queen's official residences. In the case of **Buckingham Palace (p142)**, visitors are permitted in the State Rooms but only during August and September, while **Windsor Castle (p19)** – the largest inhabited castle in the world – is open all year round.

The Palace of Holyroodhouse (p301) in Edinburgh is still used by the Royal Family, but can be visited when they are not in residence. You won't get to look around

their other Scottish home, **Balmoral Castle (p291)**, unless you move in particularly elevated circles, but public access extends to the gardens and the ballroom, where items from throughout the castle are exhibited.

Sandringham House (p173) in Norfolk, like Balmoral, is a private estate managed on the Queen's behalf, but the house is open to visitors when not in use, and there are beautiful grounds and a museum to enjoy. **Frogmore House (p18)**, in the private Home Park of Windsor Castle, can also be visited. It was one of Queen Victoria's favourite

retreats, and both she and her husband Prince Albert are buried in a mausoleum i the garden. Clarence House is now the official London residence of Prince Charles, and from 1953 until 2002 was the home of his beloved grandmother, HM Queen Elizabeth the Queen Mothe The house was open to visitors August to October 2003, but plans for any future public opening have not yet been confirmed.

The remaining London properties are St James's Palace and **Kensington Palace (p147)**, both of which are occupied by members of the Royal Famil and their offices.

Balmoral Castle

Clarence House

St James Palace

St James's is used for public functions but isn't open to the public, while Kensington Palace – a favoured residence of the reigning monarch until 1760 – is. It's managed by Historic Royal Palaces, who also look after other major attractions such as the **Tower of London (p155)**, **Hampton Court (p160)**, **Kew Palace (p160)** and **Banqueting House (p141)** – the surviving remnant of Whitehall Palace, destroyed by fire in 1698 – all formerly occupied by the monarchy. **Brighton Pavilion (p220)** and **Osborne House (p247)** on the Isle of Wight are also former royal residences, both well worth a visit.

Diana, the celebrated and much mourned People's Princess, is closely associated with her childhood home, **Althorp House (p176)** in Northamptonshire, which has been in the Spencer family since 1508. Six rooms of the house are now dedicated to an award-winning exhibition 'Diana, A Celebration'.

Chatsworth House

Stately Seats

For more exposure to gracious living take a look at the huge choice of stately homes open to the public. Many of these extraordinary buildings have been in the same family for centuries, like **Chatsworth House (p56)** in Derbyshire, still very much the home of the Duke and Duchess of Devonshire, and two great houses of North Yorkshire: **Ripley Castle (p268)**, home of the Ingilby family since 1320, and **Castle Howard (p264)** – star of many a movie but linked forever with the classic television

Ripley Castle, Yorkshire

Lacock Abbey

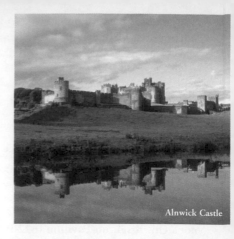

Alnwick Castle

adaptation of Evelyn Waugh's *Bridehead Revisited*.

Lyme Park (p32), Disley, the largest house in Cheshire (in the Legh family for 600 years), will also be familiar to viewers of the BBC's *Pride & Prejudice*, and Granada's *The Forsyte Saga*.

Location scouts are not slow to realise the scenic potential of our national architectural treasures. The atmospheric medieval castle at **Alnwick (p179)** (seat of the Duke of Northumberland since 1309), for example, has been used as a location for half a dozen films, including *Elizabeth* with Cate Blanchett, Joseph Fiennes and Kathy Burke (1998) but most recently and perhaps most famously in the Harry Potter movies. The scene of Harry and his classmates learning to fly their broomsticks (*Harry Potter and the Philosopher's Stone*) was shot in the castle grounds.

Durham Cathedral (p80) – also a location for *Elizabeth* – is another favourite for the Harry Potter movies, the Chapter House appearing as a Hogwart's classroom, while cloisters at Gloucester Cathedral double as school corridors. Other Hogwarts scenes are set in **Lacock Abbey (p250)**, Wiltshire, the Bodleian Library, Oxford, and Harrow Public School. However, **London Zoo Reptile House (p149)** really was the location for Harry's first experience of 'talking snake' in his shockingly close encounter with a depressed boa constrictor.

Literary links

An extraordinary number of visitor attractions throughout the guide are associated with our greatest writers and poets, whose homes have been preserved as museums and shrines, dedicated to their lives and works. The hope for us, as fleeting visitors, must be to sense the secrets of their inspiration, which in many cases is evident in their stunning surroundings:

Dylan Thomas' Boathouse

Burns House, Dumfries

Wordsworth's Dove Cottage

Brontë Parsonage Museum, Haworth, West Yorkshire (p277)
Burns House, Dumfries, Dumfries & Galloway (p308)
Charles Dickens Museum, Doughty Street, London (his former home) (p142)
Charles Dickens' Bleak House, Broadstairs, Kent (p118)
Charles Dickens' Birthplace Museum, Portsmouth (p106)
Coleridge Cottage, Nether Stowey, Somerset (p202)
Dylan Thomas' Boat House, Laugharne, Carmarthenshire (p346)
Hardy's Cottage, Higher Brockhampton, near Dorchester, Dorset (p74)
Henry James's Lamb House
        (later occupied by E F Benson), Rye, East Sussex (p224)
J M Barrie's Birthplace, Kirriemuir, Angus (p295)
James Joyce Tower, Dun Laoghaire, Co Dublin (p389)
James Joyce Centre, Dublin, Co Dublin (p388)
Jane Austen's House, Chawton, Hampshire (p101)
Keats House, Keats Grove, Hampstead, London (p147)
Milton's Cottage, Chalfont St Giles, Buckinghamshire (p22)
Rudyard Kipling's Bateman's, Burwash, East Sussex (p220)
Samuel Johnson Birthplace Museum, Lichfield, Staffordshire (p207)
Shakespeare's Birthplace, Stratford-Upon-Avon, Warwickshire (p236)
Sir Walter Scott's House, Abbotsford, Melrose, Scottish Borders (p332)
Wordsworth's House, Cockermouth, Cumbria (p48)
Wordsworth's Dove Cottage & Museum, Grasmere, Cumbria (p49)
William Butler Yeats's home, Thoor Ballylee, Gort, Co Galway (p390)

Beatles at Madame Tussaud's

Merseyside's Fab Four, who changed the face of British popular music, are celebrated in a very different kind of tourist attraction, **the Beatles Story (p163)**, in the award-winning Albert Dock development in Liverpool. Fans of the beautiful game, however should head for Preston and the **National Football Museum (p131)**. For the rest of us, who despair of getting close up and personal with the celebrity of our dreams, the next best thing is a date with his or her doppelganger at **Madame Tussaud's (p149)**.

11

How can I get away without the hassle of finding a place to stay?

Booking a place to stay can be a time-consuming process. You choose a place you like, only to find it's fully booked. That means going back to the drawing board again. Why not ask us to find the place that best suits your needs? No fuss, no worries and no booking fee.

Whatever your preference, we have the place for you. From a rustic farm cottage to a smart city centre hotel - we have them all. Choose from around 8,000 quality rated hotels and B&Bs in Great Britain and Ireland.

Just AAsk.

Hotel Booking Service
www.theAA.com

ENGLAND

View from Mutton Hill, on the South Downs, Hampshire

BEDFORDSHIRE

EVENTS & FESTIVALS

March
6th-13th Bedfordshire Festival of Music, Speech & Drama, Bedford

May
1st Ickwell May Festival, The Maypole, Ickwell Green
tbc Luton Carnival, a multi-cultural showcase

June
26th-27th Bedford International Kite Festival

July
2nd-4th Popular Flying Association International Air Rally & Exhibition, Cranfield Airfield (provisional)
3rd-4th Bedford River Festival (entertainment, parade, fete, raft races)

August
tbc Proms in the Park, Bedford Park

September
18th-19th Bedfordshire Steam & Country Fayre, Old Warden Park, near Biggleswade
29th-2nd Oct Bedford Beer Festival, Bedford Corn Exchange

October
29th Sep-2nd Bedford Beer Festival, Bedford Corn Exchange
tbc National Apple Day at Bromham Mill: apples, cider, apple bobbing, farmers market & entertainment (provisional)

November
tbc Bedford Fireworks Display, Rugby Ground, Goldington Road, Bedford
tbc Luton Fireworks Spectacular

December
tbc Bedford Victorian Christmas Fayre, Bedford town centre

above: The 16th-century Moot Hall in Elstow

AMPTHILL   Map 04 TL03

HOUGHTON HOUSE   FREE
➲ (1m NE off A421)

Now a ruin, the mansion was built for Mary Countess of Pembroke, the sister of Sir Philip Sidney. Inigo Jones is thought to have been involved in work on the house, which may have been the original 'House Beautiful' in Bunyan's *Pilgrim's Progress*.
Times: Open all reasonable times. **Facilities:** 🅿 ♿ ✿

BEDFORD   Map 04 TL04

BEDFORD MUSEUM
Castle Ln MK40 3XD
➲ (close to town bridge and Embankment)
☎ 01234 353323 ▤ 01234 273401   2 for 1
e-mail: bmuseum@bedford.gov.uk

Embark on a fascinating journey through the human and natural history of north Bedfordshire, pausing briefly to glimpse at wonders from more distant lands. Go back in time and visit the delightful rural room sets and the Old School Museum, where Blackbeard's Sword, 'Old Billy' the record breaking longest-living horse and numerous other treasures and curiosities can be found. Housed in the former Higgins and Sons Brewery, Bedford Museum is situated within the gardens of what was once Bedford Castle, beside the Great Ouse embankment. The courtyard and galleries provide an excellent setting for the varied collections.
Times: Open all year, Tue-Sat 11-5, Sun 2-5. (Closed Mon ex BH Mon afternoon, Good Fri & Xmas). **Fee:** ✱ £2.20 (ch, pen & con free). Fri free for everyone. Annual ticket £8.80. **Facilities:** 🅿 (50mtrs) 🍴 ♿ (lift available on request, subject to staff availability) toilets for disabled shop ✖ (ex guide dogs)

CECIL HIGGINS ART GALLERY & MUSEUM
Castle Ln MK40 3RP
➲ (in the centre of the town, just off the Embankment)
☎ 01234 211222 ▤ 01234 327149   2 for 1
e-mail: chag@bedford.gov.uk

A recreated Victorian mansion, with the rooms arranged as though the house was still lived in. Includes a bedroom with furniture designed by Victorian architect William Burges, and the adjoining gallery has an outstanding collection of ceramics, glass and changing exhibition of prints, drawings and watercolours. Also includes the Thomas Lester lace collection.
Times: Open all year, Tue-Sat 11-5, Sun & BH Mon 2-5. (Closed Mon, Good Fri, 25-26 Dec & 1 Jan). **Fee:** £2.20 (ch & concessions free) includes entry to Bedford Museum. Free to all visitors Fri **Facilities:** 🅿 (100yds) pay & display (free on Sun) 🍴 ♿ Wheelchair available toilets for disabled shop ✖ (ex guide dogs) ◖

LEIGHTON BUZZARD   Map 04 SP92

LEIGHTON BUZZARD RAILWAY
Pages Park Station, Billington Rd LU7 4TN
➲ (0.75m SE on A4146 signposted in and around Leighton Buzzard, near rdbt junct with A505)
☎ 01525 373888 ▤ 01525 377814   2 for 1
e-mail: info@buzzrail.co.uk

The Leighton Buzzard Railway offers a 65 minute journey into the vanished world of the English light railway, with its

continued

sharp curves, steep gradients, level crossings and unique roadside running. Built in 1919 to serve the local sand industry, the railway has carried a steam passenger service, operated by volunteers, since 1968.
Times: Open Mar-Oct, Sun & BH wknds; Jul, Wed; Aug, Tue-Thu, Sat & BH wknds. **Fee:** ✱ Return ticket £5.50 (ch 2-15 £2, pen £4.50 & ch under 2 free). Party 10+. **Facilities:** ▯ ▭ & (platform & train access for wheelchairs) toilets for disabled shop ⬏

LUTON   Map 04 TL02

JOHN DONY FIELD CENTRE
Hancock Dr, Bushmead LU2 7SF
➲ (signposted from rdbt on A6, at Barnfield College on New Bedford Rd)
☎ 01582 486983 🖹 01582 422805   FREE
e-mail: museum.gallery@luton.gov.uk
This is a purpose built study centre for exploring the landscapes, plants and animals of the Luton area. Featuring permanent displays on local archaeology, natural history and the management of the local nature reserve, it explains how ancient grasslands and hedgerows are conserved and follows 4000 years of history from Bronze Age to modern times.
Times: Open all year, Mon-Fri 9.30-4.45. Closed BHs. **Facilities:** ▯ & toilets for disabled ✖ (ex assist dogs)

LUTON MUSEUM & GALLERY
Wardown Park, Old Bedford Rd LU2 7HA
➲ (Follow brown signs from the town centre north. Turn off A6 towards   FREE
Bedford)
☎ 01582 546722 & 546739 🖹 01582 546763
e-mail: museum.gallery@luton.gov.uk
A Victorian mansion, with displays illustrating the natural and cultural history, archaeology and industries of the area, including the development of Luton's hat industry, and the Bedfordshire and Hertfordshire Regimental Collections. New 'Luton Life' displays tell the story of the town and its residents over the past 200 years. Exhibitions and events throughout the year.
Times: Open all year, Tue-Sat 10-5, Sun 1-5 (Closed Xmas, 1 Jan & Mon ex BH Mons). **Facilities:** ▯ ▭ & (parking adjacent to entrance, lift to 1st floor) toilets for disabled shop ✖ (ex guide dogs & hearing dogs)

STOCKWOOD CRAFT MUSEUM & GARDENS
Stockwood Country Park, Farley Hill LU1 4BH
➲ (signposted from M1 junct 10 and from Hitchin, Dunstable, Bedford and from Luton town centre)
☎ 01582 738714 & 546739   FREE
🖹 01582 546763
e-mail: museum.gallery@luton.gov.uk
The Museum is set in period gardens which incorporate the Ian Hamilton Finlay Sculpture Gardens. The Mossman collection of horse-drawn vehicles traces the history of transport from Roman times to the 1940s. Craft demonstrations are held at weekends in the summer. Please telephone for details of special events.
Times: Open all year; Mar-Oct, Tue-Sun 10-5; Nov-Mar, wknds 10-4. (closed Xmas & 1 Jan) **Facilities:** ▯ ▭ & (stair lift, parking, induction loop, automatic door) toilets for disabled shop ✖ (ex guide & hearing dogs)

OLD WARDEN   Map 04 TL14

THE SHUTTLEWORTH COLLECTION
Old Warden Park SG18 9EA
➲ (2m W from rdbt on A1, Biggleswade by-pass)
☎ 01767 627288 🖹 01767 626229
Housed in eight hangars on a classic grass aerodrome, 40 working historic aeroplanes span the progress of aviation with exhibits ranging from a 1909 Bleriot to a 1941 Spitfire. A garage of roadworthy motor vehicles explores the eras of the 1898 Panhard Levassor to the Railton sports car of 1937. The 19th-century coach house displays horse-drawn vehicles from 1880 to 1914. For details of flying displays ring the info line 090 6832 3310.
Times: Open Apr-Oct 10-5 (last admission 4), Nov-Mar 10-4 (last admission 3). Closed Xmas-New Year. **Fee:** ✱ £7.50 (pen £6). Most flying displays £12. (£15 1 Jun & 3 Aug). **Facilities:** ▯ ▭ ✖ licensed & toilets for disabled shop ✖ (ex guide dogs) ⬏

SANDY   Map 04 TL14

RSPB NATURE RESERVE
The Lodge SG19 2DL
➲ (1m E, on B1042 Potton road)
☎ 01767 680541 🖹 01767 683508
e-mail: claire.wallace@rspb.org.uk
The headquarters of the Royal Society for the Protection of Birds. The house and buildings are not open to the public, but there are waymarked paths and formal gardens, and two species of woodpecker, nuthatches and woodland birds may be seen, as may muntjac deer. Another feature is the specialist wildlife garden created in conjunction with the Henry Doubleday Association.
Times: Open all year, Mon-Fri 9-5, Sat, Sun & BH's 10-5. (Closed 25-26 Dec). **Fee:** ✱ £3 (ch under 16 £1, concessions £1.50). Family ticket (2 ad & 2 ch) £6. **Facilities:** ▯ & (partial access) toilets for disabled shop ✖ (ex in restricted areas) ⬏

SILSOE   Map 04 TL03

WREST PARK GARDENS
MK45 4HS
➲ (0.75m E off A6)
☎ 01525 860152
Audio tour through a century and a half of gardening styles as you explore the 90 acres of formal gardens that make up Wrest Park.
Times: Open 5 Apr-Sep, Sat, Sun & BH's only 10-6; Oct, Sat & Sun 10-5. (Last admission 1hr before closing). Dates valid until 31 Mar 2004. **Fee:** £4 (ch £2, concessions £3). Prices valid until 31 Mar 2004. **Facilities:** ▯ ✖ (ex on lead in certain areas) ✿

WHIPSNADE   Map 04 TL01

WHIPSNADE WILD ANIMAL PARK
LU6 2LF
➲ (signposted from M1 junct 9 & 12)
☎ 01582 872171 🖹 01582 872649
Set in 600 acres of countryside, Whipsnade is home to over 2,500 creatures, and is one of the largest wildlife conservation centres in Europe. Visitors can see tigers, elephants, penguins, giraffes, bears, chimps, hippos and more. Free daily demonstrations include the Elephant Walk, Birds of the World, sealions and penguin feeding.
Times: ✱ Open all year, daily. (Closed 25 Dec). Telephone 01582 872171 for opening times. **Facilities:** ▯ (charged) ▭ & (free entry for disabled cars) toilets for disabled shop ✖ ⬏

WOBURN   Map 04 SP93

WOBURN ABBEY
MK17 9WA
☎ 01525 290666 📠 01525 290271
e-mail: enquiries@woburnabbey.co.uk

Standing in 3000 acres of parkland, this palatial 18th-century mansion was originally a Cistercian Abbey, and the Dukes of Bedford have lived here since 1547. The art collection includes works by Canaletto, Rembrandt, Van Dyck, and Gainsborough. 14 state apartments are on view, and the private apartments are shown when not in use. Special events are held during the year, including the De-Havilland Tiger Moth Fly-In and a garden show.

Times: ✱ Open Jan-23 Mar; Abbey Sat & Sun only 11-4, Deer park 10.30-3.45; 24 Mar-29 Sep; Abbey weekdays 11-4, Sun & BH 11-5; 5-27 Oct Sat & Sun only; Deer Park weekdays 10-4.30, Sun & BH 10-4.45.
Facilities: 🅿 (charged) 🍴 ✖ licensed ♿ (wheelchairs accommodated by prior arrangement) toilets for disabled shop ✖ ⬤

WOBURN SAFARI PARK
Woburn Park MK17 9QN
➲ (Signposted from M1 junct 13)
☎ 01525 290407 📠 01525 290489
e-mail: info@woburnsafari.co.uk

Set in the 3000 acres of parkland belonging to Woburn Abbey, Woburn Safari Park has an extensive collection of many species. The safari road passes through an African plains area stocked with eland, zebra, hippo and rhino, then through well-keepered tiger and lion enclosures and on past bears and monkeys. Animal encounters, sea lion and parrot shows, and elephant displays, are all popular attractions. The large leisure complex also offers a boating lake, adventure playgrounds, railway train, walk-through aviary, squirrel monkey exhibit and 'the Australian Walkabout', with friendly wallabies. A new attraction is underwater viewing at Sealion Cove.

Times: ✱ Open daily, 10 Mar-27 Oct, 10-5. **Facilities:** 🅿 🍴 ✖ licensed ♿ toilets for disabled shop ✖ ⬤

Remember that prices and opening times are liable to change within the currency of this guide. It is always best to telephone in advance to check

BERKSHIRE

EVENTS & FESTIVALS

February
24th Shrove Tuesday
Great Newbury Pancake Race

May
1st-3rd Crafty Craft Race, Kennet & Avon Canal, fair & side shows in Victoria Park, Newbury
8th-22nd Newbury International Spring Festival of music and the visual arts
12th-16th Royal Windsor Horse Show

June
15th-19th Royal Ascot, Ascot Race Course (provisional)
26th-27th Newbury International Orchid Show

July
2nd-4th Bracknell Festival
17th-18th Kennet Valley Kite Festival, Thatcham (provisional)
24th De Beers Diamond Day, Ascot Race Course
25th Cartier International Polo, Smiths Lawn, Windsor Great Park (provisional)
tbc WOMAD World Music & Arts Festival, Rivermead, Reading

August
4th Cookham Regatta
7th Shergar Cup (team competition), Ascot Race Course
27th-29th Carling Reading Festival, Richfield Avenue, Reading (provisional)

September
18th-19th Newbury & Royal County of Berkshire Show, Newbury Showground
24th-26th Ascot Festival of Racing (provisional)
tbs Windsor Half Marathon
tbc Windsor Festival

October
tbc Michaelmas Fair, Northcroft, Newbury

Above: The Round Tower at Windsor Castle

BRACKNELL Map 04 SU86

The Look Out Discovery Centre

Nine Mile Ride RG12 7QW

➲ (3m S of town centre. From M3 junct 3, take A322 to Bracknell and from M4 junct 10, take A329M to Bracknell. Follow brown tourist signs)

☎ 01344 354400 2 for 1

🖷 01344 354422

e-mail: thelookout@bracknell-forest.gov.uk

A hands-on, interactive science and nature exhibition where budding scientists can spend many hours exploring and discovering over 70 fun filled exhibits within five themed zones, the topics covered linked to the National Curriculum. The newest attraction is the Sound and Music zone where visitors can see their own voice and make water dance. Other zones include Light and Colour, Forces and Movement and the Body and Perception. Climb the 88 steps to the Look Out tower and look towards Bracknell and beyond or enjoy a nature walk in the surrounding 2,600 acres of Crown Estate woodland.

Times: Open all year (Closed 25-26 Dec). **Fee:** ✱ £4.65 (ch & concessions £3.10). Family (2 adults + 2 ch or 1 adult + 3 ch) £12.40. **Facilities:** P ☕ ♿ toilets for disabled shop 🐕 (ex in grounds)

ETON Map 04 SU97

Dorney Court

Dorney SL4 6QP

➲ (signposted from M4 junct 7, via B3026)

☎ 01628 604638 🖷 01628 665772 2 for 1

e-mail: palmer@dorneycourt.co.uk

An enchanting brick and timber manor house (c1440) in a tranquil setting. With tall Tudor chimneys and a splendid great hall, it has been the home of the present family since 1510.

Times: Open BH Sun & Mons in May 1.30-4.30. Aug every afternoon ex Sat 1.30-4.30. **Fee:** £5.50 (ch £3.50, under 10's free). **Facilities:** P ☕ ♿ toilets for disabled garden centre 🐕 (ex guide dogs)

HAMPSTEAD NORREYS Map 04 SU57

The Living Rainforest

RG18 OTN (follow brown tourist signs from M4/A34)

☎ 01635 202444 🖷 01635 202440 2 for 1

e-mail: enquiries@livingrainforest.org

By providing education and supporting research into the relationship between humanity and the rainforests, this wonderful attraction hopes to promote a more sustainable future. Visitors to the Living Rainforest will see plants and wildlife that are under threat in their natural habitat, and be encouraged to take part in a large variety of activities, workshops and exhibitions.

Times: Open daily 10-5.15. (Closed from 1pm 24 Dec & 25-26 Dec) **Fee:** ✱ £4.95 (concessions £4.25, ch 5-14 £3.25 & ch 3-4 £1.95) **Facilities:** P ☕ ♿ toilets for disabled shop 🐕 (ex guide dogs)

LOWER BASILDON Map 04 SU67

Basildon Park

RG8 9NR

➲ (7m NW of Reading on W side of A329) 2 for 1

☎ 0118 984 3040 🖷 0118 976 7370

e-mail: basildonpark@nationaltrust.org.uk

This 18th-century house, built of Bath stone, fell into decay

continued

in the 20th century, but has been beautifully restored by Lord and Lady Iliffe. The classical front has a splendid central portico and pavilions, and inside there are delicate plasterwork decorations on the walls and ceilings. The Octagon drawing room has fine pictures and furniture, and there is a small formal garden.

Times: House open Apr-end Oct, Wed-Sun & BH Mon 1-5.30. Park & garden Apr-end Oct, Wed-Sun & BH Mon 12-5.30. **Fee:** ✱ House & grounds £4.50, family ticket £11.25; Grounds only £2.10, family ticket £5.25. **Facilities:** P ✕ licensed ♿ (driven buggy) toilets for disabled shop 🐕 (ex on lead in grounds)

Beale Park

Lower Basildon RG8 9NH

➲ (M4 junct 12, follow brown tourist signs to Pangbourne, A329 towards Oxford)

☎ 0118 984 5172 🖷 0118 984 5171

e-mail: bealepark@bun.com

Beale Park is home to an extraordinary bird collection including peacocks, swans, owls and parrots. It also offers a steam railway, rare breeds of farm animals, a great pet corner, meerkats, wallabies, a deer park, two splash pools, a huge adventure playground, acres of gardens, sculptures, trails and environmental education in a traditional, family park, beside the Thames. There are summer riverboat trips and excellent lake and river fishing.

Times: Open Mar-Dec. **Facilities:** P ☕ ♿ (wheelchair available, parking) toilets for disabled shop 🐕 (ex guide dogs)

NEWBURY Map 04 SU46

West Berkshire Museum

The Wharf RG14 5AS

➲ (from London take M4 junct 13, then southbound on A34, follow signs for town centre)

☎ 01635 30511 🖷 01635 38535 FREE

e-mail: heritage@westberks.gov.uk

Situated in two historic buildings in the centre of Newbury, the Cloth Hall built in 1627, and the Granary built in 1720. Apart from local history and archaeology, birds and fossils, the museum displays costume and other decorative art.

Times: Open all year: Apr-Sep, Mon-Fri (Wed during school hols only) 10-5, Sat 10-4.30. Oct-Mar, Mon-Sat (Wed during school hols only) 10-4. (Closed Sun & BHs). **Facilities:** P (15yds) ♿ shop 🐕 (ex guide dogs)

READING Map 04 SU77

Museum of English Rural Life

University of Reading, Whiteknights RG6 6AG

➲ (2m SE on A327)

☎ 0118 378 8660 🖷 0118 975 1264

e-mail: merl@reading.ac.uk

This museum houses a national collection of agricultural, domestic and crafts exhibits, including wagons, tools and a wide range of other equipment used in the English countryside over the last 150 years. Special facilities such as videos and teaching packs are available for school parties. The museum also contains extensive documentary and photographic archives, which can be studied by appointment.

Times: Open all year, Tue-Sat, 10-1 & 2-4.30. (Closed BH's & Xmas-New Year). **Fee:** ✱ £1 (ch free & pen 75p). **Facilities:** P ♿ shop 🐕

RISELEY   Map 04 SU76

WELLINGTON COUNTRY PARK

RG7 1SP

➲ (signposted off A33, between Reading & Basingstoke)

☎ 0118 932 6444 📠 0118 932 6445

e-mail: info@wellington-county-park.co.uk

350 acres of woodland and meadows, set around a lake in peaceful countryside. There is a collection of farm animals and a miniature railway. You can also fish and take a boat out on the 35-acre lake. Attractions also include crazy golf, an adventure playground and a new sandpit.

Times: Open all year Mar-Oct, daily 10-5.30, Nov-Feb wknds 10-4.30. **Fee:** £4.60 (ch £2.40) **Facilities:** 🅿 💻 ♿ (fishing platform & nature trail for disabled) toilets for disabled shop 🍽

WINDSOR   Map 04 SU97

FROGMORE HOUSE

Home Park SL4 1NJ

➲ (entrance from B3021 between Datchet & Old Windsor)

☎ 020 7766 7305 📠 020 7930 9625

e-mail: information@royalcollection.org.uk

Frogmore House, set in the private Home Park, is renowned for its beautiful landscaped garden and lake. Queen Victoria loved Frogmore so much that she broke with Royal tradition and chose to build a mausoleum for herself and Prince Albert there. The house is no longer a royal residence but is frequently used by the Royal Family for entertaining. The former library is the setting for furniture and paintings from the Royal Yacht Britannia.

Times: Open 29-31 May, 10-6 (last admission 5). 28-30 Aug, 10-5.30 (last admission 4). Prebooked guided tours Aug-Sep. **Fee:** Contact Ticket Sales and Information Office (020 7321 2233) for details of admission prices. **Facilities:** 🅿 shop 🍽 🍽

HOUSEHOLD CAVALRY MUSEUM

Combermere Barracks, St Leonards Rd SL4 3DN

➲ (on St Leonards Rd opposite King Edward VII Hospital)

☎ 01753 755112 📠 01753 755161

One of the finest military museums in Britain, with comprehensive displays of the uniforms, weapons, horse

continued

furniture (tack, regalia, etc) and armour used by the Household Cavalry from 1600 to the present day.

Times: ✱ Open all year Mon-Fri (ex BH) 9-12.30 & 2-4.30. **Facilities:** ♿ shop 🍽

LEGOLAND WINDSOR

Winkfield Rd SL4 4AY

➲ (on B3022 Windsor to Ascot road well signposted from M3 junct 3 & M4 junct 6)

☎ 08705 040404 📠 01753 626200

e-mail: sales@legoland.co.uk

With over 50 interactive rides, live shows, building workshops, driving schools and attractions. Set in 150 acres of beautiful parkland, LEGOLAND Windsor is a different sort of family theme park. An atmospheric and unique experience for the whole family, a visit to LEGOLAND Windsor is more than a day out, it's a lifetime of memories.

Times: ✱ Open daily 10 Mar-3 Nov (Closed 10-11, 17-18 & 24-25 Sep; 1-2, 8-9, & 15-16 Oct). Xmas opening 21 Dec-5 Jan. (Closed 25 Dec). **Facilities:** 🅿 💻 ✗ licensed ♿ (signing staff, wheelchair hire, parking) toilets for disabled shop 🍽 (ex guide dogs) 🍽

ST GEORGE'S CHAPEL

SL4 1NJ

➲ (M4 junct 6 & M3 junct 3)

☎ 01753 865538 📠 01753 620165

St George's Chapel, within the precincts of Windsor Castle, is one of the most beautiful ecclesiastical buildings in England. Founded by Edward IV in 1475, it is the burial place of ten monarchs, including Henry VIII and his favourite wife Jane Seymour. The Chapel is the spiritual home of the Order of the Garter, the oldest and most senior order of British Chivalry.

Times: Open Mon-Sat 10-4. (Closed 18 Oct & 23 Dec & from 1pm 24 Dec until 26 Decc & occasionally at short notice). Closed Sun, worshippers very welcome. **Fee:** ✱ Free entry to the Chapel is included in the price of entry to Windsor Castle. **Facilities:** 🅿 400 yds ♿ shop 🍽 (ex guide dogs)

FREE

Attractions with this symbol do not charge for entry.

SAVILL GARDEN (WINDSOR GREAT PARK)
Wick Ln, Englefield Green TW20 0UU
➲ (Signposted off A30 between Egham & Virginia Water)
☎ 01753 847518 📠 01753 847536
e-mail: savillgarden@crownestate.org.uk

The magnificent 35-acre garden lies within Windsor Great Park. It has spectacular woodland displays in spring, sweeping herbaceous borders in summer, fiery autumn colours and misty winter vistas. The garden's temperate house is a year-round delight.

Times: Open all year, daily 10-6 (10-4 Nov -Feb). (Closed 25-26 Dec).
Fee: Apr-May: £5.50 (ch 6-16 £2.50, pen £5); Jun-Oct: £4.50 (ch 6-16 £1.50, pen £4) Nov-Mar: £3.25 (ch £1.25, pen £2.75). Group rates available. Prices valid until 31 Mar 2004. **Facilities:** 🅿 🍴 ✗ licensed ♿ (wheelchairs available) toilets for disabled shop garden centre 🐕 (ex guide dogs) 💳

WINDSOR CASTLE
SL4 1NJ
➲ (M4 junct 6 & M3 junct 3)
☎ 020 7766 7304 📠 020 7930 9625
e-mail: windsorcastle@royalcollection.org.uk

Covering 13 acres, this is the official residence of HM The Queen and the largest inhabited castle in the world. Begun as a wooden fort by William the Conqueror, it has been added to by almost every monarch since. The Upper Ward includes the State Apartments, magnificently restored following the fire of 1992, and the Lower Ward where St George's Chapel is situated. The Doll's House designed for Queen Mary in the 1920s by Lutyens, is also on display.

Times: Open all year, daily except Good Friday & 25-26 Dec. Nov-Feb, 9.45-4.15 (last admission 3), Mar-Oct 9.45-5.15 (last admission 4). As Windsor Castle is a royal residence the opening arrangements may be subject to change at short notice. **Fee:** ✱ £11.50 (ch 5-16 £6, under 5's free, pen & students £9.50) Family ticket £29 (2 adults & 3 ch). **Facilities:** 🅿 (400yds) ♿ (ramps) toilets for disabled shop 🐕 (ex guide dogs) 💳

Above: Horseracing at Ascot

BRISTOL

EVENTS & FESTIVALS

February
tbc Bristol Beer Festival

April
15th-19th Bristolive! International festival for amateur ensembles, various venues
tbc Animated Encounters, Animation Festival, Watershed

May
tbc UK Comics Festival, Empire & Commonwealth Museum

June
13th Bristol Motor & Classic Car Show, The Downs
tbc Bristol Bike Fest, Ashton Court Estate, Long Ashton

July
3rd St Paul's Afrikan Carnival, St Paul's (provisional)
17th-18th Bristol Community Festival, Ashton Court Estate, Long Ashton
tbc Bristol Harbour Regatta Festival

August
12th-15th Bristol Balloon Fiesta, Ashton Court Estate, Long Ashton
25th-27th Bristol Flower Show, The Downs
tbc Bristol Children's Festival, The Downs

September
4th-5th International Kite Festival, Ashton Court Estate, Long Ashton

September/October
tbc Bristol Half Marathon

October
2nd-11th Poetry Festival, various venues in Bristol
10th-15th Wildscreen Festival, the world's largest festival of moving images from the natural world (provisional)

November
tbc Brief Encounters, Short Film Festival, Watershed. Bristol
tbc Firework Fiesta, Durdham Downs, Bristol

Above: Converted warehouses at Bristol docks

BRISTOL   Map 03 ST57

AT-BRISTOL
Anchor Rd, Harbourside BS1 5DB
➲ (from city centre, A4 to Anchor Rd. Located on left opposite Cathedral)
☎ 0845 345 1235 ▤ 0117 915 7200
e-mail: information@at-bristol.org.uk

For the interactive adventure of a lifetime head for At-Bristol's three attractions on the city's habourside. A clever fusion of sci-fi architecture and historic buildings are home to 'Wildwalk', a breathtaking journey through the plant and animal kingdoms; Explore, the UK's most exciting hands-on science centre; and the IMAX theatre, the largest cinema screen in the West of England.
Times: Open all year, daily 10-6. (Closed 25 Dec). **Fee:** ✱ Ticket for 3 attractions £16.50 (ch £11.45, concessions £13.45). Family ticket £52.
Facilities: ▣ (charged) ▯ licensed & (induction loop) toilets for disabled shop ✖ (ex guide dogs) ▰

BLAISE CASTLE HOUSE MUSEUM
Henbury Rd, Henbury BS10 7QS
➲ (4m NW of city, off B4057)   **FREE**
☎ 0117 903 9818 ▤ 0117 959 3475
e-mail: general_museum@bristol-city.gov.uk

Built in the 18th century for a Quaker banker, this mansion is now Bristol's Museum of Social History. Nearby Blaise Hamlet is a picturesque estate village, designed by John Nash.
Times: Open Apr-Oct, Sat-Wed, 10-5. **Facilities:** ▣ & shop ✖ (ex guide dogs)

BRISTOL CITY MUSEUM & ART GALLERY
Queen's Rd, Clifton BS8 1RL
➲ (follow signs to City Centre, then follow tourist board signs to City Museum & Art Gallery) **FREE**
☎ 0117 922 3571 ▤ 0117 922 2047
e-mail: general_museum@bristol-city.gov.uk

Regional and international collections representing ancient history, natural sciences, and fine and applied arts. Displays include dinosaurs, Bristol ceramics, silver, Chinese and Japanese ceramics. A full programme of Special Exhibitions take place throughout the year. Ring for details.
Times: Open all year, daily 10-5. (Closed 25-26 Dec). **Facilities:** ▣ (NCP 400yds) ▯ & (lift) toilets for disabled shop ✖ (ex guide dogs)

BRISTOL INDUSTRIAL MUSEUM
Prince's Wharf, Prince St, City Docks BS1 4RN **FREE**
☎ 0117 925 1470 ▤ 0117 729 7318
e-mail: general_museum@bristol-city.gov.uk

The museum is housed in a converted dockside transit shed. Motor and horse-drawn vehicles from the Bristol area are shown, with locally built aircraft and aero-engines. Railway exhibits include the industrial locomotive *Henbury*. At weekends from April to October there are trips around the harbour in either the tug *John King* or the steam tug *Mayflower* or the fire boat *Pyronant*; or trips around the dockside on the Bristol Harbour Railway. On certain weekends visitors can watch the steam crane and electric crane at work.
Times: Open Apr-Oct, Sat-Wed 10-5; Nov-Mar, Sat & Sun 10-5.
Facilities: ▣ (charged) & toilets for disabled shop ✖ (ex guide dogs)

BRISTOL ZOO GARDENS

Clifton BS8 3HA
➲ (M5 junct 17, take A4018 then follow brown elephant signs. Also signed from city centre)
☎ 0117 973 8951 ▤ 0117 973 6814
e-mail: information@bristolzoo.org.uk

Enjoy a whole day filled with excitement and discovery at Bristol Zoo Gardens. From the smallest and rarest tortoise in the world to the largest ape, there are 300 exotic and endangered species to explore. The Zoo is dedicated to conservation and involved in international breeding programmes. In Zona Brazil, visitors can experience first hand the stunning and diverse species found in the threatened coastal rainforests of Brazil. A winding wooden walkway will lead you past stunning birds, dainty agouti, grazing tapirs, and the world's largest living rodent -the capybara. Award-winning Seal & Penguin Coasts enable visitors to come face to face with penguins and seals in their natural element - beneath the waves - through transparent underwater walkways. Other favourites include Bug World, Twilight World, and the Reptile House.

Times: Open all year, daily (ex 25 Dec) from 9am. Closing times approx 5.30pm (summer) 4.30pm (winter). **Fee:** ✱ £8.90 (ch 3-14 £5, pen £7.90). **Facilities:** ▣ (charged) ▆ ✗ licensed ♿ (wheelchairs/electric scootersfor use in zoo grounds toilets for disabled shop ✖ (kennels for service dogs) ◥

BRITISH EMPIRE & COMMONWEALTH MUSEUM

Station Approach, Temple Meads BS1 6QH
➲ (in city centre, near Temple Meads station)
☎ 0117 925 4980 ▤ 0117 925 4983
e-mail: staff@empiremuseum.co.uk   2 for 1

Exploring the dramatic 500-year history of the rise and fall of the British Empire and the emergence of the modern Commonwealth, this internationally acclaimed museum uses video stations, interactive exhibits, computer games, as well as more traditional techniques. Visitors have the opportunity to dress in period costume, learn Morse code or sample exotic spices. The museum is divided into three sections: Britain's first empire 1500-1790, the British Empire at its height 1790-1914, and Independence and Beyond, and is housed in a restored railway terminus built by Brunel.

Times: Open daily 10-5. (Closed 25-26 Dec) **Fee:** ✱ £5.95 (pen & students £4.95, ch £3.95) **Facilities:** ▣ ▆ ♿ toilets for disabled shop ✖ (ex guide dogs) ◥

GEORGIAN HOUSE

7 Great George St, off Park St BS1 5RR
➲ (5 mins walk from Bristol City Centre)   FREE
☎ 0117 921 1362 ▤ 0117 922 2047
e-mail: general_museum@bristol-city.gov.uk

A carefully preserved example of a late 18th-century merchant's town house, with many original features and furnished to illustrate life both above and below stairs. A bedroom is now open, featuring a four-poster bed plus a small display recounting Bristol's involvement in the slave trade.

Times: Open Apr-Oct, Sat-Wed, 10-5. **Facilities:** ▣ (pay & display street parking) ✖ (ex guide dogs)

JOHN WESLEY'S CHAPEL(THE NEW ROOM)

36 The Horsefair, Broadmead BS1 3JE
➲ (M32 towards Broadmead)
☎ 0117 926 4740

The oldest Methodist chapel in the world, built in 1739 and extended in 1748. Above the chapel are the preacher's rooms where John Wesley, Charles Wesley and the early Methodist preachers stayed.

Times: Open all year, Mon-Sat 10-4. **Fee:** ✱ Donation requested. £2.80 for guided tour. **Facilities:** ▣ (250yds) ▆ ♿ shop ✖ (ex guide dogs) ◥

MARITIME HERITAGE CENTRE

Gas Ferry Rd BS1 6UN
➲ (M5 junct 18, follow brown signs 'Anchor')
☎ 0117 926 0680 ▤ 0117 925 5788
e-mail: commerical@ss-great-britain.com

Exploring 200 years of Bristol shipbuilding, with special reference to Charles Hill & Son, and their predecessor, James Hillhouse. At the Great Western Dock the museum forms part of the *SS Great Britain* and John Cabot's *Matthew* experience.

Times: ✱ Open all year, daily 10-5.30, 4.30 in winter. (Closed 24 & 25 Dec). **Facilities:** ▣ (charged) ▆ ♿ toilets for disabled shop ✖ (ex guide dogs) ◥

RED LODGE

Park Row BS1 5LJ
➲ (5 mins walk from Bristol City Centre)   FREE
☎ 0117 921 1360 ▤ 0117 922 2047
e-mail: general_museum@bristol-city.gov.uk

The house was built in 1590 and then altered in 1730. It has fine oak panelling and carved stone chimney pieces and is furnished in the style of both periods. The garden has now been laid out in Elizabethan style.

Times: Open Apr-Oct, Sat-Wed 10-5. **Facilities:** ▣ (NCP, adjacent) ✖ (ex guide dogs)

SS GREAT BRITAIN

Great Western Dock, Gas Ferry Rd BS1 6TY
➲ (off Cumberland Rd)
☎ 0117 926 0680 ▤ 0117 925 5788

Built and launched in Bristol in 1843, the *SS Great Britain*, designed by Isambard Kingdom Brunel, was the first ocean-going, propeller-driven, iron ship. After a life as a passenger liner, troop transport and cargo carrier, she was abandoned in the Falkland Islands in 1886. But in 1970 she was towed back to Bristol and is now being conserved in the Great Western Dock where she was built.

Times: ✱ Open all year daily 10-5.30, 4.30 in winter. (Closed 24 & 25 Dec). **Facilities:** ▣ (charged) ▆ ♿ shop ✖ ◥

FREE
Attractions with this symbol do not charge for entry.

BUCKINGHAMSHIRE

EVENTS & FESTIVALS

February
24th Shrove Tuesday Olney Pancake Day Race
April
tbc Stowe Kite Festival, Stowe Landscaped
    Gardens, Stowe Park, Buckingham
May
3rd Marlow Spring Regatta,
    Higginson Park, Marlow
June
6th Coombe Hill Run, Wendover
13th Folk on the Green, Horsefair Green,
    Stony Stratford (now part of
    Milton Keynes)
27th Milton Keynes Carnival,
    central Milton Keynes
tbc Milton Keynes International Festival
July
3rd-10th Buckingham Festival
10th North Bucks Show,—
    Stowe Park, Buckingham
August
2nd Bucks County Show,
    Weedon Park, Aylesbury
September
12th Thames Valley Grand Prix Raft Race,
    Higginson Park, Marlow
18th Marlow Carnival,
    Higginson Park, Marlow
November
tbc Milton Keynes Free Firework Display,
    central Milton Keynes
December
4th Haddenham Festival, Haddenham Village,
    between Thame & Aylesbury

Above: Mentmore House, nr Aylesbury, over the years home to Baron de Rothschild, Lord Roseberry, and the Maharishi Mahesh Yogi's University of Natural Law

BEACONSFIELD   Map 04 SU99

BEKONSCOT MODEL VILLAGE
Warwick Rd HP9 2PL
➲ (2.7m M40 junct 2, 4m M25 junct 16)
☎ 01494 672919 📠 01494 675284
e-mail: bekonscot@dial.pipex.com

A miniature world, depicting rural England in the 1930s. A Gauge 1 model railway meanders through six little villages, each with their own tiny population. Rides on the sit-on miniature railway take place weekends and school holidays. **Times:** Open mid Feb-Oct, 10-5. **Fee:** ✱ £4.80 (ch £3, students £4). **Facilities:** 🅿 💺 ♿ (wheelchair loan) toilets for disabled shop ✖ (ex guide dogs) 🍽

CHALFONT ST GILES   Map 04 SU99

CHILTERN OPEN AIR MUSEUM
Newland Park, Gorelands Ln HP8 4AB
➲ (M25 junct 17, M40 junct 2. Follow brown signs)
☎ 01494 871117 📠 01494 872774
e-mail: coamuseum@netscape.net

Saved from demolition and moved brick by brick to Newland Park, this collection of old buildings includes barns, granaries and even a tin chapel. Step back in time and get a feel of the 1940s in a fully furnished Prefab, or experience 50AD at the Iron Age House. Demonstrations including brick making, rug making, blacksmithing and storytelling. Regular living history re-enactments.
Times: Open 31 Mar-Oct, daily 10-5. **Fee:** ✱ £6 (ch £3.50, concessions £5) Family ticket (2 adults & 2 ch) £16.50. **Facilities:** 🅿 💺 ♿ (Braille guide books & taped guides available, wheelchairs) toilets for disabled shop ✖ (ex on lead) 🍽

MILTON'S COTTAGE
Dean Way HP8 4JH
➲ (0.5m W of A413. 3m N of M40 junct 2)
☎ 01494 872313
e-mail: info@miltonscottage.org

A timber-framed, 16th-century cottage, with a charming garden, the only surviving home in which John Milton lived and worked. He completed *Paradise Lost* and started

continued

Paradise Regained here. First editions of these works are among the many rare books and artefacts on display.
Times: Open Mar-Oct, Tue-Sun 10-1 & 2-6. Also open Spring & Summer BH. **Fee:** £3 (ch 15 £1). Party 20+ £2 each. **Facilities:** 🅿 ✗ licensed ♿ (special parking area closer to cottage) shop ✖ (ex guide dogs)

CLIVEDEN   Map 04 SU98
CLIVEDEN
SL6 0JA
➲ (2m N of Taplow, follow brown signs on A4)
☎ 01628 605069 ▤ 01628 669461   2 for 1
e-mail: cliveden@ntrust.org.uk

The 375 acres of garden and woodland overlook the River Thames, and include a magnificent parterre, topiary, lawns with box hedges, and water gardens. The palatial house, former home of the Astors, is now a hotel - The Great Hall and French Dining Room can be visited on certain afternoons.
Times: Open Grounds 15 Mar-Oct daily 11-6, Nov-Dec daily 11-4 (Woodlands open all year). House Apr-Oct, Thu & Sun 3-6 by timed ticket. (Last admission 5.30). **Fee:** ✱ Grounds: £6. House: £1 extra. Family ticket £15. **Facilities:** 🅿 ✗ licensed ♿ (powered vehicle & wheelchairs available, parking) toilets for disabled shop ✖ (ex in woodland) ♨ 🍴

HIGH WYCOMBE   Map 04 SU89
WYCOMBE LOCAL HISTORY & CHAIR MUSEUM
Castle Hill House, Priory Av HP13 6PX
➲ (signposted by brown tourism sign from A404 (Amersham Hill) N of High Wycombe town centre)
☎ 01494 421895 ▤ 01494 421897   FREE
e-mail: enquiries@
wycombemuseum.demon.co.uk

Situated in an 18th-century house, set in attractive grounds. The displays explore the history of the Wycombe area, focusing on the chair-making industry, with interactive displays, and changing exhibitions.
Times: Open all year, Mon-Sat 10-5, Sun 2-5. Closed on BHs except special events - ring for details. **Facilities:** 🅿 🖥 ♿ (special parking & drop off point) toilets for disabled shop ✖ (ex guide dogs)

HUGHENDEN   Map 04 SU89
HUGHENDEN MANOR
HP14 4LA
➲ (1.5m N of High Wycombe, on W side of A4128)
☎ 01494 755573 ▤ 01494 474284

Benjamin Disraeli, later the Earl of Beaconsfield and twice Prime Minister, bought the house in 1847 and lived there until his death in 1881. It still has many of his books and other possessions. The gardens are a recreation of the colourful designs of Disraeli's wife, Mary-Anne.
Times: House open 1-30 Mar, Sat & Sun only. Apr-Oct, Wed-Sun & BH Mon 1-5. Last admission 4.30. Gardens same dates as house 12-5. Park open all year. **Fee:** ✱ £4.50. Family ticket £11.50. Garden only £1.60 (ch 80p). Park free. **Facilities:** 🅿 ✗ licensed ♿ (braille leaflet, wheelchairs, ramp to house) toilets for disabled shop ✖ (ex in park & car park only) ♨

LONG CRENDON   Map 04 SP60
COURTHOUSE
HP18 9AN
➲ (2m N of Thame, via B4011 when entering village turn right into the High St. Courthouse on left at end of High St)   2 for 1
☎ 01296 381501 ▤ 01494 463310

One of the finest examples of early timber framed building in the area. Probably built as a wool store in the early 1400s, but also used as a manorial courthouse until the late 19th century, this timber-framed building stands out, even in this picturesque village. Although the windows and doors have been altered and the chimney stack is Tudor, the magnificent timber roof is original.
Times: Open, Upper storey Apr-Sep, Wed 2-6, Sat, Sun & BH Mons 11-6. **Fee:** £1 **Facilities:** 🅿 (street) (not suitable for large vehicles) ✖ ♨

MIDDLE CLAYDON   Map 04 SP72
CLAYDON HOUSE
MK18 2EY
➲ (Off A413 in Padbury, follow National Trust signs. Entrance by north drive only)
☎ 01296 730349 ▤ 01296 738511   2 for 1
e-mail: tcdgen@smtp.ntrust.org.uk

The rather sober exterior of this 18th-century house gives no clue to the extravagances that lie inside, in the form of fantastic rococo carvings. Ceilings, cornices, walls and overmantels are adorned with delicately carved fruits, birds, beasts and flowers by Luke Lightfoot. The Chinese room is particularly splendid.
Times: House open Sat-Wed 1-5 (Closed Thu & Fri). Grounds open 12-6. Last admission 4.30. Open Good Fri **Fee:** ✱ £4.50 (ch £2.20). Family ticket £11.20. Grounds £1 (ch 50p) **Facilities:** 🅿 🖥 ✗ ♿ (Braille guide, photograph albums) toilets for disabled ✖ (ex guide dogs or in park) ♨ 🍴

QUAINTON   Map 04 SP72
BUCKINGHAMSHIRE RAILWAY CENTRE
Quainton Rd Station HP22 4BY
➲ (Off A41. 7m NW of Aylesbury)
☎ 01296 655720 ▤ 01296 655720
e-mail: bucksrailcentre@btopenworld.com

Housed in a Grade 2 listed building, the Centre features an interesting and varied collection of about 20 locomotives with 40 carriages and wagons from places as far afield as South Africa, Egypt and America. Items date from the 1800s up to the 1960s. Visitors can take a ride on full-size and miniature steam trains, and stroll around the 20-acre site to see locomotives and rolling stock. The Centre runs locomotive driving courses for visitors. Regular 'Days out with Thomas' events take place throughout the year.
Times: Open with engines in steam Apr-Oct, Sun & BH Mon; Jun-Aug, Wed; 10.30-5.30. Dec Sat & Sun Santa's Magical Steamings-advanced booking recommended. Also open for static viewing Wed-Sun.
Fee: Steaming Days; £6 (ch & pen £4). Family ticket £18. BH wknds £7 (ch & pen £5). Family ticket £20. Static viewing £3 (ch & pen £2).
Facilities: 🅿 🖥 ♿ toilets for disabled shop 🍴

STOWE   Map 04 SP63

STOWE HOUSE
MK18 5EH
➲ (3m NW Buckingham)
☎ 01280 818282 🖷 01280 818186
e-mail: sses@stowe.co.uk

Set in the National Trust's landscaped gardens, Stowe is a splendid 18th-century mansion. The leading designers of the day were called in to lay out the gardens, and leading architects - Vanbrugh, Gibbs, Kent and Leoni - commissioned to decorate them with garden temples. The house is now a major public school.
Times: Open 14-16 Mar, 25-31 May, 4 Sep-19 Oct, 14-16 Nov, daily (ex Mon & Tue, but open May BH Mon) for guided tours only at 2pm; 3-27 Apr & 9 Jul-3 Sep, Wed-Sun 12-5 and daily tours at 2pm. **Fee:** ✱ £2 (ch £1). Guided tours £3 (ch £1.50). **Facilities:** 🅿 & toilets for disabled shop ✻ (ex guide dogs)

STOWE LANDSCAPE GARDENS
MK18 5EH
➲ (3m NW of Buckingham via Stoke Ave, off A422)
☎ 01280 822850
🖷 01280 822437   2 for 1
e-mail: stowegarden@nationaltrust.org.uk
One of the finest Georgian landscape gardens, made up of valleys and vistas, narrow lakes and rivers with more than 30 temples and monuments designed by many of the leading architects of the 18th century. At the centre is Stowe House, and around all is Stowe Park. The creation of the Temple family, Stowe has been described as 'a work to wonder at' in its size, splendour and variety. Many of the garden buildings have been conserved, and thousands of new trees and shrubs have been planted in recent years.
Times: Open Mar-Oct (closed 24 May), Wed-Sun, 10-5.30, last admission 4; Nov-21 Dec, Wed-Sun, last admission 3. Open all BH Mons. **Fee:** ✱ £5 (ch £2.50). Family ticket £12.50. **Facilities:** 🅿 ✕ licensed & (manual wheelchairs unsuitable, powered batricars available) toilets for disabled shop ✻ (on leads only) ✿ ➾

WADDESDON   Map 04 SP71

WADDESDON MANOR
HP18 0JH
➲ (gates off A41, 6m NW of Aylesbury)
☎ 01296 653211, 653226 & 653203
🖷 01296 653212
e-mail: twmsep@smtp.ntrust.org.uk
Waddesdon was built in the style of a French château of the 16th century and houses one of the finest collections of French 18th-century decorative arts in the world which includes French furniture, Savonnerie carpets and Sèvres porcelain. There is also a fine collection of important portraits by Gainsborough and Reynolds along with works by Dutch and Flemish masters of the 17th century. The garden is renowned for its seasonal displays, colourful shrubs, mature trees and parterre. There is a rococo-style aviary housing many exotic birds, a rose and children's garden.
Times: Open, Grounds & Aviary only, 5 Mar-21 Dec, Wed-Sun & BH Mon 10-5. House 2 Apr-2 Nov, Wed-Sun & BH Mon 11-4. Entrance by timed ticket. **Fee:** ✱ Grounds & Aviary £4 (ch £2). House & grounds £11 (ch £8). Tickets bookable in advance at booking charge (tel 01296 653226). **Facilities:** 🅿 ✕ licensed & (wheelchairs, braille guide, parking, scented plants) toilets for disabled shop ✻ (ex guide dogs) ✿ ➾

WEST WYCOMBE   Map 04 SU89

WEST WYCOMBE CAVES
HP14 3AJ   2 for 1
➲ (on A40)
☎ 01494 524411 (office) & 533739 (caves)
🖷 01494 471617
e-mail: mary@west-wycombe-estate.co.uk
The entrance to West Wycombe caves is halfway up the hill that dominates the village. On the summit stands the parish church and the mausoleum of the Dashwood family. The caves are not natural but were dug on the orders of Sir Francis Dashwood between 1748 and 1752. Sir Francis, the Chancellor of the Exchequer, was also the founder of the Hell Fire Club, whose members were reputed to have held outrageous and blasphemous parties in the caves, which extend approximately half a mile underground. The entrance, from a large forecourt, is a brick tunnel that leads into the caves, where tableaux and curiosities are exhibited.
Times: Open all year, Mar-Oct, daily 11-6; Nov-Feb, Sat & Sun 1-5. **Fee:** ✱ £3.75 (ch & pen £2.50, students £3). Party 20+. **Facilities:** 🅿 ➾ & toilets for disabled shop ✻ (ex guide dogs) ➾

WEST WYCOMBE PARK
HP14 3AJ
➲ (S of A40, at W end of West Wycombe)   2 for 1
☎ 01494 513569 🖷 01494 474284
Set in 300 acres of beautiful parkland, the house was rebuilt in the Palladian style, between 1745 and 1771, for Sir Francis Dashwood. Of particular note are the painted ceilings by

continued

Borgnis. The park was laid out in the 18th century and given an artificial lake and classical temples.

Times: Open, House & grounds Jun-Aug, Sun-Thu 2-6. Grounds only Apr-May, Sun-Thu 2-6 & Etr, May Day & Spring BH Sun & Mon 2-6. Last admission 5.15. Entry by timed tickets on wkdays. Parties must book in advance. **Fee:** ✱ House & grounds £5 (ch £2.50). Grounds only £2.60. Family ticket £12. **Facilities:** 🅿 & (partial access to ground floor & gardens) 🦮 (ex on lead in car park) 🐾

WING   Map 04 SP82

Ascott

LU7 0PS

➲ (0.5m E of Wing, 3m SW of Leighton Buzzard on S side of A418)

☎ 01296 688242   📠 01296 681904

e-mail: info@ascottestate.co.uk

A National Trust property since 1949, Ascott holds an exceptional collection of paintings, Chinese porcelain and English and French furniture. The 30-acre garden is a fine example of Victorian gardening and the grounds are stunning at any time of year.

Times: House & Gardens: Apr, 6 Aug-13 Sep daily 2-6 (ex Mon). Gardens: May-Jul every Wed & last Sun in month, 17 & 24 Sep, 2-6. **Fee:** ✱ House & Garden £5.60 (ch £2.80). Gardens only: £4 (ch £2). National Trust members free. **Facilities:** 🅿 & (wheelchrs avail, assistance required, large print guide) toilets for disabled 🦮 🐾

Above: The brightly lit Hellfire Caves of Sir Francis Dashwood at High Wycombe

CAMBRIDGESHIRE

EVENTS & FESTIVALS

January
8th-11th Cambridge Winter Ale Festival
tbc Whittlesey Straw Bear Festival

March
20th-21st National Shire Horse Show, East of
England Showground, Peterborough
27th-28th Daffodil Weekend, Thriplow

May
3rd Stilton Cheese Rolling, Stilton
7th-9th East of England Garden Show, East of
England Showground, Alwalton
7th-9th St Neots Folk Festival,
The Priory Centre, St Neots
24th-29th Cambridge Beer Festival,
Jesus Green, Cambridge
tbc Duxford Air Show, Duxford

June
5th Strawberry Fair (free festival),
Midsummer Common, Cambridge
18th-20th East of England Show, East of
England Showground, Peterborough
26th-27th Hemingford Abbots Open Gardens
& Flower Festival Weekend
30th-4th Jul Wisbech Rose Fair

July
9th-11th Ely Folk Weekend, Cresswells Lane
Site, Ely (provisional)
10th World Pea Shooting Championships &
Village Fair, Village Green, Witcham, Ely
16th-14th Aug Cambridge Summer Music
Festival, various venues
29th-1st Aug Charles Wells Cambridge Folk
Festival, Cambridge
tbc Duxford Air Show, Duxford

August
16th Jul-14th Cambridge Summer Music
Festival, various venues
24th-29th Peterborough Beer Festival

September
tbc Duxford Air Show, Duxford

October
10th The World Conker Championships,
Village Green, Ashton, Peterborough

Above: Trinity College, Cambridge

CAMBRIDGE & COUNTY FOLK MUSEUM
2/3 Castle St CB3 0AQ
➲ (Turn off A14 onto A3019, museum NW of town)
☎ 01223 355159
e-mail: info@folkmuseum.org.uk

This timber-framed inn houses items covering the everyday
life of the people of Cambridgeshire from the 17th century to
the present day. There are also temporary exhibitions.
Special exhibitions and children's activity days take place
throughout the year. Please telephone for details.
Times: Open all year, Apr-Sep, Mon-Sat 10.30-5, Sun 2-5. Oct-Mar,
Tue-Sat 10.30-5, Sun 2-5. (Last admissions 30 mins before closing).
(Closed 1 Jan, Good Fri, 24-31 Dec). Closed for refurbishment until
summer 2004, please phone for dates. **Fee:** ✱ £2.50 (ch 5-12 75p,
concessions £1.50) one free ch with every full paying adult.
Facilities: P (300yds) (pay and display on street parking) & (braille
touch tables, tape guides & large print guides) shop ✱ (ex guide dogs)

CAMBRIDGE UNIVERSITY BOTANIC GARDEN
Cory Lodge, Bateman St CB2 1JF
➲ (1m S of city centre)
☎ 01223 336265 ▤ 01223 336278
e-mail: enquiries@botanic.cam.ac.uk

The Cambridge University Botanic Garden is a 40-acre oasis
of beautifully landscaped gardens and glasshouses close to
the heart of the historic city. Opened on its present site
in 1846, the garden showcases a collection of some 8000
plant species. This Grade II heritage landscape features the
Rock Garden, displaying alpine plants, the Winter and
Autumn Gardens, tropical rainforest and seasonal displays in
the Glasshouses, the historic Systematic Beds, the Scented
Garden, Herbaceous Beds and the finest collection of trees in
the east of England.
Times: Open all year daily 10-6 (summer), 10-5 (autumn & spring),
(10-4) winter. Glasshouses 10-3.45. (Closed 25 Dec-1 Jan). Entry by
Bateman St and Station Rd gates on weekdays & by Bateman St gate
only at weekends & BH. **Fee:** £2.50 (ch & pen £2). **Facilities:** P
(0.25km) (on street parking bays-pay & display) ■ & (guiding
service, manual & motorised wheelchairs -prebooked) toilets for
disabled shop (open Mar-Oct) ✱ (ex guide dogs)

FITZWILLIAM MUSEUM
Trumpington St CB2 1RB
➲ (M11 junct 11, 12 or 13, near city centre) FREE
☎ 01223 332900 ▤ 01223 332923
e-mail: fitzmuseum-enquiries@lists.cam.ac.uk

The Fitzwilliam is the art museum of the University of
Cambridge and one of the oldest public museums in Britain.
Exhibits include ancient art and sculpture, furniture and rugs
as well as masterpieces by painters including Picasso,
Monet, Constable and Titian. Following the ongoing
redevelopment, new facilities will include education spaces,
seminar room and ceramics study centre, due for completion
in summer 2004.
Times: Open all year Tue-Sat 10-5, Sun 2.15-5 plus Etr Mon & Summer
BH. (Closed Good Fri, May Day & 23 Dec-1 Jan). Closed Xmas 2003
until after Etr 2004 for reinstallation of collections. Check website for
details. **Facilities:** P (400yds) (2hr max, metered) ■ & (full access
from summer 2004, induction loop) toilets for disabled shop ✱ (ex
guide dogs)

SCOTT POLAR RESEARCH INSTITUTE MUSEUM
Lensfield Rd CB2 1ER
➲ (1km S of City Centre)
☎ 01223 336540   ▤ 01223 336549   FREE
e-mail: rkh10@cam.ac.uk

An international centre for polar studies, including a museum featuring displays of Arctic and Antarctic expeditions, with special emphasis on those of Captain Scott. Other exhibits include Eskimo work and other arts of the polar regions, as well as displays on current scientific exploration. Public lectures run from October to December and February to April.
Times: Open all year, Mon-Fri 2.30-4. Closed some public & university hols. Occasional Saturday opening. **Facilities:** 🅿 (400mtrs) ⅔ shop 🐕 (ex guide dogs)

UNIVERSITY MUSEUM OF ARCHAEOLOGY & ANTHROPOLOGY
Downing St CB2 3DZ
➲ (located opposite Crowne Plaza Hotel)
☎ 01223 333516   ▤ 01223 333517   FREE
e-mail: cumaa@hermes.cam.ac.uk

The museum is part of the Faculty of Archaeology and Anthropology of the University of Cambridge. It was established in 1884 and is still housed in its 1916 building on the Downing Site in the city centre. It has three floors displaying renowned archaeological and anthropological collections from around the world.
Times: Open all year Tue-Sat 2-4.30. (Closed 1wk Etr & 1wk Xmas). Telephone for extended summer hours. **Facilities:** 🅿 (100yds) ⅔ (lift available) shop 🐕 (ex guide dogs)

DUXFORD   Map 05 TL44

IMPERIAL WAR MUSEUM DUXFORD
CB2 4QR
➲ (off M11 junct 10, on A505)
☎ 01223 835000   ▤ 01223 837267
e-mail: duxford@iwm.org.uk

Duxford is one of the world's most spectacular aviation heritage complexes with a collection of nearly 200 aircraft, the American Air Museum and a fine collection of military vehicles plus special exhibitions including The Battle of Britain, Normandy Experience and Monty. The Museum holds four Air Shows throughout the summer plus other special events such as the Military Vehicle Show.
Times: Open all year, mid Mar-mid Oct daily 10-6; mid Oct-mid Mar daily 10-4. (Closed 24-26 Dec) **Fee:** ✱ £8.50 (pen £6.50 & concessions £4.50). Ch under 16yrs free. Different rates apply for air shows.
Facilities: 🅿 ▆ ✗ licensed ⅔ (wheelchair available-phone in advance) toilets for disabled shop 🐕 (ex guide dogs) 🗨

ELY   Map 05 TL58

ELY CATHEDRAL
CB7 4DL
➲ (A10 or A142, 15m from Cambridge)
☎ 01353 667735   ▤ 01353 665658
e-mail: receptionist@cathedral.ely.anglican.org

The Octagon Tower of Ely Cathedral can be seen for miles as it rises above the surrounding flat fenland. A monastery was founded on the site by St Etheldreda in 673, but the present

continued

cathedral church dates from 1083 and is a magnificent example of Romanesque architecture.
Times: Open daily, Summer 7-7, Winter 7.30-6 (5pm Sun). **Fee:** ✱ £4.80 (concessions £4.20). Ch free in family group. Group reductions (15+) **Facilities:** 🅿 (walking distance) ▆ ✗ licensed ⅔ (touch tour for blind/partially sighted) toilets for disabled shop 🐕 (ex guide dogs)

OLIVER CROMWELL'S HOUSE
29 St Mary's St CB7 4HF
➲ (adjacent to St Mary's church)
☎ 01353 662062   ▤ 01353 668518
e-mail: tic@eastcambs.gov.uk

Cromwell inherited the house and local estates from a maternal uncle and moved here in 1636, along with his mother, sisters, wife and eight children. There are displays and period rooms dealing with Cromwell's life, the Civil War and domestic life in the 17th century, as well as the history of The Fens and the house itself, from its medieval origins to its role as an inn in the 19th century.
Times: Open all year: Apr-Oct, daily 10-5.30; Nov-Mar, Mon-Fri 11-4, Sat 10-5. Winter, Sun, 11.15-4. **Fee:** ✱ £3.50 (concessions £3). Family ticket £8.50. **Facilities:** 🅿 (100yds) ⅔ shop 🐕 (ex guide dogs) 🗨

THE STAINED GLASS MUSEUM
The Cathedral CB7 4DN
➲ (15m N of Cambridge via A10, situated inside Ely Cathedral)   2 for 1
☎ 01353 660347   ▤ 01353 665025
e-mail: curator@stainedglassmuseum.com

Situated in the cathedral, this museum is the only one of its kind in the country. Case exhibits show how stained-glass windows are designed and made, and there is an exhibition of approximately 100 panels dating from the 13th century to the present day, displayed at eye level in back-lit cases. The museum has recently reopened after total refurbishment.
Times: Open daily, Mon-Fri 10.30-4.30, Sat & BH 10.30-5 & Sun 12-6. **Fee:** ✱ £3.50 (ch, students & pen £2.50). Party 10+ £2.50 (concessions £2). **Facilities:** 🅿 400yds ▆ ⅔ (Inter-active video visit) toilets for disabled shop 🐕 (ex guide dogs) 🗨

HAMERTON   Map 04 TL17

HAMERTON ZOO PARK
PE28 5RE
➲ (off A1 junct 15, signed Sawtry)
☎ 01832 293362   ▤ 01832 293677
e-mail: office@hamertonzoopark.com

A wildlife breeding centre, dedicated to the practical conservation of endangered species including gibbons, marmosets, lemurs, wildcats, meerkats, sloths and many more. There is also a large and varied bird collection, with several species unique to Hamerton. Over 120 species in all. Other attractions include a children's play area, and new "creature contact" sessions.
Times: Open Summer daily 10.30-6; winter daily 10.30-4. (Closed 25 Dec) **Fee:** ✱ £6 (pen £5 & ch 3-12 £4). **Facilities:** 🅿 ▆ ⅔ toilets for disabled shop 🐕 🗨

LINTON — Map 05 TL54

CHILFORD HALL VINEYARD

Chilford Hall, Balsham Rd CB1 6LE

➲ (signposted from A1307 and A11)

☎ 01223 892641   🖂 01223 894056

e-mail: simonalper@chilfordhall.co.uk

Taste and buy award-winning wines from the largest vineyard in Cambridgeshire. See the grapes growing in the 18-acre vineyard and take a winery tour to learn how English wine is made and appreciate the subtle difference between each of the Chilford quality wines. Telephone for details of special events.

Times: Open Mar-23 Dec. **Facilities:** 🅿 ♿ & toilets for disabled shop ◄

LINTON ZOOLOGICAL GARDENS

Hadstock Rd CB1 6NT

➲ (M11 at junct 9/10, on B1052 off A1307, signposted)

☎ 01223 891308   🖂 01223 891308

Linton Zoo places emphasis on conservation and education where visitors can see a combination of beautiful gardens and a wealth of wildlife from all over the world. There are many rare and exotic creatures to see including tapirs, snow leopards, tigers, lions, Grevy's zebra, tamarin monkeys, owls, parrots, giant tortoises, snakes, tarantula spiders and many others. New arrivals include Parma wallabies and several species of rare lemur. The zoo is set in 16-acres of gardens with plenty of picnic areas, children's play area and bouncy castle.

Times: Open daily except 25-26 Dec. **Fee:** ✱ Please contact for admission prices. **Facilities:** 🅿 ♿ & toilets for disabled shop ✖ ◄

LODE — Map 05 TL56

ANGLESEY ABBEY

CB5 9EJ

➲ (6m NE of Cambridge on B1102, signposted from A14)

☎ 01223 810080   🖂 01223 810088

e-mail: angleseyabbey@ntrust.org.uk

A medieval undercroft has survived from the priory founded here in 1135, but the house dates mainly from 1600. Thomas Hobson of *Hobson's Choice* was one of the owners. A later

continued

owner was Lord Fairhaven, who amassed the huge collection of pictures, and laid out the beautiful gardens.

Times: Open House & Mill: 24 Mar-7 Nov, Wed-Sun & BH Mon's, 1-5. Gardens open 10.30-5.30 and also open in winter 10 Nov-20 Mar, daily, 10.30-4.30, closed 24-28 Dec. **Fee:** House and garden £6.60. Garden only £4.10 (£3.40 in winter). Family & party discounts available.

Facilities: 🅿 ♿ ✖ licensed & (electric buggy, wheelchairs, large print & braille guides) toilets for disabled shop garden centre ✖ (ex guide dogs) ⚜ ◄

PETERBOROUGH — Map 04 TL19

FLAG FEN BRONZE AGE CENTRE

The Droveway, Northey Rd PE6 7QJ

☎ 01733 313414   🖂 01733 349957

e-mail: office@flagfen.freeserve.co.uk

Although visitors enter this site through a 21st-century roundhouse, the rest of their day will be spent in the Bronze Age, some 3,000 years ago. Flag Fen is one of Europe's most important Bronze Age sites, and contains reconstructions of Iron Age as well as Bronze Age roundhouses. There is also a museum of artefacts found on the site over the last 20 years, as well as a Preservation Hall that contains a 60ft mural depicting the fens in ancient times.

Times: Open daily 10-4 (last admission). Site closes 5pm. (Closed 24 Dec-2 Jan) **Fee:** ✱ £4 (pen £3.50, ch & students £3) **Facilities:** 🅿 ♿ & toilets for disabled shop ✖ (ex assistance dogs) ◄

LONGTHORPE TOWER

Thorpe Rd, Longthorpe PE1 1HA

☎ 01733 268482

See the finest domestic wall paintings in northern Europe hidden in the tower for centuries until revealed by a World War II bomb.

Times: Open Apr-Oct, Sat-Sun & BH only 12-5. Dates valid until 31 Mar 2004. **Fee:** £2 (ch £1, concessions £1.50). Prices valid until 31 Mar 2004. **Facilities:** 🅿 ✖ ▓

PETERBOROUGH CATHEDRAL

PE1 1XS

➲ (access from A1 juncts with A605 or A47, follow signs)

☎ 01733 343342   🖂 01733 552465

e-mail: a.watson@
peterborough-cathedral.org.uk

With one of the most dramatic West fronts in the country, its three arches an extraordinary creation of medieval architecture, it would be easy for the interior to be an anticlimax, but it is not. The dramatic Romanesque interior is little altered since its completion 800 years ago. Particular highlights of a visit include the unique painted nave ceiling, the elaborate fan vaulting of the 'new' building, Saxon carvings from an earlier church and the burial place of two Queens. An exhibition in the North aisle tells the story of the cathedral. A range of tours can be booked in advance: please contact the Chapter office for details.

Times: Open all year, daily 9-5. **Fee:** ✱ Free - donations towards the cost of upkeep are requested & there is a charge for tours.

Facilities: 🅿 (300yds) (no parking within cathedral precincts) ♿ ✖ licensed & (touch & hearing centre, braille guide, ramps) toilets for disabled shop ✖ (ex guide dogs or in grounds)

RAMSEY   Map 04 TL28

RAMSEY ABBEY GATEHOUSE
Abbey School PE17 1DH
➲ (SE edge of Ramsey, where Chatteris Road joins B1096)   FREE
☎ 0870 609 5388   📠 01263 734924
The ruins of this 15th-century gatehouse, together with the 13th-century Lady Chapel, are all that remain of the abbey. Half of the gatehouse was taken away after the Dissolution. Built in ornate late-Gothic style, it has panelled buttresses and friezes.
Times: Open Apr-Oct, daily 10-5. **Facilities:** 🅿 ♿

WANSFORD   Map 04 TL09

NENE VALLEY RAILWAY
Wansford Station, Stibbington PE8 6LR
➲ (A1 at Stibbington, W of Peterborough, 1m south of the A47 junct)
☎ 01780 784444   📠 01780 784440
e-mail: nvrorg@aol.com
Visit Britain's International Steam Railway and see steam and diesel engines, carriages and wagons from Europe including the UK. All the sights and sounds of the golden age of steam come alive here. Travelling between Yarwell Junction, Wansford and Peterborough the 7.5 miles of track pass through the heart of the 500-acre Ferry Meadows Country Park. Nene Valley Railway is also the home of 'Thomas'- children's favourite engine.
Times: Train services operate on Sun from Jan; wknds from Apr-Oct; Wed from May, plus other mid-week services in summer. **Fee:** ✱ £10 (ch 3-15 £5, concessions £7.50). Family ticket £25. **Facilities:** 🅿 🍴 ♿ (disabled access to trains) toilets for disabled shop 🛍

WATERBEACH   Map 05 TL46

THE FARMLAND MUSEUM AND DENNY ABBEY
Ely Rd CB5 9PQ
➲ (on A10 between Cambridge and Ely)
☎ 01223 860988   📠 01223 860988   2 for 1
e-mail: f.m.denny@tesco.net
Explore two areas of rural life at this fascinating museum. The Abbey tells the story of those who have lived there, including Benedictine monks, Franciscan nuns, and the mysterious Knights Templar. The farm museum features the craft workshops of a wheelwright, a basketmaker, and a blacksmith. There are also a 1940s farmworker's cottage and a village shop.
Times: Open Apr-Oct **Fee:** ✱ £3.70 (concessions £2.80, ch £1.50)
Facilities: 🅿 🍴 ♿ toilets for disabled shop 🛍 (ex on lead in grounds)

WIMPOLE   Map 05 TL35

WIMPOLE HALL
SG8 0BW
➲ (M11 junct 12, 8 m SW of Cambridge off A603)
☎ 01223 207257   📠 01223 207838
e-mail: aweusr@smtp.ntrust.org.uk
Wimpole Hall is one of the grandest mansions in East Anglia, and has 360 acres of parkland devised and planted by no less than four celebrated landscape designers, Charles

continued

Bridgeman, `Capability' Brown, Sanderson Miller and Humphrey Repton. The house dates back to 1640, but was altered into a large 18th-century mansion with a Georgian façade. The chapel has a trompe l'oeil ceiling.
Times: ✱ Open 23 Mar-Jul & Sep-3 Nov, Tue-Thu & Sat-Sun, BH Mon's & Good Fri, 1-5; Aug Tue-Sun, BH Mon's 1-5; Nov, Sun only 1-5. Closes 4pm after 27 Oct. **Facilities:** 🅿 🍴 ✗ licensed ♿ (braille guide, battery vehicle, stairlift, wheelchairs) toilets for disabled shop 🛍 (ex park only) ♿ 🛍

WIMPOLE HOME FARM
SG8 0BW
➲ (M11 junct 12 8m SW of Cambridge off A603)
☎ 01223 208987   📠 01223 207838
e-mail: aweusr@smtp.ntrust.org.uk
When built in 1794, the Home Farm was one of the most advanced agricultural enterprises in the country. The Great Barn, now restored, holds a display of farm machinery and implements of the kind used at Wimpole over the past two centuries. On the farm there are rare breeds of domestic animals. Please ring for details of special events.
Times: ✱ Open 23 Mar-Jun & Sep-3 Nov, Tue-Thu & Sat-Sun, Good Fri & BH Mons 10.30-5; Jul & Aug, Tue-Sun 10.30-5; Nov-Mar, Sat & Sun 11-4. **Facilities:** 🅿 🍴 ✗ licensed ♿ (braille guide, wheelchairs, electric buggies) toilets for disabled shop 🛍 (ex guide dogs) ♿ 🛍

WISBECH   Map 09 TF40

PECKOVER HOUSE & GARDEN

North Brink PE13 1JR

➲ (Leave A47 & take town centre signs, then follow brown signs)

☎ 01945 583463   ▤ 01945 583463

e-mail: peckover@nationaltrust.org.uk

Dating from 1722, Peckover House is a beautiful Georgian brick townhouse with a two-acre walled town garden, one of the finest such gardens in Britain and home to over 70 types of rose. The Victorian glasshouses include a fern house, and an orangery with 300-year-old trees that still bear fruit.

Times: Open, House, Garden & Tearoom Apr-Oct, wknds, Wed & BH Mons 12.30-5 (house also open Thu May-Aug). Garden open Apr-Oct, Mon-Tue & Thu 12.30-5. **Fee:** ✻ House & garden £4 (ch £1.50). Garden £2.50 on days when only garden is open. **Facilities:** Ⓟ (400yds) blue badge holders park directly outside ▆▇ ✕ licensed ㊖ (Batricar available on loan, Large print and braille guides) toilets for disabled shop ✖ (ex guide dogs) ⛄ ◣

Special Events are held at many attractions throughout the country. As we cannot hope to list them all, please ring the places of interest for details of exhibitions, themed days, and guided walks.

CHESHIRE

EVENTS & FESTIVALS

March
13th North of England Head of the River Race, Chester

April
25th The Cheshire Run, Historic Vehicle Road Run, Lymm

May
1st Knutsford Royal May Day
19th-22nd Alderley Edge Music Festival, Festival Theatre & various venues
28th-31st Chester Folk Festival, Kelsall
tbc Chester Races May Festival, Chester Racecourse
tbc Roman Day at Chester Racecourse

June
18th-20th Folk & Boat Festival, Middlewich
22nd-23rd Cheshire County Show, The Showground, Tabley, nr Knutsford
tbc World Worm Charming Championship, Willaston Primary School, Willaston

July
10th-24th Summer Music Festival, Chester (provisional)
17th-1st Aug Fringe Festival (drama, dance & music), various venues, Chester
21st-25th Royal Horticultural Society Flower Show, Tatton Park, Knutsford
tbc Chester Horse Show, Chester Racecourse

August
22nd Family Fun Day, West Park, Macclesfield
28th Poynton Show
tbc Chester Regatta (oldest regatta in the country)

September
11th-12th Yesteryear Steam Rally, Malpas
25th-26th Vintage Fair Organ & Steam Rally, Victoria Park, Widnes

October
2nd-24th Chester Literature Festival

November
13th-28th Festival of Trees, Chester
tbc Fireworks at Chester Racecourse

Above: The orangery at Lyme Park

BEESTON

Map 07 SJ55

BEESTON CASTLE
Tarporley CW6 9TX
➲ (on minor road off A49 or A41)
☎ 01829 260464

Legend tells of a vast treasure hidden here by Richard II, but the real treasure at Beeston lies in its 4,000 years of history waiting to be discovered. Breathtaking views extend from the Pennines to the mountains of Wales.
Times: Open all year, Apr-Sep, daily 10-6 (Oct, daily 10-5); Nov-Mar, daily 10-4. (Closed 24-26 Dec & 1 Jan). Dates valid until 31 Mar 2004. **Fee:** £3.20 (ch £1.60, concessions £2.40). Prices valid until 31 Mar 2004. **Facilities:** 🅿 shop ✖ (in certain areas) ♯

CAPESTHORNE

Map 07 SJ87

CAPESTHORNE HALL
SK11 9JY
➲ (On A34 between Congleton and Wilmslow)
☎ 01625 861221 🖬 01625 861619
e-mail: info@capesthorne.com

Capesthorne has been the home of the Bromley-Davenport family and their ancestors since Domesday times. The present house dates from 1719 and was designed by the Smiths of Warwick. It was subsequently altered by Edward Blore in 1837 and after a disastrous fire in 1861 the whole of the centre portion was rebuilt by Anthony Salvin. Capesthorne contains a great variety of sculptures, paintings and other items including a collection of American Colonial furnishings.
Times: Open Apr-Oct, Wed-Sun & BH's (Closed Xmas & New Year) Park & Garden 12-5.30, Hall 1.30-3.30. **Fee:** ✷ Park, Garden & Chapel £4 (ch £2). Park, Gardens, Chapel & Hall £6.50 (ch £3 & pen £5.50). Family ticket £12. Special deal on Wed's £10 per car (up to 4 persons) £50 per coach. **Facilities:** 🅿 🍽 ✖ 㐂 (ramp access to ground floor of hall & gardens) toilets for disabled ✖ (ex guide dogs & in gardens)

CHESTER

Map 07 SJ46

CHESHIRE MILITARY MUSEUM
The Castle CH1 2DN
➲ (follow signs to Military Museum from town centre)
☎ 01244 327617 🖬 01244 401700   `2 for 1`

This military museum boasts exhibits from the history of the Cheshire Regiment, Cheshire Yeomanry, 5th Royal Inniskilling Dragoon Guards, and 3rd Carabiniers. Display of the work of George Jones, Victorian battle artist, and an exhibition of life in barracks in the 1950s. Research available by written appointment and donation. There are special events throughout the year, please phone for details.
Times: Open all year, daily 10-5 (last entry 4.30pm). (Closed 22 Dec-2 Jan). **Fee:** £2 (concessions £1). **Facilities:** 🅿 (400yds) 㐂 shop ✖ (ex guide dogs)

CHESTER CATHEDRAL
Saint Werburgh St CH1 2HU
➲ (opposite the town hall)
☎ 01244 324756 🖬 01244 341110
e-mail: office@chestercathedral.org.uk

Founded as a Benedictine monastery in 1092 on the sites of earlier churches, in 1541 it became the cathedral of the

continued

newly created Diocese of Chester and is a good example of a medieval monastic complex. Restored in the 19th century, the building contains work by Gilbert Scott, Clayton, Pugin and Kempe. There are daily services and visitors are welcome to join in. A summer music festival is held in July.
Times: Open daily 8-6 (subject to alteration). **Fee:** ✷ Donation of £3 per person requested. **Facilities:** 🅿 (200yds) (multi-storey) 🍽 ✖ licensed 㐂 (induction loop, tactile model) toilets for disabled shop ✖ (ex guide dogs)

CHESTER VISITOR CENTRE
Vicars Ln CH1 1QX
➲ (opposite Roman Amphitheatre)
☎ 01244 402111 🖬 01244 403188
e-mail: tis@chestercc.gov.uk

Among the attractions at this large visitor information centre are guided walks of Chester, brass rubbing, candle-making, World of Names which explores the history of family and first names, displays on the history of Chester, a cafe and a gift shop.
Times: ✷ Open all year Apr-Sep, Mon-Sat 9-5.30, Sun & BHs 10-4; Oct-Mar, Mon-Sat 10-5, Sun 10-4. **Facilities:** 🅿 (200yds) (short stay visitor parking) 🍽 㐂 (ramped access from Vicars Lane) toilets for disabled shop 🍷

CHESTER ZOO
Upton-by-Chester CH2 1LH
➲ (2m N of city centre off A41 & M53 Junct 10 southbound, Junct 12 all other directions)
☎ 01244 380280 🖬 01244 371273
e-mail: markcting@chesterzoo.co.uk

The largest zoological gardens in the UK, with more than 5,000 animals of more than 500 species. There are large outdoor islands for chimps, orang-utans and monkeys, penguin pool, and birds of prey. The Bat Cave is the largest enclosure in the world for endangered bat species. Features include the Spirit of the Jaguar, Dragons in Danger, Marmot Mania, Tsavo Rhino experience & Red Pandas, a huge extension to the National Elephant Centre, and the children's Fun Ark.
Times: Open all year, daily from 10. Last admission varies with season from 5.30pm high summer to 3.30pm winter. (Closed 25 Dec). **Fee:** ✷ £11 (ch 3-15 & pen £9). Family ticket (2 adult & 2 ch) £37.
Facilities: 🅿 🍽 ✖ licensed 㐂 (electric scooters, audio guide, induction loop, braille) toilets for disabled shop ✖ (ex guide & sensory dogs) 🍷

DEVA ROMAN EXPERIENCE
Pierpoint Ln, (off Bridge St) CH1 1NL
➥ (city centre)
☎ 01244 343407   📠 01244 347737

Stroll along reconstructed streets experiencing the sights, sounds and smells of Roman Chester. From the streets of Deva (the Roman name for Chester) you return to the present day on an extensive archeological 'dig', where you can discover the substantial Roman, Saxon and medieval remains beneath modern Chester.
Times: Open daily Feb-Nov 9-5, Dec-Jan 10-4 . (Closed 25-26 Dec).
Fee: £4.25 (ch £2.50, under 5's free, pen £3.75, student £3.75). Family ticket £12. Party. **Facilities:** 🅿 (200yds) & shop ✖ (ex guide dogs)

CHOLMONDELEY   Map 07 SJ55
CHOLMONDELEY CASTLE GARDENS
SY14 8AH
➥ (off A49 Tarporley to Whitchurch road)
☎ 01829 720383   📠 01829 720877
e-mail: pennypritchard@supanet.com

Dominated by a romantic Gothic Castle built in 1801 of local sandstone, the gardens are laid out with fine trees and water gardens, and have been replanted with rhododendrons, azaleas, cornus, and acer. There is also a rose and lavender garden, lakeside and woodland walks, and rare breeds of farm animals.
Times: Open Apr-Sep, Wed-Thu, Sun & BH's 11.30-5. **Fee:** ✱ £3.50 (ch £1.50). **Facilities:** 🅿 💻 & (disabled car park, part of garden accessible) toilets for disabled shop garden centre

DISLEY   Map 07 SJ98
LYME PARK
SK12 2NX
➥ (off A6, 6.5m SE of Stockport)
☎ 01663 762023   📠 01663 765035
e-mail: lymepark@nationaltrust.org.uk

Home of the Legh family for 600 years and the largest house in Cheshire, Lyme Park featured as Pemberley in the BBC's production of *Pride and Prejudice*. It also featured in Granada's production of the *Forsyte Saga*. Parts of the original Elizabethan house remain, with 18th and 19th
continued

century additions. Set in extensive historic gardens with a lake and also a 1,400 acre park, home to red and fallow deer.
Times: Open Park: Apr-Oct, daily 8-8.30; Nov-Mar, daily 8-6. Gardens: 29 Mar-Oct, Fri-Tue 11-5, Wed-Thu 1-5; Nov-18 Dec, wknds 12-3. House: 29 Mar-Oct, Fri-Tue 1-5 (last admission 4.30), BH Mon's 11-5. Cage: Apr-Oct, 2nd & 4th wknd of each month 12-4. Paddock Cottage Apr-Oct, 1st & 3rd wknd of each month, 12-4. **Fee:** ✱ Park £3.50 per car (refundable on purchase of house & garden ticket). Garden £2.50 (ch £1.25), House only £4 (ch £2), House and Garden £5.50 (ch £2.75). Family ticket £12. NT members free, ch under 5 free.
Facilities: 🅿 (charged) 💻 ✖ licensed & (close parking for house & garden) toilets for disabled shop ✖ (ex park on lead) 🍴 🍽

ELLESMERE PORT   Map 07 SJ47
BLUE PLANET AQUARIUM
Cheshire Oaks CH65 9LF
➥ (off M53 junct 10 at Cheshire Oaks. Follow signs for aquarium).
☎ 0151 357 8804   📠 0151 356 7288
e-mail: info@blueplanetaquarium.co.uk

A voyage of discovery on the longest moving walkway in the world. Beneath the waters of the Carribean Reef, see giant rays and menacing sharks pass inches from your face and stroke some favourite fish in the special rock pools or pay a visit to the incredible world of poisonous frogs. Divers hand feed the fish and sharks throughout the day and they can answer questions via state of the art communication systems.
Times: Open all year, daily from 10. (Closed Xmas). Seasonal variations in closing times, please call to confirm. **Fee:** ✱ £8.50 (ch (3-15) £6, under 3's free, concessions £6.60). Family ticket from £27.50.
Facilities: 🅿 ✖ licensed & (wheelchair hire, lifts) toilets for disabled shop ✖ (ex guide dogs) 🍽

BOAT MUSEUM
South Pier Rd CH65 4FW
➥ (M53 junct 9)
☎ 0151 355 5017   📠 0151 355 4079
e-mail: bookings@boatmuseum.freeserve.co.uk

Occupying a historic dock complex at the junction of the Shropshire Union and Manchester Ship Canals, this museum has the world's largest collection of floating canal craft, from a small weedcutter to a 300-ton coaster. Boat trips are also available. There are indoor exhibitions on canal life and local history, together with period worker's cottages, a blacksmith's forge and working engines.
Times: Open Summer daily 10-5. Winter daily (ex Thu & Fri) 11-4. (Closed 25 & 26 Dec). **Facilities:** 🅿 💻 & (tactile map for blind, wheelchair) toilets for disabled shop 🍽

GAWSWORTH   Map 07 SJ86
GAWSWORTH HALL
SK11 9RN
➥ (2.5m S of Macclesfield on A536)
☎ 01260 223456   📠 01260 223469
e-mail: gawsworth@lineone.net

This fine Tudor black-and-white manor house was the birthplace of Mary Fitton, thought by some to be the `Dark Lady' of Shakespeare's sonnets. Pictures and armour can be seen in the house, which also has a tilting ground - now
continued

thought to be a rare example of an Elizabethan pleasure garden.

Times: Open daily, Etr-Sep. Flower Festival in Dec **Fee:** ✱ £4.50 (ch £2.25). Party 20+ £3.50 each. **Facilities:** 🅿 💷 ⚐ (disabled parking in front of house) toilets for disabled shop ✖ (guide dogs in garden only) ⬛

JODRELL BANK Map 07 SJ77
VISITOR CENTRE & ARBORETUM

JODRELL BANK VISITOR CENTRE & ARBORETUM
SK11 9DL
➲ (M6 junct 18, A535 Holmes Chapel to Chelford road)
☎ 01477 571339 🖹 01477 571695
e-mail: visitorcentre@jb.man.ac.uk

At Jodrell Bank, a scientific and engineering wonder awaits you – the magnificent Lovell telescope, one of the largest radio telescopes in the world. A pathway leads you 180° around the telescope as it towers above you surveying and exploring the Universe. Then, the visitor can wander along pathways amongst the trees of the extensive arboretum. The Centre is currently under a redevelopment which will take 2-3 years to complete. At present there is a small Visitor Centre with a 3D Show.
Times: Open Nov-Feb 10.30-3, wknds 11-4.30. Mar-Oct 10.30-5.30. **Fee:** £3.50 per car, £1 for 3D Show. **Facilities:** 🅿 (charged) 💷 ⚐ (wheelchair loan) toilets for disabled shop ✖ (ex guide dogs)

KNUTSFORD Map 07 SJ77

TABLEY HOUSE
WA16 0HB
➲ (leave M6 junct 19 onto A556 S towards Chester. Entrance for cars off A5033, 2m W of Knutsford)
☎ 01565 750151 🖹 01565 653230
e-mail: enquiries@tableyhouse.co.uk

This finest Palladian House in the North West, holds the first great collection of English pictures ever made, furniture by Chippendale, Gillow and Bullock, and fascinating Leicester family memorabilia. Friendly stewards are available to talk about the Leicester's 700 years at Tabley.
Times: Open Apr-end Oct, Thu-Sun & BI ls, 2-5 (last entry 4.30). **Fee:** ✱ £4 (ch & students £1.50). **Facilities:** 🅿 💷 ⚐ (phone administrator in advance for help) toilets for disabled shop ✖ (ex guide dogs)

TATTON PARK
WA16 6QN
➲ (5m from M6 junct 19, or M56 junct 7)
☎ 01625 534400 🖹 01625 534403

Tatton is one of England's most complete historic estates, with gardens and a 1000-acre country park. The centrepiece is the Georgian mansion, with gardens laid out by Humphry Repton and Sir Joseph Paxton. More recently, a Japanese

continued

garden with a Shinto temple was created. The Tudor Old Hall is the original manor house, where a guided tour is available.

Times: Open 29 Mar-28 Sep, daily except Mon; Oct, Sat & Sun, opening times vary telephone to check. Gardens all year daily except Mon. Park Apr-Oct daily; 29 Sep-26 Mar, daily except Mon. **Facilities:** 🅿 (charged) 💷 ⚐ (old hall & areas of farm not accessible, braille guides) toilets for disabled shop garden centre ✖ (ex in parkland) 🐾 ⬛

MACCLESFIELD Map 07 SJ97

HARE HILL
SK10 4QB
➲ (4m N off B5087, follow brown signs to Hare Hill)
☎ 01625 584412

The beautiful parkland at Hare Hill also features a pretty walled garden and pergola. There are woodland paths and ponds, and, in late spring, a brilliant display of rhododendrons and azaleas.
Times: Open Apr-Oct, Wed-Thu, Sat, Sun & BH Mons 10-5.30; May daily 10-5.30; (Closed Nov-Mar). **Fee:** ✱ £2.70 (ch £1.25). £1.50 per car (refundable on entry to garden). **Facilities:** 🅿 (charged) ⚐ (wheelchair available, braille guides) ✖ (ex guide dogs) 🐾

MACCLESFIELD SILK MUSEUM
Heritage Centre, Roe St SK11 6UT
➲ (Turn off A523 & follow brown signs. Museum in town centre)
☎ 01625 613210 🖹 01625 617880   `2 for 1`
e-mail: silkmuseum@tiscali.co.uk

The story of silk in Macclesfield, told through a colourful audio-visual programme, exhibitions, textiles, garments, models and room settings. The Silk Museum is part of the Heritage centre, a restored Georgian Sunday school, which runs a full programme of musical and artistic events throughout the year. The museum opened in 2002 and has a changing temporary exhibition programme.
Times: Open all year, Mon-Sat 11-5, Sun & BH Mon 1-5. (Closed 25-26 Dec & 1 Jan). Please ring for winter opening times. **Fee:** ✱ £2.90 (concessions £2). Family ticket £7.75 Joint ticket with Paradise Mill £5.10 (concessions £2.90). Family ticket £11.15. **Facilities:** 🅿 (50mtrs) 💷 ✗ licensed ⚐ (ramps, chairlift, audio guides) toilets for disabled shop ✖ (ex guide dogs) ⬛

PARADISE MILL

Park Ln SK11 6TJ

➩ (turn off A523 'The Silk Rd' & follow brown signs)

☎ 01625 613210 ▤ 01625 617880

A working silk mill until 1981, with restored jacquard hand looms in their original location. Knowledgeable guides, many of them former silk mill workers, illustrate the silk production process with the help of demonstrations from weavers. Exhibitions and room settings give an impression of working conditions at the mill during the 1930s.
(2-for-1 Voucher applies to museum tour only.)
Times: Open all year, BH Mon & Mon-Sat from 11am. (Closed 25-26 Dec & 1 Jan). Ring for winter opening **Fee:** ✱ Telephone for details. **Facilities:** ℙ (100 yds) ♿ (care needed on uneven floors) ✖ (ex guide dogs) ☜

MOULDSWORTH   Map 07 SJ57

MOULDSWORTH MOTOR MUSEUM

Smithy Ln CH3 8AR

➩ (6m E of Chester, off B5393, close to Delamere Forest & Oulton Park Racing Circuit, signposted. Or M56 junct 12 into Frodsham then B5393 into Mouldsworth, follow brown heritage signs in village)

☎ 01928 731781

Housed in an 1937 large Art Deco building close to Delamere Forest, this is a superb collection of over 60 motor cars, motorcycles and bicycles. There is also a massive collection of automobilia - old signs, pumps, tools, mascots and badges, as well as old motoring toys, Dinky cars and pedal cars all complemented by a motoring art gallery, that has posters and advertising material. School parties are encouraged for a guided tour and structured talk. Motoring clubs visit on Sundays. There is also a Harry Potter car for children to sit in.
Times: Open Feb-Nov (Sun only), Etr wknd, early May BH Mon, Spring BH Sun-Mon & Aug BH wknd; Sun, Feb-Nov; also Wed, Jul-Aug, noon-5. **Fee:** ✱ £3 (ch £1.50, pen - reduction Wed only Jul-Aug £2.50) **Facilities:** ℙ ♿ (hands on items) shop

NANTWICH   Map 07 SJ65

STAPELEY WATER GARDENS

London Rd, Stapeley CW5 7LH

➩ (off M6 junct 16, 1m S of Nantwich on A51)

☎ 01270 623868 & 628628

▤ 01270 624919

e-mail: stapeleywg@btinternet.com

Stapeley Water Gardens consists of three main areas. The Palms Tropical Oasis is a glass pavilion which is home to Koi carp, Giant Amazon water-lilies, sharks, piranhas, parrots and exotic flowers. The two-acre Water Garden Centre houses the National Collection of water-lilies.
Times: Open Summer: Mon-Sat 9-6, BHs 10-6, Sun 10-4, Wed 9-8; Winter: Mon-Sat 9-5, BHs 10-5, Sun 10-4, (Wed 10-7 Angling dept only). The Palms Tropical Oasis open from 10am. **Fee:** ✱ The Palms Tropical Oasis £4.35 (ch £2.50, pen £3.90). Family ticket (2 ad & 2 ch) £11.65 (2 ad & 3 ch) £13.80. **Facilities:** ℙ ⬛ ✖ licensed ♿ (free wheelchair loan service) toilets for disabled shop garden centre ✖ (ex guide dogs) ☜

NESTON   Map 07 SJ27

LIVERPOOL UNIVERSITY BOTANIC GARDENS (NESS GARDENS)

Ness Gardens CH64 4AY

➩ (off A540 near Ness-on-Wirral, follow signs)

☎ 0151 353 0123 ▤ 0151 353 1004

e-mail: ejs@liv.ac.uk

A long association with plant collectors ensures a wide range of plants, providing interest for academics, horticulturists and amateurs alike. There are tree and shrub collections, water and rock gardens, herbaceous borders and glasshouses. A regular programme of lectures, courses and special events take place throughout the year for which tickets must be obtained in advance.
Times: Open all year, Nov-Feb, daily 9.30-4; Mar-Oct, daily 9.30-5. (Closed 25 Dec). **Facilities:** ℙ ⬛ ✖ licensed ♿ (wheelchair route, induction loop in lecture theatre) toilets for disabled shop garden centre ✖ (ex guide dogs) ☜

NETHER ALDERLEY   Map 07 SJ87

NETHER ALDERLEY MILL

Congleton Rd SK10 4TW

➩ (1.5m S of Alderley Edge on E side of A34)

☎ 01625 584412 ▤ 01625 587555

Built in the 15th century, this water-mill is much larger inside than it looks. Inside there are tandem overshot water-wheels, original Elizabethan timber work, and Victorian machinery which was restored to full working order in the 1960s after being derelict for 30 years. Wheat is ground occasionally for demonstration purposes, water permitting.
Times: Open Apr-Oct, Wed-Fri, Sun & BH Mon 1-4.30. Parties by arrangement. **Fee:** ✱ £2.20 (ch £1.10) **Facilities:** ℙ ✖ ♨

NORTHWICH   Map 07 SJ67

ARLEY HALL & GARDENS

CW9 6NA

➩ (5m N of Northwich on B5075. 5m NW of Knutsford A556)

☎ 01565 777353 & 777284 ▤ 01565 777465

e-mail: enquiries@arleyestate.zuunet.co.uk

Owned by the same family since medieval times, the present Arley Hall is a good example of the early Victorian Jacobean style and contains fine furniture, plasterwork, panelling and family portraits. The gardens include a walled garden, unique clipped ilex avenue, herb garden, scented garden and a woodland garden with rhododendrons, azaleas and exotic trees. Special events throughout 2004, please phone for details.
Times: Open Etr-end Sep & wknds in Oct.. **Fee:** ✱ Gardens, Grounds & Chapel £4.40 (ch 6-16 £2.20, pen £3.80) Family ticket £11 Hall £2.50 (ch 6-16 £1.60,pen £2). Party 15+. **Facilities:** ℙ ⬛ ✖ licensed ♿ (ramps, parking by entrance) toilets for disabled shop garden centre ✖ (ex in gardens on lead) ☜

SALT MUSEUM
162 London Rd CW9 8AB
➲ (on A533 0.5m S of town centre and 0.5m N of
A556. Well signposted from A556) `2 for 1`
☎ 01606 41331 🖷 01606 350420
e-mail: cheshiremuseums@cheshire.gov.uk

Britain's only Salt Museum tells the fascinating story of
Cheshire's oldest industry. Models, reconstructions, original
artefacts and audio-visual programmes throw new light on
something we all take for granted.
Times: Open Tue-Fri 10-5, wknds 2-5 (Sun 12-5 in Aug). Open BH &
Mons in Aug 10-5. **Fee:** ✱ £2.25 (ch £1.15, concessions £1.95) Family
ticket (2 adults + 2 ch) £5.65. **Facilities:** 🅿 💺 ♿ (inductory video
with induction loop facilities) toilets for disabled shop garden centre ✖
(ex guide dogs) ⬛

RUNCORN   Map 07 SJ58

NORTON PRIORY MUSEUM & GARDENS
Tudor Rd, Manor Park WA7 1SX
➲ (from M56 junct 11 in direction of Warrington,
follow brown signs)
☎ 01928 569895 🖷 01928 589743 `2 for 1`
e-mail: info@nortonpriory.org

Thirty-eight acres of peaceful woodland gardens are the
setting for the medieval priory remains, museum and Walled
Garden. Displays tell the story of the transformation of the
priory into a Tudor manor house and then into an elegant
Georgian mansion. Please telephone for details of special
events.
Times: Open all year, Apr-Oct, Mon-Fri 12-5; Sat, Sun & BHs 12-6;
Nov-Mar daily 12-4. (Closed 24-26 Dec & 1 Jan). Walled Garden open
Apr-Oct, daily 1.30-4.30) **Fee:** ✱ £3.95 (ch 5-16, students, UB40's &
pen £2.75). Family ticket (2 adults & 3 ch) £10. **Facilities:** 🅿 💺 ♿
(wheelchairs, large print & audio guides, induction loop) toilets for
disabled shop garden centre (guide dogs only wall garden)

> The AA also publishes a guide to
> Pet Friendly Places to Stay

SCHOLAR GREEN   Map 07 SJ85

LITTLE MORETON HALL
Newcastle Rd CW12 4SD
➲ (Situated on the A34, 4m S of Congleton)
☎ 01260 272018

One of the best examples of half-timbered architecture in
England. By 1580 the house was much as it is today, and the
long gallery, chapel and the great hall are very impressive.
The garden has a knot garden, orchard and herbaceous
borders. Ring for details of special events.
Times: Open late Mar-early Nov, Wed-Sun 11.30-5 or dusk if earlier,
BH Mon 11.30-5; early Nov-late Dec, weekends 11.30-4. **Fee:** ✱ £4.75
(ch £2.35) Family ticket £11.50 **Facilities:** 🅿 ✖ licensed ♿
(wheelchair, electric vehicle, braille & large print guides) toilets for
disabled shop ✖ (ex guide & assistance dogs) ⬛ ⬛

STYAL   Map 07 SJ88

QUARRY BANK MILL & STYAL ESTATE
SK9 4LA
➲ (M56 junct 5, signposted)
☎ 01625 527468 🖷 01625 539267
e-mail: quarrybankmill@ntrust.org.uk

Quarry Bank Mill is a working water and steam powered
cotton mill. Spinning and weaving from the hand processes
through the industrial revolution are demonstrated every day
and items made from the cloth are sold in the shop. Quarry
Bank Mill and its colony village is set in the beautiful Styal
Estate beside the River Bollin. Lots of practical 'hands-on'
activities plus a new children's playground and railway. The
Apprentice House and its Victorian vegetable garden show
how life was for the mill apprentices.
Times: Mill open all year, Apr-Sep daily 10.30-5.30 (last admission 4);
Oct-Mar, daily 10.30-5 (closed Mon in term time). Last admission 3.30.
Apprentice House & Garden, Tue-Fri from 11 (2-4.30 term time),
Sat-Sun & Aug from 11. Closed Mon (ex school hols). **Fee:** ✱ Mill,
Apprentice House & Gardens £7 (ch £3.80). Family ticket £17. Mill only
£5 (ch £3.50). Family ticket £14.50. Estate fee £2.50. **Facilities:** 🅿
(charged) 💺 ✖ licensed ♿ (wheelchairs) toilets for disabled shop ✖
(ex in park) ⬛ ⬛

WIDNES   Map 07 SJ58

CATALYST SCIENCE DISCOVERY CENTRE
Mersey Rd WA8 0DF
➲ (signed from M62 junct 7 and M56 junct 12)
☎ 0151 420 1121 🖷 0151 495 2030 `2 for 1`
e-mail: info@catalyst.org.uk

Discover a world where science and technology come alive,
with over 100 interactive exhibits and hands-on displays
which guarantee a fun-filled day out for all the family. Take a
trip in an all-glass lift to the Observatory, 100 feet above the
River Mersey. A range of special events is planned
throughout the year. Please ring for details.
Times: Open all year, Tue-Fri daily & BH Mon 10-5, wknds 11-5.
(Closed Mon ex BH's, 24-26 Dec & 1 Jan). **Fee:** ✱ £4.95 (ch £3.50,
concessions £3.95). Family ticket £14.95. **Facilities:** 🅿 💺 ♿ toilets
for disabled shop ✖ (ex guide dogs) ⬛

CORNWALL & THE ISLES OF SCILLY

EVENTS & FESTIVALS

March
27th-28th Falmouth Spring Flower Show,
April
4th-11th St Endellion Easter Festival of Music,
St Endellion, Port Isaac
24th Trevithick Day, Camborne
May
30th Apr-1st May Day Festival, St Ives
1st Padstow 'Obby 'Oss celebrations, Padstow
2nd Giant Bolster Festival, St Agnes, lantern
procession with giant puppets & bonfire
15th-16th Re-enactment of the Battle of
Stamford Hill, Bude (provisional)
tbc Daphne du Maurier Festival of Arts &
Literature, Fowey
June
10th-12th Royal Cornwall Show, Wadebridge
12th-13th Murdoch Weekend, Redruth
17th-27th Golowan Festival, Penzance
July
12th Stithians Show, Truro
27th-6th Aug St Endellion Summer Festival
tbs RNAS Culdrose Air Day
August
6th-7th Falmouth Classics & Regatta Week
6th-9th Re-enactment of Arthurian Battle of
Camlann, Tintagel (provisional)
27th-30th Cornwall Folk Festival, Wadebridge
28th-4th Sep Bude Jazz Festival
30th Newlyn Fish Festival (provisional)
September
4th Cornish Gorsedd, venue to be confirmed
10th-26th St Ives Fringe Festival
tbc Lanlivery Vintage Rally & Country Fair
October
13th-18th Lowender Peran, Perranporth tbc
Falmouth Oyster Festival (provisional)
November
15th-20th Camborne Music Festival
(Centenary Methodist Church)
December
23rd Tom Bawcock's Eve, Mousehole tbc City
of Lights Lantern Parade, Truro

Above: The Bodmin & Wentford Railway

BODMIN   Map 02 SX06

MILITARY MUSEUM
The Keep PL31 1EG
➲ (on B3268 beside steam railway station)
☎ 01208 72810 🖹 01208 72810
e-mail: dclimus@talk21.com
The history of a famous County Regiment with fascinating displays of uniforms, weapons, medals, badges and much more.
Times: Open all year Mon-Fri, Sun during Jul & Aug 9-5. (Closed Etr & Xmas). **Fee:** £2.50 (ch 50p). Parties 10+ £2 each. **Facilities:** 🅿 ♿ shop

PENCARROW
Washaway PL30 3AG
➲ (4m NW of Bodmin, signposted off
A389 & B3266)
☎ 01208 841369 🖹 01208 841722
e-mail: pencarrow@aol.com
Still a family home, this Georgian house has a superb collection of pictures, furniture and porcelain. The 50 acres of formal and woodland gardens include a Victorian rockery, a lake, 700 different rhododendrons and an acclaimed conifer collection. There is also a craft centre and a children's play area.
Times: Open House: 28 Mar-28 Oct, Sun-Thu 11-5 (last house tour 4pm). Gardens open daily Mar-28 Oct. **Fee:** House & Garden £7 (ch £3.50). Gardens only £3.50 (ch free). Family ticket £20. Party 20+ £6 each (ch £3), Party 31+ £5 each. **Facilities:** 🅿 💷 ♿ (2 wheelchairs for use, disabled parking at house) toilets for disabled shop ✈ (ex in gardens)

CALSTOCK   Map 02 SX46

COTEHELE
St Dominick PL12 6TA
➲ (located between Tavistock and Callington. Turn off A390 at St. Anne's Chapel, signposted 2.5m S of junct)
☎ 01579 351346 & 352739 (info)
🖹 01579 351222
e-mail: cotehele@ntrust.org.uk
A 15th-century house that contains tapestries, embroideries, furniture and armour; and outside, a beautiful garden on different levels, including a formal Italian-style garden, medieval stewpond, dovecote, and an 18th-century tower with lovely views. There is a restored water mill in the valley below, and at the Victorian riverside quay an outstation of the National Maritime Museum.
Times: Open 22 Mar-2 Nov daily ex Fri (open Good Fri), 11-5 (11-4.30 Oct & Nov). Garden open all year, daily 10.30-dusk. **Fee:** ✱ House, Garden & Mill £6.60. Garden & Mill £3.80 (ch 1/2 price, under 5's & NT members free). Family ticket £16 for House, Garden and Mill, £9 for Garden and Mill only. Party £5.60 each. **Facilities:** 🅿 💷 ✗ licensed ♿ (garden limited access,braille guide,audio loop,wheelchairs) toilets for disabled shop garden centre ♨ 🍴

FREE

Attractions with this symbol do not charge for entry.

CAMELFORD — Map 02 SX18

BRITISH CYCLING MUSEUM
The Old Station PL32 9TZ
➲ (1m N of Camelford on B3266 at junct with B3314)
☎ 01840 212811 ▤ 01840 212811
This is the nation's foremost museum of cycling history from 1818 to the present day, with over 400 cycles; more than 1000 cycling medals, fobs and badges; an extensive library; displays of gas, candle, battery and oil lighting; and many ad posters and enamel signs.
Times: Open all year, Sun-Thu 10-5. **Fee:** ✱ £2.90 (ch 5-17 £1.50). **Facilities:** ▣ & shop ✖ (ex guide dogs)

CHYSAUSTER ANCIENT VILLAGE — Map 02 SW43

CHYSAUSTER ANCIENT VILLAGE
TR20 8XA
➲ (2.5m NW of Gulval, off B3311)
☎ 07831 757934
This unique Celtic settlement includes probably the oldest known 'Village Street' in the country. Explore the remains of 2,000-year-old stone houses.
Times: Open Apr-Sep, daily 10-6 (Oct, daily 10-5). Dates valid until 31 Mar 2004. **Fee:** £2 (ch £1, concessions £1.50). Prices valid until 31 Mar 2004. **Facilities:** ▣ ✖ ⌗

The AA also publishes a guide to Pet Friendly Places to Stay

DOBWALLS — Map 02 SX26

DOBWALLS FAMILY ADVENTURE PARK
PL14 6HD
➲ (turn off A38 in centre of Dobwalls and follow the brown signs for approx 0.5m) **2 for 1**
☎ 01579 320325 & 321129
e-mail: dobwallsadventurepark@hotmail.com
Plenty to do here, with stretches of miniature American railroads to ride - there are steam and diesel locos, and visitors can take the Rio Grande ride through the forests or the Union Pacific route over the prairies. Also Adventureland - action-packed areas filled with both indoor and outdoor adventure play equipment.
Times: Open 12 Apr-10 Sep, daily 10.30-5 (10-5.30 in high season); 11 Sep-29 Sep, Sat-Thu; 1-22 Oct, Sat-Wed; 23-29 Oct, daily. **Fee:** ✱ £7.95 (ch under 2 free, pen & disabled £5.50). Family tickets available from £15.50-£52.95. Groups 10+ £5.50 each. **Facilities:** ▣ ▣ & (manual wheelchairs available) toilets for disabled shop ⬎

FALMOUTH — Map 02 SW83

NATIONAL MARITIME MUSEUM CORNWALL
Discovery Quay TR11 3QY
➲ (follow signs from A39 for park/float ride and museum)
☎ 01326 313388 ▤ 01326 317878
e-mail: enquiries@nmmc.co.uk
This exciting award winning Museum has achieved wide national and international acclaim for its architecture, hands-on displays, world renowned boats and associated video footage, maritime heritage and interactive

continued

entertainment. The Tidal Zone, the only one in Europe and one of only three in the world, offers a unique 'fish-eye' view of life under the water and enables you to see aquatic visitors! The view from the 29 metre tower is breathtaking. Travel through galleries which explain meteorology, navigation, history, tides and more.

National Maritime Museum Cornwall

Times: Open daily 10-5 (Closed 25 & 26 Dec, 5-30 Jan for exhibition rotation). **Fee:** ✱ £5.90 (concessions £3.90). Family ticket (up to 3 children) £15.50. **Facilities:** 🅿 (charged) 💭 ✗ licensed ♿ (wheelchairs provided on arrival) toilets for disabled shop ✗ (ex guide dogs) 🐾

PENDENNIS CASTLE

TR11 4LP
➲ (1m SE)
☎ 01326 316594 ▤ 01326 319911

Together with St Mawes Castle, Pendennis forms the end of a chain of castles built by Henry VIII along the south coast as protection from attack from France. Journey through 450 years of history and discover the castle's wartime secrets. **Times:** Open all year, Apr-Sep, daily 10-6; Oct, daily 10-5; Nov-Mar, daily 10-4. (Closed 24-26 Dec & 1 Jan). Dates valid until 31 Mar 2004. **Fee:** £4.20 (ch £2.10, concessions £3.20). Prices valid until 31 Mar 2004. **Facilities:** 🅿 💭 ♿ shop ✗ (ex on lead in certain areas) ♯

FOWEY   Map 02 SX15

ST CATHERINE'S CASTLE
➲ (0.75m SW of Fowey along footpath   **FREE**
off A3082)

A small sixteenth century fort built by Henry VIII to defend Fowey Harbour. It has two storeys with gun ports at ground level.
Times: Open all year, any reasonable time. **Facilities:** 🅿 (0.5m) ✗ (ex dogs on leads) ♯

GODOLPHIN CROSS   Map 02 SW63

GODOLPHIN HOUSE
TR13 9RE
➲ (situated on a minor road from Godolphin Cross to Townsend)
☎ 01736 763194 ▤ 01736 763194   **2 for 1**
e-mail: godo@euphony.net

A romantic Tudor and Stuart mansion, begun in 1475 and considerably extended over the centuries. The Godolphin
continued

family's taste is evident throughout the mansion, and of particular note are examples of 16th and 17th-century English oak furniture and Wootton's 1731 painting, *Godolphin Arabian*, one of the three Arab stallion ancestors of all British bloodstock. The gardens are Tudor, with some areas even earlier. Major repair programme on the mansion funded by English Heritage.

Times: National Trust Estate open all year. House open May-Sep, Thu & Fri 11-5 & Sun 2-5 (also Tue 11-5 in Jul & Aug). Open BH Mon 11-5. Phone for Etr opening details. **Fee:** ✱ House & gardens £5 (ch 5-15yrs £1.50). Gardens only £2 (ch free) **Facilities:** 🅿 💭 ✗ ♿ (telephone prior to visit, lift to first floor) toilets for disabled shop garden centre ✗ (ex guide dogs) 🐾

GOONHAVERN   Map 02 SW75

WORLD IN MINIATURE
Bodmin Rd TR4 9QE
➲ (turn off A30 at Boxheater junct onto B3285)
☎ 0870 458 4433 ▤ 01872 572829
e-mail: info@worldinminiature.co.uk

There are six major attractions for the price of one at this theme park. Visitors can stroll amongst famous landmarks such as the Taj Mahal and the Statue of Liberty, all in miniature scale, set in spectacular gardens. Then there is Tombstone, a wild-west town complete with saloon, bank, shops, livery stable and jail. The Adventure Dome is the original super cinema 180 direct from the USA, which shows two exciting films. The 12-acre gardens are beautifully landscaped with over 70,000 plants and shrubs. See Jurassic Adventure World, Super X Simulator and children's fairground rides.
Times: Open Etr-Oct, daily from 10am. **Fee:** ✱ £6 (ch 4-14 & pen £4.50). Family ticket (2 ad & 2 ch) £19. **Facilities:** 🅿 💭 ♿ toilets for disabled shop garden centre 🐾

GORRAN   Map 02 SW94

CAERHAYS CASTLE GARDENS
PL26 6LY
➲ (off A390 onto B3287. Right at T-junct, left at next T-junct, next left and continue to Porthluney Beach car park)
☎ 01872 501144 & 501310 ▤ 01872 501870
e-mail: estateoffice@caerhays.co.uk

For centuries this magnolia filled garden was a deer park, and it was not until the late 19th century that John Charles
continued

Williams ("JCW") inherited Caerhays and not until the early 20th that new and exotic plants were introduced here. Now the gardens are a blaze of plants from Chile, China, New Zealand, the Himalayas, and many other distant lands. Magnolias, Rhododendrons, Camellia, and japonicas can all be seen on marked walks, and the house can be visited in small groups during the spring.
Times: Open 10 Mar-May, daily 10-5.30 (last admission 4.30). House open mid Mar-Apr, telephone for details. **Fee:** ✱ £4.50 **Facilities:** 🅿 ▣ ♿ toilets for disabled ✖ (ex in garden on leads) 🍽

GWEEK   Map 02 SW72
NATIONAL SEAL SANCTUARY
TR12 6UG
➲ (pass RNAS Culdrose & take A3293 & then B3291 to Gweek, the sanctuary is signposted from village) 2 for 1
☎ 01326 221361 & 221874 🖷 01326 221210
e-mail: slcgweek@merlin-entertainments.com
Britain's largest seal rescue facility - offering a unique opportunity to learn more about these beautiful creatures. Every year it rescues, rehabilitates and releases around 30 sick or abandoned seal pups.
Times: Open all year, daily from 10am (Closed 25 Dec). **Fee:** ✱ Please call for admission prices. **Facilities:** 🅿 ▣ ♿ toilets for disabled shop 🍽

HELSTON   Map 02 SW62
FLAMBARDS VILLAGE THEME PARK
Culdrose Manor TR13 0QA
➲ (0.5m SE of Helston on A3083, Lizard road)
☎ 01326 573404 🖷 01326 573344
e-mail: info@flambards.co.uk

Three award-winning, all-weather attractions can be visited on one site here. Flambards Victorian Village is a recreation of streets, shops and houses from 1830-1910. Britain in the Blitz is a life-size wartime street featuring shops, a pub and a living room with Morrison shelter. The Science Centre is a science playground for the whole family including the new Beams of Dreams attraction. There are many rides from the gentle to the daring, including the Thunderbolt, Hornet Rollercoaster, Flambards Family Log Flume, Go Kart Circuit, Balloon Race and play areas for the very young. Creepy
continued

Crawley Show with birds, lizards snakes and giant spiders. Award-winning gardens and live entertainment.
Times: Open Etr-Oct 10.30-5. End Jul-Aug 10-6. (Closed some Mon/Fri in Oct) **Fee:** ✱ £12.25 (ch 5-14 £9.25 pen £5.95). Family of 4 £39, family of 5 £45.75 family of 6 £51. **Facilities:** 🅿 ▣ ♿ (95% accessible, free loan of wheelchairs, route guides) toilets for disabled shop garden centre ✖ (ex guide dogs) 🍽

TREVARNO ESTATE GARDEN & MUSEUM OF GARDENING
Trevarno Manor, Crowntown TR13 0RU
➲ (E of Crowntown. Leave Helston on the Penzance road signed B3302)
☎ 01326 574274 🖷 01326 574282
e-mail: enquiry@trevarnoestate.fsnet.co.uk
Victorian and Georgian gardens with the splendid fountain garden conservatory, unique range of crafts and the National Museum of Gardening. In the tranquil gardens and grounds, follow the progress of restoration projects, visit craft areas including handmade soap workshop, explore Britain's largest and most comprehensive collection of antique tools, implements, memorabilia and ephemera, creatively displayed to illustrate how gardens and gardening influences most peoples lives.
Times: Open daily 10.30-5 **Fee:** ✱ £4.75 (ch 5-14 £1.75, pen £4.20, disabled £2.50). Group 12+ **Facilities:** 🅿 ▣ ♿ limited access, parking, disabled route toilets for disabled shop 🍽

LANHYDROCK   Map 02 SX06
LANHYDROCK
PL30 5AD
➲ (2.5m SE of Bodmin, signposted from A30, A38 & B3268)
☎ 01208 265950 🖷 01208 265959
e-mail: lanhydrock@nationaltrust.org.uk
Part-Tudor, part-Victorian building that gives a vivid picture of life in Victorian times. The 'below stairs' sections have a huge kitchen, larders, dairy, bakehouse, cellars, and servants' quarters. The long gallery has a moulded ceiling showing Old Testament scenes, and overlooks the formal gardens with their clipped yews and bronze urns. The higher garden, famed for its magnolias and rhododendrons, climbs the hillside behind the house.
Times: Open Apr-Oct: House daily (ex Mon), but open BH Mon 11-5.30 (11-5 in Oct). Gardens daily from mid Feb, last admission half hour before closing. Winter: Gardens, Nov-Feb during daylight hours. **Fee:** ✱ House & Grounds £7.20 (ch £3.60). Grounds £3.90 (ch £1.95). Family ticket £18. Party £6.10 each. **Facilities:** 🅿 ▣ ✖ licensed ♿ (lift, self drive buggy (pre-book), wheelchairs) toilets for disabled shop garden centre ✖ (ex on lead in park) 🐾 🍽

LANREATH   Map 02 SX15
LANREATH FARM & FOLK MUSEUM
Churchtown PL13 2NX
➲ (A390 from Liskeard, then B3359 for Looe/Polperro, signposted)
☎ 01503 220321
A hands-on Countryside Museum reflecting bygone times in Cornwall. Implements and equipment from the farmhouse, dairy and farmyard are displayed, together with mill workings rescued from a derelict mill house. Demonstrations
continued

of local crafts are given on weekday afternoons from 2-4pm.
Play phones, pets, and models to operate make it a fun place
as well as educational.
Times: Open Etr-May & Oct, daily 11-5; Jun-Sep, daily 10-6. **Fee:** £2.50
(ch £1.50, under 5 free). Party. **Facilities:** 🅿 & shop

LAUNCESTON   Map 02 SX38

LAUNCESTON CASTLE
Castle Lodge PL15 7DR
☎ 01566 772365

Commanding the town and surrounding countryside, this
castle controlled the route onto Cornwall.
Times: Open all year, Apr-Sep, daily 10-6; Oct, daily 10-5; Nov-Mar,
Fri-Sun 10-4. (Closed between 1-2 daily, 24-26 Dec & 1 Jan). Dates
valid until 31 Mar 2004. **Fee:** £2.10 (ch £1.10, concessions £1.60). Prices
valid until 31 Mar 2004. **Facilities:** & (outer bailey only) shop ✕ ▥

LAUNCESTON STEAM RAILWAY   2 for 1
St Thomas Rd PL15 8DA
➲ (turn off A30 Launceston, well signposted)
☎ 01566 775665

The Launceston Steam Railway links the historic town of
Launceston with the hamlet of New Mills. Tickets are valid
for unlimited travel on the day of issue and you can break
your journey at various points along the track. Launceston
Station houses railway workshops, a transport museum, gift
shop and book shop.
Times: Open Good Fri 8 days inclusive; Spring, BH Sun for 6 days; Jun,
Sun-Wed; Jul-Sep, daily ex Sat; Oct half-term week. **Fee:** ✱ £5.50 (ch
£3.80, pen £5). Family ticket £18. Dogs 50p. **Facilities:** 🅿 ▂ & shop

THE TAMAR OTTER SANCTUARY
North Petherwin PL15 8GW
➲ (5m NW off B3254 Bude road)
☎ 01566 785646 ▤ 01986 892461

The Tamar Otter Sanctuary has a breeding programme for
the British otter and has to date bred and released over 100
otters into the wild. Visitors to the sanctuary can see otters
in large natural enclosures, as well as fallow and muntjac
deer, waterfowl, and wallabies.
Times: Open Apr-Oct, daily 10.30-6 **Fee:** ✱ £5 (ch £3) **Facilities:** 🅿
▂ & shop ✕ (ex guide dogs)

LOOE   Map 02 SX25

MONKEY SANCTUARY
St Martins PL13 1NZ
➲ (signposted on B3253 at No Man's Land
between East Looe & Hessenford)
☎ 01503 262532 ▤ 01503 262532
e-mail: info@monkeysanctuary.org

Visitors can see a colony of Amazonian woolly monkeys in
extensive indoor and outdoor territory. There are also
conservation gardens, children's play area, activity room, a
display room and vegetarian cafe. In addition a bat cave is
on site where visitors can watch a colony of rare 'horseshoe'
bats.
Times: Open Sun-Thu 11-4.30 from the Sun before Etr-end Sep. Also
open Autumn Half Term. **Fee:** ✱ £5 (under 5's free, ch £3 &
concession £4). Family ticket (2 ad + 2 ch) £15. **Facilities:** 🅿 ▂ &
toilets for disabled shop ✕ ◥

MARAZION   Map 02 SW53

ST MICHAEL'S MOUNT
TR17 0HT
➲ (access is by Causeway on foot at low tide. 0.5m
S of A394 at Marazion)
☎ 01736 710507 & 710265 ▤ 01736 711544
e-mail: godolphin@manor-office.co.uk

Reached on foot by causeway at low tide, or by ferry at high
tide in the summer only, St Michael's Mount rises
dramatically from the sea, a medieval castle to which a
magnificent east wing was added in the 1870s. It is home to
Lord St Leven, whose ancestor John St Aubyn acquired it in
the 17th century.
Times: Open 31 Mar-Oct, Mon-Fri 10.30-5.30. Last admission 4.45;
Nov-Mar, telephone for details. The Castle and grounds are open most
weekends during the summer season. These are special charity open
days and NT members are also asked to pay. Group
bookings 01736 710507. **Fee:** ✱ £4.80 (ch £2.40) Family ticket £13.
Party 20+ £4.40 each. **Facilities:** 🅿 (on mainland) ▂ ✕ licensed
(braille guide) shop ✕ (ex guide dogs) ◥ ◥

MAWNAN SMITH   Map 02 SW72

GLENDURGAN
TR11 5JZ
➲ (4m SW of Falmouth. 0.5m SW of Mawnan
Smith on road to Helford Passage)
☎ 01872 862090 ▤ 01872 865808
e-mail: glendurgan@nationaltrust.org.uk

This delightful garden, set in a valley above the River
Helford, was started by Alfred Fox in 1820. The informal
landscape contains trees and shrubs from all over the world,
including the Japanese loquat and tree ferns from New
Zealand. There is a laurel maze, and a Giant's Stride which is
popular with children. The house is not open.
Times: Open mid Feb-Oct, Tue-Sat & BH Mon. Last admission 4.30
(Closed Good Fri). **Fee:** ✱ £4 (ch £2). Family ticket £10. **Facilities:** 🅿
▂ & (braille guide, limited access to gardens/ground floor) toilets for
disabled shop garden centre ✕ (ex guide dogs) ◥ ◥

TREBAH GARDEN
TR11 5JZ
➲ (signposted at Treliever Cross rdbt at junct of
A39/A394 & follow brown tourist signs)
☎ 01326 250448 ▤ 01326 250781
e-mail: mail@trebah-garden.co.uk

A 25-acre wooded ravine garden, descending 200 feet from
the 18th-century house down to a private cove on the
Helford River. The cascading Water Garden has pools of
giant koi and exotic water plants, winding through two acres
of blue and white hydrangeas to the beach. There are glades
of sub-tropical tree ferns and palms, as well as
rhododendrons and many other trees and shrubs. The beach

continued

is open to visitors and there are children's trails and activities all year.

Times: Open daily 10.30-5 (last admission). **Fee:** ✱ Mar-Oct £5 (ch & disabled £3, pen £4.50, ch under 5 free); Nov-Feb £2.50 (concessions £1.50). Party 12+ £4 each. **Facilities:** 🅿 💻 ✕ licensed ♿ (2 powered wheelchairs & wheelchair route) toilets for disabled shop garden centre (dogs only on leads) ☕

NEWQUAY
Map 02 SW86

BLUE REEF AQUARIUM
Towan Promenade TR7 1DU
➲ (from A30 follow signs to Newquay, follow Blue Reef Aquarium signs to car park in town centre)
☎ 01637 878134 📠 01637 872578 **2 for 1**
e-mail: info@bluereefaquarium.co.uk

Take the ultimate undersea safari at the Blue Reef Aquarium. Discover Cornish marine life from native sharks and rays to the incredibly intelligent and playful octopus. From here journey through warmer waters to watch the magical seahorses, unusual shape shifting, jet-propelled cuttlefish and the vibrant, swaying tentacles of living sponges and anemones. Continue your safari through the underwater tunnel below a tropical sea. Here you will encounter the activities of a coral reef alive with shoals of brightly coloured fish and the graceful, black tip reef sharks which glide silently overhead. Daily talks and regular feeding demonstrations bring the experience to life.
Times: Open all year, daily 10-5. (Closed 25 Dec). Open until 6 during summer holidays. **Fee:** ✱ £5.50 (ch 3-16 £3.50, pen & student £4.75). Family ticket £16.95. **Facilities:** 🅿 (5mins walk) (prior contact for disabled parking) 💻 ♿ (lifts, wheelchair) toilets for disabled shop ✕ (ex guide dogs) ☕

DAIRY LAND FARM WORLD
Summercourt TR8 5AA
➲ (Signposted from A30 at exit for Mitchell/Summercourt)
☎ 01872 510246 📠 01872 510349
e-mail: farmworld@yahoo.com

Visitors can watch while the cows are milked to music on a spectacular merry-go-round milking machine. The life of a Victorian farmer and his neighbours is explored in the Heritage Centre, and a Farm Nature Trail features informative displays along pleasant walks. Children will have fun getting

continued

to know the farm animals in the Farm Park. They will also enjoy the playground, assault course and indoor play areas.
Times: ✱ Open daily, late Mar-Oct 10.30-5. Xmas opening telephone for details. **Facilities:** 🅿 💻 ♿ (wheelchairs for loan; disabled viewing gallery - milking) toilets for disabled shop ✕ ☕

NEWQUAY ZOO
Trenance Gardens TR7 2LZ
➲ (off A3075 and follow signs to Zoo)
☎ 01637 873342 📠 01637 851318
e-mail: info@newquayzoo.co.uk

Set in exotic lakeside gardens, monkeys and wallabies roam freely, along with otters in the oriental garden. Red pandas explore their eastern enclosure and the black apes provide entertainment with their behaviour. In the tropical house live many birds, iguanas, sloths and other animals and, it actually rains. The highlights of the day are the animal encounters and the feeding time talks.
Times: Open Apr-Oct, daily 9.30-6; Nov-Mar 10-dusk. (Closed 25 Dec)
Fee: ✱ £6.75 (ch 4+ £4.20, pen £4.95, ch under 3 free). Family ticket £19.50. Check website for more details **Facilities:** 🅿 (charged) 💻 ✕ ♿ (free wheelchairs, guided tours & sensory sculptures) toilets for disabled shop ✕ (ex guide dogs) ☕

PADSTOW
Map 02 SW97

PRIDEAUX PLACE
PL28 8RP
➲ (off B3276 Padstow to Newquay road. Follow brown heritage signs)
☎ 01841 532411 📠 01841 532945
e-mail: office@prideauxplace.fsnet.co.uk

Built by Sir Nicholas Prideaux in 1592, this impressive country house has been inhabited by his family for fourteen generations, and is still in use by them today. Visitors can see relics of the English Civil War, including a pardon from Charles II and a double-sided brooch of Cromwell and the King, as well as fascinating rooms filled with antique furniture, paintings and a 16th-century ceiling depicting the biblical story of Susannah. The house was used as a location for Trevor Nunn's film version of *Twelfth Night* and has been used in the making of many *Rosamunde Pilcher* films and television productions.
Times: Open Etr Sun-11 Apr & 12 May-3 Oct, Sun-Thu 1.30-4 (house tours). Grounds 12.30-5. Open all year to pre-booked groups (15+)
Fee: ✱ House & grounds £6 (ch £2), Grounds only £2 (ch £1)
Facilities: 🅿 💻 ♿ shop ✕ (ex on leads in grounds) ☕

PENTEWAN
Map 02 SX04

THE LOST GARDENS OF HELIGAN
PL26 6EN
➲ (signposted from A390 & B3273)
☎ 01726 845100 📠 01726 845101
e-mail: info@heligan.com

Over 200 acres of superb working Victorian gardens and pleasure grounds together with a magnificent complex of walled gardens. Summerhouses, lawns, lakes and ponds, huge productive gardens and fruithouses, and a 22-acre subtropical jungle. Heligan Home Farm and pioneering

continued

Horsemoor Hide invite visitors to witness the outer estate being brought back into "good heart". **Times:** Open daily 10-6 (last admission 4.30pm): winter 10-dusk. Closed 24-25 Dec. **Fee:** £7.50. Please telephone to confirm concessions prices. **Facilities:** ⊓ ⬛ ✗ licensed ⅋ (free loan of wheelchairs and access advice) toilets for disabled shop garden centre ✖ (ex 16 Sep-14 Jul) ▧

PENZANCE   Map 02 SW43

TRENGWAINTON GARDEN
TR20 8RZ
➲ (2m NW Penzance, 0.5m W of Heamoor off Penzance - Morvah road (B3312), 0.5m off St Just road (A3071)
☎ 01736 363148   🖷 01736 367762
e-mail: trengwainton@ntrust.org.uk
Rhododendrons and magnolias grow in profusion at Trengwainton, along with many plants that are difficult to grow in Britain. The mild climate means that seed collected on expeditions to the Far East and southern hemisphere have flourished to produce a magnificent display in this 20th-century garden. **Times:** Open 16 Feb-2 Nov, daily 10-5.30 (closed Fri-Sat) but open Good Fri 10-5.30 (Feb, Mar & Oct 10-5). Last admission 1 hr before closing.. **Fee:** ✱ £4. Family ticket £10. Party **Facilities:** ⊓ ⬛ ⅋ (braille guide, special route, 2 wheelchairs) toilets for disabled shop garden centre ▨ ▧

POOL   Map 02 SW64

CORNISH MINES & ENGINES
TR14 7AW
➲ (2m W of Redruth on A3047, signposted from A30, Pool exit)
☎ 01209 315027 & 210900   🖷 01209 315027
e-mail: info@trevithicktrust.com
Impressive relics of the tin mining industry, these great beam engines were used for pumping water from 2000ft down and for lifting men and ore from the workings below ground. The mine at East Pool has been converted into the Cornwall Industrial Heritage Centre which includes audio visual theatre giving background to all aspects of Cornwall's industrial heritage. **Times:** Open 31 Mar-2 Nov, daily (ex Sat) 11-5; Aug open daily 11-5. Nov-Mar by arrangement. **Fee:** ✱ £5 (concessions £4.60, students £3) Family ticket £13. Party. **Facilities:** ⊓ ⅋ (lift to all levels, parking by arrangement, braille guide) toilets for disabled shop ✖ (ex guide dogs) ▨ ▧

PROBUS   Map 02 SW84

TREWITHEN GARDENS
Grampound Rd TR2 4DD
➲ (on A390 between Truro & St Austell)
☎ 01726 883647   🖷 01726 882301
e-mail: gardens@trewithen-estate.demon.co.uk
The Hawkins family has lived in this charming, intimate country house since it was built in 1720. The internationally renowned landscaped garden covers some 30 acres and grows camellias, magnolias and rhododendrons as well as

continued

many rare trees and shrubs seldom seen elsewhere. The nurseries are open all year. **Times:** Open Mar-Sep, Mon-Sat 10-4.30; daily 10-4.30 Apr & May. **Fee:** ✱ £4.25 (pen £4) group 20+ £4 **Facilities:** ⊓ ⬛ ⅋ toilets for disabled garden centre ✖ (ex on lead) ▧

RESTORMEL   Map 02 SX16

RESTORMEL CASTLE
PL22 0BD
➲ (1.5m N of Lostwithiel off A390)
☎ 01208 872687
High on a moated mound, this splendid Norman stronghold offers spectacular views across the Cornish countryside. **Times:** Open all year, Apr-Sep, daily 10-6; Oct, daily 10-5. Dates valid until 31 Mar 2004. **Fee:** £2 (ch £1, concessions £1.50). Prices valid until 31 Mar 2004. **Facilities:** ⊓ ⅋ shop ✖ (ex dogs on leads) ▦

ST AUSTELL   Map 02 SX05

CHARLESTOWN SHIPWRECK & HERITAGE CENTRE
Quay Rd, Charlestown PL25 3NJ
➲ (1.25m SE A3061)
☎ 01726 69897   🖷 01726 69897
e-mail: admin@shipwreckcharlestown.com
Charlestown is a small and unspoilt village with a unique sea-lock, china-clay port, purpose built in the 18th century. The Shipwreck and Heritage Centre houses the largest display of shipwreck artefacts in the UK, along with local heritage and diving exhibits, and also a Titanic display. **Times:** Open Mar-Oct, daily 10-5 (later in high season). Last admission 1 hour before closing. **Fee:** £4.95 (ch under 10 free if accompanied by paying adult, ch under 16 £1.95, concessions £3.45). **Facilities:** ⊓ (charged) ⬛ ✗ licensed ⅋ (ramps) toilets for disabled shop ▧

THE CHINA CLAY MUSEUM - WHEAL MARTYN
Carthew PL26 8XG
➲ (2m N on B3274)
☎ 01726 850362   🖷 01726 850362
e-mail: info@wheal-martyn.com
This museum tells the story of Cornwall's most important present-day industry: china clay production. The open-air site includes a complete 19th-century clayworks, with huge granite-walled settling tanks, working water-wheels and a wooden slurry pump. There is a short audio-visual programme, nature trails and a children's adventure trail. **Times:** ✱ Open Apr-Oct, 10-6 (last admission 5pm) phone for winter opening times. **Facilities:** ⊓ ⬛ ⅋ shop ▧

EDEN PROJECT
Bodelva PL24 2SG
➲ (overlooking St Austell Bay signposted from A390/A30/A391)
☎ 01726 811911   🖷 01726 811912
e-mail: information@edenproject.com
An unforgettable experience in a breathtaking location, the Eden Project is a gateway into the fascinating world of plants and human society. Space age technology meets the lost world in the biggest greenhouse ever built. Located in a 50 metre deep crater the size of 30 football pitches are two gigantic geodesic conservatories: the Humid Tropics Biome

continued

and the Warm Temperate Biome. This is a startling and unique day out.
Times: Open daily Mar-Oct 10-6 (last admission 5pm), Nov-Feb 10-4.30 (last admission 3pm). Closed 24-25 Dec. **Fee:** ✱ £10 (ch 5-15 £4, student £5, pen £7.50). Family ticket £25. **Facilities:** 🅿 ➣ ✕ licensed ♿ (wheelchairs, car shuttle to visitor centre/biomes) toilets for disabled shop garden centre ✖ (ex guide dogs) ➤

ST IVES   Map 02 SW54
(Park your car at Lelant Station and take advantage of the park and ride service. The fee includes parking and journeys on the train between Lelant and St Ives during the day).

BARBARA HEPWORTH MUSEUM & SCULPTURE GARDEN
Barnoon Hill TR26 1AD
➲ (M5 to Exeter, A30 onto Penzance & St Ives, in town centre)
☎ 01736 796226 🖹 01736 794480
Dame Barbara Hepworth lived here from 1949 until her death in 1975, and the house is now a museum displaying sculptures and drawings, photographs, documents and other memorabilia. Visitors can also visit her workshops, which house a selection of tools and some unfinished carvings. The garden contains a number of monumental sculptures, situated amongst semi-tropical plants.
Times: Open Mar-Oct, daily 10-5.30; Nov-Feb, Tue-Sun 10-4.30.
Fee: ✱ £3.95. (ch & pen free, concessions £2.25). **Facilities:** 🅿 (880yds) ♿ (accessible with assistance) shop ✖ (ex guide dogs) ➤

TATE ST IVES
Porthmeor Beach TR26 1TG
➲ (M5 to Exeter, then A30 onto Penzance & St Ives. Located on Porthmeor Beach)
☎ 01736 796226 🖹 01736 794480
Tate St Ives offers a unique introduction to modern art, where many works can be seen in the surroundings and atmosphere, which inspired them. The gallery presents changing displays from the Tate Collection, focusing on the post-war modern movement St Ives is so famous for. Artists represented at the gallery include Alfred Wallis, Ben Nicholson, Barbara Hepworth, Naum Gabo, Peter Lanyon, Bryan Wynter, Roger Hilton, John Wells, Patrick Heron and Terry Frost. There is also a changing programme of temporary exhibitions by major contemporary artists.
Times: Open Mar-Oct, daily 10-5.30; Nov-Feb, Tue-Sun 10-4.30.
Fee: ✱ £4.25 (ch & pen free, concessions £2.50). **Facilities:** 🅿 (800yds) ➣ ✕ licensed ♿ (access ramp, lift, wheelchairs) toilets for disabled shop ✖ (ex guide dogs) ➤

> If you are dissatisfied with any aspect of an attraction, discuss the problem at the time with a member of staff

ST MAWES   Map 02 SW83
ST MAWES CASTLE
TR2 3AA
➲ (on A3078)
☎ 01326 270526
Wonderful location alongside the pretty fishing village of St Mawes, this castle is Henry VIII's most picturesque fort.
Times: Open all year, Apr-Sep, daily 10-6; Oct, daily 10-5; Nov-Mar, Wed-Sun 10-4. (Closed between 1-2, 24-26 Dec & 1 Jan). Dates valid until 31 Mar 2004. **Fee:** £3 (ch £1.50, concessions £2.30). Prices valid until 31 Mar 2004. **Facilities:** 🅿 ♿ shop ✖ (ex dogs on leads in grounds) ⚏

SANCREED   Map 02 SW42
CARN EUNY ANCIENT VILLAGE   FREE
➲ (1.25m SW of Sancreed, off A30)
The remains of an Iron-Age settlement. Surviving features include the foundations of stone huts and an intriguing curved underground passage or 'fogou'.
Times: Open any reasonable time. **Facilities:** 🅿 (600mtrs) ⚏

TINTAGEL   Map 02 SX08
TINTAGEL CASTLE
PL34 0HE
➲ (on Tintagel Head, 0.5m along uneven track from Tintagel, no vehicles)
☎ 01840 770328 🖹 01840 770328
Overlooking the wild Cornish coast, Tintagel is one of the most spectacular spots in the country associated with King Arthur and Merlin. Recent excavations revealed Dark Age connections between Spain and Cornwall, alongside the discovery of 'Arthnou' stone suggesting that this was a royal place for the Dark Age rulers of Cornwall.
Times: Open all year, Apr-13 Jul, daily 10-6; 14 Jul-26 Aug, daily 10-7; 27 Aug-Sep, daily 10-6; 1-31 Oct, daily 10-5; Nov-Mar, daily 10-4. (Closed 24-26 Dec & 1 Jan). Dates valid until 31 Mar 2004. **Fee:** £3.20 (ch £1.60, concessions £2.40). Prices valid until 31 Mar 2004. **Facilities:** 🅿 (in village) shop ✖ (ex dogs on leads) ⚏

TORPOINT   Map 02 SX45
ANTONY HOUSE
PL11 2QA
➲ (2m NW, off A374 from Trerulefoot rdbt, 2m from Torpoint Ferry)
☎ 01752 812191 🖹 01752 815724
e-mail: philip.brunsdon@nationaltrust.org.uk
A fine, largely unaltered mansion, built in brick and Pentewan stone for Sir William Carew between 1711 and 1721. The stable block and outhouses remain from an earlier 17th-century building. The house contains contemporary furniture and family portraits. The grounds include a dovecote and the Bath Pond House.
Times: Open Apr-Oct, Tue-Thu & BH Mon 1.30-5.30 (last admission 4.45). Also open Sun in Jun-Sep. **Fee:** ✱ House & Garden £4.40. Woodland garden £3. Combined Gardens only £3.70. Party rates available. **Facilities:** 🅿 ➣ ♿ (braille guide, recommended route in garden) toilets for disabled shop ✖ (ex guide dogs) ⚐ ➤

MOUNT EDGCUMBE HOUSE & COUNTRY PARK

Cremyll PL10 1HZ

➲ (from Plymouth via Cremyll Foot Ferry, Torpoint ferry or Saltash Bridge. Via Liskeard to A374, B3247 follow brown heritage signs)

☎ 01752 822236 ▤ 01752 822199

e-mail: edgcumbe@plymouth.gov.uk

Covering some 800 acres, the country park surrounding Mount Edgcumbe contains a deer park, an amphitheatre, formal gardens, sculpture, the 18th-century Earl's Garden, and woodlands containing California redwoods. The coastal footpath runs along the shores of the Park from Cremyll to Whitsand Bay. Sir Richard Edgcumbe of Cotehele built Mount Edgcumbe between 1547 and 1553. It survived a direct hit by bombs in 1941, and was restored in the 1950s. It now contains antique paintings and furniture, 16th-century tapestries, and 18th-century porcelain. In 2004 there is a special exhibition called World War II - Rame Collection, telephone for details.

Times: Open: House & Earl's Garden Apr-Sep, Thu-Sun & BH Mon's, 11-4.30. (Closed Fri & Sat). Country Park open all year. **Fee:** ✱ House & Earl's Garden £4.50 (ch 5-15 £2.25, concessions £3.50) Family ticket (2 ad & 2 ch or 1 ad & 3 ch) £10. Country Park free. **Facilities:** ▣ ᴾ ✖ licensed ᴅ toilets for disabled shop ❤

TREDINNICK   Map 02 SW97

SHIRES FAMILY ADVENTURE PARK

Trelow Farm PL27 7RA

➲ (signposted off A39)

☎ 01841 541215

e-mail: shirespark@tiscali.co.uk | 2 for 1 |

Cornwall's best kept Park is once again even more fun this year with 'The Haunted Castle', full of demons, skeletons and ghosts. Enter the 'Dragon Kingdom', the Country's largest indoor adventure zone consisting of two floors of slides, climbs, ropes, balls and towers. Take a walk through the Enchanted Forest to Greengate Meadow and meet fully animated moles, Mr Badger and their woodland friends. New attractions include Thunder Falls, double log flume ride, plus Raging River Watercoaster and Viking Warrior Pirate Ship. Acres of outdoor adventure play with the highest aerial bridges and the longest, steepest slides in Cornwall. Plus train rides around the lakes and the majestic Shire Houses including new born foals with farmyard friends.

Times: Open Good Fri-end Oct, daily 10-5. **Fee:** £8 (ch £7, pen £5) **Facilities:** ▣ ᴾ ✖ licensed ᴅ (most areas are ramped) toilets for disabled shop

---

TRELISSICK GARDEN   Map 02 SW83

TRELISSICK GARDEN

TR3 6QL

➲ (Trelissick is located 4m S of Truro on both sides of B3289, King Harry Ferry Road)

☎ 01872 862090 ▤ 01872 865808

e-mail: trelissick@nationaltrust.org.uk

Set amidst more than 500 acres of park and farmland, with panoramic views down the Carrick Roads to Falmouth and the sea. The garden is well known for its large collection of hydrangeas, camellias, rhododendrons and exotic and tender plants. The Cornish Apple Orchard contains the definitive

continued

collection of Cornish apple varieties and is particularly lovely in the spring.

Times: Open mid Feb-Oct, daily 10.30-5.30. Phone for winter opening hours. Park & woodland walks open all year. **Fee:** ✱ £4.60 (Family ticket £11.50). Party rate 15+ £3.90 each. Car park charge £2 (refundable on admission). **Facilities:** ▣ (charged) ᴾ ✖ licensed ᴅ (audio guide, wheelchairs, batricar, induction loops) toilets for disabled shop garden centre ✖ ♨ ❤

TRERICE   Map 02 SW85

TRERICE

TR8 4PG

➲ (3m SE of Newquay off A3058 at Kestle Mill)

☎ 01637 875404 ▤ 01637 879300

e-mail: trerice@nationaltrust.org.uk

The Trerice you see today was built in 1571 by Sir John Arundell IV and, having suffered no major changes since then due to a succession of absentee landlords, it is still somehow caught in the spirit of its age. The plaster ceilings in the Great Hall and Great Chamber are of particular merit and the façade of the building is now thought to be the oldest such example of Dutch influenced architecture still extant in the country. The house contains many fine pieces of furniture and a large collection of clocks. A barn houses a fascinating display of lawnmowers. The garden is planted so as to provide colour and interest throughout the year and features an orchard containing many varieties of Cornish apple trees.

Times: Open 30 Mar-2 Nov, daily (ex Tue & Sat) 11-5.30 (11-5 Oct-Nov). Open daily from 16 Jul-10 Sep. **Fee:** ✱ House: £4.50. Family ticket (2 ad & 3 ch) £11.20. Party £3.70 each. **Facilities:** ▣ ✖ licensed ᴅ (braille/large print guide, tape tour, wheelchair) toilets for disabled shop ✖ (ex guide dogs) ♨ ❤

TRURO   Map 02 SW84

ROYAL CORNWALL MUSEUM

River St TR1 2SJ

➲ (follow A390 towards town centre)

☎ 01872 272205 ▤ 01872 240514

e-mail: enquiry@
royal-cornwall-museum.freeserve.co.uk

Interesting displays on the history of the county, a world-famous collection of minerals, and paintings and drawings, including a number of Old Masters. Other galleries house displays of archaeology, Cornish history, and Egyptian artefacts. Recently completed galleries of Cornish wildlife, fashion and textiles.

Times: Open all year, Mon-Sat 10-5. Library closes 1-2. (Closed BHs) **Fee:** ✱ £3.95 (unaccompanied ch 50p, pen & students £2.50). . **Facilities:** ▣ (200 yds) (disabled parking on street) ᴾ ✖ licensed ᴅ (lift, ramps to main entrances) toilets for disabled shop ✖ (ex guide dogs) ❤

> Remember that prices and opening times are liable to change within the currency of this guide. It is always best to telephone in advance to check

WENDRON
Map 02 SW63

POLDARK MINE AND HERITAGE COMPLEX
TR13 0ER
➲ (3m from Helston on B3297
Redruth road, follow brown signs)
☎ 01326 573173 ▤ 01326 563166   `2 for 1`
e-mail: info@poldark-mine.com

The centre of this attraction is the 18th century tin mine where visitors can join a guided tour of workings which retain much of their original character. The site's Museum explains the history of tin production in Cornwall from 1800BC through to the 19th century and the fascinating story of the Cornish overseas. In addition to the Museum, the audio-visual presentation gives more insight into Cornwall's mining heritage.

Times: Open Etr-1st wk Nov, 10-5.30 (last tour 4pm). **Fee:** Guided underground tour £5.95 (ch 5-15 £3.95) Family (2 ad + 2 ch) £16.45
Facilities: 🅿 🍺 ⓓ (newly refurbished museum allowing disabled access) shop 🐾

ZENNOR
Map 02 SW43

WAYSIDE FOLK MUSEUM
TR26 3DA
➲ (4m W of St Ives, on B3306)
☎ 01736 796945

Founded in 1937, this museum covers every aspect of life in Zennor and surrounding district from 3000BC to the 1930s. Over 5000 items are displayed in 12 workshops and rooms covering wheelwrights, blacksmiths, agriculture, fishing, wrecks, mining, domestic and archaeological artefacts. A photographic exhibition entitled People of the Past tells the story of the village.

Times: Open Apr & Oct, Sun-Fri 11-5, May-Sep, daily 10.30-5.30.
Fee: ✱ £2.75 (ch £1.50, over 60's £2.50). Party rates 10+.
Facilities: 🅿 (50yds) ⓓ (not suitable for wheelchair users) shop 🐾 (ex guide dogs) 🍺

Above: The harbour at Padstow

CUMBRIA

EVENTS & FESTIVALS

March
26th-4th Apr Ulverston Walking Festival
27th-28th Flower Show, Ambleside
April
26th Mar-4th Ulverston Walking Festival
May
2nd-3rd Carlisle & Borders
  Spring Flower Show, Carlise
13th-16th Jennings Keswick Jazz Festival,
June
3rd-9th Appleby Horse Fair, Roman Road,
  Appleby-in-Westmorland
4th-5th Keswick Beer Festival, Keswick
4th-6th Cumbrian Beer Festival, Wasdale Head
12th Edwardian Festival, Grange-Over-Sands
July
17th Cumberland County Show, Carlisle
23rd-25th Maryport Blues Festival
24th-25th The Cumbria Steam Gathering,
  Cark Airfield, Flookburgh
August
4th Cartmel Show, Cartmel Park,
  Grange-Over-Sands
22nd Grasmere Lakeland Sports & Show,
  Stock Lane, Grasmere, Ambleside
September
3rd-5th Wasdale Beer Festival,
  Wasdale Head (provisional)
9th Westmorland County Show,
  Lane Farm, Crooklands, Milnthorpe
18th Egremont Crab Fair & Sports (including
  world renowned gurning competition)
tbc Powerboat Records Week,
  Lake Windermere
October
20th-23rd Westmorland Beer Festival,
  Town Hall, Kendal
November
13th-14th Kendal Mountain Film Festival,
  Highgate, Kendal
18th Biggest Liar in the World Competition,
  Santon Bridge (provisional)

Above: Catbells & Friar's Crag at Derwent Water

ALSTON   Map 12 NY74
NENT VALLEY
Nenthead Mines Heritage Centre, Nenthead CA9 3PD
➲ (5m E, on A689)
☎ 01434 382037 ▤ 01434 382294 **2 for 1**
e-mail: administration.office@virgin.net

Set in 200 acres in the North Pennines, this hands-on heritage centre contains exhibitions and displays on geology, local wildlife, and social history. Visitors can operate three enormous water wheels, gaze down a 328ft deep brewery shaft, and take an underground trip through the Nenthead mines, last worked for lead in 1915.
Times: Open Etr-Oct, daily 10.30-5. Mine tours at 1, 2.15 & 3.30 (also 11.30 on Sun) **Fee:** £4-£6.50 (pen £3.25-5.50, ch £2.50-£4.50). Family ticket £11.50-£19.80 **Facilities:** 🅿 ▦ ♿ toilets for disabled shop 🍴

SOUTH TYNEDALE RAILWAY
The Railway Station, Hexham Rd CA9 3JB
➲ (0.25m N, on A686)
☎ 01434 381696 & 382828

Running along the beautiful South Tyne valley, this narrow-gauge railway follows the route of the former Alston to Haltwhistle branch. At present the line runs between Alston and Kirkhaugh.
Times: Open Apr-Oct & Dec, wknds and BH's; 20 Jul-Aug, daily. Also open some wknds in Dec. Please enquire for times of trains. **Fee:** ✱ Return £5 (ch 3-15 £2). Single £3 (ch 3-15 £1.50). All day £12.50 (ch 3-15 £5). **Facilities:** 🅿 ♿ (railway carriage for wheelchairs, pre-booking required) toilets for disabled shop

AMBLESIDE   Map 07 NY30
ARMITT MUSEUM
Rydal Rd LA22 9BL
➲ (beyond Bridge House opposite main car park)
☎ 015394 31212 ▤ 015394 31313 **2 for 1**
e-mail: mail@armitt.com

The story of Ambleside from Roman times to present day. Explore the area through the eyes of John Ruskin, Kurt Schwitters, photographer Herbert Bell and Beatrix Potter and admire a wonderful collection of local history material. Hands on activities for all the family
Times: Open all year, daily 10-5 (last entrance 4.30pm). Closed 25-26 Dec. **Fee:** £2.50 (ch, students, pen £1.80) Family ticket £5.60.
Facilities: 🅿 (50yds) ♿ (chairlift to upstairs library, parking at establishment) toilets for disabled shop ✖ (ex guide dogs) 🍴

APPLEBY-IN-WESTMORLAND   Map 12 NY62
APPLEBY CASTLE
CA16 6XH
➲ (on A66, castle is top of the main street)
☎ 017683 51402 ▤ 017683 51082

The grounds of beautiful Castle provide a natural setting for wildlife. The fine Norman Keep and the Great Hall of the house are open to the public. Clifford family portraits and part of the Nanking Cargo are on display in the Hall. An added attraction is the introduction of a Nursery Garden in the old, walled kitchen garden.
Times: ✱ Open 4 Apr-Oct, daily 10-5 (last admission); Oct, daily 10-4.
Facilities: 🅿 ▦ ✖ ♿ (assistance available) toilets for disabled shop garden centre ✖ (ex on lead, guide dogs)

BARROW-IN-FURNESS   Map 07 SD26

FURNESS ABBEY
LH13 0TJ
➲ (1.5m NE on unclass road)
☎ 01229 823420

Located in a peaceful valley, the majestic red sandstone remains of this beautiful abbey once housed a wealthy monastic order. View the fine stone carvings and visit the exhibition to find out more about the powerful religious community that was once based here.
Times: Open all year, Apr-Sep, daily 10-6; Oct, daily 10-5; Nov-Mar, Wed-Sun 10-4. Dates valid until 31 Mar 2004. **Fee:** £3 (ch £1.50, concessions £2.30). Prices valid until 31 Mar 2004. **Facilities:** 🅿 ♿ shop 🐕 (ex on lead in certain areas) ⌗

BASSENTHWAITE   Map 11 NY23

TROTTERS WORLD OF ANIMALS
Coalbeck Farm CA12 4RD
☎ 017687 76239 📠 017687 76598
e-mail: info@trottersworld.com

Home to hundreds of friendly animals including lemurs, wallabies and other exotic animals along with reptiles and birds of prey and a family of gibbons which will keep families amused for hours. Informative, amusing demonstrations daily bring visitors closer to the animals. "Clown About" is an indoor play centre with soft play area and ballpools for toddlers upwards.
Times: ✱ Open 9 Feb-3 Nov 10-5.30. Winter Sat-Sun & daily Xmas-New Year (ex 25 Dec & 1 Jan) **Facilities:** 🅿 💷 ♿ toilets for disabled shop 🐕 (ex guide dogs) ⌐

BIRDOSWALD   Map 12 NY66

BIRDOSWALD ROMAN FORT
CA8 7DD
➲ (signposted off A69 between Brampton & Hexham)
☎ 016977 47602 📠 016977 47605   2 for 1
e-mail: birdoswald@dial.pipex.com

A visitor centre introduces you to Hadrian's Wall and the Roman Fort. This unique section of Hadrian's Wall overlooks the Irthing Gorge, and is the only point along the Wall where all the components of the Roman frontier system can be found together. Birdoswald isn't just about the Romans, though, it's also about border raids in the Middle Ages, and recent archaeological discoveries.
Times: Open Mar-9 Nov, 10-5.30. **Fee:** ✱ £3 (ch £1.75, concessions £2.50). Family ticket £7.75. English Heritage members half price.
Facilities: 🅿 💷 ♿ (ramp outside, disabled parking, lift) toilets for disabled shop ⌐

BOWNESS-ON-WINDERMERE   Map 07 SD49

BLACKWELL THE ARTS & CRAFTS HOUSE
LA23 3JR
➲ (M6 junct 36. 1.5m S of Bowness on B5360, off A5074)
☎ 015394 46139 📠 015394 88486
e-mail: info@blackwell.org.uk

Blackwell was designed by architect M H Baillie Scott (1865-1945) and completed in 1900. Part of the late 19th-century Arts and Crafts Movement it houses changing

continued

exhibitions of high quality applied arts and crafts, as well as original design features including stained glass, stonework, carved oak panelling, and plasterwork.
Times: Open 12 Feb-24 Dec daily 10-5; (Nov-Dec, Feb-Mar 10-4).
Fee: £4.50 (ch & students £2.50) Family ticket £12, groups £3.50 per person. Combined ticket with Abbot Hall £6.25. **Facilities:** 🅿 💷 ♿ (lift to upper floor) toilets for disabled shop 🐕 (ex guide dogs) ⌐

BRAMPTON   Map 12 NY56

LANERCOST PRIORY
CA8 2HQ
➲ (2.5m NE)
☎ 01697 73030

Close to Hadrian's Wall are the atmospheric ruins of this Augustinian priory founded in the 12th-century.
Times: Open Apr-Sep, daily 10-6; Oct, daily 10-5. Dates valid until 31 Mar 2004. **Fee:** £2.50 (ch £1.50, concessions £2). Prices valid until 31 Mar 2004. **Facilities:** 🅿 shop 🐕 (ex dogs on leads) ⌗

BROUGH   Map 12 NY71

BROUGH CASTLE
CA17 4EJ
➲ (8m SE of Appleby, S of A66)
☎ 0191 261 1585

Dating from Roman times the twelfth-century keep at this site replaced an earlier stronghold destroyed by the Scots in 1174. It was restored by Lady Anne Clifford in the seventeenth century. You can still see the outline of her kitchen gardens.
Times: Open any reasonable time. **Facilities:** 🅿 🐕 (ex dogs on leads) ⌗

BROUGHAM   Map 12 NY52

BROUGHAM CASTLE
CA10 2AA
➲ (1.5m SE of Penrith on minor road off A66)
☎ 01768 862488

Explore the maze of stairs and passages in the ruins of this once glorious 11th-century castle on the banks of the River Eamont. Enjoy the lively exhibition where you'll see relics from the nearby Roman Fort.
Times: Open all year, Apr-Sep, daily 10-6 (Oct, daily 10-5). Dates valid until 31 Mar 2004. **Fee:** £2.50 (ch £1.50, concessions £2). Prices valid until 31 Mar 2004. **Facilities:** 🅿 ♿ (ex keep) shop 🐕 (ex dogs on leads) ⌗

CARLISLE   Map 11 NY35

CARLISLE CASTLE
CA3 8UR
➲ (north side of city centre, close to station)
☎ 01228 591992 📠 01228 514880

Discover a thrilling and bloody past and enjoy panoramic views over the city and hills of the Lake District and Southern Scotland. Uncover an exciting history through lively exhibitions, which tell of William Rufus, Mary Queen of Scots and Bonnie Prince Charlie.
Times: Open all year, Apr-Sep, daily 9.30-6 (Oct, daily 10-5); Nov-Mar, daily 10-4. (Closed 24-26 Dec & 1 Jan). Dates valid until 31 Mar 2004.
Fee: £3.50 (ch £1.80, concessions £2.70). Prices valid until 31 Mar 2004. **Facilities:** 🅿 (400yds) ♿ (parking for disabled at Castle) shop 🐕 (ex on lead in certain areas) ⌗

CARLISLE CATHEDRAL
Castle St CA3 8TZ
➲ (M6 junct 42,43 or 44, located in City Centre)
☎ 01228 535169 & 548151 🖹 01228 547049
e-mail: office@carlislecathedral.org.uk
The Cathedral, founded in 1122 as a Norman Priory for
Augustinian canons has conducted services for nearly 900
years. Items of special interest include the East Window, with
its tracery containing some very fine 14th-century stained
glass and the Brougham Triptych, a magnificent 16th-century
carved Flemish altarpiece in St. Wilfrid's Chapel. There is an
interesting 14th-century barrel vaulted painted ceiling in the
Choir and in the north and south aisles medieval paintings
depict the Life of St. Cuthbert and St. Anthony and the
figures of the 12 Apostles.
Times: Open daily throughout the year, Mon-Sat 7.30-6.15, Sun 7.30-5,
summer BHs 9.45-6.15, winter BHs, Xmas & New Year 9.45-4.
Fee: Suggested donation of £2 per adult. **Facilities:** P (5 mins walk)
(2 disabled spaces only) ✗ licensed ৬ (parking, ramps, loop system,
large print books, chairlifts) toilets for disabled shop ✗ (ex guide dogs)

GUILDHALL MUSEUM
Green Market CA3 8JE
➲ (town centre, opposite The Crown & Mitre
Hotel)
☎ 01228 534781 🖹 01228 810249
e-mail: barbaral@carlisle-city.gov.uk
One of Carlisle's oldest buildings, c.1405 and Grade I listed.
The Guildhall was once the meeting place of Carlisle's eight
trade guilds, few of which still meet today. Experience the
cabin-like atmosphere of the shoemaker's room and the
'modernised' butcher's room with its Victorian features.
There are amazing objects such as the medieval town chest,
dating from around 1400, two small silver balls (one
dated 1599)- reputed to be the earliest surviving horse racing
prizes in the country.
Times: ✱ Open Apr-Oct, 12-4.30 **Facilities:** P (500yds) (disc parking
on street, 1 hr limit) ✗ (ex guide dogs)

TULLIE HOUSE MUSEUM & ART GALLERY
Castle St CA3 8TP
➲ (M6, junct 42, 43 or 44 follow signs to city
centre. Car park located in Devonshire Walk)
☎ 01228 534781 🖹 01228 810249
e-mail: barbaral@carlisle-city.gov.uk
Dramatic audio-visual displays, striking recreations of long
vanished scenes and imaginative hands-on displays. There is
something for everyone, no matter what age - the stunning
new underground millennium gallery or Border River
pathway linking to Carlisle Castle. This unique project
combines the museums own collections with the cutting
edge of contemporary art. The new multi-media room
features touch sensitive computer screens & a short film.
Times: ✱ Open: Nov-Mar, Mon-Sat 10-4, Sun 12-4; Apr-Jun & Sep-Oct,
Mon-Sat 10-5, Sun 12-5. Jul-Aug, Mon-Sat 10-5, Sun 11-5. (Closed 25-26
Dec & 1 Jan). **Facilities:** P (5mins walk) (disabled parking on site by
request) ✗ licensed ৬ (chair lift) toilets for disabled shop ✗ (ex guide
dogs) ▼

COCKERMOUTH Map 11 NY13

JENNINGS BREWERY TOUR AND SHOP
The Castle Brewery CA13 9NE
➲ (A66 to Cockermouth, follow tourist signs
to brewery) `2 for 1`
☎ 0845 129 7185 🖹 0845 129 7186
e-mail: maskew@jenningsbrewery.co.uk
Jennings Brothers have been brewing traditional beers
for 160 years and still use the methods used by the founder
in 1828. Situated in the shadow of Cockermouth Castle, the
water for the brewing process is still drawn from the well
which supplied the Castle with pure water.
Times: Tours: Jan-Feb & Nov- Dec, Mon-Sat, 2pm; Mar-Jun & Sep-Oct,
Mon-Sat, 2pm; Jul-Aug, daily, 11am & 12pm. **Fee:** £4.50 (ch 12-18
£1.50). **Facilities:** P shop ✗ ▼

LAKELAND SHEEP & WOOL CENTRE
Egremont Rd CA13 0QX
➲ (M6 junct 40, W on A66 to rdbt at Cockermouth
on A66/A586 junct)
☎ 01900 822673 🖹 01900 822673
e-mail: reception@sheep-woolcentre.co.uk
Come face to face with 19 different breeds of live sheep.
Stage show with 'One Man and his Dog' demonstration and
our Jersey cow. Shows four times daily, March-end Oct. All
indoors.
Times: Open all year, daily 9.30-5.30 (Closed 25 Dec & 5-18 Jan).
Fee: £4 (ch £3). **Facilities:** P ▟ ✗ licensed ৬ (hearing loop
system) toilets for disabled shop ✗ (ex guide/hearing dogs) ▼

WORDSWORTH HOUSE
Main St CA13 9RX
➲ (W end of Main Street)
☎ 01900 824805 🖹 01900 824805
e-mail: wordsworthhouse@ntrust.org.uk
William Wordsworth was born here on 7th April 1770, and
happy memories of the house had a great effect on his work.
The inside staircase, panelling and other features are
original. Portraits and other items connected with the poet
are displayed. Please ring for details of concerts and other
events during the season.
Times: Open 31 Mar-3 Oct Mon-Fri 10.30-4.30. Also Sats in Jun, Jul &
Aug. **Fee:** ✱ £3 (ch £1.50). Family ticket £8. Party. Ask for details of
discount with Dove Cottage,the Wordsworth Museum and Rydal
Mount. **Facilities:** P (100yds) ▟ ৬ (braille guide) shop ✗ (ex
assist dogs) ▨ ▼

CONISTON Map 07 SD39

BRANTWOOD
LA21 8AD
➲ (2.5m SE off B5285, unclass road. Regular ferry
services from Coniston Pier)
☎ 015394 41396 🖹 015394 41263
e-mail: enquiries@brantwood.org.uk
Brantwood, home of John Ruskin, is a beautifully situated
house with fine views across Coniston Water. Inside, there is
a large collection of Ruskin paintings and memorabilia, and

continued

visitors can enjoy delightful nature walks through the Brantwood Estate.

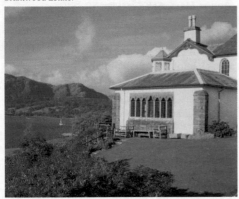

Times: Open mid Mar-mid Nov, daily 11-5.30. Winter, Wed-Sun 11-4.30. (Closed 25-26 Dec). **Fee:** ✱ House & Estate £4.75 (ch £1, student £3.50). Family ticket £10. Estate only £3. **Facilities:** 🅿 💺 ✕ licensed ♿ (wheelchairs, photo albums of inaccessible areas) toilets for disabled shop ✖ (ex guide dogs & in grounds) 🏳

RUSKIN MUSEUM
The Institute, Yewdale Rd LA21 8DU
➲ (In village centre opposite fire station, accessed from A593, A595 & B5285)
☎ 015394 41164   📠 01539 441132
e-mail: vmj@ruskinmuseum.com
John Ruskin (1819-1900) was one of Britain's most versatile and important political thinkers and artists. The museum contains many of his watercolours, drawings, letters, sketchbooks and other relics. The geology, mines and quarries of the area, Arthur Ransome's *Swallows and Amazons* country, and Donald Campbell's Bluebird are also explored in the Museum.
Times: Open all year, mid Mar-mid Nov, daily 10-5.30; Winter opening, Wed-Sun 10.30-3.30. **Fee:** ✱ £3.50 (ch £1.75). Family ticket £9. Ruskin passport gives exclusive discount for cruise on S.Y. Gondola.
Facilities: 🅿 ♿ (audio guide, handling specimens) toilets for disabled shop ✖ (ex guide dogs) 🏳

STEAM YACHT GONDOLA
Pier Cottage LA21 8AJ
➲ (A593 to Coniston, follow signs near garage 'to boats' & S Y Gondola)
☎ 015394 41288   📠 015394 41288
e-mail: rcogon@smtp.ntrust.org.uk
Launched in 1859, the graceful Gondola worked on Coniston Water until 1936. She came back into service in 1980, and visitors can once again enjoy her silent progress and old-fashioned comfort.
Times: Open Apr-Oct to scheduled daily timetable. Trips commence from 11 at Coniston Pier. Piers at Coniston & Brantwood. **Fee:** Ticket prices on application. **Facilities:** 🅿 shop 🐾 🏳

DALEMAIN
CA11 0HB
➲ (between Penrith & Ullswater on A592)
☎ 017684 86450   📠 017684 86223
e-mail: admin@dalemain.com
Originally a mediaeval pele tower, Dalemain was added to in Tudor times, and the imposing Georgian façade was completed in 1745. It has oak panelling, Chinese wallpaper, Tudor plasterwork and fine period furniture. The tower contains the Westmorland and Cumberland Yeomanry Museum, and there is a countryside collection in the 16th-century Great Barn. The gardens include a collection of old fashioned roses, and in early summer a magnificent display of blue Himalayan poppies.
Times: Open Gardens, Mediaeval Hall and agricultural & countryside collections: 28 Mar-14 Oct , Sun-Thu 10.30-5. House open 11-4.
Fee: House £5.50 (ch £3.50) Family ticket £14.50. Gardens £3.50. (ch free when accompanied). Party. **Facilities:** 🅿 💺 ✕ licensed ♿ (ramp access at entrance, setting down & collection point) toilets for disabled shop garden centre ✖ (ex guide dogs) 🏳

SOUTH LAKES WILD ANIMAL PARK
Crossgates LA15 8JR
➲ (M6 junct 36, A590 to Dalton-in-Furness, follow tourist signs)
☎ 01229 466086   📠 01229 461310
e-mail: office@wildanimalpark.co.uk
The North's leading zoo park is a unique safari on foot with many animals wandering free. Visitors can walk with kangaroos and emus in the bush, and watch parrots fly free in the trees. Hand feed (supervised at 2pm) families of seven different species of lemur, wonder at the amazing skills of gibbons, macaques and spider monkeys, and see the lions and tigers climb high into trees to catch their food. This is the only place in Britain where you can see both Amur and Sumatran tigers. Also visit the baboons, rhino, giraffes, cheetah, red panda, and over 100 other species. This is an active conservation park with partnerships all over the world to save animals and their habitats.
Times: Open all year, daily 10-5 (last admission 4.15); Nov-Feb 10-4.30 (last admission 3.45). (Closed 25 Dec). **Fee:** ✱ £7.50 (ch, pen, wheelchair users & registered blind £5). Reduced prices Nov-Mar.
Facilities: 🅿 💺 ♿ (wheelchair users may need help) toilets for disabled shop ✖

DOVE COTTAGE & THE WORDSWORTH MUSEUM
LA22 9SH
➲ (S, off A591, immediately before Grasmere village)
☎ 015394 35544   📠 015394 35748
e-mail: enquiries@wordsworth.org.uk
Dove Cottage was the inspirational home of William Wordsworth for over eight years, and it was here that he wrote some of his best-known poetry. The cottage has been open to the public since 1891, and is kept in its original

continued

condition. The museum displays manuscripts, works of art and items that belonged to the poet.
Times: Open daily 9.30-5.30, last admission 5pm. (Closed mid Jan-mid Feb & 24-26 Dec). **Fee:** ✱ Admission charge, discount and concessions available. Reciprocal discount offer with Rydal Mount, Ambleside & Wordsworth House, Cockermouth. **Facilities:** ▯ ▣ ✗ licensed &. (ramps, induction loop) toilets for disabled shop ✖ (ex guide dogs) ◥

HARDKNOTT CASTLE ROMAN FORT   Map 07 NY20

HARDKNOTT CASTLE ROMAN FORT
➲ (9m NE of Ravenglass, at W end of Hardknott Pass)

One of the most dramatic Roman sites in Britain, with stunning views of the Lakeland falls. The fort built between AD120 and AD138, controlled the road from Ravenglass to Ambleside. The remains include the headquarters building and Commandant's house, with a bath house and parade ground outside the fort.
Times: Open any reasonable time. Access may be hazardous in winter.
Facilities: ▯ ✖ (ex dogs on leads) ✾

HAWKSHEAD   Map 07 SD39

BEATRIX POTTER GALLERY
Main St LA22 0NS
☎ 015394 36355   ▤ 015394 36118
e-mail: rhabpg@smtp.ntrust.org.uk
An annually changing exhibition of Beatrix Potter's original illustrations from her children's storybooks, housed in the former office of her husband, solicitor William Heelis.
Times: ✱ Open Apr-1 Nov & Good Friday Sun-Thu 10.30-4.30 (last admission 4). Admission is by timed ticket including NT members.
Facilities: ▯ (300metres) (braille guide) shop ✖ �̷ ✾

HOLKER   Map 07 SD37

HOLKER HALL & GARDENS
Cark in Cartmel, Grange over Sands LA11 7PL
➲ (from M6 junct 36, on A590, signposted)
☎ 015395 58328   ▤ 015395 58378
e-mail: publicopening@holker.co.uk
Dating from the 16th century, the new wing of the Hall was rebuilt in 1871, after a fire. It has a notable woodcarving and many fine pieces of furniture which mix happily with family photographs from the present day. There are magnificent gardens, both formal and woodland and the Lakeland Motor Museum, exhibitions, deer park and adventure playground are further attractions.
Times: Open 28 Mar-Oct, Sun-Fri 10-6. Hall open 10.30-4.45. (Closed Sat). **Fee:** Gardens & Grounds £3.95 (ch 6-15 £2.25) Family ticket £11.95. All 3 attractions £8.25 (ch £4.65) Family ticket £23.95. Parking £1. **Facilities:** ▯ (charged) ▣ ✗ licensed &. (ramps, wheelchairs & scooters available for hire) toilets for disabled shop ◥

KENDAL   Map 07 SD59

ABBOT HALL ART GALLERY
LA9 5AL
➲ (M6 junct 36, follow signs to Kendal. Located at south end of town centre beside church)
☎ 01539 722464   ▤ 01539 722494
e-mail: info@abbothall.org.uk
The ground floor rooms of this splendid house have been restored to their former glory, with original carvings and fine panelling. The walls are hung with paintings by Romney, Gardner, Turner and Ruskin. The gallery has notable temporary exhibitions and a fine permanent collection of 18th- and 19th-century watercolours of the Lake District, and 20th-century British art, including works by Hepworth, Frink, Nicholson, Sutherland, Riley and Freud.
Times: Open 12 Feb-24 Dec, Mon-Sat 10.30-5 (Nov, Dec, Feb, Mar 10.30-4). **Fee:** £3.75 (ch & students £1.75). Family ticket £9.50. Groups £3.25 per person. Abbot Hall/Blackwell combined group ticket £6.25.
Facilities: ▯ ▣ &. (chair lifts in split level galleries, large print labels) toilets for disabled shop ✖ (ex guide dogs) ◥

KENDAL MUSEUM
Station Rd LA9 6BT
➲ (opposite railway station)
☎ 01539 721374   ▤ 01539 737976
e-mail: enquiries@kendalmuseum.org.uk
The archaeology and natural history of the Lakes is explored in this popular museum which also features a world wildlife exhibition and a display devoted to author Alfred Wainwright, who was honorary clerk to the museum.
Times: Open 12 Feb-20 Dec, Mon-Sat 10.30-5. Reduced hours Feb-Mar; Nov & Dec, 10.30-4. Closed Sun. **Fee:** ✱ £3.50 (ch, students £1.75). Family tickets £9. Groups 10+. Seasonal tickets available. Ticket provides reduced entry to Kendal Museum. **Facilities:** ▯ &. toilets for disabled shop ✖ (ex guide dogs) ◥

MUSEUM OF LAKELAND LIFE
Abbot Hall LA9 5AL
➲ (M6 junct 36, follow signs to Kendal. Located at south end of Kendal beside Abbot Hall Art Gallery)
☎ 01539 722464   ▤ 01539 722494
e-mail: info@lakelandmuseum.org.uk
The life and history of the Lake District is captured by the displays in this museum, housed in Abbot Hall's stable block. The working and social life of the area are well illustrated by a variety of exhibits including period rooms, a Victorian Cumbrian street scene and a farming display. Two of the rooms are devoted to the memory of Arthur Ransome.
Times: Open 12 Feb-24 Dec, Mon-Sat 10.30-5. (Nov, Dec, Feb, Mar 10.30-4). **Fee:** £2.75 (ch & students £1.40). Family ticket £7. Combined ticket with Abbot Hall & Lakeland Life (same day), £4.50. **Facilities:** ▯ ▣ &. (listening posts, large print labels) toilets for disabled shop ✖ (ex guide dogs) ◥

KESWICK   Map 11 NY22

CUMBERLAND PENCIL MUSEUM
Southey Works, Greta Bridge CA12 5NG
➲ (M6 N onto A66 at Penrith. Left at 2nd Keswick
exit, left at T-Junct, left over Greta Bridge)
☎ 017687 73626 📄 017687 74679
e-mail: museum@acco-uk.co.uk

Investigating the history and technology of an object most of
us take utterly for granted, this interesting museum includes
a replica of the Borrowdale mine where graphite was first
discovered, the world's largest pencil, and displays on
brass-rubbing and various artistic techniques that use
pencils.
Times: Open daily 9.30-4 (hours may be extended during peak
season). (Closed 25-26 Dec & 1 Jan) **Fee:** ✱ £2.50 (ch & pen £1.25,
students £1.75). Family ticket (2 adults, 3 children) £6.25 **Facilities:** 🅿
& toilets for disabled shop 🍽

KESWICK MUSEUM & GALLERY
Fitz Park, Station Rd CA12 4NF
➲ (M6 junct 40, A66 to Keswick, follow tourist
signs for Museum & Art Gallery when in Keswick)
☎ 017687 73263 📄 017687 80390
e-mail: keswick.museum@allerdale.gov.uk

Keswick's surprising past, from industrial mining centre to
peaceful tourist town, is revealed in this fine example of a
late Victorian museum. Set in the beautiful Fitz Park, the
collections cover local and natural history, famous
inhabitants and visitors, including the Lake Poets, and
houses the work of many artists who have been captivated
by the local landscape and history.
Times: Open Good Friday-Oct, 10-4. Tue-Thu, 10-7. **Fee:** ✱ £1.50 (ch,
pen, students, UB40's & disabled 50p). 10% discount for Parties of 10+.
Facilities: 🅿 (on road outside) (2 hour limit) & (ramp at front
entrance, with handrails) shop 🍽 (ex guide & hearing dogs)

MIREHOUSE
CA12 4QE
➲ (3m N of Keswick on A591)
☎ 017687 72287 📄 017687 72287
e-mail: info@mirehouse.com

Visitors return to Mirehouse for many reasons: the
spectacular setting of mountain and lake, the varied gardens,
changing displays on the Poetry Walk, free children's nature
notes, four woodland playgrounds, connections with many
writers and artists, live classical piano music in the house,
generous Cumbrian cooking in the tearoom, and a relaxed,
friendly welcome.
Times: Open Apr-Oct. House: Wed, Sun, (also Fri in Aug) 2-last entry
4.30. Grounds: daily 10.30-5.30. Parties by arrangement. **Fee:** ✱ House
& grounds £4 (ch £2). Grounds only £2 (ch £1). Family ticket £11.75 (2
ad & 4 ch) **Facilities:** 🅿 (charged) 🍽 & toilets for disabled 🍽 (ex
on leads & guide dogs)

> If you are dissatisfied with any
> aspect of an attraction, discuss the
> problem at the time with a
> member of staff

LAKESIDE   Map 07 SD38

AQUARIUM OF THE LAKES
LA12 8AS
➲ (M6, junct 36, take A590 to Newby Bridge. Turn
right over bridge, follow Hawkshead Road to
Lakeside. Well signposted)
☎ 015395 30153 📄 015395 30152
e-mail: aquariumofthelakes@reallive.co.uk

Set on the banks of Lake Windermere, the award-winning
Aquarium of the Lakes is the UK's largest collection of
freshwater fish. Over 30 displays recreate the journey of a
Lakeland river from mountaintop to the open sea. Naturally
themed habitats are home to everything from diving ducks
and mischievous otters to sharks and rays. An all-weather
experience for all ages.
Times: Open all year, daily from 9am. Closed 25 Dec. **Fee:** ✱ £5.95
(ch £3.75, pen £4.95). Family ticket (2 adult & 2 ch £16.95, 2 adult & 3
ch £19.95, 2 adult & 4 ch £22.95). **Facilities:** 🅿 (charged) 🍽 & (lift
to first floor, wheelchairs) toilets for disabled shop 🍽 (ex guide
dogs) 🍽

LEVENS   Map 07 SD48

LEVENS HALL
LA8 0PD
➲ (M6 junct 36. 5m S of Kendal, on A6)
☎ 015395 60321 📄 015395 60669
e-mail: email@levenshall.fsnet.co.uk

An Elizabethan mansion, built onto a 13th-century pele
tower, with fine plasterwork and panelling. The topiary
garden, laid out in 1694, has been little changed.
Times: Open: House & gardens mid Apr-mid Oct, Sun-Thu. Gardens
10-5. House 12-5. Last admission 4.30. **Fee:** ✱ House & garden £7 (ch
£3.50), garden only £5.50 (ch £2.50). **Facilities:** 🅿 🍽 & (ramps
within garden) toilets for disabled shop garden centre 🍽 (ex guide
dogs) 🍽

NEAR SAWREY   Map 07 SD39

HILL TOP
LA22 0LF
➲ (2m S of Hawkshead. Behind The Tower Bank
Arms)
☎ 015394 36269 📄 015394 36118
e-mail: rpmhtop@smtp.ntrust.org.uk

Beatrix Potter wrote many Peter Rabbit books in this little
17th-century house, which contains her furniture and china.
Times: Open 29 Mar-29 Oct, 10.30-4.30, last admission 4pm **Fee:** ✱
£4.50 (ch £1) Family ticket £10 **Facilities:** 🅿 (200 metres) (no parking
for coaches) (braille guide, handling items, accessibility by arrangement)
shop 🍽 (ex guide dogs) 🍽 🍽

PENRITH   Map 12 NY53

RHEGED - THE VILLAGE IN THE HILL
Redhills CA11 0DQ
➲ (M6 junct 40, on A66 towards Keswick)
☎ 01768 868000 📄 01768 868002
e-mail: enquiries@rheged.com

Named after Cumbria's Celtic kingdom, this incredible
attraction is the largest grass-covered building in Europe,
and is designed to look like a Lakeland hill. Inside is a
state-of-the-art Mega Systems cinema with a screen that

continued

measures 60 feet wide and 48 feet high. Alongside this cinema experience that includes films on Egypt, Cumbria and Everest, is the Helly Hansen National Mountaineering Exhibition that commemorates the 50th Anniversary of the first ascent of Everest.

Rheged – The Village in the Hill

Times: Open daily 10-5.30. (Closed 25 Dec) **Fee:** ✱ Each attraction £5.50 (ch £3.90 & pen £4.70). Family ticket £16 **Facilities:** 🅿 ▣ ✖ licensed & toilets for disabled shop ✖ (ex guide dogs) ◥

WETHERIGGS COUNTRY POTTERY
Clifton Dykes CA10 2DH
➲ (approx 2m off A6, S from Penrith, signposted)
☎ 01768 892733 ▤ 01768 892722   FREE
e-mail: info@wetheriggs-pottery.co.uk
The only steam-powered pottery in Britain, with 7.5 acres of things to do, including the Pots of Fun Studio, where you can throw or paint a pot, Designer-Makers at the work, Café, Bistro, shop. Collectibles Cabin, newt pond, play areas and pottery museum.
Times: Contact establishment for details of opening times.
Facilities: 🅿 ▣ ✖ licensed & toilets for disabled shop ✖ (ex guide dogs & dogs on lead) ◥

RAVENGLASS   Map 06 SD09
RAVENGLASS & ESKDALE RAILWAY
CA18 1SW
➲ (close to A595, Barrow to Carlisle road)
☎ 01229 717171 ▤ 01229 717011
e-mail: rer@netcomuk.co.uk
From the Lake District National Park's only coastal village of Ravenglass, small steam engines haul trains through 7 miles of outstanding, unspoilt beauty to the foot of England's highest mountains in Eskdale. Enjoy the freedom of open or cosy covered carriages. Children learn about steam with 'La'al Ratty', the Water-vole Stationmaster.
Times: Open: trains operate daily 22 Mar-early Nov. Most winter wknds, plus daily in Feb Half term. **Fee:** ✱ Return fare £7.80 (ch 5-15 £3.90). 1 adult half price with 2+ fare paying children. **Facilities:** 🅿 (charged) ▣ ✖ & (special coaches - prior notice advisable) toilets for disabled shop ◥

RYDAL   Map 11 NY30
RYDAL MOUNT AND GARDENS
LA22 9LU
➲ (1.5m from Ambleside on A591 to Grasmere)
☎ 015394 33002 ▤ 015394 31738
e-mail: rydalmount@aol.com
The family home of William Wordsworth from 1813 until his death in 1850. The house contains important family portraits, furniture, and many of the poet's personal possessions, together with first editions of his work. In a lovely setting overlooking Windermere and Rydal Water, the gardens were designed by Wordsworth himself. Evening visits for groups can be organised.
Times: Open Mar-Oct daily 9.30-5; Nov-Feb daily (ex Tue) 10-4 (Closed 8 Jan-1 Feb). **Fee:** £4.25 (ch £1.50, pen £3.50 & student £3.25). Garden only £1.75. Party 10+ (pre booked groups £3.25). Reciprocal discount ticket with Dove Cottage and Wordsworth House.
Facilities: 🅿 & shop ✖ (ex guide dogs & garden) ◥

SEDBERGH   Map 07 SD69
NATIONAL PARK CENTRE
72 Main St LA10 5AS
➲ (on Sedburgh main street at end of one way system)
☎ 015396 20125 ▤ 015396 21732   FREE
e-mail: sedbergh@yorkshiredales.org.uk
At the north-western corner of the Yorkshire Dales National Park, Sedbergh is set below the Howgill Fells. The rich natural history of the area and the beautiful scenery created a need for this visitor centre; maps, walks, guides, local information and interpretative displays can be found here, and there is a full tourist information service.
Times: Open Apr-Oct, daily 10-4; Nov-Mar Fri-Sun. **Facilities:** 🅿 (charged) & (accessible with help Radar key scheme) shop

SHAP   Map 12 NY51
SHAP ABBEY
CA10 3NB
➲ (1.5m W of Shap on bank of River Lowther)   FREE
Dedicated to St Mary Magdalene, the abbey was founded by the Premonstratensian order in 1199, but most of the ruins are of 13th-century date. The most impressive feature is the 16th-century west tower of the church.
Times: Open any reasonable time. **Facilities:** 🅿 & ✖ (ex dogs on leads)

SIZERGH   Map 07 SD48
SIZERGH CASTLE & GARDEN
LA8 8AE
➲ (3.5m S of Kendal, signed from A590)
☎ 015395 60070 ▤ 015395 60951
e-mail: sizergh@nationaltrust.org.uk
The castle has a 60-foot high tower, built in the 14th century, but most of the castle dates from the 15th to the 18th centuries. There are panelled rooms with fine carved overmantles and adze-hewn floors, and the gardens, laid out

continued

in the 18th century, contain the National Trust's largest limestone rock garden.
Times: Open Apr-Oct, Sun-Thu 1.30-5.30; Garden open Apr-Oct, from 12.30. (Last admission 5pm). **Fee:** House & Garden £5.50 (ch £2.70). Family ticket £13.70. Group rate £4.50 each. Garden only £3 (ch £1.50). **Facilities:** 🅿 💺 & (wheelchair and powered buggy for hire, braille guide) toilets for disabled shop ✖ (ex guide & hearing dogs) 🐾 🍵

SKELTON   Map 12 NY43

HUTTON-IN-THE-FOREST
CA11 9TH
➲ (6m NW of Penrith on B5305 to Wigton, 2.5m from M6 junct 41)
☎ 017684 84449   📠 017684 84571
e-mail: hutton-in-the-forest@talk21.com

A beautiful house, set in woods which were once part of the medieval forest of Inglewood. The house consists of a 14th-century pele tower with later additions, and contains a fine collection of furniture, portraits, tapestries and china, a 17th-century gallery and cupid staircase. The walled garden has a large collection of herbaceous plants, and there are 19th-century topiary terraces, a 17th-century dovecote and a woodland walk with impressive specimen trees.
Times: Open, House; 18 Apr-28 Sep Thu, Fri, Sun & BH 12.30-4. Gardens Daily ex Sat 11-5 **Facilities:** 🅿 💺 & (electric wheelchair available) shop ✖ (ex in grounds on leads)

TEMPLE SOWERBY   Map 12 NY62

ACORN BANK GARDEN AND WATERMILL
CA10 1SP
➲ (6m E of Penrith on A66)
☎ 017683 61893   📠 017683 66824
e-mail: acornbank@nationaltrust.org.uk

A delightful garden of some two and a half acres, where an extensive collection of over 180 varieties of medicinal and culinary herbs is grown. Scented plants are grown in the small greenhouse, and a circular walk runs beside the Crowdundle Beck to the partially restored watermill. Please ring for details of special events.
Times: Open late Mar-early Nov, daily (ex Tues) 10-5 (last admission 4.30pm). **Fee:** ✱ £2.60 (ch £1.30). Family ticket £6.50. Party 15+ £1.90. **Facilities:** 🅿 💺 & (braille guide, wheelchairs available) toilets for disabled shop ✖ (ex on lead on woodland walk) 🐾 🍵

TROUTBECK   Map 07 NY40

TOWNEND
LA23 1LB
➲ (3m SE of Ambleside at S end of village)
☎ 015394 32628
e-mail: rtown@smtp.ntrust.org.uk

The house is one of the finest examples of a `statesman' (wealthy yeoman) farmer's house in Cumbria, built in 1626 for George Browne, whose descendents lived here until 1943. Inside is the original home-made carved furniture, with domestic utensils, letters and papers of the farm.
Times: Open 2 Apr-Oct, Tue-Fri, Sun & BH Mon 1-5 or dusk if earlier. Last admission 4.30pm. **Fee:** ✱ £3 (ch £1.50). Family ticket £7.50. **Facilities:** 🅿 (braille guide) ✖ 🐾

WINDERMERE   Map 07 SD49

LAKE DISTRICT VISITOR CENTRE AT BROCKHOLE
LA23 1LJ
➲ (on A591, between Windermere and Ambleside follow brown tourist signs)
☎ 015394 46601   📠 015394 45555
e-mail: infodesk@lake-district.gov.uk

Set in 32 acres of landscaped gardens and grounds, on the shore of Lake Windermere, this house became England's first National Park Visitor Centre in 1969. It offers exhibitions, audio-visual programmes, lake cruises, an adventure playground and an extensive events programme.
Times: Open Etr-Oct, 10-5 daily. Grounds & gardens open all year. **Fee:** Free admission but parking charge £4 full day, £3 half day. **Facilities:** 🅿 (charged) 💺 ✖ licensed & (manual & electric wheelchairs, lifts, induction loops) toilets for disabled shop 🍵

WINDERMERE STEAMBOAT CENTRE
Rayrigg Rd LA23 1BN
➲ (0.5m N of Bowness-on-Windermere on A592)
☎ 015394 45565   📠 015394 48769   **2 for 1**
e-mail: steamboat@ecosse.net

A unique collection of Victorian and Edwardian steamboats and vintage motorboats, including the oldest steamboat in the world - the *S L Dolly* of 1850. Displays tell the social and commercial history of England's largest lake, and there are steamboat trips daily, weather permitting.
Times: Open 17 Mar-9 Nov daily, 10-5. Steamboat trips subject to availability & weather. **Fee:** £3.50 (ch £2). Family ticket £8.50, season ticket £15. **Facilities:** 🅿 💺 & toilets for disabled shop 🍵

Remember that prices and opening times are liable to change within the currency of this guide. It is always best to telephone in advance to check

DERBYSHIRE

EVENTS & FESTIVALS

February
6th-7th Beer Festival, Chesterfield
24th Shrove Tuesday Winster Pancake Races,

May-September
Well dressings throughout the county

April
13th Flagg Races, point-to-point steeplechases,
Flagg Moor

May
1st-3rd Derbyshire Steam Fair, Hartington
Moor Showground
15th-16th Chatsworth Horse Trials,
Chatsworth, nr Bakewell
22nd-24th Beer Festival, Barrow Hill
Roundhouse, Chesterfield (provisional)
tbc Brass Band Competition, Buxton
tbc Buxton Music, Speech & Drama Festival
tbc Castleton Garland Ceremony

June
27th Derbyshire County Show,
Showground, Alvaston
tbc Derbyshire Summer Garden Festival, The
Showground, Bakewell

July
2nd-4th Dove Beer & Jazz Festival,
Dove Holes, Buxton
10th-25th Buxton Festival, opera, music &
literature, Buxton (provisional)
18th Ashbourne Highland Gathering

August
4th-5th Bakewell Show, Bakewell
28th-30th Oct Matlock Bath Illuminations
30th Chesterfield Evening Fireworks

September
4th-5th Chatsworth Country Fair
11th-12th Buxton Country Music Festival
tbc Wirksworth Festival, various locations

October
14th Ilkeston Charter Fair, fun fair throughout
the streets of Ilkeston

November
7th Dovedale Dash, fun run at Thorpe
Pastures, Thorpe

above: Boundary stone in the
Peak District National Park

BOLSOVER   Map 08 SK47

BOLSOVER CASTLE
Castle St S44 6PR
➲ (on A632)
☎ 01246 822844   ▤ 01246 241569

This award winning property has the air of a romantic storybook castle, with its turrets and battlements rising from a wooded hilltop. See the stunning Venus garden with its beautiful statuary and fountain. State of the art audio tours are available.
Times: Open all year, Apr-Sep, daily 10-6 (Oct daily 10-5); Nov-Mar, Thu-Mon 10-4. (Closed 24-26 Dec & 1 Jan). Dates valid until 31 Mar 2004. **Fee:** £6.20 (ch £3.10, concessions £4.60). Prices valid until 31 Mar 2004. **Facilities:** ☐ ▣ & (keep not accessible) shop ✕ ✿

BUXTON   Map 07 SK07

POOLE'S CAVERN (BUXTON COUNTRY PARK)
Green Ln SK17 9DH
➲ (1m from Buxton town centre, off A6 and A515)
☎ 01298 26978   ▤ 01298 73563
e-mail: info@poolescavern.co.uk

Limestone rock, water, and millions of years created this natural cavern containing thousands of crystal formations. A 45-minute guided tour leads the visitor through chambers used as a shelter by Bronze-Age cave dwellers, Roman metal workers and as a hideout by the infamous robber Poole. Attractions include the underground source of the River Wye, the 'Poached Egg Chamber', Mary, Queen of Scots' Pillar, the Grand Cascade and underground sculpture formations.
Times: Open Mar-Oct, daily 10-5. (Open in winter for groups only).
Facilities: ☐ & toilets for disabled shop ✕ (ex guide dogs or in park) ▤

CALKE   Map 08 SK32

CALKE ABBEY
DE73 1LE
➲ (9m S of Derby, on A514)
☎ 01332 863822   ▤ 01332 865272
e-mail: calkeabbey@nationaltrust.org.uk

This fine baroque mansion dating from the early 18th century was built for Sir John Harpur. Among its treasures are an extensive natural history collection, a magnificent Chinese silk state bed, and a spectacular red and white

continued

drawing room. The house stands in extensive wooded parkland and also has walled flower gardens.
Times: Open 29 Mar-2 Nov Sat-Wed & BH Mon; House & church 1-5.30 Gardens from 11am. Last admission 5pm. Park open all year until 9pm (dusk if earlier). House, church & garden closed Sat 16 Aug.
Fee: ✱ £5.60 (ch £2.80). Family ticket £14. **Facilities:** 🅿 ✕ licensed ♿ (braille guide, hearing system, buggy/wheelchair available) toilets for disabled shop ✕ (ex guide dogs) ⚘

CASTLETON — Map 07 SK18

BLUE-JOHN CAVERN & MINE
Buxton Rd S33 8WP
➜ (follow brown "Blue-John Cavern" signs from Castleton)
☎ 01433 620638 & 620642 📠 01433 621586
e-mail: lesley@bluejohn.gemsoft.co.uk

A remarkable example of a water-worn cave, over a third of a mile long, with chambers 200ft high. It contains 8 of the 14 veins of Blue John stone, and has been the major source of this unique form of fluorspar for nearly 300 years.
Times: ✱ Open all year daily 9.30-5 (or dusk). Guided tours of approx 1hr every 10 mins tour. **Facilities:** 🅿 ▆ (not suitable for disabled visitors) shop ⬗

PEAK CAVERN
S33 8WS
➜ (on A6187, in centre of Castleton)
☎ 01433 620285
e-mail: info@peakcavern.co.uk

One of the most spectacular natural limestone caves in the Peak District, with an electrically-lit underground walk of about half a mile. Ropes have been made for over 500 years in the 'Grand Entrance Hall', and traces of a row of cottages can be seen. Rope-making demonstrations are included on every tour.
Times: Open Etr-Oct, daily 10-5. Nov-Etr wknds only 10-5 **Fee:** ✱ £5.50 (ch £3.50, other concessions £4.50). Family ticket £16.
Facilities: 🅿 (charged) shop ⬗

PEVERIL CASTLE
Market Place S33 8WQ
➜ (on S side of Castleton)
☎ 01433 620613

The romantic ruins of this Norman fortress are situated high on a rocky crag and the views from the great square tower of the surrounding Peak District are breathtaking. Sir Walter Scott glamourised the castle in his novel, *Peveril of the Peak*.
Times: Open all year, Apr-Sep, daily 10-6; Oct, daily 10-5; Nov-Mar, Wed-Sun 10-4. (Closed 24-26 Dec & 1 Jan). Dates valid until 31 Mar 2004. **Fee:** £2.50 (ch £1.30, concessions £1.90). Prices valid until 31 Mar 2004. **Facilities:** shop ✕ (ex dogs on leads) ▦

Speedwell Cavern
Winnats Pass S33 8WA
➲ (A625 becomes A6187 at Hathersage) 0.5m W of Castleton)
☎ **01433 620512** 🖷 **01433 621888**
e-mail: info@speedwellcavern.co.uk

Descend 105 steps to a boat that takes you on a one-mile underground exploration of the floodlit cavern.
Times: Open all year, Etr-Oct daily 9.30-5.30, Nov-Etr 10-5. (Closed 25 Dec). Phone to check Winter opening times due to weather. **Fee:** ✱ £6 (ch £4). **Facilities:** P (charged) shop

Treak Cliff Cavern
S33 8WP
➲ (0.75m W of Castleton on A6187)
☎ **01433 620571** 🖷 **01433 620519**
e-mail: treakcliff@bluejohnstone.com

An underground world of stalactites, stalagmites, flowstone, rock and cave formations, minerals and fossils. There are rich deposits of the rare and beautiful Blue John Stone, and the show caves include the Witch's Cave, Aladdin's Cave and Fairyland Grotto and some of the finest stalactites in the Peak District.
Times: Open all year, Mar-Oct, daily 10-last tour 4.20, Aug only, last tour 4.45; Nov-Feb daily 10-last tour at 3.20. Closed 24-26 & 31 Dec-1 Jan. All tours are guided & last about 40 mins. **Fee:** ✱ Adults £5.60 (ch 5-15 £3). Family ticket (2 ad & 2 ch) £15. **Facilities:** P (establishment can only cater for walking disabled) shop

CHATSWORTH — Map 08 SK27

Chatsworth
DE45 1PP
➲ (8m N of Matlock off B6012. 16m from M1 junct 29, signposted via Chesterfield, follow brown signs)
☎ **01246 582204** 🖷 **01246 583536**
e-mail: visit@chatsworth.org

Home of the Duke and Duchess of Devonshire, Chatsworth contains a massive private collection of fine and decorative arts. There is a splendid painted hall, and a great staircase leads to the chapel, decorated with statues and paintings. There are pictures, furniture and porcelain, and a trompe l'oeil painting of a violin on the music room door. The park was laid out by 'Capability' Brown, but is most famous as the work of Joseph Paxton, head gardener in the 19th century.
Times: Open 2 Apr-21 Dec, House & garden 11-5.30, Farmyard 10.30-5.30. **Fee:** ✱ House & Garden £8.50 (ch £3, students & pen £6.50). Family ticket £20. Pre-booked group discounts available. Garden only £5 (ch £2, students & pen £3.50). Family ticket £12. Farmyard & Adventure Playground £3.90 (pen & school parties £3). Groups 5+ £3.40. Family pass to all attractions £32. **Facilities:** P (charged) licensed ♿ (3 electric wheelchairs available for garden) toilets for disabled shop garden centre (ex park & gardens on lead)

CRESWELL — Map 08 SK57

Creswell Crags Museum and Education Centre
Crags Rd, Welbeck S80 3LH
➲ (on the B6042, Crags Road, between A616 and A60, 1m E of Creswell village)
☎ **01909 720378**
e-mail: info@creswell-crags.org.uk

Creswell Crags, a picturesque limestone gorge with lakes and caves, is one of Britain's most important archaeological sites. The many caves on the site have yielded Ice Age remains, including bones of woolly mammoth, reindeer, hyena and bison, and the stone tools of Ice Age hunters from over 10,000 years ago. Visit the Museum and Education Centre to learn more about your Ice Age ancestors through an exhibition, touchscreen computers and video. Join a 'Virtually the Ice Age' cave tour, picnic in Crags Meadow, or try the new activity trail.
Times: Open all year, Feb-Oct, daily, 10.30-4.30; Nov-Jan, Sun only 10.30-4.30. **Fee:** ✱ Free. Cave & site tour £2.75 (ch £2, no under 5's). £1 parking donation requested. **Facilities:** P ♿ (mobility scooter, tour may be unsuitable due to steps) toilets for disabled shop

CRICH — Map 08 SK35

Crich Tramway Village
DE4 5DP
➲ (off B5035, 8m from M1 junct 28)
☎ **0870 758 7267** 🖷 **01773 852326** 2 for 1
e-mail: info@tramway.co.uk

A mile-long scenic journey through a Period Street to open countryside with panoramic views. You can enjoy unlimited vintage tram rides, and the exhibition hall houses the largest

continued

collection of vintage electric trams in Britain. Ring for details of special events.

Times: Open Apr-Oct, daily 10-5.30 (6.30pm wknds Jun-Aug & BH wknds). Nov-Dec open wknds 10.30-4 **Fee:** ✱ £7 (ch 3-15 £3.50, pen £6). Family ticket (2 adults & 3 ch) £19. **Facilities:** Ⓟ ⬛ ✗ licensed & (Braille guidebooks, converted tram, talktype facility) toilets for disabled shop ☞

CROMFORD   Map 08 SK25
ARKWRIGHT'S CROMFORD MILL
Mill Ln DE4 3RQ
➲ (off A6, 3m S of Matlock)
☎ 01629 824297 🖷 01629 823256
e-mail: info@cromfordmill.co.uk
Sir Richard Arkwright established the world's first successful water-powered cotton spinning mill at Cromford in 1771. The Arkwright Society are involved in a major restoration to create a lasting monument to an extraordinary genius. Guided tours are available, and there is a programme of lectures and visits - ring for details. The Mill site is part of the Deswent Valley Mill World Heritage site.
Times: Open all year, daily 9-5 (Closed 25 Dec). **Facilities:** Ⓟ ✗ & toilets for disabled shop ☞

DENBY   Map 08 SK34
DENBY POTTERY VISITOR CENTRE
Derby Rd DE5 8NX
➲ (8m N of Derby off A38, on B6179,   **2 for 1**
2m S of Ripley)
☎ 01773 740799 🖷 01773 740749   **FREE**
e-mail: visitor.centre@denby.co.uk
Situated around a cobbled courtyard with shops and a restaurant. Pottery tours are available daily including hands on activities such as paint-a-plate and make a clay souvenir. Extensive cookshop with free half hour demonstrations daily. There are lots of bargains on Denby seconds in the factory shop, hand-made blown glass from the Glass Studio,

continued

Dartington Crystal Shop, local artists gallery and hand painted Denby. **(2-for-1 Voucher applies to factory tour only.)**

Times: Open all year. Factory tours, Mon-Thu 10.30 & 1. Craftroom tour, daily 11-3. Visitor Centre Mon-Sat 9.30-5, Sun 10-5. Closed 25-26 Dec. **Facilities:** Ⓟ ⬛ ✗ licensed & (lift) toilets for disabled shop garden centre ✖ (ex guide dogs) ☞

DERBY   Map 08 SK33
DERBY MUSEUM & ART GALLERY
The Strand DE1 1BS
➲ (in city centre)
☎ 01332 716659 🖷 01332 716670   **FREE**
e-mail: david.fraser@derby.gov.uk
The museum has a wide range of displays, notably of Derby porcelain, and paintings by the local artist Joseph Wright (1734-97). Also antiquities, natural history and militaria, as well as many temporary exhibitions.
Times: Open all year, Mon 11-5, Tue-Sat 10-5, Sun & BHs 2-5. Closed Xmas & New Year, telephone for details. **Facilities:** Ⓟ (50yds) & (lift to all floors, portable mini-loop, large print labels) toilets for disabled shop ✖ (ex guide dogs)

INDUSTRIAL MUSEUM
The Silk Mill, Silk Mill Ln, off Full St DE1 3AR
➲ (From Derby inner ring road, head for Cathedral & Assembly Rooms car park. 5 mins walk from here)
☎ 01332 255308 🖷 01332 716670   **FREE**
e-mail: david.fraser@derby.gov.uk
The museum is set in an early 18th-century silk mill and adjacent flour mill. Displays cover local mining, quarrying and industries, and include a major collection of Rolls Royce aero-engines from 1915 to the present. There is also a section covering the history of railway engineering in Derby.
Times: Open all year, Mon 11-5, Tue-Sat 10-5, Sun & BHs 2-5. (Closed Xmas & New Year, telephone for details). **Facilities:** Ⓟ & (lift to all floors) toilets for disabled shop ✖ (ex guide dogs)

PICKFORD'S HOUSE MUSEUM OF GEORGIAN LIFE & COSTUME

41 Friar Gate DE1 1DA

➲ (from A38 into Derby, follow signs to city centre)

☎ 01332 255363   🖷 01332 255527

e-mail: ellen.malin@derby.gov.uk   FREE

The house was built in 1770 by the architect Joseph Pickford as a combined workplace and family home. It now shows domestic life at different periods, with Georgian reception rooms and service areas and a 1930s bathroom. Other galleries are devoted to temporary exhibitions. There is also a display on the growth of Georgian Derby, and on Pickford's contribution to Midlands architecture.
Times: Open all year, Mon 11-5, Tue-Sat 10-5, Sun & BHs 2-5. (Closed Xmas & New Year, telephone for details). **Facilities:** 🅿 & (tape guides, video with sign language subtitles) shop ✖ (ex guide dogs)

ROYAL CROWN DERBY VISITOR CENTRE

194 Osmaston Rd DE23 8JZ

➲ (on A514 10 mins walk from bus & rail stations & Derby city centre)   **2 for 1**

☎ 01332 712800   🖷 01332 712899

e-mail: enquiries@royal-crown-derby.co.uk

This museum traces the history of the company from 1750 to the present day, while the factory tour demonstrates the making of Royal Crown Derby in detail from clay through to the finished product. A demonstration studio gives you the opportunity to watch craftspeople at close quarters and try out a variety of different skills.
Times: ✱ Open all year, daily. Factory tours twice daily, booking strongly advised. **Fee:** ✱ Factory tour & visitor centre £4.95, concessions £4.75. Visitor centre only £2.95, concessions £2.75.
Facilities: 🅿 🅿 ✖ licensed & (visitor entry accessible but not factory tour) toilets for disabled shop ✖ (ex guide dogs)

EYAM   Map 08 SK27

EYAM HALL

S32 5QW

➲ (in village centre)

☎ 01433 631976   🖷 01433 631603

e-mail: nicola@eyamhall.com

An intimate 17th-century manor house in the heart of the famous "plague village". Home to the Wright family since 1671, the Hall offers a glimpse of domestic history through the eyes of one family, in portraits, furniture, tapestries, costumes and memorabilia. Converted farm buildings house the Eyam Hall Craft Centre. Please telephone for details of musical and theatrical events throughout the season.
Times: Open House: Jun-Aug, Wed-Thu, Sun & BH Mon 11-4. Craft Centre open all year Tue-Sun 11-5. **Fee:** ✱ House £4.50 (ch £3.50, pen £4). Family ticket £14.50. Craft centre free admission. **Facilities:** 🅿 ✖ licensed & (disabled entrance via special gate, ramps) toilets for disabled shop ✖ (ex guide & dogs in grounds)

> The AA also publishes a guide to
> Pet Friendly Places to Stay

HADDON HALL   Map 08 SK26

HADDON HALL

DE45 1LA

➲ (1.5m S of Bakewell off A6)

☎ 01629 812855   🖷 01629 814379

e-mail: info@haddonhall.co.uk

Originally held by the illegitimate son of William the Conqueror, Haddon has been owned by the Manners family since the 16th century. Little has been added since the reign of Henry VIII, and, despite its time-worn steps, few medieval houses have so successfully withstood the ravages of time.
Times: Open Apr-Sep, daily 10.30-5; Oct, Thu-Sun 10.30-4.30. **Fee:** ✱ £7.25 (ch £3.75 & pen £6.25). Family ticket £19. Party 15+.
Facilities: 🅿 (charged) ✖ licensed & (access is impossible for those in wheelchairs) toilets for disabled shop ✖ (ex guide dogs)

HARDWICK HALL   Map 08 SK46

HARDWICK HALL

Doe Lea S44 5QJ

➲ (2m S M1 junct 29)

☎ 01246 850430   🖷 01246 854200

e-mail: hardwickhall@nationaltrust.org.uk

The romantic ruins of this impressive Elizabethan mansion have spectacular views over the country park and New Hall. An inclusive audio tour tells the story of 'Bess of Hardwick'.
Times: Open 29 Mar-26 Oct, Wed-Thu, Sat-Sun, BH Mon & Good Fri, 12.30-5 (Oct 12.30-4). Last admission 30mins before closing. Garden open 29 Mar-26 Oct daily ex Tue, 11-5.30. **Fee:** ✱ House & Garden £6.60 (ch £3.30). Family ticket £16.50. Garden only £3.50 (ch £1.70). Family £8.70. **Facilities:** 🅿 ✖ licensed & (large print & braille guide, wheelchair (pre-book)) toilets for disabled shop ✖ (ex in park on leads)

ILKESTON   Map 08 SK44

AMERICAN ADVENTURE THEME PARK

DE7 5SX

➲ (off M1 junct 26, signposted, take A610 to A608 then A6007)

☎ 0845 330 2929   🖷 01773 716140

e-mail: sales@americanadventure.co.uk

This is one of Britain's few fully themed parks, based on the legend of a whole continent. The experiences here are widely varied, from the Missile Rollercoaster in Spaceport

continued

USA, to the wet and wild excitement of the Rocky Mountain Rapids ride and the Nightmare Niagara log flume. Fort Adventure is an action packed challenge and the driving school is great for kids to find out if they've got what it takes to be an advanced driver. There's also a Mississippi paddle steamer, a horse-show in Silver City, glamorous Lazy Lil's Saloon Show Skycoaster, a 200ft free fall.
Times: ✹ Open 23 Mar-3 Nov, daily from 10. **Facilities:** 🅿 💻 ✘ licensed ♿ (free wheelchair hire, must pre book, call 0845 330 2929) toilets for disabled shop ✖ (ex guide dogs) ➷

KEDLESTON HALL   Map 08 SK34
KEDLESTON HALL
DE22 5JH
➲ (5m NW of Derby)
☎ 01332 842191 🖷 01332 841972
e-mail: kedleston@nationaltrust.org.uk
Kedleston has been the Derbyshire home of the Curzon family for over eight centuries. The original house was demolished at the end of the 17th century. In 1760 Robert Adam built the south front and designed most of the interior including the marble hall. There are pictures, furniture and china displayed in the house together with an Indian Museum containing the collection accumulated by Lord Curzon, Viceroy of India.
Times: Open all year: House; 22 Mar-2 Nov, Sat-Wed 12-4.30. Last admission 4pm. Garden; same as house but open 10-6. Park open daily, Mar-Oct 10-6, Nov-Feb 10-4. **Fee:** ✹ £5.50 (ch £2.70). Family ticket £13.70. **Facilities:** 🅿 ✘ licensed ♿ (braille guide, w/chair, self-drive vehicle) toilets for disabled shop ✖ (ex in park, must be on leads) 🐾

MATLOCK BATH   Map 08 SK25
THE HEIGHTS OF ABRAHAM CABLE CARS, CAVERNS & HILLTOP PARK
DE4 3PD
➲ (on A6, signposted from M1 junct 28 & A6. Base station next to Matlock Bath railway station)
☎ 01629 582365 🖷 01629 581128
e-mail: info@h-of-a.co.uk

The visit begins with a spectacular cable car journey across the Derwent Valley to the summit of the hill top country park. The most famous aspects of the Heights of Abraham are the two spectacular show caverns, which provide exciting tours to the underground world within the hillside.

There's the 'miners tale', in the Great Rutland Cavern-Nestus Mine and the 'story of the rock' at the Masson Cavern Pavilion. There is also an Explorer's Challenge, woodland walks and the Victoria Prospect Tower.
Times: ✹ Open daily Etr-Oct 10-5 (later in high season) for Autumn & Winter opening telephone for details. **Facilities:** 🅿 (300mtrs) 💻 ✘ licensed ♿ (please ring for details) toilets for disabled shop ✖ (ex in grounds & cable car) ➷

PEAK DISTRICT MINING MUSEUM
The Pavilion DE4 3NR
➲ (On A6 alongside River Derwent)
☎ 01629 583834
e-mail: mail@peakmines.co.uk   **2 for 1**
A large display explains the history of the Derbyshire lead industry from Roman times to the present day. The geology of the area, mining and smelting processes, the quarrying and the people who worked in the industry, are illustrated by a series of static and moving exhibits. The museum also features an early 19th-century water pressure pumping engine. There is a new recyling display in the Pump Room.
Times: Open all year, daily 11-4 (later in summer season). Closed 25 Dec. **Fee:** ✹ Museum & Mine: £4 (ch, students, disabled & pen £2.50). Family £9. Museum only or mine only £2.50 (ch, students, disabled £1.50). Family £6. Party rates. **Facilities:** 🅿 (charged) 💻 ♿ (Chair lift to Mezanine) shop ✖ (ex guide dogs)

TEMPLE MINE
Temple Rd DE4 3NR
➲ (off A6)
☎ 01629 583834
e-mail: mail@peakmines.co.uk   **2 for 1**
A typical Derbyshire mine which was worked from the early 1920s until mid 1950s for fluorspar and associated minerals and shows examples of mining methods which give an insight into working conditions underground.
Times: Open all year, Summer 10-5, Winter timed visits during afternoon. **Fee:** ✹ Museum & Mine: £4 (ch, pen, disabled £2.50). Family ticket £9. Museum only or mine only: £2.50 (ch, pen, disabled £1.50), Family £6. Party rates. **Facilities:** 🅿 (100mtrs) ✖ (ex guide dogs)

MELBOURNE   Map 08 SK32
MELBOURNE HALL & GARDENS
DE73 1EN
➲ (9m S of Derby on A514, in Melbourne take turn by bus shelter in the Market Place, follow road to Church Sq)
☎ 01332 862502 🖷 01332 862263
Sir John Coke (Charles I's Secretary of State) bought the lease of Melbourne Hall in 1628 and the house has been home to two Prime Ministers: Lord Melbourne and Lord Palmerston. The glorious formal gardens are among the finest in Britain.
Times: Open, house daily throughout Aug only (ex first three Mons) 2-5 (last admission 4.15). Prebooked parties by appointment in Aug. Gardens Apr-Sep, Wed, Sat, Sun & BH Mon 1.30-5.30. Upstairs rooms available by appointment. **Fee:** House Tue-Sat (guided tour) £3 (ch £1.50, pen £2.50), Sun & BH Mon (no guided tour) £2.50 (ch £1, pen £2). House & Garden (Aug only) £5 (ch £3, pen £4). Garden only £3 (pen £2). Family £8. **Facilities:** 🅿 (200yds) 💻 ♿ (ramp at garden entrance) shop ✖ (ex guide dogs)

continued

MIDDLETON BY WIRKSWORTH
Map 08 SK25

MIDDLETON TOP ENGINE HOUSE
Middleton Top Visitor Centre DE4 4LS
⮕ (Signed off A6 in Cromford then, 0.5m S from B5036 Cromford/Wirksworth road)
☎ 01629 823204 ◷ 01629 825336
e-mail: middletontop@derbyshire.gov.uk
A beam engine built in 1829 for the Cromford and High Peak Railway, and its octagonal engine house. The engine's job was to haul wagons up the Middleton Incline, and its last trip was in 1963 after 134 years' work. The visitor centre tells the story of this historic railway.
Times: Open: Information Centre, daily, wknds only winter. Engine House Etr-Oct 1st wknd in month (engine in motion). **Fee:** ✱ Static Engine 60p (ch 30p). Working Engine £1.20 (ch 60p). **Facilities:** 🅿 (charged) ♿ toilets for disabled shop ◁

OLD WHITTINGTON
Map 08 SK37

REVOLUTION HOUSE
High St S41 9LA
⮕ (3m N of Chesterfield town centre, on B6052 off A61, signposted)
☎ 01246 345727 ◷ 01246 345720 **FREE**
e-mail: museum@chesterfieldbc.gov.uk
Originally the Cock and Pynot alehouse, this 17th-century cottage was the scene of a meeting between local noblemen to plan their part in the Revolution of 1688. The house is now furnished in 17th-century style. A video relates the story of the Revolution and there is a small exhibition room.
Times: Open Good Fri-Sep, daily 11-4 (ex Tues). Contact museum for Xmas opening hours. **Facilities:** 🅿 (100yds) ♿ (signing available by prior arrangement) shop ◁ (ex guide dogs)

RIPLEY
Map 08 SK35

MIDLAND RAILWAY BUTTERLEY
Butterley Station DE5 3QZ
⮕ (1m N of Ripley on B6179, signposted from A38)
☎ 01773 747674 & 749788 **2 for 1**
◷ 01773 570721
e-mail: mrc@rapidial.co.uk
A regular steam-train passenger service runs here, to the centre where the aim is to depict every aspect of the golden days of the Midland Railway and its successors. Exhibits range from the steam locomotives of 1866 to an electric locomotive. There is also a large section of rolling stock spanning the last 100 years.
Times: Open all year, wknds. May-Oct also open Wed and most school hols. **Fee:** ✱ £8.50 (ch 5-16 £4.25, pen £7.50) children under 5 free. Party 15+. **Facilities:** 🅿 🍴 ♿ (special accommodation on trains) toilets for disabled shop ◁

ROWSLEY
Map 08 SK26

THE WIND IN THE WILLOWS
Peak Village DE4 2NP
⮕ (at junct of A6 & B6012) **2 for 1**
☎ 01629 733433 ◷ 01629 734850
e-mail: enquiries@windinthewillows.info
Based on the charming book written by Kenneth Grahame and illustrated by E H Shepard, this attraction brings to life the characters Mole, Ratty, Toad and Badger in an indoor recreation of the English countryside. Designed by the same team that created The World of Beatrix Potter.
Times: Open Apr-Sep, daily 10-5.30; Oct-Mar, daily 10-4.30. (Closed 25 Dec & 28-30 Jan). **Fee:** ✱ £3.75 (ch £2, under 4's free). **Facilities:** 🅿 🍴 ♿ toilets for disabled shop ◁ (ex guide dogs) ◁

SUDBURY
Map 07 SK13

SUDBURY HALL
DE6 5HT
⮕ (6m E of Uttoxeter)
☎ 01283 585305 ◷ 01283 585139
e-mail: sudburyhall@nationaltrust.org.uk
This country house was started in 1664 by Lord George Vernon. It has unusual diapered brickwork, a carved two-storey stone frontispiece, a cupola and tall chimneys. The interior features work by craftsmen including Edward Pierce and Grinling Gibbons. The Museum of Childhood contains a Victorian schoolroom, collections of toys, and displays.
Times: Open 2 Apr-2 Nov, Wed-Sun, BH Mon & Good Fri 1-5. Last admissions 30 mins before closing. Gardens open 11-6. **Fee:** ✱ House £4.50 (ch £2). Family ticket £11. Museum of Childhood £4.50. Joint ticket £7. Joint Family ticket £18. **Facilities:** 🅿 🍴 ♿ (w/chair available, large print/braille guide & touch list) toilets for disabled shop ◁ (ex in grounds) ◁

WIRKSWORTH
Map 08 SK25

WIRKSWORTH HERITAGE CENTRE
Crown Yard DE4 4ET
⮕ (on B5023 off A6 in centre of Wirksworth)
☎ 01629 825225 **2 for 1**
e-mail: heritage@crownyard.fsnet.co.uk
The Centre has been created in an old silk and velvet mill. The three floors of the mill have interpretative displays of the town's past history as a prosperous lead-mining centre. Each floor offers many features of interest including a computer game called 'Rescue the injured lead-miner', a mock-up of a natural cavern, and a Quarryman's House. During the Spring Bank Holiday you can also see the famous Well Dressings.
Times: Open mid Feb-Etr & Nov, Wed-Sat, 11-4, Sun 1.30-4; Etr-Jun & Oct, Tue-Sat, 11-4, Sun 1.30-5; Jul-Sep, Tue-Sat 10-5. Also open BH Mon. Last admission 40 mins before closing. **Fee:** ✱ £2 (ch & pen £1) Family (2 adults & 3 ch) £5. Party 20+. **Facilities:** 🅿 (80yds) (pay & display) 🍴 ✕ licensed shop ◁ (ex guide dogs)

A full guide to the Symbols & Abbreviations used in this book can be found on page 6

The AA also publishes a guide to Pet Friendly Places to Stay

DEVON

EVENTS & FESTIVALS

February
9th-21st Animated Exeter (films, workshops, exhibitions, events)

April
17th-19th RHS Plant Roadshow, Torquay (provisional)

May
20th-22nd Devon County Show, Westpoint, Clyst St Mary
tbc Blackawton International Festival of Worm Charming, Normandy Arms, Blackawton
tbc Brixham Heritage Festival (music, dance, street theatre & fireworks)
tbc Exmouth Jurassic Gateway Powerboat Grand Prix, Exmouth
tbc Torquay Powerboat Grand Prix, Torquay

July
tbc Exeter Festival of music, entertainment, jazz, comedy & dance (various venues)
tbc Okehampton Balloon Fiesta, Simmons Park, Okehampton

August
6th-8th Dartmoor Folk Festival, South Zeal, Okehampton
12th Okehampton Agricultural Show
19th Chagford Agricultural Show
27th-29th West Country Balloon Fiesta, Tavistock College, Crowndale Road, Tavistock
tbc Exeter Living History Weekend (re-enactment groups, combat displays, tournament ring)
tbc Sidmouth International Festival (various venues, folk music, dance & song)

September
14th Widecombe Fair, Old Field, Widecombe-in-the-Moor

November
tbc Plymouth American Thanksgiving Festival (various venues), Plymouth

Above: The River Tamar spanned by Brunel's railway bridge and a newer tollbridge

---

ARLINGTON   Map 02 SS64

ARLINGTON COURT
EX31 4LP
➲ (7m NE of Barnstaple, on A39)
☎ 01271 850296 📠 01271 851108
e-mail: arlingtoncourt@nationaltrust.org.uk
Arlington Court was built in 1822 and is situated in the thickly wooded Yeo Valley. The centrepiece is the Victorian mansion, surrounded by formal and informal gardens. Also open to visitors is the working stable yard, housing a collection of carriages and horse-drawn vehicles. The extensive parkland around the house is grazed by Jacob sheep and Red Devon cattle.
Times: Open 29 Mar-31 Oct, daily (ex Tue) 10.30-5.30. Last admission 4.30. Grounds open Nov-Mar during daylight hours. **Fee:** ✱ House & grounds £5.80 (ch £2.90). Grounds only £3.80. Parties 15+ £5 each.
Facilities: 🅿 ☕ ♿ (wheelchairs, ramps at house, batricar, braille guide) toilets for disabled shop ✗ (ex in grounds on lead) 🐾 🍽

BARNSTAPLE   Map 02 SS53

MARWOOD HILL GARDENS
Marwood EX31 4EB
➲ (signposted off A361 Barnstaple to Braunton road, follow brown tourist signs)
☎ 01271 342528
The 18-acre gardens with their three small lakes contain many rare trees and shrubs. There is a large bog garden and a walled garden, collections of clematis, camellias and eucalyptus. Alpine plants are also a feature, and there are plants for sale.
Times: Open daily (ex 25 Dec), dawn to dusk. **Fee:** £3 (ch under 12 free, if accompanied). **Facilities:** 🅿 ☕ ♿ garden centre ✗ (ex dogs on lead) 🍽

BEER   Map 03 SY28

PECORAMA PLEASURE GARDENS
Underleys EX12 3NA
➲ (from A3052 take B3174, Beer road, signed)
☎ 01297 21542 📠 01297 20229

The gardens are high on a hillside, overlooking Beer. A miniature steam and diesel passenger line offers visitors a stunning view of Lyme Bay as it runs through the Pleasure Gardens. Attractions include an aviary, crazy golf, children's activity area and the Peco Millennium Garden. The main

continued

building houses an exhibition of railway modelling in various small gauges. There are souvenir and railway model shops, plus full catering facilities.
Times: Open Etr-Oct , Mon-Fri 10-5.30, Sat 10-1. Open Sun Whitsun-early Sep. **Fee:** ✱ £5 (ch 4-14 £3.25, pen £4.50, over 80 & under 4 free) **Facilities:** 🅿 🍴 ✕ ৬ (access with helper, wheelchair. Garden steep in places) toilets for disabled shop ✕ (ex guide dogs) 🚩

BICTON   Map 03 SY08
BICTON PARK BOTANICAL GARDENS
East Budleigh EX9 7BJ
➲ (2m N of Budleigh Salterton on B3178, leave M5 at junct 30 & follow brown tourism signs)
☎ 01395 568465 📠 01395 568374
e-mail: info@bictongardens.co.uk

Sixty-three acres of gardens, woodland, lakes, ponds and fountains, with an Italian garden and a restored palm house where bananas and other exotica flourish. There are also fuchsia, geranium and temperate houses. A countryside museum contains farm tools, wagons and a cider press, and there's also an adventure playground and Bicton Woodland Railway.
Times: Open Winter 10-5, Summer 10-6. (Closed 25 Dec) **Fee:** £4.95 (ch £3.95, concessions £3.95). Family ticket £14.95. **Facilities:** 🅿 🍴 ✕ licensed ৬ (adapted carriage on woodland railway, wheelchairs) toilets for disabled shop garden centre 🚩

BLACKMOOR GATE   Map 03 SS64
EXMOOR ZOOLOGICAL PARK
South Stowford, Bratton Fleming EX31 4SG
➲ (off A399, follow brown tourist signs)
☎ 01598 763352 📠 01598 763352
e-mail: exmoorzoo@fsbdial.co.uk
Exmoor Zoo is both personal and friendly. Open since 1982 it is an ideal family venue, catering particularly for the younger generation. The zoo specialises in smaller animals, many endangered, such as the golden headed lion tamarins. Over 14 species of this type of primate are exhibited. Contact pens are provided throughout and children are encouraged to participate. Twice daily guided tours at feeding times along with handling sessions.
Times: ✱ Open daily, Apr-Oct 10-6; Nov-Mar 10-4. (Closed 21 Dec-1 Jan). **Facilities:** 🅿 🍴 ৬ toilets for disabled shop ✕ (ex guide dogs) 🚩

BUCKFASTLEIGH   Map 03 SX76
BUCKFAST ABBEY
TQ11 0EE
➲ (0.5m from A38, midway between Exeter and Plymouth. Turn off at 'Dart Bridge' junct and follow brown tourist signs)
☎ 01364 645500 📠 01364 643891   **FREE**
e-mail: enquiries@buckfast.org.uk
The Abbey, founded in 1018, was dissolved by Henry VIII in the 16th century. Restoration began in 1907, when four monks with little building experience began the work. The church was built on the old foundations, using local blue limestone and Ham Hill stone. The precinct contains several medieval monastic buildings, including the 14th-century guest hall which contains an exhibition of the history of the Abbey.
Times: Open all year daily. (Closed Good Fri, 24-26 Dec).
Facilities: 🅿 🍴 ৬ (braile & audio information) toilets for disabled shop ✕ (ex guide dogs) 🚩

BUCKFAST BUTTERFLY FARM & DARTMOOR OTTER SANCTUARY
TQ11 0DZ
➲ (off A38, at Dart Bridge junct, follow tourist signs)
☎ 01364 642916
e-mail: info@ottersandbutterflies.co.uk
Visitors can wander around a specially designed, undercover tropical garden, where free-flying butterflies and moths from around the world can be seen. The otter sanctuary has large enclosures with underwater viewing areas. Three types of otters can be seen including the native British otter along with Asian and North American otters.
Times: Open Good Fri-end Oct, daily 10-5.30 or dusk (if earlier). **Fee:** ✱ £4.95 (ch £3.50, pen £4.50). Family ticket £15. **Facilities:** 🅿 🍴 ৬ (wheelchair ramps) shop ✕ (ex guide dogs) 🚩

BUCKLAND ABBEY   Map 02 SX46
BUCKLAND ABBEY
PL20 6EY
➲ (off A386 0.25m S of Yelverton, signed)
☎ 01822 853607 📠 01822 855448
e-mail: bucklandabbey@nationaltrust.org.uk
Originally a prosperous 13th-century Cistercian Abbey, and then home of the Grenville family, Buckland Abbey was sold to Sir Francis Drake in 1581, who lived there until his death in 1596. Several restored buildings house a fascinating exhibition about the abbey's history. Among the exhibits is Drake's drum, which is said to give warning of danger to England. A newly created Elizabethan garden is now open.
Times: Open Apr-Oct, daily (ex Thu) 10.30-5.30. Nov-end Mar, Sat & Sun 2-5. Closed Xmas to mid-Feb. Last admissions 45mins before closing. **Fee:** ✱ Abbey & grounds £5. Grounds only £2.70. Party 15+ £4.20 each. (Car park charge refundable against purchase of admission ticket). **Facilities:** 🅿 (charged) ✕ licensed ৬ (wheelchairs & motorised buggy available) toilets for disabled shop ✕ (ex guide dogs) 🦋

CHITTLEHAMPTON · Map 03 SS62

COBBATON COMBAT COLLECTION

Cobbaton EX37 9RZ

➲ (signed from A361 & A377)

☎ 01769 540740 ⓘ 01769 540141 `2 for 1`

e-mail: info@cobbatoncombat.co.uk

World War II British and Canadian military vehicles, war documents and military equipment can be seen in this private collection. There are over 50 vehicles including tanks, one a Gulf War Centurian, and a recently added Warsaw Pact section. There is also a section on 'Mum's War' and the home front.

Times: Open Apr-Oct, daily (ex Sat) 10-5; Jul-Aug open daily. Winter open most weekdays, phone for details. **Fee:** ✱ £4.50 (ch £3, pen £4). **Facilities:** P ⬛ ♿ (most areas accessible) toilets for disabled shop ✖ (ex guide dogs) ◖

CHUDLEIGH · Map 03 SX87

CANONTEIGN FALLS

EX6 7NT

➲ (off A38 at Chudleigh/Teign Valley junction onto B3193 and follow tourist signs for 3m)

☎ 01647 252434 ⓘ 01647 52617

e-mail: canonteignfalls@lineone.net

A magical combination of waterfalls, woodlands and lakes. **Times:** Open all year, Mar-mid Nov, daily 10-5; Feb Half Term & Winter wknds. **Facilities:** P ⬛ ✖ licensed (grounds partly accessible) shop garden centre ◖

CHURSTON FERRERS · Map 03 SX95

GREENWAY GARDEN

TQ5 0ES

➲ (Turn off A3022 into Galmpton. Follow Manor Vale Road into village then follow brown signs for Greenway Garden and establishment signed)

☎ 01803 842382 ⓘ 01803 661900

e-mail: robyn.brown@nationaltrust.org

Greenway is a beautiful woodland garden set on the banks of the River Dart which time seems to have passed by. A garden held on the edge of wilderness, renowned for rare half-hardy trees and shrubs, underplanted by native wild flowers, Devon's best kept secret. The surrounding estate has many walks which give stunning views over the estuary. Travel by river to enjoy this peaceful haven. Greenway is not easily accessible, having some steep and slippery paths and all visitors are asked to wear walking shoes and to follow routes and directions according to their fitness on the day. **Times:** Open early Mar-early Oct, Wed-Sat. **Fee:** ✱ £3.70 (ch £1.80). **Facilities:** P ⬛ ♿ Part access to garden, braille guide toilets for disabled shop ✖ (ex guide dogs & in Parkland) ✽

CLOVELLY · Map 02 SS32

THE MILKY WAY ADVENTURE PARK

EX39 5RY

➲ (on A39, 2m from Clovelly)

☎ 01237 431255 ⓘ 01237 431735

e-mail: info@themilkyway.co.uk

One of the West Country's leading attractions for the biggest rides and the best shows. Attractions include Clone Zone - Europe's first interactive adventure ride featuring a

continued

suspended roller coaster; Time Warp indoor adventure play area; daily displays from the North Devon Bird of Prey Centre; archery centre; golf driving nets; railway; pets corner and more. A new attraction 'Droid Destroyers' has been added which invites pilots to save the Earth from the Vega Asteroid.

Times: ✱ Open Etr-Oct, daily 10.30-6. Telephone for winter opening times. **Facilities:** P ⬛ ♿ (ramps) toilets for disabled shop ✖ (ex if dogs on leads) ◖

CLYST ST MARY · Map 03 SX99

CREALY ADVENTURE PARK

Sidmouth Rd EX5 1DR

➲ (leave M5 junct 30 onto A3052 Exeter to Sidmouth road)

☎ 01395 233200 ⓘ 01395 233211

e-mail: fun@crealy.co.uk

Crealy Adventure Park is an experience for the whole family, with the New Animal Showtime, El Pastil Loco rollercoaster, Queen Bess Pirate Ship, Techno Race Karts, Bumper Boats, Victorian Carousel, Animal Handling, huge indoor and out door play areas and Log Flume.

Times: Open all year, Jan-Mar, daily 10-5; Apr-Oct 10-6; Nov-Dec 10-5. (Closed winter term time Mon Tue). **Fee:** ✱ £7.75-£7.95 (ch under 3 free, pen £5). Party 4+ £7.50. **Facilities:** P ⬛ ✖ licensed ♿ (Carers admitted free, rollercoaster has disabled facility) toilets for disabled shop ◖

COMBE MARTIN · Map 02 SS54

COMBE MARTIN WILDLIFE PARK & DINOSAUR PARK

EX34 0NG

➲ (M5 junct 27 then A361 towards Barnstaple and turn right onto A399)

☎ 01271 882486 ⓘ 01271 883869 `2 for 1`

e-mail: info@dinosaur-park.com

The land that time forgot. A subtropical paradise with hundreds of birds and animals and animatronic dinosaurs, so real they're alive! Fantastic sealion shows, falconry displays & animal handling sessions. Snow leopards, meerkats, apes & monkeys and lots more.

Times: Open 22 Mar-2 Nov, daily 10-4 (last admission). **Fee:** ✱ £10 (ch 3-15 £6, ch under 3 free, pen £7). Family (2 adults & 2 ch) £29. **Facilities:** P ⬛ shop ✖ (ex guide dogs)

COMPTON   Map 03 SX86

COMPTON CASTLE
TQ3 1TA
➲ (off A381 Newton Abbot to Totnes road, 4m W
of Torquay or 1.5m N of Maldon, off A380 (no
coaches on this road))
☎ 01803 875740   📠 01803 875740

A fortified house of the 14th to 16th centuries, Compton has
been the home of the Gilbert family for 600 years. The Great
Kitchen still has its bread ovens and knife-sharpening marks,
and the withdrawing room has squints through which
occupants could watch services in the chapel. Defensive
measures were added in the 16th century, when there were
French raids in the area.
Times: Open Apr-late Oct, Mon, Wed & Thu 10-12.15 & 2-5. **Fee:** ✱
Castle & garden £3 (ch £1.50) Party 15+ £2.40 (ch £1.20) each.
Facilities: 🅿 ✖ (ex guide dogs) ✺

DARTMOUTH   Map 03 SX85

BAYARD'S COVE FORT
TQ6 9AT   FREE
➲ (in Dartmouth on riverfront)

Built by the townspeople to protect the harbour, the remains
of the circular stronghold still stand at the southern end of
the harbour.
Times: Open at all reasonable times. **Facilities:** ✖ ▥

DARTMOUTH CASTLE
Castle Rd TQ6 0JN
➲ (1m SE off B3205, narrow approach road)
☎ 01803 833588   📠 01803 834445

Built at the water's edge in a superb scenic setting, the
castle's military history spans well over 600 years.
Times: Open all year, Apr-Sep, daily 10-6; Oct, daily 10-5; Nov-Mar
Wed-Sun 10-4, closed 1-2. (Closed 24-26 Dec & 1 Jan). Dates valid until
21 Mar 2004. **Fee:** £3.20 (ch £1.60, concessions £2.40). Prices valid
until 31 Mar 2004. **Facilities:** 🅿 (charged) shop ✖ ▥

WOODLANDS LEISURE PARK
Blackawton TQ9 7DQ
➲ (W, off A3122)
☎ 01803 712598   📠 01803 712680
e-mail: fun@woodlandspark.com

All weather fun with an outstanding range of indoor and
continued

outdoor attractions. Experience the biggest indoor venture
centre in the UK. Enjoy 60 acres of outdoor attractions for all
the family including three watercoasters, a 500mtr toboggan
run, Arctic Gliders, Mystic Maze and 15 massive play zones.
There is an indoor falconry centre with flying displays, and a
wide selection of animals and birds. The Master Blaster is
the newest game for the whole family. Blast, propel & vortex
thousands of balls around the alien planet.
Times: Open 26 Mar-5 Nov daily, also wknds & school holidays.
Fee: ✱ £7.90. Family ticket £29.80 (2 ad & 2 ch). **Facilities:** 🅿 💷 ♿
(ramps) toilets for disabled shop ✖ (ex guide dogs) ⬗

DREWSTEIGNTON   Map 03 SX79

CASTLE DROGO
EX6 6PB
➲ (5m S of A30 via Crockernwell (cars only).
Coaches turn off A382 at Sandy Park)
☎ 01647 433306   📠 01647 433186
e-mail: castledrogo@nationaltrust.org.uk

India tea baron Julius Drewe's dream house. This granite
castle, built between 1910 and 1930, is one of the most
remarkable works of Sir Edward Lutyens, and combines the
grandeur of a medieval castle with the comfort of the 20th
century. A great country house with terraced formal garden,
woodland spring garden, huge circular croquet lawn and
colourful herbaceous borders. Standing at more than 900ft
overlooking the wooded gorge of the River Teign with
stunning views of Dartmoor, and delightful walks.
Times: Castle open Apr-Oct, daily (ex Tues) 11-5. Garden open all
year, daily 10.30-5.30 (or dusk if earlier). **Fee:** ✱ Castle £5.90. Garden
& grounds only £3. Ch half price, under 5's free. Family ticket £14.20.
Facilities: 🅿 💷 ✖ licensed ♿ (wheelchairs available, lift to lower
ground floor) toilets for disabled shop garden centre ✖ (ex
guide/hearing dogs) ✺ ⬗

EXETER   Map 03 SX99

GUILDHALL
High St EX4 3EB
➲ (city centre)
☎ 01392 665500   FREE
e-mail: guildhall@exeter.gov.uk

This is one of the oldest municipal buildings still in use. It
was built in 1330 and then altered in 1446, and the arches
and façade were added in 1592-5. The roof timbers rest on
bosses of bears holding staves, and there are portraits of
Exeter dignitaries, guild crests, civic silver and regalia.
Times: Open when there are no mayoral functions. Times are posted
outside weekly. Special opening by arrangement. **Facilities:** 🅿
(200yds) ♿ toilets for disabled ✖ (ex guide dogs)

ST NICHOLAS' PRIORY
Mint Ln, off Fore St EX4 3AT
☎ 01392 665858   📠 01392 421252
e-mail: ramm@exeter.gov.uk

The Benedictine priory was founded in 1087. This building
was the guest wing and features a Norman undercroft, a
Tudor room, a 15th-century kitchen and a grand guest hall
with a fine 15th century arch-braced timber ceiling. Some
fine plaster decoration can be seen, and there are displays of
furniture and wood carving.
Times: Access by guide tours only, daily at 2, 2.30, 3, 3.30. **Fee:** ✱
£1.25 (concessions 75p). Family ticket £2.50. **Facilities:** 🅿 (200yds)
shop ✖ (ex guide dogs)

UNDERGROUND PASSAGES

Romangate Passage, off High St EX4 3PZ

➲ (in city centre)

☎ 01392 665887 ▤ 01392 265695

e-mail: underground.passages@exeter.gov.uk

Originally intended to bring water to the Cathedral, these passages began life in the 14th century, and were expanded in the 15th century and beyond. An outbreak of cholera in 1832 led to the construction of an alternative system, and the passages became a monument to latter-day engineering. Definitely not suitable for those inclined to claustrophobia - and flat shoes are essential. All tours are guided.

Times: Open Jun-Sep & school holidays Mon-Sat 10-5; rest of year Tue-Fri 12-5 & Sat 10-5. **Fee:** ✱ £3.75 (ch & concessions £2.75). Family ticket (2 adults & 3 ch) £11 **Facilities:** P (400mtrs) shop ✖

EXMOUTH   Map 03 SY08

THE WORLD OF COUNTRY LIFE

Sandy Bay EX8 5BU

➲ (M5 junct 30, take A376 to Exmouth. Follow signs to Sandy Bay)

☎ 01395 274533 ▤ 01392 273457

All-weather family attraction including owl displays, and a safari train that rides through a forty acre deer park. Kids will enjoy the friendly farm animals, pets centre and animal nursery. There are also a Victorian street, working models and thousands of exhibits from a bygone age, including steam and vintage vehicles.

Times: ✱ Open Etr-Oct, daily 10-5. **Facilities:** P ▣ ✖ & (all parts accessible ex 'safari train') toilets for disabled shop ✖ (ex guide dogs) ◥

GREAT TORRINGTON   Map 02 SS41

DARTINGTON CRYSTAL

EX38 7AN

➲ (Turn off A386 in centre of Great Torrington down School Lane (opposite church). Dartington Crystal is 200mtrs on left)

☎ 01805 626242 ▤ 01805 626263   `2 for 1`

e-mail: tours@dartington.co.uk

Dartington Crystal has won many international design awards in recognition of its excellence. The factory tour allows visitors to watch the glassware being crafted, from the safety of elevated viewing galleries. All age groups are encouraged to have fun in the glass activity area and to discover the fascinating story of glass and the history of Dartington in the Visitor Centre.

Times: Open all year. Visitor centre, Factory tour, Pavilion Cafe and Shops Mon-Fri 9-5 (last tour 3.15), Sat 10-5, Sun 10-4 (tours closed wknds). For Xmas, New Year and BH opening please telephone for details. **Fee:** ✱ £4.50 (ch under 16 free, pen £3.50). Max 5 ch with every full paying adult. **Facilities:** P ▣ ✖ licensed & toilets for disabled shop ✖ (ex guide dogs) ◥

RHS GARDEN ROSEMOOR

EX38 8PH

➲ (1m SE of town on A3124)

☎ 01805 624067 ▤ 01805 624717   `2 for 1`

e-mail: annet@rhs.org.uk

Rosemoor is the Royal Horticultural Society's first Regional Garden and Centre. The Formal Garden includes 200

continued

varieties of roses, and there is a herb garden, potager, cottage garden, winter garden, alpine terrace and extensive herbaceous borders.

Times: Open: Gardens all year; Visitor Centre Apr-Sep 10-6, Oct-Mar 10-5. (Closed Xmas day) **Fee:** £5 (ch under 6 free; 6-16 £1). Party 10+ **Facilities:** P ▣ ✖ licensed & (Herb garden for disabled) toilets for disabled shop garden centre ✖ (ex guide dogs) ◥

HONITON   Map 03 ST10

ALLHALLOWS MUSEUM

High St EX14 1PG

➲ (next to parish church of St Paul)

☎ 01404 44966 & 42996

e-mail: info@honitonmuseum.co.uk

The museum, housed in a chapel dating back to around 1200, has a wonderful display of Honiton lace, and there are lace demonstrations from June to August. The town's history is also illustrated.

Times: Open Mon before Etr to 31 Oct, Mon-Fri 9.30-4.30 & Sat 9.30-1. Oct, Mon-Fri 9.30-3.30, Sat 9.30-12.30. **Fee:** £2 (pen £1.50, accompanied ch free). **Facilities:** P (400yds) & (stair lift between floors, wheelchair available) shop ✖ (ex guide dogs)

ILFRACOMBE   Map 02 SS54

ILFRACOMBE MUSEUM

Runnymede Gardens, Wilder Rd EX34 8AF

➲ (Situated next to the Landmark Theatre & TIC on seafront)   `2 for 1`

☎ 01271 863541

e-mail: ilfracombe@devonmuseums.net

Ilfracombe was an important trading port from the 14th to the 16th centuries and during the Napoleonic Wars became a popular resort. The history, archaeology, geology, natural history and maritime traditions of the area are illustrated here, along with Victoriana, costumes, photographs and china.

Times: Open all year, Apr-Oct, daily 10-5; Nov-Mar, Mon-Fri 10-1. **Fee:** ✱ £1.50 (ch 50p con £1). Booked disabled school groups free. **Facilities:** P (10yds) & (ramp to front door, wide aisles) shop ✖ (ex guide dogs)

WATERMOUTH CASTLE & FAMILY THEME PARK

EX34 9SL

➲ (3m NE off A399, midway between Ilfracombe & Combe Martin)

☎ 01271 863879 ▤ 01271 865864

e-mail: enquiries@watermouthcastle.com

A popular family attraction including mechanical music demonstrations, musical water show, dungeon labyrinths, Victorian displays, bygone pier machines, animated fairy tale scenes, tube slide, mini golf, children's carousel, swingboats, aeroplane ride, water fountains, river ride, gardens and a maze.

Times: Open Apr-Oct, closed Sat. (Also closed some Mon & Fri off season). Ring for further details. **Fee:** ✱ £8.50 (ch 3-13 £7 & pen £6) **Facilities:** P ▣ & (special wheelchair route) toilets for disabled shop ✖ (ex guide dogs) ◥

KILLERTON HOUSE & GARDEN   Map 03 SS90

KILLERTON HOUSE & GARDEN
EX5 3LE
➲ (off B3181 Exeter to Culhampton road)
☎ 01392 881345 ▯ 01392 883112
Elegant 18th-century house set in an 18-acre garden with
sloping lawns and herbaceous borders. A majestic avenue of
beech trees runs up the hillside, past an arboretum of
rhododendrons and conifers. The garden has an ice house
and rustic summer house where the family's pet bear was
once kept.
Times: Open: House, daily (ex Tue), Mar & Oct, Wed-Sun, Aug daily
11-5. Gardens open all year, daily from 10.30. **Fee:** ✱ House &
grounds £5.50. Grounds only £4. **Facilities:** ▯ ▭ ✗ licensed ᕫ
(wheelchairs & motorised buggy available) toilets for disabled shop
garden centre ✖ (ex in park & guide dogs) ⅋

KINGSBRIDGE   Map 03 SX74

COOKWORTHY MUSEUM OF RURAL LIFE
The Old Grammar School, 108 Fore St TQ7 1AW
➲ (A38 onto A384, then A381 to Kingsbridge,
museum at the top of the town)
☎ 01548 853235
e-mail: wcookworthy@talk21.com
The 17th-century schoolrooms of this former grammar
school are now the setting for another kind of education.
Reconstructed room-sets of a Victorian kitchen, an
Edwardian pharmacy, a costume room and extensive
collection of local historical items are gathered to illustrate
South Devon life. A walled garden and farm gallery are also
features of this museum, founded to commemorate William
Cookworthy, `father' of the English china clay industry. The
Local Heritage Resource Centre with public access
databases, microfilm of local newspapers since 1855 and
Devon record service point are available to visitors. Please
ring for details of special events.
Times: Open all year, Apr-Sep Mon-Sat 10.30-5; Oct Mon-Fri 10.30-4.
Nov-Mar groups by arrangement. Local Heritage Resource Centre open
all year, Mon-Thu 10-12 & Wed also 2-4, other times by appointment.
Fee: £2 (ch 90p, pen £1.50).Family ticket £5 (2 ad & 4 children).Party
rates available. **Facilities:** ▯ (100mtrs) (max 3hrs) ᕫ (braille labels on
selected exhibits) toilets for disabled shop ✖ (ex guide dogs)

KINGSWEAR   Map 03 SX85

COLETON FISHACRE HOUSE & GARDEN
Brownstone Rd TQ6 0EQ
➲ (3m from Kingswear. Take Ferry Road and turn
off at Toll House, follow brown tourist signs)
☎ 01803 752466 ▯ 01803 753017
e-mail: david.mason@nationaltrust.org.uk
The house, set in a stream-fed valley on a beautiful stretch of
south Devon coastline, was designed in the 1920s for Rupert
and Lady D'Oyly Carte (of Gilbert & Sullivan fame) reflecting
the Arts & Crafts tradition, but with refreshingly modern
interiors. A luxuriant garden was created around it, and has
continued

year-round interest with a wide variety of rare and exotic
plants.
Times: Garden open 1-30 Mar, Sat & Sun only 11-5; 2 Apr-2 Nov,
Wed-Sun & BH Mon 10.30-5.30. House open 2 Apr-2 Nov, Wed-Sun &
BH Mon 11-4.30. **Fee:** ✱ House & garden £5 (ch £2.50). Family ticket
£12.50. Garden only £3.90 (ch £1.80). **Facilities:** ▯ ▭ ᕫ
(wheelchairs available, braille guides) toilets for disabled shop garden
centre ✖ (ex guide dogs) ⅋ ◥

KNIGHTSHAYES COURT   Map 03 SS91

KNIGHTSHAYES COURT
EX16 7RQ
➲ (M5 junct 27, 2m N of Tiverton off A396)
☎ 01884 254665 & 257381 ▯ 01884 243050
e-mail: knightshayes@nationaltrust.org.uk
This fine Victorian mansion, a rare example of William
Burges' work, offers much of interest to all ages. The garden
is one of the most beautiful in Devon, with formal terraces,
amusing topiary, a pool garden and woodland walks.
Times: House & garden open 27 Mar-Oct, daily (House closed Fri)
11-5.30. **Fee:** ✱ House & garden £5.70 (ch £2.80). Party rates available.
Facilities: ▯ ▭ ✗ licensed ᕫ (wheelchairs available, lift, braille &
audio guide) toilets for disabled shop garden centre ✖ (ex guide dogs
in house) ⅋

LYDFORD   Map 02 SX58

LYDFORD CASTLE AND SAXON TOWN
EX20 4BH   ▣FREE
➲ (in Lydford off A386)
Standing above the gorge of the River Lyd, this tower, dating
back to the twelfth century, was notorious as a prison. The
earthworks of the original Norman fort lie to the south.
Times: Open all reasonable times. **Facilities:** ▯ ✖ (ex dogs on leads)
⅋

LYDFORD GORGE
EX20 4BH
➲ (off A386, between Okehampton & Tavistock)
☎ 01822 820320 & 820441 ▯ 01822 822000
e-mail: dlybhx@smpt.ntrust.org.uk
The spectacular gorge has been formed by the River Lyd,
which has cut into the rock and caused swirling boulders to
scoop out potholes in the stream bed. This has created some
dramatic features, notably the Devil's Cauldron close to
Lydford Bridge. At the end of the gorge is the 90ft-high White
Lady Waterfall.
Times: ✱ Open Apr-Sep, daily 10-5.30; Oct, daily 10-4. (Nov-Mar,
waterfall entrance only, daily 10.30-3). **Facilities:** ▯ ▭ (easy access
path above gorge, audio tapes) shop ⅋

MORWELLHAM   Map 02 SX47

MORWELLHAM QUAY
PL19 8JL
➲ (4m W of Tavistock, off A390. Midway between
Gunnislake & Tavisock. Signed)
☎ 01822 832766 & 833808 ▯ 01822 833808
Morwellham was the greatest copper port in Queen
Victoria's empire. Once the mines were exhausted the port
area disintegrated into wasteland, until 1970 when a
charitable trust was set up for its restoration. Visitors can
ride by electric tramway underground into a copper mine,
continued

last worked in 1869. The staff wear Victorian costume and visitors can try on replica costumes in the Limeburner's Cottage.

Times: ✷ Open all year (ex Xmas wk) 10-5.30 (4.30 Nov-Etr). Last admission 3.30 (2.30 Nov-Etr). **Facilities:** 🅿 💷 ✗ licensed & (smooth paths, but difficult areas in Victorian village) toilets for disabled shop ✗ (ex on lead) ◥

NEWTON ABBOT   Map 03 SX87

BRADLEY MANOR
TQ12 6BN
➲ (SW of Newton Abbot on A381 Totnes road. 1m from town centre)
☎ 01626 354513

A National Trust property of 70 acres, the 15th-century house and chapel are surrounded by woodland. The River Lemon and a millstream flow through the estate.

Times: ✷ Open Apr-Sep, Wed & Thu, 2-5. **Facilities:** 🅿 ✗ ⚙ ⚘

HEDGEHOG HOSPITAL AT PRICKLY BALL FARM
Denbury Rd, East Ogwell TQ12 6BZ
➲ (1.5m from Newton Abbot on A381 towards Totnes, follow brown heritage signs)
☎ 01626 362319 & 330685 🖷 01626 330685
e-mail: hedgehog@hedgehog.org.uk

See, touch and learn about this wild animal. In mid-season see baby hogs bottle feeding. Find out how to encourage hedgehogs into your garden and how they are put back into the wild. Talks on hedgehogs throughout the day, short basic video information about hedgehogs available.

Times: Open wk before Etr-end Oct, 10.30-5. Last admission 1hr before closing. **Fee:** £4.95 (ch 4-14 £3.95, pen £4.50, ch under 3 free). **Facilities:** 🅿 💷 & (large print menu, use of wheelchair, Braille menu) toilets for disabled shop garden centre ✗ (ex guide dogs) ◥

TUCKERS MALTINGS
Teign Rd TQ12 4AA
➲ (follow brown tourist signs from Newton Abbot railway station)
☎ 01626 334734 🖷 01626 330153
e-mail: info@tuckersmaltings.com

The only working Malthouse in England open to the public, producing malt from barley for over 30 West Country breweries. Learn all about the process of malting - and taste the end product at the in-house brewery. Guided tours last an hour.

Times: Open Good Fri-end Oct, Mon-Sat (Closed Sun ex in Jul & Aug). Speciality bottled beer shop open throughout the year. Phone to check winter opening. **Fee:** ✷ £5.25 (ch 5-15 £3.25, 16-17 £3.95, pen £4.75). Family ticket £14.95. **Facilities:** 🅿 & toilets for disabled shop ◥

OKEHAMPTON   Map 02 SX59

MUSEUM OF DARTMOOR LIFE
3 West St EX20 1HQ
➲ (follow brown signs off all major roads into Okehampton. Museum on main road next to White Hart Hotel)
☎ 01837 52295 🖷 01837 659330
e-mail: dartmoormuseum@eclipse.co.uk

Housed on three floors in an early 19th century mill, the museum tells the story of how people have lived, worked

continued

and played on and around Dartmoor through the centuries. It shows how the moorland has shaped their lives just as their work has shaped the moorland. In the Cranmere Gallery, temporary exhibitions feature local history, art and crafts.

Times: ✷ Open Etr-Oct, Mon-Sat 10-5 (also Sun, Jun-Sep). Winter opening times, telephone for details. **Facilities:** 🅿 💷 shop

OKEHAMPTON CASTLE
Castle Lodge EX20 1JB
➲ (1m SW of town centre)
☎ 01837 52844

Once the largest castle in Devon set amongst the stunning Dartmoor foothills. A free audio tour brings this romantic ruin to life.

Times: Open Apr-Sep, daily 10-6; Oct, daily 10-5. Dates valid until 31 Mar 2004. **Fee:** £2.60 (ch £1.30, concessions £2). Prices valid until 31 Mar 2004. **Facilities:** 🅿 shop ✗ (ex dogs on leads) ⚏

OTTERTON   Map 03 SY08

OTTERTON MILL CENTRE
EX9 7HG
➲ (on the B3178, midway between Budleigh Salterton and Newton Poppleford)
☎ 01392 568521 🖷 01395 568521
e-mail: escape@ottertonmill.com

Mentioned in the Domesday Book, this water-powered mill grinds wholemeal flour used in the baking of bread and cakes sold on the premises. A gallery houses exhibitions through the summer and autumn, and there are sculpture, pottery, weaving, basket-making and spinning studios. There is a co-operative craft shop, and an annual exhibition of furniture from West Country workshops.

Times: Open 7 days a week 10-5. Also open from 7pm Fri & Sat. **Facilities:** 🅿 💷 ✗ licensed & (free entry to ground floor) shop ◥

PAIGNTON   Map 03 SX86

PAIGNTON & DARTMOUTH STEAM RAILWAY
Queens Park Station, Torbay Rd TQ4 6AF
➲ (from Paignton follow brown tourist signs)
☎ 01803 555872 🖷 01803 664313
e-mail: pdsr@talk21.com

Steam trains run for seven miles from Paignton to Kingswear on the former Great Western line, stopping at Goodrington Sands, Churston, and Kingswear, connecting with the ferry crossing to Dartmouth. Combined river excursions available. Ring for details of special events.

Times: Open Jun-Sep daily 9-5.30 & selected days Oct & Apr-May. **Fee:** ✷ Paignton to Kingswear £6.60 (ch £4.60, pen £6). Family £20. Paignton to Dartmouth (including ferry) £7.70 (ch £5.20, pen £7.10). Family £24. **Facilities:** 🅿 (5mins walk) 💷 & (wheelchair ramp for boarding train) toilets for disabled shop ◥

PAIGNTON ZOO ENVIRONMENTAL PARK
Totnes Rd TQ4 7EU
➲ (1m from Paignton town centre on A3022 Totnes road)
☎ 01803 697500 🖷 01803 523457
e-mail: info@paigntonzoo.org.uk

Paignton is one of Britain's biggest zoos, set in a beautiful and secluded woodland valley, where new enclosures are spacious and naturalistic. A tour will take you through some

continued

of the world's threatened habitats - Forest, Savannah, Wetland and Desert, with hundreds of species, many of them endangered and part of conservation breeding programmes. There are regular keeper talks, a children's play area, and special events include an annual Easter Egg Safari.

Paignton Zoo Environmental Park

Times: Open all year, daily 10-6 (5pm in winter). Last admission 5pm (4pm in winter). (Closed 25 Dec). **Fee:** £6.75 (ch 3-15 £4.95, students £5.50). Family ticket £21.50 **Facilities:** 🅿 💷 ✗ licensed ♿ (some steep hills, wheelchair loan-booking essential) toilets for disabled shop ✗ (ex guide dogs) 🍴

PLYMOUTH   Map 02 SX45

CITY MUSEUM & ART GALLERY
Drake Circus PL4 8AJ
➲ (turn off A38 onto A374, follow signs to city centre, museum on NW of city centre, opposite university)
☎ 01752 304774 📠 01752 304775   FREE
e-mail: museum@plymouth.gov.uk

The City Museum and Art Gallery is home to a Fine and Decorative Art Collection of paintings, prints and Reynolds family portraits, silver and Plymouth China, and the Cottonian Collection of drawings, sculpture and books. There is a lively programme of art exhibitions, as well as archaeology, local and natural history displays, and the Discovery Centre with a 'hands-on' section for children. **Times:** Open all year, Tue-Fri 10-5.30, Sat 10-5, BH Mon 10-5. (Closed Good Fri & 25-26 Dec). **Facilities:** 🅿 (200yds) ♿ (wheelchair available) toilets for disabled shop ✗ (ex guide dogs)

MERCHANT'S HOUSE MUSEUM
33 St Andrews St PL1 2AX
➲ (Turn off A38 onto A374, follow signs to city centre, house located behind St Andrew's Church).
☎ 01752 304774 📠 01752 304775
e-mail: plymouth.museum@plymouth.gov.uk

The largest and finest 16th-century house surviving in Plymouth. Inside visitors can discover various aspects of Plymouth's past, including a reconstructed Victorian pharmacy, life during World War II, and a Victorian schoolroom which is available for group bookings. **Times:** Open Apr-Sep, Tue-Fri 10-5.30, Sat 10-5, BH Mon 10-5 during summer (closed 1-2). **Fee:** ✱ £1.10 (ch 60p). **Facilities:** 🅿 (400yds) ♿ shop ✗

PLYMOUTH DOME
The Hoe PL1 2NZ
☎ 01752 603300 & 600608 (recorded message) 📠 01752 256361

This high-tech visitor centre lets you explore the sounds and smells of an Elizabethan street, walk the gun-deck of a galleon, dodge the press gang, stroll with film stars on an ocean liner, and witness the devastation of the Blitz. Examine satellite weather pictures as they arrive from space, keep up to date with shipping movements and monitor the busy harbour on radar. An excellent introduction to Plymouth and a colourful interpretation of the past. Ring for details of special events.
Times: Open Apr-Oct, daily 10-5; Nov-Mar, Tue-Sat 10-4 **Fee:** ✱ £4.50 (ch £3, ch under 5 free, pen & students £3.50). **Facilities:** 🅿 (200yds) 💷 ♿ (audio descriptions, induction loop, wheelchairs available) toilets for disabled shop ✗ (ex guide dogs) 🍴

ROYAL CITADEL
PL1 2PD
➲ (at the end of Plymouth Hoe)
☎ 01752 775841
e-mail: plymouthbbg@hotmail.com

A dramatic 17th-century fortress built to defend the coastline from the Dutch. It is still in use today.
Times: Open 27 May-Sep, daily. Access by guided tour only, book via email: plymouthbbg@hotmail.com. Dates valid until 31 Mar 2004.
Fee: £3 (concessions £2.75). Prices valid until 31 Mar 2004.
Facilities: ✗ ⚏

PLYMPTON   Map 02 SX55

SALTRAM
PL7 1UH
➲ (3.5m E of Plymouth, between A38 and A379. Take Plympton turn at Marsh Mill rdbt, turn right at 4th traffic lights to Cot Hill. At T-junct right into Merafield Rd, Saltram 0.25m on right)
☎ 01752 333500 & 01752 333503
📠 01752 336474
e-mail: saltram@nationaltrust.org.uk

This magnificent George II house still has its original contents. The collection of paintings was begun at the suggestion of Reynolds and includes many of his portraits. The saloon and dining room were designed by Robert Adam and have superb decorative plasterwork and period furniture. **Times:** Open House: late Mar-late Oct, Sat-Thu 12-4.30. Garden open all year, Mar-Nov 10.30-5.30, Nov-Feb 11-4. **Fee:** ✱ £6.30. Gardens only £3.30. **Facilities:** 🅿 💷 ✗ licensed ♿ (wheelchairs available, lift, braille & audio guides) toilets for disabled shop ✗ (ex in park on leads) 🐾 🍴

POWDERHAM   Map 03 SX98

POWDERHAM CASTLE
EX6 8JQ
➲ (signposted off A379 Exeter/Dawlish road)
☎ 01626 890243 📠 01626 890729
e-mail: castle@powderham.co.uk

Built between 1390 and 1420, this ancestral home of the Earls of Devon was damaged in the Civil War. The house was restored and altered in later times and is set in beautiful

continued

rose gardens with views over the deer park to the Exe Estuary. Ring for details of special events.
Times: Open Etr-end Oct, 10-5.30 (last admission 5pm). Closed Sat.
Fee: ✱ £6.90 (ch £3.90, pen £6.40). Family ticket £17.80. Party.
Facilities: 🅿 💺 ✕ licensed ♿ (ramps) toilets for disabled shop garden centre ➤

SALCOMBE   Map 03 SX73

OVERBECKS MUSEUM & GARDEN
Sharpitor TQ8 8LW
➲ (2.5m SW of Salcombe and 2m S of Malborough)
☎ 01548 842893 🖷 01548 845020
e-mail: dovrcx@smtp.ntrust.org.uk

The garden is on the most southerly tip of Devon, and allows many exotic plants to flourish. The Edwardian house displays toys, dolls and a natural history collection, and there is a secret room for children where they can search for 'Fred' the friendly ghost.
Times: Open Apr-Jul Sun-Fri 11-5.30; Aug daily 11-5.30; Sep Sun-Fri 11-5.30; Oct Sun-Thu 11-5. Gardens open all year, 10-8 (or sunset if earlier). **Fee:** Museum & gardens £4.60 (ch £2.30). Gardens only £3.40 (ch £1.70). Family ticket £11.50. **Facilities:** 🅿 (charged) 💺 ♿ (ramp from garden, braille guide) shop ✖ (ex guide dogs) 🚲 ♨ ➤

SOUTH MOLTON   Map 03 SS72

QUINCE HONEY FARM
EX36 3AZ
➲ (3.5m W of A361, on N edge of South Molton)
☎ 01769 572401 🖷 01769 574704   2 for 1
e-mail: info@quincehoney.co.uk

Follow the story of honey and beeswax from flower to table. The exhibition allows you to see the world of bees close up in complete safety; hives open at the press of a button revealing the honeybees' secret life. After viewing the bees at work, sample the fruits of their labour in the café or shop.
Times: Open daily, Apr-Sep 9-6; Oct 9-5; Shop only Nov-Etr 9-5. (Closed 25 Dec-4 Jan). **Fee:** ✱ £3.50 (ch 5-16 £2, pen £2.80)
Facilities: 🅿 💺 ♿ toilets for disabled shop ✖ (ex guide dogs) ➤

STICKLEPATH   Map 03 SX69

FINCH FOUNDRY
EX20 2NW
➲ (Turn off A30 at Okehampton junct, follow brown signs to Finch Foundry. Located in main street of village. Approx 4m from Okehampton).
☎ 01837 840046 🖷 01837 840046

Finch Foundry was, in the 19th century, a water-powered factory for making sickles, scythes, shovels and other hand tools. Although no longer in production, three waterwheels can still be seen driving huge hammers, shears, grindstone and other machinery, with daily working demonstrations. These demonstrations explain the key role the foundry played in the local community.
Times: Open Apr-Nov, daily ex Tue, 11-5.30. **Fee:** £3 (ch £1.50).
Facilities: 🅿 💺 ♿ (access to shop/tea room, view main foundry via shop) shop ♨ ➤

TAVISTOCK
See Morwellham

TIVERTON   Map 03 SS91

TIVERTON CASTLE
EX16 6RP
➲ (M5 junct 27, then 7m on A361 towards Tiverton to rdbt where Castle is signposted)
☎ 01884 253200 & 255200 🖷 01884 254200
e-mail: tiverton.castle@ukf.net

The original castle, built in 1106 by order of Henry I, was rebuilt late 13th-14th centuries. It resisted General Fairfax during the Civil War but fell to him when a lucky shot hit the drawbridge chain. Now a private house, the gardens are lovely and there's a fine Civil War armoury.
Times: Open Etr-Jun & Sep, Sun,Thu & BH Mon's only 2.30-5.30; Jul & Aug, Sun-Thu 2.30-5.30. **Fee:** £4 (ch 7-16 £2,under 7 free). Disabled half price if accessing ground floor only. **Facilities:** 🅿 ♿ toilets for disabled shop ✖ (ex guide dogs)

TIVERTON MUSEUM OF MID DEVON LIFE
Beck's Square EX16 6PJ
➲ (in centre of town next to Beck's Square car park)   2 for 1
☎ 01884 256295
e-mail: curator@tivertonmusuem.org.uk

This large and comprehensive museum now with 15 galleries, re-opened after extensive rebuilding and redisplayed throughout. It is housed in a 19th-century school and the exhibits include a Heathcote Lace Gallery featuring items from the local lace-making industry. There is also an agricultural section with a collection of farm wagons and implements. Other large exhibits include two waterwheels and a railway locomotive with many GWR items.
Times: Open Feb-mid Dec, Mon-Fri 10.30-4.30, Sat 10-1. **Fee:** £3.50 (ch £1, pen £2.50) **Facilities:** 🅿 (100yds) ♿ (lift) toilets for disabled shop ✖ (ex guide dogs)

TORQUAY   Map 03 SX96

BABBACOMBE MODEL VILLAGE
Hampton Av, Babbacombe TQ1 3LA
➲ (follow brown tourist signs from outskirts of town)
☎ 01803 328669 & 315315 🖷 01803 315173
e-mail: ss@babbacombemodelvillage.co.uk

Set in four acres of beautifully maintained, miniature landscaped garden, the village contains over 400 models and 1200ft of model railway. City Lights, an evening illuminations feature, depicts Piccadilly Circus in miniature. At the end of your visit, enjoy a new facility that offers breathtaking views over the model village. There are also free trips on an open-top bus. Computer presentation area; undercover display area; vintage model railway layout; and the new Aquaviva, an evening water, light and sound spectacular.
Times: Open all year, Good Fri-Jun, 9.30-10; Jul-Aug, 9-10; Sep, 9.30-10; Oct, 9.30-9; Nov-Good Fri, 10-dusk. Closed 25 Dec. **Fee:** ✱ £5.95 (ch £3.95, pen £4.80). Family ticket £18.50. **Facilities:** 🅿 (charged) 💺 ✕ ♿ (push button audio information) toilets for disabled shop garden centre ➤

'BYGONES'

Fore St, St Marychurch TQ1 4PR
➲ (follow tourist signs into Torquay and St
Marychurch)
☎ 01803 326108 ▤ 01803 326108

Step back in time in this life-size Victorian exhibition street
of over 20 shops including a forge, pub and period display
rooms, housed in a former cinema. Exhibits include a large
model railway layout, illuminated fantasyland, railwayana
and military exhibits including a walk-through World War I
trench. At Christmas the street is turned into a winter
wonderland. A new set piece features Babbacombe's John
Lee ('the man they couldn't hang') in his cell. There is
something here for all the family.
Times: Open all year, Summer 10-9.30, (Fri-Sun 10-6); Spring &
Autumn 10-6; Winter 10-4, wknds & school hols 10-5. Last entry 1hr
before closing. **Fee:** ✱ £4.50 (ch 4-14 £3, pen £3.95). Family ticket
£13. Prices may change, contact in advance. **Facilities:** Ⓟ (50yds) ▤
(ramp) shop ✖ (ex guide dogs)

KENTS CAVERN

Cavern House, 91 Ilsham Rd, Wellswood TQ1 2JF
➲ (1.25m NE off B3199, follow brown tourist signs.
1m from Torquay Harbour)
☎ 01803 215136 ▤ 01803 211034   2 for 1
e-mail: mail@kents-cavern.co.uk

Probably the most important Palaeolithic site in Britain and
recognised as one of the most significant archaeological
areas. This is not only a world of spectacular natural beauty,
but also a priceless record of past times, where a multitude
of secrets of mankind, animals and nature have become
trapped and preserved over the last 500,000 years. 170 years
after the first excavations and with over 80,000 remains
already unearthed, modern research is still discovering new
clues to our past.
Times: Open daily (ex 25 Dec). Oct-Mar 10-last tour 4pm; Apr-Jun &
Sep 10-last tour 4.30pm; Jul-Aug 9.30-last tour 5pm. Evenings: Jul-Aug
(Mon-Thu) 6-9.30. **Fee:** ✱ Daytime: £6 (ch 4-15 £3.80) Family £17.60.
Ghost evening tour: £6.30 (ch £3.90) Family £18.40. **Facilities:** Ⓟ ▤
ᵴ toilets for disabled shop ✖ (ex guide dogs) ✦

LIVING COASTS

Beacon Quay TQ1 2BG
➲ (follow A379 and brown tourist signs)
☎ 01803 202470 ▤ 01803 202471
e-mail: info@livingcoasts.org.uk

Living Coasts is an unusual and ambitious attraction that
allows visitors to take a trip around the coastlines of the
world without leaving Torquay. Specially designed
environments are home to fur seals, auks, penguins, ducks,
rats, and waders among others. Visitors can obtain special
joint tickets which will allow them to visit nearby Paignton
Zoo.
Times: Open daily from 10. (Closed 25 Dec) **Fee:** ✱ £5.50 (ch over 3
£3.90, pen £4.25). Family ticket (2 adults, 2 ch) £16.90 **Facilities:** Ⓟ
▤ ✗ licensed ᵴ toilets for disabled shop ✖ (ex assist dogs) ✦

┌─────────────────────────────────┐
│   FREE   │
│ Attractions with this symbol do │
│   not charge for entry.   │
└─────────────────────────────────┘

TORRE ABBEY HISTORIC HOUSE & GALLERY

Kings Dr TQ2 5JE
➲ (on Torquay seafront, next to Riviera Centre)
☎ 01803 293593 ▤ 01803 215948
e-mail: michael.rhodes@torbay.gov.uk

The Abbey was founded in 1196 as a monastery and later
adapted as a country house. It contains mementoes of crime
writer Agatha Christie, paintings, sculpture, antiques, and
Torquay terracotta pottery. The medieval monastic remains,
which include the great barn, guest hall, gatehouse and
undercrofts, are the most complete in Devon and Cornwall.
Times: Open daily Apr-1 Nov, 9.30-6. (Last admission 5pm).
Fee: £3.50 (ch 15 £1.70, under 8 free, pen & students £3). Family ticket
£7.75. **Facilities:** Ⓟ (100yds) (disabled parking by prior arrangement)
▤ ᵴ (hearing loops, touch tours by prior arrangement) shop ✖ (ex
guide dogs)

TOTNES   Map 03 SX86

GUILDHALL

Rampart Walk, off High St TQ9 5QH
➲ (behind St Mary's Church on the main street)
☎ 01803 862147 ▤ 01803 864275
e-mail: totnestowncouncil@btinternet.com

Originally the refectory, kitchens, brewery and bakery for the
Benedictine Priory of Totnes (1088-1536), the building was
established as the Guildhall in 1553 during the reign of
Edward VI. A magistrates' court and a prison opened
in 1624, and the council chamber is still used today.
Times: ✱ Open Apr-Oct, Mon-Fri 10.30-1 & 2-4; Other times by
appointment. **Facilities:** Ⓟ (50yds)

TOTNES CASTLE

TQ9 5NU
➲ (on hill overlooking town)
☎ 01803 864406

One of the best surviving examples of a Norman motte and
bailey castle with spectacular views. The once great ditch
that surrounded the keep is today filled with the cottages and
gardens of the town.
Times: Open Apr-Sep, daily 10-6; Oct, daily 10-5. Dates valid until 31
Mar 2004. **Fee:** £1.80 (ch 90p, concessions £1.40). Prices valid until 31
Mar 2004. **Facilities:** Ⓟ (70yds) (payment required) shop ✖ (ex dogs
on leads) ✿

TOTNES MUSEUM

70 Fore St TQ9 5RU
➲ (from bottom of Totnes Town, turn into Fore St
by Royal Seven Stars Hotel. The museum on left of
main street, just before East Gate Arch Clock
Tower)
☎ 01803 863821 ▤ 01803 863821
e-mail: totnesmuseum@btconnect.com

An Elizabethan merchant's house, dating from 1575, said to
have been built for Sir Walter Kelland, a wealthy merchant.
The building houses archaeological and social history
collection and room dedicated to Charles Babbage, inventor
of the first computer. Study centre archives located at the
rear of the museum.
Times: Open Etr-mid Oct, Mon-Fri & BHs 10.30-4.30, group bookings
only as arranged. **Fee:** £1.50 (ch 5-16 25p, students & pen £1).
Facilities: Ⓟ (440yds) (restricted parking on main street) ᵴ (personal
guided tours available) shop ✖ (ex small dogs & guide dogs)

UFFCULME Map 03 ST01

Coldharbour Mill Working Wool Museum

Coldharbour Mill EX15 3EE

(2m from M5 junct 27, off B3181. Follow signs to Willand, then brown signs to Working Wool Museum)

01884 840960 01884 840858

e-mail: info@coldharbourmill.org.uk

The Picturesque Coldharbour Mill is set in idyllic Devon countryside. It has been producing textiles since 1790 and is now a working museum, still making knitting wools and fabrics on period machinery. It has a wealth of craftwork on display. With machine demonstrations, a water wheel and steam engines, Coldharbour Mill is a wonderful and very different family day out.

Times: Open Feb-Dec, daily 10.30-5. Last tour 3.45pm **Fee:** £5.50 (ch 5-16 £2.50). Family ticket £15. Party 20+. **Facilities:** licensed (helpful guides & lift, indoor restaurant not accessible) toilets for disabled shop (ex guide dogs or in grounds)

YELVERTON Map 02 SX56

Yelverton Paperweight Centre

4 Buckland Ter, Leg O'Mutton Corner PL20 6AD

(at Yelverton off A386, Plymouth to Tavistock road)

FREE

01822 854250 01822 854250

e-mail: paperweightcentre@btinternet.com

This unusual centre is the home of the Broughton Collection - a glittering permanent collection of glass paperweights of all sizes and designs. The centre also has an extensive range of modern glass paperweights for sale. Prices range from a few pounds to over £1000. There is also a series of oil and watercolour paintings by talented local artists.

Times: Open Apr-Oct, daily 10-5; 1-24 Dec, daily; Nov & Jan-Mar wknds only or by appointment. **Facilities:** P (100yds) (ramp on request) shop

Above: The ponies of Dartmoor

DORSET

EVENTS & FESTIVALS

January
1st Annual Bath Race, Poole Quay, Poole

February
tbc Brass Monkey Winter Gold Cup
(powerboat event)

April
30th-3rd May Dorchester Festival

May
30th Apr-3rd Dorchester Festival
23rd Old Harbour Oyster Festival,
Brewers Quay, Weymouth
tbc Trawler Race & Water Carnival,
Weymouth Old Harbour, Weymouth
tbc Weymouth International Beach Kite
Festival, Weymouth Beach

June
11th-13th Wimborne Folk Festival, Wimborne
19th Dorchester Carnival (provisional)
tbc Annual Military & Veterans Festival,
Weymouth Pavilion Complex,
Weymouth Seafront
tbc Cancer Research Charity
Power Boat Race, Poole

July
18th Tolpuddle Martyrs Memorial Rally &
Festival, Tolpuddle
24th-1st August Lyme Regis Lifeboat Week,
The Cobb, Lyme Regis

August
24th Jul-1st Lyme Regis Lifeboat Week
28th-30th Abbotsbury Swannery Swan Fair
tbc Bournemouth Regatta
tbc Weymouth Carnival, Weymouth Seafront

September
1st-5th Great Dorset Steam Fair,
Tarrant Hinton
4th-5th Dorchester Show, Dorchester

October
tbc Weymouth Beach Motorcross
Championship

November
tbc Weymouth Guy Fawkes, The Beach

Above: Deckchairs on Marine Parade, Lyme Regis

ABBOTSBURY   Map 03 SY58

ABBOTSBURY SWANNERY
New Barn Rd DT3 4JG
➲ (turn off A35 at Winterborne Steepleton near
Dorchester. Abbotsbury on B3157 coastal road,
between Weymouth and Bridport)
☎ 01305 871858 📠 01305 871092
e-mail: info@abbotsbury-tourism.co.uk
Abbotsbury is the breeding ground of the only managed
colonial herd of mute swans. The swans can be seen safely
at close quarters, and the site is also home or stopping point
for many wild birds. The highlight of the year is the cygnet
season, end of May to the end of June, when there may be
over 100 nests on site. Visitors can often take pictures of
cygnets emerging from eggs at close quarters. There is an
audio-visual show, as well as mass feeding at noon & 4pm
daily, and an ugly duckling trail.
Times: Open 24 Mar-2 Nov, daily 10-6, last admission 5. **Fee:** ✱ £5.80
(ch £3.50 & pen £5.50). **Facilities:** 🅿 ➲ ✗ licensed ♿ (free
wheelchair loan, herb garden for blind) toilets for disabled shop
✗ ◗

ATHELHAMPTON   Map 03 SY79

ATHELHAMPTON HOUSE & GARDENS
DT2 7LG
➲ (off A35 Northbrook junct, follow brown tourist
signs towards Puddletown, at traffic lights turn left,
Athelhampton is approx 1m on left)
☎ 01305 848363 📠 01305 848135   **2 for 1**
e-mail: pcooke@athelhampton.co.uk
Athelhampton, one of the finest 15th-century houses in
England, contains magnificently furnished rooms including
The Great Hall of 1485 and the library. The glorious Grade I
gardens contain the world-famous topiary pyramids,
fountains, and collections of tulips, magnolias, roses,
clematis and lilies in season.
Times: Open Mar-Oct, daily 10.30-5. Also Sun in winter (ex Xmas).
(Closed Fri & Sat). **Fee:** ✱ House & Garden £7 (ch free, pen £6.30,
student & disabled £4.95). Garden only £4.95 (ch free). **Facilities:** 🅿
➲ ✗ licensed ♿ (2 motorised scooter for use in grounds) toilets for
disabled shop ✗ (ex assistance dogs) ◗

BEAMINSTER   Map 03 ST40

MAPPERTON
DT8 3NR
➲ (2m SE off A356 & B3163)
☎ 01308 862645 📠 01308 863348
e-mail: office@mapperton.com
Several acres of terraced valley gardens with specimen trees
and shrubs, and formal borders surround a manor house that
dates back to the 16th century. There are also fountains,
grottoes, stone fishponds and an orangery, and the garden
offers good views and walks. The Mapperton Courtyard Fair
is held annually in August with craft demonstrations, stalls,
house tours and local displays.
Times: Open Gardens: Mar-Oct, daily 2-6. House open Jun-9 Jul,
weekday afternoons 2-4.30. **Fee:** Gardens £4 (ch 5-18 £2, under 5
free). House £2.50. Guided tours £3.50. **Facilities:** 🅿 ➲ ♿ (ramp
from parking area to garden) toilets for disabled shop ✗ (ex guide
dogs)

BLANDFORD FORUM   Map 03 ST80

ROYAL SIGNALS MUSEUM
Blandford Camp DT11 8RH
➲ (signposted off the B3082 Blandford/Wimborne road & A354 Salisbury road.)
☎ 01258 482248 📠 01258 482084
e-mail: info@royalsignalsmuseum.com

The Royal Signals Museum depicts the history of military communications, science and technology from the Crimea to the Gulf. As well as displays on all major conflicts involving British forces, there are the stories of the ATS, the Long Range Desert Group, Air Support, Airborne, Para and SAS Signals. For children there are trails and interactive exhibits.
Times: ✱ Open Mar-Oct, Mon-Fri 10-5, Sat-Sun 10-4. Closed 10 days over Xmas & New Year **Facilities:** 🅿 💻 ♿ (ramps & chair lift) toilets for disabled shop 🐕 (ex guide dogs) ☕

BOURNEMOUTH   Map 04 SZ09

OCEANARIUM
Pier Approach, West Beach BH2 5AA
➲ (from A338 Wessex Way, follow the Oceanarium tourist signs)
☎ 01202 311993 📠 01202 311990
e-mail: oceanarium@reallive.co.uk

A voyage of global discovery during which the visitor visits many of the world's oceans and sees them in an entirely new way. The hidden beauty and drama of underwater life along and beyond these shores will be revealed as never before.
Times: ✱ Open all year, daily from 10am (Closed 25 Dec).
Facilities: 🅿 (100mtrs) 💻 ♿ (wheelchair for hire) toilets for disabled shop 🐕 (ex guide dogs) ☕

BOVINGTON CAMP   Map 03 SY88

CLOUDS HILL
BH20 7NQ
➲ (1m N of Bovington Camp & Tank Museum)
☎ 01929 405616

T E Lawrence ('Lawrence of Arabia') bought this cottage in 1925 when he was a private in the Tank Corps at Bovington. He would escape here to play records and entertain friends to feasts of baked beans and China tea. The furniture and contents were Lawrence's own and a new display tells the story of Lawrence's life.
Times: Open 1 Apr-Oct, Thu-Sun. **Fee:** £3.10. **Facilities:** 🅿 (Braille guide) 🐕 🚗 ♨

THE TANK MUSEUM
BH20 6JG
➲ (off A352 or A35, follow brown tank signs from Bere Regis & Wool)
☎ 01929 405096 📠 01929 405360
e-mail: info@tankmuseum.co.uk

The Tank Museum houses the world's finest international collection of Armoured Fighting Vehicles. Tanks in Action displays are held every Thursday at noon during July-September and every Tuesday from end July to August Bank Holiday. Armoured vehicle rides are available

continued

throughout the summer, and various special events take place - please telephone for details.
Times: Open all year, daily 10-5 (Closed from 22-26 Dec). **Fee:** ✱ £7.50 (ch £5, pen £6.50). Family saver £21 (2 adult & 2 ch); £17.50 (1 adult & 2 ch). Group rates available. **Facilities:** 🅿 💻 ✗ licensed ♿ (wheelchairs available, Braille & audio tours) toilets for disabled shop 🐕 (ex guide dogs) ☕

BROWNSEA ISLAND   Map 03 SZ08

BROWNSEA ISLAND
BH15 7EE
➲ (located in Poole Harbour)
☎ 01202 707744 📠 01202 701635

Visitors to this 250-acre nature reserve managed by the Dorset Trust for Nature Conservation can take advantage of a guided tour. The island is most famous as the site of the first scout camp, held by Lord Baden-Powell in 1907. Scouts and Guides are still the only people allowed to stay here overnight.
Times: ✱ Open Apr-1 Oct, daily 10-5 (10-6 Jul & Aug) **Facilities:** 💻 ✗ ♿ (Braille guide, 2 selfdrive vehicles- booking advisable) toilets for disabled shop 🐕 ♨

CANFORD CLIFFS   Map 04 SZ08

COMPTON ACRES GARDENS
Canford Cliffs Rd BH13 7ES
➲ (on B3065, follow brown tourist signs)
☎ 01202 700778 📠 01202 707537
e-mail: sales@comptonacres.co.uk

The ten acres of Compton Acres incorporate Japanese, Roman and Italian gardens, rock and water gardens, and heather gardens. There are fine views over Poole Harbour and the Purbeck Hills, and a collection of bronze and marble statuary. Two of the gardens have been themed to create an Egyptian Court Garden and a Spanish Water Garden.
Times: ✱ Open Apr-Dec 10-6 (last entry 5.15) **Facilities:** 🅿 💻 ✗ licensed ♿ (level paths and ramps into shops and cafe) toilets for disabled shop garden centre 🐕 (ex guide & hearing dogs) ☕

CHRISTCHURCH   Map 04 SZ19

CHRISTCHURCH CASTLE & NORMAN HOUSE
➲ (near Christchurch Priory)   FREE

Set on the river bank, the ruins of this Norman keep and constable's house date back to the twelfth century.
Times: Open any reasonable time. **Facilities:** 🐕 (ex dogs on leads) ♿

RED HOUSE MUSEUM & GARDENS
Quay Rd BH23 1BU
➲ (follow brown tourist signs from Christchurch, Red House is on the corner of Quay Rd)
☎ 01202 482860 📠 01202 481924

A museum with plenty of variety, featuring local history, archaeology, and natural history, displayed in a beautiful Georgian house. There's an excellent costume collection, some Arthur Romney-Green furniture and gardens with a woodland walk and herb garden. Regularly changing temporary exhibitions include contemporary art.
Times: ✱ Open all year, Tue-Sat 10-5 Sun 2-5 (Closed Mon ex BH). Last admission 4.30pm. **Facilities:** 🅿 (200yds) 💻 ♿ (hearing aid and loop in reception only) shop 🐕 (ex guide & hearing dogs)

CORFE CASTLE　　　Map 03 SY98

CORFE CASTLE
BH20 5EZ
➲ (follow A351 from Wareham to Swanage. Corfe Castle approx 5m along this road)
☎ 01929 481294　🖹 01929 477067
e-mail: corfecastle@nationaltrust.org.uk

Built in Norman times, the castle was added to by King John. It was defended during the Civil War by Lady Bankes, who surrendered after a stout resistance. Parliament ordered the demolition of the castle, and today it is one of the most impressive ruins in England. Ring for details of special events.
Times: Open daily, Mar 10-5; Apr-end Sep 10-6; Oct 10-5; Nov-Feb 10-4. Last admission 30 mins before closing (Closed 25-26 Dec).
Fee: £4.50 (ch £2.25). Family ticket (2 ad & 3 ch) £11.50 or (1 ad & 3 ch) £7. National Trust members free. **Facilities:** 🅿 ➡ ✕ licensed (Braille guide & menu) shop ♨ ➷

CORFE CASTLE MUSEUM
West St BH20 5HE
➲ (to side of church on left of West St upon leaving village square)
☎ 01929 480974　🖹 01929 480974
e-mail: kenwollaston@tesco.net

The tiny, rectangular building was partly rebuilt in brick after a fire in 1780, and is the smallest town hall building in England. It has old village relics, and dinosaur footprints 130 million years old. A council chamber on the first floor is reached by a staircase at one end. The Ancient Order of Marblers meets here each Shrove Tuesday.
Times: Open all year, Apr-Oct, daily 9.30-6; Nov-Mar, wknds and Xmas holidays 10-5. **Facilities:** 🅿 (200yds) ♿ ✕

DORCHESTER　　　Map 03 SY69

DINOSAUR MUSEUM
Icen Way DT1 1EW
➲ (off A35 into Dorchester, museum in town centre just off High East Street)
☎ 01305 269880　🖹 01305 268885
e-mail: info@thedinosaurmuseum.com

Britain's award-winning museum devoted to dinosaurs has an appealing mixture of fossils, skeletons, life-size reconstructions and interactive displays such as the `feelies'. There are audio-visual presentations and computer displays providing an all-round family attraction with new displays each year.
Times: Open all year, daily 9.30-5.30 (10-4.30 Nov-Mar). (Closed 24-26 Dec). **Fee:** ✱ £5.50 (ch, pen & student £3.95, under 4's free). Family ticket £15.95. **Facilities:** 🅿 (50yds) ♿ (Many low level displays) shop ➷

DORSET COUNTY MUSEUM
High West St DT1 1XA
➲ (turn off A354 signposted Dorchester, attraction on right half way up main street)
☎ 01305 262735　🖹 01305 257180
e-mail: dorsetcountymuseum@
dor-mus.demon.co.uk

Displays cover prehistoric and Roman times, including sites such as Maiden Castle, and there's a gallery on Dorset

continued

writers with sections on the poet William Barnes, Thomas Hardy (with a reconstruction of his study), and 20th-century writers. Also geology, local wildlife and social history are explored in the museum.
Times: Open all year, Mon-Sat, 10-5. Also open Sun during May-Oct. (Closed 24-26 Dec & Good Friday). **Fee:** £3.90 (concessions £2.60, ch free). **Facilities:** 🅿 (600yds) (nearby parking is not free) ♿ (Free entry for disabled visitors, ramp, audio commentary) shop ✕ (ex guide dogs) ➷

DORSET TEDDY BEAR MUSEUM
Antelope Walk, Cornhill DT1 1BE
➲ (turn off A35 and museum in town centre near Tourist Information Centre)
☎ 01305 263200　🖹 01305 268885
e-mail: info@teddybearmuseum.co.uk

A visit to the museum begins with the home of Edward Bear and his extended family of human-sized teddy bears. Then, in a more traditional museum setting, view hundreds of teddy bears from throughout the last century in atmospheric and evocative displays.
Times: Open daily, Mon-Sat 9.30-5, Sun 10-4.30. (Closed 25-26 Dec). **Fee:** ✱ £2.95 (ch £1.95, under 4's free). Family £8.95. **Facilities:** 🅿 (500mtrs) shop ✕ (ex guide dogs) ➷

HARDY'S COTTAGE
Higher Bockhampton DT2 8QJ
➲ (3m NE of Dorchester, 0.5m S of A35. Turn off A35 at Kingston Maurward rdbt towards Stinsford and Bockhampton. Left onto Bockhampton Ln, signed to Hardy's Cottage)
☎ 01305 262366

The small cob and thatch cottage where novelist and poet Thomas Hardy was born in 1840 and from where he would walk 6 miles to school in Dorchester every day. It was built by his great-grandfather and is little altered since. The interior has been furnished by the trust.
Times: Open Apr-Oct. **Fee:** £3.00. **Facilities:** 🅿 (10 min walk) (no coach parking) ♿ (car parking by arrangement, large print guide) ✕ ♨

MAIDEN CASTLE
DT1 9PR
➲ (2m S of Dorchester, access off A354, N of bypass)

The Iron Age fort ranks among the finest in Britain. It covers 47 acres, and has daunting earthworks, with a complicated defensive system around the entrances. One of its main purposes may well have been to protect grain from marauding bands. The first single-rampart fort dates from around 700BC, and by 100BC the earthworks covered the whole plateau. It was finally overrun by Roman troops in AD43.
Times: Open any reasonable time. **Facilities:** 🅿 ✕ (ex dogs on leads) ♨

THE MILITARY MUSEUM OF DEVON & DORSET
The Keep, Bridport Rd DT1 1RN
➲ (situated near the top of High West St leading out of town towards Bridport)
☎ 01305 264066　🖹 01305 250373
e-mail: keep.museum@talk21.com

Three hundred years of military history, with displays on the

continued

Devon Regiment, Dorset Regiment, Dorset Militia and Volunteers, the Queen's Own Dorset Yeomanry, and Devonshire and Dorset Regiment (from 1958). The Museum uses modern technology and creative displays to tell the stories of the Infantry, Cavalry and Artillerymen.
Times: Open Apr-Sep, Mon-Sat 9-5; Oct-Mar, Tue-Sat 9-5; (also Jul & Aug, Sun 10-4). Closed Xmas & New Year. **Fee:** ✹ £3 (ch, student & pen £2). Family ticket £9 **Facilities:** 🅿 & (lift avalible to 3 floors) toilets for disabled shop ✈ (ex guide dogs) �

TUTANKHAMUN EXHIBITION
High West St DT1 1UW
➲ (off A35 into Dorchester town centre)
☎ 01305 269571 🗎 01305 268885
e-mail: info@tutankhamun-exhibition.co.uk
The exhibition recreates the excitement of one of the world's greatest discoveries of ancient treasure. A reconstruction of the tomb and recreations of its treasures are displayed. The superbly preserved mummified body of the boy king can be seen, wonderfully recreated in every detail. Facsimiles of some of the most famous treasures, including the golden funerary mask and the harpooner can be seen in the final gallery.
Times: Open all year daily, Apr-Oct, 9.30-5.30; Nov-Mar wkdays 9.30-5, wknds 10-4.30. (Closed 24-26 Dec). **Fee:** ✹ £5.50 (ch £3.95, pen & student £4.75, under 5's free). Family ticket £15.95 **Facilities:** 🅿 (200yds) & shop ✈ (ex guide dogs) ➮

MINTERNE MAGNA   Map 03 ST60
MINTERNE GARDENS
DT2 7AU
➲ (2m N of Cerne Abbas on A352 Dorchester-Sherborne road)
☎ 01300 341370
Lakes, cascades, streams and many fine and rare trees will be found in these lovely landscaped gardens. The 18th-century design is a superb setting for the spring shows of rhododendrons, azaleas and spring bulbs, and the autumn colour.
Times: Open Mar-10 Nov, daily 10-7. **Fee:** £3 (accompanied ch free). **Facilities:** 🅿

POOLE   Map 03 SZ09
WATERFRONT MUSEUM
4 High St BH15 1BW
➲ (off Poole Quay)
☎ 01202 262600 🗎 01202 262622   **FREE**
e-mail: museums@poole.gov.uk
The museum tells the story of Poole's seafaring past. Learn of the Roman occupation and see material raised from the Studland Bay wreck. Scaplen's Court, just a few yards from the museum, is a beautifully restored domestic building dating from the medieval period. Although it is only open to the public in August, Scaplen's Court is not to be missed, with a Victorian school room, a kitchen and scullery.
Times: Museum: open Apr-Oct, Mon-Sat 10-5, Sun noon-5; Nov-Mar, Mon-Sat 10-3, Sun noon-3. Scaplen's Court: Aug, Mon-Sat 10-5, Sun noon-5. **Facilities:** 🅿 (250mtrs) & (Scaplen's Court not accessible) toilets for disabled ✈ (ex guide dogs) ➮

PORTLAND   Map 03 SY67
PORTLAND CASTLE
Castleton DT5 1AZ
➲ (overlooking Portland harbour)
☎ 01305 820539 🗎 01305 860853
Visit one of Henry VIII's finest coastal forts in use right up to the Second World War. Home to the Wrens and scene of the US troops' embarkation for the D-Day invasion in 1944. Explore the Captain's House and Gardens.
Times: Open all year, Apr-Sep, daily 10-6; Oct, daily 10-5; Nov-Mar, Fri-Sun 10-4. (Closed 24-26 Dec & 1 Jan). Dates valid until 31 Mar 2004. **Fee:** £3.50 (ch £1.80, concessions £2.60). Prices valid until 31 Mar 2004. **Facilities:** 🅿 💷 & shop ✈ ⚄

PORTLAND MUSEUM
217 Wakeham DT5 1HS
➲ (A354, through Fortuneswell to Portland Heights Hotel, then English Heritage signs)
☎ 01305 821804 🗎 01305 761654
e-mail: tourism@weymouth.gov.uk
Avice's cottage in Thomas Hardy's book *The Well-Beloved*, this building is now a museum of local and historical interest, with varied displays. Regular temporary exhibitions are held. The adjoining Marie Stopes cottage houses the shop and a display of maritime history.
Times: Open Etr-Oct, Fri-Tue (ex school holidays open daily), 10.30-5 (Closed 1-1.30 daily). **Fee:** ✹ £2. **Facilities:** 🅿 (50yds) (coach parking on roadside) & shop

SHAFTESBURY   Map 03 ST82
SHAFTESBURY ABBEY MUSEUM & GARDEN
Park Walk SP7 8JR
➲ (follow signs to Shaftesbury town centre. Shaftesbury Abbey is signed from outside Wharf's Restaurant)
☎ 01747 852910 🗎 01747 852910
e-mail: user@shaftesburyabbey.fsnet.co.uk
The Abbey at Shaftesbury was part of a nunnery founded by King Alfred in 888. It became one of the wealthiest in the country but was destroyed during the Dissolution in 1539. The excavated ruins show the foundations of the abbey church. The story is told through the use of carved stone and medieval floor tiles and illustrations from ancient manuscripts.
Times: Open Apr-Oct, daily, 10-5. **Fee:** £2 (ch 60p, concessions £1.50). **Facilities:** 🅿 (250yds) & (large print guides & audio tour) toilets for disabled shop

SHERBORNE   Map 03 ST61
SHERBORNE CASTLE
New Rd DT9 5NR
➲ (off A30, 0.5m SE of Sherborne)
☎ 01935 813182 🗎 01935 816727
e-mail: enquiries@sherbornecastle.com
Built by Sir Walter Raleigh in 1594, Sherborne Castle has been the home of the Digby family since 1617. Prince William of Orange was entertained here in 1688, and George III visited in 1789. Splendid collections of art, furniture and porcelain are on show in the Castle. Lancelot 'Capability'

continued

Brown created the lake in 1753 and beautiful gardens and grounds surround it.
Times: Open Apr-Oct, Tue-Thu, Sat-Sun & BH Mon 11-4.30. Castle opens from 2.30 on Sat. Last admission 4.30. **Fee:** ✱ £6 (pen £5.50). Gardens only £3.25. Ch under 15 free (max 4 ch per adult). Party 15+
Facilities: 🅿 💷 ♿ (braille guide book) toilets for disabled shop 🍴

SHERBORNE MUSEUM
Abbey Gate House, Church Ln DT9 3BP
➲ (From the bottom of Cheap St (main shopping street), walk through Church Ln towards the Abbey, museum on left)
☎ 01935 812252
e-mail: admin@shermus.fsnet.co.uk
The museum features a model of Sherborne's original Norman castle, as well as a fine Victorian doll's house and other domestic and agricultural bygones. There are also items of local geological, natural history and archaeological interest, including Roman material.
Times: Open Apr-Oct, Tue-Sat 10.30-4.30, Sun 2.30-4.30; BH Mon 2.30-4.30 **Fee:** ✱ £1 (ch & students free) **Facilities:** 🅿 (200yds) ♿ toilets for disabled shop 🐾 (ex guide dogs)

SHERBORNE OLD CASTLE
Castleton D19 3SA
➲ (0.5m E off B3145)
☎ 01935 812730 📠 01935 812730
The ruins of this early 12th-century castle are a testament to the 16 days Oliver Cromwell's army took capture of it during the Civil War.
Times: Open Apr-Sep, daily 10-6; Oct, daily 10-5. Dates valid until 31 Mar 2004. **Fee:** £2 (ch £1, concessions £1.50). Prices valid until 31 Mar 2004. **Facilities:** 🅿 ♿ shop 🐾 ⚹

SWANAGE   Map 03 SZ07

SWANAGE RAILWAY
Station House BH19 1HB
➲ (signed from A351)
☎ 01929 425800 📠 01929 426680
e-mail: general@swanrail.freeserve.co.uk

The railway from Swanage to Wareham was closed in 1972, and in 1976 the Swanage Railway took possession and have gradually restored the line, which now runs for 6 miles,
continued

passing the ruins of Corfe Castle. Ring for details of special events.
Times: Open every weekend throughout the year, daily Apr-Oct.
Fee: ✱ Swanage-Corfe / Norden £7 return, £4 single (ch £5 return & £2.70 single). Family ticket £21. Day Rover £14 (ch & pen £10). Group 15+ **Facilities:** 🅿 💷 ✗ licensed ♿ (special disabled persons coach) toilets for disabled shop (shop at Swanage Station) 🍴

TOLPUDDLE   Map 03 SY79

TOLPUDDLE MARTYRS MUSEUM
DT2 7EH
➲ (off A35 from Dorchester, Tolpuddle is signposted at Troytown turn off. Continue on A35, Museum has brown heritage signpost giving clear directions)
☎ 01305 848237 📠 01305 848237   FREE
e-mail: jpickering@tuc.org.uk

One dawn, in the bitter February of 1834, six Tolpuddle farm labourers were arrested after forming a trade union. A frightened squire's trumped up charge triggered one of the most celebrated stories in the history of human rights. That dawn arrest created the Tolpuddle Martyrs, who were punished with transportation as convicts to Australia. Packed with illustrative displays, this new state-of-the-art, interactive exhibition tells the Tolpuddle Martyrs story. Every summer in July, the museum holds the Tolpuddle Martyrs Festival. The weekend combines celebration with tradition offering traditional and contemporary music as well as many other attractions.
Times: Open all year, Apr-Oct, Tue-Sat 10-5.30, Sun 11-5.30; Nov-Mar, Tue-Sat 10-4, Sun 11-4. Open BH Mon. (Closed 20 Dec-2 Jan).
Facilities: 🅿 (outside museum) ♿ (interactive computers at wheelchair height & parking) toilets for disabled shop 🐾 (ex guide dogs)

WEST LULWORTH   Map 03 SY88

LULWORTH CASTLE
BH20 5QS
➲ (from Wareham, W on A352 for 1m, left onto B3070 to E Lulworth, follow tourist signs)
☎ 01929 400352 📠 01929 400563   2 for 1
e-mail: estate.office@lulworth.com
Glimpse life below stairs in the restored kitchen, and enjoy beautiful views from the top of the tower of this historic castle set in beautiful parkland. The 18th-century chapel is
continued

the first Catholic chapel built in England after the Reformation. Children will enjoy the animal farm, play area, indoor activity room and pitch and putt. **Times:** Open Castle: Summer 10.30-6; Winter 10.30-4. Lulworth Castle House open Wed 28 May-30 Jul, 2-5. **Fee:** ✱ £6 (ch 5-16 £3.50, concessions £5) Family £15. English Heritage Members half price. Lulworth Castle House £2 (ch free, concessions £2). **Facilities:** ⓟ ⬛ ♿ (limited in castle due to grade one listing) toilets for disabled shop ➽

WEYMOUTH — Map 03 SY67

DEEP SEA ADVENTURE & SHARKY'S PLAY & PARTY WAREHOUSE
9 Custom House Quay, Old Harbour DT4 8BG
➲ (follow signs on A35 to Weymouth. Follow signs to the Deep Sea Adventure, which is located on the Old Harbour between pavillion and town bridge)
☎ 0871 222 5760 ▤ 0871 222 5760
e-mail: enquiries@deepsea-adventure.co.uk
A fascinating attraction telling the story of underwater exploration and marine exploits. Discover the history of Weymouth's Old Harbour, compelling tales of shipwreck survival, explore the Black Hole and search for Ollie the Oyster. Also a unique display telling the gripping tale of the *Titanic* disaster. Sharky's Play Area is four floors of fun-packed adventure. Separate toddler area for the under fives. **Times:** Open all year, daily 9.30-7 (high season 9.30-8). (Closed 25 & 26 Dec & 1 Jan). **Fee:** ✱ Sharky's Play Zone: Adults free (ch £3.30). Deep Sea Adventure: £3.75 (ch 5-15 £2.75, pen & student £3.25). Combined ticket for both attractions, ch £4./5. **Facilities:** ⓟ (100yds) ✗ licensed ♿ (lift & sign language for deaf) toilets for disabled shop ➽ (ex guide dogs) ➽

RSPB NATURE RESERVE RADIPOLE LAKE
The Swannery Car Park DT4 7TZ
➲ (within the town, close to seafront & railway station)
☎ 01305 778313 ▤ 01305 778313
Covering 222 acres, the Reserve offers firm paths, hide and a visitor centre. Several types of warblers, mute swans, gadwalls, teals and great crested grebes may be seen, and the visitor centre has viewing windows overlooking the lake. Phone for details of special events. **Times:** ✱ Open daily 9-5 **Facilities:** ⓟ (concessions for members from centre) ♿ shop ➽

SEA LIFE PARK
Lodmoor Country Park DT4 7SX
➲ (on A353)   2 for 1
☎ 01305 788255 ▤ 01305 760165
e-mail: simongrove@merlinentertainments.biz
Set in the beautiful Lodmoor Country Park. Marvel at the mysteries of the deep and discover amazing sea creatures from around our own shores in spectacular marine displays. **Times:** Open all year, daily from 10am. (Closed 25 Dec). **Fee:** ✱ £8.50 (ch £6.25, pen & student £7.50) **Facilities:** ⓟ (charged) ⬛ ✗ ♿ toilets for disabled shop ➽ (ex guide dogs) ➽

WIMBORNE — Map 03 SZ09

KINGSTON LACY HOUSE, GARDEN & PARK
BH21 4EA
➲ (1.5m W of Wimborne, B3082)
☎ 01202 883402 (Mon-Fri) & 842913 (wknds)
▤ 01202 882402
e-mail: kingstonlacy@nationaltrust.org.uk
Kingston Lacy House was the home of the Bankes family for over 300 years. The original house is 17th century, but in the 1830s was given a stone façade. The Italian marble staircase, Venetian ceiling, treasures from Spain and an Egyptian obelisk were also added. There are outstanding pictures by Titian, Rubens, Velasquez, Reynolds and Van Dyck. No photography is allowed in the house. **Times:** Open Garden & Park, Feb-16 Mar, wknds 10.30-4; 22 Mar-2 Nov, daily 10.30-6; 7 Nov-21 Dec, Fri-Sun 10.30-4. House open 22 Mar-2 Nov, daily ex Mon & Tue 11-5 (last admission 4pm). **Fee:** ✱ House, Garden & Park £6.80 (ch £3.40). Park & Gardens only £3.50 (ch £1.75). **Facilities:** ⓟ ⬛ ✗ licensed ♿ (parking by arrangement) toilets for disabled shop ➽ (ex on leads in park & wood) ➽

KNOLL GARDENS & NURSERY
Stapehill Rd, Hampreston BH21 7ND
➲ (3m E between Wimborne and Ferndown off A31, at Canford Bottom rdbt, into B3073 signed Ham Lane)
☎ 01202 873931 ▤ 01202 870842   2 for 1
e-mail: enquiries@knollgardens.co.uk
Over 6000 plant species from all over the world thrive here, within a six-acre site. There are water gardens with waterfalls, pools and a stream, herbaceous borders, and many other features. There is also a 'Dragon' formal garden and a Mediterranean-style gravel garden. The nursery offers a wide range of plants; best known for its range of Ornamental Grasses and 'plants for the modern lifestyle'. **Times:** Open all year, Wed-Sun, 10-5 (or dusk if earlier). **Fee:** ✱ £3.50 (ch 5-15 £2, student & pen £3). Family £9.50 Party 15+. **Facilities:** ⓟ ⬛ ♿ (wheelchairs available) toilets for disabled garden centre ➽ (ex guide dogs) ➽

PRIEST'S HOUSE MUSEUM AND GARDEN
23-27 High St BH21 1HR
☎ 01202 882533 ▤ 01202 882533
e-mail: priestshouse@eastdorset.gov.uk
An award-winning local history museum, set in an historic house with a Victorian kitchen where regular cooking demonstrations are held (4th Saturday in the month, 2pm-5pm). There are nine other rooms to see, along with regular special exhibitions, a new costume and textile gallery and a beautiful 300ft-long walled garden. **Times:** Open Apr-Oct, Mon-Sat, 10-4.30. Also every Sun Jul-Aug & BH wknds 2-5. **Fee:** ✱ £2.50 (ch £2, pen & students £2). Family ticket £7. Season ticket £7. **Facilities:** ⓟ (200yds) ⬛ ♿ (hands on archaeology gallery, audio tapes) shop ➽ (ex guide dogs)

STAPEHILL ABBEY
Wimborne Rd West BH21 2EB
➲ (2.5m E off A31 at Canford Bottom rdbt) 2 for 1
☎ 01202 861686 🖹 01202 894589

This early 19th-century abbey, home for nearly 200 years to Cistercian nuns, is now a busy working crafts centre with many attractions under cover. There are award-winning landscaped gardens, parkland and picnic spots, and the Power to the Land exhibition. Telephone for details of special events.
Times: Open Etr-Sep, daily 10-5; Oct-Etr Wed-Sun 10-4. (Closed 22 Dec-Feb). **Fee:** ✱ £7.50 (ch 4-16 £4.50, students & pen £7). Family ticket (2 ad & 2 ch) £19.50. **Facilities:** 🅿 🍽 ♿ toilets for disabled shop garden centre ✖ (ex guide dogs) 🍴

WOOL   Map 03 SY88

MONKEY WORLD
Longthorns BH20 6HH
➲ (1m N of Wool on Bere Regis Rd)
☎ 01929 462537 & 0800 456600
🖹 01929 405414
e-mail: apes@monkeyworld.org

Set up in order to rescue monkeys and apes from abuse and illegal smuggling, Monkey World houses over 100 primates in 60 acres of Dorset woodland. There are 45 chimps, the largest grouping outside Africa, as well as orang-utans, gibbons, woolly monkeys, lemurs, macaques and marmosets. Those wishing to help the centre continue in its quest to rescue primates from lives of misery may like to take part in the adoption scheme which includes free admission to the park for one year.
Times: Open daily 10-5 (Jul-Aug 10-6). Last admission 1 hour before closing **Fee:** £7 (ch & concessions £5.50). Family ticket (1 ad & 2 ch) £16, (2 ad & 2 ch) £21. Group15+. **Facilities:** 🅿 🍽 ✖ ♿ toilets for disabled shop ✖ (ex guide dogs) 🍴

---

2 for 1

Attractions with this symbol by their entry are participating in our 2-for-1 voucher scheme. For details see page 6 or the vouchers at the front of the guide

---

COUNTY DURHAM

EVENTS & FESTIVALS

May
1st-3rd Teesdale Thrash – concerts, ceilidhs, music sessions and morris dancing in Bernard Castle

June
12th-13th Durham Regatta, River Wear, Durham (provisional)

July
3rd-4th Summer Festival, Durham city centre
10th Durham Miners Gala – colourful miners' banners paraded through the city of Durham (provisional)
tbc Chester-le-Street Traction Engine Rally, South Burn Grange
tbc Durham County Show, Lambton Park, nr Chester-le-Street

August
28th-29th Weardale Agricultural Show, Showfield, St John's Chapel (provisional)
29th-30th Durham Light Infantry Vehicle Rally, DLI Museum & Durham Art Gallery (provisional)
tbc Billingham International Folklore Festival, Billingham, Stockton-on-Tees
tbc Ploughing Match, Beamish, The North of England Open Air Museum

September
4th-5th Wolsingham & Wear Valley Agricultural Show, Wolsingham (provisional)
11th-12th Stanhope Agricultural Show & Country Fair, Stanhope (provisional)

December
4th-5th Victorian Christmas Festival, Durham city centre (provisional)

Above: This statue in Durham is of Charles William Vane Stewart, 3rd Marquis of Londonderry, ancestor of Winston Churchill and relative of Diana Spencer

BARNARD CASTLE   Map 12 NZ01

BARNARD CASTLE
DL12 9AT

☎ 01833 638212

Imposing remains of one of England's largest medieval castles perched high on a rugged escarpment above the banks of the River Tees.
Times: Open all year, 29 Mar-Sep, daily 10-6 (Oct, daily 10-5); Nov-Mar, Wed-Sun 10-4. (Closed 24-26 Dec & 1 Jan). Dates valid until 31 Mar 2004. **Fee:** £2.60 (ch £1.30, concessions £2). Prices valid until 31 Mar 2004. **Facilities:** ৬ shop ✖ (ex dogs on leads) ✿

THE BOWES MUSEUM
DL12 8NP
➲ (located in Barnard Castle, just of the A66)
☎ 01833 690606 ▤ 01833 637163
e-mail: info@bowersmuseum.org.uk

The Bowes museum is housed in a purpose built château in Teesdale. The château was the inspiration of John & Joséphine Bowes. Opened in 1892, the museum has a collection containing paintings by Boudin, Canaletto, Goya, Tiepolo and Turner. There are also fine textiles, ceramics and furniture. Set in 23 acres of parkland with a parterre garden, the museum is a day out for all the family.
Times: Open daily 11-5. (closed 25-26 Dec & 1 Jan) **Fee:** ✱ £6 (concessions £5, U16 free). **Facilities:** 🄿 ᕷ ৬ (lift, ramped entrance, reserved parking) toilets for disabled shop (grounds only)

EGGLESTONE ABBEY
DL12 8QN
➲ (1m S of Barnard Castle on minor road off B6277)   **FREE**

The scant, but charming remains of a small medieval monastery. The picturesque ruins of Egglestone are located above a bend in the River Tees. A large part of the church can be seen, as can remnants of monastic buildings.
Times: Open any reasonable time. **Facilities:** 🄿 ৬ ✖ (ex dogs on leads) ✿

BEAMISH   Map 12 NZ25

BEAMISH, THE NORTH OF ENGLAND OPEN-AIR MUSEUM
DH9 0RG
➲ (off A693 & A6076 signposted off A1(M) junct 63. In County Durham midway between Durham City and Newcastle-upon-Tyne)
☎ 0191 370 4000 ▤ 0191 370 4001
e-mail: museum@beamish.org.uk

Set in 200 acres of countryside, award winning Beamish recreates life in the early 1800s and 1900s. Costumed staff welcome visitors to a 1913 town street, colliery village, farm and railway station; a display of how people lived and worked. Ride on early electric tramcars, take a ride on a replica of an 1825 steam railway and visit Pockerley Manor where a yeoman farmer and his family would have lived.
Times: Open 5 Apr-2 Nov, daily 10-5; 3 Nov-2 Apr daily (ex Mon & Fri) 10-4. Closed 15 Dec-5 Jan. **Fee:** ✱ Summer £12 (ch £6, over 60's £9). Winter £4 (ch £4, over 60's £4). NB a winter visit is centered on the town and tramway only, other areas are closed. **Facilities:** 🄿 ᕷ ৬ (not ideal for wheelchairs, free entry for essential helpers) toilets for disabled shop ◥

BISHOP AUCKLAND   Map 08 NZ22

AUCKLAND CASTLE
DL14 7NR
➲ (from A1(M), exit at junct 61 and join A688 signposted to Bishop Auckland, follow signs to Bishop Auckland Market Place and then Brown Tourist sign for Auckland Castle)
☎ 01388 601627 ▤ 01388 609323
e-mail: auckland.castle@zetnet.co.uk

Serving as the principal county residence of the Prince Bishops since the 12th century, Auckland Castle is the home of the Bishop of Durham. Built on a promontory overlooking the River Wear and the Roman Fort of Binchester, the Castle has been added to and adapted over the centuries. St Peter's Chapel houses many of the treasures of past Bishops.
Times: ✱ Open Apr-Sep, Mon & Thu 12.30-5 & Sun 2-5. (Closed 13 Jun, 1 & 26 Sep). **Facilities:** 🄿 ᕷ ৬ (chair walker available by prior arrangement) toilets for disabled shop ✖ (ex guide dogs)

BOWES   Map 12 NY91

BOWES CASTLE
DL12 9LD
➲ (in Bowes village, just off A66)   `FREE`

Massive ruins of Henry II's tower keep, three story's high, set within the earthworks of a Roman fort and overlooking the valley of the River Greta.
Times: Open any reasonable time. **Facilities:** ♿ ✕ (ex dogs on leads) 🚗 ♨

THE OTTER TRUST'S NORTH PENNINES RESERVE
Vale House Farm DL12 9RH
➲ (S side of A66 Scotch Corner to Penrith Rd)
☎ 01833 628339 ▤ 01986 892461

Set in 230 acres of upland farmland, the Otter Trust reserve isn't just about otters, although there is an ongoing release programme that aims to protect the otter from extinction. Visitors can also see red and fallow deer, mouflon sheep, and a wide range of birds including curlew, oystercatchers, snipe, and black grouse. The visitor centre contains exhibits on some of the animals as well as local history, and overlooks the charming River Greta.
Times: Open Apr-Oct, daily 10.30-6 **Fee:** ✷ £5 (ch £3) **Facilities:** P ▤ ♿ toilets for disabled shop ✕ (ex guide dogs)

COWSHILL   Map 12 NY84

KILLHOPE LEAD MINING MUSEUM
DL13 1AR
➲ (beside A689 midway between Stanhope & Alston)
☎ 01388 537505 ▤ 01388 537617   `2 for 1`
e-mail: killhope@durham.gov.uk

Equipped with hard hats and lamps, you can descend into the depths of the earth and explore the working conditions of lead miners. The lead mine and 19th-century crushing mill have been restored to look as they would have done in the 1870s, and the 34ft water wheel has been restored to working order. There is also a visitor centre and mineral exhibition, based on the life of miners and their families, a woodland walk, children's play area and a red squirrel and bird hide.
Times: Open Apr-Sep, daily 10.30-5 (Oct Wknds, half term, BH's & summer school hols open until 5.30); Open 4, 5 & 11, 12 Dec.
Fee: £3.40 (ch, disabled, & UB40 £1.70). Additional charge for mine visit £1.60 (ch, disabled, UB40 80p) **Facilities:** P ▤ ♿ (electric scooter, sympathetic hearing scheme) toilets for disabled shop 🦻

DARLINGTON   Map 08 NZ21

DARLINGTON RAILWAY CENTRE & MUSEUM
North Rd Station DL3 6ST
➲ (0.75m N, off A167)
☎ 01325 460532 ▤ 01325 287746
e-mail: museum@darlington.gov.uk

Housed in the carefully restored North Road Station, this museum's prize exhibit is *Locomotion*, which pulled the first passenger train on the Stockton to Darlington railway and was built by Robert Stephenson & Co in 1825. Several other steam locomotives are also shown, together with models and other exhibits relating to the Stockton and Darlington and the North Eastern Railway companies. Recently arrived
continued

at the museum for a two year period is an A2 Pacific No60532 'Blue Peter'. Refreshments are available.

Times: Open daily 10-5 (closed 25-26 Dec & 1 Jan). **Fee:** £2.20 (ch £1.10, pen £1.50). **Facilities:** P ♿ toilets for disabled shop ✕ (ex guide dogs) 🦻

DURHAM   Map 12 NZ24

DURHAM CATHEDRAL
DH1 3EH
➲ (A1(M) to Durham, turn off at A690 into city, follow signs to car parks)
☎ 0191 386 4266 ▤ 0191 386 4267
e-mail: enquiries@durhamcathedral.co.uk

Founded in 1093 as a shrine to St Cuthbert, the cathedral is a remarkable example of Norman architecture, set in an impressive position high above the River Wear. A full programme of concerts throughout the year. St Cuthbert's Day Procession (phone for details).
Times: Open all year, daily 9.30-6.15; 21 Jun-8 Sep 9.30-8. (Sun 12.30-5). Cathedral is closed to visitors during evening recitals & concerts. **Fee:** £4 Donation requested. **Facilities:** P (in city centre) ✕ licensed ♿ (braille guide, touch/hearing centre, stairclimber) toilets for disabled shop ✕ (ex guide dogs)

DURHAM LIGHT INFANTRY MUSEUM & DURHAM ART GALLERY
Aykley Heads DH1 5TU
➲ (0.5m NW, turn right off A691)
☎ 0191 384 2214 ▤ 0191 386 1770
e-mail: dli@durham.gov.uk

The history of the Regiment is told in displays of artefacts, medals, uniforms and vehicles. The Art Gallery has a continuous programme of temporary exhibitions, and holds regular lectures and concerts.
Times: Open all year, Apr-Oct, daily 10-5; Nov-Mar, daily 10-4 (closed 25 Dec). **Fee:** ✷ £2.50 (£1.25 concessions). family ticket £6.25
Facilities: P ▤ ♿ (wheelchair available, lift, ramps) toilets for disabled shop ✕ (ex guide dogs) 🦻

> If you are dissatisfied with any aspect of an attraction, discuss the problem at the time with a member of staff

FINCHALE PRIORY
Brasside, Newton Hall DH1 5SH
➲ (3m NE)
☎ 0191 386 3828

Dating from the 13th-century, these beautiful priory ruins are in a wooded setting besides the River Wear.
Times: Open Apr-Sep, daily 10-6. Dates valid until 31 Mar 2004.
Fee: £2 (ch £1, concessions £1.70). Prices valid until 31 Mar 2004.
Facilities: 🅿 (charged) 🖭 shop ✖ (ex dogs on lead) ⚏

ORIENTAL MUSEUM
University of Durham, Elvet Hill DH1 3TH
➲ (signposted from A167 & A177)   2 for 1
☎ 0191 334 5694 ▤ 0191 334 5694
e-mail: oriental.museum@durham.ac.uk

The Marvels of China gallery opened in 2000 and introduces the visitor to contemporary China, its history and decorative arts. Other displays cover the Islamic World, Buddhism, Chinese archaeology, the story of writing, a Javanese Gamelan Orchestra and an Egyptian Gallery containing everything from mummies to magic amulets.
Times: Open Mon-Fri 10-5, wknds 12-5. (Closed Xmas-New Year).
Fee: £1.50 (concessions 75p). Family ticket £3.50. **Facilities:** 🅿 🖭 ⚅ (lifts to all floors) toilets for disabled shop ✖ 🖒

HARTLEPOOL   Map 08 NZ53
HMS TRINCOMALEE
Jackson Dock TS24 0SQ
➲ (From A19 take A689 or A179, follow signs for Hartlepool Historic Quay)
☎ 01429 223193 ▤ 01429 864385
e-mail: office@hms-trincomalee.co.uk

HMS *Trincomalee*, is the oldest ship afloat in the UK and the last of Nelson's frigates. Now fully restored in an award winning project. Come aboard for a unique experience of navy life two centuries ago.
Times: Open all year, Summer: 10-5, Winter: 10.30-4. Closed Xmas & New Year. **Facilities:** 🅿 ⚅ (3 out of the 4 decks are accessible by lift) shop ✖ (ex guide dogs) 🖒

MUSEUM OF HARTLEPOOL
Jackson Dock, Maritime Av TS24 0XZ
➲ (Historic Quay & Museum towards the Marina)
☎ 01429 860077 ▤ 01429 523477

This museum tells the story of Hartlepool from prehistory to the present day and includes many original artefacts, models, computer interactives and hands-on exhibits. See how iron and steel ships were built and climb aboard the Humber ferry *Wingfield Castle*, a paddle steamer built in Hartlepool in 1934.
Times: ✱ Open all year, daily (closed 25-26 Dec & 1 Jan).
Facilities: 🅿 🖭 ⚅ toilets for disabled shop ✖ (ex guide dogs)

> Remember that prices and opening times are liable to change within the currency of this guide. It is always best to telephone in advance to check

SHILDON   Map 08 NZ22
TIMOTHY HACKWORTH VICTORIAN & RAILWAY MUSEUM
Soho Cottages, Hackworth Close DL4 1PQ
➲ (SE of Town Centre. Signed from A6072 & B6282)
☎ 01388 777999 ▤ 01388 777999

Timothy Hackwood (1786-1850) was an important figure in the development of steam travel. He constructed *Puffing Billy* for William Hedley, ran Stephenson's Newcastle Works, and also became the first superintendent of the Stockton & Darlington Railway. The museum and house detail Hackwood's life and the steam transport revolution, as well as displaying working models and locomotives from various periods. Steam train rides are available throughout the year.
Times: ✱ Open Good Fri-end Oct, Wed-Sun & BH's 10-5
Facilities: 🅿 🖭 ⚅ toilets for disabled shop ✖ (ex guide dogs)

STAINDROP   Map 12 NZ12
RABY CASTLE
DL2 3AH
➲ (on A688, Barnard Castle to Bishop Auckland road, 1m N of Staindrop. Travelling S, leave A1(M) junct 58 on A68, turning left onto A688 towards Barnard Castle, Castle on right)
☎ 01833 660202 ▤ 01833 660169
e-mail: admin@rabycastle.com

The castle was built during Saxon times but is predominantly 14th century, with many later additions. It has an impressive gateway; nine towers; a vast medieval hall; and a splendid restored Victorian octagonal drawing-room which has re-emerged as one of the most striking interiors from the 19th century. The castle contains fine pictures, interesting furniture and ceramics, and a carriage collection.
Times: ✱ Open May & Sep, Wed & Sun only. Jun-Aug, Sun-Fri. Castle open 1-5. Park & gardens 11-5.30, (last admission 4.30pm). Open BH wknds Sat-Wed. **Facilities:** 🅿 🖭 ⚅ (most of ground floor accessible) toilets for disabled shop ✖ (ex guide dogs & on lead) 🖒

TANFIELD   Map 12 NZ15
TANFIELD RAILWAY
Old Marley Hill NE16 5ET
➲ (on A6076 1m S of Sunniside)
☎ 0191 388 7545 ▤ 0191 387 4784   2 for 1
e-mail: tanfield@ingsoc.demon.co.uk

A 3-mile working steam railway and the oldest existing railway in the world. The Causey Arch, the first large railway bridge of its era, is the centrepiece of a deep wooded valley, with picturesque walks. You can ride in carriages that first saw use in Victorian times, and visit Marley Hill shed, the home of 35 engines; inside the shed you can see the stationary steam engine at work driving some of the vintage machine tools. The blacksmith is also often at work forging new parts for the restoration work. Special events are held throughout the year, please telephone for details.
Times: Open all year, summer daily 10-5; winter daily 10-4. Trains: Sun & Summer BH's wknds; also Thu & Sat mid Jul-Aug. Santa's Specials Sat & Sun in Dec (booking essential). Mince pie specials Boxing Day.
Fee: ✱ Admission free. Train travel £4.50 (under 5 free, ch & pen £2.50). Family discount tickets avalible £11.50. **Facilities:** 🅿 🖭 ⚅ (all trains carry ramps for wheelchair access) toilets for disabled shop

ESSEX

EVENTS & FESTIVALS

January
tbc Maldon Mud Race (around 500
competitors racing 400 metres on the river
bed at low tide)

May
16th Essex Young Farmers Show, Essex County
Showground, Great Leighs
31st Redoubt Fete, Redoubt Fort, Harwich
tbc Southend Air Show
tbc Tour de Tendring Cycle Ride,
Tendring area

June
5th-6th Thaxted Morris Ring Meet, various
venues, annual meeting of Morris Men
25th-4th Jul Harwich Festival, various venues

July
25th Jun-4th Harwich Festival, various venues
10th Dunmow Flitch Trials. Dating from
1104, this custom awards a flitch of bacon
to whoever does not repent their marriage
within a year and a day. (Event held every
four years)
10th Tendring Hundred Show, Lawford House
Park, Manningtree – agricultural show
tbc Classic Car Rally London-Southend
tbc Cressing Temple Festival – jazz, classical
music, drama
tbc RNLI Sea Festival, Harwich

August
21st-25th Clacton Jazz Festival (provisional)
tbc Clacton Air Show, Clacton Seafront
tbc Clacton Carnival
tbc Southend Carnival, Chalkwell Park
tbc Southend Jazz Festival (various venues)

September
tbc Maldon Town Regatta
tbc Old Leigh Regatta
tbc Walton Folk Festival

Above: Clacton Pier

AUDLEY END   Map 05 TL53

AUDLEY END HOUSE & GARDENS
CB11 4JF
➲ (1m W of Saffron Walden on B1383)
☎ 01799 522399 ▤ 01799 521276

One of the most significant Jacobean houses in England with
31 opulent rooms on view. Set in 'Capability' Brown
landscaped park, with walled Victorian kitchen garden.
Times: Open Apr-Sep; Wed-Sun & BH; Grounds 11-6 (last entry 5pm);
House, 12-5 (last entry 4pm). Oct: Grounds 11-4 Wed-Fri (last entry
3pm), Sat-Sun 11-5; House 11-3 Sat-Sun 11-3 (last entry 2pm). Dates
valid until 31 Mar 2004. **Fee:** House & Grounds: £8 (ch £4, concessions
£6). Grounds only £4 (ch £2, concessions £3). Prices valid until 31
Mar 2004. **Facilities:** ▣ (charged) ▣ ♿ shop ✻ (ex on leads) ▦

CASTLE HEDINGHAM   Map 05 TL73

COLNE VALLEY RAILWAY & MUSEUM
Castle Hedingham Station CO9 3DZ
➲ (4m NW of Halstead on A1017)
☎ 01787 461174

The old Colne Valley and Halstead railway buildings have
been rebuilt here. Stock includes seven steam locomotives
plus 70 other engines, carriages and wagons, in steam from
Easter to December. Visitors can dine in style in restored
Pullman carriages while travelling along the line. Please
telephone for a free timetable and details of the many special
events.
Times: Open all year, daily 10-dusk. Steam days, rides from 12-4.
(Closed 23 Dec-1 Feb). Steam days every Sun and BH from Mothering
Sunday to end Oct, Wed of school summer holidays & special events.
Railway Farm Park open May-Sep. Phone 01787 461174 for timetable
information. **Fee:** ✱ Steam days: £6 (ch £3, pen £5) Family ticket £18.
Diesel days £5 (ch £2.50); Family ticket £15. **Facilities:** ▣ ▣ ✗
licensed ♿ (ramps for wheelchairs to get onto carriages) shop ✻ (ex
guide dogs) ◖

HEDINGHAM CASTLE
CO9 3DJ
➲ (on B1508, 1m off A1017
Colchester/Cambridge. Follow brown heritage
signs to Hedingham Castle)
☎ 01787 460261 ▤ 01787 461473
e-mail: hedinghamcastle@aspects.net

This impressive Norman castle was built in 1140. It was
continued

besieged by King John, and visited by Henry VII, Henry VIII and Elizabeth I, and was home to the de Veres, Earls of Oxford, for over 500 years. During the summer months Hedingham's colourful heritage comes to life with a full programme of special events. There are medieval jousts and sieges with authentic living history displays and encampments. Please telephone for details civil ceremony weddings and corporate hire. **Times:** Open Etr-Oct, Sun-Fri, 11-4. **Fee:** £4 (ch £3, concessions £3.50). Family ticket £14. **Facilities:** 🅿 🅿 shop ✖ (ex in grounds) 🌰

CHELMSFORD   Map 05 TL70

RHS Garden Hyde Hall
Rettendon CM3 8ET
➲ (from M25 junct 28 (signed A12) or 29 (signed A127). SE of Chelmsford signed from A130. Exit Rettendon Turnpike, N through Rettendon Village, follow brown tourist signs)
☎ 01245 400256 📠 01245 402100
e-mail: hydehall@rhs.org.uk

Calling itself "A garden of inspirational beauty", RHS Garden Hyde Hall is a great day out for flower-lovers, and includes highlights such as the Dry Garden, a modern rose garden designed by Robin Williams, colour themed herbaceous borders, a farmhouse garden, and the NCCPG National Collection™ of Viburnum. New areas include The Queen Mother's Garden and a Wildlife Garden.
Times: Open Jan-Sep, daily 10-6; Oct onwards 10-5. **Fee:** £4.50 (ch 6-16 £1, ch under 6 free, disabled carer/companion free). Groups 10+ £3 each. **Facilities:** 🅿 ✖ licensed ♿ (ramps and easy access to visitor centre) toilets for disabled shop garden centre ✖ (ex guide dogs) 🌰

COGGESHALL   Map 05 TL82

Paycocke's
West St CO6 1NS
➲ (Signposted from A120, on S side of West Street)
☎ 01376 561305

This timber-framed house is a fine example of a medieval merchant's home. It was completed in about 1505 and has interesting carvings on the outside timbers, including the Paycocke trade sign. Inside there are further elaborate carvings and linenfold panelling. Behind the house is a pretty garden.
Times: Open 31 Mar-13 Oct Tue, Thu, Sun & BH Mon 2-5.30. **Fee:** ✱ £2.30, joint ticket with Coggeshall Grange Barn £3.40. **Facilities:** 🅿 (400yds) ♿ ✖ (ex guide dogs) 🐾

COLCHESTER   Map 05 TL92

Beth Chatto Gardens
Elmstead Market CO7 7DB
➲ (5m E of Colchester on A133)
☎ 01206 822007 📠 01206 825933
e-mail: info@bethchatto.fsnet.co.uk

Begun almost 40 years ago, when Beth Chatto and her late husband began working on acres of wasteland. Now an area

continued

of landscaped gardens with many unusual plants grown in a variety of conditions.
Times: Open all year, Mar-Oct, Mon-Sat 9-5; Nov-Feb, Mon-Fri 9-4. (Closed Sun). **Fee:** £3.50, from May 2004 £4 (accompanied ch under 14 free) **Facilities:** 🅿 🅿 ♿ (access to parts of garden may be difficult, parking) toilets for disabled garden centre ✖ (ex guide dogs) 🌰

Colchester Castle Museum
Castle Park, High St CO1 1TJ
➲ (at E end of High St)
☎ 01206 282939 📠 01206 282925

The largest Norman castle keep in Europe - built over the remains of the magnificent Roman Temple of Claudius which was destroyed by Boudicca in AD60. Colchester was the first capital of Roman Britain, and the archaeological collections are among the finest in the country. Please telephone for details of a range of events held in the school holidays.
Times: Open all year, Mon-Sat 10-5, Sun 11-5. Closed Xmas/New Year **Fee:** ✱ £4.25 (ch u5's free, ch & concessions £2.80). **Facilities:** 🅿 (town centre) ♿ (all parts accessible except vaults) toilets for disabled shop ✖ (ex guide dogs) 🌰

Colchester Zoo
Stanway, Maldon Rd CO3 0SL
➲ (turn off A12 onto A1124 and follow elephant signs)
☎ 01206 331292 📠 01206 331392   2 for 1
e-mail: enquiries@colchester-zoo.co.uk

One of England's finest zoos, Colchester Zoo has over 200 types of animals. Visitors can meet the elephants, handle a snake, and see parrots, seals, penguins and birds of prey all appearing in informative daily displays. New enclosures include Spirit of Africa, Elephant Kingdom, Penguin Shores, the Wilds of Asia for orangutans, and Chimp World. There is also an undercover soft play complex, road train, four adventure play areas, eating places and gift shops, all set in 40 acres of gardens.
Times: Open all year, daily from 9.30. Last admission 5.30 (1hr before dusk out of season). Closed 25 Dec. **Fee:** ✱ £9.90 (ch 3-14 & pen £6.50, disabled £4). **Facilities:** 🅿 🅿 ✖ licensed ♿ (easy route developed) toilets for disabled shop garden centre ✖ 🌰

HADLEIGH   Map 05 TQ88

Hadleigh Castle
➲ (0.75m S of A13)   **FREE**
☎ 01760 755161

The subject of several of Constable's paintings, the castle has fine views of the Thames estuary. It is defended by ditches on three sides, and the north-east and south-east towers are still impressive.
Times: Open any reasonable time. **Facilities:** (limited access due to hilly surroundings) ✖ (ex dogs on leads) ♿

HARWICH   Map 05 TM23

Harwich Redoubt Fort
CO12 3TE
➲ (behind 29 Main Rd)
☎ 01255 503429 📠 01255 503429   2 for 1
e-mail: theharwichsociety@quista.net

The 180ft-diameter circular fort was built in 1808 in case of

continued

invasion by Napoleon. It has a dry moat and 8ft-thick walls, with 18 rooms for stores, ammunition and quarters for 300 men. The Redoubt is being restored by the Harwich Society, and contains three small museums. Ten guns can be seen on the battlements.
Times: Open May-Aug, daily 10-4.30; Sep-Apr, Sun only 10-4. **Fee:** ✱ £1 (accompanied ch free). **Facilities:** P (200yds) shop

HEDINGHAM
See Castle Hedingham

LAYER MARNEY   Map 05 TL91
LAYER MARNEY TOWER
CO5 9US
➲ (off B1022 Colchester to Maldon road, signposted)
☎ 01206 330784 🖹 01206 330884
e-mail: info@layermarneytower.co.uk
The tallest Tudor gatehouse in the country, intended to be the entrance to a courtyard which would have rivalled Hampton Court Palace. The death of Henry, 1st Lord Marney in 1523, and of his son in 1525, meant that the building work ceased before completion. The beautiful parish church lies within the grounds and a wildlife walk offers the chance to see a range of livestock.
Times: Open Apr-Sep, Mon-Fri 12-5, Sun 12-5 & BHs 11-5. **Fee:** ✱ £3.50 (ch £2). Family ticket £10. Guided tour £4.75. Party 20+.
Facilities: P 💷 ✗ licensed 🚻 (ramps in garden and farm) toilets for disabled shop ✖ (ex guide dogs & dogs on lead) ◥

MISTLEY   Map 05 TM13
MISTLEY TOWERS
CO11 1NJ
➲ (on B1352, 1.5m E of A137 at Lawford) FREE
☎ 01206 393884
All that remains of the grand hall and church, designed by Robert Adam, are the lodges built in 1782 for the hall, and two square towers, topped with drums and domes which came from an earlier church.
Times: Open all reasonable times. Key available from Mistley Quay Workshops & Teashop. **Facilities:** 🚻 ❖

NEWPORT   Map 05 TL53
MOLE HALL WILDLIFE PARK
Widdington CB11 3SS
➲ (M11 junct 8. Situated between Stansted & Saffron Walden, off B1383)
☎ 01799 540400 & 541359 🖹 01799 542408
e-mail: enquiries@molehall.co.uk
The Park covers 20 acres and has been lovingly developed by the Johnstone family for over 40 years. The wide variety of animals range from South American Lama Guanaco to Red squirrels, Leopard-like Serval Cat and the Formosan Sika Deer, which is extinct in the wild. Mole Hall is also home to 2 species of otter, being the first regular breeders in the UK of the North American Otter. Other residents include chimpanzees, capuchins, lemurs and much more. In the tropical butterfly pavilion, see butterflies on the wing and
continued

free flying small birds. Tarantulas, snakes, leaf-eating ants, pools of aquatic life, small monkeys, tortoises and lovebirds.
Times: Open all year, daily 10.30-6 (or dusk). (Closed 25 Dec). Butterfly House open mid Mar-Oct. **Fee:** ✱ £5 (ch £3.50 under 3's free, pen, student & disabled £4). **Facilities:** P 💷 🚻 (Difficult in wet weather for wheelchairs) toilets for disabled shop garden centre ✖ (ex guide dogs) ◥

SAFFRON WALDEN   Map 05 TL53
SAFFRON WALDEN MUSEUM
Museum St CB10 1JL
➲ (take B184/B1052 & follow signs to Saffron Walden)
☎ 01799 510333 🖹 01799 510334
e-mail: museum@uttesford.gov.uk
Built in 1834, this friendly museum lies near the castle ruins in the centre of town. Its collections include local archaeology, natural history, ceramics, glass, costume, furniture, toys, an ancient Egyptian room, a new natural history gallery and Discovery Centre. This museum has won awards for disabled access.
Times: ✱ Open all year, Mar-Oct, Mon-Sat 10-5, Sun & BHs 2-5; Nov-Feb, Mon-Sat, 10-4.30, Sun & BHs 2-4.30. (Closed 24 & 25 Dec). **Fee:** £1 (concessions 50p & ch 18 free). **Facilities:** P 🚻 (ramped entrance, wheelchairs available, stairlifts) toilets for disabled shop ✖ (ex guide dogs)

SOUTHEND-ON-SEA   Map 05 TQ88
SOUTHEND MUSEUM, PLANETARIUM & DISCOVERY CENTRE
Victoria Av SS2 6EW
➲ (take A127 or A13 towards town centre. Museum is adjacent to Southend Victoria Railway Station)
☎ 01702 434449 🖹 01702 349806
e-mail: southendmuseum@hotmail.com
A fine Edwardian building housing displays of archaeology, natural history and local history, telling the story of man in the south-east Essex area. Also the only planetarium in the South East outside London. Ring for details of special events.
Times: Open Central Museum: Tue-Sat 10-5 (Closed Sun-Mon & BH); Planetarium: Wed-Sat, shows at 11, 2 & 4. **Fee:** ✱ Central Museum free. Planetarium £2.25 (ch & pen £1.60). Family tickets £7. Party rates on request. **Facilities:** P (50mtrs) (disabled only behind museum) 🚻 (planetarium not accessible, disabled access to centre) shop ✖ (ex guide dogs)

SOUTHEND PIER MUSEUM
Western Esplanade SS1 2EL
➲ (A127 follow signs to seafront and pier)
☎ 01702 611214 & 614553
Southend Pier is one and a third miles long and was built in 1830. This living museum portrays the history of the pier, its railway, its disasters, and the people who have lived and worked there. Exhibits include ex-pier rolling stock, a reconstructed signal box with working levers, and antique slot machines.
Times: Open May-Oct **Fee:** ✱ 60p (accompanied ch under 12 free) **Facilities:** P (50yds) 🚻 shop ✖ (ex guide dogs)

STANSTED　　　　　　　　　Map 05 TL52

HOUSE ON THE HILL MUSEUM ADVENTURE
CM24 8SP
➲ (off B1383 in the centre of Stansted Mountfitchet)
☎ 01279 813567　🖹 01279 816391
e-mail: gold@enta.net

A large, privately-owned toy museum, housed on two floors covering 7,000 sq. ft. A huge variety of toys, books and games from the late Victorian period up to the 1970s. There is a space display, Teddy Bears' picnic, Action Man, Sindy, Barbie, military displays and much more. Additional displays of film, theatre and television memorabilia are on show, plus end of the pier slot machines.
Times: Open daily, 10-5; (closed for a few days over the Xmas period)
Facilities: 🅿 (charged) shop ✖ (ex guide dogs) 🍴

MOUNTFITCHET CASTLE & NORMAN VILLAGE
CM24 8SP
➲ (off B1383, in centre of village. 5 min from M11 junct 8)
☎ 01279 813237　🖹 01279 816391
e-mail: mountfitchetcastle@btopenworld.com

Norman motte and bailey castle and village reconstructed as it was in Norman England of 1066, on its original historic site. A vivid illustration of village life in Domesday England, complete with houses, church, seige tower, seige weapons, and many types of animals roaming freely. Animated wax figures in all the buildings give historical information to visitors.
Times: Open daily, mid Mar-mid Nov, 10-5. **Fee:** £6 (ch 14 £5, pen £5.50). **Facilities:** 🅿 (charged) 💭 ♿ (laser commentaries) toilets for disabled shop ✖ (ex guide dogs) 🍴

Remember that prices and opening times are liable to change within the currency of this guide. It is always best to telephone in advance to check

TILBURY　　　　　　　　　Map 05 TQ67

TILBURY FORT
No 2 Office Block, The Fort RM18 7NR
➲ (0.5 mile E off A126)
☎ 01375 858489

View the finest example of 17th-century military engineering, a spectacular sight on the River Thames. View the World War I and II gun emplacements and even fire a real anti-aircraft gun.
Times: Open all year, Apr-Sep, daily 10-6; Oct, daily 10-5; Nov-Mar, daily 10-4. (Closed between 1-2, 24-26 Dec & 1 Jan). Dates valid until 31 Mar 2004. **Fee:** £3 (ch £1.50, concessions £2.50). Prices valid until 31 Mar 2004. **Facilities:** ♿ shop ✖ (ex on lead in certain areas) 🚻

WALTHAM ABBEY　　　　　　　Map 05 TL30

LEE VALLEY PARK FARMS
Stubbings Hall Ln, Crooked Mile EN9 2EG
➲ (M25 junct 26, follow to Waltham Abbey. 2m from Waltham Abbey on B914)　【2 for 1】
☎ 01992 892781 & 892291　🖹 01992 892291
e-mail: hayeshill@leevalleypark.com

Set in the heart of Lee Valley Country Park, Hayes Hill Farm offers young and old the chance to view many types of farm animals. Meet a variety of rare breeds in the traditional-style farmyard. In the pet centre, see many creatures from meerkats to chipmonks. During summer, there are tractor and trailor rides to Holyfield Hall, a 700-acre working dairy and arable farm.
Times: Open all year, Mon-Fri 10-4.30, wknds & BH 10-5.30.
Fee: £3.50 (ch 3+ £2.50, concessions £3). **Facilities:** 🅿 💭 ♿ (graded concrete paths, signed routes) toilets for disabled shop 🍴

WALTHAM ABBEY GATEHOUSE, BRIDGE & ENTRANCE TO CLOISTERS
➲ (in Waltham Abbey off A112)　　　　　【FREE】
☎ 01992 702200

Beside the great Norman church at Waltham are the slight remains of the abbey buildings - bridge, gatehouse and part of the north cloister. The bridge is named after King Harold, founder of the abbey.
Times: Open any reasonable time. **Facilities:** ♿ (sensory trail guide) ✖ (ex dogs on leads) 🚻

GLOUCESTERSHIRE

EVENTS & FESTIVALS

February
5th-8th Cheltenham Folk Festival

March
16th-18th National Hunt Festival, Cheltenham

April
29th-2nd May Badminton Horse Trials
29th-3rd May Cheltenham International Jazz Festival

May
3rd Cheese Roll, A46 nr Brockworth
5th-16th Cheltenham Competitive Festival

June
4th Robert Dover's Cotswold Olimpick Games, Dover's Hill, Chipping Coopers Hill
18th-20th Three Counties Show, Malvern

July
1st-31st Hailes Festival
2nd-18th Cheltenham Fringe Festival
2nd-18th Cheltenham International Festival of Music
10th-11th Tewkesbury Medieval Festival, Cupshill Fields, Tewkesbury (provisional)
17th-18th Tewkesbury Water Festival
24th-25th International Kite Festival, Tewkesbury (provisional)
24th-31st Guiting Festival, Guiting Power
26th-9th Aug Musica Deo Sacra, Tewkesbury Abbey, religious choral music
tbc Cotswold Show & Country Fair, Cirencester Park, Cirencester
tbc Gloucester Festival
tbc Royal International Air Tattoo, RAF Fairford

August
31st Jul-9th Gloucester Blues & Heritage Festival, various venues
tbc Twyning to Tewkesbury Raft Race

September
25th-26th The Malvern Autumn Garden & Country Show, Malvern

October
tbc Cheltenham Festival of Literature
tbc Tewkesbury Mop Fair (street fair)

Above: The Benedictine Abbey at Tewkesbury

BERKELEY   Map 03 ST69

BERKELEY CASTLE
GL13 9BQ
➲ (just off A38 midway between Bristol & Gloucester. From M5 take junct 14 or 15)
☎ 01453 810332
e-mail: info@berkeley.castle.com

Home of the Berkeleys for almost 850 years, the castle is a rambling and romantic fortress surrounded by 14ft thick walls, with a Norman keep, a great hall, medieval kitchens, and the dungeon where Edward II was murdered. Outside there are Elizabethan terraced gardens overlooking rolling countryside towards the River Severn. See also the beautiful butterfly house; an enclosed tranquil glasshouse garden with hundreds of exotic butterflies in free flight among unusual plants and flowers.
Times: Open Apr-Sep, Wed-Sat 11-4, Sun 2-5; Oct, Sun only 2-5. Also open BH Mon 11-4. Last admission 30mins before closing. **Fee:** Castle & Gardens: £6.25 (ch 5-15 £3.25, pen £5). Family ticket (2 adult & 2 ch) £16.25. **Facilities:** ☐ ☞ shop ✖ (ex guide dogs) ☜

JENNER MUSEUM
Church Ln, High St GL13 9BH
➲ (follow tourist signs from A38 to town centre, turn left into High Street & left again into Church Lane)
☎ 01453 810631   ⌨ 01453 811690
e-mail: manager@jennermuseum.com

This beautiful Georgian house was the home of Edward Jenner, the discoverer of vaccination against smallpox. The house and the garden, with its Temple of Vaccinia, are much as they were in Jenner's day. The displays record Jenner's life as an 18th-century country doctor, his work on vaccination and his interest in natural history.
Times: Open Apr-Sep, Tue-Sat 12.30-5.30, Sun 1-5.30. Oct, Sun 1-5.30. (Closed Mon, ex BH Mon 12.30-5.30). **Fee:** ✱ £3 (ch £1.50, students & pen £2.30). Family ticket £7.50. Party 20+. **Facilities:** ☐ ♿ toilets for disabled shop ✖ (ex guide dogs)

FREE

Attractions with this symbol do not charge for entry.

BOURTON-ON-THE-WATER   Map 04 SP12

BIRDLAND
Risssington Rd GL54 2BN
➲ (on A429)
☎ 01451 820480   ☐ 01451 822398
e-mail: sb.birdland@virgin.net

Birdland is a natural setting of woodland, river and gardens, which is inhabited by over 500 birds; flamingos, pelicans, penguins, cranes, storks, cassowary and waterfowl can be seen on various aspects of the water habitat. Over 50 aviaries of parrots, falcons, pheasants, hornbills, touracos, pigeons, ibis and many more. Tropical, Toucan and Desert Houses are home to the more delicate species.
Times: Open all year, Apr-Oct, daily 10-6; Nov-Mar, daily 10-4. Last admission 1hr before closing. (Closed 25 Dec). **Fee:** ✱ £4.75 (ch 4-14 £2.65, pen £3.75). Family ticket (2 ad & 2 ch) £13.50. Party 10+.
Facilities: P (adjacent) ⬛& toilets for disabled shop ✖ (ex dogs on lead) ◥

MODEL VILLAGE
Old New Inn GL54 2AF
☎ 01451 820467   ☐ 01451 810236
e-mail: reception@theoldnewinn.co.uk

The model is built of Cotswold stone to a scale of one-ninth, and is a perfect replica of the village. It includes a miniature River Windrush, a working model waterwheel, churches and shops, with tiny trees, shrubs and alpine plants.
Times: Open all year 9-5.45 (summer), 10-dusk (winter). (Closed 25 Dec). **Fee:** ✱ £2.75 (ch £2, pen £2.50). **Facilities:** P (500yds) ⬛✖ licensed shop ✖ (ex guide dogs) ◥

CHEDWORTH   Map 04 SP01

CHEDWORTH ROMAN VILLA
Yanworth GL54 3LJ
➲ (3m NW of Fossebridge on A429)
☎ 01242 890256   ☐ 01242 890544
e-mail: chedworth@smtp.ntrust.org.uk

The remains of a Romano-British villa, excavated 1864-66. Set in a beautiful wooded combe, there are fine 4th-century mosaics, two bath houses, and a temple with spring. The museum houses the smaller finds and there is a 9-minute video programme. Telephone for further details of special events.
Times: ✱ Open 26 Feb-22 Mar, daily (ex Mon) 11-4; 23 Mar-20 Oct, daily (ex Mon) 10-5; 22 Oct-17 Nov, daily (ex Mon) 11-4. Closed Mon (ex BH Mon's). **Facilities:** P & (audio tour) toilets for disabled shop ✖ ♨ ◥

CHELTENHAM   Map 03 SO92

CHELTENHAM ART GALLERY & MUSEUM
Clarence St GL50 3JT
➲ (close to town centre and bus station)
☎ 01242 237431   ☐ 01242 262334
e-mail: artgallery@cheltenham.gov.uk

The museum has an outstanding collection relating to the Arts and Crafts Movement, including fine furniture and exquisite metalwork. The Art Gallery contains Dutch and British paintings from the 17th century to the present day. The Oriental Gallery features pottery, costumes and treasures from the Ming Dynasty to the reign of the last Chinese Emperor. There is also a display about Edward Wilson who

continued

journeyed with Captain Scott in 1911-12, together with the history of Britain's most complete Regency town and archaeological treasures from the neighbouring Cotswolds. Special exhibitions are held throughout the year.
Times: Open all year, First Thu in the month 11-5.20, Mon-Sat 10-5.20, Sun 2-4.20. (Closed BHs & Etr Sun). **Fee:** Free, donations welcome.
Facilities: P (500 metres) disabled parking on site ⬛& (handling tables; speech reinforcement system) toilets for disabled shop ✖ (ex guide dogs) ◥

HOLST BIRTHPLACE MUSEUM
4 Clarence Rd GL52 2AY
➲ (opposite gateway of Pittville Park. 10 min walk from town centre)
☎ 01242 524846   ☐ 01242 580182
e-mail: holstmuseum@btconnect.com

Gustav Holst, composer of *The Planets* was born at this Regency house in 1874. The museum contains unique displays on Holst's life, including his original piano. The rooms of the house have been carefully restored, each area evoking a different period in the history of the house from Regency to Edwardian times.
Times: Open Tue-Sat 10-4 (Closed Mon & Dec-Jan, ex pre-booked groups) **Fee:** £2.50 (ch & concessions £2). Family ticket (2 ad & 3 ch) £7. **Facilities:** P (250yds) (large print & braille guide, special hands-on tours) shop ✖ (ex guide dogs)

CIRENCESTER   Map 04 SP00

CORINIUM MUSEUM
Park St GL7 2BX
➲ (in town centre)
☎ 01285 655611   ☐ 01285 643286
e-mail: simone.clark@cotswold.gov.uk

Cirencester was the second largest town in Roman Britain and the Corinium Museum brings the period to life with full-scale re-constructions. A major and innovative development will transform the museum into a unique community resource. The proposed re-opening date is Spring 2004. The museum will boast a new Anglo-Saxon gallery, a new ground floor life-long learning centre, new displays on the Roman history and archaeology of Cirencester and the Cotswolds and new 18th and 19th century displays. For more information visit www.cotswold.gov.uk
Times: Closed for refurbishment. Proposed re-opening Spring 2004, please contact museum to confirm opening times. **Fee:** ✱ £2.50 (ch £1, students £1, pen £2). Family ticket £5. Party. Fri after 3.30pm free admission. **Facilities:** P (440yds town centre) ⬛✖ licensed & toilets for disabled shop ◥

CLEARWELL   Map 03 SO50

CLEARWELL CAVES ANCIENT IRON MINES
GL16 8JR
➲ (1.5m S of Coleford town centre, off B4228 follow brown tourism signs)
☎ 01594 832535   ☐ 01594 833362
e-mail: jw@clearwellcaves.com

These impressive natural caves have also been mined since the earliest times for paint pigment and iron ore. Today visitors explore nine large caverns with displays of local

continued

mining and geology. Colour room where ochre pigments are still produced and blacksmith shop.
Times: Open Mar-Oct daily 10-5. Jan-Feb Sat-Sun 10-5. Christmas Fantasy 1-24 Dec, daily 10-5. **Fee:** ✱ £4 (ch £2.50, concessions £3.50) Family ticket £11. **Facilities:** 🅿 🍽 & (hands-on exhibits, braille guide book, contact in advance) toilets for disabled shop 🗙 (ex guide & hearing dogs) 🍽

CRANHAM   Map 03 SO81

PRINKNASH ABBEY AND POTTERY
GL4 8EX
➲ (on A46 between Cheltenham & Stroud)
☎ 01452 812066 📄 01452 812529
e-mail: bjnicholls@prinknash.fsnet.co.uk

Set in a large park, the old priory building is a 12th to 16th-century house, used by Benedictine monks and guests of Gloucester Abbey until 1539. It became an abbey for Benedictine monks from Caldey in 1928. Rich beds of clay were discovered when foundations were being dug for the new abbey building, and so the pottery was established, employing local craftspeople.
Times: ✱ Open all year. Abbey Church: daily 5am-8pm. Pottery: Mon-Sat 11-4.30 (Sun pm). Pottery shop & tearoom 9-5.30. (Closed Good Fri, 25 & 26 Dec). **Facilities:** 🅿 🍽 & toilets for disabled shop

PRINKNASH BIRD & DEER PARK
GL4 8EX
➲ (M5 junct 11a, A417 Cirencester. Take 1st exit signposted A46 Stroud. Follow brown tourist signs)
☎ 01452 812727

Nine acres of parkland and lakes make a beautiful home for black swans, geese and other water birds. There are also exotic birds such as white and Indian blue peacocks and crown cranes, as well as tame fallow deer and pygmy goats. The Golden Wood is stocked with ornamental pheasants, and leads to the reputedly haunted monks' fishpond, which contains trout. An 80-year old, free-standing, 16ft tall Wendy House in the style of a Tudor house has recently been erected near the picnic area.
Times: Open all year, daily 10-5 (4pm in winter). Park closes at 6pm (5pm in winter). (Closed 25-26 Dec, 1 Jan & Good Fri). **Fee:** ✱ £3.80 (ch £1.90, pen £2.90). Party 10+ £2.90 (ch £1.70, pen £1.90). Prices under review. **Facilities:** 🅿 🍽 shop 🗙

DEERHURST   Map 03 SO82

ODDA'S CHAPEL
➲ (off B4213 near River Severn at Abbots Court SW of parish church)

This rare Saxon chapel was built by Earl Odda and dedicated in 1056. When it was discovered, it had been incorporated into a farmhouse. It has now been carefully restored.
Times: Open Apr-Oct, 10-6; Nov-Mar, 10-4. Closed 24-26 Dec & 1 Jan. **Facilities:** 🅿 (charged) 🗙

> The AA also publishes a guide to Family Friendly Places to Stay, Eat & Visit

DYRHAM   Map 03 ST77

DYRHAM PARK
SN14 8ER
➲ (8m N of Bath, 2m from M4 junct 18)
☎ 0117 937 2501
e-mail: wfijew@smtp.ntrust.org.uk

Dyrham Park is a splendid William and Mary house, with interiors that have hardly altered since the late 17th century. It has contemporary Dutch-style furnishings, Dutch pictures and blue-and-white Delft ware. Around the house is an ancient park with fallow deer.
Times: ✱ Open 28 Mar-2 Nov. **Facilities:** 🅿 🍽 ✗ licensed & (Braille & audio guides, stairclimber, free bus from car park) toilets for disabled shop 🗙 (ex in dog walk area) 🌿

GLOUCESTER   Map 03 SO81

GLOUCESTER CITY MUSEUM & ART GALLERY
Brunswick Rd GL1 1HP
➲ (centre of Gloucester)
☎ 01452 396131 📄 01452 410898
e-mail: city.museum@gloucester.gov.uk

An impressive range of Roman artefacts including the Rufus Sita tombstone; the amazing Iron Age Birdlip Mirror; one of the earliest backgammon sets in the world; dinosaur fossils; and paintings by famous artists such as Turner and Gainsborough. There is something for everyone, full-sized dinosaurs; wildlife from the City and the Gloucestershire countryside; beautiful antique furniture, glass, ceramics and silver; hands-on displays, computer quizzes and activity workstations throughout the galleries. There is an exciting range of temporary exhibitions from contemporary art and textiles to dinosaurs and local history; children's holiday activities and regular special events.
Times: Open all year, Tue-Sat 10-5. **Fee:** ✱ £2 (concessions £1). Free to Gloucester City residents and under 18's. **Facilities:** 🅿 (500yds) & toilets for disabled shop 🗙 (ex guide dogs) 🍽

> Special Events are held at many attractions throughout the country. As we cannot hope to list them all, please ring the places of interest for details of exhibitions, themed days, and guided walks.

GLOUCESTER FOLK MUSEUM

99-103 Westgate St GL1 2PG

➲ (accessed by A40 and A48 from the W, A38 and M5 from the N, A40 & B4073 from the E and A4173 & A38 from the S)

☎ 01452 396467 ▤ 01452 330495

e-mail: folk.museum@gloucester.gov.uk

Three floors of splendid Tudor and Jacobean timber-framed buildings dating from the 16th and 17th centuries along with new buildings housing the Dairy, Ironmonger's shop and Wheelwright and Carpenter workshops. Local history, domestic life, crafts, trades and industries from 1500 to the present, including Toys and Childhood gallery with hands-on toys and a puppet theatre, the Siege of Gloucester, a Victorian Class Room, Victorian Kitchen and laundry equipment. A wide range of exhibitions, hands-on activities, events, demonstrations and role play sessions are held throughout the year. There is an attractive cottage garden and courtyard for events, often with live animals, and outside games. **Times:** Open all year, Tue-Sat 10-5. **Fee:** ✱ £2 (concessions £1). Free to Gloucester city residents & under 18's. **Facilities:** 🅿 (500yds) ⅚ (hands-on displays, virtual tour of Protal gallery) shop ✖ (ex guide dogs) 🥡

THE NATIONAL WATERWAYS MUSEUM

Llanthony Warehouse, The Docks GL1 2EH

➲ (follow signs for historic docks off M5 and A40 and also within the city, situated to the south of the city centre)

☎ 01452 318200 ▤ 01452 318202

e-mail: bookingsnwm@thewaterwaystrust.org

Based in Gloucester Docks, this museum takes up three floors of a seven-storey Victorian warehouse, and documents the 200-year history of Britain's water-based transport. The emphasis is on hands-on experience, including working models and engines, interactive displays, actual craft, computer interactions and the national collection of inland waterways. Boat trips are also available between Easter and October.

Times: Open all year, daily 10-5. Last admissions 4pm (Closed 25 Dec). **Fee:** £5 (under 5's free ch & pen £4). Family tickets £12-£16. **Facilities:** 🅿 (charged) 🍽 ⅚ (wheelchair, lifts, limited access to floating exhibits) toilets for disabled shop ✖ (ex guide dogs) 🥡

NATURE IN ART

Wallsworth Hall, Tewkesbury Rd, Twigworth GL2 9PA

➲ (2m N of Gloucester on A38, from village follow tourist signs)

☎ 01452 731422 ▤ 01452 730937

e-mail: ninart@globalnet.co.uk

Nature is the theme at this museum and art gallery, and there are many outstanding exhibits including sculpture, tapestries and ceramics. There is a comprehensive 'artist in residence' programme for ten months of the year, and events include regular monthly talks, film showings and a full programme of temporary exhibitions and art courses. Work from over 60 countries spanning 1500 years is included in the collection which has been specially commended twice in the National Heritage Museum of the Year Awards. From Picasso to David Shepherd, Flemish masters to ethnic art, contemporary sculpture to Japanese prints - there is something for everyone. **Times:** Open all year, Tue-Sun & BH's 10-5. Mon by arrangement. (Closed 24-26 Dec). **Fee:** £3.60 (ch, pen & students £3.10, ch under 8 free). Family ticket £11. Party 15+. **Facilities:** 🅿 🍽 ⅚ (lift & ramps at entrance) toilets for disabled shop ✖ (ex guide dogs)

GUITING POWER   Map 04 SP02

COTSWOLD FARM PARK

GL54 5UG

➲ (signposted off B4077 from M5 Junct 9)

☎ 01451 850307 ▤ 01451 850423

e-mail: info@cotswoldfarmpark.co.uk

At the Cotswold Farm Park there are nearly 50 breeding

continued

herds and flocks of the rarest British breeds of sheep, cattle, pigs, goats, horses, poultry and waterfowl. Set on the very top of the Cotswold Hills, this is the perfect opportunity to get to know a Bagot goat, cuddle a Cotswold lamb, stroke a mighty Longhorn ox, and admire generations of our living agricultural heritage. New born lambs and goat kids can be seen from April to May, spring calves in May, foals and sheep shearing in June and piglets throughout the year. Lambing takes place in front of visitors from mid March to the end of April and milking during July, August and September.
Times: Open 29 Mar-14 Sep, daily 10.30-5 (then open wknds only until end Oct 10.30-4). **Fee:** ✱ £4.80 (ch £3.30, pen £4.50). Family ticket £15. **Facilities:** 🅿 💷 ♿ (ramps, wheelchair to let) toilets for disabled shop ✕ (ex guide dogs) 🍴

HAILES   Map 04 SP02

HAILES ABBEY
GL54 5PB
➲ (2m NE of Winchcombe off B4632)
☎ 01242 602398

Explore the atmospheric ruins of this great medieval pilgrimage abbey, in the midst of the Cotswolds. Built in the 13th-century Hailes become famous when presented with a phial that was said to contain the blood of Christ.
Times: Open Apr-Sep, daily 10-6; Oct, daily 10-5. Dates valid until 31 Mar 2004. **Fee:** £3 (ch £1.50, concessions £2.30). Prices valid until 31 Mar 2004. **Facilities:** 🅿 ♿ shop ✕ (ex dogs on leads) ♨ 🍴

LYDNEY   Map 03 SO60

DEAN FOREST RAILWAY
Norchard Railway Centre, New Mills, Forest Rd
GL15 4ET
➲ (At Lydney, turn off the Gloucester to Chepstow (A48) road and follow brown tourist signs to Norchard Railway Centre, on B4234 Lydney-Parkend road)
☎ 01594 843423 (info) & 845840
🖨 01594 845840

Just north of Lydney lies the headquarters of the Dean Forest Railway where a number of steam locomotives, plus lots of coaches, wagons and railway equipment are on show and guided tours are available by prior arrangement. Standard gauge passenger service on steam haulage runs from Norchard to Lydney Junction and back to Norchard, the
continued

diesel train runs from Lydney Junction to Tufts and back to Lydney Junction.
Times: Open all year, daily for static displays. Steam days: Oct, Sun only; Jun-Sep, Wed & Sun; Aug, Thu & Sat. Diesel only days: Jun-Jul, Sun only. (Additional days & school holidays telephone 01594 843423 for details). **Facilities:** 🅿 💷 ♿ (specially adapted coach for wheelchairs, phone for details) toilets for disabled shop

MICKLETON   Map 04 SP14

HIDCOTE MANOR GARDEN
Chipping Campden GL55 6LR
➲ (1m E of B4632, near the village of Mickleton)
☎ 01386 438333   🖨 01386 438817
e-mail: hidcote@nationaltrust.org.uk

One of the most delightful gardens in England, created by the horticulturist Major Laurence Johnston and comprising a series of small gardens within the whole, separated by walls and hedges of different species.
Times: Open 29 Mar-2 Nov, Mon-Wed & Sat-Sun, 10.30-6 (last admission at 5pm, from 1 Oct last admission at 4pm) **Fee:** ✱ £5.90 (ch £2.90) family £14.50. **Facilities:** 🅿 💷 ✕ licensed ♿ (partial access, limited due to stone paths) toilets for disabled shop garden centre ✕ (ex guide dogs) 🍴

KIFTSGATE COURT GARDEN
Mickleton GL55 6LN
➲ (0.5m S off A46, adjacent Hidcote NT garden)
☎ 01386 438777   🖨 01386 438777
e-mail: kiftsgte@aol.com

Kiftsgate Garden is spectacularly set on the edge of the Cotswold Escarpment, with views over the Vale of Evesham. It contains many rare plants collected by three generations of women gardeners, including the largest rose in England, the R. Filipes Kiftsgate.
Times: Open Apr-May & Aug-Sep; Wed, Thu, Sun & BH Mon 2-6. Jun-Jul Mon, Wed, Thu, Sat & Sun 12-6. **Fee:** ✱ £4.50 (ch £1). **Facilities:** 🅿 💷 garden centre ✕ (ex guide dogs)

MORETON-IN-MARSH   Map 04 SP23

BATSFORD ARBORETUM
Admissions Centre, Batsford Park GL56 9QB
➲ (1.5m NW, off A44 from Moreton-in-Marsh)
☎ 01386 701441   **2 for 1**
🖨 01386 701829
e-mail: batsarb@batsfound.freeserve.co.uk

Batsford Arboretum has one of the largest private collections of trees in Great Britain and wonderful views across the Vale of Evenlode. Visitors can stroll amongst the spring flowers that cascade down the hillside, and see many rare and unusual trees. There is an impressive display of colour during autumn, and peace and tranquillity are ever present. View the Buddha and cave and try and negotiate the waterfall without getting too wet.
Times: Open Feb-mid Nov, daily 10-5; mid Nov-Jan, wknds only 10-4. **Fee:** £5 (ch 4-15 £1, con £4). Party 12+. **Facilities:** 🅿 💷 ♿ (some steep & slippery paths not suited to wheelchairs) toilets for disabled shop garden centre 🍴

COTSWOLD FALCONRY CENTRE
Batsford Park GL56 9QB
➲ (1m W of Moreton-in-Marsh on A44)
☎ 01386 701043
e-mail: geoffdalton@yahoo.co.uk
`2 for 1`

Conveniently located by the Batsford Park Arboretum, the Cotswold Falconry gives daily demonstrations in the art of falconry. The emphasis here is on breeding and conservation, and eagles, hawks, owls and falcons can be seen.
Times: Open mid Feb-mid Nov, 10.30-5.30. (Last admission 5pm).
Fee: £5 (ch 4-15 £2.50, concession £4). Joint ticket with Batsford Arboretum £6.50 (ch 4-15 £3, concession £6). **Facilities:** 🅿 ♿ (no steps, wide doorways) toilets for disabled shop garden centre 🗙 (ex on leads in arboretum) 🍴

SEZINCOTE
GL56 9AW
➲ (1.5m out of Moreton-in-Marsh on A44, Evesham road)
☎ 01386 700444

The Indian-style house at Sezincote was the inspiration for Brighton Pavilion; its charming water garden adds to its exotic aura and features trees of unusual size.
Times: Open: House, May-Jul & Sep, Thu & Fri 2.30-6. Garden only, all year (ex Dec) Thu, Fri & BH Mon 2-6 or dusk if earlier. **Fee:** ✱ House & garden £5. Garden only £3.50 (ch £1 under 5 free). Children not allowed in the House. Groups by appointment only. **Facilities:** 🅿 ♿ 🗙 (ex guide dogs)

NEWENT   Map 03 SO72
THE NATIONAL BIRDS OF PREY CENTRE
GL18 1JJ
➲ (follow A40, right onto B4219 towards Newent. Follow brown tourist signs from Newent town)
☎ 0870 9901992 🖷 01531 821389
e-mail: jpj@nbpc.demon.co.uk

Trained birds can be seen at close quarters in the Hawk Walk and the Owl Courtyard and there are also breeding aviaries, a gift shop, bookshop, picnic areas, coffee shop and children's play area. Birds are flown three times daily in summer and winter, giving an exciting and educational display. There are over 110 aviaries on view with 85 species. The centre leads the world in the field of captive breeding.
Times: Open Feb-Oct, daily 10.30-5.30 or dusk if earlier. Also open in Nov-Dec for evening events. **Facilities:** 🅿 🍽 ♿ (special tours available, pre-booking required) toilets for disabled shop 🗙 🍴

THE SHAMBLES
Church St GL18 1PP
➲ (close to town centre near church)
☎ 01531 822144

Cobbled streets, alleyways, cottages and houses set in over an acre with display shops and trades, even a tin chapel and cottage garden all helping to recreate the feel and atmosphere of a small Victorian town.
Times: Open mid Mar-end Oct, Tue-Sun & BH's 10-5 (or dusk); Nov-Dec wknds only. **Fee:** ✱ £3.85 (ch £2.25, pen £3.25).
Facilities: 🅿 (100yds) 🍽 ♿ toilets for disabled shop 🍴

NORTHLEACH   Map 04 SP11
KEITH HARDING'S WORLD OF MECHANICAL MUSIC
The Oak House, High St GL54 3ET
➲ (at crossroads of A40 & A429)
☎ 01451 860181 🖷 01451 861133
e-mail: keith@mechanicalmusic.co.uk

A fascinating collection of antique clocks, musical boxes, automata and mechanical musical instruments, restored and maintained in the world-famous workshops, displayed in a period setting, and played during regular tours. There is an exhibition of coin operated instruments which visitors can play.
Times: Open all year, daily 10-6. Last tour 5pm. Closed 25-26 Dec.
Fee: ✱ £5 (ch £2.50, pen & students £4). Discounts for families & groups. **Facilities:** 🅿 ♿ toilets for disabled shop 🗙 (ex guide dogs) 🍴

OWLPEN   Map 03 ST79
OWLPEN MANOR
GL11 5BZ
➲ (3m E of Dursley off B4066, follow brown tourist signs)
☎ 01453 860261 🖷 01453 860819
e-mail: sales@owlpen.com

A romantic Tudor manor house, with unique 17th-century painted cloth wallhangings, furniture, pictures and textiles. The house is set in formal terraced gardens, and is part of a picturesque Cotswold manorial group including a Jacobean Court House, a Victorian church and medieval tithe barn.
Times: ✱ Open Apr-15 Oct, Tue-Sun & BH Mon, 2-5. **Facilities:** 🅿 🍽 🗙 licensed 🗙 🍴

PAINSWICK   Map 03 SO80
PAINSWICK ROCOCO GARDEN
GL6 6TH
➲ (on B4073 0.5m NW of Painswick)
☎ 01452 813204 🖷 01452 814888
e-mail: info@rococogarden.co.uk
`2 for 1`

This beautiful Rococo garden (a compromise between formality and informality) is the only one of its period to survive complete. There are ponds, woodland walks, a maze, kitchen garden and herbacious borders, all set in a Cotswold

continued

valley famous for snowdrops in the early spring. Ring for details of special events.

Painswick Rococo Garden

Times: Open 10 Jan-Oct, daily 11-5. **Fee:** ✱ £3.60 (ch £1.80, pen £3.30). **Facilities:** 🅿 🍽 ✗ licensed shop garden centre ◖

SLIMBRIDGE Map 03 SO70

WWT SLIMBRIDGE
GL2 7BT
➲ (off A38, signed from M5 junct 13 & 14)
☎ 01453 890333 ▤ 01453 890827
e-mail: slimbridge@wwt.org.uk

Slimbridge is home to the world's largest collection of exotic wildfowl - and the only place in Europe where all six types of flamingo can be seen. Up to 8,000 wild birds winter on the 800-acre reserve of flat fields, marsh and mudflats on the River Severn. Facilities include a Tropical House, Discovery Centre, shop and restaurant.
Times: Open all year, daily from 9.30-5 (winter 4pm). (Closed 25 Dec). **Fee:** ✱ £6.40 (ch £3.90, pen £5.10). Family ticket £16.70. **Facilities:** 🅿 🍽 ✗ licensed ⏦ (wheelchair loan, tapes for blind, hearing pads & loops) toilets for disabled shop ✗ (ex guide & hearing dogs) ◖

SNOWSHILL Map 04 SP03

SNOWSHILL MANOR
WR12 7JU
➲ (3m SW of Broadway, off A44)
☎ 01386 852410 ▤ 01386 842822
e-mail: snowshillmanor@nationaltrust.org.uk

This Arts and Crafts garden was designed by its owner Charles Paget Wade, in collaboration with M. H. Baillie Scott, as a series of outdoor rooms to compliment his traditional Cotswold manor house filled with his unique collection of artefacts including musical instruments, clocks, toys, bicycles and Japanese armour. This was the first National Trust garden to be managed following organic principles, it is a lively mix of cottage flowers, bright colours and delightful scents with stunning views across the Cotswold countryside. Please note that the house will be closed in 2004.
Times: ✱ Open mid Mar-Oct daily (ex Mon/Tue) 11-5.30. (Open BH Mon) House closed for 2004. **Fee:** £3.80 (ch £1.90) garden & grounds only. **Facilities:** 🅿 ✗ licensed ⏦ (Braille guides, audio tapes) toilets for disabled shop ✗ (ex guide dogs) ⛟ ◖

SOUDLEY Map 03 SO61

DEAN HERITAGE CENTRE
Camp Mill GL14 2UB
➲ (on B4227, in Forest of Dean)
☎ 01594 822170 ▤ 01594 823711   **2 for 1**
e-mail: deanmuse@btinternet.com

The Centre tells the story of this unique area, and its people, from pre-historic times to present day. Displays include a reconstructed cottage, a working beam engine from Lightmore Colliery, charcoal burners camp and art gallery. There are also nature trails with animals. There is an adventure playground that includes a maze and swing bridge. Library and research facilities are available by appointment.
Times: Open all year, daily, British Winter 10-4, British Summer 10-5.30. (Closed 24-26 Dec & 1 Jan) **Fee:** £4 (ch £2.50, pen & con £3.50). Family ticket £12. Under 5's free. **Facilities:** 🅿 🍽 ⏦ (lift, ramps, help from establishment staff) toilets for disabled shop ✗ (ex guide dogs) ◖

TETBURY Map 03 ST89

CHAVENAGE HOUSE
GL8 8XP
➲ (2m NW of Tetbury signposted   **2 for 1**
off B4014. 7m SE of Stroud off A46)
☎ 01666 502329 & 505576 ▤ 01453 836778
e-mail: info@chavenage.com

Built in 1576, this unspoilt Elizabethan house contains stained glass from the 16th-century and earlier with some good furniture and tapestries. The owner during the Civil War was a Parliamentarian, and the house contains Cromwellian relics. In more recent years, the house has been the location for *Grace and Favour, Poirot, The House of Elliot, Berkeley Square, Casualty* and *Cider with Rosie*. Tours of the house are enlivened by ghost stories.
Times: Open May-Sep, Thu, Sun & BHs 2-5. Also Etr Sun & Mon. Other days by appointment only. **Fee:** ✱ £5 (ch £2.50). **Facilities:** 🅿 ⏦ ✗ (ex guide dogs)

ULEY Map 03 ST79

ULEY LONG BARROW (HETTY PEGLER'S TUMP)
➲ (3.5m NE of Dursley on B4066)   **FREE**

This 180ft Neolithic long barrow is popularly known as Hetty Pegler's Tump. The mound, surrounded by a wall, is about 85ft wide. It contains a stone central passage, and three burial chambers.
Times: Open any reasonable time. **Facilities:** ⛊

WESTBURY ON SEVERN Map 03 SO71

WESTBURY COURT GARDEN
GL14 1PD
➲ (9m SW of Gloucester on A48)
☎ 01452 760461
e-mail: westbury@smtp.ntrust.org.uk

This formal water garden with canals and yew hedges was laid out between 1696 and 1705. It is the earliest of its kind remaining in England and was restored in 1971 and planted
continued

with species dated pre-1700, including apple, pear and plum trees.
Times: ✱ Open Mar-Jun daily (ex Mon/Tue) but open BH Mon's. Jul-Aug, daily 10-6. Sep-27Oct, Wed-Sun, 10-6. Other months by appointment. **Facilities:** 🅿 ♿ (braille guide, w/chair available) toilets for disabled shop ✖ (ex guide dogs) 💥

WESTONBIRT   Map 03 ST88

WESTONBIRT ARBORETUM
GL8 8QS
➲ (3m S Tetbury on A433)
☎ 01666 880220   📠 01666 880559

Begun in 1829, this arboretum contains one of the finest and most important collections of trees and shrubs in the world. There are 18,000 specimens, planted from 1829 to the present day, covering 600 acres of landscaped Cotswold countryside. Magnificent displays of Rhododendrons, Azaleas, Magnolias and wild flowers, and ablaze with colour in the autumn from the national collection of Japanese Maples.
Times: Open all year, daily 10-8 or sunset. Visitor centre & shop all year. (Closed Xmas & New Year) **Fee:** Jun-mid Sep £7.50 (ch £1, pen £6.50) Family ticket £15. Mid Sep-Dec £6 (ch £1, pen £5) Family ticket £12. **Facilities:** 🅿 💺 ✖ licensed ♿ (electric & manual wheelchair for loan, telephone to book) toilets for disabled shop garden centre 🍴

WINCHCOMBE   Map 04 SP02

SUDELEY CASTLE & GARDENS
GL54 5JD
➲ (B4632 to Winchcombe, Castle is signposted from town)
☎ 01242 602308   📠 01242 602959
e-mail: marketing@sudeley.org.uk

Sabina Rüber

Sudeley Castle was home to Katherine Parr, who is buried in the Chapel. Henry VIII, Anne Boleyn, Lady Jane Grey and Elizabeth I all stayed or visited here; and it was the headquarters of Prince Rupert during the Civil War. The Queen's Garden is famous for its rose collection, there are exhibitions and a children's adventure playground.
Times: Open daily Mar-2 Nov, Grounds, Gardens, exhibition, shop & plant centre 10.30-5.30. 29 Mar-2 Nov, Castle apartments & Church & restaurant 11-5. **Fee:** ✱ Castle & Gardens £6.70-£7.70 (ch 5-15 £3.70-£4.70 & concessions £5.70-£6.70). Gardens only £5-£6 (ch £2.75-£3.75 & concessions £4-£5). Family ticket (2 ad & 2 ch) £18.50-£22. Party 20+ £5.70 (ch £3.70, concessions £4.70). **Facilities:** 🅿 ✖ licensed ♿ (limited access to gardens only) toilets for disabled shop garden centre ✖ (by request on arrival) 🍴

Above: Kiftsgate Court

GREATER MANCHESTER

EVENTS & FESTIVALS

January
25th Rochdale District Annual Brass Band
Contest, Wardle High School, Rochdale
tbc Chinese New Year Celebrations, parade
from Town Hall to Chinatown

May
tbc Streets Ahead, street festival, Manchester

June
19th-20th Greater Manchester Youth Games,
Robin Park Stadium, Wigan (provisional)
tbc National Bike Week Events in Manchester

July
3rd Unity Festival, Chorlton Park
4th Italian Procession, through city centre to
St John's Cathedral, Salford
24th-25th Chadkirk Festival, Stockport
24th Jul-1st Aug Manchester Jazz Festival (various
venues including outdoors)
tbc The Manchester Show, Platt Fields Park
tbc North Manchester Mela, Heaton Park

August
24th Jul-1st Manchester Jazz Festival (various
venues including outdoors)
14th Bramhall Horticultural Show

October
20th-21st Kinofilm, International Short Film
Festival, various venues (provisional)

November
tbc Manchester District Annual Brass Band
Contest, Wardle High School, Rochdale

*Above: The Town Hall and Albert Memorial in
Manchester*

ALTRINCHAM   Map 07 SJ78
DUNHAM MASSEY
WA14 4SJ
➲ (3m SW of Altrincham (off A56), off M6 junct 19
or off M56 junct 7, then follow brown signs)
☎ 0161 941 1025 🖃 0161 929 7508
e-mail: mdmsec@smtp.ntrust.org.uk
A fine 18th-century house, garden and park, home of the
Earls of Stamford until 1976. The house contains fine
furniture and silverware, and some thirty rooms, including
the library, billiard room, fully-equipped kitchen, butler's
pantry and laundry. The garden is on an ancient site with
waterside plantings, mixed borders and fine lawns. There is
also a 300 acre deer park. Telephone for details of special
events.
Times: Open: Park, restaurant & shop open all year. House open
Apr-Oct, 12-5 (11 Sun & BH Mon, closes at 4 during late Oct). Garden
Apr-Oct, 11-5.30 (closes 4.30 in late Oct). Last entry to house 30mins
before closing time. **Fee:** ✱ House & Garden £5.80 (ch £2.90). House
only £3.80 (ch £1.90). Garden only £3.80 (ch £1.90). Family ticket
£14.50. Park only, £3 per car. **Facilities:** 🅿 (charged) ✗ licensed &
(loan of batricar/wheelchairs, lift, braille guide, parking) toilets for
disabled shop ✖ (ex on lead in Park) ✖ 🔖

ASHTON-UNDER-LYNE   Map 07 SJ99
CENTRAL ART GALLERY
Central Library Building, Old St OL6 7SG
☎ 0161 342 2650
e-mail: portland.basin@mail.gov.uk
Set in a fine Victorian Gothic building, the Central Art Gallery
has three areas, each of which offers a varied programme of
temporary exhibitions. The range covers painting, sculpture
and textiles.
Times: Open all year, Tue, Wed & Fri 10-5; Thu 1-7.30 & Sat 9-4.
Facilities: 🅿 & toilets for disabled shop ✖ (ex guide dogs)

MUSEUM OF THE MANCHESTER REGIMENT
The Town Hall, Market Place OL6 6DL
➲ (in town centre, follow signs for museum)
☎ 0161 342 3078 & 0161 342 3710
🖃 0161 343 2869
e-mail: portland.basin@mail.tameside.gov.uk
The social and regimental history of the Manchesters is
explored at this museum, tracing the story back to its origins
in the 18th century. The Manchesters fought in both World
Wars, the Boer War, and the Crimea.
Times: ✱ Open all year, Mon-Sat, 10-4. (Closed Sun). **Facilities:** 🅿
(50yds) (pay & display) & toilets for disabled shop ✖ (ex guide dogs)

PORTLAND BASIN MUSEUM
Portland Place OL7 0QA
➲ (off A635)
☎ 0161 343 2878 🖃 0161 343 2869
e-mail: portland.basin@mail.gov.uk
Exploring the social and industrial history of Tameside, this
museum is part of the recently rebuilt Ashton Canal
Warehouse, built in 1834. Visitors can walk around a 1920s
street, dress up in old hats and gloves, steer a virtual canal
continued

boat, and see the original canal powered waterwheel that once drove the warehouse machinery.
Times: Open all year, Tue-Sun 10-5. (Closed Mon, ex BH's)
Facilities: 🅿 ♿ (Wheelchair, lift, loop system) toilets for disabled shop ✖ (ex guide dogs)

BRAMHALL
Map 07 SJ88
BRAMALL HALL & PARK
SK7 3NX
➲ (from A6 turn right at Blossoms public house through Davenport village then turn right - signposted)
☎ 0161 485 3708 📠 0161 486 6959
e-mail: bramall.hall@stockport.gov.uk
This large timber-framed hall dates from the 14th century, and is one of the finest black-and-white houses in the North West. It has rare 16th-century wall paintings and period furniture, and was the home of the Davenport family for 500 years. Much of the house is open to the public and available for hire. Open air concerts and plays are a feature in summer.
Times: Open all year, Good Fri-Sep, Mon-Sat 1-5, Sun & BH's 11-5; Oct-New Year's Day Tue-Sat 1-4, Sun & BH's 11-4; 2 Jan-Good Fri Sat & Sun 12-4. Closed 25-26 Dec. **Fee:** £3.50 (concessions £2). Family ticket £8.50. **Facilities:** 🅿 (charged) 🍽 ♿ (access for wheelchair users) toilets for disabled shop ✖ (ex guide dogs) 🍴

MANCHESTER
Map 07 SJ89
CITY ART GALLERY
Mosley St/Princess St M2 3JL
☎ 0161 234 1456 📠 0161 236 7369
e-mail: cityart@mcrl.poptel.org.uk
The Mosley Street Galleries have permanent displays of European art, ceramics and silver, displayed with furniture in an elaborate decorative scheme. There's a superb collection of Victorian art, including some major Pre-Raphaelite paintings. Decorative and applied arts, including porcelain, furniture and sculpture can also be seen.
Times: ✱ Gallery now reopened after expansion scheme. Unfortunately at the time of going to print we have not received confirmation of new details **Facilities:**

GALLERY OF COSTUME
Platt Hall, Rusholme M14 5LL
➲ (situated in Platt Fields Park, access from Wilmslow Rd. 2m S of city centre)
☎ 0161 224 5217 📠 0161 256 3278
With one of the most comprehensive costume collections in Great Britain, this gallery makes captivating viewing. Housed in a fine Georgian mansion, the displays focus on the changing styles of everyday fashion and accessories over the last 400 years. Contemporary fashion is also illustrated. Because of the vast amount of material in the collection, no one period is permanently illustrated.
Times: ✱ Open Tue-Sun 10-4 (5pm during summer). Also open BH Mon's. **Facilities:** 🅿 ♿ shop ✖ (ex guide dogs)

> The AA also publishes a guide to
> Pet Friendly Places to Stay

IMPERIAL WAR MUSEUM NORTH
The Quays, Trafford Wharf Rd, Trafford Park M17 1TZ
☎ 0161 836 4000 📠 0161 836 4012
e-mail: info@iwmnorth.org.uk

This recently-opened war museum is built to resemble three shards of a shattered globe, representing conflict on land, sea, and in the air. Inside are thousands of exhibits, interactive sessions, performances, and recreations that explore the way that 20th century conflict has shaped our lives.
Times: Open daily 10-6. (Closed 24-26 Dec) **Facilities:** 🅿 (charged) 🍽 ✖ licensed ♿ toilets for disabled shop ✖ (ex guide dogs) 🍴

JOHN RYLANDS LIBRARY
150 Deansgate M3 3EH
➲ (on Deangate, a main thoroughfare in city centre, A56. Situated next to the Manchester Evening News Building)
☎ 0161 834 5343 📠 0161 834 5574
e-mail: spcoll72@fs1.li.man.ac.uk
Founded as a memorial to Manchester cotton-magnate and millionaire John Rylands, this is a public library, and also the Special Collections Division of the John Rylands University Library of Manchester. Internationally renowned, it extends to two million books, manuscripts and archival items representing some fifty cultures and ranging in date from the third millennium BC to the present day.
Times: Open all year, Mon-Fri 10-5.30, Sat 10-1. (Closed Sun, BH & Xmas-New Year). **Facilities:** 🅿 (400yds) (pay and display) shop ✖ (ex guide dogs by arrangement)

MANCHESTER MUSEUM
The University, Oxford Rd M13 9PL
➲ (S of city centre on B5117)
☎ 0161 275 2634 📠 0161 275 2676
e-mail: dot.fenton@man.ac.uk/museum
After a major recent refurbishment the Manchester Museum has leading research facilities and collections in archaeology, botany, Egyptology, ethnology, mineralogy, numismatics and zoology, among others. There are large galleries devoted to most of these departments, but the Egyptology collection is particularly impressive, and includes mummies excavated by Sir William Flinders Petrie.
Times: ✱ Open all year, Mon-Sat 10-5, Sun & BHs 11-4. **Facilities:** 🅿 (350mtrs) ♿ (Provision for disabled telephone in advance) shop ✖ (ex guide dogs)

MANCHESTER UNITED MUSEUM & TOUR CENTRE

Sir Matt Busby Way, Old Trafford M16 0RA

➲ (2m from city centre, off A56)

☎ 0870 442 1994 📠 0161 868 8861   `2 for 1`

e-mail: tours@manutd.co.uk

This museum was opened in 1986 and is the first purpose-built British football museum. It covers the history of Manchester United in words, pictures, sound and vision, from its inception in 1878 to the present day.
Times: Open daily 9.30-5 (open until 1/2hr before kick off on Match Days). (Closed some days over Xmas & New Year) **Fee:** ✱ Stadium tour & Museum: £8.50 (ch & pen £5.75) Family ticket £23.50. Museum only: £5.50 (ch & pen £3.75) Family ticket £15.50. **Facilities:** 🅿 💺 ✗ licensed ♿ (wheelchair,audio visual scrips,part of tour not accessible) toilets for disabled shop 🐕 (ex dogs only) ▬

THE MUSEUM OF SCIENCE AND INDUSTRY IN MANCHESTER

Liverpool Rd, Castlefield M3 4FP

➲ (follow brown tourist signs from city centre)

☎ 0161 832 2244 & 0161 832 1830   `FREE`

📠 0161 833 1471

e-mail: marketing@msim.org.uk

This museum is housed in the buildings of the world's oldest passenger railway station. Colourful galleries packed full of fascinating facts and amazing artefacts bring the past to life. Walk away from your own shadow in Xperiment! The mind bending science centre, see wheels of industry turning in the Power Hall, and the planes that made flying history in the Air and Space Hall. A programme of changing exhibitions.
Times: Open all year, daily 10-5. Last admission 4.30. (Closed 24-26 Dec). **Facilities:** 🅿 (charged) 💺 ✗ licensed ♿ (lifts, wheelchair loan service) toilets for disabled shop 🐕 (ex guide dogs) ▬

MUSEUM OF TRANSPORT

Boyle St, Cheetham M8 8UW

➲ (museum adjacent to Queens Rd bus depot, and is 1.25m N of City Centre.

☎ 0161 205 2122 📠 0161 205 2122

e-mail: Gmts.enquire@btinternet.com

This museum is a must-see for fans of public transport! Among the many interesting exhibits are more than 80 beautifully restored buses and coaches from the region - the biggest collection in the UK. Displays of old photographs,
continued

tickets and other memorabilia complement the vehicles, some of which date back to 1890. Please telephone for details of special events.
Times: ✱ Open all year, Wed, Sat, Sun & BH 10-5 ex Xmas.
Facilities: 🅿 💺 ♿ toilets for disabled shop ▬

URBIS

Cathedral Gardens M4 3BG

☎ 0161 907 9099 📠 0161 605 8201   `2 for 1`

e-mail: info@urbis.org.uk

Taking its starting point as 200 years of the history of Manchester, this ultra-modern museum allows visitors to explore life in five other cities, Sao Paolo, Los Angeles, Tokyo, Singapore, and Paris. All aspects of city life are covered, including transport, law, social interaction, and day-to-day personal existence.
Times: Open all year daily 10-6 **Fee:** ✱ £5 (concessions £3.50, under 8's free) **Facilities:** 🅿 (200yds) 💺 ✗ ♿ toilets for disabled shop 🐕 (ex guide dogs) ▬

THE WHITWORTH ART GALLERY

The University of Manchester, Oxford Rd M15 6ER

➲ (follow brown tourist signs, on Oxford road on B5117 to S of Manchester City Centre)

☎ 0161 275 7450 📠 0161 275 7451   `FREE`

e-mail: whitworth@man.ac.uk

The gallery houses an impressive range of modern and historic drawings, prints, paintings and sculpture, as well as the largest collection of textiles and wallpapers outside London and an internationally famous collection of British watercolours. The gallery hosts an innovative programme of touring exhibitions. A selection of tour lectures, workshops and concerts complement the exhibition programme.
Times: Open Mon-Sat 10-5, Sun 2-5. (Closed Good Fri & Xmas-New Year). **Facilities:** 🅿 💺 ✗ licensed ♿ (wheelchair available, induction loop, Braille lift buttons) toilets for disabled shop 🐕 (ex guide dogs)

PRESTWICH   Map 07 SD80

HEATON HALL

Heaton Park M25 2SW

☎ 0161 773 1231 or 0161 234 1456

📠 0161 236 2880

Designed by James Wyatt for Sir Thomas Egerton in 1772, the house has magnificent period interiors decorated with fine plasterwork, paintings and furniture. Other attractions include a unique circular room with Pompeian-style paintings, and the original Samuel Green organ still in working order.
Times: ✱ Open Etr-end Oct, but phone for time details on 0161-234 1456. **Facilities:** 🅿 (charged) ♿ (occasional 'touch tours'. Phone for details) toilets for disabled shop 🐕 (ex guide dogs)

SALFORD   Map 07 SJ89

THE LOWRY

Pier Eight, Salford Quays M50 3AZ

➲ (from M60 take junct 12 for M602. Salford Quays is 0.25m from junction 3 of the M602, follow Lowry signs)   `2 for 1`

☎ 0870 787 5774 📠 0161 876 2001   `FREE`

e-mail: info@thelowry.com

The Lowry is an award-winning building housing galleries,
continued

shops, cafés and a restaurant, plus two theatres showing everything from West End plays and musicals, comedians, ballet and live bands. With regular family activity too, you can make a whole day of your visit.
(2-for-1 voucher applies to building tour only)

Times: Open daily from 10am. (Closed 25 Dec). **Facilities:** ⓟ (charged) ⍁ ✗ licensed ♿ toilets for disabled shop ✖ (ex guide dogs) ⬗

SALFORD MUSEUM & ART GALLERY
Peel Park, Crescent M5 4WU
⮑ (from N leave M60 junct 13, A666. From S follow signs from end of M602. Museum on A6)
☎ 0161 736 2649 🖹 0161 745 9490   `FREE`
e-mail: salford.museum@salford.gov.uk

The museum features a reconstruction of a 19th-20th century northern street with original shop fronts. Upstairs in the galleries there are temporary exhibitions and a gallery displaying paintings, sculptures and ceramics. Recent additions include the lifetimes gallery, featuring audio, IT zones, temporary exhibitions, a spectacular Pilkington's display and lots of hands-on activities and dressing up areas
Times: Open all year, Mon-Fri 10-4.45, Sat & Sun 1-5. (Closed Good Fri, Etr Sat, 25 & 26 Dec, 1 Jan). **Facilities:** ⓟ ⍁ ♿ (braille & large print labels & visitor packs, hearing loop) toilets for disabled shop ✖ (guide dogs) ⬗

STALYBRIDGE   Map 07 SJ99
ASTLEY CHEETHAM ART GALLERY
Trinity St
☎ 0161 338 2708
e-mail: portland.basin@mail.tameside.uk

Built as a gift to the town in 1901 by mill owner John Frederick Cheetham, this one-time lecture hall has been an art gallery since 1932 when Cheetham left his collection to the town. Among the works are Italian paintings from the Renaissance, British masters such as Cox and Burne-Jones, and more recent gifts such as works by Turner and local artist Harry Rutherford.
Times: ✱ Open all year, Mon-Tue, Wed & Fri 1-7.30; Sat 9-4.
Facilities: ⓟ shop ✖ (ex guide dogs)

MUSEUM of TRANSPORT
Boyle Street, Cheetham, Manchester M8 8UW
Tel/Fax: 0161 205 2122

A trip down memory lane

Over 80 buses, coaches and trams representing over a century of road public transport in Greater Manchester.

Special events including a Vintage vehicle rally, themed displays, a weekend for people with disabilities and participation in the National Heritage Weekend.

The Museum has tearooms, shop, facilities for the disabled. A small exhibits area and archive and research facilities.

STOCKPORT   Map 07 SJ89

HAT WORKS MUSEUM

Wellington Mill, Wellington Rd South SK3 0EU

➲ (opposite Stockport bus station) `2 for 1`

☎ 0161 355 7770 📠 0161 480 8735

Stockport was once at the centre of a thriving hatting industry. At the end of the 19th century over 4,500 people were employed in making hats. Now the industry has faded, the city continues to celebrate its heritage with the UK's first and only museum dedicated to hats and hatmaking. Visitors can look in on original workshops, looks at hats from all over the world, see audio-visual presentations, or have a go at felt-making. Plenty of hats to try on too.

Times: Open daily Mon-Sat 10-5, Sun & BH's 11-5. (Closed 25-26 Dec & 1 Jan) **Fee:** ✱ £3.95 (concessions £2.50, ch £2.50, under 5's free). Family ticket £11 **Facilities:** P ⬤ & toilets for disabled shop ✖ (ex guide dogs) 🦮

UPPERMILL   Map 07 SD90

SADDLEWORTH MUSEUM & ART GALLERY

High St OL3 6HS

➲ (From M62 E exit at junct 22 or from M62 W exit at junct 21. On A670) `2 for 1`

☎ 01457 874093 📠 01457 870336

e-mail: **museum-curator@saddleworth.net**

Based in an old mill building next to the Huddersfield canal, the museum explores the history of the Saddleworth area. Wool weaving is the traditional industry, displayed in the 18th-century Weaver's Cottage and the Victoria Mill Gallery. The textile machinery is run regularly by arrangement. The Art Gallery has regular exhibitions.

Times: Open all year, Nov-late Mar, daily 1-4; late Mar-Oct, Mon-Sat 10-5, Sun 12-5. (Closed 24-25 Dec & 31 Dec-1 Jan). **Fee:** £2 (concessions £1) Family ticket £4. **Facilities:** P & (stairlift, ramps, braille & large print guides, wheelchair) toilets for disabled shop ✖ (ex guide dogs)

WIGAN   Map 07 SD50

WIGAN PIER

Trencherfield Mill WN3 4EF

➲ (follow brown tourist signs from motorway, M6 junct 25-27 / M61 junct 6-8)

☎ 01942 323666 📠 01942 701927 `2 for 1`

e-mail: **wiganpier@wlct.org**

Wigan Pier is a journey never to be forgotten. Part museum, part theatre, Wigan Pier is a mixture of entertainment and education. Step back in time at 'The Way We Were' heritage centre, visit Trencherfield Mill and The Machinery Hall, and then visit the newest attraction the Museum of Memories. Additional on-site attractions include walks, talks, boat trips, events and much more.

Times: Open all year, Mon-Thu 10-5; Sat & Sun 11-5. (Closed every Fri ex Good Fri, 25-26 Dec, 1 Jan). **Fee:** ✱ £7.95 (concessions £6.25). Site ticket £22.75 (2 ad & 2 concessions). **Facilities:** P ⬤ ✖ licensed & (braille guide, audio tape, large text leaflet, minicom) toilets for disabled shop ✖ (ex guide dogs) 🦮

See advert on page 97

Above: Manchester Canal

HAMPSHIRE

EVENTS & FESTIVALS

February
16th-21st Children's Festival (theatre, arts, workshops), The Tower, Romsey Road, Winchester

May
1st-3rd Heavy Horse Show, Castle Field & Southsea Common

June
tbc Butser Festival of Flight, Queen Elizabeth Country Park, Portsmouth
tbc Power in the Park, pop concert, Southampton Common
tbc Southsea Spectacular (vintage transport rally), Southsea Common

July
1st-4th Hat Fair (oldest street theatre fair in England), Winchester
2nd-4th Southampton Balloon & Flower Festival, The Common, Southampton
9th-18th Winchester Festival (multi-arts festival)
19th-25th Farnborough International Airshow, Farnborough Airfield
23rd-25th Netley Marsh Steam Engine Rally, Netley Marsh, Southampton
tbc New Forest Show

August
6th-8th Portsmouth & Southsea Show, Southsea Common
28th-30th Kite Festival, Southsea Common

September
11th Romsey Show, Broadlands Park, Romsey
tbc Great South Run – 10-mile international event, Southsea Seafront
tbc Southampton International Boat Show, Mayflower Park, Southampton

November
3rd Bonfire Night Firework Spectacular, King George V Playing Field, Cosham
25th-28th A Festival of Christmas, Historic Dockyard, Portsmouth
tbc Winchester Grand Firework Display

Above: An eerie scene in the New Forest

ALDERSHOT   Map 04 SU85

AIRBORNE FORCES MUSEUM
Browning Barracks, Queens Av GU11 2BU
➲ (from motorway take A325 to Aldershot then take next left)
☎ 01252 349619 ▤ 01252 349203
e-mail: airborneforcesmuseum@army.mod.uk.net

The museum traces the history of the Parachute Regiment and British Airborne Forces since 1940. Using weapons, equipment, dioramas and briefing models it depicts the story of airborne actions such as the early raids, D-Day, Arnhem, the Rhine Crossing, and post-war campaigns such as Suez, the Falklands and Kosovo.

Times: Open all year, Mon-Fri 10-4.30 (last admission 3.45), Sat-Sun & BH 10-4. (Closed Xmas). **Fee:** ✱ £3 (ch, pen & former members of the Regiment £1) **Facilities:** ▣ & (wheelchair ramps) shop ✖ (ex guide dogs)

ALDERSHOT MILITARY MUSEUM
Evelyn Woods Rd, Queens Av GU11 2LG
➲ (A331 exit for 'Aldershot Military Town (North)', attraction near to North Camp)
☎ 01252 314598 ▤ 01252 342942   **2 for 1**
e-mail: musmim@hants.gov.uk

Follow the development of the 'Home of the British army' and the 'Birthplace of British aviation' through brand new displays. Also discover the fascinating local history of Aldershot and Farnborough including British first powered flight.

Times: Open Mar-Oct, daily 10-5; Nov-Feb, daily 10-5. **Fee:** ✱ £2 (ch & unemployed £1, pen £1.50) **Facilities:** ▣ & shop ✖ (ex guide dogs)

AMPFIELD   Map 04 SU42

THE SIR HAROLD HILLIER GARDENS & ARBORETUM
Jermyns Ln SO51 0QA (3m NE of Romsey, signposted off A3090 & B3057)
☎ 01794 368787 ▤ 01794 368027

Established in 1953, this 180-acre public garden comprises the greatest collection of hardy trees and shrubs in the world. A garden for all seasons with stunning range of seasonal colour and interest and featuring eleven national plant collections. Champion trees, the Gurkha Memorial Garden and the largest Winter Garden in Europe.

Times: ✱ Open all year, Apr-Oct wkdays 10.30-6, wknds & BHs 9.30-6. Nov-Mar daily 10.30-5 or dusk if earlier (closed Xmas). **Facilities:** ▣ ✖ licensed & (all ability path) toilets for disabled garden centre ✖ (ex guide dogs)

ANDOVER   Map 04 SU34

FINKLEY DOWN FARM PARK
SP11 6NF
➲ (signposted from A303 & A343, 1.5m N of A303 and 2m E of Andover)
☎ 01264 352195 ▤ 01264 363172
e-mail: admin@finkleydownfarm.co.uk

A wide range of farm animals and poultry can be seen here, including some rare breeds. The pets corner has tame, hand-reared animals that can be stroked and petted. There

continued

are also a Countryside Museum, housed in a barn, Romany caravans and rural bygones to see, an adventure playground and a large picnic area.
Times: Open mid Mar-Oct, daily 10-6. Last admission 5pm. **Fee:** ✱ £4.75 (ch £3.75, pen £4.25). Family ticket £16 (2 ad & 2ch).
Facilities: 🅿 💺 ও toilets for disabled shop 🐾 (ex guide dogs) 🍴

ASHURST   Map 04 SU31
LONGDOWN DAIRY FARM
Longdown SO40 7EH
➲ (off A35 between Lyndhurst & Southampton)
☎ 023 8029 3326 🖷 023 8029 3376
e-mail: enquiries@longdownfarm.co.uk
Fun for all the family with a variety of hands-on activities every day, including small animals and pony grooming. Indoor and outdoor play areas, with trampoline and ball pools. Land Rover driving for adults, pedal tractors for children. Tearoom, picnic area and excellent gift shop.
Times: Open Feb-Dec, daily 10-5. **Fee:** ✱ £4.75 (ch 3-14 & pen £4). Saver ticket £16.50 (2 ad & 2 ch). **Facilities:** 🅿 💺 ও toilets for disabled shop 🐾 (kennels provided) 🍴

BASINGSTOKE   Map 04 SU65
MILESTONES - HAMPSHIRE'S LIVING HISTORY MUSEUM
Basingstoke Leisure Park, Churchill Way West RG21 6YR
➲ (M3 junct 6, take ringway road (West) and follow signs for Leisure Park)
☎ 01256 477766 🖷 01256 477784   `2 for 1`
e-mail: jane.holmes@hants.gov.uk

Milestones brings Hampshire's recent past to life through stunning period street scenes and exciting interactive areas, all under one roof. Nationally important collections of transport, technology and everyday life are presented in an entertaining way. Staff in period costumes, mannequins and sounds will bring the streets to life.
Times: Open Tue-Fri & BH's 10-5, Sat-Sun 11-5 (Closed 24-26 Dec & 1 Jan). Prices may increase, please telephone for details. **Fee:** ✱ £6.50 (ch £3.50, concessions £5.25). Family ticket (2 adults & 2 ch) £16.50. Group discounts 17+. **Facilities:** 🅿 💺 ও (induction loops, video screens with subtitles) toilets for disabled shop 🐾 (ex guide dogs) 🍴

BEAULIEU   Map 04 SU30
BEAULIEU : NATIONAL MOTOR MUSEUM
SO42 7ZN
➲ (M27 junct 2, A326, B3054, then follow tourist signs)
☎ 01590 612345 🖷 01590 612624
e-mail: info@beaulieu.co.uk
Set in the heart of William the Conqueror's New Forest, on the banks of the Beaulieu River, stands this 16th-century house. It has become most famous as the home of the National Motor Museum. The site also contains the picturesque abbey building ruins, which have an exhibition on life in the middle ages, and various family treasures and memorabilia. In 2002-2003 a display of James Bond boats is also on view.
Times: Open all year - Palace House & Gardens, National Motor Museum, Beaulieu Abbey & Exhibition of Monastic Life, May-Sep 10-6; Oct-Apr 10-5. (Closed 25 Dec). **Facilities:** 🅿 💺 ও (ramp access to most areas, lift to upper level) toilets for disabled shop 🍴

BISHOP'S WALTHAM   Map 04 SU51
BISHOP'S WALTHAM PALACE
SO32 1DH
➲ (on A333)
☎ 01489 892460
Discover the medieval seat of the Bishops of Winchester. Enjoy the wonderful moated grounds and an exhibition about the powerful Winchester Bishops.
Times: Open all year, Apr-Sep, daily 10-6 (Oct, daily 10-5). Dates valid until 31 Mar 2004. **Fee:** £2.50 (ch £1.30, concessions £1.90). Prices valid until 31 Mar 2004. **Facilities:** 🅿 ও shop 🐾 (ex on lead in certain areas) ⊞

BOLDRE   Map 04 SZ39
SPINNERS GARDEN AND NURSERY
School Ln SO41 5QE
➲ (off A337, between Brockenhurst & Lymington)
☎ 01590 673347
The garden has been entirely created by the owners since 1960. It has azaleas, rhododendrons, camellias and magnolias, interspersed with primulas, blue poppies and other woodland and ground cover plants. The nursery is famed for its rare trees, shrubs and plants.
Times: Open mid Apr-mid Sep, daily 10-5. Other times on application. Mid Sep-mid Apr Nursery and part of garden open, free entry. **Fee:** £2
Facilities: 🅿 garden centre 🐾 (ex guide dogs)

> Remember that prices and opening times are liable to change within the currency of this guide. It is always best to telephone in advance to check

BREAMORE
Map 04 SU11

BREAMORE HOUSE & COUNTRYSIDE
SP6 2DF
➲ (turn off A338, between Salisbury & Fordingbridge and follow signs for 1m)
☎ 01725 512468 📠 01725 512858
e-mail: breamore@ukonline.co.uk `2 for 1`

The handsome manor house was completed in around 1583 and has a fine collection of paintings, china and tapestries. The museum has good examples of steam engines, and uses reconstructed workshops and other displays to show how people lived and worked a century or so ago. There is also a children's playground.
Times: Open Apr, Tue, Sun & Etr, May-Jul & Sep, Tue-Thu & Sat, Sun & all BH, Aug, daily 2-5.30 (Countryside Museum 1pm). **Fee:** £6 (ch £4). Party £5 each. **Facilities:** 🅿 🖈 ᕕ (ramps, parking, recorded message & book about 2nd floor) toilets for disabled shop 🐾 (ex guide dogs)

BUCKLER'S HARD
Map 04 SU40

BUCKLER'S HARD VILLAGE & MARITIME MUSEUM
SO42 7XB
➲ (M27 junct 2, A326, B3054 then follow tourist signs to Beaulieu & Bucklers Hard)
☎ 01590 616203 📠 01590 612624
e-mail: info@bucklershard.co.uk

An enticing port of call, the historic and picturesque shipbuilding village of Buckler's Hard is where ships from Nelson's fleet were built. After setting a course for the Bucklers Hard Story and authentically reconstructed 18th century Historic Cottages savour the sight and sounds of the countryside on a ramble along the Riverside Walk or enjoy a cruise on the Beaulieu River on 'Swiftsure' during the summer months.
Times: Open all year, Etr-Sep 10.30-5, winter 11-4. (Closed 25 Dec).
Facilities: 🅿 🖈 ✕ licensed ᕕ shop ⬗

BURGHCLERE
Map 04 SU46

SANDHAM MEMORIAL CHAPEL
RG20 9JT
➲ (4m S Newbury off A34)
☎ 01635 278394 📠 01635 278394
e-mail: sandham@ntrust.org.uk

This red brick chapel was built in the 1920s for the artist Stanley Spencer to fill with murals inspired by his experiences in WWI. Influenced by Giotto's Avena Chapel in Padua, Spencer took 5 years to complete what is arguably his finest achievement. The chapel is set amongst lawns and orchards with views over Watership Down.
Times: ✱ Open Apr-Oct, Wed-Sun, 11.30-5 & BH Mon. Nov & Mar, Sat & Sun 11.30-4. Dec-Feb by appointment only. **Facilities:** 🅿 ᕕ (Braille guide, large print guide, ramps) 🐾 (ex on leads in garden) 🐕 ⬗

The AA also publishes a guide to Family Friendly Places to Stay, Eat & Visit

---

JANE AUSTEN'S HOUSE
CHAWTON, ALTON, HANTS
Telephone: 01420 83262

17th-century house where Jane Austen lived from 1809 to 1817

OPEN 11 – 4.00pm
1st Mar–30 Nov: daily
Dec, Jan and Feb: Sats and Suns only,
and 27 Dec- 2 Jan
(Closed Christmas Day and Boxing Day)
Adult £4, Child 50p
Groups and Concessions £3.00

Refreshments available in village   Bookshop

CHAWTON
Map 04 SU73

JANE AUSTEN'S HOUSE
GU34 1SD
➲ (1m SW of Alton, in centre of village)
☎ 01420 83262 📠 01420 83262
e-mail: museum@janeausten.demon.co.uk

Jane Austen lived and wrote here from 1809 to 1817. Restored to look as it would have done in the early 1800s, with items such as the author's donkey cart and writing table to be seen.
Times: Open daily Mar-Nov; Dec-Feb wknds only. Also open 27 Dec-1 Jan & Feb half term. **Facilities:** 🅿 (300yds) ᕕ (wheelchair ramp) toilets for disabled shop 🐾 (ex guide dogs & service dogs) ⬗

EXBURY   Map 04 SU40

EXBURY GARDENS & RAILWAY   `2 for 1`
Exbury Estate Office SO45 1AZ
⮕ (from M27 junct 2, 3m from Beaulieu, off B3054)
☎ 023 8089 1203   📠 023 8089 9940

A 200-acre landscaped woodland garden on the east bank of
the Beaulieu River, with one of the finest collections of
rhododendrons, azaleas, camellias and magnolias in the
world - as well as many rare and beautiful shrubs and trees.
A labyrinth of tracks and paths enable you to explore the
beautiful gardens and walks. Year round interest is ensured
in various parts of the gardens and a steam railway has
several features. **(2-for-1 Voucher is not valid for special
events or during the month of May)**
Times: Open Mar-early Nov, daily 10-5.30; 8 Nov-14 Dec, wknds only
10-4. **Fee:** ✱ £3.50-£5.50 (ch under 10 free, ch 10-15 £2.50-£3.50, pen
£3-£5, £4.50 Tue-Thu). Railway £2-£2.50. **Facilities:** 🅿 ✕ licensed ♿
(free wheelchair loans & access maps, buggy tours £3) toilets for
disabled shop garden centre ◀

FAREHAM   Map 04 SU50

ROYAL ARMOURIES FORT NELSON
Downend Rd PO17 6AN
⮕ (from M27 junct 11, follow brown tourist signs
for Royal Armouries).
☎ 01329 233734   📠 01329 822092   `FREE`
e-mail: fnenquiries@armouries.org.uk

Wonderfully restored 19 acre Victorian fort overlooking
Portsmouth Harbour, with spectacular views. Built in
the 1860s to deter a threatened French invasion there are
secret tunnels, underground chambers and grass ramparts to
explore. Home to the Royal Armouries' collection of artillery,
part of the National Museum of Arms and Armour, with
over 350 pieces from the Romans to the infamous Iraqi
supergun.
Times: Open all year, daily. Closed 25-26 Dec. **Facilities:** 🅿 💷 ♿
(access & audio guide, ramps, induction loop, wheelchair) toilets for
disabled shop ✕ (ex guide & hearing dogs) ◀

GOSPORT   Map 04 SZ69

EXPLOSION! MUSEUM OF NAVAL FIREPOWER
Priddy's Hard PO12 4LE
⮕ (A32 and follow signs)
☎ 023 9250 5600   📠 023 9250 5605   `2 for 1`
e-mail: info@explosion.org.uk

Explosion! The Museum of Naval Firepower set in the green
Heritage Area of Priddy's Hard in Gosport on the shores of
Portsmouth Harbour, telling the story of naval firepower from
the days of gunpowder to modern missiles. Come face to
face with the atom bomb, the Exocet missile and the Gatling
Gun and take a trip into the fascinating story of the men and
woman who supplied the Royal Navy. Walk around the
buildings that were a state secret for 200 years and discover
the Grand Magazine, an amazing vault once packed full with
gunpowder, now a stunning multimedia film show.
Times: Open all year, Apr-Oct, daily 10-5.30; Nov-Mar, daily 10-4.30.
(Closed 24-26 Dec) **Fee:** ✱ £5 (ch £3, pen £4). Family ticket £13
Facilities: 🅿 💷 ♿ toilets for disabled shop ✕ (ex guide dogs) ◀

ROYAL NAVY SUBMARINE MUSEUM & HMS ALLIANCE
Haslar Jetty Rd PO12 2AS
⮕ (M27 junct 11, follow signs for Submarine
Museum)
☎ 023 9252 9217 & 9251 0354
📠 023 9251 1349
e-mail: rnsubs@rnsubmus.co.uk

The great attraction of this museum is the chance to see
inside a submarine, and there are guided tours of *HMS
Alliance*, as well as displays exploring the development of
submarines. Two periscopes from *HMS Conqueror* can be
seen in the reconstruction of a nuclear submarine control
room, giving panoramic views of Portsmouth Harbour. A
new gallery shows the development of submarine weapons
from the tiny torpedo to the huge polaris nuclear missile.
The navy's first submarine is back on display in a new
gallery and exhibition space.
Times: ✱ Open all year, Apr-Oct 10-5.30; Nov-Mar 10-4.30. (Closed 24
Dec-1 Jan). Allow 3 hrs for visit. Last tour 1 hour before closing.
Facilities: 🅿 💷 ♿ (information in Braille, lift to upper gallery) toilets
for disabled shop ✕ (ex guide dogs) ◀

HARTLEY WINTNEY   Map 04 SU75

WEST GREEN HOUSE GARDENS
West Green RG27 8JB
⮕ (off A30, at Phoenix Green take sign to West
Green, along Thackhams Lane. House last left)
☎ 01252 844611   📠 01252 844611

The gardens are now considered to be one of the top 50
gardens in England and were the subject of a BBC television
programme. Today the Queen Anne house is surrounded by
four walled gardens, lakes, follies, the green theatre,
nymphaeum, mixed border and potager. The owner is a
noted garden writer and lecturer.
Times: Open May-Aug, Wed-Sun 11-4.30. **Fee:** ✱ £5 (ch under 7
free). **Facilities:** 🅿 ✕ ♿ (most areas accessible) shop garden centre
✕ (ex guide dogs)

HAVANT   Map 04 SU70

STAUNTON COUNTRY PARK
Middle Park Way PO9 5HB
⮕ (off B2149, between Havant & Horndean)
☎ 023 9245 3405   📠 023 9249 8156
e-mail: amanda.fallbrown@hants.gov.uk

This colourful Victorian Park offers a wonderful range of
attractions for all age groups. Meet and feed the friendly
animals at the Ornamental Farm where there is a broad
range of animals from llama and shirehorses to pigs and
pigmy goats. Explore the Victorian tropical glasshouses with
exotic flowers from around the world, including the giant
Amazonian waterlily (summer months only). 1000 acres of
parkland and lakes to explore.
Times: Open 10-5 (4pm winter). **Facilities:** 🅿 💷 ♿ (wheelchair for
visitors, most areas accessible) toilets for disabled shop ✕ (dogs in
parkland only) ◀

HIGHCLERE Map 04 SU45
HIGHCLERE CASTLE & GARDENS
RG20 9RN
➲ (4.5m S of Newbury, off A34) `2 for 1`
☎ 01635 253210 🖷 01635 255315
e-mail: theoffice@highclerecastle.co.uk

This splendid early Victorian mansion stands in beautiful parkland. It has sumptuous interiors and numerous Old Master pictures. Also shown are early finds by the 5th Earl of Carnarvon, one of the discoverers of Tutankhamun's tomb.
Times: Open Jul-Aug (may occasionally be subject to closure during this period), Tue-Fri & Sun 11-5 (last admission 4pm); Sat 11-3.30 (last admission 2.30pm). Also open BH 25-26 May & 25 Aug). Closed 5 Jul.
Fee: ✱ £7 (ch £3.50, pen £5.50). Grounds & gardens only £4 (ch £1.50). Family ticket £17. Party 15+. **Facilities:** 🅿 ⬛ ✗ licensed ⓖ (wheelchair available) toilets for disabled shop ✖ (ex guide dogs) 🍴

HINTON AMPNER Map 04 SU62
HINTON AMPNER GARDEN
SO24 0LA
➲ (off A272, 1m W of Bramdean) `2 for 1`
☎ 01962 771305 🖷 01962 793101
e-mail: hintonamper@nationaltrust.org.uk

Set in superb Hampshire countryside, this delightful garden combines formality of design with informality of planting. Full of scent and colour, the walks open up into unexpected vistas. The house, restored after a fire in 1960, displays a fine collection of Regency furniture and Italian paintings.
Times: Open Garden: Apr-Sep, Sat-Wed 12-5. House: Apr-Sep, Tue & Wed 1.30-5 (also Aug, Sat & Sun 1.30-5). **Fee:** ✱ House and Garden £5, garden only £4. **Facilities:** 🅿 ⬛ ⓖ (Braille guides, special parking, map for wheelchair users) toilets for disabled ✖ (ex guide dogs) 🐾

HURST CASTLE Map 04 SZ38
HURST CASTLE
SO4 0FF
➲ (on Pebble Spit S of Keyhaven)
☎ 01590 642344

Built by Henry VIII, Hurst Castle was the pride of Tudor England's coastal defences. Crouched menacingly on a shingle spit, the castle has a fascinating history, including involvement in the smuggling trade in the 17th and 18th centuries.
Times: Open Apr-Oct, daily 10.30-5. Dates valid until 31 Mar 2004.
Fee: £2.80 (ch £1.60, concessions £2.50). Prices valid until 31 Mar 2004. **Facilities:** ⬛ ✖ (ex on lead in certain areas) 🎏

LIPHOOK Map 04 SU83
BOHUNT MANOR
GU30 7DL
➲ (on old A3 opposite junct)
☎ 01428 727936 🖷 01428 727936
e-mail: eddie@bohuntmanor.freeserve.co.uk

Bohunt includes woodland gardens with a lakeside walk, a water garden, roses, tulips and herbaceous borders, and a collection of ornamental ducks, white swans, and geese. Several unusual trees and shrubs include a handkerchief tree and a Judas tree. The property has been given to the Worldwide Fund for Nature.
Times: Open all year, daily 10-5. **Fee:** ✱ £1.50 (ch free, pen £1).
Facilities: 🅿 ⓖ garden centre ✖ (ex guide dogs)

HOLLYCOMBE STEAM COLLECTION
Iron Hill, Midhurst Rd GU30 7LP
➲ (1m SE Liphook on Midhurst road, follow brown tourist signs)
☎ 01428 724900 🖷 01428 723682 `2 for 1`
e-mail: info@hollycombe.co.uk

A comprehensive collection of working steam-power, including a large Edwardian fairground, three railways, including one with spectacular views of the South Downs, traction engine hauled rides, steam agricultural machinery, pets corner, sawmill and even a paddle steamer engine.
Times: Open 4 Apr-10 Oct, Sun & BHs; 2-30 Aug, daily 12-5. Rides open from 1pm. **Fee:** ✱ £7.50 (ch & pen £6). Saver ticket (2 ad & 2ch) £24. Party 15+. **Facilities:** 🅿 ⬛ ⓖ toilets for disabled shop ✖ (guide dogs on request) 🍴

LYMINGTON Map 04 SZ39
BRAXTON GARDENS
Braxton Courtyard, Lymore Ln SO41 0TX
➲ (leave A337 at Everton onto B3058 then turn left into Lymore Ln, Braxton Courtyard on left)
☎ 01590 642008

Beautiful gardens set around attractive Victorian farm buildings. A courtyard with raised lily pool leads into a walled garden, which overflows with aromatic plants during the summer. A converted barn is available for private hire.
Times: ✱ Open daily 10-5. Shorter opening hours in winter, please telephone for details. **Facilities:** 🅿 ⬛ ⓖ shop garden centre ✖ (ex guide dogs) 🍴

LYNDHURST Map 04 SU30
NEW FOREST MUSEUM & VISITOR CENTRE
Main Car Park, High St SO43 7NY
➲ (leave M27 at Cadnam & follow A337 to Lyndhurst. Museum signposted)
☎ 023 8028 3444 🖷 023 8028 4236
e-mail: office@newforestmuseum.org.uk

The story of the New Forest - history, traditions, character and wildlife, told through an audio-visual show and exhibition displays. With life-size models of Forest characters, and the famous New Forest embroidery.
Times: Open daily, from 10am. Closed 25 & 26 Dec. **Fee:** £3 (ch £2 pen £2.50) Family ticket £8 (2a+2ch). **Facilities:** 🅿 ⓖ toilets for disabled shop 🍴

MARWELL
Map 04 SU52

MARWELL ZOOLOGICAL PARK
Colden Common SO21 1JH
➲ (M3 junct 11 or M27 junct 5. Zoo located on B2177, follow brown tourist signs)
☎ 01962 777407 ▤ 01962 777511
e-mail: marwell@marwell.org.uk

Marwell has over 200 species of rare and wonderful animals including tigers, snow leopards, rhino, meerkats, hippo and zebra. Highlights include The World of Lemurs, Encounter Village with unusual domesticated animals, Tropical World with its rainforest environment, Into Africa for giraffes and monkeys, Penguin World and Desert Carnivores. Recent additions include an exciting new leopard enclosure. Marwell is dedicated to saving endangered species and every visit helps conservation work. With road and rail trains, holiday activities, restaurant, gift shops and adventure playgrounds Marwell provides fun and interest for all ages. **Times:** Open all year, daily (ex 25 Dec), 10-6 (in summer), 10-4 (in winter). Last admission 90 min before closing. **Fee:** ✱ £10-£11 (ch 3-14 £7.50, pen £9). Family ticket (2 ad & 2 ch) £32.50-£35.50. **Facilities:** ▣ ▣ ✗ ৬ (wheelchairs & tours for visually impaired/disabled groups) toilets for disabled shop ✖ ▩

MIDDLE WALLOP
Map 04 SU23

MUSEUM OF ARMY FLYING & EXPLORER'S WORLD
SO20 8DY
➲ (on A343, between Andover & Salisbury)
☎ 01980 674421
▤ 01264 781694   2 for 1
e-mail: enquiries@flying-museum.org.uk
One of the country's finest historical collections of military kites, gliders, aeroplanes and helicopters. Imaginative dioramas and displays trace the development of Army flying from before the First World War to more recent conflicts in Ireland, the Falklands and the Gulf. Sit at the controls of a real Scout helicopter and test your skills on the helicopter flight simulator, plus children's science and education centre. **Times:** Open all year, daily 10-4.30. Closed week prior to Xmas. Evening visits by special arrangement. **Fee:** ✱ £5 (ch £3.50, pen & student £4) Family £15. Party 10+. **Facilities:** ▣ ▣ ✗ licensed ৬ (lifts to upper levels) toilets for disabled shop ✖ (ex guide dogs or in grounds) ▩

MINSTEAD
Map 04 SU21

FURZEY GARDENS
SO43 7GL
➲ (1m S of junct A31/M3 Cadnam off A31 or A337 near Lyndhurst)
☎ 023 8081 2464 & 8081 2297
▤ 023 8081 2297   2 for 1
e-mail: mtp@milestonenet.co.uk
A large thatched gallery is the venue for refreshments and displays of local arts and crafts, and the eight acres of peaceful glades which surround it include winter and summer heathers, rare flowering trees and shrubs and a mass of spring bulbs. There is a 16th-century cottage, lake, and the nursery, run by the Minstead Training Project for Young People with Learning Disabilities, sells a wide range of produce. **Times:** Gardens open daily 10-5 (or dusk if earlier). (Closed Xmas). Gallery Open: Mar-Oct, 10-5. **Fee:** ✱ Mar-Oct: £3.50 (ch £1.50, pen £2.80) Family £9. Nov-Feb: £1.50 (ch 50p, pen £1) Family £3. Party 10+. **Facilities:** ▣ ▣ ৬ (garden access for wheelchair visitors with assistance) toilets for disabled shop garden centre ✖ (guide dogs)

MOTTISFONT
Map 04 SU32

MOTTISFONT ABBEY GARDEN
SO51 0LP
➲ (4.5m NW Romsey, 1m W of A3057)
☎ 01794 340757 ▤ 01794 341492
e-mail: mottisfontabbey@nationaltrust.org.uk

In a picturesque setting by the River Test, Mottisfont Abbey is an 18th-century house adapted from a 12th-century priory. The north front shows its medieval church origins quite clearly, and the garden has splendid old trees and a walled garden planted with the national collection of old-fashioned roses. The estate includes Mottisfont village and surrounding farmland and woods. **Times:** Open Garden & Grounds: 17 Mar-4 Nov, Sat-Wed 11-6 (or dusk if earlier). 9-24 Jun special opening daily from 11-8.30. Last admission to grounds 1hr before closing. House: 1-5. Derek Hill Picture Collection: Sun-Tue 1-5. **Fee:** ✱ £6 (ch £3) Family ticket £15. **Facilities:** ▣ ▣ ✗ licensed ৬ (Braille guide, wheelchair available, volunteer driven buggy) toilets for disabled shop garden centre ✖ (ex guide dogs) ▩ ▩

NETLEY Map 04 SU40

Netley Abbey

SO31 5FB
➲ (4m SE of Southampton, facing Southampton Water)
FREE
☎ 02392 581059

A romantic ruin, set among green lawns and trees, this 13th-century Cistercian abbey was founded by Peter des Roches, tutor to Henry III. Nearby is the 19th-century-Gothic Netley Castle.

Times: Open any reasonable time. **Facilities:** P ♿ ✈ #

NEW ALRESFORD Map 04 SU53

Watercress Line

The Railway Station SO24 9JG
➲ (stations at Alton & Alresford signposted off A31, follow brown tourist signs)
☎ 01962 733810 📠 01962 735448
2 for 1
e-mail: info@watercressline.co.uk

The Watercress Line runs through ten miles of rolling scenic countryside between Alton and Alresford. All four stations are 'dressed' in period style, and there's a locomotive yard and picnic area at Ropley.

Times: Open May-Sep Tue-Thu & wknds; Jan-Apr & Oct wknds only. **Fee:** ✱ Unlimited travel for the day, £9 (ch £4, pen £8). Family ticket £22. **Facilities:** P (charged) ☕ ✕ licensed ♿ (ramp access to trains) toilets for disabled shop (at Alresford, Alton & Ropley stations) 💳

NEW MILTON Map 04 SZ29

Sammy Miller Motorcycle Museum

Bashley Cross Rd BH25 5SZ
➲ (signposted off A35)
☎ 01425 620777 📠 01425 619696
e-mail: info@sammymiller.co.uk

With machines dating back to 1900, some are the only surviving examples of their type. The Racing collection features World Record breaking bikes and their history, including the first bike to lap a Grand Prix Course at over 100 miles per hour. Special events include marquee days.

Times: Open all year, daily 10-4.30. **Fee:** ✱ £3.50 (ch £1.50). **Facilities:** P ☕ ✕ licensed ♿ (special rates for disabled people) toilets for disabled shop ✈ (ex guide dogs) 💳

OLD BASING Map 04 SU65

Basing House

Redbridge Ln RG24 7HB
➲ (signed from Basingstoke Ring Road)
☎ 01256 467294 📠 01256 326283

The largest house of Tudor England, almost entirely destroyed by Parliament during a two-year siege ending in 1645. Built on the site of a Norman castle in 1530, the ruins include a 300ft long tunnel. There is a re-creation of a garden of 1600 and exhibitions showing the history of the house. A fine 16th-century barn stands nearby.

Times: Open Apr-Sep, Wed-Sun & BH 2-6. **Fee:** £2 (ch & pen £1). Registered disabled free. **Facilities:** P ♿ (disabled parking by prior arangement) toilets for disabled shop

OWER Map 04 SU31

Paultons Park

SO51 6AL
➲ (exit M27 junct 2, near junct A31 & A36)
☎ 023 8081 4442 📠 023 8081 3025
e-mail: info@paultons.co.uk

Paultons Park offers a great day out for all the family with over forty different attractions. Many fun activities include Stinger Roller coaster, bumper boats, 6-lane astroglide, teacup ride, Raging River ride log flume, Pirate Ship Swingboat, Dragon Ride Roundabout, Flying Frog mini-coaster and new Wave Runner Coaster. Attractions for younger children include Kid's Kingdom, Tiny Tots Town, Rabbit Ride, the Magic Forest where nursery rhymes come to life, Wonderful World of Wind in the Willows and the Ladybird ride. In beautiful parkland setting with extensive 'Capability' Brown gardens landscaped with ponds and aviaries for exotic birds; lake and hedge maze. There is also the Romany Experience Museum with unique collection of gypsy wagons and the Village Life Museum. Something for everyone.

Times: Open mid Mar-Oct, daily 10-6; Nov & Dec, wknds only until Xmas. **Fee:** ✱ £12.50 (ch under 14). Children under 1m tall enter for free. Range of Family Supersavers. **Facilities:** P ☕ ✕ licensed ♿ (pre-booked wheelchair hire, some rides unsuitable) toilets for disabled shop ✈ (ex guide dogs) 💳

PORTCHESTER Map 04 SU60

Portchester Castle

Castle St PO16 9QW
➲ (off A27)
☎ 01705 378291

Discover 2,000 years of history from its Roman beginnings to the years of medieval splendour. Stand where Henry V rallied his troops before setting out to the battle of Agincourt in 1415.

Times: Open all year, Apr-Sep, daily 10-6; Oct, daily 10-5; Nov-Mar, daily 10-4. (Closed 24-26 Dec & 1 Jan). Dates valid until 31 Mar 2004. **Fee:** £3.50 (ch £1.80, concessions £2.60). Prices valid until 31 Mar 2004. **Facilities:** P ♿ shop ✈ (ex on lead in certain areas) #

PORTSMOUTH   Map 04 SU60

BLUE REEF AQUARIUM
Clarence Esplanade PO5 3PB
➲ (follow brown tourist signs)   `2 for 1`
☎ 023 9287 5222 ▤ 023 9229 4443
e-mail: portsmouth@bluereefaquarium.co.uk
Visitors can take an undersea safari through the oceans of
the world at this recently opened aquarium overlooking the
Solent. Mediterranean and tropical waters are recreated, and
are home to a stunning array of undersea life including
seahorses, puffer fish, coral, piranhas, and incredible
crustaceans. The huge tropical ocean tank has a
walkthrough tunnel for close encounters of an underwater
kind.
Times: Open daily from 10am. Closing times vary with season, please
telephone for details. **Fee:** ✱ £5.95 (pen £4.95, ch 3-16 £3.95)
Facilities: ℗ 🍽 ⅋ toilets for disabled shop ✖ (ex assist dogs) 🍴

CHARLES DICKENS' BIRTHPLACE MUSEUM
393 Old Commercial Rd PO1 4QL
➲ (accessible from M27, 1st left at 1st rdbt)
☎ 023 9282 7261 ▤ 023 9287 5276
e-mail: Christopher.Spendlove@
portsmouthcc.gov.uk
A small terraced house built in 1805 which became the
birthplace and early home of the famous novelist, born
in 1812. On display are items pertaining to Dickens' work,
portraits of the Dickens' family, and the couch on which he
died. Dickens readings are given in the exhibition room on
the first Sunday of each month at 3pm.
Times: Open Apr-Sep, daily 10-5.30; Oct, daily 10-5. (Last admission
5pm). **Fee:** £2.50 (ch & student £1.50, accompanied ch 13 free, pen
£1.80). Family ticket £6.50. **Facilities:** ℗ (150mtrs) shop ✖ (ex guide
& helper dogs) 🍴

CITY MUSEUM & RECORDS OFFICE
Museum Rd PO1 2LJ
➲ (M27/M275 into Portsmouth, follow museum
symbol signs)
☎ 023 9282 7261 ▤ 023 9287 5276   `FREE`
e-mail: Christopher.Spendlove@
portsmouthcc.gov.uk
Dedicated to local history, fine and decorative art, 'The Story
of Portsmouth' displays room settings showing life here from
the 17th century to the 1950s. The 'Portsmouth at Play'
exhibition features leisure pursuits from the Victorian period
to the 1970s. The museum has a fine and decorative art
gallery, plus a temporary exhibition gallery with regular
changing exhibitions. The Record Office contains the official
records of the City of Portsmouth from the 14th century.
Times: Open all year, Apr-Oct daily 10-5.30; Nov-Mar daily 10-5.
Closed 24-26 Dec and Record Office closed on public holidays.
Facilities: ℗ 🍽 ⅋ (induction loops, lift & wheelchairs available,
parking) toilets for disabled shop ✖ (ex guide & helper dogs)

FREE
Attractions with this symbol do
not charge for entry.

D-DAY MUSEUM & OVERLORD EMBROIDERY
Clarence Esplanade PO5 3NT
➲ (M27/M275 into Portsmouth follow D Day
Museum & seafront signposts)
☎ 023 9282 7261 ▤ 023 9287 5276
e-mail: Christopher.Spendlove@
portsmouthcc.gov.uk

Portsmouth's D-Day Museum tells the dramatic story of the
Allied landings in Normandy in 1944. Centrepiece is the
magnificent 'Overlord Embroidery', 34 individual panels and
83 metres in length. Experience the world's largest ever
seaborne invasion, and step back in time to scenes of
wartime Britain. Military equipment, vehicles, landing craft
and personal memories complete this special story.
Times: Open all year, Apr-Oct daily 10-5.30. Nov-Mar, 10-5. **Fee:** £5
(ch £3, pen £3.75). Family ticket £13. **Facilities:** ℗ (charged) 🍽 ⅋
(induction loops, sound aids, wheelchairs available) toilets for disabled
shop ✖ (ex guide & helper dogs) 🍴

EASTNEY BEAM ENGINE HOUSE
Henderson Rd, Eastney PO4 9JF
➲ (accessible from A3(M), A27 & A2030, turn left
at Bransbury Park traffic lights)
☎ 023 9282 7261 ▤ 023 9287 5276   `FREE`
e-mail: christopher.spendlove@
portsmouthcc.gov.uk
The main attraction here is a magnificent pair of James Watt
Beam Engines still housed in their original High-Victorian
engine house opened in 1887. One of these engines is in
steam when the museum is open. A variety of other pumping
engines, many in running order are also on display.
Times: Open last (whole) weekend of every month, 1-5 (last
admission 30 minutes before closing). (Closed Aug & Dec).
Facilities: ℗ (300mtrs) ✖ (ex guide & helper dogs)

NATURAL HISTORY MUSEUM & BUTTERFLY HOUSE
Cumberland House, Eastern Pde PO4 9RF
➲ (Can be reached via A3(M), A27 or A2030,
follow signs to seafront)
☎ 023 9282 7261 ▤ 023 9282 5276
e-mail: Christopher.Spendlove@
portsmouthcc.gov.uk
Focusing on the natural history and geology of the area, with
wildlife dioramas including a riverbank scene with fresh

continued

water aquarium. During the summer British and European butterflies fly free in the Butterfly House.
Times: Open all year daily, Apr-Oct 10-5.30; Nov-Mar 10-5.
Fee: Nov-Mar, £2 (ch £1.20, accompanied child under 13 free, pen £1.50). Apr-Oct, £2.50 (ch £1.50, accompanied ch under 13 free & pen £1.80). Family ticket £6.50. **Facilities:** P (200mtrs) shop ✻ (ex guide & helper dogs) ⏻

PORTSMOUTH HISTORIC DOCKYARD
HM Naval Base PO1 3LJ
➲ (follow brown historic ships sign from M27/M275)
☎ 023 9287 0999 ▤ 023 9229 5252
e-mail: mail@historicdockyard.co.uk
Portsmouth Historic Dockyard is home to the world's greatest historic ships: *Mary Rose*, *HMS Victory*, *HMS Warrior* and the Royal Naval Museum. Action Stations is an attraction demonstrating life aboard a modern naval frigate. Many special events held throughout the year. Telephone for details.
Times: ✻ Open all year, Apr-Oct, daily 10-5.30; Nov-Mar, daily 10-5. (Closed 25 Dec). **Facilities:** P (charged) ⏻ ✗ ⏻ toilets for disabled shop ⏻

THE ROYAL MARINES MUSEUM
Southsea PO4 9PX
➲ (signposted from seafront)   `2 for 1`
☎ 023 9281 9385 ▤ 023 9283 8420
e-mail: info@royalmarinesmuseum.co.uk
Telling the story of the 330-year history of the Marines through dramatic displays, exciting films and videos, state of the art interactives and there's even a live snake and scorpion. Also a world famous medal collection, portraits and silverware.
Times: Open all year, Jun-Aug, daily 10-5; Sep-May, daily 10-4.30. (Closed 24-26 Dec). **Fee:** ✻ £4.75 (ch £2.25, pen £3.50). Family ticket (2 ad & 4 ch) £12. **Facilities:** P ⏻ ⏻ (wheelchairs, hearing loops, special tours-prior notice) toilets for disabled shop ✻ (ex guide dogs or in grounds) ⏻

SOUTHSEA CASTLE
Clarence Esplanade PO5 3PA
➲ (accessible from M27, A27, A3M, A2030, follow castle signposts)
☎ 023 9282 7261 ▤ 023 9287 5276
e-mail: Christopher.Spendlove@portsmouthcc.gov.uk
Part of Henry VIII's national coastal defences, this fort was built in 1544. In the 'Time Tunnel' experience, the ghost of the castle's first master gunner guides you through the dramatic scenes from the castle's eventful history. Audio-visual presentation, underground passages, Tudor military history displays, artillery, and panoramic views of the Solent and Isle of Wight.
Times: Open all year, Apr-Sep, daily 10-5.30; Oct-Mar, daily 10-5.
Fee: £2.50 (ch & students £1.50, ch accompanied under 13 free, pen £1.80). Family ticket £6.50. **Facilities:** P (charged) ⏻ (wheelchair available) shop ✻ (ex guide & helper dogs) ⏻

SPITBANK FORT
P O Box 129 PO12 2XY
➲ (ferries depart from HM Naval Base Portsmouth, Portsmouth Hard & Gosport Ferry Pontoon)
☎ 01329 664286 & 07977 066560
Built in the 1860s as part of the coastal defences against the French, this massive granite and iron fortress stands a mile out to sea, with magnificent views across the Solent. The interior is a maze of passages connecting over 50 rooms on two levels.
Times: ✻ Open May-Sep, Tue-Sun. (Weather permitting).
Facilities: P ⏻

RINGWOOD   Map 04 SU10
MOORS VALLEY COUNTRY PARK
Horton Rd, Ashley Heath BH24 2ET
➲ (1.5m from Ashley Heath rdbt on A31 near Three Legged Cross)
☎ 01425 470721 ▤ 01425 471656
e-mail: mvalley@eastdorsetdc.gov.uk
Fifteen hundred acres of forest, woodland, heathland, lakes, river and meadows provide a home for a wide variety of plants and animals, and there's a Visitor Centre, Adventure Playground, picnic area, Moors Valley Railway, and Tree Top Trail. Cycle hire is also available.
Times: Open all year (ex 25 Dec), 8-dusk. Visitor centre open 9.30-4.30 (later in summer). **Fee:** ✻ No admission charge but parking up to £5 per day. **Facilities:** P (charged) ⏻ ✗ ⏻ (visitor centre & park mostly accessible, wheelchairs) toilets for disabled shop ✻ (ex in park on lead)

ROCKBOURNE   Map 04 SU11
ROCKBOURNE ROMAN VILLA
SP6 3PG
➲ (from Salisbury exit A338 at Fordingbridge, take B3078 westwards through Sandleheath & follow signs. Or turn off A354 Salisbury to Blandford road, W of Coombe Bissett.)
☎ 01725 518541
Discovered in 1942, the site features the remains of a 40-room Roman villa and is the largest in the area. Displays include mosaics and a very rare hypocaust system. The museum displays the many artefacts found on the site during excavations. Roman re-enactments are performed - please ring for details.
Times: Open Apr-Sep, daily 10.30-6. Last admission 5.30pm. **Fee:** ✻ £1.95 (concessions £1.10). **Facilities:** P ⏻ ⏻ (ramps in & out of museum) toilets for disabled shop ✻ (ex guide/hearing dogs)

ROMSEY   Map 04 SU32
BROADLANDS
SO51 9ZD
➲ (main entrance on A3090 Romsey by-pass)
☎ 01794 505010 ▤ 01794 505040
e-mail: admin@broadlands.net
Famous as the home of the late Lord Mountbatten, Broadlands is now home to his grandson Lord Romsey. An elegant Palladian mansion in a beautiful landscaped setting on the banks of the River Test, Broadlands was also the

continued

country residence of Lord Palmerston, the great Victorian statesman.
Times: Open daily, 9 Jun-7 Sep, 12-5.30. Last admission 4pm. **Fee:** ✱ £6.50 (ch 12-16 £3.95, concessions £5.50). Party 15+. **Facilities:** 🅿 🍴 ♿ toilets for disabled shop 🐕 (ex guide dogs) 🍴

SELBORNE   Map 04 SU73

GILBERT WHITE'S HOUSE & THE OATES MUSEUM
High St GU34 3JH
➲ (on village High St)
☎ 01420 511275

Charming 18th-century house, home of famous naturalist, the Rev. Gilbert White, author of *The Natural History and Antiquities of Selborne*. There are also exhibitions on two famous members of the Oates family - Captain Oates who accompanied Scott to the South Pole, and Frank Oates, a Victorian explorer. Special events include a Gilbert White day in July.
Times: ✱ Open daily Jan-24 Dec, 11-5. **Fee:** £4 (ch £1, pen £3.50). **Facilities:** 🅿 (200yds) 🍴 ♿ shop 🐕 (ex guide dogs) 🍴

SHERBORNE ST JOHN   Map 04 SU65

THE VYNE
RG24 9HL
➲ (4m N of Basingstoke, off A340, signposted from A33, A339 & A340)
☎ 01256 883858   🖷 01256 881720
e-mail: thevyne@ntrust.org.uk
Built in the early 16th-century for Lord Sandy's, Henry VIII's Lord Chamberlain, the house acquired a classical portico in the mid 17th-centry (the first of its kind in England) and contains a fascinating Tudor chapel with renaissance glass, a palladian staircase and a wealth of old panelling and fine furniture. The attractive grounds feature herbaceous borders and a wild garden, with lawns, lakes and woodland walks
Times: Open House & Gardens 29 Mar-2 Nov daily ex Thu & Fri 1-5, wknds 11-5. Gardens also open wknds in Feb & Mar, 11-5. **Fee:** House & Grounds £6.70 (ch £3.25). Group £5.20. Grounds & Gardens only £3.70 (ch £1.95). NT members free. **Facilities:** 🅿 🍴 ✗ licensed ♿ (Braille guides & touch tours) toilets for disabled shop 🐕 (ex guide & hearing dogs) 🐾 🍴

SILCHESTER   Map 04 SU66

CALLEVA MUSEUM
Bramley Rd RG7 2LU   ⟦FREE⟧
➲ (between Basingstoke & Reading.
Reached from A340, follow brown tourist signs)
Little remains of the Roman town of Calleva Atrebatum except the 1.5 miles of city wall, still an impressive sight, and the ampitheatre. This small museum shows what life may have been like in a Roman town, while the main artefacts from the site can be seen in the Silchester Gallery at Reading Museum.
Times: Open daily 9am-sunset. Closed 25 Dec. **Facilities:** 🅿 ♿

SOUTHAMPTON   Map 04 SU41

MUSEUM OF ARCHAEOLOGY
God's House Tower, Winkle St SO14 2NY
➲ (near the waterfront close to Queen's Park and the Town Quay)
☎ 023 8063 5904 & 8083 2768   ⟦FREE⟧
🖷 023 8033 9601
e-mail: historic.sites@southampton.gov.uk
The museum housed in an early fortified building, dating from the 1400s and taking its name from the nearby medieval hospital. Exhibits on the Roman, Saxon and medieval towns of Southampton are displayed.
Times: Open Tue-Fri 10-12 & 1-5; Sat 10-12 & 1-4; Sun 2-5. Also open BH Mon. **Facilities:** 🅿 (400 yds) (designated areas only, parking charges) ♿ shop 🐕 (ex guide dogs)

SOUTHAMPTON CITY ART GALLERY
Civic Centre, Commercial Rd SO14 7LP
➲ (situated on the Watts Park side of the Civic Centre, a short walk from the station, on Commercial Rd)   ⟦FREE⟧
☎ 023 8083 2277   🖷 023 8083 2153
e-mail: art.gallery@southampton.gov.uk
The largest gallery in the south of England, with the finest collection of contemporary art in the country outside London. Varied displays of landscapes, portrait paintings or recent British art are always available, as well as a special display, selected by members of the public.
Times: Open all year, Tue, Wed & Fri 10-5, Thu 10-5, Sat 10-5, Sun 1-4. (Closed 25-27 & 31 Dec). **Facilities:** 🅿 (50yds) (nearby street parking is 1hr only) 🍴 ✗ licensed ♿ (free BSL signed tours by arrangement, 'touch tour') toilets for disabled shop 🐕 (ex guide dogs)

SOUTHAMPTON MARITIME MUSEUM
The Wool House, Town Quay SO14 2AR
➲ (on the waterfront, near to the Town Quay)
☎ 023 8022 3941 & 8063 5904   ⟦FREE⟧
🖷 023 8033 9601
e-mail: historic.sites@southampton.gov.uk
The Wool House was built in the 14th century as a warehouse for wool, and now houses a maritime museum, with models and displays telling the history of the Victorian and modern port of Southampton. There are exhibitions of the *Titanic, Queen Mary* and an interactive area for children.
Times: Open all year, Tue-Fri 10-12 & 1-5, Sat 10-12 & 1-4, Sun 2-5. Also open BH Mon. **Facilities:** 🅿 (400yds) (metered parking adjacent) ♿ shop 🐕 (ex guide dogs)

STRATFIELD SAYE   Map 04 SU66
STRATFIELD SAYE HOUSE
RG7 2BZ
➲ (off A33 between Reading & Basingstoke)
☎ 01256 882882   🖳 01256 881466
Stratfield Saye House was bought for the 1st Duke of
Wellington as his country house. The family still live here.
The house contains the personal possessions, collections of
painting and furniture of the great Duke. The Duke's
magnificent funeral carriage is on display in the grounds.
Times: Open 7 Jul-3 Aug, daily. **Fee:** ✱ £6 (ch £3, concession £5).
Facilities: 🅿 💷 🖒 toilets for disabled shop 🐾 (ex in grounds)

TITCHFIELD   Map 04 SU50
TITCHFIELD ABBEY
PO15 5RA
➲ (0.5m N off Titchfield, off A27)   **FREE**
☎ 01329 842133
Also known as 'Palace House', in Tudor times this was the
seat of the Earl of Southampton, built on the site of the
abbey founded in 1232. He incorporated the gatehouse and
the nave of the church into his house.
Times: Open Apr-Sep, daily 10-6; Oct, daily 10-5; Nov-Mar, daily 10-4.
Dates valid until 31 Mar 2004. **Facilities:** 🅿 🖒 🐾 (ex dogs on leads)

WEYHILL   Map 04 SU34
THE HAWK CONSERVANCY AND COUNTRY PARK
SP11 8DY
➲ (3m W of Andover, signposted from A303)
☎ 01264 772252   🖳 01264 773772
e-mail: info@hawk-conservancy.org
This is the largest centre in the south for birds of prey from
all over the world including eagles, hawks, falcons, owls,
vultures and kites. Exciting birds of prey demonstrations are
held daily at noon, 2pm, and 3.30pm, including the 'Valley of
the Eagles' at 2pm. Different birds are flown at these times
and visitors may have the opportunity to hold a bird and
adults can fly a Harris hawk.
Times: Open Feb half-term-Oct half-term, daily from 10.30 (last
admission 4pm). **Fee:** ✱ £6.95 (ch £4.35, pen & student £6.35). Family
ticket £21.50. **Facilities:** 🅿 💷 🖒 (wheelchair area in flying grounds,
viewing areas in hides) toilets for disabled shop 🐾 🍴

WHITCHURCH   Map 04 SU44
WHITCHURCH SILK MILL
28 Winchester St RG28 7AL
➲ (halfway between Winchester & Newbury
signposted clearly on the A34. Located in centre of
the town)
☎ 01256 892065   🖳 01256 893882
e-mail: silkmill@btinternet.com
The mill is idyllically located on the river Test. Whitchurch Silk
Mill is the oldest surviving textile mill in Southern England.
Fine silks and ribbons are still woven for interiors and
fashion. See the 19th-century waterwheel pounding and learn
about winding, warping and weaving. There is a programme
of exhibitions, workshops and children's activities.
Times: Open Tue-Sun & BH Mon 10.30-5 (last admission 4.15). Closed
24 Dec-1 Jan. **Fee:** £3.50 (ch £1.75, pen & students £3). Family ticket (2
adults & 3 ch) £8.75. **Facilities:** 🅿 💷 🖒 (disabled parking adjacent
site) toilets for disabled shop 🐾 (ex guide dogs) 🍴

WINCHESTER   Map 04 SU42
GURKHA MUSEUM
Peninsula Barracks, Romsey Rd SO23 8TS
➲ (M3 junct 9 to Winchester, follow round traffic
circuit into High St 1st left after Westgate)
☎ 01962 842832   🖳 01962 877597
e-mail: curator@thegurkhamuseum.co.uk
This museum tells the fascinating story of the Gurkha's
involvement with the British Army. Travel from Nepal to the
North-West Frontier and beyond, with the help of life-sized
dioramas, interactive exhibits and sound displays.
Times: Open all year, BH Mon, Tue-Sat 10-5, Sun 12-4. Telephone for
Xmas opening times. (Closed 25-26 Dec, 1 Jan and Tue following BH
Mon) **Facilities:** 🅿 🖒 (lift & chair lift) toilets for disabled shop 🐾 (ex
guide dogs)

HOSPITAL OF ST CROSS
St Cross SO23 9SD
➲ (1.5m S of city, on A3335)
☎ 01962 851375   🖳 01962 878221
e-mail: visitors@stcrosshospital.co.uk
Founded in 1132 for the benefit of 13 poor men, and still
functioning as an almshouse. Throughout the Middle Ages
the Hospital handed out the Dole - bread and beer - to
travellers, and this is still done. The Church of St Cross,
Brethren's Hall and medieval kitchen, and the walled Master's
Garden are all worthy of note.
Times: Open all year, Apr-Oct, Mon-Sat 9.30-5; Nov-Mar 10.30-3.30.
(Closed Sun, Good Fri & 25 Dec). **Facilities:** 🅿 (200yds) (2 hrs) 💷
🖒 (A resident Brother can act as guide and assistant) toilets for
disabled shop 🐾 (ex guide dogs) 🍴

INTECH - HAMPSHIRE TECHNOLOGY CENTRE
Telegraph Way, Morn Hill SO21 1HX
➲ (on B3404 Alresford road)
☎ 01962 863791   🖳 01962 868524
e-mail: htct@intech-uk.com
This purpose-built 3500 square metre building houses 100
interactive exhibits, which demonstrate the science and
technology of the world around us in an engaging and
exciting way. The philosophy is most definitely 'hands-on',
and the motto of the centre is 'Doing is Believing'. Exhibits
deal with things like viscosity, tornados, and Newton's Cradle
among others.
Times: Open daily 10-4. (Closed Xmas & 1 Jan) **Fee:** ✱ £5.50 (pen £4,
ch £3.50) **Facilities:** 🅿 💷 🖒 shop 🐾

THE KING'S ROYAL HUSSARS REGIMENTAL MUSEUM   **FREE**
Peninsula Barracks, Romsey Rd SO23 8TS
➲ (exit M3 junct 9/10 follow signs for city centre,
then hospital A&E red signs to Romsey road.
Vehicle access is from Romsey road. A3090/B3040
at centre of city before heading uphill towards
Royal Hampshire Hospital)
☎ 01962 828539 & 828541   🖳 01962 828538
e-mail: beresford@krhmuseum.freeserve.co.uk
The Royal Hussars were formed by the amalgamation of two
regiments raised at the time of the Jacobite Rebellion
continued

in 1715, the Royal Hussars and the 14th/20th King's Hussars. This museum tells their story.
Times: Open 5 Jan-18 Dec, Tue-Fri 10-4, wknds, BH's & 1/2 term Mon, 12-4. Closed daily between 12.45-1.15. **Facilities:** 🅿 � (lift to first floor) toilets for disabled shop ✖ (ex guide dogs)

ROYAL HAMPSHIRE REGIMENT MUSEUM & MEMORIAL GARDEN
Serle's House, Southgate St SO23 9EG
➲ (Museum near city centre, 150m from traffic lights in High St)   **FREE**
☎ 01962 863658   ▯ 01962 888302
Regimental Museum of the Royal Hampshire Regiment 1702-1992, set in an 18th-century house by the regiment's Memorial Garden. The museum tells the history of the regiment, its regulars, militia, volunteers and Territorials.
Times: Normally open all year (ex 2 wks Xmas & New Year), Mon-Fri 11-3.30; Apr-Oct wknds & BH 12-4. Closed for building work Jul 2003-Apr 2004. **Facilities:** 🅿 (800mtrs) ⏺ shop ✖ (ex guide dogs)

THE GREAT HALL
Castle Av SO23 8PJ
➲ (Great Hall situated at top of High St. Pedestrians only- turn left into Castle Ave nearest public car park is Tower St. Park & Ride recommended)   **FREE**
☎ 01962 846476   ▯ 01962 841326
The only surviving part of Winchester Castle, once home to the Domesday Book, this 13th-century hall was the centre of court and government life. Built between 1222-1235 during the reign of Henry III, it is one of the largest and finest five bay halls in England to have survived to present day. The Round Table based on the Arthurian Legend and built between 1230-1280 hangs in the hall. Queen Eleanor's Garden, a re-creation of a late 13th century ornamental garden, was opened in 1986 by the Queen Mother.
Times: Open all year, Mar-Oct daily 10-5; Nov-Feb, daily 10-5, wknds 10-4. (Closed 25-26 Dec). **Facilities:** 🅿 (200yds) ⏺ toilets for disabled shop ✖ (ex guide/hearing dogs) ⬐

---

2 for 1

Attractions with this symbol by their entry are participating in our 2-for-1 voucher scheme. For details see page 6 or the vouchers at the front of the guide

---

WINCHESTER CATHEDRAL
SO23 9LS
➲ (in city centre - follow city heritage signs)
☎ 01962 857200 & 866854   ▯ 01962 857201
e-mail: cathedral.office@   **FREE**
winchester-cathedral.org.uk
The longest medieval church in Europe, founded in 1079 on a site where Christian worship had already been offered for over 400 years. Among its treasures are the 12th-century illuminated Winchester Bible, the font, medieval wall paintings and Triforium Gallery Museum.
Times: Open all year, daily 8.30-6.30. Subject to services and special events. **Facilities:** 🅿 (500mtrs) ⬐ ✖ licensed ⏺ (chair lift to east end of Cathedral, touch & hearing model) toilets for disabled shop ✖ (ex guide dogs)

WINCHESTER CITY MILL
Bridge St SO23 8EJ
➲ (by the city bridge between King Alfred's statue & Chesil St)
☎ 01962 870057   ▯ 01962 870057
e-mail: swigen@smtp.ntrust.org.uk
Built over the fastflowing River Itchen in 1744, the mill has a delightful small island garden and an impressive millrace.
Times: ✱ Open Apr-Oct, Wed-Sun & BH Mons 11-4.45; Mar wknds only. Last admission 15 mins before closing. **Facilities:** 🅿 (200 yds) shop ⬥ ⬐

WINCHESTER COLLEGE
College St SO23 9NA
➲ (In Winchester City Centre S of Cathedral Close, beyond Kingsgate arch. Limited vehicle access along College St)
☎ 01962 621209   ▯ 01962 621166
e-mail: enterprises@wincoll.ac.uk
Founded in 1382, Winchester College is believed to be the oldest continuously running school in England. The College has greatly expanded over the years but the original buildings remain intact. Visitors can follow in the footsteps of John Keats, and see the College's many historic buildings, including a schoolhouse thought to have been designed by Christopher Wren. Also the 14th-century gothic chapel with one of the earliest examples of a Fan vaulted roof constructed from wood rather than stone, the original scholars dining room and the cloister containing memorials to former members of the college including one to Mallory the Mountaineer.
Times: Open all year (ex Xmas & New Year). Guided tours available Mon, Wed, Fri & Sat; 10.45, 12, 2.15 & 3.30. Tue & Thu 10.45 & 12. Sun 2.15 & 3.30. Groups of 10+ at times to suit by arrangement only.
Fee: £3.50 (ch, pen & students £3). **Facilities:** 🅿 (250yds) (Street parking max stay 1hr) ⏺ (access ramps) toilets for disabled shop ✖ (ex guide dogs) ⬐

HEREFORDSHIRE

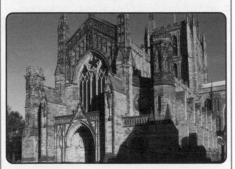

EVENTS & FESTIVALS

May
2nd-3rd Blossom Time Weekend,
  Putley, nr Ledbury
4th-6th Hereford May Fair (provisional)
June
4th-13th Jun Leominster Festival,
  mixed arts, various venues
25th-27th Music Festival, Dore Abbey,
  Abbeydore
July
2nd-11th Ledbury Poetry Festival
August
tbc Eardisland Annual Duck Races
tbc Ross-on-Wye International Festival
September
10th-12th Bromyard Folk Festival
October
2nd-30th Herefordshire Photography Festival
16th-17th Big Apple Weekend,
  Much Marcle, nr Ledbury

Top: Hereford Cathedral
Above: 17th-century Grange Court at Leominster

ASHTON   Map 03 SO56

BERRINGTON HALL
Berrington HR6 0DW
➲ (3m N of Leominster, on A49)   **2 for 1**
☎ 01568 615721 ▤ 01568 613263
e-mail: berrington@nationaltrust.org.uk

An elegant neo-classical house of the late 18th century, designed by Henry Holland and set in a park landscape by `Capability' Brown. There is a restored bedroom suite, a nursery, a Victorian laundry and a tiled Georgian dairy.
Times: Open 29 Mar-29 Oct, Sat-Wed & Good Fri 1-5 (4.30pm in Oct/Nov). Last admission 30min before closing. Garden open 12-6 (4.30pm in Oct). Park walk open Jul-29 Oct, same times as house.
Fee: ✱ £4.60 (ch £2.30) Family ticket £11.50. Garden only £3.20. Joint ticket with Croft Castle £5.50 **Facilities:** ₽ ✗ licensed ₠ (by arrangement, wheelchairs/batricar, steps to entrance toilets for disabled shop ⋈ (ex guide dogs) ⋓ ⬒

BROCKHAMPTON   Map 03 SO65

BROCKHAMPTON ESTATE
WR6 5TB
➲ (2m E of Bromyard on A44)
☎ 01885 482077 & 488099 ▤ 01885 482151
e-mail: brockhampton@nationaltrust.org.uk

Lower Brockhampton on the Brockhampton Estate near Bromyard is a late 14th-century moated manor house, with an attractive half-timbered 15th-century gatehouse, a rare example of this type of structure, and the ruins of a 12th-century chapel. It is part of a larger National Trust property covering over 1700 acres of Herefordshire/Worcestershire countryside with various walks including a Sculpture Trail.
Times: Open Apr-3 Nov daily (ex Mon/Tue) but open BH Mon's Apr-2 Nov 12-5 (12-4 in Oct/Nov). Woodland walks open to dusk throughout the year. **Fee:** ✱ Lower Brockhampton £3.20 (ch £1.60) Family £8.
Facilities: ₽ ⬛ ₠ (special parking for disabled) toilets for disabled shop ⋈ (ex in woodland area) ⋓

CROFT   Map 03 SO46

CROFT CASTLE
HR6 9PW
➲ (off B4362)
☎ 01568 780246 ▤ 01568 780462   **2 for 1**
e-mail: croft@nationaltrust.org.uk

Home of the Croft family since Domesday (with a break of 170 years from 1750); walls and towers date from the 14th and 15th centuries; the interior is mainly 18th century. There is a splendid avenue of 350-year-old Spanish chestnuts, and an Iron Age Fort (Croft Ambrey) may be reached by footpath.
Times: Park open all year, daily. Gardens & Tea Room open 29 Mar-Jun, Wed-Sun 12-5; Jul-Aug, Tue-Sun 12-5; Sep, Wed-Sun 12-5; Oct-2 Nov, Sat-Sun 12-5. Castle open 18 Apr-Jun & Sep, Wed-Sun 1-5; Jul-Aug, Tue-Sun 1-5; Oct-2 Nov, Sat-Sun 1-5. **Fee:** ✱ Garden only £3 (ch £1.50). Castle & Garden £4.20 (ch £2.10). Family ticket £10.50. Joint ticket with Berrington Castle £5.50. Car park £2.20. **Facilities:** ₽ (charged) ⬛ ₠ (parking available, braille guide) toilets for disabled shop ⋈ (ex guide dogs & in park) ⋓

GOODRICH   Map 03 SO51

GOODRICH CASTLE
HR9 6HY
➲ (5m S of Ross-on-Wye, off A40)
☎ 01600 890538

A magnificent red sandstone fortress rising out of a rocky outcrop above the Wye Valley. Climb the huge towers for exhilarating views and explore a maze of small rooms and passageways. Hear about the doomed civil war lovers on our audio tour.
Times: Open all year, Apr-Sep, daily 10-6; Oct, daily 10-5; Nov-Mar, Wed-Sun 10-4. (Closed 24-26 Dec & 1 Jan). Dates valid until 31 Mar 2004. **Fee:** £3.70 (ch £1.90, concessions £2.80). Prices valid until 31 Mar 2004. **Facilities:** 🅿 shop ✖ ♯

HEREFORD   Map 03 SO53

CIDER MUSEUM & KING OFFA DISTILLERY
21 Ryelands St HR4 0LW (off A438 Hereford to Brecon road)
☎ 01432 354207   🖷 01432 371641
e-mail: info@cidermuseum.co.uk

Explore the fascinating history of cider making - old cidermaking equipment, the cooper's workshop and Vat house with hydraulic presses and bottling machinery. An annual International cider competition is held and cidermaking festival weekends take place.
Times: Open all year, Apr-Oct, daily 10-5.30; Nov-Dec, daily 11-3. Jan-Mar, Tue-Sun 11-3. Pre-booked groups at anytime. **Fee:** £2.80 (concessions £2.30). Party 15+, 50p reduction per person.
Facilities: 🅿 ♿ & (audiotapes, large print guide sheets) shop ✖ (ex guide dogs)

HEREFORD CATHEDRAL
HR1 2NG
➲ (A49 signed from city inner ring roads)
☎ 01432 374200   🖷 01432 374220
e-mail: office@herefordcathedral.co.uk

The first bishop was appointed to the See of Hereford in 676AD. The cathedral is mainly Norman with a 13th-century Lady Chapel. Hereford's two outstanding treasures are exhibited together in the museum building at the West front. The Mappa Mundi - drawn in 1289, and the famous Chained Library - containing over 1400 chained books and 227 manuscripts dating from the 8th century.
Times: ✱ Cathedral open daily for visitors 9.30-5; Mappa Mundi & Chained Library Exhibition Summer: Mon-Sat 10-4.15, Sun 11-3.15. Winter: Mon-Sat 11-3.15 (closed Sun). **Facilities:** 🅿 (0.25m) ♿ & (touch facility for blind, braille & large print info) toilets for disabled shop ✖ (ex guide dogs) ◗

OLD HOUSE
High Town HR1 2AA
➲ (located in the centre of the High Town)
☎ 01432 260694

The Old House is a fine Jacobean building dating from around 1621, and was once in a row of similar houses. Its rooms are furnished in 17th-century style and give visitors the chance to learn what life was like in Cromwell's time.
Times: Open all year, 10-5. Apr-Sep, Tue-Sat 10-5, Sun & BH Mon 10-4.
Facilities: 🅿 & shop (very small) ✖ (ex guide dogs)

KINGTON   Map 03 SO25

HERGEST CROFT GARDENS
HR5 3EG
➲ (turn off A44 W of Kington and follow signs)
☎ 01544 230160   🖷 01544 232031   **2 for 1**
e-mail: gardens@hergest.kc3.co.uk

From spring bulbs to autumn colour, this is a garden for all seasons. A fine collection of trees and shrubs surrounds the Edwardian house. There's an old fashioned kitchen garden with spring and summer borders, and Park Wood, a hidden valley with splendid rhododendrons.
Times: Open Mar-Oct, 12.30-5.30; May-Jun noon-6. **Fee:** £4 (ch under 16 free). Party 20+ £3.50 **Facilities:** 🅿 ♿ & (portable ramp & wheelchair available) toilets for disabled shop garden centre ✖ (ex dogs on lead) ◗

LEDBURY   Map 03 SO73

EASTNOR CASTLE
Eastnor HR8 1RL
➲ (the castle is 2.5m E of Ledbury on the A438 Tewkesbury road)
☎ 01531 633160   🖷 01531 631776
e-mail: eastnorcastle@eastnorcastle.com

A magnificent Georgian castle in a lovely setting, with a deer park, arboretum and lake. Inside are tapestries, fine art and armour, and the Italianate and Gothic interiors have been beautifully restored. There's an adventure playground, nature trails and lakeside walks.
Times: Open 11 Apr-3 Oct, Sun & BH Mon; Jul & Aug, Sun-Fri 11-5.
Fee: Castle & grounds £6.50 (ch £4, pen £6) Family £17. Grounds only £4.50 (ch £3, pen £4). **Facilities:** 🅿 ♿ & (please telephone for access & facilities details) shop ◗

SWAINSHILL   Map 03 SO44

THE WEIR GARDENS
HR4 7QF
➲ (5m W of Hereford, on A438)   **2 for 1**
☎ 01981 590509

A delightful riverside garden which is at its best in spring when there are lovely displays of naturalised bulbs set in woodland and grassland walks. Cliff garden walks can be taken here, with fine views of the River Wye and the Welsh hills.
Times: Open Jan-mid Feb wknds only, 11-4. Mid Feb-Oct, Wed-Sun & BH's, 11-6. **Fee:** ✱ £3. Family £7. **Facilities:** 🅿 ✖ ♨

HERTFORDSHIRE

EVENTS & FESTIVALS

May
6th-9th Living Crafts, Hatfield House
22nd-23rd Herts Garden Show,
    Knebworth House
29th-30th Herts County Show,
    Herts County Showground, Redbourn

June
tbc Hertford Carnival

July
2nd-18th St Albans Festival
tbc Fireworks & Laser Concert,
    Knebworth House

August
6th-8th Art in Clay, Hatfield House
30th St Albans Carnival (provisional)

September
29th-2nd Oct St Albans Beer Festival
tbc Hoddeson Carnival
tbc Homes, Gardens & Flower Show,
    Hatfield House

October
29th Sep-2nd St Albans Beer Festival
tbc Apple Day Fair & Market,
    city centre, St Albans

November
tbc Firework display, Verulamium Park,
    St Albans

Top: Hatfield House, Hatfield
Above: Statue at Knebworth House

AYOT ST LAWRENCE — Map 04 TL11

SHAW'S CORNER
AL6 9BX
➲ (A1(M) junct 4 or M1 junct 10. Follow B653
signed Wheathampstead & follow NT signs to
Shaw's Corner in village)
☎ 01438 820307 ▤ 01438 820307
e-mail: shawscorner@nationaltrust.org.uk
George Bernard Shaw lived here from 1906 until his death
in 1950. He gave the house to the National Trust in 1946, and
the contents are much as they were in his time. Among the
displays are his hats, including a soft homburg he wore for
60 years, his bicycle exercise machine, fountain pens,
spectacles and several pictures. His writing hat is hidden at
the bottom of the garden
Times: ✱ Open 20 Mar-Oct, Wed-Sun & BH Mon. Gardens noon-5.30.
House 1-5. **Fee:** £3.80 (ch £1.90) Family £9.50. **Facilities:** ▯ &
(braille guide to house, scented plants, items to touch) ✖ (ex on lead
in car park) ⛝ ◥

BERKHAMSTED — Map 04 SP90

BERKHAMSTED CASTLE
HP4 1HF   **FREE**
➲ (by Berkhamsted station)
Roads and a railway have cut into the castle site, but its huge
banks and ditches remain impressive. The original
motte-and-bailey was built after the Norman Conquest, and
there is a later stone keep, owned by the Black Prince, eldest
son of King Edward III, where King John of France was
imprisoned.
Times: Open all year, daily, summer 10-6; winter 10-4. (Closed 25 Dec
& 1 Jan). Dates valid until 31 Mar 2004. **Facilities:** ✖ (ex dogs on
leads) ⌗

HATFIELD — Map 04 TL20

HATFIELD HOUSE, PARK AND GARDENS
AL9 5NQ
➲ (2m from junct 4 A1(M) on A1000, 7m from M25
junct 23. House is opposite Hatfield railway
station)
☎ 01707 287010 ▤ 01707 287033
e-mail: curator@hatfield-house.co.uk

Home of the Cecil family for 400 years, this celebrated
Jacobean house is steeped in Elizabethan and Victorian
continued

political history and is famous for its exquisite furniture, tapestries and paintings. The extensive formal gardens which reflect their historic origins, are designed by Lady Salisbury and managed entirely organically. A children's play area and nature trails are also open to the public.
Times: Open Etr Sat-Sep. House: daily 12-4, guided tours only on weekdays. Park & gardens: daily 11-5.30. **Fee:** House Park & Gardens: £7.50 (ch £4). Park only £2 (ch £1). Park & gardens: £4.50 (ch 3.50). Fri (Connoisseurs' Day), £10.50 (no concessions). **Facilities:** ◨ ✗ licensed ⓹ (lift to 1st floor) toilets for disabled shop garden centre (not in garden) ⬤

KNEBWORTH   Map 04 TL22

KNEBWORTH HOUSE, GARDENS & COUNTRY PARK
SG3 6PY
➲ (direct access from A1(M) junct 7 Stevenage South)
☎ 01438 812661 ▤ 01438 811908
e-mail: info@knebworthhouse.com

Home of the Lytton family since 1490, the original Tudor Manor was transformed in 1843 by the spectacular high Gothic decoration of Victorian novelist Sir Edward Bulwer Lytton. The formal gardens, laid out by Edwin Lutyens in 1908, include a Gertrude Jekyll herb garden, a maze, recently restored walled garden and wilderness walks. The 250-acre park includes a miniature railway, an adventure playground and a deer park.
Times: Open daily 3-18 Apr, end May-early Jun & early Jul-end Aug. Wknds & BH's 27-28 Mar, 24 Apr-23 May, 12-27 Jun & 4-26 Sep. Park, Playground & Gardens 11-5.30; House & Exhibition noon-5 (last admission 4.15). **Fee:** Please contact for details. **Facilities:** ◨ ⬤ ⓹ (with prior notice visitors can be driven to front door) toilets for disabled shop (2 shops) garden centre ✗ (ex guide dogs & in park) ⬤

LETCHWORTH   Map 04 TL23

MUSEUM & ART GALLERY
Broadway SG6 3PF
➲ (Museum is situated next door to the Public Library, in the Town Centre, near the Broadway Cinema) **FREE**
☎ 01462 685647 ▤ 01462 481879
e-mail: letchworth.museum@north-herts.gov.uk
Opened in 1914 to house the collections of the Letchworth
continued

Naturalists' Society, this local museum has exhibits on local wildlife, geology, arts and crafts, and archaeology. There is also a museum shop and a regular programme of workshops.
Times: Open all year Mon-Tue, Thu-Sat (Closed BHs), 10-5.
Facilities: ℗ (100yds) ⓹ (special provisions on request) shop ✗ (ex guide dogs)

LONDON COLNEY   Map 04 TL10

DE HAVILLAND AIRCRAFT HERITAGE CENTRE
Salisbury Hall AL2 1EX
➲ (signposted from junct 22 of M25. Follow signs for 'Mosquito Aircraft Museum' onto B556).
☎ 01727 822051 & 826400
▤ 01727 826400

The oldest aircraft museum in Britain, opened in 1959 to preserve and display the de Havilland Mosquito prototype on the site of its conception. A working museum with displays of 20 de Havilland aircraft and sections together with a comprehensive collection of de Havilland engines and memorabilia. Selective cockpits are open to enter. Education storyboard 'maze style' now open.
Times: Open first Sun Mar-last Sun Oct, Sun & BH Mons 10.30-5.30, Tue, Thu & Sat 2-5.30. **Fee:** £5 (ch under 5 free, ch & pen £3) Family ticket £13 (2 adults & 2 ch) **Facilities:** ℗ ⬤ ⓹ (wheelchairs available) toilets for disabled shop (not accessible for wheelchairs) ✗ (ex on lead & under control) ⬤

ST ALBANS   Map 04 TL10

CLOCK TOWER
Market Place AL3 3DR
➲ (City centre, junct of High St (A1081) & Market Place)
☎ 01727 855843
This early 15th-century curfew tower, which faces the High Street, provides fine views over the city (especially of the abbey) and the surrounding countryside. This is one of the only two medieval curfew towers in the country. It has a bell, older than the tower itself, which strikes on the hour.
Times: Open Good Fri-mid Sep, Sat, Sun & BH 10.30-5. **Fee:** ✱ 30p (ch 5-11 15p, accompanied ch under 5 free) **Facilities:** ℗ (400yds) shop ✗

GARDENS OF THE ROSE (ROYAL NATIONAL ROSE SOCIETY)
Chiswell Green Ln AL2 3NR
➲ (2m S off B4630 Watford Rd in Chiswell Green Ln)
☎ 01727 850461 🖷 01727 850360   2 for 1
e-mail: mail@rnrs.org.uk

The gardens of the Royal National Rose Society, which include the International Trial Ground for new roses. The gardens contain over 30,000 plants in 1,650 different varieties. These include old-fashioned roses, modern roses and the roses of the future. The National Miniature Rose Show takes place during July.
Times: Open 31 May-late Sep, Mon-Sat 10-5 (Sun & BH Mon 10-6).
Fee: ✱ £4 (ch 5-15 £1.50, pen & UB40 £3.50) Party 20+ £3.50 each.
Facilities: 🅿 ➓ & (ramps where necessary) toilets for disabled shop garden centre ✖ (ex guide dogs) ◥

GORHAMBURY
AL3 6AH
➲ (entry via lodge gates on A414)
☎ 01727 855000 🖷 01727 843675

This house was built by Sir Robert Taylor between 1774 and 1784 to house an extensive picture collection of 17th-century portraits of the Grimston and Bacon families and their contemporaries. Also of note is the 16th-century enamelled glass collection and an early English pile carpet.
Times: Open May-Sep, Thu 2-5. **Fee:** ✱ £6 (ch £3, pen £4). Party.
Facilities: 🅿 shop ✖

MUSEUM OF ST ALBANS
Hatfield Rd AL1 3RR
➲ (city centre on A1057 Hatfield road)
☎ 01727 819340 🖷 01727 837472   FREE
e-mail: museum@stalbans.gov.uk

Exhibits include the Salaman collection of craft tools, and reconstructed workshops. The history of St Albans is traced from the departure of the Romans up to the present day. There is a special exhibition gallery with a surprising variety of exhibitions and a wildlife garden with picnic area.
Times: Open all year, daily 10-5, Sun 2-5. (Closed 25 & 26 Dec).
Facilities: 🅿 & toilets for disabled shop ✖ (ex guide dogs) ◥

Knebworth
HOUSE, GARDENS & PARK

Home of the Lytton family for over 500 years, where Elizabeth I visited, Dickens acted and Churchill painted. Extensive Gardens, Maze, Indian Raj Display Adventure Playground, Miniature Railway, Gift Shop and Garden Terrace Tea Room, set in 250 acres of deer park.

FULL PROGRAMME OF EXCITING EVENTS IN THE PARK, EASTER TILL SEPT, PLEASE TELEPHONE FOR DETAILS.

OPEN DATES 2004 *(SUBJECT TO SPECIAL EVENTS)*
Daily: 3 -18 April; 29 May - 6 June; 3 July - 31 Aug ind.
Weekends & Bank Hols only: 27 - 28 Mar; 24 Apr - 23 May; 12 - 27 June; 4 - 26 Sept incl.

OPENING TIMES 2004
Park, Playground & Gardens: 11.00am - 5.30pm
House & Exhibition: 12.00 noon - 5.00pm (last admission 4.15pm)
For further information, please contact:

The Estate Office, Knebworth Park, Nr Stevenage, Herts SG3 6PY
Tel: 01438 812661   Fax: 01438 811908
email: info@knebworthhouse.com   website: www.knebworthhouse.com
Immediate access off the A1(M), via our own slip road at Junction 7, 15 miles from M25 (J23).

ROMAN THEATRE OF VERULAMIUM
St Michaels AL3 6AH
➲ (off A4147)
☎ 01727 835035 🖷 01727 843675

The theatre was discovered in 1847 and excavated in 1935. It is unique in England. First constructed around AD160, it is semicircular in shape, 180ft across and could hold over 2000 spectators.
Times: ✱ Open all year, daily 10-5 (4 in winter). Closed 25-26 Dec. 1 Jan by appointment only. **Facilities:** 🅿 & (limited access to viewing path) shop (on leads only)

ST ALBANS CATHEDRAL
Sumpter Yard AL1 1BY
➲ (M25 junct 22a, in the centre of St Albans)
☎ 01727 860780 🖷 01727 850944
e-mail: admin@stalbanscathedal.org.uk

An imposing Norman abbey church built on the site of the execution of St Alban, Britain's first martyr (c250AD). The cathedral is constructed from recycled Roman brick taken from nearby Verulamium.
Times: Open daily, 9-5.45, closed 25 Dec (pm) **Fee:** Admission free. Suggested donation £2.50 per adult. **Facilities:** 🅿 (200mtrs) ➓ & (touch & hearing centre, braille guides) toilets for disabled shop ✖ (ex assist dogs)

VERULAMIUM MUSEUM

St Michaels AL3 4SW

➲ (follow signs for St Albans, museum signposted)

☎ 01727 751810   ▌ 01727 859919   `2 for 1`

e-mail: a.coles@stalbans.gov.uk

Verulamium was one of the largest and most important
Roman towns in Britain - by the lst century AD it was
declared a 'municipium', giving its inhabitants the rights of
Roman citizenship, the only British city granted this honour.
A mosaic and underfloor heating system can be seen, and
the museum has wall paintings, jewellery, pottery and other
domestic items. On the second weekend of every month
legionaries occupy the galleries and describe the tactics and
equipment of the Roman Imperial Army and the life of a
legionary.

Times: Open all year wkdys 10-5.30, Sun 2-5.30. (Closed 25-26 Dec).
Fee: ✱ £3.30 (ch, pen & students £2). Family ticket £8. Subject to
change. **Facilities:** ▐ (charged) ♿ (ramp access to main entrance)
toilets for disabled shop ✖ (ex guide dogs) ◥

TRING   Map 04 SP91

THE WALTER ROTHSCHILD ZOOLOGICAL MUSEUM

Akeman St HP23 6AP

➲ (signposted from A41)

☎ 020 7942 6171   ▌ 020 7942 6150   `FREE`

e-mail: tring-enquiries@nhm.ac.uk

An unusual museum, founded in the 1890s by Lionel Walter,
2nd Baron Rothschild, scientist, eccentric and natural history
enthusiast. Now part of the Natural History Museum, it
houses more than 4000 specimens from whales to fleas, and
humming birds to tigers.

Times: Open all year, Mon-Sat 10-5, Sun 2-5. (Closed 24-26 Dec).
Facilities: ▐ 💻 ♿ (ramps to shop & cafe, disabled parking space)
toilets for disabled shop ✖ (ex guide dogs)

WARE   Map 05 TL31

SCOTT'S GROTTO

Scott's Rd SG12 9JQ

➲ (off A119)

☎ 01920 464131   ▌ 0870 120 6902   `FREE`

e-mail: jg@ware-herts.org.uk

Scott's Grotto, built in the 1760s by the Quaker poet John
Scott, has been described by English Heritage as 'one of the
finest in England'. Recently restored by the Ware Society, it
consists of underground passages and chambers decorated
with flints, shells, minerals and stones, and extends 67ft into
the side of the hill. Please wear flat shoes and bring a torch.

Times: Open Apr-end Sep, Sat & BH Mon 2-4.30. Other times by
appointment only. **Facilities:** ▐ (on street) 🛴

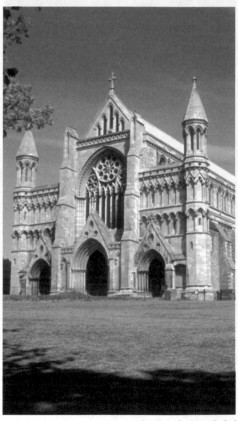

Above: St Alban's Cathedral

KENT

EVENTS & FESTIVALS

April
24th-25th Weald of Kent Garden Show, The
    Hop Farm Country Park, Paddock Wood

May
29th-31st Kent Garden Show, Kent & County
    Showground (provisional)
tbc Tonbridge Carnival

June
19th-27th Broadstairs Dickens Festival
20th Whitstable Community Fun Day,
    Tankerton Slopes, Marine Parade
tbc Canterbury Carnival
tbc Stour Music Festival, Canterbury

July
16th-18th Kent County Show, Maidstone
25th-31st Deal Regatta Week
28th Party on the Prom, Deal
29th Deal Carnival
tbc Dover Carnival
tbc Whitstable Regatta, Whitstable

August
6th-13th Broadstairs Folk Week
7th Swale Barge & Smack Race, Whitstable
8th Broadstairs & St Peters Carnival
14th Herne Bay Carnival
14th-15th Autorama vintage/classic car show,
    Dunorlan Park, Tunbridge Wells
18th Broadstairs Water Gala
28th-30th Southeast Garden Show, Hop Farm
    Country Park, Paddock Wood
30th Sedan Chair Race, Tunbridge Wells
tbc Dover Regatta
tbc Margate Summer Carnival
tbc Sandwich Festival
tbc Whitstable Oyster Festival

September
tbc Deal Maritime Folk Festival
tbc Sandwich Carnival

October
9th-23rd Canterbury Festival, Canterbury

December
4th Tankerton Christmas Street Market,
    Whitstable (provisional)

*Above: Church of St Thomas
Becket on Romney Marsh*

AYLESFORD Map 05 TQ75

AYLESFORD PRIORY
The Friars ME20 7BX
➲ (M20 junct 6 onto A229, M2 junct 3 onto A229,
signposted)
☎ 01622 717272 📠 01622 715575
e-mail: friarsevents@hotmail.com

Built in the 13th and 14th centuries, the Priory has been
restored and is now a house of prayer, guesthouse,
conference centre and a place of pilgrimage and retreat. It
has fine cloisters, and displays sculpture and ceramics by
modern artists.
Times: Open all year, daily 9-dusk. Gift & book shop May-Sep, 10-5;
Oct-Apr, 10-4 (Sun 11am). Guided tours of the priory by arrangement.
Fee: ✱ Free, donations welcome. £2 for annual fund-raising day, 29
Jun. **Facilities:** 🅿 ⬛ ♿ (wheelchairs available, ramps) toilets for
disabled shop ✖ (ex guide & hearing dogs)

BEKESBOURNE Map 05 TR15

HOWLETTS WILD ANIMAL PARK
CT4 5EL
➲ (off A2, 3m S of Canterbury, follow brown
tourist signs)
☎ 01303 264647 📠 01303 264944
e-mail: info@howletts.net

Howletts is a wild animal park founded by John Aspinall and
has the world's largest breeding gorilla colony in captivity. It
also has tigers, small cats, free-running deer and antelope,
snow leopards, bison, honey badgers, African elephants, and
many endangered species of monkey.
Times: ✱ Open all year, daily 10-5 last admission 4.30, (3pm in
winter). Park closes at dusk. Closed 25 Dec. **Fee:** ✱ £11.95 (ch 4-14
£8.95) Family £34 (2 ad + 2 ch), £39 (2 ad + 3 ch). **Facilities:** 🅿 ⬛
✖ ♿ toilets for disabled shop ✖ ⬛

BELTRING Map 05 TQ64

HOP FARM & COUNTRY PARK
TN12 6PY
➲ (on A228 at Paddock Wood)
☎ 01622 872068 📠 01622 872630
e-mail: enquiry@thehopfarm.co.uk

The Hop Farm is one of the South East's most popular family
visitor attractions and event locations. Set amongst the
largest collection of Victorian Oast houses attractions
include; museums and exhibitions, indoor and outdoor play
areas, animal farm and shire horses, and restaurant and gift
shop.
Times: Open all year from 10am (Closed 24-26 Dec & for the Party in
the Park concert) **Fee:** ✱ £6.50 (ch under 4 free, ch 4-15 & pen £5.50).
Family ticket £20 (2 ad & 2 ch). **Facilities:** 🅿 ⬛ ✖ licensed ♿ toilets
for disabled shop ⬛

BIDDENDEN Map 05 TQ83

BIDDENDEN VINEYARDS & CIDER WORKS
Little Whatmans, Gribble Bridge Ln TN27 8DF
➲ (0.5m S off A262, between Biddenden &
Tenterden)
☎ 01580 291726 📠 01580 291933
e-mail: info@biddendenvineyards.co.uk

The present vineyard was established in 1969 and now

continued

covers 22 acres. Visitors are welcome to stroll around the vineyard and to taste wines, ciders and apple juice available at the shop.

Times: Open all year, Shop: Mon-Fri 10-5, Sat 10-5, Sun & BH 11-5. Closed noon 24 Dec-2 Jan & Sun in Jan & Feb. **Fee:** Non-guided groups and individuals free. Pre-booked guided tours (minimum 15 adults) £3.30 (ch 10-18 £1, ch under 10 free). **Facilities:** shop (ex guide dogs)

BIRCHINGTON Map 05 TR36

POWELL-COTTON MUSEUM, QUEX HOUSE & GARDENS

Quex Park CT7 0BH

(W of Margate on A28. Drive in to Birchington and turn right into Park Lane before rdbt in centre of town. The entrance to Quex Park 600 yds on left)

01843 842168 01843 846661

e-mail: powell-cotton.museum@virgin.net

Major Powell-Cotton spent much of his life on the study of African animals and many different cultures. This museum, founded in 1895, is his legacy, consisting of animal dioramas, photographs, extensive notes, and artefacts from around the world. Also on display in Quex House, the family home, are collections of Eastern and Asian furniture, Kashmir walnut wall carvings, Chinese silk embroidery, and English period furniture.

Times: Open Apr-Oct Tue-Thu, Sun & BH 11-5, Quex House 2-4.30. Nov & Mar Sun 11-4, Quex House closed. (Closed Dec-Feb). **Fee:** * Summer £4 (ch & pen £3, under 5's free), Family ticket (2 adults & 3 children) £12. Winter £3 (ch & pen £2.50), Family ticket (2 adults & 3 children) £8. Garden only £1 (ch & pen 50p). **Facilities:** licensed (two wheelchairs available) toilets for disabled shop (ex assistance dogs)

BOROUGH GREEN Map 05 TQ65

GREAT COMP GARDEN

TN15 8QS

(2m E off B2016)

2 for 1

01732 882669

e-mail: greatcompgarden@aol.com

A beautiful seven-acre garden created since 1957 by Mr and Mrs R Cameron for low maintenance and year-round interest. There is a plantsmans' collection of trees, shrubs, heathers and herbaceous plants in a setting of fine lawns and grass paths. The 17th-century house is not open. Chamber music, classical concerts and other events are organised by the Great Comp Society, details from the Secretary, Great Comp Society at the above address.

Times: Open Apr-Oct, daily 11-5.30. **Fee:** £4 (ch £1). Annual ticket £12 (pen £8). **Facilities:** (wheelchair for hire) toilets for disabled garden centre (ex guide dogs)

BRASTED Map 05 TQ45

EMMETTS GARDEN

Ide Hill TN14 6AY

(1m S of A25, Sundridge-Ide Hill road)

01732 868381 & 866368 01732 868193

e-mail: kchxxx@smtp.ntrust.org.uk

Emmetts is a charming hillside shrub garden, with bluebells, azaleas and rhododendrons in spring and fine autumn colours. It has magnificent views over Bough Beech Reservoir and the Weald. Emmetts Blues Concert in July.

Times: Open 22 Mar-29 Jun, Wed-Sun & BH 11-5 (last admission 4.15); 2 Jul-2 Nov Wed, Sat & Sun **Facilities:** (wheelchairs & buggy service from car park to garden) toilets for disabled shop

BROADSTAIRS Map 05 TR36

BLEAK HOUSE DICKENS MARITIME & SMUGGLING

Fort Rd CT10 1EY

(off Eastern Esplanade, near Viking Bay)

01843 862224

The house was a favourite seaside residence of Charles Dickens, and he wrote all of *David Copperfield* and other works here, and drafted the idea for *Bleak House*. There are also exhibitions of relics salvaged from the Goodwin Sands and Kent's only smuggling museum.

Times: * Open mid Feb-mid Dec, daily; Jan-mid Feb wknds only.10-6 **Facilities:** P (100 yds) (provisions made for blind) shop

DICKENS HOUSE MUSEUM

2 Victoria Pde CT10 1QS

(on the seafront)

01843 863453 01843 863453

2 for 1

e-mail: aleeault@aol.com

The house was immortalised by Charles Dickens in *David Copperfield* as the home of the hero's aunt, Betsy Trotwood, whom Dickens based on owner Miss Mary Pearson Strong. Dickens' letters and possessions are shown, with local and Dickensian prints, costumes and general Victoriana.

Times: Open Etr-Oct, daily 2-5, also Sat-Sun mid Jun-Aug 10.30-5. **Fee:** * £2 (ch & student £1). Family ticket (2 ad & 2 ch) £5. **Facilities:** P (400yds) (pay & display) shop (ex guide dogs)

CANTERBURY Map 05 TR15

CANTERBURY ROMAN MUSEUM

Butchery Ln, Longmarket CT1 2RA

(in the centre close to the cathedral and city centre car parks)

01227 785575 01227 455047

e-mail: museums@canterbury.gov.uk

Step below today's Canterbury to discover an exciting part of the Roman town including the real remains of a house with fine mosaics. Experience everyday life in the reconstructed

continued

market place and see exquisite silver and glass. Try your skills on the touch screen computer, and in the hands-on area with actual finds. Use the computer animation of Roman Canterbury to join the search for the lost temple. **Times:** Open all year, Mon-Sat 10-5 & Sun (Jun-Oct) 1.30-5. Last admission 4pm. (Closed Good Fri & Xmas period). **Fee:** ✱ £2.70 (ch 5-18, disabled, pen & students £1.70). Family ticket £7. **Facilities:** P (500mtrs) ♿ (lift) toilets for disabled shop ✸

THE CANTERBURY TALES

Saint Margaret's St CT1 2TG

➲ (In heart of city centre, follow finger sign-posting)

☎ 01227 479227 ▤ 01227 765584

e-mail: info@canterburytales.org.uk

Step back in time to experience the sights sounds and smells of the Middle Ages in this reconstruction of 14th century England. Travel from the Tabard Inn, in London, to St. Thomas Becket's Shrine in Canterbury with Chaucer's colourful pilgrims. Their tales of chivalry, romance and intrigue are vividly brought to life for you along your journey. **Times:** Open all year, Mar-Jun 10-5, Jul-Aug 9.30-5, Sep-Oct 10-4 & Nov-Feb 10-4.30. **Fee:** ✱ £6.75 (ch £5.25, pen & student £5.75) Family ticket (2 ad & 2 ch) £22. **Facilities:** P (200mtrs) ♨ ♿ (notice required for wheelchairs) toilets for disabled shop ✸ (ex guide dogs) ♥

CANTERBURY WEST GATE MUSEUM

Saint Peter's St CT1 2RA

➲ (at the end of the main street beside the river, the entrance is under the main arch)

☎ 01227 789576 ▤ 01227 455047

e-mail: museums@canterbury.gov.uk

The last of the city's fortified gatehouses sits astride the London road with the river as a moat. Rebuilt in around 1380 by Archbishop Sudbury, it was used as a prison for many years. The battlements give a splendid panoramic view of the city and are a good vantage point for photographs. Arms and armour can be seen in the guardroom, and there are cells in the towers. Brass rubbings can be made and children can try on replica armour. **Times:** Open all year (ex Good Fri & Xmas period), Mon-Sat; 11-12.30 & 1.30-3.30. Last admission 15 mins before closure. **Fee:** ✱ £1 (ch, disabled, pen, students & UB40 65p). Family ticket £2.50. Party 10+. **Facilities:** P (100yds) shop ✸

DRUIDSTONE PARK & ART PARK

Honey Hill, Blean CT2 9JR

➲ (3m NW on A290 from Canterbury)

☎ 01227 765168 ▤ 01227 768860

Idyllic garden setting for a range of sculptures. Enchanted woodland walks where dwells the sleeping dragon. See the mystical Oak circle with the old man of the oaks. Children's farmyard, play areas, gift shop & cafeteria. **Times:** Open Etr-Nov, daily, 10-5.30. **Fee:** ✱ £4.10 (ch £3 & pen £3.60). Family ticket £12.20. **Facilities:** P ♨ ♿ toilets for disabled shop ✸ (ex guide dogs)

MUSEUM OF CANTERBURY

Stour St CT1 2RA

➲ (in the Medieval Poor Priests' Hospital, just off St Margaret's St or High St)

☎ 01227 475202 ▤ 01227 455047

e-mail: museums@canterbury.gov.uk

Are you up to the challenge of the medieval discovery gallery? Or want to know what life was like during the wartime Blitz? What clues are there about Marlowe's life in the Elizabethan treasure chest? And why are Rupert Bear, Bagpuss and Basil Brush here? Find out - and much more, in the new, interactive displays for all the family. Set in the Poor Priest's Hospital, one of the city's finest medieval buildings. **Times:** Open all year, Mon-Sat 10.30-5 & Sun (Jun-Sep) 1.30-5 (last admission 4pm). (Closed Good Fri & Xmas period). **Fee:** ✱ £3 (concessions £2). Family ticket £8. **Facilities:** P ♿ toilets for disabled shop ✸

ROYAL MUSEUM & ART GALLERY WITH BUFFS MUSEUM

High St CT1 2RA

➲ (in the Beaney Institute (1st floor) in the High St)

☎ 01227 452747 ▤ 01227 455047   FREE

e-mail: museums@canterbury.gov.uk

A splendid Victorian building, houses decorative arts and the city's picture collections- including a gallery for T.S. Cooper, England finest cattle painter. The art gallery is the major space in the arena for the visual arts with a varied exhibition programme. Here too is the Buffs Museum, which tells the story of one of England's oldest infantry regiments and its worldwide service. **Times:** Open all year, Mon-Sat 10-5. (Closed Good Fri and Xmas period). **Facilities:** P (500mtrs) shop ✸

ST AUGUSTINE'S ABBEY

CT1 1TF

➲ (off A28)

☎ 01227 767345

Part of the Canterbury World Heritage site, this is considered by many as the birthplace of Christianity in England. Visit the fascinating museum and take the free interactive audio tour. **Times:** Open all year, Apr-Sep, daily 10-6; Oct, daily 10-5; Nov-Mar, daily 10-4. (Closed 24-26 Dec & 1 Jan). Dates valid until 31 Mar 2004. **Fee:** £3 (ch £1.50, concessions £2.30). Prices valid until 31 Mar 2004. **Facilities:** P ♿ shop ✸ (ex dogs on leads) ⊞

CHARTWELL Map 05 TQ45

Chartwell

TN16 1PS

➲ (2m S of Westerham, off B2026)

☎ **01732 866368 (info line) & 868381**

📠 **01732 868193**

e-mail: kchxxx@smpt.ntrust.org.uk

The former home of Sir Winston Churchill is filled with reminders of the great statesman, from his hats and uniforms to gifts presented by Stalin, Roosevelt & de Gaulle. There are paintings of Churchill and other works by notable artists, and also many paintings by Churchill himself.

Times: Open 22 Mar-9 Nov, house, garden & studio, Wed-Sun 11-5. Tue Jul/Aug Open BH Mon's & Tue in Jul/Aug. Last admission 4.15pm (5.30pm BH) **Facilities:** P ✕ licensed ♿ (2 steps to lift, grounds partially accessible, parking) toilets for disabled shop (ex guide dogs or in garden)

CHATHAM Map 05 TQ76

Fort Amherst

Dock Rd ME4 4UB

➲ (adjacent to the A231 dock road, 0.5m from Chatham Dockyard)

☎ **01634 847747** 📠 **01634 830612**

e-mail: amherstman2@hotmail.com

A fine Georgian fortress set in over 15 acres of attractive parkland. A fascinating collection of caves, tunnels, gun-batteries and barracks gives visitors an insight into the life of the Napoleonic soldier. Please telephone for details of special events, including historic re-enactments.

Times: Open daily Nov-Mar Sat/Sun 10-3.30. Apr-Oct daily 10-4 **Facilities:** P ♿ (wheelchair provided, road access up to fort) toilets for disabled shop (ex guide dogs)

The Historic Dockyard Chatham

ME4 4TZ

➲ (from M20 & M2 junct 3, follow signs for Chatham on A229. Then take A230 and A231, following brown tourist signs. Brown anchor signs lead to visitors entrance)

☎ **01634 823800** 📠 **01634 823801** **2 for 1**

e-mail: info@chdt.org.uk

The Historic Dockyard celebrates over 400 years of naval history in one 80-acre site. Exhibits include Battle Ships with WWII destroyer *HMS Cavalier* and the spy sub *Ocelot*. Lifeboat with a display of 15 full size boats, archive film and artefacts; and Wooden Walls which looks at the life of a carpenter's apprentice in the 18th century. The naval architecture is spectacular.

Times: Open mid Feb-early Nov, daily 10-6. Last entry 4pm. **Fee:** * £9.50 (ch 5-15 £6, concession £7). Family ticket (2 ad & 2 ch) £25, additional child £3. **Facilities:** P ✕ licensed ♿ (wheelchair available, braille guides, virtual tours) toilets for disabled shop

CHIDDINGSTONE Map 05 TQ54

Chiddingstone Castle

TN8 7AD

➲ (off B2027, at Bough Beech)

☎ **01892 870347**

The 'castle' is a 17th-century house, almost completely rebuilt in the castle style c1800 by William Atkinson.

continued

It contains Stewart and Jacobite paintings and other relics, Egyptian and Oriental antiquities, and a fine collection of Japanese lacquer and swords. The interior has recently been refurbished with extra rooms open to visitors.

Times: * Open Apr-May, Oct, Easter & Public Holidays, Jun-Sep, Wed-Fri & Sun. Weekdays 2-5.30; Sun & BH 11.30-5.30. **Facilities:** P ♿ shop (ex guide dogs on lead)

DEAL Map 05 TR35

Deal Castle

Victoria Rd CT14 7BA

➲ (SW of Deal town centre)

☎ **01304 372762**

Discover the history of this formidable fortress as you explore the long, dark passages that once linked a garrison of 119 guns.

Times: Open all year, Apr-Sep, daily 10-6; Oct, daily 10-5; Nov-Mar, Wed-Sun 10-4. (Closed 24-26 Dec & 1 Jan). Dates valid until 31 Mar 2004. **Fee:** £3.50 (ch £1.80, concessions £2.60). Prices valid until 31 Mar 2004. **Facilities:** ♿ (parking available) shop

Walmer Castle

Kingsdown Rd CT14 7LJ

➲ (1m S on coast, off A258)

☎ **01304 364288**

Originally built by Henry VIII as a formidable and austere fortress, the castle has since been transformed into an elegant stately home, formerly used by HM The Queen Mother. Many of her rooms are open to view, but the special highlight is the magnificent gardens.

Times: Open all year, Apr-Sep, daily 10-6; Oct, daily 10-5; Nov-Dec & Mar, Wed-Sun 10-4 (Jan-Feb, Sat & Sun only 10-4). (Closed 24-26 Dec, 1 Jan). Dates valid until 31 Mar 2004. **Fee:** £5.50 (ch £2.80, concessions £4.10). Prices valid until 31 Mar 2004. **Facilities:** P ♿ (parking available) shop

DOVER Map 05 TR34

Crabble Corn Mill

Lower Rd, River CT17 0UY

➲ (M20 into Dover towards Eastern Docks onto A2. Take road as far as Whitfield rdbt. At rdbt 2nd turning down Whitfield Hill towards North Dover. At bottom of hill left. At traffic lights right into River Crabble, under railway bridge and 1st right, Mill 500mtrs on left)

☎ **01304 823292** 📠 **01304 823292** **2 for 1**

e-mail: miller@ccmt.org.co.uk

Visit this beautifully restored working Kentish water mill dating from 1812. Regular demonstrations of waterwheel working and making stoneground wholemeal flour from Kentish organic wheat. Flour for sale, also home-baked produce in cafe. Exhibition space displays work of local artists and craftspeople.

Times: Open all year, Mar-Sep, daily 11-5; Winter, Sun only (except by appointment). Open all year for groups by arrangement. Closed Xmas & Jan. **Fee:** Self guided tours: £2.50 (ch 5-15 yrs £1.50, pen & students £2). Family ticket £6. Guide tours: £3 (ch 5-15 yrs £2.20, pen & students £2.50). Family ticket £6.50. **Facilities:** P ♿ shop (ex guide dogs)

DOVER CASTLE & SECRET WARTIME TUNNELS
CT16 1HU

☎ 01304 211067 📄 01304 214739

Various exhibitions demonstrate how Dover Castle has served as a vital strategic centre for the Iron Age onwards. In May 1940 the tunnels under the castle became the nerve centre for 'Operation Dynamo' - the evacuation of Dunkirk. These wartime secrets are now revealed for all to see.
Times: Open all year, Apr-Sep, daily 10-6; Oct, daily 10-5; Nov-Mar, daily 10-4. (Closed 24-26 Dec & 1 Jan). Dates valid until 31 Mar 2004.
Fee: £8 (ch £4, concessions £6). Prices valid until 31 Mar 2004.
Facilities: 🅿 ✕ ᵹ shop 🐾 (ex on lead in certain areas) ⚌

ROMAN PAINTED HOUSE
New St CT17 9AJ

➲ (follow A20 to York St bypass, located in town centre)

☎ 01304 203279

Visit five rooms of a Roman hotel built 1800 years ago, famous for its unique, well-preserved Bacchic frescos. The Roman underfloor heating system and part of a late-Roman defensive wall are also on view. There are extensive displays on Roman Dover, and special events are held throughout the year.
Times: Open Apr-Sep, Tue-Sun 10-5, also BH Mon & Mon Jul & Aug.
Fee: £2 (ch & pen 80p) **Facilities:** 🅿 ᵹ (touch table, glass panels on gallery for wheelchairs) shop 🐾

DUNGENESS   Map 05 TR01

DUNGENESS POWER STATIONS' VISITOR CENTRE
TN29 9PP

➲ (follow A259 to New Romney, right turn signposted B2075 to Lydd, power station signposted)

☎ 01797 321815 📄 01797 321844

The 'A' and 'B' power stations at Dungeness make an extraordinary sight in a landscape of shingle, fishing boats and owner-built houses. There is a high-tech information centre, with 'hands-on' interactive videos and many other displays and models including an environmental exhibition which depicts Dungeness from the Ice Age through to today.
Times: ✱ Open Mar-Oct, Mon-Fri, 10-4. Nov-Feb by appointment only.
Facilities: 🅿 ᵹ (information centre only/shortened tour by appointment) toilets for disabled shop 🐾 (ex guide dogs)

DYMCHURCH   Map 05 TR12

DYMCHURCH MARTELLO TOWER
High St CT16 1HU

➲ (access from High St not seafront)

☎ 01304 211067

This artillery tower formed part of a chain of strongholds intended to resist invasion by Napoleon.
Times: Telephone for opening details. **Fee:** £1.50 (ch 80p, concessions £1.10). Prices valid until 31 Mar 2004. **Facilities:** 🐾 ⚌

EDENBRIDGE
See Hever

EYNSFORD   Map 05 TQ56

EYNSFORD CASTLE   [FREE]
➲ (in Eynsford, off A225)

One of the first stone castles to be built by the Normans. The moat and remains of the curtain wall and hall can still be seen.
Times: Open all year, Apr-Sep, daily 10-6; Oct-Feb, daily 10-4. Dates valid until 31 Mar 2004. **Facilities:** 🅿 ᵹ 🐾 (ex dogs on leads) ⚌

LULLINGSTONE CASTLE
DA4 0JA

➲ (1m SW of Eynsford via A225 & Lullingstone Roman Villa)

☎ 01322 862114 📄 01322 862115

The house was altered extensively in Queen Anne's time, and has fine state rooms and beautiful grounds. The 15th-century gate tower was one of the first gatehouses in England to be made entirely of bricks, and there is a church with family monuments. Please telephone for details of special events.
Times: Open, House May-Aug, Sat, Sun & BH 2-6. Parties by arrangement. **Fee:** ✱ House & Gardens £5 (ch £2 & pen £4) family £10. **Facilities:** 🅿 ᵹ shop 🐾

LULLINGSTONE ROMAN VILLA
Lullingstone Ln DA4 0JA

➲ (0.5m SW off A225)

☎ 01322 863467

One of the most exciting finds with wonderful mosaic floors, wall paintings and skeletal remains. Audio tours offer a fascinating insight into the life of a well-to-do Roman family.
Times: Open all year, Apr-Sep, daily 10-6; Oct, daily 10-5; Nov-Mar, daily 10-4. (Closed 24-26 Dec & 1 Jan). Dates valid until 31 Mar 2004.
Fee: £3 (ch £1.50, concessions £2.30). Prices valid until 31 Mar 2004.
Facilities: 🅿 🐾 ⚌

FAVERSHAM   Map 05 TR06

FLEUR DE LIS HERITAGE CENTRE
10-13 Preston St ME13 8NS

➲ (3 minutes drive from M2 junct 6)

☎ 01795 534542   [2 for 1]
e-mail: faversham@btinternet.com

Recently expanded and updated, and housed in 16th-century premises, the Centre features colourful displays and room settings that vividly evoke the 2000 year history of Faversham. Special features include the 'Gunpowder Experience' and a working old-style village telephone exchange, one of only two remaining in Britain. In July, during the Faversham Open House Scheme, over 20 historic properties in the town are opened to the public.
Times: Open all year, Mon-Sat, 10-4; Sun 10-1. **Fee:** £2 (ch & pen £1)
Facilities: 🅿 (200yds) ᵹ toilets for disabled shop ◥

GILLINGHAM   Map 05 TQ76

ROYAL ENGINEERS MUSEUM
Prince Arthur Rd ME4 4UG
➲ (follow brown signs from Gillingham &
Chatham town centres)
☎ 01634 406397   🖷 01634 822371   **2 for 1**
e-mail: remuseum.rhqre@gtnet.gov.uk

The museum covers the diverse and sometimes surprising
work of the Royal Engineers. Learn about the first military
divers, photographers, aviators and surveyors; see
memorabilia relating to General Gordon and Field Marshal
Lord Kitchener, Wellington's battle map from Waterloo and a
Harrier jump-jet. The superb medal displays include 25
Victoria Crosses.
Times: Open all year, Mon-Thu 10-5, Sat-Sun & BH Mon 11.30-5.
(Closed Good Fri, 25-26 Dec & 1 Jan). **Fee:** £5 (ch, pen & UB40s
£2.50). Family ticket £12. **Facilities:** 🅿 & (help available if required,
chair lift to upper level) toilets for disabled shop ✕ (ex guide
dogs) ⌫

GOUDHURST   Map 05 TQ73

FINCHCOCKS
TN17 1HH
➲ (off A262)
☎ 01580 211702   🖷 01580 211007   **2 for 1**
e-mail: katrina@finchcocks.co.uk

This fine early Georgian house stands in a spacious park
with a beautiful garden, and contains an outstanding
collection of keyboard instruments from the 17th century
onwards. They have been restored to playing condition, and
there are musical tours on all open days and private visits.
Visually handicapped visitors may touch the instruments as
well as hear them.
Times: Open Etr-Sep, Sun & BH Mon 2-6; Aug, Wed, Thu & Sun only
2-6. Private groups on other days by appointment Apr-Oct. **Fee:** £7.50.
Facilities: 🅿 ⬛ ✕ licensed & (wheelchair available) toilets for
disabled shop garden centre ✕ (ex guide dogs)

GROOMBRIDGE PLACE   Map 05 TQ53

**GROOMBRIDGE PLACE GARDENS &
ENCHANTED FOREST**
TN3 9QG
➲ (turn off A264 onto B2110 0.5m from Langton
Green. Follow signs to Groombridge. Entrance at
bottom of Groombridge Hill in Groombridge
village)
☎ 01892 861444 (office) & 863999 (info line)
🖷 01892 863996
e-mail: office@groombridge.co.uk

These award winning gardens, set in 200 acres, feature
magnificent walled gardens and herbaceous borders, rose
gardens, secret gardens, drunken topiary and much more,
against the romantic backdrop of a 17th century moated
continued

manor. In the ancient woodland of the 'Enchanted Forest'
there's mystery, innovation and excitement for all ages.

Times: Open Apr-5 Nov, daily 9.30-6 or dusk. **Fee:** £8.50 (ch 3-12 £7,
pen £7.20). Family ticket (2 ad & 2 ch) £28.50. Groups 20+ available on
request. **Facilities:** 🅿 ⬛ & (ramps, canal boat) toilets for disabled
shop ✕ (ex guide/hearing dogs) ⌫

HAWKINGE   Map 05 TR23

KENT BATTLE OF BRITAIN MUSEUM
Aerodrome Rd CT18 7AG
➲ (off A260, 1m along Aerodrome road)
☎ 01303 893140
e-mail: kentbattleofbritainmuseum@
btinternet.com

Once a Battle of Britain Station, today it houses the largest
collection of relics and related memorabilia of British and
German aircraft involved in the fighting. Also shown full-size
replicas of the Hurricane, Spitfire and Me109 used in Battle
of Britain films. The year 2000 was the 60th anniversary of
the Battle of Britain and a new memorial has been dedicated.
Artefacts on show, recovered from over 600 battle of Britain
aircraft all form a lasting memorial to all those involved in
the conflict.
Times: Open Etr-Sep, daily 10-5; Oct, daily 11-4. Last admission 1 hour
before closing. **Facilities:** 🅿 ⬛ & shop ✕ (ex guide dogs)

HEVER   Map 05 TQ44

HEVER CASTLE & GARDENS
TN8 7NG
➲ (M25 junct 5 or 6, 3m SE of Edenbridge, off
B2026)
☎ 01732 865224   🖷 01732 866796
e-mail: mail@hevercastle.co.uk

This enchanting, double-moated, 13th-century castle was the
childhood home of Anne Boleyn. Restored by the American
millionaire William Waldorf Astor at the beginning of the
20th century, it shows superb Edwardian craftsmanship.
Astor also transformed the grounds, creating a lake, a
spectacular Italian garden filled with antique sculptures; and
a maze. Recent additions to the gardens include a 110 metre
herbaceous border and a 'splashing' water maze on the
continued

Sixteen Acre Island, as well as a woodland walk known as Sunday Walk.

Times: Open Mar-Nov, daily. Castle 12-6, Gardens 11-6. Last admission 5pm. (Closes 4pm Mar & Nov). **Fee:** ✱ Castle & Gardens £8.40 (ch 5-14 £4.60, pen £7.10). Family ticket £21.40. Gardens only £6.70 (ch 5-14 £4.40, pen £5.70). Family ticket £17.80. Party 15+. **Facilities:** 🅿 🍽 ✗ licensed ♿ (wheelchairs available, book in advance) toilets for disabled shop garden centre 🐕 (ex on leads, and guide dogs) ☕

HYTHE	**Map 05 TR13**

ROMNEY, HYTHE & DYMCHURCH RAILWAY
TN28 8PL
➲ (off M20 junct 11, off A259 signed New Romney)
☎ 01797 362353 & 363256 📠 01797 363591
e-mail: rhdr@romneyrail.fsnet.co.uk

The world's smallest public railway has its headquarters here. The concept of two enthusiasts coincided with Southern Railway's plans for expansion, and so the thirteen-and-a-half mile stretch of 15 inch gauge railway

continued

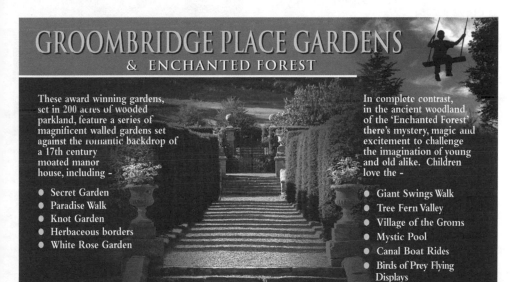

came into being, running from Hythe through New Romney and Dymchurch to Dungeness Lighthouse.
Times: Open daily Etr-Sep, also wknds in Mar & Oct. For times apply to: The Manager, RH & DR., New Romney, Kent. **Fee:** Charged according to journey. **Facilities:** ▣ (charged) 🍴 ♿ (stairlift to Toy & Model Museum) toilets for disabled shop (Dymchurch & Dungeness high season only) 🍴

IGHTHAM   Map 05 TQ55
IGHTHAM MOTE
TN15 0NT
➲ (2.5m S off A227, 6m E of Sevenoaks)
☎ 01732 810378 & 811145 (info line)
🖷 01732 811029
e-mail: igthammote@nationaltrust.org.uk

This moated manor house, nestling in a sunken valley, dates from 1330. The main features of the house span many centuries and include the Great Hall, old chapel and crypt, Tudor chapel with painted ceiling, drawing room with Jacobean fireplace, frieze and 18th century handpainted Chinese wallpaper and the billiards room. There is an extensive garden and interesting walks in the surrounding woodland.
Times: ✶ Open Apr-Nov, daily ex Tue & Sat, 10-5.30. Open Good Fri. Last admission 5pm. **Facilities:** ▣ 🍴 ✗ licensed ♿ (wheelchairs available,special parking ask at ticket office) toilets for disabled shop 🗙 🥾

LAMBERHURST   Map 05 TQ63
BAYHAM ABBEY
TN3 8DE
➲ (off B2169, 2m W in East Sussex)
☎ 01892 890381

Explore the romantic ruins of this 13th-century abbey built by French monks in an 18th-century landscaped setting.
Times: Open Apr-Sep, daily 10-6 (Oct, daily 10-5); Nov-Mar, Sat & Sun 10-4. (Closed 24-26 Dec & 1 Jan). Dates valid until 31 Mar 2004.
Fee: £2.50 (ch £1.30, concessions £1.90). Prices valid until 31 Mar 2004. **Facilities:** ▣ ♿ ✿

SCOTNEY CASTLE GARDEN
TN3 8JN
➲ (1m S, of Lamberhurst on A21)
☎ 01892 891081   🖷 01892 890110
e-mail: kscxxx@smtp.ntrust.org.uk

The beautiful gardens at Scotney were planned in the 19th century around the remains of the old, moated Scotney Castle. There is something to see at every time of year, with spring flowers followed by rhododendrons, azaleas and a mass of roses, and then superb autumn colours. Estate walks all year through 770 acres of woodlands and meadows, walker's guide available.
Times: ✶ Open Garden: Apr-end Oct. Old Castle open May-mid Sep, Wed-Sun, 11-6 or sunset if earlier. BH Mon 11-6. (Closed Good Fri). Last admission 1hr before closing. **Facilities:** ▣ ♿ (wheelchair hire, braille & large print guidebook,audio tape) toilets for disabled shop 🗙 (ex guide & hearing dogs) 🥾 🍴

LYDD   Map 05 TR02
RSPB NATURE RESERVE
Boulderwall Farm, Dungeness Rd TN29 9PN
➲ (off Lydd to Dungeness road, 1m SE of Lydd, follow tourist signs)
☎ 01797 320588   🖷 01797 321962
e-mail: dungeness@rspb.org.uk

This coastal reserve comprises 2106 acres of shingle beach and flooded pits. An excellent place to watch breeding terns, gulls and other water birds. Wheatears, great crested and little grebes also nest here, and outside the breeding season there are large flocks of teals, shovelers, and goldeneyes, goosanders, smews and both Slavonian and red-necked grebes.
Times: Visitor Centre open all year, daily 10-5 (10-4 Nov-Feb). Reserve open all year, daily 9-9 (or sunset if earlier). (Closed 25-26 Dec).
Fee: ✶ £3 (ch £1, concessions £2). **Facilities:** ▣ ♿ (access by car to some hides) toilets for disabled shop 🗙 (ex guide dogs) 🍴

LYMPNE   Map 05 TR13
PORT LYMPNE WILD ANIMAL PARK, MANSION & GARDEN
CT21 4PD
➲ (off M20 junct 11, follow brown tourist signs. Also follow brown tourist signs from A20 between Ashford and Folkestone)
☎ 01303 264647   🖷 01303 264944
e-mail: info@howletts.net

A 400-acre wild animal park that houses hundreds of rare animals: Indian elephants, rhinos, wolves, bison, snow leopards, Siberian and Indian tigers, gorillas and monkeys. The mansion designed by Sir Herbert Baker is surrounded by 15 acres of spectacular gardens. Inside, the most notable features include the restored Rex Whistler Tent Room, Moroccan Patio and hexagonal library where the Treaty of Paris was signed after World War I. Visit the Spencer Roberts Mural room and the Martin Jordan animal mural room.
Times: Open all year, daily 10-6 (closes at dusk in summer), last admission 4.30pm summer, 3pm winter. (Closed 25 Dec). **Fee:** ✶ £11.95 (ch 4-14 & pen £8.95). Family ticket £34 (2 adults & 2 ch) £39 (2 adults & 3 ch). **Facilities:** ▣ 🍴 ✗ licensed ♿ (very limited access for disabled, special route available) toilets for disabled shop garden centre (in season) 🗙 🍴

MAIDSTONE   Map 05 TQ75

LEEDS CASTLE

ME17 1PL

➲ (7m E of Maidstone at junct 8 of M20/A20, clearly signposted)

☎ 01622 765400 📄 01622 735616

e-mail: enquiries@leeds-castle.co.uk

Set on two islands in the centre of a lake, Leeds Castle has been called the 'loveliest castle in the world', and was home to six medieval Queens of England, as well as being Henry VIII's Royal Palace. Among the treasures inside are many paintings, tapestries and furnishings. Attractions in the grounds include formal gardens, two mazes, exotic bird aviary, dog collar museum, vineyard, woodland walks and show greenhouses.

Times: Open all year daily, Mar-Oct 10-5 (Castle 11-5.30). Nov-Feb 10-3 (Castle 10.15-3.30). Closed 28 Jun; 5 Jul; 8 Nov; 25 Dec

Facilities: 🅿 💺 ✕ licensed ♿ (Braille information, induction loops & wheelchair, lift) toilets for disabled shop garden centre ✖ (ex guide dogs) 💬

MAIDSTONE MUSEUM & BENTLIF ART GALLERY

Saint Faith's St ME14 1LH

➲ (close to County Hall & Maidstone E train stn)

☎ 01622 602838 📄 01622 685022   **FREE**

e-mail: alexgurr@maidstone.gov.uk

Set in an Elizabethan manor house which has been much extended over the years, this museum houses an outstanding collection of fine and applied arts, including watercolours, furniture, ceramics, and a collection of Japanese art and artefacts. The museum of the Queen's Own Royal West Kent Regiment is also housed here. Please apply for details of temporary exhibitions, workshops etc.

Times: Open all year, Mon-Sat 10-5.15, Sun & BH Mon 11-4. (Closed 25-26 Dec). **Facilities:** 🅿 (150 mtrs) 💺 ♿ shop ✖ (ex guide dogs) 💬

> If you are dissatisfied with any aspect of an attraction, discuss the problem at the time with a member of staff

MUSEUM OF KENT LIFE

Lock Ln, Sandling ME14 3AU

➲ (from M20 junct 6 onto A229 Maidstone road, follow signs for Aylesford)   **2 for 1**

☎ 01622 763936 📄 01622 662024

e-mail: enquiries@museum-kentlife.co.uk

Kent's award-winning open air museum is home to an outstanding collection of historic buildings which house exhibitions on life in Kent over the last 100 years. An early 20th-century village hall and reconstruction of cottages from the 17th & 20th-centuries are more recent buildings to be viewed.

Times: Open Feb-1 Nov, daily 10-5.30, in winter open every wknd 10-3. **Fee:** ✱ £5.50 (ch £3.50, pen £4). Family ticket £16. **Facilities:** 🅿 💺 ✕ licensed ♿ (wheelchairs available, ramps, transport available) toilets for disabled shop 💬

Tyrwhitt Drake Museum of Carriages
The Archbishop's Stables, Mill St ME15 6YE
➲ (close to River Medway & Archbishops Palace, just off A229 in town centre)
☎ 01622 602838 ▤ 01622 682451

A wide array of horse-drawn carriages and vehicles is displayed in these late-medieval stables, which are interesting in themselves. The exhibits include state, official and private carriages, and some are on loan from royal collections.
Times: Open all year 10.30-4.30. Last admission 3.45. **Fee:** £2 (ch 15 & pen £1.60), family ticket £4. **Facilities:** Ⓟ (50 yds) ♿ shop ✖ (ex guide dogs)

MINSTER-IN-THANET   Map 05 TR36
Minster Abbey
CT12 4HF
➲ (turn off A253 at Minster rdbt. Down the hill through the village. Turn left at St. Mary's Church).
☎ 01843 821254

One of the first nunneries in England was built on this site in the 7th century. Rebuilt in later centuries, it is still home to a religious community, run by Benedictine nuns. The ruins of the old abbey and the cloisters are open to the public. One wing dates back to 1027, and there is a 12th-century carving of Christ.
Times: ✱ Open all year, May-Sep, Mon-Fri 11-12 & 2.30-4, Sat 11-12; Oct-Apr, Mon-Sat 11-12. **Facilities:** Ⓟ ♿ toilets for disabled shop (ex guide dogs)

PENSHURST   Map 05 TQ54
Penshurst Place & Gardens
TN11 8DG
➲ (from M25 junct 5 take A21 Hastings road then exit at Hildenborough, then follow signs)
☎ 01892 870307 ▤ 01892 870866
e-mail: enquiries@penshurstplace.com

Built between 1340 and 1345, the original house is perfectly preserved. Enlarged by successive owners during the 15th, 16th and 17th centuries, the great variety of architectural styles creates a dramatic backdrop for the extensive collections of English, French and Italian furniture, tapestries and paintings. The chestnut-beamed Baron's Hall is the oldest and finest in the country, and the house is set in
continued

magnificent formal gardens. There is a toy museum, venture playground, woodland trail and 10 acres of walled formal gardens.
Times: Open: 6-26 Mar wknds only, 27 Mar-Oct daily. Grounds open 10.30-6pm, House opens noon-5.30pm (4pm on Sat) **Fee:** ✱ House & Grounds £6.50 (ch 5-16 £4.50, pen & students £6). Family £18. Grounds only £5 (ch 5-16 £4, pen & students £4.50) Family £15. Party 20+. Garden season ticket £30. **Facilities:** Ⓟ ✖ licensed ♿ (ramp into Barons Hall, Braille room guides) toilets for disabled shop garden centre ✖ (ex guide dogs) 🍴

RAMSGATE   Map 05 TR36
Maritime Museum
Clock House, Pier Yard, Royal Harbour CT11 8LS
➲ (follow Harbour signs)
☎ 01843 587765 & 570622
▤ 01843 582359   `2 for 1`
e-mail: museum@ekmt.fsnet.co.uk

The Maritime Museum Ramsgate is housed in the early 19th-century Clock House, and contains four galleries depicting various aspects of the maritime heritage of the East Kent area. The adjacent restored dry dock and floating exhibits from the museum's historic ship collection include the steam tug *Cervia* and the Dunkirk little ship motor yacht *Sundowner*.
Times: Open Easter-Sep, Tue-Sun 10-5. Oct-Easter Thu-Sun 10-4.30.
Fee: ✱ Combined ticket for museum & steam tug £1.50. (ch & pen 75p). Family £4. **Facilities:** Ⓟ (charged) ♿ (restricted) shop ✖

RECULVER   Map 05 TR26
Reculver Towers & Roman Fort
CT6 6SU
➲ (3m E of Herne Bay)   `FREE`
☎ 01227 740676

An imposing 12th-century landmark: twin towers and with the walls of a Roman fort.
Times: Open any reasonable time. **Facilities:** Ⓟ ♿ (long slope form carpark to fort) ✖ (ex dogs on leads) ⌗

RICHBOROUGH   Map 05 TR36
Richborough Castle
CT13 9JW
➲ (1.5m N of Sandwich off A257)
☎ 01304 612013

Explore the site of the first Roman landing in Britain and visit the museum with its collection of artefacts uncovered on site. See the remains of the huge triumphal arch, once 25 metres high.
Times: Open all year, Apr-Sep, daily 10-6; Oct, daily 10-5; Nov-Feb, Sat-Sun 10-4; Mar, Wed-Sun 10-4. (Closed 24-26 Dec & 1 Jan). Dates valid until 31 Mar 2004. **Fee:** £3 (ch £1.50, concessions £2.30). Prices valid until 31 Mar 2004. **Facilities:** Ⓟ ♿ shop ✖ (ex on lead in certain areas) ⌗

ROCHESTER   Map 05 TQ76
Charles Dickens Centre
Eastgate House, High St ME1 1EW
☎ 01634 844176 ▤ 01634 827980

A fine late Tudor building with an early 20th-century extension, which houses a series of displays relating to the life and works of Charles Dickens. In the garden is Dicken's
continued

Swiss chalet study from Gads Hill Place. Eastgate House appeared as Westgate House in *Pickwick Papers* and The Nun's House in *Edwin Drood*.
Times: ✱ Open all year, daily 10-5.30. (Closed Xmas). Last admission 4.45pm. **Facilities:** P (250 yds) shop ✖ ➧

GUILDHALL MUSEUM
High St ME1 1PY
➲ (follow signs from A2 to Rochester city centre, museum is at N end of High St)
☎ 01634 848717 ▤ 01634 832919
e-mail: guildhall.museum@medway.gov.uk
Housed in two adjacent buildings, one dating from 1687 and the other from 1909. The collections are arranged chronologically from Prehistory to the Victorian and Edwardian periods. They cover local history and archaeology, fine and decorative art. There is a gallery devoted to the prison hulks of the River Medway. The museum stages a regular programme of temporary exhibitions.
Times: Open all year, daily 10-4.30. Last admissions 4 (Closed Xmas & New Year). **Facilities:** P (250 yds) ⅋ shop ✖ (ex guide & hearing dogs)

ROCHESTER CASTLE
ME1 1SX
➲ (by Rochester Bridge, A2, junct 1 M2, junct 2 M25)
☎ 01634 402276
Built on the Roman City Wall, this Norman bishop's castle was a vital royal stronghold.
Times: Open all year, Apr-Sep, daily 10-6; Oct-Mar, daily 10-4. (Closed 24-26 Dec & 1 Jan). Dates valid until 31 Mar 2004. **Fee:** Telephone for details of admission charges. **Facilities:** shop ✖ ✿

ROLVENDEN   Map 05 TQ83

C M BOOTH COLLECTION OF HISTORIC VEHICLES
Falstaff Antiques, 63 High St TN17 4LP
➲ (on A28, 3 miles from Tenterden)
☎ 01580 241234
e-mail: info@morganmuseum.co.uk   `2 for 1`
Not just vehicles, but various other items of interest connected with transport. There is a unique collection of three-wheel Morgan cars, dating from 1913, and the only known Humber tri-car of 1904, as well as a 1929 Morris van, a 1936 Bampton caravan, motorcycles and bicycles. There is also a toy and model car display.
Times: Open all year, Mon-Sat 10-6. (Closed 25-26 Dec). **Fee:** £2 (ch £1) **Facilities:** P (roadside) shop ➧

SEVENOAKS   Map 05 TQ55

KNOLE
TN15 0RP
➲ (S end of Sevenoaks, E of A225)
☎ 01732 462100 & 450608 (info line)
▤ 01732 465528
e-mail: knole@.ntrust.org.uk
In the 15th century Thomas Bourchier, Archbishop of Canterbury, transformed Knole from a simple medieval manor house into a palace. A century later Henry VIII

continued

extended it to even grander proportions. In the middle of the 16th century Elizabeth I gave it to Thomas Sackville and the Sackvilles kept the house for ten generations.
Times: Open mid Mar-early Nov, Wed-Sun & BH, 11-4. **Facilities:** P (charged) ▃ ⅋ Audio loop/Braille guide toilets for disabled shop ✖ (ex in park on lead) ⅋ ➧

SISSINGHURST   Map 05 TQ73

SISSINGHURST CASTLE GARDEN
TN17 2AB
➲ (1m E of Sissinghurst village on A262)
☎ 01580 710700 ▤ 01580 710702
e-mail: ksixxx@smtp.ntrust.org.uk
The Tudor mansion of Sissinghurst Castle was bought in a neglected state in 1930 by Sir Harold Nicolson and his wife, the writer Vita Sackville-West. They set about restoring house and gardens and the gardens now rank among the most attractive and popular in England.
Times: ✱ Open: Gardens Apr-14 Oct, Tue-Fri 1-6.30; Sat, Sun & Good Fri 10-6.30 (last admission 5.30) Closed Mon incl BH Mon. Limited capacity timed tickets in operation so visitors may have to wait for admission, garden may be closed when its capacity has been reached. Garden is least crowded in Apr, Sep & Oct. **Facilities:** P ✖ licensed ⅋ (Admission restricted to 2 wheelchairs at any one time) toilets for disabled shop ✖ (ex guide dogs) ⅋ ➧

SITTINGBOURNE   Map 05 TQ96

DOLPHIN SAILING BARGE MUSEUM
Crown Quay Ln ME10 3SN
➲ (N on A2, signed)
☎ 01795 423215 & 421549
The museum presents the history of the Thames spritsail sailing barge, many of which were built along the banks of Milton Creek. Tools of the trade, photographs and associated artefacts can be seen at the barge yard along with the sailing barge Cambria. Privately owned barges are repaired - there's a forge, shipwright's shop and sail loft.
Times: ✱ Open Etr-Oct, Sun & BHs 11-5. Other times by arrangement. **Facilities:** P ⅋ toilets for disabled shop

SMALLHYTHE   Map 05 TQ83

SMALLHYTHE PLACE
TN30 7NG
➲ (2m S of Tenterden, on E side of the Rye Road on B2082)
☎ 01580 762334 ▤ 01580 762334
e-mail: smallhytheplace.ntrust.org.uk
Once a Tudor harbour master's house, this half-timbered, 16th-century building was Dame Ellen Terry's last home, and is now a museum of Ellen Terry memorabilia. The barn is situated in the grounds and is now a theatre and is open most days courtesy of the Barn Theatre Society.
Times: Open Apr-Oct, Sat-Wed 11-5, also Good Fri. Last admission 30 mins before closing. **Facilities:** P ⅋ (album of descriptions & photos of upstairs, braille guide) ✖ (ex guide dogs) ⅋

> ### The AA also publishes a guide to Pet Friendly Places to Stay

SWINGFIELD MINNIS   Map 05 TR24

THE BUTTERFLY CENTRE

McFarlanes Garden Centre CT15 7HX

➲ (on A260 by junction with Elham-Lydden road)

☎ 01303 844244

A tropical greenhouse garden with scores of colourful free-flying butterflies from all over the world among exotic plants such as bougainvillea, oleander and banana. The temperate section houses British butterflies, with many favourite species and some rarer varieties.

Times: ✱ Open Apr-1 Oct, daily 10-5. Closed Easter Sunday.

Facilities: 🅿 💺 ⚹ shop garden centre ✖ (ex guide dogs) 🍴

TUNBRIDGE WELLS   Map 05 TQ53
(ROYAL)

A DAY AT THE WELLS

The Corn Exchange, The Pantiles TN2 5QJ

➲ (1hr from London, in the heart of Kent, accessible via A26/A21/A267).   [2 for 1]

☎ 01892 546545 📠 01892 513857

Take a gentile walk through Georgian England. Experience the sights, sounds and smells of a summer's day in 1740s Tunbridge Wells. Meet the 18th-century socialites of this popular spa town and watch as they sample the spring waters, parade and waltz around the ballrooms.

Times: Open daily, Apr-Oct 10-5, Nov-Mar 10-4. **Fee:** ✱ £5.50 (ch, pen & student £4.50). Family (2 ad & 2 ch) £17.50 (2 ad & 1 ch) £13.

Facilities: 🅿 (charged) ⚹ (specially designed flat route tour available) shop ✖ (ex guide dogs) 🍴

TUNBRIDGE WELLS MUSEUM AND ART GALLERY

Civic Centre, Mount Pleasant TN1 1JN

➲ (adjacent to Town Hall, off A264)

☎ 01892 554171 & 526121 📠 01892 534227

The museum displays local history, along with Tunbridge ware, archaeology, toys and dolls, and domestic and agricultural bygones. The art gallery has regularly changing art and craft exhibitions and touring displays from British and European museums.

Times: Open all year, daily 9.30-5. (Closed Sun, BH's & Etr Sat).

Facilities: 🅿 (200 yds) ⚹ parking adjacent to building shop ✖ (ex guide dogs)

UPNOR   Map 05 TQ77

UPNOR CASTLE

ME2 4XG

➲ (on unclass road off A228)

☎ 01634 718742 & 338110

16th-century gun fort built to protect Elizabeth I's warships. It saw action in 1667, when the Dutch navy sailed up the Medway to attack the dockyard at Cahtham.

Times: Open Apr-Sep, daily 10-6; Oct, daily 10-4. Dates valid until 31 Mar 2004. **Fee:** Telephone for details of admission fees. **Facilities:** 🅿 ⚹ ✖ (ex on leads in certain areas) 🎫

WESTERHAM   Map 05 TQ45

QUEBEC HOUSE

TN16 1TD

➲ (at E end of village on N side of A25 facing junct with B2026 Edenbridge Road.)

☎ 01892 890651 📠 01892 890110

Westerham was the birthplace of General Wolfe, who spent his childhood in this multi-gabled, square brick house, now renamed Quebec House. The house probably dates from the 16th century and was extended and altered in the 17th century. It contains a Wolfe museum and an exhibition on Wolfe and the Quebec campaign.

Times: ✱ Open Apr-Oct, Tue & Sun only 2-6 (last admission 5.30pm). Parties by written arrangement. **Facilities:** 🅿 (150m) ⚹ (tactile items) toilets for disabled ✖ (ex guide dogs) 🐾

SQUERRYES COURT MANOR
HOUSE & GARDENS

TN16 1SJ

➲ (0.5m W of town centre, signposted off A25)

☎ 01959 562345 & 563118 📠 01959 565949

e-mail: squerryes.court@squerryes.co.uk

This beautiful manor house, built in 1681, has been the home of the Wardes since 1731. It contains a fine collection of pictures, furniture, porcelain and tapestries. The lovely garden was landscaped in the 18th century and has a lake, restored formal garden, and woodland walks.

Times: Open Apr-Sep, Wed, Sat, Sun & BH Mon's. Garden open 12-5.30, House 1.30-5.30 (last entry 5pm) **Fee:** ✱ House & grounds £4.80 (ch 14 £2.60 & pen £4.20). Family ticket £12.20. Grounds £3.20 (ch 14 £1.60 & pen £2.70) **Facilities:** 🅿 💺 ⚹ (telephone in advance, part of grounds accessible) toilets for disabled shop ✖ (ex on leads in grounds)

WEST MALLING   Map 05 TQ65

ST LEONARD'S TOWER

ME19 6PE

➲ (on unclass road W of A228)   [FREE]

☎ 01732 870872

Early example of a Norman tower keep, built c.1080 by Gundulf, Bishop of Rochester. The tower stands almost to its original height and takes its name from a chapel dedicated to St Leonard that once stood nearby.

Times: Open any reasonable time for exterior viewing. Contact West Malling Parish Council for interior viewing - 01732 870872.

Facilities: ⚹ ✖ (ex dogs on leads) 🎫

Remember that prices and opening times are liable to change within the currency of this guide. It is always best to telephone in advance to check

LANCASHIRE

Events & Festivals

January
25th Rochdale District Annual Brass Band Contest, Wardle High School, Rochdale

February
15th Action Research Young Entertainment (brass band contest), Blackpool

March
14th Brass Band Championships, Blackpool
26-27th Lancashire Food Festival, Accrington

April
9th-12th Easter Maritime Festival, Lancaster

May
tbc Lancashire Clog-Dancing Festival & Competition, Accrington Town Centre

June
tbc Blackpool Marathon

July
15th-18th Wasted, punk festival, Morcambe
tbc Morecambe Festival of Light & Water
tbc Town Criers Championship

August
3rd-5th Fylde 2004 (folk festival), Fleetwood
30th Lancaster Georgian Festival & National Sedan Chair Carrying Championships

September
3rd-7th Nov Blackpool Illuminations, Promenade from Starr Gate to Bispham
tbc Heritage Gala, including Bradford to Morecambe Historic Vehicle Run
tbc Jazz Festival Lancaster

October
tbc Lancaster Litfest, literary festival
tbc Morecambe Festival of Comedy

November
3rd Sep-7th Blackpool Illuminations, Promenade from Starr Gate to Bispham
tbc Fireworks Spectacular over historic Lancaster & Beacon Lighting
tbc Jacobite Day, Lancaster

December
tbc Annual Lancaster Festival of Christmas Trees

Above: Blackpool Pleasure Beach

BLACKPOOL — Map 07 SD33

Blackpool Zoo Park

East Park Dr FY3 8PP
(M55 junct 4, follow brown tourist signs)
☎ 01253 830830 Fax 01253 830800
e-mail: zookeeper@blackpool-zoo.freeserve.co.uk

This modern zoo, built in 1972, houses over four hundred animals within its 32 acres of landscaped gardens. There is a miniature railway, the chance to ride with dolphins in the 'Swimulator', a children's play area, animal feeding times and keeper talks throughout the day.

Times: Open all year daily, summer 10-6; winter 10-5 or dusk. (Closed 25 Dec). **Fee:** * £7.50 (ch £5.50). Family (2 ad & 2 ch) £24, (2 ad & 3 ch) £29. Concessions for seniors, disabled people, carers and groups are available. **Facilities:** licensed (wheelchair loan, braille factsheets, sensory experiences) toilets for disabled shop

CHARNOCK RICHARD — Map 07 SD51

Camelot Theme Park

PR7 5LP
(from M6 junct 27/28, or M61 junct 8 follow brown tourism signs)
☎ 01257 453044 Fax 01257 452320
e-mail: kingarthur@camelotthemepark.co.uk

With five Magical Lands full of thrilling rides for all ages, like Excalibur 2 a fearsome ride that spins you two ways simultaneously at over 75 feet in the air and Pendragon's Plunge Water Slides plus spectacular shows, including our famous Jousting Tournament. Camelot offers the whole family a full day of excitement and fun.

Times: Open Etr-Oct. Telephone for further details. **Facilities:** (disabled car parking) toilets for disabled shop (ex guide dogs)

CHORLEY — Map 07 SD51

Astley Hall Museum & Art Gallery

Astley Park PR7 1NP
(2m W of Chorley off A581 Southport road)
☎ 01257 515555 Fax 01257 515556
e-mail: astleyhall@lineone.net

A charming Tudor/Stuart building set in beautiful parkland, this lovely Hall retains a comfortable 'lived-in' atmosphere. There are pictures and pottery to see, as well as fine furniture and rare plasterwork ceilings.

Times: * Open Apr-Oct, Tue-Sun 12-5; Nov-Mar Sat-Sun 12-4. **Facilities:** (video of upper floors, print/braille guide, CD audio guide) shop (ex guide dogs)

CLITHEROE — Map 07 SD74

Clitheroe Castle Museum

Castle Gate, Castle St BB7 1BA
(follow Clitheroe signs from A59 by-pass. Museum located in castle grounds near town centre).
☎ 01200 424635
e-mail: museum@ribblevalley.gov.uk

The museum has a good collection of carboniferous fossils, and items of local interest. Displays include local history and the industrial archaeology of the Ribble Valley, while special

continued

features include the restored Hacking ferry boat believed to be the inspiration for "Buckleberry Ferry" featured in JRR Tolkien's *Fellowship of the Ring*, printer's and clogger's shops and Edwardian kitchen. The area is renowned for its early 17th-century witches, and the museum has a small display on witchcraft.

Clitheroe Castle Museum

Times: Open 11-4.30; Mar-Etr, Sat-Wed; Etr-Oct, daily inc BH; Nov, Dec & Feb, wknds & school half terms. (Closed Jan) **Facilities:** P (500yds) (disabled only parking at establishment) & shop ✸ (ex guide dogs)

LANCASTER   Map 07 SD46

CITY MUSEUM (ALSO 15 CASTLE HILL)

Market Sq LA1 1HT

➲ (In city centre just off A6)   `2 for 1`

☎ 01524 64637   ▤ 01524 841692

e-mail: paul.thompson@mus.lancscc.gov.uk

The fine Georgian town hall is the setting for the museum, which explores the history and archaeology of the city from prehistoric and Roman times onwards. Also housed here is the museum of the King's Own Royal Lancaster Regiment. The Cottage Museum, furnished in the style of an artisan's house of around 1820, faces Lancaster Castle.

Times: Open all year, Mon-Sat 10-5, (Closed 25 Dec-1 Jan). 15 Castle Hill, Etr-Sep, daily 2-5. **Fee:** ✱ City Museum free. 15 Castle Hill £1 (concessions 25p). **Facilities:** P (5 mins walk) & (ramp to entrance/ground floor, 2 stairlifts) shop ✸ (ex guide dogs)

LANCASTER MARITIME MUSEUM

St George's Quay LA1 1RB

➲ (close to M6, junct 33 & 34. From A6 follow signs to Lancaster town centre)   `2 for 1`

☎ 01524 64637   ▤ 01524 841692

e-mail: paul.thompson@mus.lancscc.gov.uk

Graceful Ionic columns adorn the front of the Custom House, built in 1764. Inside, the histories of the 18th-century transatlantic maritime trade of Lancaster, the Lancaster Canal and the fishing industry of Morecambe Bay are well illustrated.

Times: Open all year, daily, Etr-Oct 11am-5pm; Nov-Etr 12.30-4pm. **Fee:** ✱ £3 (concessions £1). **Facilities:** P ▣ & (ramped access, lift to all floors, ground floor entry) toilets for disabled shop ✸ (ex guide dogs)

SHIRE HALL

Lancaster Castle, Castle Pde LA1 1YJ

➲ (follow brown tourist signs from M6 junct 33/34)

☎ 01524 64998   ▤ 01524 847914

e-mail: christine.goodier@ property.lancscc.gov.uk

Founded on the site of three Roman forts, Lancaster Castle dominates Castle Hill, above the River Lune. The Norman keep was built in about 1170 and King John added a curtain wall and Hadrian's Tower. The Shire Hall, noted for its Gothic revival design, contains a splendid display of heraldry. The Crown Court was notorious as having handed out the greatest number of death sentences of any court in the land. **Times:** Open daily ex Xmas/New Year 10.30 (1st tour)-4 (last tour). Court sittings permitting -it is advisable to telephone before visiting. **Fee:** ✱ £4 (ch, pen & students £2.50). Family ticket £11. **Facilities:** P (100mtrs) (voucher system) & shop ✸ (ex guide dogs) ▰

LEIGHTON HALL   Map 07 SD47

LEIGHTON HALL

LA5 9ST

➲ (off M6 at junct 35 onto A6 & follow signs)

☎ 01524 734474   ▤ 01524 720357

e-mail: info@leightonhall.co.uk

Early Gillow furniture is displayed among other treasures in the fine interior of this neo-Gothic mansion. Outside a large collection of birds of prey can be seen, and flying displays are given each afternoon. There are also fine gardens, a maze and a woodland walk.

Times: Open May-Sep, Sun, Tue-Fri & BH Mon from 2pm. For Aug only open from 12.30. (Last admission 4.30pm). **Fee:** £5 (ch 5-16 £3.50, pen & student £4.50). Family ticket £15. **Facilities:** P ▣ & shop garden centre ✸ (ex guide dogs & in park)

LEYLAND   Map 07 SD52

BRITISH COMMERCIAL VEHICLE MUSEUM

King St PR5 1LE

➲ (0.75m from junct 28 M6, in town centre)

☎ 01772 451011   ▤ 01772 623404

A unique line-up of historic commercial vehicles and buses spanning a century of truck and bus building. There are more than 50 exhibits on permanent display.

Times: Open Apr-Sep, Sun, Tue-Thu & BH Mons (Oct open Sun only). **Fee:** £4 (ch & pen £2). Family ticket (2 ad & 3 ch) £10. **Facilities:** P ▣ & (ramps to decked viewing area) toilets for disabled shop ✸ (ex guide dogs)

MARTIN MERE   Map 07 SD41

WWT MARTIN MERE

L40 0TA

➲ (signposted from M61, M58 &M6, 6m from Ormskirk, off A59)

☎ 01704 895181   ▤ 01704 892343   `2 for 1`

e-mail: info@martinmere.co.uk

One of Britain's most important wetland sites, where you can get really close to a variety of ducks, geese and swans from all over the world as well as two flocks of flamingos. Thousands of wildfowl, including pink-footed geese, Bewick's and Whooper swans, winter here. Other features include a children's adventure playground, exhibition gallery,

continued

craft area and an educational centre. The Annual North West Bird Fair takes place during November and wild swans by floodlight from 1st November to 31st January.
Times: Open all year, daily 9.30-5.30 (5 in winter). (Closed 25 Dec).
Fee: ✱ £5.50 (ch £3.30, pen £4.50). Family ticket £14.50.
Facilities: 🅿 💷 ♿ (wheelchair loan, Braille trail, heated hide, audio tours) toilets for disabled shop ✖ (ex guide dogs) 🍴

PADIHAM   Map 07 SD73

GAWTHORPE HALL
BB12 8UA
⮑ (off A671)
☎ 01282 771004 📠 01282 770178
e-mail: rpmgaw@smtp.ntrust.org.uk

An early 17th-century manor house, built around Britain's most southerly pele tower, restored in 1850. A collection of portraits from the National Portrait Gallery and the Kay Shuttleworth Collections of costume, embroidery and lace are on show in the expanded exhibition areas.
Times: ✱ Open 31 Mar-Oct, Garden: daily 10-6. Hall: Tue-Thu, Sat & Sun 1-5. Also open BH Mon & Good Fri. (Last admission 4.30).
Facilities: 🅿 💷 ♿ toilets for disabled shop ✖ (ex in grounds) 🐾

PRESTON   Map 07 SD52

HARRIS MUSEUM & ART GALLERY
Market Square PR1 2PP
⮑ (exit M6 at junct 31, follow signs for Preston city centre)
☎ 01772 258248 📠 01772 886764   FREE
e-mail: harris.museum@preston.gov.uk

An impressive grade 1 listed Greek Revival building containing extensive collections of fine and decorative art including a gallery of Clothes and Fashion. The Story of Preston covers the city's history and the lively exhibition programmes of contemporary art and social history are accompanied by events and activities throughout the year.
Times: Open all year, Mon-Sat 10-5, Sun 11-4. (Closed BHs).
Facilities: 🅿 (5 mins walk) (blue badge disabled parking only) 💷 ♿ (Wheelchair available. Chair lift to mezzanine galleries) toilets for disabled shop ✖ (ex guide/assistance dogs) 🍴

THE NATIONAL FOOTBALL MUSEUM
Sir Tom Finney Way, Deepdale PR1 6RY
⮑ (2m from M6 juncts 31, 31A or 32. Follow brown tourist signs in Preston)
☎ 01772 908442 📠 01772 908433
e-mail: enquiries@nationalfootballmuseum.com

What location could be more fitting for a National Football Museum than Deepdale Stadium, the home of Preston North End, first winners of the professional football league in 1888-9? This fascinating trip through football past and present includes the FIFA Museum Collection, a fine display of memorabilia and artefacts; interactive displays that allow visitors to commentate on matches, and take virtual trips to every League ground in the country; and an art gallery dedicated to the Beautiful Game.
Times: ✱ Open Tue-Sat 10-5, Sun 11-5. (Closed Mon ex BH's). Contact for opening times on match days. **Facilities:** 🅿 💷 ♿ (Lifts, multi-sensory exhibitions) toilets for disabled shop ✖ (ex guide dogs) 🍴

ROSSENDALE   Map 07 SD72

WHITAKER PARK & ROSSENDALE MUSEUM
Whitaker Park, Haslingden Rd, Rawtenstall BB4 6RE
⮑ (off A681, 0.25m W of Rawtenstall centre)
☎ 01706 244682 📠 01706 250037

Former mill owner's house, built in 1840 and set in the delightful Whitaker Park. Displays include fine and decorative arts, a Victorian drawing room, natural history, costume, local and social history.
Times: Open Mon-Fri, 1-5; Sat 10-5 (Apr-Oct), 10-4 (Nov-Mar); Sun noon-5 (Apr-Oct), noon-4 (Nov-Mar). BH's 1-5. (Closed 24-26 Dec & 1 Jan). **Facilities:** 🅿 ♿ (large print, audio guides, induction loop) toilets for disabled shop ✖ (ex guide dogs)

RUFFORD   Map 07 SD41

RUFFORD OLD HALL
L40 1SG
⮑ (off A59, 7m North of Ormskirk)
☎ 01704 821254 📠 01704 821254

There is a story that William Shakespeare performed here for the owner Sir Thomas Hesketh in the magnificent Great Hall. Built in 1530, it was the Hesketh family seat for the next 250 years. The Carolean Wing, altered in 1821, features fine collections of 16th and 17th-century oak furniture, arms, armour and tapestries.
Times: Open 12 Apr-late Oct, Sat-Wed. Hall 1-5 (last admission 4.30pm). Garden, restaurant & shop 11-5. **Fee:** ✱ House and garden: £4.30 (ch £2). Family ticket £10.50. Groups £2.75 each. Garden only £2 (ch £1). No groups Sun and BH Mon. **Facilities:** 🅿 ✖ licensed ♿ (braille guide, wheelchairs, large print guide) toilets for disabled shop 🐾

SAMLESBURY   Map 07 SD53

SAMLESBURY HALL
Preston New Rd PR5 0UP (M6 junct 31/A677 for 3m)
☎ 01254 812010 & 812229 📠 01254 812174
e-mail: samlesburyhall@btconnect.co.uk

A well restored half-timbered manor house, built during the 14th and 15th centuries, and set in 5 acres of beautiful grounds. Sales of antiques and collector's items, craft shows and temporary exhibitions are held all year round.
Times: Open all year, daily, 11-4.30. Closed 25-26 Dec and on Sat for weddings, newer part of hall open Sat for antiques sales **Fee:** ✱ £3 (ch 4-16 £1). **Facilities:** 🅿 💷 ✖ licensed ♿ toilets for disabled garden centre ✖ (ex guide dogs) 🍴

SILVERDALE   Map 07 SD47

RSPB NATURE RESERVE
Myers Farm LA5 0SW
⮑ (M6 junct 35, head west on A501(M) for 0.5m to end. Turn right and head N on A6. Follow brown tourist signs)
☎ 01524 701601 📠 01524 701601
e-mail: leighton.moss@rspb.org.uk

A large reed swamp with meres with willow and alder scrub in a valley with woodland on its limestone slopes. The reserve covers 321 acres, and is home to the North West's largest concentration of bitterns, together with bearded tits, reed, sedge and grasshopper warblers, shovelers, pochards, tufted ducks and marsh harriers. Black terns and ospreys regularly pass through in spring and greenshanks and

continued

various sandpipers in the autumn. Wintering wildfowl include large flocks of mallards, teals, wigeons, and shovelers.

Times: Reserve: open daily 9am-Dusk (or sunset if earlier). Visitor Centre daily 9.30-5. Feb-Oct 9.30-4.30 Nov-Jan. Closed 25 Dec.

Fee: £4.50 (ch £1, concessions £3) Family £9. RSPB members Free

Facilities: 🅿 ➡ ✕ ♿ (Stairlift available to tea room) toilets for disabled shop ✖ (ex guide dogs) 🍽

TURTON BOTTOMS   Map 07 SD71

TURTON TOWER

BL7 0HG (on B6391, off A666 or A676)

☎ 01204 852203   🖷 01204 853759

e-mail: turtontower.lcc@btinternet.com

A historic house incorporating a 15th-century tower house and Elizabethan half-timbered buildings, and displaying a major collection of carved wood furniture. During the 19th century, the house became associated with the Gothic revival and later typified the idealism of the Arts and Crafts movement. The gardens are being restored in late-Victorian style. The exhibition gallery houses three exhibitions per season, usually consisting of one high profile, one by regional artists and finally a touring show from elsewhere in the country.

Times: Open May-Sep, Mon-Thu 11-5, wknds 1-5; Mar-Oct, Mon-Wed 1-5, wknds 1-4; Apr Sat-Wed 1-5; Nov & Feb, Sun 1-4. Other times by prior arrangement. **Facilities:** 🅿 ➡ ♿ toilets for disabled shop ✖ (ex in grounds) 🍽

WHALLEY   Map 07 SD73

WHALLEY ABBEY

BB7 9SS

➲ (Just off A59 4m S of Clitheroe).

☎ 01254 828400   🖷 01254 828401

The ruins of a 14th-century Cistercian abbey, set in the delightful gardens of the Blackburn Diocesan Retreat and Conference House, a 17th-century manor house with gardens reaching down to the River Calder. The remains include two gateways, a chapter house and the abbot's lodgings and kitchen.

Times: ✱ Grounds open all year; coffee shop, shop & exhibition area, Jan-Dec daily 11-5. (Closed 24 & 25 Dec 2002 & 6-9 Jan 2003).

Facilities: 🅿 ➡ ✕ licensed ♿ (chair lifts, ramps) toilets for disabled shop ✖ (ex guide dogs)

LEICESTERSHIRE

EVENTS & FESTIVALS

February
6th-15th Comedy Festival, Leicester

May
2nd-3rd Leicestershire County Show, Dishley Grange, Loughborough
8th Heart Link Street Organ Festival, various venues, Leicester (provisional)
22nd-12th Jun Leicester Early Music Festival

June
22nd May-12th Leicester Early Music Festival
tbc International Music Festival, Leicester

July
tbc Belgrave Mela, Abbey Park, Leicester

August
6th-8th Leicestershire Country Music Festival, Sapcote Playing Fields
7th Caribbean Carnival, Victoria Park, Leicester
tbc Abbey Park Music Festival, Leicester
tbc Castle Park Festival, Leicester
tbc City of Leicester Horticultural Show

October
tbc Dashera, Hindu festival, Leicester
tbc Navrati, Asian religious festival, Leicester

October/November
tbc Diwali Celebrations, Leicester

November
tbc Abbey Park Bonfire & Fireworks Display

Above: Carvings on the Clock Tower, Leicester
Top: Ruins of Lord Hastings' manor,
Ashby-de-la-Zouch

ASHBY-DE-LA-ZOUCH Map 08 SK31

ASHBY-DE-LA-ZOUCH CASTLE
South St LE65 1BR
☎ 01530 413343
Impressive ruins of a late medieval castle. The magnificent 24 metre Hastings Tower offers panoramic views of the surrounding countryside. Ashby was used for the famous jousting scene in Sir Walter Scott's classic romance *Ivanhoe*.
Times: Open Apr-Sep, daily 10-6; Oct, daily 10-5; Nov-Mar, Wed-Sun 10-4. (Closed 24-26 Dec & 1 Jan). Dates valid until 31 Mar 2004.
Fee: £3.20 (ch £1.60, concessions £2.40). Prices valid until 31 Mar 2004. **Facilities:** 🅿 & shop ✖ (ex on leads) ✿

BELVOIR Map 08 SK83

BELVOIR CASTLE
NG32 1PD
➲ (between A52 & A607, follow the brown heritage signs from A1, A52, A607 & A46)
☎ 01476 871007 📠 01476 871018   2 for 1
e-mail: info@belvoircastle.com
Although Belvoir Castle has been the home of the Dukes of Rutland for many centuries, the turrets, battlements, towers and pinnacles of the house are a 19th-century fantasy. Amongst the many treasures to be seen inside are paintings by Murillo, Holbein and other famous artists. Also here is the museum of the Queens Royal Lancers. Lovingly restored gardens are also open to visitors. Special events planned every weekend throughout the season, phone for details.
Times: Open 16-20 Feb; 1 Apr-30 Sep, daily (closed Mon & Thu); Mar & Oct Sun only. **Fee:** £8 (ch £5 pen £7). **Facilities:** 🅿 💷 ✖ licensed & (permitted to be driven/drive right up to castle entrance) toilets for disabled shop ✖ (ex guide dogs) 🍴

CASTLE DONINGTON Map 08 SK42

DONINGTON GRAND PRIX COLLECTION
Donington Park DE74 2RP
➲ (2m from M1 junct 23a/24 and M42/A42 close to Nottingham Derby and Leicester)
☎ 01332 811027 📠 01332 812829
e-mail: enquiries@doningtoncollection.co.uk
From the turn of the twentieth century to the new millennium, it's all here. The largest collection of Mclaren racing cars on public display. The worlds only complete collection of the famous Racing Green Vanwalls, every William F1 car from 1983 to 1999, a superb BRM display, more rare four wheel drive racing cars than you'll see anywhere else, Ferraris driven by Asvar; and Ickx, Senna's winning McLaren from the 1993 European Grand Prix at Donington, Stirling Moss's Lotus which defeated the might of the works Ferraris at Monaco in 1961, Jim Clark's beautiful Lotus 25, Ronnie Peterson's Unique six wheel Tyrell, together with several other examples of his famous marque-including Jacky Stewart's Tyrell 001, they're all here, and many, many more.
Times: Open daily 10-5 (last admission 4pm). Open later on race days. (Closed over Xmas period - telephone to confirm opening times over this period). **Facilities:** 🅿 💷 ✖ licensed & shop ✖ (ex guide dogs) 🍴

COALVILLE Map 08 SK41

SNIBSTON DISCOVERY PARK
County Hall LE3 8TB
➲ (4.5m from M1 junct 22/2m or from A42/M42 junct 13 on A511 on the West side of Coalville)
☎ 01530 278444 📠 01530 813301   2 for 1
e-mail: snibston@leics.gov.uk
At Leicestershire's all-weather science and industry museum, visitors can try to solve over 50 hands-on experiments, or explore our rich heritage in the Transport, Extractive, Engineering and Textile and Fashion Galleries. Ex-miners give tours of Snibston's colliery buildings, and kids can let off steam in the outdoor science and water playgrounds.
Times: Open all year, 10-5 (Closed 12-16 Jan & 25-26 Dec). **Fee:** £5.50 (ch £3.50, concessions £3.75). Family ticket £15. Party. **Facilities:** 🅿 💷 & (Braille labels, touch tables, parking available) toilets for disabled shop ✖ (ex guide dogs) 🍴

DONINGTON-LE-HEATH Map 05 SK41

DONINGTON-LE-HEATH MANOR HOUSE
Manor Rd LE67 2FW
➲ (S of Coalville)
☎ 01530 831259 📠 01530 831259   FREE
e-mail: museum@leics.gov.uk
This is a rare example of a medieval manor house, tracing its history back to about 1280. It has now been restored as a period house, with fine oak furnishings. The surrounding grounds include period gardens, and the adjoining stone barn houses a restaurant.
Times: Open Apr-Sep, 11-5; Oct, Nov & Mar 11-3. Dec-Feb wknds only **Facilities:** 🅿 💷 ✖ & shop ✖ (ex guide dogs)

KIRBY MUXLOE Map 04 SK50

KIRBY MUXLOE CASTLE
Oakcroft Av LE9 9MD
➲ (off B5380)
☎ 01162 386886
A picturesque, moated, brick-built castle begun in 1480 by William, Lord Hastings who was executed by Richard III in 1483. Work stopped and the castle stands much as Hastings left it.
Times: Open Apr-Oct, wknds & BH's only 12-5. Dates valid until 31 Mar 2004. **Fee:** £2.20 (ch £1.10, concessions £1.70). Prices valid until 31 Mar 2004. **Facilities:** 🅿 shop ✖ ✿

LEICESTER Map 04 SK50

ABBEY PUMPING STATION
Corporation Rd, Abbey Ln LE4 5PX
➲ (off A6, 1m N from city centre)   FREE
☎ 0116 299 5111 📠 0116 299 5125
Built as a sewage pumping station in 1891, this fascinating museum features some of the largest steam beam engines in the country, and an exhibition on the history and technology of toilets, water and hygiene. There are also a steam shovel and a passenger carrying a narrow gauge railway.
Times: Open Apr-Sep, Mon-Sat 10-5, Sun 1-5; Oct-Mar, Mon-Sat 10-4, Sun 1-4 (Closed 24-26 & 31 Dec-1 Jan). **Facilities:** 🅿 & (loan of wheelchairs, wheelchair lift) toilets for disabled shop ✖ (ex guide dogs) 🍴

BELGRAVE HALL & GARDENS
Church Rd, off Thurcaston Rd, Belgrave LE4 5PE
➲ (off Belgrave/Loughborough road, 1m from city centre)
☎ 0116 266 6590 📠 0116 261 3063 FREE

A delightful three-storey Queen Anne house dating from 1709 with beautiful period and botanic gardens. Authentic room settings contrast Georgian elegance with Victorian cosiness and include the kitchen, drawing room, music room and nursery.
Times: Open all year, Apr-Sep, Mon-Sat 10-5, Sun 1-5; Oct-Mar, Mon-Sat 10-4, Sun 1-4. Closed 24-26 Dec & 31 Dec-1 Jan. **Facilities:** 🅿 🚻 (loan of wheelchair) toilets for disabled shop ✖ (ex guide dogs)

THE GUILDHALL
Guildhall Ln LE1 5FQ
➲ (Next to Leicester Cathedral)
☎ 0116 253 2569 📠 0116 253 9626

A preserved medieval building dating back to the 14th century, The Guildhall is the city's oldest building still in use. Over the centuries it has served as the Hall of the Guild of Corpus Christi, the Civic Centre and Town Hall, a judicial centre for court sessions and home to Leicester's first police force. The Guildhall now houses one of the oldest libraries in the country, as well as hosting events, activities and performances.
Times: Open all year: Apr-Sep, Mon-Sat 10-5, Sun 1-5; Oct-Mar, Mon-Sat 10-4, Sun 1-4. (Closed 24-26 Dec & 1 Jan) **Fee:** Admission free. Donations welcome. **Facilities:** 🅿 (100yds) 🚻 🚻 wheelchair loan, induction loop, voice minicom toilets for disabled shop ✖ (ex guide dogs) 🦮

JEWRY WALL MUSEUM & SITE
St Nicholas Circle LE1 4LB
➲ (opposite The Holiday Inn)
☎ 0116 225 4971 📠 0116 225 4966

Behind the massive fragment of the Roman Jewry wall and a Roman Baths site of the 2nd century AD is the Museum of Leicestershire Archaeology, which covers finds from the earliest times to the Middle Ages.
Times: Open Apr-Sep, Mon-Sat 10-5, Sun 1-5; Oct-Mar, Mon-Sat 10-4, Sun 1-4 (Closed 24-26 Dec & 1 Dec-1 Jan). **Fee:** ✱ Admission free, however a charge is made for some events. Donations welcome. **Facilities:** 🅿 (300yds) (limited on-street parking) 🚻 toilets for disabled shop ✖ (ex guide dogs)

LEICESTERSHIRE MUSEUM & ART GALLERY
53 New Walk LE1 7EA
➲ (situated on New Walk. Access by car from A6 onto Waterloo way at Railway Stn. Right into Regent Rd, right onto West St, right onto Princess Rd which leads to car park) FREE
☎ 0116 225 4900 📠 0116 225 4927

This major regional venue houses local and national collections. There's an internationally famous collection of German Expressionism and other displays include the Rutland Dinosaur and the Egyptian Gallery. An Extensive Natural History collection augmented by art from the renaissance to contemporary.
Times: Open all year, Apr-Sep, Mon-Sat 10-5, Sun 1-5. Oct-Mar, Mon-Sat 10-4, Sun 1-4. (Closed 24-26 Dec & 31 Dec-1 Jan). **Facilities:** 🅿 🚻 🚻 (wheelchairs for loan, minicom, induction loop) toilets for disabled shop ✖ (ex guide dogs) 🦮

NATIONAL SPACE CENTRE
Exploration Dr LE4 5NS
➲ (off A6, 2m N of city centre)
☎ 0116 261 0261 📠 0116 258 2100
e-mail: info@spacecentre.co.uk

Offering five themed galleries, cutting-edge audio-visual technology and glimpses into genuine space research, the National Space Centre is a unique experience. Learn about the planets, astronaut life, weather forecasting, space-stations and satellites. Visit the Space Theatre and the Newsdesk, and take a look at the scientists and astronomers doing genuine research in the Space Science Research Unit.
Times: ✱ Open all year, Tue-Fri 9.30-last entry 4pm, Sat-Sun 9.30-4.30. School holidays, Mon 12-4.30 & Tue-Sun 9.30-4.30. **Facilities:** 🅿 🚻 ✖ licensed 🚻 toilets for disabled shop ✖ (ex guide dogs) 🦮

NEWARKE HOUSES
The Newarke LE2 7BY
➲ (opposite De Montfort University) FREE
☎ 0116 225 4980 📠 0116 225 4982

This museum follows Leicestershire's social history from the 15th century to the present, showing everyday life and social change throughout the county. Clocks, toys, domestic objects, greetings cards and Asian arts are among the many collections. A reconstructed street scene gives a glimpse of Victorian life and the fascinating story of Daniel Lambert, the famous 52-stone gaoler of the 18th century, is also told.
Times: Open Apr-Sep, Mon-Sat 10-5, Sun 1-5; Oct-Mar, Mon-Sat 10-4, Sun 1-4 (Closed 24-26 Dec & 31 Dec-1 Jan). **Facilities:** 🅿 (200yds) 🚻 (car parking can be arranged) shop ✖ (ex guide dogs)

THE RECORD OFFICE FOR LEICESTERSHIRE & RUTLAND
Long St, Wigston Magna LE18 2AH
➲ (Old A50, S of Leicester City)
☎ 0116 257 1080 📠 0116 257 1120 FREE
e-mail: museums@leics.gov.uk

Housed in a converted 19th-century school in Wigston, the Record Office holds photographs, electoral registers and archive film, files of local newspapers, history tapes and sound recordings, all of which can be studied.
Times: Open all year, Mon, Tue & Thu 9.15-5, Wed 9.15-7.30, Fri 9.15-4.45, Sat 9.15-12.15. (Closed Sun & BH wknds Sat-Tue). **Facilities:** 🅿 🚻 toilets for disabled ✖ (ex guide dogs) 🚲

UNIVERSITY OF LEICESTER HAROLD MARTIN BOTANIC GARDEN
Beaumont Hall, Stoughton Dr South, Oadby LE2 2NA
➲ (3m SE A6, entrance at 'The Knoll', Glebe Rd, Oadby)
☎ 0116 271 7725

The grounds of four houses, now used as student residences and not open to the public, make up this 16-acre garden. A great variety of plants in different settings provide a delightful place to walk, including rock, water and sunken gardens, trees, borders, heathers and glasshouses.
Times: Open Mon-Fri 10-4 (ex 25-26 Dec & 1 Jan), Sat & Sun 10-4 (from 3rd weekend in Mar to 2nd weekend in Nov inclusive). **Facilities:** 🅿 (adjacent) 🚻 toilets for disabled ✖ (ex guide dogs)

LOUGHBOROUGH
GREAT CENTRAL RAILWAY
Great Central Rd LE11 1RW
➲ (signposted from A6)
☎ 01509 230726 📠 01509 239791
e-mail: booking_office@gcrailway.co.uk

Map 08 SK51

This private steam railway runs over eight miles from Loughborough Central to Leicester North, with all trains calling at Quorn & Woodhouse and Rothley. The locomotive depot and museum are at Loughborough Central. A buffet car runs on most trains.
Times: Open all year Sat, Sun & BH Mon & daily during 17-20 Feb, 12-16 Apr, 1 Jun-27 Aug. **Fee:** ✱ Runabout (all day unlimited travel) £11 (ch & pen £7.50). Family ticket £25. **Facilities:** 🅿 💻 ✗ licensed ♿ (disabled coach available on most trains, check beforehand) toilets for disabled shop 🍴

MARKET BOSWORTH
THE BATTLEFIELD LINE
Shackerstone Station, Shackerstone, Nuneaton CV13 6NW
➲ (from A444/A447 take B585 to Market Bosworth and follow signs for Congerstone/Shackerstone. Follow brown tourist signs from M42 Junct 11).
☎ 01827 880754 📠 01827 881050
e-mail: robertlep@aol.com

Map 04 SK40

Together with a regular railway service (mainly steam) from Shackerstone to Shenton, there is an extensive railway museum featuring a collection of rolling stock and many other relics from the age of steam.
Times: Open all year, Passenger steam train service operates Apr-Oct, Sat, Sun & BH Mon. Heritage Railcar Wed Jul-Aug **Facilities:** 🅿 💻 ✗ ♿ toilets for disabled shop 🍴

BOSWORTH BATTLEFIELD VISITOR CENTRE & COUNTRY PARK
Ambion Hill, Sutton Cheney CV13 0AD
➲ (follow brown tourist signs from A447, A444 & A5)
☎ 01455 290429 📠 01455 292841
e-mail: bosworth@leics.gov.uk

The Battle of Bosworth Field was fought in 1485 between the armies of Richard III and the future Henry VII. The visitor

continued

centre offers a comprehensive interpretation of the battle, with exhibitions, models and a film theatre. Special medieval attractions are held in the summer months.

Times: ✱ Open all year, Country Park and Battle Trails daily 11-5. Nov & Dec Sun 11-dusk; Mar wknds 11-5. Visitor Centre open Apr-Oct. Parties all year by arrangement. **Facilities:** 🅿 (charged) 💻 ♿ (wheelchair & electric scooter hire, tactile exhibits) toilets for disabled shop 🍴

MOIRA
CONKERS
Millennium Av, Rawdon Rd DE12 6GA
➲ (located on B5003 in Moira, signposted from A444 and A42)
☎ 01283 216633 📠 01283 210321
e-mail: info@visitconkers.com

Map 08 SK31

Conkers, located at the heart of the National Forest, is a unique mix of indoor and outdoor hands on experiences. Indoors at the Discovery Centre there are 4 discovery zones designed for children and adults of all ages where you can get really close to the forest and experience its life and energy - for example see the world through the eyes of a spider or crawl through a living leaf. At Waterside, a new indoor play centre for children and the Gallery Restaurant have just opened. Visitors can travel between the centres on a miniature railway. Outdoors there are 23 different activities including nature trails, an assault course, playgrounds and mazes.
Times: Open daily, summer 10-6, winter 10-5. (Closed 25 Dec).
Fee: ✱ £5.50 (ch £3.50, concessions £4.50). Family ticket (2 ad & 2 ch) £15.95. **Facilities:** 🅿 💻 ✗ licensed ♿ (multi access walks & trails accessible to wheelchairs) toilets for disabled shop garden centre ✗ (ex guide dogs) 🍴

SWINFORD
STANFORD HALL
LE17 6DH
➲ (7.5m NE of Rugby, 1.5m from Swinford. 2m from the M1, M6, A14 junct)
☎ 01788 860250 📠 01788 860870
e-mail: enquiries@stanfordhall.co.uk

Map 04 SP57

A beautiful William and Mary house, built in 1697 by Sir Roger Cave, ancestor of the present owner. The house contains antique furniture, paintings (including the Stuart

continued

Collection) and family costumes. Special events include car and motorcycle owners' club rallies.

Times: Open Etr Sun-end Sep, Sun & BH Mon 1.30-5; grounds open noon on BH & earlier on Event Days. Open any day or evening during season for pre-booked parties of 20+. **Fee:** House & Grounds £5 (ch £2); Grounds only £3 (ch £1); Motorcycle Museum £1 (ch 35p). Party 20+ £4.75 each. **Facilities:** 🅿 ⬛ ♿ (please contact for details) toilets for disabled shop ✖ (ex guide dogs & in park)

TWYCROSS
Map 04 SK30

TWYCROSS ZOO PARK
CV9 3PX
➲ (On A444 Burton to Nuneaton road, directly off M42 Junct 11)
☎ 01827 880250 📄 01827 880700

Set in 50 acres of parkland, the zoo is home to around 1000 animals, most of which are endangered species. Twycross is the only zoo in Britain to house Bonobos - humans' 'closest living relative'. There are also various other animals such as lions, elephants and giraffes, and a pets' corner for younger children. Other attractions include a Penguin Pool with underwater viewing and a Children's Adventure Playground. **Times:** Open all year, daily 10-6 (4pm in winter). (Closed 25 Dec). **Fee:** ✱ Please telephone for prices. **Facilities:** 🅿 (charged) ⬛ ♿ toilets for disabled shop ✖ (ex guide dogs) 🍴

FREE
Attractions with this symbol do not charge for entry.

LINCOLNSHIRE

EVENTS & FESTIVALS

January
  25th The Great Australian Breakfast (celebrating Australia Day), Lawn Visitor Centre, Lincoln

April
  4th Lincoln 10km Run (provisional)

May
  1st-3rd Spalding Flower Parade & Springfields Country Fair
  28th-31st Folk Festival, Cleethorpes
  tbc Lincoln Grand Prix Cycle Race

June
  19th-20th Royal Air Force Waddington International Air Show, RAF Waddington
  23rd-24th Lincolnshire Show, Lincolnshire Showground, Grange-de-Lings, Lincoln

July
  24th-25th Heckington Show, Estate Showground, Heckington (provisional)
  tbc Lincoln Water Carnival, Brayford Pool

August
  21st-22nd Lincolnshire Steam & Vintage Rally, Lincolnshire Showground, Grange-de-Lings, Lincoln

November
  tbc Bonfire night celebrations, Cleethorpes

December
  tbc Lincoln Christmas Market, Up-Hill, Lincoln

Above: Wesleyan Chapel, New York
Top: St Botolph's steeple by the River Haven, Boston

BELTON — Map 08 SK93

BELTON HOUSE PARK & GARDENS
NG32 2LS
➥ (3m NE Grantham on A607)
☎ 01476 566116 🖷 01476 579071
e-mail: belton@nationaltrust.org.uk

The ground floor of the house has a succession of state rooms, with the Marble Hall as its centrepiece. Splendid furnishings and decorations throughout the house include tapestries and hangings, family portraits, porcelain and fine furniture.
Times: Open 29 Mar-2 Nov, Wed-Sun & BH Mon. House open 12.30-5 (last admission 4.30). Garden & Park open 11-5.30, 10.30-5.30 in Aug. Garden open 8 Nov-21 Dec, Sat & Sun 12-4. **Fee:** ✱ £5.80 (ch £2.90). Family ticket £14.50. **Facilities:** 🅿 ✗ licensed க (braille guide, hearing scheme, audio guide) toilets for disabled shop ✕ (ex in grounds) ✍

CLEETHORPES — Map 08 TA30

PLEASURE ISLAND FAMILY THEME PARK
Kings Rd DN35 0PL
➥ (Follow signs to Pleasure Island from A180)
☎ 01472 211511 🖷 01472 211087   **2 for 1**
e-mail: pleasureisland@btinternet.com

Pleasure Island is packed with over seventy rides and attractions. Hold on tight as the colossal wheel of steel rockets you into the sky at a G-force of 2.5, then hurtles you around 360 degrees, sending riders into orbit and giving the sensation of complete weightlessness. It's not just grown ups and thrill seekers who are catered for at Pleasure Island. For youngsters there's hours of fun in Tinkaboo Town, an indoor themed area full of rides and attractions.
Times: Open 6 Apr-7 Sep, daily from 10. Plus wknds during Sep-Oct & daily during half term (25 Oct-2 Nov). **Fee:** ✱ £11.50 (ch under 4 free, pen £7.50). **Facilities:** 🅿 ✗ licensed க toilets for disabled shop ✍

CONINGSBY — Map 08 TF25

BATTLE OF BRITAIN MEMORIAL FLIGHT VISITOR CENTRE
LN4 4SY
➥ (on A153)
☎ 01526 344041 🖷 01526 342330   **2 for 1**
e-mail: bbmf@lincolnshire.gov.uk

View the aircraft of the Battle of Britain Memorial Flight, comprising the only flying Lancaster in Europe, five Spitfires, two Hurricanes, a Dakota and two Chipmunks. Because of operational commitments, specific aircraft may not be available. Ring for information before planning a visit.
Times: Open all year, Mon-Fri, conducted tours 10-3.30. (Closed 2 wks Xmas). (Phone prior to visiting to check security situation) **Fee:** ✱ Free entry to visitor centre, charge for guided tour. **Facilities:** 🅿 ✗ க (electric wheelchairs not allowed in hangar) toilets for disabled shop ✕ (ex guide dogs) ✍

> The AA also publishes a guide to Pet Friendly Places to Stay

EPWORTH — Map 08 SE70

OLD RECTORY
1 Rectory St DN9 1HX
➥ (on A161, 3m S of M180 junct 2)
☎ 01427 872268
e-mail: curator@epswortholdrectory.org.uk

John and Charles Wesley were brought up in this handsome rectory, built in 1709. Maintained by the World Methodist Council as 'The Home of the Wesleys', the house displays items which belonged to John and Charles Wesley and their parents Samuel and Susanna. The house is a registered museum.
Times: Open daily Mar-Oct, Mon-Sat 10-12 & 2-4, Sun 2-4 (only in Mar, Apr & Oct) May-Sep Mon-Sat 10-4.30. Sun 2-4.30. Other times by prior arrangement. **Facilities:** 🅿 ✗ க shop ✕ (ex guide dogs) ✍

GAINSBOROUGH — Map 08 SK88

GAINSBOROUGH OLD HALL
Parnell St DN21 2NB
➥ (turn off A1 onto A57 to Gainsborough. Follow brown heritage signs in city centre. Old Hall is adjacent to town centre.)
☎ 01427 612669 🖷 01427 612779   **2 for 1**
e-mail: gainsboroughholdhall@lincolnshire.gov.uk

A complete medieval manor house dating back to 1460-80 and containing a remarkable Great Hall and original kitchen with a variety of room settings. Richard III, Henry VIII, the Mayflower Pilgrims and John Wesley all visited the Old Hall.
Times: Open all year, Mon-Sat 10-5; Etr-Oct, Sun 2-5.30. (Closed 24-26 & 31 Dec & 1 Jan). **Fee:** ✱ £2.60 (concession £1.50). Family ticket (2 ad & 3 ch) £6.70. **Facilities:** 🅿 (100yds) (unrestricted parking 100yds from Hall) க (audio tour, induction loop, wheelchair for visitors use) ✕ (ex guide dogs)

GRIMSBY — Map 08 TA20

NATIONAL FISHING HERITAGE CENTRE
Alexandra Dock DN31 1UZ
➥ (follow signs off M180)
☎ 01472 323345 🖷 01472 323555

Sign on as a crew member for a journey of discovery, and experience the harsh reality of life on board a deep sea trawler built inside the Centre. Through interactive games and displays, your challenge is to navigate the icy waters of the Arctic in search of the catch.
Times: ✱ Open Apr-Sep, Mon-Thu 10-4, Sat-Sun 11-5 (10.30-5.30 Jul-Sep). **Facilities:** 🅿 க (easy access route) toilets for disabled shop ✕ (ex guide dogs) ✍

GRIMSTHORPE — Map 08 TF02

GRIMSTHORPE CASTLE
PE10 0NB
➥ (on A151, 8m E of Colsterworth rbt on A1)
☎ 01778 591205 🖷 01778 591259   **2 for 1**
e-mail: ray@grimsthorpe.co.uk

Seat of the Willoughby de Eresby family since 1516, the
continued

castle has a medieval tower and a Tudor quadrangular house with a Baroque north front by Vanbrugh. There are eight state rooms and two picture galleries, and an important collection of furniture, pictures and tapestries.
Times: Open early Apr-late Sep, Sun, Thu & BH Mon. Daily in Aug ex Fri & Sat. Park & Gardens 11-6, Castle 1-5 (last admission 4.30). **Fee:** ✱ Park & Gardens £3 (ch £2, concessions £2.50). Combined ticket £6.50 with castle (ch £3.50, concessions £5.50). **Facilities:** P ◪ ✗ licensed ⅋ toilets for disabled shop ◥

HECKINGTON   Map 08 TF14

THE PEAROOM
Station Yard, Station Rd NG34 9JJ
➲ (4m E of Sleaford, off A17)
☎ 01529 460765 ▤ 01529 460948

The Pearoom has a craft shop, galleries and workshops for ten resident craft workers. Their products include pottery, textiles and calligraphy; and also there is a weaver-feltmaker. An active programme of craft exhibitions runs throughout the year accompanied by a programme of weekend course activities. A commissioning centre shows the work of many local makers willing to work to commission.
Times: ✱ Open all year, Mon-Sat & BHs 10-5, Sun 12-5. **Facilities:** P ◪ ⅋ toilets for disabled shop ✘ (ex guide dogs)

LINCOLN   Map 08 SK97

GREYFRIARS EXHIBITION CENTRE
Broadgate LN2 1HQ
➲ (located on the lower part of Lincoln, between Central Library and St Swithins close to the Waterside Shopping Centre)
☎ 01522 530401 ▤ 01522 552811   FREE
e-mail: greyfriars@lincolnshire.co.uk
The county's main archaeology museum, housed in a magnificent medieval building, forms part of Greyfriars.
Times: Open all year, Tue-Sat (closed Xmas/New Year). **Facilities:** ⅋ shop ✘ (ex guide dogs)

LINCOLN CASTLE
Castle Hill LN1 3AA
☎ 01522 511068 ▤ 01522 512150
Situated in the centre of Lincoln, the Castle, built in 1068 by William the Conqueror, dominates the Bailgate area alongside the great Cathedral. In addition to its many medieval features, Lincoln Castle has strong 19th-century connections and the unique Victorian prison chapel is perhaps the most awe-inspiring. The beautiful surroundings are ideal for historical adventures, picnics and special events that include jousting, Roman re-enactments, and Vintage vehicle rallies. The Castle is the home of the Magna Carta and there is an exhibition interpreting and displaying this important document.
Times: ✱ Open - Summer: Mon-Sat 9.30-5.30, Sun 11-5.30. Winter: Mon-Sat 9.30-4.30, Sun 11-4.30. (Closed 24-26 & 31 Dec & 1 Jan).
Facilities: P (100yds) ◪ ⅋ (hearing loop) toilets for disabled shop ✘ (ex guide dogs) ◥

MUSEUM OF LINCOLNSHIRE LIFE
Burton Rd LN1 3LY
➲ (100mtr walk from Lincoln Castle)   2 for 1
☎ 01522 528448 ▤ 01522 521264
e-mail: lincolnshirelife_museum@ lincolnshire.gov.uk
A large and varied social history museum, where two centuries of Lincolnshire life are illustrated by enthralling displays of domestic implements, industrial machinery, agricultural tools and a collection of horse-drawn vehicles. The exciting and interactive Royal Lincolnshire Regiment Museum contains videos, an audio tour, and touch screen computers.
Times: Open all year, May-Sep, daily 10-5.30; Oct-Apr, Mon-Sat 10-5.30, Sun 2-5.30. **Fee:** ✱ £2 (concessions £1.20). Family (2ad+3ch) £5.20. **Facilities:** P ◪ ⅋ (wheelchair available, parking space) toilets for disabled shop ✘

USHER GALLERY
Lindum Rd LN2 1NN
➲ (in city centre, signed)   FREE
☎ 01522 527980 ▤ 01522 560165
e-mail: usher.gallery@lincolnshire.gov.uk
Built as the result of a bequest by Lincoln jeweller James Ward Usher, the Gallery houses his magnificent collection of watches, porcelain and miniatures, as well as topographical works, watercolours by Peter de Wint, Tennyson memorabilia and coins. The gallery has a popular and changing display of contemporary visual arts and crafts. There is a lively lecture programme and children's activity diary.
Times: Open all year, Tue-Sat 10-5.30 (last entry 4.30), Sun 2.30-5. (Closed 24-26 Dec & 1 Jan). Open BHs. **Facilities:** P (150yds) ◪ ⅋ (large print exhibition guides, induction loop, parking) toilets for disabled shop ✘ (ex guide dogs) ◥

SCUNTHORPE   Map 08 SE81

NORMANBY HALL COUNTRY PARK
Normanby DN15 9HU
➲ (4m N of Scunthorpe off B1430)   2 for 1
☎ 01724 720588 ▤ 01724 721248
e-mail: normanbyhall@northlincs.gov.uk

A whole host of activities and attractions are offered in
continued

the 300 acres of grounds that surround Normanby Hall, including riding, nature trails and a farming museum. Inside the Regency mansion the fine rooms are decorated and furnished in period style. Fully restored and working Victorian kitchen garden. There is also a Victorian walled garden with a new nursery selling a wide range of Victorian and other unusual plants.
Times: Open, Park all year, daily 9am-dusk. Walled garden: daily 10.30-5 (4pm winter). Hall & Farming Museum: Apr-Sep daily 1-5.
Fee: ✱ Mar-1 Oct £4 (concessions £3). Family ticket £11. Season ticket (resident) £8 (non resident) £16, Oct-Mar £2.20 per car. **Facilities:** 🅿 (charged) 💻 ✖ licensed ♿ (audio tour & sensory bed in walled garden) toilets for disabled shop garden centre ✖ (ex guide dogs & park on lead) 🍴

SKEGNESS   Map 09 TF56
CHURCH FARM MUSEUM
Church Rd South PE25 2HF
➲ (follow brown museum signs on entering Skegness)
☎ 01754 766658 ▤ 01754 898243   2 for 1
e-mail: churchfarmmuseum@lincolnshire.gov.uk
A farmhouse and outbuildings, restored to show the way of life on a Lincolnshire farm at the end of the 19th century, with farm implements and machinery plus household equipment on display. Temporary exhibitions are held in the barn with special events throughout the season. A timber framed mud & stud cottage is restored on site.
Times: Open Apr-Oct, daily 10.30-5.30 **Fee:** ✱ £1 (ch 50p).
Facilities: 🅿 💻 ♿ (wheelchair available, grounds accessible with care) toilets for disabled shop ✖ (ex guide dogs)

SKEGNESS NATURELAND SEAL SANCTUARY
North Pde PE25 1DB
➲ (N end of seafront)
☎ 01754 764345 ▤ 01754 764345
e-mail: natureland@fsbdial.co.uk
Natureland houses seals, penguins, tropical birds, aquarium, reptiles, pets' corner etc. Also free-flight tropical butterflies (May Oct). Natureland is well known for its rescue of abandoned seal pups, and has successfully reared and returned to the wild a large number of them. The hospital unit incorporates a public viewing area, and a large seascape seal pool (with underwater viewing).
Times: Open all year, daily at 10am. Closing times vary according to season. (Closed 25-26 Dec & 1 Jan). **Fee:** ✱ £4.75 (ch u3 free, ch £3.10, pen £3.80). Family ticket £14.10. **Facilities:** 🅿 (100yds) 💻 ♿ (low windows on seal pools) toilets for disabled shop 🍴

SPALDING   Map 08 TF22
BUTTERFLY & WILDLIFE PARK
Long Sutton PE12 9LE   2 for 1
➲ (off A17 at Long Sutton)
☎ 01406 363833 & 363209 ▤ 01406 363182
e-mail: butterflypark@hotmail.com
The Park contains one of Britain's largest walk-through tropical houses, in which hundreds of butterflies and birds from all over the world fly freely. Outside are 15 acres of butterfly and bee gardens, wildflower meadows, nature trail, farm animals, a pets' corner and a large adventure

continued

playground. At The Lincolnshire Birds of Prey Centre, there are daily birds of prey displays. See an ant room where visitors can observe leaf-cutting ants in their natural working habitat. New to the park is Reptile Land, home to crocodiles and snakes.
Times: Open end Mar-end Oct, daily 10-5. (Sep & Oct 10-4). **Fee:** ✱ £5 (ch 3-16 £3.70, pen £4.70). Family ticket £16.50-£19.50. Party rates on application. **Facilities:** 🅿 ✖ licensed ♿ (wheelchairs available) toilets for disabled shop ✖ (ex guide dogs) 🍴

STAMFORD   Map 04 TF00
BURGHLEY HOUSE
PE9 3JY
➲ (1.5m off A1 at Stamford)
☎ 01780 752451 ▤ 01780 480125
e-mail: burghley@burghley.co.uk
This great Elizabethan palace, built by William Cecil, has all the hallmarks of that ostentatious period. The vast house is three storeys high and the roof is a riot of pinnacles, cupolas and paired chimneys in classic Tudor style. However, the interior was restyled in the 17th century, and the state rooms are now Baroque, with silver fireplaces, elaborate plasterwork and painted ceilings. These were painted by Antonio Verrio, whose Heaven Room is quite awe-inspiring.
Times: Open end Mar-Oct, daily. Please telephone for details. **Fee:** ✱ £7.50 (ch 5-11 £3.70 or free with every paying adult, pen £6.80) **Facilities:** 🅿 💻 ✖ licensed ♿ (chairlift access, some mobility required) toilets for disabled shop 🍴 (ex guide dogs) 🍴

STAMFORD MUSEUM
Broad St PE9 1PJ
➲ (from A1 follow town centre signs from any Stamford exit)   FREE
☎ 01780 766317 ▤ 01780 480363
e-mail: stamford_museum@lincolnshire.gov.uk
Displays illustrate the history of this fine stone town and include Stamford Ware pottery, the visit of Daniel Lambert and the Town's more recent industrial past. The new Stamford Tapestry depicts the history of the town in wool.
Times: Open all year, Apr-Sep, Mon-Sat 10-5, Sun 2-5; Oct-Mar Mon-Sat 10-5. (Closed 24-26 & 31 Dec & 1 Jan). **Facilities:** 🅿 (200yds) (on street parking is limited waiting) ♿ (info on 1st floor gallery available) shop 🍴 (ex guide dogs)

TATTERSHALL   Map 08 TF25
TATTERSHALL CASTLE
LN4 4LR
➲ (S of A153, 15m NE of Sleaford)
☎ 01526 342543
e-mail: tattershallcastle@nationaltrust.org.uk
This large fortified house was built in 1440 by Ralph Cromwell, Treasurer of England, and has a keep 100ft high. Restored in 1911-14, it contains four great chambers with large Gothic fireplaces, tapestries and brick vaulting. Spectacular views from battlements and museum room in guardhouse.
Times: Open Mar-14 Dec, Mar, Sat & Sun 12-4, Apr-Oct, Sat-Wed 11-5.30; Nov-14 Dec, Sat & Sun 12-4. **Fee:** ✱ £3.40 (ch £1.70). Family ticket £8.50. **Facilities:** 🅿 ♿ (braile guide) toilets for disabled shop 🍴 (ex guide dogs) 🦮

THORNTON — Map 08 TA11

THORNTON ABBEY AND GATEHOUSE

DN39 6TU

➲ (7m SE of Humber Bridge, on a road E of A1077) **FREE**

This abbey, founded in 1139 for a community of Augustinian cannons, was reconstructed from the 1260s as its prestige and riches grew. The remains of a beautiful octagonal chapter-house are notably fine. Most impressive is the fourteenth-century gatehouse, recognised as one of the grandest in England.

Times: Open Abbey Grounds: Apr-Sep, 10-6. Gatehouse: Apr-Sep, 1st & 3rd Sun of month, 12-6; Oct-Mar, 3rd Sun of month 12-4. Dates valid until 31 Mar 2004. **Facilities:** ℗ ⅋ (mostly accessible apart from gatehouse) ✖ (ex on lead in certain areas) ✿

WOOLSTHORPE — Map 08 SK92

WOOLSTHORPE MANOR

23 Newton Way NG33 5NR

➲ (7m S of Grantham, 1m W of A1)

☎ 01476 860338 📠 01746 860338

e-mail: woolsthorpemanor@ nationaltrust.org.uk

A fine stone-built, 17th-century farmhouse which was the birthplace of the scientist and philosopher Sir Isaac Newton. He also lived at the house from 1665-67 during the Plague. An early edition of his Principia Mathematica (1687) is in the house. Science Discovery Centre and exhibition.

Times: Open Mar-Oct, Mar & Oct, Sat-Sun 1-5; Apr-Sep Wed-Sun, BH Mon & Good Fri 1-5, Jul-Aug 1-6 **Fee:** ✱ £3.60 (ch £1.80). Family ticket £9. **Facilities:** ℗ (braile & large print guide, wheelchair available) ✖ (ex guide dogs) ⅋

LONDON

EVENTS & FESTIVALS

January
1st New Year's Day Parade, Parliament Square, SW1, to Berkeley Square
tbc Chinese New Year Celebrations, Gerrard Street & Leicester Square

March
20th Head of the River Race, River Thames, Mortlake to Putney
28th Oxford & Cambridge Boat Race

April
18th London Marathon

May
25th-28th Chelsea Flower Show

June
5th-6th Biggin Hill International Air Fair, Biggin Hill Airfield (provisional)
6th London to Brighton Classic Car Run
12th Trooping the Colour for the Queen's Birthday, Horse Guards Parade
tbc Beating Retreat by the Household Division Massed Bands, Horse Guards Parade

July
6th-11th Hampton Court Palace Flower Show, Hampton Court Palace, East Mosley
tbc Soho Festival, St Anne's Gardens & Wardour Street

August
29th-30th Notting Hill Carnival

September
6th-7th City of London Flower Show, Guildhall, Gresham Street
11th-12th Mayor's Thames Festival, South Bank

October
3rd Pearly Harvest Festival, St Martin in the Fields
24th Trafalgar Day Parade, Trafalgar Square

November
7th London to Brighton Veteran Car Run, Hyde Park
13th Lord Mayor's Show, City of London
14th Remembrance Day Service & Parade, Cenotaph, Whitehall

Above: Statue on the top of the Bank of England

W1

APSLEY HOUSE, THE WELLINGTON MUSEUM

Hyde Park Corner WIJ 7NT

➲ (Underground - Hyde Park Corner, **2 for 1**
exit 1 overlooking rdbt)

☎ 020 7499 5676 ▤ 020 7493 6576

Number One, London, is the popular name for one of the Capital's finest private residences, 19th-century home of the first Duke of Wellington. Built in the 1770s, its rich interiors have been returned to their former glory, and house the Duke's magnificent collection of paintings, silver, porcelain, sculpture and furniture. **Times:** Open Tue-Sun 11-5. (Closed Mon ex BH Mon, Good Fri, May Day BH, 24-26 Dec & 1 Jan). Last admission 4.30pm. Current arrangement may be subject to change from Apr 2004, call before you visit. **Fee:** ✱ £4.50 (ch under 18 & pen free, disabled & UB40 £3). Includes the use of a soundguide. Prices may change Apr 2004, contact before visit. **Facilities:** ℗ (NCP 10mins walk) ら (lift) shop ✖ (ex guide dogs) ◥

EC2

BANK OF ENGLAND MUSEUM

Threadneedle St EC2R 8AH

➲ (muscum housed in Bank of London, entrance in Bartholomew Lane)

☎ 020 7601 5545 ▤ 020 7601 5808 **FREE**
e-mail: museum@bankofengland.co.uk

Located in the heart of The City, this museum traces the history of the Bank from its foundation in 1694, and includes a collection of gold bars, old and new which can be held by visitors. New interactive programme. **Times:** Open all year, Mon-Fri 10-5. (Closed wknds & BH's). Open on the day of the Lord Major's Show. **Facilities:** ℗ (10 mins walk) ら (special need presentation, advance notice helpful) toilets for disabled shop

SE1

BANKSIDE GALLERY

48 Hopton St SE1 9JH

➲ (E of Blackfriars Bridge, South Bank of the Thames, adjacent to Tate Modern and the Millennium Bridge)

☎ 020 7928 7521 ▤ 020 7928 2820 **2 for 1**
c-mail: info@bankside gallery.com

Bankside Gallery is the home of the Royal Watercolour Society (RWS) and the Royal Society of Painter-Printmakers (RE). A series of regularly changing exhibitions throughout the year displays the work of both societies. **Times:** Opening dates vary according to exhibitions programme - Tue-Fri 10-5, Sat & Sun 11-5. (Closed Mon) **Fee:** ✱ £3.50 (concessions £2). Some exhibitions are free. ℗ ら shop ✖ ◥

SW1

BANQUETING HOUSE AT WHITEHALL PALACE

Whitehall SW1A 2ER

➲ (Underground - Westminster, Charing Cross or Embankment)

☎ 020 7930 4179 ▤ 020 7930 8268
e-mail: valerie.jarvis@hrp.org.uk

Designed by Inigo Jones, this is the only surviving building of the vast Whitehall Palace, destroyed by fire 300 years ago. The Palace has seen many significant royal events, including

continued

the execution of Charles I in 1649. The Banqueting House's Rubens ceiling paintings are stunning examples of the larger works of the Flemish Master and its classical Palladian style set the fashion for much of London's later architecture. **Times:** Open all year, Mon-Sat 10-5. (Closed Good Fri, 24 Dec-1 Jan & BH's). Liable to close at short notice for Government functions. **Fee:** £4 (ch 5-16 £2.60 (under 5 free) concessions £3). ℗ (5 mins) (no parking in Whitehall) ら toilets for disabled shop ✖ (ex guide/hearing dogs) ◥

SE1

BRITISH AIRWAYS LONDON EYE

Riverside Building, County Hall, Westminster Bridge Rd SE1 7PB

➲ (Underground - Waterloo/Westminster)

☎ 0870 500 0600 ▤ 0870 990 8882
e-mail: customer.services@ba-londoneye.com

The British Airways London Eye is one of the most inspiring and visually dramatic additions to the London skyline. At 135m high, it is the world's tallest observation wheel, allowing you to see one of the world's most exciting cities from a completely new perspective. The Eye takes you on a gradual, 30 minute, 360 degree rotation, revealing parts of the city, which are simply not visible from the ground. For Londoners and visitors alike, it is the best way to see London and it's many celebrated landmarks. The Eye provides the perfect location for private parties and entertaining and offers a wide variety of in flight hospitality packages, like champagne and canapés, which are available to enjoy from the privacy of a private capsule. **Times:** Open May, Mon-Thu 9.30-8, Fri-Sun 9.30-9, (24-31 May last flight 10pm); June, Mon-Thu 9.30-9, Fri-Sun 9.30-10; July-Aug daily 9.30-10; Sep, Mon-Thu 9.30-8, Fri-Sun 9.30-9, (1-7 Sep last flight 10pm); Oct-Dec, daily 9.30-8. (Closed 25 Dec) **Fee:** ✱ £11 (ch under 5 free, ch £5.50, disabled visitors £9, pen £10). Fast track entry £30. ℗ (500yds) ▣ ら (braile guidebooks, wheelchair hire, carer ticket) toilets for disabled shop ✖ (ex guide & hearing dogs) ◥

W12

BBC TELEVISION CENTRE TOURS

BBC Television Centre, Wood Ln W12 7RJ

➲ (Underground - Central Line/White City)

☎ 0870 603 0304 ▤ 020 8576 7466
e-mail: bbctours@bbc.co.uk

Take a look behind the scenes at the world's most famous TV centre. As the BBC TV Centre is a working building, no

continued

guarantees can be made as to what visitors will see, although dressing rooms, the News Centre, the Weather Centre, and various studios are all possible. The uncertain nature of the visit means that no two are the same, and that only pre-booked guided tours are available.
Times: Open Mon-Sat. Tours at 10, 10.20, 1.15, 1.30, 3.30 & 3.45. (Closed 24 Dec-2 Jan). All tours must be pre-booked. **Fee:** £7.95 (concessions £6.95, student £5.95). Family ticket £21.95 P (5min walk) (no parking on road outside) & (wheelchair available) toilets for disabled shop ✖ (ex guide/hearing dogs) ◥

WC1
BRITISH MUSEUM
Great Russell St WC1B 3DG
➲ (Underground - Russell Sq, Tottenham Court Rd, Holborn)
☎ 020 7323 8000 ▯ 020 7323 8616
e-mail: information@thebritishmuseum.ac.uk
Behind its imposing Neo-Classical façade the British Museum displays the rich and varied treasures which make it one of the great museums of the world. Founded in 1753, displays cover the works of humanity from pre-historic to modern times. The galleries are the responsibility of ten departments, which include Egyptian, Greek and Roman, Japanese, Medieval and later, Prints and Drawings, and Ethnography. Among the treasures to be seen are the Egyptian mummies, the sculptures from the Parthenon, the Anglo-Saxon treasure from the Sutton Hoo ship burial and the Vindolanda Tablets from Hadrian's Wall. There is a regular programme of gallery talks, guided tours and lectures, and young visitors can enjoy special children's trails.
Times: ✱ Open all year, Gallery: Mon-Sat 10-5.30 & Thu-Fri 10-8.30. Great Court: Mon 9-6, Tue-Wed & Sun 9-9, Thu-Sat 9am-11pm. (Closed Good Fri, 24-26 Dec & 1 Jan). **Facilities:** P (5 mins walk) ◢✖ licensed & (parking by arrangement) toilets for disabled shop ✖ (ex guide/companion dogs)

SW1
BUCKINGHAM PALACE
Buckingham Palace Rd SW1 1AA
➲ (Underground - Victoria, Green Park, St James' Park)
☎ 020 7766 7300 ▯ 020 7930 9625
e-mail: buckinghampalace@
royalcollection.org.uk
Buckingham Palace has been the official London residence of Britain's sovereigns since 1837. Today it serves as both the home and office of Her Majesty the Queen. Its nineteen State Rooms, which open for eight weeks a year, form the heart of the working palace and more than 50,000 people visit each year as guests at State, ceremonial and official occasions and garden parties. After visiting the State Rooms, visitors can enjoy a walk along the south side of the garden, which offers 'superb views of the west front of the Palace and the 19th century lake.
Times: Open 5 Aug-29 Sep 9.30-4.30 last admission 4.15. Entry by timed-ticket **Fee:** ✱ £12 (ch under 17 £6, pen & student £10) Family ticket (2 adults & 3 ch) £29. Tickets bought in advance £1 booking fee P (200yds) (very limited, driving not recommended) & (ex gardens, pre-booking essential) toilets for disabled shop ✖ (ex guide dogs) ◥

SW1
CABINET WAR ROOMS
Clive Steps, King Charles St SW1A 2AQ
➲ (Underground - Westminster (exit 6) or St James Park)
☎ 020 7930 6961 ▯ 020 7839 5897   `2 for 1`
e-mail: cwr@iwm.org.uk
The underground emergency accommodation used to protect the Prime Minister, Winston Churchill, his War Cabinet and the Chiefs of Staff during WWII provides a fascinating insight into those tense days and nights. Among the 21 rooms are the Cabinet Room, the Map Room (where information about operations on all fronts was collected) and the Prime Minister's room, all carefully preserved since the end of the war.
In 2003 a further 9 secret historic rooms, including the Churchill's kitchen, dining room and Mrs Churchill's bedroom, were revealed to the public for the first time. These rooms provide an insight into the domestic side of Britain's wartime Prime Minister, they were intended to provide a sheltered space where the people he valued most could eat, sleep and work in safety, while the bombs rained down outside.
Times: Open all year, daily 9.30-6. (10-6 Oct-Mar) last admission 5.15 (Closed 24-26 Dec). **Fee:** ✱ £7 (ch under 16 free, students & pen £5.50). Party 10+ £5.80 per person. P (10 mins walk) ◢& (education service, object handling session, induction loop) toilets for disabled shop ✖ (ex guide dogs) ◥

SW3
CARLYLE'S HOUSE
24 Cheyne Row SW3 5HL
➲ (Underground - Sloane Square. Off Cheyne Walk between Battersea & Albert Bridges).
☎ 020 7352 7087 ▯ 020 7352 5108
e-mail: carlyleshouse@nationaltrust.org.uk
'The Sage of Chelsea' - distinguished essayist and writer of historical works, Thomas Carlyle - lived here from 1834 until his death in 1881. Such literary notables as Tennyson, Thackeray, Browning, George Eliot and Dickens were frequent visitors.
Times: Open Apr-Oct, Wed-Fri 2-5. Sat-Sun & BH Mons 11-5. Last admission 4.30. (Closed Mon-Tue). **Fee:** ✱ £3.70 (ch 5-16, £1.80). P (street metered) ✖ (ex guide dogs) ⬥ ⬥

WC1
THE CHARLES DICKENS MUSEUM
48 Doughty St WC1N 2LX
➲ (Underground - Russell Square or Chancery Lane)
☎ 020 7405 2127 ▯ 020 7831 5175   `2 for 1`
e-mail: info@dickensmuseum.com
Charles Dickens lived in Doughty Street in his twenties and it was here he worked on his first full-length novel, *The Pickwick Papers*, and later *Oliver Twist* and *Nicholas Nickleby*. Pages of the original manuscripts are on display, together

continued

with valuable first editions, his marriage licence and many other personal mementoes.

Times: Open all year, Mon-Sat 10-5, Sun 11-5. **Fee:** ✱ £4 (ch under 16 £2, concession £3). Family ticket £9. Ⓟ (in street) (metered, 2 hrs max) ♿ shop 🐕 💳

SW3

Chelsea Physic Garden

66 Royal Hospital Rd, (entrance in Swan Walk) SW3 4HS

➲ (Underground - Sloane Square)

☎ 020 7352 5646 🖹 020 7376 3910

Begun in 1673 for the study of plants used by the Society of Apothecaries. This garden is one of Europe's oldest botanic gardens and is the only one to retain the title 'Physic' after the old name for the healing arts. The garden is still used for botanical and medicinal research, and offers displays of many fascinating plants in lovely surroundings.

Times: Open Apr-Oct, Wed 12-5, Sun 2-6. Additional opening during Chelsea Flower Show week, late May & Chelsea Festival week late Jun. Groups at other times by appointment. **Fee:** ✱ £5 (ch 5-15, students & UB40 £3, ch under 5 free). **Facilities:** Ⓟ (0.5m) (west end of Battersea Park) ☕ ♿ (disabled parking) toilets for disabled shop 🐕 (ex guide dogs)

W4

Chiswick House

Burlington Ln, Chiswick W4 2RD

➲ (Underground - Gunnersbury)

☎ 020 8995 0508 🖹 020 8742 3104

Discover the story of this celebrated Palladian villa, a fine example of 18th-century English architecture with lavish interiors and classical landscaping.

Times: Open Apr-Sep, Wed-Sun & BH's 10-6 (Oct, Wed-Sun 10-5). Closed Nov-Mar but exclusive group visits are available, please telephone for details. Dates valid until 31 Mar 2004. **Fee:** £3.50 (ch £2, concessions £3). Prices valid until 31 Mar 2004. **Facilities:** Ⓟ ☕ ♿ (telephone in advance for wheelchair facilities) shop 🐕 (ex on lead in some areas) ⌗

The AA also publishes a guide to Family Friendly Places to Stay, Eat & Visit

WC2

Courtauld Gallery

Somerset House, Strand WC2R 0RN

➲ (Underground - Temple, Embankment)

☎ 020 7848 2526 🖹 020 7848 2589 2 for 1

e-mail: galleryinfo@courtauld.ac.uk

The Galleries contain the superb collection of paintings begun by Samuel Courtauld in the 1920s and 1930s and presented to the University of London in memory of his wife. This is the most important collection of Impressionist and post-Impressionist works in Britain and includes paintings by Monet, Renoir, Degas, Cézanne, Van Gogh and Gauguin. There are also works by Michelangelo, Rubens, Goya, and other notable Masters, as well as early Italian paintings.

Times: Open daily 10-6. Last admission 5.15. **Fee:** ✱ £5 (concessions £4). Ⓟ (NCP Drury Lane) ☕ ♿ (parking by arrangement only, call 020 7836 8686, lift) toilets for disabled shop 🐕 (ex guide dogs) 💳

SE10

Cutty Sark Clipper Ship

King William Walk, Greenwich SE10 9HT

➲ (situated in dry dock beside Greenwich Pier)

☎ 020 8858 3445 & 020 8858 2698

🖹 020 8853 3589

e-mail: info@cuttysark.org.uk

The fastest tea clipper ever, built in 1869, she once sailed 363 miles in a single day. Preserved in dry dock since 1957, her graceful lines dominate the riverside at Greenwich. Exhibitions and a video presentation the story of the ship, and restoration work can be seen.

Times: Open all year, daily 10-5 (Closed 24-26 Dec). Last ticket 30 mins before closing. **Facilities:** Ⓟ (500mtrs) ♿ shop 🐕 (ex guide dogs) 💳

SE1

Dali Universe

County Hall, Riverside Building SE1 7PB

➲ (Adjacent to the London Eye and opposite Big Ben)

☎ 020 7620 2720 🖹 020 7620 3120 2 for 1

e-mail: info@daliuniverse.com

The Dali Universe is a conceptual exhibition dedicated to one of the 20th century's most important artistic forces, Salvador Dali (1904-1989). Arranged thematically to cover the major influences in his life and work, The Dali Universe boasts over 500 works of art, from sculpture to rare etchings, from furniture to gold jewellery. Highlights include the Lobster Telephone and the Mae West Lips sofa.

Times: Open daily 10-5.30 (ex 25 Dec) **Fee:** ✱ £8.50 (children under 5 free, ch 10-16 £4.95, concessions £7.50)under 10's free Ⓟ (5 mins) ♿ (elevator, ramp access) toilets for disabled shop 🐕 💳

SE1

Design Museum

Shad Thames SE1 2YD

➲ (Turn off Tooley St onto Shad Thames. Underground - London Bridge & Tower Hill)

☎ 0870 909 9009 🖹 0870 909 1909

The Design Museum is the first museum in the world to be dedicated to 20th and 21st century design. Since opening in 1989, it has become one of London's most inspiring

continued

attractions and has won international acclaim for its ground-breaking exhibition and education programmes. The museum aims to excite everyone about design by stimulating the public interest in design, fashion, creative technology and architecture. Permanent collections of design classics and temporary exhibitions ranging from retrospectives on the work of great designers to thematic shows on Bauhaus, Dessau and Erotic design. As well as exploring the history of modern design, the Design Museum showcases the best of contemporary designs and technologies, which will shape our future.

Times: Open all year, daily 10-5.45 (last entry 5.15). Late opening on Fri, 9pm (last entry 8.30pm). Closed 25 Dec only. **Fee:** ✱ £6 (concessions £4) Family ticket £16. **Facilities:** P (3 mins) (Gainsford St car park is chargeable) ▃ ✗ licensed ♿ (ramped entrance, wheelchair & lift) toilets for disabled shop ✗ (ex guide dogs) ◗

EC4
DR JOHNSON'S HOUSE
17 Gough Square EC4A 3DE
⮑ (Underground - Temple, Blackfriars, Chancery Lane)
☎ 020 7353 3745 🖷 020 7353 3745
e-mail: curator@drjohnsonshouse.org

The celebrated literary figure, Dr Samuel Johnson, lived here between 1748 and 1759. He wrote his English Dictionary here, and a facsimile third edition is on display at the house. The dictionary took nine and a half years to complete and contained 40,000 words. Johnson then undertook the formidable task of editing the complete works of Shakespeare. The house is a handsome example of early 18th-century architecture, and includes a collection of prints, letters and other Johnson memorabilia.

Times: Open all year, May-Sep, daily 11-5.30; Oct-Apr 11-5. (Closed Sun, BH's, Good Fri & 24 Dec). **Fee:** ✱ £4 (ch £1, under 10 free, students & pen £3). Family £9. P (500yds) (limited meters) (Large print info sheets, handrails, seating) shop ✗ (ex guide dogs)

SE21
DULWICH PICTURE GALLERY
Gallery Rd, Dulwich SE21 7AD
⮑ (off South Circular A205 follow signs to Dulwich village) `2 for 1`
☎ 020 8693 5254 🖷 020 8299 8700
e-mail: info@dulwichpicturegallery.org.uk

This is the oldest public picture gallery in England, housing a magnificent collection of Old Masters, including works by Poussin, Claude, Rubens, Murillo, Van Dyck, Rembrandt, Watteau and Gainsborough. The gallery was designed by Sir John Soane in 1811. The collection, the building and the critically acclaimed loan exhibitions make the gallery a must see for art lovers.

Times: Open all year, Tue-Fri 10-5, wknds & BH Mon 11-5. (Closed Mon). **Fee:** £4 (pen £3, students, UB40, disabled & ch free). P ✗ licensed ♿ (wheelchairs available, hearing loop) toilets for disabled shop ✗ (ex guide dogs) ◗

> The AA also publishes a guide to
> Pet Friendly Places to Stay

SE9
ELTHAM PALACE HOUSE & GARDENS
Court Yard SE9 5QE
☎ 020 8294 2548

Stephen and Virginia Courtauld's stunning country house shows the glamour and allure of 1930's Art Deco style and is a feast of luxurious design ideas. The house incorporates the medieval Great Hall and stunning moated gardens.

Times: Open Apr-Sep, Wed-Fri, Sun & BH's 10-6; Oct, Wed-Fri & Sun 10-5; Nov-Mar, Wed-Fri & Sun 10-4. (Closed 22 Dec-31 Jan). Dates valid until 21 Mar 2004. **Fee:** House & Gardens: £6.50 (ch £3.50, concessions £5). Gardens only: £4 (ch £2, concessions £3). Prices valid until 31 Mar 2004. **Facilities:** P ♿ shop ✗ 🚗 ⌗

SE1
THE FASHION & TEXTILE MUSEUM
83 Bermondsey St SE1 3XF
☎ 020 7403 0222 🖷 020 7407 8664
e-mail: info@ftmlondon.org

Set on the South Bank, and opened in 2002, the FTM is the first exhibition space in London to dedicate itself to the global fashion industry. The Museum will hold two or three major exhibitions a year, manage an education and outreach programme, and host an extensive digital fashion and textile archive.

Times: Open Tue-Sun 11-5.45 (last admission 5.15pm) **Fee:** £6 (concessions £4) P ♿ toilets for disabled shop ✗ ◗

NW3
FENTON HOUSE
Windmill Hill NW3 6RT
⮑ (Underground - Hampstead, right out of station. Cross Heath St, up Holly Hill. Take right fork at top of hill into Hampstead Grove. Entrance on left of Hampstead Grove) `2 for 1`
☎ 020 7435 3471 🖷 020 7435 3471
e-mail: fentonhouse@nationaltrust.org.uk

A William and Mary merchants house built about 1686 and set in a walled garden, Fenton House is now owned by the National Trust. It contains outstanding displays of Oriental and European porcelain, 17th century needlework pictures and Georgian furniture as well as the Benton Fletcher collection of early keyboard instruments.

Times: Open Mar, Sat & Sun 2-5; Apr-Oct, Sat-Sun & BH Mon 11-5pm, Wed-Fri 2-5pm. Last admission 4.30pm. **Fee:** ✱ £4.50 (ch £2.25). Family ticket £11.50. Group 15+ £3.80. ♿ (photographs of upper floors which are not accessible) ✗ ⛺

SE18
FIREPOWER
Royal Arsenal, Woolwich SE18 6ST
⮑ (A205, right at Woolwich ferry onto A206, Firepower is signposted from there).
☎ 020 8855 7755 🖷 020 8855 7100
e-mail: info@firepower.org.uk

Firepower is the Royal Artillery Museum in the historic Royal Arsenal spans 2000 years of artillery and shows how it developed from Roman catapult to guided missile to *continued* self-propelled gun. Put science into action with touchscreen displays and be awed by the big guns. **Times:** Open from Wed-Sun & BH's 11-5.30. Phone for winter opening times. **Facilities:** P (charged) �& (wheelchairs available) toilets for disabled shop ✗ (ex guide dogs) ☜

SE1
FLORENCE NIGHTINGALE MUSEUM
Gassiot House, 2 Lambeth Palace Rd SE1 7EW
➲ (Underground - Westminster, Waterloo. On the site of St Thomas' Hospital)
☎ 020 7620 0374 ▤ 020 7928 1760
e-mail: info@florence-nightingale.co.uk
Florence Nightingale needs no introduction, but this museum shows clearly that she was more than 'The Lady with the Lamp'. Beautifully designed, the museum creates a personal setting in which a large collection of Florence's personal items including childhood souvenirs, her dress, furniture from her houses and honours awarded to her in old age are displayed. There is a small military history collection of souvenirs from the Crimean War, including military medals and a military nursing uniform. **Times:** Open all year, Mon-Fri 10-5; wknds & BH's 11.30-4.30. Last admission 1hr before closing. (Closed Good Fri, Etr Sun & 24 Dec-2 Jan). **Fee:** £4.80 (ch 5-18, student, pen & disabled visitor £3.80). Family ticket (up to 4) £12. Discounted rates for pre-booked groups of 15+. P (20mtrs) (hospital parking limited and charged) �& toilets for disabled shop ✗ (ex guide dogs) ☜

NW3
FREUD MUSEUM
20 Maresfield Gardens, Hampstead NW3 5SX
➲ (Underground - Finchley Road)
☎ 020 7435 2002 & 7435 5167   2 for 1
▤ 020 7431 5452
e-mail: freud@gn.apc.org
In 1938, Sigmund Freud left Vienna as a refugee from the Nazi occupation and chose exile in England, transferring his entire domestic and working environment to this house. He worked here until his death a year later. His extraordinary collection of Egyptian, Greek, Roman and Oriental antiquities, his working library and papers, and his fine furniture including the famous desk and couch are all here. **Times:** Open all year, Wed-Sun 12-5 (Closed BH's, telephone for Xmas Holiday times). **Fee:** £5 (ch 12-18, students, UB40 & pen £2, ch under 12 free). P �& (personal tours can be arranged if booked in advance) shop ✗ (ex guide dogs) ☜

E2
GEFFRYE MUSEUM
136 Kingsland Rd, Shoreditch E2 8EA
➲ (establishment at the Southern end of Kingsland Rd A10 in Shoreditch)
☎ 020 7739 9893 ▤ 020 7729 5647   FREE
e-mail: info@geffrye-museum.org.uk
The only museum in the UK to specialise in the domestic interiors and furniture of the urban middle classes. Displays span the 400 years from 1600 to the present day, forming a sequence of period rooms which capture the nature of English interior style. The museum is set in elegant, 18th-century buildings, surrounded by delightful gardens including an award-winning walled herb garden and a series

of historical gardens which highlight changes in urban middle-class gardens from the 17th to 20th centuries. One of the museum's historic almshouses has recently been fully restored to its original condition and is open on selected days (ring for details). **Times:** Open all year, Tue-Sat 10-5, Sun & BH Mons 12-5 (Closed Mon, Good Fri, 24-26 Dec & New Year). **Facilities:** P (150yds) (meter parking) ✗ licensed �& (ramps, lift, wheelchair available) toilets for disabled shop ✗ (ex guide dogs)

WC2
GILBERT COLLECTION
Somerset House, Strand WC2R 1LA
➲ (Underground - Temple, Covent Garden)
☎ 020 7420 9400 ▤ 020 7420 9440   2 for 1
e-mail: info@gilbert-collection.org.uk
An outstanding collection of decorative arts and an important bequest to the nation. The Gilbert Collection is the gift of Sir Arthur Gilbert and is on permanent display at Somerset House. The museum includes European silver, gold snuff boxes and Italian mosaics, the displays also include furniture, clocks and portrait miniatures. Temporary exhibitions run throughout the year. **(2-for-1 Voucher applies to permanent collection only)** **Times:** Open daily 10-6, last admission 5.15. **Fee:** ✱ £5 (concessions £4, under 18, uk students, unemployed free). Combined ticket with Courtauld & Hermitage Gallery. P (400mtrs) ▄ ✗ licensed �& (lifts, hearing loop, wheelchair hire, disabled parking) toilets for disabled shop ✗ (ex guide dogs) ☜

SE1
GOLDEN HINDE EDUCATIONAL MUSEUM
St Mary Overie Dock, Cathedral St SE1 9DE
➲ (On the Thames path between Southwark Cathedral and the new Globe Theatre)
☎ 020 7403 0123 ▤ 020 7407 5908   2 for 1
e-mail: info@goldenhinde.co.uk
A full size replica of Sir Francis Drake's famous 16th century galleon. Just like the original, this *Golden Hinde* has circumnavigated the globe. You can explore the five decks, and replica furnishings add to the atmosphere. Special events include Living History re-enactments. There are holiday workshops for children and the ship is also available for private hire. **Times:** Open all year, 9.30-5.30. Visitors are advised to check opening times as they may vary due to closures for functions. **Fee:** ✱ £2.75 (ch 4-13 £2, under 4's free, concessions £2.35). Family (2 ad & 3 ch) £8. P (on street parking) ▄ shop ✗ (ex guide dogs) ☜

EC2
THE GUILDHALL
Gresham St EC2V 5AE
➲ (Underground - Bank, St Paul's)
☎ 020 7606 3030 ▤ 020 7260 1119   FREE
The Court of Common Council (presided over by the Lord Mayor) administers the City of London and meets in the Guildhall. Dating from 1411, the building was badly damaged in the Great Fire and again in the Blitz. The great hall, traditionally used for the Lord Mayor's Banquet and other important civic functions, is impressively decorated with the banners and shields of the livery companies, of which there are more than 90. The Clock Museum, which has a collection

continued

continued

of 700 exhibits, charts the history of 500 years of time-keeping.
Times: Open all year, May-Sep, daily 10-5; Oct-Apr, Mon-Sat 10-5. (Closed Xmas, New Year, Good Fri, Etr Mon & infrequently for Civic occasions). Please contact 020 7606 3030 ext 1463 before visit to be certain of access. **Facilities:** & shop ✖

W1
HANDEL HOUSE MUSEUM
25 Brook St W1K 4HB
➲ (off Park Lane into Brook Gate, then Upper Brook Street. Pass Claridge's Hotel on right. The entrance is Lancashire Court)
☎ 020 7495 1685 🖥 020 7495 1759
e-mail: mail@handelhouse.org
Home to George Frideric Handel from 1723 until his death in 1759, the Handel House Museum celebrates Handel's career and times. It was here that Handel composed, *Messiah, Zadok the Priest* and *Fireworks Music*. Over 200 years later, live music, educational projects and public events still bring the address to life.
Times: Open Tue, Wed & Sat 10-6, Thu 10-8, Sun 12-6. (Closed BH Mon 25-26 Dec & 1 Jan) **Fee:** ✱ £4.50 (ch £2, concessions £3.50) P & toilets for disabled shop ✖ (ex guide dogs) ◥

N6
HIGHGATE CEMETERY
Swains Ln N6 6PJ
➲ (Underground - Archway, see directions posted at exit)
☎ 020 8340 1834
Highgate Cemetery is the most impressive of a series of large, formally arranged and landscaped cemeteries which were established around the perimeter of London in the mid-19th century. There's a wealth of fine sculpture and architecture amongst the tombstones, monuments and mausoleums as well as the graves of such notables as the Rossetti family, George Eliot, Michael Faraday and Karl Marx. It is also a Grade II listed park.
Times: Open all year. Eastern Cemetery: daily 10 (11 wknds)-5 (4 in winter). Western Cemetery by guided tour only: Sat & Sun 11-4 (3 in winter); midweek tours at 2pm, advisable to book. (Closed 25-26 Dec & during funerals). **Fee:** ✱ East cemetery £2. Tour of West cemetery £3 (ch 8-16 £1, no ch under 8 on tours). Donations encouraged to assist restoration. Camera permits for private use £1 on each side (no video or flash). **Facilities:** P (300yds) (on site parking for grave owners only) ✖

SE1
HMS BELFAST
Morgans Ln, Tooley St SE1 2JH
➲ (Underground - London Bridge/Tower Hill/Monument. Rail: London Bridge)
☎ 020 7940 6300 🖥 020 7403 0719
e-mail: hmsbelfast@iwm.org.uk
Europe's last surviving big gun armoured warship from the Second World War, *HMS Belfast* was launched in 1938 and served in the North Atlantic and Arctic with the Home Fleet. She led the Allied naval bombardment of German positions on D-Day, and was saved for the nation in 1971. A tour of the ship will take you from the Captain's Bridge through nine
continued

decks to the massive Boiler and Engine Rooms. You can visit the cramped Messdecks, Officers' Cabins, Galley, Sick Bay, Dentist and Laundry.
Times: Open all year, daily. Mar-Oct 10-6, last admission 5.15; Nov-28 Feb 10-5, last admission 4.15. (Closed 24-26 Dec). **Fee:** £6 (ch under 16 free, concessions £3.80). Party £4.80 per person. P (150yds) ▣ & (wheelchair lift for access on board) toilets for disabled shop ✖ (ex guide dogs) ◥

W4
HOGARTH HOUSE
Hogarth Ln, Great West Rd W4 2QN
➲ (50yds W of Hogarth rdbt on Great West Road A4).
☎ 020 8994 6757   FREE
🖥 0845 456 2880
This 18th-century house was the country home of artist William Hogarth (1697-1764) during the last 15 years of his life. The house contains displays on the artist's life, and many of his satirical engravings. The gardens contain Hogarth's famous mulberry tree.
Times: Open Apr-Oct, Tue-Fri 1-5, Sat-Sun 1-6; Nov-Mar, Tue-Fri 1-4, Sat-Sun 1-5. (Closed Mon (ex BH's), Jan, 25-26 Dec, Good Fri).
Facilities: P (25 & 50yds) (spaces marked in Axis Centre car park) & toilets for disabled shop ✖ (ex guide dogs)

SE23
THE HORNIMAN MUSEUM & GARDENS
London Rd, Forest Hill SE23 3PQ
➲ (situated on A205)
☎ 020 8699 2339 (rec info) 020 8699 1872
🖥 020 8291 5506
e-mail: marketing@horniman.ac.uko.uk
Founder Frederick Horniman, a tea merchant, gave the museum to the people of London in 1901. The collection covers Natural History - including Vanishing Birds; African Worlds; and The Music Room, which is currently undergoing redevelopment. There are 16 acres of gardens, and the museum hosts a variety of workshops and activities.
Times: ✱ Open all year, Mon-Sat 10.30-5.30, Sun 2-5.30 (Closed 24-26 Dec). Gardens close at sunset. **Facilities:** P (opposite museum) ▣ & (chair lift to parts of upper floor) toilets for disabled shop ✖ (ex guide dogs or in gardens)

SW1
HOUSES OF PARLIAMENT
Westminster SW1A 0AA
➲ (Underground - Westminster)
☎ 020 7219 4272 🖥 020 7219 5839
Visitors to the Houses of Parliament will receive a guided tour through the Queen's Robing Room, Royal Gallery, Prince's Chamber, Chamber of the House of Lords, Central Lobby, Chamber of the House of Commons, Division Lobby, St Stephen's Hall and the 900 year old Westminster Hall. No large items of luggage or prams/pushchairs permitted.
Times: Open 26 Jul-30 Aug, Mon, Tue, Fri & Sat, 9.15-4.30, Wed & Thu, 1.15-4.30; 19 Sep-4 Oct, Mon, Fri & Sat, 9.15-4.30, Tue-Thu 1.15-4.30. Times are for 1st and last tours of the day. **Fee:** ✱ £7 (ch 5-16 £5, concessions £5) Family ticket £22. Foreign language tours £7.50-£9. Group rates on application. **Facilities:** P (50mtrs) (limited parking, metered) ▣ & (touch & sound model for visually impaired) toilets for disabled shop ✖ (ex guide dogs) 🚲 ◥

SE1
IMPERIAL WAR MUSEUM
Lambeth Rd SE1 6HZ

➲ (Underground - Lambeth North, Elephant & Castle or Waterloo)

☎ 020 7416 5000 🖹 020 7416 5374 **FREE**
e-mail: mail@iwm.org.uk

Founded in 1917, this museum illustrates and records all aspects of the two World Wars and other military operations involving Britain and the Commonwealth since 1914. There are always special exhibitions and the programme of events includes film shows and lectures. The museum has a wealth of military reference material, although some reference departments are open to the public by appointment only. **Times:** Open all year, daily 10-6. (Closed 24-26 Dec). **Facilities:** P (on street 100mtrs) (metered Mon-Fri) ▰ ✗ licensed ⚹ (parking & wheelchair hire book in advance, study room) toilets for disabled shop ✖ (ex guide dogs) ◥

N3
THE JEWISH MUSEUM
The Sternberg Centre, 80 East End Rd, Finchley N3 2SY

➲ (Underground - Finchley Central, 10 mins walk via Station Rd & Manor View) **2 for 1**

☎ 020 8349 1143 🖹 020 8343 2162
e-mail: enquiries@jewishmuseum.org.uk

The Jewish Museum traces the story of Jewish immigration and settlement in London, including a reconstruction of an East End tailoring workshop. It also has a Holocaust Education Gallery with an exhibition on Leon Greenman - British Citizen and Auschwitz survivor. There is a regular programme of changing exhibitions and events. **Times:** Open all year, Sun 10.30-4.30, Mon-Thu 10.30-5. Closed Jewish festivals, public holidays & 24 Dec-4 Jan. Also closed Sun in Aug & BH wknds. **Fee:** £2 (concessions £1, ch free) P (50mtrs) (on street parking) ▰ ⚹ toilets for disabled shop ✖

NW1
THE JEWISH MUSEUM
Raymond Burton House, 129-131 Albert St, Camden Town NW1 7NB

➲ (Underground - Camden Town, 3 mins walk from station)

☎ 020 7284 1997 🖹 020 7267 9008 **2 for 1**
e-mail: admin@jmus.org.uk

The museum explores the history and religious life of the
continued

Jewish community in Britain and beyond. The History Gallery traces Jewish roots in Britain from the Norman Conquest until recent times, and the Ceremonial Art Gallery illustrates Jewish religious life. There are social history displays and re-constructions, and, at a different address, a moving exhibition on a British-born Holocaust survivor. **Times:** Open Mon-Thu, 10-4, Sun 10-5. Closed Jewish Festivals & public holidays. **Fee:** £3.50 (ch, students, disabled & UB40 £1.50, pen £2.50) Family ticket £8. P (outside museum) (pay & display parking) ⚹ (induction loop in lecture room linked to audio-visual unit) toilets for disabled shop ✖ (ex guide dogs) ◥

NW3
KEATS HOUSE
Keats Grove, Hampstead NW3 2RR

➲ (Underground - Hampstead, about 15mins walk from station)

☎ 020 7435 2062 🖹 020 7431 9293
e-mail: keatshouse@corpoflondon.gov.uk

The poet John Keats lived in this house from 1818-1820 and wrote some of his most famous poems, including *Ode to a Nightingale* here. His fiancee, Fanny Brawne, lived next door, and they often walked together on nearby Hampstead Heath. The house contains many of his personal items including inkstand, engagement ring, paintings, jewellery and manuscripts. **Times:** ✱ Open 23 Apr-10 Dec, Tue-Sat 12-5. Tue-Sat between 10-12 guided tours, schools & visits by appointment take place. Wed between 5-8 a programme of tours & lectures are available. Sun & BH'S 12-5. **Facilities:** P (500yds) (residents parking in operation) ⚹ shop ✖ (ex guide dogs)

W8
KENSINGTON PALACE STATE APARTMENTS & ROYAL CEREMONIAL DRESS COLLECTION
Kensington Gardens W8 4PX

➲ (Underground - High Street Kensington or Notting Hill Gate)

☎ 0870 751 5170 🖹 020 7376 0198

Highlights of a visit to Kensington include the recently restored Kings Apartments with a fine collection of Old Masters; Tintoretto and Van Dyke amongst them. The Royal Ceremonial Dress Collection includes a selection of HM The Queen's dresses, representations of tailor's and dressmaker's workshops, and a display of dresses belonging to Diana, Princess of Wales. **Times:** Open Mar-Oct 10-6, last admission 5; Nov-end Feb 10-5, last admission 4. (Closed 24-26 Dec). **Fee:** £10 (ch 5-16 £6.50, under 5's free, students & pens £7.50). Family ticket (2 ad & 3 ch) £30. **Facilities:** P (500yds) ▰ ⚹ (cafeteria has wheelchair access ramp) toilets for disabled shop ✖ (ex guide dogs) ◥

NW3
KENWOOD HOUSE
Hampstead Ln NW3 7JR

➲ (Underground - Hampstead) **FREE**
☎ 020 8348 1286 🖹 020 7973 3891

In splendid grounds beside Hampstead Heath, this outstanding neo-classical house contains one of the most important collections of paintings ever given to the nation. Works by Rembrandt, Vermeer, Turner, Gainsborough and Reynolds are all set against a backdrop of sumptuous rooms.
continued

Scenes from *Notting Hill* and *Mansfield Park* were both filmed here.
Times: Open all year, Apr-Sep, daily 10-5.30; Oct, daily 10-5; Nov-Mar, daily 10-4. On Wed & Fri house opens at 10.30. (Closed 24-26 Dec & 1 Jan). Dates valid until 31 Mar 2004. **Facilities:** 🅿 💷 ✕ licensed & toilets for disabled shop ✕ (ex on lead in certain areas) ✱

W14
LEIGHTON HOUSE MUSEUM & ART GALLERY
12 Holland Park Rd W14 8LZ
⊃ (Underground - High Street Kensington. Museum is N of Kensington High Street, off Melbury Rd).   `2 for 1`
☎ 020 7602 3316
e-mail: museums@rbkc.gov.uk

An opulent and exotic example of high Victorian taste, Leighton House was built for the President of the Royal Academy, Frederic Lord Leighton. The main body of the house was built in 1866 but the fabulous Arab Hall, an arresting 'Arabian Nights' creation, was not completed until 13 years later.
Times: Open all year, daily 11-5. (Closed Tue). **Fee:** ✱ £3 (concessions £1). Joint tours £10. 🅿 (100mtrs) (metered) shop ✕ 🏳

W8
LINLEY SAMBOURNE HOUSE
18 Stafford Ter W8 7BH
⊃ (Underground - High Street Kensington)
☎ 020 7602 3316   🖹 020 7602 3316

The home of Linley Sambourne (1844-1910), chief political cartoonist at *Punch* magazine, has had its magnificent artistic interior preserved, almost unchanged, since the late 19th century. Also displayed are many of Sambourne's own drawings and photographs.
Times: ✱ Telephone for details. **Facilities:** 🅿 (metered parking) shop ✕

SE1
LONDON AQUARIUM
County Hall, Riverside Building, Westminster Bridge Rd SE1 7PB
⊃ (Underground-Waterloo & Westminster. On south bank next to Westminster Bridge, nr Big Ben & London Eye)
☎ 020 7967 8000   🖹 020 7967 8029
e-mail: info@londonaquarium.co.uk

The London Aquarium is one of Europe's largest displays of global aquatic life with over 350 species in over 50 displays, ranging from the mystical seahorse to the deadly stonefish. The huge Pacific display is home to a variety of jacks, stingrays and eight sharks. Come and witness the spectacular Atlantic feed where our team of divers hand feed rays and native British sharks. The rainforest feed incorporates a frenzied piranha feed with the amazing marksmanship of the archerfish. There is also a range of education tours and literature to enhance any visit.
Times: Open all year, daily 10-6. Last admission 1hr before closing. Closed 25 Dec. late opening over summer months see website for details **Fee:** ✱ £8.75 (ch 3-14 £5.25, concessions £6.50, ch under 3's free, registered disabled £3.50). Family ticket (2 ad & 2 ch) £25. 🅿 (300mtrs) 💷 & (wheelchairs available) toilets for disabled shop ✕ (ex guide & hearing dogs) 🏳

N1
THE LONDON CANAL MUSEUM
12/13 New Wharf Rd N1 9RT
⊃ (Underground - Kings Cross. Follow York Way along East side of King's Cross Stn, turn right at Wharfedale Rd, then left into New Wharf Rd).
☎ 020 7713 0836 & 🖹 020 7689 6679
e-mail: info@canalmuseum.org.uk

The museum covers the development of London's canals (particularly Regent's Canal), canal vessels and trade, and the way of life of the canal people. Housed in a former ice warehouse and stables, it also illustrates horse transport and the unusual trade of importing ice from Norway; there are two large ice wells under the floor. Facilities include temporary moorings, so you can arrive by boat if you want. There are regular special exhibitions.
Times: Open all year, Tue-Sun & BH Mon 10-4.30 (last admission 3.45). Closed 24-26 & 31 Dec. **Fee:** ✱ £2.50 (ch, students, pen & UB40s £1.25, under 8's free). Groups 10+ 🅿 (0.25m) (parking Mon-Fri before 6.30pm,Sat 1.30) & (large print guides) toilets for disabled shop ✕ (ex guide dogs) 🏳

SE1
LONDON DUNGEON
28-34 Tooley St SE1 2SZ
⊃ (Next to London Bridge Station)
☎ 020 7403 7221   🖹 020 7378 1529   `2 for 1`
e-mail: londondungeon@
merlin-entertainments.com

Blood and guts, torture and terror, in re-enactments of some of the most gruesome events in British history. Brave the Great Fire of London, sail down the Thames towards Traitor's Gate, or visit Executioners corner. You can also meet some especially Wicked Women in a new exhibition. Step back to 1665 to dodge the rats inhabiting London's newest feature, 'The Great Plague'.
Times: Open all year, daily, Apr-Sep 10-5.30; Oct-Mar 10.30-5. Late night opening in the Summer. Telephone for exact times. **Fee:** ✱ £12.95 (ch 14 £8.25, stu & pen £11.25). Group 20+ 🅿 (NCP 200yds) 💷 & toilets for disabled shop ✕ (ex guide dogs) 🏳

WC2
LONDON'S TRANSPORT MUSEUM
The Piazza, Covent Garden WC2E 7BB
⊃ (Underground - Covent Garden, Leicester Sq or Holburn)
☎ 020 7379 6344 & 020 7565 7299
🖹 020 7565 7250
e-mail: resourced@ltmuseum.co.uk

Covent Garden's original Victorian flower market is home to this excellent museum which explores the colourful story of London and its famous transport system from 1800 to the present day. There are buses, trams, tube trains, and posters, as well as touch-screen displays, videos, working models and tube simulators to bring the story to life.
Times: Open all year, daily 10-6, Fri 11-6. Last admission 5.15pm. (Closed 24-26 Dec). **Facilities:** 🅿 (5 mins walk) (parking meters) 💷 & (lift & ramps, touch & sign tours) toilets for disabled shop ✕ (ex guide dogs) 🏳

SW13
LONDON WETLAND CENTRE
Queen Elizabeth Walk SW13 9WT
➲ (underground - Hammersmith).
☎ 020 8409 4400 ▤ 020 8409 4401
e-mail: info@wetlandcentre.org.uk
An inspiring wetland landscape that stretches over 105 acres, almost in the heart of London, in Barnes SW13. 30 wild wetland habitats have been created from reservoir lagoon to ponds, lakes and reedbeds and all are home to a wealth of wildlife.
Times: Winter 9.30-4, Summer 9.30-5. **Fee:** ✱ £6.75 (ch £4 & pen £5.50). Family ticket £17.50. Groups 10+. Car park £2 charge on Sun & BH's per vehicle. ▣ (charged) ⬤✗ licensed ⓓ (ramps, lifts) toilets for disabled shop ✖ (ex guide dogs)

NW1
LONDON ZOO
Regents Park NW1 4RY
➲ (Underground - Camden Town or Regents Park)
☎ 020 7722 3333 ▤ 020 7586 5743
e-mail: marketing@zsl.org
London Zoo is home to over 12,000 animals, insects, reptiles and fish. First opened in 1828, the Zoo can claim the world's first aquarium, insect and reptile house. Daily events such as Animals in Action, feeding times and Animal Encounters give an insight into animal behaviour. Exhibits include the Aquarium, Reptile House, and the Moonlight World where day and night are reversed. The 'Web of Life' exhibition introduces the amazing range of life forms found in Earth's major habitats, through live animal exhibits and interactive displays.
Times: ✱ Open all year, daily from 10am. (Closed 25 Dec).
Facilities: ▣ (charged) ⬤✗ licensed ⓓ (wheelchairs & booster scooter available) toilets for disabled shop ✖ ▤

NW8
LORD'S TOUR & M.C.C. MUSEUM
Lord's Ground NW8 8QN
➲ (Underground - St John's Wood)
☎ 020 7616 8595 & 7616 8596
▤ 020 7266 3825
e-mail: tours@mcc.org.uk
Established in 1787, Lord's is the home of the MCC and cricket. Guided tours take you behind the scenes, and highlights include the Long Room and the MCC Museum, where the Ashes and a large collection of paintings and memorabilia are displayed. The Museum is open on match days for spectators. **(2-for-1 Voucher applies to public guided tours only, not match day admission to museum)**
Times: Open all year, Oct-Mar tours at 12 & 2pm. Apr-Sep 10am, 12 & 2pm (restrictions on some match days). Telephone for details & bookings. **Fee:** Guided tour £7 (ch £4.50, students & pen £5.50). Family ticket (2 ad & 2 ch) £19. Party 25+. Museum only £2.50 (concessions £1) plus ground admission (match days only). ▣✗ licensed ⓓ (by arrangement) toilets for disabled shop ✖ (ex guide dogs) ▤

NW1
MADAME TUSSAUD'S & THE LONDON PLANETARIUM
Marylebone Rd NW1 5LR
➲ (Underground - Baker Street)
☎ 020 7935 6861 ▤ 020 7465 0862
e-mail: firstname.lastname@
madame-tussauds.com
Madame Tussaud's world-famous waxwork collection was founded in Paris in 1770. It moved to England in 1802 and found a permanent home in London's Marylebone Road in 1884. The 21st century has brought new innovations and new levels of interactivity. Listen to Kylie Minogue whisper in your ear, become an A-list celeb in the 'Blush' nightclub, and take your chances in a high security prison populated by dangerous serial killers. Madame Tussaud's has recently been combined with the equally memorable London Planetarium, where visitors can now interact with characters from Disney's *Treasure Planet*.
Times: Open all year 10-5.30 (9.30am wknds, 9am summer) **Fee:** ✱ £14.95 (ch under 16 £10.50, pen £11.80). (Includes entry into London Planetarium) ▣ (200mtrs) ✗ licensed ⓓ (All parts accessible except Spirit of London ride) toilets for disabled shop ✖ (ex guide dogs) ▤

SW1
MALL GALLERIES
The Mall SW1Y 5BD
➲ (Underground - Charing Cross, situated on the Mall, near Trafalgar Square and Admiralty Arch)
☎ 020 7930 6844 ▤ 020 7839 7830
e-mail: info@mallgalleries.com
The venue for the annual open exhibitions of eight national art societies. There is also a wide range of individual and group shows.
Times: Open all year, daily 10-5. Closed between exhibitions and at Christmas. Some late night opening, please phone for details
Fee: £2.50 Depending on exhibition (ch & pen £1). groups 10+ £1 p.p ▣ (50 yds) (no parking at the Mall) ⓓ (chairlift to galleries) toilets for disabled ✖ (ex guide dogs) ▤

EC4
MIDDLE TEMPLE HALL
The Temple EC4Y 9AT
➲ (Underground - Temple, Blackfriars. Turn left at the embankment & left into Middle Temple lane. Hall half way up on left)
☎ 020 7427 4800 ▤ 020 7427 4801
e-mail: library@middletemple.org.uk
Between Fleet Street and the Thames are the Middle and Inner Temples, separate Inns of Court, so named after the Knights Templar who occupied the site from about 1160. Middle Temple Hall is a fine example of Tudor architecture and was completed in about 1570. The hall has a double hammerbeam roof and beautiful stained glass. The 29ft-long high table was made from a single oak tree from Windsor Forest. Sir Francis Drake was a visitor to and friend of the Middle Temple, and a table made from timbers from the *Golden Hind* - the ship in which he sailed around the world - is shown.
Times: ✱ Open all year, Mon-Fri 10-12 & 3-4 (Closed BH & legal vacations). **Facilities:** ⓓ ✖ ⚘

EC3
THE MONUMENT
Monument St EC3R 8AH
➲ (Underground - Monument)
☎ 020 7626 2717   📠 020 7403 4477

Designed by Wren and Hooke and erected in 1671-7, the Monument commemorates the Great Fire of 1666 which is reputed to have started in nearby Pudding Lane. The fire destroyed nearly 90 churches and about 13,000 houses. This fluted Doric column stands 202ft high (Pudding Lane is exactly 202ft from its base) and you can climb the 311 steps to a platform at the summit, and receive a certificate as proof of your athletic abilities.
Times: ✱ Open Mon-Sun, 10-6. Last admission 5.40pm. **Facilities:** ✖

E2
MUSEUM OF CHILDHOOD AT BETHNAL GREEN
Cambridge Heath Rd E2 9PA
➲ (Underground - Bethnal Green)
☎ 020 8980 2415   📠 020 8983 5225
e-mail: bgmc@vam.ac.uk

The Museum of Childhood houses a multitude of childhood delights. Toys, dolls and dolls' houses, model soldiers, puppets, games, model theatres, children's costume and nursery antiques are all included in its well planned displays. Art cart and soft play every weekend throughout the school holidays. Permanent under 5's play area and games zone with board games and giant snakes & ladders.
Times: ✱ Open all year, Mon-Thu & Sat-Sun 10-5.50 (Closed Fri, 24-26 Dec & 1 Jan). **Facilities:** P (Metered parking) 🏪 ♿ (disabled parking by arrangment) toilets for disabled shop ✖

SE1
MUSEUM OF GARDEN HISTORY
Lambeth Palace Rd SE1 7LB
➲ (Underground - Waterloo/Lambeth North, next to Lambeth Palace opposite Houses of Parliament)
☎ 020 7401 8865   📠 020 7401 8869
e-mail: info@museumgardenhistory.org

Adjacent to the south gateway of Lambeth Palace is the former church of St Mary-at-Lambeth, now the Museum of Garden History. There is a permanent exhibition on the history of gardens and a collection of ancient tools. The shop sells souvenirs, books, gifts and seeds from the plant collection. Admiral Bligh of the *Bounty* is buried in the garden.
Times: Open 2 Feb-mid Dec, daily, 10.30-5. **Facilities:** P (100yds) (metered) 🏪 ♿ shop ✖ (ex guide dogs) ▼

EC2
MUSEUM OF LONDON
150 London Wall EC2Y 5HN
➲ (Underground - St Paul's, Barbican)
☎ 020 7600 3699   📠 020 7600 1058
e-mail: info@museumoflondon.org.uk

Dedicated to the story of London and its people, the Museum of London exists to inspire a passion for London in all who visit it. As well as the permanent collection, the Museum has a varied exhibition programme with three major temporary exhibitions and six topical displays each year. There are also
continued

smaller exhibitions in the newly-developed foyer gallery. A wide programme of lectures and activities are provided.
Times: ✱ Open all year, Mon-Sat 10-5.50, Sun 12-5.50 (closed 24-26 Dec & 1 Jan). **Facilities:** P 🏪 ♿ (wheelchairs available, lifts & induction loops, parking) toilets for disabled shop ✖ (ex guide dogs) ▼

EC1
MUSEUM OF THE ORDER OF ST JOHN
St John's Gate, St John's Ln, Clerkenwell EC1M 4DA
➲ (Underground - Farringdon, Barbican)
☎ 020 7253 6644   📠 020 7336 0587

One of the most obscure and fascinating museums in London, St John's Gate displays treasures that once belonged to the Knights Hospitaller, the crusading knights who are now better known as first aiders. Maltese silver, Italian furniture, paintings, coins and pharmacy jars are among the objects on view. Guided tours are available.
Times: ✱ Open all year, Mon-Sat 10-5, Sat 10-4 (Closed Etr, Xmas wk & BH wknds). Guided tours 11 & 2.30 Tue, Fri & Sat. **Facilities:** P (meters/ NCP 300yds) ♿ toilets for disabled shop ✖ (ex guide dogs)

WC2
MUSEUMS OF THE ROYAL COLLEGE OF SURGEONS
35-43 Lincoln's Inn Fields WC2A 3PE
➲ (Underground - Holborn)
☎ 020 7869 6560   📠 020 7869 6564   `FREE`
e-mail: museums@rcseng.ac.uk

Two museums are housed here - the Hunterian Museum contains the anatomical and pathological specimens collected by John Hunter FRS (1728-1793), a renowned surgeon and teacher of anatomy, and displays relating to the work of Sir Joseph Lister, pioneer of antiseptic surgery. The Odontological Museum contains an extensive collection of human and animal skulls and teeth as well as dental instruments. The museums are being combined and refurbished, due to re-open at the end of 2004.
Times: Closed for refurbishment until the end of 2004, please telephone for details **Facilities:** P (25mtrs) (pay & display 8-6pm) ♿ (prior notice required) shop ✖ (ex guide dogs)

SW3
NATIONAL ARMY MUSEUM
Royal Hospital Rd, Chelsea SW3 4HT
➲ (Underground - Sloane Square)
☎ 020 7730 0717   📠 020 7823 6573
e-mail: info@national-army-museum.ac.uk

The museum offers a unique insight into the lives of Britain's soldiers, with displays including weapons, paintings, equipment, models, medals, and uniforms.
Times: ✱ Open all year, daily 10-5.30. (Closed Good Fri, May Day, 24-26 Dec & 1 Jan). **Facilities:** P 🏪 ♿ (wheelchair lift to access lower ground floor) toilets for disabled shop ✖ (ex guide dogs)

> A full guide to the Symbols &
> Abbreviations used in this book
> can be found on page 6

WC2
NATIONAL GALLERY
Trafalgar Square WC2N 5DN

➲ (Underground - Charing Cross, Leicester Square, Embankment & Piccadilly Circus. Rail: Charing Cross. Located on N side of Trafalgar Sq)

☎ 020 7747 2885 🖷 020 7747 2423

e-mail: information@ng-london.org.uk

All the great periods of Western European painting from 1260-1900 are represented here. The Gallery's particular treasures include Velázquez's *Toilet of Venus*, Leonardo da Vinci's Cartoon *(The Virgin and Child with Saints Anne and John the Baptist)*, Rembrandt's *Belshazzar's Feast*, Van Gogh's *Sunflowers*, and Titian's *Bacchus and Ariadne*. The British paintings include Gainsborough's *Mr and Mrs Andrews* and Constable's *Haywain*.

Times: Open all year, daily 10-6, (Wed until 9pm). Special major charging exhibitions open normal gallery times. Closed 24-26 Dec & 1 Jan. **Facilities:** P (100yds) 💷 ✖ licensed ዼ (wheelchair, induction loop, lift, deaf/blind visitor tours) toilets for disabled shop ✖ (ex guide & hearing dogs) 🔊

SE10
NATIONAL MARITIME MUSEUM
Romney Rd SE10 9NF

➲ (central Greenwich)

☎ 020 8312 6565 🖷 020 8312 6632

Britain's seafaring history displayed in an impressive modern museum. Themes include exploration and discovery, Nelson, trade and empire, passenger shipping and luxury liners, maritime London, costume, art and the sea, and the future of the sea. There are interactive displays for children.

Times: Open all year, daily 10-5. (Closed Xmas/New Year) **Fee:** Free, except special exhibtions. **Facilities:** P (50 yds) (parking in Greenwich limited) 💷 ✖ licensed ዼ (wheelchairs, advisory service for hearing/sight impaired) toilets for disabled shop ✖ (guide dogs) 🔊

WC2
NATIONAL PORTRAIT GALLERY
St Martin's Place WC2H 0HE

➲ (Underground - Charing Cross, Leicester Square)

☎ 020 7306 0055 🖷 020 7306 0056

The National Portrait Gallery is home to the largest collection of portraiture in the world featuring famous British men and woman who have created history from the Middle Ages until the present day. Over 1000 portraits are on display across three floors form Henry VIII and Florence Nightingale to The Beatles and The Queen. And, if you want to rest those weary feet, visit the fabulous Portrait Restaurant on the top floor with roof-top views across London.

Times: Open all year, Mon-Wed & Sat-Sun 10-6, Thu-Fri 10-9. (Closed Good Fri, 24-26 Dec & 1 Jan). Gallery closure commences 10mins prior to stated time. **Facilities:** P (200yds) 💷 ✖ licensed ዼ (stair climber,touch tours,audio guide,large print captions) toilets for disabled shop ✖ (ex guide dogs) 🔊

SW7
THE NATURAL HISTORY MUSEUM
Cromwell Rd SW7 5BD

➲ (Underground - South Kensington)

☎ 020 7942 5000 🖷 020 7942 5075   FREE

e-mail: marketing@nhm.ac.uk

This vast and elaborate Romanesque-style building, with its terracotta facing showing relief mouldings of animals, birds and fishes, covers an area of four acres. A multitude of fascinating galleries cover every aspect of natural history. A major permanent exhibition on dinosaurs includes skeletons and displays on how dinosaurs lived, why they became extinct, and how they were dug up and studied by scientists. 'The Power Within' offers the opportunity to experience an earthquake and the 'Earth's Treasury' exhibition displays the museum's collection of gems and minerals. Don't miss the opportunity to see behind the scenes and talk to some of the museum's scientists in the new Darwin Centre.

Times: Mon-Sat 10-5.50, Sun 11-5.50 (last admission 5.30). Closed 24-26 Dec. **Facilities:** P (180yds) (limited parking,advise public transport) 💷 ✖ licensed ዼ (top floor/one gallery not accessible, wheelchair hire) toilets for disabled shop ✖ (ex guide dogs) 🔊

SE10
OLD ROYAL NAVAL COLLEGE
Greenwich SE10 9NN

➲ (In centre of Greenwich, off the one way system, (college approach), located on the Thames next to the Cutty Sark and Greenwich Pier)   FREE

☎ 020 8269 4791 🖷 020 8269 4757

e-mail: info@greenwichfoundation.org.uk

The grade one listed Old Royal Navy College buildings are now in the care of the Greenwich Foundation. They occupy the site of the Tudor palace where Henry VIII and Elizabeth I were born. The former Greenwich Hospital buildings incorporate a magnificent painted hall by Thornhill and a chapel by James Stuart. Also open to the public are the beautiful grounds of the estate, and a visitor centre featuring an exhibition on the world heritage site of maritime Greenwich and the history of the site.

Times: Open all year (Painted Hall and Chapel only), daily 10-5 (last admission 4.15). Chapel closed until 12.30 on Sundays. **Facilities:** P (200mtrs) (all local streets, yellow line roads) 💷 ✖ licensed ዼ (can be given access if prior notice given) toilets for disabled shop ✖ (ex guide dogs) 🔊

WC1
PETRIE MUSEUM OF EGYPTIAN ARCHAEOLOGY
Malet Place, Univerity College London WC1E 6BT

➲ (on 1st floor of the D M S Watson building, in Malet Place, off Torrington Place)

☎ 020 7679 2884 🖷 020 7679 2886   FREE

e-mail: petrie.museum@ucl.ac.uk

One of the largest and most inspiring collections of Egyptian archaeology anywhere in the world. The displays illustrate life in the Nile Valley from prehistory, through the era of the Pharoahs to Roman and Islamic times. Especially noted for its collection of the personal items that illustrate life and death in Ancient Egypt, including the world's earliest surviving dress (c 2800BC).

Times: Open all year, Tue-Fri 1-5, Sat 10-1. Closed for 1 wk at Xmas/Etr.
Facilities: 💷 ✖ ዼ toilets for disabled shop ✖ (ex guide dogs)

W1
POLLOCK'S TOY MUSEUM
1 Scala St W1T 2HL
➲ (Underground - Goodge Street)
☎ 020 7636 3452
e-mail: info@pollocksmuseum.co.uk

Teddy bears, wax and china dolls, dolls' houses, board games, toy theatres, tin toys, mechanical and optical toys, folk toys and nursery furniture, are among the attractions to be seen in this appealing museum. Items from all over the world and from all periods are displayed in two small, interconnecting houses with winding staircases and charming little rooms. Toy theatre performances available for groups.
Times: Open all year, Mon-Sat 10-5. (Closed BH's, Sun & Xmas).
Fee: ✱ £3 (ch 3-18 £1.50) P (100yds) (Central London restrictions) ♿ shop ❦

SW1
THE QUEEN'S GALLERY
Buckingham Palace, Buckingham Palace Rd SW1A 1AA
➲ (Underground - Victoria, Green Park & St. James' Park)
☎ 020 7766 7301 📠 020 7930 9625
e-mail: buckinghampalace@royalcollection.org.uk

The Gallery hosts changing exhibitions of works of art from the Royal Collection. The collection has largely been formed since the restoration of the Monarchy in 1660 and included paintings, drawings and watercolours, furniture, ceramics, clocks, silver, sculpture, jewellery, books, manuscripts, prints and maps, arms and armour, fans, and textiles. Works of art from the Royal Collection are also on display at the principal royal residences. Exhibitions in 2004 include 'Fabergé' and 'George III and Queen Charlotte: Patronage, Collecting and Court Taste'.
Times: Open all year, daily, 10-5.30. Last admission 4.30. (Closed 9 Apr, 25 & 26 Dec) Entry by timed ticket. **Fee:** ✱ £6.50 (ch under 5 free, ch under 17 £3, pen £5). Family Ticket (2 ad & 3 ch) £16. P (200yds) ♿ toilets for disabled shop ✖ (ex guide dogs) ❦

SE10
THE QUEENS HOUSE
Romney Rd, Greenwich SE10 9NF
➲ (central Greenwich)
☎ 020 8312 6565 📠 020 8312 6632

The first Palladian-style villa in England, designed by Inigo Jones for Anne of Denmark and completed for Queen Henrietta Maria, wife of Charles I. Restoration means that the house can be seen as it appeared when new, with bright silks and furnishings. The Great Hall, the State Rooms and a Loggia overlooking Greenwich Park are notable features.
Times: (Please telephone for opening times) **Fee:** (Free, except special exhibitions) **Facilities:** P (50 yds) ✖ licensed ♿ (Blind kit/stairclimber/wheelchairs) toilets for disabled shop ✖ ❦

Attractions with this symbol do not charge for entry.

W1
ROYAL ACADEMY OF ARTS
Burlington House, Piccadilly W1J 0BD
➲ (Underground - Piccadilly Circus, head towards Green Park)
☎ 020 7300 8000 📠 020 7300 5886

Known principally for its exhibitions, the Royal Academy of Arts was founded in 1768 and is Britain's oldest Fine Arts institution. Two of its founding principles were to provide a free school and to mount 'an annual exhibition open to all artists of distinguished merit', now known as the Summer Exhibition. Both continue today. The Royal Academy's most prized possession, Michelangelo's Tondo, *The Virgin and Child with the Infant St John,* one of only four marble sculptures by the artist outside Italy, is on permanent display in the Sackler Wing.
Times: Open daily 10-6. (Closed 25 Dec & Good Fri) late night opening Fridays 10-10. **Fee:** ✱ £6-£8 (ch, students, pen & group visitors reduced price). Prices vary for each exhibition **Facilities:** 💻 ✖ licensed ♿ toilets for disabled shop ✖ (ex guide dogs) ❦

NW9
ROYAL AIR FORCE MUSEUM
Grahame Park Way, Hendon NW9 5LL
➲ (within easy reach of the A5, A41, M1 and North circular A406 roads. Tube on Northern Line to Colindale. Rail to Mill Hill Broadway station. Bus route 303 passes the door)
☎ 020 8205 2266 📠 020 8358 4981 FREE
e-mail: groupbusiness@rafmuseum.org

Take off to the Royal Air Force Museum and soar through the history of aviation from the earliest balloon flights to the latest Eurofighter. Gaze at a world-class collection of over 80 aircraft, aviation/wartime memorabilia and artefacts, together with an awe inspiring sound and light show that takes the visitor back in time to the Battle of Britain. Other exciting features include a 'walk through' Sunderland flying boat, a touch and try Jet Provost, a simulator ride, film shows, art gallery and outdoor activity area. The museum also runs many temporary exhibitions, fairs and functions as well as outdoor summer events. **(2-for-1 Voucher applies to simulator ride only)**
Times: Open daily 10-6. Closed 8-17 Dec & Xmas/New Year.
Facilities: P 💻 ✖ licensed ♿ (lifts, ramps & wheelchairs available) toilets for disabled shop ✖ (ex guide dogs) ❦

SW3
ROYAL HOSPITAL CHELSEA
Royal Hospital Rd SW3 4SR
➲ (near Sloane Square, off A3216 & A3031)
☎ 020 7881 5204 📠 020 7881 5463 FREE
e-mail: info@chelsea-pensioners.org.uk

Founded in 1682 by Charles II as a retreat for army veterans who had become unfit for duty, the Royal Hospital Chelsea was built on the site of an intended theological college founded by James I in 1609. The buildings were designed and built by Sir Christopher Wren, and then added to by Robert Adam and Sir John Soane. The most recent parts are a new infirmary opened by the present Queen in 1961, and a social centre opened by Prince Charles in 1985. The hospital houses some 400 'In-Pensioners' who also do voluntary

continued

work as tour guides, clerical assistants and ground staff. Visitors can stroll around the grounds, gain admission to the Chapel, Great Hall and Museum, and visit the Council Chamber on application to the Adjutant.

Times: Open Mon-Sat 10-12 & 2-4, Sun 2-4. (Museum closed Oct-Mar)
Facilities: ▣ & toilets for disabled shop ✖ (ex with prior notice)

SW1
THE ROYAL MEWS
Buckingham Palace, Buckingham Palace Rd SW1W 0QH
➲ (Underground - Victoria, Green Park, St. James Park)
☎ 020 7766 7302 🖹 020 7930 9625
e-mail: buckinghampalace@royalcollection.org.uk

Designed by John Nash and completed in 1825, the Royal Mews houses the State Coaches, horse drawn carriages and motor cars used for coronations, state visits, royal weddings and the State Opening of Parliament. These include the Gold State Coach, made in 1762, with panels painted by the Florentine artist Cipriani. As one of the finest working stables in existence, the Royal Mews provides a unique opportunity for you to see a working department of the Royal Household.

Times: Open Mar-Oct, 11-4 (Aug-Sep 10-5). (Last admission 3.15; Aug-Sep 4.15). **Fee:** ✱ £5 (ch under 5 free, ch 5-16 £2.50, pen & students £4) Family ticket (2 ad & 3 ch) £12.50. ▣ (200yds) & (telephone for access information) toilets for disabled shop ✖ (ex guide dogs) ◀

SE10
ROYAL OBSERVATORY GREENWICH
Greenwich Park, Greenwich SE10 9NF
➲ (off A2, Greenwich Park)   FREE
☎ 020 8312 6565 🖹 020 8312 6632

Charles II founded the Royal Observatory in 1675 'for perfecting navigation and astronomy'. It stands at zero meridian longitude and is the original home of Greenwich Mean Time. It houses an extensive collection of historic timekeeping, astronomical and navigational instruments. Planetarium shows throughout the year. Events are planned for the school holidays.

Times: Open all year, daily 10-5 (Closed 24-26 Dec & 1 Jan)
Facilities: ▣ & toilets for disabled shop ✖ ◀

EC4
ST PAUL'S CATHEDRAL
St Pauls Courtyard EC4M 8AD   2 for 1
☎ 020 7246 8348 🖹 020 7248 3104
e-mail: chapterhouse@stpaulscathedral.org.uk

Completed in 1710, Sir Christopher Wren's architectural masterpiece is the cathedral church of the Bishop of London, and arose, like so much of this area of London, from the ashes of the Great Fire of London in 1666. Among the worthies buried here are Nelson and the Duke of Wellington, while Holman Hunt's masterpiece, *Light of the World* hangs in the nave. Impressive views of London can be seen from the Golden Gallery.

Times: Open Mon-Sat 8.30-4.15pm. Cathedral may close for special services. **Fee:** ✱ £6 (ch £3, concessions £5) ▣ 💻 ✖ licensed & toilets for disabled shop ✖ (ex guide dogs) ◀

SW7
SCIENCE MUSEUM
Exhibition Rd, South Kensington SW7 2DD
➲ (Underground - South Kensington, Signposted from tube stn)
☎ 020 7942 4000 🖹 020 7942 4421
e-mail: sciencemuseum@nmsi.ac.uk

Ideal for children and adults too, the displays feature many working models with knobs to press, handles to turn and buttons to push to various different effects: exhibits are set in motion, light up, rotate and make noises. The collections cover science, technology, engineering and industry through the ages; there are galleries dealing with printing, chemistry, nuclear physics, navigation, photography, electricity, communications and medicine. The new Wellcome Wing includes an IMAX cinema, 6 new galleries and a restaurant.

Times: ✱ Open all year, daily 10-6. (Closed 24-26 Dec).
Facilities: 💻 ✖ licensed & (personal 2hr tour of museum) toilets for disabled shop ✖ (ex guide dogs) ◀

W2
SERPENTINE GALLERY
Kensington Gardens W2 3XA
➲ (Underground - Knightsbridge, Lancaster Gate, South Kensington)
☎ 020 7402 6075 🖹 020 7402 4103   FREE
e-mail: press@serpentinegallery.org

The Serpentine Gallery, named after the lake in Hyde Park, is situated in the heart of Kensington Gardens in a 1934 tea pavilion, and was founded in 1970 by the Arts Council of Great Britain. Today the Gallery attracts over 400,000 visitors a year and is one of the best places in London for modern and contemporary art and architecture.

Times: Open daily 10-6. **Facilities:** ▣ (charged) & toilets for disabled shop ✖ (ex guide dogs) ◀

SE1
SHAKESPEARE'S GLOBE EXHIBITION AND THEATRE TOUR
21 New Globe Walk, Bankside SE1 9DT
➲ (Underground - London Bridge, walk along Bankside. Mansion House, walk across Southwark Bridge. St Pauls, walk across Millennium Bridge)
☎ 020 7902 1500 🖹 020 7902 1515   2 for 1
e-mail: info@shakespearesglobe.com

Guides help to bring England's theatrical heritage to life at the 'unparalleled and astonishing' recreation of this famous theatre. Discover what an Elizabethan audience would have been like, find out about the rivalry between the bankside theatres, the bear baiting and the stews, hear about the penny stinkards and find out what a bodger is.

Times: Open all year, May-Sep, daily 9-12 (12-5 virtual theatre tour); Oct-Apr 10-6. **Fee:** £8 (ch £5.50, pen & students £6.50). Group rates available. ▣ (0.5m) (very limited on-street parking) 💻 ✖ licensed & (parking spaces, 'touch tours' available by appointment) toilets for disabled shop ✖ (ex guide & hearing dogs) ◀

WC2
SIR JOHN SOANE'S MUSEUM
13 Lincoln's Inn Fields WC2A 3BP
➲ (Underground - Holborn)
☎ 020 7405 2107 ▤ 020 7831 3957 FREE

Sir John Soane was responsible for some of the most splendid architecture in London, and his house, built in 1812, contains his collections of antiquities, sculpture, paintings, drawings and books. Amongst his treasures are the *Rake's Progress* and *Election* series of paintings by Hogarth.
Times: Open all year, Tue-Sat 10-5. Also first Tue of month 6-9pm. (Closed BH). Lecture tour Sat 2.30 (limited no of tickets sold from 2pm) **Facilities:** P (200yds) (metered parking) ♿ (wheelchair available, phone for details of accessibility) shop ✘ (ex guide dogs) ➲

SE5
SOUTH LONDON GALLERY
65 Peckham Rd SE5 8UH
➲ (from Vauxhall take A202 to Camberwell Green. SLG is halfway between Camberwell Green and Peckham).
☎ 020 7703 6120 & 020 7703 9799-taped info
▤ 020 7252 4730 FREE
e-mail: mail@southlondongallery.org

The gallery presents a programme of up to eight exhibitions a year of cutting-edge contemporary art, and has established itself as South East London's premier venue for contemporary visual arts. The Gallery also aims to bring contemporary art of the highest standards to audiences in South London and to assist in the regeneration of the area by attracting audiences from across Britain and abroad.
Times: Gallery closed for refurbishment Autumn 2003-Spring 2004. **Facilities:** P on-street parking ♿ (disabled access from Spring 2004) toilets for disabled ✘ (ex guide dogs)

SE1
SOUTHWARK CATHEDRAL
Montague Close SE1 9DA
➲ (Adjacent to London Bridge (Rd & Station), off Borough High Street.
☎ 020 7367 6700 ▤ 020 7367 6730
e-mail: cathedral@dswark.org.uk

Originally an Augustinian priory, this is London's oldest gothic church building, and has been a place of worship for more than 1,000 years. It became a cathedral for the Diocese of Southwark in 1905, and has links with Chaucer, Dickens and Shakespeare. John Gower and Shakespeare's brother Edmund are buried here. John Harvard of US university fame was baptised here in 1607, and there is a chapel to his memory. Visitors can view part of a Roman road, 14th-century cloister work, and kilns used for Southwark delftware in the 17th/18th centuries.
Times: ✱ Open daily: Cathedral 9-6, Cathedral exhibition 10-6. (No tourism permitted on Good Fri & 25 Dec) **Facilities:** P ✘ licensed ♿ toilets for disabled shop ✘ (ex service dogs) ➲

E9
SUTTON HOUSE
2 & 4 Homerton High St E9 6JQ
➲ (10 minute walk from Hackney Central train station) 2 for 1
☎ 020 8986 2264
e-mail: suttonhouse@nationaltrust.org.uk

In London's East End, the building is a rare example of a Tudor red-brick house. Built in 1535 by Sir Rufe Sadleir, Principal Secretary of State for Henry VIII, the house has 18th-century alterations and later additions.
Times: Open 23 Jan-19 Dec, Fri & Sat 1-5.30; Sun & BH Mon 11.30-5.30. **Fee:** ✱ £2.20. Family ticket £4.90. P (on street parking) (meters) ▣ ♿ (induction loop, braille guide) toilets for disabled shop ✘ (ex guide dogs) ☙

SW1
TATE BRITAIN
Millbank SW1P 4RG
➲ (Underground - Pimlico)
☎ 020 7887 8000 & rec info 020 7887 8008
e-mail: information@tate.org.uk

Tate Britain is the national gallery of British art from 1500 to the present day, from Tudors to the Turner Prize. Tate holds the greatest collection of British art in the world, including works by Blake, Constable, Epstein, Gainsborough, Gilbert and George, Hatoum, Hirst, Hockney, Hodgkin, Hogarth, Moore, Rossetti, Sickert, Spencer, Stubbs and Turner. The gallery is the world centre for the understanding and enjoyment of British art. The opening of the Tate Centenary provides Tate Britain with ten new and five refurbished galleries used for special exhibitions and the permanent collection.
Times: Open daily 10-5.50. (Closed 24-26 Dec). **Facilities:** P (100mtrs) (1hr stay) ▣ ✘ licensed ♿ (wheelchairs on request, parking by prior arrangement) toilets for disabled shop ✘ (ex guide & hearing dogs) ➲

SE1
TATE MODERN
Bankside SE1 9TG
➲ (Underground - Southwark, Blackfriars)
☎ 020 7887 8008 (info) & 020 7887 8888
▤ 020 7401 5052 FREE
e-mail: information@tate.org.uk

Tate Modern, on the bank of the River Thames, is the world's most popular art museum. Presenting a permanent collection of modern and contemporary art and hosting special exhibitions. It has welcomed over 13 million visitors since it opened in May 2000.
Times: Open all year, Sun-Thu 10-6, Fri & Sat 10am-10pm. (Closed 24-26 Dec). **Facilities:** P (very limited) ▣ ✘ licensed ♿ (parking & wheelchairs available call 020 7887 8888) toilets for disabled shop ✘ (ex guide dogs) ➲

SE18
THAMES BARRIER INFORMATION & LEARNING CENTRE

1 Unity Way SE18 5NJ

➪ (Turn off A102(M) onto A206, turn onto Eastmoor St and follow signs)   **2 for 1**
☎ 020 8305 4188 📠 020 8855 2146
e-mail: sonia.gill@environment-agency.gov.uk

Spanning a third of a mile, the Thames Barrier is the world's largest movable flood barrier. The visitors' centre and exhibition on the South Bank explains the flood threat and the construction of this £535 million project, now valued at £1 billion. Each month a test closure of all ten gates, lasting over 2 hours, is carried out and the annual full day closure of all ten gates takes place in the autumn.

Times: Open 31 Mar-29 Sep, 10.30-4.30. **Fee:** £1 (ch 50p, pen 75p). Car park £1. Coach park free. 🅿 (charged) 💻 ♿ (lift from river pier approach) toilets for disabled shop ✖ (ex guide dogs) ▼

WC2
THEATRE MUSEUM

Russell St, Covent Gardent WC2E 7PR

➪ (Underground - Covent Garden, Leicester Sq)
☎ 020 7943 4700 📠 020 7943 4777   **FREE**
e-mail: tmenquiries@vam.ac.uk

Major developments, events and personalities from the performing arts, including stage models, costumes, prints, drawings, posters, puppets, props and a variety of other theatre memorabilia. There are guided tours, demonstrations on the art of stage make-up, and you can dress up in costumes from National Theatre companies. Groups are advised to book in advance.

Times: Open all year, Tue-Sun 10-6. (closed 24-26 Dec & 1 Jan)
Facilities: 🅿 (meters, NCP 250yds) ♿ toilets for disabled shop ✖ (ex guide dogs) ▼

SE1
THE TOWER BRIDGE EXHIBITION

Tower Bridge Rd SE1 2UP

➪ (Underground - Tower Hill or London Bridge)
☎ 020 7940 3985 📠 020 7357 7935
e-mail: enquiries@towerbridge.org.uk

One of the capital's most famous landmarks, its glass-covered walkways stand 142ft above the Thames, affording panoramic views of the river. Much of the original machinery for working the bridge can be seen in the engine rooms. The Tower Bridge Exhibition uses state-of-the-art effects to present the story of the bridge in a dramatic and exciting fashion.

Times: Open all year, 9.30-6 (last ticket sold 5pm). (Closed 1 Jan & 24-25 Dec). **Fee:** ✱ £4.50 (concessions £3.50) Family tickets from £11. 🅿 (100yds) ♿ toilets for disabled shop ✖ ▼

EC3
TOWER OF LONDON

Tower Hill EC3N 4AB

➪ (Underground - Tower Hill)
☎ 0870 756 6060

Perhaps the most famous castle in the world, the Tower of London has played a central part in British history. The White Tower, built by William the Conqueror as a show of strength to the people of London, remains one of the most

continued

outstanding examples of Norman military architecture in Europe. For hundreds of years the Tower was used, among other things, as the State Prison. It was here that Henry VIII had two of his wives executed, here that Lady Jane Grey died and here that Sir Walter Raleigh was imprisoned. The Yeoman Warders, or 'Beefeaters' play an important role in the protection of the Tower - home of the Crown Jewels - and are informative and entertaining. Look out for the ravens, whose continued residence is said to ensure that the Kingdom does not fall. The Crowns and Diamonds exhibition features a number of crowns never displayed to the public before and more than 12,000 rough and polished diamonds. Also open to the public are the Royal Armouries, which received their first recorded visitor as long ago as 1489. The displays include an extensive range of arms and armour dating from the Norman ages, a collection of Spanish arms and the Line of Kings.

Times: Open all year, Mar-Oct, Mon-Sat 9-6, Sun 10-6 (last admission 5pm); Nov-Feb, Tue-Sat 9-5, Sun 10-5 (last admission 4pm). (Closed 24-26 Dec & 1 Jan). **Fee:** £12 (ch £7.00 under 5's free, concessions £9). Family ticket (2 ad & 3 ch) £36. **Facilities:** 🅿 (100yds) (NCP Lower Thames St) 💻 ✖ licensed ♿ (access guide can be obtained in advance call 020 7488 5694) toilets for disabled shop ✖ (ex guide dogs) ▼

SW7
VICTORIA AND ALBERT MUSEUM

Cromwell Rd, South Kensington SW7 2RL

➪ (Underground - South Kensington)
☎ 020 7942 2000   **FREE**
e-mail: vanda@vam.ac.uk

The world's finest museum of the applied and decorative arts, with collections spanning 3000 years, and comprising sculpture, furniture, fashion and textiles, paintings, silver, glass, ceramics, jewellery, books, prints, and photographs from Britain and all over the world. Highlights include the national collection of paintings by John Constable, the Dress Court showing fashion from 1500 to the present day, a superb Asian collection, the Jewellery Gallery including the Russian Crown Jewels, and the 20th Century Gallery, devoted to contemporary art and design. The stunning British Galleries 1500-1900 tell the story of British design from the Tudor age to the Victorian era.

Times: Open all year, Mon-Sun 10-5.45. (Closed 24-26 Dec). Wed & last Fri of month open late, 10-10. **Facilities:** 🅿 (500yds) (limited, charged parking) 💻 ✖ licensed ♿ (braille guide, tour tape. For further info please phone) toilets for disabled shop ✖ (ex guide dogs) ▼

SE1
VINOPOLIS, CITY OF WINE
1 Bank End SE1 9BU

➲ (Underground-London Bridge. Borough High Street West exit, right into Stoney St, then left into Park St)

☎ 0870 241 4040 ▤ 020 7940 8302
e-mail: sales@vinopolis.co.uk

Vinopolis is a journey through the world of wine that covers two and a half acres. Discover wine cultures from around the world and the origins of the art of wine making. New to Vinopolis is the 'Bombay Sapphire Experience'.
Times: Open all year, Mon, Fri & Sat 12-9, Tue-Thu & Sun 12-6, (last admission 2 hrs before closing). Please call for opening hours in Dec and BH's. **Fee:** ✱ Mon, Fri-Sun, £12.50, (ch U16 free, seniors (60+) £11.50), Tue-Thu £11, (ch U16 free, seniors (60+) £10). ℙ (5-10 min walk) (NCP parking) 🍽 ✗ licensed ⅋ (lifts & ramps) toilets for disabled shop ✗ (ex guide dogs) ⬤

W1
WALLACE COLLECTION
Hertford House, Manchester Square W1U 3BN

➲ (Underground - Bond Street, Baker Street, Oxford Circus)

☎ 020 7563 9500 ▤ 020 7224 2155   FREE
e-mail: enquiries@wallacecollection.org

An elegant 18th-century town house is an appropriate gallery for this outstanding collection of art. Founded by the 1st Marquis of Hertford, it was bequeathed to the nation in 1897 and came on public display three years later. As well as an unrivalled representation of 18th-century French art with paintings by Boucher, Watteau and Fragonard, Hertford House is the home of Frans Hals' *Laughing Cavalier* and of paintings by Gainsborough, Rubens, Delacroix and Titian. It also houses the largest collection of arms and armour outside the Tower of London.
(2-for-1 Voucher applies to guided audio tours only)
Times: Open all year, Mon-Sat 10-5, Sun 12-5. (Closed Good Fri, May BH, 24-26 Dec & 1 Jan). **Facilities:** ℙ (NCP & meters) (meters are free on Sun) 🍽 ✗ licensed ⅋ (lift, ramp, wheelchair available upon request) toilets for disabled shop ✗ ⬤

SE3
THE WERNHER COLLECTION AT RANGER'S HOUSE
Chesterfield Walk, Blackheath SE10 8QY

☎ 020 8853 0035 ▤ 020 8853 0090

Handsome 18th-century house with lovely views over London, Greenwich Park, Blackheath and the Thames. View the 'Wernher Collection' of self-made millionaire Julius Wernher, who made his fortune in the diamond mines of South Africa.
Times: Open Apr-Sep, Wed-Sun & BH's 10-6; Oct, Wed-Sun 10-5; Nov-Mar, Wed-Sun 10-4. (Closed 22 Dec-2 Mar). Dates valid until 31 Mar 2004. **Fee:** £4.50 (ch £2.50, concessions £3.50). Prices valid until 31 Mar 2004. **Facilities:** ℙ ⅋ toilets for disabled shop ✗ (in certain areas) ⌗

EC1
WESLEY'S CHAPEL, HOUSE & MUSEUM OF METHODISM
49 City Rd EC1Y 1AU

➲ (Underground - Old Street- exit number 4)

☎ 020 7253 2262   FREE
▤ 020 7608 3825

Wesley's Chapel has been the Mother Church of World Methodism since its construction in 1778. The crypt houses a museum which traces the development of Methodism from the 18th century to the present day. Wesley's house - built by him in 1779 - was his home when not touring and preaching. Special events are held on May 24 (the anniversary of Wesley's conversion), and November 1st (the anniversary of the Chapel's opening).
Times: Open all year, Mon-Sat & BH 10-4 (Closed BH's, 25 & 26 Dec). Main service 11am Sun followed by an opportunity to tour the museum and house. **Facilities:** ℙ (NCP at Finsbury Square) ⅋ (lift to the crypt of the chapel) toilets for disabled shop ✗ (ex guide dogs) ⬤

SW1
WESTMINSTER ABBEY
Broad Sanctuary SW1P 3PA

➲ (Underground - Westminster, St James's Park. Next to Parliament Square and opposite the Houses of Parliament)

☎ 020 7222 5152 7654 4900 ▤ 020 7233 2072
e-mail: info@westminster-abbey.org

Westminster Abbey was originally a Benedictine monastery. In the 11th century, it was re-founded by St. Edward the Confessor. The great Romanesque abbey Edward built next to his royal palace became his burial place shortly after it was completed. Over the centuries that followed, many more kings and queens have been buried, and many great figures commemorated, in the abbey. The abbey has been the setting for nearly every coronation since that of William the Conqueror in 1066, and for numerous other royal occasions.

continued

The present building, begun by Henry III in 1245, is one of the most visited churches in the world.
Times: Abbey: Mon-Fri 9.30-3.45, Sat 9-1.45. Wed late night opening 6-7pm. Last admission 60 mins before closing. Cloister: daily 8-6. No tourist visiting on Sundays, however visitors are welcome at services. The Abbey may at short notice be closed for special services & other events. **Fee:** ✱ £6 (ch 11-15 £4, under 11's free, pen & students £4). Family ticket (2 ad & 2 ch) £12. ⬛ & (areas accessible induction loop) shop ✖ (ex guide dogs) ◥

SW1
WESTMINSTER CATHEDRAL
Victoria St SW1P 1QW
➲ (300 yds from Victoria Station)
☎ 020 7798 9055 ▤ 020 7798 9090   FREE
e-mail: barrypalmer@rcdow.org.uk
Westminster Cathedral is a fascinating example of Victorian architecture. Designed in the Early Christian Byzantine style by John Francis Bentley, its strongly oriental appearance makes it very distinctive. The foundation stone was laid in 1895 but the interior decorations are not fully completed. The Campanile Bell Tower is 273ft high and has a four-sided viewing gallery with magnificent views over London. The lift is open daily 9am-5pm Mar-Nov but shut Mon-Wed from Dec-Feb.
Times: Open all year, daily 7-7. **Facilities:** ℗ (0.25m) (2hr metered parking) ⬛ & (all parts accessible except side chapels) shop ✖ (ex guide dogs)

SW1
WESTMINSTER HALL
Westminster SW1A 0AA
➲ (Underground - Westminster Hall)
☎ 020 7219 4272
The great Westminster Hall, where Charles I was tried in 1649, has survived virtually intact since it was remodelled at the end of the 14th century. It escaped the fire in 1834 which destroyed much of the medieval Palace of Westminster, and the magnificent hammerbeam roof is the earliest surviving example of its kind.
Times: ✱ Westminster Hall can only be viewed by those on a tour of the Houses of Parliament, which must be arranged by an MP or Peer.
Facilities: & toilets for disabled shop ✖

> If you want to tell us about an attraction you think should be included in this book, please use the Readers' Report form at the back of the book, or e-mail: lifestyleguides@theAA.com

E17
WILLIAM MORRIS GALLERY
Lloyd Park, Forest Rd E17 4PP
➲ (Underground -Blackhorse Rd, take bus no. 123 along Forest Rd, get off at the Lloyd Park stop)
☎ 020 8527 3782   FREE
▤ 020 8527 7070
Victorian artist, craftsman, poet and free thinker William Morris lived here from 1848 to 1856, and the house has been devoted to his life and work. Displays include fabrics, stained glass, wallpaper and furniture, as well as Pre-Raphaelite paintings, sculpture by Rodin, ceramics and a collection of pictures by Frank Brangwyn, who worked briefly for Morris.
Times: Open all year, Tue-Sat and 1st Sun in each month 10-1 & 2-5. (Closed Mon & BH's). Telephone for Xmas/New Year opening times.
Facilities: ℗ & shop ✖ (ex guide dogs) ◥

SW19
WIMBLEDON LAWN TENNIS MUSEUM
Centre Court, Church Rd SW19 5AE
➲ (Underground - Southfields, 15mins walk)
☎ 020 8946 6131 ▤ 020 8944 6497   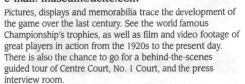 2 for 1
e-mail: museum@aeltc.com
Pictures, displays and memorabilia trace the development of the game over the last century. See the world famous Championship's trophies, as well as film and video footage of great players in action from the 1920s to the present day. There is also the chance to go for a behind-the-scenes guided tour of Centre Court, No. 1 Court, and the press interview room.
Times: Open daily all year, 10.30-5. (Closed middle Sun of Championships, Mon immediately following the Championships, 24-26 Dec & 1 Jan). **Fee:** ✱ £5.50 (ch under 5 free, ch £3.50, con £4.50). Party 15+. ℗ ⬛ ✗ licensed & (lift, stairlift to cafe) toilets for disabled shop ✖ (ex guide dogs) ◥

SE1
WINSTON CHURCHILL'S BRITAIN AT WAR EXPERIENCE
64/66 Tooley St SE1 2TF
➲ (Mid way down Tooley St, between London Bridge & Tower Bridge. 2min walk from London Bridge Stn).
☎ 020 7403 3171 ▤ 020 7403 5104   2 for 1
e-mail: britainatwar@dial.pipex.com
The Britain at War Experience pays tribute to the ordinary people who lived through the Second World War. Huddle in the Anderson shelter, share the excitement and anxiety of the evacuees as they wait to be transported to new homes and experience the fury of the London Blitz. An exciting adventure for all ages.
Times: Open all year, Apr-Sep 10-5.30pm; Oct-Mar 10-4.30. (Closed 24-26 Dec) **Fee:** ✱ £7.50 (ch 5-16 £4, student & pen £4.50). Family ticket (2 ad+2 ch) £16. ℗ (100mtrs) & (wheelchair for loan) toilets for disabled shop (small) ✖ (ex guide dogs) ◥

Above: Hampton Court

BARNET   Map 04 TQ29

MUSEUM OF DOMESTIC DESIGN & ARCHITECTURE

Middlesex University, Cat Hill EN4 8HT
➲ (from M25, junct 24 signposted A111 Cockfosters to Cat Hill)
☎ 020 8411 5244 📠 020 8411 6639
e-mail: moda@mdx.ac.uk

Located on Middlesex University's Cat Hill campus, the MoDA houses one of the most comprehensive collections of late 19th and 20th century decorative design for the home. A wide ranging exhibition programme is offered throughout the year, alongside the permanent exhibit, Exploring Interiors: Decoration of the Home 1900-1960.

Times: Open Tue-Sat 10-5, Sun 2-5. (Closed Mon, Etr, Xmas & New Year). **Facilities:** 🅿 ♿ toilets for disabled shop ✘ (ex guide dogs)

BEXLEY   Map 05 TQ47

HALL PLACE

Bourne Rd DA5 1PQ
➲ (near junct of A2 & A233)   **FREE**
☎ 01322 526574 📠 01322 522921

Hall Place is an attractive Grade I listed mansion of chequered flint and brick, with wonderful gardens. There is topiary in the form of the `Queen's Beasts'; rose, rock, peat and water gardens; and a herb garden with a fascinating range of plants (labelled in braille) for medicine and cooking. There is also a conservatory, a local studies centre and museum. Please telephone for details of the programme of temporary exhibitions, lectures and concerts in the museum and Great Hall.

Times: Open all year, House: Mon-Sat 10-5, Sun & BHs 11-5 (summer); Tue-Sat 10-4.15 (winter). Gardens: Mon-Fri 7.30-dusk, Sat & Sun 9-dusk. **Facilities:** 🅿 🍽 ✘ licensed ♿ toilets for disabled shop garden centre (award winning Greenflag) ✘ (ex guide/hearing dogs)

BRENTFORD   Map 04 TQ17

KEW BRIDGE STEAM MUSEUM

Green Dragon Ln TW8 0EN
➲ (Underground - Kew Gardens, District line then 391 bus. Museum 100yds from N side of Kew Bridge. From M4 junct 2 follow A4 to Chiswick rdbt, take A315 to Kew Bridge, Green Dragon Ln 1st right after lights)
☎ 020 8568 4757 📠 020 8569 9978
e-mail: info@kbsm.org

This Victorian pumping station has steam engines and six beam engines, of which five are working and one is the largest in the world. A diesel house and waterwheel can also be seen along with London's only steam narrow-gauge railway, which operates every Sunday (Mar-Nov). The Water for Life Gallery tells the story of London's water supply from Pre-Roman times. The newest exhibit is a water pump, once powered by horses.

Times: Open all year, daily 11-5. Engines in steam wknds & BHs. (Closed Good Fri, Xmas wk & New Year) **Fee:** Weekdays £3.60, wknds £4.60 (reductions for pen, students & ch). **Facilities:** 🅿 🍽 ♿ (tours for partially sighted, wheelchairs, large print guide) toilets for disabled shop 🍴

MUSICAL MUSEUM
368 High St TW8 0BD
➲ (Underground - Gunnersbury, nr Kew Bridge)
☎ 020 8560 8108

This museum will take you back to a bygone age to hear and see a marvellous working collection of automatic musical instruments from small music boxes to a mighty Wurlitzer theatre organ. Working demonstrations.
Times: ✱ Open Apr-Oct, Sat & Sun 2-5. Also Jul-Aug, Wed 2-4.
Facilities: 🅿 (200 yds) ♿ shop ✖ (guide dogs)

CHESSINGTON   Map 04 TQ16

CHESSINGTON WORLD OF ADVENTURES
Leatherhead Rd KT9 2NE
➲ (M25 junct 9/10, on A243)
☎ 0870 444 7777 📠 01372 725050

Feel the fantasy of Hocus Pocus Hall - the new magical 4-D experience home to a wacky wizard and mischievous goblins and where magical mayhem is literally brought to life in front of your eyes! Plus don't miss the fang-tastic Vampire, quick fire challenge of Tomb Blaster or fun-filled Dennis's Madhouse in Beanoland. Take a safari trip down Trail of the Kings then journey into Toytown with Toadie's Crazy Cars, Berry Bouncers and Tiny Truckers. Or, for the more daring, face a power of the mighty Samurai, or find Rameses waiting to seek his Revenge. There's so much to feed the imagination and excite the senses!
Times: Open 10 Apr-2 Nov (excluding some off peak days) either 10-5, 10-6 or 10-7 (telephone for details). Open until 7.30 during Halloween Hocus Pocus. **Fee:** ✱ £18-£24 (ch under 4 free, ch 4-11 £14.50-£18). Family ticket (2 ad & 2 ch) from £52. Advance booking provides added benefits. **Facilities:** 🅿 💺 ✖ licensed ♿ (some rides not accessible, disabled guide available) toilets for disabled shop ✖ (ex guide dogs & hearing dogs) ◗

CHISLEHURST   Map 05 TQ47

CHISLEHURST CAVES
Old Hill BR7 5NB
➲ (off A222 near Chislehurst railway stn. Turn into station road , then right & right again into Caveside Close)   **2 for 1**
☎ 020 8467 3264 📠 020 8295 0407
e-mail: enquiries@chislehurstcaves.co.uk

Miles of mystery and history beneath your feet. Grab a lantern and get ready for an amazing adventure! Visit the
continued

caves and your whole family can travel back in time as you explore the maze of passageways dug through the chalk deep beneath Chislehurst. Accompanied by an experienced guide on a 45 minute tour you'll see the tunnels made famous as a shelter during the Second World War, visit the cave's church, druid altar, the haunted pool and much more!
Times: Open all year, Wed-Sun, 10-4. Daily during school hols (incl half terms). Closed Xmas. **Fee:** £4 (ch & pen £2). **Facilities:** 🅿 💺 ✖ licensed (ramps) shop ✖ (ex guide dogs) ◗

DOWNE   Map 05 TQ46

DOWN HOUSE - HOME OF CHARLES DARWIN
BR6 7JT
➲ (Off A233, signposted)
☎ 01689 859119

Charles Darwin, perhaps the most influential scientist of the 19th-century, lived at Down House for over 40 years. He wrote the revolutionary book, *On the Origin of Species* here. Explore the exhibition on the first floor and visit the ground floor study, which was the centre of his life.
Times: Open Apr-Sep, Wed-Sun & BH's 10-6; Oct, Wed-Sun 10-5; Nov-Mar, Wed-Sun 10-4. (Closed 22 Dec-3 Feb). Dates valid until 31 Mar 2004. **Fee:** £6 (ch £3, concessions £4.50). Prices valid until 31 Mar 2004. **Facilities:** 🅿 ♿ shop ✖

ESHER   Map 04 TQ16

CLAREMONT LANDSCAPE GARDEN
Portsmouth Rd KT10 9JG
➲ (E of A307)
☎ 01372 467806 📠 01372 464394
e-mail: claremont@ntrust.org.uk

Laid out by Vanbrugh and Bridgeman before 1720, extended and naturalised by Kent, this is the earliest surviving example of an English landscaped garden. Its 50 acres include a lake with an island pavilion, a grotto and a turf amphitheatre. Telephone 01372 451596 for details of events.
Times: ✱ Open all year Apr-end of Oct daily, Nov-end Dec & Jan-end Mar daily (ex Mon). Apr-Oct Mon-Fri 10-6, Sat-Sun & BH Mon 10-7 (closed all day 10 & 11 Jul closes 2pm 12-15 Jul); Nov-Mar 10-5 or sunset if earlier. Closed 25 Dec & 1 Jan. House open Feb-Nov, 1st wknd of month 2-3 (ex 1st Sat in Jul). House not National Trust.
Facilities: 🅿 💺 ♿ (wheelchairs available, Braille guide) toilets for disabled shop ✖ (ex on leads, Nov-Mar only) 🐾

HAM   Map 04 TQ17

HAM HOUSE   **2 for 1**
TW10 7RS
➲ (W of A307, between Kingston & Richmond)
☎ 020 8940 1950 📠 020 8332 6903
e-mail: hamhouse@nationaltrust.org.uk

Built in 1610 and extended in the 1670s, Ham House is one of the most outstanding Stuart houses from that period. It was home to the Duchess of Lauderdale, who was renowned as a political schemer, and during the 17th century the house was at the heart of Civil War politics and Restoration court intrigues. The beautiful gardens include the Cherry Garden featuring lavender parterres flanked by two Berceaux of pleached Hornbeam and a statue of Bacchus at its centre. There are also eight grass plats, including, a 17th Century Orangery; a tea terrace; an outer courtyard with walnut and chestnut trees that act as a roost and nesting site for a large
continued

flock of green parakeets; and formal listed avenues of over 250 trees.
Times: Open Gardens: all year, Sat-Wed 11-6 or dusk if earlier. (Closed 25-26 Dec & 1 Jan). House: 3 Apr-Oct, Sat-Wed 1-5. Last admission 4.30. **Fee:** ✱ House £7 (ch £3.50). Family ticket £17.50. Garden only £3 (ch £1.50). Family ticket £7.50. **Facilities:** ⓟ (400yds) 🅿 & (Braille guide, wheelchairs, stairclimber, lift, parking) toilets for disabled shop ✖ (ex guide/hearing dogs) ⏚ ☎

HAMPTON COURT   Map 04 TQ16

HAMPTON COURT PALACE
KT8 9AU
➲ (on A308, close to A3, M3 & M25 exits. Train from Waterloo - Hampton Court, 2mins walk from station)
☎ 0870 752 7777 & 8781 9501
🖷 020 8781 9669

With over 500 years of royal history Hampton Court Palace has something to offer everyone, from the magnificent State Apartments to the domestic reality of the Tudor Kitchens. Costumed guides and audio tours bring the palace to life and provide an insight into how life in the palace would have been in the time of Henry VIII and William III.
Times: Open mid Mar-mid Oct, daily, 9.30-6 (10.15-6 on Mon); mid Oct-mid Mar, daily, 9.30-4.30 (10.15-4.30 on Mon). **Fee:** £11 (ch 5-16 £7.25, pen & students £8.25). Family £33. **Facilities:** ⓟ (charged) 🅿 ✖ licensed & (lifts, buggies for gardens, wheelchairs, wardens to assist) toilets for disabled shop (4 shops on site) ✖ (ex guide/hearing dogs) ☎

ISLEWORTH   Map 04 TQ17

SYON HOUSE
TW8 8JF
➲ (via A310 Twickenham road into Park Rd)
☎ 020 8560 0882 020 8560 0883
🖷 020 8568 0936
e-mail: info@syonpark.co.uk   `2 for 1`
Set in 200 acres of parkland, Syon House is the London home of the Duke of Northumberland, whose family have lived here since the late 16th century. During the second half of the 18th century the first Duke of Northumberland engaged Robert Adam to remodel the interior and `Capability' Brown to landscape the grounds. Adam was also responsible for the furniture and decorations, and the result is particularly spectacular in the superbly coloured Ante-Room and Long Gallery.
Times: Open 24 Mar-Oct, Wed-Thu, Sun & BH 11-5 (last ticket 4.15pm). **Fee:** ✱ Combined ticket for house and gardens £6.95 (ch £5.95 concessions £6.50). Family ticket £15. **Facilities:** ⓟ 🅿 & (only accessible if visitor can walk 9 stairs to entrance) toilets for disabled shop garden centre ✖ ☎

SYON PARK
TW8 8JF
➲ (A310 Twickenham Road into Park Rd)
☎ 020 8560 0882 🖷 020 8568 0936   `2 for 1`
e-mail: info@syonpark.co.uk
Contained within the 40 acres that make up Syon Park Gardens is one of the inspirations for the Crystal Palace at the Great Exhibition of 1851: a vast crescent of metal and glass, the first construction of its kind in the world and
continued

known as the Great Conservatory. Although the horticultural reputation of Syon Park goes back to the 16th century, its beauty today is thanks to the master of landscape design, `Capability' Brown.
Times: Open all year, daily 10-5.30 or dusk if earlier. (Closed 25 & 26 Dec). **Fee:** ✱ £3.50 (concessions £2.50). Combined ticket for house & gardens £6.95 (ch £5.95 concessions £6.50). Family ticket £15. **Facilities:** ⓟ 🅿 & toilets for disabled shop garden centre ✖ (ex guide dogs) ☎

KEW   Map 04 TQ17

KEW GARDENS (ROYAL BOTANIC GARDENS)
TW9 3AB
➲ (Underground - Kew Gdns)
☎ 020 8332 5655 🖷 020 8332 5197
e-mail: info@kew.org

Kew Gardens is a paradise throughout the seasons. Lose yourself in the magnificent conservatories and discover plants from the world's deserts, mountains and oceans. Wide-open spaces, stunning vistas, listed buildings and wildlife contribute to the Garden's unique atmosphere. As well as being famous for its beautiful gardens, Kew is world renowned for its contribution to botanical and horticultural science.
Times: Open all year, Gardens daily 9.30-between 4 & 6.30pm on weekdays, between 4-7.30pm Suns & BH's, depending on the time of sunset.(Closed 25 Dec & 1 Jan) **Fee:** ✱ £7.50 (concessions £5.50, ch under 17 free). **Facilities:** ⓟ (charged) 🅿 ✖ licensed & (16 seat bus tour: enquiries ring 020 8332 5643) toilets for disabled shop ✖ (ex guide dogs) ☎

KEW PALACE
Royal Botanic Gardens TW9 3AB
➲ (Underground - Kew Bridge)
☎ 020 8781 9540
A favourite country residence during the reign of the first three Hanoverian Kings, Kew was the site of several royal houses. A fairly modest red-brick building, built in the Dutch style with gables, Kew Palace was built in 1631 and used for nearly a century until 1818 when Queen Charlotte died. Family paintings and personal relics, furniture and tapestries are on display, and a charming 17th-century garden has been recreated.
Times: Closed for major repairs. Please telephone 020 8332 5655 or visit www.hrp.org.uk for further details. **Fee:** Prices not confirmed for 2004.

THE NATIONAL ARCHIVES
Ruskin Av TW9 4DU
➲ (Underground - Kew Gardens)
☎ 020 8392 5202 & 020 8487 9202
🖷 020 8487 9202   `FREE`
e-mail: events@pro.gov.uk
The National Archives houses one of the finest, most complete archives in Europe, comprising the records of the central government and law courts from the Norman Conquest to the present century. It is a mine of information and some of the most interesting material including Domesday Book.
Times: Open Mon, Wed & Fri, 9-4.45; Tue, 10-7; Thu, 9-7 (closed 1st wk in Dec, Sun & public holiday wknds). **Facilities:** ⓟ 🅿 & (hearing loops & large print text in museum) toilets for disabled shop ✖ (ex guide dogs)

QUEEN CHARLOTTE'S COTTAGE
Royal Botanic Gardens TW9 3AB
➲ (Underground - Kew Bridge)   FREE
☎ 020 8332 5189

Typical of the fashionable rustic style popular with the gentry in the 18th century, the cottage was built for George III and Queen Charlotte as a home for their menagerie of exotic pets, as well as a picnic spot and summer house.
Times: Open weekends only between May & Sep. **Facilities:** shop ✖

OSTERLEY   Map 04 TQ17

OSTERLEY PARK HOUSE
TW7 4RB
➲ (Underground - Osterley)
☎ 020 8560 7714 🖷 020 8568 7714
e-mail: tsogen@smtp.ntrust.org.uk

This Elizabethan mansion has been transformed into an 18th-century villa, its elegant interior decoration designed in neo-classical style by Robert Adam. The State Apartments include a Gobelin tapestry ante-room and a dressing-room decorated in the Etruscan style.
Times: ✱ Open all year: Park & pleasure grounds, daily 9-7.30 or sunset if earlier. House: Apr-1 Nov, Wed-Sun 2-5, BH Sun & Mon 1-5. Last admission 4.30. (Closed Good Fri & 25-26 Dec). **Facilities:** 🅿 (charged) 🝐 & toilets for disabled shop ✖ (ex on lead in park) 🐾

TWICKENHAM   Map 04 TQ17

MARBLE HILL HOUSE
Richmond Rd TW1 2NL
☎ 020 8892 5115 🖷 020 8607 9976

A magnificent Thames-side Palladian villa built for Henrietta Howard, mistress of King George II, set in 66 acres of riverside parklands.
Times: Open Apr-Sep, Wed-Sun & BH's 10-6; Oct, Wed-Sun 10-5. (Closed Nov-Mar but exclusive group visits are available by arrangement). Dates valid until 31 Mar 2004. **Fee:** £3.50 (ch £2, concessions £3). Prices valid until 31 Mar 2004. **Facilities:** 🅿 🝐 ✖ licensed & toilets for disabled shop ✖ (ex on lead in certain areas) ⚏

MUSEUM OF RUGBY & TWICKENHAM STADIUM TOURS
Rugby Football Union, Rugby Rd TW1 1DZ
➲ (A316 following signs to museum)   2 for 1
☎ 020 8892 8877 🖷 020 8892 2817
e-mail: museum@rfu.com

Located beneath the East Stand of the Twickenham Stadium, home of the England team and headquarters of the Rugby Football Union, the museum uses interactive displays, period set pieces and video footage to bring the history of the game to life. The tour includes a visit to the England dressing room, and magnificent views of the stadium from the top of the north stand.
Times: Open, Tue-Sat 10-5 (last admission 4.30pm), Sun 11-5 (last admission 4.30pm). (Closed post Twickenham match day Sundays, Etr Sun, 24-26 Dec & 1 Jan). **Fee:** Museum Tour: £8 (concessions £5). **Facilities:** 🅿 🝐 ✖ licensed & toilets for disabled shop ✖ (ex guide dogs) 🝐

ORLEANS HOUSE GALLERY
Riverside TW1 3DJ
➲ (From Twickenham drive along Richmond road (A305), Orleans Rd is on right just past Orleans Park School)
☎ 020 8892 0221 🖷 020 8744 0501
e-mail: m.denovellis@richmond.gov.uk

Stroll beside the Thames and through the woodland gardens of Orleans House, where you will find stunning 18th century interior design and an excellent public art gallery. Visitors of all ages can try out their own artistic talents in pre-booked workshops, and wide-ranging temporary exhibitions are held throughout the year - please telephone for details.
Times: ✱ Open Oct-Mar, Tue-Sat 1-4.30, Sun & BH 2-4.30; Apr-Sep Tue-Sat 1-5.30, Sun & BH 2-5.30. **Facilities:** 🅿 & (handling objects & large print labels for some exhibitions) toilets for disabled shop ✖ (ex guide dogs)

Above: Kew Gardens

MERSEYSIDE

EVENTS & FESTIVALS

February
tbc Chinese New Year celebrations, in and around Chinatown, Liverpool

April
1st-3rd Martell Cognac Grand National Festival, Aintree Racecourse, Liverpool

May
16th Liverpool Women's 10k Run, Liverpool City Centre

June
14th-18th The Mersey River Festival, River Mersey & Albert Dock, Liverpool

July
4th Liverpool-Chester-Liverpool Bike Ride
10th-11th Wirral Show, Promenade, New Brighton, Wirral (provisional)
30th-1st Aug St Helens Show, Sherdley Park, St Helens
tbc Halton Show, Spike Island Halton
tbc Merseyside International Street Festival

August
30th Jul-1st St Helens Show, Sherdley Park, St Helens
19th-22nd Southport Flower Show, Victoria Park, Rotten Row, Southport
28th-30th International Beatles Week & Convention, various venues in Liverpool city centre
tbc British Musical Firework Championships, Kings Gardens, Southport
tbc Creamfields Festival, Old Liverpool Airfield, Speke Boulevard

September
12th Liverpool Corporate Cup Run, 5km course in the city centre
tbc The Southport Airshow, The Promenade, Southport

November
tbc British Ministrada Festival of Gymnastics & Dance, Liverpool

Above: Inside the Cathedral of Christ the King

BIRKENHEAD   Map 07 SJ38

BIRKENHEAD PRIORY
Priory St CH41 5JH
☎ 0151 666 1249

Founded in 1150, the Priory provided accommodation for the Prior and 16 Benedictine monks. Most of the buildings were neglected after the Dissolution, but not all are ruined. An interpretive centre traces the history and development of the site. St Mary's, the first parish church of Birkenhead, was opened in 1821 adjacent to the Priory: only the tower now stands.
Times: ✱ Open all year, Sat & Sun 1-5 (in summer), 12-4 (in winter) & Tue-Sun 1-5 (school holidays), 12-4 (Oct & Feb half term). Telephone to confirm. **Facilities:** 🅿 ♿ toilets for disabled shop ✈ (ex guide dogs)

HISTORIC WARSHIPS
East Float, Dock Rd CH41 1DJ
⮌ (end of M53 all docks turn off follow tourist signs. From Liverpool Wallasey tunnel 1st exit after toll & follow brown heritage signs)
☎ 0151 650 1573   **2 for 1**
🖷 0151 650 1473
e-mail: manager@warships.freeserve.co.uk

HMS Onyx served in the Falklands and is the only submarine afloat in the UK that visitors can explore. *HMS Plymouth*, an anti-submarine frigate also served in the Falklands. The U534 is the only WWII German U-Boat to be raised from the sea bed. Pre-booking required, adults only admitted to U-Boat.
Times: Open all year, Sep-Mar daily 10-4, Apr-Aug daily 10-5. (Closed 24-26 Dec, only open wknds for the first 6 wks of the year). **Fee:** ✱ £5.50 (ch £3.50, pen £4.50). Family ticket £15. Combined ships & U-Boat £13.50 (adults only). U-Boat £8. **Facilities:** 🅿 ▦ ♿ museum only, access to HMS Plymouth, multimedia tour of U534 shop ✈ (ex guide dogs) ◥

WILLIAMSON ART GALLERY & MUSEUM
Slatey Rd CH43 4UE
☎ 0151 652 4177   🖷 0151 670 0253
e-mail: wag@museum-service.freeserve.co.uk

English watercolours and works by the Liverpool school are an outstanding feature of the gallery. There is a large collection of pictures by P Wilson Steer, and also on view are sculpture, ceramics, glass, silver and furniture. The museum is linked to the gallery, and has displays on the history of the town and its port. Birkenhead was a hamlet before the 19th century, but grew large and rich through ship-building and the docks. Also on view are the Baxter Motor Collection, cars and motorbikes in a period garage setting.
Times: ✱ Open all year, Tue-Sun & BHs 1-5, (Closed Xmas & Good Fri). **Facilities:** 🅿 ♿ toilets for disabled shop ✈

If you are dissatisfied with any aspect of an attraction, discuss the problem at the time with a member of staff

LIVERPOOL   Map 07 SJ39

THE BEATLES STORY
Britannia Pavilion, Albert Dock L3 4AA
☎ 0151 709 1963 ▤ 0151 708 0039

Relive the story of the four lads from Liverpool who took the world by storm and changed the face of popular music for ever.
Times: ✳ Open Apr-Oct daily 10-6, Nov-Mar daily 10-5 (last admission always 1hr before close). **Facilities:** 🅿 ♿ toilets for disabled shop ✕ (ex guide dogs) 🍴

CENTRAL LIBRARY
William Brown St L3 8EW
➲ (Adjacent to St. George's Hall, which is opposite Lime St. Station. Central Library is located betwen the museum and the art gallery)
☎ 0151 233 5858 ▤ 0151 233 5824
e-mail: refham.central.library@liverpool.gov.uk
The Picton, Hornby and Brown buildings, situated in the Victorian grandeur of William Brown Street, house Liverpool's collection of over one million books, forming one of Britain's largest and oldest public libraries. The Liverpool Record Office is one of the country's largest and most significant County Record offices.
Times: ✳ Open all year, Mon-Thu 9-7.30, Fri 9-5, Sat 10-4 & Sun 12-4. Closed BHs. **Facilities:** 🅿 (50 yds) (pay & display parking only) ♿ (lift, text magnification, reading machine) toilets for disabled ✕ (ex guide dogs)

CONSERVATION CENTRE
White Chapel L1 6HZ
☎ 0151 478 4999 ▤ 0151 478 4990
Award winning centre, the only one of its kind, gives the public an insight into the world of museum and gallery conservation.
Times: Mon-Sat 10-5, Sun 12-5, Closed 23-26 Dec & 1 Jan **Facilities:** 🅿 (charged) 🍽♿ toilets for disabled shop ✕ ex guide dogs 🍴

FINGERPRINTS OF ELVIS
Unit 17, The Colonnades, Albert Dock L3 4AA
➲ (in Albert Dock next to Tate Liverpool)
☎ 0151 709 1790 ▤ 0151 709 5510
Elvis comes to Liverpool, or at least his fingerprints do. Along with his Harley Davidson, a collection of his jewellery, *continued*

guitars, karate belts, and stage suits, the actual fingerprints taken from Elvis for his gun licence application can be seen. Fans can also view army insignia from the King's days in the 1st Battalion, 32d Armor Regiment, 3d Armored Division, and law enforcement badges awarded to and collected by Elvis. This is the only major collection of Presley memorabilia outside the USA, and features an audio narration supplied by his stepbrother, David Stanley.
Times: Open all year. (Closed 25-26 Dec) **Fee:** £7.95 (concessions £5.45). Family ticket £23 **Facilities:** 🅿 ♿ shop ✕ (ex guide dogs) 🍴

THE GRAND NATIONAL EXPERIENCE
Aintree Racecourse, Ormskirk Rd L9 5AS
☎ 0151 522 2921 ▤ 0151 522 2920
e-mail: aintree@rht.net
A fascinating look at Britain's most famous horserace, the Martell Grand National. Visitors can sit in the jockey's weighing-in chair, walk around the dressing rooms, watch video presentations, and view a gallery of paintings and photography depicting the race.
Times: Open 26 May-17 Oct **Facilities:** 🅿 ♿ toilets for disabled shop ✕ (ex guide dogs) 🍴

HM CUSTOMS & EXCISE NATIONAL MUSEUM
Merseyside Maritime Museum, Albert Dock L3 4AQ
☎ 0151 478 4499 ▤ 0151 478 4590
Enter the exciting world of smuggle busting where everyday items reveal their hidden secrets. Find a fake, rummage for hidden goods and spot a suspect traveller. Look into the *continued*

illustrious history of HM Customs & Excise, it's the longest battle in history and it's still going on today! **Times:** Open daily 10-5. (Closed 23-26 Dec & 1 Jan) **Facilities:** 🅿 💻 ✖ licensed ♿ (restricted wheelchair access, no access to basement) toilets for disabled shop ✖ (ex guide dogs) 🍽

LIVERPOOL CATHEDRAL
St James' Mount L1 7AZ
➲ (0.75m S of city centre)
☎ 0151 709 6271 🖷 0151 702 7292
e-mail: info@liverpoolcathedral.org.uk

Although it appears at first sight to be as old as any other monumental cathedral in Britain, Liverpool Cathedral is in fact a 20th century structure, that was only completed in 1978. Its foundation stone was laid in 1904, and through two World Wars the building continued. It is the largest Anglican Cathedral in Europe, and has the largest pipe organ and the heaviest ringing peal of bells in the world. **Times:** Open daily 8-6 **Fee:** ✱ Free. Donations invited. Tower £2.50 (concessions £1.50) **Facilities:** 🅿 (charged) 💻 ✖ ♿ toilets for disabled shop ✖ (ex guide dogs)

LIVERPOOL FOOTBALL CLUB VISITORS CENTRE TOUR
Anfield Rd L4 0TH
☎ 0151 260 6677 🖷 0151 264 0149
e-mail: stephen.done@liverpoolfc.tv

See all the first team kit set out for a match day, listen to a recorded 'team talk' from Gerard Houllier, and then touch the famous 'This is Anfield' sign to the sound of 45,000 cheering fans - a marvellous experience for any Liverpool fan! **Times:** Open all year: Museum daily 10-5 last admission 4pm. (Closed 25-26 Dec). Match days 9am until last admission - 1hr before kick off. Museum & Tour - tours are run subject to daily demand. Advance booking is essential to avoid disappointment. **Fee:** Museum only, £5 (ch under 6 & pen £3) Family £13. Museum & Tour £8.50 (ch under 16 & pen £5.50) Family £23. **Facilities:** 🅿 💻 ✖ licensed ♿ (lifts to all areas for wheelchairs) toilets for disabled shop ✖ (ex guide dogs) 🍽

LIVERPOOL MUSEUM
William Brown St L3 8EN
➲ (in city centre next to St George's Hall and Lime St)   FREE
☎ 0151 478 4393
e-mail: themuseum@liverpoolmuseums.org.uk

One of Britain's most interesting museums, the Liverpool Museum has diverse collections ranging from the Amazonian rain forests to the mysteries of outer space. Special attractions include the award-winning hands-on Natural History Centre and the Planetarium. The museum is currently undergoing extensive building improvements and refurbishment, and many new features are due in 2005. Please note that during construction work some galleries may be closed.
Times: Open Mon-Sat 10-5, Sun noon-5. (Closed 23-26 Dec & 1 Jan)
Facilities: 🅿 💻 ♿ toilets for disabled shop ✖ (ex guide dogs)

MERSEYSIDE MARITIME MUSEUM
Albert Dock L3 4AQ
➲ (The Albert Dock is situated near Liverpool's historic waterfront. Entry into the dock is from the Strand).
☎ 0151 478 4499 🖷 0151 478 4590

Set in the heart of Liverpool's magnificent waterfront, the Merseyside Maritime Museum offers a unique insight into the history of the great port of Liverpool, its ships and its people. **Times:** Open daily 10-5 (Closed 23-26 Dec & 1 Jan). **Facilities:** 🅿 ✖ licensed ♿ (lifts, wheelchairs, ramps, ex pilot boat & basement) toilets for disabled shop ✖ (ex guide dogs) 🍽

METROPOLITAN CATHEDRAL OF CHRIST THE KING
Mount Pleasant L3 5TQ
➲ (5 mins walk from either Liverpool Lime Street or Liverpool Central Railway Station. 'Smart' buses stop outside)
☎ 0151 709 9222 🖷 0151 708 7274
e-mail: met.cathedral@boltblue.com

A modern Roman Catholic cathedral which provides a focal point on the Liverpool skyline. The imposing structure of curving concrete ribs and stained glass was designed by Sir Frederick Gibberd and consecrated in 1967. Monumental crypt of brick and granite by Sir Edwin Lutyens 1933 **Times:** Open daily 8-6 (Sun 5pm in winter). **Fee:** Free admission, although donations welcome. **Facilities:** 🅿 (charged) ♿ (lift, loop system, no access to Crypt) toilets for disabled shop ✖ (ex guide dogs) 🍽

MUSEUM OF LIVERPOOL LIFE
Pier Head L3 4AA
➲ (follow signs for Albert Dock, museum is on Pier Head side)   FREE
☎ 0151 478 4080 🖷 0151 478 4090
e-mail: liverpoollife@liverpoolmuseums.org.uk

The Museum of Liverpool Life celebrates the contribution of the people of Liverpool to national life. Recently expanded to include three new galleries, City Lives exploring the richness of Liverpool's cultural diversity, The River Room featuring life around the river Mersey and City Soldiers about the King's Regiment. Other galleries include Mersey Culture from Brookside to the Grand National, Making a Living and Demanding a Voice. **Times:** Open daily 10-5. (Closed 23-26 Dec & 1 Jan). **Facilities:** 🅿 (charged) ♿ (wheelchairs, audio handsets, subtitles on video terminals) toilets for disabled shop ✖ (ex guide/hearing dogs)

NATIONAL WILDFLOWER CENTRE
Court Hey Park L16 3NA
➲ (M62 junct 5, take A5080 to rdbt. Exit into Roby Rd, entrance 0.5m on left)   2 for 1
☎ 0151 737 1819 🖷 0151 737 1820
e-mail: info@nwc.org.uk

Set in a public park on the outskirts of Liverpool, the National Wildflower Centre promotes the creation of wildflower habitats around the country and provides educational materials, wildflower seeds and interactive facilities. The Centre has demonstration areas, children's activities, a working nursery, compost display and rooftop

continued

walk. The centre has a comprehensive programme of events through the summer.

Times: Open Apr-Sep, daily 10-5. **Fee:** ✱ £3 (ch 5-16, pen, students & unemployed £1.50). Family ticket (2 adults & 2 ch) £7.50. Season tickets & group discount tickets available. **Facilities:** ⓟ ⬛ & Electric buggy & wheelchair available for use. toilets for disabled shop garden centre ✱ (ex guide dogs & in park) ◗

SUDLEY HOUSE
Mossley Hill Rd L18 8BX
➲ (near Aigburth Station and Mossley Hill Station)
☎ 0151 724 3245   [FREE]
e-mail: sudley@liverpoolmuseums.org.uk
The former family home of the Liverpool merchant George Holt in the Liverpool suburb of Mossley Hill. Works on show are drawn mainly from his collection of British paintings including Landseer, Turner, Gainsborough, Reynolds and Romney as well as major pre-Raphaelite painters. Many of the original Victorian features of the building survive, including tiles, ceramics, stained glass and wallpaper.
Times: Open Mon-Sat 10-5, Sun noon-5. (Closed 23-26 Dec & 1 Jan).
Facilities: ⓟ ⬛ & ✱ (ex guide dogs)

TATE LIVERPOOL
Albert Dock L3 4BB
➲ (within walking distance of Liverpool Lime Street train station)
☎ 0151 702 7400 & 0151 702 7402
▤ 0151 702 7401
e-mail: liverpoolinfo@tate.org.uk
A converted Victorian warehouse with stunning views across the River Mersey, Tate Liverpool displays the best of the National Collection of 20th-Century Art. A changing programme of exhibitions draws on works from public and private collections across the world.
Times: Open Tue-Sun, 10-5.30. (Closed Mon ex BH Mon, 25-26 Dec, 1 Jan & Good Fri). **Facilities:** ⓟ ⬛ & (wheelchairs available, leaflets in Braille, hearing loop) toilets for disabled shop ✱ ◗

WALKER ART GALLERY
William Brown St L3 8EL
➲ (follow brown and white signs)
☎ 0151 478 4199 ▤ 0151 478 4390
For over 120 years, visitors have been surprised, charmed & moved by The Walker's world-famous collection including masterpieces by Rembrandt, Poussin, Rubens & Murillo. Newly refurbished galleries will display an exciting and varied programme of must see exhibitions.
Times: Open Mon-Sat 10-5, Sun 12-5 (closed 23-26 & 1 Jan)
Facilities: ⓟ (charged) ⬛ ✕ & (prior notice appreciated, wheelchair on request) toilets for disabled shop ✱ (ex guide dogs)

PORT SUNLIGHT   Map 07 SJ38

LADY LEVER ART GALLERY
CH62 5EQ
➲ (Follow brown heritage signs)
☎ 0151 478 4136 ▤ 0151 478 4140
e-mail: ladyleverartgallery@nmgm.org
The Lady Lever Art Gallery houses many world famous works of art, including Pre-Raphaelite masterpieces by Millais, Burne-Jones and Rossetti. Dramatic landscapes by the great British painters, Turner & Constable are also displayed alongside portraits by Gainsborough, Romney & Reynolds.
Times: ✱ Open all year, Mon-Sat 10-5, Sun 12-5. (Closed 23-26 Dec & 1 Jan) **Facilities:** ⓟ (charged) ⬛ & (prior notice appreciated, wheelchair on request) toilets for disabled ✱ (ex guide dogs)

PRESCOT   Map 07 SJ49

KNOWSLEY SAFARI PARK
L34 4AN
➲ (M62 junct 6 onto M57 junct 2. Follow 'safari park' signs)
☎ 0151 430 9009 ▤ 0151 426 3677
e-mail: safari.park@knowsley.com
A five-mile drive through the reserves enables visitors to see lions, tigers, elephants, rhinos, monkeys and many other animals in spacious, natural surroundings. Also a children's amusement park, reptile house, pets' corner plus sealion shows. Other attractions include an amusement park and a miniature railway.
Times: Open all year, Mar-Oct., daily 10-4. Winter Nov-Feb 11-3.
Fee: ✱ £8 (ch & pen £5). **Facilities:** ⓟ ⬛ & toilets for disabled shop ✱ (kennels provided) ◗

PRESCOT MUSEUM
34 Church St L34 3LA
➲ (situated on corner of High St (A57) & Church St. Follow the brown heritage signs)   [FREE]
☎ 0151 430 7787 ▤ 0151 430 7219
e-mail: prescot.museum.dlcs@knowsley.gov.uk
Permanent exhibitions reflecting the local history of the area, including the important clock and watch making heritage. There is a programme of special exhibitions, events and holiday activities, telephone for details.
Times: Open all year, Tue-Sat 10-5 (closed 1-2), Sun 2-5 (closed BH's)
Facilities: ⓟ (100 yds) & (ramp to ground floor) shop ✱ (ex guide dogs)

SOUTHPORT   Map 07 SD31

ATKINSON ART GALLERY
Lord St PR8 1DH
➲ (located in centre of Lord Street, next to the Town Hall)
☎ 01704 533133 ext 2110
🖷 0151 934 2110
e-mail: atkinson.gallery@leisure.sefton.gov.uk
The gallery specialises in 19th-and 20th-century oil paintings, watercolours, drawings and prints, as well as 20th-century sculpture. Temporary exhibitions are shown regularly at the art gallery.
Times: Open all year, Mon-Wed & Fri 10-5, Thu & Sat 10-1. (Closed 25-26 Dec & 1 Jan). **Facilities:** P (next street) (pay & display) ✗ licensed ᨒ shop ✈ (ex guide dogs)

THE BRITISH LAWNMOWER MUSEUM
106-114 Shakespeare St PR8 5AJ
➲ (From M6, M58 or M57 follow signs towards town centre, then brown heritage signs to museum)
☎ 01704 501336 🖷 01704 500564   **2 for 1**
e-mail: info@lawnmowerworld.co.uk
This award-winning museum houses a private collection of over 200 rare exhibits of garden machinery of special interest dating from 1799. There is also the largest collection of vintage toy lawnmowers and games in the world. See the lawnmowers of the rich and famous as well as machines made by Rolls Royce, Royal Enfield, Sidley and many more. A tribute to the garden machine industry over the last 200 years.
Times: Open daily, 9-5.30, ex Sun & BH Mon. **Fee:** £1 (ch 50p). Guided tour £4. **Facilities:** P shop ✈ 🍴

PLEASURELAND
Marine Dr PR8 1RX
➲ (signed from Southport Town Centre)   **2 for 1**
☎ 0870 220 0204 🖷 01704 537936
e-mail: mail@pleasurelandltd.freeserve.co.uk
Home to five rollercoasters, including TRAUMAtizer, the UK's tallest, fastest suspended coaster. Lucozade Space Shot 125ft is a vertical reality thrill ride. Over 100 rides and attractions, providing fun for the whole family.
Times: Open Mar-Nov opening times vary please call for information. **Fee:** £16 all day (juniors £11). Entry for 4 (adults and/or children) £50. **Facilities:** P (charged) 🍴 ✗ licensed ᨒ (access on some rides) toilets for disabled shop ✈ (ex guide dogs) 🍴

> Remember that prices and opening times are liable to change within the currency of this guide. It is always best to telephone in advance to check

SOUTHPORT ZOO & CONSERVATION TRUST
Princes Park PR8 1RX
➲ (from outskirts of Southport follow brown heritage signs, situated next to Pleasureland Town Centre)
☎ 01704 538102 & 548894 🖷 01704 538102
e-mail: info@southportzoo.com

Among the animals here are lions, snow leopards, lynx, chimpanzees, parrots, otters and llamas. An extension houses a pets' corner barn, a giant tortoise house, primate house and porcupines. There is also a reptile house with an aquarium. During the summer there are snake handling sessions with talks. There is an education centre for schools who have booked in advance. There is also new primate house and a new otter pool.
Times: Open Summer: 10-6; Winter: 10-4. Closed 25 Dec. **Fee:** ✱ £5 (ch & pen £4). Party 20+ £4.50 (ch £3.50) each. **Facilities:** P (100yds) (metered) 🍴 ᨒ (wide pathways, wide doorways) toilets for disabled shop

SPEKE   Map 07 SJ48

SPEKE HALL
The Walk L24 1XD
➲ (follow signs for Liverpool Airport and brown heritage signs marked 'Speke Hall')
☎ 0151 427 7231 🖷 0151 427 9860
A remarkable timber-framed manor house set in tranquil gardens and grounds. The house has a Tudor Great Hall, Stuart plasterwork, and William Morris wallpapers. Outside are varied grounds, including a rose garden, bluebell woods and woodland walks. Special events include Open Air Shakespeare, hands-on family activities, guided walks and tours.
Times: House open: Wed-Sun (open BH Mon) 1-5.30; Nov-mid Dec, Sat & Sun 1-4.30. Garden open daily (ex Mon & closed 24-26 Dec, 31 Dec, 1 Jan & Good Fri). **Fee:** ✱ Hall & Gardens: £5.50 (ch £3.50). Gardens only: £2.50 (ch £1.50). Family ticket £16. **Facilities:** P (charged) 🍴 ✗ ᨒ (Wheelchairs & Electric car) toilets for disabled shop ✈ (on estate only) 🐾 🍴

NORFOLK

EVENTS & FESTIVALS

May
 1st King's Lynn May Garland Procession,
  town centre, King's Lynn
 tbc Norwich Bike Ride, 50/100-mile ride
  around Norfolk (provisional)
 tbc Norfolk & Norwich Festival
  (music and the arts)

June
 30th-1st Jul Royal Norfolk Show, Royal
  Norfolk Showground

July
 30th Jun-1st Royal Norfolk Show, Royal
  Norfolk Showground
 3rd-4th Morris & Folk Festival, Sheringham
 17th-18th Weeting Steam Rally, Weeting
 31st Sandringham Flower Show (provisional)
 31st-1st Aug Worstead Village Festival
 tbc Lord Mayor's Celebrations, Norwich
 tbc Norwich Music Festival

August
 31st Jul-1st Worstead Village Festival
 1st-7th Mundesley Festival
 30th Aylsham Agricultural Show
 tbc Deepdale Jazz Festival, Marsh Barn,
  Burnham Deepdale (provisional)
 tbc West Norfolk CAMRA
  Rhythm & Booze Festival

September
 11th-12th Great Yarmouth Maritime Festival,
  South Quay, Great Yarmouth

October
 tbc CAMRA Norwich Beer Festival

November
 tbc Sparks in the Park, fireworks set to music
  plus funfair, Earlham Park, Norwich

December
 tbc Norwegian Christmas Fayre, Market Place,
  Great Yarmouth

Above: Cromer at dusk

BACONSTHORPE — Map 09 TG13

BACONSTHORPE CASTLE
NR25 6LN
➲ (0.75m N of Baconsthorpe off unclass road,
3m E of Holt) **FREE**
☎ 01799 322399

The remains of a fifteenth-century castle, built by Sir John Heydon during the Wars of the Roses. The exact date when the building first begun is not known, since Sir John did not apply for the statutory royal licence necessary to construct a fortified house. In the 1560s, Sir John's grandson added the outer gatehouse, which was inhabited until the 1920s, when one of the turrets fell down. The remains of red brick and knapped flint are reflected in the lake, which partly embraces the castle as a moat.
Times: Open all year, any reasonable time. **Facilities:** 🅿 ✈ (ex dogs on leads) ♨

BANHAM — Map 05 TM08

BANHAM ZOO
The Grove NR16 2HE
➲ (on B1113, signed off A11 and A140. Follow brown tourist signs)
☎ 01953 887771 & 887773 ▤ 01953 887445

Set in 35 acres of magnificent parkland, see hundreds of animals ranging from big cats to birds of prey and siamangs to shire horses. Tiger Territory is a purpose-built enclosure for Siberian tigers, including a rock pool and woodland setting. See also Lemur Island and Tamarin and Marmoset Islands. The Heritage Farm Stables & Falconry displays Norfolk's rural heritage with majestic shire horses and birds of prey. Other attractions include Children's Farmyard Barn and Adventure Play Area.
Times: ✱ Open all year, daily from 10-5 (10-4.30 Jan-mid Mar & Nov-Dec, 10-5.30 Jul-Sep). (Closed 25-26 Dec). Last admission 1 hour before closing. **Facilities:** 🅿 ▰ ✕ licensed ♿ (3 wheelchairs for hire, special parking) toilets for disabled shop ✈ ➹

BLICKLING — Map 09 TG12

BLICKLING HALL
NR11 6NF
➲ (on B1354, 1.5m NW of Aylsham, signposted off A140 Norwich to Cromer road)
☎ 01263 738030 ▤ 01263 731660
e-mail: blickling@nationaltrust.org.uk

Flanked by dark yew hedges and topped by pinnacles, the warm red brick front of Blickling is a memorable sight. The grounds include woodland and a lake, a formal parterre, and a dry moat filled with roses, camellias and other plants.
Times: Hall open 31 Mar-28 Oct, Wed-Sun & BH, 1-4.30 (1-3.30 Oct). Also open Tue in Aug. Garden, shop & restaurant same days as hall 10.15-5.15. **Fee:** ✱ £6.90 (ch £3.45). **Facilities:** 🅿 ▰ ✕ licensed ♿ (wheelchairs & batricars, Braille guide, lift, parking) toilets for disabled shop garden centre ✈ (ex guide dogs) ➷ ➹

BRESSINGHAM   Map 05 TM08

BRESSINGHAM STEAM MUSEUM & GARDENS
IP22 2AB
➲ (on A1066 2.5m W of Diss. Between Thetford & Diss)
☎ 01379 686900 & 687386   ✉ 01379 688085
e-mail: info@bressingham.co.uk

Alan Bloom is an internationally recognised nurseryman and a steam enthusiast, and has combined his interests to great effect at Bressingham. There are three miniature steam-hauled trains, including a 15in gauge running through two and a half miles of the wooded Waveney Valley. The Dell Garden has 5000 species of perennials and alpines; Foggy Bottom has wide vistas, pathways, trees, shrubs, conifers and winter colour (restricted opening). A steam roundabout is another attraction, and the Norfolk fire museum is housed here. Various events are held, including Friends of Thomas the Tank Engine, please telephone for details.
Times: ✱ Open: Steam Museum, Dad's Army collection, Foggy Bottom & Dell Garden Apr-Sep, daily 10.30-5.30 (10.30-4.30 Mar & Oct). Museum & collections open all year (ex 24 Dec-8 Jan). Last admission 1 hour before closing time. **Facilities:** 🅿 🍴 ✗ licensed & (wheelchairs can be taken onto Nursery & Waveney lines) toilets for disabled shop garden centre ✗ (ex guide dogs) ◗

BURGH CASTLE   Map 05 TG40

BERNEY ARMS WINDMILL
NR30 1SB
☎ 01493 700605

One of the largest and best-preserved Victorian windmills in Norfolk, with seven floors to explore. Built to grind cement, its superb machinery is still fully operational.
Times: Open Apr-Oct, daily 9-5. (Closed between 1-2 daily). Dates valid until 31 Mar 2004. **Fee:** £2 (ch £1, concessions £1.50). Prices valid until 31 Mar 2004. **Facilities:** shop ✗ (ex dogs on leads) ✿

BURGH CASTLE
NR31 9PZ
➲ (at far W end of Breydon Water on unclass road, 3m W of Great Yarmouth)   FREE

Burgh Castle was built in the third century AD by the Romans, as one of a chain of forts along the Saxon Shore - the coast where Saxon invaders landed. Sections of the massive walls still stand.
Times: Open any reasonable time. **Facilities:** ✗ (ex dogs on leads) ✿

CAISTER-ON-SEA   Map 09 TG51

CAISTER ROMAN SITE   FREE
➲ (3m N of Great Yarmouth)

The name Caister has Roman origins, and this was in fact a Roman naval base. The remains include the south gateway, a town wall built of flint with brick courses and part of what may have been a seamen's hostel.
Times: Open any reasonable time. **Facilities:** ✗ (ex dogs on leads) ✿

CASTLE ACRE   Map 09 TF81

CASTLE ACRE PRIORY AND CASTLE
Stocks Green PE32 2XD
☎ 01760 755394   ✉ 01760 755594

Britain's best-preserved Cluniac priory with walled herb garden where visitors can find out about the medieval uses of herbs. Nearby Castle Acre Castle is also well worth a visit.
Times: Open all year Apr-Sep, daily 10-6 (Oct daily 10-5); Nov-Mar, Wed-Sun 10-4. (Closed 24-26 Dec & 1 Jan). Dates valid until 31 Mar 2004. **Fee:** £4 (ch £2, concessions £3). Prices valid until 31 Mar 2004. **Facilities:** 🅿 & shop ✗ (ex dogs on leads) ✿

CASTLE RISING   Map 09 TF62

CASTLE RISING CASTLE
PE31 6AH
➲ (off A149)
☎ 01553 631330

A fine twelfth-century domestic keep, set amid huge defensive earthworks, once the palace and home to Isabella, the 'She Wolf' of France, dowager Queen of England. The keep walls stand to their original height.
Times: Open all year, Apr-Sep, daily 10-6; Oct, daily 10-5; Nov-Mar, Wed-Sun 10-4. (Closed 24-26 Dec & 1 Jan). Dates valid until 31 Mar 2004. **Fee:** £3.75 (ch £2.10, concessions £3). Prices valid until 31 Mar 2004. **Facilities:** 🅿 & (exterior only) toilets for disabled shop ✗ (ex dogs on leads) ✿

CROMER   Map 09 TG24

CROMER MUSEUM
East Cottages, Tucker St NR27 9HB
➲ (located in town centre)   2 for 1
☎ 01263 513543   ✉ 01263 511651
e-mail: cromer.museum@norfolk.gov.uk

The museum is housed in five 19th-century fishermen's cottages, one of which has period furnishings. There are pictures and exhibits from Victorian Cromer, with collections illustrating local natural history, archaeology, social history and geology. Items to discover include the scandal of mixed bathing, the daring rescues of Henry Blogg and the Cromer Lifeboatmen, and the incredible story of the West Runton elephant, Britain's oldest and most complete elephant fossil.
Times: Open all year, Mon-Sat 10-5, Sun 2-5. Closed Mon 1-2. May be closed for refurbishment during winter months **Fee:** ✱ £1.80 (concessions £1.40, ch 90p, under 5's free) **Facilities:** 🅿 (100mtrs) & shop ✗ (ex guide dogs)

HENRY BLOGG MUSEUM
No 2 Boathouse, The Promenade NR27 9HE
➲ (located at the bottom of East Gangway)
☎ 01263 511294   ✉ 01263 513018
e-mail: rfmuirhead@csma-netlink.co.uk

A lifeboat has been stationed at the Cromer since 1804, and the museum in No 2 boat house at the bottom of The Gangway covers local lifeboat history and the RNLI in general. The main exhibit is the WWII Watson Class lifeboat *H F Bailey*, the boat Henry Blogg coxed. In ten years he helped to save over 500 lives.
Times: ✱ Open Etr-Oct, daily 10-4. Or by appointment with the Curator. **Facilities:** 🅿 (pay & display in town) & shop

ERPINGHAM Map 09 TG13
WOLTERTON PARK
NR11 7LY
➲ (signposted from A140 Norwich to Cromer)
☎ 01263 584175 `FREE`
🖥 01263 761214

Covering some 800 hectares this estate contains managed conservation areas, 18th-century landscaped gardens, and Wolterton Hall, built in the 1720s. Special events include gardening demonstrations, concerts, plays, opera, craft fairs, guided walks and history lectures.
Times: Open: Park daily; Hall, late Apr-end Oct, Fri 2-5 (last entry 4). **Facilities:** P (charged) & toilets for disabled shop ✖ (ex on lead & guide dogs)

FAKENHAM Map 09 TF93
See also Thursford Green

PENSTHORPE WATERFOWL PARK & NATURE RESERVE
Pensthorpe NR21 0LN
➲ (just outside Fakenham on the A1067 to Norwich)
☎ 01328 851465 🖥 01328 855905 `2 for 1`
e-mail: info@pensthorpe.com

Covering 200 acres of beautiful Norfolk countryside, with five lakes which are home to the largest collection of waterfowl and waders in Europe. Spacious walk-through enclosures and a network of hardsurfaced pathways ensures close contact with birds at the water's edge.
Times: Open all year, daily 10-4.30 **Fee:** ✱ £5.50 (ch £3, pen £5)
Facilities: P ◻ ✖ licensed & (network of hard surfaced pathways ensures access) toilets for disabled shop ✖ (ex guide dogs)

FELBRIGG Map 09 TG23
FELBRIGG HALL
NR11 8PR
➲ (off B1436 between A148 Cromer to Kings Lynn & A140 Cromer to Norwich)
☎ 01263 837444 🖥 01263 837032
e-mail: felbrigg@nationaltrust.org.uk

Felbrigg is a 17th-century house built on the site of an existing medieval hall. It contains a superb collection of 18th-century furniture and pictures and an outstanding library. A 550-acre wood shelters the house from the North Sea and contains waymarked walks and a working dovecot.
Times: Open house and garden: late Mar-early Nov, Sat-Wed, house 1-5, garden 11-5.30. BH Mon 11-5. Park walks available daily dawn-dusk. **Fee:** ✱ House & garden £6 (ch £3). Garden only £2.50.
Facilities: P ◻ ✖ licensed & (battery operated wheelchair for garden, Braille guide) toilets for disabled shop ✖ (ex guide or on lead in park) 🐾

> The AA also publishes a guide to Family Friendly Places to Stay, Eat & Visit

FILBY Map 09 TG41
THRIGBY HALL WILDLIFE GARDENS
NR29 3DR
➲ (on unclass road off A1064, between Acle & Caister on Sea)
☎ 01493 369477 🖥 01493 368256
e-mail: mail@thrigbyhall.co.uk

The 250-year-old park of Thrigby Hall is now the home of animals and birds from Asia, and the lake has ornamental wildfowl. There are tropical bird houses, a unique blue willow pattern garden and tree walk and a summer house as old as the park. The enormous jungled swamp hall has special features such as underwater viewing of large crocodiles.
Times: Open all year, daily from 10. **Fee:** ✱ £6.50 (ch 4-14 £4.50, pen £5.50). **Facilities:** P ◻ & (wheelchairs available) toilets for disabled shop ✖ (ex guide dogs)

FLEGGBURGH Map 09 TG41
THE VILLAGE
Burgh St. Margaret NR29 3AF
➲ (7m from Great Yarmouth, on A1064 between Acle and Caister-on-Sea)
☎ 01493 369770 🖥 01493 369318

The Village Experience is set in over 30 acres of woodland. Working steam and traditional fairground rides, exploratorium, live shows including a puppet show and a cinema-organ concert. Other attractions include a fairground, a children's drawing studio, a soft play area and a maze.
Times: ✱ Open 24 Mar-end Oct, daily 10-5. Other times not confirmed. Saturday is grounds only day (admission reduced accordingly) **Facilities:** P ◻ ✖ licensed & toilets for disabled shop ✖ (ex guide dogs)

GREAT BIRCHAM Map 09 TF73
BIRCHAM WINDMILL `2 for 1`
PE31 6SJ
➲ (0.5m W off unclassified Snettisham road).
☎ 01485 578393
e-mail: birchamwindmill@btinternet.com

This windmill is one of the last remaining in Norfolk. Sails turn on windy days, and the adjacent tea room serves home-made cakes, light lunches and cream teas. There is also a bakery shop and cycle hire.
Times: Open Etr-Sep, 10-5. **Fee:** £2.75 (ch £1.50, pen £2.50)
Facilities: P ◻ & toilets for disabled shop

GREAT YARMOUTH Map 05 TG50
ELIZABETHAN HOUSE MUSEUM
4 South Quay NR30 2QH
☎ 01493 855746

A wealthy merchant built this house in 1596. It has been completely re-displayed to show a wealthy household through time from the 16th to 19th centuries. Visitors can see a Victorian kitchen, scullery and parlour, a Tudor bedroom and dining room, a Stuart (Civil War) 'conspiracy' room and a children's toy room.
Times: Open 25 Apr- Oct, Mon-Fri 10-5; Sat & Sun 1.15-5. **Fee:** £2.60 (ch £1.30, concessions £2). Family ticket £6. **Facilities:** P (100yds) & shop ✖

MERRIVALE MODEL VILLAGE
Wellington Pier Gardens, Marine Pde NR30 3JG
➲ (Marine parade seafront. Next to Wellington Pier)
☎ 01493 842097

Set in attractive landscaped gardens, this comprehensive miniature village is built on a scale of 1:12. The layout includes a two and a half inch gauge model railway, radio-controlled boats, and over 200 models set in an acre of landscaped gardens. There are additional amusements and remote-controlled cars and boats.
Times: ✻ Open Etr 9.30-6, Jun-Oct 9.30-10. **Facilities:** P (opposite) 🍽 ⅃ shop ✻ (ex on leads)

ROW 111 HOUSES/OLD MERCHANT'S HOUSE AND GREYFRIARS CLOISTERS
South Quay NR30 2RQ
➲ (follow signs to dock and south quay)
☎ 01493 857900

Visit these 17th-century houses unique to Great Yarmouth, and the remains of a Franciscan friary with rare early wall paintings. Guided tours explain how the rich and poor lived in these properties over various time periods.
Times: Open Apr-Oct, daily 10-5. Guided tours depart from Row 11 House at 10, 12, 2 & 5. All tours include Old Merchant's House and Greyfriar's Cloisters. Dates valid until 31 Mar 2004. **Fee:** £3 (ch £1.50, concessions £2). Prices valid until 31 Mar 2004. **Facilities:** shop ✻ ⅃⅃

TOLHOUSE MUSEUM
Tolhouse St NR30 2SH
☎ 01493 858900 🖹 01493 745459

This late 13th-century building was once the town's court house and gaol and has dungeons which can be visited. The rooms above contain exhibits on local history. The museum has become a brass rubbing centre and has a wide range of replica brasses from which rubbings can be made. Prices start at 50p and include materials and instructions.
Times: Open Apr-Oct, Mon-Fri 10-5; Sat & Sun 1.15-5. **Fee:** £2.60 (ch £1.30, concessions £2). Family ticket £6. **Facilities:** P (100yds) (lift to ground & 2nd floor) shop ✻

GRESSENHALL   Map 09 TF91
ROOTS OF NORFOLK
Beech House NR20 4DR
➲ (A47, B1110 through East Dereham towards Holt, onto B1146 to Fakenham, museum is 1.5m on right)
☎ 01362 860563 🖹 01362 860385
e-mail: gressenhall.museum@norfolk.gov.uk

Housed in a former workhouse, the museum reflects the rural history of the county over the past 200 years. Displays include Cherry Tree Cottage and garden, a typical farm labourer's home of the early 20th century, as well as reconstructed craftsmen's workshops. Union Farm is a working farm, which is worked with heavy horses and stocked with rare breeds of sheep, cattle, pigs and poultry. Farm trail, woodland and riverside walk, osier beds. Special events and demonstrations throughout the season.
Times: Open Mar-Oct, Tue-Sun, also BH & School Hol Mon, 10.30-5.30; Nov & Dec Sun only 11-4. **Fee:** £5.45 (ch £4.35, concessions £4.95). Family ticket £17.60. **Facilities:** P 🍽 ⅃ (sound guide & wheelchair loan) toilets for disabled shop ✻ 🍽

GRIMES GRAVES   Map 05 TL88
GRIMES GRAVES
IP26 5DE
➲ (7m NW of Thetford off A134)
☎ 01842 810656

These unique and remarkable Neolithic flint mines are the earliest major industrial site in Europe.
Times: Open all year, Apr-Sep, daily 10-6; Oct, daily 10-5; Nov-Mar, Wed-Sun 10-4 (closed between 1-2). (Closed 24-26 Dec & 1 Jan). Dates valid until 31 Mar 2004. **Fee:** £2.50 (ch £1.50, concessions £2). Prices valid until 31 Mar 2004. **Facilities:** P ⅃ (exhibition area, grounds only; access track rough) shop ✻ (ex on lead in certain areas) ⅃⅃

HEACHAM   Map 09 TF63
NORFOLK LAVENDER
Caley Mill PE31 7JE
➲ (on A149 at junct with B1454)
☎ 01485 570384 🖹 01485 571176
e-mail: admin@norfolk-lavender.co.uk

This is the largest lavender-growing and distilling operation in Britain. Different coloured lavenders are grown in strips and harvested in July and August. There are also herb gardens and a fragrant Plant Centre, and guided tours of the distillery and gardens.
Times: Open all year, daily, Apr-Oct 10-5; Nov-Mar 10-4. (Closed 25-26 Dec & 1 Jan). **Fee:** ✻ Admission to grounds free. Guided tours £1.95 (May-Sep). Trip to Lavender Field £3.95, mid Jun-mid Aug.
Facilities: P 🍽 ✗ licensed ⅃ (wheelchairs for loan) toilets for disabled shop garden centre 🍽

HOLKHAM   Map 09 TF84
HOLKHAM HALL & BYGONES MUSEUM
NR23 1AB
➲ (off A149, 2m W of Wells-next-the-Sea)
☎ 01328 710227 🖹 01328 711707
e-mail: i.herrieveh@holkham.co.uk

This classic Palladian mansion was built between 1734 and 1764 by Thomas Coke, 1st Earl of Leicester, and is home to his descendants. It has a magnificent alabaster entrance hall and the sumptuous state rooms house Greek and Roman statues, fine furniture and paintings by Rubens, Van Dyck, Gainsborough and others. The Bygones Museum, housed in the stable block, has over 5,000 items of domestic and agricultural display - from gramophones to fire engines.
Times: Open May-Sep, Thu-Mon 1-5; Etr, May & Summer BHs also open Sat-Mon 11.30-5. **Fee:** Hall £6.50 (ch £3.25). Bygones £5 (ch £2.50). Combined ticket Hall & Bygones: £10 (ch £5). Family ticket £25. **Facilities:** P 🍽 ⅃ (wheelchair ramps at all entrances) toilets for disabled shop garden centre (ex guide & on lead in park) ⅃⅃ (prior booking advised) 🍽

HORSEY   Map 09 TG42
HORSEY WINDPUMP
NR29 4EF
➲ (15m N of Great Yarmouth, on the B1159 4m NE of Martham)
☎ 01493 393904

Set in a remote part of the Norfolk Broads, the windpump mill was built 200 years ago to drain the area, and then rebuilt in 1912 by Dan England, a noted Norfolk millwright.

continued

It has been restored since being struck by lightning in 1943, and overlooks Horsey Mere and marshes, noted for their wild birds and insects, as a site of International Importance for Nature Conservation.
Times: Open 10.30-4.30, last admission 4pm; Mar, Sat-Sun only; Apr-Jun, Wed-Sun; Jul-Aug, daily; Sep-Oct, Wed-Sun; Open bank holidays. **Fee:** £2 (ch £1). National Trust members free entry & parking. Mooring fees payable to the Horsey Estate (inc NT members).
Facilities: ▣ (charged) ▦ ও (parking, ramps to ground floor) toilets for disabled shop ✖ (ex guide dogs) ❊

HORSHAM ST FAITH   Map 09 TG21
CITY OF NORWICH AVIATION MUSEUM
Old Norwich Rd NR10 3JF
➲ (follow brown tourist signs from A140 Norwich to Cromer Road)
☎ 01603 893080 ▤ 01603 893080
e-mail: derek.waters@virgin.net

A massive Avro Vulcan bomber, veteran of the Falklands War, dominates the collection of military and civilian aircraft at this museum. There are several displays relating to the aeronautical history of Norfolk, including some on the role played by Norfolk-based RAF and USAAF planes during World War II, and a section dedicated to the operations of RAF Bomber Command's 100 group.
Times: Open all year, Apr-Oct Tue-Sat, 10-5. Sun 12-5. Open BH Mon 12-5 & Mon late Jul-Aug 10-5. Nov-Mar, Wed & Sat 10-4. Sun 12-4.
Fee: £2.80 (ch & concessions £1.50, pen £2.30) Family ticket £8.
Facilities: ▣ ▦ ও (assistance available) shop ✖ (ex guide dogs) ❧

HOUGHTON   Map 09 TF72
HOUGHTON HALL
PE31 6UE
➲ (1.25m off A148)
☎ 01485 528569 ▤ 01485 528167
e-mail: administrator@houghtonhall.com
Houghton Hall built in the 1920's by Sir Robert Walpole, Britain's first Prime Minister, is one of the grandest surviving Palladian Houses in England. Now owned by the 7th Marquess of Cholmondeley. The spectacular 5-acre walled garden, recently restored by Lord Cholmondeley in memory of his grandmother, has been divided into areas for fruit and vegetables, spacious herbaceous borders, and formal rose gardens with over 150 varieties. A collection of Model Soldiers contains over 20,000 models laid out in various battle formations.
Times: Open Etr Sun-last Sun Sep, Wed, Thu, Sun & BH's. House open 2-5.30, grounds 1-5.30. **Fee:** £6.50 (ch 5-16 £3, ch under 5 free). Excluding house £4 (ch 5-16 £2). **Facilities:** ▣ ▦ ✖ licensed ও (lift) toilets for disabled shop ✖

HUNSTANTON   Map 09 TF64
SEA LIFE AQUARIUM & MARINE SANCTUARY
Southern Promenade PE36 5BH
☎ 01485 533576 ▤ 01485 533531
With over 30 fascinating displays of marine life, this fascinating aquarium offers close encounters with starfish, sharks, octopus, eels and many other underwater wonders.
continued

Feeding demonstrations, talks and special presentations. Latest addition: Otters.
Times: ✱ Open all year, daily from 10. (Closed 25 Dec) **Facilities:** ▣ (charged) ▦ ✖ ও toilets for disabled shop ✖ (ex guide dogs) ❧

KING'S LYNN   Map 09 TF62
AFRICAN VIOLET CENTRE
Terrington St Clement PE34 4PL
➲ (situated beside A17 5m from Kings Lynn and 3m from A47/A17 junct)
☎ 01553 828374 ▤ 01553 828376
e-mail: info@africanvioletcentre.ltd.uk
A warm and friendly welcome awaits you at the African Violet Centre. As a major plant specialist the centre offers a wide variety of plants for any enthusiast. Best known for their vast selection and display of African violets. The African Violet Centre is a winner of many Chelsea Gold Medals.
Times: Open daily Mon-Sat 9-5, Sun 10-5. (Closed Xmas & New Year).
Facilities: ▣ ▦ ও (ramps & wide doors) toilets for disabled shop garden centre ✖ (ex guide dogs) ❧

KING'S LYNN ARTS CENTRE
27-29 King St PE30 1HA
➲ (located just off Tuesday Market Place in King Street, next to Globe Hotel)
☎ 01553 765565 & 01553 764864
▤ 01553 762141
Although it has been used for many purposes, the theatrical associations of this 15th-century Guildhall are strongest: Shakespeare himself is said to have performed here. The annual King's Lynn Festival takes place towards the end of July.
Times: Open Mon-Fri, 10-2. Closed show days, Sun, BHs, Good Fri & 24 Dec-1st Mon in Jan. **Facilities:** ▣ ▦ ✖ ও (hearing loop, ramp) toilets for disabled ✖ ❊

LYNN MUSEUM
Market St PE30 1NL
➲ (Town Centre)
☎ 01553 775001 ▤ 01553 775001
e-mail: lynn.museum@norfolk.gov.uk
Once it was a walled city of considerable importance; its two great churches, two marketplaces and two Guildhalls testify to its size. King's Lynn was also a noted port and a stop on the Pilgrim's Way to Walsingham. The geology, archaeology and natural history of the area are the main collections in the local museum. Objects in the archaeology gallery include Bronze Age weapons and the skeleton of a Saxon warrior. Relics from the medieval town of Lynn include an important collection of pilgrim badges. Also see the Snarling Tiger, the Medieval Stonemason, the Victorian Ironmonger's Shop and the beautiful 19th century fairground roundabout horses of Frederick Savage.
Times: Open all year, Tue-Sat, 10-5. **Fee:** £1 (ch 60p, concessions 80p). **Facilities:** ▣ (500yds) ও shop ✖

> The AA also publishes a guide to
> Pet Friendly Places to Stay

LENWADE   Map 09 TG01
DINOSAUR ADVENTURE PARK
Weston Park NR9 5JW
➲ (9m from Norwich. Follow Weston Park signs
from A47 or A1067)
☎ 01603 876310 🖷 01603 876315
e-mail: info@dinosaurpark.co.uk
Children will have great fun coming face to face with lots of
friendly farm animals (real), and giant dinosaurs (thankfully
not real). Alongside the animals there are adventure play
areas, a fossil workshop, raptor racers, Jurassic putt, a
Victorian walled garden, and the Neanderthal walk.
Times: Open Etr-8 Sep & Oct half term, daily; 9 Sep-20 Oct, Fri, Sat &
Sun. **Fee:** ✻ £6.75 (ch & pen £5.75). **Facilities:** 🅿 💷 ఈ toilets for
disabled shop ✖ (ex guide dogs) 🍽

LITTLE WALSINGHAM   Map 09 TF93
WALSINGHAM ABBEY GROUNDS
& SHIREHALL MUSEUM
NR22 6BP
➲ (Follow B1105 from Fakenham. Entrance to
museum through tourist info centre in village)
☎ 01328 820510 & 820259 🖷 01328 820098
e-mail: walsingham.museum@farmline.com
In the grounds of the Abbey are the ruins of the original
Augustinian priory built in the 1100s. The priory was built
over the shrine of Our Lady of Walsingham which had been
established in 1061. Shirehall Museum consists of an original
Georgian Courthouse, displays on the history of Walsingham
and local artefacts. The museum is situated in 20 acres of
tranquil and picturesque gardens with access to woodland
and river walks across the historic parkland.
Times: Open Apr-late Oct, daily 10-4.30; Nov-Dec, wknds only 10-4;
late Jan-late Feb, daily 10-4. Other times through Estate office Mon-Fri,
10-4. Closed between 1-2. **Fee:** ✻ £3 (concessions £1.50)
Facilities: 🅿 (100yds) ఈ toilets for disabled shop garden centre ✖
(ex on leads) 🍽

NORTH CREAKE   Map 09 TF83
CREAKE ABBEY
NR21 9LF   **FREE**
➲ (off B1355)
The ruins of the church of an Augustinian almshouse, later
converted to an abbey.
Times: Open any reasonable time. **Facilities:** ✖ (ex dogs on leads) 🎫

NORWICH   Map 05 TG20
BRIDEWELL MUSEUM
Bridewell Alley NR2 1AQ
➲ (in town centre)
☎ 01603 667228 🖷 01603 765651
e-mail: museums@norfolk.gov.uk
Built in the late 14th century, this flint-faced merchant's
house was used as a prison from 1583 to 1828. It now
houses displays illustrating the trades and industries of
Norwich during the past 200 years, including a large
collection of locally made boots and shoes. There are also a
reconstructed 1920s pharmacy, a 1930s pawnbrokers shop
and a blacksmith's smithy. Special for children: "Hunt the
Animals" quiz trail.
Times: Open Apr-Oct. **Fee:** £2 (ch £1.20, concessions £1.60) Family
ticket £5. **Facilities:** 🅿 5min walk shop ✖ (ex guide dogs)

NORWICH CASTLE MUSEUM
Castle Meadow NR1 3JU
➲ (located in city centre)
☎ 01603 493625 🖷 01603 493623
e-mail: museums@norfolk.gov.uk
The Castle keep was built in the 12th century, and the
museum houses displays of art, archaeology, natural history,
Lowestoft porcelain, Norwich silver, a large collection of
paintings (with special emphasis on the Norwich School of
Painters) and British ceramic teapots. There are also guided
tours of the dungeons and battlements. A programme of
exhibitions, children's events, gallery and evening talks takes
place throughout the year. Please ring for details.
Times: Open all year, Mon-Fri 10-4.30, Sat 10-5, Sun 1-5; School
holidays: School holidays Mon-Sat 10-6, Sun 1-5. (Closed 23-26 Dec &
1 Jan). **Fee:** All galleries £4.95 (ch 4-16 £3.95, conc £4.50). Adult in
family grp £4.45 (ch £3.55). **Facilities:** 🅿 (200mtrs) 💷 ఈ (lift to first
floor, special parking by prior arrangement) toilets for disabled shop ✖
(ex guide dogs)

NORWICH CATHEDRAL
The Close NR1 4DH
➲ (A47, A11 to city centre, inner ring road to
Barrack St rdbt, take road towards city centre to
Tombland)
☎ 01603 218321 🖷 01603 766032
e-mail: vis-profficer@cathedral.org.uk
The splendour and tranquillity of Norwich Cathedral have
attracted visitors and pilgrims for nearly 1000 years. Norwich
has the second highest spire, and the largest monastic
cloister in England, and the 1,000 carved medieval roof
bosses are amazing. The building remains a place of quiet
reflection and prayer as well as for participation in daily
worship or the rich pageantry of the Church's festivals.
Times: Open daily, 7.30-7 (6pm mid Sep-mid May). **Fee:** Donations
welcomed £3 (ch £1). Guided tours £3 (ch £1). **Facilities:** 🅿 (440yds)
✖ licensed ఈ (lift, touch & hearing centre, audio-induction loop)
toilets for disabled shop ✖ (allowed in some areas)

ROYAL NORFOLK REGIMENTAL MUSEUM
Shirehall, Market Av NR1 3JQ
➲ (adjacent to Norwich Castle Museum)
☎ 01603 493623 🖷 01603 493623
Museum displays deal with the social as well as military
history of the county regiment from 1685, including the daily
life of a soldier. Audio-visual displays and graphics
complement the collection and there's a programme of
temporary exhibitions.
Times: ✻ Open all year, Mon-Sat 10-5, Sun 2-5. (Closed Xmas period
& 1 Jan). **Facilities:** 🅿 (400yds) ఈ (stair lift available, ring for details)
shop ✖ (ex guide dogs)

SAINSBURY CENTRE FOR VISUAL ARTS
University of East Anglia NR4 7TJ
➲ (From A11, take A47 Southern bypass W
towards Swaffham. 1st exit onto B1108, follow
brown signs on this road)
☎ 01603 593199 🖷 01603 259401   **2 for 1**
e-mail: scva@uea.ac.uk
The collection of Sir Robert and Lady Sainsbury was given to
the University in 1973. This outstanding collection is housed
in two buildings designed by Norman Foster and combines

continued

modern Western art with fine and applied arts from Africa, the Pacific, the Americas, Asia, Egypt, Medieval Europe and the ancient Mediterranean.
Times: Open Tue & Thu-Sun 11-5, Wed 11-8. (Closed Mon & University closure at Xmas). Phone in advance to check for gallery closures during refurbishment work. **Fee:** Collection & exhibition £2 (concessions £1). **Facilities:** ▣ ▣ ✕ licensed ৬ (parking at main entrance, wheelchair available on loan) toilets for disabled shop ✖ (guide dogs by arrangement) ◥

OXBOROUGH   Map 05 TF70
OXBURGH HALL
PE33 9PS
➲ (7m SW of Swaffham. Signposted from A134 at Stoke ferry & Swaffham).
☎ 01366 328258 ▤ 01366 328066
e-mail: oxburghhall@nationaltrust.org.uk
The outstanding feature of this 15th-century moated building is the 80ft high Tudor gatehouse which has remained unaltered throughout the centuries. Henry VII lodged in the King's Room in 1487. A parterre garden of French design stands outside the moat. Rare needlework by Mary Queen of Scots and Bess of Hardwick is on display. A particular attraction is a genuine 17th century priests hole, which is accessible to members of the public.
Times: Open House: 22 Mar-2 Nov, daily (ex Thu & Fri) 1-5, BH Mon 11-5, last admission 4.30. Garden: 1-16 Mar, wknds, 11-4; 23 Mar-3 Nov daily (ex Thu & Fri) 11-5.30; Aug daily 11-5.30. **Fee:** ✱ House & Gdns £5.50 (ch £2.80), Family ticket £14.50. Gdns only £2.80 (ch £1.40). Party 15+ £4.50. **Facilities:** ▣ ✕ licensed ৬ (braille guide, wheelchairs available, touch tour) toilets for disabled shop ✖·(ex guide dogs) ⚘ ◥

REEDHAM   Map 05 TG40
PETTITTS ANIMAL ADVENTURE PARK
NR13 3UA
➲ (off A47 at Acle)
☎ 01493 700094 & 701403 ▤ 01493 700933
Three parks in one, aimed at the younger child. Rides include a railway and roller coaster; the adventure play area has a golf course, ball pond and tearoom; and entertainment is provided by clowns, puppets and live musicians. Among the animals that can be seen are small horses, wallabies, birds of prey, goats, chickens and ducks.
Times: Open daily 12 Apr-2 Nov, 10-5/5.30. **Fee:** ✱ £7.75 (ch 3-15 £7.25, pen/disabled £5.85). **Facilities:** ▣ ▣ ৬ (ramps to all areas) toilets for disabled shop ✖ ◥

ST OLAVES   Map 05 TM49
ST OLAVE'S PRIORY   `FREE`
➲ (5.5m SW of Great Yarmouth on A143)
Remains of an Augustinian priory founded nearly 200 years after the death in 1030 of the patron saint of Norway, after whom it was named.
Times: Open any reasonable time. **Facilities:** ✖ (ex on lead in certain areas) ⚘

SANDRINGHAM   Map 09 TF62
SANDRINGHAM HOUSE, GROUNDS, MUSEUM & COUNTRY PARK
PE35 6EN
➲ (off A148)
☎ 01553 772675 & 612908 ▤ 01485 541571
e-mail: visits@sandringhamestate.co.uk
The private country retreat of Her Majesty The Queen, this neo-Jacobean house was built in 1870 for King Edward VII. The main rooms used by the Royal Family when in residence are all open to the public. Sixty acres of glorious grounds surround the House and offer beauty and colour throughout the season. Sandringham Museum contains fascinating displays of Royal memorabilia.
Times: Open Etr Sat-mid Jul & early Aug-Oct. House open 11-4.45, Museum 11-5 & Grounds 10.30-5. **Fee:** ✱ House, Museum & Grounds: £6.50 (ch £4, pen £5). Family ticket £17. **Facilities:** ▣ ▣ ✕ licensed ৬ (wheelchair loan, free transport in grounds, Braille guide) toilets for disabled shop garden centre ✖ (ex guide dogs) ◥

SAXTHORPE   Map 09 TG13
MANNINGTON GARDENS & COUNTRYSIDE
Mannington Hall NR11 7BB
➲ (signposted from Corpusty/Saxthorpe on B1149 Norwich-Holt road. Follow brown signs) `2 for 1`
☎ 01263 584175 ▤ 01263 761214
The moated manor house, built in 1460 and still a family home, forms a centre-piece for the pretty gardens which surround it. Visitors can take in the Heritage rose garden, lakes, a scented garden, a ruined church, and horse graves.
Times: Open: Gardens Jun-Aug, Wed-Fri 11-5; also Sun noon-5; 30 Apr-1 Oct. Walks open every day from 9am. Hall open by prior appointment only. **Fee:** ✱ Garden £3 (accompanied ch 16 free, students & pen £2.50). Walks free (car park for walkers £1).
Facilities: ▣ ▣ ৬ (boardwalk across meadow, wheelchair ramps) toilets for disabled shop ✖ (ex guide dogs)

SHERINGHAM   Map 09 TG14
NORTH NORFOLK RAILWAY
Sheringham Station, Station Approach NR26 8RA
➲ (from A148 take A1082. Next to large car park by rdbt in town centre)
☎ 01263 820800 ▤ 01263 820801
e-mail: enquiries@nnrailway.com
A steam railway with trains operating on most days (Apr-Sep), with extra days as the season progresses and a daily service in the summer. At Weybourne Station there is a collection of steam locomotives and rolling stock, some of which are undergoing or awaiting restoration. There is also a museum of railway memorabilia.
Times: Open Apr-Sep; daily during summer season; Dec (Santa specials). Telephone for details of other running days. **Fee:** £8 (ch under 4 free, ch 4-15 £4.50, pen £7). Family ticket £23 (free brochure while stocks last). **Facilities:** ▣ ▣ ৬ (ramps to trains, carriage converted for wheelchair access) toilets for disabled shop ◥

SNETTISHAM   Map 09 TF63

PARK FARM
PE31 7NQ

➲ (signposted on A149, Park Farm is close to the church)

☎ 01485 542425   🖶 01485 543503

e-mail: parkfarm@supanet.com

You can see farming in action here with lambing in the spring, sheep shearing in May and deer calving in June and July. Sheep, goats, lambs, rabbits, turkeys, ducks, chickens, ponies, piglets etc can be seen in the paddocks, and the sheep centre has over 40 different breeds. Other attractions include a large adventure playground, horse and pony rides, 2.5 miles of farm trails, visitor centre and craft workshops, including leather worker.

Times: Open Mar-Oct, daily 10-5; Nov-Feb (ring for details). Closed 25 Dec & 1st Jan. **Fee:** £4.75 (ch £3.75, pen £4). Family ticket £15.

Facilities: 🅿 ♨ ♿ (gravel paths, ramps where needed) toilets for disabled shop ✖ (ex on farm trails) 🍽

SOUTH WALSHAM   Map 09 TG31

FAIRHAVEN WOODLAND & WATER GARDEN
School Rd NR13 6EA

➲ (follow brown heritage signs from A47 onto B1140 to South Walsham. Drive through village towards Gt Yarmouth. Turn left into school road, 100yds past South Walsham Hall)   **2 for 1**

☎ 01603 270449   🖶 01603 270449

e-mail: fairhavengardens@norfolkbroads.com

These delightful woodland and water gardens offer a combination of cultivated and wild flowers. In spring there are masses of primroses and bluebells, with azaleas and rhododendrons in several areas. Candelabra primulas and some unusual plants grow near the waterways, and in summer the wild flowers provide a habitat for butterflies, bees and dragonflies.

Times: Open daily 10-5, extended opening until 9pm Wed & Thu, May-Aug. (Closed 25 Dec). **Fee:** £3.50 (ch £1.25, under 5 free, pen & concessions £3). Single membership tickets £12.50. Family membership ticket £30. **Facilities:** 🅿 ♨ ♿ (ramp, grab rail) toilets for disabled shop garden centre ✖ (ex on lead) 🍽

THETFORD   Map 05 TL88

ANCIENT HOUSE MUSEUM
White Hart St IP24 1AA

➲ (in town centre)

☎ 01842 752599

e-mail: ancient.house.museum@norfolk.gov.uk

An early Tudor timber-framed house with beautifully carved beamed ceilings, it now houses an exhibition on Thetford and Breckland life. This has been traced back to very early times, and there are examples from local Neolithic settlements. Brass rubbing facilities are available and there is a small period garden recreated in the rear courtyard.

Times: Open all year, Mon-Sat, 10-5 (Closed Mon 12.30-1); Jun-Aug also Sun 2-5. (Closed Good Fri, Xmas period & New Year's Day). **Fee:** Free (ex Jul & Aug £1, ch 60p, concessions 80p). **Facilities:** 🅿 (20yds) shop garden centre ✖

THETFORD PRIORY   **FREE**
➲ (on W side of Thetford near station)

A glimpse of medieval religious life before the dissolution of the monasteries. The Priory of Our Lady of Thetford belonged to the Order of Cluny, and was founded in 1103 by Roger Bigod, an old soldier and friend of William the Conqueror.

Times: Open all year, any reasonable time. **Facilities:** ✖ (ex dogs on leads) ⚏

THETFORD WARREN LODGE   **FREE**
➲ (2m W of Thetford, off B1107)

The remains of a two-storey hunting lodge, built in 15th-century of flint with stone dressings.

Times: Open any reasonable time. Currently closed for repair, contact regional office on 01233 582700 before visiting. **Facilities:** ✖ (ex dogs on leads) ⚏

THURSFORD GREEN   Map 09 TF93

THURSFORD COLLECTION
NR21 0AS

➲ (1m off A148. Halfway between Fakenham and Holt)   **2 for 1**

☎ 01328 878477   🖶 01328 878415

e-mail: admin@thursfordcollection.co.uk

This exciting collection specialises in organs, with a Wurlitzer cinema organ, fairground organs, barrel organs and street organs among its treasures. There are live musical shows every day. The collection also includes showmen's engines, ploughing engines and farm machinery. There is a children's play area and a breathtaking 'Venetian gondola' switchback ride.

Times: Open Good Fri-last Sun in Sep, daily, 12-5. Closed Sat. **Fee:** £5.30 (ch under 4 free, ch 4-14 £2.80, students £4.55 pen £5). Party 15+ £4.55 each. **Facilities:** 🅿 ♨ ✖ licensed ♿ toilets for disabled shop (five different giftshops) ✖ (ex guide dogs) 🍽

> ## The AA also publishes a guide to Pet Friendly Places to Stay

TITCHWELL   Map 09 TF74

RSPB NATURE RESERVE
PE31 8BB
➲ (6m E of Hunstanton on A149, signposted entrance)
☎ 01485 210779 ▤ 01485 210779
e-mail: titchwell@rspb.org.uk

A firm path takes you to three hides and on to the beach where a platform overlooking the sea is suitable for wheelchairs. A colony of avocets nest on the enclosed marsh with gadwalls, tufted ducks, shovelers and black-headed gulls. During the season many migrants visit the marsh including wigeon, black-tailed godwits, curlews, and sandpipers.

Times: ✱ Open at all times. Visitor Centre daily 10-5 (4pm Nov-Mar). **Facilities:** ▣ (charged) ▆ ﬔ (ramps to hides, wheelchair bays in hides) toilets for disabled shop ▼

WEETING   Map 05 TL78

WEETING CASTLE
IP27 0RQ
➲ (2m N of Brandon off B1106)   **FREE**

This ruined 11th-century fortified manor house stands in a moated enclosure. There are interesting but slight remains of a three-storey cross-wing.

Times: Open any reasonable time. **Facilities:** ✖ (ex dogs on leads) ⌗

WELLS-NEXT-THE-SEA   Map 09 TF94

WELLS & WALSINGHAM LIGHT RAILWAY
NR23 1QB
➲ (A149 Cromer road)
☎ 01328 711630

The railway covers the four miles between Wells and Walsingham, and is the longest ten and a quarter inch gauge track in the world. The line passes through some very attractive countryside, particularly noted for its wild flowers and butterflies. This is the home of the unique Garratt Steam Locomotive specially built for this line.

Times: Open daily Good Fri-Oct. **Fee:** ✱ £6 return (ch £4.50 return). **Facilities:** ▣ ▆ ﬔ shop

> Special Events are held at many attractions throughout the country. As we cannot hope to list them all, please ring the places of interest for details of exhibitions, themed days, and guided walks.

WELNEY   Map 05 TL59

WWT WELNEY
Hundred Foot Bank PE14 9TN
➲ (off A1101, N of Ely)
☎ 01353 860711 ▤ 01353 860711   **2 for 1**
e-mail: welney@wwt.org.uk

This important wetland site on the beautiful Ouse Washes is famed for the breathtaking spectacle of wild ducks, geese and swans which spend the winter here. Impressive observation facilities, including hides, towers and an observatory, offer outstanding views of the huge numbers of wildfowl which include Bewick's and whooper swans, wigeon, teal and shoveler. Floodlit evening swan feeds take place between November and February. There are two hides for wheelchair users.

Times: Open all year, daily 10-5. (Closed 25 Dec). **Fee:** ✱ £3.65 (ch £2, pen £2.90). Family ticket £9.25. **Facilities:** ▣ ▆ ﬔ toilets for disabled shop ✖ (ex guide/hearing dogs) ▼

WEST RUNTON   Map 09 TG14

NORFOLK SHIRE HORSE CENTRE
West Runton Stables NR27 9QH
➲ (off A149)
☎ 01263 837339 ▤ 01263 837132
e-mail: bakewell@norfolkshirehorse.fsnet.co.uk

The Shire Horse Centre has a collection of draught horses and some breeds of mountain and moorland ponies. There are also exhibits of horse-drawn machinery, waggons and carts, and harnessing and working demonstrations are given twice every day. Other attractions include a children's farm, a photographic display of draught horses past and present, talks and a video show. There is a riding school on the premises as well.

Times: Open Etr-last Fri in Oct, Sun-Fri; also Sats BHs. Last admission 3.45pm **Fee:** ✱ £5 (ch £3, pen £4). **Facilities:** ▣ ▆ ﬔ toilets for disabled shop ✖ (ex on lead) ▼

WEYBOURNE   Map 09 TG14

THE MUCKLEBURGH COLLECTION   **2 for 1**
Weybourne Military Camp NR25 7EG
➲ (on A149, coast road, 3m W of Sheringham)
☎ 01263 588210 & 588608 ▤ 01263 588425
e-mail: info@muckleburgh.co.uk

The largest privately-owned military collection of its kind in the country, which incorporates the Museum of the Suffolk and Norfolk Yeomanry. Exhibits include restored and working tanks, armoured cars, trucks and artillery of WWII, and equipment and weapons from the Falklands and the Gulf War. Live tank demonstrations are run daily (except Saturdays) during school holidays.

Times: Open 10 Feb-2 Nov, daily 10-5. **Fee:** £5.50 (ch £3 & pen £4.50). Family ticket £13.50. **Facilities:** ▣ ▆ ✖ ﬔ (ramped access, wheelchairs available) toilets for disabled shop ✖ (ex guide, kennels provided) ▼

NORTHAMPTONSHIRE

Events & Festivals

May
29th-31st British Waterways Annual Boat Show, Crick (provisional)
21st-23rd Moulton Village Festival (Sat main day of event)

June
tbc Northampton Music & Arts Festival

July
3rd-4th Hollowell Steam & Heavy Horse Show, Hollowell nr Northampton
tbc Northampton Town Show, Abington Park, Northampton

August
tbc Northampton Hot Air Balloon Festival, Northampton Racecourse, Northampton

October
10th World Conker Championship, Village Green, Ashton, near Oundle

Top: Cottesbrooke Hall, nr Northampton
Above: Sir Thomas Tresham's symbolic Triangular Lodge near Rushton

ALTHORP   Map 04 SP66

ALTHORP
NN7 4HQ
➔ (M1 junct 16 and follow signs to Althorp)
☎ 01604 770107 0870 167 9000
🖨 01604 770042
e-mail: mail@althorp.com

Althorp House has been the home of the Spencer family since 1508. The house was built in the 16th century, but has been changed since, most notably by Henry Holland in the 18th century. Recently restored by the present Earl, the house is carefully maintained and in immaculate condition. The award-winning exhibition 'Diana, A Celebration' is located in six rooms and depicts the life and work of Diana, Princess of Wales. There is in addition, a room which depicts the work of the Diana, Princess of Wales Memorial Fund.
Times: Open Jul-Sep, daily 10-5. Closed 31 Aug.(not confirmed)
Fee: ✱ £11.50 (ch £5.50 & pen £9.50). Family ticket £28.50. Tickets discounted if pre-booked. (not confirmed) **Facilities:** 🅿 🍴 ♿ (disabled parking, wheelchairs, audio tour, shuttle) toilets for disabled shop ✖ (ex guide dogs) ♥

CANONS ASHBY   Map 04 SP55

CANONS ASHBY HOUSE
NN11 3SD
➔ (easy access from either M40, junct 11 or M1, junct 16)
☎ 01327 861900   🖨 01327 861909
e-mail: canonashby@nationaltrust.org.uk

Home of the Dryden family since the 16th century, this is an exceptional small manor house, with Elizabethan wall paintings and Jacobean plasterwork. It has restored gardens, a small park and a church - part of the original 13th-century Augustinian priory.
Times: Open Apr-29 Oct, Sat-Wed & BH Mon 1-5.30 (12-4.30 Oct) or dusk if earlier. Closed Good Fri. **Fee:** ✱ £5.40 (ch £2.70). Family ticket £13.50 **Facilities:** 🅿 🍴 ♿ (Braille/large print guide, taped guide, w/lchair available) toilets for disabled shop ✖ (ex on lead in home paddock) 🐾

DEENE   Map 04 SP99

DEENE PARK
NN17 3EW
➔ (0.5m off A43, between Kettering & Stamford)
☎ 01780 450278 & 450223 🖨 01780 450282
e-mail: admin@deenepark.com

A mainly 16th-century house of great architectural importance, and home of the Brudenell family since 1514 (including the 7th Earl of Cardigan who led the Charge of the Light Brigade). There's a large lake and park, and extensive gardens with old-fashioned roses, rare trees and shrubs. Phone for details of garden openings and any other special events.
Times: Open 2-5 BH's (Sun & Mon) Etr, May, Spring & Aug; Jun-Aug, Sun. Party 20+ by prior arrangement with House Keeper. **Fee:** ✱ House & Gardens: £5.50 (ch 10-14 £2.50, concessions £5). Gardens only: £3 (ch £1.50). Children under 10 free admission with accompanying adult. **Facilities:** 🅿 🍴 ♿ (ramps to cafeteria and gardens) toilets for disabled shop ✖ (ex guide dogs in garden only)

KIRBY HALL
NN17 5EN
➲ (on unclass road off A43, 4m NE of Corby)
☎ 01536 203230

An outstanding Elizabethan mansion with unusually strict symmetry and amazing Renaissance detail. The beautiful formal gardens gained a reputation in the 17th-century as being the finest in England.
Times: Open all year, Apr-Sep, daily 10-6; Oct, daily 10-5; Nov-Mar, Sat-Sun 10-4. (Closed 24-26 Dec & 1 Jan). Dates valid until 31 Mar 2004. **Fee:** £3.50 (ch £1.80, concessions £2.60). Prices valid until 31 Mar 2004. **Facilities:** 🅿 & shop ✖ (in certain areas) ♯

HOLDENBY   Map 04 SP66
HOLDENBY HOUSE, GARDENS & FALCONRY CENTRE
NN6 8DJ
➲ (7m NW of Northampton, off A5199 or A428)
☎ 01604 770074   ▤ 01604 770962
e-mail: sarah@holdenby.com

Just across the fields from Althorp, this former palace and prison of Charles I provides a stately backdrop to a beautiful garden and host of attractions. Falconry, 17th-century farmstead, children's amusements, shop and tearoom.
Times: ✱ Open; Gardens & Falconry Centre Apr-end Sep, Sun 1-5. 14 Jul to end Aug open daily 1-5 (ex Sat). House open Etr, Whitsun & Aug BH. Contact for details of additional Falconry Centre opening days.
Facilities: 🅿 🏪 & (gravel paths with ramps) toilets for disabled shop (on leads)

KETTERING   Map 04 SP87
ALFRED EAST GALLERY
Sheep St NN16 OAN (A43/A6, located in town centre)
☎ 01536 534274   ▤ 01536 534370   FREE
e-mail: museum@kettering.gov.uk

The Gallery has a permanent exhibition space showing work by Sir Alfred East, Thomas Cooper Gotch and other local artists, as well as selections from the Gallery's contemporary collection, including Sir Howard Hodgkin and John Bevan. Two further display spaces are dedicated to monthly changing sales exhibitions of art, craft and photography.
Times: Open all year, Mon-Sat 9.30-5 (closed BHs) **Facilities:** 🅿 (300yds) & shop ✖ (ex guide dogs)

LYVEDEN NEW BIELD   Map 04 SP98
LYVEDEN NEW BIELD
PE8 5AT
➲ (4m SW Oundle via A427)
☎ 01832 205358
e-mail: lyvedennewbield@nationaltrust.org.uk

An incomplete Elizabethan garden house and moated garden. Building began in 1595 by Sir Thomas Tresham, to symbolise his Catholic faith, and Lyveden remains virtually unaltered since work stopped when he died in 1605. The house has fascinating Elizabethan detail and in the grounds is one of the oldest garden layouts in Britain.
Times: House, Elizabethan Water Garden & Visitor Information Room open 2 Apr-2 Nov Wed-Sun 10.30-5, 3 Nov-Mar Sat & Sun 10.30-4. Open daily throughout Aug. **Fee:** ✱ £2.50 (ch £1.20). Family £6.20.
Facilities: 🅿 (0.5 m along track) ✖ (ex on leads) ⅏

NASSINGTON   Map 04 TL09
PREBENDAL MANOR HOUSE
PE8 6QG
➲ (turn off A605 Warrington rdbt and follow brown heritage signs, the manor is opposite the church)
☎ 01780 782575
e-mail: info@prebendal-manor.demon.co.uk

Dating from the early 13th-century, this is the oldest manor in Northamptonshire. There's a 15th-century dovecote and tithe barn museum, and the largest re-created medieval garden in Europe, boasting fishponds, herbers, arbours, turf seats, trellised herbers, medieval vegetable garden and vineyard.
Times: Open Etr Mon-Sep, Wed & Sun & BH Mon 1-5.30. **Fee:** ✱ House & garden £4.50 (ch £2). Garden only £4. **Facilities:** 🅿 🏪 & (ramps) shop ✖ (guide dogs)

NORTHAMPTON   Map 04 SP76
NORTHAMPTON MUSEUM & ART GALLERY
Guildhall Rd NN1 1DP
➲ (situated in the town centre)   FREE
☎ 01604 838111   ▤ 01604 838720
e-mail: museums@northhampton.gov.uk

Reflecting Northampton's proud standing as Britain's boot and shoe capital, the museum houses a collection of boots and shoes which is considered one of the finest in the world. Other displays include the History of Northampton, Decorative Arts, the Art Gallery, and special temporary exhibitions.
Times: Open all year, Mon-Sat 10-5, Sun 2-5. **Facilities:** 🅿 (200 yds) & (wheelchairs available, large print catalogues) toilets for disabled shop ✖ (ex guide/assistance dogs) ◤

ROCKINGHAM   Map 04 SP89
ROCKINGHAM CASTLE
LE16 8TH
➲ (2m N of Corby, off A6003)   2 for 1
☎ 01536 770240   ▤ 01536 771692
e-mail: a.norman@rockinghamcastle.com

Set on a hill overlooking five counties, the castle was built by William the Conqueror. The site of the original keep is now a rose garden, but the outline of the curtain wall remains as do the foundations of the Norman hall, and the twin towers of the gatehouse. A royal residence for 450 years, the castle was granted to Edward Watson in the 16th century, and the Watson family have lived there ever since.
Times: Open Jul-Aug, Tue & Thu, BH Mon 1-5. Grounds open at 11.30 am on Sun & BH Mon. **Fee:** ✱ £6 (ch £4 & pen £5.50). Family ticket £16. **Facilities:** 🅿 🏪 & (may alight at entrance, parking, ramps) toilets for disabled shop ✖ (ex in grounds) ◤

RUSHTON   Map 04 SP88
TRIANGULAR LODGE
NN14 1RP
☎ 01536 710761

A delightful Elizabethan folly designed to symbolise the Holy Trinity, with its three sides, three floors, trefoil windows and three triangular gables on each side.
Times: Open Apr-Sep, daily 10-6; Oct, daily 10-5. Dates valid until 31 Mar 2004. **Fee:** £2 (ch £1, concessions £1.50). Prices valid until 31 Mar 2004. **Facilities:** 🅿 shop ✖ (ex on lead in some areas) ♯

STOKE BRUERNE   Map 04 SP74

CANAL MUSEUM

NN12 7SE

⮡ (A508, 4m S of junct 15 of M1. 5m from Towcester A43/A5 junct)

☎ 01604 862229 ▤ 01604 864199   `2 for 1`
e-mail: canal.museum@
thewaterwaystrust.co.uk

Housed on three floors of an old cornmill, the colourful collection vividly portrays the many aspects of inland waterways from their origins to the present day, complementing the flight of locks and long canal tunnel outside.

Times: Open Etr-Oct daily, 10-5; Nov-Etr Tue-Sun, 10-4. Closed 25-26 Dec. Last admission 30 mins before closing time. **Fee:** ✱ £3 (ch, pen & student £2). Family ticket £8 (2 adults & 2 ch) **Facilities:** ▱ (charged) & toilets for disabled shop ✖ (ex guide dogs) ▰

SULGRAVE   Map 04 SP54

SULGRAVE MANOR

Manor Rd OX17 2SD

⮡ (off B4525 Banbury to Northampton road. 6m from M40 junct 11, 15m From M1 junct 15a)

☎ 01295 760205 ▤ 01295 768056   `2 for 1`
e-mail: sulgrave-manor@talk21.com

Home to George Washington's ancestors until 1656 when his great grandfather, John, emigrated to Virginia. Inside the house there are many relics of George Washington. Though much of the house is a 20th-century restoration, original parts include the porch (with a carving of the original American flag), a screens passage, the great hall and the great Chamber.

Times: Open Apr-Oct 2-5.30. Closed Mon & Fri ex BH's and special event days. Other times by appointment (closed 25-26 Dec & Jan) **Fee:** £5 (ch £2.50). Party 20+. £4.50 (ch £2.25) Special event days £6.50 (ch £3.25). Family ticket £17.50. **Facilities:** ▱ ▰ & (induction loop available in shop or ticket office) toilets for disabled shop ✖ (ex guide & outside on leads) ▰

NORTHUMBERLAND

EVENTS & FESTIVALS

April
  tbc Morpeth Northumbrian Gathering, Morpeth Town Hall

May
  1st Riding the Bounds, Berwick-upon-Tweed (traditional horseback ride)
  31st Northumberland County Show, Tynedale Park, Corbridge
  tbc Border Marches, Berwick-upon-Tweed
  tbc Teeside Garden Festival, Preston Park, Stockton-on-Tees

June
  19th Ovingham Goose Fair, Ovingham Village Green
  27th-4th Jul Alnwick Fair
  tbc Allendale Fair, Market Square,

July
  27th-4th Jul Alnwick Fair
  3rd-4th Amble Sea Fair, Amble
  16th-18th Rothbury Traditional Music Festival, Rothbury
  25th Alnwick Castle Tournament, Alnwick

August
  7th Powburn Show & Sheepdog Trials
  7th-13th Alnwick International Music Festival (provisional)
  7th Slaley Show, Townhead Field, Slaley
  tbc Military Tattoo, Barracks, Berwick-upon-Tweed

September
  4th Alnwick District Horticultural Show

November
  6th Northumbrian Gathering

Above: Forest at Dallington Heath

ALNWICK   Map 12 NU11

ALNWICK CASTLE
NE66 1NQ
➲ (off A1 on outskirts of town, follow signs for
The Alnwick Garden & Castle)
☎ 01665 510777   🖹 01665 510876
e-mail: enquiries@alnwickcastle.com
Alnwick Castle is the main seat of the Duke of
Northumberland whose family have lived here since 1309.
The stern, medieval exterior belies the treasure house within,
furnished in Renaissance style, with paintings by Titian, Van
Dyck and Canaletto, and an exquisite collection of Meissen
china. The Regiment Museum of Royal Northumberland
Fusiliers is housed in the Abbot's Tower of the Castle.
Recently refurbished towers include museums of local
archaeology and the Percy Tenantry volunteers.
Times: ✱ Open 28 Mar-25 Oct, daily 11-5 (last admission 4.15).
Facilities: 🅿 💷 ♿ (Castle lift for those able to walk a little) toilets
for disabled shop ✘ (ex guide dogs) ♥

BAMBURGH   Map 12 NU13

BAMBURGH CASTLE
NE69 7DF
➲ (A1 Belford by-pass, E on B1342 to Bamburgh)
☎ 01668 214515 & 214208   🖹 01668 214060
e-mail: bamburghcastle@aol.com
Rising dramatically from a rocky outcrop, Bamburgh Castle is
a huge, square Norman castle. Last restored in the 19th
century, it has an impressive hall and an armoury with a
large collection of armour from the Tower of London. Guide
services are available.
Times: Open 15 Mar-Oct, daily 11-5 (last admission 4.30pm). Other
times by prior arrangement. **Facilities:** 🅿 (charged) 💷 ♿ shop ✘
(ex guide dogs)

GRACE DARLING MUSEUM
Radcliffe Rd NE69 7AE
➲ (follow A1, turn off at Bamburgh & follow
signposts to Northumbria Coastal route, museum
on right)
☎ 01668 214465   🖹 01668 214465
Pictures, documents and other reminders of the heroine are
on display, including the boat in which Grace Darling and her
father, keeper of Longstone Lighthouse, Farne Islands,
rescued nine survivors from the wrecked SS Forfarshire
in 1838.
Times: Open Etr-Oct, daily 10-5 (Sun 12-5). **Fee:** ✱ Free. Voluntary
contribution of £1 (ch 50p) is requested. **Facilities:** 🅿 (400yds) ♿
(ramps) shop ✘ (ex guide dogs)

BARDON MILL   Map 12 NY76

VINDOLANDA (CHESTERHOLM)
Vindolanda Trust NE47 7JN
➲ (signposted from A69 or B6318)
☎ 01434 344277   🖹 01434 344060
e-mail: info@vindolanda.com
Vindolanda was a Roman fort and frontier town. It was
started well before Hadrian's Wall, and became a base
for 500 soldiers. The civilian settlement lay just west of the

continued

fort and has been excavated. The excellent museum in the
country house of Chesterholm nearby has displays and
reconstructions. There are also formal gardens and an
open-air museum with Roman Temple, shop, house and
Northumbrian croft.
Times: Open mid Feb-mid Nov, daily. Feb & Nov 10-4, Mar & Oct 10-5,
Apr & Sep 10-5.30, May-Jun 10-6, Jul-Aug 10-6.30. **Fee:** ✱ £4.10 (ch
£2.90, student & pen £3.50, free admission for disabled). Saver ticket
for joint admission to sister site - The Roman Army Museum £6 (ch
£4.30, pen £5.20) Party. **Facilities:** 🅿 💷 ♿ toilets for disabled shop
✘ (ex guide dogs) ♥

BELSAY   Map 12 NZ07

BELSAY HALL, CASTLE AND GARDENS
NE20 0DX
➲ (on A696)
☎ 01661 881636   🖹 01661 881043
Beautiful neo-classical hall, built from its own quarries with
a spectacular garden deservedly listed Grade 1 in the
Register of Gardens. It is slightly unclear who built the
'Grecian-style hall', however it was designed by Sir Charles
in 1807, in Greek Revival style. The magnificent 30 acres of
grounds contain the ruins of a 14th-century castle.
Times: Open all year, Apr-Sap, daily 10-6 (Oct 10-5); Nov-Mar, daily
10-4. Closed 24-26 Dec & 1 Jan. Dates valid until 31 Mar 2004.
Fee: £4.50 (ch £2.30, concessions £3.40). Prices valid until 31
Mar 2004. **Facilities:** 🅿 💷 ♿ toilets for disabled shop ✘ (ex on
lead in certain areas) ✪

BERWICK-UPON-TWEED   Map 12 NT95

BERWICK-UPON-TWEED BARRACKS
TD15 1DF
➲ (on the Parade, off Church St, Berwick town
centre)
☎ 01289 304493
Take an informative journey into our military past at the
famous border town's barracks.
Times: Open all year, Apr-Sep, daily 10-6 (Oct daily 10-5); Nov-Mar,
Wed-Sun 10-4. (Closed between 1-2 daily, 24-26 Dec & 1 Jan). Dates
valid until 31 Mar 2004. **Fee:** £3 (ch £1.50, concessions £2.30). Prices
valid until 31 Mar 2004. **Facilities:** 🅿 (town centre) shop (ex on lead
in certain areas) ✪

PAXTON HOUSE
TD15 1SZ
➲ (3m from A1 Berwick-upon-Tweed bypass on
B6461 Kelso road)
☎ 01289 386291   🖹 01289 386660   **2 for 1**
e-mail: info@paxtonhouse.com
Built in 1758 for the Laird of Wedderburn, the house is a fine
example of neo-Palladian architecture. Much of the house is
furnished by Chippendale and there is a large picture gallery.
The house is set in 80 acres beside the River Tweed, and the
grounds include an adventure playground.
Times: Open daily from Apr-Oct, House & gallery 11-5 (last tour of
house 4.15pm). Grounds 10-sunset. **Fee:** House & Grounds: £6 (ch £3)
Family ticket £16. Grounds only: £3 (ch £1.50) Family ticket £8.
Facilities: 🅿 💷 ✗ licensed ♿ (lifts to main areas of house, parking
close to reception) toilets for disabled shop ✘ (ex guide/on lead in
grounds) ♥

CAMBO   Map 12 NZ08

WALLINGTON HOUSE WALLED GARDEN & GROUNDS
NE61 4AR
➲ (6m NW of Belsay)
☎ 01670 773600 🖷 01670 774420
e-mail: nwaplr@smtp.ntrust.org.uk

The house is set in a great moorland estate of over 12,000 acres. It features delicate plasterwork, Capability Brown gardens and William Bell Scott murals. In the 19th century Ruskin and other writers and artists came here as guests. Special events include open air concerts and theatre productions.

Times: Open: House Apr-Sep, daily (ex Tue) 1-5.30, Oct daily (ex Tue) 1-4.30. Last admission half hour before closing. Walled garden Apr-Oct, daily 10-7 or dusk; Nov-Mar, 10-4 or dusk if earlier. Grounds open all year. **Facilities:** 🅿 ◢ ✕ ♿ (Vessa Ventura scooter, Braille guide) toilets for disabled shop garden centre ❦ ❧

CARRAWBROUGH   Map 12 NY87

TEMPLE OF MITHRAS (HADRIAN'S WALL) FREE
➲ (3.75m W of Chollerford on B6318)

This fascinating Mithraic temple was uncovered by a farmer in 1949. Its three altars to the war god, Mithras date from the third century AD, and are now in the Museum of Antiquities in Newcastle, but there are copies on site.

Times: Open any reasonable time. **Facilities:** 🅿 ✿

CHILLINGHAM   Map 12 NU02

CHILLINGHAM CASTLE
NE66 5NJ
➲ (signposted from A1 & A697)
☎ 01668 215359 🖷 01668 215463
e-mail: enquiries@chillingham.castle.com

This remarkable castle with its alarming dungeons and torture chamber is now undergoing restoration. Romantic grounds laid out by Sir Jeffry Wyatville command views over the Cheviots and include topiary gardens and woodland walks. Weddings, private functions and meals can be arranged, and fishing is available. Please ring for details of special events.

Times: Open Etr wknd & May-Sep, Sun-Fri (Last admission 4.30pm). Other times by prior arrangement. Castle 1-5, grounds & tearoom 12-5. **Fee:** ✱ £5 (ch £2, pen £4.50). Party 10+. **Facilities:** 🅿 ◢ ♿ shop ✕ ❧

CHILLINGHAM WILD CATTLE PARK
NE66 5NP
➲ (off B6348, follow brown tourist signs off A1 and A697)
☎ 01668 215250 🖷 01668 215250

The park, a registered charity, at Chillingham boasts an extraordinary survival: a herd of wild white cattle descended from animals trapped in the park when the wall was built in the 13th century; they are the sole surviving pure-bred examples of their breed in the world. Binoculars are recommended for a close view. Visitors are accompanied into the park by the Warden.

Times: Open Apr-Oct, daily 10-12 & 2-5, Sun 2-5. (Closed Tue). **Fee:** ✱ £3 (ch £1 & pen £2.50). **Facilities:** 🅿 shop ✕

CORBRIDGE   Map 12 NY96

CORBRIDGE ROMAN SITE AND MUSEUM
NE45 5NT
➲ (0.5m NW of Corbridge on minor road - signposted)
☎ 01434 632349

Originally a fort, which evolved into a prosperous town during the Roman era. An excellent starting point to explore Hadrian's Wall. The museum houses a fascinating collection of finds.

Times: Open all year, Apr-Sep, daily 10-6; Oct, daily 10-5; Nov-Mar, Wed-Sun 10-4. (Closed 24-26 Dec & 1 Jan). Dates valid until 31 Mar 2004. **Fee:** £3.10 (ch £1.60, concessions £2.30). Prices valid until 31 Mar 2004. **Facilities:** 🅿 ♿ toilets for disabled ✕ (ex in certain areas) ✿

EMBLETON   Map 12 NU22

DUNSTANBURGH CASTLE
Craster NE66 2RD
➲ (1.5m E on footpaths from Craster or Embleton)
☎ 01665 576231

An easy 12 mile coastal walk leads to the eerie skeleton of this wonderful 14th century castle situated on a basalt crag more than 30 metres high with breathtaking views. The castle was built by Thomas Earl of Lancaster, nephew to King Edward II.

Times: Open all year, Apr-Sep, daily 10-6; Oct, daily 10-5; Nov-Mar, Wed-Sun 10-4. (Closed 24-26 Dec & 1 Jan). Dates valid until 31 Mar 2004. **Fee:** £2.20 (ch £1.10, concessions £1.70). Prices valid until 31 Mar 2004. **Facilities:** 🅿 (charged) ✕ (ex dogs on leads) ✿

HOLY ISLAND (LINDISFARNE)   Map 12 NU14

LINDISFARNE CASTLE
TD15 2SH
➲ (8m S Berwick from A1 on Holy Island)
☎ 01289 389244 🖷 01289 389349

The 16th-century castle was restored by Sir Edwin Lutyens in 1903 for the owner of *Country Life* magazine. The austere outside walls belie the Edwardian comfort within, and there is a little garden designed by Gertrude Jekyll.

Times: Open Apr-Oct, daily (closed Fri ex Good Fri) as Lindisfarne is a tidal island, the Castle will open 4.5 hrs which will always include 12-3 and then either earlier opening or later closing as the tide allows. **Facilities:** 🅿 (1m in village) ✕ ❦

LINDISFARNE PRIORY
TD15 2RX
➲ (Can only be reached at low tide across a causeway. Tide tables posted at each end of the causeway)
☎ 01289 389200

One of the holiest Anglo-Saxon sites in England, renowned for the original burial place of St Cuthbert whose corpse was discovered 11 years after his burial and found to be mysteriously undecayed. An award-winning museum.

Times: Open all year, Apr-Sep, daily 10-6; Oct, daily 10-5; Nov-Mar, daily 10-4. (Closed 24-26 Dec & 1 Jan). Dates valid until 31 Mar 2004. **Fee:** £3 (ch £1.50, concessions £2.30). Prices valid until 31 Mar 2004. **Facilities:** shop ✕ (ex on leads in certain areas) ✿

HOUSESTEADS
Map 12 NY76

HOUSESTEADS ROMAN FORT
Haydon Bridge NE47 6NN
➲ (2.5m NE of Bardon Mill on B6318)
☎ 01434 344363

The jewel in the crown of Hadrian's Wall and the most complete Roman fort in Britain. These superb remains offer a fascinating glimpse into the past glories of one of the world's greatest empires.
Times: Open all year, Apr-Sep, daily 10-6; Oct, daily 10-5; Nov-Mar, daily 10-4. (Closed 24-26 Dec & 1 Jan). Dates valid until 31 Mar 2004.
Fee: £3.10 (ch £1.60, concessions £2.30). Prices valid until 31 Mar 2004. **Facilities:** P (0.25m from fort) (charge payable) (disabled parking) shop ✖ (ex on leads in certain areas) ✿

LONGFRAMLINGTON
Map 12 NU10

BRINKBURN PRIORY
NE65 8AF
➲ (off B6344)
☎ 01665 570628

This late 12th-century church is a fine example of early gothic architecture set in beautiful riverside surroundings. Look out for some unusual modern sculptures.
Times: Open Apr-Sep, daily 10-6, (Oct, daily 10-5). Dates valid until 31 Mar 2004. **Fee:** £2 (ch £1, concessions £1.50). Prices valid until 31 Mar 2004. **Facilities:** P shop ✖ (ex dogs on lead) ✿

MORPETH
Map 12 NZ28

MORPETH CHANTRY BAGPIPE MUSEUM
Bridge St NE61 1PJ
➲ (off A1)   FREE
☎ 01670 500717
e-mail: amoore@castlemorpeth.gov.uk

This unusual museum specialises in the history and development of Northumbrian small pipes and their music. They are set in the context of bagpipes from around the world, from India to Inverness.
Times: Open all year, Mon-Sat, 10-5, open Sun in Aug & Dec. (Closed 25-26 Dec, 1 Jan & Etr Mon). **Facilities:** P (100 metres) & (induction loop, not suitable for wheelchairs) shop 🎧

NORHAM
Map 12 NT94

NORHAM CASTLE
TD15 2JY
☎ 01289 382329

A mighty border fortress built in 1160, was one of the strongest of the border castles. Take an audio tour conjuring up four centuries of sieges and war with the Scots.
Times: Open Apr-Sep, daily 10-6. Dates valid until 31 Mar 2004.
Fee: £2 (ch £1, concessions £1.50). Prices valid until 31 Mar 2004.
Facilities: P & ✖ ✿

FREE

Attractions with this symbol do not charge for entry.

PRUDHOE
Map 12 NZ06

PRUDHOE CASTLE
NE42 6NA
➲ (on minor road off A695)
☎ 01661 833459

Explore the romantic remains of this 13th-century fortress perched on a steep wooded spur rising above the Tyne and set in lovely grounds.
Times: Open Apr-Sep, daily 10-6; Oct, daily 10-5. Dates valid until 31 Mar 2004. **Fee:** £2 (ch £1, concessions £1.50). Prices valid until 31 Mar 2004. **Facilities:** P shop ✖ (ex on lead in certain areas) ✿

ROTHBURY
Map 12 NU00

CRAGSIDE
NE65 7PX
➲ (1m NW of Morpeth on A697, turn left onto B6341, entrance 1m N of Rothbury).
☎ 01669 620333 & 620150 🖨 01669 620066
e-mail: ncrvmx@smtp.ntrust.org.uk

This Victorian mansion was the first building in the world to be lit by hydro-electricity. In the 1880s the house had hot and cold running water, central heating, telephones and a passenger lift. There is a vast forest garden to explore containing one of Europe's largest rock gardens, formal gardens, lakes and an adventure play area.
Times: ✱ Open, Estate & Gardens: 23 Mar-4 Nov, Tue-Sun & BH Mons 10.30-7 last admission 5;. House: 23 Mar-Sep 1-5.30. Oct-3 Nov 1-4. Last admission 1hr before closing. **Facilities:** P ✖ licensed & (ltd access, Braille guide, wheelchair path, lift) toilets for disabled shop ✖ (ex in grounds on lead) 🐾

WALWICK
Map 12 NY97

CHESTERS ROMAN FORT & MUSEUM
Chollerford NE46 4EP
➲ (0.5m W of Chollerford on B6318)
☎ 01434 681379

The best-preserved Roman cavalry fort in Britain. The museum holds displays of carved stones, altars and sculptures from all along Hadrian's Wall.
Times: Open all year, Apr-Sep, daily 10-6; Oct, daily 10-5; Nov-Mar, daily 10-4. (Closed 24-26 Dec & 1 Jan). Dates valid until 31 Mar 2004. **Fee:** £3.10 (ch £1.60, concessions £2.30). Prices valid until 31 Mar 2004. **Facilities:** P ▣ & (wheelchair access limited) shop ✖ (ex on lead in some areas) ✿

WARKWORTH
Map 12 NU20

WARKWORTH CASTLE & HERMITAGE
NE66 0UJ
☎ 01665 711423

The magnificent eight-towered keep of Warkworth Castle stands on a hill high above the River Coquet, dominating all around it. A complex stronghold, it was home to the Percy family, which at times wielded more power in the North than the King himself.
Times: Open Apr-Sep, daily 10-6; Oct, daily 10-5; Nov-Mar, daily 10-4. (Closed between 1-2 in winter, 24-26 Dec & 1 Jan). Dates valid until 31 Mar 2004. **Fee:** £3 (ch £1.50, concessions £2.30). Prices valid until 31 Mar 2004. **Facilities:** P & (limited access) shop ✖ (ex on lead in certain areas) ✿

NOTTINGHAMSHIRE

EVENTS & FESTIVALS

February
tbc Eid Mela, Nottingham (Muslim festival
with music, dance & children's activities)

March
17th St Patrick's Day Parade, Nottingham

May
8th-9th Newark & Nottingham County Show,
Newark & Nottingham Showground,
Winthorpe

June
tbc Newark on Water Festival

July
4th Mansfield Fun Run
9th-11th Americana International Festival,
Newark Showground, Winthorpe, Newark
tbc Annual Robin Hood Festival, Sherwood
Forest Country Park & Visitor Centre
tbc Newark Festival, Riverside Park, Newark

August
2nd-8th Annual Robin Hood Festival,
Sherwood Forest Country Park & Visitor
Centre, Edwinstowe
tbc Caribbean Carnival, Forest Recreation
Ground, Nottingham
(& parade through city)
tbc Riverside Festival, Victoria Embankment,
Nottingham (world & roots music, street
theatre, children's entertainers)

September
26th Robin Hood Marathon, Nottingham
(from Victoria Embankment)
29th-2nd Oct Goose Fair, Forest Recreation
Ground, Nottingham (Europe's largest
travelling fair)

October
29th Sep-2nd Goose Fair, Forest Recreation
Ground, Nottingham (Europe's largest
travelling fair)
tbc Dusshera Mela, Nottingham Castle,
Nottingham (Hindu festival)

November
tbc Robin Hood Pageant, Nottingham Castle

Above: Newark Castle by the River Trent

EASTWOOD   Map 08 SK44

D H LAWRENCE HERITAGE
Durban House Heritage Centre, Mansfield Rd NG16 3DZ
➲ (M1 J26, then take A610, follow brown tourist
signs from this road)   `2 for 1`
☎ 01773 717353   ▤ 01773 713509
Tread in the footsteps of D H Lawrence and go on a
fascinating journey through the development of his
hometown - Eastwood - exploring the landscape, people and
their influence on the writer in an astounding re-creation of
a Victorian family home and exciting interactive exhibition.
Times: Open all year, Apr-Oct, daily 10-5; Nov-Mar, daily 10-4. Closed
24 Dec-1 Jan. **Fee:** ✱ Free Mon-Fri. Single site £2 (concessions £1.20).
Both sites £3.50 (concessions £1.80). **Facilities:** 🅿 ▣ ✖ 㤙 (lift to
exhibition) toilets for disabled shop ✖ (ex guide dogs) ◗

EDWINSTOWE   Map 08 SK66

SHERWOOD FOREST COUNTRY PARK & VISITOR CENTRE
NG21 9HN
➲ (on B6034 N of Edwinstowe
between A6075 and A616)   `FREE`
☎ 01623 823202 & 824490   ▤ 01623 823202
e-mail: sherwood.forest@nottscc.gov.uk

At the heart of the Robin Hood legend is Sherwood Forest.
Today it is a country park and visitor centre with 450 acres of
ancient oaks and shimmering silver birches. Waymarked
pathways guide you through the forest. A year round
programme of events includes the spectacular Robin Hood
Festival.
Times: Country Park: open daily dawn to dusk. Visitor Centre: open
daily 10-5 (4.30pm Nov-Mar) **Facilities:** 🅿 (charged) ✖ 㤙 toilets for
disabled shop (ex guide dogs) ◗

FARNSFIELD   Map 08 SK65

WHITE POST MODERN FARM CENTRE
NG22 8HL
➲ (12m N of Nottingham on A614)
☎ 01623 882977 & 882026   ▤ 01623 883499
e-mail: tim@whitepostfarmcentre.co.uk
This award-winning working farm gives an introduction to a
variety of modern farming methods. It explains how farms
work, with exhibits such as llamas, deer, pigs, cows, snails,

continued

quails, snakes and fish. There's a lot to see indoors, including the incubator room, mousetown and a reptile house. There is also a large indoor play area including a sledge run, trampoline and a large bouncy slide.

Times: Open daily 10-5 **Facilities:** 🅿 💺 ♿ (sign language, free hire wheelchairs, book if more than 6) toilets for disabled shop ✖ (ex guide dogs) 🍴

NEWARK-ON-TRENT　　　Map 08 SK75

MILLGATE MUSEUM
48 Millgate NG24 4TS
➲ (easy access from A1 & A46)
☎ 01636 655730　📄 01636 655735　**FREE**
e-mail: museums@nsdc.info

Fascinating exhibitions - recreated streets, shops and houses in period settings. The museum displays illustrate the working and domestic life of local people, from Victorian times to 1950. The mezzanine gallery, home to a number of temporary exhibitions showing the work of local artists, designers and photographers.
Times: Open all year, Mon-Fri 10-5, Sat & Sun & BH 1-5. Last admission 4.30. **Facilities:** 🅿 (250yds) 💺 ♿ toilets for disabled shop ✖ (ex aid dogs)

NEWARK AIR MUSEUM
The Airfield, Winthorpe NG24 2NY
➲ (easy access from A1, A46, A17 & Newark relief road, follow tourism signs)
☎ 01636 707170　📄 01636 707170　**2 for 1**
e-mail: newarkair@lineone.net

A diverse collection of transport, training and reconnaissance aircraft, jet fighters, bombers and helicopters, now numbering more than sixty. An Undercover Aircraft Display Hall and an Engine Hall make the museum an all-weather attraction. Everything is displayed around a WWII airfield.
Times: Open all year, Mar-Sep daily 10-5; Oct-Feb, daily 10-4. (Closed 24-26 Dec). Other times by appointment. **Fee:** ✱ £4.25 (ch £2.50, pen £3.50). Family ticket £11.50. Party 10+. **Facilities:** 🅿 💺 ♿ toilets for disabled shop (sells aviation books, kits & videos) 🍴

Sherwood Forest

Explore the legendary home of England's world-famous outlaw

- See the mighty Major Oak
- Explore the way-marked Forest Trails
- Visit the Exhibitions and shops
- Take a break in the Forest Table Restaurant
- Enjoy family events – including the Annual Robin Hood Festival

Sherwood Forest Country Park & Visitor Centre, Edwinstowe, Notts NG21 9HN Tel: 01623 823202
e-mail: *sherwood.forest@nottscc.gov.uk*
www.sherwood-forest.org.uk

Nottinghamshire County Council Community Services

VINA COOKE MUSEUM OF DOLLS & BYGONE CHILDHOOD
The Old Rectory, Cromwell NG23 6JE
➲ (5m N of Newark off A1)　**2 for 1**
☎ 01636 821364

All kinds of childhood memorabilia are displayed in this 17th-century house: prams, toys, dolls' houses, costumes and a large collection of Victorian and Edwardian dolls including Vina Cooke hand-made character dolls.
Times: Open Apr-Sep, Sat-Thurs 10.30-12 & 2-5. Oct-Mar, opening times vary. **Fee:** ✱ £3 (ch £1.50, pen £2.50). **Facilities:** 🅿 ♿ shop ✖ (ex on lead)

NEWSTEAD　　　Map 09 SK55

NEWSTEAD ABBEY
Newstead Abbey Park NG15 8NA
➲ (off A60, between Nottingham & Mansfield)
☎ 01623 455900　📄 01623 455904

This beautiful house is best known as the home of poet Lord Byron. Visitors can see Byron's own rooms, mementoes of the poet and other splendidly decorated rooms. The grounds of over 300 acres include waterfalls, ponds, water gardens and Japanese gardens. Special events include outdoor theatre and opera, Christmas events and Ghost Tours.
Times: Open: Grounds all year, daily 9-dusk (ex last Fri in Nov & 25 Dec); House Apr-Sep, daily 12-5. Last admission 4pm. **Fee:** ✱ House & Grounds £5 (ch £1.50, concessions £2.50) Family ticket £12. Grounds only £2.50 (ch & concessions £1.50) Family ticket £7. Subject to change.
Facilities: 🅿 💺 ✖ licensed ♿ (audio tour & wheelchair for loan Apr-Sep) toilets for disabled shop (open Apr-Sep) ✖ (ex guide or garden on lead) 🍴

NOTTINGHAM   Map 08 SK53

BREWHOUSE YARD MUSEUM
Castle Boulevard NG7 1FB
☎ 0115 915 3600 & 0115 915 3640   `2 for 1`
🖥 0115 915 3601

Nestled in the rock below Nottingham Castle and housed in a row of 17th century cottages, the museum presents a realistic glimpse of life in Nottingham over the last 300 years. Discover the caves behind the museum and peer through 1920s shop windows.
Times: Open daily, 10-4.30. Last admission 4pm **Fee:** ✱ Free Mon-Fri but donations appreciated. Weekends & BH's £1.50 (con 80p). Family ticket £3.80. **Facilities:** P (100yds) ♿ (call 0115 915 3700 for info on access) toilets for disabled shop ✖ (ex guide dogs)

THE CAVES OF NOTTINGHAM
Upper Level, Broadmarsh Shopping Centre NG1 7LS
➲ (within Broadmarsh Shopping Centre, on the first floor)
☎ 0115 924 1424   🖥 0115 924 1430
e-mail: info@cavesofnottingham.co.uk

A unique 750-year-old cave system situated beneath a modern day shopping centre. A digital audio tour guides you through the only remaining underground medieval tannery in England, beer cellars, an air raid shelter and the remains of Drury Hill, one of the oldest streets in Nottingham.
Times: Open daily 10-5, Sun 11-5 (last admission 4.15pm, Sun 4pm). (Closed 24-26 Dec, 1 Jan & Etr Sun). **Facilities:** P (charged) ♿ (non-accessible to wheelchairs,induction loop,textual guide) shop ✖ (ex guide dogs)

GALLERIES OF JUSTICE
The Shire Hall, High Pavement, Lace Market NG1 1HN
➲ (follow signs to City Centre, brown heritage signs to Lace Market & Galleries of Justice)
☎ 0115 952 0555   🖥 0115 993 9828   `2 for 1`
e-mail: info@galleriesofjustice.org.uk

The Galleries of Justice are located on the site of an original Court and County Gaol. Visitors can take an authentic tour through three centuries of Crime and Punishment and witness a trial re-created in the authentic Victorian courtroom before being 'sent down' to the original cells and medieval caves. In the genuine Edwardian police station, an interactive forensic science display allows visitors to 'crack the case'. A series of innovative and stimulating temporary exhibitions run throughout the year. Special activities for all the family run in school holidays.
Times: Open all year, Tue-Sun & BH Mon's 10-5 (also open Mon in school hols). Last admission one hour before closing. Contact for Xmas opening times. **Fee:** ✱ £6.95 (ch £5.25, concessions £5.95). Family ticket £19.95 (2 adult & 2 ch). Ticket vaild for one visit to all exhibitions for 12 months from date of purchase. **Facilities:** P (5 mins walk) 🚍 ♿ (Braille control lifts, induction loop, large print lables) toilets for disabled shop ✖ (ex guide dogs)

THE LACE CENTRE
Severns Building, Castle Rd NG1 6AA
➲ (follow signs for the Castle, situated opposite the Robin Hood statue)   `FREE`
☎ 0115 941 3539   🖥 0115 941 3539

Exquisite Nottingham lace fills this small building, with panels also hanging from the beamed ceiling. There are weekly demonstrations of lace-making on Thursday afternoons from Easter to October. Telephone for details.
Times: Open Jan-Mar, daily 10-4; Apr-Nov, 10-5. Every Sun 11am-4pm. (Closed Xmas & New Year) **Facilities:** P (100yds) (metered street parking) shop 🛍

THE LACE MARKET CENTRE
3-5 High Pavement, The Lace Market NG1 1HF
➲ (Follow signs for Lace Market Parking in the city centre) Mon-Sat
☎ 0115 988 1849   🖥 0115 950 5166   `FREE`
e-mail: info@nottinghamlace.org

'Nottingham Lace and its People' is a free exhibition that includes a photographic story, hand-lace and machine-lace demonstrations. The Lace Market Trail, which takes about an hour, guides you to all the points of interest around this historical part of the city.
Times: Open Mon-Sat, 10-5: Sun 10.30-4 (Closed Xmas). **Facilities:** P (100yds) ♿ (counters at lower level, lift, audio & written tour) shop ✖ (ex guide dogs) 🛍

NOTTINGHAM CASTLE
NG1 6EL   `2 for 1`
☎ 0115 915 3700   🖥 0115 915 3653

This 17th-century building is both museum and art gallery, with major temporary exhibitions, by historical and contemporary artists, as well as the permanent collections. There is a 'Story of Nottingham' exhibition and a gallery designed especially to entertain young children. Guided tours of the underground passages take place on most days.
Times: Open all year, daily 10-5. Grounds 8-dusk. (Closed 25 & 26 Dec). **Fee:** ✱ Mon-Fri free, wknds & BH's £2 (ch & concessions £1). Family ticket £5. **Facilities:** P (400yds) 🚍 ♿ (parking at castle, for more info call 0115 915 3700) toilets for disabled shop ✖ (ex guide dogs)

NOTTINGHAM INDUSTRIAL MUSEUM
Courtyard Buildings, Wollaton Park NG8 2AE
➲ (4m from Nottingham City Centre off A6514)
☎ 0115 915 3910   🖥 0115 915 3941

Nottingham's industrial history is on display in this 18th-century stable block. Lace, hosiery, pharmaceuticals (Nottingham was the home of the founder of Boots the Chemists), tobacco and much else are among the exhibits. There is a beam engine and other steam engines, regularly in steam.
Times: ✱ Open Apr-Sep, daily 11-5; Oct-Mar only open on steaming days, contact for details. **Facilities:** P (charged) ♿ (hand & powered wheelchairs available) toilets for disabled shop ✖ (ex guide dogs)

TALES OF ROBIN HOOD

30-38 Maid Marian Way NG1 6GF

➲ (in Nottingham city centre, follow brown & white signs. Situated minutes from Nottingham Castle)

☎ 0115 948 3284   🖷 0115 950 1536

e-mail: robinhoodcentre@mail.com

Special effects and adventure cars transport the visitor back to medieval Nottingham and Sherwood Forest, legendary home of Robin Hood. There is commentary in seven languages via portable CD players. Medieval banquets and other events take place throughout the year.

Times: Open all year, daily 10-6. Last admission 4.30pm. (Closed 25-26 Dec). **Fee:** £6.95 (ch £4.95, pen & students £5.95) Family ticket from £19.99. Party. **Facilities:** 🅿 (NCP 200 yds) 🍴 ♿ (specially adapted 'car', lift) toilets for disabled shop ✘ (ex guide dogs) 🍷

WOLLATON HALL & PARK

Wollaton NG8 2AE

➲ (M1 junct 25 signed from A52, A609, A6154, A60 and city centre)

☎ 0115 915 3900   🖷 0115 915 3932

e-mail: info@wollatonhall.org.uk

Built in the late 16th century, and extended in the 19th, Wollaton Hall and Park holds Nottingham's Natural History Museum, Nottingham's Industrial Museum, the Wollaton Park Visitor Centre, and the Yard Gallery, which has changing exhibitions exploring art and the environment. The Hall itself is set in 500 acres of deer park, with herds of red and fallow deer roaming wild. There are also formal gardens, a lake, nature trails, adventure playgrounds, a sensory garden and a water garden. The many events throughout the year include pop concerts, opera, and twilight bat walks. **(2-for-1 Voucher applies to joint tickets only, i.e. Hall and Industrial Museum)**

Times: Open Hall, visitor centre, shop, yard gallery daily, Oct-Mar 11-4, Apr-Sep 11-5. Industrial Museum open Apr-Sept, daily 11-5. Park & grounds weekdays 8am-dusk, weekends 9am-dusk. **Fee:** ✱ Free weekdays. Ticket for either Hall or Museum £1.50 (ch & concessions 80p), family ticket £3.80. Ticket for Hall & Museum £2 (concessions £1) family ticket £5. Charge made at wknds & BH's only. **Facilities:** 🅿 (charged) 🍴 ♿ (call 0115 915 3700 for info on access) toilets for disabled shop ✘ (ex guide dogs/leads in park) 🍷

OLLERTON   Map 08 SK66

RUFFORD ABBEY AND COUNTRY PARK

NG22 9DF

➲ (2m S of Ollerton, adjacent to A614)

☎ 01623 822944   🖷 01623 824840

e-mail: marilyn.louden@nottscc.gov.uk

At the heart of the wooded country park stand the remains of a 12th-century Cistercian Abbey, housing an exhibition on the life of a monk at Rufford. Many species of wildlife can be

continued

seen on the lake, and there are lovely formal gardens, with sculptures and Britain's first centre for studio ceramics.

Times: Open all year 10.30-5.30 (closes 4pm Jan & Feb). For further details of opening times telephone establishment. **Facilities:** 🅿 (charged) 🍴 ✘ licensed ♿ (lift to craft centre gallery, free parking, wheelchair loan) toilets for disabled shop garden centre ✘ (ex guide dogs or in park) 🍷

SOUTHWELL   Map 08 SK65

THE WORKHOUSE
Upton Rd NG25 0PT
☎ 01636 817250 📠 01636 817251
e-mail: theworkhouse@nationaltrust.org.uk
Enter this 19th-century brick institution and discover the
thought-provoking story of the 'welfare' system of the New
Poor Law. The least altered workhouse in existence today, it
survives from hundreds that once covered the country.
Explore the segregated stairs and rooms, use the audio
guide, based on archive records, to bring the 19th-century
inhabitants to life in the empty rooms, then try the
interactive displays exploring poverty through the years and
across the country.
Times: Open 29 Mar-2 Nov, Thu-Mon noon-5 (Aug 11-5). Last
admission 1hr before closing. Wk beginning 26 May, daily & wk
beginning 27 Oct, daily (ex Wed) **Fee:** ✱ £4.20 (ch £2.10). Family ticket
£10.50 **Facilities:** 🅿 ♿ toilets for disabled ✖ (ex guide dogs) 🦮

SUTTON-CUM-LOUND   Map 08 SK68

WETLANDS WATERFOWL RESERVE & EXOTIC
BIRD PARK
Off Loundlow Rd DN22 8SB
➲ (Signposted on A638)   `2 for 1`
☎ 01777 818099
The Reserve is a 32-acre site for both wild and exotic
waterfowl. Visitors can see a collection of birds of prey,
parrots, geese, ducks, and wigeon among others. There are
also many small mammals and farm and wild animals,
including llamas, wallabies, emus, monkeys, red squirrels,
deer and goats.
Times: Open all year, daily 10-5.30 (or dusk - whichever is earlier).
(Closed 25 Dec). **Fee:** ✱ £2.50 (ch & pen £2). **Facilities:** 🅿 🍴 ♿
(wheelchair available) shop ✖ (ex guide dogs)

WORKSOP   Map 08 SK57

CLUMBER PARK
The Estate Office, Clumber Park S80 3AZ
➲ (4.5m SE of Worksop, signposted from A1).
☎ 01909 476592 📠 01909 500721
e-mail: clumberpark@nationaltrust.org.uk
An impressive, landscaped park, laid out by Capability
Brown. An outstanding feature is the lake running through
the park, a haven for wildfowl, covering an area of 80 acres.
The park is a mixture of woodland, open grass and
heathland.
Times: Open: Walled Garden, Victorian Apiary, Fig House, Vineries &
Garden Tools exhibition Apr-Sep Wed, Thu & Fri 10.30-5.30, Sat, Sun &
BH Mon 10.30-6. Oct Wed-Sun 10.30-4. Chapel: Apr-Sep, daily
10.30-5.30 (until 6 Sat & Sun); Oct-Jan daily 10.30-4. Contact warden
for conservation centre opening times. **Fee:** ✱ Pedestrians free; cars,
motorbikes & caravanettes £3.60, mini-coaches and cars with caravans
£4.60, coaches: free. **Facilities:** 🅿 (charged) 🍴 ✖ licensed ♿
(powered self-drive vehicle available if booked) toilets for disabled
shop garden centre 🦮

OXFORDSHIRE

EVENTS & FESTIVALS

March
28th Poohsticks World Championships,
    Little Wittenham
6th-3rd Apr Abingdon Arts Festival,
    various venues

April
6th Mar-3rd Abingdon Arts Festival,
    various venues

May
1st May 6am Choir singing from Magdalen
    Tower, Magdalen College, Oxford
31st Lord Mayor's Parade, Oxford
tbc Oxford Annual Balloon Fiesta,
    Cutterslowe Park

June
23th Encaenia (Oxford University graduation
    event with gowned procession through the
    city)
30th-4th Jul Henley Royal Regatta,
    Henley-on-Thames
tbc Oxford Canal Festival, Aristotle Lane
    Recreation Ground

July
30th Jun-4th Henley Royal Regatta,
    Henley-on-Thames
7th-11th Henley Festival (various venues)
tbc Swan Upping, River Thames,
    Sunbury-Abingdon

September
6th-7th St Giles Fair, Oxford
11th Henley Show
16th Thame & Oxfordshire County Show
26th-27th Great British Cheese Festival,
    Blenheim Palace

October
3rd Ploughing Match, Bishopsland Farm,
    Dunsden, nr Reading
tbc Banbury Folk & Good Music Day

Above: The Bridge of Sighs, Oxford

BANBURY   Map 04 SP44

BANBURY MUSEUM
Spiceball Park Rd OX16 2PQ
➲ (M40 junct 11 straight across at first rdbt into
Hennef Way, left at next rdbt into Concord Avenue,
right at next rdbt & left at next rdbt, Castle Quay
Shopping Centre & Museum on right)   **FREE**
☎ 01295 259855 🖹 01295 269469
e-mail: banburymuseum@cherwell-dc.gov.uk
Come and visit Banbury's stunning new museum! Opening
this summer, it is situated in an attractive canal-side location
in the centre of Banbury. Exciting modern displays tell of
Banbury's origins and historic past. The Civil War; the plush
manufacturing industry; the Victorian market town; costume
from the 17th century to the present day; Tooley's Boatyard
and the Oxford Canal, are just some of the subjects
illustrated in the new museum.
Times: ✱ Open all year, Mon-Sat, 10-5, Sun 10.30-4.30. **Facilities:** P
(500yds) 💺 ✗ licensed ♿ toilets for disabled shop ✖ (ex guide
dogs) ▼

BROUGHTON   Map 04 SP43

BROUGHTON CASTLE
OX15 5EB
➲ (2m W of Banbury Cross on B4035
Shipston-on-Stour)   **2 for 1**
☎ 01295 276070 🖹 01295 276070
e-mail: admin@broughtoncastle.demon.co.uk
Built by Sir John de Broughton, then owned by William of
Wykeham, and later by the first Lord Saye and Sele, the
castle is an early 14th-and mid 16th-century house with a
moat and gatehouse. Period furniture, paintings and Civil
War relics are displayed. There are fine borders in the knot
garden.
Times: Open Etr Sun& Mon, May-16 Sep, Wed, Sun & BH Mon, 2-5
(also open Thu in Jul & Aug). **Fee:** £5.50 (ch 5-15 £2.50, pen &
students £4.50). **Facilities:** P 💺 ♿ toilets for disabled shop ✖ (ex
in grounds on leads)

BURFORD   Map 04 SP21

COTSWOLD WILDLIFE PARK
OX18 4JW
➲ (2m S of Burford on the A361)
☎ 01993 823006 🖹 01993 823807

This 160-acre landscaped zoological park, surrounds a listed
continued

Gothic-style manor house. There is a varied collection of
animals from all over the world, many of which are
endangered species such as Asiatic Lions, Leopards, White
Rhinos and Red Pandas. There's an adventure playground, a
children's farmyard, and train rides during the summer. The
park has also become one of the Cotswold's leading
attractions for garden enthusiasts, with its exotic summer
displays and varied plantings offering interest all year.
Times: Open all year, daily (ex 25 Dec) from 10am, last admission
4.30pm Mar-Sep, 4pm Oct, 3.30pm Nov-Feb. **Fee:** £7.50 (ch & pen £5).
Party rate £6.50 (ch £4 pen £4.50). **Facilities:** P 💺 ✗ licensed ♿
(parking, free hire of wheelchairs) toilets for disabled shop ▼

BUSCOT   Map 04 SU29

BUSCOT PARK
SN7 8BU
➲ (on A417 between Faringdon & Lechdale)
☎ 01367 240786 🖹 01367 241794
e-mail: estbuscot@aol.com
An 18th-century Adam-style house with park and water
garden. Home of the Faringdon collection of paintings and
furniture. The park is landscaped with extensive water
continued

Remember that prices and
opening times are liable to change
within the currency of this guide.
It is always best to telephone in
advance to check

gardens designed by Harold Peto with parkland walks and a walled garden boasting seasonal herbaceous borders.

Buscot Park

Times: Grounds only open Apr-Sep, Mon & Tue 2-6. House & grounds open Apr-Sep, Wed-Fri 2-6. Also open BH's, 2nd & 4th wknd in month plus 1st & 5th wknd in May. (Last entry 5.30pm). **Fee:** House & Grounds £6.50; Grounds only £4.50 (ch half price). **Facilities:** 🅿 💺 ♿ (motorised mobility vehicle-must pre-book) toilets for disabled ✈ ☘ ⚓

DEDDINGTON   Map 04 SP43
DEDDINGTON CASTLE
OX5 4TE   FREE
➲ (S of B4031 on E side of Deddington)

The large earthworks of the outer and inner baileys can be seen; the remains of 12th-century castle buildings have been excavated, but they are not now visible.
Times: Open any reasonable time. **Facilities:** ✈ (ex dogs on leads) ⚏

DIDCOT   Map 04 SU58
DIDCOT RAILWAY CENTRE
OX11 7NJ
➲ (on A4130 at Didcot Parkway Station)
☎ 01235 817200   📠 01235 510621   2 for 1
e-mail: didrlyc@globalnet.co.uk

Based around the original GWR engine shed, the Centre is home to the biggest collection anywhere of Great Western Railway steam locomotives, carriages and wagons. A typical GWR station has been re-created and a section of Brunel's original broad gauge track relaid.
Times: Open all year, Sat & Sun. 4-18 Apr, 29 May-5 Sep, daily 10-5. Steamdays first and last Sun from Mar, BH's, all Sun Jul-Aug, Wed 14 Jul-25 Aug & Sat in Aug, 10-5 (Nov-Feb, 10-4). **Fee:** ✱ £4-£8 depending on event (ch £3-£7.50, over 60's £3.50-£6.50). **Facilities:** 🅿 (100yds) 💺 ♿ (advance notice recommended, some awkward steps) toilets for disabled shop ⚓

GREAT COXWELL   Map 04 SU29
GREAT COXWELL BARN
➲ (2m SW of Faringdon between A420 & B4019)
☎ 01793 762209
e-mail: tbcjaw@smtp.ntrust.org.uk

William Morris said that the barn was `as noble as a cathedral'. It is a 13th-century stone-built tithe barn, 152ft

continued

long and 44ft wide, with a beautifully crafted framework of timbers supporting the lofty stone roof. The barn was built for the Cistercians.
Times: Open all reasonable times. For details please contact Estate Office. **Fee:** ✱ 50p **Facilities:** 🅿 ✈ (ex on leads) ☘

HENLEY-ON-THAMES   Map 04 SU78
GREYS COURT
Rotherfield Greys RG9 4PG
➲ (M4 junct 8 or 9, take A404 (M) to Henley-on-Thames. From Nettlebed mini rdbt on A4130 take B481. Property is signposted 3m on left. Can also be accessed from Henley town centre by following signs to Peppard/Greys for 3m)
☎ 01491 628529
e-mail: tgrgen@smtp.ntrust.org.uk   2 for 1

A picturesque house, originating from the 14th century but with later additions. There is a beautiful courtyard and the surviving tower which dates from 1347. The outbuildings include a Tudor wheelhouse - one supplying water to the house, walled gardens and an ornamental vegetable garden.
Times: Open: House: part of ground floor only, Apr-Sep Wed-Fri & BH Mons (closed Good Fri). Garden Mar-Oct. **Fee:** ✱ House & Garden £4.80. Family ticket £12. Garden only £3.40 Family ticket £8.30.
Facilities: 🅿 💺 ♿ (ground floor & gardens partly accessible) shop (bookshop) ✈ (ex on lead in car park) ☘

RIVER & ROWING MUSEUM
Mill Meadows RG9 1BF
➲ (off A4130, signposted to Mill Meadows)
☎ 01491 415600   📠 01491 415601   2 for 1
e-mail: museum@rrm.co.uk

The award-winning River and Rowing Museum is the only museum in the world with galleries dedicated to rowing and the 'Quest for Speed', from the Greek Trireme to Modern Olympic rowing boats; the River Thames from source to sea with its rich history and varied wildlife. See the boats that won gold in Sydney and the riverside town of Henley featuring the Royal Regatta.
Times: Open Summer: May-Aug 10-5.30. Winter: Sep-Apr 10-5. (museum closed 24-25 & 31 Dec & 1 Jan). **Fee:** ✱ £4.95 (concessions £3.75). Family ticket from £13.95. Party 10+. **Facilities:** 🅿 💺 ✗ licensed ♿ Lift access to upstairs galleries, ramps at entrance toilets for disabled shop ✈ (ex guide dogs) ⚓

LONG WITTENHAM   Map 04 SU59

PENDON MUSEUM

OX14 4QD

➲ (follow brown signs from A4130 Didcot-Wallingford or A415 Abingdon-Wallingford road)

☎ 01865 407365

This charming exhibition shows highly detailed and historically accurate model railway and village scenes transporting the visitor back into 1930s country landscapes. Skilled modellers can often be seen at work on the exhibits. **Times:** Open Sat & Sun 2-5, BH wknds 11-5 also Wed in Jul, Aug & Oct half term. (Closed Dec). **Fee:** ✱ £4 (ch £2, pen £3.50, under 6's free). Family ticket (2 ad & 3 ch) £12. **Facilities:** 🅿 💷 ♿ (phone in advance, special seating with handrails) toilets for disabled shop ✕ (ex guide dogs) ➰

MAPLEDURHAM   Map 04 SU67

MAPLEDURHAM HOUSE
RG4 7TR

➲ (off A4074, follow brown heritage signs from Reading)

☎ 0118 972 3350 🖃 0118 972 4016
e-mail: mtrust1997@aol.com

The small community at Mapledurham includes the house, a watermill and a church. The fine Elizabethan mansion, surrounded by quiet parkland that runs down to the River Thames, was built by the Blount family in the 16th century. The estate has literary connections with the poet Alexander Pope, with Galsworthy's *Forsyte Saga* and Kenneth Graham's *Wind in the Willows*, and was a location for the film *The Eagle has Landed*. **Times:** Open Etr-Sep, Sat, Sun & BH's 2-5.30 Picnic area 2-5.30. Last admission 5pm. Group visits midweek by arrangement. **Fee:** ✱ Combined house, watermill & grounds £6 (ch £3). House & grounds £4 (ch £2). Watermill & grounds £3 (ch £1.50). **Facilities:** 🅿 💷 ♿ shop ✕ (ex park area) ➰

MAPLEDURHAM WATERMILL
RG4 7TR

➲ (off A4074, follow brown heritage signs from Reading)

☎ 0118 972 3350 🖃 0118 972 4016
e-mail: mtrust1997@aol.com

Close to Mapledurham House stands the last working corn and grist mill on the Thames, still using traditional wooden machinery and producing flour for local bakers and shops. The watermill's products can be purchased in the shop. When Mapledurham House is open the mill can be reached by river launch. **Times:** Open Etr-Sep, Sat, Sun & BHs 2-5.30. Picnic area 2-5.30. Last admission 5. Groups midweek by arrangement. **Fee:** ✱ Watermill & grounds £3 (ch £1.50) **Facilities:** 🅿 💷 ♿ shop ✕ (ex in country park) ➰

MINSTER LOVELL   Map 04 SP31

MINSTER LOVELL HALL & DOVECOT
OX8 5RN

➲ (adjacent to Minster Lovell church, [FREE] 3m W of Witney off A40)

Home of the ill-fated Lovell family, the ruins of the 15th-century house are steeped in history and legend. One of the main features of the estate is the medieval dovecote. **Times:** Open any reasonable time. **Facilities:** ✕ (ex dogs on leads) ♨

NORTH LEIGH   Map 04 SP31

NORTH LEIGH ROMAN VILLA
OX8 6QB   [FREE]

➲ (2m N of North Leigh)

This is the remains of a large and well-build Roman courtyard villa. The most important feature is an almost complete mosaic tile floor, which is intricately patterned in reds and browns. **Times:** Open, grounds all year. Viewing window for mosaic tile floor. Pedestrian access only from the main road - 600 yds. **Facilities:** 🅿 ✕ (ex dogs on leads) ♨

OXFORD   Map 04 SP50

ASHMOLEAN MUSEUM OF ART & ARCHAEOLOGY
Beaumont St OX1 2PH

➲ (city centre, opposite The Randolph Hotel)

☎ 01865 278000 🖃 01865 278018

The oldest museum in the country, opened in 1683, the Ashmolean contains Oxford University's priceless collections. Many important historical art pieces and artefacts are on display, including work from Ancient Greece through to the twentieth century. **Times:** Open all year, Tue-Sat 10-5, Sun & BH Mons 2-5. (Closed Etr & during St.Giles Fair in early Sep, Xmas & 1 Jan). **Fee:** Free. Guided tours by arrangement. **Facilities:** 🅿 (100-200mtrs) (pay & display) 💷 ✕ licensed ♿ (entry ramp from Beaumont St. Tel. before visit) toilets for disabled shop ✕ ➰

HARCOURT ARBORETUM
Nuneham Courtenay OX44 9PX

➲ (400 yds S of Nuneham Courtenay on A4074)

☎ 01865 343501 🖃 01865 341828
e-mail: piers.newth@botanic-garden.ox.ac.uk

The gardens consist of 75 acres of mixed woodland, meadow, pond, rhododendron walks and fine specimen trees. **Times:** Open May-Oct, daily 10-5; Nov-Apr, Mon-Fri 10-4.30. Closed 22 Dec-4 Jan & Good Fri-Etr Mon. **Fee:** ✱ £2 pay & display for car park or £5 for 1yr season ticket. **Facilities:** 🅿 (charged) ♿ ✕ (ex guide dogs)

MUSEUM OF OXFORD
St Aldate's OX1 1DZ

☎ 01865 252761 🖃 01865 252254
e-mail: museum@oxford.gov.uk

Permanent displays depict the archaeology and history of the city through the ages. There are temporary exhibitions, facilities for school parties and groups, and an audio tour. **Times:** ✱ Open all year, Tue-Fri 10-4, Sat 10-5 & Sun 12-4. (Closed 25-26 Dec, Good Fri & Etr Sun). **Facilities:** shop ✕ (ex guide dogs) ➰

MUSEUM OF THE HISTORY OF SCIENCE
Old Ashmolean Building, Broad St OX1 3AZ

➲ (Next to Sheldonian Theatre in city centre, on Bond Street)

☎ 01865 277280 🖃 01865 277288   [FREE]
e-mail: museum@mhs.ox.ac.uk

The first purpose built museum in Britain, containing the world's finest collection of early scientific instruments used in astronomy, navigation, surveying, physics and chemistry. **Times:** Open Tue-Sat 12-4, Sun 2-5 (closed Xmas wk). **Facilities:** 🅿 (300mtrs) (limited street parking, meters) ♿ (lift) toilets for disabled shop ✕ (ex guide dogs) ➰

THE OXFORD STORY
6 Broad St OX1 3AJ
➲ (Follow signs)
☎ 01865 728822 ▤ 01865 791716
e-mail: info@oxfordstory.co.uk

The Oxford Story offers the very best introduction to the city's world famous University. Climb aboard our indoor 'dark' ride to travel through the university's 900 years of history. In our interactive exhibition, 'innovate' you can quiz experts from Oxford University on modern day issues, from heart disease to climate change.
Times: Open Jan-Jun & Sep-Dec, Mon-Sat 10-4.30 & Sun 11-4.30. Jul & Aug daily 9.30-5. Closed 25 Dec. **Fee:** ✱ £6.75 (ch £5.25, pen & students £5.75), Family ticket (2 ad & 2 ch) £22. **Facilities:** P (300mtrs) ৬ (advisable to phone in advance) toilets for disabled shop ✖ (ex guide dogs) 🍽

OXFORD UNIVERSITY MUSEUM OF NATURAL HISTORY
Parks Rd OX1 3PW
➲ (opposite Keble College)
☎ 01865 272950 ▤ 01865 272970
e-mail: info@oum.ox.ac.uk
Built between 1855 and 1860, this museum of "the natural sciences" was intended to satisfy a growing interest in biology, botany, archaeology, zoology, entomology and so on. The museum reflects Oxford University's position as a 19th-century centre of learning, with displays of early dinosaur discoveries, Darwinian evolution and Elias Ashmole's collection of preserved animals. Although visitors to the Pitt-Rivers Museum must pass through the University Museum, the two should not be confused.
Times: Open daily 12-5. Times vary at Xmas & Etr. **Facilities:** P (200mtrs) (meter parking) ৬ toilets for disabled shop ✖

PITT RIVERS MUSEUM
South Parks Rd OX1 3PP
➲ (10 min walk from Oxford city centre)
☎ 01865 270927 ▤ 01865 270943
e-mail: prm@prm.ox.ac.uk
The museum is one of the city's most popular attractions, it is part of the University of Oxford and was founded in 1884. The collections held at the museum are internationally acclaimed, and contain many objects from different cultures of the world and from various periods, all grouped by type, or purpose. Special exhibitions during 7th Sep 2003 to

Nov 2004 "Seeing Lhasa: depictions of the Tibetan Capital 1936-1947". Rare photographs, albums and film. Plus a site-specific installation by Gonkar Gyatso, a contemporary Tibetan artist.
Times: Open Mon-Sat 12-4.30 & Sun 2-4.30. (Closed Xmas & Etr, open BH's) **Facilities:** ৬ (audio guide, wheelchair trail and map to ground floor) toilets for disabled shop ✖ (ex guide dogs)

ST EDMUND HALL
College of Oxford University OX1 4AR
➲ (Queen's Lane Oxford at the end of the High St).
☎ 01865 279000 ▤ 01865 279090
e-mail: bursary@seh.ox.ac.uk
This is the only surviving medieval academic hall and has a Norman crypt, 17th-century dining hall, chapel and quadrangle. Other buildings are of the 18th and 20th centuries.
Times: Open all year. (Closed 24 Dec-4 Jan, 9-18 Apr & 28-31 Aug). **Facilities:** ▬ ৬ toilets for disabled ✖ (ex guide dogs)

UNIVERSITY OF OXFORD BOTANIC GARDEN
Rose Ln OX1 4AZ
➲ (E end of High St on banks of river Cherwell)
☎ 01865 286690 ▤ 01865 286693
e-mail: postmaster@botanic-garden.ox.ac.uk
Founded in 1621, this botanic garden is the oldest in the country. There is a collection of over 8000 species of plants from all over the world.
Times: Open all year, daily 9-5 (9-4.15 Oct-Mar), Greenhouses, daily 10-4.30 (9-4 Oct-Mar). Last admission 4.15. (Closed Good Fri & 25 Dec). **Fee:** Apr-Sept £2.50, otherwise by donation. Accompanied ch under 12 free. **Facilities:** P (0.5m) park and ride system ৬ toilets for disabled ✖ (ex guide dogs)

ROUSHAM   Map 04 SP42
ROUSHAM HOUSE
OX25 4QX
➲ (1m E of A4260. 0.5m S of B4030)
☎ 01869 347110 ▤ 01869 347110
This attractive mansion was built by Sir Robert Dormer in 1635. During the Civil War it was a Royalist garrison. The house contains over 150 portraits and other pictures, and also much fine contemporary furniture. The gardens are a masterpiece by William Kent, and are his only work to survive unspoiled.
Times: Open all year, garden only, daily 10-4.30. House, Apr-Sep, Wed, Sun & BH Mon 2-4.30 (last entry). **Fee:** House £3, Garden £3. Groups by arrangement. No children under 15. **Facilities:** P ৬ ✖ (ex guide dogs)

RYCOTE   Map 04 SP60
RYCOTE CHAPEL
OX9 2PE
➲ (off B4013)
This small private chapel was founded in 1449 by Richard Quatremayne. It has its original font, and a particularly fine 17th-century interior. The chapel was visited by both Elizabeth I and Charles I.
Times: Open Apr-Sep, Fri-Sun & BH's 2-6. Dates valid until 31 Mar 2004. **Fee:** £2.20 (ch £1.10, concessions £1.70). Prices valid until 31 Mar 2004. **Facilities:** P ৬ (if assisted) shop ✖ ⌗

continued

STONOR   Map 04 SU78
STONOR HOUSE & PARK
RG9 6HF

➲ (M40 junct 6, through Wattington, towards
Nettlebed. At top of hill, left along B480 towards
Henley. Stonor approx 3m further on left just
before Stonor village)

☎ 01491 638587 ▤ 01491 639348
e-mail: jweaver@stonor.com

The house dates back to 1190 but features a Tudor façade. It
has a medieval Catholic chapel which is still in use today,
and shows some of the earliest domestic architecture in
Oxfordshire. Its treasures include rare furniture, paintings,
sculptures and tapestries from Britain, Europe and America.
The house is set in beautiful gardens commanding views of
the surrounding deer park.

Times: Open Apr-Sep, Sun 2-5.30; Jul & Aug, also Wed 2-5.30; BH
Mons. Parties by appointment Tue-Thu, Apr-Sep. **Fee:** £6 (ch 14
accompanied free). Gardens only £3.50. Private guided tours £7 each.
Facilities: ▣ 💺 ও shop ✖ (ex in grounds on lead)

UFFINGTON   Map 04 SU38
UFFINGTON CASTLE, WHITE
HORSE & DRAGON HILL   FREE
➲ (S of B4507)

The 'castle' is an Iron Age fort on the ancient Ridgeway Path.
It covers about eight acres and has only one gateway. On the
hill below the fort is the White Horse, a 375ft prehistoric
figure carved in the chalky hillside and thought to be
about 2000 years old.

Times: Open all year, any reasonable time. **Facilities:** ▣ ✖ (ex dogs
on leads) ✤

WATERPERRY   Map 04 SP60
WATERPERRY GARDENS
OX33 1JZ   2 for 1
➲ (2.5m from A40, turn off at Wheatley)
☎ 01844 339226 & 339254 ▤ 01844 339883

The manor of Waterperry is mentioned in the Domesday Book.
The present house (not open) was rebuilt by Sir John Curson
in 1713. The peaceful gardens and nurseries which surround
the house were the home of a celebrated horticultural school
between 1932 and 1971, and have fine herbaceous borders, a
rock garden, riverside walk, shrub borders, lawns and trees.
Please phone for details of special events.

Times: Open all year, Gardens (ex Xmas & New Year & during "Art in
Action" 15-18 Jul). Apr-Oct 9-5.30, Nov-Mar 9-5 daily. **Fee:** Apr-Oct,
£3.75 (ch 10-16 £2, ch under 10 free, pen £3.25). Nov-Mar £1.75 Party
20+. **Facilities:** ▣ 💺 ✖ licensed ও (grounds mostly accessible)
toilets for disabled shop garden centre (ex on leads) 🍴

> **If you are dissatisfied with any
> aspect of an attraction, discuss the
> problem at the time with a
> member of staff**

WITNEY   Map 04 SP31
COGGES MANOR FARM MUSEUM
Church Ln, Cogges OX28 3LA

➲ (0.5m SE off A4022)
☎ 01993 772602 ▤ 01993 703056
e-mail: info@cogges.org

The museum includes the Manor, dairy and walled garden,
and has breeds of animals typical of the Victorian period.
The first floor of the manor contains period rooms. Special
events take place through the season.

Times: Open Apr-Nov, Tue-Fri & BH Mon 10.30-5.30, Sat & Sun
12-5.30. Early closing Oct. (Closed Good Fri). **Fee:** £4.20 (ch £2.30,
pen, students & UB40 £2.85). Family ticket £12.90 (2 ad & 2 ch).
Facilities: ▣ 💺 ও (wheelchair available,commentary/history file for
1st floor) toilets for disabled shop 🍴

WOODSTOCK   Map 04 SP41
BLENHEIM PALACE
OX20 1PX

➲ (M40 junct 9, follow signs to Blenheim, on A44
8m N of Oxford)
☎ 01993 811091 & 811325 (information line)
▤ 01993 813527
e-mail: admin@blenheimpalace.com

Home of the 11th Duke of Marlborough and birthplace of Sir
Winston Churchill, Blenheim Palace is an English Baroque
masterpiece. Fine furniture, sculpture, paintings and
tapestries are set in magnificent gilded staterooms that
overlook sweeping lawns and formal gardens. 'Capability'
Brown landscaped the 2100-acre grounds, which are open to
visitors for pleasant walks and beautiful views.

Times: Palace & Gardens mid Mar-Oct, daily 10.30-5.30 (last admission
4.45pm). Park daily all year. **Facilities:** ▣ 💺 ✖ licensed ও (ramps
to front door, disabled parking) toilets for disabled shop 🍴 (ex in park
on leads) 🍴

OXFORDSHIRE MUSEUM
Fletcher's House OX20 1SN

➲ (A44 Evesham-Oxford, follow signs for
Blenheim Palace. Museum opposite church)
☎ 01993 811456 ▤ 01993 813239
e-mail: oxon.museum@oxfordshire.go.uk

Situated in the heart of the historic town of Woodstock, the
award-winning redevelopment of Fletcher's House provides
a home for the new country museum. Set in attractive
gardens, the new museum celebrates Oxfordshire in all its
diversity and features collections of local history, art,
archaeology, landscape and wildlife as well as a gallery
exploring the Country's innovative industries from nuclear
power to nanotechnology. Interactive exhibits offer new
learning experiences for visitors of all ages. The museum's
purpose built Garden Gallery houses a variety of touring
exhibitions of regional and national interest.

Times: Open all year, Tue-Sat 10-5. Last admission 4.30. (Closed Good
Fri, 25-26 Dec & 1 Jan). Galleries are closed on Mon (but open BH
Mon's, 2-5). **Facilities:** ▣ (outside entrance) (3hr free, no return
within 1hr) 💺 ✖ licensed ও (chair lifts to all galleries) toilets for
disabled 🍴 (ex guide dogs)

RUTLAND

EVENTS & FESTIVALS

August
tbc British Birdwatching Fair, Egleton
tbc Models & Miniatures, Stapleford Steam
Railway, nr Melton Mowbray

Above: Circular maze at Wing
Top: Normanton Church in Rutland Water

LYDDINGTON   Map 04 SP89

LYDDINGTON BEDE HOUSE
Blue Coat Ln LE15 9LZ
☎ 01572 822438
Once a prominent medieval palace later converted into an
almshouse for the poor. Its history is bought to life in an
evocative audio tour.
Times: Open Apr-Sep, daily 10-6; Oct, daily 10-5). Dates valid until 31
Mar 2004. **Fee:** £3.20 (ch £1.60, concessions £2.40). Prices valid until
31 Mar 2004. **Facilities:** ఈ ✹ ⚏

OAKHAM   Map 04 SK80

OAKHAM CASTLE
Catmos St LE15 6HW
➲ (off Market place)
☎ 01572 758440   ▤ 01572 758445   **FREE**
e-mail: museum@rutland.gov.uk
An exceptionally fine Norman Great Hall of a 12th-century
fortified manor house. Earthworks, walls and remains of an
earlier motte can be seen along with medieval sculptures
and unique presentation horseshoes forfeited by peers of the
realm and royalty to the Lord of the Manor. Licensed for Civil
Marriages. Please enquire for details of the Oakham Festival.
Times: Open all year, Mon-Sat 10.30-5 (closed 1-1.30), Sun 2-4. Closed
good Fri & Xmas. **Facilities:** ℙ (400yds) (disabled parking only by
notification) ఈ shop ✹ (ex guide dogs)

RUTLAND COUNTY MUSEUM
Catmos St LE15 6HW
➲ (on A6003, S of town centre)
☎ 01572 758440   ▤ 01572 758445   **FREE**
e-mail: museum@rutland.gov.uk
Rutland County Museum has displays of farming equipment,
machinery and wagons, rural tradesmen's tools, domestic
collections and local archaeology, all housed in a splendid
late 18th-century cavalry riding school.
Times: Open all year, Mon-Sat 10.30-5, Sun 2-4. Closed Good Fri &
Xmas. **Facilities:** ℙ (adjacent) (pay & display, free on Sun) ఈ
(induction loop in meeting room) toilets for disabled shop ✹ (ex guide
dogs)

SHROPSHIRE

EVENTS & FESTIVALS

June
6th-27th Much Wenlock Festival
13th Royal Air Force Show, Royal Air Force
    Museum Cosford
19th Shrewsbury Carnival & Show,
    Quarry Park
19th-4th Jul Ludlow Festival in the ruins of
    Ludlow Castle
25th-26th Shropshire & West Midlands Show,
    Showground, Berwick Road, Shrewsbury
tbc International Kite & Boomerang Festival,
    Shrewsbury

July
19th Jun-4th Ludlow Festival in the ruins of
    Ludlow Castle
17th-18th Wem Sweet Pea Festival, New Town
    Hall, High Street, Wem
17th-19th Festival at the Edge (storytelling),
    Stokes Barn, Much Wenlock

August
13th-14th Shrewsbury Flower Show
27th-30th Bridgnorth Folk Festival
29th-30th County of Salop Steam Rally
29th-30th Shropshire Game Fair, Chetwynd
    Park, Newport, Telford

September
18th-19th The Midland Game & Country Fair,
    Weston Park, Weston-under-Lizard, Nr
    Shifnel
tbc Shrewsbury Real Ale Festival

Above: Iron Age hillfort near town of New Invention
Top: Ironbridge, Telford

ACTON BURNELL   Map 07 SJ50

ACTON BURNELL CASTLE
SY5 7PE
➲ (located in Acton Burnell on   **FREE**
unclass road 8m S of Shrewsbury)
The warm red sandstone shell of a fortified
thirteenth-century manor house. The site of the first
parliament at which the commons were fully represented.
Times: Open at all reasonable times. **Facilities:** & ✗ (ex dogs on
leads) ✿

ATCHAM   Map 07 SJ50

ATTINGHAM PARK
SY4 4TP
➲ (4m SE of Shrewsbury on B4380)
☎ 01743 708123   ▤ 01743 708175   **2 for 1**
e-mail: attingham@nationaltrust.org.uk
Attingham Park is centred on one of Britain's finest regency
mansions, set in a landscaped deer park. Close by one can
meet the animals at one of Britain's only organic open farms.
Times: House open mid Mar-Oct, Fri-Tue 1-4.30, BH Mon 11-5. Deer
park & grounds daily Mar-Oct 9am-8pm, Nov-Feb 9am-5pm. **Fee:** ✱
£5 (ch £2.50) Family ticket £12.50. Park & Grounds £2.30 (ch £1.15).
Facilities: ▣ ▣ & (2 electric self drive buggies) toilets for disabled
shop (ex guide & hearing dogs) ⅍

BENTHALL   Map 07 SJ60

BENTHALL HALL
TF12 5RX
➲ (on B4375)
☎ 01952 882159
e-mail: benthall@ntrust.org.uk
The main part of the house was built around 1585. A wing at
the back, which has been altered at various times, dates
originally from about 1520. It is an attractive sandstone
building with mullioned windows, fine oak panelling and a
splendid carved staircase.
Times: Open Apr-Sep, Tue, Wed, BH Mon & Sun before BH Mon's;
Jul-Sep open every Sun. House 2-5.30, Garden 1.30-5.30. **Fee:** ✱
House £3.60 (ch £1.80). Garden only £2.30. **Facilities:** ▣ & (braille
sheets) toilets for disabled ✗ (ex guide dogs) ⅍ ⬥

BOSCOBEL   Map 07 SJ80

BOSCOBEL HOUSE AND THE ROYAL OAK
Brewood ST19 9AR
➲ (on unclass road between A41 and A5)
☎ 01902 850244   ▤ 01902 850295
This fully restored and refurbished lodge and famous Royal
Oak tree is where King Charles II sought refuge from
Cromwell's troops in 1651. The house was built around 1632.
Times: Open Mar-Sep, daily 11-6 (Oct-Nov, daily 11-5). (Closed
Dec-Feb). Entry to house by guided tour only. (Last admission 30mins
before closing). Dates valid until 31 Mar 2004. **Fee:** £4.40 (ch £2.20,
concessions £3.30). Prices valid until 31 Mar 2004. **Facilities:** ▣ ▣
shop ✗ ✿

WHITELADIES PRIORY

➔ (1m SW of Boscobel House, off an
unclass road between A41 and A5) **FREE**

Only the ruins are left of this Augustinian nunnery, which
dates from 1158 and was destroyed in the Civil War. After
the Battle of Worcester Charles II hid here and in the nearby
woods before going on to Boscobel House.

Times: Open any reasonable time. **Facilities:** ✖ (ex dogs on leads) ✿

BUILDWAS   Map 07 SJ60

BUILDWAS ABBEY

Iron Bridge TF8 7BW

➔ (on S bank of River Severn on B4378)
☎ 01952 433274

Set beside the River Severn, against a backdrop of wooded
grounds, are the extensive remains of this Cistercian abbey
founded in 1135.

Times: Open Apr-Sep, daily 11-5. Dates valid until 31 Mar 2004.
Fee: £2.20 (ch £1.10, concessions £1.70). Prices valid until 31 Mar 2004.
Facilities: 🅿 ♿ shop ✖ ✿

BURFORD   Map 03 SO56

BURFORD HOUSE GARDENS

WR15 8HQ

➔ (off A456, 1m W of Tenbury Wells, 8m from
Ludlow)
☎ 01584 810777 📠 01584 810673
e-mail: info@burford.co.uk

Burford Garden Company's store at Burford House Gardens
has been designed to inspire and delight all garden lovers.
Together with everything imaginable for the English garden,
Burford House Gardens specialise in Clematis, the Queen of
climbers, which in popularity, is second only to the Rose in
Britain. Hundreds of varieties are for sale, many of which
have were bred and are grown on site in the Treasure's
Clematis Nursery.

Times: Open all year 9-6 or dusk if earlier. **Fee:** ✱ £3.95 (ch £1). Party
20+ £3 each. **Facilities:** 🅿 💷 ✖ licensed ♿ (ramp into gardens,
sloping paths) toilets for disabled shop garden centre ✖ (ex in Plant
Centre) 🍽

COSFORD   Map 07 SJ70

ROYAL AIR FORCE MUSEUM

TF11 8UP

➔ (on A41, 1m S of M54 junct 3)
☎ 01902 376200 📠 01902 376211 **FREE**
e-mail: cosford@rafmuseum.org

This is one of the largest aviation collections in the UK.
Exhibits include the Victor and Vulcan bombers, the
Hastings, York and British Airways airliners, the Belfast
freighter and the last airworthy Britannia. The research and
development collection includes the notable TSR2, Fairey
Delta, Bristol 188 and many more important aircraft.

Times: Open all year daily, 10-6 (last admission 4). Closed 24-26 Dec
& 1 Jan **Facilities:** 🅿 ✖ licensed ♿ (free loan of 3 manual
wheelchairs) toilets for disabled shop ✖ (ex guide dogs)

CRAVEN ARMS   Map 07 SO48

SECRET HILLS, THE SHROPSHIRE HILLS
DISCOVERY CENTRE   **2 for 1**

School Rd SY7 9RS

➔ (on A49, on southern edge of Craven Arms)
☎ 01588 676000 📠 01588 676030
e-mail: jill.jarrett@shropshire-cc.gov.uk

This new attraction explores the history, nature and
geography of the Shropshire Hills, through a series of
interactive displays and simulations. These include
Landscape of Contrasts, Ancient Landscape, a simulated
Balloon Flight, and Land of Inspiration. The Centre has 23
acres of meadow lands sloping down to the river Onny for
all visitors to explore. There is a network of cycle routes and
walks and during the summer a shuttle bus service operates
from the centre, at weekends, which allows visitors to
explore the local landscape, hills, villages and market towns.
The Centre also houses the Secret Hills Gallery which
features changing displays of craft and artworks which
celebrates Shropshire's creative industry. There is also a
shop, restaurant and visitors information centre.

Times: Open all year, daily from 10am. Last admission 3.30 (Nov-Mar),
4.30 (Apr-Oct). **Fee:** ✱ £4.25 (ch £2.75 & pen £3.75, ch under 5 free).
Family ticket £12.20. Groups 20+ £3.75 each, ch £2.50 each.
Facilities: 🅿 💷 ✖ licensed ♿ (wheelchair available) toilets for
disabled shop ✖ (ex assistance dogs) 🍽

HAUGHMOND ABBEY Map 07 SJ51

HAUGHMOND ABBEY
Upton Magna SY4 4RW
➲ (off B5062)
☎ 01743 709661

Absorb these extensive 12th-century Augustinian abbey ruins, and visit the small museum.
Times: Open Apr-Sep, daily 11-5. Dates valid until 31 Mar 2004.
Fee: £2.20 (ch £1.10, concessions £1.70). Prices valid until 31 Mar 2004.
Facilities: 🅿 ⛄ (limited access for wheelchair users) shop ✕ (ex dogs on leads) ⚏

HODNET Map 07 SJ62

HODNET HALL GARDENS
TF9 3NN
➲ (M6 junct 12/15 or M54 junct 3. Hodnet is on the A442, Telford-Whitchurch road and A53 Shrewsbury-Market Drayton road).
☎ 01630 685202 🖷 01630 685853

Sixty acres of landscaped gardens offer tranquillity among pools, lush plants and trees. Big game trophies adorn the 17th-century tearooms, and plants are usually for sale in the kitchen gardens. The house, rebuilt in Victorian-Elizabethan style, is not open.
Times: Open Apr-Sep, Tue-Sun & BH Mon 12-5. **Facilities:** 🅿 ⛄ ⛄ (2 wheelchairs available) toilets for disabled shop garden centre

IRONBRIDGE Map 07 SJ60

IRONBRIDGE GORGE MUSEUMS
Coach Rd TF8 7DQ
➲ (M54 junct 4, signposted)
☎ 01952 433522 & 0800 590258
🖷 01952 432204
e-mail: info@ironbridge.org.uk

Ironbridge is the site of the world's first iron bridge, it was cast and built here in 1779, to span a narrow gorge over the River Severn. Now Ironbridge is the site of a remarkable series of museums relating the story of the bridge, recreating life in Victorian times and featuring ceramics and social history displays.
Times: Open all year, 10-5. Some small sites closed Nov-Mar. Telephone or write for exact winter details. **Fee:** £12.95 (ch £8.25, pen £11.25). Family £40. Passport to all sites, until all have been visited. It is therefore possible to return to Ironbridge on different days to ensure the whole atmosphere of the museums are captured. **Facilities:** 🅿 ⛄ ✕ licensed ⛄ (wheelchairs, potters wheel, braille guide, lifts, hearing loop) toilets for disabled shop ✕ (ex Blists Hill & guide dogs) ⚏

LILLESHALL Map 07 SJ71

LILLESHALL ABBEY
TF10 9HW
➲ (off A518 on unclass road) ⬛FREE⬛
☎ 0121 625 6820

In the beautiful grounds of Lilleshall Hall, ruined Lilleshall Abbey was founded shortly before the middle of the 12th century and from the high west front visitors can look down the entire 228ft length of the abbey church.
Times: Open Apr-Sep, any reasonable time. Dates valid until 31 Mar 2004. **Facilities:** ✕ (ex dogs on leads) ⚏

LUDLOW Map 07 SO57

LUDLOW CASTLE
Castle Square SY8 1AY
➲ (A49, turn off into Ludlow Town centre).
☎ 01584 873355

Ludlow Castle dates from about 1086. In 1473, Edward IV sent the Prince of Wales and his brother - later to become the Princes in the Tower - to live here and Ludlow Castle became a seat of government. John Milton's *Comus* was first performed at Ludlow Castle in 1634; now contemporary performances of Shakespeare's plays, together with concerts, are put on in the castle grounds during the Ludlow Festival (end June-early July).
Times: Open all year, Jan Sat-Sun 10-4; Feb-Mar daily 10-4; Apr-Jul daily 10-5; Aug daily 10-7; Sep daily 10-5; Oct-Dec daily 10-4 (last admission 30 minutes before closing). **Fee:** £3.50 (ch under 6 free, ch £1.50, pen £3). Family ticket £9.50. **Facilities:** 🅿 (100yds) ⛄ toilets for disabled shop ◀

LYDBURY NORTH Map 07 SO38

WALCOT HALL
SY7 8AZ
➲ (3m E. of Bishops Castle, on B4385, beside the Powis Arms)
☎ 01568 610693 🖷 01568 610693
e-mail: lesley@walcothall.com

Re-designed by Sir William Chambers for Lord Clive of India in 1763. The Georgian House possesses a free-standing and recently restored ballroom, stableyard with matching clock towers and extensive walled garden. There is an Arboretum, noted for its rhododendrons and azaleas, specimen trees, pools and a lake. The ballroom is available for hire and the Hall holds a licence for civil weddings.
Times: Open 25 & 26 May. Arboretum & gardens open Apr-Oct .
Facilities: 🅿 ⛄ (lift to 1st floor)

MORETON CORBET Map 07 SJ52

MORETON CORBET CASTLE ⬛FREE⬛
➲ (off B5063, in Moreton Corbet)

Inherited by the Corbets in 1235, who are thought to have remodelled the great keep, this castle may already have been standing for over 100 years. It was remodelled in the 16th century and then partially demolished to make way for a great Elizabethan mansion House. Although damaged in the civil war, the castle and mansion stand today as one of the most picturesque ruins of the Shropshire Marches.
Times: Open all reasonable times. **Facilities:** 🅿 ⛄ ✕ (ex dogs on leads) ⚏

MUCH WENLOCK Map 07 SO69

MUCH WENLOCK PRIORY
TA3 6HS
☎ 01952 727466

Experience the ruins of this large Cluniac priory and the atmospheric remains of the 13th-century church and Norman chapter house. The audio tour offers a fascinating insight into its history. Impressive topiary figures guard the priory ruins.
Times: Open all year, Apr-Sep, daily 10-6; Oct, daily 10-5; Nov-Mar, Wed-Sun 10-4. (Closed between 1-2 in winter, 24-26 Dec & 1 Jan. Dates valid until 31 Mar 2004. **Fee:** £3 (ch £1.50, concessions £2.30). Prices valid until 31 Mar 2004. **Facilities:** 🅿 ⚏

OSWESTRY Map 07 SJ22

OLD OSWESTRY HILL FORT

➲ (1m N of Oswestry, off an unclass road off A483) **FREE**

An impressive Iron Age hill-fort of 68 acres, defended by a series of five ramparts, with an elaborate western entrance and unusual earthwork cisterns.

Times: Open any reasonable time. **Facilities:** ⊞

QUATT Map 07 SO78

DUDMASTON

WV15 6QN

➲ (4m SE of Bridgnorth on A442)
☎ 01746 780866 ▤ 01746 780744
e-mail: mouefe@smtp.ntrust.org.uk

The 17th-century flower paintings which belonged to Francis Darby of Coalbrookdale are exhibited in this house of the same period, with modern works, botanical art and fine furniture. The house stands in an extensive parkland garden and there are dingle and lakeside walks.

Times: ✱ Open Apr-Sep, Teu, Wed & Sun & BH Mons, 2-5.30. Garden noon-6. Closed Good Fri. **Facilities:** 🅿 ▣ ৬ (Braille guides, taped tours) toilets for disabled shop ✖ (ex in grounds) ✤ ▤

SHREWSBURY Map 07 SJ41

SHREWSBURY CASTLE AND SHROPSHIRE REGIMENTAL MUSEUM

The Castle, Castle St SY1 2AT

➲ (located in town centre, adjacent to railway station)
☎ 01743 358516 ▤ 01743 354811
e-mail: shropsrm@zoom.co.uk

The museum of The King's Shropshire Light Infantry and The Shropshire Yeomanry is housed in the main surviving building of Shrewsbury Castle which once dominated the town. The grounds contain the medieval 'motte' and the romantic 'Laura's Tower'.

Times: ✱ Open Tue-Sat 10-4.30, also Sun from Etr-1 Oct & BH Mon. Closed Dec & Jan. Telephone for winter opening times. Castle grounds open Mon-Sat & Sun as above, 9-5 **Facilities:** 🅿 (3 mins NCP) (on street parking by voucher only) ৬ (please ask staff for assistance) toilets for disabled shop ✖ (ex guide dogs)

STOKESAY Map 07 SO48

STOKESAY CASTLE

SY7 9AH

➲ (1m S of Craven Arms off A49)
☎ 01588 672544

Most perfectly preserved 13th-century fortified manor house. See its superb timber-framed Jacobean gatehouse and stroll through the impressive great hall. Delightful cottage gardens.

Times: Open all year, Apr-Sep, daily 10-6; Oct, daily 10-5; Nov-Mar, daily 10-4 (Closed between 1-2, 24-26 Dec & 1 Jan). Dates valid until 31 Mar 2004. **Fee:** £4.50 (ch £2.30, concessions £3.40). Prices valid until 31 Mar 2004. **Facilities:** 🅿 ৬ (tape tour for visually handicapped, ramp for wheelchairs) toilets for disabled ✖

TELFORD Map 07 SJ60

HOO FARM ANIMAL KINGDOM

Preston-on-the-Weald Moors TF6 6DJ

➲ (M54 junct 6, follow brown tourist signs)
☎ 01952 677917 ▤ 01952 677944
e-mail: info@hoofarm.com **2 for 1**

Hoo Farm is a real children's paradise where there is always something happening. A clean, friendly farm that appeals to all ages and offers close contact with a wide variety of animals from fluffy yellow chicks and baby lambs to foxes, llamas, deer and ostriches. A daily programme of events encourages audience participation in the form of bottle feeding lambs, pig feeding and collecting the freshly laid eggs. New for this year is ferret racing! The Craft Area offers the chance to try your hand at candle dipping, glass or pottery painting or even throwing a pot on the potters wheel. There are Junior Quad Bikes and a Rifle Range, Pony Rides, powered mini tractors as well as indoor and outdoor play areas and a new games room.

Times: Open 23 Mar-8 Sep, daily 10-6 (last admission 5). 10 Sep-22 Nov, Tue-Sun 10-5 (last admission 4. Closed Mon ex Halloween). 23 Nov-24 Dec daily 10-5 (closes at 1pm 24 Dec). (Closed 25 Dec-mid Mar). **Fee:** ✱ £4.25 (ch £3.50 & pen £3.75). Family ticket (2 ad & 3 ch) £16. **Facilities:** 🅿 ▣ ৬ toilets for disabled shop ✖ (ex guide dogs) ▤

WESTON-UNDER-REDCASTLE Map 07 SJ52

HAWKSTONE HISTORIC PARK & FOLLIES

SY4 5UY

➲ (3m from Hodnet off A53, follow the brown heritage signs)
☎ 01939 200611 ▤ 01939 200311
e-mail: info@hawkstone.co.uk

Created in the 18th century by the Hill family, Hawkstone was once one of the greatest historic parklands in history. After almost one hundred years of neglect it has now been restored and designated a Grade 1 historic park. Visitors can once again experience the magical world of intricate pathways, arches and bridges, towering cliffs and follies, and an awesome grotto. The Grand Valley and woodlands have centuries-old oaks, wild rhododendrons and lofty monkey puzzles. The park covers nearly 100 acres of hilly terrain and visitors are advised to wear sensible shoes and clothing and to bring a torch. Allow 3-4 hours for the tour, which is well

continued

signposted and a route map is provided in the admission price. Attractions include 'Hear King Arthur' and meeting the Duke of Wellington in the White Tower to discuss the Battle of Waterloo.

Times: Open Sat & Sun Jan-Mar; Wed-Sun, Apr -May & Sep-Oct,: Jun-Aug, daily. Closed Nov & Dec. Open from 10am **Facilities:** 🅿 💻 ✖ licensed 🕭 (no access to follies due to terrain access Valley only) toilets for disabled shop ✖ (ex on lead) ➾

WROXETER   Map 07 SJ50

WROXETER ROMAN CITY
SY5 6PH
➱ (5m E of Shrewsbury, 1m S of A5)
☎ 01743 761330

Discover what urban life was like 2,000 years ago in the forth largest city in Roman Britain. See the remains of the impressive 2nd-century municipal baths and view the excavated treasures in the museum.

Times: Open all year, Apr-Sep, daily 10-6; Oct, daily 10-5; Nov-Mar, daily 10-4. (Closed between 1-2 & 24-26 Dec & 1 Jan). Dates valid until 31 Mar 2004. **Fee:** £3.70 (ch £1.90, concessions £2.80). Prices valid until 31 Mar 2004. **Facilities:** 🅿 🕭 shop ✖ (ex dogs on leads) ⌗

Remember that prices and opening times are liable to change within the currency of this guide. It is always best to telephone in advance to check

Above: Timber-framed houses in Shrewsbury

SOMERSET

EVENTS & FESTIVALS

February
28th-7th Mar Bath Literature Festival

March
28th Feb-7th Bath Literature Festival
tbc Bath Shakespeare Festival

May
1st-3rd Bath Annual Spring Flower Show,
Royal Victoria Park
21st-6th Jun Bath International Music Festival
(various venues)
28th-13th Jun Bath Fringe Festival
(various venues)
28th-31st The Royal Bath & West Show, Royal
Bath & West Showground, Shepton Mallet

June
21st May-6th Bath International Music
Festival (various venues)
28th May-13th Bath Fringe Festival
(various venues)
25th-27th Glastonbury Festival, Worthy Farm,
Pilton, Glastonbury (provisional)

July
10th Glastonbury Pilgrimage,
Glastonbury Abbey
tbc Glastonbury International Dance Festival
(various venues)

August
4th-5th Taunton Flower Show,
Vivary Park, Taunton
tbc Glastonbury Children's Festival

October
16th Taunton Carnival

November
tbc Bridgwater Guy Fawkes Carnival,
Bridgwater
tbc Glastonbury Chilkwell Guy Fawkes
Carnival

Above: Clock on Wells Cathedral

AXBRIDGE   Map 03 ST45

KING JOHN'S HUNTING LODGE
The Square BS26 2AP
☎ 01934 732012

Nothing to do with King John or with hunting, this jettied and timber-framed house was built around 1500. It gives a good indication of the wealth of the merchants of that time and is now a museum of local history, with old photographs, paintings and items such as the town stocks and constables' staves.

Times: ✱ Open 29 Mar-Sep, daily 1-4. **Facilities:** ᵬ shop ✖ ❧

BARRINGTON   Map 03 ST31

BARRINGTON COURT GARDEN
TA19 0NQ
➲ (5m NE of Ilminster on B3168)
☎ 01460 241938 🖷 01460 241938
e-mail: barringtoncourt@ntrust.org.uk

The house dates from the 17th century, but the gardens were created in the 1920s, with the help (through the post) of Gertrude Jekyll. They are laid out in `rooms' and there is a large walled kitchen garden supplying fresh fruit and vegetables to the restaurant.

Times: Open Mar & Oct: Thu, Fri, Sat & Sun 11-4.30: Apr-Sep: daily (ex Wed) 11-5.30; Oct Tue, Fri, Sat & Sun 11-4.30. **Facilities:** 🅿 💻 ✖ licensed ᵬ (batricars available, Braille guides, wheelchairs) toilets for disabled shop garden centre ✖ ❧

BATH   Map 03 ST76

AMERICAN MUSEUM
Claverton Manor BA2 7BD
➲ (2.5m SE)
☎ 01225 460503 🖷 01225 480726
e-mail: info@americanmuseum.org

Claverton Manor is just two miles south east of Bath, in a beautiful setting above the River Avon. The house was built in 1820 by Sir Jeffrey Wyatville, and is now a museum of American decorative arts. The gardens are well worth seeing, and include an American arboretum and a replica of George Washington's garden at Mount Vernon. The Folk Art Gallery and the New Gallery are among the many exhibits in the grounds along with seasonal exhibitions.

Times: Open 24 Mar-4 Nov, Tue-Sun 2-5. Gardens 1-6. BH Sun & Mon 11-5. **Fee:** ✱ £6 (ch £3.50, pen £5.50). **Facilities:** 🅿 💻 ᵬ toilets for disabled shop ⬢

BATH ABBEY
BA1 1LT   `FREE`
➲ (centre of Bath, next to Pump Rooms)
☎ 01225 422462 & 446300 🖷 01225 429990
e-mail: office@bathabbey.org

The 15th-century abbey church was built on the site of the Saxon abbey where King Edgar was crowned in 973. The church is Perpendicular style with Norman arches and superb fan-vaulting. The famous West Front carvings represent the founder-bishop's dream of angels ascending and descending from heaven.

Times: Open all year, Etr-Oct, Mon-Sat 9-6; Nov-Etr 9-4.30. Sun all year 1-2.30 & 4.30-5.30. **Facilities:** 🅿 (5 mins) (limited street parking) ᵬ toilets for disabled shop ✖ (ex guide & hearing dogs)

BATH POSTAL MUSEUM

8 Broad St BA1 5LJ

➲ (M4 junct 18. Follow A46 to Bath, on entering city fork left at mini rdbt. After all traffic lights into Walcot St. Podium car park facing)

☎ 01225 460333 ▤ 01225 460333

e-mail: info@bathpostalmuseum.org

`2 for 1`

Discover how 18th-century Bath influenced and developed the Postal System, including the story of the Penny Post. The first letter sent with a stamp was sent from this very building. Visitors can explore the history of written communication from Egyptian clay tablets, thousands of years ago, to the first Airmail flight from Bath to London in 1912. See the Victorian Post Office and watch three continuous video films including the in-house production entitled 'History of Writing'. Visit the children's activity room, tearoom and shop. **Times:** Open all year, Mon-Sat 11-4.30. Last admission Mar-Oct 4.30pm; Oct-Mar 4pm (Closed Sun, 25-26 Dec & 1 Jan). **Fee:** £2.90 (ch under 5 free, ch £1.50, students £1.90 & pen £2.60). Family and Party 10+ tickets available. **Facilities:** ℙ (150yds) (no on street parking) 💻 ♿ (films and computer games for hearing impaired) toilets for disabled shop 🐕 (ex guide dogs)

THE BUILDING OF BATH MUSEUM

Countess of Huntingdons Chapel, The Vineyards, The Paragon BA1 5NA

➲ (M4 junct 18 down A46 towards Bath city centre. Take A4, 2nd exit at mini rdbt. Along road on right)

☎ 01225 333895 ▤ 01225 445473

e-mail: cathryn@bathmuseum.co.uk

This new museum relates the fascinating story of how Georgian Bath was created. 17th century Bath was a medieval market town but in the space of 100 years it was transformed into one of the most beautiful and glamorous cities in Europe. The exhibition depicts elegant society life in "Beau" Nash's spa resort and explains how the houses were constructed. After a visit, the street scene outside seems like an extension of the exhibition. Ring for details of special events such as concerts and lectures. **Times:** ✱ Open 15 Feb-1 Dec, Tue-Sun & BH's 10.30-5. **Facilities:** ℙ (500mtrs) ♿ shop 🐕 (ex guide dogs) 🍴

HOLBURNE MUSEUM OF ART

Great Pulteney St BA2 4DB

➲ (M4 junct 18 to A4 and follow brown signs)

☎ 01225 466669 ▤ 01225 333121

e-mail: holburne@bath.ac.uk

This elegant building shows 17th and 18th-century collections of fine and decorative art, notably silver, porcelain, glass, furniture and Old Master paintings. There is an annual programme of events and lively lectures. The biggest Gainsborough painting in Britain, of The Byam Family, previously unseen by the general public is on loan to the museum for three years.

Times: Open mid Feb-mid Dec, Tue-Sat 10-5, Sun 2.30-5.30. (Closed Mon ex group bookings by appointment). **Fee:** ✱ £4 (ch £1.50, pen £3.50, concessions available). Group rates available. **Facilities:** ℙ 💻 ♿ (lift to all floors) toilets for disabled shop 🐕 (ex guide dogs)

MUSEUM OF BATH AT WORK

Julian Rd BA1 2RH

➲ (from city centre, off Lansdown Rd into Julian Rd. Museum is next to church on right)

☎ 01225 318348 ▤ 01225 318348

e-mail: mobaw@hotmail.com

`2 for 1`

The centre houses the Bowler collection, and the entire stock-in-trade of various Victorian craftsmen. Also here is 'The Story of Bath Stone', with a replica of a mine face before mechanisation, and a Bath cabinet-maker's workshop. Horstmann Car Gallery is a new feature, plus a computerised information point of Bath's heritage at work. **Times:** Open all year, Etr-1 Nov, daily 10-5; Nov-Etr, wknds 10-5. (Closed 25-26 Dec). **Fee:** ✱ £3.50 (ch, pen & students £2.50). Family ticket £10. **Facilities:** ℙ (0.25m) 💻 ♿ shop 🐕 (ex guide dogs)

MUSEUM OF COSTUME

Bennett St BA1 2QH

➲ (M4 junct 18, follow A46 into Bath. Museum near city centre)

☎ 01225 477785 ▤ 01225 477743

e-mail: costume_bookings@bathnes.gov.uk

The Museum of Costume is one of the finest collections of fashionable dress in the world, covering the period from the late 16th-century to the present day. It is housed in Bath's famous 18th-century Assembly Rooms designed by John

continued

Wood the Younger in 1771. Entrance to the Assembly Rooms is free.
Times: Open all year, daily 10-4.30 (Closed 25 & 26 Dec). **Fee:** ✱ £5.50 (ch £3.75). Family ticket £15. Combined ticket with Roman Baths, £11 (ch £6.20). **Facilities:** P (5 mins walk) (park & ride recommended) 🚃 & (audio guides available) toilets for disabled shop ✗ (ex guide dogs) 🏴

No 1 Royal Crescent
BA1 2LR
☎ 01225 428126   📄 01225 481850
e-mail: no1@bptrust.demon.co.uk
Bath is very much a Georgian city, but most of its houses have naturally altered over the years to suit changing tastes and lifestyles. Built in 1768 by John Wood the Elder, No 1 Royal Crescent has been restored to look as it would have done some 200 years ago. Visitors can see a grand townhouse of the late 18th-century with authentic furniture, paintings and carpets. On the ground floor are the study and dining room and on the first floor a lady's bedroom and drawing room. In the basement a period kitchen and museum shop.
Times: Open 10 Feb-23 Oct, Tue-Sun 10.30-5; 24 Oct-28 Nov, Tue-Sun 10.30-4. Open BH Mon. Open wknds 6, 7, 13 & 14 Dec (Closed Good Fri). Last admission 30 mins before closing. **Fee:** £4 (concessions £3.50). Family ticket £12. Party 10+ £3 each. **Facilities:** P (5 mins walk) (street parking with card £1 per hour) (large print handouts, handling items, guides) shop ✗ (ex guide dogs)

Roman Baths & Pump Room
Abbey Church Yard BA1 1LZ
➲ (M4 junct 18, A46 into city centre)
☎ 01225 477785   📄 01225 477743
e-mail: romanbaths_bookings@bathnes.gov.uk

The remains of the Roman baths and temple give a vivid impression of life nearly 2000 years ago. Built next to Britain's only hot spring, the baths served the sick, and the pilgrims visiting the adjacent Temple of Sulis Minerva. Above the Temple Courtyard, the Pump Room became a popular meeting place in the 18th century. The site still flows with
continued

natural hot water and no visit is complete without a taste of the famous hot spa water.
Times: Open all year, Mar-Jun & Sep-Oct, daily 9-5; Jul & Aug daily 9am-9pm; Jan-Feb & Nov-Dec, daily 9.30-4.30. (Closed 25 & 26 Dec). Last exit 1hr after closing. **Fee:** ✱ £8.50 (ch £4.80). Family ticket £22. Combined ticket with Museum of Costume £11 (ch £6.20). Disabled visitors free admission to ground floor areas. **Facilities:** P (5 mins walk) (park & ride recommended) ✗ licensed & (sign language & audio tours) toilets for disabled shop ✗ (ex guide dogs) 🏴

Sally Lunn's Refreshment House & Museum
4 North Pde Passage BA1 1NX
➲ (Centre of Bath, follow signs, next to Bath Abbey)
☎ 01225 461634   📄 01225 447090
e-mail: info@sallylunns.co.uk
This Tudor building is Bath's oldest house and was a popular 17th-century meeting place. The traditional 'Sally Lunn' is similar to a brioche, and it is popularly believed to carry the name of its first maker who came to Bath in 1680. The bun is still served in the restaurant, and the original oven, Georgian cooking range and a collection of baking utensils are displayed in the museum.
Times: Open all year, Museum - Mon-Fri 10-6, Sat 10-5, Sun 11-5. (Closed 25-26 Dec & 1 Jan). **Fee:** ✱ 30p (concessions free). **Facilities:** P (2-3 min walk) (cards required for street parking) 🚃 ✗ licensed & (Braille menu for the blind) shop ✗ (ex guide dogs) 🏴

CASTLE CARY   Map 03 ST63

Hadspen Garden & Nursery
Hadspen House BA7 7NG
➲ (2m SE off A371)
☎ 01749 813707   📄 01749 813707
Situated within a 17th-century curved wall, this five acre garden has borders planted with roses and herbaceous plants, many of which have been developed here. Plants grown in the garden are available in the adjoining nursery.
Times: Open 4 Mar-26 Sep, Thu-Sun & BHs 10-5. **Fee:** £4 (ch 50p). Free admission for wheelchair users. **Facilities:** P ✗ & garden centre ✗ (ex guide dogs) 🏴

CHARD   Map 03 ST30

Forde Abbey
TA20 4LU
➲ (5m SE of Chard, signposted from A30 and A358)
☎ 01460 221290   📄 01460 220296
e-mail: forde.abbey@virgin.net
As one of the top gardens in England, Forde Abbey has much to offer keen gardeners. The 30 acres include a colourful bog garden, a walled kitchen garden, cascades, ponds, Ionic temple, rockery, herbaceous borders and much more. The privately owned magnificent 12th century house contains outstanding Mortlake tapestries, spectacularly decorated plaster ceilings and fine furniture and paintings.
Times: Gardens, open all year, daily 10-4.30. House Apr-Oct, Tue-Fri, Sun & BH 12-4. **Fee:** ✱ Gardens £5.25 (ch free, pen £4.75). House & Gardens £7 (ch free, pen £6.50). **Facilities:** P 🚃 ✗ licensed & (wheelchair and batricar available) toilets for disabled shop garden centre ✗ (on leads in the garden) 🏴

CLEVEDON   Map 03 ST47

CLEVEDON COURT
Tickenham Rd BS21 6QU
➲ (off B3130 1.5m E of Clevedon)
☎ 01275 872257

Clevedon Court is a remarkably complete manor house of around 1320. Additions have been made in each century, so it has a pleasing variety of styles, with an 18th-century, terraced garden.
Times: ✱ Open 31 Mar-29 Sep, Wed-Thu, Sun & BH Mon 2-5.
Facilities: ⓟ ⓺ (ground floor accessible via 4 steps) ✖ ✿

CRICKET ST THOMAS   Map 03 ST30

THE WILDLIFE PARK AT CRICKET ST THOMAS
TA20 4DB
➲ (3m E of Chard on A30, follow brown heritage signs. Clearly signposted from M5 junct 25)
☎ 01460 30111   `2 for 1`
▤ 01460 30817
e-mail: teresa.white2@bourne-leisure.co.uk

The Wildlife Park offers you the chance to see more than 60 species of animals at close quarters. Visitors can learn about what is being done to save endangered species, take a walk through the Lemur Wood, ride on the Safari Train or visit the Children's Farm. During peak season, park mascot Larry the Lemur stars in his own show.
Times: Open all year, daily 10-dusk, last admission 4pm in summer. (Closed 25 Dec). **Fee:** £6.95 (ch 3-14 £4.95 & pen £5.95, under 3's free). Family ticket £21. **Facilities:** ⓟ ⓹ ✖ licensed ⓺ (some steep slopes) toilets for disabled shop ✖ (ex guide dogs) ⬕

DUNSTER   Map 03 SS94

DUNSTER CASTLE
TA24 6SL
➲ (3m SE of Minehead, approach from A39. Approx 2m from Dunster Stn)
☎ 01643 821314   ▤ 01643 823000
e-mail: wdugen@smtp.ntrust.org.uk

The castle's picturesque appearance is largely due to 19th-century work, but older features can also be seen, the superb 17th-century oak staircase for example. Sub-tropical plants flourish in the 28-acre park and the terraced gardens are noted for exotica such as a giant lemon tree, yuccas, mimosa and palms.
Times: ✱ Open: Castle: 31 Mar-Sep, Sat-Wed 11-5; Oct-4 Nov, Sat-Wed 11-4. Garden & Park: Apr-29 Sep daily 10-5; Oct-Mar 11-4.
Facilities: ⓟ ⓺ (Braille & audio guides, large print guides & Batricar) toilets for disabled shop ✖ (in park only) ✿

EAST HUNTSPILL   Map 03 ST34

SECRET WORLD-BADGER & WILDLIFE RESERVE CENTRE
New Rd TA9 9PZ
➲ (Signposted from A38, 1m S of Highbridge)
☎ 01278 783250   ▤ 01278 793109
e-mail: enquiries@secretworld.org

This wildlife rescue centre enables visitors to see foxes, badgers, owls and other animals in natural surroundings. The 17th-century farmhouse is now a tearoom, serving

continued

meals throughout the day. There are farm demonstrations and talks as well.
Times: ✱ Open Mar-Nov, daily 10-6. Nov-Dec, daily 10-5. Feb- Mar, daily 10-5. **Facilities:** ⓟ ⓹ ✖ ⓺ toilets for disabled shop garden centre

EAST LAMBROOK   Map 03 ST41

EAST LAMBROOK MANOR GARDEN
TA13 5HH
➲ (signed off A303, at South Petherton rdbt)
☎ 01460 240328   ▤ 01460 242344   `2 for 1`
e-mail: enquiries@eastlambrook.com

It was the late Margery Fish who created the concept of 'cottage gardening' in the 1940s. Her wonderful Grade I listed gardens are known to garden lovers throughout the world. The gardens now house the National Collection of Geraniums, a specialist plant nursery, a tea shop and art gallery.
Times: Open Feb-Oct, daily 10-5. **Fee:** ✱ £3.95 (ch £1 & pen £3.50). Group rate available. **Facilities:** ⓟ ⓹ ⓺ (gardens partly accessible) shop garden centre ✖ (ex guide dogs) ⬕

FARLEIGH HUNGERFORD   Map 03 ST85

FARLEIGH HUNGERFORD CASTLE
BA2 7RS
➲ (3.5m W of Trowbridge on A366)
☎ 01225 754026

Set in a picturesque valley, this castle hides many secrets and a sinister past. An audio tour reveals all.
Times: Open all year, Apr-Sep, daily 10 6; Oct, daily 10-5; Nov-Mar, Wed-Sun 10-4. (Closed 24-26 Dec & 1 Jan). Dates valid until 31 Mar 2004. **Fee:** £2.50 (ch £1.30, concessions £1.90). Prices valid until 31 Mar 2004. **Facilities:** ⓟ ⓺ shop ✖ ✿

GLASTONBURY   Map 03 ST43

GLASTONBURY ABBEY
Abbey Gatehouse, Magdalene St BA6 9EL
➲ (Located on A361 between Frome & Taunton. M5 junct 23 then take A39 to Glastonbury)
☎ 01458 832267   ▤ 01458 832267   `2 for 1`
e-mail: info@glastonburyabbey.com

Few places in Britain are as rich in myth and legend as Glastonbury. Tradition maintains that the impressive ruins mark the birth place of Christianity in Britain. Joseph of Arimathea is said to have founded a chapel here in AD61, planting his staff in the ground where it flowered both at Christmas and Easter. Later, it is said, King Arthur and Guinevere were buried here, and the abbey has been a place of pilgrimage since the Middle Ages. The present abbey ruins date mostly from the 12th and 13th centuries, fell into decay after the Dissolution. The display area contains artefacts and a model of the Abbey as it might have been in 1539. During the summer months meet Brother Thomas, who will tell you how the monks used to live.
Times: Open all year, daily, Jun-Aug 9-6; Sep-May 9.30-6 or dusk, whichever is the earliest. Dec-Feb open at 10am. (Closed 25 Dec).
Fee: ✱ £3.50 (ch 5-15 £1.50, pen & students £3). Family ticket £8 (2ad+2ch) **Facilities:** ⓟ (charged) ⓹ ⓺ (no access in Lady Chapel,audio tape,deaf loop,wheelchairs) toilets for disabled shop ✖ (ex on lead) ⬕

KINGSDON Map 03 ST52

LYTES CARY MANOR

TA11 7HU

➲ (off A303, signposted from Padimore rdbt at junction of A303 & A37, take A372)

☎ 01458 224471 📠 01458 224471

e-mail: lytescarymanor@ntrust.co.uk

Fine medieval manor house and delightful 14th-century chapel, surrounded by gardens with an enchanting mixture of formality and simplicity. Much of the present house was built in the 16th century although the oldest part, the chapel, dates from 1343. The Great Hall was a 15th-century addition. Unfortunately the gardens did not survive, but the present formal gardens are being restocked with plants that were commonly grown at the time of building. Large borders and hidden paths are enclosed by high yew topiary hedges.

Times: Open Apr-Oct, Sun, Mon, Wed & Fri 11-5. **Fee:** ✱ £4.60 (ch £2). **Facilities:** 🅿 ♿ (Braille guide, scented plants) toilets for disabled ✖ (ex guide dogs) 🐾

MONTACUTE Map 03 ST41

MONTACUTE HOUSE

TA15 6XP

➲ (off A3088)

☎ 01935 823289 📠 01935 826921

e-mail: wmogen@smtp.ntrust.org.uk

Set amidst formal gardens, Montacute House was built by Sir Edward Phelips. He was a successful lawyer, and became Speaker of the House of Commons in 1604. Inside there are decorated ceilings, ornate fireplaces, heraldic glass and fine wood panelling. The Long Gallery displays a permanent collection of Tudor and Jacobean portraits from the National Portrait Gallery in London.

Times: Open, Garden & Park: Apr-30 Oct daily (ex Tue) 11-5.30. Nov-Mar Wed-Sun 11-5. House: Apr-30 Oct, daily (ex Tue) 11-5 **Facilities:** 🅿 💻 ✖ licensed ♿ (Braille guide) toilets for disabled shop garden centre ✖ (ex in park) 🐾

MUCHELNEY Map 03 ST42

MUCHELNEY ABBEY

TA10 0DQ

☎ 01458 250664 📠 01458 253842

The monastery was first established at Muchelney by Ine, a 7th-century king of Wessex. It did not survive the Viking invasions, but the abbey was re-founded about AD950 and lasted for nearly six centuries. The present remains date largely from the 12th century. The best preserved feature of the site today is the Abbot's lodging, which had only just been completed in 1539 when the abbey was surrendered to Henry VIII.

Times: Open Apr-Sep, daily 10-6; Oct, daily 10-5. Dates valid until 31 Mar 2004. **Fee:** £2.50 (ch £1.30, concessions £1.90). Prices valid until 31 Mar 2004. **Facilities:** 🅿 ♿ shop ✖ ✿

NETHER STOWEY Map 03 ST13

COLERIDGE COTTAGE

35 Lime St TA5 1NQ

➲ (At W end of Nether Stowey, on S Side of A39, 8m W of Bridgwater).

☎ 01278 732662

It was in this small cottage that Coleridge was most inspired as a poet and here that he wrote *The Rime of the Ancient*

continued

Mariner, part of *Christabel* and *Frost at Midnight.* The Coleridge family moved to Nether Stowey in 1797 and became friendly with the Wordsworths who lived nearby.

Times: ✱ Open Apr-Sep, Tue-Thu & Sun 2-5. **Facilities:** 🅿 ✖ 🐾

NUNNEY Map 03 ST74

NUNNEY CASTLE `FREE`

➲ (3.5m SW of Frome, off A361)

Built in 1373, and supposedly modelled on France's Bastille, this crenellated manor house has one of the deepest moats in England. It was ruined by Parliamentarian forces in the Civil War.

Times: Open any reasonable time. **Facilities:** ♿ ✖ (ex dogs on leads) ✿

SPARKFORD Map 03 ST62

HAYNES MOTOR MUSEUM

BA22 7LH

➲ (from A303 follow A359 road towards Castle Cary, the museum is clearly signposted) `2 for 1`

☎ 01963 440804 📠 01963 441004

e-mail: info@haynesmotormuseum.co.uk

Spectacular collection of historic cars, motorcycles and motoring memorabilia. Vehicles range from a 1903 Oldsmobile to sports cars of the 50s and 60s and modern day classics. Also at the Museum is a 70 seat video cinema, the Hall of Motorsports, a millennium hall and a picnic area and children's adventure playground.

Times: Open all year, Mar-Oct, daily 9.30-5.30; Nov-Feb, 10-4.30. Etr-summer hols open to 6.30pm. (Closed 25 & 26 Dec & 1 Jan). **Fee:** Adult £6.50 (ch £3.50, concessions £5). Family £8.50 (1 ad & 1 ch), £19 (2 ad & 3 ch). **Facilities:** 🅿 ✖ licensed ♿ (ramps & loan wheelchairs available) toilets for disabled shop ✖ (ex guide dogs & in grounds) 🍴

STOKE ST GREGORY Map 03 ST32

WILLOW & WETLANDS VISITOR CENTRE

Meare Green Court TA3 6HY

➲ (between North Curry & Stoke St Gregory, signed from A361 & A378)

☎ 01823 490249 📠 01823 490814 `2 for 1`

e-mail: phcoate@globalnet.co.uk

The centre is owned and run by Somerset Basketmakers and willow growers P H Coate & Son. The environmental exhibition gives a fascinating insight into the Somerset Levels and Moors. Guided tours are available.

Times: Open all year, Mon-Fri 9-5 (guided tours 10-4), Sat (no tours) 9-5. Closed Sun. **Fee:** ✱ Admission free, tour charge £3.50 (ch £1.75, pen £3). Family ticket £8. Credit cards accepted if total admission price exceeds £10. **Facilities:** 🅿 💻 ♿ toilets for disabled shop 🍴

STOKE-SUB-HAMDON Map 03 ST41

STOKE-SUB-HAMDON PRIORY

North St TA4 6QP

➲ (between A303 & A3088)

☎ 01985 843600

A complex of buildings, begun in the 14th century for the priests of the Chantry Chapel of St Nicholas (now destroyed).

Times: ✱ Open 29 Mar-2 Nov, daily 10-6 or dusk if earlier. **Facilities:** 🅿 (5mtrs) 🚲 (on road parking only) 🐾

STREET — Map 03 ST43

THE SHOE MUSEUM
C & J Clark Ltd, High St BA16 0YA
➲ (M5 Junct 23, take A39 to Street, follow signs for Clarks Village) **FREE**
☎ 01458 842169 🖹 01458 442226

The museum is in the oldest part of the shoe factory set up by Cyrus and James Clark in 1825. It contains shoes from Roman times to the present, buckles, engravings, fashion plates, machinery, hand tools and advertising material. **Times:** Open all year. Mon-Fri 10-4.45, Sat 10-1.30 & 2-5, Sun 11-1.30 & 2-5. (Closed 10 days over Xmas) **Facilities:** P ✗ ᚔ (access weekdays only) shop ✗ (ex guide dogs)

TAUNTON — Map 03 ST22

HESTERCOMBE GARDENS
Cheddon Fitzpaine TA2 8LG
➲ (3m N of Taunton near Cheddon Fitzpaine. Signposted from all main roads)
☎ 01823 413923 🖹 01823 413747
e-mail: info@hestercombegardens.com

There are three period gardens to enjoy at Hestercombe: the 40-acre Georgian pleasure grounds with woodland walks, temples, Witch House and Great Cascade; the Victorian terrace and newly established Victorian shrubbery; and the Edwardian gardens, where the work of Gertrude Jekyll and architect Edwin Lutyens are shown off to full effect. **Times:** Open every day, 10-6 (last admission 5). **Fee:** ✱ £5 (ch 5-15 £1.20, pen £4.70). Family ticket £11. **Facilities:** P ᚔ ᚔ (gardens partially accessible) toilets for disabled shop garden centre (open Apr-Oct) ✗ (ex on lead) 🐾

TINTINHULL — Map 03 ST41

TINTINHULL HOUSE GARDEN
BA22 9PZ
➲ (0.5m S off A303. Follow signs to Tintinhull village, garden is well signposted from village)
☎ 01935 822545 🖹 01935 826357
e-mail: floyd.summerhayes@nationaltrust.org.uk

An attractive, mainly 17th-century farmhouse with a Queen Anne façade, it stands in two acres of beautiful formal

continued

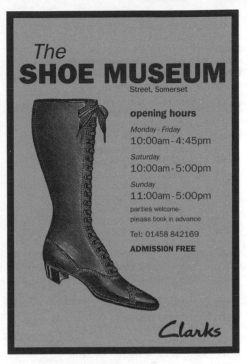

gardens. The gardens were largely created by Mrs Reiss, who gave the property to the National Trust in 1953. **Times:** Open Apr-Sep, Wed-Sun & BH Mons 12-6. **Fee:** ✱ £4 (ch £2). **Facilities:** P ᚔ ✗ (ex guide dogs) 🐾

WASHFORD — Map 03 ST04

CLEEVE ABBEY
TA23 0PS
➲ (0.25m S of A39)
☎ 01984 640377

This 13th-century monastic site features some of the finest cloister buildings in England; medieval wall paintings, a mosaic tiled floor and an interesting exhibition. **Times:** Open all year, Apr-Sep, daily 10-6; Oct, daily 10-5 ; Nov-Mar daily 10-1 & 2-4. (Closed 24-26 Dec & 1 Jan). Dates valid until 31 Mar 2004. **Fee:** £3 (ch £1.50, concessions £2.30). Prices valid until 31 Mar 2004. **Facilities:** P ᚔ shop ✗ (ex on leads in certain areas) 🏳

TROPIQUARIA ANIMAL AND ADVENTURE PARK
TA23 0QB
➲ (on A39, between Williton and Minehead)
☎ 01984 640688 🖹 01984 641105
e-mail: office@tropiquaria.co.uk

Housed in a 1930s BBC transmitting station, the main hall has been converted into an indoor jungle with a 15-foot waterfall, tropical plants and free-flying birds. (Snakes, lizards, iguanas, spiders, toads and terrapins are caged!) Downstairs is the submarine crypt with local and tropical marine life. Other features include landscaped gardens, the Shadowstring Puppet Theatre, and 'Wireless in the West' museum. Also two new full size pirate adventure ships are

continued

moored on the front lawn accessible to pirates of all ages!.The park has an indoor playcastle for adventure and fun whatever the weather.
Times: Open Apr-Sep, daily 10-6 (last entry 4.30); Oct daily 11-5 (last entry 4); Nov-Mar wknds 11-4 (last entry 3). **Fee:** ✱ £6 (ch & pen £5). **Facilities:** P ⬛ ♿ (ramp to pirate galleon & indoor castle) toilets for disabled shop ✖ (ex guide dogs) 🔊

WELLS   Map 03 ST54

THE BISHOP'S PALACE
Henderson Rooms BA5 2PD
➲ (next to cathedral off the Market Sq)
☎ 01749 678691 📠 01749 678691

Close to the cathedral is the moated bishop's palace. The early part of the palace, the bishop's chapel and the ruins of the banqueting hall date from the 13th century and the undercroft remains virtually unchanged from this time. There are several state rooms and a long gallery which houses portraits of former Bishops. Events include a Living History re-enactment.
Times: ✱ Open Apr-Oct, Tue-Fri & BH's; daily in Aug 10.30-5 Sun 1-5. Gates close at exactly 6pm. **Facilities:** P (100yds) ⬛ ✖ licensed ♿ (free use of electric wheelchair) shop

WESTON-SUPER-MARE   Map 03 ST36

THE HELICOPTER MUSEUM
The Heliport, Locking Moor Rd BS24 8PP
➲ (outskirts of town on A371, nr M5 Junct 21)
☎ 01934 635227 📠 01934 645230
e-mail: office@helimuseum.fsnet.co.uk

The world's largest rotary-wing collection and the only helicopter museum in Britain. More than 70 helicopters and autogyros are on display - including examples from France, Germany, Poland, Russia and the United States, from 1935 to the present day - with displays of models, engines and other components explaining the history and development of the rotocraft. Special events include `Open Cockpit Days', when visitors can learn more about how the helicopter works.
Times: Open all year, Nov-Mar Wed-Sun 10-4.30. Apr-Oct 10-5.30. (closed 24-26 Dec & 1 Jan) Open daily during Etr & Summer school hols 10-6.30. **Fee:** ✱ £4.95 (ch under 5 free, ch 5-16 £2.95, pen £3.95). Family ticket (2ad+2ch) £13, (2ad+3ch) £15. Party 12+. **Facilities:** P ⬛ ♿ (large print and braille information sheet) toilets for disabled shop 🔊

> The AA also publishes a guide to Pet Friendly Places to Stay

NORTH SOMERSET MUSEUM
Burlington St BS23 1PR
☎ 01934 621028 📠 01934 612526
e-mail: nickgoff@n-somerset.org.uk

This museum, housed in the former workshops of the Edwardian Gaslight Company, has displays on the seaside holiday, an old chemist's shop, a dairy and Victorian pavement mosaics. Adjoining the museum is Clara's Cottage, a Westonian home of the 1900s with period kitchen, parlour, bedroom and back yard. One of the rooms has an additional display of Peggy Nisbet dolls. Other displays include wildlife gallery, Mendip minerals, mining and local archaeology, costume, ceramics and cameras.
Times: Open all year: Mon-Sat 10-4.30, (Closed 25-26 Dec & 1 Jan). **Facilities:** P (800 yds) (some disabled parking outside museum) ⬛ ♿ toilets for disabled shop garden centre ✖ (ex guide dogs) 🔊

WOOKEY HOLE   Map 03 ST54

WOOKEY HOLE CAVES & PAPERMILL
BA5 1BB
➲ (M5 junct 22 follow signs via A38 & A371, from Bristol & Bath A39 to Wells then 2m to Wookey Hole)
☎ 01749 672243 📠 01749 677749   **2 for 1**
e-mail: witch@wookey.co.uk

A 40 minute guided tour leads visitors through this amazing complex of caves, with stalagmites, stalactites and other interesting geological features. There is also a Victorian papermill, with handmade papermaking and an old penny pier with mirror maze and penny arcade.
Times: Open all year, Mar-Oct 10-5; Nov-Feb 10.30-4.30. (Closed 17-25 Dec). **Fee:** ✱ £8.80 (ch £5.50). **Facilities:** P ✖ licensed ♿ (papermill only accessible) toilets for disabled shop ✖ (ex guide dogs) 🔊

YEOVILTON   Map 03 ST52

FLEET AIR ARM MUSEUM
Royal Naval Air Station BA22 8HT
➲ (on B3151)
☎ 01935 840565 📠 01935 842630
e-mail: info@fleetairarm.com

The size of four football pitches, the Fleet Air Arm Museum has over 40 aircraft on display, hands-on interactive displays, an aircraft carrier's flight deck, a helicopter simulator, and displays on the history and technology of manned flight.
Times: Open all year, daily (ex 24-26 Dec) 10-5.30. (4.30 Nov-Mar). **Fee:** ✱ £8.50 (ch 5-16 £5.75, concessions £6.75). **Facilities:** P ⬛ ✖ licensed ♿ (wheelchairs available) toilets for disabled shop ✖ (ex guide dogs) 🔊

STAFFORDSHIRE

EVENTS & FESTIVALS

January
15th-18th Manchester Dog Show,
Staffordshire Show Ground
30th-31st Winter Beer & Wine Festival,
Lichfield

June
2nd-3rd Staffordshire County Show, County
Showground
18th-20th Lichfield Folk Festival
(various venues)

July
3rd-11th Stafford Festival, Stafford
9th-11th FUSE, the Event in a Tent, Beacon
Park, Lichfield
24th-27th Lichfield Real Ale,
Jazz & Blues Festival
tbc Lichfield International Arts Festival
(various venues)
tbc Staffordshire Bull Terrier Show,
Staffordshire County Showground

August
tbc Victorian Street Market & Circus,
Shugborough Estate

September
6th Abbots Bromley Horn Dance
(throughout village)

November
5th-6th National Chrysanthemum Show,
Staffordshire County Showground

Above: Dr Johnson at Lichfield
Top: Hill-top folly owned by the National Trust

ALTON
Map 07 SK04

ALTON TOWERS
ST10 4DB
➲ (signposted from M1 junct 23A, M6 junct 15, M1
junct 28 or M6 junct 16)
☎ 08705 204060 ▤ 01538 704097
e-mail: info@alton-towers.com

Alton Towers offers rides, shows and attractions guaranteed
to suit every member of the family. There are enchanting
children's areas and the theme park has more thrill rides
than any other in Europe. The Alton Towers Hotel displays a
wonderful array of artefacts and memorabilia from a bygone
age. On top of all this, there are 200 acres of landscaped
gardens and the majestic ruins of the Towers themselves.
Times: ✱ Open 16 Mar-3 Nov, daily 9.30-5/7 depending on season.
Facilities: ▣ (charged) ▆ ✗ licensed ♿ (disabled guest guide
books) toilets for disabled shop ✖ (ex guide dogs) ◥

BIDDULPH
Map 07 SJ85

BIDDULPH GRANGE GARDEN
Grange Rd ST8 7SD
➲ (off A527, 0.5m N of Biddulph)
☎ 01782 517999 ▤ 01782 510624
e-mail: mbgwxm@smtp.ntrust.org.uk

This exciting and rare survival of a high Victorian garden has
undergone extensive restoration. Conceived by James
Bateman, the fifteen acres are divided into a number of
smaller gardens which were designed to house specimens
from his extensive plant collection.
Times: ✱ Open mid Mar-Oct, Wed-Fri 12-5.30. Sat-Sun & BH Mon
11-5.30 (last admission 5.30 or dusk if earlier); early Nov-mid Dec,
Sat-Sun 12-4 or dusk. **Facilities:** ▣ ▆ (not suitable for people with
mobility problems) shop ✖ (ex guide dogs) ◥

BURTON-UPON-TRENT
Map 08 SK22

THE BASS MUSEUM
PO Box 220, Horninglow St DE14 1YQ
➲ (off A38 at Burton-on-Trent, well signposted
through town)
☎ 0845 600 0598 ▤ 01283 513613
e-mail: enquiries@bass-museum.com

Located in Burton-on-Trent, Britain's brewing capital, the
Bass Museum brings together a unique collection of artefacts
and memorabilia tracing the fascinating history of the
brewing industry. Experience Virtual Britain - a unique
interactive journey revealing life as it was back in the census
year of 1881. And after drinking-in the story of brewing, past
and present, there's still plenty to explore - meet the famous
Coors shire horses, witness the authentic art of coopering or
visit the museum shop. End the day by sampling the fine
beers brewed by the micro brewery or enjoy home cooked
food in the Wheelwright's Restaurant.
Times: Open all year, daily 10-5. Last admission 4pm. (Closed 25-26
Dec & 1 Jan). **Fee:** ✱ £5.50 (ch £3, pen £4). Family ticket £16.50.
Brewery tours by arrangement only, at extra charge (all admissions inc
free glass of beer/lager/soft drink). **Facilities:** ▣ ✗ licensed ♿ (lift)
toilets for disabled shop ✖ (ex guide dogs) ◥

CHEDDLETON Map 07 SJ95

CHEDDLETON FLINT MILL
Beside Caldon Canal, Leek Rd ST13 7HL
➲ (3m S of Leek on A520)
☎ 01782 502907

FREE

Two water mills complete with wheels are preserved here, and both are in running order. The 17th-century south mill was used to grind corn, while the north mill was built to grind flint for the pottery industry. The restored buildings have displays on aspects of the pottery industry. Exhibits include examples of motive power, such as a Robey steam engine, and of transport, such as the restored 70ft horse-drawn narrow boat 'Vienna'. There is a learning room suitable for school and adult parties.
Times: Open all year, Sat & Sun 2-5, Mon-Fri 10-5 (by arrangement). **Facilities:** P &

CHURNET VALLEY RAILWAY
The Station ST13 7EE
➲ (3m S from Leek, 3m N from Cellarhead along the A520)
☎ 01538 360522 ▤ 01538 361848   2 for 1
e-mail: mgt@cheddcur.freeserve.co.uk
The Churnet Valley Railway runs through the hidden countryside between Cheddleton, with its grade II Victorian station, and Froghall, with the newly built station and Canal Wharf. The journey incorporates Consall, which has a sleepy rural station and nature reserve, and Leekbrook with one of the longest tunnels on a preserved railway.
Times: Open Sun, Mar-mid Oct; Wed & Sat, July & Aug; Tue, Thu & Sat, Aug (& BH Mon). **Fee:** ✱ Return ticket £7 (ch £4, pen £6). **Facilities:** P ▨ & ramps shop ◥

HALFPENNY GREEN Map 07 SO89

HALFPENNY GREEN VINEYARDS
DY7 5EP
➲ (0.5m off B4176 Dudley to Telford road)
☎ 01384 221122 ▤ 01384 221101
e-mail: enquiries@
halfpenny-green-vineyards.co.uk

FREE

Using German, French and hybrid varieties that can prosper even in the poorest British summer, this vineyard offers "The complete English wine experience." This includes a
continued

self-guided vineyard trail as well as guided tours, wine-tasting, a craft centre and a visitor centre. Visitors can purchase wines with personalised labels for special occasions. Coarse fishing is also available.
Times: Open all year, daily 10.30-5. **Facilities:** P ▨ ✗ licensed & toilets for disabled shop ✖ (ex guide dogs) ◥

HIMLEY Map 07 SO89

HIMLEY HALL & PARK
DY3 4DF
➲ (off A449, on B4176)
☎ 01902 324093 & 326665 ▤ 01902 894163
e-mail: himley.hall@dudley.gov.uk
The extensive parkland offers a range of attractions, including a nine-hole golf course and coarse fishing. The hall is open to the public when exhibitions are taking place. Permanent orienteering course, a charge is made for the maps. Guided tours at the hall available by prior arrangement. The Hall is available for private hire. There are also a large variety of outdoor events and concerts.
Times: Open Hall: early Apr-mid Sep, 2-5. Closed Mon ex BH. Park open all year. **Fee:** free admission except for special events
Facilities: P (charged) ▨ & toilets for disabled ✖ (ex guide dogs & in park)

LICHFIELD Map 07 SK10

ERASMUS DARWIN HOUSE
Beacon St WS13 7AD
➲ (signposted to Lichfield Cathedral. Access by foot through the cathedral close, at West end)
☎ 01543 306260 ▤ 01543 306261   2 for 1
e-mail: erasmus.d@virgin.net
The House is dedicated to Erasmus Darwin, the grandfather of Charles Darwin, and a talented doctor, inventor, philosopher, poet and founder member of the Lunar Society. A resident of Lichfield for more than 20 years, the displays are contained within his beautiful 18th-century home, and recreate the story of Erasmus' life, ideas and inventions, through period rooms, audio visual and interactive displays.
Times: Open Thu-Sat 10-4.30, Sun & BH Mon noon-4.30. Last admission 3.45. (Closed Good Fri, Xmas & New Year) **Fee:** ✱ £2.50 (concessions £2). Family ticket (2 adults & 2 children) £6. **Facilities:** P (200mtrs) & (audio tour) toilets for disabled shop ✖ (ex guide dogs)

LICHFIELD CATHEDRAL
WS13 7LD
➲ (signposted from all major roads and within city A38, A5, A461 & A51)
☎ 01543 306240 & 306100 ▤ 01543 306109
e-mail: enquiries@lichfield-cathedral.org
The Cathedral's three spires, known as the Ladies of the Vale, dominate the landscape. The first cathedral here was founded in AD700 to house the shrine of St Chad. The present building, with its elaborate carvings, has been much restored since it was attacked during the Civil War. Among its treasures are an 8th-century illuminated manuscript, the Lichfield Gospels and a collection of modern silver. Many musical events take place here.
Times: Open daily 7.45-6.30. **Fee:** Suggested donation of £3 for each adult visitor. **Facilities:** P (200mtrs) (no parking ex disabled in close) ▨ ✗ licensed & (touch & hearing centre for blind) toilets for disabled shop ✖ (ex guide/hearing dogs)

LICHFIELD HERITAGE CENTRE

Market Square WS13 6LG

➲ (situated on Market Sq in centre of city, easily accessible from A38, A5 and A51)

☎ 01543 256611 ▤ 01543 414749

e-mail: info@lichfieldheritage.org.uk

A colourful new exhibition, 'The Lichfield Story' gives a vivid account of Lichfield's rich and varied history over 2000 years. It is the home to the Staffordshire Millennium Embroideries which are displayed within their own gallery. In addition, the Exhibition houses fine examples of City, Diocesan and Regimental silver, ancient Charters and archives. Two audio visual presentations, a Family Trail and for younger children a Mouse Hole Trail provide interest and fun for all the family as they tour the Exhibition.

Times: Open all year, daily 10-5, Sun 10.30-5. Last admission 4pm. (Closed Xmas & New Year) **Fee:** ✽ £3.50 (ch 5-15 £1, concessions £2.50, under 5's free). Family ticket (2 ad & 2 ch) £8. Viewing platform (when available) £2 (ch £1, concessions £1.50). Groups and school parties welcome by arrangement, contact the administrators office for information on prices. **Facilities:** ℙ (200yds) ⬤♿ (lift to first floor) toilets for disabled shop ✖ (ex guide dogs) ◥

SAMUEL JOHNSON BIRTHPLACE MUSEUM

Breadmarket St WS13 6LG

➲ (located in city centre market place)

☎ 01543 264972 ▤ 01543 414779

e-mail: sjmuseum@lichfield.gov.uk

Dr Samuel Johnson, author of the famous English dictionary of 1755, lexicographer, poet, critic, biographer & personality. One of England's greatest writers, Dr Johnson was born in this house in 1709. The birthplace now houses a museum dedicated to his extraordinary life, work and personality. Five floors of exhibits featuring period room settings, introductory video and personal items owned by Johnson, his family and his famous friends.

Times: Open daily Apr-Sep 10.30-4.30; Oct-Mar 12-4.30. Last admission 4pm. **Fee:** £2.20 (concessions £1.30). Family ticket £5.80. **Facilities:** ℙ (500yds) (large print text literature, induction loop system) shop ✖ (ex guide dogs)

SHUGBOROUGH   Map 07 SJ92

SHUGBOROUGH ESTATE

ST17 0XB

➲ (6m E of Stafford off A513, signposted from M6 junct 13)

☎ 01889 881388 ▤ 01889 881323

e-mail: shugborough.promotions@ staffordshire.gov.uk

Set on the edge of Cannock Chase, Shugborough is the magnificent 900-acre seat of the Earls of Lichfield. The 18th-century mansion house contains fine collections of ceramics, silver, paintings and French furniture. Part of the house is still lived in by the Lichfield family. Visitors can enjoy the Grade I listed historic garden and a unique collection of neo-classical monuments. Other attractions include the museum and the original servants' quarters, the laundry, kitchens, brewhouse and coachhouses which have all been restored and are fully operational. Shugborough

continued

Park Farm is a Georgian farmstead with an agricultural museum, working corn mill and rare breeds centre.

Times: Open 27 Mar-26 Sep, daily (ex Mon, but open BH Mon) 11-5. Sun only during Oct. Site open all year to pre-booked parties. **Fee:** House & Museum, £6 (concessions £4). Family Ticket £18. Farm £2 (concessions £1). Family ticket £5. All sites, family ticket £20. Farm Rover, family ticket £30. **Facilities:** ℙ (charged) ⬤✖ licensed ♿ (step climber for wheelchairs, 2 Batricars) toilets for disabled shop ✖ (ex guide dogs & in parkland) ◥ ◥

STAFFORD   Map 07 SJ92

SHIRE HALL GALLERY

Market Square ST16 2LD

➲ (M6 junct 13, follow signs to Stafford town centre & gallery is signed from there). **FREE**

☎ 01785 278345 ▤ 02785 278327

e-mail: shirehallgallery@staffordshire.gov.uk

A fine gallery housed in the 18th-century Shire Hall - one of Staffordshire's most magnificent buildings. It holds exhibitions of contemporary arts, contains historic courtrooms and a Crafts Council selected craft shop.

Times: Open all year Mon-Sat, 9.30-5. Gallery closes for exhibition changes and at BH's, please call for further details. **Facilities:** ℙ (5 mins walk) ✖ ♿ toilets for disabled shop ✖ (ex guide dogs) ◥

STOKE-ON-TRENT   Map 07 SJ84

CERAMICA

Market Place, Burslem ST6 3DS

➲ (exit M6 junct 15/16 take A500 leave at A4527 (signposted Tunstall) After 0.5 mile turn right onto B5051 for Burslem. Ceramica is in Old Town Hall in centre of town.)

☎ 01782 832001 ▤ 01782 823300

e-mail: info@ceramicauk.com

A unique experience for all the family, Ceramica is housed in the Old Town Hall in the centre of Burslem, Mother Town of the Potteries. Explore the hands-on activities in Bizarreland, and learn how clay is transformed into china. Dig into history with the time team and take a magic carpet ride over the town. Discover the past, present and future of ceramics with the interactive displays in the Pavillions. Explore the Memory Bank and read the local news on Ceramica TV.

Times: Open Mon, Wed-Sat 9.30-5, Sun 10.30-4.30. (closed Jan). **Fee:** ✽ £3.50, (concessions £2.50, under 5's free). Family ticket (2ad+2ch) £9. **Facilities:** ℙ (charged) ♿ (ramps, lift to all floors, tactile displays) toilets for disabled shop ✖ (ex guide dogs) ◥

GLADSTONE WORKING POTTERY MUSEUM

Uttoxeter Rd, Longton ST3 1PQ

➲ (M6 junct 15, follow A500 to A50 then follow brown heritage signs. From M1 follow A50 westbound then follow brown signs)

☎ 01782 319232 ▤ 01782 598640 **2 for 1**

e-mail: gladstone@stoke.gov.uk

Located at the heart of the Potteries, Gladstone Pottery Museum is the last remaining Victorian Pottery industry. Whilst touring the original factory building discover what it was like for the men, women and children to live and work in a potbank during the era of the coal firing bottle ovens. In original workshops working potters can be found demonstrating traditional pottery skills. There are also lots of

continued

opportunities for you to have a go at pottery making, throw your own pot on the potters wheel, make china flowers and decorate pottery items to take home. Also explore Flushed with pride and The Tile Gallery.
Times: Open all year, daily 10-5 (last admission 4pm). Limited opening Xmas & New Year. **Fee:** £4.95 (ch £3.50, students & pen £3.95). Family ticket £14 (2 ad & 3 ch 4-16yrs). **Facilities:** 🅿 💷 ✗ licensed & (special potters wheel for wheelchair users) toilets for disabled shop ✗ (ex guide dogs) 🔔

Royal Doulton Visitor Centre
Nile St, Burslem ST6 2AJ
➲ (M6 junct 15 from S or 16 from N. Join A500 leaving at exit for Tunstall A527, follow tourist signs)
☎ 01782 292434   🖷 01782 292424
e-mail: visitor@royal-doulton.com
The centre has extensive displays of both current products and out of production pieces together with ranges from the museum tracing the history of Royal Doulton. Live demonstrations showing the skill and craftsmanship in the creation and hand painting of figurines. Behind the scenes look at the working factory weekdays only, prior booking advised.
Times: ✱ Open all year, Mon-Sat 9.30-5, Sun 10.30-4.30. Factory tours by advance booking Mon-Fri 10.30-2 (1.30 Fri). (Closed Xmas week). No tours during factory holidays. **Fee:** ✱ Visitor Centre only £3 (concessions £2.25); Factory Tour & Visitor Centre £6.50 (concessions £5). Parties 12+ Visitor Centre £2. Factory tour and visitor centre £4.50. **Facilities:** 🅿 💷 ✗ & (only Visitor Centre accessible) toilets for disabled shop ✗ (ex guide dogs) 🔔

Spode
Church St ST4 1BX
➲ (M6 junct 15/A500 to Stoke. Ignore city centre signs. Turn left at Stoke rdbt, follow brown tourist signs)
☎ 01782 744011   🖷 01782 744012
e-mail: visitorcentre@spode.co.uk
Spode is the oldest English pottery company still on its original site. Here Josiah Spode first perfected the formula for fine bone china. The Spode site houses a restaurant, factory shops, concession outlets, and a visitors centre with exhibits on the history and heritage of the ceramics industry. Fully guided factory tours are available, pre-booking essential.
Times: ✱ Visitor Centre, Museum, Factory Shops, concessions & licensed restaurant. Mon-Sat 9-5, Sun 10-4. Factory Tours by prior appointment weekdays only, not available during factory closures-please ring for details. **Facilities:** 🅿 (charged) ✗ licensed & (ramps) toilets for disabled shop ✗ (ex guide dogs) 🔔

The Potteries Museum & Art Gallery
Bethesda St, Hanley ST1 3DW
➲ (M6 junct 15/16 take A500 to Stoke-on-Trent. Follow signs for city centre (Hanley), cultural quarters & the Potteries museum)
☎ 01782 232323   🖷 01782 232500
e-mail: museums@stoke.gov.uk
The history of the Potteries under one roof, including a dazzling display of the world's finest collection of Staffordshire ceramics. Other displays introduce natural,

local and archaeological history from in and around The Potteries, and a Mark 16 Spitfire commemorating its locally born designer - Reginald Mitchell.

Times: Open Mar-Oct Mon-Sat 10-5 Sun 2-5; Nov-Feb Mon-Sat 10-4, Sun 1-4; closed 25 Dec-1Jan **Facilities:** 🅿 (500mtrs) 💷 & (lift, induction loop, 2 wheelchairs available) toilets for disabled shop ✗ (ex guide/helping dogs) 🔔

Wedgwood Visitor Centre
Barlaston ST12 9ES
➲ (follow tourist signs southwards on the A34, from M6 junct15)
☎ 01782 282986   🖷 01782 374083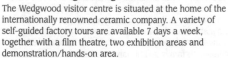
e-mail: bookings@wedgewood.com
The Wedgwood visitor centre is situated at the home of the internationally renowned ceramic company. A variety of self-guided factory tours are available 7 days a week, together with a film theatre, two exhibition areas and demonstration/hands-on area.
Times: Open all year, Mon-Fri 9-5, Sat & Sun 10-5; (Closed 24 Dec-1 Jan). **Fee:** ✱ £7.95-£8.95 (concession £5.95-6.95). Family ticket £26.95-29.95. **Facilities:** 🅿 ✗ licensed & (fully wheelchair accessible) toilets for disabled shop ✗ (ex guide dogs) 🔔

TAMWORTH	Map 07 SK20

Drayton Manor Theme Park & Zoo
B78 3TW
➲ (M42, junct 9, follow brown tourist board signs on A4091)
☎ 01827 287979   🖷 01827 288916
e-mail: info@draytonmanor.co.uk
A popular family theme park with over 100 brilliant rides and attractions set in 250 acres of parkland and lakes. Drayton Manor features world-class rides like 'Apocalypse'- the world's first stand-up tower drop, 'Stormforce 10' - the best water ride in the country and 'Shockwave' - Europe's only stand-up rollercoaster. Fantastic family thrills in 'Excalibur - a Dragon's Tale' and 'Private Adventure' - plus a host of children's rides, zoo, museum, shops and attractions.
Times: Park open end Mar-end Oct. Rides from 10.30-5 or 6. Zoo open all year. **Fee:** Please telephone for details. **Facilities:** 🅿 💷 ✗ & (ramps or lifts to most rides, some rides limited access) toilets for disabled shop garden centre ✗ (ex in park) 🔔

continued

TAMWORTH CASTLE

The Holloway, Ladybank B79 7NA
➲ (from M42 junct 10 & M6 junct 12, access via A5)
☎ 01827 709629 & 709626 ▤ 01827 709630
e-mail: heritage@tamworth.gov.uk

The dramatic Norman motte and bailey castle was once the home of England's Royal Champions and today is (reputedly) haunted by two lady ghosts. Quizzes, dressing-up and brass-rubbing make it a great family destination.
Times: Open Tue-Sun 12-5.15. Last admission 4.30. Telephone to confirm opening times before visiting. **Fee:** £4.30 (ch £2.20). Family £11.90. Prices subject to change. **Facilities:** P (100yds & 400yds) ▆ & (one wheelchair for use inside the castle) shop ✕ (ex guide dogs & hearing dogs)

WALL   Map 07 SK10

WALL ROMAN SITE

Watling St WS14 0AW
➲ (off A5)
☎ 01543 480768

Explore the haunting remains of a 2,000 year old wayside staging post situated along Watling Street, the famous Kent to North Wales Roman road.
Times: Open all year, Apr-Sep, daily 10-6; Oct, daily 10-5. Dates valid until 31 Mar 2004. **Fee:** £2.60 (ch £1.30, concessions £2). Prices valid until 31 Mar 2004. **Facilities:** P shop ✕ (ex dogs on leads) ⛿ ⛟

WESTON PARK   Map 07 SJ81

WESTON PARK

TF11 8LE
➲ (on A5 at Weston-under-Lizard, 30min from central Birmingham 3m off M54 junct 3 and 8m off M6 junct 12).
☎ 01952 852100 ▤ 01952 850430   2 for 1
e-mail: enquiries@weston-park.com

Built in 1671, this fine mansion stands in elegant gardens and a vast park designed by 'Capability' Brown. Three lakes, a miniature railway, and a woodland adventure playground are to be found in the grounds, and in the house itself there is a magnificent collection of pictures, furniture and tapestries. There is also an animal centre and Deer Park.
Times: Open wknds from 19 Apr-Jul, then daily until 7 Sep. **Fee:** Park & Gardens £2.50 (ch 3-14 £1.50, pen £2). House, £2.25 (ch 3-14 £1.25, pen £1.75). Family ticket (2 ad & 3 ch) inc house, park & gardens £9.50. **Facilities:** P ▆ ✕ licensed & (disabled route, access to restaurant & shop) toilets for disabled shop ▬

WHITTINGTON   Map 07 SK10

STAFFORDSHIRE REGIMENT MUSEUM, WHITTINGTON BARRACKS

Whittington Barracks WS14 9PY   2 for 1
➲ (on A51 between Lichfield/Tamworth)
☎ 0121 311 3240/3229 ▤ 0121 311 3205
e-mail: museum@rhqstaffords.fsnet.co.uk

Located next to Whittington Barracks, the museum tells the story of the soldiers of the Staffordshire Regiment and its predecessors. Exhibits include vehicles, uniforms, weapons, medals and memorabilia relating to three hundred years of regimental history, including distinguished service in the First and Second World Wars and the Gulf War. Visitors can experience a World War I trench system with sound effects and a World War II Anderson shelter.
Times: Open all year, Tue-Fri 10-4.30 (last admission 4); also Apr-Oct wknds and BH 1-4.30. (Closed Xmas-New Year). Parties at other times by arrangement. **Fee:** ✱ £2 (concessions £1) Family ticket £5. Regimental Association Members & Serving Soldiers free. **Facilities:** P & (ramps, lowered kerbs, graded access to attraction) toilets for disabled shop ✕ (outside only ex guide dogs)

WILLOUGHBRIDGE   Map 07 SJ74

THE DOROTHY CLIVE GARDEN

TF9 4EU
➲ (on A51 between Nantwich & Stone)
☎ 01630 647237 ▤ 01630 647902

This 200-year-old gravel quarry has been converted into a delightful woodland garden. The quarry is at the top of a small hill and the garden has fine views of the countryside and adjoining counties. There is a variety of rare trees and shrubs. The garden provides colour and interest throughout the seasons from spring to glowing autumn tints.
Times: Open Apr-Oct, daily 10-5.30. **Fee:** ✱ £3.50 (ch under 11 free, ch 11-16 £1, pen £3). Party 20+ £3 each. **Facilities:** P ▆ & (wheelchairs for use, special route) toilets for disabled (on leads only)

> Remember that prices and opening times are liable to change within the currency of this guide. It is always best to telephone in advance to check

SUFFOLK

EVENTS & FESTIVALS

April
tbc East Anglian Beer Festival, Corn Exchange, Bury St Edmunds

May
9th South Suffolk Show, Point-to-Point Course, Ampton Park, Ingham
14th-30th Bury St Edmunds Festival, arts festival, various venues
tbc Sagitta Guineas Festival, Newmarket Racecourse, Newmarket

June
2nd-3rd Suffolk Show, Suffolk Showground, Bucklesham Road, Ipswich
11th-27th Aldeburgh Festival of Music & the Arts, Snape Maltings Concert Hall, Snape

June/July
tbc East Coast Regatta, Lowestoft

July
4th Ipswich Music Day
tbc Suffolk Coast Bike Ride

August
1st-31st August Proms, Snape Maltings Concert Hall, Snape
29th-30th Eye Show, Eye Show Ground, Eye
tbc Lowestoft Seafront Air Festival

November
tbc November Big Night Out, fireworks, bonfire & fair, Melford Hall Park, Long Melford

Above: The Rotunda at Ickworth Park
Top: Beach huts at Southwold

BUNGAY   Map 05 TM38

OTTER TRUST
Earsham NR35 2AF
➲ (off A143, 1m W of Bungay)
☎ 01986 893470 📠 01986 892461
The Otter Trust's main aim is to breed this endangered species in captivity in sufficient numbers so that it can re-introduce young otters into the wild wherever suitable habitat remains. This re-introduction programme has been running since 1983. The Otter Trust covers 23 acres on the banks of the River Waveney. As well as otter pens, there are three lakes with a large collection of European waterfowl.
Times: Open Apr (or Good Fri if earlier)-Oct, daily 10.30-6. **Fee:** ✱ £5 (ch over 3 £3, pen £4). Disabled person in wheelchair free.
Facilities: 🅿 🍴 ♿ toilets for disabled shop 🐕 (ex guide dogs)

BURY ST EDMUNDS   Map 05 TL86

MANOR HOUSE MUSEUM
Honey Hill IP33 1HF
➲ (Edge of Town Centre, follow signs to Police Station, opposite is museum car park) [2 for 1]
☎ 01284 757076 📠 01284 747231
e-mail: stedmundsbury@burybo.stedbc.gov.uk
The Georgian mansion specialises in costumes, textiles, horology and fine and decorative art from the 17th to the 20th centuries. There is a temporary exhibition gallery as well as workshops in textiles and horology - new features are feely pictures and boxes.
Times: Open all year Wed-Sun, 11-4. (Closed: Good Fri, 25 & 26 Dec & 1 Jan). Other times by arrangement. **Fee:** ✱ £2.50 (ch & concessions £2). **Facilities:** 🅿 (charged) 🍴 ✗ ♿ (Special tours can be arranged for disabled groups) toilets for disabled shop 🐕 (ex guide dogs) 🍴

MOYSE'S HALL MUSEUM   [2 for 1]
Cornhill IP33 1DX
➲ (Take Bury central exit from A14, follow signs for town centre, museum situated in town centre)
☎ 01284 706183 📠 01284 765373
e-mail: maggie.goodger@stedsbc/gov.uk
Moyse's Hall is a 12th-century Norman house built of flint and stone which now serves as a local history museum, and among the fascinating exhibits are memorabilia of the notorious William Corder "Murder in the Red Barn".
Times: Open all year, Mon-Fri 10.30-4.30, Sat & Sun 11-4. (Closed 25-26 Dec, 1 Jan & Good Fri) **Fee:** £2.50 (ch & concessions £2). Free for residents of St Edmundsbury. **Facilities:** 🅿 (200yds) ♿ (stairlift, lift, hearing loop, Braille pictures) toilets for disabled shop 🐕 (ex guide dogs) 🍴

CAVENDISH   Map 05 TL84

THE SUE RYDER CARE VISITOR CENTRE
PO Box 5736 CO10 8RN
➲ (on A1092 Long Melford to Clare road)
☎ 01787 282591 📠 01787 282991
The museum was conceived by Sue Ryder as a tribute to those whose suffering and courage during World War II brought the charity into being. On site is a chapel open daily for private prayer, beautiful and peaceful gardens overlooking the lake, gift and care shop and a coffee shop.
Times: Open all year, daily 10-5. (Closed 24-27 Dec). **Fee:** ✱ £1 (ch & pen 50p). Parties by appointment. **Facilities:** 🅿 🍴 ♿ toilets for disabled shop 🐕 (access to gardens only)

EASTON   Map 05 TM25

EASTON FARM PARK

IP13 0EQ

➲ (signed from A12 at Wickam Market, and
from A1120)

☎ 01728 746475 ▤ 01728 747861   `2 for 1`

e-mail: easton@eastonfarmpark.co.uk

Award winning Farm Park on the banks of the River Deben.
There are lots of breeds of farm animals, including Suffolk
Punch horses, ponies, pigs, lambs, calves, goats, rabbits,
guinea pigs & poultry. Chicks hatching and egg collecting
daily. Free pat-a-pet & pony rides every day.

Times: Open Mar-end Sep, daily 10.30-6. Also open Feb & Oct half
term hols. **Fee:** ✱ £5.25 (ch under 1 free, ch 1-16 £3.75 pen £4.25).
Facilities: 🅿 ▣ ♿ (special parking) toilets for disabled shop ⬗

EUSTON   Map 05 TL87

EUSTON HALL

IP24 2QP

➲ (on A1088, 3m S of Thetford)

☎ 01842 766366 ▤ 01842 766764

e-mail: lcampbell@euston-estate.co.uk

Home of the Duke and Duchess of Grafton, this 18th-century
house is notable for its fine collection of pictures, by Stubbs,
Lely, Van Dyck and other Masters. The grounds were laid out
by John Evelyn, William Kent and `Capability' Brown, and
include a 17th-century church in the style of Wren and a
river walk to the newly restored watermill.

Times: Open 17 Jun-16 Sep, Thu only. Also open Sun 27 Jun, 18 Jul &
5 Sep, 2.30-5. **Fee:** £4 (ch 5-16 £2, students & pen £3). Parties 12+ £3
each. Ground only £2. **Facilities:** 🅿 ▣ ♿ toilets for disabled shop
✶ (ex guide dogs)

FLIXTON   Map 05 TM38

NORFOLK & SUFFOLK AVIATION MUSEUM

Buckeroo Way; The Street NR35 1NZ

➲ (off A143, take B1062, 2m W of Bungay)

☎ 01986 896644   `FREE`

e-mail: nsam.flixton@virgin.net

Situated in the Waveney Valley, the museum has over 40
historic aircraft. There is also a Bloodhound surface-to-air
missile, the 446th Bomb Group Museum, RAF Bomber
Command Museum, the Royal Observer Corps Museum, RAF
Air-Sea Rescue and Coastal Command and a souvenir shop.
Among the displays are Decoy Sites and Wartime Deception,
and Fallen Eagles - Wartime Luftwaffe Crashes.

Times: Open Apr-Oct, Sun-Thu 10-5 (last admission 4); Nov-Mar 10-4
(last admission 3) Tue, Wed, Sun. New Year closed 2 weeks either side.
Facilities: 🅿 ▣ ♿ (helper advised. ramps to all buildings) toilets for
disabled shop ✶ (ex guide dogs)

> Special Events are held at many
> attractions throughout the country.
> As we cannot hope to list them all,
> please ring the places of interest for
> details of exhibitions, themed days,
> and guided walks.

FRAMLINGHAM   Map 05 TM26

FRAMLINGHAM CASTLE

IP8 9BT

➲ (on B1116)

☎ 01728 724189

Walk the 12th-century battlements that encircle the castle
site with their impressive thirteen towers. Exceptional views
over the countryside and a very popular audio tour.

Times: Open all year, Apr-Sep, daily 10-6; Oct, daily 10-5; Nov-Mar,
daily 10-4. (Closed 24-26 Dec & 1 Jan). Dates valid until 31 Mar 2004.
Fee: £4 (ch £2, concessions £3). Prices valid until 31 Mar 2004.
Facilities: 🅿 ♿ shop ✶ (ex dogs on lead) ⚏

HORRINGER   Map 05 TL86

ICKWORTH HOUSE, PARK & GARDENS

The Rotunda IP29 5QE

➲ (2.5m S of Bury St Edmunds in the village of
Horringer on the A143)

☎ 01284 735270 ▤ 01284 735175

e-mail: ickworth@ntrust.org.uk

The eccentric Earl of Bristol created this equally eccentric
house, begun in 1795, to display his collection of European
art. The Georgian Silver Collection is considered the finest in
private hands. 'Capability' Brown designed the parkland, and
also featured are a deer enclosure, waymarked walks and an
adventure playground.

Times: ✱ Open: House 24 Mar-28 Oct, Tue, Wed, Fri, wknds & BH
Mons 1-5 (4.30 in Oct) last admission 4.30; Garden open daily 24
Mar-28 Oct 10-5. 29 Oct-Mar 10-4 wkdays; Park daily 7am-7pm.
Facilities: 🅿 ✗ licensed ♿ (braille guide batricars stairlift to shop &
restaurant) toilets for disabled shop garden centre ✶ (ex guide dogs &
in park) ✿

IPSWICH   Map 05 TM14

CHRISTCHURCH MANSION

Soane St IP4 2BE

➲ (South side of Christchurch Park)

☎ 01473 253246 & 213761 ▤ 01473 210328

e-mail: mansion@ipswich.gov.uk

The house was built in 1548 on the site of an Augustinian
priory. Set in a beautiful park, it displays period rooms and
an art gallery which has changing exhibitions. The Suffolk
Artists' Gallery has a collection of paintings by Constable and
Gainsborough.

Times: ✱ Open all year, Tue-Sat 10-5 (dusk in winter), Sun 2.30-4.30
(dusk in winter). (Closed Good Fri & 24-26 Dec & 1-2 Jan). Open BH
Mon. **Facilities:** 🅿 ♿ (tape guide for partially sighted) shop ✶

IPSWICH MUSEUM

High St IP1 3QH

➲ (Follow tourist signs to Crown St car park.
Museum 3 mins walk from here)

☎ 01473 433550 ▤ 01473 433558

e-mail: museum.service@ipswich.gov.uk

The Museum has sections on Victorian Natural History,
Suffolk wildlife, Suffolk geology, Roman Suffolk,
Anglo-Saxon Ipswich and Peoples of the World. There is also
one of the best bird collections in the country.

Times: ✱ Open all year, Tue-Sat 10-5. (Closed Sun, BH's, 24-26 Dec &
1 Jan). **Facilities:** 🅿 (3 min walk) ♿ (lift) toilets for disabled shop ✶
(ex guide dogs)

LAVENHAM   Map 05 TL94

LAVENHAM GUILDHALL
Market Place CO10 9QZ
➲ (Lavenham Market Place. A1141 & B1071)
☎ 01787 247646 🖷 01787 246345
e-mail: jane.gosling@nationaltrust.org.uk
The Guildhall of Corpus Christi is one of the finest timber framed buildings in Britain. It was built around 1530 by the prosperous Corpus Christi Guild, for religious rather than commercial reasons. The hall now houses a local history museum telling the story of Lavenham's 15th- and 16th-century cloth-trade riches. Visitors can also see the walled garden with its 19th-century lock-up and mortuary. **Times:** Open Mar & Nov, Sat & Sun 11-4; Apr, Wed-Sun 11-5; May-Oct daily 11-5. (Closed Good Fri but open BH Mon) **Fee:** ✱ £3 (accompanied ch free). Parties £2.50 each. School parties by arrangement 60p per ch. **Facilities:** 🅿 (adjacent) 🍴 (photo album of upstairs floors) shop 🐾 (ex guide dogs) ♨

LEISTON   Map 05 TM46

LEISTON ABBEY   FREE
➲ (N of Leiston, off B1069)
For hundreds of years this 14th-century abbey was used as a farm and its church became a barn. A Georgian house, now used as a retreat house, was built into its fabric and remains of the choir, the church transepts and parts of the cloisters still stand. **Times:** Open any reasonable time. **Facilities:** 🅿 ♿ 🐾 (ex dogs on leads)

LONG SHOP STEAM MUSEUM
Main St IP16 4ES
➲ (Turn off A12, follow B1119 from Saxmundham to Leiston. Museum is in the middle of town)
☎ 01728 832189 🖷 01728 832189   2 for 1
e-mail: longshop@care4free.net
Discover the Magic of Steam through a visit to the world famous traction engine manufacturers. Trace the history of the factory and Richard Garrett engineering. See the traction engines and road rollers in the very place that they were built. Soak up the atmosphere of the Long Shop, built in 1852 as one of the first production line engineering halls in the world. An award-winning museum with five exhibition halls full of items from the glorious age of steam and covering 200 years of local, social and industrial history. **Times:** Open Apr-Oct, Mon-Sat 10-5, Sun 11-5. **Fee:** £3.50 (ch under 5 free, ch £1, concessions £3) **Facilities:** 🅿 ♿ (wheelchair available) toilets for disabled shop 🐾 (ex guide dogs)

LINDSEY   Map 05 TL94

LINDSEY CHAPEL
Rose Green (on unclass road 0.5m E
of Rose Green)   FREE
Built mainly in the 13th century, this small thatched, flint-and-stone chapel incorporates some earlier work. **Times:** Open all year, daily 10-4. Dates valid until 31 Mar 2004. **Facilities:** ♿ 🐾 ♨

LONG MELFORD   Map 05 TL84

KENTWELL HALL
CO10 9BA
➲ (signposted off A134, between Bury St Edmunds & Sudbury)
☎ 01787 310207 🖷 01787 379318   2 for 1
e-mail: info@kentwell.co.uk
Kentwell Hall is a moated red brick Tudor manor with gardens, woodland walks and a rare breeds farm. The house and grounds are open to the public at certain times of the year, and recreations of Tudor and 1940s life take place at weekends. Ring for details. **Times:** Open: Gardens & Farm Sun during Mar, Apr-Jun. House, Gardens & Farm 14 Jul-early Sep daily; Oct, Sun only. Also open BH wknds & school hols. Historical recreations on selected wknds throughout year. **Fee:** ✱ Inclusive ticket £6.75 (ch £4.25, pen £5.75). Garden & Farm only £4.75 (ch £3, pen £4). Special prices apply for recreations. **Facilities:** 🅿 🍴 ♿ (wheelchair ramp & 2 wheelchairs for loan) toilets for disabled shop 🐾 (ex guide dogs) 🍽

MELFORD HALL
CO10 9AA
➲ (off A134, 3m N of Sudbury, next to village green).
☎ 01787 880286 🖷 01787 880286
e-mail: kathy.lintin@nationaltrust.org.uk
Queen Elizabeth I was a guest at this turreted, brick-built Tudor house in 1578. It features an 18th-century drawing room, a Regency library and a Victorian bedroom. There is also a large collection of Chinese porcelain, and a display on Beatrix Potter, who was related to the owners and often stayed here. The garden has a Tudor pavilion, which may have been built as a banqueting house. **Times:** Open Etr wknd & Etr Mon; Apr & Oct wknds only; May-Sep, daily Wed-Sun (open BH Mon) 2-5.30. **Fee:** ✱ £4.50, National Trust Members free. **Facilities:** 🅿 ♿ (stairlift, ramp, Braille & large print guides) toilets for disabled 🐾 (ex guide dogs & dogs in park) ♨

FREE
Attractions with this symbol do not charge for entry.

LOWESTOFT   Map 05 TM59

EAST ANGLIA TRANSPORT MUSEUM
Chapel Rd, Carlton Colville NR33 8BL
➲ (3m SW of Lowestoft, follow brown signs from A12, A146 & B1384)
☎ 01502 518459 🖷 01502 584658
e-mail: enquiries@eatm.org.uk
A particular attraction of this museum is the reconstructed 1930s street scene which is used as a setting for working vehicles: visitors can ride by tram, trolley bus and narrow gauge railway. Other motor, steam and electrical

continued

vehicles are exhibited. There is also a woodland picnic area served by trams.

Times: Open Good Fri & Etr Sat 2-4, Etr Sun-Etr Mon 11-5. May-Sep, Sun & BH's 11-5; Wed & Sat 2-5 (last entry 1 hour before closing). **Fee:** £5 (ch 5-15 & pen £3.50). Price includes rides. Party rates available. **Facilities:** 🅿 💷 ♿ toilets for disabled shop 🍽

MARITIME MUSEUM
Sparrow Nest Gardens, Whapload Rd NR32 1XG
➲ (on A12, 100 mtrs N of Lowestoft Lighthouse, turn right down Ravine)   `2 for 1`
☎ 01502 561963
Models of ancient and modern fishing and commercial boats, fishing gear and shipwrights' tools are among the exhibits. Exhibition of the evolution of lifeboats, a replica of the aft cabin of a steam drifter. There is also an art gallery.
Times: Open Good Fri, Sat, Sun & Mon (9-12 Apr); May-10 Oct, daily 10-5. **Fee:** 75p (ch & students 25p, pen 50p). **Facilities:** 🅿 ♿ shop 🍽 (ex guide & small dogs)

NEW PLEASUREWOOD HILLS
Leisure Way, Corton NR32 5DZ
➲ (off A12 at Lowestoft)
☎ 01502 586000 (admin) & 508200 (info)
📠 01502 567393
e-mail: info@pleasurewoodhills.co.uk
There are over 40 rides, shows and attractions at New Pleasurewood Hills, set in 50 acres of beautiful parkland. Old favourites such as the Tidal Wave Watercoaster and the Fairytale Fantasy Ride combine with more recent attractions such as Formula K Raceway Go-Karts, the new 100ft Drop Tower, the Crazy Coaster and the Double Decker Carousel.
Times: Open Apr-Oct & Xmas. Telephone for details. **Fee:** ✱ £13 over 1.25mtr, £11 under 1.25mtr, under 1mtr free, family ticket (2 ad & 2 ch) £46. Telephone for details. **Facilities:** 🅿 💷 ✗ licensed ♿ (all shows accessible, most ride operators able to assist) toilets for disabled shop 🍽 (ex guide dogs) 🍽

NEWMARKET   Map 05 TL66
NATIONAL HORSERACING MUSEUM AND TOURS
99 High St CB8 8JL
➲ (located in centre of Newmarket High St).
☎ 01638 667333   📠 01638 665600
This friendly award-winning museum tells the story of the people and horses involved in racing in Britain. Have a go on

the horse simulator in the hands-on gallery and chat to retired jockey's and trainers about their experiences. Special mini bus tours visit the gallops, a stable and yard and horses' swimming pool.
Times: Open 15 Apr-3 Nov, Tue-Sun (also BH Mons & Mons in Jul & Aug) 11-5. 10am opening on race days. **Fee:** ✱ £4.50 (ch £1.50, concessions £3.50). Family ticket £10 (2 ad & 2 ch). **Facilities:** 🅿 (300yds) (coach drop off in front of museum) 💷 ✗ licensed ♿ (ramps) toilets for disabled shop 🍽 (ex guide dogs) 🍽

ORFORD   Map 05 TM45
ORFORD CASTLE
IP12 2ND
➲ (on B1084)
☎ 01394 450472
A great keep of Henry II with three huge towers and commanding views over Orford Ness. Climb the spiral staircase leading to a maze of rooms and passageways.
Times: Open all year, Apr-Sep, daily 10-6; Oct, daily 10-5; Nov-Mar, Wed-Sun, 10-4. (Closed between 1-2, 24-26 Dec & 1 Jan). Dates valid until 31 Mar 2004. **Fee:** £4 (ch £2, concessions £3). Prices valid until 31 Mar 2004. **Facilities:** 🅿 shop 🍽 ⊞

SAXTEAD GREEN   Map 05 TM26
SAXTEAD GREEN POST MILL
The Mill House IP13 9QQ
➲ (2.5m NW of Framlingham on A1120)
☎ 01728 685789
A post mill since 1287, Saxtead Green Post Mill is still in working order. Climb the wooden stairs to the various floors full of fascinating mill machinery. An audio tour explains the workings of the mill.
Times: Open Apr-Sep, Mon-Sat 10-6; Oct, Mon-Sat 10-5. (Closed between 1-2). Dates valid until 31 Mar 2004. **Fee:** £2.50 (ch £1.50, concessions £2). Prices valid until 31 Mar 2004. **Facilities:** (exterior only) shop 🍽 ⊞

STOWMARKET   Map 05 TM05
MUSEUM OF EAST ANGLIAN LIFE
IP14 1DL
➲ (located in centre of Stowmarket opposite ASDA Supermarket & is signposted from A14 & B1115)
☎ 01449 612229   📠 01449 672307
e-mail: meal@meal.fsnet.co.uk
This 70-acre, all-weather museum is set in an attractive river-valley site. There are reconstructed buildings, including a water mill, a smithy and also a wind pump, and the Boby Building houses craft workshops. There are displays on Victorian domestic life, gypsies, farming and industry. These include working steam traction engines, the only surviving pair of Burrell ploughing engines of 1879, and a working Suffolk Punch horse. New: william Bone Building illustrating history of ransomes of Ipswich.
Times: ✱ Open Apr-Oct. **Facilities:** 🅿 (adjacent) 💷 ♿ (wheelchairs available, special vehicle facilities) toilets for disabled shop 🍽

continued

SUDBURY   Map 05 TL84

GAINSBOROUGH'S HOUSE

46 Gainsborough St CO10 2EU

➲ (Gainsborough's House is situated in the centre of Sudbury. Follow pedestrian signs from the town centre car parks or from the train stn)

☎ 01787 372958 ▤ 01787 376991
e-mail: mail@gainsborough.org

The birthplace of Thomas Gainsborough RA (1727-88). The Georgian-fronted town house, with an attractive walled garden, displays more of the artist's work than any other gallery, together with 18th-century furniture and memorabilia. There's a varied programme of exhibitions throughout the year including fine art, craft, photography, printmaking and sculpture.
Times: Open all year, House: Mon-Sat 10-5, Sun & BH Mons 2-5. (Closed Good Fri & Xmas-New Year). **Fee:** £3.50 (ch, students & disabled £1.50, pen £2.80). Party rates available. **Facilities:** P (300yds) (no parking in Gainsborough Street) & toilets for disabled shop ✗ (ex guide dogs) ➡

SUFFOLK WILDLIFE PARK Map 05 TM58

SUFFOLK WILDLIFE PARK

Kessingland NR33 7TF

➲ (25min S of Gt. Yarmouth, just S of Lowestoft off the A12)

☎ 01502 740291 ▤ 01502 741104

Enjoy the atmosphere and excitement of your very own African Adventure at Suffolk Wildlife Park. Spend the whole day exploring 100 acres of dramatic coastal parkland, filled with animals from the African continent and around the world. Guide your expedition to giraffe, lion, buffalo, hyena and many more exciting animals. Capture the true splendour and atmosphere of the park by going walkabout amongst the large open paddocks or join the children's favourite - the Safari Roadtrain with its live commentary of fascinating animal facts.
Times: Open all year, daily from 10am. (Closed 25-26 Dec). Closes at 4pm Jan-mid Mar & Nov-Dec, 5pm mid Mar-Jun & Oct, 5.30pm Jul-Sep.
Fee: ✳ £5.95-£7.95 (ch 3-14 £4.50-£5.95). **Facilities:** P ▣ ✗ & (wheelchairs available for hire) toilets for disabled shop ✗ ➡

WESTLETON   Map 05 TM46

RSPB NATURE RESERVE MINSMERE

IP17 3BY

➲ (signposted from A12 & Westleton)

☎ 01728 648281 ▤ 01728 648770
e-mail: minsmere@rspb.org.uk

Set on the beautiful Suffolk coast, Minsmere offers an enjoyable day out for all. Nature trails take you through a variety of habitats to the excellent birdwatching hides. Spring, is a time for birdsong, including nightingales and booming bitterns. In summer, you can watch breeding avocets and marsh harriers. Autumn is excellent for migrants, and in winter, hundreds of wildfowl visit the reserve. Look out for otters and red deer. The visitor centre has a well-stocked shop and licensed tearoom, and you can

continued

find out more about the reserve. There is a programme of events throughout the year, including several for children and families.
Times: Open daily (ex closed Tue) 9-9 (or dusk if earlier). Visitor centre open 9-5 (Nov-Jan 9-4). (Closed 25-26 Dec). **Fee:** ✳ £5 (ch £1.50, concessions £3). Family ticket £10. **Facilities:** P ▣ & (batricar available for loan, booking advised) toilets for disabled shop ✗ (ex guide dogs) ➡

WEST STOW   Map 05 TL87

WEST STOW ANGLO SAXON VILLAGE

West Stow Country Park, Icklingham Rd IP28 6HG

➲ (off A1101, follow brown heritage signs located 7m North West of Bury St Edmunds

☎ 01284 728718 ▤ 01284 728277
e-mail: weststow@stedsbc.gov.uk

The village is a reconstruction of a pagan Anglo-Saxon settlement dated 420-650 AD. Seven buildings have been reconstructed on the site of the excavated settlement. There is a Visitors' Centre and a children's play area. A new Anglo-Saxon Centre houses the original objects found on the site. The village is located in the West Stow Country Park. The park is 125 acres with river, lake, woodland and heath and has many trails and paths.
Times: Open all year, daily 10-5. Last entry 4pm (3.30 in Winter) **Fee:** ✳ £5 (ch £4). Family ticket £15. (prices subject to changes for special events) **Facilities:** P ▣ & (ramps) toilets for disabled shop ✗ (ex guide dogs) ➡

WOODBRIDGE   Map 05 TM24

WOODBRIDGE TIDE MILL

Tide Mill Way IP12 (follow signs for Woodbridge off A12, 7m E of Ipswich - Tide Mill is on riverside).

☎ 01473 626618
e-mail: geoffgostling@aol.com

The machinery of this 18th-century mill has been completely restored. There are photographs and working models on display. Situated on a busy quayside, the unique building looks over towards the historic site of the Sutton Hoo Ship Burial. Every effort is made to run the machinery for a while whenever the mill is open and the tides are favourable.
Times: Open Etr, then daily May-Sep; Apr, Oct wknds only, 11-5.
Fee: ✳ £1.50 (concessions £1, accompanied ch free). **Facilities:** P (400yds) (no parking or turning in Tide Mill Way) & shop ✗ (ex guide dogs)

SURREY

EVENTS & FESTIVALS

May
31st Surrey County Show, Stoke Park,
Guildford

June
4th-5th Derby Festival,
town & racecourse, Epsom
22nd-24th Wisley Flower Show, Royal
Horticultural Society Garden, Wisley
26th-31st Jul Guildford Summer Festival
(various events throughout the month)

July
26th Jun-31st Guildford Summer Festival
(various events throughout the month)
2nd-4th Guilfest, live music festival
(provisional)

August
1st Cranleigh Show, Showground, Cranleigh
17th-19th Wisley Flower Show, Royal
Horticultural Society Garden, Wisley

September
tbc Ballooning Festival, Loseley Park,
Guildford

October/November
tbc Guildford Book Festival

Above: Flowers at Thursley
Top: Surrey Docks, Rotherhithe

ASH VALE   Map 04 SU85

ARMY MEDICAL SERVICES MUSEUM
Keogh Barracks GU12 5RQ
➲ (M3 junct 4 on A331 to Mytchett then follow
tourist signs)
☎ 01252 868612 🗎 01252 868832
e-mail: museum@keogh72.freeserve.co.uk

The museum traces the history of Army medicine, nursing
and dentistry and veterinary science from 1660 until the
present day. Medical equipment and ambulances
complement displays including uniforms and medals.
Times: ✱ Open all year, Mon-Fri 10-3.30. (Closed Xmas, New Year &
BH). Wknds & BH by appointment only. **Facilities:** 🅿 ♿ hand rails,
wide doors toilets for disabled shop (large shop selling souvenirs) ✖
(ex guide dogs)

CHERTSEY   Map 04 TQ06

THORPE PARK
Staines Rd KT16 8PN
➲ (M25 junct 11 or 13 and follow signs via A320 to
Thorpe Park)
☎ 0870 444 4466 🗎 01932 566367

New for 2003 one of the world's most intense, disorienting,
exhilarating rollercoasters - Nemesis Inferno - the legendary
feet-free, suspended coaster with volcanic theming and
effects, plus the wrenching Quantum. Back for a second
sense-ational season, Colossus, the world's first 10-looping
rollercoaster will continue to demonstrate the mighty power
of Ten. Experience the trio of "must ride" thrill sensations -
explosive Detonator, awesome Vortex and spinning Zodiac.
Plus Tidal Wave, one of Europe's highest water drop rides,
the white water thrills of Ribena Rumba Rapids, X:/No Way
Out, Loggers Leap, Pirates-4D, Neptune's Beach, Thorpe farm
and lots more besides - it's the most sizzling season yet!
Times: Open from 5 Apr-2 Nov (ex some off-peak days) 9/10-5/6
(times vary), 7.30pm from 25 Jul-7 Sep, until 8pm on fireworks night &
from noon-11 on Fri nights. **Fee:** ✱ £19-£25 (ch under 4 free, ch 4-11
£15.50-£18.50). Family ticket (2 ad & 2 ch under 11) £54-67.
Facilities: 🅿 ➦ ✖ licensed ♿ (some rides not accessible,
wheelchair hire available) toilets for disabled shop ✖ (ex guide
dogs) ➥

EAST CLANDON   Map 04 TQ05

HATCHLANDS PARK
GU4 7RT
➲ (E off Guildford, off A246)
☎ 01483 222482 🗎 01483 223176
e-mail: hatchlands@ntrust.org.uk

Built in the 1750's for Admiral Boscawen, hero of the battle
of Louisburg and set in a beautiful 430 acre Repton Park
offering a variety of park and woodlands walks, Hatchlands
boasts the earliest known decorative works by Robert Adam.
Hatchlands is home to the Cobbe collection, the world's
largest group of keyboard instrument associated with famous
composers. There is also a small garden by Gertrude Jekyll,
flowering from late May to early July and a beautiful bluebell
wood in May.
Times: House & Gardens: Apr-Oct, Tue-Thu & Sun, 2-5.30 (also open
BH & Fri in Aug). Park Walks open Apr-Oct, daily, 11-6. **Facilities:** 🅿
✖ licensed ♿ (wheelchair available & special parking) toilets for
disabled shop ✖ (ex guide dogs) 🐾

FARNHAM   Map 04 SU84

BIRDWORLD & UNDERWATERWORLD
Holt Pound GU10 4LD
➲ (3m S of Farnham on A325)
☎ 01420 22140 ▯ 01420 23715
e-mail: bookings@birdworld.co.uk   `2 for 1`

Birdworld is the largest bird collection in the country and includes toucans, pelicans, flamingoes, ostriches and many others. Underwater World is a tropical aquarium with brilliant lighting that shows off collections of marine and freshwater fish, as well as the swampy depths of the alligator exhibit. Visitors can also visit some beautiful gardens, the Jenny Wren farm and the Heron Theatre.
Times: Open daily, 10-6 (summer), 10-4.30 (winter). **Fee:** £9.75 (ch 3-14 £6.95, pen £7.50). Family ticket (2 ad & 2 ch) £29.95.
Facilities: ▯ ▯ & (wheelchairs available) toilets for disabled shop garden centre ✕ (ex guide dogs) ◗

FARNHAM CASTLE KEEP
Castle Hill GU6 0AG
➲ (0.5m N on A287)
☎ 01252 713393
A motte and bailey castle, once one of the seats of the bishop of Winchester, has been in continuous occupation since the 12th-century.
Times: Open Apr-Sep, daily 10-6 (Oct, daily 10-5). Dates valid until 31 Mar 2004. **Fee:** £2.50 (ch £1.30, concessions £1.90). Dates valid until 31 Mar 2004. **Facilities:** ▯ shop ✕ (ex dogs on leads) ✣

GODSTONE   Map 05 TQ35

GODSTONE FARM
RH9 8LX
➲ (M25 junct 6, south of village, signposted)
☎ 01883 742546 ▯ 01883 740380
e-mail: havefun@godstonefarm.co.uk
An ideal day out for children, Godstone Farm has lots of friendly animals, big sand pits and play areas. The Indoor Play Barn costs 80p extra on rainy days.
Times: Open Mar-Oct, 10-6 (last admission 5); Nov-Feb 10-5 (last admission 4). Closed 25 & 26 Dec. **Fee:** Contact for admission prices. **Facilities:** ▯ ▯ & toilets for disabled shop ✕ (ex guide dogs) ◗

GREAT BOOKHAM   Map 04 TQ15

POLESDEN LACEY
RH5 6BD
➲ (2m S off A246 from village of Bookham)
☎ 01372 452048 ▯ 01372 452023
e-mail: spljxd@smtp.n.trust.org.uk
King George VI and Queen Elizabeth (the Queen Mother) spent part of their honeymoon here, and photographs of other notable guests can be seen. The house is handsomely furnished and full of charm, and it is set in spacious grounds. There is also a summer festival, where concerts and plays are performed. Please phone 01372 452048 for details of special events.
Times: ✱ Open all year. Grounds, Garden & Landscape walks: daily 11-6. House: 23 Mar-3 Nov, Wed-Sun 11-5. Also BH Mon 11-5 (last admission 30mins before closing) **Facilities:** ▯ ▯ ✕ licensed & (Braille guide & disabled parking by arrangement) toilets for disabled shop garden centre ✕ (ex guide dogs or in grounds) ◗

GUILDFORD   Map 04 SU94

DAPDUNE WHARF
Wharf Rd GU1 4RR
➲ (off Woodbridge Road to rear of Surrey County Cricket Ground)
☎ 01483 561389 ▯ 01483 531667
e-mail: riverwey@ntrust.org.uk
The visitor centre at Dapdune Wharf is the centrepiece of one of the National Trust's most unusual properties, the River Way Navigations. A series of interactive exhibits and displays allow you to discover the fascinating story of Surrey's secret waterway, one of the first British rivers to be made navigable. See where huge Wey barges were built and climb aboard Reliance, one of the last surviving barges. Children's trails and special events run throughout the season.
Times: ✱ Open Apr-Oct, Thu-Mon 11-5. River trips Thu-Mon 11-5 (conditions permitting) **Facilities:** ▯ ▯ & (braille guide) toilets for disabled shop ✕ (ex on lead) ◗

GUILDFORD HOUSE GALLERY
155 High St GU1 3AJ   `FREE`
➲ (N side of High St, opposite Sainsbury's)
☎ 01483 444740 ▯ 01483 444742
e-mail: guildfordhouse@guildford.gov.uk
An impressive building in its own right, Guildford House dates from 1660 and has been Guildford's art gallery since 1959. A changing selection from the Borough's Art Collection is on display, including pastel portraits by John Russell, topographical paintings and contemporary craftwork, as well as temporary exhibitions.
Times: Open Tue-Sat 10-4.45. **Facilities:** ▯ (100yds) ▯ ✕ & shop ✕ (ex guide dogs)

LOSELEY PARK
GU3 1HS
➲ (2m SW of Guildford, off A3 onto B3000)
☎ 01483 304440 & 505501 ▯ 01483 302036
e-mail: enquiries@loseley-park.com
Magnificent Elizabethan mansion, home of the More-Molyneux family for over 450 years. Set in magnificent parkland scenery. Based on a Gertude Jekyll design. The

continued

walled garden contains five gardens each with its own theme and character. These include the award-wining Rose Garden, Vine Walk, Fruit, Flower Garden & the Serene White Fountain Garden.
Times: Open Walled Garden: 3 May-26 Sep, Wed-Sun & BH Mon 11-5. House open 30 May-30 Aug, Wed-Sun & BH Mon 1-5 (last tour 4.15pm). **Fee:** ✱ House & Gardens £6 (ch £3, ch under 5 free, concessions £5). Gardens only £3 (ch £1.50, concessions £2.50). Party. Garden summer ticket £15, admits ticket holder & guest from May-Sep. **Facilities:** 🅿 💷 ✗ licensed ♿ (wheelchair available, parking outside shop) toilets for disabled shop garden centre ✖ (ex guide dogs)

HASCOMBE   Map 04 SU94
WINKWORTH ARBORETUM
Hascombe Rd GU8 4AD
➲ (2m NW on B2130, follow brown tourist signs from Godalming)
☎ 01483 208477 📠 01483 208252
e-mail: swagen@smtp.ntrust.org.uk
This lovely woodland covers a hillside of nearly 100 acres, with fine views over the North Downs. The best times to visit are April and May, for the azaleas, bluebells and other flowers, and October for the autumn colours. A delightful Victorian boathouse is open Apr-Oct with fine views over Rowes Flashe lake. With many rare trees and shrubs in group plantings for spring and autumn colour effect.
Times: Open all year, daily during daylight hours. (Could close when weather is bad) **Facilities:** 🅿 💷 ♿ (suggested route, free entry for helpers) toilets for disabled shop ✖ (ex on leads) 🐾 🍽

OUTWOOD   Map 04 TQ34
OUTWOOD WINDMILL
Outwood Common RH1 5PW
➲ (M25 Junct 6, take A25 through Godstone towards Redhill, after 1m turn S off A25 at Bletchingly, between The Prince Albert & the White Hart. Mill is 3m on left)
☎ 01342 843458 & 843644 📠 01342 843458
e-mail: sheila@outwoodwindmill.co.uk
This award-winning example of a post-mill dates from 1665 and is the oldest working windmill in England and one of the best preserved in existence. Standing 400ft above sea level, it is surrounded by common land and National Trust property. Ducks and geese wander freely in the grounds, and there is a small museum of bygones.
Times: Open Etr Sun-last Sun in Oct, Sun & BH Mons only 2-6. Other days & evening tours by arrangement. **Fee:** ✱ £2 (ch £1).
Facilities: 🅿 (10yds) ♿ toilets for disabled shop ✖ (dogs on leads only)

PAINSHILL PARK   Map 04 TQ06
PAINSHILL LANDSCAPE GARDEN
KT11 1JE
➲ (W of Cobham, on A245, in Between Streets)
☎ 01932 868113 📠 01932 868001
e-mail: info@painshill.co.uk
Painshill, created by the Hon. Charles Hamilton between 1738 and 1773, it was a pleasure ground for fashionable society. The garden has been described as landscape theatre in which the spectator moves from scene to scene. Staged around a huge serpentine lake, surprises

continued

come at every turn-a Gothic Temple, Chinese Bridge, Ruined Abbey, Grotto, Turkish Tent, Gothic Tower, spectacular waterwheel, 18th century planting and a working vineyard.
Times: Open Mar-Oct, Tue-Sun & BH, 10.30-6. (last entry 4.30pm). Nov-Feb, Wed-Sun, & BH 11-4 (gates close 3pm). Closed 25 Dec.
Fee: ✱ £6 (ch 5-16 £3.50, concessions £5.25). Pre-booked adult groups 10+ £5. Please telephone 01932 868113 for 2004 prices
Facilities: 🅿 💷 ✗ ♿ (wheelchairs & buggies available - pre-booked) toilets for disabled shop ✖ (ex guide dogs) 🍽

REIGATE   Map 04 TQ24
REIGATE PRIORY MUSEUM
Bell St RH2 7RL
➲ (off A217)   FREE
☎ 01737 222550
The Priory Museum is housed in Reigate Priory which was originally founded before 1200, this Grade I listed building was converted to a mansion in Tudor times. Notable features include the magnificent Holbein fireplace, 17th century oak staircase and murals. The small museum has changing exhibitions on a wide range of subjects, designed to appeal to both adults and children. The collection includes domestic bygones, local history and costume.
Times: Open Etr-early Dec Wed & Sat, 2-4.30 in term time.
Facilities: 🅿 (50yds) ♿ (hands on facilities) shop ✖

TILFORD   Map 04 SU84
RURAL LIFE CENTRE
Reeds Rd GU10 2DL
➲ (off A287, 3m S of Farnham, signposted)
☎ 01252 795571 📠 01252 795571   2 for 1
e-mail: rural.life@lineone.net
The museum covers village life from 1750 to 1960. It is set in over ten acres of garden and woodland and incorporates purpose-built and reconstructed buildings, including a chapel. Displays show village crafts and trades, such as wheelwrighting, thatching, ploughing and gardening. The historic village playground provides entertainment for children and there is an arboretum featuring over 100 trees from around the world.
Times: Open Apr-Sep, Wed-Sun & BH 11-6. Winter Wed only 11-4
Fee: £5 (ch £3 & pen £4). Family ticket £12 (2 adults & 2 ch). Family ticket £14 in 2004 **Facilities:** 🅿 💷 ✗ ♿ (3 wheelchairs for use) toilets for disabled shop 🍽

WEST CLANDON   Map 04 TQ05
CLANDON PARK
GU4 7RQ
➲ (E of Guildford on A247)
☎ 01483 222482 📠 01483 223479
e-mail: clandonpark@ntrust.org.uk
A grand Palladian mansion built c.1730 by the Venetian architect Giacomo Leoni, and notable for its magnificent marble hall. The house is filled with the superb Gubbay collection of 18th century furniture, porcelain, textiles and carpets. The attractive gardens contain a parterre, grotto, sunken Dutch garden and a Maori meetinghouse.
Times: House and garden open Apr-Oct, Tue-Thu & Sun 11-5 (also BH's) **Facilities:** 🅿 ✗ licensed ♿ (wheelchairs, Braille guide & disabled parking) toilets for disabled shop ✖ (ex guide dogs) 🐾 🍽

WEYBRIDGE   Map 04 TQ06

BROOKLANDS MUSEUM

Brooklands Rd KT13 0QN

➲ (M25 junct 10/11, museum off B374)

☎ 01932 857381   🖷 01932 855465

e-mail: info@brooklandsmuseum.com

Brooklands racing circuit was the birthplace of British
motorsport and aviation. From 1907 to 1987 it was a
world-renowned centre of engineering excellence. The
Museum features old banked track and the 1-in-4 Test Hill.
Many of the original buildings have been restored including
the Clubhouse, the Shell and BP Petrol Pagodas, and the
Malcolm Campbell Sheds in the Motoring Village. Many
motorcycles, cars and aircraft are on display. Ring for details
of special events.

Times: Open Tue-Sun & BHs 10-5 (4pm in winter). **Fee:** ✱ £7 (ch u5
free, ch 6-16 £5, pen & students £6). Family ticket (2ad+3ch) £18.
Facilities: 🅿 🍴 ♿ toilets for disabled shop ✖ (ex guide dogs) 🤟

WISLEY   Map 04 TQ05

RHS GARDEN WISLEY

GU23 6QB

➲ (on A3, close to M25 junct 10)

☎ 01483 224234   🖷 01483 211750

Covering over 240 acres, Wisley is the flagship of the Royal
Horticultural Society demonstrating the very best in
gardening practices. The gardens have a wide variety of
trees, shrubs and plants, many of which are unusual in
Britain. Whatever the season the garden serves as a working
encyclopedia for gardeners of all levels.

Times: Open all year, Mon-Fri 10-6 (4.30pm Nov-Feb), Sat-Sun, 9-6
(4.30pm Nov-Feb). (Closed 25 Dec). Glasshouses close at 4.15 **Fee:** ✱
£6 (ch 6-16 £2, ch under 6 free). Party 10+ **Facilities:** 🅿 🍴 ✖
licensed ♿ (free wheelchairs, electric buggies, wheelchair route) toilets
for disabled shop garden centre ✖ (ex guide dogs) 🤟

EAST SUSSEX

EVENTS & FESTIVALS

May
1st-23rd Brighton International Festival,
   various venues (England's largest mixed
   arts festival)
9th MG Regency Run, London to Brighton
   run for MG cars (provisional)
20th-29th Aug Glyndebourne Festival Opera,
   Glyndebourne, Glynde, Lewis
30th-31st Battle Medieval Fair, Abbey Green,
   High Street, Battle
tbc Hastings Traditional Jack in the Green
   Morris Dance Festival (various venues)

June
6th London to Brighton Classic Car Run
13th London to Brighton Bike Race

July
1st Battle Abbey Classic Car Show & Country
   Fayre, High Street, Battle (provisional)
tbc Hastings Beer & Music Festival, The Tennis
   Lawns, Alexandra Park, Dordrecht Way,
   Hastings
tbc The Siege of Rye, longbow event

August
14th Pride in Brighton & Hove, gay pride
   parade, Preston Park
tbc Hastings Old Town Week
tbc Rye Medieval Festival

September
4th-19th Rye Festival (provisional)

October
9th-17th Hastings Week (various venues)

November
7th London to Brighton Veteran Car Run,
   Hyde Park
tbc Hastings Borough Bonfire Celebrations
   (provisional)

December
tbc Burning of the Clocks Parade with
   lanterns and fireworks, Brighton seafront

Above: View of the cliffs at Seven Sisters

ALFRISTON   Map 05 TQ50

Alfriston Clergy House
The Tye BN26 5TL
➲ (4m NE of Seaford, E of B2108, next to church)
☎ 01323 870001 🖹 01323 871318
e-mail: ksdxxx@smtp.ntrust.org.uk
Step back into the Middle Ages with a visit to this 14th
century thatched Wealden Hall House. Trace the history of
this magnificent building - the first to be acquired by the
National Trust in 1896 - and discover why the chalk floor is
soaked in sour milk! Explore the colourful cottage garden,
and savour the idyllic setting beside Alfriston's famous parish
church, with stunning views across the meandering River
Cuckmere.
Times: ✽ Open Apr-Oct Sat-Mon, daily (ex Tue & Fri), 10-5.
Facilities: 🅿 (0.25 mile) (Braille guide) shop ✱ (ex guide dogs)
✽ 🍽

Drusillas Park
BN26 5QS
➲ (off A27 near Alfriston between Brighton &
Eastbourne)
☎ 01323 874100 🖹 01323 874101
e-mail: drusilla@drusilla.demon.co.uk

Situated amidst the stunning scenery of the Cuckmere Valley
at Alfriston, Drusillas is widely recognised as the Best Small
Zoo in England. There are over 100 animal species in
naturalistic environments, including meerkats, bats,
penguins, monkeys, reptiles and creepy crawlies. The large
adventure play area is paradise for anyone who needs to let
off steam. There are also beautiful gardens, Panning for
Gold, a Wacky Workshop, Jungle Adventure Golf, Explorers
Lagoon, Mokomo's Jungle Rock, a train that goes through the
llama paddock and the Discovery Centre.
Times: Open all year, daily 10-6 (winter 10-5). (Closed 24-26 Dec).
Fee: ✽ Family super saver tickets: Family of 3 £25.45, family of 4
£33.95, family of 5 £41.15. **Facilities:** 🅿 🍽 ✗ licensed ♿ (rear train
carriage & sensory trails) toilets for disabled shop ✱ (ex guide
dogs) 🍽

BATTLE   Map 05 TQ71

Battle Museum of Local History
The Almonry, High St TN33 0EA
➲ (A21 towards Hastings. Turn right onto A2001
on entering Battle at rdbt, cross & park on Market
Sq. Museum on High St adjacent to Market Sq, N
end of town)
☎ 01424 775955 🖹 01424 772827
e-mail: ann@battlehill.freeserve.co.uk
The focal point of this museum is the only battle-axe head
yet from the Battle of Hastings and a reproduction of the
Bayeux Tapestry. There are also local history exhibits. There
is a special exhibition displaying the wealth of finds at the
Beauport Park Roman Bath House excavated just outside
Battle. The museum holds two or three temporary
exhibitions each year.
Times: Open Apr-Oct, daily 10.30-4.30 (Sun 2-5). **Fee:** £1 (ch 20p, ch
accompanied free). **Facilities:** 🅿 (20yds) 🍽 ✗ licensed ♿ (stair lift)
toilets for disabled shop ✱ (ex guide dogs)

Buckleys Yesterday's World
89-90 High St TN33 0AQ
➲ (A21 onto A2100 towards Battle, opposite
Battle Abbey)
☎ 01424 775378 🖹 01424 775174
e-mail: info@yesterdaysworld.co.uk
A fun day out for all the family, as the past is brought to life.
Walk down the cobbled streets of yesteryear and meet the
colourful characters in over 30 shop and room settings
including a 1930's grocer's and a Victorian kitchen. The
exhibition contains many rarities from the 1850's onwards,
including some of Queen Victoria's personal effects and
letters written by the present queen. The museum is housed
in beautiful gardens with children's play village, miniature
golf and summer tea rooms.
Times: Open all year, Mar-Oct, daily 10-6; Oct-Mar, daily 10-5.30.
(Closed 25-26 Dec & 1 Jan). **Fee:** ✽ £4.95 (ch £3.50, pen & students
£4.50). Family ticket £15.75. Discount for special needs visitors &
groups of 15+. **Facilities:** 🅿 (100yds) (£1.50 per day) 🍽 ♿ (limited
access for wheelchairs) toilets for disabled shop 🍽

1066 Battle of Hastings Abbey & Battlefield
TN33 0AD
➲ (A21 onto A2100)
☎ 01424 773792 🖹 01242 775059
Explore the site of the Battle of Hastings where on 14th
October 1066, one of the most famous events in English
history took place. Free interactive wand tour of the
battlefield and atmospheric abbey ruins.
Times: Open all year, Apr-Sep, daily 10-6 (Oct 10-5); Nov-Mar, daily
10-4. (Closed 24-26 Dec & 1 Jan). Dates valid until 31 Mar 2004.
Fee: £5 (ch £2.50, concessions £3.80). Prices valid until 31 Mar 2004.
Facilities: 🅿 (charged) ♿ shop ✱ (ex in certain areas) ▓

BODIAM   Map 05 TQ72

BODIAM CASTLE
TN32 5UA
➲ (2m E of A21 Hurst Green)
☎ 01580 830436   📠 01580 830398
e-mail: kboxxx@smtp.ntrust.org.uk

With its tall round drum towers at each corner, Bodiam is something of a fairytale castle. It was built in 1386 by Sir Edward Dalnygrigge, for comfort and defence. The walls measure some 6ft 6in thick, and the great gatehouse was defended by gun loops and three portcullises.
Times: * Open 16 Feb-Oct, daily 10-6 or dusk if earlier; Nov-15 Feb, Sat & Sun 10-4 or dusk. Last admission 1 hour before closing.
Facilities: 🅿 (charged) 🍴 ♿ (Braille/large print guides, special parking on request) toilets for disabled shop ✗ (ex in grounds on a lead) ⛟ ♥

BRIGHTON   Map 04 TQ30

BOOTH MUSEUM OF NATURAL HISTORY
194 Dyke Rd BN1 5AA
➲ (from A27 Brighton by pass, 1.5m NW of town centre, opposite Dyke Rd Park)
☎ 01273 292777   📠 01273 292778   **FREE**
e-mail: boothmus@pavilion.co.uk

The museum was built in 1874 to house the bird collection of Edward Thomas Booth (1840-1890). His collection is still on display, but the museum has expanded considerably since Booth's day and now includes thousands of butterfly and insect specimens, geology galleries with fossils, rocks and local dinosaur bones and a magnificent collection of animal skeletons, largely collected by F W Lucas (1842-1932), a Brighton solicitor.
Times: Open all year, Mon-Sat (ex Thu) 10-5, Sun 2-5. (Closed Good Fri, Xmas & 1 Jan). **Facilities:** 🅿 (road opposite) (two hour limit) ♿ shop ✗ (ex guide dogs)

MUSEUM & ART GALLERY
Church St BN1 1UE
➲ (A23/M23 from London, in City centre near seafront. New entrance in the Royal Pavilion Gardens)   **FREE**
☎ 01273 290900   📠 01273 292841

A £10 million redevelopment has transformed Brighton museum into a State-of-the-art visitor attraction. Dynamic and innovative new galleries, including fashion, 20th century design and world art, featuring exciting interactive displays appealing to all ages. The museum also benefits from a spacious new entrance located in the Royal Pavilion gardens and full disabled access.
Times: Open all year, Tue 10-7, Wed-Sat 10-5 & Sun 2-5. (closed Mon ex BHs). **Facilities:** 🅿 (5 mins walk) (Church St NCP & on street) 🍴 ♿ (lift,tactile exhibits,induction loops,ramps,automatic door) toilets for disabled shop ✗ (ex guide dogs)

PRESTON MANOR
Preston Drove BN1 6SD
➲ (off A23, 2m N of Brighton)
☎ 01273 292770   📠 01273 292771
e-mail: visitor.services@brighton-hove.gov.uk

This charming Edwardian manor house is beautifully furnished with notable collections of silver, furniture and

continued

paintings and presents a unique opportunity to see an Edwardian home both `upstairs' and `downstairs'. The servants' quarters can also be seen, featuring kitchen, butler's pantry and boot hall. The house is set in beautiful gardens, which include a pet cemetery and the 13th-century parish church of St Peter. The newly restored walled garden enables disabled people to explore the garden for the first time.
Times: Open all year, Tue-Sat 10-5, Sun 2-5, Mon 1-5 (BH Mons 10-5). (Closed Good Fri & 25-26 Dec). **Fee:** * £3.70 (ch 5-15 £2.15, pen, students & UB40 £3). Family ticket £5.85-£9.95. Party 20+ £3.15 each. Joint ticket with Royal Pavilion £8.20. **Facilities:** 🅿 ♿ (access to ground floor with prior notice) shop ✗ (ex guide dogs)

ROYAL PAVILION
BN1 1EE
➲ (M23/A23 from London, situated in Brighton City Centre near seafront. 15 min walk from Brighton train station)
☎ 01273 290900   📠 01273 292871
e-mail: visitor.services@brighton-hove.gov.uk

Acclaimed as one of the most exotically beautiful buildings in the British Isles, the Royal Pavilion was the magnificent seaside residence of George IV. The breathtaking Regency palace is decorated in Chinese style, with a romanticised Indian exterior, and surrounded by restored Regency gardens.
Times: Open all year, Apr-Sep, daily 9.30-5.45 (last admission 5); Oct-May, daily 10-5.15 (last admission 4.30). **Fee:** * £5.80 (ch £3.40, concessions £4) Family ticket £9.20-£15. Joint ticket with Preston Manor £8.20 Groups 20+£4.90 each. **Facilities:** 🅿 (5 mins walk) (NCP & on street) 🍴 ♿ (tours for the blind by arrangement, wheelchairs) toilets for disabled shop ✗ (ex guide dogs) ♥

SEA LIFE CENTRE
Marine Pde BN2 1TB
➲ (Situated next to Brighton Pier between Marine Parade and Madeira Drive)   **2 for 1**
☎ 01273 604234   📠 01273 681840
e-mail: slcbrighton@merlinentertainments.biz

Experience spectacular marine displays, set in the world's oldest functioning aquarium. Take a look at over 100 species in their natural habitat, including seahorses, sharks and rays. Over forty exhibits include Adventures at 20,000 Leagues complete with NASA-designed walkthrough observation tunnel. Features also include a Captain Pugwash quiz trail, a soft play area, a cafe and a giftshop.
Times: Open all year, daily (ex 25 Dec), 10-6. Last admission 5. (Open later on wknds in summer & school holidays) **Fee:** £7.50 (ch £4.50, students & pen £6.50, ch under 3 free). **Facilities:** 🅿 (200yds) (pay & display) 🍴 ♿ toilets for disabled shop ✗ (ex guide dogs) ♥

BURWASH   Map 05 TQ62

BATEMAN'S
TN19 7DS
➲ (0.5m SW off A265)
☎ 01435 882302   📠 01435 882811
e-mail: kbaxxx@smtp.ntrust.org.uk

Rudyard Kipling lived for over 34 years in this 17th-century manor house and it remains much the same as it was during his lifetime. His 1928 Rolls Royce Phantom is on display, and

continued

the watermill at the bottom of the garden grinds wheat into flour on Saturday afternoons.

Times: ✱ Open Apr-1 Nov, Sat-Wed 11-5.30, also open Good Fri, (last admission 4.30pm). House closes at 5pm. **Facilities:** 🅿 💺 ✘ licensed ♿ (Braille guide, touch test, computerised tour of upper floors) toilets for disabled shop ✖ (ex guide/hearing dogs) 🐾 🍴

EASTBOURNE Map 05 TV69

"HOW WE LIVED THEN" MUSEUM OF SHOPS & SOCIAL HISTORY

20 Cornfield Ter BN21 4NS
➲ (just off seafront, between town centre & theatres)
☎ 01323 737143
e-mail: howwelivedthen@btconnect.com

Over the last 40 years, Jan and Graham Upton have collected over 100,000 items which are now displayed on four floors of authentic old shops and room-settings, transporting visitors back to their grandparents' era. Other displays, such as seaside souvenirs, wartime rationing and Royal mementoes, help to capture 100 years of social history.
Times: Open daily all year, 10-5.30 (last entry 5pm). Winter times subject to change, telephone establishment. **Fee:** £3.50 (ch 5-15 £2.50, under 5's free, pen £3). Party 10+. **Facilities:** 🅿 (outside) ♿ (no charge for disabled) shop

WISH TOWER PUPPET MUSEUM

Martello Tower No 73, King Edward Pde BN21 4BU
➲ (on seafront, W of pier)
☎ 01323 417776 📠 01323 644440
e-mail: puppet.workshop@virgin.net

This museum hosts a unique display of puppets from all over the world. From early shadow puppets of Asia, through over 300 years of Punch and Judy in England to television and film puppets of today. Puppet shows sometimes take place during the summer.
Times: Open May-mid Jul & Sep, wknds 11-5; mid Jul-Aug, daily 11-5. **Fee:** ✱ £1.80 (ch16 & pen £1.25, students £1.50). Family ticket (2ad & 2ch) £5. **Facilities:** 🅿 (100mtrs) shop ✖ 🍴

FIRLE Map 05 TQ40

FIRLE PLACE

BN8 6LP
➲ (off A27, Eastbourne to Brighton road)
☎ 01273 858307 📠 01273 858188
e-mail: firleestate@aol.com

Home of the Gage family for over 500 years, the house has a Tudor core but was remodelled in the 18th century. Its treasures include important European and English Old Master paintings, fine English and French furniture, and porcelain, including notable examples from Sèvres and English factories. There are family monuments and brasses in the church at West Firle.
Times: Open 12 May-Sep, Sun, Wed, Thu & BHs 1.45-4.15.
Facilities: 🅿 ✘ licensed ♿ toilets for disabled shop ✖ (ex in garden)

GLYNDE Map 05 TQ40

GLYNDE PLACE

BN8 6SX
➲ (off A27 between Lewes & Eastbourne)
☎ 01273 858224 📠 01273 858224
e-mail: hampden@glyndeplace.co.uk

A lovely Elizabethan manor with 18th-century additions, in a beautiful downland setting. Glynde Place is the family home of Viscount and Viscountess Hampden whose forebears built the house in 1669 using a mixture of flint and stone. Portraits, furniture, silver, embroidery and books testify to 400 years of family life.
Times: Open Jun-Sep, Wed, Sun & Aug BH 2-4.45. **Fee:** £5.50 (ch £2.75). Parties 25+ £4 each. **Facilities:** 🅿 💺 shop ✖ (guide dogs)

HAILSHAM Map 05 TQ50

MICHELHAM PRIORY

Upper Dicker BN27 3QS
➲ (off A22 & A27, 2m W of Hailsham, 8m NW of Eastbourne, signposted from A27 & A22).
☎ 01323 844224 📠 01323 844030
e-mail: adminmich@sussexpast.co.uk

Set on a moated island surrounded by glorious gardens, Michelham Priory is one of the most beautiful historic houses in Sussex. Founded in 1229 for Augustinian canons, the Priory is approached through a 14th-century gatehouse spanning the longest water-filled medieval moat in the country. Most of the original priory was demolished during

continued

the Dissolution, but the remains were incorporated into a Tudor farm that became a country house. Outside, the gardens are enhanced by a working watermill, physic garden, smithy, rope museum and the dramatic Elizabethan Great Barn.
Times: Open Mar-Oct, Tue-Sun (daily in Aug & BH Mons). Mar & Oct 10.30-4, Apr-Jul & Sep 10.30-5, Aug 10.30-5.30. **Fee:** ✱ £5 (ch 5-15 £2.60, pen & student £4.30). Family ticket (2 ad & 2 ch) £12.90.
Facilities: ▣ ▆ ✗ licensed ৬ (pre-booked wheelchairs, Braille guide & tactile tours) toilets for disabled shop ✖ (ex guide dogs) ◥

HALLAND   Map 05 TQ51

BENTLEY WILDFOWL & MOTOR MUSEUM
BN8 5AF
➲ (7m NE of Lewes, signposted off A22, A26 & B2192) |2 for 1|
☎ 01825 840573 ▯ 01825 841322
e-mail: barrysutherland@pavilion.co.uk
Hundreds of swans, geese and ducks from all over the world can be seen on lakes and ponds along with flamingoes and peacocks. There is a fine array of Veteran, Edwardian and Vintage vehicles, and the house has splendid antiques and wildfowl paintings. The gardens specialise in old fashioned roses. Other attractions include woodland walks, a nature trail, Education Centre, adventure playground and a miniature train.
Times: Open 17 Mar-Oct, daily 10.30-4.30. House open from noon, Apr-Nov, Feb & part of Mar, wknds only. Estate closed Dec & Jan. House closed all winter. **Fee:** ✱ Summer £5.50 (ch 4-15 £3.80, pen & students £4.50). Family ticket (2 ad & 4 ch) £17.50. Winter £4.20. Special rates for disabled. **Facilities:** ▣ ▆ ৬ (wheelchairs available) toilets for disabled shop ✖ (ex guide dogs) ◥

HASTINGS   Map 05 TQ80

OLD TOWN HALL MUSEUM OF LOCAL HISTORY
Old Town Hall, High St TN34 3EW
➲ (off A259 coast road into High St in Hastings old town. Signposted) |FREE|
☎ 01424 781166 ▯ 01424 781165
e-mail: oldtownmuseum@hastings.gov.uk
Situated in the heart of Hastings Old Town, the museum was originally a Georgian Town Hall built in 1823. Refurbished displays tell the story of Hastings Old Town as a walk back in time, with features including a Cinque Ports ship, and interactive displays.
Times: Open Apr-Sep, daily 10-5; Oct-Mar, daily 11-4. **Facilities:** ▣ (150yds) (parking metres in operation) ৬ (lift, evac chair, low-level displays, audio tour) toilets for disabled shop ✖ (ex guide dogs)

> If you want to tell us about an attraction you think should be included in this book, please use the Readers' Report form at the back of the book, or e-mail: lifestyleguides@theAA.com

SMUGGLERS ADVENTURE
St Clements Caves, West Hill TN34 3HY
➲ (follow brown and cream signs along A259 coast road through Hastings. Use seafront carpark and then take West cliff railway or follow signed footpath) |2 for 1|
☎ 01424 422964 ▯ 01424 721483
e-mail: smugglers@discoverhastings.co.uk
A Smuggler's Adventure is a themed experience housed in a labyrinth of caverns and passages deep below the West Hill. Visitors first tour a comprehensive exhibition and museum, followed by a video theatre, before embarking on the Adventure Walk - a trip through several acres of caves with life-size tableaux, push-button automated models and dramatic scenic effects depicting life in the days of 18th-century smuggling.
Times: Open all year daily, Etr-Sep 10-5.30; Oct-Etr 11-4.30. (Closed 24-26 Dec). **Fee:** ✱ £5.75 (ch £3.65, concessions £4.75). Family ticket £15.75. **Facilities:** ▣ (500yds) (parking meters on some streets) shop ✖ (ex guide dogs) ◥

1066 STORY IN HASTINGS CASTLE
Castle Hill Rd, West Hill TN34 3RG
➲ (close to A259 seafront, 2m from B2093)
☎ 01424 781111 & 781112 (info line)
▯ 01424 781186
The ruins of the Norman castle stand on the cliffs, close to the site of William the Conqueror's first motte-and-bailey castle in England. It was excavated in 1825 and 1968, and old dungeons were discovered in 1894. An unusual approach to the castle can be made via the West Hill Cliff Railway.
Times: Open Mar-Sep 10-5 (5.30 summer school hols); Oct-Feb 11-3.30 (Closed 24-26 Dec). **Facilities:** ▣ (seafront) (time restrictions, pay & display) ৬ (ramps) shop ✖ (ex guide dogs)

HERSTMONCEUX   Map 05 TQ61

THE OBSERVATORY SCIENCE CENTRE
BN27 1RG
➲ (2m E of village on Boreham Street to Pevensey Road)
☎ 01323 832731 ▯ 01323 832741
e-mail: info@the-observatory.org
From the 1950s to the 1980s this was part of the Royal Greenwich Observatory, and was used by astronomers to observe and chart movements in the night sky. Visitors can learn about not only astronomy, but also other areas of science in a series of interactive and engaging displays. There are also exhibitions, a discovery park, and a collection of unusual giant exhibits.
Times: ✱ Open 9-17 Feb & 23 Mar-3 Nov, 10-6 (last admission 5 in Feb, Oct & Nov) **Facilities:** ▣ ▆ ৬ ramps+ disabled entrance toilets for disabled shop ✖ (ex guide dogs) ◥

THE TRUGGERY
Coopers Croft BN27 1QL
➲ (from A22 at Hailsham, Boship rdbt, take A271 towards Bexhill for 4m)
☎ 01323 832314 ▯ 01323 832314 |FREE|
e-mail: sarah@truggery.fsnet.co.uk
The art of Sussex trug making can be seen through all the

continued

work processes including preparing timber, use of the draw knife and assembly of trug.

Times: Open Tue-Fri 10-5, Sat 10-1. Closed Sun & Mon. Jan-Apr opening times may vary. **Facilities:** P & shop 🚐 🍴

HOVE Map 04 TQ20

BRITISH ENGINEERIUM-MUSEUM OF STEAM & MECHANICAL ANTIQUITIES
off Nevill Rd BN3 7QA
➲ (signposted off A27 from Worthing & Eastbourne)
☎ 01273 559583 🖨 01273 566403
e-mail: info@britishengineerium.com

This restored Victorian water pumping station has an original working beam engine of 1876, and a French Corliss horizontal engine which won first prize at the Paris International Exhibition of 1889. There are also traction engines, fire engines, and many other full-size and model engines. Also an exhibition of craftsmen's tools and domestic appliances. Boilers are fired up and in steam on special days. **Times:** Open all year, daily 10-4. In steam first Sun in month & Sun & Mon of BH's. Telephone for details of days closed prior to Xmas. **Facilities:** P & shop 🍴 (ex guide dogs)

LEWES Map 05 TQ41

ANNE OF CLEVES HOUSE
52 Southover High St BN7 1JA
➲ (S of town centre off A27/A26/A275)
☎ 01273 474610 🖨 01273 486990
e-mail: anne@sussexpast.co.uk

Henry VIII gave this beautiful timber-framed house to Anne of Cleves, his fourth wife, as part of her divorce settlement. Today there are collections of early English furniture, Sussex pottery and stone from Lewes Priory, plus a local social history exhibition. The Wealden Iron Gallery tells the story of the industrial past of Sussex and contains a large collection of iron artefacts. **Times:** Open Jan-Feb & Nov-Dec, Tue-Sat 10-5; Mar-Oct, Tue-Sat 10-5, Sun, Mon & BH's 11-5. Closed 24-26 Dec. **Fee:** ✱ £2.80 (ch 5-15 £1.40, pen & student £2.50). Family ticket £7 (2 ad & 2 ch), £5.50 (1 ad & 4 ch). **Facilities:** P (25yds) (on street-2hr restriction) & shop 🍴 (ex guide dogs) 🍴

LEWES CASTLE & BARBICAN HOUSE MUSEUM
169 High St BN7 1YE
➲ (N of High St off A27/A26/A275)
☎ 01273 486290 🖨 01273 486990
e-mail: castle@sussexpast.co.uk

High above the medieval streets stands Lewes Castle, begun soon after the Norman Conquest by William de Warenne as his stronghold in Sussex and added to over the next 300 years, culminating in the magnificent Barbican. Thomas Read Kemp and his family owned and updated the ruins during Georgian times. Barbican House is next to the castle, and now houses a museum covering the area from pre-history to the late medieval period. Visitors can climb to the top of the castle, from where they are rewarded by stunning views. A 'sound and light' show in the museum below tells the story of the town of Lewes through the ages. **Times:** Open daily, Tue-Sat 10-5.30, Sun & Mon 11-5.30. Last admission 30 mins before closing. Closed Mon's in Jan & Xmas. **Fee:** ✱ £4.20 (ch £2.10, pen & student £3.70). Family ticket (2 ad & 2 ch) £11.40, (1 ad & 4 ch) £8.40. **Facilities:** P (on street parking) (touch screen) shop 🍴 (ex guide dogs) 🍴

NEWHAVEN Map 05 TQ40

PARADISE PARK & GARDENS
Avis Rd BN9 0DH
➲ (signposted off A26 & A259)
☎ 01273 512123 🖨 01273 616005   **2 for 1**
e-mail: enquiries@paradisepark.co.uk

A perfect day out for plant lovers whatever the season. Discover the unusual garden designs with waterfalls, fountains and lakes, including the Caribbean garden and the tranquil Oriental garden. The Conservatory Gardens complex contains a large variety of the world's flora divided into several zones. There's also a Sussex history trail and Planet Earth with moving dinosaurs and interactive displays, plus rides and amusements for children. **Times:** Open all year, daily 9-6 (Closed 25-26 Dec). **Fee:** £5.99 (ch £4.99). Family ticket £19.99 (2 ad & 3 ch). **Facilities:** P 💷 ✕ licensed & (all areas level or ramped) toilets for disabled shop garden centre 🍴 (ex guide dogs) 🍴

NORTHIAM Map 05 TQ82

GREAT DIXTER
TN31 6PH
➲ (off A28, signposted)
☎ 01797 252878 🖨 01797 252879
e-mail: office@greatdixter.co.uk

Birthplace and home of Christopher Lloyd, gardening writer, Great Dixter was built in 1460 and boasts one of the largest timber-framed buildings in the country. Lutyens was employed to restore both the house and gardens in 1910. The gardens are now a combination of meadows, ponds, topiary and notably the Long Border and Exotic Garden. **Times:** Open 29 Mar-26 Oct, Tue-Sun & BH Mon, 2-5.30 (last admission 5); Gardens only open from 11am on Sun & Mon BH wknds only. **Fee:** House & Gardens £6.50 (ch £2). Gardens only £5 (ch £1.50). Party 25+. **Facilities:** P & (one wheelchair available free of charge) toilets for disabled shop garden centre 🍴 (ex guide dogs) 🍴

PEVENSEY Map 05 TQ60
PEVENSEY CASTLE
BN24 5LE
➲ (off A259)
☎ 01323 762604

William the Conqueror landed here in 1066 and established his first stronghold. Discover the history of the Norman castle and the remains of an unusual keep through the free audio tour.
Times: Open all year, Apr-Sep, daily 10-6; Oct, daily 10-5; Nov-Mar, Wed-Sun 10-4. (Closed 24-26 Dec & 1 Jan). Dates valid until 31 Mar 2004. **Facilities:** P (charged) 🅿️ & shop ✕ (ex on lead in certain areas) ⊞

RYE Map 05 TQ92
LAMB HOUSE
West St TN31 7ES
➲ (facing W end of Church)
☎ 01892 890651 📠 01892 890110

This 18th-century house was the home of novelist Henry James from 1898 until his death in 1916, and was later occupied by the writer, E F Benson. Some of James' personal posessions can be seen. There is also a charming walled garden.
Times: ✱ Open Apr-2 Nov; Wed & Sat 2-6, (last admission 5.30).
Facilities: P (200mtrs) (scented plants & herbs) ✕ (ex guide dogs) 🌱

RYE CASTLE MUSEUM
3 East St TN31 7JY
➲ (In town centre, on A259)   `2 for 1`
☎ 01797 226728

Part of the museum is housed in a stone tower built as a fortification in 1249. The museum's collection of ironwork, medieval pots and smuggling items are on display here, while the East Street site contains the rest of the collection, including pottery made in Rye, fashions, an eighteenth-century fire engine, toys, cinque port regalia, a special exhibition on Rye in WWII and descriptions of the changes to the harbour and shipbuilding in Rye. The museum tells the story of Rye's long and illustrious history.
Times: Open all year Nov-Mar wknds only 10.30-3; Apr-Oct Thu-Mon 10.30-5. (last entry 4.30). Closed between 1-2pm. **Fee:** Entrance to both sites: £2.90 (ch under 7 free, ch 7-16 £1.50, concessions £2, ch U7 free). Family ticket £5.90. Single entry only: £1.90 (ch under 7 free, ch 7-16) £1, concessions £1.50). Family ticket £4.50. Party 8+.
Facilities: P (30yds) (street limited to 1hr) & (only East Street accessible) toilets for disabled shop ✕ (ex guide dogs)

> Remember that prices and opening times are liable to change within the currency of this guide. It is always best to telephone in advance to check

SHEFFIELD PARK Map 05 TQ42
SHEFFIELD PARK GARDEN
TN22 3QX
➲ (5m E of Haywards Heath off A275)
☎ 01825 790231 📠 01825 791264
e-mail: kshxxx@smtp.ntrust.org.uk

Sheffield Park was originally landscaped by 'Capability' Brown, in about 1775 to create a beautiful park with four lakes and cascades. Further extensive planting was done at the beginning of the 20th century, to give emphasis to autumn colour among the trees. In May and June masses of azaleas and rhododendrons bloom and later there are magnificent waterlilies on the lakes. Autumn brings stunning colours from the many rare trees and shrubs. Special events throughout the season.
Times: ✱ Open Jan-Feb Sat-Sun 10.30-4; Mar-Oct Tue-Sun (open BH Mons) 10.30-6; Nov-Dec Tue-Sun 10.30-4 (Last admission 1 hour before closing). **Facilities:** P 🅿️ & (powered self drive cars & wheelchairs available) toilets for disabled shop ✕ (ex guide/hearing dogs) 🌱 ⬤

SHEFFIELD PARK STATION Map 05 TQ42
BLUEBELL RAILWAY
Sheffield Park Station TN22 3QL   `2 for 1`
➲ (4.5m E of Haywards Heath, off A275)
☎ 01825 720800 & 722370 📠 01825 720804
e-mail: info@bluebell-railway.co.uk

A volunteer-run heritage steam railway with nine miles of track running through pretty Sussex countryside. Please note that there is no parking at Kingscote Station. If you wish to board the train here, catch the bus (service 473) which connects Kingscote and East Grinstead.
Times: Open all year, Sat & Sun, daily May-Sep & during school holidays. Santa Specials run Dec. For timetable and information regarding trains contact above. **Fee:** ✱ 3rd class return fare £8.50 (ch £4.20). Family ticket £23. Admission to Sheffield Park Station only £1.60 (ch 80p). Other tickets available on request. **Facilities:** P 🅿️ ✕ licensed & (special carriage for wheelchairs & carers with lift) toilets for disabled shop ⬤

TICEHURST Map 05 TQ63
PASHLEY MANOR GARDENS
TN5 7HE
➲ (on B2099 between A21 and Ticehurst village, brown tourist signposted)
☎ 01580 200888 📠 01580 200102
e-mail: info@pashleymanorgardens.com

Once belonging to the family of Anne Boleyn, Pashley Manor has a beautiful traditional English garden that has been open to the public since 1992. Visitors can wander among fine old trees, fountains, springs and large ponds, all surrounded by romantic landscaping and imaginative plantings. Statues and sculptures by Europe's leading sculptors are on display both in the gardens and in the Great Hall. A series of craft and plant fairs take place throughout the year.
Times: Open 5 Apr-27 Sep, Tue-Thu, Sat & BH Mon 11-5; Garden only Oct, Mon-Fri 10-4. **Fee:** ✱ £6 (pen £5.50) **Facilities:** P ✕ licensed & toilets for disabled shop ✕ (ex guide dogs) ⬤

WEST SUSSEX

EVENTS & FESTIVALS

April
9th British & World Marbles Championships,
Greyhound pub, Crawley

May
3rd Spring Garden & Leisure Show,
Showground, Ardingly, Haywards Heath
15th-16th Sussex Garden Show, Borde Hill
Garden, Haywards Heath

June
2nd-5th Flower Festival, Chichester Cathedral
7th Spring Carnival, Southgate Playing Field,
Southgate Avenue, Crawley
9th-10th Corpus Christi Carpet of Flowers &
Floral Festival, Cathedral of Our Lady & St
Philip Howard, Arundel
10th-12th South of England Show,
Showground, Ardingly, Haywards Heath
19th-20th Parham Steam Rally, Pulborough
25th-27th Crawley Folk Festival, Crawley

July
2nd Pop in the Park, Tilgate Park, Crawley
3rd Prom in the Park, Crawley
15th-18th Southern Cathedrals Festival,
choirs of Chichester, Salisbury &
Winchester cathedrals, Chichester
Cathedral
30th-1st Aug Crawley International Mela, The
Hawth, Crawley
tbc Bognor Birdman (attempts at self-powered
flight), esplanade & seafront, Bognor Regis
tbc Chichester Festivities, various venues
tbc Petworth Festival (various Venues)

August
14th-15th Crawley Circus Festival, The
Hawth, Crawley (provisional)
tbc Arundel Festival
tbc Littlehampton Regatta, River Arun, Arun
Parade & Oyster Pond, Littlehampton

September
11th Findon Great Sheep Fair, Nepcote Green,
Findon (provisional)

October
2nd-3rd South of England Autumn Show,
Ardingly, Haywards Heath

Above: Chichester Harbour

AMBERLEY   Map 04 TQ01

AMBERLEY WORKING MUSEUM
BN18 9LT
➲ (on B2139, between Arundel and Storrington,
adjacent to Amberley railway station)
☎ 01798 831370 ▧ 01798 831831
e-mail: office@amberleymuseum.co.uk

36 acre open-air museum dedicated to the industrial heritage
of the south east of England. Traditional craftspeople on site
(including a blacksmith and potter), working narrow-gauge
railway and vintage bus collection, connected Earth
telecommunications display, Seeboard Electricity Hall,
stationary engines, print workshop, woodturners,
wheelwrights, nature trails, restaurant, shop and much more.
Times: Open 12 Mar-2 Nov, Wed-Sun & BH Mon 10-5.30 (last
admission 4.30). Also open daily during school holidays. **Fee:** ✱ £7.20
(ch 5-16 £4, pen & students £6.20). Family ticket (2 ad & 3 ch) £20.
Facilities: 🅿 💷 ᕟ (wheelchairs available for loan & large print
guides) toilets for disabled shop 🍽

ARDINGLY   Map 05 TQ32

WAKEHURST PLACE & MILLENNIUM SEED BANK
RH17 6TN
➲ (1.5m NW of Ardingley, on B2028)
☎ 01444 894066 ▧ 01444 894069
e-mail: wakehurst@kew.org

Woodland and lakes linked by a pretty watercourse make
this large garden a beautiful place to walk, and it also has an
amazing variety of interesting trees and shrubs, a winter
garden, and a rock walk. It is administered and maintained
by the Royal Botanic Gardens at Kew.
Times: Open all year, Nov-Jan 10-4; Feb & Oct 10-5; Mar 10-6; Apr-Sep
10-7. (Closed 25 Dec & 1 Jan). Last admission 30 mins before closing.
Mansion Restaurant, shop & exhibition closes one hour before garden
& car park. **Facilities:** 🅿 💷 ✗ licensed ᕟ (wheelchair available)
toilets for disabled shop garden centre 🍽 (ex guide dogs) 🍽

ARUNDEL   Map 04 TQ00

ARUNDEL CASTLE
BN18 9AB
➲ (on A27 between Chichester & Worthing)
☎ 01903 883136 ▧ 01903 884581
e-mail: info@arundelcastle.org

Set high on a hill in West Sussex, this magnificent castle and
stately home, seat of the Dukes of Norfolk for nearly 1000
years, commands stunning views across the river Arun and
out to sea. Climb to the keep and battlements; marvel at a
fine collection of 16th-century furniture; portraits by Van
Dyke, Gainsborough, Canaletto and others; tapestries and the
personal possessions of Mary, Queen of Scots; wander in the
grounds and renovated Victorian flower and vegetable
gardens.
Times: Open Apr-Oct, Sun-Fri 11-5 (Castle open 12-5). Last admission
4pm (Closed all Sat & Good Fri). **Fee:** ✱ £9 (ch 5-16 £5.50, pen £7).
Family ticket £24.50. Party 20+. **Facilities:** 🅿 💷 ᕟ toilets for
disabled shop 🍽 (ex guide dogs) 🍽

WWT ARUNDEL
Mill Rd BN18 9PB
➲ (signposted from A27 & A29)
☎ 01903 883355 📠 01903 884834 **2 for 1**
e-mail: arundel@wwt.org.uk

More than a thousand ducks, geese and swans from all over the world can be found here, many of which are so friendly that they will eat from your hand. The wild reserve attracts a variety of birds and includes a reedbed habitat considered so vital to the wetland wildlife it shelters that it has been designated a Site of Special Scientific Interest. Visitors can walk right through this reedbed on a specially designed boardwalk. There is a packed programme of events and activities throughout the year.
Times: Open all year, daily. Summer 9.30-5; Winter 9.30-4.30. Last admission Summer 5pm; Winter 4pm. (Closed 25 Dec). **Fee:** ✱ £5.50 (ch £3.50, pen £4.50). Family ticket £14.50. **Facilities:** 🅿 💷 ✗ licensed ♿ (level paths, free wheelchair loan) toilets for disabled shop ✗ (ex guide/hearing dogs) ⬤

ASHINGTON Map 04 TQ11

HOLLY GATE CACTUS GARDEN
Billingshurst Rd RH20 3BB
➲ (off A24, towards Ashington then B2133 towards Billingshurst for 0.5m)
☎ 01903 892930 **2 for 1**
e-mail: info@hollygatecactus.co.uk

A mecca for the cactus enthusiast, with more than 30,000 succulent and cactus plants, including many rare types. They come from both arid and tropical parts of the world, and are housed in over 10,000 sq ft of greenhouses.
Times: Open all year, daily 9-5. (Closed 25-26 Dec). **Fee:** ✱ £2 (ch & pen £1.50). Family ticket £6. Party 20+ 25p deduction. **Facilities:** 🅿 ♿ shop garden centre ✗ (ex guide dogs)

BIGNOR Map 04 SU91

BIGNOR ROMAN VILLA & MUSEUM
RH20 1PH
➲ (between A29 & A285, signposted)
☎ 01798 869259 📠 01798 869259
e-mail: bignorromanvilla@care4free.net

Rediscovered in 1811, this Roman house was built on a grand scale. It is one of the largest known, and has spectacular mosaics. The heating system can also be seen, and various finds from excavations are on show. The longest mosaic in Britain (82ft) is on display here in its original position.
Times: Open Mar-Apr Tue-Sun & BH 10-5, May 10-5 daily, Jun-Sep 10-6 daily, Oct 10-5 daily **Fee:** £3.80 (ch 5-15 £1.60, pen £2.70). Party 10+. Guided tours by arrangement. **Facilities:** 🅿 💷 ♿ Most areas accessible shop ✗ (ex guide dogs) ⬤

BRAMBER Map 04 TQ11

BRAMBER CASTLE
BN4 3FB **FREE**
➲ (on W side of village off A283)

The remains of a Norman motte and bailey castle. The gatehouse, still standing almost to its original height, and walls are still visible.
Times: Open any reasonable time. **Facilities:** 🅿 ⚘

CHICHESTER Map 04 SU80

CHICHESTER CATHEDRAL
West St PO19 1PX
➲ (in city centre) **FREE**
☎ 01243 782595 📠 01243 812499
e-mail: visitors@chichestercathedral.org.uk

The beauty of the 900-year-old cathedral, site of the shrine of St Richard, is enhanced by many art treasures, ancient and modern.
Times: Open daily end Mar-end Sep 7.15-7; end Sep-end Mar 7.15-6.
Facilities: 🅿 (within city walls) 💷 ✗ ♿ (touch & hearing centre, loop system) toilets for disabled shop ✗ (ex guide dogs)

MECHANICAL MUSIC & DOLL COLLECTION
Church Rd, Portfield PO19 4HN
➲ (1m E of Chichester, signposted off A27)
☎ 01243 372646 📠 01243 370299

A unique opportunity to see and hear barrel organs, polyphons, musical boxes, fair organs etc - all fully restored and playing. A magical musical tour to fascinate and entertain all ages. The doll collection contains fine examples of Victorian china and wax dolls, and felt and velvet dolls of the 1920s.
Times: Open Jun-Sep, Wed 1-4; Group bookings anytime in the year by prior arrangement. **Fee:** ✱ £2.50 (ch £1.25). **Facilities:** 🅿 ♿ shop ✗ (ex guide dogs)

PALLANT HOUSE GALLERY
9 North Pallant PO19 1TJ
➲ (from city centre (the Cross) take East St turning right at Superdrug. Gallery at end of North Pallant on left)
☎ 01243 774557 📠 01243 536038
e-mail: info@pallant.org.uk

A Queen Anne townhouse and a modern building have been combined to house a fine collection of 20th century British art. The permanent collection includes pieces by: Auerbach, Blake, Bomberg, Caulfield, Freud, Hamilton, Hitchens, Lege, Moore, Nash, Nicholson, Piper, Richards, Severini, Sickert and Sutherland. Telephone for details of temporary exhibitions.
Times: Closed until Spring 2004 for refurbishment **Fee:** ✱ £4 (ch & W Sussex students free, other students & unemployed £2.50, concessions £3). **Facilities:** 🅿 (100 yds) 💷 ✗ licensed ♿ toilets for disabled shop ✗ (ex guide dogs) ⬤

EAST GRINSTEAD Map 05 TQ33

STANDEN
RH19 4NE
➲ (2m S of East Grinstead, signposted from B2110)
☎ 01342 323029 📠 01342 316424
e-mail: standen@ntrust.org.uk

Standen is a showpiece of the 19th-century Arts and Crafts movement. It was designed by Philip Webb for the Beale family, and was intended for decoration with William Morris wallpapers and fabrics. The interior has been carefully preserved. Webb also designed some of the furniture and details. There is a beautiful hillside garden. Telephone for details of special events.
Times: ✱ House open Apr-Nov, Wed-Sun & BH 11-5. Garden open same dates as house 11-6 & Nov-mid Dec, Fri-Sun 11-3. Last entry to house 4.30 **Facilities:** 🅿 ✗ licensed ♿ (Braille guide & touch list) shop ✗ (ex guide dogs & on wood walk) ⚘ ⬤

FISHBOURNE — Map 04 SU80

FISHBOURNE ROMAN PALACE
Salthill Rd PO19 3QR
➲ (off A27 onto A259 into Fishbourne. Turn right
into Salthill Rd & right into Roman Way)
☎ 01243 785859 ▤ 01243 539266
e-mail: adminfish@sussexpast.co.uk

This is the largest known Roman residence in Britain. It was
occupied from the 1st to the 3rd centuries AD, and has
mosaic floors and painted walls. 25 of these mosaic floors
can still be seen in varying states of completeness, including
others rescued from elsewhere in the area. Outside, part of
the garden has been replanted to its original 1st-century
plan. The museum displays a collection of finds from the
excavations and tells the story of the site's discovery. An
audio-visual presentation helps bring the site back to life, as
it would have been many centuries ago.
Times: Open all year, daily Feb-15 Dec. Feb, Nov-Dec 10-4; Mar-Jul &
Sep-Oct 10-5; Aug 10-6. Winter wknds 10-4. **Fee:** ✱ £5 (ch £2.60, pen
& students £4.30, registered disabled £3.90). Family ticket £12.90 (2 ad
& 2 ch). Group rates available. **Facilities:** ▣ ▣ ₺ (self guiding tapes
& tactile objects for the blind) toilets for disabled shop garden centre
✕ (ex guide dogs) ▧

FONTWELL — Map 04 SU90

DENMANS GARDEN
Denmans Ln BN18 0SU
➲ (5m E of Chichester off A27 W between
Chichester and Arundel, adjacent to Fontwell
racecourse) **2 for 1**
☎ 01243 542808 ▤ 01243 544064
e-mail: denmans@denmans-garden.co.uk

A unique 20th-century garden artistically planted with an
emphasis on colour, shape and texture. Plants within the
garden are allowed to self-seed and ramble. The garden
makes much use of gravel throughout, including a gravel
'stream'. A remarkable collection of plants, including glass
areas for tender plants, a walled garden and plenty of quiet
sitting areas.
Times: Open Mar-Oct daily 9-5. **Fee:** ✱ £2.95 (ch £1.75, ch under 4
free, pen £2.65). Party 15+ £2.50 each. **Facilities:** ▣ ▣ ₺ shop
garden centre ✕ (ex guide dogs) ▧

GOODWOOD — Map 04 SU81

GOODWOOD HOUSE
PO18 0PX
➲ (3m NE of Chichester)
☎ 01243 755000 ▤ 01243 755005
e-mail: curator@goodwood.co.uk

Ancestral home of the Dukes of Richmond for 300 years.
Following refurbishment the State Apartments have taken on
new life, including the restored tapestry drawing room.
Goodwood was the country home of the scandalous and
glamorous Lennox sisters, immortalised in the BBC TV
production of *Aristocrats*. Unrivalled as an English ancestral
collection, the paintings include works by Van Dyck,
Reynolds, Stubbs and Canaletto.
Times: Open 30 Mar-6 Oct, Sun & Mon; 3-28 Aug, Sun-Thu 1-5.
(Closed 13 Apr, 22 Jun, 6, 7, 13 & 14 Jul & 7 Sep). **Fee:** ✱ £7 (ch,
disabled & student £3, pen £6). Groups 20+ £6 each. **Facilities:** ▣
▣ ₺ (ramp at front of house, disabled parking area) toilets for
disabled shop ✕ ▧

HANDCROSS — Map 04 TQ22

NYMANS GARDEN
RH17 6EB
➲ (on B2114)
☎ 01444 400321 & 400777 ▤ 01444 400253

Set in the Sussex Weald, Nymans has flowering shrubs and
roses, a flower garden in the old walled orchard, and a
secret sunken garden. There are some fine and rare trees.
Summer events are held in the garden. For details please call
regional box office (01372) 451596.
Times: ✱ Open Garden: Mar-29 Oct, daily Wed, Thu & wknds, (also
open BH Mon) 11-6 or sunset if earlier. Nov-Mar, wknds, 11-4, restricted
according to ground conditions. Closed 25-26 & 30-31 Dec. Phone for
more information. House open 29 Mar-29 Oct 12-4. **Facilities:** ▣ ▣
₺ (wheelchair route, wheelchair available, braille guide) toilets for
disabled shop ✕ (ex guide dogs & hearing dogs) ▨

HAYWARDS HEATH — Map 05 TQ32

BORDE HILL GARDEN
Balcombe Rd RH16 1XP
➲ (0.5m N of Haywards Heath on Balcombe Road,
3m from A23)
☎ 01444 450326 ▤ 01444 440427
e-mail: info@bordehill.co.uk

Beauty for all seasons with formal 'garden rooms' such as
the Rose and Italian Garden, combine with informal areas
like the Azalea Ring, the Garden of Allah and the Round Dell.
A plantsman's paradise, with rare trees and shrubs
introduced in the early 1900s by the Great Plant Collectors
from all corners of the world. Spring is heralded early by a
magnificent collection of magnolias, rhododendron and
azaleas, blending into summer with fragrant roses and
herbaceous plants, developing into rich autumn borders
before winter's architectural splendour. Magical woodland
and parkland walks with outstanding views across the
impressive Victorian viaduct.
Times: Open all year, daily 10-6 or dusk if earlier. **Fee:** £6 (ch £3.50).
Party 20+ £5 (ch £3) each. **Facilities:** ▣ ▣ ✕ licensed ₺
(wheelchairs available, audio/Braille guides) toilets for disabled shop
garden centre (must be on lead) ▧

LITTLEHAMPTON   Map 04 TQ00

LOOK & SEA! VISITOR CENTRE
63-65 Surrey St BN17 5AW
➲ (on harbour front)
☎ 01903 718984 🖹 01903 718036
e-mail: info@lookandsea.co.uk

An interactive museum exploring the history and geography of Littlehampton and the surrounding area. Inside the modern waterfront building you can meet the 500,000 year old Boxgrove Man, become a ship's captain in an interactive computer game, and enjoy spectacular panoramic views of the Sussex coast from the circular glass tower.
Times: Open May-Oct, daily 10-5; Nov-Mar, Fri-Mon 11-4 **Fee:** ✱ £4.50 (ch £2.70, pen & student £3.50). Family ticket (2 adults + 2 ch) £14 **Facilities:** 🅿 💻 🚻 toilets for disabled shop ✖ (ex guide dogs) 🍴

LOWER BEEDING   Map 04 TQ22

LEONARDSLEE GARDENS
RH13 6PP
➲ (4m SW from Handcross, at junct of B2110 & A281)
☎ 01403 891212 🖹 01403 891305
e-mail: gardens@leonardslee.com
This Grade I listed garden is set in a peaceful valley with walks around seven beautiful lakes. It is a paradise in spring, with banks of rhododendrons and azaleas along paths lined with bluebells. Wallabies live in parts of the valley, deer in the parks and wildfowl on the lakes. Enjoy the Rock Garden, the fascinating Bonsai, the new 'Behind the Doll's House' exhibition and the collection of Victorian Motorcars (1889-1900).
Times: ✱ Open Apr-Oct, daily 9.30-6 **Facilities:** 🅿 💻 ✖ licensed (No wheelchair access) shop garden centre ✖

FREE

Attractions with this symbol do not charge for entry.

PETWORTH   Map 04 SU92

PETWORTH HOUSE & PARK
GU28 0AE
➲ (in town centre, A272/283)
☎ 01798 342207 & 343929 🖹 01798 342963
e-mail: petworth@ntrust.org.uk
Petworth house is an impressive 17th-century mansion set in a 700 acre Deer Park, landscaped by 'Capability' Brown, and immortalised in Turner's paintings. At Petworth you will find the National Trust's finest art collection including work by Van Dyck, Titian, and Turner as well as sculpture ceramics and fine furniture. Fascinating servants' quarters show the domestic side of life of this great estate.
Times: ✱ Open 23 Mar-3 Nov (closed Thu & Fri) 11-5.30 last entry 5
Facilities: 🅿 💻 ✖ licensed ♿ (wheelchairs available, Braille guide) toilets for disabled shop ✖ (ex guide/hearing dogs) 🍴 🍴

PULBOROUGH   Map 04 TQ01

PARHAM HOUSE & GARDENS
Parham Park RH20 4HS
➲ (midway between A29 & A24, off A283 between Pulborough & Storrington)
☎ 01903 744888 & 742021 🖹 01903 746557
e-mail: enquiries@parhaminsussex.co.uk
Surrounded by a deer park, fine gardens and 18th-century Pleasure Grounds in a beautiful downland setting, this Elizabethan family home contains an important collection of paintings, furniture, carpets and rare needlework. A brick and turf maze has been created in the grounds - designed with children in mind, it is called `Veronica's Maze'.
Times: Open Etr Sun-Sep, Wed, Thu, Sun & BH (also open Tue & Fri in Aug). Gardens open 12-6; House 2-6 (last entry 5). Guided tours on Wed & Thu mornings & Tue & Fri afternoons by special arrangement.
Fee: ✱ House & Gardens £6 (ch 5-15 £2, pen & disabled visitors £5.50). Family ticket £14. Gardens only £4 (ch £1). Party rates available.
Facilities: 🅿 💻 ♿ (wheelchairs, ramps, recorded tour tape, parking) toilets for disabled shop garden centre ✖ (ex guide dogs & in grounds) 🍴

RSPB PULBOROUGH BROOKS NATURE RESERVE
Uppertons Barn Visitor Centre, Wiggonholt RH20 2EL
➲ (signposted on A283, 2m SE of Pulborough & 2m NW of Storrington)
☎ 01798 875851
e-mail: pulborough.brooks@rspb.org.uk
Set in the scenic Arun Valley and easily reached via the visitor centre at Wiggonholt, this is an excellent reserve for year-round family visits. A nature trail winds through hedgerow-lined lanes to viewing hides overlooking water-meadows. Breeding summer birds include nightingales and warblers, ducks and wading birds, and nightjars and hobbies on nearby heathland. Unusual wading birds and hedgerow birds regularly pass through on spring and autumn migration.
Times: Open daily, Reserve: 9-9, (or sunset if earlier). Visitor centre: 10-5. Reserve closed 26 Dec, Visitor Centre closed 25-26 Dec.
Fee: ✱ £3.50 (ch £1 concession £2.50) Family ticket £7. **Facilities:** 🅿 💻 ♿ (ramps at some hides/batricar bookable/easy gradient trail) toilets for disabled shop ✖ (ex guide dogs) 🍴

SINGLETON Map 04 SU81

WEALD & DOWNLAND OPEN AIR MUSEUM

PO18 0EU

➲ (6m N of Chichester on A286)

☎ 01243 811348 🖃 01243 811475

e-mail: office@wealddown.co.uk

A showcase of English architectural heritage, where historic buildings have been rescued from destruction and rebuilt in a parkland setting. Vividly demonstrating the evolution of building techniques and use of local materials, these fascinating buildings bring to life the homes, farms and rural industries of the south east of the past 500 years.
Times: Open all year, Mar-Oct, daily 10.30-6 (last admission 5); Nov-Feb, Sat & Sun 10.30-4, also 26 Dec-1 Jan daily & Feb half term, 10.30-4. **Fee:** ✹ £7 (ch & students £4, pen £6.50). Family ticket (2 adults & 3 ch) £19. Party. **Facilities:** 🅿 🖭 ♿ (separate entrance and ramps available for some buildings) toilets for disabled shop (ex on leads) ⬗

SOUTH HARTING Map 04 SU71

UPPARK

GU31 5QR

➲ (A3 take A272, B2146 to South Harting, follow signs to Uppark.)

☎ 01730 825415 825857 🖃 01730 825873

e mail: uppark@ntrust.org.uk

On 30th August 1989 this late 17th-century house was partially destroyed by fire. The attic and the first floor were completely gutted, but virtually all of the 18th-century contents were saved. Following an ambitious restoration project, Uppark has been restored to its state 'the day before the fire'.
Times: ✹ Open 24 Mar-Oct, Sun-Thu. House 1-5. Car park, woodland walk, garden & Exhibition 11-5. Last admission to house 4pm. Timed tickets will be in operation on BH Sun & Mon & Sun in Aug. House open 12-5 on Sun in Aug. **Facilities:** 🅿 🖭 ✕ licensed ♿ (ramps, lift to basement, chair lift in exhibition) toilets for disabled shop ✖ (ex woodland walk & car park) ✿ ⬗

TANGMERE Map 04 SU90

TANGMERE MILITARY AVIATION MUSEUM TRUST

PO20 2ES

➲ (off A27, 3m E of Chichester on the Arundel side)

☎ 01243 775223 🖃 01243 789490

e-mail: admin@tangmere-museum.org.uk

Based at an airfield that played an important role during the World Wars, this museum spans 80 years of military aviation. There are photographs, documents, aircraft and aircraft parts on display along with a Hurricane replica, Spitfire replica and cockpit simulator. A hangar houses a Supermarine Swift and the record-breaking aircraft Meteor and Hunter.
Times: Open Mar-Oct, daily 10-5.30; Feb & Nov, daily 10-4.30. **Fee:** ✹ £4 (ch £1.50 & pen £3) Family £9.50 (2 ad & 2 ch). **Facilities:** 🅿 🖭 ♿ (wheelchairs available) toilets for disabled shop ✖ (ex guide dogs)

WEST DEAN Map 04 SU81

WEST DEAN GARDENS

Estate Office PO18 0QZ

➲ (on A286, 6m N of Chichester)

☎ 01243 818210 & 811301 🖃 01243 811342

e-mail: gardens@westdean.org.uk

Award winning historic garden of 35 acres in a tranquil downland setting. Noted for its 300ft long Harold Peto pergola, mixed and herbaceous borders, rustic summerhouses and specimen trees. Walled kitchen garden with magnificent collection of 16 Victorian glasshouses and frames. The visitors' centre provides a high level of facilities with a beautiful prospect of the River Lavant and West Dean Park.
Times: Open Mar, Apr & Oct, daily 11-5; May-Sep 10.30-5. Last ticket 4.30pm. **Fee:** ✹ £5 (ch £2, pen £4.50). Party+ £4.50. **Facilities:** 🅿 ✕ licensed ♿ (reserved parking, 2 wheelchairs available) toilets for disabled shop ✖ (ex guide dogs) ⬗

TYNE & WEAR

EVENTS & FESTIVALS

April
  10th-12th Gateshead Spring Flower Show,
    Gateshead Central Nursery (provisional)

July
  2nd-4th Whitby Bay
    International Jazz Festival
  24th-25th Sunderland International Air Show,
    Promenade, Seaburn, Sunderland
    (provisional)
  30th-1st Aug Gateshead Summer Flower Show,
    Gateshead Central Nursery

August
  30th Jul-1st Gateshead Summer Flower Show,
    Gateshead Central Nursery (provisional)
  29th-30th Newcastle Mela (free Asian festival),
    Exhibition Park, Newcastle-upon-Tyne
  tbc North of England Motorshow, Gosforth
    Park Racecourse, Newcastle

September/October
  tbc Great North Run (Newcastle-upon-Tyne to
    South Shields)
  tbc Junior Great North Run, Gateshead
    International Stadium, Gateshead

November
  tbc Newcastle Comedy Festival (various
    venues), Newcastle-upon-Tyne

Above: The Tyne Bridge, Newcastle
Top: Angel of the North, Gateshead

GATESHEAD   Map 12 NZ26

BALTIC THE CENTRE FOR CONTEMPORARY ART
South Shore Rd NE8 3BA
➲ (on quayside)
☎ 0191 478 1810   ▤ 0191 478 1922   FREE
e-mail: info@balticmill.com

Once a 1950s grain warehouse, part of the Baltic Flour Mills,
this industrial brick building now accommodates 3000
square metres of gallery space, studios, and archives, along
with a shop and three eating places. The exhibitions, and the
work of artists-in-residence here are unashamedly
contemporary, and include film, photography, sculpture,
painting, and sound.
Times: Open Mon-Wed, Fri & Sat 10-7, Thu 10-10 and Sun 10-5.
Facilities: 🅿 (charged) 💺✗ licensed ⓰ toilets for disabled shop ✖
(ex guide dogs)

JARROW   Map 12 NZ36

BEDES WORLD & ST PAUL'S CHURCH
Church Bank NE32 3DY
➲ (off A185 near south end of Tyne tunnel)
☎ 0191 489 2106   ▤ 0191 428 2361   2 for 1
e-mail: visitor.info@bedesworld.co.uk

The Venerable Bede lived over 1300 years ago and was one
of early Britain's greatest scholars, author of the "Historia
Ecclesiastica Gentis Anglorum" - the definitive history of the
early medieval period. As well as exhibits detailing Bede's
monastic life and work, the museum re-creates an
Anglo-Saxon farm and incorporates the ruins of the
medieval monastery.
Times: Open all year, Apr-Oct, Mon-Sat 10-5.30, Sun noon-5.30;
Nov-Mar, Mon-Sat 10-4.30 & Sun 12-4.30; Xmas-New Year opening
times vary. Church open Mon-Sat 10-4 & Sun 2.30-4, unless service
being held. **Fee:** ✱ £4.50 (ch & concessions £2.50). Family ticket £9.
UB40 Family ticket £6. Party rates 15+. **Facilities:** 🅿 💺 ⓰
(wheelchair & elec. wheelchair on request, disabled parking) toilets for
disabled shop ✖ (ex guide dogs) ☜

NEWCASTLE UPON TYNE   Map 12 NZ26

HANCOCK MUSEUM
Barras Bridge NE2 4PT
➲ (Follow exit signs for city centre A167 off
the A1)
☎ 0191 222 7418   ▤ 0191 222 6753
e-mail: hancock.museum@ncl.ac.uk

Newcastle's premier Natural History museum unravels the
natural world, through sensational galleries and close
encounters with resident reptiles and insects. For more than
one hundred years the Hancock Museum has provided
visitors with a glimpse of the animal kingdom and the
powerful and often destructive forces of nature. From the
Dinosaurs to live animals, the Hancock is home to creatures
past and present and the odd Egyptian mummy or two.
Times: Open all year, Mon-Sat, 10-5, Sun 2-5. Closed 25 & 26 Dec & 1
Jan. **Fee:** £2.50 (ch & concessions £1.75). Family ticket (2 ad & 2 ch)
£7.25. Prices vary with special exhibitions, call 0191 222 7418 for details.
Facilities: 🅿 💺 ⓰ (stair lift, audio & Braille guide, sign language)
toilets for disabled shop ✖ (ex guide dogs) ☜

LIFE SCIENCE CENTRE
Times Square NE1 4EP
➲ (A1m, A69, A184, A1058 & A167, follow signs to the Life Science Centre or Central station)
☎ 0191 243 8223 & 0191 243 8210
▤ 0191 2438201
e-mail: bookings@lifesciencecentre.co.uk

The Life Science Centre is an interactive, action-packed day out that takes the visitor to the beginning of life and back again. From single-celled organisms to dinosaurs, from 4 billion years ago to today, this is a fascinating attraction that deals with perhaps the most fundamental subject of all: Life Itself.
Times: Open daily Mon-Sat 10-6, Sun 11-6 . Closed 25 Dec & 1 Jan. (Last entry subject to seasonal demand). **Fee:** ✱ £6.95 (ch £4.50, concessions £5.50). Family ticket £19.95. **Facilities:** ▣ (charged) ▭ ✗ licensed ♿ (ramps, wheelchairs, induction loops) toilets for disabled shop ✈ (ex guide dogs) ▰

MUSEUM OF ANTIQUITIES
The University NE1 7RU
➲ (on campus of Newcastle University)
☎ 0191 222 7849   ▤ 0191 222 8561   FREE
e-mail: m.o.antiquities@ncl.ac.uk

Artefacts from north east England from prehistoric times to AD 1600 are on display here. The principal museum for Hadrian's Wall, this collection includes models of the wall, life-size Roman soldiers and a recently refurbished reconstruction of the Temple of Mithras.
Times: Open all year, daily (ex Sun), 10-5 (Closed Good Fri, 24-26 Dec & 1 Jan). **Facilities:** ▣ (400yds) ♿ (Large print guide) shop ✈ (ex guide dogs) ▰

ROWLANDS GILL   Map 12 NZ15
GIBSIDE
NE16 6BG
➲ (turn off A1 western Bypass following brown tourist signs from Gibside & Gibside Chapel, 3m W of Metro Centre & 6m SW of Gateshead, on B6314)
☎ 01207 542255
e-mail: tony.walton@ntrust.org.uk

The important early 18th-century landscaped park contains a chapel - an outstanding example of Palladian architecture, built to a design by James Paine as the mausoleum for members of the Bowes family. It stands at one end of the Great Walk of Turkey oaks, looking towards the column of British Liberty.
Times: Open: Grounds all year (ex Mon), 10-4.30. Open BH Mon (Mar-Oct 10-5, Nov-Feb 10-3.30). Chapel: Apr-Oct as grounds 11-5, otherwise by prior arrangment. **Facilities:** ▣ ▭ ♿ (Braille guide, wheelchairs & wheelchair carrier) toilets for disabled shop ❅ ▰

SOUTH SHIELDS   Map 12 NZ36
ARBEIA ROMAN FORT & MUSEUM
Baring St NE33 2BB
➲ (5 mins walk from South Shields Town Centre)
☎ 0191 456 1369 & 454 4093
▤ 0191 427 6862

In South Shields town are the extensive remains of Arbeia, a Roman fort in use from the 2nd to 4th century. It was the supply base for the Roman army's campaign against
continued

Scotland. On site there are full size reconstructions of a fort gateway, a barrack block and part of the commanding officer's house. Archaeological evacuations are in progress throughout the summer.
Times: Open all year, Etr-Sep, Mon-Sat 10.30-5.30, Sun 1-5; Oct-Etr, Mon-Sat 10-4. Closed 25-26 Dec, 1 Jan & Good Fri. **Facilities:** ▣ ♿ (Minicom system) toilets for disabled shop ▰

SUNDERLAND   Map 12 NZ35
MUSEUM & WINTER GARDENS
Burdon Rd SR1 1PP
➲ (situated in Sunderland City Centre)
☎ 0191 553 2323   ▤ 0191 553 7828
e-mail: sunderland.museum@ tyne-wear-museums.org.uk

This award-winning attraction re-opened in 2001. The wide-ranging displays, with many hands-on exhibits, cover the archaeology and geology of Sunderland, the coal mines and shipyards of the area and the spectacular glass and pottery made on Wearside. Other galleries show the changes in the lifestyles of Sunderland women over the past century, works by LS Lowry and wildlife from all corners of the globe. The Winter Gardens is a horticultural wonderland where the exotic plants from around the world can be seen growing to their full natural height in a spectacular glass and steel rotunda.
Times: Open all year, Mon 10-4, Tue-Sat 10-5, Sun 2-5. **Facilities:** ▣ (150 yds) ✗ licensed ♿ (lifts to all floors, induction loops) toilets for disabled shop ✈ (ex guide dogs) ▰

NATIONAL GLASS CENTRE
Liberty Way SR6 0GL
☎ 0191 515 5555   ▤ 0191 515 5556   2 for 1
e-mail: info@nationalglasscentre.com

Housed in a striking modern building, the National Glass Centre celebrates the unique material and explains its history. Visitors can see the changing exhibitions of glass art, featuring pieces by leading artists. There is also the opportunity to witness the glass-making process and learn more about the substance and how it impacts on our lives. The brave can even walk on the glass roof 30 feet above the riverside.
Times: Open daily 10-5 (last admission to glass tour 4pm). Closed 25 Dec & 1 Jan. **Fee:** £5 (concessions £3). Family ticket £12. **Facilities:** ▣ ✗ licensed ♿ (lifts, ramps, parking facilites) toilets for disabled shop ✈ (ex guide dogs) ▰

TYNEMOUTH   Map 12 NZ36
BLUE REEF AQUARIUM   2 for 1
Grand Pde NE30 4JF
➲ (from A19 take A1058, situated on seafront)
☎ 0191 258 1031   ▤ 0191 257 2116
e-mail: tynemouth@bluereefaquarium.co.uk

From its position overlooking one of the North East's prettiest beaches, Blue Reef is home to a dazzling variety of creatures including seahorses, puffer fish, octopi, and even the deadly piranha. Visitors can walk through an underwater tunnel in a 250,000 litre tropical ocean tank. This offers close encounters with all manner of undersea wonders like sharks and stingrays.
Times: Open daily from 10am. (Closed 25 Dec) **Fee:** ✱ £4.95 (pen & student £4.25, ch £3.25). Family ticket (2 adults + 3 ch) £14.95 **Facilities:** ▣ ▭ ♿ toilets for disabled shop ✈ (ex guide dogs) ▰

TYNEMOUTH PRIORY AND CASTLE
NE30 4BZ
⮕ (near North Pier)
☎ 0191 257 1090

Discover a rich and varied history as you explore the priory, castle and underground chambers beneath a World War I gun battery.
Times: Open all year, Apr-Sep, daily 10-6; Oct, daily 10-5; Nov-Mar, Wed-Sun 10-4. Closed between 1-2 in winter, 24-26 Dec & 1 Jan). Dates valid until 31 Mar 2004. **Fee:** £2.50 (ch £1.30, concessions £1.90). Prices valid until 31 Mar 2004. **Facilities:** �& (wheelchair access to priory) shop ✲ (ex dogs on leads) ⌗

WALLSEND   Map 12 NZ26
SEGEDUNUM ROMAN FORT, BATHS & MUSEUM
Buddle St NE28 6HR
⮕ (A187 from Tyne Tunnel, signposted)   2 for 1
☎ 0191 236 9347   📠 0191 295 5858
e-mail: segedunum@twmuseums.org.uk

Hadrian's Wall was built by the Roman Emperor, Hadrian in 122AD, Segedunum was built as part of the Wall, serving as a garrison for 600 soldiers until the collapse of Roman rule around 410AD. This major historical venture shows what life would have been like then, using artefacts, audio-visuals, reconstructed buildings and a 34m high viewing tower.
Times: Open all year, Apr-Oct, daily 10-5; Nov-Mar, daily 10-3.30. (Closed 25-26 Dec & 1 Jan) **Fee:** ✱ £3.50 (ch, pen & concessions £1.95). Family ticket £9 **Facilities:** 🅿 ➡ & (lifts) toilets for disabled shop ✲ (ex guide dogs) ◖

WASHINGTON   Map 12 NZ35
WASHINGTON OLD HALL
The Avenue, Washington Village NE38 7LE
⮕ (from A1 and A19 follow signs to Washington, then District 4. The Avenue, next to Holy Trinity Church)
☎ 0191 416 6879   📠 0191 4192065
e-mail: nwohal@smtp.ntrust.org.uk

The home of George Washington's ancestors from 1183 to 1613, the Old Hall was originally an early medieval manor, but was rebuilt in the 17th century. The house has been restored and filled with period furniture. Exhibitions include stepping back in time and enjoying the peace and quite in the beautifully-planted Knot Parterre gardens, The Jacobean Great Hall, Kitchen, Panelled room and the Liberty Room celebrating American Independence and the life of George Washington.
Times: Open Apr-Oct, Sun-Wed & Good Fri 11-5. Last admission 4.30.
Facilities: 🅿 ➡ & (Braille guide, sensory scented gardens, handrails, ramps) toilets for disabled shop ✲ (ex guide dogs) ◣

WWT WASHINGTON
District 15 NE38 8LE
⮕ (signposted off A195, A1231 & A182)
☎ 0191 416 5454   📠 0191 416 5801   2 for 1
e-mail: washington@wwt.org.uk

In a parkland setting, on the north bank of the River Wear, WWT Washington is the home of a wonderful collection of exotic wildfowl from all over the world. There is also a heronry where visitors can watch a colony of wild Grey Herons on CCTV. The 100-acre site includes an area for wintering wildfowl which can be observed from hides, and a flock of Chilean Flamingos. Other features include a discovery centre, waterfowl nursery, picture windows and a viewing gallery from which to observe the birds.
Times: Open all year, daily 9.30-5 (summer) or 9.30-4 (winter). Closed 25 Dec. **Fee:** ✱ £5.50 (ch £3.50, concessions £4.50). Family £14.50.
Facilities: 🅿 ➡ ✕ licensed & (lowered windows in certain hides, wheelchairs to hire free) toilets for disabled shop ✲ (ex guide/hearing dogs) ◖

WHITBURN   Map 12 NZ46
SOUTER LIGHTHOUSE
Coast Rd SR6 7NH
⮕ (On A183 coast road, 2m S of South Shields, 3m N of Sunderland).
☎ 0191 529 3161 & 01670 773966
📠 0191 529 0902
e-mail: nslhse@smtp.ntrust.org.uk

When it opened in 1871, Souter was the most advanced lighthouse in the world. Painted red and white and standing at 150ft high, it is a dramatic building and hands-on displays and volunteers help bring it to life. The Engine and Battery Rooms are all in working order and are included in the guided tour, along with the light tower and museum cottage.
Times: ✱ Open Apr-Oct daily ex Fri, (open Good Fri), 11-5. Last admission 4.30. Please contact for opening at other times.
Facilities: 🅿 ✕ & Braille guide, induction loops, tactile exhibits toilets for disabled shop ✲ (ex guide dogs) ◣ ◖

WARWICKSHIRE

EVENTS & FESTIVALS

March
20th-21st Spring Craft Fair, Ragley Hall,
Alcester (provisional)

April
10th-11th Gardeners Weekend, Ragley Hall,
Alcester (provisional)
30th-9th May Leamington Festival

May
30th-31st Transport Show, Ragley Hall,
Alcester (provisional)
30th Apr-9th Leamington Festival

July
1st-11th Warwick Festival, various venues
4th-7th The Royal Show, National Agricultural
Centre, Stoneleigh Park
23rd-25th Warwick Folk Festival
(various venues)

August
8th Caspian Horses Show, Ragley Hall,
Alcester (provisional)
14th-15th Warwickshire & West Midlands
Game Fair, Ragley Hall, Alcester
(provisional)
28th-30th Town & Country Festival, NAC
Stoneleigh

September
11th-12th Harvest Gardening Festival, Ragley
Hall, Alcester (provisional)

October
tbc Autumn Craft Fair, Ragley Hall, Alcester
(provisional)

November
27th-28th Yuletide Craft Fair, Ragley Hall,
Alcester (provisional)

*Above: Memorial to William Shakespeare, Bancroft
Gardens, Stratford-on-Avon*

ALCESTER   Map 04 SP05
RAGLEY HALL
B49 5NJ
➲ (8m SW of Stratford upon Avon,off A46/A435,
follow brown tourist signs)
☎ 01789 762090 🖷 01789 764791
e-mail: info@ragleyhall.com
Built in 1680, Ragley is the family home of the Marquess and
Marchioness of Hertford and houses a superb collection of
18th century paintings, porcelain and furniture. Set in 27
acres of gardens and 400 acres of parkland, The House
contains a stunning mural by Graham Rust "The Temptation"
and England's finest Baroque plasterwork dated 1750. Ticket
includes the House, Terrace Tea Rooms overlooking the Rose
Garden, Gift Shop, Adventure Playground, unique 3D Maze,
Lakeside Picnic area, Woodland Walk and Stables containing
equestrian memorabilia. Location for BBC production of
Scarlet Pimpernel.
Times: Open mid Apr-end Sep, Thu-Sun & BH Mon. Park & Garden
open daily, mid Jul-end Aug. **Fee:** ✱ House (including garden & park)
£6 (ch £4.50, pen £5). £1 entry to state rooms. **Facilities:** 🅿 💷 ♿
(lift to first floor) toilets for disabled shop (on leads in park only)

BADDESLEY CLINTON   Map 04 SP27
BADDESLEY CLINTON HALL
B93 0DQ
➲ (0.75m W off A4141, 7.5m NW of Warwick)
☎ 01564 783294   `2 for 1`
🖷 01564 782706
e-mail: baddesleyclinton@nationaltrust.org.uk
A romantically-sited medieval moated house, dating from the
14th century, that has changed very little since 1634. With
family portraits, priest holes, chapel, garden, ponds, nature
trail and lake walk. An autumn lecture programme is
planned.
Times: Open Garden, Restaurant & Shop: 5 Mar-30 Apr & Oct-2 Nov,
Wed-Sun 12-5; May-Sep, Wed-Sun 12-5.30; 5 Nov-14 Dec, Wed-Sun
12-4.30. House: 5 Mar-30 Apr & Oct-2 Nov, Wed-Sun 1.30-5; May-Sep,
Wed-Sun 1.30-5.30. **Fee:** ✱ Garden only £3 (ch £1.50). House &
Garden £6 (ch £3). Family ticket £15. Joint ticket with Packwood House
£8.60 (ch £4.30). Family ticket £21.50. Joint ticket for gardens only
£4.30 (ch £2.15). National Trust members and children under 5 free.
Facilities: 🅿 ✗ licensed ♿ (wheelchairs for hire, Braille guides, tactile
route) toilets for disabled shop ✈ (ex guide dogs) 🍷 🍴

CHARLECOTE   Map 04 SP25
CHARLECOTE PARK
CV35 9ER
➲ (5m E of Stratford, 1m W of Wellesbourne on
B4086)
☎ 01789 470277 🖷 01789 470544
e-mail: charlecote@smtp.ntrust.org.uk
Built in the 1550s and later visited by Queen Elizabeth I,
Charlecote Park was landscaped by 'Capability' Brown.
Fallow deer, reputedly poached by Shakespeare, and a flock
of Jacob sheep first introduced in 1756. The principal rooms
are decorated in Elizabethan Revival style.
Times: Open 6 Mar-2 Nov; 12-5. Fri-Tue 12-5. Gardens 11-6
Facilities: 🅿 💷 ✗ licensed ♿ (Braille guides & hearing scheme
available) toilets for disabled shop ✈ 🍷 🍴

COUGHTON   Map 04 SP06
COUGHTON COURT
B49 5JA
➲ (2m N of Alcester on E side of A435)
☎ 01789 762435 400702 ▤ 01789 765544

During the Civil War this formerly moated and mainly Elizabethan house was attacked by both Parliamentary and Royalist forces. There are exhibitions on the Gunpowder Plot and Children's Clothes. Outdoor concert with fireworks in July.
Times: Open Apr-Jun, Wed-Sun; Jul-Aug, Tue-Sun; Sep, Wed-Sun; Oct wknds only. Also open BH Mons. (Closed 21 Jun). **Fee:** ✱ £7.95 (ch £3.95). Family ticket £23-£26.50. Garden only £5.10 (ch £2.50). Family ticket £15-£17.25. **Facilities:** ⬛ (charged) ✗ licensed ⴺ (Braille guide, wheelchair available) toilets for disabled shop ✕ (ex guide dogs)
⬥ ⬤

FARNBOROUGH   Map 04 SP44
FARNBOROUGH HALL
OX17 1DU
➲ (6m N of Banbury, 0.5m W of A423)
☎ 01295 690002

A classical mid 18th-century stone house with notable plasterwork; the entrance hall, staircase and two principal rooms are shown. The grounds contain charming 18th-century temples, a 3/4-mile terrace walk and an obelisk.
Times: ✱ House, grounds & terrace walk open Apr-Sep, Wed & Sat, 5 & 6 May 2-6. Terrace walk Thu & Fri by appointment only, 2-6. Last admission 5.30pm. (Closed Good Friday) **Fee:** ✱ House, Garden & Terrace walk £3.60 (ch £1.80), Family £9. Terrace walk £1.80. Terrace walk only (Thu & Fri) £1. **Facilities:** ⬛ ⴺ ✕ (ex guide dogs) ⬥

GAYDON   Map 04 SP35
HERITAGE MOTOR CENTRE
Banbury Rd CV35 0BJ
➲ (M40 Junct 12 and take B4100. Heritage motor centre is signposted from this junct)
☎ 01926 641188 ▤ 01926 641555
e-mail: enquiries@heritage-motor-centre.co.uk

Home to the largest collection of historic British cars anywhere in the world, the Heritage Motor Centre is set in 65 acres of grounds. Attractions at the Centre include the Time Road, a fascinating journey through Britain's motoring and

continued

social history, the motoring cinema, and the 'Get Behind the Wheel' zone, where visitors get the chance to sit in a variety of cars from the collection. Outside, there are go-kart tracks and a children's electric roadway.
Times: Open daily 10-5. (Closed 24-26 Dec). **Fee:** ✱ £8 (ch 5-16 £6, under 5 free, & pen £7). Family ticket £25. Additional charges apply to outdoor activities **Facilities:** ⬛ ⬤ ⴺ (lift to all floors, limited number of manual wheelchairs) toilets for disabled shop ✕ (ex guide/hearing dogs) ⬤

KENILWORTH   Map 04 SP27
KENILWORTH CASTLE
CV8 1NE
☎ 01926 852078 ▤ 01926 851514

Explore the largest and most extensive castle ruin in England, with a past rich in famous names and events in history. Its massive red sandstone towers, keep and wall glow brightly in the sunlight. Discover the history of Kenilworth through the interactive model in Leicester's Barn.
Times: Open all year, Apr-Sep, daily 10-6; Oct, daily 10-5; Nov-Mar daily 10-4. (Closed 24-26 Dec & 1 Jan). Dates valid until 31 Mar 2004.
Fee: £4.50 (ch £2.30, concessions £3.40). Prices valid until 31 Mar 2004. **Facilities:** ⬛ ⬤ ⴺ shop ✕ (ex dogs on leads) ⧉

STONELEIGH ABBEY
CV8 2LF
➲ (Entrance to the abbey is off the B4115 close to the junction of the A46 and A452)
☎ 01926 858535 & 858585 ▤ 01926 850724
e-mail: enquire@stoneleighabbey.org

Stoneleigh Abbey is one of the finest country house estates in the Midlands and has seen the subject of considerable restoration work. The abbey, founded in the reign of Henry II, is now managed by a charitable trust. Visitors will experience a wealth of architectural styles spanning more than 800 years. The magnificent state rooms and chapel, the medieval Gatehouse and the Regency stables are some of the major areas to be admired. Set in 690 acres of parkland.
Times: Open Good Fri-Oct, Tue-Thu, Sun & BHs for guided tours at 11, 1 & 3pm. Grounds open 10-5. **Fee:** ✱ £5 (one child free with every paying adult, additional ch £2.50, pen £3.50) Party rates available.
Facilities: ⬛ ⬤ ⴺ (West Wing, Ground Level and grounds) toilets for disabled shop (guide dogs)

MIDDLETON   Map 07 SP19
ASH END HOUSE CHILDRENS FARM
Middleton Ln, Middleton B78 2BL
➲ (signposted from A4091)
☎ 0121 329 3240 ▤ 0121 329 3240
e-mail: childrensfarm@ashendhouse.fsnet.co.uk

Ideal for young children, this is a small family-owned farm with many friendly animals to feed and stroke, including some rare breeds. Cafe, shop, gift shop, play areas, picnic barns and lots of undercover activities.
Times: Open daily 10-5 or dusk in winter. (Closed 25 Dec-1 Jan and weekdays in Jan). **Fee:** £2.50 (ch £5 includes animal feed, pony ride, farm badge & all activities). **Facilities:** ⬛ ⬤ ⴺ toilets for disabled shop ✕ (ex guide dogs) ⬤

MIDDLETON HALL

B78 2AE

➲ (M42 junct 9, on A4091 midway between Belfry & Drayton Manor, follow brown heritage signs)

☎ 01827 283095 ▤ 01827 285717

e-mail: middletonhall@btconnect.com

Once the home of two great 17th-century naturalists, Francis Willughby and John Ray, the Hall shows several architectural styles, from c1300 to a Georgian west wing. The grounds include a nature reserve, lake, meadow, orchard and woodland, all Sites of Special Scientific Interest.
Times: ✱ Open Apr-13 Oct, Sun 2-5, BH 11-5. **Facilities:** ▣ ▆ ♿ (wheelchair available) toilets for disabled shop

NUNEATON   Map 04 SP39

ARBURY HALL

CV10 7PT

➲ (2m SW of Nuneaton, off B4102 Meriden road)

☎ 024 7638 2804 ▤ 024 7664 1147

e-mail: brenda.newell@arburyhall.net

The 16th-century Elizabethan house, Gothicised in the 18th century, has been the home of the Newdegate family for over 450 years. It is the finest complete example of Gothic revival architecture in existence, and contains pictures, furniture, and beautiful plasterwork ceilings. The 17th-century stable block, with a central doorway by Wren, houses the tearooms and lovely gardens with lakes and wooded walks.
Times: Open Etr-Sep 2-5.30 (last admission 5pm). Hall & gardens: Sun & Mon of BH weekends only. For other opening days & times, contact the Administrator. **Fee:** ✱ £6.50 (ch f4) gardens only £4.50 (ch £3) **Facilities:** ▣ ▆ ♿ shop ✖ (ex guide dogs & in grounds)

PACKWOOD HOUSE   Map 07 SP17

PACKWOOD HOUSE

B94 6AT

➲ (on unclass road off A34)

☎ 01564 782024 ▤ 01564 787920   [2 for 1]

e-mail: packwood@nationaltrust.org.uk

Dating from the 16th century, Packwood House has been extended and much changed over the years. An important collection of tapestries and textiles is displayed. Equally important are the stunning gardens with renowned herbaceous borders, attracting many visitors, and the almost surreal topiary garden based on the Sermon on the Mount.
Times: Open Gardens: 6 Mar-3 Nov Wed-Sun, BH Mon, Good Fri. Mar/Oct/Nov 11-4.30. May-Sep 11-5.30; House Mar-Nov 12-4. **Fee:** ✱ House & Garden £5.40 (ch £2.70). Family ticket £13.50. Garden only £2.70 (ch £1.35). **Facilities:** ▣ ♿ (w/chairs available, tactile tour, Braille guide) toilets for disabled shop ✖ (ex guide dogs) ⬥ ▀

RUGBY   Map 04 SP57

THE JAMES GILBERT RUGBY FOOTBALL MUSEUM

5 Saint Matthew's St CV21 3BY

➲ (On A428 opposite Rugby school).

☎ 01788 333889 ▤ 01788 540795

e-mail: museum@james-gilbert.com

An intriguing collection of Rugby football memorabilia is housed in the shop in which Gilbert's have made their world

continued

famous Rugby balls since 1842. Visitors can watch a craftsman at work, hand-stitching the footballs. Situated near to Rugby School and its famous playing field.
Times: ✱ Open all year, Mon-Sat 9-5. Phone for holiday opening times. **Facilities:** ▣ (500 yds) ♿ shop ✖ (ex guide dogs)

RYTON-ON-DUNSMORE   Map 04 SP37

RYTON ORGANIC GARDENS

CV8 3LG

➲ (5m SE of Coventry signposted off A45, on the road to the village of Wolston)

☎ 024 7630 3517 ▤ 024 7663 9229   [2 for 1]

e-mail: enquiry@hdra.org.uk

Eight acres of glorious gardens show how you can grow flowers, fruit and vegetables nature's way without added chemicals. More than thirty individual gardens to look at and enjoy. New in 2003 'The Vegetable Kingdom' - learn all about vegetables, their history, varieties, and how they help to keep us healthy, in a fully interactive visitor centre. Special events, tours, restaurant and coffee shop.
Times: Daily 10-5. (Closed Xmas). **Fee:** £3.95 (child £1.50). **Facilities:** ▣ ▆ ✖ licensed ♿ (wheelchairs available) toilets for disabled shop garden centre ✖ (ex guide dogs) ▀

SHOTTERY   Map 04 SP15

ANNE HATHAWAY'S COTTAGE

Cottage Ln CV37 9HH

➲ (House in Shottery Village, 1m from Stratford)

☎ 01789 292100 ▤ 01789 296083

e-mail: info@shakespeare.org.uk

This world famous picturesque thatched cottage, childhood house of Shakespeare's wife, continued to be owned by Anne Hathaway's descendants until the late 19th century. It still contains the Hathaway bed. Outside lies a beautiful cottage garden and a tree and sculpture garden including a maze.
Times: Open daily Apr-May & Oct-Nov, Mon-Sat 9.30-5, Sun 10-5; Jun-Aug, Mon-Sat 9-5, Sun 9.30-5; Nov-Mar, daily 10-4 except 23-26 Dec **Fee:** ✱ £5 (ch £2, concessions £4, Family £12. All 5 Shakespeare houses £13 (ch £6.50, concessions £12) Family £29. **Facilities:** ▣ ▆ ♿ toilets for disabled shop ✖ (ex assist dogs) ▀

STRATFORD-UPON-AVON   Map 04 SP25

HALL'S CROFT
Old Town CV37 6BG
➲ (Located in the centre of Stratford upon Avon)
☎ 01789 292107   ▤ 01789 296083
e-mail: info@shakespeare.org.uk
16th century house with Jacobean additions displaying outstanding furniture and paintings where Shakespeare's daughter Susanna, and her husband, Dr John Hall, lived before moving to New Place on the dramatist's death. There is an exhibition on Tudor medicine, and fine walled gardens can also be seen.
Times: Open Nov-Mar, daily 11-4; Apr-May & Sep-Oct, daily 11-5; Jun-Aug, Mon-Sat 9.30-5, Sun 10-5. **Fee:** ✱ £3.50 (ch £1.70. All 5 Shakespeare houses £13 (ch £6.50, concessions £4) Family ticket £29.
Facilities: ℙ 💻 ♿ toilets for disabled shop ✖ (ex assist dogs) ▨

NEW PLACE / NASH'S HOUSE
Chapel St CV37 6EP
➲ (Located in the centre of Stratford upon Avon).
☎ 01789 292325   ▤ 01789 292083
e-mail: info@shakespeare.org.uk
Once owned by Thomas Nash, who married Shakespeare's daughter Elizabeth. In addition to exceptional furnishings of Shakespeare's time, the house also contains displays on the history of Stratford. Outside lies the site of Shakespeare's final Stratford home - discover why it was demolished. Stroll in the Elizabethan style knott garden, as well as Shakespeare's Great Garden.
Times: Open Nov-Mar, daily 11-4; Apr-May & Sep-Oct, daily 11-5; Jun-Aug, Mon-Sat 9.30-5, Sun 10-5.30. **Fee:** ✱ £3.50 (ch £1.70 & concessions £3). Family ticket £29. All 5 Shakespeare houses £13 (ch £6.50, concessions £12) 3 in town (Shakespeare's Birthplace, Nash's House & New Place & Hollin's Croft £9 (ch £4.50 concessions £8) Family ticket £20. **Facilities:** ℙ (250yds) ♿ toilets for disabled ✖ (ex assist dogs) ▨

ROYAL SHAKESPEARE COMPANY COLLECTION
Royal Shakespeare Theatre, Waterside CV37 6BB
➲ (M40 junct 14 take A46 S. At 1st rdbt take 1st exit (A439). Parking in town centre, follow RSC signposted)
☎ 01789 262870   ▤ 01789 262870
e-mail: info@rsc.org.uk
The RSC gallery opened in 1881, and was part of the first Shakespeare Memorial Theatre. In 1926 fire destroyed the theatre leaving only a semi circular wall and the gallery. The exhibition space now displays costumes from past RSC productions, paintings and other Theatre Memorabilia.
Times: Open all year, Mon-Fri 1.30-6.30, Sat 10.30-6.30 & Sun 11.30-4.30. (Closed 24 & 25 Dec).Theatre tours usually Mon-Fri (ex matinee days), 1.30 & 5.30, Sun 12, 1, 2 & 3. **Fee:** ✱ Exhibition £1.50 (ch, pen & students £1). Family ticket £4. Theatre Tours £4 (ch, pen & students £3) - advisable to book in advance. **Facilities:** ℙ (charged) 💻 ✖ ♿ services for hearing impaired, Braille books/reading room toilets for disabled shop ✖ (ex guide dogs)

SHAKESPEARE'S BIRTHPLACE
Henley St CV37 6QW
➲ (In town centre)
☎ 01789 204016   ▤ 01789 292083
e-mail: info@shakespeare.org.uk

Shakespeare was born in the half-timbered house in 1564, the house remained the family home until the 19th century. It contains numerous exhibits of the Elizabethan period and Shakespeare memorabilia, and the acclaimed exhibition, Shakespeare; His Life and Background.
Times: Open Nov-Mar, Mon-Sat 10-4, Sun 10.30-4; Apr-May & Sep-Oct, Mon-Sat 10-5, Sun 10.30-5; Jun-Aug, Mon-Sat 9-5, Sun 9.30-5. **Fee:** ✱ £6.50 (ch £2.50, concessions £5.50). Family ticket £15. All 5 Shakespeare houses £13 (ch £6.50, concessions £12). Family ticket £29, 3 in town (Shakespeare's Birthplace, Nash's House & New Place & Hollins Croft £9 (ch £4.50, concessions £8). Family ticket £20.
Facilities: ℙ ♿ toilets for disabled shop ✖ (ex assist dogs) ▨

STRATFORD BUTTERFLY FARM
Tramway Walk, Swan's Nest Ln CV37 7LS
➲ (south bank of River Avon opposite RSC)
☎ 01789 299288   ▤ 01789 415878
e-mail: sales@butterflyfarm.co.uk
Europe's largest live Butterfly and Insect Exhibit. Hundreds of the world's most spectacular and colourful butterflies, in the unique setting of a lush tropical landscape, with splashing waterfalls and fish-filled pools. See also the strange and fascinating Insect City, a bustling metropolis of ants, bees, stick insects, beetles and other remarkable insects. See the dangerous and deadly in Arachnoland!
Times: Open daily 10-6 (winter 10-dusk). Closed 25 Dec. **Fee:** ✱ £4.25 (ch £3.25, pen & students £3.75). Family £12.50 **Facilities:** ℙ (opposite entrance) (site parking orange badge holders only) ♿ toilets for disabled shop ✖ ▨

THE TEDDY BEAR MUSEUM
19 Greenhill St CV37 6LF
➲ (M40 follow signs to Stratford Town Centre)
☎ 01789 293160
e-mail: info@theteddybearmuseum.com
Collection of some of the oldest and rarest teddy bears in the world, housed in a small house once owned by Henry VIII. Lots of modern teddy bear stars too, including the original

continued

Fozzie Bear, Paddington Bear from the earliest television series, Mr Bean's bear, and many more.

Times: ✱ Open all year, daily 9.30-5.30. Closed 25-26 Dec. **Facilities:** 🅿 (30yds & 200yds) (access to ground floor shop only) shop ✖ (ex guide dogs) 🍴

UPTON HOUSE   Map 04 SP34

UPTON HOUSE
OX15 6HT
➲ (on A422, 7m NW of Banbury, 12m SE of Stratford)
☎ 01295 670266 ▤ 01295 670266
e-mail: upton@smtp.ntrust.org.uk
The house, built of mellow local stone, dates from 1695, but

continued

its outstanding collections are the chief attraction. They include paintings by English and Continental Old Masters, Brussels tapestries, Sèvres porcelain, Chelsea figures, 18th-century furniture, and a collection of original artwork used to advertise Shell oil during the 1920s and 30s. Viscount Bearsted, the donor of Upton, was chairman of Shell at one time.
Times: ✱ Open 23 Mar-3 Nov daily (ex Thu/Fri) 1-5, last admission 4.30. **Facilities:** 🅿 🍴 ♿ (Braille guide, parking nr house, buggy for lower garden) toilets for disabled shop ✖ (ex guide dogs) 🐾

WARWICK   Map 04 SP26

WARWICK CASTLE
CV34 4QU
➲ (2m from M40 exit 15)
☎ 0870 442 2000 ▤ 01926 401692
e-mail: customer.information@
warwick-castle.com
From the days of William the Conqueror to the reign of Queen Victoria, Warwick Castle has provided a backdrop for many turbulent times. Attractions include the gloomy Dungeon and Torture Chamber, the grand State Rooms, the Great Hall, and a reconstruction of the Royal Weekend Party of 1898, where "Daisy", Countess of Warwick held sway.
Times: Open all year, daily 10-6 (5pm Nov-Mar, 7pm Aug). Closed 25 Dec. **Fee:** ✱ £11.25-£15.50 (ch 4-16 £6.95-£10, pen £8-£11.75, student £8.50-£12). Family ticket (2 ad & 2 ch) £32-£44. Wheelchair bound visitors free. Group discounts are available. **Facilities:** 🅿 (charged) 🍴 ✖ licensed ♿ (free parking, wheelchair hire) toilets for disabled shop ✖ (ex assistance dogs) 🍴

WARWICKSHIRE YEOMANRY MUSEUM

The Court House Vaults, Jury St CV34 4EW
➲ (situated on the corner of Jury Street & Castle Street, 2m E of M40 junct 15)
☎ 01926 492212 ▤ 01926 494837

The vaults of the courthouse display militaria from the county Yeomanry, dating from 1794 to 1945. It includes regimental silver, paintings, uniforms and weapons. A small room in the cellars now houses the HUJ Gun project, a field gun captured by the Yeomanry in 1917.

Times: Open Good Fri-Sep, Fri-Sun & BHs 10-1 & 2-4. Other times by prior arrangement. **Fee:** Donations welcome. **Facilities:** Ⓟ (300yds) (2hr max in nearby streets) shop ✖

WILMCOTE   Map 04 SP15

MARY ARDEN'S HOUSE AND THE SHAKESPEARE COUNTRYSIDE MUSEUM

Station Rd CV37 9UN
➲ (3m NW off A34)
☎ 01789 293455 ▤ 01789 292083
e-mail: info@shakespeare.org.uk

Mary Arden, Shakespeare's mother, lived here before she married John Shakespeare. The site includes many farm buildings, activities and rare breeds and gives an insight into the traditions of the countryside from Shakespeare's time to the early 20th century. Falconry displays take place throughout the day.

Times: Open Nov-Mar, Mon-Sat 10-4, Sun 10.30-4; Apr-May & Sep-Oct, Mon-Sat 10-5, Sun 10.30-5; Jun-Aug, Mon-Sat 9.30-5, Sun 10-5. **Fee:** ✱ £5.50 (ch £2.50, concession £5). Family ticket £13.50. All 5 Shakespeare houses £13 (ch £6.50, concession £12). Family ticket £29. **Facilities:** Ⓟ
🍴 & toilets for disabled shop ✖ (ex assist dogs) 🍵

WEST MIDLANDS

EVENTS & FESTIVALS

March
4th-7th Crufts Dog Show, National Exhibition Centre, Birmingham
17th St Patrick's Day Pageant, Coventry

June
16th-20th BBC Gardeners' World Live, NEC, Birmingham
tbc Coventry Classic Car Run, War Memorial Park, Coventry
tbc Godiva Festival, War Memorial Park, Coventry

July
2nd City of Wolverhampton Show (provisional)
24th-25th Wolvestock Music Festival, Hickman Park, Bilston (provisional)
tbc Birmingham International Jazz Festival

August
tbc Coventry Jazz Festival
tbc Italian Festival, School Street, Wolverhampton
tbc Steam & Vintage Rally, West Park, Wolverhampton

September
11th-12th Birmingham Artsfest, city centre

November
tbc Coombe Fireworks, Coventry
tbc Firework Display, West Park, Wolverhampton

Above: Birmingham Museum & Art Gallery
Top: Birmingham Botanical Gardens

BIRMINGHAM   Map 07 SP08

ASTON HALL
Trinity Rd, Aston B6 6JD
➲ (M6 junct 6 follow A38(M) Aston Expressway
towards city centre. Leave at Aston Waterlinks and
follow brown signs to Aston Hall)
☎ 0121 327 0062 ▤ 0121 327 7162
e-mail: bmag-enquiries@birmingham.gov.uk
Built by Sir Thomas Holte, Aston Hall is a fine Jacobean
mansion complete with a panelled Long Gallery, balustraded
staircase and magnificent plaster friezes and ceilings. King
Charles I spent a night here during the Civil War and the
house was damaged by Parliamentary troops. It was also
leased to James Watt Junior, the son of the great industrial
pioneer.
Times: ✱ Open Etr-Oct, Tue-Fri 1-4; Sat & Sun 12-4. Closed Mon ex
BH's. **Facilities:** 🅿 ■ ♿ (ground floor only partially accessible) shop
✖ (ex guide dogs)

BIRMINGHAM BOTANICAL GARDENS & GLASSHOUSES
Westbourne Rd, Edgbaston B15 3TR
➲ (2m W of city centre, follow signs for
Edgbaston, then brown heritage signs)
☎ 0121 454 1860 ▤ 0121 454 7835
e-mail: admin@
birminghambotanicalgardens.org.uk

Originally opened in 1832, the gardens include the Tropical
House, which has 24ft-wide lily pool and lush vegetation.
The Mediterranean house features a wide variety of citrus
fruits and the Arid House has a desert scene with its giant
agaves and opuntias. Outside, a tour of the gardens includes
rhododendrons and azalea borders and a collection of
over 200 trees. Young children's discovery garden & a
sculpture trail.
Times: Open daily all year, wkdays 9-7 or dusk, Sun 10-7 or dusk
whichever is earlier. (Closed 25 Dec). **Fee:** ✱ £5.50 (concessions £3);
£6 summer Sun & BH's. Family £15 (£16 summer & BH's) Groups 10+
£4.50 (concessions £2.70) **Facilities:** 🅿 ■ ✖ licensed ♿ (3
wheelchairs, 2 electric scooters & Braille guides) toilets for disabled
shop garden centre ✖ (ex guide dogs) ▱

THE BIRMINGHAM BOTANICAL GARDENS & GLASSHOUSES
Garden of the World
Open in 1832, the Gardens are a 15 acre "Oasis of
Delight" with over 200 trees and the finest collection
of plants in the Midlands. Tropical, Mediterranean
and Arid glasshouses. National Bonsai Collection.
Children's Playground, Children's Discovery Garden,
exotic birds, art gallery and Sculpture Trail. Gift
shop. Plant sales. Restaurant. Bands play summer
Sunday afternoons and Bank Holidays. Open Daily.

Westbourne Road, Edgbaston, Birmingham
West Midlands B15 3TR
Tel: 0121 454 1860 Fax: 0121 454 7835
Group bookings by prior appointment
Email: admin@birminghambotanicalgardens.org.uk
Internet: www.birminghambotanicalgardens.org.uk

BIRMINGHAM MUSEUM & ART GALLERY
Chamberlain Sq B3 3DH
☎ 0121 303 2834 ▤ 0121 303 1394
One of the world's best collections of Pre-Raphaelite
paintings can be seen here, including important works by
Burne-Jones, a native of Birmingham. Also on display are
fine silver, ceramics and glass. The archaeology section has
prehistoric Egyptian, Greek and Roman antiquities, and also
objects from the Near East, Mexico and Peru.
Times: ✱ Open all year Mon-Thu & Sat 10-5, Fri 10.30-5 and Sun
12.30-5. **Facilities:** 🅿 ■ ✖ licensed ♿ (lift) toilets for disabled shop
✖ ▱

THE JEWELLERY QUARTER DISCOVERY CENTRE
75-79 Vyse St, Hockley B18 6HA
➲ (off A41 into Vyse St, museum on left hand side
after 1st side street).
☎ 0121 554 3598 ▤ 0121 554 9700
e-mail: louise_evans@birmingham.gov.uk
The Museum tells the story of jewellery making in
Birmingham from its origins in the Middle Ages right through
to the present day. Discover the skill of the jeweller's craft
and enjoy a unique tour of an original jewellery factory
frozen in time. For over eighty years the family firm of Smith
and Pepper produced jewellery from the factory. This
perfectly preserved 'time capsule' workshop has changed
little since the beginning of the century. The Jewellery
Quarter is still very much at the forefront of jewellery

continued

manufacture in Britain and the Museum showcases the work of the city's most exciting new designers.
Times: ✱ Open all year, Mon-Fri 10-4, Sat 11-5. (Closed Sun). Open BHs but closed Xmas/New Year **Facilities:** P (limited 2hr stay/pay & display) ♨ ♿ (tours for hearing/visually impaired booked in advance) toilets for disabled shop ✖ (ex guide dogs) ☞

RSPB SANDWELL VALLEY NATURE RESERVE
20 Tanhouse Av, Great Barr B43 5AG
➲ (off B4167 Hamstead Road into Tanhouse Avenue)
☎ 0121 357 7395 ▤ 0121 358 3013 FREE

Opened in 1983 on the site of an old colliery, Sandwell Valley is home to hundreds of bird, animal and insect species in five different habitats. Summer is the best time to see the yellow wagtail or reed warblers, while wintertime attracts goosanders, snipe, and redshanks. There are guided walks and bug hunts for the kids in summer, and a shop and visitor centre all year round.
Times: Open Tue-Fri 9-5, Sat & Sun 10-5, closes at dusk in winter. (Closed Mon, 24 Dec-2 Jan) **Facilities:** P ♿ toilets for disabled shop ✖ (ex on lead)

SAREHOLE MILL
Cole Bank Rd, Hall Green B13 0BD
➲ (M42 Junct 4. Take A34 towards Birmingham. After 5m turn left on B4146 Sarehole Mill on left)
☎ 0121 777 6612 ▤ 0121 303 2891

Home to Birmingham's only working watermill; Sarehole Mill was built in the 1760's. Used for both flour production and metal rolling up to the last century, the Mill can still be seen in action during the summer months. Restored with financial backing from JRR Tolkien, who grew up in the area and cites Sarehole as an influence for writing the Hobbit and Lord of the Rings.
Times: ✱ Open Apr-Oct, Tue-Fri 1-4, Sat-Sun & BH 12-4. (Closed Mon) **Facilities:** P ✖ (ex guide dogs)

SELLY MANOR MUSEUM
Maple Rd, Bournville B30 2AE
➲ (off A38)
☎ 0121 472 0199 ▤ 0121 471 4101
e-mail: gillianellis@bvt.org.uk

These two timber-framed manor houses date from the 13th and early 14th centuries, and have been re-erected in the 'garden suburb' of Bournville. There is a herb garden and events are held all year.
Times: ✱ Open mid Jan-mid Dec, Tue-Fri & BH 10-5 (Apr-Sep, Sat-Sun 2-5), phone for details. **Facilities:** P ♿ toilets for disabled shop

SOHO HOUSE
Soho Av, Handsworth B18 5LB
➲ (from city centre follow A41 to Soho Rd, follow brown heritage signs to Soho Ave)
☎ 0121 554 9122 ▤ 0121 554 5929
e-mail: soho.house.bmag@dnet.co.uk

Soho House was the elegant home of industrial pioneer Matthew Boulton between 1766 and 1809. Here, he met with some of the most important thinkers and scientists of his day. The house has been carefully restored and contains many of Boulton's possessions including furniture, clocks,

continued

silverware and the original dining table where the Lunar Society met.
Times: ✱ Open all year, Tue-Sat 10-5 & Sun 12-5; also BH Mon. **Facilities:** P ♨ ♿ (induction loop) toilets for disabled shop ✖ (ex guide dogs) ☞

THINKTANK AT MILLENNIUM POINT
Millennium Point, Curzon St B4 7XG
☎ 0121 202 2222 ▤ 0121 202 2280 2 for 1
e-mail: findout@thinktank.ac

Thinktank is the Birmingham Museum of Science and Discovery, and has four floors with ten themed galleries that are packed with interactive exhibits that explore everything from locomotives and aircraft to intestines and spit glands! The special LEGO lab offers kids the chance to programme their own LEGO robots and find out how LEGO itself evolved.
Times: Open daily 10-5 (last entry 4). (Closed 24-26 Dec) **Fee:** ✱ £6.95 (ch £4.95). Family ticket (1 adult + 1 ch) £9, (2 adults + 2 ch) £18 **Facilities:** P (charged) ♨ ♿ toilets for disabled shop ✖ (ex guide dogs) ☞

<hr>

BOURNVILLE   Map 07 SP08

CADBURY WORLD
Linden Rd B30 2LD
➲ (1m S of A38 Bristol Rd, on A4040 Ring Rd)
☎ 0121 451 4159 ▤ 0121 451 1366
e-mail: cadbury.world@csplc.com

Lots of recent changes have meant Cadbury World now has much more to see, do and taste. There is the chance to get involved in the chocolate making process, and to find out how the chocolate is used to make famous confectionery. Visitors can learn about the early struggles and triumphs of the Cadbury business, and follow the history of Cadbury television advertising. Besides all this, visitors can relax on the gentle Cadabra ride, and be a big kid in CadburyLand, the Fantasy Factory, and on the Cocoa Road.
Times: Contact information line 0121 451 4180 for opening times. **Fee:** ✱ £8.75 (ch £6.60, concessions £7) **Facilities:** P ♨ ✖ ♿ (adapted ride & lift to 2nd floor, subtitles) toilets for disabled shop ✖ (ex guide dogs) ☞

<hr>

COVENTRY   Map 04 SP37

COVENTRY CATHEDRAL & VISITOR CENTRE
7 Priory Row CV1 5ES
➲ (signposted on all approaches to the city)
☎ 024 7622 7597 ▤ 024 7663 1448
e-mail: information@coventrycathedral.org

Coventry's old cathedral was bombed during an air raid of November 1940 which devastated the city. The remains have been carefully preserved. The new cathedral was designed by Sir Basil Spence and consecrated in May 1962. It contains outstanding modern works of art, including a huge tapestry designed by Graham Sutherland, the west screen (a wall of glass engraved by John Hutton with saints and angels), bronzes by Epstein, and the great baptistry window by John Piper.
Times: Open all year, daily, Etr-Oct 8.30-6, Oct-Etr 8.30-5.30. **Fee:** Cathedral £3 donation. Camera charge £2. Video charge £5. **Facilities:** P (250yds) ♨ ♿ (lift, touch and hearing centre, paved wheelchair access) toilets for disabled shop ✖ (ex guide dogs)

COVENTRY TRANSPORT MUSEUM

Hales St CV1 1PN

➲ (just off junc 1 Coventry ring road, Tower Street in City Centre)

☎ 024 7683 2425 ▤ 024 7683 2465 **FREE**

e-mail: museum@mbrt.co.uk

Coventry is the traditional home of the motor industry. The Coventry Transport Museum displays the largest collection of British cars, buses, cycles and motorcycles in the world. Visitors can learn about motoring's early days in 'landmarques', how Royalty travelled, and see Thrust 2 and Thrust SSC, the world land speed record cars.

Times: Open all year, daily 10-5. (Closed 24-26 Dec). **Facilities:** P (adjacent) (pay & display) ▆ よ (audio tour, tactile floor & models, wheelchairs for hire) toilets for disabled shop ✖ (ex guide dogs) ▰

HERBERT ART GALLERY & MUSEUM

Jordan Well CV1 5QP

➲ (located in city centre near Cathedral)

☎ 024 7683 2381 & 7683 2565 **FREE**
▤ 024 7683 2410

e-mail: artsandheritage@coventry.gov.uk

'Godiva City', tells Coventry's story over 1,000 years, through interactive exhibits, objects, pictures and words. Changing displays of art, craft, social and industrial history. It is Coventry's premier museum hosting a range of exhibitions and events.

Times: Open all year, Mon-Sat 10-5.30, Sun 12-5. (Closed 24-26,31 Dec & 1 Jan) **Facilities:** P (500yds) ▆ よ (disabled parking, automatic doors, tactile/audio displays) toilets for disabled shop ✖ (ex guide/assistance dogs)

JAGUAR DAIMLER HERITAGE CENTRE

Browns Ln, Allesley CV5 9DR

➲ (on A45, follow signs for Browns Lane Plant)

☎ 024 7620 3322 ▤ 024 7620 2835 **FREE**

e-mail: jagtrust@jaguar.com

A new museum that explores the history of Daimler and Jaguar motor vehicles, from the 1897 Daimler Grafton-Paeton to the 1990 Jaguar XJ220.

Times: Open Mon-Thu 9-4, Fri 9-3 & last Sun of month 10-4. **Facilities:** P よ toilets for disabled shop ✖ (ex guide dogs)

LUNT ROMAN FORT

Coventry Rd, Baginton CV8 3AJ

➲ (S side of city, off Stonebridge highway, A45)

☎ 024 7683 2381 & 7683 2565
▤ 024 7683 2410

e-mail: artsandheritage@coventry.co.uk

The turf and timber Roman fort from around the end of the 1st century has been faithfully reconstructed. An Interpretation Centre is housed in the granary.

Times: Open 27 Mar-Oct, Sat-Sun & BH Mon's 10-5; Mid Jul-end Aug, Thu-Tue 10-5; Spring BH wk, Thu-Tue 10-5. **Fee:** £2 (concessions £1). **Facilities:** P よ (ramp to Granary Interpretation Centre) toilets for disabled shop ✖ (ex guide/assistance dogs)

PRIORY VISITOR CENTRE

Priory Row CV1 5EX

➲ (in city centre near Cathedral)

☎ 024 7683 2381 ▤ 024 7683 2410 **FREE**

e-mail: artsandheritage@coventry.gov.uk

Earl Leofric and his wife Lady Godiva founded a monastery in Coventry in the 11th century. This priory disappeared somewhere beneath the cathedral that was built on the site, until this cathedral was in turn demolished by Henry VIII in the 16th century. Soon after that most of the buildings on the site had been reduced to ground level, leaving modern archaeologists to discover the outlines of history. This visitor centre displays finds from the site as well as telling the story of Coventry's first cathedral.

Times: Open Mon-Sat 10-5.30, Sun noon-4 **Facilities:** P (500yds) よ toilets for disabled shop ✖ (ex guide/assistance dogs)

ST MARY'S GUILDHALL

Bayley Ln CV1 5QP

➲ (in city centre near ruined Cathedral)

☎ 024 7683 2381 ▤ 024 7683 2410 **FREE**

e-mail: artsandheritage@coventry.gov.uk

This impressive medieval Guildhall has stood in the heart of Coventry for over 650 years, and has played its part in the history of the area. It served as Henry VI's court during the War of the Roses, was a prison to Mary Queen of Scots, and was used as a setting by George Eliot in her novel 'Adam Bede'. The Great Hall contains a Tournai tapestry commissioned for the visit of Henry VII and Queen Elizabeth in 1500.

Times: Open Etr Sun-Sep, Sun-Thu 10-4 **Facilities:** P (600 yds) よ shop ✖ (ex guide/assistance dogs)

DUDLEY   Map 07 SO99

BLACK COUNTRY LIVING MUSEUM

Tipton Rd DY1 4SQ

➲ (on A4037, nr Showcase cinema)

☎ 0121 557 9643 & 0121 520 8054
▤ 0121 557 4242

e-mail: info@bclm.co.uk

On the 26-acre site is a recreated canal-side village, with shops, houses and workplaces. Meet the costumed guides and find out what life was like around 1900. Ride on a tramcar, take a trip down the underground mine, venture into the limestone caverns or visit the olde tyme fairground (additional charge). There are also demonstrations of chainmaking, glass engraving and sweet-making. Watch a silent movie in the Limelight cinema, taste fish and chips cooked on a 1930s range, and finish your visit with a glass of real ale in the Bottle and Glass Inn.

Times: ✱ Open all year, Mar-Oct daily 10-5; Nov-Feb, Wed-Sun 10-4. (Telephone for Christmas closing) **Facilities:** P (charged) ▆ ✖ licensed よ (ramps available) toilets for disabled shop ✖ (ex guide dogs) ▰

DUDLEY ZOOLOGICAL GARDENS

2 The Broadway DY1 4QB

➩ (M5 junct 2 towards Wolverhampton/Dudley. Signposted)

☎ 01384 215313 🖃 01384 456048

e-mail: marketing@dudleyzoo.org.uk

Set in 40 acres, the castle ruins are an impressive example of feudal splendour, whilst the zoo houses one of the most diverse collections of animals in the country. Home to many endangered species, there is the opportunity to see and learn about animals from every continent.

Times: Open all year, Etr-mid Sep, daily 10-4; mid Sep-Etr, daily 10-3. (Closed 25 Dec). **Fee:** ✱ £7.95 (ch 4-15 £5, concessions £5.50). Family ticket £27 (2ad+3ch) **Facilities:** 🅿 (charged) 🍴✗ licensed ♿ (land train from gates-castle, wheelchair hire) toilets for disabled shop ✖ 🍹

MUSEUM & ART GALLERY

St James's Rd DY1 1HU

➩ (M5 northbound, exit at junct 2. Take A4123 signposted to Dudley)

☎ 01384 815575 🖃 01384 815576

e-mail: museum.pls@mbc.dudley.gov.uk

The museum houses the Brooke Robinson collection of 17th, 18th and 19th century European painting, furniture, ceramics and enamels. A fine geological gallery, 'The Time Trail' has spectacular displays of fossils from the local Wenlock limestone and coal measures.

Times: ✱ Open all year, Mon-Sat 10-4. (Closed BHs). **Facilities:** 🅿 (25mtrs) ♿ (Braille & large print text. Tactile objects) shop ✖ (ex guide dogs)

SOLIHULL   Map 07 SP17

NATIONAL MOTORCYCLE MUSEUM

Coventry Rd, Bickenhill B92 0EJ

➩ (near junct 6, of M42, off A45 near NEC)

☎ 01675 443311 🖃 0121 711 3153

Five exhibition halls showing British motorcycles built during the Golden Age of motorcycling. Spanning 90 years, the immaculately restored machines are the products of

continued

around 150 different factories. Over 700 machines are on show, most are owned by the museum, others are from collections or private owners. Restoration work is carried out by enthusiasts, and new motorcycles are acquired from all over the world.

Times: Open all year, daily 10-6. (Closed 24-26 Dec). **Fee:** ✱ £4.95 (ch 12 & pen £3.75). Party 20+ **Facilities:** 🅿 ✗ licensed ♿ toilets for disabled shop ✖ (ex guide dogs) 🍹

STOURBRIDGE   Map 07 SO88

THE FALCONRY CENTRE

Hurrans Garden Centre, Kidderminster Rd South, Hagley DY9 0JB

➩ (off A456)

☎ 01562 700014 🖃 01562 700014

The centre houses some 70 birds of prey including owls, hawks and falcons and is also a rehabilitation centre for sick and injured birds of prey. Spectacular flying displays are put on daily from midday. There are picnic areas, special fun days and training courses available.

Times: Open all year, daily 10-5 & Sun 11-5. (Closed 25, 26 Dec & Etr Sun). **Fee:** £3 (ch, pen & disabled £2). Party 25+ 10% discount. **Facilities:** 🅿 🍴 ♿ toilets for disabled shop garden centre ✖ (ex guide dogs) 🍹

WALSALL   Map 07 SP09

NEW ART GALLERY WALSALL

Gallery Square WS2 8LG signposted from all main routes

☎ 01922 654400 🖃 01922 654401   **FREE**

e-mail: info@artatwalsall.org.uk

Largely funded by National Lottery money, this new modern art gallery was opened in February 2000. Its unusual tower has a variety of oddly shaped windows, while the main building has six floors of art on display. Includes the Garman Ryan permanent collection and a Discovery Gallery.

Times: Open all year Tue-Sat 10-5, Sun noon-5. Closed Mon ex BH Mon's. **Facilities:** 🅿 🍴✗ ♿ (lift access to facilties, induction loop, large print) toilets for disabled shop ✖ (ex guide dogs)

WALSALL LEATHER MUSEUM

Littleton St West WS2 8EQ

➩ (On Walsall ring-road on North side of town)

☎ 01922 721153 🖃 01922 725827   **FREE**

e-mail: leathermuseum@walsall.gov.uk

Award winning working museum in the saddlery and leathergoods 'capital' of Britain. Watch skilled craftsmen and women at work in this restored Victorian leather factory. Displays tell the story of Walsall's leatherworkers past and present. Large shop stocks range of Walsall made leathergoods, many at bargain prices. Saddle Room Cafe serves delicious home-cooked cakes and light lunches. Groups very welcome, guided tours available.

Times: Open all year, Tue-Sat 10-5 (Nov-Mar 4pm), Sun noon-5 (Nov-Mar 4pm). Open BH Mon. (Closed 24-26 Dec, 1 Jan, Good Fri, Etr Sun & May Day). **Facilities:** 🅿 (10metres) 🍴 ♿ (staff with sign language skills,tactile activities,parking) toilets for disabled shop ✖ (ex guide dogs) 🍹

WOLVERHAMPTON   Map 07 SO99

MOSELEY OLD HALL

Fordhouses WV10 7HY   2 for 1

➲ (4m N of Wolverhampton, off A460 and A449)

☎ 01902 782808   🖷 01902 782808

e-mail: mosleyoldhall@nationaltrust.org.uk

Charles II sheltered in Moseley Old Hall after the Battle of Worcester in 1651. There are numerous pictures and other reminders of the king. The house itself is an Elizabethan timber-framed building which was encased in brick in the 19th century. The small garden has a nut walk, period herbs and plants, and a formal knot garden. For details of special events please send a 9" x 4" envelope.

Times: Open 22 Mar-14 Dec; Mar-Nov Wed, Sat-Sun, BH Mon and Tue 1-5 (BH 11-5). Nov & Dec: Sun 1-4 **Fee:** ✱ £4.40 (ch £2.20). Family ticket £11. Party 15+ £3.70. **Facilities:** 🅿 ⬛ ♿ (Braille & large print, 1 wheelchair, thick handled cutlery) toilets for disabled shop ➤ (ex guide dogs) ⚋ 🍽

WIGHTWICK MANOR

WV6 8EE

➲ (3m W, beside Mermaid Inn off A454 Bridgenorth)   2 for 1

☎ 01902 761400   🖷 01902 764663

e-mail: wightwickmanor@ntrust.org.uk

This house was begun in 1887 and is one of the finest examples of 19th-century decorative style. All aspects of William Morris's talents are shown in the house - wallpapers, textiles, carpets, tiles, embroidery and even books. The garden reflects late Victorian and Edwardian design.

Times: Open Mar-24 Dec, Thu, Sat & BH Sun & Mon 1.30-5. Last admission 4.30. Garden & servant tours throughout the year, please phone for details. **Fee:** ✱ £5.70 (accompanied ch & students £2.85). Gardens only £2.50 ch free in garden **Facilities:** 🅿 ⬛ ♿ (car parking call 01902 761400 for details) shop ➤ (except on leads) ⚋

Above: The dome of the Church of St Lazar, a Serbian orthodox church in Bournville

ISLE OF WIGHT

EVENTS & FESTIVALS

April
9th-11th Easter Challenge yacht racing – start
of the yachting season

May
tbc International Fly In, Bembridge Airport

June
4th-6th Old Gaffers Festival, Yarmouth,
festival of gaff-rigged vessels,
entertainment & stalls
19th Midsummer Fair, Northcourt Manor,
Shorwell
26th Round the Island Yacht Race
tbc Isle of Wight Festival, Seaclose Park,
Newport

July
24th-25th Isle of Wight County Show

August
7th-14th Cowes Week, international yachting
regatta, music & street theatre
27th-30th The Island Steam Show,
Havenstreet
tbc Cowes Powerboat Festival
tbc Isle of Wight Garlic Festival, Newchurch

Above: The Needles
Top: Yachting at Cowes

ALUM BAY   Map 04 SZ38

THE NEEDLES OLD BATTERY
West High Down PO30 0JH
➲ (at Needles Headland, W of Freshwater Bay and
Alum Bay, B3322)
☎ 01983 754772 🖷 01983 756978
e-mail: jean.pitt@nationaltrust.org.uk

The threat of a French invasion prompted the construction
in 1862 of this spectacularly sited fort, which still retains its
original gun barrels. The laboratory, searchlight
position-finding cells have all been restored and a 65m
tunnel leads to stunning views of the Hampshire and Dorset
coastline.
Times: Open 28 Mar-Jun & Sep-Oct daily (closed Fri ex Good Fri)
10.30-5; Jul-Aug daily 10.30-5; Property closes in bad weather.
Telephone on day of visit to check. **Fee:** ✱ £3.50 (ch £1.50). Family
ticket £7.50. **Facilities:** Ⓟ (0.75m) 🍴 ♿ (ramp & audio tours) toilets
for disabled 🐾 ⬅

THE NEEDLES PARK
PO39 0JD
➲ (signposted, on B3322)
☎ 0870 458 0022 🖷 01983 755260
e-mail: info@theneedles.co.uk

Overlooking the Needles on the western edge of the Island,
the park has attractions for all the family: included in the
wide range facilities is the spectacular chair lift to the beach
to view the famous coloured sandcliffs, Needles Rocks and
continued

lighthouse. Other popular attractions include Alum Bay Glass and the Isle of Wight Sweet Manufactory.

Times: Open 29 Mar-early Nov, daily 10-5. Hours extended in high season. **Fee:** ✱ No admission charged for entrance to Park. All day car park charge £3. Pay as you go attractions or Supersaver Attraction discount ticket £7.50 (ch £5.50). **Facilities:** 🅿 (charged) 💻 ✕ licensed ♿ toilets for disabled shop ☜

ARRETON Map 04 SZ58

HASELEY MANOR
Heasley Ln PO30 3AN
➲ (on Sandown to Newport road)
☎ 01983 865420 ▤ 01983 867547

This is the oldest and largest manor open to the public on the Island. Parts of the south wing have some of the original building, c1300, but the rest of the house is a mixture of styles. The manor has since been carefully restored and 20 rooms can be viewed. Outside, there is a reconstructed 18th-century farm complete with animals. There is also a children's play area with a tree house, and a small lake with an island castle.

Times: ✱ Open Etr-Sep, Mon-Fri 10-5.30. (Closed Sat & Sun).
Facilities: 🅿 💻 ✕ licensed ♿ (wheelchair ramps) toilets for disabled shop ☜

ROBIN HILL COUNTRY PARK
Downend PO30 2NU
➲ (0.5m from Allerton village next door to the Hare and Hounds pub)
☎ 01983 527352 ▤ 01983 527347

Set in 88 acres of downland and woods, Robin Hill offers a Tree Top Trail, Mazes, Snake Slides, Troll Island, Toboggan Run Ride, Squirrel Tower, Forest Sculptures and a Countryside Centre and the 3 largest rides on the island the Hoom Toboggan Rub, Motion Platform Cinema.

Times: ✱ Open 25 Mar-3 Nov, daily 10-5 (last admission 4).
Facilities: 🅿 💻 ✕ ♿ (most areas are accessible. ramps access) toilets for disabled shop ✖ (ex on leads) ☜

BEMBRIDGE Map 04 SZ68

BEMBRIDGE WINDMILL
PO30 4EB
➲ (0.5m S of Bembridge on B3395)
☎ 01983 873945

The only windmill on the island to survive, Bembridge mill
continued

was built about 1700 and was in use until 1913. The stone-built tower with its wooden cap and machinery have been restored since it was given to the National Trust in 1961.

Times: Open 28 Mar-Jun & Sep-24 Oct, Sun-Fri, 10-5 (Closed Sat ex Etr Sat); Jul-Aug, daily 10-5. **Fee:** ✱ £1.90 (ch 95p). **Facilities:** 🅿 (200yds) shop ✖ (ex guide dogs) ♨ ☜

BLACKGANG Map 04 SZ47

BLACKGANG CHINE FANTASY PARK
PO38 2HN
➲ (follow signs from Ventnor for Whitnell & Niton. From the village of Niton follow signs for Blackgang)
☎ 01983 730330 ▤ 01983 731267
e-mail: vectisventureltd@btinternet.com

Opened as scenic gardens in 1843 covering some 40 acres, the park has imaginative play areas, water gardens, maze and coastal gardens. Set on the steep wooded slopes of the chine are the themed areas Smugglerland, Nurseryland, Dinosaurland, Fantasyland and Frontierland. St Catherine's Quay has a maritime exhibition showing the history of local and maritime affairs.

Times: Open 31 Mar-2 Nov daily, 10-5. Whitsun & high season open until 10pm. **Fee:** Combined ticket to chine, sawmill & quay £7.50. Saver ticket (4 people) £26. **Facilities:** 🅿 (charged) 💻 ✕ ♿ (some paths steep) toilets for disabled shop ☜

BRADING Map 04 SZ68

ISLE OF WIGHT WAX WORKS
46 High St PO36 0DQ
➲ (on A3055, in Brading High St)
☎ 01983 407286 ▤ 01983 402112
e-mail: waxworks@
bradingisleofwight.fsnet.co.uk

Set in 3/4 acre in the historic 'Kynge's Towne' of Brading, this attraction comprises the Rectory mansion filled with famous and infamous characters from the past, the chamber of horrors, world of nature, Professor Copperthwaithe's extraordinary collection of oddities and the art of candle carving

Times: Open all year, Summer 10-5, extended in high season. Telephone for Dec & Jan opening times. **Fee:** ✱ £5.25 (ch £3.50, under 5 free, pen £4). Family £16 (2ad+2ch), Family £19 (2ad+3ch). Party 20+. **Facilities:** 🅿 💻 ♿ (Disabled route planner) toilets for disabled shop ☜

LILLIPUT ANTIQUE DOLL & TOY MUSEUM
High St PO36 0DJ
➲ (A3055 Ryde/Sandown road, in Brading High Street)
☎ 01983 407231 ▤ 01983 404663
e-mail: lilliput.museum@btconnect.com

This private museum contains one of the finest collections of antique dolls and toys in Britain. There are over 2000 exhibits, ranging in age from 2000BC to 1945 with examples of almost every seriously collectable doll, many with royal connections. Also dolls' houses, teddy bears and rare and unusual toys.

Times: Open all year, daily, 10-5. **Fee:** ✱ £1.95 (ch & pen £1, ch under 5 free). Party on request. **Facilities:** 🅿 (200 yds) ♿ (ramps provided on request) shop ☜

MORTON MANOR

PO36 0EP

➲ (off A3055 in Brading, well signposted)

☎ 01983 406168

The manor dates back to 1249, but was rebuilt in 1680 with further changes during the Georgian period. The house contains furniture of both the 18th and 19th centuries, but its main attraction lies in the gardens and vineyard. The garden is landscaped into terraces, with ornamental ponds, a sunken garden and a traditional Elizabethan turf maze. There is also an established vineyard and winery.

Times: ✱ Open Apr-Oct, daily 10-5.30 (Closed Sat) Last admissions 4.30. **Facilities:** 🅿 ⬛ ✕ licensed ♿ shop garden centre 🦮 (ex in garden on lead)

NUNWELL HOUSE & GARDENS

Coach Ln PO36 0JQ

➲ (Off Ryde-Sandown Rd, A3055)   **2 for 1**

☎ 01983 407240

Set in beautiful gardens, Nunwell is an impressive, lived-in and much loved house where King Charles I spent his last night of freedom. It has fine furniture and interesting collections of family militaria. In summer, concerts are occasionally held in the music room.

Times: Open House & Gardens: 30-31 May then 5 Jul-8 Sep, Mon-Wed 1-5. Tours of the house at 1.30, 2.30 and 3.30. **Fee:** £4 inc guide book. **Facilities:** 🅿 shop 🦮 (ex guide dogs)

CARISBROOKE   Map 04 SZ48

CARISBROOKE CASTLE

PO30 1XY

➲ (1.25m SW of Newport, off B3401)

☎ 01983 522107   🖨 01983 528632

A royal fortress and prison to King Charles I, Carisbrooke is set on a sweeping ridge at the heart of the Isle of Wight. Don't miss the donkeys that can be seen working a 16th-century wheel to draw water from the well.

Times: Open all year, Apr-Sep, daily 10-6 (Oct, daily 10-5); Nov-Mar, daily 10-4. (Closed 24-26 Dec & 1 Jan). Dates valid until 31 Mar 2004. **Fee:** £5 (ch £2.50, concessions £3.80). Prices valid until 31 Mar 2004. **Facilities:** 🅿 ⬛ ♿ shop ♯

FRESHWATER   Map 04 SZ38

DIMBOLA LODGE

Terrace Ln, Freshwater Bay PO40 9QE

➲ (off A3054)

☎ 01983 756814   🖨 01983 755578

e-mail: administrator@dimbola.co.uk

Home of Julia Margaret Cameron, the pioneer Victorian portrait photographer. The house has the largest permanent collection of Cameron prints on display in the UK, as well as galleries exhibiting work by young, up and coming, and acclaimed modern photographers; and a large display of cameras and accessories.

Times: ✱ Open all year 10-5 (Closed 5 days at Xmas). **Facilities:** 🅿 ✕ ♿ chairlifts toilets for disabled shop 🦮 (ex guide dogs) 🍴

HAVENSTREET   Map 04 SZ58

ISLE OF WIGHT STEAM RAILWAY

The Railway Station PO33 4DS

➲ (Situated between Ryde & Newport. Railway well signposted)

☎ 01983 882204   🖨 01983 884515

e-mail: havenstreet@iwsteamrailway.co.uk

When the Newport to Ryde railway was closed, Haven Street Station was taken over by a private company, the Isle of Wight Steam Railway. A number of volunteers restored the station, locomotives and rolling stock, and steam trains now run the five miles from Wootton, via Haven Street to Smallbrook Junction where there is a direct interchange with the Ryde-Shanklin electric trains.

Times: ✱ Open selected days Mar-Oct (Jun-Sep daily) **Facilities:** 🅿 ⬛ ♿ (with assistance) toilets for disabled shop 🍴

MOTTISTONE   Map 04 SZ48

MOTTISTONE MANOR GARDEN

PO30 4ED

➲ (2m W of Brighstone on B3399)

☎ 01983 741302

The garden of this 16th and 17th-century manor house, which is tenanted, is noted for its colourful herbaceous border, grassy terraces planted with fruit trees and lovely sea views. There are also some delightful walks between the Downs and the coast.

Times: Open 28 Mar-Oct, Tue & Wed 11-5.30 & Sun 2-5.30 **Fee:** ✱ £2.80 (ch £1.30) **Facilities:** 🅿 ⬛ ♿ (limited access) toilets for disabled shop 🍴

NEWTOWN   Map 04 SZ49

OLD TOWN HALL

Town Ln PO30 4PA

➲ (1m N of A3054 between Yarmouth & Newport)

☎ 01983 531785

The small, now tranquil, village of Newtown once sent two members to parliament and the Town Hall was the setting for often turbulent elections. An exhibition inside depicts the

continued

exploits of 'Ferguson's gang', an anonymous group of trust benefactors in the 1920s and 1930s.

Times: Open 28 Mar-end Jun & Sep-24 Oct, Mon, Wed & Sun, 2-5 (also open Good Fri & Etr Sat); Jul & Aug Sun-Thu, 2-5. **Fee:** ✱ £1.60 (ch 80p). **Facilities:** 🅿 ♿ shop ✖ (ex guide dogs) 🦮

OSBORNE HOUSE   Map 04 SZ59

OSBORNE HOUSE
PO32 6JY
➲ (1m SE of East Cowes)
☎ 01983 200022   🖷 01983 281380

The beloved seaside retreat of Queen Victoria offers a glimpse into the private life of Britain's longest reigning monarch. The royal apartments are full of treasured mementos. The Dunbar Room evokes the atmosphere of India as experienced by Queen Victoria. Visit the gardens and the charming Swiss Cottage.
Times: Open House: Apr-Sep, daily 10-6; Oct, daily 10-5 (last admission 4). Gardens: Apr-Oct, daily 10-6 (last admission 4). For winter & spring pre-booked guided tours, contact site for details. Dates valid until 31 Mar 2004. **Fee:** House & Gardens: £8 (ch £4, concessions £6). Garden only: £4.50 (ch £2.30, concessions £3.40). Prices valid until 31 Mar 2004. **Facilities:** 🅿 🍴 ♿ shop ✖ ⚏

PORCHFIELD   Map 04 SZ49

COLEMANS ANIMAL FARM
Colemans Ln PO30 4LX
➲ (from A3054 Newport-Yarmouth Rd, follow brown tourist signs)
☎ 01983 522831   🖷 01983 522434
e-mail: info@colemansfarm.net

Ideal for young children, this extensive petting farm has donkeys, goats, rabbits, guinea pigs, pigs, Highland cattle, Shetland ponies, chickens, ducks and geese. There is also a fun barn with slides and swings, an adventure playground, a Tractor Fun Park, and an Old Barn Café for adults who need to relax. Visitors can cuddle, stroke and feed the animals at special times throughout the day.
Times: Open 22 Mar-2 Nov, Tue-Sun 10-5. (Closed Mon, ex during school and bank holidays) **Fee:** ✱ £3.95 (ch & concessions £2.95)
Facilities: 🅿 🍴 ♿ toilets for disabled shop

SHANKLIN   Map 04 SZ58

SHANKLIN CHINE
12 Pomona Rd PO37 6PF
➲ (turn off A3055 into Chine Hollow, Shanklin Old Village (between Crab Inn & Pencil Cottage) to Upper entrance or turn off A3055 at lights, left into Hope Rd & continue onto Esplanade. Lower entrance Western end.
☎ 01983 866432   🖷 01983 866145   **2 for 1**
e-mail: jill@shanklinchine.co.uk

This historic gorge at Shanklin is a magical world of unique beauty and a rich haven of rare plants, woodland and wildlife, including red squirrels and enchanting waterfalls. A path winds down through the ravine with overhanging trees, ferns and other flora covering steep sides. The Exhibition "The Island - Then and Now", introduced in 2003, is in the Heritage Centre, together with PLUTO (Pipe Line Under The Ocean) which carried petrol to the Allied troops in Normandy. Also featured is the 40 Royal Marines Commando display, commemorating their link with the Chine - they trained here during the war in preparation for the Dieppe Raid of 1942. After dusk, during the summer months, subtle illuminations create a different world.
Times: Open daily, 1 Apr-20 May 10-5; 21 May-26 Sep 10-10; 27 Sep-31 Oct 10-5. (weather conditions may influence opening times, illuminated after dusk). **Fee:** £3.50 (ch under 16 £2, pen & students £2.50). Family ticket £9 (2 adult & 2 ch), £11 (2 adult & 3 ch). Group rates available. **Facilities:** 🅿 (450yds) 🍴 (access via lower entry only) shop (on lead at all times)

SHORWELL   Map 04 SZ48

YAFFORD WATER MILL FARM PARK
PO30 3LH
➲ (on B3399, Shorwell to Brightstone Road)
☎ 01983 740610 & 741125   🖷 01983 740610

The mill is situated in attractive surroundings with a large mill pond. The great overshot wheel still turns and all the milling machinery is in working order. An unusual attraction is the millpond, which is home to a seal. The millstream has pools and falls with flowers and trees along its banks. Old farm wagons, agricultural machinery and a narrow gauge railway can also be seen along with rare breeds of sheep, pigs and cattle.
Times: Open all year, daily 10-6 or dusk in winter. (Last admission 5pm). **Facilities:** 🅿 🍴 ♿ toilets for disabled shop ✖ (ex guide dogs)

VENTNOR   Map 04 SZ57

SMUGGLING MUSEUM
Botanic Gardens PO38 1UL
➲ (on A3055, 1m W of Ventnor)   **2 for 1**
☎ 01983 853677

Situated underground in extensive vaults, this unique museum shows methods of smuggling used over a 700-year period right up to the present day.
Times: Open Apr-Sep, daily 10-5. **Fee:** £2.80 (ch & pen £1.40). Parties by arrangement. **Facilities:** 🅿 (charged) shop

VENTNOR BOTANIC GARDEN

Undercliff Dr PO38 1UL
(on A3055 coastal road)
☎ **01983 855397** Fax **01983 856756**
e-mail: alison.ellsbury@iow.gov.uk

Due to the unique microclimate of the 'Undercliff', plants that can only survive in a Mediterranean climate thrive on the Isle of Wight. Built on the site of a Victorian hospital for TB sufferers, the garden was founded in 1970 by Sir Harold Hillier, and opened in 1972 by Earl Mountbatten. The garden has plants from Australasia, Africa, America, the Mediterranean, and the Far East, and is a great day out for anyone remotely interested in exotic flora.

Times: Gardens: open all year; Visitor Centre & Green House: Mar-Oct, daily 10-5 & Nov-Feb, wknds only **Fee:** Free admission to Gardens & Visitor Centre; Green House £1 **Facilities:** P (charged) toilets for disabled shop garden centre (ex in garden)

WROXALL Map 04 SZ57

APPULDURCOMBE HOUSE

PO38 3EW
(off B3327, 0.5 miles W)
☎ **01983 852484**

The shell of Appuldurcombe, once the grandest house on the Isle of Wight, stands in its own grounds, designed by 'Capability' Brown. An exhibition of prints and photographs depicts the house and its history.

Times: Open 15 Feb-Apr, daily 10-4; May-Sep, daily 10-5; Oct-15 Dec, daily 10-4 (last admission to property 1hr before closing). Dates valid until 31 Mar 2004. **Fee:** £2.50 (ch £1.50 & concessions £2.25). Family ticket £7. Prices valid until 31 Mar 2004. **Facilities:** P shop (ex dogs on leads)

YARMOUTH Map 04 SZ38

YARMOUTH CASTLE

Quay St PO4 1OP
(adjacent to car ferry terminal)
☎ **01983 760678**

The last addition to Henry VIII's coastal defences completed in 1547, the Tudor castle is set in a beautiful old seaside town. See the Isle of Wight paintings and memorable photographs of Old Yarmouth.

Times: Open Apr-Sep, daily 10-6; Oct, daily 10-5. Dates valid until 31 Mar 2004. **Fee:** £2.50 (ch £1.30, concessions £1.90). Prices valid until 31 Mar 2004. **Facilities:** P (200yds) shop (ex dogs on leads)

WILTSHIRE

EVENTS & FESTIVALS

May
- 1st Downton Cuckoo Fair, medieval fair in village centre
- 1st-15th Swindon Festival of Literature, various venues
- tbc Chippenham Folk Festival
- tbc Salisbury Festival (various venues)
- tbc Swindon Kite Festival

June
- tbc Corsham Festival

July
- 16th-18th Larmer Tree Festival, Larmer Tree Victorian Pleasure Gardens, Cranbourne Chase (festival of world music)
- tbc Calne Country Music Festival
- tbc Marlborough International Jazz Festival
- tbc North Wiltshire Business & Community Fesival, Monkton Park, Chippenham

August
- tbc Wiltshire Festival (music), Lydiard Park, Lydiard Tregoze, West Swindon

October
- 1st-10th Calne Music & Arts Festival
- tbc Cricklade Festival

Above: Bowood House, Calne
Top: Stonehenge, Salisbury

AVEBURY · Map 04 SU06

ALEXANDER KEILLER MUSEUM
High St SN8 1RF
➲ (Turn off A4 onto A4361/B4003)
☎ 01672 539250 ▤ 01672 539388
e-mail: wavgen@smtp.ntrust.org.uk

This is one of the most important prehistoric sites in Europe, and was built before Stonehenge. An avenue of great stones leads to the site, which may have been a place of great religious significance. The museum has recently had the addition of the barn gallery. This interactive museum uses the latest interpretative techniques to explain the history of the Avebury landscape.
Times: ✱ Open Apr-Oct, daily 10-6 or dusk if earlier; Nov-Mar, 10-4. (Closed 24-26 Dec & 1 Jan). **Facilities:** ▯ ▆ ✗ licensed ⅋ toilets for disabled shop ✖ (ex guide dogs) ⚏ ⅏ ◥

AVEBURY MANOR
SN8 1RF
➲ (from A4 take A4361/B4003)
☎ 01672 539250 ▤ 01672 539388
e-mail: aveburyofficerservices@
nationaltrust.org.uk

Avebury Manor has a monastic origin, and has been much altered since then. The present buildings date from the early 16th century, with notable Queen Anne alterations and Edwardian renovation. The flower gardens contain medieval walls, and there are examples of topiary.
Times: Open: House 2 Apr-Oct, Tue-Wed, Sun & BH Mon 2-5.30 (last admission 5pm or dusk if earlier). Garden 2 Apr-Oct daily ex Mon & Thu (open BH Mon). **Fee:** ✱ Manor & garden £3.70 (ch £1.90). Garden £2.80 (ch £1.40). **Facilities:** ▯ (charged) ⅋ shop ✖ ⅏ ◥

BRADFORD-ON-AVON · Map 03 ST86

BRADFORD-ON-AVON TITHE BARN `FREE`
➲ (0.25m S of town centre, off B3109)
This impressive tithe barn, over 160ft long by 30ft wide, once belonged to Shaftesbury Abbey. The roof is of stone slates, supported outside by buttresses and inside by massive beams and a network of rafters.
Times: Open all year, daily 10.30-4. (Closed 25 Dec). Dtaes valid until 31 Mar 2004. **Facilities:** ▯ (charged) ⅋ ✖ ⚏

GREAT CHALFIELD MANOR
SN12 8NJ
➲ (3m SW of Melksham) `2 for 1`
☎ 01225 782239
Built during the Wars of the Roses, the manor is a beautiful, mellow, moated house, restored in the 1920s.
Times: Open Mar-Oct, Tue-Thu, guided tours only at 12.15, 2.15, 3.45, 4.30. **Fee:** £4.40 (ch £2.20) Family ticket £11. **Facilities:** ▯ ✖ ⅏

CORSHAM COURT
HOME OF THE METHUEN FAMILY

Corsham Court is one of England's finest Stately Homes. It was a Royal Manor in the days of the Saxon Kings, and the present building is based upon an Elizabethan Manor dating from 1582. Magnificent Georgian State Rooms were added in 1760. It houses one of the oldest and most distinguished collections of Old Masters and Furniture in the country, and with its 'Capability' Brown gardens and arboretum, and architecture by John Nash and Thomas Bellamy, Corsham Court provides the visitor with a wonderful opportunity to enjoy the many delights of the historic and beautiful Stately Home.

Tel/Fax: 01249 701610
For opening times see gazetteer entry

CALNE · Map 03 ST97

BOWOOD HOUSE & GARDENS
SN11 0LZ
➲ (off A4 Chippenham to Calne rd, in Derry Hill village)
☎ 01249 812102 ▤ 01249 821757
e-mail: houseandgardens@bowood.org

Built in 1624, the house was finished by the first Earl of Shelburne, who employed celebrated architects, notably Robert Adam, to complete the work. Adam's library is particularly admired, and also in the house is the laboratory where Dr Joseph Priestley discovered the existence of oxygen in 1774. The house overlooks terraced gardens towards the 40-acre lake and some beautiful parkland. The gardens were laid out by 'Capability' Brown in the 1760s, and are carpeted with daffodils, narcissi and bluebells in spring. There is also an adventure playground and new soft play area.
Times: Open Apr-Oct, daily 11-6, including BH. Rhododendron Gardens (separate entrance off A342) open 6 weeks during mid Apr-early Jun, 11-6. **Fee:** ✱ House & Gardens £6.25 (ch 2-4 £3.15; 5-15 £4; pen £5.15). Rhododendrons only £3.50 **Facilities:** ▯ ▆ ✗ licensed ⅋ (parking by arrangement) toilets for disabled shop ✖ (ex guide & hearing dogs) ◥

CORSHAM   Map 03 ST87
CORSHAM COURT
SN13 0BZ
➲ (4m W of Chippenham off the A4)
☎ 01249 701610 🖷 01249 701610

The Elizabethan manor was built in 1582, and then bought by the Methuen family in the 18th century to house their collections of paintings and statues. 'Capability' Brown made additions to the house and laid out the park, and later John Nash made further changes. There is furniture by Chippendale, Adam, Cobb and Johnson inside, as well as the Methuen collection of Old Master paintings. The garden has flowering shrubs, herbaceous borders, a Georgian bath house and peacocks.
Times: Open Summer: 20 Mar-Sep daily ex Mon Fri, but incl BH's 2-5.30. Winter: Oct-19 Mar open wknds only 2-4.30pm. Last admission 30 minutes before closing. (Closed Dec). Open throughout year by appointment for groups 15+. **Fee:** Prices not confirmed for 2004.
Facilities: 🅿 💺 ♿ shop ✕ (on leads only)

HOLT   Map 03 ST86
THE COURTS
BA14 6RR
➲ (3m N of Trowbridge, on B3107)   `2 for 1`
☎ 01225 782340 🖷 01225 782340
Weavers came to The Courts to have their disputes settled until the end of the 18th century. The house is not open, but it makes an attractive backdrop to the gardens - a network of stone paths, yew hedges, pools and borders with a strange, almost magical atmosphere.
Times: Open 27 Mar-17 Oct daily (ex Wed) 11-5.30 out of season by appointment only. **Fee:** £4.50 (ch £2.25) Family ticket £11.50 Group £4.
Facilities: 🅿 💺 ♿ ✕ (ex guide dogs) ⛝

LACOCK   Map 03 ST96
LACKHAM COUNTRY PARK
Wiltshire College, Lackham SN15 2NY
➲ (3m S of Chippenham, on A350. 6m S of M4 Junct 17)
☎ 01249 466800 🖷 01249 444474   `2 for 1`
e-mail: adavies@wiltscoll.ac.uk
Various visitor attractions are situated within the 210-hectare estate of Wiltshire College - Lackham. Thatched and refurbished farm buildings accommodate the farm museum and the grounds feature a walled garden, glasshouses, and a
continued

farm park. Also grown in this garden was the largest citron (large lemon) which earned a place in the Guinness Book of Records. There is also a self-guided picturesque woodland walk available.
Times: Open Etr-Aug, Sun & BH Mon, Tue-Thu in Aug 10-5. Last admission 4pm. **Fee:** £2 (concessions £1.50, up to 2 ch under 16 free).
Facilities: 🅿 💺 ♿ (wheelchair available) toilets for disabled shop garden centre

LACOCK ABBEY, FOX TALBOT MUSEUM & VILLAGE
SN15 2LG
➲ (3m S of Chippenham, E of A350)
☎ 01249 730227 (abbey) 🖷 01249 730501
Lacock Abbey was the venue for a series of innovative photographic experiments by William Henry Fox Talbot. The Abbey was founded in the 13th century. At the Dissolution it was sold to William Sharington, who destroyed the church and turned the rest into a grand home.
Times: Museum, Cloisters & Grounds, Mar-Oct, daily 11-5.30. Closed Good Fri. Abbey, 29 Mar-2 Nov daily, ex Tue, 1-5.30. Closed Good Fri. Museum open winter wknds, but closed 25 Dec-2 Jan. **Fee:** Museum Abbey, grounds & cloisters £7 (ch £3.50) Family ticket £17.90. Party: grounds, cloisters & museum only £4.80 (ch £2.20) Family ticket £11.20. Abbey & garden only £5.60 (ch £2.80). Family ticket £14.30. Telephone 01249 730141 for events leaflet. **Facilities:** 🅿 ♿ (taped guides) toilets for disabled shop ✕ ⛝

LONGLEAT   Map 03 ST84
LONGLEAT
The Estate Office BA12 7NW
➲ (Turn off A36 Bath-Salisbury onto A362 Warminster-Frome).
☎ 01985 844400 🖷 01985 844885
e-mail: longleat@longleat.co.uk

Nestling within magnificent 'Capability' Brown landscaped grounds in the heart of Wiltshire, Longleat House is widely regarded as one of the most beautiful stately homes open to the public. Longleat House was built by Sir John Thynne and completed in 1580. It has remained the home of the same family ever since. Many treasures are contained within the house: paintings by Tintoretto and Wooton, exquisite Flemish tapestries, fine French furniture and elaborate ceilings by John Dibblee Crace. The murals in the family apartments in the West Wing were painted by Alexander Thynne, the present Marquis, and are fascinating and remarkable
continued

additions to the collection. Apart from the ancestral home, Longleat is also renowned for its safari park, the first of its kind in the UK. Here, visitors have the rare opportunity to see hundreds of animals in natural woodland and parkland settings. Among the most magnificent sights are the famous pride of lions, white tigers, wolves, rhesus monkeys, elephants and zebra. Other attractions which ensure a fun family day out include the 'World's Longest Hedge Maze', the 'Adventure Castle', 'Longleat Railway', 'Pets' Corner' and the 'Safari Boats'.

Times: Open Attractions: 5 Mar-2 Nov. House: daily (ex Xmas Day). Ring to confirm opening arrangements out of season. **Fee:** ✱ Longleat passport: £16 (ch 3-4 yrs & pen £13) **Facilities:** 🅿 💷 ✗ licensed ♿ (Informative leaflet available or see website) toilets for disabled shop (free kennels for Safari park) ➤

LUDGERSHALL   Map 04 SU25

LUDGERSHALL CASTLE AND CROSS
SP11 9QR   [FREE]
➲ (7m NW of Andover on A342)

Ruins of an early 12th-century royal hunting palace and medieval cross. The visitor can see large earthworks of the Norman motte-and-bailey castle and the flint walls of the later hunting palace. The stump of a medieval cross stands in the village street.

Times: Open all reasonable times. **Facilities:** 🅿 ♿ ✗ (ex dogs on leads) ⌗

LYDIARD PARK   Map 04 SU18

LYDIARD PARK
Lydiard Tregoze SN5 9PA
➲ (from M4 junct 16. Follow brown
Tourist Information signs)
☎ 01793 770401 🖷 01793 877909

Set in country parkland, Lydiard Park belonged to the St John family (the Bolingbrokes) for 500 years up until 1943 when the Swindon Corporation purchased it. Since then the house has been restored and many of the original furnishings returned, together with a family portrait collection dating from Elizabethan to Victorian times. Exceptional plasterwork, early wallpaper, a rare painted glass window, and a room devoted to the talented 18th-century amateur artist, Lady Diana Spencer (Beauclerk), can also be seen.

Times: Open all year, House: Mon-Sat 10-5, Sun 2-5. Winter closing 4pm (Nov-Feb). Park: all year, daily closing at dusk each day. **Fee:** ✱ £1.50 (ch 75p). **Facilities:** 🅿 💷 ♿ (telephone 01793 770401 for access information sheet) toilets for disabled shop ✗ (ex guide dogs in house)

MARLBOROUGH   Map 04 SU16

CROFTON BEAM ENGINES
Crofton Pumping Station, Crofton SN8 3DW
➲ (signposted from A338/A346/B3087 at Burbage
and from A4 at Froxfield)
☎ 01672 870300
e-mail: administration@katrust.org

The oldest working beam engine in the world still in its original building and still doing its original job, the Boulton and Watt 1812, can be found in this rural spot. Its companion is a Harvey's of Hayle of 1845. Both are steam driven, from a
continued

hand-stoked, coal-fired boiler, and pump water into the summit level of the Kennet and Avon Canal with a lift of 40ft.

Times: ✱ Open daily from Etr-late Sep, 10.30-5 (last entry 4.30). Steaming on Bank Holiday weekends and last wknd of Jun, Jul & Sep **Facilities:** 🅿 💷 ♿ (phone warden in advance, sighted guides provided) shop ✗

MIDDLE WOODFORD   Map 04 SU13

HEALE GARDENS, PLANT CENTRE & SHOP
SP4 6NT
➲ (4m N of Salisbury, between A360 & A345)
☎ 01722 782504 🖷 01722 782504

Heale House and its eight acres of beautiful garden lie beside the River Avon at Middle Woodford. Much of the house is unchanged since King Charles II sheltered here after the Battle of Worcester in 1651. The garden provides a wonderfully varied collection of plants, shrubs, and musk and other roses, growing in the formal setting of clipped hedges and mellow stonework.

Times: Gardens & Plant centre open all year, daily 10-5. Closed Mon (ex BH Mons). **Fee:** £3.75 (ch 5-15 £1.50 under 5's free). **Facilities:** 🅿 💷 ♿ shop garden centre ✗ (ex guide dogs) ➤

SALISBURY   Map 04 SU12

THE MEDIEVAL HALL (SECRETS OF SALISBURY)
Cathedral Close SP1 2EY
➲ (look for signs within Salisbury Cathedral Close)
☎ 01722 412472 & 324731 🖷 01722 339983
e-mail: medieval.hall@ntworld.com

Visit the historic 13th century Medieval Hall and watch the fascinating 40 minute sound and picture guide to the city and region. A witty and informative soundtrack, (sometimes available in other languages) specially composed music and some startling effects accompany hundreds of images to provide an insight into Salisbury's extraordinary past, the colourful city of today, and many more of the attractions in the area. Enjoy refreshments 'while you watch'. Contact the Hall for full details of special events.

Times: Open Apr-Sep, from 11-5. Also open throughout year for pre-booked groups. **Fee:** ✱ £2 (ch 7-18 £1, ch under 6 free). Family tickets available **Facilities:** 🅿 (charged) ♿ (ramp access) shop

MOMPESSON HOUSE
Chorister's Green, Cathedral Close SP1 2EL
➲ (from Salisbury centre, walk through gateway at top of high street into Cathedral Close, turn right, house on right).
☎ 01722 335659 🖷 01722 321559
e-mail: mompessonhouse@nationaltrust.org.uk

With its superb wrought-iron railings and perfect proportions, this Queen Anne house makes an impressive addition to the elegant Cathedral Close in Salisbury. Inside are stucco ceilings, a carved oak staircase and period furniture plus an important collection of 18th-century glasses, china and some outstanding paintings.

Times: Open 9 Apr-31 Oct, daily (ex Thu & Fri) 11-5. **Fee:** ✱ £3.90 (ch £1.95). Group rate £3.40. Garden only 80p. **Facilities:** 🅿 (260 yds) (limited disabled parking available) 💷 ♿ toilets for disabled shop (ramps, braille guide) ✗ ➤

OLD SARUM
Castle Rd SP1 3SD
➲ (2m N on A345)
☎ 01722 335398 ▤ 01722 416037
The site of the original city of Salisbury. The 56-acre ruins of this once bustling town are rich in history and woodland. Founded in the Iron Age and occupied until the 16th century. Romans, Saxons and Normans have all left their mark.
Times: Open all year, Apr-Sep, daily 10-6 (9-6 Jul-Aug); Oct, daily 10-5; Nov-Mar daily 10-4. (Closed 24-26 Dec & 1 Jan). Dates valid until 31 Mar 2004. **Fee:** £2.50 (ch £1.30, concessions £1.90). Prices valid until 31 Mar 2004. **Facilities:** ᴾ & (assess to outer bailey and grounds only) shop ✖ (ex dogs on leads) ♯

SALISBURY CATHEDRAL
33 The Close SP1 2EJ
➲ (South of the city centre & Market Sq)
☎ 01722 555120 ▤ 01722 555116
e-mail: visitors@salcath.co.uk

Built in one phase between 1220 and 1258, the Cathedral is probably Britain's finest piece of medieval architecture. The spire is 123 metres tall, making it the tallest in England. The Chapter House displays a frieze depicting scenes from Genesis and Exodus, also the finest surviving Magna Carta. The Choir continues a tradition that began around 800 years ago, with performances at daily services. They are accompanied by Europe's finest romantic church organ. The surrounding Cathedral Close contains two museums, two small stately homes and acres of lawn.
Times: Open all year, daily 7.15-6.15; Jun-Aug, Mon-Sat 7.15-7.15.
Fee: Suggested Voluntary Donations: £3.80 (ch 5-17 £2, pen & students £3.30). Family £8.50. **Facilities:** ᴾ (100yds) ▆✖ licensed & (loop system, interpretative model for blind, wheelchairs) toilets for disabled shop (closed 25 Dec) ➾

SALISBURY & SOUTH WILTSHIRE MUSEUM
The King's House, 65 The Close SP1 2EN
➲ (in Cathedral Close)   **2 for 1**
☎ 01722 332151 ▤ 01722 325611
e-mail: museum@salisburymuseum.org.uk
One of the most outstanding of the beautiful buildings in Cathedral Close houses this local museum. Galleries feature Stonehenge, History of Salisbury, the Pitt Rivers collection, ceramics and pictures and the Wedgwood room, a reconstruction of a pre-NHS surgery, and a costume, lace and embroidery gallery.
Times: Open all year Mon-Sat 10-5; also Suns Jul & Aug, 2-5. (Closed Xmas). **Fee:** £3.50 (under 5's free, ch £1, pen, students & UB40s £2.30). Party. Season saver tickets available. **Facilities:** ᴾ (100 metres) (nearby parking charge) ✖ & parking by prior arrangement,induction loop in lecture hall toilets for disabled shop ✖ (ex guide dogs) ➾

STONEHENGE   Map 04 SU14

STONEHENGE
SP4 7DE
➲ (2m W of Amesbury on junct A303 and A344/A360)
☎ 01980 624715
Britain's greatest prehistoric monument and a World Heritage Site. What visitors see today are the substantial remains of the last in a series of monuments erected between c3000 and 1600BC.
Times: Open all year, 16 Mar-May, daily 9.30-6; Jun-Aug, daily 9-7; Sep-15 Oct, daily 9.30-6. 16-15 Mar, daily 9.30-4. (Closed 24-26 Dec & 1 Jan). Dates valid until 31 Mar 2004. **Fee:** £5 (ch £2.50, concessions £3.80). Prices valid until 31 Mar 2004. **Facilities:** ᴾ ▆ & shop ✖ (ex guide & hearing dogs) ♯

STOURHEAD   Map 03 ST73

STOURHEAD GARDEN & HOUSE
Estate Office BA12 6QD
➲ (At Stourton off B3092, 3m NW Mere, follow brown tourist signs)
☎ 01747 841152 ▤ 01747 842005
e-mail: wstest@smtp.ntrust.org.uk
Enchanting 18th century landscape garden set around a lake with classical temples, a grotto and rare tress and plants. Fine palladian mansion built by Colen Campbell containing fine works of art and furniture by Chippendale the younger.
Times: Garden open all year 9-7 (or dusk if earlier). House open 28 Mar-31 Oct ,11-5 (closed on Wed & Thu); King Alfred tower open 28 Mar-31 Oct, daily 12-5. **Facilities:** ᴾ ▆✖ licensed & (wheelchairs, electric buggy, telephone in advance) toilets for disabled shop garden centre ✖ (ex in gardens Nov-Feb only) ♨ ➾

STOURTON   Map 03 ST73

STOURTON HOUSE FLOWER GARDEN
Stourton House BA12 6QF
➲ (3m NW of Mere, on A303)
☎ 01747 840417
Set in the attractive village of Stourton, the house has more than four acres of beautifully maintained flower gardens. Many grass paths lead through varied and colourful shrubs and trees. Stourton House also specialises in unusual plants

continued

and dried flowers, many of which are for sale. It also has collections of daffodils, delphiniums and hydrangeas.

Times: ✳ Open Apr-end Nov, Wed, Thu, Sun & BH Mon 11-6 (or dusk if earlier). Also open Dec-Mar, wkdays for plant/dried flower sales. **Facilities:** 🅿 💻 ♿ (wheelchairs available) toilets for disabled shop (plants for sale) garden centre ✈ (ex by arrangement)

SWINDON   Map 04 SU18

STEAM - MUSEUM OF THE GREAT WESTERN RAILWAY
Kemble Dr SN2 2TA
➲ (from junct 16 of M4 & A420 follow brown signs to 'Outlet Centre' and Museum)
☎ 01793 466646 🖷 01793 466615
e-mail: steampostbox@swindon.gov.uk

Nominated for European Museum of the Year, this fascinating day out tells the story of the men and women who built, operated and travelled on the Great Western Railway. Hands-on displays, world-famous locomotives, archive film footage and the testimonies of ex-railway workers bring the story to life. A reconstructed station platform, posters and holiday memorabilia recreate the glamour and excitement of the golden age of steam. Located next door to the McArthurGlen Designer Outlet Great Western, Steam offers a great day out for all. Good value group packages, special events and exhibitions, shop and café.
Times: Open Nov-Mar, Mon-Sat 10-5, Sun 11-5. Apr-Oct, Mon-Sat 10-5.30, Sun 11-5.30. **Fee:** ✳ £5.95 (ch £3.80, pen £3.90) Family ticket £14.70 (2ad+2ch) **Facilities:** 🅿 (100 yds) (disabled parking 20yds) 💻 ♿ audio guide, wheelchair or scooter can be pre-booked toilets for disabled shop ✈ (ex guide dogs) 🍴

TEFFONT MAGNA   Map 03 ST93

FARMER GILES FARMSTEAD
SP3 5QY
➲ (11m W of Salisbury, off A303 at Teffont)
☎ 01722 716338 🖷 01722 716993
e-mail: tdeane6995@aol.com
Set in 175 acres of Wiltshire downland, this is a real working dairy farm. You can watch the cows being milked, bottle feed lambs and get to know a host of other animals and pets. There is an adventure playground with tractors and a relaxing walk along the picturesque Beech belt, meeting
continued

Highland cattle and Shire horses along the way. There are also exhibition areas and a restaurant.

Times: ✳ Open 18 Mar-5 Nov, daily 10-6, wknds in winters, 10-dusk. Party bookings all year. **Facilities:** 🅿 ✕ licensed ♿ (complete access for disabled/wheelchairs available for use) toilets for disabled shop 🍴

TISBURY   Map 03 ST92

OLD WARDOUR CASTLE
SP3 6RR
➲ (2m SW)
☎ 01747 870487
This 14th-century castle stands in a romantic lakeside setting. Landscaped grounds and elaborate rockwork grotto surround the unusual hexagonal ruins. Scenes from *Robin Hood, Price of Thieves*, starring Kevin Costner, were filmed here.
Times: Open all year, Apr-Sep, daily 10-6; Oct, daily 10-5; Nov-Mar, Wed-Sun 10-4 (Closed between 1-2, 24-26 Dec & 1 Jan). Dates valid until 31 Mar 2004. **Fee:** £2.60 (ch £1.30, concessions £2). Prices valid until 31 Mar 2004. **Facilities:** 🅿 ♿ ⚙

WESTBURY   Map 03 ST85

BROKERSWOOD COUNTRY PARK
Brokerswood BA13 4EH
➲ (turn off A36 at Bell Inn, Standerwick. Follow brown heritage signs)
☎ 01373 822238 & 823880 🖷 01373 858474
e-mail: woodland.park@virgin.net
Brokerswood Country Park's nature walk leads through 80 acres of woodlands, with a lake and wildfowl. Facilities include a woodland visitor centre (covering wildlife and forestry), two children's adventure playgrounds (Etr-Oct school holidays & wkends only), indoor soft play area, guided walks and the woodland railway, over a third of a mile long.
Times: Open all year; Park open daily 10-5. Closed Christmas Day, Boxing Day & New Year's Day. Ring for museum opening hours. **Fee:** ✳ £3 (ch 5-17yrs £1.50, pen £2.50) **Facilities:** 🅿 💻 ♿ (ramp access to cafe) shop 🍴

The AA also publishes a guide to Pet Friendly Places to Stay

WESTWOOD   Map 03 ST85

WESTWOOD MANOR

BA15 2AF

➲ (1.5m SW of Bradford on Avon, off B3109)

☎ 01225 863374   ▤ 01225 867316

This late 15th-century stone manor house has some particularly fine Jacobean plasterwork. The house, situated by the parish church, was altered in 1610 but still retains its late Gothic and Jacobean windows.

Times: Open Apr-Sep, Tue, Wed & Sun, 2-5. **Fee:** £4.40 (ch £2.20) Family ticket £11.20. **Facilities:** ▣ ✖ ⚘

WILTON (NEAR SALISBURY) Map 04 SU03

WILTON HOUSE

SP2 0BJ

➲ (3m W of Salisbury, on the A30, 10m from Stonehenge & A303)

☎ 01722 746720 & 746729(24 hr line)

▤ 01722 744447

e-mail: tourism@wiltonhouse.com

This fabulous Palladian mansion amazes visitors with its treasures, including magnificent art, fine furniture and interiors by Inigo Jones. The traditional and modern gardens, some designed by Lord Pembroke himself, are fabulous throughout the season and continue to delight visitors, whilst the adventure playground is a firm favourite with children.

Times: Open 11 Apr-26 Oct daily 10.30-5.30. Last admission 4.30. House closed Mon, ex BH's. **Fee:** ✱ £9.25 (ch 5-15 £5, under 5 £1, students & pen £7.50). Family ticket £22. **Facilities:** ▣ ▣ ᴇ (induction loop) toilets for disabled shop garden centre ✖ (ex service dogs) ⬤

WOODHENGE   Map 04 SU14

WOODHENGE

➲ (1.5m N of Amesbury, off A345 just S of Durrington)   [FREE]

A Neolithic ceremonial monument dating from about 2300 BC, consisting of six concentric rings of timber posts, now marked by concrete piles. The long axis of the rings, which are oval, points to the rising sun on Midsummer Day.

Times: Open all reasonable times. **Facilities:** ▣ ᴇ ✖ (ex dogs on leads) ▒

The AA also publishes a guide to Pet Friendly Places to Stay

WORCESTERSHIRE

EVENTS & FESTIVALS

May
7th-9th Spring Garden Show, Three Counties Showground, Malvern
tbc Oakapple Day, The Commandery, Worcester
tbc Upton Folk Festival (various venues), Upton-upon-Severn

June
18th-20th Three Counties Show, Three Counties Showground, Malvern
25th-27th Upton Jazz Festival (various venues), Upton-upon-Severn

July
16th-18th Upton Blues Festival, Upton-upon-Severn (provisional)
tbc Worcester Carnival

September
25th-26th The Malvern Autumn Show, Three Counties Showground, Malvern

December
tbc Victorian Christmas Fayre

Above: Worcester's Guildhall
Top: Queen Victoria Memorial Beacon, Malvern

BEWDLEY Map 07 SO77

SEVERN VALLEY RAILWAY
Comberton Hill DY10 1QN
☎ 01299 403816 🖷 01299 400839
(For full entry see Kidderminster)

WEST MIDLAND SAFARI & LEISURE PARK
Spring Grove DY12 1LF
➲ (on A456 between Kidderminster & Bewdley)
☎ 01299 402114 🖷 01299 404519
e-mail: info@wmsp.co.uk
Located in the heart of rural Worcestershire, this 200-acre site is the home to a drive-through safari and Tiger World. There are a variety of rides, amusements and live shows suitable for all members of the family. Other features include Pets Corner, Hippo Lakes, Goat Walk, Seal Aquarium Creepy Crawlies exhibit, animal and reptile encounters and Sealion Theatre.
Times: Open Apr-Oct, daily from 10am including BH's. **Fee:** ✱ £6.75 (ch 4 free). Multi ride wristband £8. Junior restricted £6.50 (restricted rides only). Ride tickets £3 for two tickets from machines (various no of tickets per ride). **Facilities:** 🅿 💷 ✕ licensed ♿ (most area accessible slopes/tarmac paths) shop ✖ (ex guide dogs) 🥤

BROADWAY Map 04 SP03

BROADWAY TOWER & ANIMAL PARK
WR12 7LB
➲ (off A44, 1m SE of village)
☎ 01386 852390 🖷 01386 858038
e-mail: broadway-cotswold.co.uk/tower.html
The 65ft tower was designed by James Wyatt for the 6th Earl of Coventry, and built in 1799. The unique building now houses exhibitions depicting its colourful past and various uses such as holiday retreat to artist and designer William Morris. The viewing platform is equipped with a telescope, giving wonderful views over 13 counties. Around the Tower is a park with adventure playground, children's farm, BBQs, giant chess and draughts, and animal enclosures.
Times: ✱ Open Apr-Oct, daily 10.30-5. Nov-Mar (tower only) wknds weather permitting 11-3 or by prior booking. **Facilities:** 🅿 💷 ✕ licensed ♿ toilets for disabled shop 🥤

BROMSGROVE Map 07 SO97

AVONCROFT MUSEUM OF HISTORIC BUILDINGS
Stoke Heath B60 4JR
➲ (2m S, off A38)
☎ 01527 831886 🖷 01527 876934 `2 for 1`
e-mail: avoncroft1@compuserve.com
A visit to Avoncroft takes you through nearly 700 years of history. Here you can see 25 buildings rescued from destruction and authentically restored on a 15 acre rural site. There are 15th and 16th-century timber framed buildings, 18th-century agricultural buildings and a cockpit. There are industrial buildings and a working windmill from the 19th century, and from the 20th a fully furnished pre-fab.
Times: Open Jul-Aug daily 10.30-5; Apr-Jun & Sep-Oct 10.30-4.30 (wknds 5.30), (Closed Mon); Mar & Nov 10.30-4, (Closed Mon & Fri). Open BHs. **Fee:** ✱ £5.50 (ch £2.75, pen £4.50). Family ticket £14.50. **Facilities:** 🅿 💷 ♿ (ramps, wheelchair available) toilets for disabled shop 🥤

EVESHAM Map 04 SP04

THE ALMONRY HERITAGE CENTRE
Abbey Gate WR11 4EJ
➲ (on A4184, opposite Merstow Green, main North/South route through Evesham)
☎ 01386 446944 🖷 01386 442348
e-mail: almonry@eveshamtc.ndirect.co.uk
The 14th-century stone and timber building was the home of the Almoner of the Benedictine Abbey in Evesham. It now houses exhibitions relating to the history of Evesham Abbey, the Battle of Evesham, and the culture and trade of Evesham. Evesham Tourist Information Centre is also located here.
Times: Open all year, Mon-Sat & BHs (ex Xmas & Sun in Nov-Feb) 10-5, Sun 2-5. **Fee:** £2.50 (ch 16 free, pen & students £1.50). **Facilities:** 🅿 (110yds) shop ✖

GREAT WITLEY Map 03 SO76

WITLEY COURT
WR6 6JT
➲ (on A433)
☎ 01299 896636
Discover the spectacular ruins of this once-great house destroyed by fire in 1937. Explore the magnificent landscaped gardens, which feature the stunning Perseus & Andromeda fountains and are home to contemporary sculpture. Step back in time with the audio tour.
Times: Open all year, Apr-Sep, daily 10-6; Oct, daily 10-5; Nov-Mar, Wed-Sun, 10-4. (Closed 24-26 Dec & 1 Jan). Dates valid until 31 Mar 2004. **Fee:** £4.60 (ch £2.30, concessions £3.50). Prices valid until 31 Mar 2004 **Facilities:** 🅿 💷 ♿ shop ✖ 🚻

HANBURY Map 03 SO96

HANBURY HALL
School Rd WR9 7EA
➲ (4.5m E of Droitwich, 1m N of B4090 and 1.5m W of B4091)
☎ 01527 821214 🖷 01527 821251 `2 for 1`
e-mail: hanbury@smtp.ntrust.org.uk

This William and Mary style red-brick house, completed in 1701, was built by a prosperous local family. The house contains outstanding painted ceilings and staircase by Thornhill, and the Watney collection of porcelain. The 18th-century garden has recently been restored with many

continued

features including parterre, bowling green and working orangery.
Times: Open 22 Mar-29 Oct Sat-Wed 12-5.30 or dusk if earlier. Garden & tearoom opens 12 noon. **Fee:** ✱ House & Garden £5 (ch £3). Family ticket £12.50. Garden only £3 (ch £1.60). **Facilities:** 🅿 🍴 ♿ (Braille guide) toilets for disabled shop ✖ (ex in park) 🐾 ⛟

KIDDERMINSTER   Map 07 SO87

SEVERN VALLEY RAILWAY
Comberton Hill DY10 1QN
➲ (on A448, clearly signposted)
☎ 01299 403816   🖷 01299 400839

The leading standard gauge steam railway, with one of the largest collections of locomotives and rolling stock in the country. Services operate from Kidderminster and Bewdley to Bridgnorth through 16 miles of picturesque scenery along the River Severn. Special steam galas and "Day out with Thomas" Weekends take place during the year along with Santa Specials.
Times: Trains operate wknds throughout year, daily early May to end Sep, plus school holidays & half terms, Santa Specials, phone for details. **Fee:** ✱ Subject to Review. (Train fares vary according to journey. Main through ticket £10.50 return, Family ticket £28)
Facilities: 🅿 (charged) 🍴 ♿ (some specially adapted trains, call for details) toilets for disabled shop (at Kidderminster/Bridgnorth) ⛟

WORCESTERSHIRE COUNTY MUSEUM
Hartlebury Castle, Hartlebury DY11 7XZ
➲ (4m S of Kidderminster clearly signed from A449)
☎ 01299 250416   🖷 01299 251890   `2 for 1`
e-mail: museum@worcestershire.gov.uk
Housed in the north wing of Hartlebury Castle, the County Museum contains a delightful display of crafts and industries. There are unique collections of toys, costume, domestic life, room settings and horse-drawn vehicles as well as a reconstructed forge, schoolroom, wheelwright's and tailor's shop.
Times: Open Feb-Nov, Mon-Thu 10-5, BH's 11-5, Fri & Sun 2-5. (Closed Sat & Good Fri). **Fee:** ✱ £2.50 (ch & pen £1.20). Family ticket £6.50.
Facilities: 🅿 🍴 ♿ (car parking spaces, close to main building) toilets for disabled shop ✖ (ex guide dogs & in grounds) ⛟

REDDITCH   Map 03 SP06

FORGE MILL NEEDLE MUSEUM & BORDESLEY ABBEY VISITOR CENTRE
Forge Mill, Needle Mill Ln, Riverside B98 8HY
➲ (N side of Redditch, off A441. M42 junct 2)
☎ 01527 62509   `2 for 1`
e-mail: museum@redditchbc.gov.uk
The Needle Museum tells the fascinating and sometimes gruesome story of how needles are made. Working, water-powered machinery can be seen in an original needle-scouring mill. The Visitor Centre is an archaeological museum showing finds from excavations at the nearby Bordesley Abbey.
Times: Open Etr-Sep, Mon-Fri 11-4.30, Sat-Sun 2-5; Feb-Etr & Oct-Nov, Mon-Thu 11-4 & Sun 2-5. Parties by arrangement. **Fee:** ✱ £3.50 (ch 50p, pen £2.50). Family ticket £7.50. Reduced admission charge for holders of a Reddicard. **Facilities:** 🅿 ♿ (wheelchair available, audio tour of museum) toilets for disabled shop ✖ (ex guide dogs) ⛟

SPETCHLEY   Map 03 SO85

SPETCHLEY PARK GARDENS
Spetchley Park WR5 1RS
➲ (3m E of Worcester, off A422)
☎ 01905 345213 or 345224   🖷 01453 511915
e-mail: hb@spetchleygardens.co.uk
The 110-acre deer park and the 30-acre gardens surround an early 19th-century mansion (not open), with sweeping lawns and herbaceous borders, a rose lawn and enclosed gardens with low box and yew hedges. There is a large collection of trees (including 17th-century Cedars of Lebanon), shrubs and plants, many of which are rare or unusual.
Times: Open Apr-Sep, Tue-Fri 11-5, Sun 2-5; BH Mons 11-5, (last admission 4pm). Other days by appointment. **Fee:** ✱ £4 (ch £2). Party 25+ £3.80. **Facilities:** 🅿 🍴 ♿ (most of garden accessible) ✖ (ex guide dogs)

STONE   Map 07 SO87

STONE HOUSE COTTAGE GARDENS
DY10 4BG
➲ (2m SE of Kidderminster, on A448)
☎ 01562 69902   🖷 01562 69960   `2 for 1`
e-mail: louisa@shcn.co.uk
A beautiful walled garden with towers provides a sheltered area of about one acre for rare shrubs, climbers and interesting herbaceous plants. Adjacent to the garden is a nursery with a large selection of unusual plants.
Times: Open Gardens & nursery Mar-end Sep, Wed-Sat 10-5.30.
Fee: ✱ £2.50 (ch free). **Facilities:** 🅿 ♿ garden centre ✖

WORCESTER   Map 03 SO85

CITY MUSEUM & ART GALLERY
Foregate St WR1 1DT
➲ (Located in City Centre, 150m from Foregate St Train Station)
☎ 01905 25371   🖷 01905 616979   `FREE`
e-mail: artgalleryandmuseum@ cityofworcester.gov.uk
The gallery has temporary art exhibitions from both local and national sources. Museum exhibits cover geology, local and natural history. Of particular interest is a complete

continued

19th-century chemist's shop. There are collections relating to the Worcestershire Regiment and the Worcestershire Yeomanry Cavalry.
Times: Open all year, Mon, Tue-Fri 9.30-5.30, Sat 9.30-5.(Closed 25-26 Dec & 1 Jan also Good Fri) **Facilities:** P (city centre) 🚽 ♿ (lift, induction loop) toilets for disabled shop ✗ ☞

THE COMMANDERY
Sidbury WR1 2HU
➲ (M5 junct 7, A44, signposted)
☎ 01905 361821 📄 01905 361822
e-mail: thecommandery@cityof
worcester.gov.uk
The headquarters of Charles II's army during the Battle of Worcester in 1651. The Commandery is an impressive complex of medieval timber framed buildings. Various exhibitions include 'Civil War',which details the events of England's bloody revolution.
Times: ✱ Open all year, Mon-Sat 10-5, Sun 1.30-5. (Closed 25-26 Dec & 1 Jan) **Facilities:** P (100yds) shop ✗ (ex guide dogs) ☞

ELGAR'S BIRTHPLACE MUSEUM
Crown East Ln, Lower Broadheath WR2 6RH
➲ (3m W, signposted off A44 to Leominster).
☎ 01905 333224 📄 01905 333426 `2 for 1`
e-mail: birthplace@elgarmuseum.org
In 2000, the Elgar Centre was opened, to complement the historic Birthplace Cottage and to provide additional exhibition space for more treasures from this unique collection, telling the story of Elgar's musical development and inspirations. Listen to his music as the audio tour guides you round the easily accessible displays.
Times: Open daily 11-5, Feb-Xmas. Last admission 4.15. (Closed 23 Dec-end Jan). **Fee:** ✱ £4.50 (ch £2 & pen £4). Family ticket £11. Party rates available. **Facilities:** P ♿ (large print guides, audio facilities, wheelchair) toilets for disabled shop ✗ (ex guide dogs) ☞

HAWFORD DOVECOTE
➲ (3m N on A449)
☎ 01684 855300
An unusual square, half-timbered 16th-century dovecote. Access on foot only via the entrance drive to the adjoining house.
Times: ✱ Open Apr-Oct, daily 9-6 or sunset. (Closed Good Fri). Other times by prior appointment only. **Facilities:** P (on street parking) ✗ 🐾

MUSEUM OF LOCAL LIFE
Friar St WR1 2NA
➲ (City centre, 5min walk from Cathedral)
☎ 01905 722349
This interesting 500-year-old timber-framed house has a squint and an ornate plaster ceiling. It is now a museum of local life and displays show life here over the last 200 years.
Times: Open all year, Mon-Wed & Fri-Sat 10.30-5. Also BH's. (Closed 25-26 Dec & 1 Jan). **Facilities:** P (200yds) ♿ toilets for disabled shop ✗ (ex guide dogs) ☞

MUSEUM OF WORCESTER PORCELAIN
Severn St WR1 2NE
➲ (M5 Junct 7, follow signs to city centre, at 7th set of lights take 1st left into Edger Street & bear left with road into Severn St. At T Junct bear right & after 700yds take 1st left. Museum on left)
☎ 01905 746000 📄 01905 617807 `2 for 1`
e-mail: museum@royal-worcester.co.uk
The Victorian buildings lead into the heart of a world famous porcelain industry and was founded in 1751. The guided tours and the Museum of Worcester Porcelain take visitors on a design journey through time. Exhibits include room settings, dining scenes and shop fronts in the Georgian, Victorian and 20th century galleries.
Times: Open all year, Mon-Sat 9-5.30, Sun 11-5. closed 25, 25 Dec & Etr Sun. **Fee:** ✱ Museum: £3.50 (concessions £2.75), family £7.50. Special all-in-one £9 (concessions £7.25), family £21.50. **Facilities:** P (charged) ♿ (ex factory) toilets for disabled shop ✗ ☞

WORCESTER CATHEDRAL
WR1 2LH
➲ (Worcester city centre, signed from M5 junct 7)
☎ 01905 28854 & 21004 📄 01905 611139
e-mail: info@worcestercathedral.org.uk
Worcester Cathedral is one of England's loveliest cathedrals, with Royal Tombs, medieval cloisters, an ancient crypt and Chapter House and magnificent Victorian stained glass. The tower is open in the summer. There are a number of different celebrations each year, including the Heart of England Food Fair and many concerts.
Times: Open all year, daily 7.30-6. **Fee:** ✱ Donations. (Suggested £3 per adult). **Facilities:** P (500yds) 🚽 ♿ (Access from College Green) toilets for disabled shop ✗ (ex guide dogs)

EAST RIDING OF YORKSHIRE

EVENTS & FESTIVALS

May
24th-31st Bridlington Arts Festival
(various venues)
27th-31st Beverley & East Riding Early Music
Festival, Beverley Minster & various East
Riding churches

June
tbc Beverley & East Riding Folk Festival,
(various venues)

July
2nd-4th Hornsea Music Festival,
(various venues)
21st Driffield Agricultural Show, Driffield
Showground

August
tbc International Sea Shanty Festival, Hull
Marina, Hull

September
tbc Beverley & East Riding Chamber
Music Festival
tbc Hull Show, East Park, Hull
tbc International Sequence Dance Festival,
Royal Hall Ballroom, Bridlington

October
tbc Hull Fair, Walton Street Fairground, Hull

November
tbc Hull Literature Festival (various venues)

Above: Rowing boats on Hornsea Mere
Top: Flamborough Cliffs

BEMPTON   Map 08 TA17

RSPB NATURE RESERVE
YO15 1JD
➲ (take cliff road from B1229, Bempton Village
and follow brown tourist signs)
☎ 01262 851179   ▤ 01262 851533

Part of the spectacular chalk cliffs that stretch from
Flamborough Head to Speeton. This is one of the best sites
in England to see thousands of nesting seabirds including
gannets and puffins at close quarters. Viewpoints overlook
the cliffs, which are best visited from April to July. Over 2
miles of chalk cliffs rising to 400ft with numerus cracks and
ledges. Enormous numbers of seabirds nest on these cliffs
including guillemots, razorbills, kittiwakes, fulmars, herring
gulls and several pairs of shag. This is the only gannetry in
England and is growing annually. Many migrants pass
off-shore including terns, skuas and shearwaters. Wheatears,
ring ouzels and merlins frequent the clifftop on migration.
Grey seal and porpoise are sometimes seen offshore.
Times: Open for visitor centre daily, Mar-Nov 10-5. Winter wknds only
9.30-4. Closed Jan. **Facilities:** ▯ (charged) ▯▯ ₺ toilets for disabled
shop (must be on lead) ⌇

BEVERLEY   Map 08 TA03

THE GUILDHALL
Register Sq HU17 9AU
➲ (in Register Square, next to the post office)
☎ 01482 884414   ▤ 01482 884747   `2 for 1`
e-mail: museum@sewerby.clara.net

A Guildhall has been on this site since 1500, although parts
of the building date back to a private dwelling of 1320.
Largely remodelled in the Palladian style in the 1760s, the
Courtroom features a magnificent stucco work ceiling, and
the Magistrate's Room houses rare 17th-century Civic
furniture.
Times: Open every Fri, 10-4. Please phone for guide tours at other
times **Fee:** ✱ Free on Fri. Charge for guided tours at other times
Facilities: ▯ (100yds) ₺ ✖ (ex guide dogs)

MUSEUM OF ARMY TRANSPORT
Flemingate HU17 0NG
➲ (follow brown tourist signs once in Beverley. 5
mins walk from Minster)
☎ 01482 860445   ▤ 01482 872767

The museum tells the story of army transport from horse
drawn waggons to the Gulf conflict: everything from
prototype vehicles to Montgomery's Rolls Royce and the last
Blackburn Beverley aircraft. There are also other exhibits to
be explored including `Monty's Men and D-Day Dodgers".
Times: Open all year, daily 10-5. (Closed 24 Dec-2 Jan). **Fee:** ✱ £4.50
(ch 5-15, pen & student £3). Family ticket £12 (2 adults & 2 ch). Under
5's free. **Facilities:** ▯ (charged) ▯▯ ₺ (parking next to entrance)
toilets for disabled shop ✖ (ex guide dogs)

BURTON AGNES   Map 08 TA16

BURTON AGNES HALL
Estate Office YO25 0ND
➲ (on A614)
☎ 01262 490324   ▤ 01262 490513
e-mail: burton.agnes@farmline.com

Built in 1598, this is a magnificent Elizabethan house, with
continued

furniture, pictures and china amassed by the family owners over four centuries. There is a walled garden with maze, potager, herbaceous borders, clematis, campanula and geranium collections, and jungle garden, as well as woodland walks.

Times: Open Apr-Oct, daily 11-5. **Fee:** ✱ Hall & grounds £5.20 (ch £2.60, pen £4.70). Grounds only £2.60 (ch £1.15, pen £2.35). Party 30+. **Facilities:** 🅿 🍴 & (scented garden for the blind) toilets for disabled shop garden centre ⬗

BURTON AGNES MANOR HOUSE
➲ (in Burton Agnes, 5m SW of Bridlington on A166) FREE

A rare and well-preserved example of a Norman house. Some interesting Norman architectural features can still be seen, but the building was encased in brick during the 17th and 18th centuries. The house is near Burton Agnes Hall and the gardens are privately owned and not managed by English Heritage.
Times: Open Apr-Oct, 11-5. Dates valid until 31 Mar 2004.
Facilities: 🐾 (ex dogs on leads) ⌗

HORNSEA Map 08 TA14
HORNSEA MUSEUM
11 Newbegin HU18 1AB
➲ (turn off A165 onto B1244)
☎ 01964 533443

A former farmhouse whose outbuildings now illustrate local life and history. There are 19th-century period rooms and a dairy, plus craft tools and farming implements. Photographs, local personalities and industries are also featured.
Times: Open Etr-mid Oct, Tue-Sat 11-5, Sun 2-5 (last admission 4). **Fee:** ✱ £2 (concessions £1.50). Family ticket £6 **Facilities:** 🅿 (50yds) & (audio interpretation for blind/partially sighted) toilets for disabled shop 🐾 (ex guide dogs)

KINGSTON UPON HULL Map 08 TA02
MAISTER HOUSE
160 High St HU1 1NL
➲ (city centre)
☎ 01482 324114 📠 01482 227003

The house is a mid-18th-century rebuilding, notable for its splendid stone and wrought-iron staircase, ornate stucco
continued

work and finely carved doors. Only the staircase and entrance hall are open.
Times: Open all year, Mon-Fri 10-4 (Closed BH). **Fee:** ✱ 80p (incl guide book). **Facilities:** 🅿 🐾 🍴 ⬗

MARITIME MUSEUM
Queen Victoria Square HU1 3DX
➲ (from M62 follow A63 to town centre, museum is within pedestrian area of town centre)
☎ 01482 613902 📠 01482 613710
e-mail: museums@hullcc.gov.uk

Hull's maritime history is illustrated here, with displays on whales and whaling, ships and shipping, and other aspects of this Humber port. There is also a Victorian court room which is used for temporary exhibitions. The restored dock area, with its fine Victorian and Georgian buildings, is well worth exploring too.
Times: ✱ Open all year, Mon-Sat 10-5 & Sun 1.30-4.30. (Closed 25-2 Jan & Good Fri). **Facilities:** 🅿 (100yds) & shop 🐾 (ex guide dogs)

'STREETLIFE' - HULL MUSEUM OF TRANSPORT
High St HU1 1PS
➲ (A63 from M62, follow signs for Old Town)
☎ 01482 613902 📠 01482 613710
e-mail: museums@hullcc.gov.uk

This purpose built museum uses a 'hands-on' approach to trace 200 years of transport history. With a vehicle collection of national importance, state-of-the-art animatronic displays and authentic scenarios, you can see Hull's Old Town brought vividly to life. The mail coach ride uses the very latest in computer technology to recreate a Victorian journey by four-in-hand.
Times: ✱ Open all year, Mon-Sat 10-5, Sun 1.30-4.30. (Closed 24-25 Dec & Good Fri). **Facilities:** 🅿 (500mtrs) & toilets for disabled shop 🐾 (ex guide dogs)

THE DEEP
HU1 4DP
➲ (follow signs from Hull City Centre)
☎ 01482 381000 📠 01482 381010
e-mail: info@thedeep.co.uk

Billing itself as "The World's Only Submarium", this fascinating aquarium centre is Europe's deepest, containing 2.5 million litres of water and 87 tonnes of salt. Dynamic displays recreate the birth of the universe, allow visitors to pilot a submarine and walk the ocean floor, and ride in the world's only underwater glass lift surrounded by sharks, eels, Napoleon Wrasse, and hundreds of other creatures.
Times: Open daily 10-6. (Closed 24-25 Dec) **Fee:** £6.50 (ch under 16 £4). Family ticket (2 adults & 3 ch) £21 **Facilities:** 🅿 (charged) 🍴 & (signing for the deaf if booked in advance) toilets for disabled shop 🐾 (ex guide dogs) ⬗

WILBERFORCE HOUSE
23-25 High St HU1 1NE
➲ (A63 from M62 or A1079 from York, follow signs for Old Town)
☎ 01482 613902 📠 01482 613710
e-mail: museums@hullcc.gov.uk

The early 17th-century Merchant's house was the birthplace of William Wilberforce, who became a leading campaigner against slavery. There are Jacobean and Georgian rooms and
continued

displays on Wilberforce and the anti-slavery campaign. The house also has secluded gardens. There are special exhibitions throughout the year.
Times: Open all year, Mon-Sat 10-5 & Sun 1.30-4.30. (Closed 25-26 Dec, 1 Jan & Good Fri). **Facilities:** P (500mtrs) (meters on street) & (large print, video area & audio guides) shop ✖ (ex guide dogs)

POCKLINGTON   Map 08 SE84

BURNBY HALL GARDEN & STEWART COLLECTION
The Balk YO42 2QF
➲ (off A1079 at turning for Pocklington off B1247)
☎ 01759 302068
e-mail: burnbyhallgardens@hotmail.com
The two lakes in this garden have an outstanding collection of 80 varieties of hardy water lilies, designated a National Collection. The lakes stand within nine acres of beautiful gardens including heather beds, a rock garden, a spring and summer bedding area, woodland walk and Victorian garden. The museum contains sporting trophies and ethnic material gathered on world-wide travels.
Times: ✱ Open 29 Mar-Sep, daily 10-1 & 2-6. Oct, daily 10-1, 2-5 (last admission 5pm). **Facilities:** P ♨ & (free wheelchair hire, viewing platform for wheelchairs) toilets for disabled shop ✖ (ex guide dogs) ☜

SEWERBY   Map 08 TA16

SEWERBY HALL & GARDENS
YO15 1EA
➲ (1m NE of Bridlington on B1255 towards Flamborough)
☎ 01262 673769 ▤ 01262 673090
e-mail: sewerby.hall@eastring.gov.uk
Sewerby Hall and Gardens, set in 50 acres of parkland overlooking Bridlington Bay, dates back to 1715. The Georgian House, with its 19th century Orangery, contains art galleries, archaeological displays and an Amy Johnson Room with a collection of her trophies and mementoes. The grounds include magnificent walled Old English and Rose gardens and host many events throughout the year. Activities for all the family include a Children's Zoo and play areas, golf, putting, bowls, plus woodland and clifftop walks. Phone for details of special events.
Times: ✱ Estate open all year, dawn-dusk. Hall - contact office for further details **Facilities:** P ♨ & toilets for disabled shop ☜

SPROATLEY   Map 08 TA13

BURTON CONSTABLE HALL
HU11 4LN
➲ (1.5m N of Sproatley. 14m from Beverley, follow A165 Bridlington road)
☎ 01964 562400 ▤ 01964 563229   `2 for 1`
e-mail: enquiries@burtonconstable.com
This superb Elizabethan house was built in 1570, but much of the interior was remodelled in the 18th century. There are magnificent reception rooms and a Tudor long gallery with a pendant roof: the contents range from pictures and furniture to a unique collection of 18th-century scientific instruments. Outside are 200 acres of parkland landscaped by `Capability' Brown, with oaks and chestnuts, and a lake with an island.
Times: Open, Hall & grounds Etr Sun-end Oct. Grounds 12.30-5, Hall 1-5. Last admission 4pm. Closed Fri. **Fee:** ✱ House £5 (ch £2, pen £4.50). Family ticket £11. **Facilities:** P ♨ & (stair lift to first foor, wheelchairs) toilets for disabled shop

NORTH YORKSHIRE

EVENTS & FESTIVALS

January
    tbc Harrogate Winter Antiques Fair, Great Yorkshire Showground, Harrogate
March
    tbc Langholm & Eskdale Festival of the Arts, Whitby Pavilion Complex, Whitby
April
    tbc Harrogate International Youth Music Festival (various venues)
    tbc Harrogate Spring Antiques & Fine Art Fair, Great Yorkshire Showground, Harrogate
    tbc Harrogate Spring Flower Show
May
    1st-3rd Ripon Spring Festival
    tbc Moor & Coast Festival (music, song, dance & arts), Whitby
June
    tbc Grassington Festival, Grassington
    tbc Nidderdale Festival
    tbc North Yorkshire County Show, Otterington Hall, South Otterington
July
    2nd-11th York Early Music Festival
    13th-15th Great Yorkshire Show, Great Yorkshire Showground, Harrogate
    22nd-7th Aug Harrogate International Festival (various venues)
    17th-18th Masham Steam Engine & Fair Organ Rally
August
    22nd Jul-7th Harrogate International Festival (various venues)
    8th-9th Feva 2004, Knaresborough Festival
    14th Ripley Show, Ripley Castle Park, Ripley
September
    tbc Harrogate Autumn Show, Great Yorkshire Show Ground, Harrogate
    tbc Ripon International Festival of Music & the Arts
October
    tbc Captain Cook Festival (various venues), Whitby

Above: The lake at Studley Royal

ALDBOROUGH Map 08 SE46

ALDBOROUGH ROMAN SITE
YO5 9ES
➲ (0.75m SE of Boroughbridge, on minor road off B6265 within 1m of junction of A1 & A6055)
☎ 01423 322768

View two spectacular mosaic pavements and discover the remains of the once principal Roman town.
Times: Open Apr-Sep, daily 10-1 & 2-6 (Oct 10-1 & 2-5). (Closed Nov-Mar). Dates valid until 31 Mar 2004. **Fee:** £2 (ch £1, concessions £1.50). Prices are valid until 31 Mar 2004. **Facilities:** shop ✖ (ex on leads/restricted areas) ♨

AYSGARTH Map 07 SE08

NATIONAL PARK CENTRE
DL8 3TH
➲ (off A684, Leyburn to Hawes road at Falls junct & continue down hill over river, centre 500yds on left)
☎ 01969 663424   🖹 01969 663105   FREE
e-mail: aysgarth@ytbtic.co.uk

A visitor centre for the Yorkshire Dales National Park, with maps, guides, walks and local information. Displays explain the history and natural history of the area.
Times: Open Apr-Oct, daily 10-5; Winter open Fri-Sun, 10-4.
Facilities: 🅿 (charged) 🍺 ✖ ♿ toilets for disabled shop ✖ (ex guide dogs) 🚲 🍴

BEDALE Map 08 SE28

BEDALE MUSEUM
DL8 1AA
➲ (on A684, 1.5m W of A1 at Leeming Bar. Opposite church, at N end of town)
☎ 01677 423797   🖹 01677 425393   FREE

Situated in a building dating back to the 17th century, the Bedale is a fascinating museum. The central attraction is the Bedale fire engine, which dates back to 1742. Other artefacts include documents, toys, craft tools and household utensils, which all help to give an absorbing picture of the lifestyle of the times.
Times: Open Tue & Fri 10-12.30 & 2-4, Wed 2-4, Thu-Sat 10-12
Facilities: 🅿 ♿ ✖ (ex guide dogs)

BENINGBROUGH Map 08 SE55

BENINGBROUGH HALL
YO6 1DD
➲ (off A19, 8m NW of York. Entrance at Newton Lodge)
☎ 01904 470666   🖹 01904 470002
e-mail: ybbrgb@smtp.ntrust.org.uk

Beningbrough was built around 1716. It houses 100 pictures from the National Portrait Gallery in London. Ornately carved wood panelling is a feature of several of the rooms. The other side of country house life can be seen in the restored Victorian laundry.
Times: ✱ Open 23 Mar-3 Nov daily (ex Thu/Fri) open Good Friday, Jul/Aug daily ex Thu 12-5. Grounds 11-5.30. **Facilities:** 🅿 ✖ licensed ♿ (access to Victorian laundry, shop & restaurant) toilets for disabled shop ✖ ♨

BRIMHAM Map 08 SE26

BRIMHAM ROCKS
Summerbridge HG3 4DW
➲ (10m NW of Harrogate, off B6265)
☎ 01423 780688   🖹 01423 781020
e-mail: yorkbm@smtp.ntrust.org.uk

A Victorian guidebook described the rocks as 'a place wrecked with grim and hideous forms defying all description and definition'. The rocks have remained a great attraction, and stand on National Trust open moorland at a height of 950ft. An old shooting lodge in the area is now an information point and shop.
Times: Open 8-dusk, (facilities may close in bad weather): shop with exhibition room, kiosk 27 Mar/Apr/May/Oct, Sat/Sun, B Hols and local school hols 11-5. 29 May/Jun-Sep, daily 11-5, Nov/Dec Suns 26 Dec & 1 Jan **Fee:** Cars (up to 4hrs £2.50, over 4hrs £3.50). Minibuses £6. Coaches £12. Motorcycles free. **Facilities:** 🅿 🍺 ♿ (specially adapted path(steep in places), braille guide) toilets for disabled shop ♨

CASTLE BOLTON Map 07 SE09

BOLTON CASTLE
DL8 4ET
➲ (off A684, 6m W of Leyburn)
☎ 01969 623981   🖹 01969 623332
e-mail: harry@boltoncastle.co.uk

Medieval castle completed in 1399, overlooking Wensleydale. Stronghold of the Scrope family. Mary Queen of Scots was imprisoned here for 6 months. The castle was besieged and taken by Parliamentary forces in 1645. Tapestries, tableaux, arms and armour can be seen. Medieval gardens have been developed.
Times: Open Apr-Oct 10-5, Nov-Mar 10-4. **Fee:** ✱ £4 (ch & pen £3). Family ticket £10. **Facilities:** 🅿 🍺 shop ✖ 🍴

CASTLE HOWARD

See Malton

CLAPHAM Map 07 SD76

CLAPHAM NATIONAL PARK CENTRE
LA2 8ED
➲ (signposted off A65 at Clapham)
☎ 015242 51419

A comprehensive information centre with displays on the local countryside and limestone scenery. A wide range of maps, guides, information leaflets, gifts and souvenirs are stocked and knowledgeable staff are on duty to answer questions.
Times: ✱ Open Apr-Oct, daily 10-5.Limited opening Nov-Mar.
Facilities: 🅿 (charged) (Radar key scheme) shop 🍴

> Remember that prices and opening times are liable to change within the currency of this guide. It is always best to telephone in advance to check

COXWOLD   Map 08 SE57
BYLAND ABBEY
YO6 4BD
⮑ (2m S of A170 between Thirsk & Helmsley, near Coxwold village)
☎ 01347 868614
A hauntingly beautiful monastic ruin set in peaceful meadows in the shadow of the Hambleton Hills. Marvel at the collection of medieval floor tiles still in their original setting.
Times: Open Apr-Sep, Thu-Mon 10-6 (Oct 10-5); Jul & Aug open daily. Dates valid until 31 Mar 2004. **Fee:** £2 (ch £1, concessions £1.50). Prices valid until 31 Mar 2004. **Facilities:** 🅿 ⅃ (garden/grounds partly accessible) toilets for disabled ✖ (ex dogs on lead) ⚏ ⬛

DANBY   Map 08 NZ70
MOORS CENTRE
Lodge Ln YO21 2NB
⮑ (turn S off A171 signed "the Moors Centre Danby". Turn left at cross road in Danby village and follow road for 2m, The Moors Centre is at a bend on the right)
☎ 01287 660654   📠 01287 660308
e-mail: moorscentre@ytbtic.co.uk
The ideal place to start exploring the North York Moors National Park. There is an exhibition about the area as well as events, video, a shop and local walks. The Moorsbus service also operates from this site - phone for details.
Times: Open all year, Apr-Oct, daily 10-5. Nov, Dec & Mar daily 11-4. Jan & Feb wknds only 11-4. **Facilities:** 🅿 (charged) ⅃ ⅃ (woodland & garden trails, motorised & manual wheelchairs) toilets for disabled shop ✖ (ex guide dogs & in grounds)

EASBY   Map 08 NZ10
EASBY ABBEY   FREE
⮑ (1m SE of Richmond off B6271)
Set beside the River Swale, this Premonstratensian Abbey was founded in 1155 and dedicated to St Agatha. Extensive remains of the monks' domestic buildings can be seen.
Times: Open Apr-Sep, 10-6; Oct 10-5; Nov-Mar, 10-4. (Closed 24-25 Dec). Dates valid until 31 Mar 2004. **Facilities:** 🅿 ✖ (ex dogs on leads) ⚏

ELVINGTON   Map 08 SE74
YORKSHIRE AIR MUSEUM & ALLIED AIR FORCES MEMORIAL
Halifax Way YO41 4AU
⮑ (from York take A1079 then immediate right onto B1228, museum is signposted on right)
☎ 01904 608595   📠 01904 608246
e-mail: museum@yorkshireairmuseum.co.uk
This award-winning museum and memorial is based around the largest authentic former WWII Bomber Command Station open to the public. There is a restored tower, an air gunners museum, archives, an Airborne Forces display, Squadron memorial rooms, and much more. Among the exhibits are replicas of the pioneering Cayley Glider and Wright Flyer,

continued

along with the Halifax Bomber and modern jets like the Harrier GR3.

Times: Open daily, 10-5 (summer), 10-3.30 (winter). Closed 25 & 26 Dec. **Fee:** ✱ £5 (ch £3 & pen £4). **Facilities:** 🅿 ⅃ ✖ licensed ⅃ toilets for disabled shop ⬛

FAIRBURN   Map 08 SE42
RSPB NATURE RESERVE
Fairburn Ings, The Visitor Centre, Newton Ln WF10 2BH
⮑ (W of A1, N of Ferrybridge. Signed from Allerton Bywater off A656. Signed Fairburn Village off A1)
☎ 01977 603796
e-mail: chris.drake@rspb.org.uk
One-third of the 700-acre RSPB reserve is open water, and over 270 species of birds have been recorded. A visitor centre provides information, and there is an elevated boardwalk, suitable for disabled visitors.
Times: ✱ Access to the reserve via car park, open 9-dusk. Centre open 10-5 weekends and 11-4 weekdays (closed 25-26 Dec). **Facilities:** 🅿 ⅃ (raised boardwalk for wheelchair) toilets for disabled shop (ex guide dogs)

GRASSINGTON   Map 07 SE06
NATIONAL PARK CENTRE
Hedbden Rd BD23 5LB
⮑ (situated on B6265 in the main Grassington car park)
☎ 01756 752774   📠 01756 753358   FREE
e-mail: grassington@ytbtic.co.uk
The centre is a useful introduction to the Yorkshire Dales National Park. It has a video and a display on 'Wharfedale - Gateway to the Park', and maps, guides and local information are available. There is also a 24-hr public access information service through computer screens and a full tourist information service.
Times: Open Apr-Oct daily, 10-5; Nov-Mar Wed, Fri, & Sat-Sun, 10-4 (also daily in school hols). **Facilities:** 🅿 (charged) ⅃ toilets for disabled shop

GUISBOROUGH   Map 08 NZ61
GISBOROUGH PRIORY
TS14 6HG
➲ (next to parish church)
☎ 01287 633801

The remains of the east end of the 14th-century church make a dramatic sight here. The priory was founded in the 12th century for Augustinian canons.
Times: Open all year Apr-Sep, Tue-Sun 9-5; Oct-Mar, Wed-Sun 9-5. (Closed 24 Dec-1 Jan). Dates valid until 31 Mar 2004. **Fee:** £1.10 (ch 55p, concessions 75p). Prices valid until 31 Mar 2004. **Facilities:** 🅿 ▣ ⅋ ✖ (ex dogs on leads)

HARROGATE   Map 08 SE35
RHS GARDEN HARLOW CARR
Crag Ln, Otley Rd HG3 1QB
➲ (off B6162 (Otley Rd), 1.5 miles from Harrogate centre)
☎ 01423 565418 📠 01423 530663
e-mail: admin-harlowcarr@rhs.org.uk

Established in 1950, RHS Garden Harlow Carr provides a beautiful garden setting to assess the suitability of plants for growing in the North. The 58 acres includes a breathtaking streamside garden, peaceful woodland and arboretum, scented, herb and foliage gardens and National Collections. There is also a Museum of Gardening and a library on site.
Times: Open all year, daily 9.30-6, or dusk if sooner. **Fee:** £5 (ch under 11 free, 11-16 £1, pen £4.50 **Facilities:** 🅿 ▣ ✖ licensed ⅋ (3 electric and 2 push wheelchairs available) toilets for disabled shop garden centre ✖ (ex guide dogs) ♥

THE ROYAL PUMP ROOM MUSEUM
Crown Place HG1 2RY
➲ (Take A61 into Harrogate town centre and follow brown heritage signs to museum)
☎ 01423 556188 📠 01423 556130
e-mail: lg23@harrogate.gov.uk

Housed in delightful early Victorian pump room over the town's sulphur wells, the museum tells the story of Harrogate's heyday as England's European spa. Visitors discover some of the amazing spa treatments; taste the sulphur water; and explore stories of Russian royalty, communal ox-roasts and early bicycles, among many others. Changing exhibitions complement permanent displays
Times: Open all year, Apr-Oct, Mon-Sat 10-5, Sun 2-5, (Nov-Mar close at 4pm). (Closed 24-26 Dec & 1 Jan). **Fee:** ✱ £2.50 (ch £1.25, concession £1.50). Family rate £6.50 (2 adults & 2 ch). Party. Combined seasonal tickets available for The Royal Pump Room Museum & Knaresborough Castle & Museum. **Facilities:** 🅿 (100yds) (restricted to 3hrs, need parking disc) ⅋ toilets for disabled shop ✖ (guide dogs only)

HAWES   Map 07 SD88
DALES COUNTRYSIDE MUSEUM CENTRE
Station Yard DL8 3NT
➲ (Off A684 in the Old Station Yard).
☎ 01969 667450 & 667494 📠 01969 667165
e-mail: hawes@ytbtic.co.uk

Fascinating museum telling the story of the people and
continued

landscape of the Yorkshire Dales. Static steam loco and carriages with video and displays. Interactive area.
Times: Open all year 10-5. **Fee:** ✱ Museum: £3 (ch free, concessions £2) . National park centre free. **Facilities:** 🅿 (charged) ⅋ (lifts, ramps and parking) toilets for disabled shop ✖ (ex guide dogs) ♥

HELMSLEY   Map 08 SE68
DUNCOMBE PARK
YO62 5EB
➲ (Duncombe Park is located within the North York Moors National Park, 25m N of York, off the A170 Thirsk-Scarborough road, 1m from Helmsley market place).
☎ 01439 770213 📠 01439 771114   **2 for 1**
e-mail: sally@duncombepark.com

Duncombe Park stands at the heart of a spectacular 30-acre early 18th-century landscape garden which is set in 300 acres of dramatic parkland around the River Rye. The house, originally built in 1713, was gutted by fire in 1879 and rebuilt in 1895. Its principal rooms are a fine example of the type of grand interior popular at the turn of the century. Home of the Duncombes for 300 years, for much of this century the house was a girls' school. In 1985 the present Lord and Lady Feversham decided to make it a family home again and after major restoration, opened the house to the public in 1990. Part of the garden and parkland were designated a 250-acre National Nature Reserve in 1994. Special events include a Country Fair (May), an Antiques Fair (June), Steam Fair (July), Antiques Fair (November). Please telephone for details.
Times: Open: 28 Apr-27 Oct Sun-Thu; Gardens, Parkland Centre tea room & shop & Parkland walks 11-5.30. House by guided tour only every hour from 12.30 - 3.30. **Fee:** ✱ House & Gardens £6 (ch 10-16, £3, concessions £5) Gardens & Parkland £3 (ch £1.50, concessions £3) Parkland only £2 (ch £1). **Facilities:** 🅿 ✖ licensed ⅋ portable ramp, lift, wheelchair for loan) toilets for disabled shop ✖ (ex park) ♥

HELMSLEY CASTLE
YO6 5AB
☎ 01439 770442

An atmospheric ruin with formidable double earthworks. Also, an exhibition of the history of the castle.
Times: Open all year, Apr-Sep, daily 10-6; Oct, daily 10-5; Nov-Mar, Wed-Sun 10-1 & 2-4. (Closed 24-26 Dec & 1 Jan). Dates valid until 31 Mar 2004. **Fee:** £2.60 (ch £1.30, concessions £2). Prices valid until 31 Mar 2004. **Facilities:** 🅿 (charged) shop ✖ (ex dogs on leads) ⌗

KIRBY MISPERTON   Map 08 SE77
FLAMINGO LAND THEME PARK & ZOO
The Rectory YO17 6UX
➲ (turn off A64 onto A169, Pickering to Whitley road)
☎ 01653 668287 📠 01653 668280   **2 for 1**
e-mail: info@flamingoland.co.uk

Set in 375 acres of North Yorkshire countryside, with over 100 rides and attractions there's something for everyone at Flamingo Land. Enjoy the thrills and spills of 12 white knuckle rides or enjoy a stroll through the extensive
continued

zoo where you'll find tigers, giraffes, hippos and rhinos. The theme park also boasts 6 great family shows.

Times: Open end Mar-2 Nov from 10. Closing times vary depending upon season. **Fee:** ✱ £14.50 (ch under 4 free, pens £7.25). Family ticket (4 people) £54. **Facilities:** 🅿 ⏺ ✕ licensed ♿ (parking, wheelchair hire) toilets for disabled shop 🍽

KIRKHAM   Map 08 SE76

KIRKHAM PRIORY
Whitwell-on-the-Hill YO6 7JS
➲ (5m SW of Malton on minor road off A64)
☎ 01653 618768

Discover the ruins of this Augustinian priory, which includes a magnificent carved gatehouse, set in a peaceful and secluded valley by the River Derwent.

Times: Open Apr-Sep, daily 10-6; Oct, daily 10-5. (Closed between 1 & 2, daily). Dates valid until 31 Mar 2004. **Fee:** £2 (ch £1, concessions £1.50). Prices valid until 31 Mar 2004. **Facilities:** 🅿 ♿ ✕ (ex dogs on leads) 🎫

KNARESBOROUGH   Map 08 SE35

KNARESBOROUGH CASTLE & MUSEUM
Castle Yard HG5 8AS
➲ (turn off the High St towards the Market Square. continue past the Market Square the turn right at the police station into the Castleyard.)
☎ 01423 556188 🖷 01423 556130
e-mail: lg23@harrogate.gov.uk

High above the town of Knaresborough, the ruins of this 14th-century castle look down over the gorge of the River Nidd. This imposing fortress was once the hiding place of Thomas Becket's murderers and served as a prison for Richard II. Remains include the keep, the sally-port, parts of the curtain wall and the Old Court of Knaresborough. It now houses a local museum, and entrance is part of the combined ticket price.

Times: Open Good Fri-end Sep, daily 10.30-5. Guided tours regulary available. **Fee:** £2.50 (ch £1.25, concessions £1.50). Family ticket (2 adults & 2 ch) £6.50. Party 10+. Joint & season tickets available for Knaresborough Castle & Museum & The Royal Pump Room Museum. **Facilities:** 🅿 (charged) ♿ toilets for disabled shop ✕ (ex guide dogs)

MALHAM   Map 07 SD96

MALHAM NATIONAL PARK CENTRE
BD23 4DA
➲ (Turn off A65 at Gargrave opp. petrol stn. Malham 7m).
☎ 01729 830363
e-mail: malham@ytbtic.org

The national park centre has maps, guides and local information together with displays on the remarkable natural history of the area, local community and work of conservation bodies. Audio-visuals are provided for groups and a 24-hour teletext information service is available..

Times: ✱ Open Apr-Oct, daily 10-5. Limited winter opening. **Facilities:** 🅿 (charged) ♿ (Radar key scheme for toilet) toilets for disabled shop 🍽

MALTON   Map 08 SE77

CASTLE HOWARD
YO60 7DA
➲ (15m NE of York, off A64, follow the brown heritage signs to Castle Howard)
☎ 01653 648333 🖷 01653 648529
e-mail: house@castlehoward.co.uk   [2 for 1]

In its dramatic setting of lakes, fountains and extensive gardens, this 18th-century palace was designed by Sir John Vanbrugh. Castle Howard was begun in 1699 for the 3rd Earl of Carlisle, Charles Howard. The interior has a 192ft Long Gallery, as well as a Chapel with magnificent stained glass windows by the 19th-century artist, Edward Burne-Jones. The Castle contains a portrait of Henry VIII by Holbein and works by Rubens, Reynolds and Gainsborough. The grounds include the domed Temple of the Four Winds by Vanbrugh, and the family Mausoleum.

Times: Open mid Feb-Oct, grounds, exhibition wing, plant centre & stable court yard, daily from 10. House 11. Last admissions 4. Grounds close 6.30. **Fee:** ✱ £9 (ch £6, pen £8). Grounds only £5.50 (ch £3.50). **Facilities:** 🅿 ⏺ ✕ licensed ♿ (wheelchair lift, free adapted transport to house) toilets for disabled shop garden centre (ex guide dogs) 🍽

EDEN CAMP MODERN HISTORY THEME MUSEUM
Eden Camp YO17 6RT
➲ (junct of A64 & A169, between York & Scarborough)
☎ 01653 697777 🖷 01653 698243
e-mail: admin@edencamp.co.uk

The story of the people's war unfolds in this museum devoted to civilian life in World War II. The displays, covering the blackout, rationing, the Blitz, the Home Guard and others, are housed in a former prisoner-of-war camp built in 1942 for German and Italian soldiers. Hut 13, part of a Millennium project, covers the conflicts that Britain has been involved with from 1945 to present day.

Times: Open 2nd Mon in Jan-23 Dec, daily 10-5. Last admission 4pm. Allow at least 3-4hrs for a visit. **Fee:** ✱ £4 (ch & pen £3) Party 10+. **Facilities:** 🅿 ⏺ ♿ (taped tours, braille guides) toilets for disabled shop

MALTON MUSEUM
Old Town Hall, Market Place YO17 7LP
➲ (leave A64, follow signs for Malton town centre)
☎ 01653 695136

The extensive Roman settlements in the area are represented and illustrated in this museum, including collections from the Roman fort of Derventio. There are also displays of local prehistoric and medieval finds plus changing exhibitions of local interest.
Times: Open Etr Sat-Oct, Mon-Sat 10-4. **Fee:** ✱ £1.50 (ch, pen & students £1) Family ticket £4 (2 adults & 2 ch) **Facilities:** P (adjacent) (pay & display-2hrs) ᴕ shop ✘ (ex guide dogs)

MASHAM   Map 08 SE28

THEAKSTON WORKING BREWERY & VISITOR CENTRE
The Brewery HG4 4YD
➲ (on A6108)
☎ 01765 680000 ▤ 01765 684330   2 for 1
e-mail: bookings@theakstons.co.uk

Visit the Theakston Brewery in Masham, home of the legendary 'Old Peculier' and witness the creation of real taste first-hand. Discover how traditional brewing techniques are still being applied to create today's award winning pint. As these tours are thirsty work, you'll be invited, to round off your visit in the bar with a glass of real British beer at its best.
Times: Open 1 Apr-5 Nov, daily 10.30-5.30; 06 Nov-12 Dec, Wed, Sat, Sun 10.30-5.30. **Fee:** ✱ £4.50 (ch 2-17 £2, including soft drink, student & pen £3.50). **Facilities:** P (400yds) ᴕ (ex brewery tours) toilets for disabled shop ✘ (ex guide dogs) ⬗

MIDDLEHAM   Map 07 SE18

MIDDLEHAM CASTLE
DL8 4RJ
➲ (2m S of Leyburn on A6108)
☎ 01969 623899

Explore the maze of rooms and passageways at this impressive castle, once the boyhood home of the ill-fated Richard III. Oak viewing Gallery of the magnificent views of the 12th-century keep and exhibition.
Times: Open all year, Apr-Sep, daily 10-6; Oct, daily 10-5; Nov-Dec, daily, 10-1 & 2-4; Jan-Mar, Wed-Sun 10-1& 2-4. (Closed 24-26 Dec & 1 Jan). Dates valid until 31 Mar 2004. **Fee:** £3 (ch £1.50, concessions £2.30). Prices valid until 31 Mar 2004. **Facilities:** P ᴕ (ex tower) shop ⌗

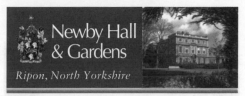

MIDDLESBROUGH   Map 08 NZ42

CAPTAIN COOK BIRTHPLACE MUSEUM
Stewart Park, Marton TS7 6AS
➲ (3m S on A172)
☎ 01642 311211 ▤ 01642 317419
e-mail: jeanette_grainger@
middlesbrough.gov.uk

Opened to mark the 250th anniversary of the birth of the voyager in 1728, this museum illustrates the early life of James Cook and his discoveries with permanent and temporary exhibitions. Located in spacious and rolling parkland, the site also offers outside attractions for the visitor. Recently refurbished, the museum has a special resource centre which has fresh approaches to presentation with computers, films, special effects, interactives and educational aids.
Times: ✱ Open all year: Tue-Sun, Summer hrs 10am-5.30pm. Winter hrs 9am-4pm. Last entry 45 mins before closure. (Closed Mon except BH, 25-26 Dec & 1 Jan). **Facilities:** P ⬛ ᴕ (lift to all floors, car parking) toilets for disabled shop ✘ (ex guide dogs) ⬗

NEWBY HALL & GARDENS   Map 08 SE36

NEWBY HALL & GARDENS
HG4 5AE
➲ (4m SE of Ripon & 2m W of A1M, off B6265, between Boroughbridge and Ripon)
☎ 01423 322583 ▤ 01423 324452
e-mail: info@newbyhall.com

A late 17th-century house with beautifully restored Robert Adam interiors containing an important collection of classical sculpture and Gobelin tapestries. 25 acres of

continued

award-winning gardens include a miniature railway, an adventure garden for children and a woodland discovery walk.

Newby Hall & Gardens

Times: Open Apr-Sep, Tue-Sun & BH's; Gardens 11-5.30; House 12-5. Last admission 5pm (gardens), 4.30pm (house). **Fee:** ✱ House & Garden £7.20, (ch £4.70, pen £6.20). Gardens only £5.70 (ch £4.20, pen £4.70). Party rates and family tickets on application. **Facilities:** 🅿 💺 ✗ licensed 👩‍🦽 (wheelchairs available, maps of wheelchair routes) toilets for disabled shop garden centre ✗ (ex guide dogs) ☞

NORTH STAINLEY   Map 08 SE27

LIGHTWATER VALLEY THEME PARK
HG4 3HT
➲ (3m N of Ripon on the A6108)
☎ 0870 458 0060 & 458 0040
📠 01765 635359   `2 for 1`
e-mail: leisure@lightwatervalley.co.uk

The family sized theme park with thrills of all sizes, from Europe's longest rollercoaster; 'The Ultimate' and 'The Grizzly Bear' log flume to family favourites such as the 'ladybird' rollercoaster and Grand Prix Go Karting along with spinning teacups, vintage cars and much more for younger children. You just pay once and enjoy the fun all day long!
Times: Open 23 Mar-7 Apr, weekends only; 13 Apr-26 May inc BH Mon; daily from Jun-2 Sep, weekends only 7 Sep-13 Oct. daily 19 Oct-27 Oct. **Fee:** ✱ £13.50 over 1.2 metres, £12 under 1.2 metres, free under 1m; senior citizens £5.95. Family ticket £48 (2ad + 2ch) or (1ad + 3ch u16). **Facilities:** 🅿 💺 ✗ licensed 👩‍🦽 (even pathways) toilets for disabled shop ✗ (ex guide dogs) ☞

NUNNINGTON   Map 08 SE67

NUNNINGTON HALL
YO6 5UY
➲ (4.5m SE of Helmsley)
☎ 01439 748283 📠 01439 748284
e-mail: yorknu@smtp.ntrust.org.uk

This large 16th to 17th-century house has panelled rooms and a magnificent staircase. The Carlisle collection of miniature rooms is on display.
Times: ✱ Open 23 Mar-3 Nov, Mar-May & Sep-Nov, daily (ex Mon/Tue) open BH Mons 1.30-4.30 (last admission 5pm May & Sep); Jun-Aug; daily ex Mon (open BH Mon) 1.30-5. **Facilities:** 🅿 💺 👩‍🦽 (w/chairs, Braille guide, scented garden) toilets for disabled shop 🐾

ORMESBY   Map 08 NZ51

ORMESBY HALL
TS7 9AS
➲ (3m SE of Middlesborough, W of A19 take the A174 to the A172 . Follow signs for Ormesby Hall. Car entrance on Ladgate Lane)
☎ 01642 324188 📠 01642 300937
e-mail: ormesbyhall@ntrust.org.uk

An 18th-century mansion, Ormesby Hall has stables attributed to John Carr of York. Plasterwork, furniture and 18th-century pictures are on view.
Times: Open 24 Mar-2 Nov: daily ex Mon, Fri & Sat (open Good Fri & BH Mons) 1.30-4.30. **Fee:** ✱ House & Gardens £3.70 (ch £1.80) Family ticket £9 (2+3). Garden only £2.50 (ch £1). Party. **Facilities:** 🅿 💺 👩‍🦽 (parking, Braille guide, special tours) toilets for disabled shop 🐾 🌿

OSMOTHERLEY   Map 08 SE49

MOUNT GRACE PRIORY
DL6 3JG
➲ (1m NW)
☎ 01609 883494 📠 01609 883361

The best preserved Carthusian monastery in the country, set in breathtakingly beautiful woodland surroundings and garden, including fully reconstructed Monks' cells and herb garden, illustrating the solitary life of the monk.
Times: Open Apr-Sep, daily 10-6; Oct, daily 10-5; Nov-Mar, Wed-Sun 10-4. Last admission 30 minutes before closing time. (Closed 24-26 Dec & 1 Jan). Dates valid until 31 Mar 2004. **Fee:** £3.20 (ch £1.60, concessions £2.40). Prices valid until 31 Mar 2004. **Facilities:** 🅿 shop ✗ ⚙ 🌿

PARCEVALL HALL   Map 07 SEO6
GARDENS

PARCEVALL HALL GARDENS
BD23 6DE
➲ (Off B6265 between Grassington and Pateley Bridge)
☎ 01756 720311 📠 01756 720441
e-mail: info@parcevallhallgardens.co.uk

Enjoying a hillside setting east of the main Wharfedale Valley, these beautiful gardens surround a Grade II listed house which is used as the Bradford Diocesan Retreat House (not open to the public).
Times: Open Apr-Oct, daily 10-6. Winter visitors by appointment. **Fee:** £3 (ch up to 16 50p). **Facilities:** 🅿 💺 shop

PATELEY BRIDGE   Map 07 SE16

STUMP CROSS CAVERNS
Greenhow HG3 5JL
➲ (situated on the B6265 between Pateley Bridge and Grassington)
☎ 01756 752780 📠 01756 752780

Discovered by the brothers Mark and William Newbould in 1860, Stump Cross Caverns have been an attraction for visitors since 1863 when one shilling was charged for entrance. Among the few limestone show caves in Britain, these require no special clothing, experience or equipment, as walkways are gravel and concrete and floodlighting is

continued

provided. Stalagmites, stalagtites and calcite precipitation make this an eerie day out.
Times: Open daily, mid Mar-02 Nov, then wknds (winter months) 10-5. **Fee:** ✱ £4.75 (ch £2.50 ch under 4 free) **Facilities:** 🅿 🖃 shop ✖ (ex guide dogs) 🍴

PICKERING Map 08 SE78

NORTH YORKSHIRE MOORS RAILWAY
Pickering Station YO18 7AJ
➲ (from A169 take roads towards Kirkbymoorside at traffic lights turn right, Stn 400 yds on left)
☎ 01751 472508 🖹 01751 476970
e-mail: admin@nymr.pickering.fsnet.co.uk
Operating through the heart of the North York Moors National Park between Pickering and Grosmont, steam trains cover a distance of 18 miles. The locomotive sheds at Grosmont are open to the public. Events throughout the year include Day Out with Thomas events, Steam Gala, Santa Specials.
Times: Open 29 Mar-2 Nov, daily; Dec, Santa specials and Christmas to New Year running. Further information available from Pickering Station. **Fee:** ✱ Return: £12 (ch £6, pen £10.50). Family ticket £27 (2ad+3ch), others on request. **Party** 20+. **Facilities:** 🅿 (charged) 🖃 ✖ licensed ♿ (ramp for trains) toilets for disabled shop (at Pickering, Goathland & Grosmont) 🍴

PICKERING CASTLE
YO6 5AB
☎ 01751 474989
Splendid 12th-century castle, on the edge of the Yorkshire Moors, originally built by William the Conqueror. Visit the exhibition on the castle's history and take in the views from the keep.
Times: Open Apr-Sep, daily 10-6; Oct, daily 10-5; Nov-Mar, Wed-Sun 10-1& 2-4. (Closed 24-26 Dec & 1 Jan). Dates valid until 31 Mar 2004. **Fee:** £2.60 (ch £1.30, concessions £2). Prices valid until 31 Mar 2004.
Facilities: 🅿 ♿ (ex motte) shop ✖ (ex dogs on leads) ⌗

REDCAR Map 08 NZ62

RNLI ZETLAND MUSEUM
5 King St TS10 3AH
➲ (on corner of King St and The Promenade)
☎ 01642 485370 & 471813   FREE
The museum portrays the lifeboat, maritime, fishing and local history of the area, including its main exhibit 'The Zetland' - the oldest lifeboat in the world, dating from 1802. There is also a replica of a fisherman's cottage c1900 and almost 2000 other exhibits. The museum is housed in an early lifeboat station, now a listed building.
Times: Open May-Sep, Mon-Fri 1-4, Sat & Sun 12-4. Also Etr. Other times by appointment. **Facilities:** 🅿 (20m) (50p per hour) ♿ (ground floor accessible only) shop

> If you are dissatisfied with any aspect of an attraction, discuss the problem at the time with a member of staff

RICHMOND Map 07 NZ10

GREEN HOWARDS MUSEUM
Trinity Church Square, Market Place DL10 4QN
➲ (Take any turning on the A1, between Catterick & South Corner, signposted to Richmond. Located in centre cobbled market square, in Holy Trinity Church).
☎ 01748 822133 🖹 01748 821924   2 for 1
e-mail: green.howards@virgin.net
This award-winning museum traces the military history of the Green Howards from the late 17th century onwards. The exhibits include uniforms, weapons, medals and a special Victoria Cross exhibition. Regimental and civic plate is displayed, and there is CD ROM and touch screen video of the First World War Western Front and the Green Howards in the Second World War. Audio guide available.
Times: Open Feb, Mon-Fri 10-4.30; Mar, Mon-Fri 10-4.30; mid Apr-Oct, Mon-Sat 9.30-4.30 & Sun 2-4.30; Nov, Mon-Sat 10-4.30. **Fee:** ✱ £2.50 (unaccompanied ch £1.50, pen £2). Family ticket £5. Richmondshire residents and accompanied children free. **Facilities:** 🅿 (in market place) (disk parking, 2hr max) ♿ (stairlift for access to all floors, lightweight wheelchair) shop ✖ (guide dogs only)

RICHMOND CASTLE
DL10 4QW
☎ 01748 822493
Overlooking the River Swale and market town of Richmond, the views from the keep are stunning. Built by William the Conqueror to subdue the rebellious North, the castle now houses an exciting interactive exhibition.
Times: Open all year, Apr-Sep, daily 10-6; Oct, daily 10-5; Nov-Mar, daily 10-4. (14-22 Feb, daily, 10-5). (Closed 24-26 Dec & 1 Jan). Dates valid until 31 Mar 2004. **Fee:** £3 (ch £1.50, concessions £2.30). Prices valid until 31 Mar 2004. **Facilities:** 🅿 (800 yds) ♿ toilets for disabled shop ✖ (ex dogs on leads) ⌗

RIEVAULX Map 08 SE58

RIEVAULX ABBEY
➲ (2.25m W of Helmsley on minor road off B1257)
☎ 01439 798228
Explore the magnificent romantic ruin set in a tranquil wooded valley of the River Rye. Find out about monastic life with the help of our audio tour and exhibition.
Times: Open Apr-Sep, daily 10-6; Oct, daily 10-5; Nov-Mar, daily 10-4 (14-22 Feb, daily 10-5). Dates valid until 31 Mar 2004. **Fee:** £3.80 (ch £1.90, concessions £2.90). Dates valid until 31 Mar 2004. **Facilities:** 🅿 ♿ shop ✖ (ex dogs on leads) 🚲 ⌗

RIEVAULX TERRACE & TEMPLES
YO62 5LJ
➲ (2m NW of Helmsley on B1257)
☎ 01439 798340 🖹 01439 748284
This curved terrace, half a mile long, overlooks the abbey, with views of Ryedale and the Hambleton Hills. It has two mock-Greek temples, one built for hunting parties, the other for quiet contemplation. There are also remarkable frescoes by Borgnis, and an exhibition on English landscape design.
Times: ✱ Open 23 Mar-3 Nov: daily 10.30-6 (5pm Oct & Nov). Last admission 1hr before closing. **Facilities:** 🅿 ♿ (w/chair/runaround vehicle/Braille guide/ramp) shop 🌿

RIPLEY Map 08 SE26

RIPLEY CASTLE
HG3 3AY
➲ (off A61, Harrogate to Ripon road)
☎ 01423 770152 ▤ 01423 771745   2 for 1
e-mail: enquiries@ripleycastle.co.uk

Ripley Castle has been home to the Ingilby family since 1320, and stands at the heart of an estate with deer park, lake and Victorian walled gardens. The Castle has a rich history and a fine collection of Royalist armour housed in the 1555 tower. There are also walled gardens, tropical hot houses, woodland walks, pleasure grounds and the National Hyacinth collection in spring.
Times: Open Sep-May, Tue, Thu, Sat & Sun 10.30-3; Jun-Aug daily 10.30-3, also BH and school holidays. Groups by arrangement. **Fee:** ✱ Castle & Gardens £6 (ch £3.50, pen £5). Gardens only £3.50 (ch £1.50, pen £2.50). Party **Facilities:** 🅿 💺 ✕ licensed ♿ (mobility buggy is available for hire) toilets for disabled shop garden centre ✖ (ex guide dogs) 💊

RIPON Map 08 SE37

FOUNTAINS ABBEY & STUDLEY ROYAL
HG4 3DY
➲ (4m W of Ripon off B6265)
☎ 01765 608888 ▤ 01765 608889
Founded by Cistercian monks in 1132, Fountains Abbey is the largest monastic ruin in Britain. It was acquired by William Aislabie in 1768, and became the focal point of his landscaped gardens at Studley. Other interesting features include Fountains Hall, built between 1598 and 1611 using the stone from the abbey ruins.
Times: ✱ Open all year, daily (except Fri in Nov, Dec & Jan); Apr-Sep, 10-6 (closes at 4pm 12/13Jul & one day in Aug); Oct-Mar 10-4 or dusk if earlier. Last admission one hour before closing. **Facilities:** 🅿 💺 ✕ licensed ♿ (W/chairs, Braille/large print guides) toilets for disabled shop 💊

NORTON CONYERS HALL
HG4 5EQ
➲ (from Ripon take A61 to Thirsk. At top of hill just outside Ripon, turn sharp left onto Wath Road)
☎ 01765 640337 ▤ 01765 692772
This late medieval house with Stuart and Georgian additions has belonged to the Grahams since 1624. It was visited by

Charles I and James II. Another visitor was Charlotte Brontë a family legend of a mad woman confined in the attics is said to have given her the idea for the mad Mrs Rochester in *Jane Eyre*. Family costumes are on display. Please note that ladies are requested not to wear stiletto-heeled shoes.
Times: Open - House & Garden, Etr Sun & Mon, BH Sun & Mon; 25 Apr-27 June & 4 July-29 Aug Sun only; 28 Jun-3 July daily, House 2-5, Garden 12-5. Gardens open Thu 12-4, throughought year. **Fee:** £4 (ch 10-16, pen, concessions £3). Garden entry is free, with donations welcome, although a charge is made at garden charity openings. Parties by arrangement. **Facilities:** 🅿 ♿ (ramp at entrance) toilets for disabled shop ✖ (ex guide dogs or lead)

SALTBURN-BY-THE-SEA Map 08 NZ62

SALTBURN SMUGGLERS HERITAGE CENTRE
Old Saltburn TS12 1HF
➲ (adjoining Ship Inn, on A174) 2 for 1
☎ 01287 625252 ▤ 01287 625252
Set in old fisherman's cottages, this centre skillfully blends costumed characters with authentic sounds and smells. Follow the story of John Andrew "King of Smugglers", who was at the heart of illicit local trade 200 years ago.
Times: Open Apr-Sep, daily 10-6: Winter open by arrangement only telephone 01642 444318. **Fee:** ✱ £1.90 (ch £1.40). Family ticket £5.65. Party. **Facilities:** 🅿 (200 mtrs) (charged) shop ✖

SCARBOROUGH Map 08 TA08

SCARBOROUGH CASTLE
Castle Rd YO11 1HY
➲ (E of town centre)
☎ 01723 372451
This 12th-century fortress housed many important figures in history. Enjoy the spectacular coastal view and see the remains of the great keep still standing over three storeys high. Discover the castle's exciting history through the free audio tour.
Times: Open all year, Apr-Sep, daily 10-6; Oct, daily 10-5; Nov-Mar, daily 10-4. (14-22 Feb, daily, 10-5). (Closed 24-26 Dec & 1 Jan). Dates valid until 31 Mar 2004. **Fee:** £3 (ch £1.50, concessions £2.30). Prices valid until 31 Mar 2004. **Facilities:** 🅿 (100 yds) ♿ (ex in keep) ⚏

SEA LIFE & MARINE SANCTUARY
Scalby Mills Rd, North Bay YO12 6RP
➲ (follow brown and white signs after entering Scarborough. Centre is in 'North Bay Leisure Parks' area of town)
☎ 01723 376125 ▤ 01723 376285
Now in its 10th year, this fascinating marine sanctuary has just launched a pan-European SOS Conservation & Rescue campaign as part of its continued conservation programme. The centre is home to seahorses, a seal hospital, otters, seapool creatures, sharks and a home for convalescent Sea Turtles.
Times: ✱ Open daily ex 25 Dec. **Facilities:** 🅿 (charged) 💺 ♿ (lift to cafe) toilets for disabled shop ✖ 💊

> The AA also publishes a guide to
> Pet Friendly Places to Stay

continued

SKINNINGROVE Map 08 NZ71
CLEVELAND IRONSTONE MINING MUSEUM
Deepdale TS13 4AP
➲ (Located in Skinningrove Valley, just off A174 between Middlesbrough and Whitby)
☎ 01287 642877 ▤ 01287 642970 **2 for 1**
e-mail: visits@ironstonemuseum.co.uk
On the site of the old Loftus Mine, this museum offers visitors a glimpse into the underground world of Cleveland's ironstone mining past. Discover the special skills and customs of the miners who helped make Cleveland the most important ironstone mining district in Victorian and Edwardian England.
Times: Open Apr-Oct, daily from 1 (last admission 3.30pm). Nov-Mar, schools & parties only. Parties by arrangement. **Fee:** £3.50 (ch £2). Family ticket (2ad+2c) £10. **Facilities:** ▣ & (telephone for details) toilets for disabled shop ✖ (ex guide dogs)

SKIPTON Map 07 SD95
SKIPTON CASTLE
BD23 1AQ
➲ (Centre of Skipton at the head of the high street)
☎ 01756 792442 ▤ 01756 796100
e-mail: info@skiptoncastle.co.uk

Skipton is one of the most complete and well-preserved medieval castles in England. Some of the castle dates from the 1650s when it was rebuilt after being partially damaged following the Civil War. However, the original castle was erected in Norman times and became the home of the Clifford family in 1310 and remained so until 1676. Illustrated tour sheets are available in a number of languages.
Times: Open daily from 10am (Sun noon). Last admission 6pm (4pm Oct-Feb). (Closed 25 Dec). **Fee:** ✱ £4.80 (inc illustrated tour sheet) (ch under 18 £2.40, under 5 free, concessions £4.20). Family ticket £12.50. Party 15+. **Facilities:** ▣ (200m) ▣ shop 🍴

A full guide to the Symbols & Abbreviations used in this book can be found on page 6

SUTTON-ON-THE-FOREST Map 08 SE56
SUTTON PARK
YO61 1DP **2 for 1**
➲ (off A1237onto B1363 York to Helmsley Road. 8m North of York City Centre)
☎ 01347 810249 & 811239 ▤ 01347 811251
e-mail: suttonpark@fsbdial.co.uk
The early Georgian house contains fine furniture, paintings and porcelain. The grounds have superb, award-winning terraced gardens, a lily pond and a Georgian ice house. There are also delightful woodland walks as well as spaces for caravans.
Times: Gardens 2 Apr-end Sept, daily 11am-5pm. House open 2 Apr-27 Sep, Wed & Sun, also Good Fri, Etr Mon and all BH Mons. **Fee:** ✱ Gardens only £2.50 (ch 50p, pen £1.50). House & Gardens £5 (ch £2.50, pen £4) **Facilities:** ▣ ▣ & ✖ (ex guide dogs in garden)

WHITBY Map 08 NZ81
WHITBY ABBEY
YO22 4JT
➲ (on clifftop E of Whitby town centre)
☎ 01947 603568 ▤ 01947 825561
Uncover the full story of these atmospheric ruins in their impressive clifftop location above the picturesque fishing town with associations ranging from Victorian jewellery and whaling, to Count Dracula.
Times: Open all year, Apr-Sep, daily 10-6; Oct, daily 10-5; Nov-Mar, daily 10-4. (14-22 Feb, daily, 10-5). (Closed 24-26 Dec & 1 Jan). Dates valid until 31 Mar 2004. **Fee:** £3.80 (ch £1.90, concession £2.90). Prices valid until 31 Mar 2004. **Facilities:** ▣ (charged) ▣ (parking available) shop ✖ (ex on lead in grounds) ⚡

WINTRINGHAM Map 08 SE87
WOLDS WAY LAVENDER
Deer Farm Park, Sandy Ln, Wintringham YO17 8HW
➲ (Off A64 between Malton & Scarborough)
☎ 01944 758641 **FREE**
e-mail: admin@deerparkfarm.com
The medicinal and therapeutic benefits of lavender are extolled at this 12-acre site close to the Yorkshire Wolds. Four acres are currently planted with lavender, and a wood-burning still for the extraction of lavender oil will soon be in place (2005). Visitors can be calmed by the Sensory Areas, enjoy a cuppa at Lavender Lil's Tearoom, and purchase all manner of lavender items at the farm shop.
Times: Open daily, week before Etr-Sep, 10-5. **Facilities:** ▣ ▣ & garden centre Lavender & herb plants ✖ (ex guide dogs) 🍴

YORK Map 08 SE65
THE ARC
St Saviourgate YO1 8NN
➲ (City centre, follow pedestrian signposts for Archaeological Resource Centre)
☎ 01904 543403 ▤ 01904 627097 **2 for 1**
e-mail: enquiries@vikingjorvik.com
The ARC is the perfect place to visit to experience an unusual way to discover York's Viking history. Visitors have the opportunity to become an archaeologist and handle genuine 1000 year-old objects that once belonged to the Vikings themselves. With the help of a special detective

continued

guidebook, it is possible to deduce what life was really like at that time.
Times: Open: School holidays Mon-Sat 11-3.30. Closed mid Dec-early Jan. Open for schools & groups all year Mon-Fri 10-3.30. **Fee:** ✱ £4.50. (ch, students & pen £4) Family £15. Group rates available on request. **Facilities:** P (50yds) & (induction loop, sensory garden, hearing posts) toilets for disabled shop ✗ (ex guide dogs) ◤

CLIFFORD'S TOWER
Tower St YO1 1SA
☎ 01904 646940
Visit this proud symbol of the might of England's medieval kings - and enjoy magnificent views over York. The original wooden tower was built to help William the Conqueror subdue the North. It was burned down during the persecution of the Jewish community in 1190 and rebuilt in a rare design of interlocking circles by Henry III in the 13th century.
Times: Open Apr-Sep, daily 10-6; Oct, daily 10-5; Nov-Mar, daily 10-4. (15-23 Feb, daily 10-5). (Closed 24-26 Dec & 1 Jan). Dates valid until 31 Mar 2004. **Fee:** £2.50 (ch £1.30, concessions £1.90). Prices valid until 31 Mar 2004. **Facilities:** P shop ✗ ⇔ ✿

FAIRFAX HOUSE
Castlegate YO1 9RN
➲ (city centre, close to Jorvik Centre and Cliffords Tower)
☎ 01904 655543 ▤ 01904 652262   **2 for 1**
e-mail: peterbrown@fairfaxhouse.co.uk
An outstanding mid 18th-century house with a richly decorated interior, Fairfax House was acquired by the York Civic Trust in 1983 and restored. The house contains fine examples of Georgian furniture, porcelain, paintings and clocks which were donated by Mr Noel Terry, the great grandson of the founder of the York-based confectionery business. There is a special display of a recreated meal dating from 1763 in the dining room and kitchen.
Times: Open 20 Feb-5 Jan, Mon-Sat 11-5, (Fri guided tours only at 11am & 2pm). Sun 1.30-5. Last admission 4.30pm. **Fee:** ✱ £4.50 (ch £1.50, pen & student £3.75) **Facilities:** P (50yds) (3hr short stay) & (with assistance, phone before visit) shop ✗ (guide dogs) ◤

GUILDHALL
Coney St YO1 9QN
➲ (5mins walk from the rail station)   **FREE**
☎ 01904 613161 ▤ 01904 551052
The present Hall dates from 1446 but in 1942 an air raid virtually destroyed the building. The present Guildhall was carefully restored as an exact replica and was re-opened in 1960. There is an interesting arch-braced roof decorated with colourful bosses and supported by 12 solid oak pillars. There are also some beautiful stained-glass windows.
Times: Open all year, May-Oct, Mon-Fri 9-5, Sat 10-5, Sun 2-5; Nov-Apr, Mon-Fri 9-5.(Closed Good Fri, Spring BH, 25-26 Dec & 1 Jan). **Facilities:** P (15-20 mins walk) & (electric chair lift & ramps) toilets for disabled ✗ (ex guide dogs) ⇔

JORVIK
Coppergate YO1 9WT
➲ (situated in the Coppergate shopping area in city centre, follow the signs to Jorvik)
☎ 01904 543403 ▤ 01904 627097
e-mail: enquiries@vikingjorvik.com

Explore York's Viking history on the very site where archaeologists discovered remains of the city of Jorvik. Encounter Viking residents, learn what life was like here 1000 years ago, and journey through a reconstruction of actual Viking streets. During 2003 and 2004 a special exhibition 'Fearsome Craftsmen' will focus on different Viking-Age arts and crafts.
Times: Open all year, Apr-Oct daily 10-5; and Viking festival Nov-Mar daily 10-4 (Closed 25 Dec). Opening times subject to change, please telephone for up to date details. **Fee:** ✱ £7.20 (ch 5-15 £5.10, under 5 free, student & pen £6.10) Family £21.95. Telephone bookings on 01904 543403 (£1 booking fee per person at peak times). **Facilities:** P (400 yds) (limited to 3 hours) ▣ & (lift & time car designed to take wheelchair, hearing loop) toilets for disabled shop ✗ (ex guide dogs) ◤

MERCHANT ADVENTURERS' HALL
Fossgate YO1 9XD
➲ (located in town centre, between Piccadilly and Fossgate)   **2 for 1**
☎ 01904 654818 ▤ 01904 654818
e-mail: enquiries@theyorkcompany.co.uk
The medieval guild hall of the powerful Merchant Adventurers' Company was built 1357-1361 and is one of the finest in Europe. The Hall contains early furniture, one piece dating from the 13th century, paintings, silver, and weights and measures.
Times: Open 5 Jan-28 Mar & 4 Oct-21Dec, Mon-Sat 9-3.30; 29 Mar-3 Oct, Mon-Thu 9-5, Fri-Sat 9-3.30, Sun 12-4. **Fee:** £2 (ch under 7 free, ch 70p, pen & students £1.70). **Facilities:** P (500yds) & (access from Fossgate) toilets for disabled ✗ (ex guide dogs)

NATIONAL RAILWAY MUSEUM
Leeman Rd YO26 4XJ
➲ (NRM is situated behind the railway station. Signposted from all major approach roads)
☎ 01904 621261   ▤ 01904 611112
e-mail: nrm@nmsi.ac.uk

Among the impressive exhibits are a reconstruction of Stephenson's Rocket; the record-breaking Mallard; a life-size section of the Channel Tunnel; a Japanese bullet train and Royal Palaces on Wheels. The recently added wing features the Workshop, the Warehouse, and the Working Railway Gallery.

Times: Open all year, Mon-Sun 10-6. (Closed 24-26 Dec).
Fee: Admission may be charged for special events. **Facilities:** ▣ (charged) ⬛ ✗ licensed ♿ ("Please Touch" evenings) toilets for disabled shop ✖ (ex guide/hearing dogs) ⬛

ST WILLIAMS COLLEGE
5 College St YO1 7JF
➲ (adjacent to York Minster at east end)
☎ 01904 557233   ▤ 01904 557234
e-mail: info@yorkminster.org

St Williams College, a 15th-century timber-framed building, housed chantry priests until 1549. It now contains York Minster's Conference & Banquet Centre, shop, restaurant and the medieval rooms are open to view when not being used for functions an ideal venue for wedding receptions and medieval banquets. Craft Fairs most weekends.

Times: ✱ Open all year 10-5 for viewing of medieval rooms subject to private bookings - phone for details. Closed 24-26 Dec & Good Fri.
Facilities: ▣ ⬛ ✗ licensed shop ✖

TREASURER'S HOUSE
Chapter House St YO1 7JL
➲ (in Minster Yard, on N side of Minster
☎ 01904 624247   ▤ 01904 647372
e-mail: yorkth@smtp.ntrust.org.uk

Named after the Treasurer of York Minster and built over a Roman Road, the house is not all it seems. Come & discover why! Nestled behind the Minster, the size, splendour and contents of the house are a constant surprise to visitors - as are the famous ghost stories. Children's trails and access to the tea room free.

Times: Open Apr-Oct, daily except Fri, 11-5. **Fee:** ✱ £4 (ch £2). Family ticket £10 (2+3). **Facilities:** ▣ (800 mtrs) ⬛ ✗ ♿ (Braille guide/tactile pictures/induction loop/scented path) ✖ (ex guide dogs) ⬛

THE YORK BREWERY CO LTD
12 Toft Green YO1 6JT
➲ (within City Walks)
☎ 01904 621162   ▤ 01904 621216   `2 for 1`
e-mail: tony@yorkbrew.co.uk

One of the North's finest independent breweries now offers a tour of its premises inside the city walls. Visitors can observe all the processes that go into producing beers like Centurion's Ghost, Full Bloom, Guzzler, and Silly Mid Off. Those made intolerably thirsty by the sight of all this brewing expertise will be glad to know that the adult ticket price includes one pint of beer.

Times: Open daily tours at 12.30, 2, 3.30 and 5 **Fee:** ✱ £4.25 (pen £3.75, ch 14-17 £3) **Facilities:** ▣ 50yds shop ✖ (ex guide dogs) ⬛

YORK CASTLE MUSEUM
The Eye of York YO1 1RY (city centre, next to Clifford's Tower)
☎ 01904 653611   ▤ 01904 671078

Fascinating exhibits that bring memories to life, imaginatively displayed through reconstructions of period rooms and two indoor streets, complete with cobbles, a Hansom cab and a park. The museum is housed in the city's former prison and is based on an extensive collection of 'bygones' acquired at the beginning of the twentieth century. It was one of the first folk museums to display a huge range of everyday objects in an authentic scene. The Victorian street includes a pawnbroker, a tallow candle factory and a haberdasher's. There is even a reconstruction of the original sweet shop of the York chocolate manufacturer, Joseph Terry. An extensive collection of many other items ranging from musical instruments to costumes and a gallery of domestic gadgets from Victorian times to the 1960s (entitled 'Every home should have one') are further attractions to this remarkable museum. The museum also has one of Britain's finest collections of Militaria; this includes a superb example of an Anglo-Saxon helmet - one of only three known. A special exhibition called 'Seeing it Through' explores the life of York citizens during the Second World War. The museum includes the cell where highwayman Dick Turpin was held. Please contact the museum for deatils of exhibition and events.

Times: ✱ Open all year, Apr-Oct Mon-Sat 9.30-5.30, Sun 10-5.30; Nov-Mar, Mon-Sat 9.30-4, Sun 10-4. (Closed 25-26 Dec & 1 Jan).
Facilities: ⬛ ♿ toilets for disabled shop ✖ ⬛

YORK CITY ART GALLERY
Exhibition Square YO1 7EW
➲ (3min walk from the minster in the centre of York).
☎ 01904 551861   ▤ 01904 551866
e-mail: art.gallery@york.gov.uk

The gallery is remarkable for the range and quality of its collections that provide a survey of most developments in Western European painting over the past six centuries, something that most regional galleries cannot claim to do. Works by Parmigianino, Bellotto, Lely, Reynolds, Frith, Boudin, Lowry and Nash and nudes by Etty are on permanent display. There are also fine collections of watercolours and pottery.

Times: ✱ Open all year, daily 10-5. (Closed 25 & 26 Dec & 1 Jan).
Facilities: ▣ (500mtrs) ♿ (chair lift) toilets for disabled shop ✖ (ex guide dogs) ⬛

THE YORK DUNGEON
12 Clifford St YO1 9RD
➲ (A64/A19/A59 - head for city centre)
☎ 01904 632599   ▤ 01904 612602   `2 for 1`
e-mail: yorkdungeons@
merlinentertainments.biz

Deep in the heart of historic York, buried beneath it's very paving stones, lies The York Dungeon, bringing more than 2,000 years of gruesomely authentic history vividly back to life...and death. As you delve into the darkest chapters of our grim and bloody past, recreated in all its dreadful detail remember - everything you experience really happened... A warning - in the dungeon's dark catacombs it always pays to

continued

keep your wits about you. The 'exhibits' have an unnerving habit of coming back to life... The journey-includes features of Dick Turpin, Guy Fawkes, Witch Trails, Clifford's Tower, Pit of Despair and Gorvik - the real viking experience. **Times:** Open all year, daily 10.30-5 (closes 4.30 Oct-Mar). Closed 25 Dec. **Fee:** ✳ £8.50 (ch £5.95, students & pen £7.50). Family ticket (2 adult & 2 ch) £25. **Facilities:** P (500yds) ♿ (wheelchair ramps, stairlifts, award winning access) toilets for disabled shop 🗨

YORK MINSTER
Deangate YO1 7EW
➲ (Easy access via A19, A1 or A64)
☎ 01904 557216 📠 01904 557218
e-mail: visitors@yorkminster.org

Enjoy the peaceful atmosphere of the largest Gothic cathedral in Northern Europe, a place of worship for over 1,000 years, and a treasure house of stained glass. Take an audio tour of the Undercroft to find out more about the Minster's fascinating history and climb the Tower for an amazing view. **Times:** Open from 7am for services. Visitors Mon-Sat 9-4.45 (9.30 in winter), Sun noon-3.45. Phone for 2004 details. **Fee:** ✳ £4.50 (ch16 free, concessions £3). Small charge also for the Undercroft and Tower). **Facilities:** P (440yds) ♿ (tactile model, braille & large print guide) toilets for disabled shop 🐕 (ex guide dogs) 🗨

YORKSHIRE MUSEUM
Museum Gardens YO1 7FR
➲ (park & ride service from 4 sites near A64/A19/A1079 & A166, also 3 car parks within short walk)
☎ 01904 551800 📠 01904 551802
e-mail: yorkshire.museum@york.gov.uk
The Yorkshire Museum is set in 10 acres of botanical gardens in the heart of the historic City of York, and displays some of the finest Roman, Anglo-Saxon, Viking and Medieval treasures ever discovered in Britain. The Middleham jewel, a fine example of English Gothic jewellery, is on display, and in the Roman Gallery, visitors can see a marble head of Constantine the Great. The Anglo-Saxon Gallery houses the delicate silver-gilt Ormside bowl and the Gilling sword. **Times:** ✳ Open all year, daily 10-5. **Facilities:** P (5 mins walk) ♿ (ramps & lift) toilets for disabled shop 🐕 🗨

SOUTH YORKSHIRE

EVENTS & FESTIVALS

January
6th The Ancient Haxey Hood Game,
   Doncaster

May
3rd Sheffield Mayfest, folk festival with live
   music & dance

June
tbc Firth Park Festival, Firth Park, Sheffield
tbc Grenoside Gala, Grenoside Park, Sheffield
tbc Sheffield Children's Festival
tbc Sheffield Festival of Transport
tbc Sheffield Motor Show,
   Hillsborough Park, Sheffield

July
4th Abbey Field Park Multicultural Festival
tbc City Centre Carnival, Sheffield
tbc Dore Gala, Sheffield
tbc Eccelsfield Gala,
   Hillsborough Park, Sheffield
tbc Hillsborough Gala,
   Hillsborough Park, Sheffield
tbc Sharrow Festival
   (family festival with music & art)
tbc South Yorkshire Festival,
   Wortley Hall, Sheffield

August
tbc 3DOM Festival (free urban festival),
   Devon Green, Sheffield
tbc The Sheffield Show, Graves Park, Sheffield

September
tbc Sheffield Fayre, Norfolk Park

October
13th-19th Sheffield International
   Documentary Festival
16th-30th Off the Shelf Literature Festival,
   Sheffield

Above: Damflask Reservoir, Loxley Valley

BARNSLEY Map 08 SE30

MONK BRETTON PRIORY
S71 5QD
➲ (1m E of Barnsley town centre, off A633) FREE

The priory was an important Cluniac house, founded in 1153. The considerable remains of the gatehouse, church and other buildings can be seen.

Times: Open all year, Apr-Sep, daily 10-6; Oct, daily 10-5; Nov-Mar, daily 10-4. (Closed 24-26 Dec & 1 Jan). Dates valid until 31 Mar 2004.
Facilities: 🅿 ✹ (ex dogs on leads) ⊞

CONISBROUGH Map 08 SK59

CONISBROUGH CASTLE
DN12 3HH
➲ (NE of town centre off A630)
☎ 01709 863329

The white, circular keep of this 12th-century castle is a spectacular structure. Made of magnesian limestone, it is the oldest of its kind in England. Recently restored, with two new floors and a roof, it is a fine example of medieval architecture and was the inspiration for Sir Walter Scott's classic novel *Ivanhoe*.

Times: Opening times vary, please telephone site for details.
Fee: Prices vary, telephone site for details. **Facilities:** 🅿 💺 ♿ (wheelchair access limited) shop ✹ ⊞

CUSWORTH Map 08 SE50

THE MUSEUM OF SOUTH YORKSHIRE LIFE CUSWORTH H HALL
Cusworth Ln DN5 7TU
➲ (3m NW of Doncaster)
☎ 01302 782342 📠 01302 782342 FREE
e-mail: museum@doncaster.gov.uk

The Museum of South Yorkshire is located in Cusworth Hall, an 18th-century country house set in a landscaped park. It has displays which illustrate the way local people here lived, worked and entertained themselves over the last 200 years.
Times: Open Mon-Fri 10-5, Sat 11-5 & Sun 1-5. (4pm Dec & Jan). Closed Good Fri, Xmas & 1 Jan. Hall & Park undergoing restoration and at times some areas may not be open to the public. Telephone for details. **Facilities:** 🅿 💺 ♿ (wheelchair available) toilets for disabled shop ✹ (ex guide dogs)

DONCASTER Map 08 SE50

BRODSWORTH HALL & GARDENS
Brodsworth DN5 7XJ
➲ (between A635 & A638)
☎ 01302 722598 📠 01302 337165

This Victorian country house has survived largely intact. Imagine how the serving classes fared below stairs, then experience, in contrast, the opulent 'upstairs' apartments.
continued

Outside, visitors can enjoy a leisurely stroll around the extensive newly restored gardens.

Times: Open, House: Apr-26 Oct, Tue-Sun & BH, 1-6 (last admission 5pm). Gardens: Apr-26 Oct, Tue-Sun & BH's 12-6, Mon 11-4; Nov-Mar, wknds only. (Closed 24-26 Dec & 1 Jan). Dates valid until 31 Mar 2004.
Fee: House & Gardens £6 (ch £3, concessions £4.50). Gardens only during summer £3.50 (ch £1.80, concessions £2.60), during winter £2 (ch £1, concessions £1.50). Prices valid until 31 Mar 2004.
Facilities: 🅿 💺 ♿ toilets for disabled shop (12-6) ✹ ⊞ 🢇

DONCASTER MUSEUM & ART GALLERY
Chequer Rd DN1 2AE
➲ (off inner ring road)
☎ 01302 734293 📠 01302 735409 FREE
e-mail: museum@doncaster.gov.uk

The wide-ranging collections include fine and decorative art and sculpture. Also ceramics, glass, silver, and displays on history, archaeology and natural history. The historical collection of the Kings Own Yorkshire Light Infantry is housed here. Temporary exhibitions are held.
Times: Open all year, Mon-Sat 10-5, Sun 2-5. (Closed Good Fri, 25-26 Dec & 1 Jan). **Facilities:** 🅿 ♿ (lift, hearing loop in lecture room) toilets for disabled shop ✹ (ex guide dogs)

EARTH CENTRE
Denaby Main DN12 4EA
➲ (follow brown signs from A1M. From junct 36 follow brown Earth Centre signs along A630, then A6023 towards Mexborough. Earth Centre next right after Coniston Train Stn)
☎ 01709 513933 📠 01709 512010
e-mail: info@earthcentre.org.uk

Earth Centre is a park for active leisure and learning with outdoor activities such as climbing, archery and canoeing. New in 2003 were Shipwreck Island, an adventure golf course, Blue Beard's Galleon and Amazon Adventure. Visitors can also enjoy a guided tour on Hope's Express, the bright red road train.
Times: Open all year, daily (ex Xmas day) 10-5 (peak), 10-4 (off peak), 10-7 (school holidays). **Fee:** £4.50 (ch & concessions £3.50, ch under 5 & essential carers free). Some activities incur an additional charge of £2.50. **Facilities:** 🅿 (charged) 💺 ✕ licensed ♿ (prebooked wheelchairs/electric cars for hire) toilets for disabled shop ✹ (ex guide dogs) 🢇

MALTBY   Map 08 SK59

ROCHE ABBEY
S66 8NW
➲ (1.5m S off A634)
☎ 01709 812739

Visit the enchanting valley designed by 'Capability' Brown and discover the fascinating ruins of Roche Abbey, founded in 1147 by the Cistercians.
Times: Open all year, Apr-Sep, daily 10-6; Oct, daily 10-5. Dates valid until 31 Mar 2004. **Fee:** £2 (ch £1, concessions £1.50). Prices valid until 31 Mar 2004. **Facilities:** 🅿 & shop ✖ (ex dogs on leads) ♯

ROTHERHAM   Map 08 SK49

MAGNA SCIENCE ADVENTURE CENTRE
Sheffield Rd, Templeborough S60 1DX
➲ (M1 junct 34 , follow Templeborough sign off rdbt, then follow brown heritage signs)
☎ 01709 720002   ▤ 01709 820092   [2 for 1]
e-mail: jeyre@magnatrust.co.uk

Magna is the UK's first Science Adventure Centre, an exciting exploration of Earth, Air, Fire, Water and Power. A chance for visitors to create their own adventure through hands-on interactive challenges. Visit the five Adventure Pavilions, two shows and the outdoor adventure park and have fun unearthing the mysteries of our world.
Times: Please phone for 2004 details **Fee:** ✱ £8 (ch & concessions £6). Family (2ad+2ch) ticket £24, (2ad+3ch) £26. **Facilities:** 🅿 🍽 ✖ licensed & (lifts, portable seating, wheelchair hire) toilets for disabled shop ✖ (ex guide dogs) 🍵

SHEFFIELD   Map 08 SK38

BISHOPS HOUSE
Meersbrook Park, Norton Lees Ln S8 9BE
➲ (2m S of Sheffield, on A61 Chesterfield road)
☎ 0114 278 2600
e-mail: info@sheffieldgalleries.org.uk

This 15th and 16th-century yeoman's house has been restored and opened as a museum of local and social history. Several rooms have been furnished and there are displays of life in Tudor and Stuart times. Special educational facilities can be arranged for schools and colleges. Please ring for details.
Times: Open Sat 10-4.30. Sun 11-4.30 **Facilities:** 🅿 (roadside parking on nearby streets) & shop ✖ (ex guide dogs)

KELHAM ISLAND MUSEUM
Alma St S3 8RY
➲ (0.5m NW of city centre, take A61 N to West Bar, follow signposts)
☎ 0114 272 2106   ▤ 0114 275 7847
e-mail: postmaster@simt.co.uk

The story of Sheffield, its industry and life, with the most powerful working steam engine in Europe, reconstructed workshops, and craftspeople demonstrating traditional 'made in Sheffield' skills - this is a 'living' museum. During the year Kelham Island stages events, displays and temporary exhibitions culminating in the annual Christmas Victorian Market.
Times: Open Mon-Thu 10-4, Sun 11-4.45.Closed Fri and Sat. Check opening days/times at Christmas & New Year before travelling. **Fee:** ✱ £3.50 (ch £2, pen £2.50). Family ticket £8. **Facilities:** 🅿 🍽 & (wheelchair on request) toilets for disabled shop ✖

MILLENNIUM GALLERIES
Arundel Gate S1 2PP
☎ 0114 278 2600   ▤ 0114 278 2604
e-mail: info@sheffieldgalleries.org.uk

With four different galleries under one roof, the Millennium Galleries has something for everyone. Enjoy new blockbuster exhibitions drawn from the collections of Britain's national galleries and museums, including the Victoria & Albert Museum and Tate Gallery. See the best of contemporary craft and design in a range of exhibitions by established and up-and-coming makers. Be dazzled by Sheffield's magnificent and internationally important collection of decorative and domestic metalwork and silverware. Discover the Ruskin Gallery with its wonderful array of treasures by Victorian artist and writer John Ruskin.
Times: ✱ Open daily Mon-Sat 10-5, Sun 11-5. **Facilities:** 🅿 🍽 ✖ licensed & (hearing loop) toilets for disabled shop ✖ (ex guide dogs) 🍵

> Special Events are held at many attractions throughout the country. As we cannot hope to list them all, please ring the places of interest for details of exhibitions, themed days, and guided walks.

WEST YORKSHIRE

EVENTS & FESTIVALS

March
tbc Bradford Film Festival, National Museum of Photography, Film & Television
tbc Daffodil Week, Haworth

April
3rd-4th Complementary Medicine Festival, Kings Hall Winter Gardens, Ilkley
12th World Coal Carrying Championship, Royal Oak Pub, Owl Lane, Ossett

May
9th-16th Wharfedale Music Festival, various venues in Ilkley (competitive festival of music, dance, poetry, speech and drama)
tbc Todmorden Gang Show, Todmorden

June
19th Todmorden Agricultural Show, Central Vale Park, Burnley Road, Todmorden
tbc Wetherby Agricultural Show, Grange Park, Wetherby

July
2nd-4th Cleckheaton Folk Festival, various venues (provisional)
18th Arthington Show, Old Showfield, Pool Bank, Bramhope
tbc Bradford Festival & Mela, Peel Park

October
tbc Leeds International Film Festival, Town Hall, Leeds (provisional)

November
13th-14th Complementary Medicine Festival, Kings Hall Winter Gardens, Ilkley
19th-28th Huddersfield Contemporary Music Festival

November/December
tbc Haworth Victorian Christmas Festival

Above: Haworth's Parsonage, home of the Brontës

BOLLING HALL
Bowling Hall Rd BD4 7LP
➲ (1m from city centre off A650)
☎ 01274 723057 ▤ 01274 726220
e-mail: abickley@legend.co.uk

A classic West Yorkshire manor house, complete with galleried 'housebody' (hall), Bolling Hall dates mainly from the 17th century but has medieval and 18th-century sections. It has panelled rooms, plasterwork in original colours, heraldic glass and a rare Chippendale bed.
Times: ✱ Open all year, Wed-Fri 11-4, Sat 10-5, Sun 12-5. (Closed Mon ex BH, Good Fri, 25 & 26 Dec). **Facilities:** ⊞ & shop ✖

BRADFORD INDUSTRIAL MUSEUM AND HORSES AT WORK
Moorside Mills, Moorside Rd, Eccleshill BD2 3HP
➲ (off A658)
☎ 01274 631756 ▤ 01274 636362

Moorside Mills is an original spinning mill, now part of a museum that brings vividly to life the story of Bradford's woollen industry. There is the machinery that once converted raw wool into cloth, and the mill yard rings with the sound of iron on stone as shire horses pull trams, haul buses and give rides. Daily demonstrations and changing exhibitions.
Times: ✱ Open all year, Tue-Sat 10-5, Sun 12-5. (Closed Mon ex BH)
Facilities: ⊞ ▣ & (induction loop in lecture theatre) toilets for disabled shop ✖

CARTWRIGHT HALL ART GALLERY
Lister Park BD9 4NS
➲ (1m from city centre on A650)
☎ 01274 751212 ▤ 01274 481045

Built in dramatic Baroque style in 1904, the gallery has permanent collections of 19th and 20th-century British art, contemporary prints, and older works by British and European masters.
Times: ✱ Open all year Apr-Sep, Tue-Sat 10-5, Sun 1-5. (Closed Mon ex BH, Good Fri, 25 & 26 Dec). **Facilities:** ▣ & (wheelchair available) toilets for disabled shop ✖

COLOUR MUSEUM
Perkin House, 1 Providence St BD1 2PW
➲ (from city centre follow signs B6144 (Haworth), then follow brown heritage signs)
☎ 01274 390955 ▤ 01274 392888   **2 for 1**
e-mail: museum@sdc.org.uk

Europe's only Museum of Colour comprises two galleries packed with visitor-operated exhibits demonstrating the effects of light and colour, including optical illusions, and the story of dyeing and textile printing. There is a programme of special exhibitions and events. Please telephone for details.
Times: Open 2 Jan-18 Dec, Tue-Sat, 10-4. **Fee:** ✱ £2 (concessions £1.50). Family ticket £4 **Facilities:** ℙ (300 yds) & (lift from street level, ramps at door) toilets for disabled shop ✖ (ex guide dogs) ◥

NATIONAL MUSEUM OF PHOTOGRAPHY, FILM & TELEVISION

BD1 1NQ

➲ (2m from end of M606, follow signs for city centre)

☎ 0870 7010200 🖨 01274 394540

e-mail: talk.nmpft@nmsi.ac.uk

Experience the past, present and future of photography, film and television with amazing interactive displays and spectacular 3D IMAX cinema. **Times:** Open all year, Tue-Sun, BH's & main school hols 10-6. (Closed Mon). **Fee:** Admission to permanent galleries free, IMAX Cinema £5.95 (concessions £4.20). Groups 20% discount. **Facilities:** P (adjacent) 🅿🖤 ✖ licensed 🚻 (tailored tours, Braille signs,induction loop,cinema seating) toilets for disabled shop ✖ (ex guide dogs) 🍴

BRAMHAM   Map 08 SE44

BRAMHAM PARK

LS23 6ND

➲ (on A,14m S of Wetherby, take Bramham/Thorner slip road and follow signs)

☎ 01937 846000 🖨 01937 846007

e-mail: lucy.finucane@bramhampark.co.uk

This fine Queen Anne house was built by Robert Benson and is the home of his descendants. The garden has ornamental ponds, cascades, temples and avenues. **Times:** ✱ Open Apr-Sep, daily 10.30-5.30. **Facilities:** P 🚻 toilets for disabled woodlands only

GOMERSAL   Map 08 SE22

RED HOUSE

Oxford Rd BD19 4JP

➲ (M62 Junct 26, take A58 towards Leeds then right onto A651 towards Gomersal. Red House is on the right hand side)

☎ 01274 335100 🖨 01274 335105

Delightful redbrick house displayed as the 1830s home of a Yorkshire wool clothier and merchant. The house and family was frequently visited by Charlotte Brontë in the 1830s and featured in her novel *Shirley*. The gardens have been reconstructed in the style of the period and there are exhibitions on the Brontë connection and local history in the restored Barn and Cartsheds. **Times:** ✱ Open all year, Mon-Fri 11-5, Sat-Sun 12-5. Telephone for Xmas opening. (Closed Good Fri & 1 Jan). **Facilities:** P 🚻 (Braille & T-setting hearing aid available) toilets for disabled shop ✖ (ex guide dogs) 🍴

HALIFAX   Map 07 SE02

BANKFIELD MUSEUM

Boothtown Rd, Akroyd Park HX3 6HG

➲ (museum is on A647 Bradford via Queensbury road, 0.5m from Halifax town centre)

☎ 01422 354823 & 352334

🖨 01422 349020   FREE

e-mail: bankfield-museum@calderdale.gov.uk

Built by Edward Akroyd in the 1860s, this Renaissance-style building is set in parkland on a hill overlooking the town. It has an outstanding collection of costumes and textiles from many periods and parts of the world, including a new gallery featuring East European textiles. There is also a section on

continued

toys, and the museum of the Duke of Wellington's Regiment is housed here. Temporary exhibitions are held and there is a lively programme of events, workshops and activities. Please ring for details.

Times: Open all year, Tue-Sat 10-5, Sun 2-5, BH Mon 10-5.(extended closing times at Xmas and New Year, phone for details) **Facilities:** P 🚻 (audio guide & tactile objects) toilets for disabled shop ✖ (ex guide dogs) 🍴

EUREKA! THE MUSEUM FOR CHILDREN

Discovery Rd HX1 2NE

➲ (M62 junct 24 follow brown heritage signs to Halifax centre (A629))

☎ 01422 330069 & 01426 983191

🖨 01422 330275

e-mail: info@eureka.org.uk

With over 400 'must touch'exhibits, interactive activities and challenges, visitors are invited to embark upon a journey of discovery through four main gallery spaces: Me and My Body, Living and Working Together, Our Global Garden and Invent, Create, Communicate (this gallery being redeveloped for 2004.). Children can find out how their bodies and senses work, discover the realities of daily life, travel from the familiar 'backyard' to amazing and faraway places and explore the world of communications. **Times:** Open all year, daily 10-5 (except 24-26 Dec) **Fee:** ✱ £5.95. Family Saver ticket £27.50 **Facilities:** P (charged) 🅿🚻 (lift, staff trained in basic sign language, large print) toilets for disabled shop ✖ (ex guide dogs) 🍴

PIECE HALL

HX1 1RE

➲ (follow brown tourist signs, close to Halifax railway station)

☎ 01422 358087 🖨 01422 349310

e-mail: karen.belshaw@calderdale.gov.uk

The merchants of Halifax built the elegant and unique hall in 1779, and it has over 300 merchant's rooms around a courtyard, now housing an industrial museum, art galleries and shops selling antiques, books etc. There is an open market on Friday and Saturday, and a flea market on Thursday. There is a lively programme of exhibitions, workshops, activities and events throughout the year, and a festival in the summer, please ring for details. **Times:** ✱ Open all year daily (Closed 25-26 Dec). Art Gallery). Tue-Sun & BH Mons 10-5. **Facilities:** P (50 yds) 🅿🚻 (lifts, shopmobility on site & audio guide available) toilets for disabled shop 🍴

SHIBDEN HALL

Lister's Rd HX3 6XG   2 for 1

➲ (2km E of Halifax on A58)

☎ 01422 352246 & 321455 🖨 01422 348440

e-mail: shibden.hall@calderdale.gov.uk

The house dates back to the early 15th century, and its rooms have been laid out to illustrate life in different periods of its history. Craft weekends, featuring over 30 craftworkers demonstrating historic skills, are held, and there's a lively programme of craft events, workshops and family activities. Please apply for details. **Times:** Open Mar-Nov, Mon-Sat 10-5, Sun 12-5. Dec-Feb, Mon-Sat 10-4, Sun 12-4. **Fee:** ✱ £3.50 (ch & concessions £2.50) Family ticket £10. **Facilities:** P 🅿🚻 (garden only partially accesible) toilets for disabled shop ✖ (ex guide dogs) 🍴

HAREWOOD   Map 08 SE34
HAREWOOD HOUSE & BIRD GARDEN
LS17 9LQ

➲ (junc A61/A659 Leeds/Harrogate Rd)

☎ 0113 218 1010 ▤ 0113 218 1002

e-mail: business@harewood.org

Designed in 1759 by John Carr, Harewood House is the home of the Queen's cousin, the Earl of Harewood. His mother, HRH Princess Mary, Princess Royal lived at Harewood for 35 years and much of her memorabilia is still displayed. The House, renowned for its stunning architecture and exquisite Adam interiors, contains a rich collection of Chippendale furniture, fine porcelain and outstanding art collections from Italian Renaissance masterpieces and Turner watercolours to contemporary works. The old kitchen contains the best collection of noble household copperware in the country giving visitors a glimpse into below stairs life. The grounds include a restored parterre terrace, oriental rock garden, walled garden, lakeside and woodland walks, a bird garden and for youngsters, an adventure playground.
Times: Open 12 Mar-16 Nov, daily Bird Garden from 10am, House from 11am. Grounds & Bird Garden open wknds 22-23 Nov-13-14 Dec.
Fee: ✱ 'Freedom ticket' (house, grounds, bird garden, terrace gallery) Mon-Sat £9.50 (ch £5.25, pen £7.75) Family £29. Sun & BH £10.50 (ch £5.75, pen £8.75) Family £32. Bird Garden & Grounds: £6.75 (ch £4.25 pen £5.75) Family £21. Sun & BH £7.75 (ch £4.75, pen £6.75) Family £24. **Facilities:** ▱ ⬛ ✕ licensed ⅙ (electric ramp, lift, free audio tour) toilets for disabled shop garden centre ✖ (ex guide dogs or in gardens) ⬔

HAWORTH   Map 07 SE03
BRONTË PARSONAGE MUSEUM
BD22 8DR

➲ (A629 & A6033 follow signs for Haworth, take Rawdon Rd, pass 2 car parks, next left, then right)

☎ 01535 642323 ▤ 01535 647131

e-mail: bronte@bronte.org.uk

Haworth Parsonage was the lifelong family home of the Brontës. An intensely close-knit family, the Brontës saw the parsonage as the heart of their world and the moorland setting provided them with inspiration for their writing. The house contains much personal memorabilia, including the furniture Charlotte bought with the proceeds of her literary success, Branwell's portraits of local worthies, Emily's writing desk and Anne's books and drawings.
Times: Open Apr-Sep, daily 10-5.30; Oct-Mar daily 11-5 (final admission 30 min before closing). Closed 24-27 Dec & 2-31 Jan.
Fee: ✱ £4.80 (ch 5-16 £1.50, concessions £3.50). Family ticket £10.50.
Facilities: ▱ (charged) ⅙ (Information in large type & Braille) shop ✖ (ex guide dogs) ⬔

KEIGHLEY & WORTH VALLEY RAILWAY & MUSEUM
Keighley BD22 8NJ

➲ (1m from Keighley on A629 Halifax road, look out for 'Brown Sign').

☎ 01535 645214 & 677777 ▤ 01535 647317

The line was built mainly to serve the valley's mills, and goes through the heart of Brontë country. Beginning at Keighley (shared with Railtrack), it climbs up to Haworth, and terminates at Oxenhope, which has a storage and restoration

continued

building. At Haworth there are locomotive workshops and at Ingrow West, an award-winning museum.
Times: All year weekend service, but daily all BH wks & 19 Jun-1 Sep.
Fee: ✱ Full line return ticket £6 reduced fares for ch & pen. Family return ticket £16. Day rover (unlimited travel) £8, Family day rover £20. Under 5's free. Party rates. **Facilities:** ▱ (charged) ⬛ ⅙ (wheelchairs can be accommodated in brake car). toilets for disabled shop ⬔

HUDDERSFIELD   Map 07 SE11
TOLSON MEMORIAL MUSEUM
Ravensknowle Park, Wakefield Rd HD5 8DJ

➲ (on A629), 1m from town centre.   **FREE**

☎ 01484 223830 ▤ 01484 223843

Displays on the development of the cloth industry and a collection of horse-drawn vehicles, together with natural history, archaeology, toys and folk exhibits. There is a full programme of events and temporary exhibitions.
Times: Open all year. Mon-Fri 11-5, Sat & Sun noon-5. (Closed Xmas).
Facilities: ▱ ⅙ mini-com, partial stairlift, induction loop, parking toilets for disabled shop ✖ (ex registered guide dogs) ⬔

ILKLEY   Map 07 SE14
MANOR HOUSE GALLERY & MUSEUM
Castle Yard, Church St LS29 9DT

➲ (behind Ilkley Parish Church, on A65)

☎ 01943 600066 ▤ 01943 817079

This Elizabethan manor house, one of Ilkley's few buildings to pre-date the 19th century, was built on the site of a Roman fort. Part of the Roman wall can be seen, together with Roman relics and displays on archaeology. There is a collection of 17th and 18th-century farmhouse parlour and kitchen furniture, and the art gallery exhibits works by contemporary artists and craftsmen.
Times: ✱ Open all year, Wed-Sat 11-5, Sun 1-4. (Closed Good Fri, 25-28 Dec). **Facilities:** ⅙ shop ✖

KEIGHLEY   Map 07 SE04
CLIFFE CASTLE MUSEUM & GALLERY
Spring Gardens Ln BD20 6LH

➲ (NW of town off A629)

☎ 01535 618230 ▤ 01535 610536

French furniture from the Victoria and Albert Museum is displayed, together with collections of local and natural history, ceramics, dolls, geological items and minerals. The grounds of this 19th-century mansion have a play area and an aviary.
Times: ✱ Open all year, Tue-Sat 10-5, Sun 12-5. Also open BH Mon. (Closed Good Fri & 25-28 Dec). **Facilities:** ▱ ⬛ ⅙ toilets for disabled shop ✖

EAST RIDDLESDEN HALL
Bradford Rd BD20 4EA

➲ (1m NE of Keighley on south side of Bradford Rd)

☎ 01535 607075 ▤ 01535 691462

e-mail: yorker@smtp.ntrust.org.uk

This charming 17th-century Yorkshire manor house is typical of its kind, although the plasterwork and oak panelling are contemporary. A small secluded garden is found in the

continued

grounds, which also feature one of the largest medieval tithe barns in the north of England.
Times: ✳ Open 23 Mar-3 Nov daily (ex Mon/thu/Fri) open Good Fri, BH Mons and Mons in Jul/Aug 12-5 (Sat 1-5) **Facilities:** 🅿 💷 ♿ shop ✖ ♨

LEEDS   Map 08 SE33

ABBEY HOUSE MUSEUM
Abbey Walk, Abbey Rd, Kirkstall LS5 3EH
➲ (3m W of Leeds city centre on A65)
☎ 0113 230 5492 🖷 0113 230 5499
e-mail: abbeyhouse.museum@virgin.net

Displays at this museum include an interactive childhood gallery, a look at Kirkstall Abbey, and an exploration of life in Victorian Leeds. Three reconstructed streets allow the visitor to immerse themselves in the sights and sounds of the late 19th century, from the glamourous art furnishers shop to the impoverished widow washerwoman.
Times: Open all year Tue-Fri 10-5, Sat noon-5, Sun 10-5. Closed Mon ex BH Mon (open 10-5) **Fee:** ✳ £3 (ch £1 accompanied by an adult, concessions £2). Family ticket £5 **Facilities:** 🅿 💷 ✖ licensed ♿ (Braille plaques on wall, tactile tours by request) toilets for disabled shop ✖ (ex guide dogs) ♨

CITY ART GALLERY   FREE
The Headrow LS1 3AA
➲ (city centre, next to town hall and library)
☎ 0113 247 8248 🖷 0113 244 9689

Home to one of the best collections of 20th-century British art outside London, as well as Victorian and late 19th-century pictures, an outstanding collection of English watercolours, a display of modern sculpture and temporary exhibitions focusing on the contemporary.
Times: Open all year, Mon-Sat 10-5, Wed until 8, Sun 1-5.Closed BHs.
Facilities: 🅿 💷 ✖ licensed ♿ (restricted access to upper floor) toilets for disabled shop ✖ (ex guide dogs)

KIRKSTALL ABBEY
Abbey Rd, Kirkstall LS5 3EH
➲ (off A65, W of city centre).
☎ 0113 275 5821   FREE

The most complete 12th-century Cistercian Abbey in the country stands on the banks of the River Aire. Many of the original buildings can still be seen, including the cloister, church and refectory. Regular tours take visitors to areas not normally accessible to the public. During the summer the Abbey hosts plays, fairs and musical events.
Times: Open all year. Abbey site open dawn-dusk. **Facilities:** 🅿 ♿ toilets for disabled shop ✖

LEEDS INDUSTRIAL MUSEUM AT ARMLEY MILLS
Canal Rd, Armley LS12 2QF
➲ (2m W of city centre, off A65)   2 for 1
☎ 0113 263 7861

Once the world's largest woollen mill, Armley Mills evokes memories of the 18th-century woollen industry, showing the progress of wool from the sheep to knitted clothing. The museum has its own 1930s cinema illustrating the history of cinema projection, including the first moving pictures taken in Leeds. There are demonstrations of static engines and

continued

steam locomotives, a printing gallery and a journey through the working world of textiles and fashion.
Times: Open all year, Tue-Sat 10-5, Sun 1-5. Last entry 1 hr before closing. (Closed Mon ex BHs). **Fee:** £2 (ch 50p pen, students & UB40's £1) Friends & Family ticket £5 (2 adults & 3 ch) **Facilities:** 🅿 ♿ (chair-lifts between floors) toilets for disabled shop ✖ ♨

MIDDLETON RAILWAY
Moor Rd, Hunslet LS10 2JQ
➲ (M621 junct 5 or follow signs from A61)
☎ 0113 271 0320 (ansaphone)   2 for 1
🖷 01977 620585
e-mail: info@middletonrailway.org.uk

This was the first railway authorised by an Act of Parliament (in 1758) and the first to succeed with steam locomotives (in 1812). Steam trains run each weekend in season from Tunstall Road roundabout to Middleton Park. There is a programme of special events.
Times: Moor Road Station open for viewing every wknd. Trains run Sat, Sun & BH, Apr-Dec. **Fee:** ✳ Entry to station free. £2.50 (ch £1.50) Return train fare. Family ticket £7. **Facilities:** 🅿 💷 ♿ (ramped access to all areas) toilets for disabled shop ♨

ROYAL ARMOURIES MUSEUM
Armouries Dr LS10 1LT
➲ (off A61 close to Leeds centre, follow brown heritage signs)
☎ 0113 220 1999 & 0990 106 666   FREE
🖷 0113 220 1934
e-mail: enquiries@armouries.org.uk

The museum is an impressive contemporary home for the renowned national collection of arms and armour. The collection is divided between five galleries: War, Tournament, Self-Defence, Hunting and Oriental. The Hall of Steel features a 100ft-high mass of 3000 pieces of arms and armour. Extensive interactive displays, dramatisations of jousting tournaments etc. and the chance to see leather workers and armourers at work all make for an exciting day out.
Times: Open daily, from 10-5. (Closed 24-25 Dec) **Facilities:** 🅿 (charged) 💷 ✖ licensed ♿ (induction loops, wheelchairs, signers, low level counter) toilets for disabled shop ✖ (ex guide/hearing dogs) ♨

TEMPLE NEWSAM HOUSE & PARK
LS15 0AE
➲ (off A63)   2 for 1
☎ 0113 264 7321 (House) & 264 5535 (Park)
🖷 0113 260 2285

This Tudor and Jacobean mansion boasts extensive collections of decorative arts in their original room settings, including an incomparable Chippendale collection. Set in 1,200 acres of parkland (landscaped by `Capability' Brown), there is a Rare Breeds Centre, and the gardens have a magnificent display of rhododendrons.
Times: Open all year. House: Tue-Sat 10-5, Sun 1-5; Nov-28 Dec & Mar, Tue-Sat 10-4, Sun 12-5. Open Bank Hols. Home Farm: Tue-Sun, 10-4 (3 in winter); Gardens: 10-dusk. Estate: daily, dawn-dusk. Closed Jan-Feb re-opens 28 Feb. **Fee:** Joint ticket £5 (ch £3). Family tickets £13 (2 ad+2 ch). **Facilities:** 🅿 (charged) 💷 ♿ (ramps giving full accesss to parkland,wheelchairs for hire) toilets for disabled shop ✖ ♨

THACKRAY MUSEUM

Beckett St LS9 7LN

➲ (M1 junct 43, onto M621 junct 4. Follow signs for Harrogate & St James Hospital, follow brown tourist signs)

☎ 0113 244 4343   📠 0113 247 0219

e-mail: info@thackraymuseum.org

Housed in a large Victorian building, next to the famous St James's Hospital, the Thackray Museum offers a unique hands-on experience. A cow from Gloucester, green mould and smelly toilets - all these things have helped transform our lives. Find out how by walking back in time and exploring the sights, sounds and smells of Victorian slum life. **Times:** Open all year, daily 10-5. Closed 24-26 & 31 Dec & 1 Jan **Fee:** ✱ £4.90 (ch 4-16 £3.50, pen, students & unemployed £3.90). Family ticket (2 adults & 3 ch) £16. Group rates available. **Facilities:** 🅿 (charged) 💻 ♿ (wheelchairs, induction loop) toilets for disabled shop ✖ (ex guide dogs) 🍴

THWAITE MILLS WATERMILL

Thwaite Ln, Stourton LS10 1RP

➲ (2m S of city centre, off A61)

☎ 0113 249 6453   📠 0113 246 5561

A guide will take you on a tour of this water-powered mill which sits between the River Aire and the Aire and Calder Navigation. Two great wheels drive a mass of cogs and grinding wheels which crushed stone for putty and paint throughout the 19th century. This was the hub of a tiny island community, and the Georgian mill-owner's house has been restored to house displays on the mill's history. **Times:** Open Tues-Sat 10am-5pm & Sun 1-5pm. Nov-Dec & March Tues-Sat 10am-4pm, Sun 12-4pm. Open BH Mon. Closed Jan & Feb. **Fee:** ✱ £2 (ch 50p, £1 concessions). Family & Friends ticket £5 (2 adults & 3 ch) **Facilities:** 🅿 ♿ (wheelchair lifts) toilets for disabled shop ✖ 🍴

TROPICAL WORLD

Canal Gardens, Roundhay Park LS8 2ER

➲ (3m N of city centre off A58 at Oakwood)

☎ 0113 266 1850   📠 0113 237 0077

The atmosphere of the tropics is recreated here as visitors walk among exotic trees. A waterfall cascades into a rock-pool and other pools contain terrapins and carp. There are reptiles, insects and more than 30 species of butterfly. There is also a Nocturnal House, a South American Rainforest, and a Desert House. **Times:** Open daily, 10-early evening (dusk in winter), special times at Christmas. Closed 25 Dec **Fee:** ✱ £1.50 (ch 8-15 75p, ch under 8 & Leeds card holders free). **Facilities:** 🅿 💻 ♿ toilets for disabled shop ✖ (ex guide dogs) 🍴

LOTHERTON HALL   Map 08 SE43

LOTHERTON HALL

Aberford LS25 3EB

➲ (off the A1, 0.75m E of junct with B1217)

☎ 0113 281 3259

Built in Edwardian times, the museum contains furniture, pictures, silver and ceramics from the Gascoigne collection, and works of art on loan from Leeds galleries. Outside, the

continued

Edwardian garden, bird garden and deer park are delightful places in which to stroll. **Times:** Open Tue-Sat 10-5. Sun 1-5. Bank Hols. Nov-Dec & Mar Tue-Sat 10-4, Sun 12-4. **Fee:** Hall, £2 (ch, pen & students £1, unaccompanied ch 50p). Family & Friends ticket £5 (2 adults & 3 ch). Party 15+. Free admission to Bird Garden, Gardens & Parkland. Free admission to house for driver. **Facilities:** 🅿 (charged) 💻 ✖ licensed ♿ shop ✖ (ex in park) 🍴

MIDDLESTOWN   Map 08 SE21

NATIONAL COAL MINING MUSEUM FOR ENGLAND

Caphouse Colliery, New Rd WF4 4RH

➲ (on A642 between Wakefield & Huddersfield)

☎ 01924 848806   📠 01924 844567   FREE

e-mail: info@ncm.org.uk

A unique opportunity to go 140 metres underground down one of Britain's oldest working mines, guided by an ex-miner, where models and machinery depict methods and conditions of mining from the early 1800s to the present day. You are strongly advised to wear sensible footwear and warm clothing. **Times:** Open all year, daily 10-5. (Closed 24-26 Dec & 1 Jan). **Facilities:** 🅿 💻 ✖ licensed ♿ (nature trail not accessible) toilets for disabled shop ✖ (ex guide dogs) 🍴

NOSTELL PRIORY   Map 08 SE41

NOSTELL PRIORY

Doncaster Rd WF4 1QE

➲ (5m SE of Wakefield towards Doncaster, on A638)

☎ 01924 863892   📠 01924 865282

e-mail: yorknp@smtp.ntrust.org.uk

Built by Paine in the middle of the 18th century, the priory has an additional wing built by Adam in 1766. It contains a notable saloon and tapestry room, and displays pictures and Chippendale furniture. There is a lake in the grounds. Events held include the Royal British Legion Rally and a Country Fair. **Times:** ✱ Open 2-17 Mar, Sat & Sun only, grounds, shop & tearoom 11-4. House closed 23 Mar-3 Nov, daily ex Mon/Tue (open Good Fri & BH Mon) 1-5.30. grounds open 11-6, shop & tesroom 11.30-5.30. 9 Nov-15 Dec: Sat/Suns only 12-4. Grounds, shop & tea room 11-4.30 **Facilities:** 🅿 💻 ♿ (lift, Braille guide/tactile books, w/hchair) toilets for disabled shop (ex around vista) 🐾

OAKWELL HALL   Map 08 SE22

OAKWELL HALL
Nutter Ln, Birstall WF17 9LG
➲ (6m SE of Bradford, off M62 junct 26/27, follow
brown heritage signs, turn off A652 onto Nutter
Lane)
☎ 01924 326240 🖶 01924 326249
e-mail: oakwell.hall@kirklees.gov.uk

A moated Elizabethan manor house, furnished as it might
have looked in the 1690s. Extensive 110-acre country park
with visitor information centre, period gardens, nature trails,
arboretum and children's adventure playground.
Times: Open all year, daily Mon-Fri 11-5; Sat & Sun 12-5. (ex Good Fri,
24 Dec-1 Jan). **Fee:** ✱ Hall £1.40 (ch & wheelchair users 50p). Family
ticket £3. Charges Mar -Oct. Free admission Nov-Feb. Vistor centre and
park free all year. **Facilities:** 🅿 💻 ♿ (herb garden for the blind,
large print & Braille guide) toilets for disabled shop 🛪 (park only ex
guide dogs) 🍴

WAKEFIELD   Map 08 SE32

WAKEFIELD ART GALLERY
Wentworth Ter WF1 3QW
➲ (N of city centre by Wakefield College and
Clayton Hospital)   **FREE**
☎ 01924 305796 🖶 01924 305770

Wakefield was home to two of Britain's greatest modern
sculptors - Barbara Hepworth and Henry Moore. The art
gallery, which has an important collection of 20th-century
paintings and sculptures, has a special room devoted to
these two local artists. There are frequent temporary
exhibitions of both modern and earlier works.
Times: Open all year, Tue-Sat 10.30-4.30, Sun 2-4.30. **Facilities:** 🅿
(on street) (on street parking restricted to 2hrs) ♿ shop 🛪 (ex guide
dogs)

WEST BRETTON   Map 08 SE21

YORKSHIRE SCULPTURE PARK
WF4 4LG
➲ (From M1 J38, follow Brown Heritage signs to
the A637. Turn left at the rdbt signposted to
Yorkshire Sculpture Park)
☎ 01924 830302 🖶 01924 832600   **FREE**
e-mail: office@ysp.co.uk

Set in the beautiful grounds and gardens of a 500 acre, 18th
century country estate, Yorkshire Sculpture Park is one of the
world's leading open-air galleries and presents a changing
programme of international sculpture exhibitions. The
landscape provides a variety of magnificent scenic vistas of
the valley, lakes and 18th century estate buildings and
bridges. By organising a number of temporary exhibitions
each year, the park ensures that there is always something
new to see. A new Visitor's Centre opened in 2002 providing
all-weather facilities including a large restaurant, shop,
coffee bar, audio-visual auditorium and meeting rooms.
Times: Open all year 10-6 (summer) 10-4 (winter). (Closed 24, 25 &
31 Dec) **Facilities:** 🅿 (charged) 💻 ✕ licensed ♿ (free scooters,
parking, trail accessible for wheelchairs) toilets for disabled shop 🛪
(assist dogs only inside)

Above: Cobbled streets in Haworth

GUERNSEY

Events & Festivals

February
20th-21st Mar Guernsey Eisteddfod Festival

March
20th Feb-21st Guernsey Eisteddfod Festival

May
9th Liberation Day Celebrations, St Peter Port

June
5th-13th Floral Guernsey Festival Week, featuring Floral Guernsey Show (provisional)
20th Healthspan Half Marathon, Pleinmont to Bulwer Avenue
tbc Little Russell Regatta

July
5th Le Viaer Marchi (the Old Market), traditional arts, crafts, dance and music, Saumarez Park (provisional)
31st-7th Aug St Peter Port Town Carnival
tbc North Regatta, St Sampsons Harbour

August
31st Jul-7th St Peter Port Town Carnival
11th-12th South Show, agricultural show (provisional)
18th-19th West Show, agricultural show (provisional)
25th-26th North Show, agricultural show & Battle of Flowers (provisional)

September
10th-12th Guernsey International Air Rally (provisional)

October
1st Guernsey Jazz Festival, Duke of Richmond Hotel, St Peter Port (provisional)
tbc Guernsey Lily International Amateur Film Festival & Video Festival, Carlton Hotel, St Martins

Above: Grandes Rocques beach

FOREST — Map 16

German Occupation Museum

GY8 0BG
(Behind Forest Church near the airport)
☎ 01481 238205

The museum has the Channel Islands' largest collection of Occupation items, with tableaux of a kitchen, bunker rooms and a street during the Occupation. Liberation Day 9th May will be celebrated with special events and exhibitions.

Times: ✱ Open Apr-Oct 10-5, Nov-Mar 10-1 (Closed Mon). **Fee:** £3.50 (ch £2). **Facilities:** P (ramps & handrails)

ROCQUAINE BAY — Map 16

Fort Grey and Shipwreck Museum

GY7 9BY
(on coast road at Rocquaine Bay) **2 for 1**
☎ 01481 265036 Fax 01481 263279
e-mail: education@museum.guernsey.net

The fort is a Martello tower, built in 1804, as part of the Channel Islands' extensive defences. It is nicknamed the `cup and saucer' because of its appearance, and houses a museum devoted to ships wrecked on the treacherous Hanois reefs nearby.

Times: Open Apr-Oct, 10-5 **Fee:** Fort Grey, £2.50 (pen £1.25), 3 Venue Ticket £9 (pen £5) **Facilities:** P (opposite fort) shop (ex guide dogs)

ST ANDREW — Map 16

German Military Underground Hospital & Ammunition Store

La Vassalerie GY6 8XR
(St Andrews Parish, centre of island)
☎ 01481 239100

The largest structure created during the German Occupation of the Channel Islands, a concrete maze of about 75,000 sq. ft, which took slave workers three-and-a-half years to complete, at the cost of many lives. Most of the equipment has been removed, but the central heating plant, hospital beds and cooking facilities can still be seen.

Times: Open Jul-Aug, daily 10-noon & 2-4.30; May-Jun & Sep, daily 10-noon & 2-4; Apr & Oct, daily 2-4; Mar & Nov, Sun & Thu 2-3. **Fee:** ✱ £2.80 (ch 80p). **Facilities:** P shop

ST MARTIN — Map 16

Sausmarez Manor

Sausmarez Rd GY4 6SG
(Halfway between airport & St Peter Port)
☎ 01481 235571 Fax 01481 235572
e-mail: peter@artparks.co.uk

The Manor has been owned and lived in by the same family for centuries. The style of each room is different, with collections of Oriental, French and English furniture and paintings. Outside the Formal Garden has herbaceous borders, and the Woodland Garden, set around two small lakes and a stream, is planted with colourful shrubs, bulbs

continued

and wild flowers from the subtropics. Also on view, a comprehensive sculpture park.
Times: Open Etr-Oct 10.30 & 11.30, Mon-Thu; Jun-Aug 10.30, 11.30 & 2 Mon-Thu; or by appointment. **Fee:** ✱ House £5.40 (ch £2, pen £4.50). Woodland Garden £3 (accompanied ch & pen £2.50, disabled free). Dolls House Collection £2.50 (ch £1.50, stu & pen £2). Family ticket £7. Sculpture Park £3 (accompanied ch & pen £2.50, disabled free).
Facilities: 🅿 💺 ♿ (free admission, partial access to garden, wheelchair loan) shop (Specialises in dolls houses etc) ✈ (ex dogs for blind and deaf)

ST PETER PORT   Map 16
CASTLE CORNET
GY1 UG (0.5m from town centre)
☎ 01481 721657 🖷 01481 715177
e-mail: education@museum.guernsey.net

The history of this magnificent castle spans eight centuries and its buildings now house several museums, the Refectory Cafe and a shop. Soldiers fire the noonday gun in a daily ceremony. Look for the Maritime Museum that charts Guernsey's nautical history, the 'Story of Castle Cornet' with its mystery skeleton, and special exhibitions in the Royal Guernsey Militia Museum.
Times: Open Apr-Oct, daily 10-5. **Fee:** £6 (pen £4). 3 venue ticket £9 (pen £5) **Facilities:** 🅿 (100 yds) (2 hr time zone, 10hr within 200 yards) 💺 shop ✈ (ex guide dogs) 🍴

GUERNSEY MUSEUM & ART GALLERY
Candie Gardens GY1 1UG
➲ (On the outskirts of St Peter Port set in the Victorian 'Candie gardens').
☎ 01481 726518 🖷 01481 715177
e-mail: education@museum.guernsey.net

The museum tells the story of Guernsey and its people. There is an audio-visual theatre and an art gallery, and special exhibitions are arranged throughout the year. It is surrounded by beautiful gardens with superb views over St Peter Port harbour.
Times: Open Apr- Oct daily 10-5 **Fee:** £3.50 (pen £2.50). 3 venue ticket £9 (pen £5) **Facilities:** 🅿 (outside museum) (2hr & 5hr) 💺♿ toilets for disabled shop ✈ (ex guide dogs) 🍴

VALE   Map 16
ROUSSE TOWER
Rousse Tower Headland (On Island's W coast, signposted)
☎ 01481 726518 & 726965   FREE
🖷 01481 715177
e-mail: peter@museum.guernsey.net

One of the original fifteen towers built in 1778-9 in prime defensive positions around the coast of Guernsey. They were designed primarily to prevent the landing of troops on nearby beaches. Musket fire could be directed on invading forces through the loopholes. An interpretation centre displays replica guns.
Times: Open Apr-Oct 9-dusk, Nov-Mar Wed, Sat & Sun 9-4.
Facilities: 🅿 ✈ (ex guide dogs)

JERSEY

EVENTS & FESTIVALS

March
26th-4th Apr Spring Garden Festival
April
26th Mar-4th Spring Garden Festival
May
9th Liberation Day
15th-22nd Spring Walking Week
29th-31st Country Fayre –
    traditional country fayre
June
1st-6th Jun, Jersey Heritage – Time Travellers
12th-13th Early Summer Flower Show
25th-27th Jersey Revels, medieval event
    marking Jersey's 800-year allegiance to the
    British Crown
tbc Maritime Festival
July
3rd-10th Summer Walking Week
tbc Jersey Garden Festival – open gardens,
    guided walks & demonstrations
August
9th-13th Jersey Battle of Flowers –
    spectacular carnival
20th-22nd Summer Flower Show, Howard
    Davis Park
September
9th International Air Display
18th-25th Autumn Walking Week
October
8th-10th Autumn Fruit & Flower Festival
20th-27th La Fais'sie d'cidre (Cider Festival)
November/December
tbc Fête dé Noué (Christmas festival)

Above: Sunset over Seymour Tower

GOREY   Map 16

MONT ORGUEIL CASTLE
JE3 6ET
⮑ (A3 or coast road to Gorey)
☎ 01534 853292 ▤ 01534 854303
e-mail: marketing@jerseyheritagetrust.org
Standing on a rocky headland, on a site which has been fortified since the Iron Age, this is one of the best-preserved examples in Europe of a medieval concentric castle, and dates from the 12th and 13th centuries.
Times: ✱ Open daily throughout the year 9.30-6; Last admission 5pm. Times in winter change (Fri-Mon 10-dusk) **Facilities:** ℗ (200 yds) (discs required at harbour) shop ✖ (ex guide dogs) ◥

LA GREVE DE LECQ   Map 16

GREVE DE LECQ BARRACKS
⮑ (on right hand side of valley, overlooking the beach)
☎ 01534 483193 482238   **FREE**
▤ 01534 485873
e-mail: nationaltrust@jerseymail.co.uk
Originally serving as an outpost of the British Empire, these barracks, built in 1810, were used for civilian housing from the end of WWI to 1972, when they were bought by the National Trust and made into a museum that depicts the life of soldiers who were stationed here in the 19th century. Also includes a collection of old horse-drawn carriages.
Times: Open Etr wknd & 6 May-28 Sep, Tue-Sat 11-5 & Sun 2-5. (Closed Mon). **Facilities:** ℗ & (wheelchair ramps) toilets for disabled shop ✖ (ex guide dogs) ⇴

GROUVILLE   Map 16

LA HOUGUE BIE
JE2 7UA
⮑ (A6 or A7 to Five Oaks then Prines Tower Rd)
☎ 01534 853823 ▤ 01534 856472
e-mail: marketing@jerseyheritagetrust.org
This Neolithic burial mound stands 40ft high, and covers a stone-built passage grave that is still intact and may be entered. The passage is 50ft long, and built of huge stones, the mound is made from earth, rubble and limpet shells. On top of the mound are two medieval chapels, one of which has a replica of the Holy Sepulchre in Jerusalem below. Also on the site is an underground bunker built by the Germans as a communications centre. Contact the Jersey Museum for information on special events.
Times: ✱ Open 29 Mar-Oct, daily 10-5. **Facilities:** ℗ & shop ✖ (ex guide dogs) ◥

ST BRELADE   Map 16

JERSEY LAVENDER FARM
Rue du Pont Marquet JE3 8DS
⮑ (on the B25 from St Aubin's Bay to Redhouses)
☎ 01534 742933 ▤ 01534 745613
e-mail: admin@jerseylavender.co.uk
At Jersey Lavender we grow nine acres of lavender, distil out the essential oil and create a range of fine toiletry products. Visitors are able to see the whole process from cultivating, through to harvesting, distillation and the production of the final product. There is a national collection of lavenders, extensive gardens, herb beds and walks among the lavender
continued

fields. There are also other herbs that are grown and distilled, namely eucalyptus, rosemary and tea tree.
Times: Open 20 May-21 Sep, Mon-Sat 10-5. **Fee:** ✱ £3 (ch under 14 free). **Facilities:** ℗ ▦ & (wheelchair loan, wide doors, grab rails etc) toilets for disabled shop garden centre ◥

ST CLEMENT   Map 16

SAMARÈS MANOR   **2 for 1**
JE2 6QW
⮑ (2m E of St Helier on St Clements Inner Road)
☎ 01534 870551 ▤ 01534 768949
The manor stands in 14 acres of beautiful gardens. The Japanese Garden occupies an artificial hill, and has a series of waterfalls cascading over Cumberland limestone. There's a craft centre, farm animals and a children's play area. Falconry and Parrot displays mornings and afternoons except Sundays.
Times: ✱ Open 3 Apr-14 Oct. **Fee:** £4.95 (ch under 16 £1.95, pen £4.50). Sat prices: £3.95 (ch under 16 £1.75, pen £3.50) **Facilities:** ℗ ▦ ✖ licensed & toilets for disabled shop garden centre ✖ (ex guide dogs) ◥

ST HELIER   Map 16

ELIZABETH CASTLE
JE2 3WU
⮑ (access by causeway or amphibious vehicle)
☎ 01534 723971 ▤ 01534 610338
e-mail: marketing@jerseyheritagetrust.org
The original Elizabethan fortress was extended in the 17th and 18th centuries, and then refortified by the Germans during the Occupation. Please telephone for details of events.
Times: ✱ Open 29 Mar-Oct, daily 9.30-6. Last admission 5. **Facilities:** ℗ ▦ & shop ✖ (ex guide dogs) ◥

JERSEY MUSEUM
The Weighbridge JE2 3NF
⮑ (near bus station on weighbridge)
☎ 01534 633300 ▤ 01534 633301
e-mail: marketing@jerseyheritagetrust.org
Home to 'The Story of Jersey', Jersey's art gallery, an exhibition gallery which features a changing programme, a lecture theatre, and an audio-visual theatre. Special exhibitions take place throughout the year.
Times: ✱ Open all year, daily 10-5. Winter daily 10-4. (Closed 24-26 Dec & 1 Jan). **Facilities:** ℗ (100yds) (paycard at most public parking) ✖ licensed & (audio loop, audio guide for partially sighted, car park) toilets for disabled shop ✖ (ex guide dogs) ◥

MARITIME MUSEUM & OCCUPATION TAPESTRY GALLERY
New North Quay JE2 3ND
⮑ (alongside Marina, opposite Liberation Square)
☎ 01534 811043 ▤ 01534 874099
e-mail: marketing@jerseyheritagetrust
This converted 19th-century warehouse houses the tapestry consisting of 12 two-metre panels that tells the story of the occupation of Jersey during World War II. Each of the 12 parishes took responsibility for stitching a panel, making it the largest community arts project ever undertaken on the island. The Maritime Museum celebrates the relationship of
continued

islanders and the sea, including an award winning hand-on experience, especially enjoyed by children.
Times: ✳ Open all year, daily 10-5 (winter closing at 4pm).
Facilities: P (paycards in public car parks) ♿ (braille books, audio guide etc) toilets for disabled shop ✖ (ex guide dogs) 🍴

ST LAWRENCE   Map 16

German Underground Hospital
Les Charrieres Malorey JE3 1FU
➲ (bus route 8A from St Helier)
☎ 01534 863442 📄 01534 865970
e-mail: info@germanundergroundhospital.co.uk
On 1 July 1940 the Channel Islands were occupied by German forces, and this vast complex dug deep into a hillside is the most evocative reminder of that Occupation. A video presentation, along with a large collection of memorabilia, illustrates of the lives of the islanders at war and a further exhibition records their impressions during 1945, the year of liberation.
Times: Open 10 Feb-11 Nov, daily 9.30-5.30 Last admission 4.15. 16 Nov-8 Dec 9.30-1.30 last admission 12 **Facilities:** P 🍴 ✖ licensed ♿ (ramp to restaurant & lift in Visitor Centre to restaurant) toilets for disabled shop ✖ (ex guide dogs) 🍴

Hamptonne Country Life Museum
La Rue de la Patente JE3 1HS
➲ (5m from St Helier on A1, A10 & follow signs)
☎ 01534 863955 📄 01534 863935
e-mail: marketing@jerseyheritagetrust.org
Here you will find a medieval 17th-century home, furnished in authentic style and surrounded by 19th-century farm buildings. Guided tours every weekday. Perpetual living history interpretation and daily demonstrations.
Times: ✳ Open 29 Mar-Oct, daily 10-4. **Facilities:** P 🍴 ♿ toilets for disabled shop ✖ (ex guide dogs) 🍴

ST OUEN   Map 16

The Channel Islands Military Museum
Five Mile Rd
➲ (Northern end of the 5 Mile Rd, at the rear of the Jersey Woollen Mill & across the road from Jersey Pearl).
☎ 01534 723136
e-mail: damienhorn@jerseymail.co.uk
The museum is housed in a German coastal defence bunker, which formed part of Hitler's Atlantic Wall. It has been restored, as far as possible, to give the visitor an idea of how it looked. The visitor can also see German uniforms, motorcycles, weapons, documents, photographs and other items from the 1940-45 occupation.
Times: Open week before Etr-Oct **Fee:** ✳ £3 (ch £1.50). **Facilities:** P 🍴 ♿ (All parts accessible ex 1 small room) toilets for disabled shop ✖ (ex guide dogs)

Kempt Tower Visitor Centre
Five Mile Rd
☎ 01534 483651 & 483140 📄 01534 485289
The centre has displays on history and the wildlife of St Ouen's Bay, including Les Mielles, which is Jersey's miniature national park. Nature walks are held every Thursday (May to September). Check local press for details.
Times: ✳ Open BH's & Apr & Oct, Thu & Sun only 2-5; May-Sep, daily (ex Mon) 2-5. **Facilities:** P shop ✖

ST PETER   Map 16

The Living Legend
Rue de Petit Aleval JE3 7ET
➲ (From main town of St Helier. Go along main esplanade-turn right to Bel Royal. Turn left and follow road to The Living Legend signposted from the German Underground Hospital)
☎ 01534 485496 📄 01534 485855
e-mail: info@jerseyslivinglegend.co.je
Pass through the granite archways into the landscaped gardens and the world of the Jersey Experience where Jersey's exciting past is recreated in a three dimensional spectacle. Learn of the heroes and villains, the folklore and the story of the island's links with the UK and her struggles with Europe. Other attractions include an adventure playground, street entertainment, the Jersey Craft and Shopping Village, a range of shops and the Jersey Kitchen Restaurant.
Times: Open Apr-Oct, daily 9.30-5; Mar & Nov, Mon-Wed & Sat-Sun 10-5. **Fee:** ✳ £6.80 (ch 7-13 £4.60 , pen £6.20, student £5.25, disabled £5.35). **Facilities:** P 🍴 ✖ licensed ♿ (wheelchair available) toilets for disabled shop ✖ (ex guide dogs) 🍴

Le Moulin de Quetivel
St Peters Valley, Le Mont Fallu JE3 3EN
➲ (travel out of St Helier via first tower (A1) heading W. Take the A11 through St Peter's Valley. The mill is located on the left, with the junct of Le Mont Fallu B58)
☎ 01534 483193 01534 745408
📄 01534 485873
e-mail: nationaltrust@jerseymail.co.uk
There has been a water mill on this site since 1309. The present granite-built mill was worked until the end of the 19th century, when it fell into disrepair; during the German Occupation it was reactivated for grinding locally grown corn, but after 1945 a fire destroyed the remaining machinery, roof and internal woodwork. In 1971 the National Trust for Jersey began restoration, and the mill is now producing stoneground flour again.
Times: Open 20 May-25 Sep, Tue-Thu 10-4. **Fee:** ✳ £2 (pen & students £1.50, Ch under 16 free). **Facilities:** P ♿ shop ✖ (ex guide dogs) 🐾

TRINITY   Map 16
DURRELL WILDLIFE CONSERVATION TRUST
Les Augres Manor, La Profunde Rue JE3 5BP
☎ 01534 860000 ▤ 01534 860001

Gerald Durrell's unique sanctuary and breeding centre for many of the world's rarest animals. Visitors can see these remarkable creatures, some so rare that they can only be found here, in modern, spacious enclosures in the gardens of the 16th-century manor house. Major attractions are the magical Aye-Ayes from Madagascar and the world-famous family of Lowland gorillas. There is a comprehensive programme of keeper talks, animal displays and activities.
Times: ✱ Open all year, daily 9.30-6 (dusk in winter). (Closed 25 Dec). **Facilities:** ▱ ✗ licensed ♿ (trail for the blind, auditory loop in pavilion) toilets for disabled shop ✈ ▰

Above: St Ouen's Bay, Jersey

ISLE OF MAN

EVENTS & FESTIVALS

April
8th-12th Mananan Guitar Festival, Erin Arts
Centre, Port Erin
10th Manx Mountain Marathon, from Ramsey
to Port Erin over 12 peaks

May
29th-11th Jun Isle of Man TT Motorcycle
Festival (various venues)

June
29th May-11th Isle of Man TT Motorcycle
Festival (various venues)
24th-4th Jul Mananan Summer Festival of
Music & the Arts (various venues)

July
24th Jun-4th Mananan Summer Festival of
Music & the Arts (various venues)
18th-24th Yn Chruinnaght Inter-Celtic
Festival, various venues, Ramsey
30th-1st Aug Manx International Car Rally
(various venues)

August
30th Jul-1st Manx International Car Rally
(various venues)
13th-14th Royal Manx Agricultural Show,
Sulby
tbc Manx Grand Prix bike racing on mountain
circuit
tbc Manx Traditional Boat Festival, Peel

September
5th-11th Mananan Opera Festival, Erin Arts
Centre, Port Erin (provisional)

November
12th-14th Mananan Summer Festival of Music
& the Arts (various venues)

*Above: Standing stones at the Cashtal-Yn-Ard
burial chamber*

BALLASALLA   Map 06 SC27
RUSHEN ABBEY
IM9 3DB
➲ (In Ballasalla turn right at the Whitestone Inn,
left at next rdbt, then 1st right over the bridge, car
park on left)
☎ 01624 648000 📠 01624 648001
e-mail: enquiries@mnh.gov.im

The most substantial and important medieval religious site in
the Isle of Man. Remains of medieval buildings, exhibitions
and displays, set in beautifully landscaped gardens.
Times: Open Apr-late Oct, daily 10-5. **Fee:** ✱ £3 (ch £1.50) family
ticket £7.50 **Facilities:** 🅿 ♿ toilets for disabled shop ✖ (ex guide
dogs) ☕

BALLAUGH   Map 06 SC39
CURRAGHS WILD LIFE PARK
IM7 5EA
➲ (on main road halfway between Kirk Michael
& Ramsey)
☎ 01624 897323 📠 01624 897327
e-mail: curraghswlp@gov.im

This park has been developed adjacent to the reserve area of
the Ballaugh Curraghs and a large variety of animals and
birds can be seen. A walk through enclosure lets visitors
explore the world of wildlife, including local habitats along
the Curraghs nature trail. The miniature railway runs on
Sundays.
Times: Open all year Etr-Oct, daily 10-6. Last admission 5pm. Oct-Etr,
Sat & Sun 10-4. **Fee:** ✱ £4 (ch £2, pen £2.70). Party. **Facilities:** 🅿 🍔
♿ (loan of wheelchair & electric wheelchair) toilets for disabled shop
✖ (ex guide dogs by arrangement)

CASTLETOWN   Map 06 SC26
CASTLE RUSHEN
The Quay IM9 1LD
➲ (centre of Castletown)
☎ 01624 648000 📠 01624 648001
e-mail: enquiries@mnh.gov.im

One of Britain's most complete medieval castles, Castle
Rushen is a limestone fortress rising out of the heart of the
old capital of the island, Castletown. Once the fortress of the
Kings and Lords of Mann, Castle Rushen is bought alive with
rich decorations, and the sounds and smells of a bygone era.
In summer battles are re-enacted and the lifestyle of the
period recreated by enthusiasts.
Times: Open daily, 10-5, Apr-late Oct. **Fee:** ✱ £4.25 (ch £2.25) Family
£10.75. Group bookings available from £3.40. **Facilities:** 🅿 (100 yds)
Disc Zone Parking ♿ shop ✖ (ex guide dogs) ☕

NAUTICAL MUSEUM
➲ (From Castletown Centre, cross the footbridge over
the harbour. Museum is on the right)
☎ 01624 648000 📠 01624 648001
e-mail: enquiries@mnh.gov.im

Set at the mouth of Castletown harbour this museum is
home to an 18th-century armed yacht, The Peggy, built by a
Manxman in 1791. A replica sailmaker's loft, ship model and
continued

photographs bring alive Manx maritime life and trade in the days of sail.
Times: Open daily 10-5, Apr-late Oct. **Fee:** ✱ £3 (ch £1.50). Family £7.50. Group bookings available **Facilities:** 🅿 ⚹ shop ✖ (ex guide dogs) 🐾

OLD GRAMMAR SCHOOL
IM9 1LE
➲ (centre of Castletown, opposite the castle)
☎ 01624 648000 🖹 01624 648001
e-mail: enquiries@mnh.gov.im   **FREE**
Built around 1200AD, the former capital's first church, St Mary's, has had a significant role in Manx education. It was a school from 1570 to 1930 and evokes memories of Victorian school life.
Times: Open daily 10-5, Apr-late Oct. **Facilities:** 🅿 shop ✖ (ex guide dogs)

THE OLD HOUSE OF KEYS
IM9 1LA
➲ (opposite Castletown Rushen in centre of Castletown)
☎ 01624 648000 🖹 01624 648001
e-mail: enquiries@mnh.gov.im
The Old House of Keys is a portrayal of the long and often turbulent history of Manx politics. It has been restored to its appearance in 1866 and visitors are invited to participate in a lively debate with interactive Members of Tynwald, the Manx parliament.
Times: Open Apr-late Oct, daily 10-5. **Fee:** ✱ £3 (ch £1.50) Family ticket £7.50 **Facilities:** 🅿 30yds disc zone parking ⚹ ✖ (ex guide dogs)

CREGNEISH   Map 06 SC16
CREGNEASH VILLAGE FOLK MUSEUM
➲ (2m from Port Erin/Port St Mary, signposted)
☎ 01624 648000 🖹 01624 648001
e-mail: enquiries@mnh.gov.im
The Cregneash story begins in Cummal Beg - the village information centre where you can experience what life was really like in a Manx crofting village during the early 19th century. As you stroll around this attractive village, set in beautiful countryside, call into Harry Kelly's cottage, a Turner's shed, a Weaver's house, and the Smithy. The Manx Four-horned Loghtan Sheep can be seen grazing along with other animals from the village farm.
Times: Open Apr-late Oct, daily 10-5. **Fee:** ✱ £3 (ch £1.50) Family £7.50. Group rates from £2.40 **Facilities:** 🅿 🍴 shop ✖ (ex guide dogs) 🐾

DOUGLAS   Map 06 SC37
MANX MUSEUM
IM1 3LY
➲ (Signposted in Douglas)
☎ 01624 648000 🖹 01624 648001
e-mail: enquiries@mnh.gov.im   **FREE**
The Island's treasure house provides an exciting introduction to the "Story of Mann" where a specially produced film portrayal of Manx history complements the award winning displays. Galleries depict natural history, archaeology and the social development of the Island. There are also examples of

continued

famous Manx artists in the National Art Gallery together with the Island's National archive and reference library
Times: Open daily all year, Mon-Sat 10-5. (Closed 25/26 Dec & 1 Jan). **Facilities:** 🅿 ✖ licensed ⚹ (Lift) toilets for disabled shop ✖ (ex guide dogs) 🐾

SNAEFELL MOUNTAIN RAILWAY
Banks Circus IM1 5PT
➲ (Manx Electric Railway from Douglas and change at Laxey)
☎ 01624 663366 🖹 01624 663637
Snaefell is the Isle of Man's highest mountain. Running up it is Britain's oldest working mountain railway, which was laid in 1895. From the top of Snaefell, on a clear day, England, Ireland, Scotland and Wales are all visible.
Times: Open 29 Apr-29 Sep **Fee:** ✱ Various fares charged. **Facilities:** 🅿 🍴 shop 🐾

LAXEY   Map 06 SC48
GREAT LAXEY WHEEL & MINES TRAIL
➲ (signposted in Laxey village)
☎ 01624 648000 🖹 01624 648001
e-mail: enquiries@mnh.gov.im
Built in 1854, the Great Laxey Wheel, 22 metres in diameter, is the largest working water wheel in the world. It was designed to pump water from the lead and zinc mines and is an acknowledged masterpiece of Victorian engineering. The wheel was christened by Lady Isabella, the wife of the Lieutenant Governor of the Isle of Man.
Times: Open Apr-late Oct, daily 10-5. **Fee:** ✱ £3 (ch £1.50) Family £7.50. Group rates available **Facilities:** 🅿 ⚹ shop ✖ (ex guide dogs) 🐾

PEEL   Map 06 SC28
HOUSE OF MANANNAN
Mill Rd IM5 1TA
➲ (In Peel follow signs to the house)
☎ 01624 648000 🖹 01624 648001
e-mail: enquiries@mnh.gov.im
This £6 million centre is an unforgettable experience. Reconstructions, interactive displays, audio visual presentations and original material explore the Celtic, Viking and maritime traditions of the Isle of Man. A visit will leave you in awe of the diversity of Manx heritage and eager to learn more.
Times: Open daily, 10-5. (Closed 25-26 Dec & 1 Jan). **Fee:** ✱ £5 (ch £2.50) Family £12.50. Group rates available **Facilities:** 🅿 ⚹ toilets for disabled shop ✖ (ex guide dogs) 🐾

PEEL CASTLE
IM5 1TB
➲ (on St Patrick's Isle, facing Peel Bay, signposted in Peel)
☎ 01624 648000 🖹 01624 648001
e-mail: enquiries@mnh.gov.im
One of the Island's principle historic centres, this great natural fortress with its imposing curtain wall set majestically at the mouth of Peel Harbour is steeped in Viking heritage. The sandstone walls of Peel Castle enclose

continued

an 11th century church and Round Tower, the 13th century St German's Cathedral and the later apartments of the Lords of Mann.
Times: Open Apr-late Oct, daily 10-5. **Fee:** ✱ £3 (ch £1.50). Family £7.50. Group rates available **Facilities:** 🅿 shop ✖ (ex guide dogs)

RAMSEY   Map 06 SC49

'THE GROVE' RURAL LIFE MUSEUM
IM8 3UA
⮕ (on W side of Andreas Road. Signposted in Ramsey)
☎ 01624 648000 🖷 01624 648001
e-mail: enquiries@mnh.gov.im

This Victorian time capsule was a country house built as a summer retreat for a Liverpool shipping merchant. Rooms are filled with period furnishings together with a costume exhibition. In the adjacent farmyard are buildings containing displays on farming and 19th century vehicles. Around the grounds you may see Loghtan sheep, ducks and perhaps a Manx cat.
Times: Open Apr-late Oct, daily 10-5. **Fee:** ✱ £3 (ch £1.50). Family £7.50, group rates available **Facilities:** 🅿 🍴 ♿ shop ✖ (ex guide dogs) 🍴

If you want to tell us about an attraction you think should be included in this book, please use the Readers' Report form at the back of the book, or e-mail:
lifestyleguides@theAA.com

Above: The Laxey Wheel

SCOTLAND
EVENTS & FESTIVALS

January
31st Dec 03-1st Stonehaven Fireballing Festival
(various venues), Stonehaven
1st Men's & Boy's 'Ba', mass football game,
Kirkwall, Orkney Isles
14th-1st Feb Celtic Connections Festival, Glasgow
25th Burns Night
27th Up Helly Aa, Lerwick, Shetland Islands

February
14th Jan-1st Celtic Connections Festival, Glasgow
24th-29th Scottish Curling Championships, Dewar's
Centre, Ice Rink, Perth

April
2nd-13th Edinburgh International Science Festival
(various venues), Edinburgh
16th-17th Scottish Grand National, Ayr Racecourse,
Ayr (provisional)

May
26th-27th Angus Show, Haughmuir by Brechin,
Angus
29th-30th Atholl Gathering & Highland Games,
Blair Atholl, Perth & Kinross
tbc Dundee Jazz Festival, Dundee
tbc Inverkip Scottish Powerboat Grand Prix
tbc Scottish International Children's Festival,
Edinburgh
tbc Shetland Folk Festival, Lerwick

June
6th Borders Historic Motoring Extravaganza,
Mellerstain House, Borders
13th Forfar Highland Games, Forfar, Angus
24th-27th Royal Highland Show, Ingliston,
Edinburgh

18th-23rd St Magnus Festival, Orkney
tbc Glasgow International Jazz Festival
tbc Lanimer Day, Lanark, South Lanarkshire

July
11th Stirling Highland Games, Stirlingshire
28th Stranraer Show, Dumfries & Galloway
30th Langholm Common Riding, Dumfries &
Galloway
tbc Dundee Blues Bonanza, Dundee

August
4th-14th Aberdeen International Youth Festival
6th-9th Border Gathering, Dumfries & Galloway
College
7th Aboyne Highland Games, Aboyne
12th Highland Games, Monaltrie Park, Ballater,
Aberdeenshire
14th-15th Arbroath Seafest, Arbroath, Angus
15th Perth Highland Games, Perth
15th-4th Sep Edinburgh International Festival
22nd Crieff Highland Games, Market Park, Crieff,
Perthshire
tbc Edinburgh International Film Festival
tbc Edinburgh Military Tattoo

September
15th Aug-4th Edinburgh International Festival
3rd-5th City of Dundee Summer Flower Show
4th Braemar Gathering, Princess Royal & Duke of
Fife Memorial Park, Braemar, Aberdeenshire
12th-19th Techfest, Aberdeen, various venues

November
26th-28th Dundee Mountain Film Festival, Bonar
Hall, Dundee

Glen Coe, the Highlands of Scotland.

ABERDEEN CITY

ABERDEEN   Map 15 NJ90

ABERDEEN ART GALLERY
Schoolhill AB10 1FQ
➲ (located in city centre)
☎ 01224 523700 🖷 01224 632133   FREE
e-mail: info@aagm.co.uk

One of the city's most popular tourist attractions Aberdeen's splendid art gallery houses an important fine art collection with many 19th and 20th century works.
Times: Open all year ex Xmas/New Year. Mon-Sat 10-5, Sun 2-5.
Facilities: 🅿 (500yds) 🍽 ♿ (ramp, lift) toilets for disabled shop ✺ (ex guide dogs)

ABERDEEN MARITIME MUSEUM
Shiprow AB11 5BY
➲ (located in city centre)
☎ 01224 337700 🖷 01224 213066   FREE
e-mail: info@aagm.co.uk

The museum is in Provost Ross's House, Aberdeen's oldest building (1593). It highlights the city's maritime history, its oil industry, and its shipbuilding.
Times: Open all year (ex Xmas & New Year). Mon-Sat 10-5, Sun 12-3.
Telephone for details. **Facilities:** 🅿 (250yds) 🍽 ✕ licensed ♿ (ramps, lifts) toilets for disabled shop ✺ 🍴

CRUICKSHANK BOTANIC GARDEN
University of Aberdeen, St Machar Dr AB24 3UU
➲ (enter by gate in Chanonry, in Old Aberdeen)
☎ 01224 272704 🖷 01224 272703   FREE
e-mail: pss@abdn.ac.uk

Developed at the end of the 19th century, the 11 acres include rock and water gardens, a rose garden, a fine herbaceous border, an arboretum and a patio garden. There are collections of spring bulbs, gentians and alpine plants, and a fine array of trees and shrubs.
Times: Open all year, Mon-Fri 9-4.30; also Sat & Sun, May-Sep 2-5.
Facilities: 🅿 (200metres) ♿ ✺

THE GORDON HIGHLANDERS MUSEUM
St Lukes, Viewfield Rd AB15 7XH
☎ 01224 311200 🖷 01224 319323
e-mail: museum@gordonhighlanders.com

Presenting a large collection of artefacts, interactive displays, audio-visual theatre, and reconstructions, the Gordon Highlanders Museum is the perfect day out for anyone interested in British military history. The grounds also contain a tea-room, the home and paintings of Scottish artist, Sir George Reid, and gardens.
Times: Open Apr-Oct Tue-Sat 10.30-4.30, Sun 1.30-4.30. (Closed Mon). Open by appointment only at other times. **Fee:** ✱ £2.50 (ch £1, con £1.50) **Facilities:** 🅿 🍽 ♿ low level cases, hearing loop toilets for disabled shop ✺ (ex guide dogs) 🍴

PROVOST SKENE'S HOUSE
Guestrow, (off Broad St) AB10 1AS
☎ 01224 641086
e-mail: info@aagm.co.uk   FREE

Experience the epitome of style and elegance in this 16th-century townhouse, furnished and decorated in the styles of earlier times. See changing fashions in the Costume Gallery and view an important cycle of religious paintings in the gallery.
Times: Open all year Mon-Sat 10-5, Sun 1-4. closed Xmas & New Year). Telephone for details. **Facilities:** 🅿 (200yds) 🍽 ♿ ✺ (ex guide dogs)

SATROSPHERE ("HANDS-ON" SCIENCE & TECHNOLOGY CENTRE)
179 Constitution St AB24 5TU
➲ (located 5min from town centre, and very close to Aberdeen Beach Esplanade)
☎ 01224 640340 🖷 01224 622211
e-mail: info@satrosphere.net

Satrosphere, the Discovery Place, is different from many museums or exhibition centres. It is an Interactive Centre where everything is 'hands-on'. Displays aren't locked in glass cases and there are certainly no "Do Not Touch" signs. The emphasis is on doing and finding out, not just looking and standing back. Over 100 exhibits, interactive shows, workshops and special weekend events.
Times: ✱ Open all year, Mon-Sat 10-5, Sun 11.30-5. (Closed 25-26 Dec & 1-2 Jan). **Facilities:** 🅿 🍽 ♿ toilets for disabled shop ✺ (ex guide dogs) 🍴

PETERCULTER   Map 15 NJ80

DRUM CASTLE
AB31 5EY
➲ (3m W, off A93)
☎ 01330 811204 🖷 01330 811962
e-mail: drum@nts.org.uk

The great 13th-century Square Tower is one of the three oldest tower houses in Scotland and has associations with Robert the Bruce. The handsome mansion, added in 1619, houses a collection of family memorabilia. The grounds contain the 100-acre Old Wood of Drum, a natural oak wood and an old rose garden.
Times: Open Apr-May & Sep, daily 12.30-5.30, Jun-Aug, daily 10-5.30. Grounds all year, daily 9.30-sunset. **Fee:** ✱ £7 (concession £5.25) Family ticket £19. Groups adult £5.60, child/school £1. Please book groups in advance. Garden & grounds only £2.50 (concession £1.90) Groups adult £2, child/school £1 Admission free to NTS members. For other details please phone (0131) 243 9387 or check website.
Facilities: 🅿 🍽 ♿ (wheelchair available) shop ✺ (ex guide dogs) 🍶

ABERDEENSHIRE

ALFORD   Map 15 NJ51

ALFORD VALLEY RAILWAY
AB33 8AD
➲ (A944 Alford Village)
☎ 019755 62326 & 62811 🖷 019755 63182

Narrow-gauge passenger railway in two sections: Alford-Haughton Park and Haughton Park-Murray Park approx one mile each. Steam on peak weekends. Diesel traction. Exhibitions.
Times: Open Apr, May & Sep wknds 1-5, Jun-Aug daily from 1pm (30 min service). Party bookings also available at other times. **Fee:** ✱ £2 (ch £1) return fare. **Facilities:** 🅿 ♿ (ramps at station platforms) toilets for disabled shop

continued

CRAIGIEVAR CASTLE
AB33 8JF
➲ (On A980, 6m S of Alford)
☎ 013398 83635

A fairytale like castle, the Great Tower completed in 1626. The collection includes family portraits and 17th and 18th century furniture.
Times: Open Apr-Sep, Fri-Tue 12-5.30. Guided tours only. Grounds all year, daily 9.30-sunset. **Fee:** ✱ £9 (concession £6.50). Family ticket £23. Admission free to NTS members. For other details phone 0131 243 9387 or check website. **Facilities:** ▣

BALMORAL   Map 15 NO29
BALMORAL CASTLE GROUNDS & EXHIBITION
AB35 5TB
➲ (on A93 between Ballater & Braemar)
☎ 013397 42534 ▤ 013397 42034
e-mail: info@balmoralcastle.com

Queen Victoria and Prince Albert first rented Balmoral Castle in 1848, and Prince Albert bought the property four years later. He commissioned William Smith to build a new castle, which was completed by 1856 and is still the Royal Family's Highland residence. Country walks and pony trekking can be enjoyed, and an exhibition of paintings and other works of art can be seen in the castle ballroom, together with a Travel and Carriage exhibition and a wildlife exhibition.
Times: Open Apr-Jul, daily 10-5. **Fee:** £5 (ch under 16 £1, pen £4)
Facilities: ▣ (100yds) ▃ & (wheelchairs & battricars available, reserved parking) toilets for disabled shop ✖ (ex guide dogs/in grounds) ◥

BANCHORY   Map 15 NO69
BANCHORY MUSEUM
Bridge St AB31 5SX
➲ (located in Bridge St beside tourist information centre, 100yards from main car park and 25 yards from High St through Scott Skinner Square)
☎ 01771 622906 ▤ 01771 622884
e-mail: heritage@aberdeenshire.gov.uk

The museum has displays on Scott Skinner (The 'Strathspey King'), natural history, royal commemorative china, local silver artefacts and a variety of local history displays.
Times: Open May, Jun & Sep, Mon-Sat 11-1 & 2-4.30; Jul-Aug, Mon-Sat 11-1, 2-4.30 & Sun 2-4.30. Tel. for Apr & Oct opening times.
Facilities: ▣ (100yds) (limited) & (toilet in staff area, ask museum asst) toilets for disabled shop ✖ (ex guide dogs)

BANFF   Map 15 NJ66
BANFF MUSEUM
High St AB45 1AE
☎ 01771 622906 ▤ 01771 622884
e-mail: heritage@aberdeenshire.gov.uk

Displays of geology, natural history, local history, Banff silver, arms and armour, and displays relating to James Ferguson (18th-century astronomer) and Thomas Edward (19th-century Banff naturalist).
Times: Open Jun-Sep, Mon-Sat 2-4.30. **Facilities:** ▣ (200yds) & shop ✖ (ex guide dogs)

DUFF HOUSE
AB45 3SX
➲ (0.5m S, access south of town)
☎ 01261 818181

The house was designed by William Adam for William Duff, later Earl of Fife. The main block was roofed in 1739, but the planned wings were never built. Although it is incomplete, the house is still considered one of Britain's finest Georgian baroque buildings. Duff House is a Country House Gallery of the National Galleries of Scotland.
Times: ✱ Telephone for details of opening dates and times.
Facilities: ▣ ✖ & toilets for disabled shop ✖▮

CORGARFF   Map 15 NJ20
CORGARFF CASTLE
AB36 8YL
➲ (8m W of Strathdon village)
☎ 01975 651460

The 16th-century tower was besieged in 1571 and is associated with the Jacobite risings of 1715 and 1745. It later became a military barracks. Its last military use was to control the smuggling of whisky between 1827 and 1831.
Times: ✱ Open all year, Apr-Sep, daily 9.30-6.30; Oct-Mar, wknds only. (Closed 25-26 Dec). Telephone for 2004 details **Facilities:** ▣ shop ▮

CRATHES   Map 15 NO79
CRATHES CASTLE & GARDEN
AB31 5QJ
➲ (On A93, 3m E of Banchory)
☎ 01330 844525 ▤ 01330 844797
e-mail: crathes@nts.org.uk

This impressive 16th-century castle with magnificent interiors has royal associations dating from 1323. There is a large walled garden and a notable collection of unusual plants, including yew hedges dating from 1702. The grounds contain six nature trails, one suitable for disabled visitors, and an adventure playground.
Times: Open: Castle & Visitor Centre: Apr-Sep, daily 10-5.30, Oct daily 10-4.30. To help enjoy your visit & for safety reasons, admission to the castle is by timed ticket (limited numbers: entry may be delayed). Garden & grounds all year, daily 9-sunset. **Fee:** ✱ £9 (concession £6.50) Admission free to NTS members. For other details please phone 0131 243 9387 or check website. **Facilities:** ▣ ✖ licensed & (tape for visually impaired) toilets for disabled shop ✖ (ex guide dogs) ◈

FETTERCAIRN   Map 15 NO67
FASQUE
AB30 1DN
➲ (0.5m N on B974)
☎ 01561 340569 & 340202
▤ 01561 340325 & 340569

Fasque has been the home of the Gladstone family since 1829, and W E Gladstone, four times Prime Minister, lived here from 1830 to 1851. There are impressive state rooms and a handsome, sweeping staircase, as well as extensive servants' quarters. The spacious park has red deer and Soay sheep.
Times: ✱ Open Jul-Aug, daily 11-5. (Closed 5.30). Groups at all other times by arrangement at any other time all year round. **Facilities:** ▣ ▃ & (wheelchairs available) shop ✖

HUNTLY   Map 15 NJ53

BRANDER MUSEUM
The Square AB54 8AE
➲ (In centre of Huntly, sharing building with
library, museum on ground floor)
☎ 01771 622906   📠 01771 622884
e-mail: heritage@aberdeenshire.gov.uk
The museum has displays of local and church history, plus
the 19th-century Anderson Bey and the Sudanese
campaigns. Exhibits connected with George MacDonald,
author and playwright can also be seen.
Times: Open all year, Tue-Sat 2-4.30. **Facilities:** P (25yds) ♿ (access
difficult due to 3 large steps at entrance) shop ✶ (ex guide dogs)

HUNTLY CASTLE
AB54 4SH
☎ 01466 793191
The original medieval castle was rebuilt a number of times
and destroyed, once by Mary, Queen of Scots. It was rebuilt
for the last time in 1602, in palatial style, and is now an
impressive ruin, noted for its ornate heraldic decorations. It
stands in wooded parkland.
Times: ✱ Open all year, Apr-Sep, daily 9.30-6.30; Oct-Mar, Mon-Sat
9.30-4.30, Sun 2-4.30. (Closed Thu pm, Fri & Sun in winter & 25-26
Dec). **Facilities:** P shop ▮

INVERURIE   Map 15 NJ72

CARNEGIE MUSEUM
Town House, The Square AB51 3SN
➲ (In centre of Inverurie, on left hand side of
townhouse building, above library)
☎ 01771 622906   📠 01771 622884
e-mail: heritage@aberdeenshire.gov.uk
This fine museum contains displays on local history and
archaeology, including Pictish stones, Bronze Age material
and the Great North of Scotland Railway.
Times: Open all year, Mon & Wed-Fri 2-4.30, Sat 10-1 & 2-4. (Closed
Tue & public holidays) **Facilities:** P (50yds) shop ✶ (ex guide dogs)

KEMNAY   Map 15 NJ71

CASTLE FRASER
AB51 7LD
➲ (off A944, 4m N of Dunecht)
☎ 01330 833463
e-mail: castlefraser@nts.org.uk
The massive Z-plan castle was built between 1575 and 1636
and is one of the grandest of the Castles of Mar. The interior
was remodelled in 1838 and decoration and furnishings of
that period survive in some of the rooms. A formal garden
inside the old walled garden, estate trails, a children's play
area and a programme of concerts are among the
attractions.
Times: Apr-Jun & Sep, Fri-Tue 12-5.30, Jul-Aug, daily 11-5.30 **Fee:** ✱
£7 (concession £5.25) Groups adult £5.60, child £1, please book groups
in advance. Admission free to NTS members. For other details please
phone 0131 243 9387. **Facilities:** P 🍴 ♿ shop garden centre ✶ (ex
guide dogs, certain areas) ♨

KILDRUMMY   Map 15 NJ41

KILDRUMMY CASTLE
AB54 7XT
➲ (10m SW of Alford)
☎ 01975 571331
An important part of Scottish history, at least until it was
dismantled in 1717, this fortress was the seat of the Earls of
Mar. Now it is a ruined, but splendid, example of a
13th-century castle, with four round towers, hall and chapel
all discernible. Some parts of the building, including the
Great Gatehouse, are from the 15th and 16th centuries.
Times: ✱ Open Apr-Sep, daily 9.30-6.30. **Facilities:** P ♿ toilets for
disabled shop ▮

KILDRUMMY CASTLE GARDENS
AB33 8RA
➲ (on A97 off A944. Ten miles west of Alford)
☎ 019755 71277 & 71203   📠 019755 71277
e-mail: information@
kildrummy-castle-gardens.co.uk
With the picturesque ruin as a backdrop, these beautiful
gardens include an alpine garden in an ancient quarry and a
water garden. There's a small museum and a children's play
area.
Times: Open Apr-Oct, daily 10-5. **Fee:** ✱ £2.50 (ch free)
Facilities: P 🍴 ♿ toilets for disabled shop garden centre

MACDUFF   Map 15 NJ76

MACDUFF MARINE AQUARIUM
11 High Shore AB44 1SL
➲ (off A947 to Macduff, aquarium signposted)
☎ 01261 833369   📠 01261 831052   `2 for 1`
e-mail: macduff.aquarium@
aberdeenshire.gov.uk

Exciting displays feature local sealife. The central exhibit,
unique in Britain, holds a living kelp reef. Divers feed the fish
in this tank. Other displays include an estuary exhibit, splash
tank, rock pools, deep reef tank and ray pool. Young visitors
especially enjoy the touch pools. There are talks, video
presentations and feeding shows throughout the week.
Times: Open 10-5 daily (last admission 4.15). (Closed 25-26 Dec & 31
Dec-2 Jan) **Fee:** ✱ £4.20 (ch £1.80, concessions £2.35). Family ticket
(2 adults & 2 ch) £10.70. Groups 10+ **Facilities:** P ♿ (audio tour for
visually impaired) toilets for disabled shop ✶ (ex guide dogs) 🍴

MARYCULTER   Map 15 NO89
STORYBOOK GLEN
AB12 5FT
➲ (5m W of Aberdeen on B9077)
☎ 01224 732941 📠 01224 732941

This is a child's fantasy land, where favourite nursery rhyme and fairytale characters are brought to life. Grown-ups can enjoy the nostalgia and also the 20 acres of Deeside country, full of flowers, plants, trees and waterfalls.
Times: ✱ Open Mar-Oct, daily 10-6; Nov-Feb, daily 10-4.
Facilities: 🅿 💷 ✗ licensed ♿ toilets for disabled shop garden centre ✗ (ex guide dogs) ▼

METHLICK   Map 15 NJ83
HADDO HOUSE
AB41 7EQ
➲ (off B999, 4m N of Pitmedden)
☎ 01651 851440 📠 01651 851888
e-mail: haddo@nts.org.uk

Haddo House is renowned for its association with the Haddo Choral Society and is the venue for international concerts. It is a splendid Palladian-style mansion built in the 1730s to designs by William Adam. Home to the Earls of Aberdeen, the house was refurbished in the 1880s in the 'Adam Revival' style. The adjoining country park offers beautiful woodland walks.
Times: Open, House: Jun, Fri-Mon 11-4.30; Jul-Aug, daily 11-4.30. Guided tours only, departing set times. Garden open all year, daily 9.30-6. **Fee:** ✱ £7 (concession £5.25). Family ticket £19. Groups adult £5.60, child/school £1. Admission free to NTS members. For other details please phone 0131 243 9387. **Facilities:** 🅿 ✗ ♿ (lift to first floor of house & wheelchair) toilets for disabled shop ✗ (ex in grounds & guide dogs) ▼

MINTLAW   Map 15 NJ94
ABERDEENSHIRE FARMING MUSEUM
Aden Country Park AB42 5FQ
➲ (1m W of Mintlaw on A950)
☎ 01771 622906 📠 01771 622884
e-mail: heritage@aberdeenshire.gov.uk

Housed in 19th-century farm buildings, once part of the estate which now makes up the Aden Country Park. Two centuries of farming history and innovation are illustrated, and the story of the estate is also told. The reconstructed farm of Hareshowe shows how a family in the north-east farmed during the 1950s - access by guided tour only.
Times: Open May-Sep, daily 11-4.30; Apr & Oct, wknds only noon-4.30. Last admission 30 mins before closing. Park open all year, Apr-Sep 7-10, winter 7-7. To be confirmed. **Facilities:** 🅿 (charged) 💷 ♿ (sensory garden) toilets for disabled shop ✗ (ex guide dogs)

OLD DEER   Map 15 NJ94
DEER ABBEY
➲ (2m W of Mintlaw on A950)   FREE
☎ 01466 793191

The remains of the Cistercian Abbey, founded in 1218, include the infirmary, Abbot's House and the southern claustral range. The University Library at Cambridge now houses the famous Book of Deer.
Times: Open at all reasonable times. **Facilities:** 🅿 ✗ ▌

OYNE   Map 15 NJ62
ARCHAEOLINK
Berryhill AB52 6QP
➲ (1m off A96 on B9002)
☎ 01464 851500 📠 01464 851544   2 for 1
e-mail: info@archaeolink.co.uk

A stunning audio-visual show, a Myths and Legends Gallery and a whole range of interpretation techniques help visitors to explore what it was like to live 6000 years ago. In addition there are landscaped walkways, and outdoor activity areas including an Iron Age farm, Roman marching camp and Stone Age settlement in the 40-acre park.
Times: Open Apr-Oct, daily 11-5. **Fee:** ✱ £4.25 (ch 3-6 £2.50, 7-16 £3, concessions £3.50) Family £13-£19. **Facilities:** 🅿 💷 ✗ licensed ♿ (induction loop in theatre, wheelchair) toilets for disabled shop ✗ (ex guide dogs) ▼

PETERHEAD   Map 15 NK14
ARBUTHNOT MUSEUM & ART GALLERY
St Peter St AB42 1QD
➲ (in centre of Peterhead, at St Peter Street & Queen Street x-roads, above library)
☎ 01771 622906 📠 01771 622884
e-mail: heritage@aberdeenshire.gov.uk

Specialising in local exhibits, particularly those relating to the fishing industry, this museum also displays Arctic and whaling specimens and a British coin collection. The regular programme of exhibitions changes approximately every six weeks.
Times: Open all year, Mon, Tue & Thu-Sat 11-1 & 2-4.30, Wed 11-1. (Closed Sun and BHs). **Facilities:** 🅿 (150 yds) shop ✗ (ex guide dogs)

PITMEDDEN   Map 15 NJ82
PITMEDDEN GARDEN
AB41 7PD
➲ (1m W of Pitmedden on A920)
☎ 01651 842352 📠 01651 843188
e-mail: aclipson@nts.scot.demon.co.uk

The fine 17th-century walled garden, with sundials, pavilions and fountains dotted among the parterres, has been authentically restored, and there is a Museum of Farming Life and a woodland walk.
Times: Open - May-Sep, daily 10-5.30. Grounds: all year, daily. **Fee:** ✱ £5 (concession £3.75) Family ticket £13.50. Groups adult £4, child/school £1. Please book groups in advance. Admission free to NTS members. For other details please phone 0131 243 9387. **Facilities:** 🅿 💷 ♿ (2 wheelchairs available) toilets for disabled shop ▼

TOLQUHON CASTLE
AB41 7LP
➲ (2m NE off B999)
☎ 01651 851286

Now roofless, this late 16th-century quadrangular mansion encloses an early 15th-century tower. There is a fine gatehouse and a splendid courtyard.
Times: ✱ Open all year, Apr-Sep, daily 9.30-6.30; Oct-Mar, wknds only. (Closed 25-26 Dec). telephone for 2004 details **Facilities:** 🅿 ♿ toilets for disabled shop ✗ ▌

RHYNIE   Map 15 NJ42

LEITH HALL & GARDEN
Kennethmont AB54 4NQ
➲ (on B9002, 1m W of Kennethmont)
☎ 01464 831216   🖷 01464 831594
e-mail: leithhall@nts.org.uk

Home of the Leith family for over 300 years, the house dates back to 1650, and has a number of Jacobite relics and fine examples of needlework. It is surrounded by charming gardens and extensive grounds.

Times: Open - House: Good Fri-Etr Mon, daily 12-5; May-Sep, Fri-Tue 12-5. Garden & grounds all year, daily 9.30-sunset. **Fee:** ✻ £7 (concession £5.25) Family ticket £19. Garden & grounds only £2.50 (concession £1.90) Admission free to NTS members. For other details please phone 0131 243 9387. **Facilities:** 🅿 💷 ⅁ (parking next to hall, scented garden for the blind) toilets for disabled ✖ (ex guide dogs) ♨

STONEHAVEN   Map 15 NO88

DUNNOTTAR CASTLE
AB39 2TL
➲ (2m S of Stonehaven on A92)
☎ 01569 762173

This once-impregnable fortress, now a spectacular ruin, was the site of the successful protection of the Scottish Crown Jewels from the might of Cromwell. A must for anyone who takes Scottish history seriously.

Times: Open all year, summer Mon-Sat 9-6, Sun 2-5; winter open Fri-Mon only. Last entry 30mins before closing. (Closed 25-26 Dec & New Year). **Fee:** ✻ £3.50 (ch 5-15 £1) **Facilities:** 🅿 ✖ (ex on lead)

TOLBOOTH MUSEUM
Old Pier AB39 2JU
➲ (On Harbour Front, Stonehaven)
☎ 01771 622906   🖷 01771 622884
e-mail: heritage@aberdeenshire.gov.uk

Built in the late 16th century as a storehouse for the Earls Marischal at Dunnottar Castle, the building was the Kincardineshire County Tollbooth from 1600-1767. Displays feature local history and fishing.

Times: Open May-Oct, Wed-Mon, 1.30-4.30. (Closed Tue). **Facilities:** 🅿 (20yds) ⅁ shop ✖ (ex guide dogs)

TURRIFF   Map 15 NJ75

FYVIE CASTLE
Fyvie AB53 8JS
➲ (8m SE of Turriff on A947)
☎ 01651 891266   🖷 01651 891107
e-mail: aclipson@nts.scot.demon.co.uk

This superb castle, founded in the 13th century, has five towers, each built in a different century, and is one of the grandest examples of Scottish Baronial. It contains the finest wheel stair in Scotland, and a 17th-century morning room, lavishly furnished in Edwarian style. The collection of portraits is exceptional, and there are also displays of arms and armour and tapestries.

Times: Open Apr-Jun & Sep, Fri-Tue 12-5; Jul- Aug, daily 11-5. Grounds all year, daily, 9.30-sunset. **Fee:** ✻ £7 (concession £5.25) Family ticket £19. Groups adult £5.60, child/school £1. Please book groups in advance. Admission free to NTS members. For other details please phone 0131 243 9387. **Facilities:** 🅿 💷 ⅁ (small lift, braille sheets) toilets for disabled shop ✖ (ex guide dogs) ♨

ANGUS

ARBROATH   Map 12 NO64

ARBROATH ABBEY
DD11 1EG
☎ 01241 878756

The 'Declaration of Arbroath' - declaring Robert the Bruce as king - was signed at the 12th-century abbey on 6 April 1320. The abbot's house is well preserved, and the church remains are also interesting.

Times: ✻ Open all year, Apr-Sep, daily 9.30-6.30; Oct-Mar, Mon-Sat 9.30-4.30, Sun 2-4.30. (Closed Thu pm, Fri & Sun am in winter). please phone for 2004 details **Facilities:** 🅿 ⅁ ✖ █

ARBROATH MUSEUM
Signal Tower, Ladyloan DD11 1PU
➲ (on A92 adjacent to harbour. 16m NE of Dundee)
☎ 01241 875598   🖷 01241 439263   **FREE**
e-mail: signal.tower@angus.gov.uk

Fish and Arbroath Smokies, textiles and engineering feature at this local history museum housed in the 1813 shore station of Stevenson's Bell Rock lighthouse.

Times: Open all year, Mon-Sat 10-5; Jul-Aug, Sun 2-5. (Closed 25-26 Dec & 1-2 Jan). **Facilities:** 🅿 ⅁ (induction loop) shop ✖ (ex guide dogs)

BRECHIN   Map 15 NO66

PICTAVIA VISITOR CENTRE
DD9 6RL
➲ (off A90)
☎ 01356 626813   🖷 01356 626814
e-mail: laffertyc@angus.gov.uk

Find about more about the ancient pagan nation of the Picts, who lived in Scotland nearly 2000 years ago. Visitors can learn about Pictish culture, art and religion through film, interactive displays and music. There are also nature and farm trails, a pets' corner, and an adventure playground.

Times: ✻ Open daily; Summer Mon-Sat 9-6, Sun 10-5; Winter Mon-Sat 9-5, Sun 10-5. (Closed 25-26 Dec & 1 Jan) **Facilities:** 🅿 💷 ✗ licensed ⅁ toilets for disabled shop garden centre

CARNOUSTIE   Map 12 NO53

BARRY WATER MILL
Barry DD7 7RJ
➲ (N of Barry village between A92 & A930, 2m W of Carnoustie)
☎ 01241 856761

This restored 18th-century mill works on a demonstration basis. Records show that the site has been used for milling since the 16th century. Displays highlight the important place the mill held in the community. There is a waymarked walk and picnic area.

Times: Open Apr-Oct, Fri-Tue, 12-5 **Fee:** £5 (concession £3.75) Adult group £4, child/school group £1. Family ticket £13.50. Admission free to NTS members. For other details please phone 0131 243 9387. **Facilities:** 🅿 ⅁ ramp from car park to mill toilets for disabled (grounds only) ♨

EDZELL
Map 15 NO56

EDZELL CASTLE
DD9 7UE
➲ (on B966)
☎ 01356 648631

The 16th-century castle has a remarkable walled garden built in 1604 by Sir David Lindsay. Flower-filled recesses in the walls are alternated with heraldic and symbolic sculptures of a sort not seen elsewhere in Scotland. There are ornamental and border gardens and a garden house.
Times: ✱ Open all year, Apr-Sep, daily 9.30-6.30; Oct-Mar, Mon-Sat 9.30-4.30, Sun 2-4.30. (Closed Thu pm, Fri in winter & 25-26 Dec). Telephone for 2004 details **Facilities:** 🅿 ⛄ shop ▮

FORFAR
Map 15 NO45

THE MEFFAN ART GALLERY & MUSEUM
20 West High St DD8 1BB
➲ (Turn off A90, 13m N of Dundee, drive into Forfar town centre. The Meffan is right in the town centre).
☎ 01307 464123 467017   FREE
📠 01307 468451
e-mail: the.meffan@angus.gov.uk

This lively, ever-changing contemporary art gallery and museum are full of surprises. Walk down a cobbled street full of shops, ending up at a witch-burning scene! Carved Pictish stones and a diorama of an archaeological dig complete the vibrant displays.
Times: Open all year. (Closed 25-26 Dec & 1-2 Jan). **Facilities:** 🅿 (150yds) 30 mins limit on street ⛄ handrails and wide door toilets for disabled shop ▸✖ (ex guide dogs) 🐾

GLAMIS
Map 15 NO34

ANGUS FOLK MUSEUM
Kirkwynd Cottages DD8 1RT
➲ (off A94, in Glamis)
☎ 01307 840288   📠 01307 840233

A row of stone-roofed, late 18th-century cottages now houses the splendid Angus Folk Collection of domestic equipment and cottage furniture. Across the wynd, an Angus stone steading houses 'The Life on the Land' exhibition.
Times: Open Apr-Jun & Sep, Fri-Tue 12-5; Jul & Aug 12-5. **Fee:** ✱ £5 (concession £3.75) Groups adult £4, child/school group £1, groups please book in advance. Family ticket £13.50. Admission free to NTS members. For other details please phone 0131 243 9387. **Facilities:** 🅿 ⛄ toilets for disabled ▸✖ (ex guide dogs) 🐾

GLAMIS CASTLE
DD8 1RJ
➲ (5m W of Forfar on A94)
☎ 01307 840393   📠 01307 840733
e-mail: admin@glamis-castle.co.uk

Glamis Castle is the family home of the Earls of Strathmore and Kinghorne and has been a royal residence since 1372. It is the childhood home of The Queen Mother, the birthplace of Princess Margaret and the setting for Shakespeare's play
continued

Macbeth. Though the Castle is open to visitors it remains the home of the Strathmore family.
Times: Open 29 Mar-Oct, 10.30-5.30. Last admission 4.45pm. **Fee:** ✱ Castle & grounds £6.70 (ch £3.50, pen & students £5). Family ticket £18. Grounds only £3.50 (ch, pen & students £2.50). Group 20+ **Facilities:** 🅿 ✖ licensed ⛄ toilets for disabled shop ▸✖ (ex in grounds) 🍴

KIRRIEMUIR
Map 15 NO35

J M BARRIE'S BIRTHPLACE
9 Brechin Rd DD8 4BX
➲ (on A90/A926 6m NW of Forfar)
☎ 01575 572646
e-mail: aclipson@nts.scot.demon.co.uk

The creator of Peter Pan, Sir James Barrie, was born in Kirriemuir in 1860. The upper floors of No 9 Brechin Road are furnished as they may have been when Barrie lived there, and the adjacent house, No 11, houses an exhibition about him. The wash-house outside was his first 'theatre' and gave him the idea for Wendy's house in *Peter Pan*.
Times: Open Apr-Jun & Sep, Fri-Tue 12-5; Jul-Aug, daily 12-5. **Fee:** ✱ £5 (concession £3.75) Groups adult £4, child/school £1, please book groups in advance. Family ticket £13.50. Admission free to NTS members. For other details please phone 0131 243 9387.
Facilities: 🅿 (100yds) 🔊 ⛄ (stairlift, audio programmes) shop ▸✖ (ex guide dogs) 🐾

MONTROSE
Map 15 NO75

HOUSE OF DUN
DD10 9LQ
➲ (on A935, 3m W of Montrose)
☎ 01674 810264   📠 01674 810722
e-mail: houseofdun@nts.org.uk

This Georgian house, overlooking the Montrose Basin, was built for Lord Dun in 1730 and is noted for the exuberant plasterwork of the interior. Family portraits, fine furniture and porcelain are on display, and royal mementos connected with a daughter of King William IV and the actress Mrs Jordan, who lived here in the 19th century. There is a walled garden and woodland walks.
Times: Open - House: Apr-Jun, & Sep, Fri-Tue 12-5, Jul-Aug, daily 12-5. Garden & grounds all year daily 9.30-sunset. **Fee:** ✱ £7 (concession £5.25) Family ticket £19. Groups adult £5.60, child/school £1. Please book groups in advance. Admission free to NTS members. For other details please phone 0131 243 9387. **Facilities:** 🅿 ✖ ⛄ (braille sheets, house wheelchair & stair lift) toilets for disabled shop ▸✖ (ex guide dogs) 🐾

MONTROSE MUSEUM & ART GALLERY
Panmure Place DD10 8HE
➲ (opposite Montrose Academy in town centre, approach via A92 from Aberdeen
or Dundee)   FREE
☎ 01674 673232
e-mail: montrose.museum@angus.gov.uk

Extensive local collections cover the history of Montrose from prehistoric times, the maritime history of the port, the natural history of Angus, and local art.
Times: Open all year, Mon-Sat 10-5. (Closed 25-26 Dec & 1-2 Jan). **Facilities:** 🅿 ⛄ shop ▸✖ (ex guide dogs)

ARGYLL & BUTE

ARDUAINE   Map 10 NM71
ARDUAINE GARDEN
PA34 4XQ
➲ (20m S of Oban, on A816)
☎ 01852 200366 ▤ 01852 200233
An outstanding 18-acre garden on a promontory bounded by
Loch Melfort and the Sound of Jura, climatically favoured by
the North Atlantic Drift. It is famous for its rhododendrons
and azalea species and other rare trees and shrubs.
Times: Open all year, daily 9.30-sunset. Reception Apr-Sep 9.30-4.30.
Fee: ✱ £3.50 (concession £2.60) Groups adult £2.80, child/school £1,
please book in advance. Family ticket £9.50. Admission free to NTS
members. For other details please phone 0131 243 9387.
Facilities: ▣ ♿ toilets for disabled ✖ (ex guide dogs) ⍾

ARROCHAR   Map 10 NN20
ARGYLL FOREST PARK
Forest Enterprise, Ardgartan Visitor Centre G83 7AR
➲ (on A83 at the foot of "The Rest and Be
Thankful")
☎ 01301 702597 ▤ 01301 702597
e-mail: fekilmun@forestry.gov.uk
This park extends over a large area of hill ground and forest,
noted for its rugged beauty. Numerous forest walks and
picnic sites allow exploration; the Arboretum walks and the
route between Younger Botanic Gardens and Puck's Glen are
particularly lovely. Guided walks and other ranger-led
activities are planned; also deer watches and 4x4 safaris.
Times: ✱ Open all year. **Facilities:** ▣ shop ⍾

AUCHINDRAIN   Map 10 NN00
AUCHINDRAIN TOWNSHIP-OPEN AIR MUSEUM
PA32 8XN
➲ (6m SW of Inverarary on A83)
☎ 01499 500235
Auchindrain is an original West Highland township of great
antiquity, and the only communal tenancy township to have
survived on its centuries-old site. The buildings are furnished
and equipped to present a fascinating glimpse of Highland
life in the last century.
Times: Open Apr-Sep, daily 10-5. **Fee:** ✱ £3.80 (ch £1.80, pen £3).
Family ticket £9.50. **Facilities:** ▣ shop

BARCALDINE   Map 10 NM94
BARCALDINE CASTLE
Benderloch PA37 1SA
➲ (9m N of Oban on A828 Oban/Fort William
road. Take left turn to Tralee in Benderloch)
☎ 01631 720598 ▤ 01631 720598
e-mail: barcaldine.castle@tesco.net
The 16th-century home of the Campbells of Barcaldine. The
last of the seven castles built by Black Duncan to be held in
Campbell hands, and associated with the Appin Murder and
Glencoe Massacre. Said to be haunted by the Blue Lady, the
castle has secret passages and bottle dungeon; there is also
a family quiz trail.
Times: Open Jul-Aug afternoons. **Fee:** ✱ £3.65 (ch £1.95, concessions
£3) **Facilities:** ▣ ▣ shop ✖ � ⍾

SCOTTISH SEA LIFE SANCTUARY
PA37 1SE
➲ (10m N of Oban on A828, Oban to
Fort William rd)
☎ 01631 720386 ▤ 01631 720529
e-mail: obansealife@merlinentertainments.biz
Set in one of Scotland's most picturesque locations, the
Scottish Sea Life Sanctuary provides dramatic views of
native undersea life including stingrays, seals, octopus and
catfish. There are daily talks and feeding demonstrations and
during the summer young seals can be viewed prior to their
release back into the wild. Recent additions include Otter
Creer - a large naturally landscaped enclosure with deep
diving pool with underwater viewing and cascading streams
through other pools 'into the deep', a themed interactive
area displaying living creatures from the deep. There is a
restaurant, gift shop, children's play park and a nature trail.
Times: Open all year, mid Feb-Nov, daily 10-5. Dec & Jan, Sat, Sun &
school holidays only. **Fee:** ✱ £6.95 (ch £4.95, pen £5.95). Group 15+.
Facilities: ▣ ▣ ✖ ♿ (assistance available for wheelchairs) toilets
for disabled shop ✖ (ex guide dogs) ⍾

BENMORE   Map 10 NS18
BENMORE BOTANIC GARDEN
PA23 8QU
➲ (7m N of Dunoon on A815)
☎ 01369 706261 ▤ 01369 706369
e-mail: benmore@rbge.org.uk
From the formal gardens, through the hillside woodlands,
follow the paths to a stunning viewpoint with a spectacular
outlook across the garden and the Holy Loch to the Firth of
Clyde and beyond. Amongst many highlights are the stately
conifers, the magnificent avenue of Giant Redwoods, and an
extensive magnolia and rhododendron collection.
Times: Open Mar-Oct, daily, 10am; Mar & Oct, close 5pm, Apr -Sep,
close 6pm. **Fee:** £3.50 (ch £1, concessions £3). Family £8. Party rates.
Facilities: ▣ ▣ ✖ licensed ♿ toilets for disabled shop garden
centre ✖ (on short lead) ⍾

CARNASSERIE CASTLE   Map 10 NM80
CARNASSERIE CASTLE
PA31 8RQ   ╎FREE╎
➲ (2m N of Kilmartin off A816)
A handsome combined tower house and hall, home of John
Carswell, first Protestant Bishop of the Isles and translator of
the first book printed in Gaelic. Very fine architectural details
of the late 16th century.
Times: Open at all reasonable times. **Facilities:** ✖ ▮

GIGHA ISLAND   Map 10 NR64
ACHAMORE GARDENS
PA41 7AD
☎ 01583 505267 & 505254 ▤ 01583 505244
e-mail: william@isle-of-gigha.co.uk
Wonderful woodland gardens of rhododendrons and azaleas,
created by Sir James Horlick, who bought the little island of
Gigha in 1944. Many of the plants were brought in laundry
baskets from his former home in Berkshire. Sub-tropical
plants flourish in the rich soil and virtually frost-free climate,
and there is a walled garden for some of the finer specimens.
Times: ✱ Open all year, daily. **Facilities:** ▣ ♿

HELENSBURGH   Map 10 NS28

THE HILL HOUSE

Upper Colquhoun St G84 9AJ

➲ (off B832, between A82 & A814)

☎ 01436 673900   🖹 01436 674685

The Hill House is a handsome example of Charles Rennie Mackintosh's work, modern but part-inspired by Scottish tower houses. It was commissioned by the publisher Walter Blackie. The gardens are being restored to Blackie's design, with features reflecting the suggestions of Mackintosh. There is also a special display about Mackintosh.
Times: Open Apr-Oct, daily 1.30-5.30. Morning visits available for pre-booked groups. **Fee:** ✱ £7 (concession £5.25). Family ticket £19.
Facilities: 🅿 💷 shop ✖ ❦

INVERARAY   Map 10 NN00

BELL TOWER OF ALL SAINTS' CHURCH

The Avenue PA32 8YX

➲ (through the arches on Front St, into Avenue car park)

☎ 01546 602315   🖹 01546 602519

e-mail: dean.sedati@virgin.net

The tower was built in the 1920s and stands at 126ft. It has the world's second heaviest ring of ten bells, installed as a Campbell War Memorial in 1931. An exhibition on campanology is mounted inside and visiting bell ringers give recitals, usually once a month. A splendid view rewards those who climb to the roof.
Times: Open Etr-Sep, daily 10-1 & 2-5. **Fee:** ✱ £2 (ch & pen 75p).
Family ticket £4 **Facilities:** 🅿 (adjacent to tower) ♿ ✖ (ex guide dogs)

INVERARAY CASTLE

PA32 8XE

➲ (on A83 Glasgow to Campbeltown road)

☎ 01499 302203   🖹 01499 302421

e-mail: enquiries@inveraray-castle.com

The third Duke of Argyll engaged Roger Morris to build the present castle in 1743; in the process the old Burgh of Inveraray was demolished and a new one built nearby. The 5th Duke commissioned the beautiful interior decoration. The great armoury hall and staterooms are of particular note.
Times: Open 5 Apr - 26 Oct. Apr-Jun, Sep & Oct, Mon-Thu & Sat 10-1 & 2-5.45. Sun 1-5.45; Jul & Aug, Mon-Sat 10-5.45, Sun 1-5.45. Last admission 12.30 & 5. **Facilities:** 🅿 💷 ♿ shop ✖ (ex guide dogs) 🍴

INVERARAY JAIL

Church Square PA32 8TX

➲ (on main Campbeltown Road, A82/A83)

☎ 01499 302381   🖹 01499 302195

e-mail: inverarayjail@btclick.com

Enter Inveraray Jail and step back in time. See furnished cells and experience prison sounds and smells. Ask the `prisoner' how to pick oakum. Turn the heavy handle of an original crank machine, take 40 winks in a hammock or listen to Matron's tales of day-to-day prison life. Visit the magnificent 1820 courtroom and hear trials in progress.

continued

Imaginative exhibitions including `Torture, Death and Damnation' and `In Prison Today'.
Times: Open all year, Nov-Mar, daily 10-5 (last admisssion 4); Apr-Oct, daily 9.30-6 (last admission 5). (Closed 25 Dec & 1 Jan). **Fee:** ✱ £5.75 (ch £2.80, pen £3.75). Family ticket £15.70. **Facilities:** 🅿 (100 yds) ♿ (wheelchair ramp at rear, induction loop in courtroom) toilets for disabled shop 💷

KILMARTIN   Map 10 NR89

DUNADD FORT   `FREE`

➲ (2m S of Kilmartin on A816)

Dunadd was one of the ancient capitals of Dalriada from which the Celtic kingdom of Scotland was formed. Near to this prehistoric hill fort (now little more than an isolated hillock) are carvings of a boar and a footprint; these probably marked the spot where early kings were invested with their royal power.
Times: Open at all reasonable times. **Facilities:** ✖ ▮

KILMARTIN HOUSE MUSEUM

PA31 8RQ

➲ (in centre of village, adjacent to church)

☎ 01546 510278   🖹 01546 510330

e-mail: museum@kilmartin.org

Kilmartin may seem to be a quiet Scottish village, but at least 150 prehistoric sites lie within six miles it. There are mysterious carved rocks, enigmatic standing stones, fascinating burial cairns and the fortress of the earliest Scottish Kings. Thousands of years of history are traced in a museum that explores ancient peoples' struggles for survival, their attempts to understand the world around them, early agriculture, and social strife in the shape of aggression and conflict. There is also an audio-visual extravaganza that uses 12 projectors to project 600 slides in 16 minutes. The presentation deals with the history and beauty of the landscape of Mid Argyll.
Times: Open daily 10-5.30. (Closed 25 Dec & 1 Jan) **Fee:** £4.50 (ch £1.50, concessions £3.50). Family ticket £10 **Facilities:** 🅿 💷 ♿ toilets for disabled shop ✖ (ex guide dogs) 🚐 💷

LOCHAWE   Map 10 NN12

CRUACHAN POWER STATION

Dalmally PA33 1AN

➲ (A85 18m E of Oban)

☎ 01866 822618   🖹 01866 822509

A vast cavern hidden 1km inside Ben Cruachan, which contains a 400,000-kilowatt hydro-electric power station, driven by water drawn from a high-level reservoir up the mountain. A guided tour takes you inside the mountain and reveals the generators in their underground cavern.
Times: ✱ Open Etr-Nov, daily 9.30-5 (last tour 4.15). Aug 9.30-6 (last tour 5.15) **Facilities:** 🅿 💷 ♿ toilets for disabled shop ✖ (ex guide dogs) 💷

MINARD   Map 10 NR99

CRARAE GARDENS

PA32 8YA

➲ (10m S of Inveraray on the A83)

☎ 01546 886614   🖹 01546 886614

Set beside Loch Fyne, these gardens are among Scotland's loveliest, noted for their rhododendrons, azaleas, conifers

continued

and ornamental shrubs, which include a number of rare species.
Times: Open all year, daily, 9-sunset. Visitor centre, Etr-Oct, daily 10-5.
Fee: ✱ £3.50 (concession £2.60). Family ticket £9.50. Groups adult £2.80, child/school £1. Please book groups in advance. Admission free to NTS members. For other details phone 0131 243 9387. **Facilities:** P ➐ & toilets for disabled shop garden centre ➐

OBAN   Map 10 NM83

CAITHNESS GLASS VISITOR CENTRE
The Waterfront, Railway Pier PA34 4LW
➲ (centre of Oban on the pier beside the train station)
☎ 01631 566523 ▤ 01631 566523
Factory shop selling a wide range of perfect and slightly imperfect paperweights and glassware, as well as ceramics, crystal and jewellery.
Times: Open all year, Mon-Sat 9-5 (open late Jun-Sep). Etr-Oct Sun 10-4; **Facilities:** P (100yds) & shop ✖ (ex guide dogs)

DUNSTAFFNAGE CASTLE
PA37 1PZ
➲ (3m N on peninsula)
☎ 01631 562465
Now ruined, this four-sided stronghold has a gatehouse, two round towers and walls 10ft thick. It was once the prison of Flora MacDonald.
Times: ✱ Open all year, Apr-Sep, daily 9.30-6.30; Oct-Mar, Sat-Wed Sun 9.30-4.30. (Closed 25-26 Dec). **Facilities:** P shop ▮

TAYNUILT   Map 10 NN03

BONAWE IRON FURNACE
PA35 1JQ
➲ (0.75m NE off B845)
☎ 01866 822432
The furnace is a restored charcoal blast-furnace for iron-smelting and making cast-iron. It was established in 1753 and worked until 1876. The works exploited the Forest of Lorne to provide charcoal for fuel.
Times: ✱ Open Apr-Sep, daily 9.30-6.30. **Facilities:** P & toilets for disabled shop ▮

EDINBURGH

BALERNO   Map 11 NT16

MALLENY GARDEN
EH14 7AF
➲ (off Lanark Rd (A70))
☎ 0131 449 2283
The delightful gardens are set round a 17th-century house (not open to the public). Shrub roses, a woodland garden, and a group of four clipped yews, survivors of a group planted in 1603, are among its notable features. The National Bonsai Collection for Scotland is also at Malleny.
Times: Garden: all year daily 10-6 or dusk if earlier. House not open.
Fee: ✱ £2 (concession £1). Admission free to NTS Members. For other details please phone 0131 243 9387. **Facilities:** P & ✖ (ex guide dogs) ➥

EDINBURGH   Map 11 NT27

BRASS RUBBING CENTRE
Trinity Apse, Chalmers Close, High St EH1 1SS
➲ (located on the Royal Mile)
☎ 0131 556 4364 ▤ 0131 557 3364
Housed in the 15th-century remnant of Trinity Apse, the Centre offers the chance to make your own rubbing from a wide range of replica monumental brasses and Pictish stones. Tuition is available.
Times: Open Apr-Sep, Mon-Sat 10-5 (during Edinburgh Festival Sun 12-5). **Fee:** Free entry. Charge for brass rubbing. **Facilities:** P (250mtrs) (parking meters, few spaces) shop ✖ (ex guide dogs)

CAMERA OBSCURA & WORLD OF ILLUSIONS
Castlehill, Royal Mile EH1 2ND
➲ (next to Edinburgh Castle)
☎ 0131 226 3709 ▤ 0131 225 4239
e-mail: info@camera-obscura.co.uk
A unique view of Edinburgh - as the lights go down, a brilliant moving image of the surrounding city appears. The scene changes as a guide operates the camera's system of revolving lenses and mirrors.
Times: Open all year, daily, Apr-Oct 9.30-6; Nov-Mar 10-5. (Closed 25 Dec). Open later Jul-Aug, phone for details. **Fee:** ✱ £5.75 (ch £3.70, students & pen £4.60) **Facilities:** P (300mtrs) shop ✖ (ex guide dogs) ➐

CITY ART CENTRE
2 Market St EH1 1DE
➲ (located, opposite rear of Waverley Stn on Market Street)
☎ 0131 529 3993 ▤ 0131 529 3986
e-mail: enquiries@city-art-centre.demon.uk
The City Art Centre houses the city's permanent fine art collection and stages a constantly changing programme of temporary exhibitions from all parts of the world. It has six floors of display galleries (linked by an escalator).
Times: Open Mon-Sat 10-5 (& Sun 12-5 Jul-Aug). **Fee:** Free. Admission charged for some exhibitions. **Facilities:** P (500yds) (single yellow lines) ➐ & (induction loop, lifts, braille signage, escalator) toilets for disabled shop ✖ (ex guide dogs) ➐

CRAIGMILLAR CASTLE
EH16 4SY
➲ (2.5m SE, off A68)
☎ 0131 661 4445
Mary Queen of Scots retreated to this 14th-century stronghold after the murder of Rizzio. The plot to murder Darnley, her second husband, was also hatched here. There are 16th and 17th century apartments.
Times: ✱ Open all year, Apr-Sep, daily 9.30-6.30; Oct-Mar, Mon-Sat 9.30-4.30. Sun 2-4.30. (Closed Thu pm & Fri in winter & 25-26 Dec).
Facilities: P & toilets for disabled shop ▮

DEAN GALLERY
73 Belford Rd EH4 3DS
➲ (20 min walk from Edinburgh Haymarket stn & Princes St)
☎ 0131 624 6200 ▤ 0131 343 3250
e-mail: enquiries@nationalgalleries.org
Opened in March 1999, the Dean Gallery provides a home for
continued

the Eduardo Paolozzi gift of sculpture and graphic art, the Gallery of Modern Art's renowned Dada and Surrealist collections, a major library and archive centre, along with temporary exhibition space for modern and contemporary art.
Times: Open all year, Mon-Sat 10-5, Sun 12-5. Extended opening during Edinburgh Festival. (Closed 25-26 Dec). **Fee:** ✱ Admission to permanent collections free, charge may be made for special exhibitions. **Facilities:** 🅿 💻 ♿ (ramps & lift) toilets for disabled shop ✖ (ex guide dogs) ◀

DYNAMIC EARTH
Holyrood Rd EH8 8AS
➲ (on the edge of Holyrood Park, opposite the Palace of Holyrood House)
☎ 0131 550 7800 📠 0131 550 7801
e-mail: enquiries@dynamicearth.co.uk
A new attraction that takes you on a fantastic journey of discovery back through time to learn why the Earth has changed. Amazing interactive displays let you see, hear, smell and feel the planet as it was in the past, as it is today and how it will be in the future.
Times: Open Apr-Oct, daily 10-6; Nov-Mar, Wed-Sat 10-5. (Closed 24-26 Dec). **Fee:** ✱ £8.45 (ch £4.95). Family ticket (2ad & 2ch) £22.50. **Facilities:** 🅿 (charged) 💻 ✖ licensed ♿ (audio guides, large print gallery guides) toilets for disabled shop ✖ (ex guide dogs) ◀

EDINBURGH CASTLE
EH1 2NG
☎ 0131 225 9846
This historic stronghold stands on the precipitous crag of Castle Rock. One of the oldest parts is the 11th-century chapel of the saintly Queen Margaret, but most of the present castle evolved later, during its stormy history of sieges and wars, and was altered again in Victorian times. The Scottish crown and other royal regalia are displayed in the Crown Room. Also notable is the Scottish National War Memorial.
Times: ✱ Open Apr-Sep, daily 9.30-6; Oct-Mar, daily 9.30-5. Last ticket sold 45 mins before closing time. (Closed 25-26 Dec). **Facilities:** 🅿 (charged) 💻 ✖ licensed ♿ (free transport to top of Castle Hill lift) toilets for disabled shop ✖ 🚼

THE EDINBURGH DUNGEON
31 Market St EH1 1QB
☎ 0131 240 1000 & 240 1002   2 for 1
📠 0131 240 1002
e-mail: edinburghdungeon@merlinentertainments.biz
From the team that brought you The London Dungeon, there comes a Scottish "feast of fun with history's horrible bits". A mixture of live actors, rides, shows and special effects take the brave visitor back into a dark past that includes such delights as the 18th-century Judgement of Sinners, the 17th-century Plague, and the new attraction, Clan Wars, which attempts to recreate the horror of the Glencoe Massacre of 1692.
Times: Open all year (ex 25 Dec). Contact for times of admission. **Fee:** ✱ £8.50 (ch 4-14 £5.95, concessions £7.50) **Facilities:** 🅿 (100mtrs) ♿ toilets for disabled shop ✖ (ex guide dogs) ◀

EDINBURGH ZOO
Murrayfield EH12 6TS
➲ (3m W of Edinburgh City Centre on A8 towards Glasgow)
☎ 0131 334 9171 📠 0131 314 0382
e-mail: marketing@rzss.org.uk
Scotland's largest wildlife attraction, set in 80 acres of leafy hillside parkland, just ten minutes from the city centre. With over 1,000 animals ranging from the tiny poison arrow frog to massive white rhinos, including many threatened species. See the world's largest penguin pool with underwater viewing, and the Darwin Maze, based on the theme of evolution.
Times: Open all year, Apr-Sep, daily 9-6; Oct & Mar, daily 9-5; Nov-Feb, daily 9-4.30. **Fee:** ✱ £8 (ch 3-14 & disabled £5, student £6, pen £4.50). **Facilities:** 🅿 (charged) 💻 ✖ licensed ♿ (wheelchair loan free, 1 helper free - phone in advance) toilets for disabled shop ✖ (ex guide dogs) ◀

GEORGIAN HOUSE
7 Charlotte Square EH2 4DR
➲ (2 mins walk W end of Princes Street)
☎ 0131 226 3318 📠 0131 226 3318
e-mail: thegeorgianhouse@nts.org.uk
The house is part of Robert Adam's splendid north side of Charlotte Square, the epitome of Edinburgh New Town architecture. The lower floors of No 7 have been restored in the style of the early 1800s, when the house was new. There also videos of life in the New Town, and this house in particular.
Times: Open Apr-Oct, daily 10-5; Mar & Nov-24 Dec daily 11-3. **Fee:** ✱ £5 (concession £3.75) Family ticket £13.50. Groups adult £4, child/school £1. Please book groups in advance. Admission free for NTS members. For other details please phone 0131 243 9387. **Facilities:** 🅿 (100 yds) (meters. disabled directly outside) ♿ (induction loop, braille guide) shop ✖ (ex guide dogs) 🚼

GLADSTONE'S LAND
477b Lawnmarket EH1 2NT
➲ (5 mins walk from Princes Street via Mound)
☎ 0131 226 5856 📠 0131 226 4851
Built in 1620, this six-storey tenement, once a merchant's house, still has its arcaded front - a rare feature now. Visitors can also see unusual tempera paintings on the walls and ceilings. It is furnished as a typical 17th-century merchant's home, complete with ground-floor shop front and goods of the period.
Times: Apr-Oct, Mon-Sat, 10-5, Sun 2-5 **Fee:** ✱ £3.50 (concession £2.60) Family ticket £9.50. Groups adult £2.80, child/school £1. Please book groups in advance. Admission free to NTS members. For other details please phone 0131 243 9387. **Facilities:** 🅿 (440yds) (outside for disabled) ♿ (tours for the blind can be arranged) shop ✖ (ex guide dogs) 🚼

JOHN KNOX HOUSE
The Netherbow, 43-45 High St EH1 1SR
➲ (between The Castle and Holyrood House)
☎ 0131 556 9579 📠 0131 557 5224
John Knox the Reformer is said to have died in the house, which was built by the goldsmith to Mary, Queen of Scots.

continued

Renovation work has revealed the original floor in the Oak Room, and a magnificent painted ceiling.
Times: Open all year, Mon-Sat 10-5 & Sun in Jul -Aug 12-5. (Closed Xmas). Closed Oct-Dec 2003 for refurbishment. Phone for details.
Fee: ✱ £2.25 (ch 75p, under 7's free, concessions £1.75).
Facilities: P (5 min walk) (paying car park) ﹠ (transcript of tapes for deaf, tours for blind, with notice) toilets for disabled shop ✖ (ex guide dogs) ⬤

LAURISTON CASTLE
Cramond Rd South, Davidson's Mains EH4 5QD
➲ (NW outskirts of Edinburgh, 1m E of Cramond overlooking the Forth at Silverknowles)
☎ 0131 336 2060 ▤ 0131 312 7165
The castle is a late 16th-century tower house with 19th-century additions but is most notable as a classic example of the Edwardian age. It has a beautifully preserved Edwardian interior and the feel of a country house, and the spacious grounds are very pleasant.
Times: Open all year by guided tour only; Apr-Oct, 11-1 & 2-5; Nov-Mar, wknds 2-4. (Closed Fri). **Fee:** ✱ £4.50 (ch, pen & concessions £3). **Facilities:** P ﹠ toilets for disabled shop ✖ (ex guide dogs)

MUSEUM OF CHILDHOOD
42 High Street, Royal Mile, EH1 1TG
➲ (On the Royal Mile)   **FREE**
☎ 0131 529 4142 ▤ 0131 558 3103
One of the first museums of its kind, it was reopened after major expansion. It has a wonderful collection of toys, games and other belongings of children through the ages, to delight visitors both old and young. Ring for details of special events.
Times: Open all year, Mon-Sat, Jun-Sep 10-6; Oct-May 10-5; (also Sun 12-5 in Jul-Aug). **Facilities:** P ﹠ (3 floors only) toilets for disabled shop ✖ (ex guide dogs)

MUSEUM OF EDINBURGH
142 Canongate, Royal Mile EH8 8DD
➲ (located on the Royal Mile)   **FREE**
☎ 0131 529 4143 ▤ 0131 557 3346
Housed in one of the best-preserved 16th-century buildings in the Old Town. It was built in 1570 and later became the headquarters of the Incorporation of Hammermen. Now a museum of local history, it has collections of silver, glassware, pottery, and other items such as street signs.
Times: Open all year, Mon-Sat 10-5. (During Festival period only, Sun 2-5). **Facilities:** P (200yds) (parking meters, limited spaces) ﹠ shop ✖ (ex guide dogs)

MUSEUM OF SCOTLAND
Chambers St EH1 1JF
☎ 0131 247 4219 ▤ 0131 220 4819   **FREE**
e-mail: info@nms.ac.uk
The museum is a striking new landmark in Edinburgh's historic Old Town. It houses more than 10,000 of the nation's most precious artefacts, as well as everyday objects which throw light on life in Scotland through the ages. Admission
continued

to the Royal Museum which is adjacent to the Museum of Scotland is also free. Telephone for details of special events.

Times: Open all year, Mon, Wed-Sat 10-5, Tue 10-8 & Sun 12-5.
Facilities: P ▆ ✖ licensed ﹠ toilets for disabled shop ✖ (ex assist dogs) ⬤

NATIONAL GALLERY OF SCOTLAND
The Mound EH2 2EL
➲ (off Princes Street)
☎ 0131 624 6200 ▤ 0131 343 3250
e-mail: enquiries@nationalgalleries.org
Occupying a handsome neo-classical building designed by William Playfair, the gallery is home to Scotland's greatest collection of European paintings and sculpture from the Renaissance to Post-Impressionism. It contains notable collections of works by Old Masters, Impressionists and Scottish artists.
Times: Open all year, Mon-Sat 10-5, Sun 12-5. Extended opening hours during the Edinburgh Festival period. (Closed 25-26 Dec).
Fee: ✱ Free. Admission charged to some major exhibitions.
Facilities: P (150yds) ﹠ (ramps & lift, room A1 not accessible) toilets for disabled shop ✖ (ex guide dogs) ⬤

NATIONAL WAR MUSEUM OF SCOTLAND
Edinburgh Castle EH1 2NG
☎ 0131 225 7534 ▤ 0131 225 3848
e-mail: info@nms.ac.uk
Explore the Scottish experience of war and military service over the last 400 years.
Times: Open all year, Apr-Oct, daily 9.45-5.45; Nov-Mar, daily 9.45-4.45. **Facilities:** P ﹠ toilets for disabled shop ✖ (ex assist dogs)

NELSON MONUMENT
Calton Hill EH7 5AA Calton Hill
➲ (Overlooking end of city)
☎ 0131 556 2716 ▤ 0131 557 3346
Designed in 1807 the monument dominates the east end of Princes Street. The views are superb, and every day except Sunday the time ball drops at 1pm as the gun at the castle goes off.
Times: Open all year, Apr-Sep, Mon 1-6 & Tue-Sat 10-6; Oct-Mar Mon-Sat 10-3. **Fee:** ✱ £2 **Facilities:** P shop ✖ (ex guide dogs)

PALACE OF HOLYROODHOUSE

EH8 8DX
➲ (at east end of Royal Mile)
☎ 0131 556 5100 📠 020 7930 9625
e-mail: information@royalcollection.org.uk

The Palace grew from the guest house of the Abbey of the Holyrood, said to have been founded by David I after a miraculous apparition. Mary, Queen of Scots had her court here from 1561 to 1567, and 'Bonnie' Prince Charlie held levees at the Palace during his occupation of Edinburgh. The Palace is still used by the Royal Family, but can be visited when they are not in residence. The picture gallery is notable for its series of Scottish Monarchs.
Times: Open daily, Apr-Oct 9.30-6 (last admission 5.15); Nov-Mar 9.30-4.30 (last admission 3.45). Closed 25-26 Dec and when The Queen is in residence. **Fee:** ✱ £7.50 (ch under 17 £3.30, pen & students £6). Family ticket (2ad+3ch) £19. Under 5 free **Facilities:** 🅿 (charged) ♿ (first floor by lift, wheelchair available) toilets for disabled shop ✖ (ex guide dogs) 📶

PARLIAMENT HOUSE

Supreme Courts, 2-11 Parliament Square EH1 1RQ
➲ (behind St Giles Cathedral)
☎ 0131 225 2595 📠 0131 240 6755

Scotland's independent parliament last sat in 1707, in this 17th-century building hidden behind an 1829 façade, now the seat of the Supreme Law Courts of Scotland. A large stained glass window depicts the inauguration of the Court of Session in 1540.
Times: Open all year, Mon-Fri 10-4. **Facilities:** 🅿 (400 mtrs) metered parking in high street 🍴 ✖ ♿ toilets for disabled ✖ (ex guide dogs)

THE PEOPLE'S STORY

Canongate Tolbooth, 163 Canongate, Royal Mile EH8 8BN
➲ (On the Royal Mile) `FREE`
☎ 0131 529 4057 📠 0131 556 3439

The museum, housed in the 16th-century tolbooth, tells the story of the ordinary people of Edinburgh from the late 18th century to the present day. Reconstructions include a prison cell, 1930s pub and 1940s kitchen supported by photographs, displays, sounds and smells.
Times: Open, Mon-Sat 10-5. Also, open Sun during Edinburgh Festival 2-5. **Facilities:** 🅿 (100yds) (parking meters) ♿ (lift, induction loop in video room, touch facilities) toilets for disabled shop ✖ (ex guide dogs)

THE REAL MARY KING'S CLOSE

2 Warriston's Close, High St EH1 1PG
➲ (opposite St Giles Cathedral)
☎ 08702 430160 📠 0131 225 0671
e-mail: info@realmarykingsclose.co.uk

Beneath Edinburgh's Royal Mile lies a warren of hidden streets, the remnants of old streets that were partly demolished in the 18th century. For many years people lived, worked and died in these subterranean streets, and now they

continued

are finally open to the public, as an eerie reminder of Edinburgh's underground communities.

Times: Open all year daily, tours run every 20mins from 10am. Last tour Apr-Oct 9pm, Nov-Mar 4pm. (Closed 25 Dec) **Fee:** ✱ £7 (ch £5, pen & student £6). Family ticket (2 adults + 2 ch) £21 **Facilities:** 🅿 ♿ toilets for disabled shop ✖ (ex guide dogs) 📶

ROYAL BOTANIC GARDEN EDINBURGH

20A Inverleith Row EH3 5LR
➲ (1m N of city centre, off the A902)
☎ 0131 552 7171 📠 0131 248 2901 `FREE`
e-mail: info@rbge.org.uk

Established in 1670, on an area the size of a tennis court, the Garden is now over 70 acres of beautifully landscaped grounds. Spectacular features include the Rock Garden and the Chinese Hillside. The amazing glasshouses feature Britain's tallest palm house and the magnificent woodland gardens and arboretum.
Times: Open all year, daily; Apr-Sep, 10-7; Mar & Oct, 10-6; Nov-Feb, 10-4. (Closed 25 Dec & 1 Jan). Facilities close 30 mins before the Garden. **Facilities:** 🅿 (restricted at certain times) 🍴 ✖ licensed ♿ (wheelchairs available at east/west gates) toilets for disabled shop garden centre ✖ (ex guide dogs) 📶

ROYAL MUSEUM

Chambers St EH1 1JF
➲ (5min from Edinburgh Castle `FREE`
and the Royal Mile in city centre)
☎ 0131 247 4219 (info) 📠 0131 220 4819
e-mail: info@nms.ac.uk

This magnificent museum houses extensive international collections covering the Decorative Arts, Natural History, Science, Technology and Working Life, and Geology. Temporary exhibitions, films, lectures and concerts take place throughout the year.
Times: Open all year, Mon-Sat 10-5, Sun 12-5 (Tue late opening till 8). (Closed 25 Dec. Phone for times on 26 Dec/1 Jan). **Facilities:** 🅿 🍴 ✖ licensed ♿ (induction loops) toilets for disabled shop ✖ (ex assist dogs) 📶

THE ROYAL YACHT BRITANNIA
Ocean Terminal, Leith EH6 6JJ
➲ (Situated within Ocean Terminal)
☎ 0131 555 5566 🖷 0131 555 8835
e-mail: enquiries@tryb.co.uk

Visit the Royal Yacht Britannia, now in Edinburgh's historic port of Leith. The experience starts in the Visitor Centre where you can discover Britannia's fascinating story. Then step aboard for a self-led audio tour which takes you around five decks giving you a unique insight into what life was like for the Royal Family, Officers and Yachtsmen. Highlights include the State Apartments, Admirals Cabin, Engine Room, Laundry, Sick Bay and Royal Marine Barracks.
Times: Open Jan-Mar & Oct-Dec: 10-3.30 (close 5). Apr-Sep 9.30-4.30 (close 6) **Fee:** ✱ £8 (ch under 5 free, 5-17 £4, pen £6). Family ticket (2adults & 3 ch) £20. **Facilities:** 🅿 & (lift to ship, all areas ramped) toilets for disabled shop ✖ (ex guide dogs) ◥

SCOTCH WHISKY HERITAGE CENTRE
354 Castlehill, The Royal Mile EH1 2NE
☎ 0131 220 0441 🖷 0131 220 6288
e-mail: enquiry@whisky-heritage.co.uk
This fascinating heritage centre reveals the history of the Scottish Whisky industry. The tour has four main areas: The Making of Scotch Whisky, The Distillery, The Blender's Ghost, and Whisky Barrel Ride. The Whisky Bond Bar has over 270 different whiskies available.
Times: ✱ Open daily, 10-5.30 (extended in summer). (Closed 25 Dec). **Facilities:** 🅿 (0.25m) ◕ & (braille script) toilets for disabled shop ✖ (ex guide dogs) ◥

SCOTTISH NATIONAL GALLERY OF MODERN ART
Belford Rd EH4 3DR
➲ (in the West End, 20min walk from Haymarket station)
☎ 0131 624 6200 🖷 0131 343 3250
e-mail: enquiries@nationalgalleries.org
An outstanding collection of 20th-century painting, sculpture and graphic art. Includes major works by Matisse, Picasso, Bacon, Moore and Lichtenstein and an exceptional group of

continued

Scottish paintings. Set in leafy grounds with a sculpture garden.
Times: Open all year, Mon-Sat 10-5 & Sun 12-5. Extended opening hours during the Edinburgh Festival. (Closed 25-26 Dec). **Fee:** ✱ Free. Admission charged to some major exhibitions. **Facilities:** 🅿 ◕ & (ramps & lift) toilets for disabled shop ✖ (ex guide dogs) ◥

SCOTTISH NATIONAL PORTRAIT GALLERY
1 Queen St EH2 1JD
➲ (parallel to Princes Street, just behind St Andrew Square)
☎ 0131 624 6200 🖷 0131 558 3691   **FREE**
e-mail: enquiries@nationalgalleries.org
The collection provides a visual history of Scotland from the 16th century to the present day, told through the portraits of the people who shaped it. Among the most famous are Mary, Queen of Scots, Ramsay's portrait of David Hume and Raeburn's Sir Walter Scott. The building also houses the National Collection of Photography.
Times: Open all year, daily, Mon-Sat 10-5, Sun 12-5. Extended opening hours during the Edinburgh Festival. (Closed 25-26 Dec). **Facilities:** 🅿 (200yds) ◕ & (ramps & lift) toilets for disabled shop ✖ (ex guide dogs) ◥

THE WRITERS' MUSEUM
Lady Stair's House, Lady Stair's Close, Lawnmarket EH1 2PA
➲ (off the Royal Mile)   **FREE**
☎ 0131 529 4901 🖷 0131 220 5057
e-mail: enquiries@writersmuseum.demon.co.uk
Situated in the historic Lady Stair's House which dates from 1622, the museum houses various objects associated with Robert Burns, Sir Walter Scott and Robert Louis Stevenson. Temporary exhibitions are planned throughout the year.
Times: Open all year, Mon-Sat 10-5. (During Festival period only, Sun 2-5). **Facilities:** 🅿 (500mtrs) (parking meters) shop ✖ (ex guide dogs)

GOGAR   Map 11 NT17

SUNTRAP GARDEN
43 Gogarbank EH12 9BY
➲ (between A8 & A71 W of city bypass)
☎ 0131 339 7283 🖷 0131 339 2891
e-mail: suntrap@btopenworld.com
The three-acre garden comprises of many gardens within a single garden, including Italian, Rock, Peat and Woodland.
Times: Open all year: Oct-Apr, 10-4; May-Sep, 10-6 **Fee:** £1 (accompanied ch and NT members free). **Facilities:** 🅿 & toilets for disabled garden centre (open Mon-Fri) ✖ (ex on lead)

SOUTH QUEENSFERRY   Map 11 NT17

DALMENY HOUSE
EH30 9TQ
☎ 0131 331 1888 🖷 0131 331 1788
e-mail: events@dalmeny.co.uk
This is the home of the Earl and the Countess of Rosebery, whose family have lived here for over 300 years. The house, however, dates from 1815 when it was built in Tudor Gothic style. There is fine French furniture, tapestries and porcelain from the Rothschild Mentmore collection. Early Scottish furniture is also shown, with 18th-century portraits, Rosebery

continued

racing mementoes, a display of pictures and one of the world's most important Napoleonic collections.
Times: Open Jul-Aug, Sun, Mon & Tue 2-5.30. Last admission 4.30. Open other times by arrangement for groups. **Fee:** ✷ £4 (ch 10-16 £2, pen £3.50, students £3). Party 20+. **Facilities:** 🅿 💺 ♿ toilets for disabled ✖ (ex guide dogs or in grounds)

HOPETOUN HOUSE
EH30 9SL
➲ (2m W of Forth Road Bridge, off A904)
☎ 0131 331 2451 ▤ 0131 319 1885
e-mail: marketing@hopetounhouse.com
Hopetoun House at South Queensferry is just a short drive from Edinburgh and has all the ingredients for a great family day out. Whether it is a leisurely stroll, afternoon tea or a touch of nostalgia you crave, Hopetoun will fit the bill. Built some 300 years ago, it is a delight to wander the corridors and historical rooms of one of the most splendid examples of the work of Scottish architects Sir William Bruce and William Adam. It shows some of the finest examples in Scotland of carving, wainscoting and ceiling painting. With 100 acres of parkland including a deep park, the gardens are a colourful carpet of seasonal flowers. After a gentle walk, indulge yourself with a traditional tea and a browse through our shop.
Times: Open daily Apr-Sep **Facilities:** 🅿 💺 ✖ licensed ♿ (ramps) toilets for disabled shop ✖ (ex on leads) ⌖

INCHCOLM ABBEY
Inchcolm Island (1.5m S of Aberdour Access by ferry Apr-Sep)
☎ 01383 823332
Situated on a green island on the Firth of Forth, the Augustinian abbey was founded in about 1192 by Alexander I. The well-preserved remains include a fine 13th-century octagonal chapter house and a 13th-century wall painting.
Times: ✷ Open Apr-Sep, daily 9.30-6.30. **Facilities:** ♿ toilets for disabled shop ✖ ▮

QUEENSFERRY MUSEUM
53 High St EH30 9HP
☎ 0131 331 5545 ▤ 0131 557 3346
The museum commands magnificent views of the two great bridges spanning the Forth and traces the history of the people of Queensferry and Dalmeny, the historic passage to Fife, the construction of the rail and road bridges and the wildlife of the Forth estuary. An ancient annual custom, in August, is Burry Man, who is clad from head to toe in burrs, and parades through the town.
Times: Open all year, Mon & Thu-Sat 10-1, 2.15-5 (Sun noon-5)
Facilities: 🅿 (0.25m) shop ✖ (ex guide dogs)

GLASGOW

GLASGOW	Map 11 NS56

BURRELL COLLECTION
Pollok Country Park G43 1AT
➲ (2m S of city centre)   FREE
☎ 0141 287 2550 ▤ 0141 287 2597
Set in Pollok Country Park, this award-winning building

makes the priceless works of art on display seem almost part of the woodland setting. Shipping magnate Sir William Burrell's main interests were medieval Europe, Oriental art and European paintings. Colourful paintings and stained glass show the details of medieval life. Furniture, paintings, sculpture, armour and weapons help to complete the picture. Rugs, ceramics and metalwork represent the art of Islam. There is also a strong collection of Chinese and other Oriental ceramics. Paintings on display include works by Bellini, Rembrandt and the French Impressionists.
Times: Open all year, Mon-Thu & Sat 10-5, Fri & Sun 11-5.
Facilities: 🅿 (charged) 💺 ♿ (wheelchairs available, tape guides for blind) toilets for disabled shop ✖

CLYDEBUILT
Braehead Shopping Centre, King Inch Rd G51 4BN
➲ (M8 junct 25A, 26, follow signs for Braehead Shopping Centre)
☎ 0141 886 1013 ▤ 0141 886 1015
e-mail: clydebuilt@tinyworld.co.uk
On the banks of the River Clyde, home of the Scottish shipbuilding industry, visitors can discover how Glasgow's famous ships were built, from the design stages through to the launch. There are also displays on the textile and cotton industries, iron and steel, and tobacco. Hands-on activities allow you to operate a real ship's engine, become a ship's riveter, and steer a virtual ship up the Clyde.
Times: Open Mon-Thu & Sat 10-6; Sun 11-5. (Closed Fri) **Fee:** ✷ £3.50 (ch & concessions £1.75). Family ticket £8 **Facilities:** 🅿 ♿ lift toilets for disabled shop ✖ (ex guide dogs)

GALLERY OF MODERN ART
Royal Exchange Square G1 3AH
➲ (centre of Glasgow, just off Buchanan St and close to Central Station)   FREE
☎ 0141 229 1996 ▤ 0141 204 5316
Set in an elegant neo-classical building the gallery houses Glasgow's collection of post modern and contemporary art over four floors, named after the natural elements of Fire, Earth, Water and Air. A thought-provoking programme of temporary exhibitions and workshops focus on contemporary social issues, often featuring groups marginalized in today's society.
Times: Open all year, Mon-Tue & Sat 10-5, Thu 10-8, Fri & Sun 11-5.
Facilities: 🅿 (200yds) 💺 ♿ toilets for disabled shop ✖

GLASGOW BOTANIC GARDENS
730 Great Western Rd G12 0UE
➲ (From M8 jnct 17 onto A82 Dumbarton. Approx 2-3m the Botanic Gardens are on the right)   FREE
☎ 0141 334 2422 ▤ 0141 339 6964
e-mail: gbg@land.glasgow.gov.uk
Home of the national collections of Dendrobium Orchids, Begonias and tree ferns. The Victorian Kibble Palace has marble statuary secreted among the plant collections. The Gardens consist of an arboretum, herbaceous borders, an herb garden and unusual vegetables.
Times: Open all year. Gardens open daily 7am-dusk, Glasshouses 10-4.45 (4.15 in winter). **Facilities:** 🅿 street parking 💺 ♿ toilets for disabled (ex in grounds)

continued

GLASGOW CATHEDRAL

Castle St G4 0QZ

➲ (M8 junct 15, in centre of Glasgow)
☎ 0141 552 6891

The only Scottish mainland medieval cathedral to have survived the Reformation complete (apart from its western towers). Built during the 13th to 15th centuries over the supposed site of the tomb of St Kentigern. Notable features in this splendid building are the elaborately vaulted crypt, which included an introductory display and collection of carved stones, the stone screen of the early 15th century and the unfinished Blackadder Aisle.

Times: Open all year, Apr-Sep, Mon-Sat 9.30-6 (last admission 5.30), Sun 1-5; Oct-Mar, Mon-Sat 9.30-4 (last admission 3.30), Sun 1-4.
Facilities: ও (telephone for disabled access details) shop ✈ ▮

GLASGOW SCIENCE CENTRE

50 Pacific Quay G51 1EA

➲ (Follow brown signs from M8 junct 24 or M77 junct 21)
☎ 0141 420 5000 ▤ 0141 420 5010
e-mail: admin@gsc.org.uk

This ground-breaking new venue comprises three landmark buildings that form a stunning complex on the south bank of the River Clyde. Scotland's first IMAX cinema; the 10,500 sq metre Science Mall which houses exhibits including a planetarium, laboratories and a science theatre; and the Glasgow Tower, a remarkable 100mtr high free-standing structure that gives breathtaking views of the city.

Times: Science Mall: Open, daily 10-6. Imax open from 12-6, Thu-Sat late night opening. **Fee:** ✷ Science Mall: £6.95 (ch & concessions £4.95). Family ticket £17.95. Imax: £5.95 (ch & concessions £4.45). Family Ticket £17.95. Discounts available for tickets to more than one attraction. **Facilities:** ▣ ▣ ও (induction loops) toilets for disabled shop ✈ (guide/hearing dogs) ▰

GREENBANK GARDEN

Flenders Rd, Clarkston G76 8RB

➲ (off A726 on southern outskirts of the city)
☎ 0141 639 3281

The spacious, walled woodland gardens are attractively laid out in the grounds of an elegant Georgian house, and best seen between April and October. A wide range of flowers and shrubs are grown, with the idea of helping private gardeners to look at possibilities for their own gardens. A greenhouse and garden designed for the disabled gardener also displays specialised tools.

Times: Open daily 9.30-sunset **Fee:** ✷ £3.50 (concession £2.60) Family ticket £9.50. Groups adult £2.80, child/school £1. Please book groups in advance. Admission free to NTS members. For other details please phone 0131 243 9387 **Facilities:** ▣ ▣ ও (wheelchairs available) toilets for disabled shop (& plant sales) ✈ (ex guide dogs) ♨

HOLMWOOD HOUSE

61-63 Netherlee House, Cathcart G44 3YG

➲ (Off Clarkston Rd)
☎ 0141 637 2129 ▤ 0141 571 0184

Built in the mid 19th-century, the architectural style of the house is an adaptation of classical Greek. Many rooms are richly ornamented in wood, plaster and marble.

Times: Open - Apr-Oct, daily 12-5. Morning visits available for pre-booked groups. **Fee:** ✷ £3.50 (concession £2.60). Family ticket £9.50. Groups adult £2.80, child/school £1. Please book groups in advance.

HOUSE FOR AN ART LOVER

10 Dumbreck Rd, Bellahouston Park G41 5BW

➲ (Exit M8 W junct 23 marked B768, left at top of slip road onto Dumbreck Road. Bellahouston Park on right)
☎ 0141 353 4770 ▤ 0141 353 4771
e-mail: info@houseforanartlover.co.uk

Originally designed by Glasgow's most celebrated architect, Charles Rennie Mackintosh, in 1901, this unusual cultural, corporate and academic resource began construction in 1989 and was completed in 1996. Contains art galleries and rooms that can be hired for conferences, private parties and weddings.

Times: ✷ Open Apr-Sep, Sun-Thu 10-4 & Sat 10-3; Oct-Mar, Sat-Sun 10-4, telephone for wkday opening details. **Facilities:** ▣ ▣ ✕ licensed ও (lift to 2nd floor) toilets for disabled shop ✈ (ex guide dogs) ▰

HUNTERIAN ART GALLERY

The University of Glasgow G12 8QQ
☎ 0141 330 5431 ▤ 0141 330 3618
e-mail: hunter@museum.gla.ac.uk

The founding collection is made up of paintings bequeathed in the 18th century by Dr William Hunter, including works by Rembrandt and Stubbs. The Gallery now has works by James McNeill Whistler, major displays of paintings by the Scottish Colourists, and a graphics collection holding some 300,000 prints. A popular feature of the Charles Rennie Mackintosh collection is the re-construction of the interiors of The Mackintosh House.

Times: ✷ Open all year. Main gallery Mon-Sat 9.30-5. Mackintosh House Mon-Sat 9.30-12.30 & 1.30-5. Telephone for BH closures.
Facilities: ▣ (500 yds) (pay & display) ও (lift, wheelchair available) toilets for disabled shop ✈ (ex guide dogs) ▰

HUNTERIAN MUSEUM

The University of Glasgow G12 8QQ

➲ (2m W of city centre)
☎ 0141 330 4221 ▤ 0141 330 3617
e-mail: rpurss@museum.gla.ac.uk

Named after the 18th-century physician, Dr William Hunter, who bequeathed his large and important collections of coins, medals, fossils, geological specimens and archaeological and ethnographic items to the university. The exhibits are shown in the main building of the university, and temporary exhibitions are held.

Times: ✷ Open all year, Mon-Sat 9.30-5. (Closed certain BH's phone for details). **Facilities:** ▣ (100yds) ও (access by lift by prior arrangement) toilets for disabled shop ✈ (ex guide dogs) ▰

HUTCHESONS' HALL

158 Ingram St G1 1EJ

➲ (near SE corner of George Square)
☎ 0141 552 8391 ▤ 0141 552 7031
e-mail: hutchesonshall@nts.org.uk

This handsome early 19th-century building was designed by David Hamilton and houses a visitor centre and shop. There is a video about Glasgow's merchant city, and the Hall can be booked for functions. Telephone for details of concerts, recitals, etc.

Times: Gallery: open Mon-Sat, 10-5. Closed 24 Dec-mid Jan. Hall: open subject to functions. **Facilities:** ▣ (on street) (meters)(outside for disabled) ও toilets for disabled shop ✈ ♨

McLellan Galleries

270 Sauchiehall St G2 3EH
➲ (N side of Sauchiehall St, close to the Glasgow School of Art)
☎ 0141 565 4100 📠 0141 565 4111 `FREE`

The McLennan Galleries first opened in 1854 and featured the personal collection of Glasgow industrialist and coachbuilder Archibald McLennan. With over 1,200 sq metres of top gallery space, the McLellan Galleries provide Glasgow Museums with the opportunity to bring to Glasgow major exhibitions and establish Glasgow as Britain's second art city. With Kelvingrove Art Gallery closed for refurbishment, the McLennan Galleries provides a high-quality temporary exhibition space for some of the highlights from Kelvingrove's fine and decorative art collections.
Times: Open all year, Mon-Thu & Sat 10-5, Fri & Sun 11-5.
Facilities: 🅿 (500mtrs) 💺 ♿ (assistance available) toilets for disabled shop ✖

Museum of Transport

1 Burnhouse Rd G3 8DP
➲ (1.5m W of city centre)
☎ 0141 287 2720 📠 0141 287 2692 `FREE`

Walk into the Museum of Transport and the first impression is of gleaming metalwork and bright paint. All around you there are cars, caravans, carriages and carts, fire engines, buses, trams and steam locomotives. The museum uses its collections of vehicles and models to tell the story of transport by land and sea, with a unique Glasgow flavour. Visitors can even go window shopping along the recreated Kelvin Street of 1938. Upstairs 250 ship models tell the story of the great days of Clyde shipbuilding. The Museum of Transport has something for everyone.
Times: Open all year, Mon-Thu & Sat 10-5, Fri & Sun 11-5.
Facilities: 🅿 (charged) 💺 ♿ (assistance available) toilets for disabled shop ✖

Open Museum

161 Woodhead Rd, South Nitshill Ind Estate G53 7NN
☎ 0141 552 2356 `FREE`
📠 0141 552 2356
e-mail: morag.macpherson@cls.glasgow.gov.uk

This unusual museum is actually a kind of storage facility for objects from the Kelvingrove Art Gallery and Museum, which is undergoing refurbishment. This may explain the Open Museum's location on an industrial estate. This new facility will contain a learning centre, a library, and an activity room, although visitors should be aware that tours and research visits must be booked in advance.
Times: Open all year Mon-Thu & Sat 10-5, Fri-Sun 11-5.

People's Palace

Glasgow Green G40 1AT
➲ (1m SE of city centre)
☎ 0141 554 0223 📠 0141 550 0892 `FREE`

Glasgow grew from a medieval town by the Cathedral to the Second City of the British Empire. Trade with the Americans, and later industry, made the city rich. But not everyone shared in Glasgow wealth. The People's Palace on historic Glasgow Green shows how ordinary Glaswegians worked,

continued

lived and played. Visitors can discover how a family lived in a typical one-room Glasgow 'single end' tenement flat, see Billy Connolly's amazing banana boots, learn to speak Glesga, take a trip 'doon the watter' and visit the Winter Gardens.
Times: Open all year, Mon-Thu & Sat 10-5, Fri & Sun 11-5.
Facilities: 🅿 💺 ♿ toilets for disabled shop garden centre ✖

Pollok House

Pollok Country Park, 2060 Pollokshaws Rd G43 1AT
➲ (2m S of city centre)
☎ 0141 616 6410 📠 0141 616 6521
e-mail: pollokhouse@nts.org.uk

Given to the city at the same time as the land for Pollok Country Park, the house contains the remarkable Stirling Maxwell collection of Spanish paintings, including works by El Greco, Murillo and Goya. Silver, ceramics and furniture collected by the family over the generations are also on display.
Times: House: open daily 10-5, closed 25 & 26 Dec & 1 & 2 Jan.
Fee: ✱ Apr-Oct £5 (concession £3.75) Family ticket £13.50. Groups adult £4, child/school £1. Please book groups in advance. Admission free to NTS members. For other details please phone 0131 243 9387.
Facilities: 🅿 💺 ♿ shop ✖

Provand's Lordship

3 Castle St G4 0RB
➲ (1m E of city centre)
☎ 0141 552 8819 📠 0141 552 4744 `FREE`

Provand's Lordship is the only house to survive from Medieval Glasgow. For over five hundred years it has watched the changing fortunes of the city and the nearby Cathedral. Bishop Andrew Muirhead built the house as part of St Nicholas' Hospital in 1971. The prebendary of Barlanark later bought it for use as a manse. Inside, the displays recreate home life in the middle ages. Behind the house is the St Nicholas Garden, built in 1997. It is a medical herb garden, in keeping with the original purpose of the house.
Times: Open all year, Mon-Thu & Sat 10-5, Fri & Sun 11-5.
Facilities: 🅿 (50 yds) 💺 (please contact for details) shop ✖

St Mungo Religious Life & Art Museum

2 Castle St G4 0RH
➲ (1m NE of city centre)
☎ 0141 553 2557 📠 0141 552 4744 `FREE`

The award-winning St Mungo Museum explores the importance of religion in peoples' everyday lives and art. It aims to promote understanding and respect between people of different faiths and of none. Highlights of the collection include the Salvador Dali painting *Christ of St John of the Cross*. The museum also features stained glass, objects, statues and video footage. Within the grounds is Britain's first Japanese Zen garden.
Times: Open all year, Mon-Thu & Sat 10-5, Fri & Sun 11-5.
Facilities: 🅿 (50yds) 💺 ♿ (taped information & lift) toilets for disabled shop ✖

The AA also publishes a guide to
Pet Friendly Places to Stay

THE SCOTTISH FOOTBALL MUSEUM

The National Stadium, Hampden Park G42 9BA

➲ (3m S of city centre, follow brown tourist signs)

☎ 0141 616 6139   **2 for 1**

🖷 0141 616 6101

e-mail: info@scottishfootballmuseum.org.uk

Using 2500 pieces of footballing memorabilia, the Scottish Football Museum covers such themes as football's origins, women's football, fan culture, other games influenced by football, and even some social history. The exhibits include the world's oldest football, trophy and ticket, a reconstructed 1903 changing room and press box, and items of specific import, such as Kenny Dalglish's silver cap, Jimmy McGrory's boots, and the ball from Scotland's 5-1 win over England in 1928. **Times:** Open Mon-Sat 10-5, Sun 11-5. (Closed match days, special events and Xmas/New Year, please telephone in advance for confirmation) **Fee:** ✱ Museum or stadium tour £5 (concessions & ch under 16 £2.50). Combined ticket £7.50 (concessions & ch under 16 £3.75) **Facilities:** 🅿 💷 ♿ toilets for disabled shop ✖ (ex guide dogs) ◥

THE TALL SHIP AT GLASGOW HARBOUR

100 Stobcross Rd G3 8QQ

➲ (from M8 junct 19 onto A814 follow signs for 'the tall ship')

☎ 0141 222 2513   🖷 0141 222 2536   **2 for 1**

e-mail: info@thetallship.com

Visit The Tall Ship at Glasgow Harbour and step back in time to the days of sail. Experience Glasgow's maritime history at first hand and explore the UK's only remaining Clydebuilt sailing ship, the Glenlee. Exhibitions on board and in our visitor centre on the quayside tell the story of the ship and the Glasgow Harbour area. If you have ever wondered what it would have been like to be a sailor on a tall ship, this is your chance to find out! Children can have fun by joining in the hunt for Jock, the ship's cat. An unmissable experience, The Tall Ship offers guided tours, changing exhibitions, children's activities, a nautical gift shop and cafe. **Times:** Open daily Mar-Oct 10-5, Nov-Feb 11-4. **Fee:** £4.50 (concessions £3.25, 1 ch free with paying adult/concession, additional ch £2.50). **Facilities:** 🅿 💷 ✖ licensed ♿ toilets for disabled ◥

TENEMENT HOUSE

145 Buccleuch St, Garnethill G3 6QN

➲ (N of Charing Cross)

☎ 0141 333 0183

e-mail: tenementhouse@nts.org.uk

This shows an unsung but once-typical side of Glasgow life: it is a first-floor flat, built in 1892, with a parlour, bedroom, kitchen and bathroom, furnished with the original recess beds, kitchen range, sink, and coal bunker, among other articles. The home of Agnes Toward from 1911 to 1965, the flat was bought by an actress who preserved it as a 'time capsule'. The contents vividly portray the life of one section of Glasgow society. **Times:** Open Mar-Oct, daily 2-5. Weekday morning visits available for pre-booked educational & other groups. **Fee:** ✱ £3.50 (concession £2.60) Family ticket £9.50. Groups adult £2.80, child/school £1. Admission free to NTS members. For other details please phone 0131 243 9387. **Facilities:** 🅿 (100yds) (restricted, recommend parking in town) (braille guide) ✖ (ex guide dogs) ¥

UNIVERSITY OF GLASGOW VISITOR CENTRE

University Av G12 8QQ

➲ (M8 junct 19 (E) or junct 18(W))

☎ 0141 330 5511   🖷 0141 330 5225

e-mail: visitorcentre@gla.ac.uk

The Visitor Centre is spacious and pleasant, with leaflets, publications and video displays explaining how the university works and its history, plus what courses are available and which university events are open to the public. It forms the starting point for guided tours of the university's historic attractions, including the Hunterian Museum, Memorial Chapel, Bute and Randolph Halls, Professors' Square and Lion and Unicorn Staircase. **Times:** Open all year, Mon-Sat 9.30-5. Also May-Sep, Sun 2-5. In summer guided tours of the university start from the Visitor Centre at 2pm on Mon-Sat, telephone 0141 330 5511. **Fee:** ✱ Free. Charge made for tour. **Facilities:** 🅿 (880yds) (few spaces available) 💷 ♿ toilets for disabled shop ✖ ¥

CLACKMANNANSHIRE

ALLOA   Map 11 NS89

ALLOA TOWER

Alloa Park FK10 1PP

➲ (on A907)

☎ 01259 211701   🖷 01259 218744

Beautifully restored, the tower, completed in 1467, is the only remaining part of the ancestral home of the Earls of Mar. The structure retains rare medieval features, notably the complete timber roof structure and groin vaulting. A superb loan collection of portraits and chattels of the Erskine family includes paintings by Raeburn. **Times:** Open Apr-Oct, daily 1-5. Weekday morning visits available for pre-booked groups. **Fee:** ✱ £3.50 (concessions £2.60) Groups adult £2.80, child/school group £1. Family ticket £9.50. Admission free to NTS members. For other details please phone (0131) 243 9387. **Facilities:** 🅿 ♿ toilets for disabled ✖ ¥

ALVA   Map 11 NS89

MILL TRAIL VISITOR CENTRE

Glentana Mill, West Stirling St FK12 5EN

➲ (situated on A91 approx 8m E of Stirling)

☎ 01259 769696   🖷 01259 763100

In the heart of Scotland's woollen mill country, the Centre recounts the history of Scotland's woollen and tweed traditions, and features machines from spinning wheels to large motorised looms of the type in use today. Hear 12 year old Mary describe her working day as a mill girl 150 years ago, and then contrast her story with our modern working woollen mill. Factory bargains and local crafts. Tourist information centre, café. **Times:** Open all year, Jan-Jun 10-5; Jul-Aug 9-5; Sep-Dec 10-5. **Facilities:** 🅿 💷 ♿ toilets for disabled shop ✖ (ex guide dogs) ◥

DOLLAR   Map 11 NS99

CASTLE CAMPBELL

FK14 7PP

➲ (10m E of Stirling on A91)

☎ 01259 742408

Traditionally known as the 'Castle of Gloom', the 15th to 17th-century tower stands in the picturesque Ochil Hills,

continued

gives wonderful views, and can be reached by a walk through the magnificent Dollar Glen. Care must be taken in or after rain when the path may be dangerous.
Times: ✱ Open all year, Apr-Sep, daily 9.30-6.30; Oct-Mar, Mon-Sat 9.30-4.30, Sun 2-4.30. (Closed Thu & Fri in winter & 25-26 Dec).
Facilities: ☐ ✗ shop █ ♨

DUMFRIES & GALLOWAY

ARDWELL   Map 10 NX14
ARDWELL HOUSE GARDENS
DG9 9LY
➲ (10m S of Stranraer, on A716)
☎ 01776 860227   ▤ 01776 860288
Country house gardens and grounds with flowering shrubs and woodland walks. Plants for sale. House not open to the public.
Times: Open Mar-Oct, 10-5. Walled garden & greenhouses close at 5pm. **Fee:** ✱ £2 (ch & pen £1). **Facilities:** ☐ garden centre

CAERLAVEROCK   Map 11 NY06
CAERLAVEROCK CASTLE
Glencaple DG1 4RU
➲ (8m SE of Dumfries, on B725)
☎ 01387 770244
This ancient seat of the Maxwell family is a splendid medieval stronghold dating back to the 13th century. It has high walls and round towers, with machicolations added in the 15th century.
Times: ✱ Open all year, Apr-Sep, daily 9.30-6.30; Oct-Mar, Mon-Sat 9.30-4.30, Sun 2-4.30. (Closed Thu pm, Fri & Sun am in winter).
Facilities: ☐ ✗ ♿ toilets for disabled shop █

WWT CAERLAVEROCK
Eastpark Farm DG1 4RS
➲ (9m SE of Dumfries, signposted from A75)
☎ 01387 770200   ▤ 01387 770539   `2 for 1`
e-mail: caerlaverock@wwt.org.uk
This internationally important wetland is the winter habitat of the entire Svalbard population of Barnacle Geese which spends the winter on the Solway Firth. Observation facilities include twenty hides, three towers and a heated observatory. A wide variety of other wildlife can be seen, notably the rare Natterjack Toad and a family of Barn Owls which can be observed via a CCTV system.
Times: Open daily 10-5. (Closed 25 Dec). **Fee:** ✱ £4 (ch £2.50 & concessions £3.25). Family ticket £10.50 **Facilities:** ☐ ▱ ♿ toilets for disabled shop ✙ (ex guide dogs)

CARDONESS CASTLE   Map 11 NX55
CARDONESS CASTLE
DG7 2EH
➲ (1m SW of Gatehouse of Fleet off A75)
☎ 01557 814427
A 15th-century stronghold overlooking the Water of Fleet. It was once the home of the McCullochs of Galloway. The architectural details inside the tower are of very high quality.
Times: ✱ Open all year, Apr-Sep, daily 9.30-6.30; Oct-Mar, wknds only. (Closed 25-26 Dec). **Facilities:** ☐ shop █

CASTLE DOUGLAS   Map 11 NX76
THREAVE CASTLE
DG7 1RX
➲ (3m W on A75)
☎ 0411 223101
Archibald the Grim built this lonely castle in the late 14th century. It stands on an islet in the River Dee, and is four storeys high with round towers guarding the outer wall. The island is reached by boat.
Times: ✱ Open Apr-Sep, daily 9.30-6.30. **Facilities:** ☐ ✙ █

THREAVE GARDEN & ESTATE
DG7 1RX
➲ (1m W of Castle Douglas off A75)
☎ 01556 502575   ▤ 01556 502683
e-mail: threave@nts.org.uk
The best time to visit is in spring when there is a dazzling display of daffodils. The garden is a delight in all seasons, however, and is home to the National Trust for Scotland's School of Practical Gardening.
Times: Estate & Garden: all year, daily 9.30-sunset. Walled Garden & Glasshouse daily 9.30-5. Visitor Centre, Countryside Centre & exhibition Feb-Mar & Nov-23 Dec, daily 10-4; Apr-Oct, daily 9.30-5.30. House Mar-Oct, Wed-Fri & Sun, 11-4 (guided tours only, admission by timed ticket) **Fee:** ✱ £9 (concession £6.50) Family ticket £23. Garden only £5 (concession £3.75) Admission free for NTS members. For other details please phone 0131 243 9387. **Facilities:** ☐ ✗ licensed ♿ (wheelchairs available incl. electric wheelchair) toilets for disabled shop garden centre ✙ (ex guide dogs) ♨

CREETOWN   Map 11 NX45
CREETOWN GEM ROCK MUSEUM
Chain Rd DG8 7HJ
➲ (follow signs from A75 at Creetown bypass)
☎ 01671 820357 & 820554   `2 for 1`
▤ 01671 820554
e-mail: gem.rock@btinternet.com
A spectacular collection of gems, crystals, minerals and fossils. Interactive computer displays provide an opportunity to learn more, and audiovisual displays explain how minerals are formed. World-class British specimens e.g. Fluorite, calcite and hemalite.
Times: Open Etr-Sep, daily 9.30-5.30; Oct-Nov & Mar-Etr, daily 10-4; Dec-Feb, wknds 10-4 or by appointment wkdays. (Closed 23 Dec-Jan). **Fee:** £3.25 (ch £1.75, concessions £2.25, pen £2.75). Family ticket £8.25 (2ad+3ch). Party. **Facilities:** ☐ ▱ ♿ toilets for disabled shop ✙ (ex guide dogs) ◄

DRUMCOLTRAN TOWER   Map 11 NX86
DRUMCOLTRAN TOWER
➲ (7m NE of Dalbeattie, among   `FREE`
farm buildings off A711)
A well-preserved tower of mid 16th-century date simply planned and built, sitting within a busy modern farmyard.
Times: Open at any reasonable time. **Facilities:** ☐ ✙ █

DUMFRIES Map 11 NX97

BURNS MAUSOLEUM

St Michael's Churchyard

☎ 01387 255297 ▤ 01387 265081 `FREE`

e-mail: dumfriesmuseum@dumgal.gov.uk

The mausoleum is in the form of a Greek temple, and contains the tombs of Robert Burns, his wife Jean Armour, and their five sons. A sculptured group shows the Muse of Poetry flinging her cloak over Burns at the plough.
Times: Unrestricted access. **Facilities:** P (50yds) & (visitors with mobility difficulties tel 01387 255297)

DUMFRIES MUSEUM & CAMERA OBSCURA

The Observatory, Rotchell Rd DG2 7SW

➲ (Take A75 from S Carlisle or SW from Castle Douglas, museum is situated in Maxwellton area of Dumfries)

☎ 01387 253374 ▤ 01387 265081

e-mail: dumfriesmuseum@dumgal.gov.uk

Situated in and around the 18th-century windmill tower, the museum's collections were started over 150 years ago and exhibitions trace the history of the people and landscape of Dumfries and Galloway. The Camera Obscura is to be found on the top floor of the windmill tower.
Times: Open all year, Apr-Sep Mon-Sat 10-5, Sun, 2-5; Oct-Mar, Tue-Sat 10-1 & 2-5. **Fee:** ✱ Free except Camera Obscura £1.50 (concessions 75p) **Facilities:** P & (camera obscura not accessible, parking available) toilets for disabled shop

OLD BRIDGE HOUSE MUSEUM

Mill Rd DG2 7BE

➲ (at western end of Devorgilla's Bridge) `FREE`

☎ 01387 256904 ▤ 01387 265081

e-mail: dumfriesmuseum@dumgal.gov.uk

The Old Bridge House was built in 1660, and is the oldest house in Dumfries. A museum of everyday life in the town, it has an early 20th-century dentist's surgery, a Victorian nursery and kitchens of the 1850s and 1900s.
Times: Open Apr-Sep, Mon-Sat 10-5 & Sun 2-5. **Facilities:** P & shop

ROBERT BURNS CENTRE

Mill Rd DG2 7BE on Westbank of River Nith

☎ 01387 264808 ▤ 01387 265081 `FREE`

e-mail: dumfriesmuseum@dumgal.gov.uk

This award-winning centre explores the connections between Robert Burns and the town of Dumfries. Situated in the town's 18th-century watermill, the centre tells the story of Burns' last years spent in the busy streets and lively atmosphere of Dumfries in the 1790s. In the evening the centre shows feature films in the Film Theatre.
Times: Open all year, Apr-Sep, daily 10-8 (Sun 2-5); Oct-Mar, Tue-Sat 10-1 & 2-5. **Facilities:** P 🍴 ✕ & (induction loop hearing system in auditorium, chairlift) toilets for disabled shop ◥

ROBERT BURNS HOUSE

Burns St DG1 2PS

☎ 01387 255297 ▤ 01387 265081 `FREE`

e-mail: dumfriesmuseum@dumgal.gov.uk

It was here that Robert Burns spent the last three years of his short life; he died here in 1796. The house retains much of its
continued

18th-century character and contains many fascinating items connected with the poet. There is the chair in which he wrote his last poems, many original letters and manuscripts, and the famous Kilmarnock and Edinburgh editions of his work.
Times: Open all year, Apr-Sep, Mon-Sat 10-5, Sun 2-5; Oct-Mar Tue-Sat 10-1 & 2-5. **Facilities:** P (opposite) shop

DUNDRENNAN Map 11 NX74

DUNDRENNAN ABBEY

DG6 4QH

➲ (6.5m SE of Kirkcudbright, on A711)

☎ 01557 500262

The now ruined abbey was founded for the Cistercians. The east end of the church and the chapter house are of exceptional architectural quality. Mary, Queen of Scots is thought to have spent her last night in Scotland here on 15 May 1568, before seeking shelter in England, where she was imprisoned and eventually executed.
Times: ✱ Open, Apr-Sep, daily 9.30-6.30; Oct-Mar weekends 9.30-4.30, closed Thu pm & Fri. (Closed 25-26 Dec). **Facilities:** P & 🍴 █

GLENLUCE Map 10 NX15

GLENLUCE ABBEY

DG8 0AF

➲ (2m NW, off A75)

☎ 01581 300541

The abbey was founded for the Cistercians in 1192 by Roland, Earl of Galloway. The ruins include a vaulted chapter house, and stand in a beautiful setting.
Times: ✱ Open all year, Apr-Sep, daily 9.30-6.30; Oct-Mar, wknds only. (Closed 25-26 Dec). **Facilities:** P 🍴 & 🍴 █

KIRKCUDBRIGHT Map 11 NX65

BROUGHTON HOUSE & GARDEN

12 High St DG6 4JX

➲ (off A711/A755)

☎ 01557 330437

e-mail: aclipson@nts.scot.demon.co.uk

An 18th-century house where Edward A Hornel, one of the 'Glasgow Boys' group of artists, lived and worked from 1901-1933. It features a collection of his work, an extensive library of local history, including rare editions of Burns' works, and a Japanese-style garden that he created.
Times: House may be closed part 2004. Garden Feb-Mar & 1-20 Oct, Mon-Fri 11-4; Apr-Sep, Mon-Sat 11-5, Sun 1-5. **Fee:** ✱ £2 (concession £1). Admission free for NTS members. For other price details please phone 0131 243 9387. **Facilities:** P (on street) (limited space) 🍴 (ex guide dogs) ♿

MACLELLAN'S CASTLE

➲ (in Kirkcudbright on A711)

☎ 01557 331856

This handsome structure has been a ruin since the mid-18th-century. It was once an imposing castellated mansion, elaborately planned with fine architectural detail. Something of its 16th-century grandeur still remains.
Times: ✱ Open Apr-Sep, daily 9.30-6.30.
Facilities: P shop 🍴 🚲 █

STEWARTRY MUSEUM
St Mary St DG6 4AQ
➲ (from A711 through town, pass the parish church, museum in approx 200 mtrs on right)
☎ 01557 331643 🖷 01557 331643   **FREE**
e-mail: david@dumgal.gov.uk
A large and varied collection of archaeological, social history and natural history exhibits relating to the Stewartry district.
Times: Open Mar-Oct, Mon-Sat 11-4 (5pm in May, Jun & Sep; 6pm in Jul & Aug also Sun 2-5); Nov-Feb, Mon-Sat 11-4. **Facilities:** P (outside) & shop ✖ (ex guide dogs)

TOLBOOTH ART CENTRE
High St DG6 4JL
➲ (From A711, through town pass parish church & Stewartry Museum, take 1st right into High St)
☎ 01557 331556 🖷 01557 331643   **FREE**
e-mail: DavidD@dumgal.gov.uk
Dating from 1629, the Tolbooth was converted into an art centre and provides an interpretive introduction to the Kirkcudbright artists's colony, which flourished in the town from the 1880s. It also provides studio and exhibition space for contemporary local and visiting artists. There is a programe of exhibitions from March to October.
Times: Open Mar & Oct, Mon-Sat 11-4; May-Jun & Sep, Mon-Sat 10-6; Nov-Feb, Mon-Sat 11-4. Open Sun Jun-Sep 2-5. **Facilities:** P (on street parking) ♿ & (lift for access to upper floors) toilets for disabled shop ✖ (ex guide dogs)

NEW ABBEY   Map 11 NX96
NEW ABBEY CORN MILL
DG2 8BX
➲ (7m S of Dumfries on A710)
☎ 01387 850260
Built in the late 18th century, this water-driven corn mill is still in working order, and regular demonstrations are held.
Times: ✱ Open all year, Apr-Sep, daily 9.30-6.30; Oct-Mar, Mon-Sat 9.30-4.30, Sun 2-4.30. (Closed Thu pm & Fri in winter & 25-26 Dec). **Facilities:** P (100yds) shop ✖ ▌

SHAMBELLIE HOUSE MUSEUM OF COSTUME
DG2 8HQ
➲ (7m S of Dumfries, on A710)
☎ 01387 850375 🖷 01387 850461   **2 for 1**
e-mail: info@nms.ac.uk
Shambellie House is a beautiful Victorian country house set in attractive wooded grounds. You are invited to step back in time and experience Victorian and Edwardian grace and refinement. See period costume from the 1850s to the 1950s displayed in appropriate room settings with accessories, furniture and decorative art. Telephone for details of special events.
Times: Open Apr (or Good Fri if earlier)-Oct, 10-5. **Fee:** £2.50 (ch free, concession £1.50). **Facilities:** P ♿ & (house inaccessible for wheelchair users) shop ✖ (ex guide/hearing dogs)

SWEETHEART ABBEY
DG2 8BU
➲ (on A710)
☎ 01387 850397
Lady Devorgilla of Galloway founded Balliol College, Oxford in memory of her husband John Balliol; she also founded this abbey in his memory in 1273. When she died in 1289 she was buried in front of the high altar with the heart of her husband resting on her bosom; hence the name 'Sweetheart Abbey'. The abbey features an unusual precinct wall of enormous boulders.
Times: ✱ Open all year, Apr-Sep, daily 9.30-6.30; Oct-Mar, Mon-Sat 9.30-4.30, Sun 2-4.30. (Closed Thu pm & Fri & Sun am in winter & 25-26 Dec). Telephone for 2004 details **Facilities:** P & (with assistance) ✖ ▌

PALNACKIE   Map 11 NX85
ORCHARDTON TOWER   **FREE**
➲ (6m SE of Castle Douglas on A711)
A charming little tower house of mid-15th-century date. It is, uniquely, circular in plan.
Times: Open all reasonable times. (Closed 25-26 Dec). **Facilities:** P ✖ ▌

PORT LOGAN   Map 10 NX04
LOGAN BOTANIC GARDEN
DG9 9ND
➲ (on B7065, 14m S of Stranraer)
☎ 01776 860231 🖷 01776 860333
e-mail: logan@rbge.org.uk
Logan's exceptionally mild climate allows a colourful array of tender plants to thrive out-of-doors. Amongst the many highlights are tree ferns, cabhage palms, unusual shrubs, climbers and tender perennials found within the setting of the walled, water, terrace and woodland gardens.
Times: Open Mar-Oct, Mar & Oct daily 10-5. Apr-Sep 10-6 **Fee:** £3.50 (ch £1, concessions £3). Family £8 **Facilities:** P ✗ licensed & (access limited, wheelchairs available for loan) toilets for disabled shop garden centre ✖ (ex guide dogs)

RUTHWELL   Map 11 NY16
RUTHWELL CROSS   **FREE**
➲ (sited within the parish church on B724)
Now in a specially built apse in the parish church, the carved cross dates from the 7th or 8th centuries. Two faces show scenes from the Life of Christ; the others show scroll work, and parts of an ancient poem in Runic characters. It was broken up in the 18th century, but pieced together by a 19th-century minister.
Times: Open all reasonable times. Contact Key Keeper for access on 01387 870249. **Facilities:** P ✖ ▌

SAVINGS BANKS MUSEUM
DG1 4NN
➲ (off B724, 10m E of Dumfries & 6m W of Annan)
☎ 01387 870640   **FREE**
e-mail: tsbmuseum@btinternet.com
Housed in the building where Savings Banks first began, the museum traces their growth and development from 1810 up

continued

to the present day. The museum also traces the life of Dr
Henry Duncan, father of savings banks, and restorer of the
Ruthwell Cross. Multi-lingual leaflets available.
Times: Open all year, daily (ex Sun & Mon Oct-Etr), 10-1 & 2-5.
Facilities: ▣ & (touch facilities for blind, guide available) ✗ (ex
guide dogs)

SANQUHAR   Map 11 NS70
SANQUHAR TOLBOOTH MUSEUM
High St DG4 6BN
➲ (High Street Sanquhar, on A76
Dumfries-Kilmarnock Trunk Rd)   **FREE**
☎ 01659 250186 ▤ 01387 265081
e-mail: dumfriesmuseum@dumgal.gov.uk
Housed in the town's fine 18th-century tolbooth, the
museum tells the story of the mines and miners of the area,
its earliest inhabitants, native and Roman, the history and
customs of the Royal Burgh of Sanquhar and local traditions.
Times: Open Apr-Sep, Tue-Sat 10-1 & 2-5, Sun 2-5. **Facilities:** ▣ shop

STRANRAER   Map 10 NX06
CASTLE KENNEDY GARDENS
Stair Estates, Rephad DG9 8BX
➲ (5m E of Stranraer on A75, signposted at Castle
Kennedy Village)
☎ 01776 702024 ▤ 01776 706248
e-mail: info@castlekennedygardens.co.uk
Situated on a peninsula between two lochs, the gardens
around the Old Castle were first laid out in the early 18th
century. Noted for their rhododendrons and azaleas (at their
best May and early Jun) and walled kitchen garden with fine
herbaceous borders (best in Aug and Sep). The gardens
contain many avenues and walks amid beautiful scenery.
Times: Open Apr-Sep, daily 10-5. **Fee:** ✱ £3 (ch 15 £1, pen £2). Party
20+. **Facilities:** ▣ ▣ & toilets for disabled shop garden centre ◗

GLENWHAN GARDENS
Dunragit DG9 8PH
➲ (7m E of Stranraer)
☎ 01581 400222 ▤ 01581 400222
e-mail: tess@glenwhan.freeserve.co.uk
Enjoying spectacular views over the Mull of Galloway and
Luce Bay, Glenwhan is a beautiful 12 acre garden set on a
hillside. There are two lakes filled with rare species, alpines,
scree plants, heathers, conifers, roses, woodland walks and
fascinating garden sculpture.
Times: ✱ Open Apr-Sep 10-5 **Facilities:** ▣ ▣ ✗ licensed &
(wheelchairs provided) toilets for disabled shop garden centre ✗ (ex
on lead)

THORNHILL   Map 11 NX89
DRUMLANRIG CASTLE
DG3 4AQ
➲ (4m N of Thornhill off A76)
☎ 01848 330248 ▤ 01848 331682
e-mail: bre@drumlanrigcastle.org.uk
This unusual pink sandstone castle was built in the late 17th
century in Renaissance style. It contains a collection of
paintings by Rembrandt, Da Vinci, Holbein, and many others.
There is also French furniture, as well as silver and relics of
Bonnie Prince Charlie. The old stable block has a craft centre
continued

with resident craft workers, and the grounds offer extensive
gardens, working forge and woodland walks. For details of
special events phone 01848 331555.

Times: Open early May-late Aug, Castle open seven days a week.
Guided tours and restricted route may operate at various times, please
verify before visiting. **Fee:** ✱ £6 (ch £2 & pen £4. Grounds only £3.
Party 20+ £4 each. **Facilities:** ▣ ✗ licensed & (lift for wheelchair
users) toilets for disabled shop ✗ (ex in park on lead) ◗

WANLOCKHEAD   Map 11 NS81
MUSEUM OF LEAD MINING
ML12 6UT
➲ (Signposted from M74 and A76)
☎ 01659 74387 ▤ 01659 74481
e-mail: ggodfrey@goldpan.co.uk   **2 for 1**

Wanlockhead is Scotland's highest village, set in the
beautiful Lowther Hills. Visitors can see miners' cottages, the
miners' library as well as the 18th-century lead mine. Visitors
can also pan for gold.
Times: Open Apr-2 Nov, daily 10.30-4.30; Jul & Aug 10-5. **Fee:** ✱
£4.95 (ch £3.25, concessions £3.50). Family ticket £12 **Facilities:** ▣
▣ ✗ licensed & (induction loops) toilets for disabled shop ✗ (ex
guide dogs) ◗

The AA also publishes a guide to
Family Friendly Places to
Stay, Eat & Visit

WHITHORN   Map 10 NX44

WHITHORN-CRADLE OF CHRISTIANITY
45-47 George St DG8 8NS

➲ (Follow directions S from junct at Newton Stewart & Glenluce A75. Centre is on main street in centre of Whithorn)

☎ 01988 500508

e-mail: enquiries@whithorn.com

The Whithorn Dig is the site of the first Christian settlement in Scotland - the Candida Casa of St Ninian. Friendly guides explain the excavation, and there's a museum of Early Christian stones.

Times: ✱ Open daily, Apr-Oct 10.30-5. **Facilities:** 🅿 💻 ♿ (one short staircase with 'stairmatic') toilets for disabled shop 🍴

WHITHORN PRIORY
DG8 8PY

➲ (on A746)

☎ 01988 500508

The first Christian church in Scotland was founded here by St Ninian in 397AD, but the present ruins date from the 12th century. The ruins are sparse but there is a notable Norman door, the Latinus stone of the 5th century and other early Christian monuments.

Times: ✱ Open Apr-Sep daily 10-5 **Facilities:** 🅿 ♿ ✖ ▮

DUNDEE

DUNDEE   Map 11 NO43

BROUGHTY CASTLE MUSEUM
Broughty Ferry DD5 2TF

➲ (Turn S off A930 at traffic lights by Eastern Primary School in Broughty Ferry)

☎ 01382 436916 📠 01382 436951   `FREE`

e-mail: broughty@dundeecity.gov.uk

The 15th-century castle was rebuilt to defend the Tay estuary in the 19th century. It now houses fascinating displays on Dundee's whaling history, arms and armour, local history and seashore life. There are superb views across the Tay estuary from the observation room.

Times: Open all year Apr-Sep, Mon-Sat 10-4, Sun 12.30-4; Oct-Mar, Tue-Sat 10-4, Sun 12.30-4. (Closed Mons, 25-26 Dec & 1-3 Jan). **Facilities:** 🅿 (unsuitable for wheelchairs) shop ✖ (ex guide dogs)

CAMPERDOWN COUNTRY PARK
DD2 4TF

➲ (A90 to Dundee and turn onto A923 Coupar Angus rd, turn left at 1st rdbt to Camperdown Country Park)

☎ 01382 432659 📠 01382 433211

The 19th-century mansion of Camperdown House was built for the son of Admiral Lord Duncan, who defeated the Dutch at the Battle of Camperdown in 1797. The house is set in nearly 400 acres of fine parkland, which includes a wildlife centre, an adventure play area and an extensive network of footpaths and forest trails to follow.

Times: ✱ Open all year - park. Wildlife Centre - daily, Apr-Sep 10-3.45, Oct-Mar 10-2.45. **Facilities:** 🅿 ♿ (ramps) toilets for disabled shop ✖ (ex guide dogs)

DRUMLANRIG CASTLE

Dumfriesshire home of the
Duke of Buccleuch and Queensberry KT.
17th century house, with extensive gardens and Country Park. Renowned art collection, including works by Leonardo, Holbein and Rembrandt. French furniture.
Bonnie Prince Charlie relics.

Castle shop with quality goods – Tearoom
Working Forge – Craft Workshops
Adventure Playground – Visitor Centre

*18 miles north of Dumfries on A76
16 miles from Elvanfoot off M74*

Tel: 01848-330248

DISCOVERY POINT & RRS DISCOVERY
Discovery Quay DD1 4XA

➲ (in Dundee follow the brown heritage signs for Historic Ships)

☎ 01382 201245 📠 01382 225891

e-mail: info@dundeeheritage.sol.co.uk

Discovery Point is the home of RRS Discovery, Captain Scott's famous Antarctic ship. Spectacular lighting, graphics and special effects re-create key moments in the Discovery story. The restored bridge gives a captain's view over the ship and the River Tay. Learn what happened to the ship after the expedition, during the First World War and the Russian Revolution, and find out about her involvement in the first survey of whales' migratory patterns.

Times: Open Apr-Oct, Mon-Sat 10-6. Sun 11-6; Nov-Mar, Mon-Sat 10-5. Sun 11-5. **Fee:** ✱ £6.25 (ch £3.85, pen & concessions £4.70). Group £5.15 (ch £3.50, pen & concessions £4) **Facilities:** 🅿 (charged) 💻 ♿ (in-house wheelchairs & lifts, parking, ramps onto ship) toilets for disabled shop ✖ (ex guide & hearing dogs) 🍴

HM FRIGATE UNICORN
Victory Dock DD1 3JA

➲ (From W follow A85 from A90 at Invergowrie. From E follow A92. Located near N end of Tay Road Bridge).

☎ 01382 200900 & 200893   `2 for 1`

📠 01382 200923

e-mail: frigateunicorn@hotmail.com

The *Unicorn* is the oldest British-built warship afloat, and Scotland's only example of a wooden warship. Today she

continued

houses a museum of life in the Royal Navy during the days of sail, with guns, models and displays.
Times: Open all year Apr-Oct daily 10-5; Nov-Mar, Wed-Fri 12-4, Sat & Sun 10-4 (closed Mon/Tue & 2 weeks at Xmas & New Year). **Fee:** £3.50 (concessions £2.50). Family ticket £7.50-£9.50. Groups 10+ £2 each.
Facilities: 🅿 💺 ♿ (audio visual presentations, introductory video) shop ✸ 🍴

McManus Galleries
Albert Square DD1 1DA
➲ (Turn off A90 & follow signs for Dundee city centre, located in city centre).   **FREE**
☎ 01382 432084 🖷 01382 432052
e-mail: mcmanus.galleries@dundeecity.gov.uk
A remarkable Gothic building housing one of Scotland's most impressive collections of fine and decorative art. There are also displays on local archaeology, civic and social history, trades and industries and wildlife and the environment. Touring exhibitions are a regular feature.
Times: Open all year. Mon-Sat 10.30-5, Thu 10.30-7, Sun 12.30-4. (closed 25-26 Dec & 1-3 Jan) **Facilities:** 🅿 (100 yds) 💺 ♿ (wheelchair available, lift, high arm chairs & audio loop) toilets for disabled shop ✸ (ex guide dogs)

Mills Observatory
Balgay Park, Glamis Rd DD2 2UB
➲ (located 1m West of Dundee city centre, in Balgay Park, on the wooded summit of Balgay Hill)
☎ 01382 435846 🖷 01382 435962
e-mail: mills.observatory@dundeecity.gov.uk
The observatory was built in 1935, and has a Victorian 10in Cooke refracting telescope among its instruments. The gallery has displays on astronomy and space exploration; visitors can view a safe projection of the sun on bright days. There is a small planetarium for booked groups only. Open nights during the winter months, children's activities during the summer holidays.
Times: Open all year, Apr-Sep, Tue-Fri 11-5, Sat & Sun 12.30-4; Oct-Mar, Mon-Fri 4-10, Sat & Sun 12.30-4. (Closed 25-26 Dec & 1-3 Jan). **Fee:** Free except for planetarium shows extra, £1 (ch 50p) Groups £10. **Facilities:** 🅿 💺 ♿ (portable telescopes available, images on screen) shop ✸ (ex guide dogs)

Verdant Works
West Henderson's Wynd DD2 5BT
➲ (follow brown tourist signs once in Dundee)
☎ 01382 225282 🖷 01382 221612
e-mail: info@dundeeheritage.sol.co.uk
Dating from 1830, this old Jute Mill covers 50,000 sq ft and has been restored as a living museum of Dundee and Tayside's textile history and award winning European Industrial Museum. Phase I explains what jute is, where it comes from and why Dundee became the centre of its production. Working machinery illustrates the production process from raw jute to woven cloth. Phase II deals with the uses of jute and its effects on Dundee's social history.
Times: Open Apr-Oct, Mon-Sat 10-5, Sun 11-5. Nov-Mar, Mon-Sat 10-4, Sun 11-4. Venue closes 1hr after last entry. Please check for winter opening times. (Closed 25 & 26 Dec & 1-2 Jan). **Fee:** ✱ £5.95 (ch £3.85, pen & con £4.45). Family ticket (2ad+2ch) £17. **Facilities:** 🅿 (charged) ♿ (wheelchairs, induction loops) toilets for disabled shop ✸ (ex guide & hearing dogs) 🍴

EAST AYRSHIRE

GALSTON   Map 11 NS53
Loudoun Castle Theme Park
KA4 8PE
➲ (signposted from A74(M), from A77 and from A71)
☎ 01563 822296 🖷 01563 822408
e-mail: loudouncastle@btinternet.com
Castle ruins, woodland and country walks at Scotland's largest theme park, with roller coasters, go karts, log flume and Britain's largest carousel. Many other attractions, including the recently opened 'Drop Zone' a 140ft drop through the trees, and King Rory's Animal Kingdom.
Times: ✱ Open Apr-Aug & following days in Sep 3, 9-10, 16-17, 22-25, 29-30. Also 1-2, 7-8, 14-22 Oct. **Facilities:** 🅿 💺 ✕ licensed ♿ toilets for disabled shop ✸ (ex guide dogs) 🍴

KILMARNOCK   Map 10 NS43
Dick Institute Museum & Art Galleries
Elmbank Ave KA1 3BU
➲ (Follow brown tourist signs from A77 S of Glasgow, into Kilmarnock town centre.
☎ 01563 554343 🖷 01563 554344
Temporary and permanent exhibitions spread over two floors of this grand Victorian building. Fine art, social and natural history feature upstairs, whilst the downstairs galleries house temporary exhibitions of art and craft.
Times: Open all year, Gallery & Museum: Mon-Tue, Thu-Fri 10-8, Wed & Sat 10-5. (Closed Sun & PH's). **Fee:** Free except for special exhibitions when a charge may be made. **Facilities:** 🅿 ♿ (wheelchair available) toilets for disabled shop ✸ (ex guide dogs)

EAST DUNBARTONSHIRE

BEARSDEN   Map 11 NS57
Antonine Wall: Bearsden Bath-house
Roman Rd G61 2SG
➲ (signed from Bearsden Cross on A810)   **FREE**
Considered to be the best surviving visible Roman building in Scotland, the bath-house was discovered in 1973 during excavations for a construction site. It was originally built for use by the Roman garrison at Bearsden Fort, which is part of the Antonine Wall defences. This building dates from the 2nd century AD. Visitors should wear sensible footwear.
Times: Open all reasonable times. **Facilities:** ♿ ✸ 🚩

MILNGAVIE   Map 11 NS57
Mugdock Country Park
Craigallian Rd G62 8EL
➲ (N of Glasgow on A81, signed)
☎ 0141 956 6100 🖷 0141 956 5624
e-mail: lain@mcp.ndo.co.uk
This country park incorporates the remains of Mugdock and Craigend castles, set in beautiful landscapes as well as an exhibition centre, craft shops, orienteering course and many walks.
Times: ✱ Open all year, daily. **Facilities:** 🅿 💺 ♿ shop garden centre

EAST LOTHIAN

ABERLADY Map 12 NT47

MYRETON MOTOR MUSEUM

EH32 0PZ

(1.5m from A198, 2m from A1)

☎ 01875 870288 & 07947 066666 **2 for 1**

01368 860199

The museum has on show a large collection, from 1899, of cars, bicycles, motor cycles and commercials. There is also a large collection of period advertising, posters and enamel signs etc.

Times: Open, Apr-Oct daily 11-4, Nov-Mar Sun only 1-3 **Fee:** £5 (ch 16 £2). **Facilities:** (ex guide dogs)

DIRLETON Map 12 NT58

DIRLETON CASTLE

EH39 5ER

(on A198)

☎ 01620 850330

The oldest part of this romantic castle dates from the 13th century. It was besieged by Edward I in 1298, rebuilt and expanded, and then destroyed in 1650. Now the sandstone ruins have a beautiful mellow quality. Within the castle grounds is a garden established in the 16th century, with ancient yews and hedges around a bowling green.

Times: * Open all year, Apr-Sep, daily 9.30-6.30; Oct-Mar, Mon-Sat 9.30-4.30, Sun 2-4.30. (Closed 25-26 Dec). **Facilities:** shop

EAST FORTUNE Map 12 NT57

MUSEUM OF FLIGHT

East Fortune Airfield EH39 5LF

(Signposted from A1 near Haddington. Turn onto B1347, past Athelstaneford)

☎ 01620 880308 01620 880355 **2 for 1**

e-mail: info@nms.ac.uk

Situated on 63 acres of one of Britain's best preserved wartime airfields, the museum has three hangars, with more than 50 aeroplanes, plus engines, rockets and memorabilia. Items on display include two Spitfires, a Vulcan bomber and

continued

Britain's oldest surviving aeroplane, built in 1896; recent exhibits include a Phantom jet fighter and Harrier jump-jet.

Times: Open daily, Apr-Oct, 10-5; Nov-Mar wknds only, 11-4. **Fee:** £3 (ch free. concession £1.50). **Facilities:** toilets for disabled shop (ex assist dogs)

EAST LINTON Map 12 NT57

HAILES CASTLE

FREE

(1.5m SW of East Linton on A1)

A beautiful sited ruin incorporating a fortified manor of 13th-century date, extended in the 14th and 15th centuries. There are two vaulted pit-prisons.

Times: Open at all reasonable times. **Facilities:**

PRESTON MILL & PHANTASSIE DOOCOT

EH40 3DS

(signposted from A1)

☎ 01620 860426

This attractive mill, with conical, pantiled roof, is the oldest working water-driven meal mill to survive in Scotland, and was last used commercially in 1957. Nearby is the charming Phantassie Doocot (dovecote), built for 500 birds.

Times: Open Apr-Sep, Thu-Mon 12-5, Sun 1-5 **Fee:** * £3.50 (concession £2.60) Family ticket £9.50. Groups adult £2.80, child/school £1). Admission free to NTS members. For other deails please phone 0131 243 9387 **Facilities:** toilets for disabled shop (ex guide dogs)

INVERESK Map 11 NT37

INVERESK LODGE GARDEN

EH21 7TE

(A6124 S of Musselburgh)

☎ 01721 722502

This charming terraced garden, set in the historic village of Inveresk, specialises in plants, shrubs and roses suitable for growing on small plots. The 17th-century house makes an elegant backdrop.

Times: Open all year daily 10-6 or dusk if earlier. **Fee:** * £2 (concession £1). Admission free to NTS members. For other details please phone 0131 243 9387. **Facilities:** (ex guide dogs)

NORTH BERWICK Map 12 NT58

SCOTTISH SEABIRD CENTRE

The Harbour EH39 4SS

(follow the A1 from Edinburgh, take the A198 to North Berwick. Brown heritage signs clearly marked from the A1)

☎ 01620 890202 01620 890222 **2 for 1**

e-mail: info@seabird.org

Get close to nature with a visit to this award-winning centre. With panoramic views over the islands of the Firth of Forth and sand fringed bays of North Berwick, the area is a haven for wildlife. Use state-of-the-art 'Big Brother' cameras to see wide variety of wildlife action live - including gannet colony, hundreds of puffins seals and sometimes bottlenose dolphins close to shore.

Times: Open - Summer, daily 10-6; Winter, daily 10-4. **Fee:** * £4.95 (ch & concessions £3.50). Family ticket (4 persons) £13.50.

Facilities: 1 w/chair, parking on site, walking frame available toilets for disabled shop (ex guide dogs)

TANTALLON CASTLE
EH39 5PN
➲ (3m E, off A198)
☎ 01620 892727

A famous 14th-century stronghold of the Douglases facing towards the lonely Bass Rock from the rocky Firth of Forth shore. Nearby 16th-and 17th-century earthworks.
Times: ✱ Open all year, Apr-Sep, daily 9.30-6.30; Oct-Mar, Mon-Sat 9.30-4.30, Sun 2-4.30. (Closed Thu pm, Fri & Sun am in winter & 25-26 Dec). Telephone for details **Facilities:** 🅿 shop ✖ ▌

PRESTONPANS   Map 11 NT37
PRESTONGRANGE MUSEUM
Prestongrange (on B1348)
☎ 0131 653 2904 🖹 01620 828201
e-mail: elms@eastlothian.gov.uk   **FREE**

The oldest documented coal mining site in Scotland, with 800 years of history, this museum shows a Cornish Beam Engine and on-site evidence of associated industries such as brickmaking and pottery. It is located next to a 16th-century customs port. Special Events - weekend events for families and children in July/August.
Times: Open end Mar-mid Oct, daily 11-4. Last tour 3pm.
Facilities: 🅿 💺 ♿ (grounds partly accessible) toilets for disabled shop ✖ (ex guide dogs or outside)

FALKIRK

BIRKHILL   Map 11 NS97
THE BIRKHILL FIRECLAY MINE
EH51 9AQ
➲ (via A706 from Linlithgow, A904 from Grangemouth, follow brown signs to Steam Railway & Fireclay Mine)
☎ 01506 825855 🖹 01506 828766
e-mail: mine@srps.org.uk

Tour guides will meet you at Birkhill Station and lead you down into the ancient woodland of the beautiful Avon Gorge, and then into the caverns of the Birkhill Fireclay mine. See how the clay was worked, what it was used for and find the 300-million-year-old fossils in the roof of the mine.
Times: Open 3 Apr-31 Oct wknds only; Jul-Aug Tue-Sun. **Fee:** Mine & Train £7.50 (ch £4, concession £6) Family ticket (2ad & 2ch) £19. Mine only £3 (ch £2, concession £2.50) Family ticket £10. Mine only £3 (ch £1.70, pen £2.20) Family ticket £8. **Facilities:** 🅿 🍴

BO'NESS   Map 11 NT08
BO'NESS & KINNEIL RAILWAY
Bo'ness Station, Union St EH51 9AQ
➲ (A904 from all directions, signposted)
☎ 01506 822298 🖹 01506 828233
e-mail: railway@srps.org.uk

Historic railway buildings, including the station and train shed, have been relocated from sites all over Scotland. The Scottish Railway Exhibition tells the story of the development of railways and their impact on the people of Scotland. Take a seven mile return trip by steam train to the tranquil country
continued

station at Birkhill. Special events take place throughout the year.
Times: Open Apr-Jun & Sep-Oct, Sat-Sun; Jul-Aug, Tue-Sun. Steam trains daily, depart 11, 12.15, 1.45 & 3, diesel departs at 4.15. Ring for details of special events. **Fee:** Return fare £4.50 (ch 5-15 £2, concessions £3.50). Family ticket £11. Ticket for return train fare & tour of Birkhill Fireclay Mine £7.50 (ch £4, concessions £6), Family ticket £19.
Facilities: 🅿 💺 ✖ ♿ (ramps to station & adapted carriage) toilets for disabled shop (ex in cafe) 🍴

KINNEIL MUSEUM & ROMAN FORTLET
Duchess Anne Cottages, Kinniel Estate EH51 0PR
➲ (Follow tourist signs from Heritage Railway, off M9. Establishment is at the E end of town accessed via Dean Rd)
☎ 01506 778530

The museum is in a converted stable block of Kinneil House. The ground floor has displays on the industrial history of Bo'ness, while the upper floor looks at the history and environment of the Kinneil estate. The remains of the Roman fortlet can be seen nearby. An audio visual presentation shows 2000 years of history.
Times: ✱ Open all year, Mon-Sat 12.30-4. **Facilities:** 🅿 ♿ shop ✖ (ex guide dogs)

FALKIRK   Map 11 NS88
CALLENDAR HOUSE
Callendar Park FK1 1YR
➲ (from W M80 junct 4; from E M9 junct 4/5; A803 to Falkirk, follow signs into Callendar Park)
☎ 01324 503770 🖹 01324 503771

Mary, Queen of Scots, Oliver Cromwell, Bonnie Prince Charlie, noble earls and wealthy merchants all feature in the history of Callendar House. Costumed interpreters describe early 19th-century life in the kitchens and the 900-year history of the house is illustrated in the 'Story of Callendar House' exhibition. The house is set in parkland, offering boating and woodland walks. Christmas at Callendar House will include spitroasting goose in the kitchen, traditional tree and carols in the main hall.
Times: ✱ Open all year, Mon-Sat 10-5. Apr-Sep Sun 2-5. **Facilities:** 🅿 💺 ✖ ♿ (ramps & lift) toilets for disabled shop ✖ (ex guide dogs) 🍴

ROUGH CASTLE

➲ (1m E of Bonnybridge, signposted from B816) `FREE`

The impressive earthworks of a large Roman fort on the Antonine Wall can be seen here. The buildings have disappeared, but the mounds and terraces are the sites of barracks, and granary and bath buildings. Running between them is the military road, which once linked all the forts on the wall and is still well defined.

Times: Open any reasonable time. **Facilities:** 🅿 ✈ ▮

FIFE

ABERDOUR   Map 11 NT18

ABERDOUR CASTLE
KY3 0SL

➲ (In Aberdour, 5m E of Forth Bridges on A921)
☎ 01383 860519

The earliest surviving part of the castle is the 14th-century keep. There are also later buildings, and the remains of a terraced garden, a bowling green and a fine 16th-century doocot (dovecote).

Times: ✳ Open all year, Apr-Sep, daily 9.30-6.30; Oct-Mar, Mon-Sat 9.30-4.30, Sun 2-4.30. (Closed Thu pm, Fri & Sun am in winter).
Facilities: 🅿 ✗ ♿ (wheelchairs) toilets for disabled shop ▮

ANSTRUTHER   Map 12 NO50

SCOTTISH FISHERIES MUSEUM
St Ayles, Harbour Head KY10 3AB

➲ (from Edinburgh A90 take A92 to Kirkcaldy & then A915 to Upper Largo, A917 then B942 through Colinsburgh to Pittenweem, then A917 to Anstruther) `2 for 1`
☎ 01333 310628 🖩 01333 310628
e-mail: info@scottish-fisheries-museum.org

This award-winning National museum tells the story of Scottish fishing and its people from the earliest times to the present. With 10 galleries, 2 large boatyards, and a restored fisherman's cottage to see, which contain many fine paintings and photographs, boat models and actual boats, clothing and items of daily life, a visit to the museum makes for an exceptional day out.

Times: Open all year, Apr-Sep, Mon-Sat 10-5.30, Sun 11-5; Oct-Mar, Mon-Sat 10-4.30, Sun 12-4.30. (Closed 25 26 Dec & 1-2 Jan). Last admission 1 hr before closing. **Fee:** ✳ £3.50 (concessions £2.50). Party 12+ £3 (con £2, primary ch £1) Accompanied ch free. **Facilities:** 🅿 (20yds) (charge in summer) 🖳 ♿ (ramps) toilets for disabled shop ✈ (ex guide dogs)

BURNTISLAND   Map 11 NT28

BURNTISLAND EDWARDIAN FAIR MUSEUM
102 High St KY3 9AS

➲ (in the centre of Burntisland)
☎ 01592 412860 🖩 01592 412870

Burntisland Museum has recreated a walk through the sights and sounds of the town's fair in 1910, based on a painting of the scene by local artist Andrew Young. See reconstructed rides, stalls and side shows of the time.

Times: ✳ Open all year, Mon, Wed, Fri & Sat 10-1 & 2-5; Tue & Thu 10-1 & 2-7pm. Closed public holidays. **Facilities:** 🅿 (on street parking) ✈

CULROSS   Map 11 NS98

CULROSS PALACE, TOWN HOUSE & THE STUDY
West Green House KY12 8JH

➲ (off A985, 3m E of Kincardine Bridge)
☎ 01383 880359 🖩 01383 882675

A royal burgh, Culross dates from the 16th and 17th centuries and has remained virtually unchanged since. It prospered from the coal and salt trades, and when these declined in the 1700s, Culross stayed as it was. It owes its present appearance to the National Trust for Scotland, which has been gradually restoring it. In the Town House is a visitor centre and exhibition; in the building called The Study can be seen a drawing room with a Norwegian painted ceiling, and The Palace has painted rooms and terraced gardens.

Times: Open - Palace, Study & Town House: Good Fri-Sep, daily 12-5.. Garden all year 10-6 or sunset if earlier. **Fee:** ✳ £5 (concession £3.75). Family ticket £13.50. Groups adult £4, child/school £1. Please book groups in advance. Admission free to NTS members. For other details phone 0131 243 9387. **Facilities:** 🅿 🖳 ♿ toilets for disabled shop ✈ (ex guide dogs) ♨

CUPAR   Map 11 NO31

HILL OF TARVIT MANSIONHOUSE & GARDEN
KY15 5PB

➲ (2.5m S of Cupar, off A916)
☎ 01334 653127 🖩 01334 653127

Built in the first decade of the 20th century, the Mansionhouse is home to a notable collection of paintings, tapestries, furniture and Chinese porcelain. The grounds include formal gardens, and there is a regular programme of concerts and art exhibitions.

Times: Open - Apr-Sep, daily 1-5; Oct wknds 1-5. Garden & grounds all year, daily 9.30-sunset. **Fee:** ✳ £5 (concession £3.75). Family ticket £13.50. Groups adult £4, child/school £1. Please book groups in advance. Garden & grounds £2. Admission free to NTS members. For other details please phone 0131 243 9387. **Facilities:** 🅿 🖳 ♿ toilets for disabled shop ✈ (ex guide dogs) ♨

THE SCOTTISH DEER CENTRE
Bow-of-Fife KY15 4NQ

➲ (3m W of Cupar on A91)
☎ 01337 810391 🖩 01337 810477

Guided tours take about 30 minutes and allow you to meet and stroke deer. There are indoor and outdoor adventure play areas. Other features include regular falconry displays, viewing platform and a tree top walkway.

Times: Open daily, Etr-Oct 10-6, Nov-Etr 10-5. **Fee:** ✳ £4.75 (ch 3-15 £3.25) **Facilities:** 🅿 🖳 ♿ (special parking bay, loan of wheelchairs) toilets for disabled shop ✈ (ex guide dogs) ◥

DUNFERMLINE   Map 11 NT08

ABBOT HOUSE HERITAGE CENTRE
Abbot House, Maygate KY12 7NE

➲ (Dunfermline City Centre)
☎ 01383 733266 🖩 01383 624908
e-mail: dht@abbothouse.fsnet.co.uk

For the better part of a millennium, pilgrims have beaten a path to Dumfermline's door. Today visitors can still share the

continued

rich royal heritage of the capital of Fife's Magic Kingdom. The volunteer-run Abbot House Heritage Centre - dubbed 'The People's Tardis' – propels the traveller through time from the days of the Picts – a time warp peopled by a veritable Who's Who of characters from Dumfermline's past: Scotland's royal saint, Braveheart's Wallace and Bruce, Scotland's Chaucer, steel magnate Andrew Carnegie and a whole panoply of kings, ending with the birth of ill-starred Charles I.

Times: Open daily 10-5. Last entry to upper exhibitions 4.15pm. (Closed 25 Dec & 1 Jan). **Fee:** £3 (accompanied ch under 16 free, ch 5-16 £1.25 & concessions £2). Party 20+ **Facilities:** P (150yds) (disabled parking at establishment) ▣ & (parking on site, videos of inaccesible areas) toilets for disabled shop ✖ (ex guide dogs) ☜

ANDREW CARNEGIE BIRTHPLACE MUSEUM
Moodie St KY12 7PL
➲ (400yds S from Dunfermline Abbey)
☎ 01383 724302 ▤ 01383 721862
e-mail: carnegiebirthplace@hotmail.com

The museum tells the story of the handloom weaver's son, born here in 1835, who created the biggest steel works in the USA and then became a philanthropist on a huge scale. The present-day work of the philanthropic Carnegie Trust is also explained.

Times: Open Apr-Oct, Mon-Sat 11-5, Sun 2-5. **Fee:** £2 (ch under 16 free, concessions £1). **Facilities:** P & toilets for disabled shop ✖ (ex guide dogs)

DUNFERMLINE ABBEY
Pittencrieff Park
☎ 01383 739026

The monastery was a powerful Benedictine house, founded by Queen Margaret in the 11th century. A modern brass in the choir marks the grave of King Robert the Bruce. The monastery guesthouse became a royal palace, and was the birthplace of Charles I.

Times: ✱ Open all year, Apr-Sep, daily 9.30-6.30: Oct-Mar, Mon-Sat 9.30-4.30, Sun 2-4.30. (Closed Thu pm, Fri in winter & 25-26 Dec). Telephone for 2004 details. **Facilities:** P shop ✖ ▮

PITTENCRIEFF HOUSE MUSEUM
Pittencrieff Park KY12 8QH   FREE
➲ (turn off A994 on to Coal Rd, turn left into Pittencriefff Park Car Park. Attraction on W edge of town.
☎ 01383 722935 & 313838 ▤ 01383 313837

A fine 17th-century mansion house, standing in a park with lawns, greenhouses and gardens. In the house are galleries with displays on the history of the house, park and the town. Temporary exhibitions are shown in the top gallery. The house and park were given to the town by Andrew Carnegie.

Times: Open daily Apr-Sep, 11-5 **Facilities:** P (800yds) & (ramp) toilets for disabled shop ✖ (ex guide dogs)

FALKLAND   Map 11 NO20
FALKLAND PALACE & GARDEN
KY15 7BU
➲ (off A912, 11m N of Kirkaldy)
☎ 01337 857397 ▤ 01337 857980

The hunting palace of the Stuart monarchs, this fine building, with a French-Renaissance style south wing, stands in the

continued

shelter of the Lomond Hills. The beautiful Chapel Royal and King's Bedchamber are its most notable features, and it is also home to the oldest royal tennis court in Britain (1539). The garden has a spectacular delphinium border. Recorded sacred music is played hourly in the Chapel. Please telephone for details of concerts, recitals etc.

Times: Open Mar-Oct, Mon-Sat 10-6, Sun 1-5 **Fee:** ✱ £7 (concession £5.25). Family ticket £19. Groups adult £5.60, child/school £1. Garden only £3.50 (concession £2.60). Family ticket £9.50. Groups adult £2.80, child/school £1. Admission free to NTS members. For other details please phone 0131 243 9387. **Facilities:** ▣ & shop ✖ (ex guide dogs) ☙

KELLIE CASTLE &   Map 12 NO50
GARDENS
KELLIE CASTLE & GARDENS
KY10 2RF
➲ (3m NW of Pittenweem on B9171)
☎ 01333 720271 ▤ 01333 720326
e-mail: aclipson@nts-scot.demon.co.uk

The oldest part dates from about 1360, but it is for its 16th and 17th-century domestic architecture that Kellie is renowned. It has notable plasterwork and painted panelling, and there are also interesting Victorian gardens.

Times: Open - Good Fri-Etr Mon & Jun-Sep, daily 1-5. Garden & grounds all year, daily 9.30-sunset. **Fee:** ✱ £5 (concession £3.75) Family ticket £13.50. Group adult £4, child/school £1). Please book groups in advance. Admission free to NTS members. For other details please phone 0131 243 9387. **Facilities:** P ▣ & (Induction loop for the hard of hearing) shop ✖ (ex guide dogs) ☙

KIRKCALDY   Map 11 NT29
KIRKCALDY MUSEUM & ART GALLERY
War Memorial Gardens KY1 1YG
➲ (next to Kirkcaldy train station)
☎ 01592 412860 ▤ 01592 412870

Set in the town's lovely memorial gardens, the museum houses a collection of fine and decorative art, including 18th to 21st-century Scottish paintings among them the works of William McTaggart and S J Peploe. An award-winning display 'Changing Places' tells the story of the social, industrial and natural heritage of the area.

Times: ✱ Open all year, Mon-Sat 10.30-5, Sun 2-5. (Closed local hols). **Facilities:** P ▣ & (ramp to main entrance & lift to 1st floor galleries) toilets for disabled shop ✖ (ex guide dogs)

NORTH QUEENSFERRY   Map 11 NT17
DEEP SEA WORLD
KY11 1JR
➲ (from N, M90 take exit for Inverkeithing. From S follow signs to Forth Road bridge, first exit left)
☎ 01383 411880 ▤ 01383 410514
e-mail: info@deepseaworld.co.uk

The world's longest underwater tunnel gives you a diver's eye view of an underwater world. Come face to face with Sand Tiger sharks, and watch divers hand feed a wide array of sea life. Visit the Amazon experience with ferocious Piranhas and electric eels and the amazing amphibian

continued

display featuring the world's most poisonous frog. The really brave will enjoy the dangerous animals tank. **Times:** Open all year, daily, 27 Mar-Jun Mon-Fri 10-6; Jul-Aug, Mon-Fri 10-6.30; Sep-1 Nov, Mon-Fri 10-6; 2 Nov-26 Mar, Mon-Fri 11-5. Wknds, BH & school holidays 10-6. **Fee:** ✱ £7.50 (ch 3-5 £5.50, concessions £6). Family ticket & group discounts available. **Facilities:** 🅿 ⬛ ⬛ ♿ (ramps & disabled parking) toilets for disabled shop ✖ (ex guide dogs) ⬛

ST ANDREWS   Map 12 NO51

BRITISH GOLF MUSEUM
Bruce Embankment KY16 9AB
➲ (opposite Royal & Ancient Golf Club)
☎ 01334 460046 🖶 01334 460064
e-mail: hilarywebster@randagc.org

British Golf Museum
Bruce Embankment,
St Andrews, Fife KY16 9AR
www.britishgolfmuseum.co.uk
Tel: 01334 460046

Where better to find out about golf than in St Andrews, the home of golf. Using diverse displays and exciting interactive, The British Golf Museums explores the history of British golf from its origins to the personalities of today. The 18th Hole is fun for all the family, with dressing up, a mini-putting green and loads to do! **Times:** Open all year, Etr-mid Oct daily 9.30-5.30; mid Oct-Etr Thu-Mon 11-3. (closed Tue & Wed). **Fee:** ✱ £4 (ch 15 £2, pen & students £3). Family ticket £9.50. Group 10+ **Facilities:** 🅿 (charged) ♿ toilets for disabled shop ✖ (ex guide dogs)

CASTLE & VISITOR CENTRE
KY16 9AR
☎ 01334 477196
This 13th-century stronghold castle was the scene of the murder of Cardinal Beaton in 1546. The new visitor centre incorporates an exciting multi-media exhibition describing the history of the castle and nearby cathedral. **Times:** ✱ Open all year, Apr-Sep, daily 9.30-6.30; Oct-Mar, Mon-Sat 9.30-4.30, Sun 2-4.30 (winter open 9.30am on Sun). (Closed 25-26 Dec). **Facilities:** 🅿 ♿ toilets for disabled shop ✖ ▮

CATHEDRAL (& MUSEUM)
KY16 9QU
☎ 01334 472563
The cathedral was the largest in Scotland, and is now an extensive ruin. The remains date mainly from the 12th and 13th centuries, and large parts of the precinct walls have survived intact. Close by is St Rule's church, which the cathedral was built to replace. St Rule's probably dates from
continued

before the Norman Conquest, and is considered the most interesting Romanesque church in Scotland. **Times:** ✱ Open all year, Apr-Sep, daily 9.30-6.30; Oct-Mar, Mon-Sat 9.30-4.30, Sun 2-4.30 (winter open 9.30am Sun). (Closed 25-26 Dec). **Facilities:** 🅿 shop ✖ ▮

ST ANDREWS AQUARIUM
The Scores KY16 9AS
➲ (Signposted in town centre)
☎ 01334 474786 🖶 01334 475985
This continually expanding aquarium is home to shrimps, sharks, eels, octopi, seals and much much more. Special features include the Seahorse Parade, and the Sea Mammal Research Unit, which is committed to the care of sea mammals and their environment. **Times:** Open daily from 10. Please phone for winter opening **Fee:** ✱ £4.85 (ch & student £3.75, pen £4). Family ticket (2 adults & 2 ch) £14 **Facilities:** 🅿 (charged) ⬛ ✖ licensed ♿ toilets for disabled shop ✖ (ex guide dogs) ⬛

HIGHLAND

AVIEMORE   Map 14 NH81

STRATHSPEY STEAM RAILWAY
Aviemore Station, Dalfaber Rd PH22 1PY
➲ (off B970)
☎ 01479 810725
e-mail: information@strathspey-railway.co.uk
This steam railway covers the ten miles from Aviemore via Boat of Garten to Broomhill. The journey takes about 40 minutes, but allow around two hours for the round trip. Shorter trips are possible and timetables are available from the station and the tourist information centre. Special events include visits from Thomas the Tank Engine, telephone for details of dates. **Times:** Open late Mar-Oct, Wed-Thu, Sat-Sun; May-Sep, daily. Closed Sat in Apr (ex Etr). **Facilities:** 🅿 ⬛ ♿ (ramps) toilets for disabled shop ⬛

BALMACARA   Map 14 NG82

BALMACARA ESTATE & LOCHALSH WOODLAND GARDEN
IV40 8DN
➲ (3m E of Kyle of Lochalsh, off A87)
☎ 01599 566325 🖶 01599 566359
e-mail: balmacara@nts.org.uk
The Balmacara estate comprises some 5600 acres and seven crofting villages, including Plockton, a conservation area. There are excellent views of Skye, Kintail and Applecross. The main attraction is the Lochalsh Woodland Garden, but the whole area is excellent for walking. **Times:** Open - Estate: all year. Woodland garden daily 9-sunset. Balmacara Square Visitor Centre, Apr-Sep, daily, 9-5 (Fri 9-4). **Fee:** ✱ Garden £2 (concession £1). Visitor Centre £1 (honesty box). Admission free to NTS members. For other details please phone 0131 243 9387. **Facilities:** 🅿 ⬛

The AA also publishes a guide to Pet Friendly Places to Stay

BETTYHILL   Map 14 NC76

STRATHNAVER MUSEUM
KW14 7SS
☎ 01641 521418
e-mail: strathnavermus@ukonline.co.uk

The museum has displays on the Clearances, with a fine collection of Strathnaver Clearances furnishings, domestic and farm implements, and local books. There is also a Clan Mackay room. The museum's setting is a former church, a handsome stone building with a magnificent canopied pulpit dated 1774. The churchyard contains a carved stone known as the Farr Stone, which dates back to the 9th-century and is a fine example of Pictish art.
Times: Open Apr-Oct, Mon-Sat 10-1 & 2-5; Nov-Mar restricted opening. **Facilities:** ⯀ ⅋ shop ✗ (ex guide dogs)

BOAT OF GARTEN   Map 14 NH91

LOCH GARTEN OSPREY CENTRE
RSPB Reserve Abernethy Forest, Forest Lodge, Nethybridge PH25 3EF
➲ (Signposted from B970 & A9 at Aviemore, follow 'RSPB Ospreys' signs)
☎ 01479 831476 ▤ 01479 821069

Home of the Loch Garten Osprey site, this reserve holds one of most important remnants of Scots Pine forest in the Highlands. Within its 30,760 acres are forest bogs, moorland, mountain top, lochs and crofting land. In addition to the regular pair of nesting ospreys, there are breeding Scottish crossbills, capercaillies, black grouse and many others. The ospreys can be viewed through telescopes and there is a live TV link to the nest.
Times: Reserve open at all times. Osprey Centre daily, Apr-Aug 10-6. **Fee:** £2.50 (ch 50p, concessions £1.50). **Facilities:** ⯀ ⅋ (low level viewing slots & optics) toilets for disabled shop ✗ (ex guide dogs in centre) ◥

CARRBRIDGE   Map 14 NH92

LANDMARK FOREST THEME PARK
PH23 3AJ
➲ (off A9 between Aviemore & Inverness)
☎ 01479 841613 & 0800 731 3446
▤ 01479 841384
e-mail: landmarkcentre@btconnect.com

This innovative centre is designed to provide a fun and educational visit for all ages. Microworld takes a close up look at the incredible microscopic world around us. There is a 65ft forest viewing tower and a treetop trail. There are demonstrations of timber sawing, on a steam-powered sawmill and log hauling by a Clydesdale horse throughout the day. Attractions include a 3-track Watercoaster, a maze and a large covered adventure play area, mini electric cars, remote controlled truck arena.
Times: Open all year, daily, Apr-mid Jul 10-6; mid Jul-mid Aug 10-7; Sep-Oct 10-5.30; Nov-Mar 10-5. **Fee:** Apr -Oct: £7.45 (ch £5.60); Nov-Mar £2.45 (ch £2.25). Family tickets available. **Facilities:** ⯀ ⬛ ✗ licensed ⅋ (ramps to shop/resturants) toilets for disabled shop ◥

CAWDOR   Map 14 NH85

CAWDOR CASTLE
IV12 5RD
➲ (on B9090 off A96)
☎ 01667 404615 ▤ 01667 404674
e-mail: info@cawdorcastle.com

Home of the Thanes of Cawdor since the 14th century, this lovely castle has a drawbridge, an ancient tower built round a tree, and a freshwater well inside the house. Gardens Weekend takes place in June - guided tours of gardens and Bluebell Walk in Cawdor Big Wood.
Times: Open May-10 Oct, daily 10-5.30. (Last admission 5pm). **Fee:** ✱ £6.30 (ch 5-15 £3.50, pen £5.30). Family ticket £18.60. Party 20+ £5.50 each. Gardens, grounds & nature trails only £3.50. **Facilities:** ⯀ ⬛ ✗ licensed ⅋ (ramps to restaurants, shops and gardens) toilets for disabled shop ✗ (ex guide dogs) ◥

CLAVA CAIRNS   Map 14 NH74

CLAVA CAIRNS
➲ (6m E of Inverness, signposted from B9091) `FREE`
☎ 01667 460232

A well-preserved Bronze Age cemetery complex of passage graves, ring cairns, kerb cairn and standing stones in a beautiful setting. In addition, the remains of a chapel of unknown date can be seen at this site.
Times: Open at all reasonable times. **Facilities:** ⯀ ✗ ▮

CROMARTY   Map 14 NH76

HUGH MILLER'S COTTAGE
Church St IV11 8XA
➲ (A382)
☎ 01381 600245

The cottage houses an exhibition on the life and work of Hugh Miller, a stonemason born here in 1802 who became an eminent geologist and writer. It was built by his great-grandfather around 1698, and now has a charming cottage garden.
Times: Open Good Fri-Sep, daily 12-5; Oct, Sun-Wed 12-5. **Fee:** ✱ £2.50 (concession £1.90) Family ticket £7. Groups adult £2, child/school £1. Admission free to NTS members. For other details please phone 0131 243 9387. **Facilities:** ⯀ (5mins) (disabled is directly outside) ⅋ ✗ (ex guide dogs) ⬛

CULLODEN MOOR   Map 14 NH74

CULLODEN BATTLEFIELD
IV2 5EU
➲ (B9006, 5m E of Inverness)
☎ 01463 790607 ▤ 01463 794294
e-mail: culloden@nts.org.uk

A cairn recalls this last battle fought on mainland Britain, on 16 April 1746, when the Duke of Cumberland's forces routed 'Bonnie' Prince Charles Edward Stuart's army. The battlefield has been restored to its state on the day of the battle, and in summer there are 'living history' enactments. This is a most
continued

atmospheric evocation of tragic events. Telephone for details of guided tours.
Times: Open - site always. Visitor Centre: Feb-Mar & Nov-Dec, daily 11-4; Apr-Jun & Sep-Oct, daily 9-6; Jul-Aug, daily 9-7. **Fee:** ✱ £5 (concession £3.75) Family ticket £13.50. Group adult £4, child/school £1. Please book groups in advance. Admission free to NTS members. For other details please phone (0131) 243 9387. **Facilities:** 🅿 ✕ ♿ (wheelchair, induction loop, raised map) toilets for disabled shop 🍴 (ex guide dogs) 🌱

DRUMNADROCHIT Map 14 NH52

OFFICIAL LOCH NESS MONSTER EXHIBITION CENTRE
IV3 6TU
➲ (on A82, 12m S Inverness)
☎ 01456 450573 & 450218 📠 01456 450770
e-mail: brem@loch-ness-scotland.com

A fascinating and popular multi-media presentation lasting 30 minutes. Seven themed areas cover the story from the pre-history of Scotland, through the cultural roots of the legend in Highland folklore, and into the 50-year controversy which surrounds it. Using latest technology in computer animation, lasers and multi-media projection systems.
Times: Open all year; Etr-May 9.30-5.30; Jun-Sep 9.30-6 (9-8.30 Jul & Aug); Winter 10-4. Last admission 30mins before closing. **Fee:** ✱ £5.95 (ch £3.50, pen & students £4.50, ch under 7 & disabled free). Family ticket £14.95. Group. **Facilities:** 🅿 🍽 ✕ licensed ♿ (parking) toilets for disabled shop 🍴 (ex in grounds/guide dogs) 🍵

URQUHART CASTLE
IV63 6XJ
➲ (on A82)
☎ 01456 450551

The castle was once Scotland's biggest and overlooks Loch Ness. It dates mainly from the 14th century, when it was built on the site of an earlier fort, and was destroyed before the 1715 Jacobite rebellion.
Times: ✱ Open all year, Apr-Sep, daily 9.30-6.30; Oct-Mar, daily 9.30-4.30. Last admission 45mins before closing. (Closed 25-26 Dec). **Facilities:** 🅿 shop 🍴 ◾

DUNBEATH Map 15 ND12

LAIDHAY CROFT MUSEUM
KW6 6EH
➲ (1m N on A9 off Dunbeath)
☎ 01593 731244

The museum gives visitors a glimpse of a long-vanished way of life. The main building is a thatched Caithness longhouse, with the dwelling quarters, byre and stable all under one roof. It dates back some 200 years, and is furnished as it might have been 100 years ago. A collection of early farm tools and machinery is also shown. Near the house is a thatched winnowing barn with its roof supported on three 'Highland couples', or crucks.
Times: Open Etr-Oct, daily 10-6. **Fee:** £2 (ch 50p) **Facilities:** 🅿 🍽 ♿ toilets for disabled

ELPHIN Map 14 NC21

HIGHLAND & RARE BREEDS FARM
IV27 4HH
➲ (on A835 in Elphin) 2 for 1
☎ 01854 666204 📠 01854 666204

There are highland cattle, traditional 4-horned sheep with coloured fleeces, traditional Scottish ewes and lambs, rare breeds of pigs and goats. Many types of poultry, duck ponds, and a farm walk among the animals. Also on display are farm tools, crofting history, wool crafts and hand-spinning.
Times: Open Jul & Aug only **Fee:** ✱ £3.50 (ch £2.50, students & pen £3) **Facilities:** 🅿 ♿ (assistance available) toilets for disabled shop 🍴 🍵

FORT GEORGE Map 14 NH75

FORT GEORGE
IV1 2TD
➲ (11m NE of Inverness)
☎ 01667 462777

Built following the Battle of Culloden as a Highland fortress for the army of George II, this is one of the outstanding artillery fortifications in Europe and still an active army barracks.
Times: ✱ Open all year, Apr-Sep, daily 9.30-6.30; Oct-Mar, Mon-Sat 9.30-4.30, Sun 2-4.30. Last admission 45mins before closing. (Closed 25-26 Dec). **Facilities:** 🅿 ✕ ♿ toilets for disabled shop 🍴 ◾

QUEEN'S OWN HIGHLANDERS REGIMENTAL MUSEUM COLLECTION
IV2 7TD
➲ (turn off A96 5 miles out of Inverness)
☎ 01463 224380 📠 01463 224380

Fort George has been a military barracks since it was built in 1748-69, and was the Depot of the Seaforth Highlanders until 1961. The museum of the Queen's Own Highlanders (Seaforth and Camerons) is sited in the former Lieutenant Governor's house, where uniforms, medals and pictures are displayed.
Times: Open Apr-Sep, daily 10-6; Oct-Mar, Mon-Fri 10-4. (Closed Xmas, New Year & BH). **Fee:** ✱ Free. (Admission charged by Historic Scotland for entry to Fort George). **Facilities:** 🅿 ♿ (stair lift to 1st floor, wheelchair on 1st floor) toilets for disabled shop 🍴 (ex guide dogs)

FORT WILLIAM Map 14 NN17

INVERLOCHY CASTLE
PH33 6SN FREE
➲ (2m NE of Fort William, off A82)

A fine well-preserved 13th-century castle of the Comyn family; in the form of a square, with round towers at the corners. The largest tower was the donjon or keep. This is one of Scotland's earliest castles.
Times: Open at all reasonable times. **Facilities:** 🅿 🍴 ◾

West Highland Museum
Cameron Square PH33 6AJ
➲ (follow signs to tourist office, museum is next door)
☎ 01397 702169 📠 01397 701927
e-mail: info@westhighlandmuseum.org.uk

The displays illustrate traditional Highland life and history, with numerous Jacobite relics. One of them is the 'secret portrait' of Bonnie Prince Charlie, which looks like meaningless daubs of paint but reveals a portrait when reflected in a metal cylinder.

Times: Open all year Jun-Sep, Mon-Sat 10-5 (also Sun 2-5 Jul-Aug); Oct-May, Mon-Sat 10-4. **Fee:** ✱ £2 (ch 50p, concessions £1.50) **Facilities:** P (100yds) (charge May-Oct, max. 2hrs stay) ♿ toilets for disabled shop (ex guide dogs)

GAIRLOCH — Map 14 NG87

Gairloch Heritage Museum
Achtercairn IV21 2BP
➲ (On junc of A382 & B8021 nr police station & public car park/toilets) 2 for 1
☎ 01445 712287
e-mail: info@gairlochheritagemuseum.org.uk

A converted farmstead now houses the award-winning museum, which shows the way of life in this typical West Highland parish from early times to the 20th century. There are hands-on activities for children and reconstructions of a croft house room, a school room, a shop, and a smugglers' cave. You can also view Gairloch through one of the largest lenses assembled by the Northern Lighthouse Board.

Times: Open Apr-Sep, Mon-Sat 10-5; Oct, Mon-Fri 10-1.30 last admission 4.30. Winter months by arrangement. **Fee:** £3 (ch 50p, students & pen £2). Group rates available **Facilities:** P ♿ shop (ex guide dogs)

GLENCOE — Map 14 NN15

Glencoe & North Lorn Folk Museum
PH49 4HS
➲ (Turn off A82 at Glencoe crossroads then immediately right again into Glencoe village)
☎ 01855 811664

Two heather-thatched cottages in the main street of Glencoe now house items connected with the Macdonalds and the Jacobite risings. A variety of local domestic and farming exhibits, dairying and slate-working equipment, costumes and embroidery are also shown.

Times: Open mid May-Sep, Mon-Sat 10-5.30. **Fee:** ✱ £2 (ch free, concessions £1.50). **Facilities:** P ♿ shop

Glencoe Visitor Centre
PA39 4HX
➲ (on A82, 17m S of Fort William)
☎ 01855 811307 & 811729 📠 01855 811772

Glencoe has stunning scenery and some of the most challenging climbs and walks in the Highlands. Red deer, wildcats, eagles and ptarmigan are among the wildlife. It is also known as a place of treachery and infamy. The Macdonalds of Glencoe were hosts to a party of troops who, under government orders, fell upon them, men, women and

continued

children, in a bloody massacre in 1692. The Visitor Centre tells the story.

Times: ✱ Open - Site all year, daily. Visitor Centre May-Aug, daily 9.30-5.30; Mar-Apr & Sep-Oct, daily 10-5; (last admission 30 mins before closing). **Facilities:** P ☕ ♿ (induction loop in video programme room) toilets for disabled shop (ex guide dogs)

GLENFINNAN — Map 14 NM98

Glenfinnan Monument
PH37 4LT
➲ (on A830, 18.5m W of Fort William)
☎ 01397 722250
e-mail: glenfinnan@nts.org.uk

The monument commemorates Highlanders who fought for Bonnie Prince Charlie in 1745. It stands in an awe-inspiring setting at the head of Loch Shiel. There is a visitor centre with information (commentary in four languages) on the Prince's campaign.

Times: ✱ Site open all year, daily. Visitor centre: 25 Mar-18 May & 2 Sep-27 Oct, daily 10-5, 19 May-1 Sep, daily 9.30-6. **Facilities:** P ☕ ♿ (information centre only) shop

GOLSPIE — Map 14 NH89

Dunrobin Castle
KW10 6SF
➲ (1m NE on A9, from Golspie)
☎ 01408 633177 & 633268 📠 01408 634081
e-mail: info@dunrobincastle.net

The ancient seat of the Earls and Dukes of Sutherland is a splendid, gleaming, turreted structure, thanks largely to 19th-century rebuilding, and has a beautiful setting overlooking the sea. Paintings, furniture and family heirlooms are on display, and the gardens are on a grand scale to match the house. There are also falconry displays in the gardens.

Times: Open Apr-15 Oct, Mon-Sat 10.30-5.30, Sun 12-5.30. Closes 1 hr earlier Apr, May & Oct. Last admission half hour before closing. **Fee:** ✱ £6.50 (ch £4.50 & pen £5.70). Family ticket £17. Party. **Facilities:** P ☕ (access by arrangement only) shop

HELMSDALE — Map 14 ND01

Timespan
Dunrobin St KW8 6JX
➲ (off A9 in centre of village, by Telford Bridge)
☎ 01431 821327 📠 01431 821058
e-mail: admin@timespan.org.uk

Located in a historic fishing village, this museum relates to the social and natural history of the area, and the art gallery has changing exhibitions of contemporary art and works by local artists. The garden has over 100 varieties of herbs and plants. There is a gift shop, and a café with beautiful views of the Telford Bridge.

Times: Open 1 Apr- 31 Oct, Mon-Sat 9.30-5, Sun 2-5. **Fee:** £4 (ch £2 pen & student £3). Family ticket £10. **Facilities:** P (150 mtrs) ☕ ♿ (lift) toilets for disabled shop garden centre (ex guide dogs)

KINCRAIG   Map 14 NH80
HIGHLAND WILDLIFE PARK
PH21 1NL
➲ (on B9152, 7m S of Aviemore)
☎ 01540 651270 🖹 01540 651236
e-mail: info@highlandwildlifepark.org

As you drive through the main reserve, you can see awe-inspiring European bison grazing alongside wild horses, red deer and highland cattle plus a wide variety of other species. Then in the walk-round forest, woodland and moorland habitats prepare for close encounters with animals such as wolves, capercaillie, arctic foxes, wildcats, pine martens, otters and owls. Special events every weekend April to October.
Times: Open throughout the year, weather permitting. Apr-Oct, 10-6; Jun-Aug 10-7; Nov-Mar 10-4. last entry 2 hours before closing. **Fee:** ✱ £7.50 (child £5, pen £6). **Facilities:** 🅿 💺 ♿ toilets for disabled shop ✗ ➾

KINGUSSIE   Map 14 NH70
HIGHLAND FOLK MUSEUM
Duke St PH21 1JG
➲ (12m SW of Aviemore off A9 at Kingussie)
☎ 01540 661307 🖹 01540 661631
e-mail: highland.folk@highland.gov.uk

First established on Iona in 1935 this was Britain's first open air museum. It has an extensive collection of everyday domestic objects together with major exhibits providing an insight into the social history of the Highland people. Visitors will see domestic and agricultural items and trade and craft tools.
Times: ✱ Open Apr-Sep, Mon-Sat 9.30-5.30; Oct Mon-Fri 9.30-4.30; Nov-Mar guided tours Mon-Fri, check for details. **Facilities:** 🅿 ♿ (ramp) toilets for disabled shop ✗ (ex guide dogs) ➾

RUTHVEN BARRACKS
➲ (1m SE from Kingussie, signposted from A9 and A86)   `FREE`
☎ 01667 460232

An infantry barracks erected in 1719 following the Jacobite rising of 1715, with two ranges of quarters and a stable block. Captured and burnt by Prince Charles Edward Stuart's army in 1746.
Times: Open at any reasonable time. **Facilities:** 🅿 ✗ ▮

KIRKHILL   Map 14 NH54
MONIACK CASTLE (HIGHLAND WINERY)
IV5 7PQ
➲ (7m from Inverness on A862, near village of Beauly, on S side of Beauly Firth)   `2 for 1`
☎ 01463 831283 🖹 01463 831419

Commercial wine-making is not a typically Scottish industry, but nevertheless a wide range of 'country'-style wines is produced, including elderflower and silver birch; mead and sloe gin, are also made here. A selection of related products and tours of the production area are available at this unique attraction, situated in a 16th-century castle.
Times: Open all year, Apr-Oct Mon-Sat 10-5. Nov-Mar, Mon-Fri 11-4. **Fee:** £2. **Facilities:** 🅿 shop ✗ ➾

NEWTONMORE   Map 14 NN79
CLAN MACPHERSON HOUSE & MUSEUM
Main St PH20 1DE
➲ (off A9 at junct of Newtonmore and Kingussie, museum on left after entering village)
☎ 01540 673332

Containing relics and memorials of the clan chiefs and other Macpherson families as well as those of Prince Charles Edward Stuart, this museum also displays the Prince's letters to the Clan Chief of 1745 and one to the Prince from his father the Old Pretender, along with royal warrants and the green banner of the clan. Other interesting historic exhibits include James Macpherson's fiddle, swords, pictures, decorations and medals.
Times: Open Apr-Oct, Mon-Sat 10-5, Sun 2-5. Other times by appointment. **Fee:** Free. Donations welcome. **Facilities:** 🅿 ♿ (ramp entrance from car park) toilets for disabled shop ✗ (ex guide dogs)

HIGHLAND FOLK MUSEUM
Aultlarie Croft PH20 1AY
➲ (on A86, follow signs off A9)
☎ 01540 661307 🖹 01540 661631
e-mail: highland.folk@highland.gov.uk

An early 18th-century farming township with turf houses has been reconstructed at this award-winning museum. A 1930s school houses old world maps, little wooden desks and a Coates library. Other attractions include a working croft with rare breed animals and tailor's workshop. Vintage buses run throughout the site.
Times: Open Apr-Aug, Mon-Sun 10.30-5.30; Sep-Oct, Mon Fri 11-4.30. **Fee:** ✱ £5 (ch & pen £3) **Facilities:** 🅿 💺 ♿ (vintage bus with full disabled access) toilets for disabled shop ✗ (ex guide dogs) ➾

POOLEWE   Map 14 NG88
INVEREWE GARDEN
IV22 2LG
➲ (6m NE of Gairloch, on A832)
☎ 01445 781200 🖹 01445 781497
e-mail: inverewe@nts.org.uk

The influence of the North Atlantic Drift enables this remarkable garden to grow rare and sub-tropical plants. At its best in early June, but full of beauty from March to October, Inverewe has a backdrop of magnificent mountains and stands to the north of Loch Maree.
Times: Open - Garden all year, Apr-Oct, daily 9.30-9 (or sunset if earlier). Nov-Mar, 9.30-4. Visitor Centre Apr-Sep, daily 9.30-5; Oct, daily 9.30-4. **Fee:** ✱ £7 (concession £5.25) Family ticket £19. Groups adult £5.60, child/school £1. Admission free to NTS members. For other details please phone 0131 243 9387. **Facilities:** 🅿 ✗ licensed ♿ (some paths difficult) toilets for disabled shop ✗ (ex guide dogs) ♨

ROSEMARKIE   Map 14 NH75
GROAM HOUSE MUSEUM
High St IV10 8UF
➲ (Turn off A9 at Tore onto A832)
☎ 01381 620961 & 01381 621730   `FREE`
🖹 01381 621730
e-mail: groamhouse@ecosse.net

Opened in 1980, this community based museum explores the history, culture and crafts of the mysterious Picts, who faded

continued

from history over a thousand years ago. Visitors can see the Rosemarkie Stones, large slabs that show Pictish carvings; paintings, a replica Pictish harp, and a collection of photographs of Pictish stones all over the country and interactive Computer programmes.
Times: Open Etr week, daily 2-4.30; May-Sep, Mon-Sat, 10-5, Sun 2-4.30; Oct-Apr, Sat-Sun 2-4.30. Other times by appointment.
Facilities: ▣ shop ✖ (ex guide dogs) ☜

STRATHPEFFER   Map 14 NH45
HIGHLAND MUSEUM OF CHILDHOOD
The Old Station IV14 9DH
➲ (take A9 N of Inverness, then the Tore rdbt, follow signs to Dingwall. Strathpeffer lies 5m W of Dingwell on A834).
☎ 01997 421031 ▤ 01997 421031
e-mail: info@hmoc.freeserve.co.uk
Located in a renovated Victorian railway station of 1885, the museum tells the story of childhood in the Highlands amongst the crofters and townsfolk; a way of life recorded in oral testimony, displays, and evocative photographs. An award-winning video, "A Century of Highland Childhood" is shown. There are also doll and toy collections.
Times: Open Apr-Oct, daily 10-5, (Sun 2-5) also Jul & Aug evenings open to 7pm. Other times by arrangement. **Fee:** ✱ £2 (ch, pen & students £1.50). Family ticket £5 (2ad+3ch). **Facilities:** ▣ ▣ ⅊ ⅋ (tape tour with induction loop for partially sighted) shop ✖ (ex guide dogs) ☜

TORRIDON   Map 14 NG85
TORRIDON COUNTRYSIDE CENTRE
The Mains IV22 2EZ
➲ (N of A896)
☎ 01445 791221 ▤ 01445 791378
e-mail: aclipson@nts.scot.demon.co.uk.
Set amid some of Scotland's finest mountain scenery, the centre offers audio-visual presentations on the local wildlife. At the Mains nearby there are live deer to be seen.
Times: ✱ Open - Countryside Centre May-29 Sep, daily 10-6. Estate and Deer Museum daily all year. **Facilities:** ▣ ⅋ toilets for disabled ⅋

WICK   Map 15 ND35
CAITHNESS GLASS FACTORY & VISITOR CENTRE
Airport Industrial Estate KW1 5BP
➲ (on N side of Wick, beside Airport on A99 to John O'Groats)
☎ 01955 602286 ▤ 01955 605200
e-mail: visitor@caithnessglass.co.uk
All aspects of glassmaking are on view, from the initial processing of the raw materials to the finished article.
Times: ✱ Open all year, Factory shop & Restaurant Mon-Sat 9-5 (Sun, Etr-Dec 11-5). Glassmaking Mon-Fri 9-4.30. **Facilities:** ▣ ✖ licensed ⅋ toilets for disabled shop ✖ (ex guide dogs) ☜

CASTLE OF OLD WICK
➲ (1m S of Wick on Shore Road)   FREE
☎ 01667 460232
The ruin of the best-preserved Norse castle in Scotland. Dating from the 12th-century this spectacular site is on a spine of rock protecting the sea, between two deep, narrow gullies. Visitors must take great care and wear sensible shoes.
Times: Open at all reasonable times. **Facilities:** ✖ ▮

WICK HERITAGE CENTRE
20 Bank Row KW1 5HS
➲ (close to the harbour)
☎ 01955 605393 ▤ 01955 605393
The heritage centre is near the harbour in a complex of eight houses, yards and outbuildings. The centre illustrates local history from Neolithic times to the herring fishing industry. In addition, there is a complete working 19th-century lighthouse, and the famous Johnston collection of photographs.
Times: Open Jun-Sep, Mon-Sat 10-5. (Closed Sun). **Fee:** ✱ £2 (ch 50p). **Facilities:** ▣ ⅋ toilets for disabled

INVERCLYDE

GREENOCK   Map 10 NS27
McLEAN MUSEUM & ART GALLERY
15 Kelly St PA16 8JX
➲ (close to Greenock West Railway Station and Greenock Bus Station)   FREE
☎ 01475 715624 ▤ 01475 715626

James Watt was born in Greenock, and various exhibits connected with him are shown. The museum also has an art collection, and displays on shipping, local and natural history, Egyptology and ethnography.
Times: Open all year, Mon-Sat 10-5. (Closed local & national PH).
Facilities: ▣ (200mtrs) ⅋ (induction loop) toilets for disabled shop ✖ (ex guide & service dogs)

PORT GLASGOW   Map 10 NS37
NEWARK CASTLE
PA14 5NH
➲ (In Port Glasgow on the A8)
☎ 01475 741858
The one-time house of the Maxwells, dating from the 15th and 17th centuries. The courtyard and hall are preserved. Fine turrets and the remains of painted ceilings can be seen, and the hall carries an inscription of 1597.
Times: ✱ Open Apr-Sep, daily 9.30-6.30. **Facilities:** ▣ shop ▮

MIDLOTHIAN

CRICHTON   Map 11 NT36
CRICHTON CASTLE
EH37 5QH
⮕ (2.5m SW of Pathhead, off A68)
☎ 01875 320017
The castle dates back to the 14th century, but most of what remains today was built over the following 300 years. A notable feature is the 16th-century wing built by the Earl of Bothwell in Italian style, with an arcade below.
Times: ✱ Open Apr-Sep, daily 9.30-6.30. **Facilities:** 🅿️ ▮

DALKEITH   Map 11 NT36
EDINBURGH BUTTERFLY & INSECT WORLD
Dobbies Garden World, Lasswade EH18 1AZ
⮕ (0.5m S of Edinburgh city bypass at Gilmerton junct or Sherrifhall rdbt)   2 for 1
☎ 0131 663 4932 ▯ 0131 654 2774
e-mail: info@edinburgh-butterfly-world.co.uk
Richly coloured butterflies from all over the world can be seen flying among exotic rainforest plants, trees and flowers. The tropical pools are filled with giant waterlilies and colourful fish, and are surrounded by lush vegetation. Also scorpions, leaf cutting ants, beetles, tarantulas and other remarkable creatures. There is a unique honeybee display and daily insect handling sessions.
Times: Open Summer daily 9.30-5.30; winter daily 10-5. (Closed 25-26 Dec & 1 Jan). **Fee:** ✱ £4.50 (ch, concessions & students £3.50). Family ticket £14 (2ad+2ch). Party 10+. **Facilities:** 🅿️ 💺 ♿ toilets for disabled shop garden centre ✖ (ex guide dogs) ▩

NEWTONGRANGE   Map 11 NT36
SCOTTISH MINING MUSEUM
Lady Victoria Colliery EH22 4QN
⮕ (10m S of Edinburgh City on A7, signposted from Edinburgh City bypass)   2 for 1
☎ 0131 663 7519 ▯ 0131 654 1618
e-mail: enquiries@scottishminingmuseum.com
Based at Scotland's National Coalmining Museum offering an outstanding visit to Britains' finest Victorian colliery. Guided tours with miners, magic helmets, exhibitions, theatres, interactive displays and a visit to the coal face. Home to Scotland's largest steam engine.
Times: Open all year, daily 10-5. Last entry 3.30pm **Fee:** ✱ £4 (ch & concessions £2.20). Family ticket £10. Party 20+. **Facilities:** 🅿️ 💺 ✖ ♿ (Tactile Opportunites, interactive, audio tours) toilets for disabled shop ✖ (ex guide dogs) ▩

PENICUIK   Map 11 NT26
EDINBURGH CRYSTAL VISITOR CENTRE
Eastfield EH26 8HB
⮕ (on A701 road from Edinburgh to Peebles)
☎ 01968 675128   2 for 1
▯ 01968 674847
e-mail: visitorcentre@edinburgh-crystal.co.uk
Watch skilled craftsmen as they take molten crystal and turn it into intricately decorated glassware. Not only can you talk to the craftsmen themselves but there is also video footage, story boards, artefacts and audio listening posts to help you
continued

understand the 300-year-old history of glassmaking. The shop includes the largest selection of Edinburgh crystal plus seconds at bargain prices. Coffee shop.
Times: Open Mon-Sat 10-5, Sun 11-5. **Fee:** ✱ Tours £3.50 (concessions £2.50). Family ticket £9. Party 12+. **Facilities:** 🅿️ 💺 ♿ (ramp to first floor) toilets for disabled shop ✖ (ex guide dogs) ▩

MORAY

BALLINDALLOCH   Map 15 NJ13
THE GLENLIVET DISTILLERY
Glenlivet AB37 9DB
⮕ (off B9008 10m N of Tomintoul)
☎ 01340 821720 ▯ 01340 821718   FREE
e-mail: betty.munro@chivas.com
The visitor centre includes a guided tour of the whisky production facilities and a chance to see inside the vast bonded warehouses where the spirit matures. The new multimedia exhibition and interactive presentations communicate the unique history, and traditions of Glenlivet Scotch Whisky.
Times: Open Apr-Oct, Mon-Sat 10-4, Sun 12.30-4. **Facilities:** 🅿️ 💺 ♿ (cafeteria, lift to exhibition) toilets for disabled shop ✖ (ex guide dogs) ▩

BRODIE CASTLE   Map 14 NH95
BRODIE CASTLE
IV36 2TE
⮕ (4.5m W of Forres, off A96)
☎ 01309 641371 ▯ 01309 641600
e-mail: brodiecastle@nts.org.uk
The Brodie family lived here for hundreds of years before passing the castle to the NTS in 1980. It contains many treasures, including furniture, porcelain and paintings. The extensive grounds include a woodland walk and an adventure playground. Wheelchairs for disabled visitors are available. Please telephone for details of recitals, concerts, open air theatre etc.
Times: Open 1-30 Apr & Jul-Aug, daily 12-4; May-Jun & Sep, Sun-Thu 12-4; May. Grounds all year, daily, 9.30-sunset. **Fee:** ✱ £5 (concession £3.75) Groups adults £4, child/school £1, please book groups in advance. Family ticket £13.50. Garden, grounds & car parking £1. Admission free to NTS members. For other details please phone 0131 243 9387. **Facilities:** 🅿️ 💺 ♿ (audio tape & information sheet in Braille) toilets for disabled shop ✖ (ex guide dogs) ▩

BUCKIE   Map 15 NJ46
BUCKIE DRIFTER MARITIME HERITAGE CENTRE
Freuchny Rd AB56 1TT
⮕ (off A98 at March Rd Industrial Estate. Follow road N to rdbt, straight ahead and follow road to left. Buckie Drifter car park is on right at bottom of hill)
☎ 01542 834646 ▯ 01542 835995
e-mail: buckie.drifter@moray.gov.uk
An exciting maritime heritage centre, where you can discover what life was like in the fishing communities of Moray District during the herring boom years of the 1890s and 1930s. Sign on as a crew member of a steam drifter and
continued

find out how to catch herring. Try your hand at packing fish in a barrel.

Buckie Drifter Maritime Heritage Centre

Times: Open end Mar-end Oct **Facilities:** 🅿 💺 ♿ (car parking, touch display on lower floor) toilets for disabled shop ✖ (ex assistance dogs) 🍴

CRAIGELLACHIE   Map 15 NJ24

SPEYSIDE COOPERAGE VISITOR CENTRE
Dufftown Rd AB38 9RS
➲ (1m S of Craigellachie on A941)
☎ 01340 871108 📠 01340 881437
e-mail: info@speyside-coopers.demon.co.uk

A working cooperage with unique visitor centre, where skilled coopers and their apprentices practise this ancient craft. Each year they repair around 100,000 oak casks which will be used to mature many different whiskies. The 'Acorn to Cask' exhibition traces the history and development of the coopering industry.

Times: Open all year, Mon-Fri 9.30-4. (Closed Xmas & New Year).
Fee: £3.10 (ch £1.80 & pen £2.50). Family ticket £8.50. Party 15+.
Facilities: 🅿 💺 ♿ (Special picnic table) toilets for disabled shop ✖ (ex guide dogs) 🍴

DUFFTOWN   Map 15 NJ34

BALVENIE CASTLE
AB55 4DH
➲ (At Dufftown on the A941)
☎ 01340 820121

The ruined castle was the ancient stronghold of the Comyns, and became a stylish house in the 16th century.

Times: ✱ Open Apr-Sep, daily 9.30-6.30. **Facilities:** 🅿 ♿ toilets for disabled 🍴

GLENFIDDICH DISTILLERY
AB55 4DH
➲ (N of town, off A941)
☎ 01340 820373 📠 01340 822083

Set close to Balvenie Castle, the distillery was founded in 1887 by William Grant and has stayed in the hands of the family ever since. Visitors can see the whisky-making

continued

process in its various stages, including bottling, and then sample the finished product.

Times: ✱ Open all year Mon-Fri 9.30-4.30, also Etr-mid Oct Sat 9.30-4.30, Sun 12-4.30. (Closed Xmas & New Year). **Facilities:** 🅿 ♿ (ramp access to production area & warehouse gallery) toilets for disabled shop ✖ (ex guide dogs)

DUFFUS   Map 15 NJ16

DUFFUS CASTLE
➲ (5m NW of Elgin on B9012 to Burghead)   **FREE**
☎ 01667 460232

One of the finest examples of a motte and bailey castle in Scotland with a later, very fine, stone hall house and curtain wall. The original seat of the Moray family.

Times: Open at all reasonable times. **Facilities:** 🅿 ✖ 🍴

ELGIN   Map 15 NJ26

ELGIN CATHEDRAL
North College St IV30 1EL
☎ 01343 547171

Founded in 1224, the cathedral was known as the Lantern of the North and the Glory of the Kingdom because of its beauty. In 1390 it was burnt, along with most of the town. Although it was rebuilt, it fell into ruin after the Reformation. The ruins are quite substantial, however, and there is still a good deal to admire, including the fine west towers and the octagonal chapter house.

Times: ✱ Open all year, Apr-Sep, daily 9.30-6.30; Oct-Mar, Mon-Sat 9.30-4.30, Sun 2-4.30. (Closed Thu pm, Fri in winter & 25-26 Dec). **Facilities:** 🅿 ♿ shop 🍴

ELGIN MUSEUM
1 High St IV30 1EQ
➲ (East end of High Street, opp 'Safeway'. Follow brown heritage signs)
☎ 01343 543675 📠 01343 543675
e-mail: curator@elginmuseum.org.uk

This award-winning museum is internationally famous for its fossil fish and fossil reptiles, and for its Pictish stones. The displays relate to the natural and human history of Moray.

Times: Open Apr-Oct, Mon-Fri 10-5, Sat 11-4, Sun 2-5. **Fee:** ✱ £2 (ch 50p, pen, students & UB40 £1). Family ticket £4.50. **Facilities:** 🅿 (50mtrs) ♿ (handrails, case displays at sitting level with large fonts) toilets for disabled shop ✖ (ex guide dogs)

PLUSCARDEN ABBEY
IV30 8UA
➲ (6m SW on unclass road)
☎ 01343 890257 📠 01343 890258   **FREE**
e-mail: monks@pluscardenabbey.org

The original monastery, founded by Alexander II in 1230, was burnt, probably by the Wolf of Badenoch who also destroyed Elgin Cathedral. It was restored in the 14th and 19th centuries, and reoccupied in 1948 by Benedictines from Prinknash. Once more a religious community, retreat facilities are available for men and women. All services (with Gregorian chant) are open to the public. Pluscarden Pentecost Lectures held annually on Tuesday, Wednesday and Thursday after Pentecost.

Times: Open all year, daily 4.45-8.30. **Facilities:** 🅿 ♿ (induction loop, ramps to shop, garden partially accessible) toilets for disabled shop garden centre 🍴

FOCHABERS   Map 15 NJ35

BAXTERS HIGHLAND VILLAGE
IV32 7LD
➲ (1m W of Fochabers on A96)
☎ 01343 820666 ▤ 01343 821790   FREE
e-mail: highland.village@Baxters.co.uk

The Baxters food firm started here over 130 years ago and now sells its products in over 60 countries. Visitors can see the shop where the story began, watch an audio-visual display, and visit five shops. See the great hall, audio-visual theatre and cooking theatre. A food tasting area is a new addition.
Times: Open all year, Jan-Mar 10-5; Apr-Dec 9-5.30. **Facilities:** ▣ ✗ licensed ♿ (parking facilities) toilets for disabled shop ✖ (ex guide dogs) ◥

FORRES   Map 14 NJ05

DALLAS DHU DISTILLERY
IV36 2RR
➲ (1m S of Forres, off A940)
☎ 01309 676548

A perfectly preserved time capsule of the distiller's art. It was built in 1898 to supply malt whisky for Wright and Greig's 'Roderick Dhu' blend. Visitors are welcome to wander at will through this fine old Victorian distillery, or to take a guided tour, dram included.
Times: ✱ Open all year, Apr-Sep, daily 9.30-6.30; Oct-Mar, Mon-Sat 9.30-4.30, Sun 2-4.30. (Closed Thu pm, Fri in winter & 25-26 Dec). **Facilities:** ▣ ♿ toilets for disabled shop ✖ ▮

FALCONER MUSEUM
Tolbooth St IV36 1PH
➲ (11 miles W of Elgin, 26 miles E of Iverness)
☎ 01309 673701 ▤ 01309 675863   FREE
e-mail: museums@moray.gov.uk

Founded by bequests made by two brothers, Alexander and Hugh Falconer. Hugh was a distinguished scientist, friend of Darwin, recipient of many honours and Vice-President of the Royal Society. On display are fossil mammals collected by him, and items relating to his involvement in the study of anthropology. Other displays are on local wildlife, geology, archaeology and history. Also you can see the Forres Quincentennial Time Capsule.
Times: Open all year - Apr-Oct, Mon-Sat 10-5; Nov-Mar, Mon-Thu 11-12.30 & 1-3.30. (Closed Good Fri & May Day). **Facilities:** ▣ ♿ (induction loop system) shop ✖ (ex guide dogs)

SUENO'S STONE
➲ (E end of Forres, off A96)
☎ 01667 460232   FREE

The most remarkable sculptured monument in Britain, probably a cenotaph, standing over 20 feet high and dating back to the end of the first millennium AD. Covered by a protective glass enclosure.
Times: Open at all reasonable times. **Facilities:** ▣ ✖ ▮

KEITH   Map 15 NJ45

STRATHISLA DISTILLERY
Seafield Av AB55 5BS
➲ (follow A96 Aberdeen to Inverness road, Strathisla is signposted midway through the town)
☎ 01542 783044 ▤ 01542 783039   2 for 1
e-mail: jeanett.grant@chivas.com

Tour the oldest distillery in the highlands, founded in 1786. Discover the art of the blender before sipping a dram in luxurious comfort.
Times: Open Apr-Oct, Mon-Sat 10-4, Sun 12.30-4 **Fee:** £5 per person (ch18 free, children under 8 are not admitted to production areas, but are welcome in the centre) **Facilities:** ▣ (access is very limited) shop ✖ (ex guide dogs) ◥

MARYPARK   Map 15 NJ13

GLENFARCLAS DISTILLERY
AB37 9BD
➲ (4m W of Aberlour on A95 to   2 for 1
Grantown-on-Spey)
☎ 01807 500245 & 500257 ▤ 01807 500234
e-mail: J&GGrant@glenfarclas.demon.co.uk

Established in 1836, Glenfarclas Distillery is proud of its independence. There is guided tour illustrating the whisky's history and production, followed by a dram in the splendour of the Ships Room or a chance to browse in the gift shop.
Times: Open Jan-Mar, Mon-Fri 10-4; Apr-Sep, Mon-Fri 10-5, Jul-Sep also open Sat 10-5; Oct-Dec, Mon-Fri 10-4. (Closed Sun). **Fee:** ✱ £3.50. Free admission to under 18's. Party rates available. **Facilities:** ▣ ♿ (only visitor centre is accessible) toilets for disabled shop ✖ (ex guide dogs in vis. centre) ◥

ROTHES   Map 15 NJ24

GLEN GRANT DISTILLERY
AB38 7BS
➲ (On A941, in Rothes)
☎ 01340 832118 ▤ 01340 832104   FREE
e-mail: jennifer.robertson@chivas.com

Founded in 1840 in a sheltered glen by the two Grant brothers. Discover the secrets of the distillery, including the delightful Victorian garden originally created by Major Grant, and now restored to its former glory, where you can enjoy a dram.
Times: Open Apr-Oct, Mon-Sat 10-4, Sun 12.30-4. **Facilities:** ▣ ♿ (reception centre & still house) toilets for disabled shop ✖ (ex guide dogs) ◥

SPEY BAY   Map 15 NJ36

THE MORAY FIRTH WILDLIFE CENTRE
IV32 7PJ
➲ (off A96 onto B9014 at Fochabers, follow road approx 5m to village of Spey Bay. Turn left at Spey Bay Hotel and follow road for 500mtrs)
☎ 01343 820339 ▤ 01343 829109
e-mail: enquiries@mfwc.co.uk

Established in 1997, this family run visitor centre is housed in a former salmon fishing station at the mouth of the Spey. The centre contains exhibitions on dolphins, otters, birds, seals and other local wildlife, a gift shop and a restaurant.

continued

Visitors can take to sea on the "Dolphinicity", a survey boat that observes and records sightings of wildlife.
Times: ✱ Open Apr-Oct 10.30-5 **Facilities:** 🅿 💺 ✗ ♿ toilets for disabled shop ✖ (ex guide dogs) 🍴

TOMINTOUL   Map 15 NJ11

TOMINTOUL MUSEUM
The Square AB37 9ET
➲ (on A939, 13m E of Grantown)
☎ 01309 673701 📠 01309 675863   FREE
e-mail: museums@moray.gov.uk
Situated in one of the highest villages in Britain, the museum features a reconstructed crofter's kitchen and smiddy, with other displays on the local wildlife, the story of Tomintoul, and the local skiing industry.
Times: Open 25 Mar-May, Mon-Fri 9.30-12 & 2-4; Jun-Aug, Mon-Sat, 9.30-12 & 2-4.30; Sep, Mon-Sat, 9.30-12 & 2-4; 30 Sep-25 Oct, Mon-Fri, 9.30-12 & 2-4. Closed May Day & Good Fri. **Facilities:** 🅿 ♿ (Induction loop and sound commentaries) shop (gifts, postcards & books) ✖ (ex guide dogs)

NORTH AYRSHIRE

IRVINE   Map 10 NS34

THE BIG IDEA
The Harbourside KA12 8XX
➲ (Turn off A78 Irvine & follow signs for Irvine Harbourside & The Big Idea. The Big Idea is located on the right hand side)
☎ 08708 404030 📠 08708 403130   2 for 1
e-mail: net@bigidea.org.uk
The Big Idea is a permanent Millennium exhibition on the Ardeer Peninsula linked to Irvine harbourside by a retractable pedestrian bridge. It features 100 years of Nobel Laureates, and 1,000 years of invention and creative genius. Visitors can explore the history of mankind's inventions, creations and innovations.
Times: Open Mon-Fri, 10-5, Sat & Sun 10-6. Please phone for winter opening hours (Nov-Feb). **Fee:** ✱ £7.95 (ch, pen & concessions £5.95). Family ticket (2 adults & 2 ch) £24. **Facilities:** 🅿 💺 ♿ (wheelchairs) toilets for disabled shop ✖ (ex guide dogs or outside) 🍴

SCOTTISH MARITIME MUSEUM
Harbourside KA12 8QE
➲ (Follow AA signs from Irvine)   2 for 1
☎ 01294 278283 📠 01294 313211
The museum has displays that reflect all aspects of Scottish maritime history. Vessels can be seen afloat in the harbour and undercover. Experience life in a 1910 shipyard worker's tenement flat. Visit the Linthouse Engine Shop originally built in 1872, which is being developed and holds a substantial part of the museum's collection in open store.
Times: Open all year, daily 10-5, (ex Xmas & New Year). **Fee:** ✱ £2.50 (ch & pen £1.75). Family ticket £5. **Facilities:** 🅿 💺 ♿ (audio tapes for blind) toilets for disabled shop ✖ (ex guide dogs)

VENNEL GALLERY
10 Glasgow Vennel KA12 0BD
☎ 01294 275059 📠 01294 275059   FREE
e-mail: vennel@north-ayrshire.gov.uk
The Vennel Gallery has a reputation for exciting and varied exhibitions, ranging from international to local artists. Behind the museum is the Heckling Shop where Robert Burns, Scotland's most famous poet, spent part of his youth learning the trade of flax dressing. In addition to the audio-visual programme on Burns, there is a reconstruction of his lodgings at No.4 Glasgow Vennel, Irvine.
Times: Open all year Thu-Sun 10-1 & 2-5 **Facilities:** 🅿 (residential area) ♿ shop ✖ (ex guide dogs)

LARGS   Map 10 NS25

KELBURN CASTLE AND COUNTRY CENTRE
Fairlie KA29 0BE
➲ (on A78 2m S of Largs)   2 for 1
☎ 01475 568685 📠 01475 568121
e-mail: admin@kelburncountrycentre.com
Historic home of the Earls of Glasgow, Kelburn is famous for its romantic Glen, family gardens, unique trees and spectacular views over the Firth of Clyde. Glen walks, riding and trekking centre, adventure course, activity workshop, Kelburn Story Cartoon Exhibition and a family museum. The "Secret Forest" at the centre, Scotland's most unusual attraction, is a chance to explore the Giant's Castle, maze of the Green Man and secret grotto.
Times: Open all year, Etr-end Oct, daily 10-6; Nov-Mar, Grounds only. **Fee:** £5 (concessions £3.50). Family tickets £15. **Facilities:** 🅿 💺 ✗ licensed ♿ (Ranger service to assist disabled) toilets for disabled shop 🍴

VIKINGAR!
Greenock Rd KA30 8QL
➲ (Situated opposite the RNLI lifeboat stn on A78, 0.5m into Largs)
☎ 01475 689777 📠 01475 689444
e-mail: anyone@vikingar.co.uk
A multi-media experience that takes you from the first Viking raids in Scotland to their defeat at the Battle of Largs.
Times: Open daily, Apr-Sep, Mon-Fri & Sun 10.30-5.30, Sat 12.30-3.30; Oct-Mar, Mon-Fri & Sun 10.30-3.30, Sat 10.30-3.30; Nov & Feb, wknds only, Sat 12.30-3.30, Sun 10.30-3.30. (Closed Dec & Jan). **Fee:** ✱ £4 (ch 4-15 £3). Family ticket £12.20 **Facilities:** 🅿 💺 ♿ toilets for disabled shop ✖ (ex guide dogs) 🍴

SALTCOATS   Map 10 NS24

NORTH AYRSHIRE MUSEUM
Manse St, Kirkgate KA21 5AA   FREE
☎ 01294 464174 📠 01294 464174
e-mail: namuseum@north-ayrshire.gov.uk
This museum is housed in an 18th-century church, and features a rich variety of artefacts from the North Ayrshire area, including archaeological and social history material. There is a continuing programme of temporary exhibitions.
Times: Open all year, Mon-Sat (ex Sun & Wed) 10-1 & 2-5.
Facilities: 🅿 (100mtrs) ♿ toilets for disabled shop ✖ (ex guide dogs)

NORTH LANARKSHIRE

COATBRIDGE Map 11 NS76
SUMMERLEE HERITAGE TRUST
Heritage Way, West Canal St ML5 1QD
➲ (Follow main routes torwards town centre,
adjacent to Coatbridge central station) **FREE**
☎ 01236 431261 ▤ 01236 440429

A 20-acre museum of social and industrial history centring
on the remains of the Summerlee Ironworks which were put
into blast in the 1830s. The exhibition hall features displays
of social and industrial history including working machinery
and recreated workshop interiors. Outside, Summerlee
operates the only working tram in Scotland, a coal mine and
reconstructed miners' rows with interiors dating from 1840.
Times: Open daily 10-5. (Closed 25-26 Dec & 1-2 Jan). Nov-Mar 10-4.
Facilities: 🅿 🏪 ₲ (wheelchair available & staff assistance) toilets for
disabled shop ✖ (ex guide dogs)

MOTHERWELL Map 11 NS75
MOTHERWELL HERITAGE CENTRE
High Rd ML1 3HU
➲ (M74 junct 6, A723 for town centre. At top of
hill, turn left,after pedestrian crossing and just
before railway bridge) **FREE**
☎ 01698 251000 ▤ 01698 268867

This award winning audio-visual experince, 'Technopolis',
traces the history of the area from Roman times to the rise of
19th-century industry and the post-industrial era. There is
also a fine viewing tower, an exhibition gallery and family
history research facilities. A mixed programme of community
events and touring exhibitions occur throughout the year.
Times: Open Wed-Sat 10-5 (Thu 10-7), Sun 12-5. **Facilities:** 🅿 ₲
toilets for disabled shop ✖ (ex guide dogs)

PERTH & KINROSS

ABERFELDY Map 14 NN84
DEWAR'S WORLD OF WHISKY
Aberfeldy Distillery PH15 2EB
➲ (from A9 turn off for Aberfeldy on A827 at
Ballinluig)
☎ 01887 822010 ▤ 01887 822012 **2 for 1**
e-mail: worldofwhisky@dewars.com

Tradition and the latest technology are combined here to tell
the story of Dewar's White Label Whisky. Visitors are able to
sample the product in the Nosing and Tasting Bar, and have
a guided tour of the Aberfeldy distillery, where they can see
traditional techniques being employed by skilled craftsmen.
Times: Open Apr-Oct, Mon-Sat 10-6, Sun noon-4; Nov-Mar, Mon-Fri
10-4. (Closed Xmas & New Year). **Fee:** ✱ £5 (ch £2.50, concession £3).
Family ticket £12. Party by arrangement. **Facilities:** 🅿 🏪 ₲ (visitor
centre only accessible) toilets for disabled shop ✖ (ex guide dogs) 🍴

BLAIR ATHOLL Map 14 NN86
BLAIR CASTLE
PH18 5TL
➲ (7m NW of Pitlochry, off A9)
☎ 01796 481207 ▤ 01796 481487
e-mail: office@blair-castle.co.uk

Home of the Dukes of Atholl and the Atholl Highlanders, the
Duke's unique private army. The castle dates back to the
13th century but was altered in the 18th, and later given a
castellated exterior. The oldest part is Cumming's Tower,
built in about 1270. There are paintings, Jacobite relics, lace,
tapestries, and Masonic regalia. The extensive grounds
include a deer park, and a restored 18th-century walled
garden. Events are held throughout the year, including the
annual parade of the Duke's Private Army (ring for details).
Times: Open, 1 Apr-29 Oct, 9.30-4.30. **Fee:** £6.70 (ch £4.20, senior
£5.70). Family ticket £17. Party 5.40 Prices to be confirmed
Facilities: 🅿 🏪 ✖ licensed ₲ (toilets not suitable for severely
disabled, parking) shop ✖ (ex guide dogs) 🍴

CRIEFF Map 11 NN82
INNERPEFFRAY LIBRARY
PH7 3RF
➲ (4.5m SE on B8062)
☎ 01764 652819
e-mail: library@innerpeff.fsnet.co.uk

This is Scotland's oldest free lending library. It was founded
in 1680 and is still open every day except Thursdays. It is
housed in a late 18th-century building, and contains a
notable collection of bibles and rare books. Adjacent is St
Mary's Chapel, the original site for the library and the
Drummond family burial place.
Times: Open all year, Mon-Wed & Fri-Sat 10-12.45 & 2-4.45, Sun 2-4.
(Closed Thu). Nov-Feb appointment only. **Fee:** £2.50 (ch under 15
50p) **Facilities:** 🅿 🏪 ✖ (ex guide dogs)

THE FAMOUS GROUSE EXPERIENCE
The Hosh PH7 4HA
➲ (1.5m NW off A85)
☎ 01764 656565 ▤ 01764 654366
e-mail: enquiries@famousgrouse.com

A trip to Crieff is incomplete without a visit to The Famous
Grouse Experience, set in Scotland's oldest, most visited and
award-winning distillery. Opened in July 2002, this new
attraction is a fun and interesting day out which combines
the traditional distillery visit with a unique exciting sensory
experience. Spend a relaxing few hours absorbing the history
of the brand. Test your senses and see if you have what it
takes to become a 'Whisky Nose'. Have lunch, a snack or
even a barbecue at the family restaurant. Visit the
well-stocked shop or enjoy a peaceful woodland walk over
The Brig O' Dram.
Times: Open daily 9-6 (last tour 4.30). closed 25 & 26 Dec. **Fee:** ✱
Distillery visit, grouse experience show £6, (ch £3) Family £16.
Facilities: 🅿 🏪 ✖ licensed ₲ Lifts in all areas toilets for disabled
shop ✖ (ex guide dogs) 🍴

DUNKELD — Map 11 NO04

THE ELL SHOP & LITTLE HOUSES

The Cross PH8 0AN

➲ (off A9, 15m N of Perth)

☎ 01350 727460

e-mail: dunkeld@nts.org.uk

The National Trust owns two rows of 20 houses in Dunkeld, and has preserved their 17th/18th-century character. They are not open to the public, but there is a display and audio-visual show in the Information Centre.

Times: ✱ Open Ell Shop 25 Mar-Sep, Mon-Sat, 10-5.30, Sun 12.30-5.30. Oct-24 Dec, Mon-Sat 10-4.30, Sun 12.30-4.30. **Facilities:** P (300yds) ♿ toilets for disabled shop ✖ ❦

GLENGOULANDIE DEER PARK — Map 14 NN75

GLENGOULANDIE DEER PARK

PH16 5NL

➲ (8m NW of Aberfeldy on B846).

☎ 01887 830261   ▤ 01887 830261

e-mail: helenmcadam@supanet.com

Various native birds and animals are kept in surroundings as similar to their natural environment as possible, and there are herds of red deer and Highland cattle. Pets must not be allowed out of cars.

Times: ✱ Open May-Oct, 9am-1hr before sunset. **Facilities:** P (charged) shop ✖

KILLIECRANKIE — Map 14 NN96

KILLIECRANKIE VISITOR CENTRE

NTS Visitor Centre PH16 5LG

➲ (3m N of Pitlochry on B8079)

☎ 01796 473233   ▤ 01796 473233

e-mail: killiecrankie@nts.org.uk

The visitor centre features an exhibition on the battle of 1689, when the Jacobite army routed the English, although the Jacobite leader, `Bonnie Dundee', was mortally wounded in the attack. The wooded gorge is a notable beauty spot, admired by Queen Victoria, and there are some splendid walks.

Times: ✱ Visitor Centre: 25 Mar-Jun & 2 Sep-31 Oct, daily 10-5.30, Jul-1 Sep, daily 9.30-7. Site: open all year daily. **Facilities:** P ❡ ♿ (visitor centre only) toilets for disabled shop ❦

KINROSS — Map 11 NO10

KINROSS HOUSE GARDENS

KY13 8ET

➲ (M90 Edinburgh to Perth, junct 6 to Kinross, and signposted in village)

☎ 01577 862900   ▤ 01577 863372

e-mail: jm@kinrosshouse.com

Yew hedges, roses and herbaceous borders are the elegant attractions of these formal gardens. The 17th-century house was built by Sir William Bruce, but is not generally open to the public.

Times: Gardens only open Apr-Sep, daily 10-7. **Facilities:** P ♿ ✖ (ex guide dogs)

LOCH LEVEN CASTLE

Castle Island KY13 7AR

➲ (on an island in Loch Leven accessible by boat from Kinross)

☎ 01786 450000

Mary Queen of Scots was imprisoned here in this five-storey castle in 1567 - she escaped 11 months later and gave the 14th-century castle its special place in history.

Times: ✱ Open Apr-Sep, daily 9.30-6.30. Telephone for 2004 details. **Facilities:** P shop ✖ ◪

RSPB NATURE RESERVE VANE FARM

By Loch Leven KY13 9LX

➲ (on S shore of Loch Leven, entered off B9097 to Glenrothes, 2m E junct 5 M90)

☎ 01577 862355   ▤ 01577 862013

e-mail: vane.farm@rspb.org.uk

Well placed beside Loch Leven, with a nature trail and hides overlooking the Loch and a woodland trail with stunning panoramic views. Noted for its pink-footed geese. The area also attracts whooper swans, greylag geese and great spotted woodpeckers amongst others. Details of special events are available from the Visitors Centre.

Times: Open daily, 10-5. Closed 25-26 Dec, 1-2 Jan. **Fee:** £3 (ch 50p, concessions £2). Family £6. **Facilities:** P ❡ ♿ (wheelchair extensions, ramps, telescopes) toilets for disabled shop ✖ (ex guide dogs) ❧

MILNATHORT — Map 11 NO10

BURLEIGH CASTLE

KY13 7XZ   `FREE`

➲ (0.5m E of Milnathort on A911)

The roofless but otherwise complete ruin of a tower house of about 1500, with a section of defensive barmkin wall and a remarkable corner tower with a square cap-house corbelled out. This castle was visited often by James IV.

Times: Open summer only. Keys available locally, telephone 01786 45000. **Facilities:** ✖ ◪

MUTHILL — Map 11 NN81

DRUMMOND CASTLE GARDENS

PH7 4HZ

➲ (2m S of Crieff on A822)

☎ 01764 681257 & 681433   ▤ 01764 681550

e-mail: thegardens@drummondcastle.sol.co.uk

The gardens of Drummond Castle were originally laid out in 1630 by John Drummond, 2nd Earl of Perth. In 1830, the parterre was changed to an Italian style. The multi-faceted sundial was designed by John Mylne, Master Mason to Charles I. These are Scotland's largest formal gardens and amongst the finest in Europe.

Times: Open Gardens May-Oct, daily 2-6 (Last admission 5pm). Also Etr for 4 days. **Facilities:** P ♿ toilets for disabled shop

PERTH   Map 11 NO12

BLACK WATCH REGIMENTAL MUSEUM
Balhousie Castle, Hay St PH1 5HR
➲ (Follow signs to Perth & Black Watch Museum, approach via Dunkeld Road)
☎ 0131 310 8530 🖹 01738 643245
e-mail: rhq@theblackwatch.co.uk
The treasures of the 42nd/73rd Highland Regiment from 1739 to the present day are on show in this museum, together with paintings, silver, colours, uniforms and weapons.
Times: Open all year. May-Sep, Mon-Sat 10-4.30 (Closed last Sat in Jun); Oct-Apr, Mon-Fri, 10-3.30 (Closed 23 Dec-6 Jan). Other times & Parties 16+ by appointment. **Fee:** ✱ Donations. **Facilities:** 🅿 & (1 bay parking for disabled) shop ✖ (ex guide dogs)

BRANKLYN GARDEN
116 Dundee Rd PH2 7BB
➲ (on A85)
☎ 01738 625535
e-mail: aclipson@nts.scot.demon.co.uk
The gardens cover two acres and are noted for their collections of rhododendrons, shrubs and alpines. Garden tours and botanical painting courses are held.
Times: 1-30 Apr & Jul-Sep, Fri-Tue 10-5; May-Jun, daily, 10-5. **Fee:** ✱ £5 (concession £3.75) Group adult £4, child/school £1, groups please book in advance. Family ticket 13.50. Admission free to NTS members. For other details please phone (0131) 243 9387. **Facilities:** 🅿 ✖ (ex guide dogs) ✇

CAITHNESS GLASS FACTORY & VISITOR CENTRE
Inveralmond Industrial Est PH1 3TZ
➲ (on Perth Western Bypass, A9, at Inveralmond Roundabout)
☎ 01738 637373 🖹 01738 492300
e-mail: visitor@caithnessglass.co.uk
All aspects of paperweight-making can be seen from the purpose-built viewing galleries. Visitors can now enter the glasshouse on a route which enables them to watch the glassmakers closely. There is also a factory shop, a best shop, children's play area and tourist information centre with internet access.
Times: Open all year, Factory shop & restaurant, Mon-Sat 9-5, Sun 10-5 (Dec-Feb 12-5). Glassmaking Mon-Fri 9-4.30. **Facilities:** 🅿 ✖ licensed & (wheelchair available) toilets for disabled shop ✖ (ex guide dogs) ✇

HUNTINGTOWER CASTLE
PH1 3JL
➲ (2m W)
☎ 01738 627231
Formerly known as Ruthven Castle and famous as the scene of the so-called 'Raid of Ruthven' in 1582, this structure was built in the 15th and 16th centuries and features a painted ceiling.
Times: ✱ Open all year, Apr-Sep, daily 9.30-6.30; Oct-Mar, Mon-Sat 9.30-4.30, Sun 2-4.30. (Closed Thu pm, Fri in winter & 25-26 Dec).
Facilities: 🅿 shop ✖ ▮

PERTH MUSEUM & ART GALLERY
78 George St PH1 5LB
➲ (situated in the centre of Perth)
☎ 01738 632488 🖹 01738 443505   `FREE`
e-mail: museum@pkc.gov.uk
Visit Perth Museum and Art Gallery for a fascinating look into Perthshire throughout the ages. Collections cover silver, glass, art, natural history, archaeology and human history.
Times: Open all year, Mon-Sat 10-5. (Closed Xmas-New Year).
Facilities: 🅿 (adjacent) & toilets for disabled shop ✖ (ex guide dogs)

PITLOCHRY   Map 14 NN95

EDRADOUR DISTILLERY
PH16 5JP
➲ (2.5m E of Pitlochry on A924)
☎ 01796 472095 🖹 01796 472002
e-mail: lwilliamson@campbell-distillers.co.uk
It was in 1825 that a group of local farmers founded Edradour, naming it after the bubbling burn that runs through it. It is Scotland's smallest distillery and is virtually unchanged since Victorian times. Have a dram of whisky while watching an audio-visual in the malt barn and then take a guided tour through the distillery itself.
Times: ✱ Open, early Mar-end Oct, Mon-Sat 9.30-5, Sun 12-5. Winter months, Mon-Sat 10-4, shop only. Tours by arrangement in winter months. **Facilities:** 🅿 & toilets for disabled shop ✖ (ex guide & hearing dogs)

SCOTTISH & SOUTHERN ENERGY VISITOR CENTRE, DAM & FISH PASS
PH16 5ND
➲ (Turn off A9, 24m N of Perth)
☎ 01796 473152 🖹 01882 634 709
The visitor centre features an exhibition showing how electricity is brought from the power station to the customer, and there is access to the turbine viewing gallery. The salmon ladder viewing chamber allows you to see the fish as they travel upstream to their spawning ground.
Times: Open Apr-Oct, Mon-Fri 10-5.30. (Weekend opening Jul, Aug & BH's). **Fee:** ✱ £2.50 (ch £1.25, concessions £1.50). Family ticket £5.
Facilities: 🅿 & (monitor viewing of salmon fish pass) toilets for disabled shop ✖ (ex guide dogs) ◥

QUEEN'S VIEW   Map 14 NN85

QUEEN'S VIEW VISITOR CENTRE
PH16 5NR
➲ (7m W of Pitlochry on B8019)
☎ 01350 727284 🖹 01350 728635
e-mail: peter.fullarton@forestry.gsi.gov.uk
Queen Victoria admired the view on a visit here in 1866; it is possibly one of the most famous views in Scotland. The area, in the heart of the Tay Forest Park, has a variety of woodlands that visitors can walk or cycle in. A new exhibition and audio-visual display 'The Cradle of Scottish Forestry' tells the history of the people and the forests of highland Perthshire.
Times: ✱ Open Apr-Oct, daily 10-6. **Facilities:** 🅿 (charged) ▣ & toilets for disabled shop ◥

SCONE　　　　　　　　　　　Map 11 NO12

SCONE PALACE
PH2 6BD
➲ (2m NE of Perth on A93)
☎ 01738 552300 ▤ 01738 552588
e-mail: visits@scone-palace.co.uk 　2 for 1

Scottish kings were crowned at Scone until 1651 and it was the site of the famous coronation Stone of Destiny from the 9th century until the English seized it in 1296. The castellated edifice of the present palace dates from 1803 but incorporates the 16th-century and earlier buildings. The interior houses objet d'art, including French & Scottish furniture, an extensive porcelain collection and paintings. The grounds include a pinetum, the original Douglas Fir, the unique Murray Star Maze, woodland walks and herbaceous plantings. Also David Douglas Trail.
Times: Open Apr-Oct. **Fee:** ✴ Palace & Grounds £6.35 (ch £3.75, students & pen £5.50). Family ticket £25, Season ticket £15. Grounds only £3.25 (ch £1.80, students and pen £2.65) Family £10.
Facilities: ▣ ▣ ✗ licensed ᕕ (stairlift which gives access to all state rooms) toilets for disabled shop ▦

WEEM　　　　　　　　　　　Map 14 NN84

CASTLE MENZIES
PH15 2JD
➲ (Follow signs from A9)
☎ 01887 820982 ▤ 01887 820982
e-mail: menziesclan@tesco.net

Restored seat of the Chiefs of Clan Menzies, and a fine example of a 16th-century Z-plan fortified tower house. Prince Charles Edward Stuart stayed here briefly on his way to Culloden in 1746. The whole of the 16th-century building can be explored, and there's a small clan museum.
Times: Open Apr-13 Oct, Mon-Sat 10.30-5, Sun 2-5. **Fee:** £3.50 (ch £2, concessions £3). **Facilities:** ▣ ᕕ toilets for disabled shop ✖ (ex guide dogs)

RENFREWSHIRE

KILBARCHAN　　　　　　　　Map 10 NS46

WEAVER'S COTTAGE
The Cross PA10 2JG
➲ (off A737, 12m SW of Glasgow)
☎ 01505 705588
e-mail: aclipson@nts.scot.demon.co.uk

The weaving craft is regularly demonstrated at this delightful 18th-century cottage museum, and there is a collection of weaving equipment and other domestic utensils.
Times: Open Apr-Sep, Fri-Tue, 1-5; morning visits available for pre-booked groups. **Fee:** ✴ £3.50 (concession £2.60) Family ticket £9.50. Groups adult £2.80, child/school £1. Please book groups in advance. Admission free to NTS members. For other details please phone 0131 243 9387. **Facilities:** ▣ ✖ (ex guide dogs) ♗

LANGBANK　　　　　　　　Map 10 NS37

FINLAYSTONE COUNTRY ESTATE
PA14 6TJ
➲ (on A8 W of Langbank, 10m W of Glasgow Airport, follow Thistle signs)
☎ 01475 540505 ▤ 01475 540285 　2 for 1
e-mail: info@finlaystone.co.uk

A beautiful country estate, historic formal gardens which are renowned for their natural beauty, woodland walks and play areas. The 'Dolly Mixture', an international collection of dolls, can be seen in the Visitor Centre.
Times: Open all year. Woodland & Gardens daily, 10-5. **Fee:** Garden & Woods £3 (ch & pen £2). 'The Dolly Mixture' Doll Museum free.
Facilities: ▣ ▣ ᕕ (lift to second floor pathways for wheelchairs) toilets for disabled shop ▦

LOCHWINNOCH　　　　　　Map 10 NS35

RSPB LOCHWINNOCH NATURE RESERVE
Largs Rd PA12 4JF
➲ (on A760, Largs road, opposite Lochwinnoch station, 16m SW of Glasgow)
☎ 01505 842663 ▤ 01505 843026
e-mail: Lochwinnoch@rspb.org.uk

The reserve, part of Clyde Muirshiel Regional Park and a Site of Special Scientific Interest, comprises two shallow lochs fringed by marsh which in turn is fringed by scrub and woodland. There are two trails leading to three hides and a visitor centre with a viewing.
Times: Open all year, daily 10-5. (Closed 1-2 Jan & 25-26 Dec).
Fee: Trails £2 (concessions £1, ch 50p). Family ticket £4. **Facilities:** ▣ ᕕ (hides are all wheelchair accessible) toilets for disabled shop ✖ ▦

PAISLEY　　　　　　　　　　Map 11 NS46

COATS OBSERVATORY
49 Oakshaw St West PA1 2DE
➲ (M8 junct 27, 28 or 29)
☎ 0141 889 2013 ▤ 0141 889 9240

Victorian astronomical observatory, built in 1883, designed by John Honeyman. Displays on earthquakes, weather, astronomy and astronautics.
Times: ✴ Open all year, Tue-Sat 10-5, Sun 2-5. Last entry 15 minutes before closing. **Facilities:** ▣ 150yds (meters/limited street parking) shop ✖ (ex guide dogs)

PAISLEY MUSEUM & ART GALLERIES
High St PA1 2BA
☎ 0141 889 3151 ▤ 0141 889 9240

Pride of place here is given to a world-famous collection of Paisley shawls. Other collections illustrate local industrial and natural history, while the emphasis of the art gallery is on 19th-century Scottish artists and an important studio ceramics collection.
Times: ✴ Open all year, Tue-Sat 10-5, Sun 2-5. BH 10-5. **Facilities:** ▣ (200yds) ᕕ (parking on site) toilets for disabled shop ✖ (ex guide dogs)

SCOTTISH BORDERS

COLDSTREAM · Map 12 NT84

HIRSEL
Douglas & Angus Estates, Estate Office, The Hirsel
TD12 4LP
➲ (0.5m W on A697, on northern outskirts of
Coldstream)
☎ 01890 882834 & 882965 📠 01890 882834
e-mail: rogerdodd@btconnect.com

The seat of the Home family, the grounds of which are open
all year. The focal point is the Homestead Museum, craft
centre and workshops. From there, nature trails lead around
the lake, along the Leet Valley and into woodland noted for
its rhododendrons and azaleas.
Times: Garden & Grounds open all year, daylight hours. Museum 10-5.
Craft Centre Mon-Fri, 10-5, wknds noon-5. **Fee:** £2 per car
Facilities: P (charged) 💷 ✕ 🚻 toilets for disabled shop (on leads)

DRYBURGH · Map 12 NT53

DRYBURGH ABBEY
TD6 0RQ
➲ (5m SE of Melrose on B6404)
☎ 01835 822381

The abbey was one of the Border monasteries founded by
David I, and stands in a lovely setting on the River Tweed.
The ruins are equally beautiful, and the church has the
graves of Sir Walter Scott and Earl Haig.
Times: ✱ Open all year, Apr-Sep, daily 9.30-6.30; Oct-Mar, Mon-Sat
9.30-4.30, Sun 2-4.30. (Closed 25-26 Dec). **Facilities:** P 🚻 shop ✕ ⚑

DUNS · Map 12 NT75

MANDERSTON
TD11 3PP
➲ (2m E of Duns on the A6105)
☎ 01361 883450 📠 01361 882010
e-mail: palmer@manderston.co.uk

This grandest of grand houses gives a fascinating picture of
Edwardian life above and below stairs. Completely
remodelled for the millionaire racehorse owner Sir James
Miller, the architect was told to spare no expense, and so the
house boasts the world's only silver staircase. The
staterooms are magnificent, and there are fine formal
gardens, with a woodland garden and lakeside walks.
Manderston has been the setting for a number of films, most
recently *The Edwardian Country House.*
Times: Open mid May-end Sep, Thu & Sun 2-5 (also late May & Aug
English BH Mons). Gardens are open until dusk. **Fee:** House & Gardens
£6.50 (ch £3) gardens only: £3.50 (ch £1.50). **Facilities:** P 💷 🚻
shop ✕ (ex guide dogs & in gardens)

EYEMOUTH · Map 12 NT96

EYEMOUTH MUSEUM
Auld Kirk, Manse Rd TD14 5JE
➲ (Turn off A1 onto A1107, follow signs to town
centre. Attraction located in town centre).
☎ 018907 50678

The museum was opened in 1981 as a memorial to the 129
local fishermen lost in the Great Fishing Disaster of 1881. Its

continued

main feature is the 15ft Eyemouth tapestry, which was made
for the centenary. There are also displays on local history.
Times: Open Apr-Jun & Sep, Mon-Sat 10-5, Sun 1-4; Jul-Aug, Mon-Sat
10-5; Sun 1-5; Oct, Mon-Sat 10-4, (closed Sun). **Fee:** ✱ £2
(concessions £1.50). Accompanied ch free. Party. **Facilities:** P
(250yds) (45min on street outside) 🚻 shop

GALASHIELS · Map 12 NT43

LOCHCARRON OF SCOTLAND VISITOR CENTRE
Waverley Mill, Huddersfield St TD1 3BA
➲ (32m S of Edinburgh on A7 follow signs to mill)
☎ 01896 752091 & 751100
📠 01896 758833
e-mail: quality@lochcarron.com

The museum brings the town's past to life and the focal
point is a display on the woollen industry. Guided tours of
the mill take about 40 minutes.
Times: Open all year, Mon-Sat 9-5, Sun (Jun-Sep) 12-5. Mill tours
Mon-Thu at 10.30, 11.30, 1.30 & 2.30, Fri am only. **Fee:** ✱ Museum
free. Mill tour £2.50 (ch 14 free). **Facilities:** P 🚻 toilets for disabled
shop ⚑

GORDON · Map 12 NT64

MELLERSTAIN HOUSE
TD3 6LG
➲ (signposted on A6089 Kelso-Gordon road,
1m W)
☎ 01573 410225 📠 01573 410636
e-mail: enquiries@mellerstain.com

One of Scotland's finest Georgian houses, begun by William
Adam and completed by his son Robert in the 1770s. It has
beautiful plasterwork, period furniture and pictures, terraced
gardens and a lake.
Times: Open Etr & May-Sep, Sun, Mon & Wed-Fri 12.30-5 (Last
admission 4.30pm). & wknds in Oct **Fee:** ✱ £5.50 (ch free) Party 20+.
Facilities: P 💷 🚻 shop garden centre ✕ (ex guide dogs) ⚑

HERMITAGE · Map 12 NY59

HERMITAGE CASTLE
TD9 0LU
➲ (5.5m NE of Newcastleton, on B6399)
☎ 01387 376222

A vast, eerie ruin of the 14th and 15th centuries, associated
with the de Soulis, the Douglases and Mary Queen of Scots.
Much restored in the 19th century.
Times: ✱ Open Apr-Sep, daily 9.30-6.30. **Facilities:** P 🚻 ⚑

INNERLEITHEN · Map 11 NT33

ROBERT SMAIL'S PRINTING WORKS
7/9 High St EH44 6HA
☎ 01896 830206
e-mail: smails@nts.org.uk

These buildings contain a Victorian office, a paper store with
reconstructed waterwheel, a composing room and a press
room. The machinery is in full working order and visitors
may view the printer at work and experience typesetting in
the composing room.
Times: Open Good Fri-Etr Mon & Jun-Sep,Thu-Mon 12-5, Sun 1-5
Fee: ✱ £3.50 (concession £2.60) Family ticket £9.50. Groups adult
£2.80, child/school £1. Admission free for NTS members. For other
details please phone 0131 243 9387. **Facilities:** P (300yds) 🚻 shop
✕ (ex guide dogs) ♨

JEDBURGH   Map 12 NT62

JEDBURGH ABBEY
☎ 01835 863925

Standing as the most complete of the Border monasteries (although it has been sacked and rebuilt many times) Jedburgh Abbey has been described as 'the most perfect and beautiful example of the Saxon and early Gothic in Scotland'. David I founded it as a priory in the 12th century and remains of some of the domestic buildings have been uncovered during excavations.
Times: ✸ Open all year, Apr-Sep, daily 9.30-6.30; Oct-Mar, Mon-Sat 9.30-4.30, Sun 2-4.30. (Closed 25-26 Dec). **Facilities:** 🅿 & (limited access) toilets for disabled shop ✖ 🏵

KELSO   Map 12 NT73

FLOORS CASTLE
Roxburghe Estates Office TD5 7SF
➲ (from town centre follow Roxburghe Street to main gates)
☎ 01573 223333 📠 01573 226056
e-mail: marketing@floorscastle.com

The home of the 10th Duke of Roxburghe, the Castle's lived-in atmosphere enhances the superb collection of French furniture, tapestries and paintings. The house was designed by William Adam in 1721 and enjoys a magnificent setting overlooking the River Tweed and the Cheviot Hills beyond.
Times: Open 5 Apr-26 Oct, daily 10-4.30. (last admission 4). **Facilities:** 🅿 🍴 ✖ licensed & (lift) toilets for disabled shop garden centre ➰

KELSO ABBEY
☎ 0131 668 8800   `FREE`

Founded by David I in 1128 and probably the greatest of the four famous Border abbeys, Kelso became extremely wealthy and acquired extensive lands. In 1545 it served as a fortress when the town was attacked by the Earl of Hertford, but now only fragments of the once-imposing abbey church give any clue to its long history.
Times: Open at any reasonable time. **Facilities:** & 🏵

LAUDER   Map 12 NT54

THIRLESTANE CASTLE
TD2 6RU
➲ (off A68, S of Lauder)
☎ 01578 722430 📠 01578 722761
e-mail: admin@thirlestanecastle.co.uk

One of the seven "Great Houses of Scotland" this fairy-tale castle has been the home of the Maitland family, the Earls of Lauderdale, since the 12th century. Some of the most splendid plasterwork ceilings in Britain may be seen in the 17th-century state rooms. The family nurseries house a sizeable collection of antique toys and dolls. Vaulted dungeon display. The informal riverside grounds, with their views of the grouse moors, include a woodland walk, picnic tables and adventure playground.
Times: ✸ Open Apr-Oct **Facilities:** 🅿 🍴 shop ✖ (ex guide dogs) ➰

MELROSE   Map 12 NT53

ABBOTSFORD
TD6 9BQ
➲ (2m W off A6091, on B6360)
☎ 01896 752043 📠 01896 752916
e-mail: abbotsford@melrose.bordernet.co.uk

Set on the River Tweed, Sir Walter Scott's romantic mansion remains much the same as it was in his day. Inside there are many mementoes and relics of his remarkable life and also his historical collections, armouries and library, with some 9000 volumes. Scott built the mansion between 1811 and 1822, and lived here until his death ten years after its completion.
Times: Open daily from 3rd Mon in Mar-Oct, Mon-Sat 9.30-5. Sun in Mar-May & Oct 2-5. Sun Jun-Sep 9.30-5. **Fee:** ✸ £4.20 (ch £2.10). Party £3.40 (ch £1.70). **Facilities:** 🅿 🍴 & (parking at private entrance, ramps at entrance) toilets for disabled shop ✖ (ex guide dogs & hearing dogs)

HARMONY GARDEN
St Mary's Rd TD6 9LJ
➲ (Opposite Melrose Abbey)
☎ 01721 722502 📠 01721 724700

Set around the early 19th century Harmony Hall (not open to visitors), this attractive walled garden has magnificent views of Melrose Abbey and the Eildon Hills. The garden comprises lawns, herbaceous and mixed borders, vegetable and fruit areas, and a rich display of spring bulbs.
Times: Open Good Fri-Etr Mon & Jun-Sep, Mon-Sat 10-5, Sun 1-5 **Fee:** ✸ £2 (concession £1). Admission free for NTS members. For other price details please phone 0131 243 9387. **Facilities:** 🅿 & ✖ 🏵

MELROSE ABBEY & ABBEY MUSEUM
TD6 9LG
☎ 01896 822562

The ruin of this Cistercian abbey is probably one of Scotland's finest, and has been given added glamour by its connection with Sir Walter Scott. The abbey was repeatedly wrecked during the Scottish wars of independence, but parts survive from the 14th century. The heart of Robert the Bruce is buried somewhere within the church.
Times: ✸ Open all year, Apr-Sep, daily 9.30-6; Oct-Mar, Mon-Sat 9.30-6 (Closed 25-26 Dec). **Facilities:** 🅿 & shop ✖ 🏵

PRIORWOOD GARDEN & DRIED FLOWER SHOP
TD6 9PX
➲ (off A6091, in Melrose, adjacent to the Abbey. On National Cycle Route 1)
☎ 01896 822493 📠 01896 822965
e-mail: priorwooddriedflowers@nts.org.uk

This small garden specialises in flowers suitable for drying. It is formally designed with herbaceous and everlasting annual borders, and the attractive orchard has a display of `apples through the ages'. Dried flowers are on sale in the shop.
Times: Open Good Fri-Etr Mon, May-Jun & Sep-24 Dec, Mon-Sat 12-5, Sun 1-5; Jul-Aug, Mon-Sat 10-5, Sun 1-5. **Fee:** £2.50 (concession £1.90. Family ticket £7. Groups adult £2, child/school £1. Please book groups in advance. Admission free for NTS members. For other details please phone 0131 243 9387 **Facilities:** 🅿 & (ramps, paths) shop 🏵

PEEBLES Map 11 NT24

KAILZIE GARDENS
EH45 9HT
➲ (2.5m SE on B7062)
☎ 01721 720007 📠 01721 720007

These extensive grounds, with their fine old trees, provide a burnside walk flanked by bulbs, rhododendrons and azaleas. A walled garden contains herbaceous, shrub rose borders, greenhouses and a formal rose garden. A garden for all seasons, don't miss the snowdrops. A large stocked trout pond and rod hire available, and an 18-hole putting green. Some recent features at Kailzie are the open bait pond, ornamental duck pond and osprey viewing centre.
Times: Open 25 Mar-Oct, daily 11-5.30. Grounds close 5.30pm. Garden open all year. **Fee:** mid Mar-Jun £2.50, Jun-Oct £3 (end Oct-mid Mar £2 honesty box) ch 5-12 80p **Facilities:** 🅿 💺 ✗ licensed ♿ (ramps in garden) toilets for disabled shop

NEIDPATH CASTLE
EH45 8NW
➲ (0.5m of Peebles W on A72)
☎ 01721 720333 📠 01721 729573
e-mail: keith.roxburgh@eidosnet.uk

Occupying a spectacular position on the Tweed, this 14th-century stronghold was adapted to 17th-century living; it contains a rock-hewn well, a pit prison, a small museum, and a tartan display. There are fine walks and a picnic area.
Times: Open 23 Jun-14 Sep, Mon-Sat 10.30-5, Sun 12.30-5 **Fee:** ✱ £3 (ch £1, concessions £2.50). Family ticket £7.50. Party 20+. **Facilities:** 🅿 (charged) shop

SELKIRK Map 12 NT42

BOWHILL HOUSE AND COUNTRY PARK
TD7 5ET
➲ (3m W of Selkirk off A708)
☎ 01750 22204 📠 01750 22204
e-mail: bht@buccleuch.com

An outstanding collection of pictures, including works by Van Dyck, Canaletto, Reynolds, Gainsborough and Claude Lorraine, are displayed here. Memorabilia and relics of people such as Queen Victoria and Sir Walter Scott, and a restored Victorian kitchen add further interest inside the house. Outside, the wooded grounds are perfect for walking. A small theatre provides a full programme of music and drama.
Times: Open, Park: Apr-Aug daily 12-5 (ex Fri). House & park: Jul, daily 1-4.30. **Fee:** House & grounds £6 (ch under 5 & wheelchair users free, pen & groups £4). Grounds only £2. **Facilities:** 🅿 💺 ✗ licensed ♿ (guided tours for the blind) toilets for disabled shop ✗ (ex in park on leads) 💺

Remember that prices and opening times are liable to change within the currency of this guide. It is always best to telephone in advance to check

HALLIWELLS HOUSE MUSEUM
Halliwells Close, Market Place TD7 4BC
➲ (off A7 in town centre)
☎ 01750 20096 📠 01750 23282
e-mail: museums@scotborders.gov.uk

A row of late 18th-century town cottages converted into a museum. Displays recreate the building's former use as an ironmonger's shop and home, and tell the story of the Royal Burgh of Selkirk. The Robson Gallery hosts a programme of contemporary art and craft exhibitions.
Times: Open Apr-Sep, Mon-Sat 10-5, Sun 10-12; Jul-Aug, Mon-Sat 10-5.30, Sun 10-12; Oct, Mon-Sat 10-4. **Facilities:** 🅿 (charged) ♿ (lift to first floor, large print, interpretation) toilets for disabled shop ✗ (ex guide dogs) 💺

SIR WALTER SCOTT'S COURTROOM
Market Place TD7 4BT
➲ (on A7 in town centre)
☎ 01750 20096 📠 01750 23282
e-mail: museums@scotborders.gov.uk

Built in 1803-4 as a sheriff court and town hall this is where the famous novelist, Sir Walter Scott dispensed justice when he was Sheriff of Selkirkshire from 1804-1832. Displays tell of Scott's time as Sheriff, and of his place as a novelist as well as those of his contemporaries, writer, James Hogg and the explorer, Mungo Park.
Times: Open Apr-Sep, Mon-Fri 10-4, Sat 10-2; May-Aug also Sun 10-2; Oct, Mon-Sat 1-4. **Facilities:** 🅿 (100mtrs) (30min on street, car park 50p for 2hrs) shop ✗ (ex guide dogs) 💺

SMAILHOLM Map 12 NT63

SMAILHOLM TOWER
TD5 7RT
➲ (6m W of Kelso on B6937)
☎ 01573 460365

An outstanding example of a classic Border tower-house, probably erected in the 15th century. It is 57ft high and well preserved. The tower houses an exhibition of dolls and a display based on Sir Walter Scott's book *Minstrels of the Border*.
Times: ✱ Open Apr-Sep, daily 9.30-6.30; Oct-Mar, Sat-Sun only. (Closed 25-26 Dec). **Facilities:** 🅿 shop ✗ 🏳

STOBO Map 11 NT13

DAWYCK BOTANIC GARDEN
EH45 9JU
➲ (8m SW of Peebles on B712)
☎ 01721 760254 📠 01721 760214
e-mail: dawyck@rbge.org.uk

From the landscaped walks of this historic arboretum an impressive collection of mature specimen trees can be seen - some over 40m tall and including the unique Dawyck beech-stand. Notable features include the Swiss Bridge, a fine estate chapel and stonework/terracing produced by Italian craftsmen in the 1820s.
Times: Open daily 14 Feb-14 Nov. Feb & Nov 10-4. Mar-Oct 10-5. Apr-Sep 10-6 **Fee:** £3.50 (ch £1, concessions £3). Family ticket £8 **Facilities:** 🅿 💺 ♿ toilets for disabled shop garden centre ✗ (ex guide dogs) 💺

TRAQUAIR   Map 11 NT33

TRAQUAIR HOUSE
EH44 6PW
➲ (At Innerleithen take B709, house
is 1m S of Innerleithen)   **2 for 1**
☎ 01896 830323 & 830785 📄 01896 830639
e-mail: enquiries@traquair.co.uk
Said to be Scotland's oldest inhabited house, dating back to
the 12th century, 27 Scottish monarchs have stayed at
Traquair House. William the Lion Heart held court here, and
the house has associations with Mary, Queen of Scots and
the Jacobite risings. The Bear Gates were closed in 1745, not
to be reopened until the Stuarts should once again ascend
the throne. There is croquet, a maze and woodland walks by
the River Tweed, craft workshops and a children's mini
adventure playground. Also a brewery museum and shop,
and antique shop.
Times: Open 12 Apr-Oct. **Fee:** ✱ £5.60 (ch £3.10 pen £5.30) Family
£16.50 (2ad+3ch). Grounds only £2.50 (ch £1.25). **Facilities:** 🅿 💷
✗ licensed & toilets for disabled shop (must be on lead) ◥

SOUTH AYRSHIRE

ALLOWAY   Map 10 NS31

BURNS NATIONAL HERITAGE PARK
Murdoch's Lone KA7 4PQ
➲ (2m S of Ayr)
☎ 01292 443700 📄 01292 441750   **2 for 1**
The birthplace of Robert Burns, Scotland's National Poet. An
introduction to the life of Robert Burns, with an audio-visual
presentation -a multi-screen 3D experience describing the
Tale of Tam O'Shanter. This attraction consists of the
museum, Burn's Cottage, visitor centre, tranquil landscaped
gardens and historical monuments. Please telephone for
details.
Times: Open all year, Apr-Sep 9.30-5.30, Oct-Mar 10-5. Closed 25-26
Dec & 1 Jan **Fee:** ✱ Adult passport £5 (pen & ch passport £2.50).
Facilities: 🅿 💷 ✗ licensed & (wheelchair available) toilets for
disabled shop ✖ (ex guide & hearing dogs) ◥

BARGANY

See Old Dailly

CULZEAN CASTLE   Map 10 NS21

CULZEAN CASTLE & COUNTRY PARK
KA19 8LE
➲ (4m W of Maybole, off A77)
☎ 01655 884455 📄 01655 884503
e-mail: culzean@nts.org.uk
This 18th-century castle stands on a cliff in spacious grounds
and was designed by Robert Adam for the Earl of Cassillis. It
is noted for its oval staircase, circular drawing room and
plasterwork. The Eisenhower Room explores the American
general's links with Culzean. The 563-acre country park has
continued

A full guide to the Symbols &
Abbreviations used in this book
can be found on page 6

a wide range of attractions - shoreline, woodland walks,
parkland, an adventure playground and gardens.
Times: Open - Castle: Apr-Oct, daily 10.30-5 (last entry 4). Visitor
centre: Apr-Oct, daily 9-5.30; Nov-Mar, wknds 11-4. Country Park: open
all year 9.30-sunset. **Fee:** ✱ £9 (concession £6.50). Groups adult £9
(concession £6.50) Family ticket £23. Country Park only Apr-Oct £5
(concession £3.75). Family ticket £13.50. Group adult £4, child/school
£1 Admission free to NTS members. For other details please
phone 0131 243 9387. **Facilities:** 🅿 💷 ✗ licensed & (wheelchairs,
lift in castle, braille guides) toilets for disabled shop garden centre (ex
castle, ex guide dogs) ◥

KIRKOSWALD   Map 10 NS20

SOUTER JOHNNIE'S COTTAGE
Main Rd KA19 8HY
➲ (on A77, 4m SW of Maybole)
☎ 01655 760603
e-mail: aclipson@nts.scot.demon.co.uk
'Souter' means cobbler and the village cobbler who lived in
this 18th-century cottage was the inspiration for Burns'
character Souter Johnnie, in his ballad *Tam O'Shanter*. The
cottage is now a Burns museum and life-size stone figures of
the poet's characters can be seen in the restored ale-house
in the cottage garden.
Times: Open - Apr-Sep, Fri-Tue 11.30-5 **Fee:** ✱ £2.50 (concession
£1.90) Family ticket £7. Groups adult £2 child/school £1. Please book in
advance for groups. Admission free to NTS members. For other details
please phone 0131 243 9387. **Facilities:** 🅿 (75yds) & (only one small
step into cottage) ✖ (ex guide dogs) ◥

MAYBOLE   Map 10 NS20

CROSSRAGUEL ABBEY
KA19 5HQ
➲ (2m S)
☎ 01655 883113
The extensive remains of this 13th-century Cluniac
monastery are impressive and architecturally important. The
monastery was founded by Duncan, Earl of Carrick and the
church, claustral buildings, abbot's house and an imposing
castellated gatehouse can be seen.
Times: ✱ Open Apr-Sep, daily 9.30-6.30. **Facilities:** 🅿 ✖ 🇩

OLD DAILLY   Map 10 NX29

BARGANY GARDENS
KA26 9PH
➲ (4m NE on B734 from Girvan)
☎ 01465 871249 📄 01465 871282
Woodland walks with a fine show of azaleas and
rhododendrons. Plants on sale from the gardens.
Times: Open Gardens Sat, Sun & Mon, May weekends only 10-5.
Fee: ✱ £2 (ch under 12 free). **Facilities:** 🅿 & (only rock garden not
accessible)

TARBOLTON   Map 10 NS42

BACHELORS' CLUB
Sandgate St KA5 5RB
➲ (on B744, 7.5m NE of Ayr)
☎ 01292 541940
In this 17th-century thatched house, Robert Burns and his
friends formed a debating club in 1780. Burns attended
continued

dancing lessons and was initiated into freemasonry here in 1781. The house is furnished in the period.
Times: Open Apr-Sep, Fri-Tue 1-5. Morning visits available for pre-booked groups. **Fee:** ✱ £2.50 (concession £1.90) Groups adult £2, child/school £1. Family ticket £7. Admission free for NTS members. For other details please phone 0131 243 9387. **Facilities:** P (in village) & ✈ (ex guide dogs) ✿

SOUTH LANARKSHIRE

BIGGAR
Map 11 NT03

GLADSTONE COURT MUSEUM
ML12 6DT
➲ (On A702 40m from Glasgow, 30m from Edinburgh, entrance by 113 High St)
☎ 01899 221050 📠 01899 221050
e-mail: margaret@bmtrust.freeserve.co.uk
An old-fashioned village street is portrayed in this museum, which is set out in a century-old coach-house. On display are reconstructed shops, complete with old signs and advertisements - a bank, telephone exchange, photographer's booth and other interesting glimpses into the recent past.
Times: Open Etr-Oct, Mon-Sat 11-4.30, Sun 2-4.30. **Fee:** ✱ £2 (ch £1, pen £1.50). Family ticket £4. Party £1.25 each. **Facilities:** P & shop ✈ (ex guide dogs)

GREENHILL COVENANTERS HOUSE
Burn Braes ML12 6DT
➲ (On A702, 30m from Edinburgh, 40m from Glasgow) **2 for 1**
☎ 01899 221050 📠 01899 221050
e-mail: margaret@bmtrust.freserve.co.uk
This 17th-century farmhouse was brought, stone by stone, ten miles from Wiston and reconstructed at Biggar. It has relics of the turbulent 'Covenanting' period, when men and women defended the right to worship in Presbyterian style. Audio presentations.
Times: Open mid May-Sep, wknds only 2-4.30. **Fee:** ✱ £1 (ch 50p, pen 70p). Family ticket £2.50. Party 70p each. **Facilities:** P & ✈ (ex guide dogs)

MOAT PARK HERITAGE CENTRE
ML12 6DT
➲ (On A702, 30m from Edinburgh, 40m from Glasgow)
☎ 01899 221050 📠 01899 221050 **2 for 1**
e-mail: margaret@bmtrust.co.uk
The centre illustrates the history, archaeology and geology of the Upper Clyde and Tweed valleys with interesting displays.
Times: Open all year, Apr-Oct, daily 11.30-4.30, Sun 2-4.30; Nov-Feb, wkdays during office hours. Other times by prior arrangement. **Fee:** ✱ £2 (ch £1, pen £1.50). Family ticket £4. Party £1.25 each. **Facilities:** P & (upper floor with assistance on request) toilets for disabled shop ✈ (ex guide dogs)

> The AA also publishes a guide to
> Pet Friendly Places to Stay

BLANTYRE
Map 11 NS65

DAVID LIVINGSTONE CENTRE
165 Station Rd G72 9BT
➲ (M74 junc 5 onto A725, then A724, follow signs for Blantyre, right at lights, Centre is at foot of hill)
☎ 01698 823140 📠 01698 821424
Share the adventurous life of Scotland's greatest explorer, from his childhood in the Blantyre Mills to his explorations in the heart of Africa, dramatically illustrated in the historic tenement where he was born. Various events are planned throughout the season.
Times: Open Apr-24 Dec, Mon-Sat 10-5, Sun 12.30-5 **Fee:** ✱ £3.50 (concession £2.60) Family ticket £9.50. Groups adult £2.80, child/school £1. Please book groups in advance. Admission free to NTS members. For other details please phone 0131 243 9387.
Facilities: P ▣ & toilets for disabled shop ✈ (ex guide dogs/lead grounds) ✿ ⬛

BOTHWELL
Map 11 NS75

BOTHWELL CASTLE
G71 8BL
➲ (approach from Uddingston off B7071)
☎ 01698 816894
Besieged, captured and 'knocked about' several times in the Scottish-English wars, the castle is a splendid ruin. Archibald the Grim built the curtain wall; later, in 1786, the Duke of Buccleuch carved graffiti - a coronet and initials - beside a basement well.
Times: ✱ Open all year, Apr-Sep, daily 9.30-6.30; Oct- Mar, Mon-Sat 9.30-4.30, Sun 2-4.30. (Closed Thu pm, Fri & Sun am in winter).
Facilities: P shop ▮

EAST KILBRIDE
Map 11 NS65

MUSEUM OF SCOTTISH COUNTRY LIFE
Wester Kittochside G76 9HR
➲ (From Glasgow take A749 to East Kilbride. From Edinburgh follow M8 to Glasgow, turn off junct 6 on the A725 to East Kilbride. Kittochside is signposted before East Kilbride)
☎ 01355 224 181 📠 01355 571290
e-mail: info@nms.ac.uk

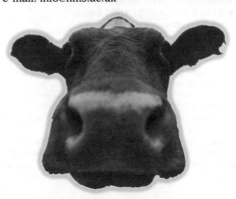

A fascinating museum built on a 170-acre farm and offering an insight into the working lives of people in rural Scotland. The museum runs a programme of events throughout the
continued

year, demonstrating its working collection and contrasting modern and traditional farming methods.
Times: Open daily 10-5 (Closed 25/26 Dec & 1/2 Jan). **Fee:** £3 (ch free, concessions £1.50). **Facilities:** 🅿 💺 ♿ (disabled parking, exhibition building is fully accessible) toilets for disabled shop ✖ (ex assist dogs) 🍴

HAMILTON   Map 11 NS75

CHATELHERAULT COUNTRY PARK
Ferniegair ML3 7UE
➲ (2.5km SE of Hamilton on A72 Hamilton-Larkhall/Lanark Clyde Valley tourist route)
☎ 01698 426213 ▯ 01698 421532   **FREE**

Designed as a hunting lodge by William Adam in 1732, Chatelherault, built of unusual pink sandstone, has been described as a gem of Scottish architecture. Situated close to the motorway, there is a visitor's centre, shop and adventure playground. Also a herd of white Cadzow cattle.
Times: Open all year, Mon-Sat 10-5, Sun 12-5. House closed all day Fri.
Facilities: 🅿 💺 ♿ (ramps, parking, large print guide) toilets for disabled shop garden centre ✖ (ex in grounds & guide dogs) 🍴

LOW PARKS MUSEUM
129 Muir St ML3 6BJ
➲ (By Asda superstore, off M74 junct 6)
☎ 01698 328232 ▯ 01698 328412

The museum tells the story of Hamilton and the Clyde Valley, created by linking the former District Museum and The Cameronians (Scottish Rifles) Museum. Housed in the town's oldest building, dating from 1696, the museum features a restored 18th-century assembly room and exhibitions on Hamilton Palace and The Covenanters.
Times: ✳ Open Mon-Sat 10-5, Sun 12-5. **Facilities:** 🅿 ♿ shop ✖ (ex guide dogs)

NEW LANARK   Map 11 NS84

NEW LANARK VISITOR CENTRE
New Lanark Visitor Centre, Mill 3, New Lanark Mills ML11 9DB
➲ (signposted from all major routes, 1 hr from Glasgow (M74/A72) and Edinburgh (A70))
☎ 01555 661345 ▯ 01555 66538
e-mail: trust@newlanark.org

Founded in 1785, New Lanark became well known in the early 19th century as a model community managed by enlightened industrialist and educational reformer Robert Owen. Surrounded by woodland and situated close to the Falls of Clyde, this unusual heritage site explores the philosophies of Robert Owen, using theatre, interactive displays, and the 'New Millennium Experience', a magical chair ride through history. Accommodation is also available at the New Lanark Mill Hotel.
Times: Open daily 11-5 (ex Xmas day & New Years Day) **Fee:** £5.95 (ch, concessions £3.95) family ticket (2ad+2ch) £16.95 **Facilities:** 🅿 💺 ✖ licensed ♿ ramps, disabled parking toilets for disabled shop ✖ (ex guide dogs) 🍴

BANNOCKBURN   Map 11 NS89

BANNOCKBURN HERITAGE CENTRE
Glasgow Rd FK7 0LJ
➲ (2m S of Stirling off M80/M9 junct 9)
☎ 01786 812664 ▯ 01786 810892   **FREE**

The Heritage Centre stands close to what is traditionally believed to have been Robert the Bruce's command post before the 1314 Battle of Bannockburn, a famous victory for the Scots and a turning point in Scottish history.
Times: Site open all year, daily. Heritage Centre Apr-Oct, daily 10-5.30; Feb-Mar & Nov-24 Dec, daily 10.30-4. Last audio-visual show half-an-hour before closing. **Facilities:** 🅿 💺 ♿ (Induction loop for the hard of hearing) toilets for disabled shop ✖ (ex site only) 🍴

BLAIR DRUMMOND   Map 11 NS79

BLAIR DRUMMOND SAFARI & LEISURE PARK
FK9 4UR
➲ (M9 exit 10, 4m along A84 towards Callander)
☎ 01786 841456 & 841396 ▯ 01786 841491
e-mail: enquiries@safari-park.co.uk

Drive through the wild animal reserves where zebras, North American bison, antelope, lions, tigers, white rhino and camels can be seen at close range. Other attractions include the sea lion show, a ride on the boat safari through the waterfowl sanctuary and around Chimpanzee Island, an adventure playground, giant astraglide, and pedal boats. There are also African elephants, giraffes and ostriches.
Times: ✳ Open Apr-1 Oct, daily 10-5.30. Last admission 4.30.
Facilities: 🅿 💺 ✖ licensed ♿ (special menus & waitress service if booked in advance) toilets for disabled shop ✖ (ex guide dogs)

CALLANDER   Map 11 NN60

ROB ROY AND TROSSACHS VISITOR CENTRE
Ancaster Square FK17 8ED
➲ (on A84)
☎ 01877 330342 ▯ 01877 330784   **2 for 1**
e-mail: robroy&t@aillst.ossian.net

The fascinating story of Scotland's most famous outlaw, Rob Roy MacGregor is vividly portrayed through an exciting multi-media theatre and explained in the carefully researched 'Life and Times' exhibition. Also full tourist information centre covering the beautiful Trossachs area, Scottish bookshops and specially themed souvenirs. Evening entertainment, including traditional Scottish music evenings, celidhs and illustrated talks, is arranged 6 nights a week from June to October; telephone for details. School pack available.
Times: Open Jan-Feb, Mon-Fri 11-3, wknds 11-4; Mar-May & Oct-Dec, daily 10-5; Jun, daily 9.30-6; Jul-Aug, daily 9-6; Sep, daily 10-6. **Fee:** ✳ £3.25 (ch & pen £2.25, students £2.50). Family ticket £8.75.
Facilities: 🅿 ♿ toilets for disabled shop ✖ 🍴

DOUNE — Map 11 NN70

DOUNE CASTLE
FK16 6EA
⮕ (8m S of Callander on A84)
☎ 01786 841742

The 14th-century stronghold with its two fine towers has been restored. It stands on the banks of the River Teith, and is associated with 'Bonnie Prince Charlie' and Sir Walter Scott. **Times:** ✱ Open all year, Apr-Sep, daily 9.30-6.30; Oct-Mar, Mon-Sat 9.30-4.30, Sun 2-4.30. (Closed Thu pm, Fri in winter & 25-26 Dec). **Facilities:** P shop ▮

KILLIN — Map 11 NN53

BREADALBANE FOLKLORE CENTRE
Falls of Dochart FK21 8XE
⮕ (on A85)
☎ 01567 820254 ▤ 01567 820764
e-mail: killin@aillst.ossian.net

Overlooking the beautiful Falls of Dochart, the Centre gives a fascinating insight into the legends of Breadalbane - Scotland's 'high country'. Learn of the magical deeds of St Fillan and hear tales of mystical giants, ancient prophesies, traditional folklore and clan history. Housed in historic St Fillans Mill which features a restored waterwheel. Tourist Information and gift shop. **Times:** Open Mar-May & Oct, daily 10-5; Jun & Sep, daily 10-6; Jul-Aug, daily 9.30-6.30. (Closed Nov-Feb). **Fee:** ✱ £2 (ch & pen £1.25, students £1.50). Family ticket £5.25. **Facilities:** P (30mtrs) & shop ✗ ➠

PORT OF MENTEITH — Map 11 NN50

INCHMAHOME PRIORY
FK8 3RA
⮕ (4m E of Aberfoyle, off A81)
☎ 01877 385294

Walter Comyn founded this Augustinian house in 1238, and it became famous as the retreat of the infant Mary Queen of Scots in 1547. The ruins of the church and cloisters are situated on an island in the Lake of Monteith. **Times:** ✱ Open Apr-Sep, daily 9.30-6.30. Ferry subject to cancellation in adverse weather conditions. **Facilities:** P shop ▮

STIRLING — Map 11 NS79

MAR'S WARK
Broad St FK8 1EE

A remarkable Renaissance mansion built by the Earl of Mar, Regent for James VI in 1570 and later used as the town workhouse. It was never completed and now the façade can be seen. **Times:** Open all reasonable times. **Facilities:** ✗ ▮

MUSEUM OF ARGYLL & SUTHERLAND HIGHLANDERS
The Castle FK8 1EH
⮕ (museum is located within Stirling Castle)
☎ 01786 475165 ▤ 01786 446038
e-mail: museum@argylls.co.uk

Situated in the King's Old Building in Stirling Castle, the museum tells the history of the Regiment from 1794 to the

continued

present day. Displays include uniforms, medals, silver, paintings, colours, pipe banners, and commentaries. **Times:** Open Etr-Sep, daily 9.30-5; Sep-Etr, daily 10-4.15. **Fee:** ✱ Entry to museum free but entry fee to castle. **Facilities:** P (castle esplanade) shop ✗

NATIONAL WALLACE MONUMENT
Abbey Craig, Causewayhead FK8 2AD
⮕ (reached from A907, Stirling to Alloa road, follow brown tourist signs)
☎ 01786 472140 ▤ 01786 461322
e-mail: nationalwallacemonument@ aillst.ossian.net

The 220ft tower was completed in 1869, and Sir William Wallace's two-handed sword is preserved inside. Seven battlefields and a fine view towards the Highlands can be seen in one of the most awe inspiring views in Scotland. Exhibitions on three floors. **Times:** Open all year Jan-Feb & Nov-Dec, daily 10.30-4; Mar-May & Oct, daily 10-5; Jun, daily 10-6; Jul-Aug, daily 9.30-6.30; Sep, daily 9.30-5. **Fee:** ✱ £5 (ch & pen £3.25, student £3.75). Family ticket £13.25. **Facilities:** P ▣ & (limited access) shop ✗ ➠

OLD TOWN JAIL
Saint John St FK8 1EA
⮕ (follow signs for castle up the hill, jail on left at top of Saint John's St)
☎ 01786 450050 ▤ 01786 471301
e-mail: otjva@aillst.ossian.net

Built in 1847 to replace the old Tolbooth jail, this is an outstanding example of Victorian architecture. A living history performance means the visitor can learn about the daily life of the prisoners and the strict regime practised in the prison. **Times:** Open Apr-Sep, daily 9.30-5.30; Oct & Mar, daily 9.30-4.30; Nov-Feb, daily 9.30-3.30. **Fee:** ✱ £5 (ch & pen £3.25, student £3.75). Family ticket £13.25. **Facilities:** P & toilets for disabled shop ✗ ➠

SMITH ART GALLERY & MUSEUM
Dumbarton Rd FK8 2RQ
⮕ (M9 junct 10, follow Stirling Castle)
☎ 01786 471917 ▤ 01786 449523
e-mail: museum@smithartgallery.demon.co.uk

This award-winning museum and gallery presents a variety of exhibitions drawing on its own rich collections and works from elsewhere. A range of programmes and events take place, ring for details. **Times:** Open all year, Tue-Sat 10.30-5, Sun 2-5 (Closed Mon, 25-26 Dec & 1 Jan). **Facilities:** P ▣ & (wheelchair lift, induction loop in theatre) toilets for disabled shop

STIRLING CASTLE
Upper Castle Hill FK8 1EJ
☎ 01786 450000

Sitting on top of a 250ft rock, Stirling Castle has a strategic position on the Firth of Forth. As a result it has been the scene of many events in Scotland's history. James II was born at the castle in 1430. Mary Queen of Scots spent some years there, and it was James IV's childhood home. Among

continued

its finest features are the splendid Renaissance palace built by James V, and the Chapel Royal, rebuilt by James VI.
Times: ✱ Open all year, Apr-Sep, daily 9.30-6; Oct-Mar, daily 9.30-4.15. Last ticket sold 45 mins prior to closing time. Telephone for details. **Facilities:** 🅿 (charged) ✗ licensed & toilets for disabled shop ✗🅿

WEST DUNBARTONSHIRE

BALLOCH   Map 10 NS38
BALLOCH CASTLE COUNTRY PARK
G83 8LX
➲ (A82 for Dumbarton, Balloch from Glasgow. A811 for Balloch from Stirling.)
☎ 01389 758216 📋 01389 720922
Set at the southern end of Loch Lomond, the park encompasses varying habitats, a walled garden, and lawns for picnics giving wonderful views of the loch. Overlooking the lawns is Balloch Castle, built in 1808. Its visitor centre gives an introduction to local history and wildlife.
Times: ✱ Open: Visitor Centre, Apr-Oct daily 10-5.45. Country Park open all year, 8-dusk. **Facilities:** 🅿 ▣ & toilets for disabled shop ◥

DUMBARTON   Map 10 NS37
DUMBARTON CASTLE
G82 1JJ
☎ 01389 732167
The castle, set on the 240ft Dumbarton Rock above the River Clyde, dominates the town (the capital of the Celtic kingdom of Strathclyde) and commands spectacular views. Most of what can be seen today dates from the 18th and 19th centuries, but there are a few earlier remains.
Times: ✱ Open all year, Apr-Sep, daily 10-6.30. Oct-Mar, Sun 2-4.30. **Facilities:** 🅿 shop ✗🅿

WEST LOTHIAN

LINLITHGOW   Map 11 NS97
BLACKNESS CASTLE
EH49 7AL
➲ (4m NE)
☎ 01506 834807
Once, this was one of the most important fortresses in Scotland. Used as a state prison during covenanting time and in the late 19th-century as a powder magazine, it was one of four castles left fortified by the Articles of Union. Most impressive are the massive 17th-century artillery emplacements.
Times: ✱ Open all year, Apr-Sep, daily 9.30-6.30; Oct-Mar, Mon-Sat 9.30-4.30, Sun 2-4.30. (Closed Thu pm, Fri & Sun am in winter). **Facilities:** 🅿 shop 🅿

HOUSE OF THE BINNS
EH49 7NA
➲ (4m E of Linlithgow off A904)
☎ 01506 834255
e-mail: houseofthebinns@nts.org.uk
An example of changing architectural tastes from 1612 onwards, this house reflects the transition from fortified

continued

stronghold to spacious mansion. The original three-storey building, with small windows and twin turrets, evolved into a fine crenellated house with beautiful moulded plaster ceilings - the ancestral home of the Dalyell family. There is a magnificent display of snowdrops and daffodils in spring.
Times: House: Jun-Sep, Sat-Mon 2-5. Parkland: Apr-Oct, daily 10-7, Nov-Mar, daily 10-4. **Fee:** ✱ £5 (concession £3.75) Family ticket £13.50. Groups adult £4, child/school £1. Admission free to NTS members. For other details please telephone 0131 243 9387
Facilities: 🅿 & (braille sheets) 🅿 (ex guide dogs) ♨

LINLITHGOW PALACE
EH49 7AL
➲ (off M9)
☎ 01506 842896
The magnificent ruin of a great Royal Palace, set in its own park or 'peel'. All the Stewart kings lived here, and work commissioned by James I, III, IV, and VI can be seen. The great hall and the chapel are particularly fine. James V was born here in 1512 and Mary, Queen of Scots in 1542.
Times: ✱ Open all year, Apr-Sep, daily 9.30-6.30; Oct-Mar, Mon-Sat 9.30-4.30, Sun 2-4.30. (Closed 25-26 Dec). **Facilities:** 🅿 shop 🅿🅿

LIVINGSTON   Map 11 NT06
ALMOND VALLEY HERITAGE CENTRE
Millfield EH54 7AR
➲ (2m from M8 junct 3)
☎ 01506 414957 📋 01506 497771
e-mail: info@almondvalley.co.uk
A combination of fun and educational potential ideal for children, Almond Valley has a petting zoo of farm animals, an interactive museum on the shale oil industry, a narrow gauge railway, and tractor rides. Special events throughout the year. Ring for details.
Times: Open all year, daily 10-5. **Fee:** £3 (ch £2). Family (2+4) £10.
Facilities: 🅿 ▣ & toilets for disabled shop ◥

SCOTTISH ISLANDS

ARRAN, ISLE OF

BRODICK   Map 10 NS03
BRODICK CASTLE, GARDEN & COUNTRY PARK
KA27 8HY
➲ (Ferry from Ardrossan-Brodick. From N end of Arran-Kintyre frequent in Summer, limited in winter)
☎ 01770 302202 & 302462 📋 01770 302312
e-mail: brodick@nts.org.uk
The site has been fortified since Viking times, but the present castle dating from the 13th century was a stronghold of the Dukes of Hamilton. Splendid silver, fine porcelain and paintings acquired by generations of owners can be seen, including many sporting pictures and trophies. There is a magnificent woodland garden, started by the Duchess of

continued

Montrose in 1923, world famous for its rhododendrons and azaleas.
Times: ✳ Open Apr-Oct, daily 11-4.30 (closes 3.30 in Oct). Country Park: open all year, daily 9.30-sunset **Fee:** ✳ £7 (concession £5.25) Groups adult £5.60, child/school £1, please book groups in advance. Family ticket £19. Garden & Country Park only Apr-Oct £3.50 (concession £2.60) Groups adult £2.80, child/school £1. Family ticket £9.50. Nov-Mar admission free, car parking £2. Admission free to NTS members. **Facilities:** 🅿 ✗ ♿ Braille, wheelchairs motorised buggy & stairlift toilets for disabled shop 🎫 (ex guide dogs) 🍴

ISLE OF ARRAN HERITAGE MUSEUM
Rosaburn KA27 8DP
➲ (Right at Brodick Pier, approx 1m)
☎ 01770 302636
e-mail: tom.macleod@arranmuseum.co.uk
The setting is an 18th-century croft farm, including a cottage restored to its pre-1920 state and a 'smiddy' where a blacksmith worked until the late 1960s. There are also occasional demonstrations of horseshoeing, sheepshearing, weaving and spinning, a veteran car rally and a golf tournament - please ring for details. **Times:** Open Apr-Oct, daily 10.30-4.30. **Facilities:** 🅿 💺 ♿ shop

LOCHRANZA   Map 10 NR95
ISLE OF ARRAN DISTILLERY VISITOR CENTRE
KA27 8HJ
➲ (from Brodick Ferry Terminal take coast road N for 14 m. Distillery located on edge of village of Lochranza)
☎ 01770 830264   🖷 01770 830364
e-mail: visitorcentre@arranwhisky.com
Located amidst beautiful surroundings, the distillery was built recently to revive the dormant traditions of Arran single malt whisky production. After a guided tour of the distillery, visitors can now taste some of the first whiskies to be ready after production began in 1995.
Times: Open daily Mar-Oct; Nov-Dec, open 4 days a week. (Closed Jan). **Facilities:** 🅿 ✗ licensed ♿ (ex working distillery, chair lift in visitor centre) toilets for disabled shop 🎫 (ex guide dogs) 🍴

BUTE, ISLE OF

ROTHESAY   Map 10 NS06
ARDENCRAIG
PA20 9HA
➲ (1m off A844, S of Rothesay)
☎ 01700 504225   🖷 01700 504225
e-mail: allan.macdonald@argyll-bute.co.uk
Particular attention has been paid to improving the layout of the garden and introducing rare plants. The greenhouse and walled garden produce plants for floral displays throughout the district. A variety of fish is kept in the ornamental ponds and the aviaries have some interesting birds.
Times: ✳ Open May-Sep. **Facilities:** 🅿 💺 ♿ 🎫 (ex guide dogs)

BUTE MUSEUM
Stuart St PA20 0EP
➲ (The road behind the castle)
☎ 01700 505067
e-mail: Ivor@butemuseum.fsnet.co.uk
Local and natural history displays, including birds, mammals and seashore items; varied collections of recent bygones, a collection of early Christian crosses, and flints and pots from various Mesolithic and Neolithic burial cairns.
Times: Open all year, Apr-Sep, Mon-Sat 10.30-4.30, Sun 2.30-4.30; Oct-Mar, Tue-Sat 2.30-4.30 (Closed Sun & Mon). **Fee:** £1.50 (ch 50p, pen £1) **Facilities:** 🅿 (3 mins walk) ♿ (touch table for blind, ramps) shop

ROTHESAY CASTLE
PA20 0DA
☎ 01700 502691
The focal point of Rothesay is this 13th-century castle. It has lofty curtain walls defended by drum towers that enclose a circular courtyard.
Times: ✳ Open all year, Apr-Sep, daily 9.30-6.30; Oct-Mar, Mon-Sat 9.30-4.30, Sun 2-4.30. (Closed Thu pm, Fri in winter & 25-26 Dec). **Facilities:** 🅿 shop 🚩

GREAT CUMBRAE ISLAND

MILLPORT   Map 10 NS15
MUSEUM OF THE CUMBRAES
Garrison House KA28 0DG
➲ (Ferry to Millport, from Largs Cal-Mac Terminal. Bus meets each ferry.)   **FREE**
☎ 01475 531191   🖷 01475 531191
e-mail: namuseum@north-ayrshire.gov.uk
A small museum which displays the history and life of the Cumbraes. There is also a fine collection of local photographs.
Times: Open Apr-Sep, Thu-Mon 10-1, 2-5. **Facilities:** 🅿 ♿ shop 🎫 (ex guide dogs)

LEWIS, ISLE OF

ARNOL   Map 13 NB34
BLACK HOUSE MUSEUM
PA86 9DB
➲ (11m NW of Stornoway on A858)
☎ 01851 710395
A traditional Hebridean dwelling, built without mortar and roofed with thatch on a timber framework. It has a central peat fire in the kitchen, no chimney and a byre under the same roof.
Times: ✳ Open all year, Apr-Sep, Mon-Sat 9.30-6.30; Oct-Mar, Mon-Thu & Sat 9.30-4.30. (Closed 25-26 Dec). **Facilities:** 🅿 ♿ toilets for disabled shop 🎫 🚩

CALLANISH   Map 13 NB23

CALLANISH STANDING STONES
PA86 9DY
➲ (12m W of Stornoway off A859)
☎ 01851 621422

An avenue of 19 monoliths leads north from a circle of 13 stones with rows of more stones fanning out to south, east and west. Probably constructed between 3000 and 1500BC, this is a unique cruciform of megaliths.
Times: ✱ Site accessible at all times. Visitor Centre open Apr-Sep, Mon-Sat 10-7; Oct-Mar, Mon-Sat 10-4. **Facilities:** 🅿 ✕ & toilets for disabled shop ▮

CARLOWAY   Map 13 NB24

DUN CARLOWAY BROCH   `FREE`
➲ (1.5m S of Carloway on A858)

Brochs are late-prehistoric circular stone towers, and their origins are mysterious. One of the best examples can be seen at Dun Carloway, where the tower still stands about 30ft high.
Times: Open at all reasonable times. **Facilities:** 🅿 ▮

MULL, ISLE OF

CRAIGNURE   Map 10 NM73

MULL & WEST HIGHLAND NARROW GAUGE RAILWAY
Craignure (old pier) Station PA65 6AY
➲ (0.25 mile from Craignure Ferry Terminal, just off the road to Iona)
☎ 01680 812494 (in season) or 01680 300389
🖹 01680 300595
e-mail: mullrail@dee-emm.co.uk

The first passenger railway on a Scottish island, opened in 1984. Both steam and diesel trains operate on the ten-and-a-quarter inch gauge line, which runs from Craignure to Torosay Castle. The 1.25 mile line offers dramatic woodland and mountain views taking in Ben Nevis, Glencoe and the isle of Lismore.
Times: Open Etr-mid Oct **Fee:** Return £3.75 (ch £2.75); Single £2.75 (ch £1.75). Family ticket return £9.95, single £6.75. **Facilities:** 🅿 & (provision to carry person seated in wheelchair on trains) shop 🛒

TOROSAY CASTLE & GARDENS
PA65 6AY
➲ (1.5m S of Ferry Terminal at Craignure)
☎ 01680 812421 🖹 01680 812470
e-mail: torosay@aol.com

The Scottish baronial architecture of this Victorian castle is complemented by the magnificent setting, and inside the house there are displays of portraits and wildlife pictures, family scrapbooks and a study of the Antarctic. The gardens include a statue walk and water garden, an avenue of Australian gum trees, and an Oriental garden. Within the grounds there is a narrow gauge steam and diesel railway.
Times: Open end Mar-end Oct, daily 10.30-5. Gardens all year. **Fee:** ✱ House & Gardens: £5 (ch £1.75, student & pen £4) Family £12. Gardens only: £4 (ch £1.25, student & pen £3) Family £10. **Facilities:** 🅿 🖵 & toilets for disabled shop (specialising in locally produced goods) garden centre 🛒 (Exc guide/hearing dogs) 🛒

ORKNEY

BIRSAY   Map 16 HY22

EARL'S PALACE
KW15 1PD
➲ (on A966)   `FREE`
☎ 01856 721205 & 841815

The gaunt remains of the residence of the 16th-century Earl of Orkney, constructed round a courtyard.
Times: Open at all reasonable times. **Facilities:** 🛒 ▮

DOUNBY   Map 16 HY22

BROUGH OF BIRSAY
➲ (off A966)
☎ 01856 841815

This ruined Romanesque church stands next to the remains of a Norse village. The nave, chancel and semicircular apse can be seen, along with claustral buildings. Crossings must be made on foot at low-water - there is no boat.
Times: Open when tides permit, 11 Jun-Sep, daily 9.30-6.30. **Fee:** £1.80 (ch 50p, concessions £1.50). **Facilities:** ▮

CLICK MILL
➲ (2.5m from Dounby on B905).
☎ 01856 841815   `FREE`

The last surviving horizontal water mill in Orkney, of a type well represented in Shetland and Lewis. The mill is in working condition and visitors should wear sensible footwear.
Times: Open at all reasonable time. **Facilities:** ▮

SKARA BRAE
KW16 3LR
➲ (19m W of Kirkwall on B9056)
☎ 01856 841815

Engulfed in drift sand, this remarkable group of well-preserved Stone Age dwellings is the most outstanding survivor of its kind in Britain. Stone furniture and a fireplace can be seen.
Times: ✱ Open all year, Apr-Sep, daily 9.30-6.30; Oct-Mar, Mon-Sat 9.30-4.30, Sun 2-4.30. (Closed 25-26 Dec). **Facilities:** 🅿 ✕ & toilets for disabled shop 🛒 ▮

FINSTOWN   Map 16 HY31

MAES HOWE CHAMBERED CAIRN
➲ (9m W of Kirkwall, on A965)
☎ 01856 761606

The masonry of Britain's finest megalithic tomb is in a remarkably good state of preservation. Dating from neolithic times, it contains Viking carvings and runes.
Times: ✱ Open all year, Apr-Sep, daily 9.30-6.30; Oct-Mar, Mon-Sat 9.30-4.30, Sun 2-4.30. (Closed Sun am in winter & 25-26 Dec). **Facilities:** 🅿 ✕ shop 🛒 ▮

STONES OF STENNESS CIRCLE AND HENGE
➲ (5m NE of Stromness on B9055)   `FREE`
☎ 01856 841815

Dating back to the second millennium BC, the remains of this stone circle are near the Ring of Brogar - a splendid circle of upright stones surrounded by a ditch.
Times: Open at any reasonable time. **Facilities:** 🅿 ▮

HARRAY
Map 16 HY31

CORRIGALL FARM & KIRBUSTER MUSEUM
KW17 2JR

☎ **01856 771411 & 771268**   `FREE`

▤ **01856 874615**

The museum consists of two Orkney farmhouses with outbuildings. Kirbuster (Birsay) has the last surviving example of a `Firehoose' with its central hearth; Corrigall (Harray) represents an improved farmhouse and steading of the late 1800s.

Times: Open Mar-Oct, Mon-Sat 10.30-1 & 2-5, Sun 2-7. **Facilities:** P ⎏ shop ✖ (ex guide dogs) ⬤

KIRKWALL
Map 16 HY41

BISHOP'S & EARL'S PALACES
KW15 1PD

➲ (In Kirkwall on A960)

☎ **01856 875461**

The Bishop's Palace is a hall-house of the 12th century, later much altered, with a round tower built by Bishop Reid in 1541-48. A later addition was made by the notorious Patrick Stewart, Earl of Orkney, who built the adjacent Earl's Palace between 1600 and 1607 in a splendid Renaissance style.

Times: ✱ Open Apr-Sep, daily 9.30-6.30. Telephone for 2003 details. **Facilities:** shop ⚑

SCAPA FLOW VISITOR CENTRE & MUSEUM
Hoy KW15 1DH

➲ (on A964 to Houton, ferry crossing takes 45 mins, visitors centre 2 mins from ferry terminal)

☎ **01856 791300**   ▤ **01856 871560**   `FREE`

e-mail: museum@orkney.gov.uk

Also known as the Lyness Interpretation Centre, this fascinating museum is home to a large collection of military equipment used in the defence of the Orkneys during the First and Second World Wars. There are also guns salvaged from the German ships scuppered in WWII. Visitors arrive at the island after a short boat trip from the Orkney mainland.

Times: Open all year: Mon-Fri 9-4.30 (mid May-Oct also Sat, Sun 10.30-3.30). **Facilities:** P ⬛ ⎏ toilets for disabled shop ✖ (ex guide dogs) ⬤

THE ORKNEY MUSEUM
Broad St KW15 1DH

➲ (town centre)

☎ **01856 873191**   ▤ **01856 874616**   `FREE`

e-mail: museum@orkney.gov.uk

One of the finest vernacular town houses in Scotland, this 16th-century building now contains a museum of Orkney history, including the islands' fascinating archaeology.

Times: Open, Oct-Mar Mon-Sat, 10.30-12.30 & 1.30-5, Apr-Sep, 10.30-5 Mon-Sat. **Facilities:** P (50yds) ⎏ shop ✖ (ex guide dogs) ⬤

STROMNESS
Map 16 HY20

ORKNEY MARITIME & NATURAL HISTORY MUSEUM
52 Alfred St KW16 3DF

☎ **01856 850025**

The museum focuses on Orkney's broad maritime connections, including fishing, whaling, the Hudson's Bay

continued

Company, the German Fleet in Scapa Flow, and the award winning Pilot's House extension. The Natural History Gallery is fully restored, displaying a fine collection of curios and rare and interesting exhibits.

Times: Open Apr-Sep, Mon-Sun 10-5; Oct-Mar, Mon-Sat 11-3.30. (Closed Xmas, New Year & 3 wks Feb-Mar). **Fee:** ✱ £2.50 (ch 50p con £2). Family ticket £5. **Facilities:** P (50yds) ⎏ toilets for disabled shop ✖ (ex guide dogs)

PIER ARTS CENTRE
KW16 3AA

☎ **01856 850209**   ▤ **01856 851462**

e-mail: info@pierartscentre.com

The collection is housed in a warehouse standing on its own stone pier. There is a constantly changing programme of exhibitions.

Times: ✱ Open all year, Tue-Sat 10.30-12.30 & 1.30-5. **Facilities:** P (100yds) ⎏ shop ✖ (ex guide dogs)

WESTRAY
Map 16 HY44

NOLTLAND CASTLE
➲ (1m W of Pierowall village)   `FREE`

☎ **01856 841815**

A fine, ruined Z-plan tower, built between 1560 and 1573 but never completed. The tower is remarkable for its large number of gun loops and impressive staircase.

Times: Open 11 Jun-Sep, daily 9.30-6.30. **Facilities:** ✖ ⚑

SHETLAND

LERWICK
Map 16 HU44

CLICKIMIN
ZE1 0QX

➲ (1m SW of Lerwick on A970)   `FREE`

☎ **01466 793191**

The remains of a prehistoric settlement that was fortified at the beginning of the Iron Age with a stone-built fort. The site was occupied for over 1000 years. The remains include a partially demolished broch (round tower) which still stands to a height of 17ft.

Times: Open at all reasonable times. **Facilities:** ⚑

FORT CHARLOTTE
ZE1 0JN

➲ (in centre of Lerwick)   `FREE`

☎ **01466 793191**

A five-sided artillery fort with bastions projecting from each corner. The walls are high and massive. It was built in 1665 to protect the Sound of Bressay from the Dutch, but taken by them and burned in 1673. It was rebuilt in 1781.

Times: Open at all reasonable times. Key available locally. **Facilities:** ⚑

SHETLAND MUSEUM
Lower Hillhead ZE1 0EL

☎ **01595 695057**   ▤ **01595 696729**   `FREE`

e-mail: shetland.museum@sic.shetland.gov.uk

The massive brass propeller blade outside the building is from the 17,000-ton liner *Oceanic*, wrecked off Foula in 1914. The archaeology gallery covers Neolithic burials, axe-making, Bronze Age houses, Iron Age farming and domestic life. There are also agricultural and social history

continued

displays, including peat-working, corn harvest, local businesses, medals, bootmaking and Shetland weddings. Changing displays of local contemporary art.
Times: Open all year Mon, Wed, Fri 10-7, Tue, Thu, Sat 10-5.
Facilities: ☐ ৬ (lift, wheelchair available) toilets for disabled shop ✗ (ex guide dogs) ☞

MOUSA ISLAND   Map 16 HU42

MOUSA BROCH
➲ (accessible by boat from Sandwick)   `FREE`
☎ 01466 793191

This broch is the best-preserved example of an Iron Age drystone tower in Scotland. The tower is nearly complete and rises to a height of 40ft. The outer and inner walls both contain staircases that may be climbed to the parapet.
Times: Open at all reasonable time. **Facilities:** ▮

SCALLOWAY   Map 16 HU33

SCALLOWAY CASTLE
ZE1 0TP
➲ (6m from Lerwick on A970)   `FREE`
☎ 01466 793191

The ruins of a castle designed on the medieval two-step plan. The castle was actually built in 1600 by Patrick Stewart, Earl of Orkney. When the Earl, who was renowned for his cruelty, was executed in 1615, the castle fell into disuse.
Times: Open at all reasonable time. **Facilities:** ☐ ▮

SUMBURGH   Map 16 HU30

JARLSHOF PREHISTORIC SITE
➲ (At Sumburgh Head, approx 22m S of Lerwick)
☎ 01950 460112

One of the most remarkable archaeological sites in Europe. There are remains of Bronze Age, Iron Age and Viking settlements as well as a medieval farm. There is also a 16th-century Laird's House, once the home of the Earls Robert and Patrick Stewart, and the basis of 'Jarlshof' in Sir Walter Scott's novel *The Pirate*.
Times: ✱ Open Apr-Sep, daily 9.30-6.30. **Facilities:** ☐ shop ▮

ARMADALE   Map 13 NG60

ARMADALE CASTLE GARDENS & MUSEUM OF THE ISLES
IV45 8RS
➲ (16m S of Broadford on A851. Signposted with Clan Donald Centre or Armadale Castle Gardens & Museum of the Isles. Easily reached by Skye Bridge or the Mallaig A830 to Armdale Ferry)
☎ 01471 844305 & 844227 ▤ 01471 844275
e-mail: office@cland.demon.co.uk

Armadale Castle and Gardens were built in 1815 as the home of Lord Macdonald. The warming effect of the Gulf Stream allows exotic trees and plants to flourish. Within the 40 acres of gardens is the Museum of the Isles, where visitors can discover the history of the Highlands.
Times: Open daily 9.30-5.30. Garden & Museum open Apr-Oct.
Facilities: ☐ � ✗ licensed ৬ (wheelchairs available) toilets for disabled shop (on lead) ☞

DUNVEGAN   Map 13 NG24

DUNVEGAN CASTLE
IV55 8WF
➲ (Follow A87 over Skye Bridge. Turn onto A863 at Sligachan and continue o to Dunvegan Castle)
☎ 01470 521206 ▤ 01470 521205
e-mail: info@dunvegancastle.com

This fortress stronghold set on the sea loch of Dunvegan has been the home of the Chief of Macleod for 800 years. On view are books, pictures, arms and treasured relics of the clan. A pedigree Highland Cattle fold is also an attraction, as is the boat trip to the nearby Seal Colony.
Times: Open 24 Mar-31 Oct, daily 10-5.30 (last entry 5pm). Castle & Gardens, Nov-Mar, daily 11-4 (last entry 3.30pm). Closed 25-26 Dec & 1-2 Jan. **Fee:** ✱ Castle & Gardens: £6.50 (ch 5-15 yrs £3.50, pen & students £5.50). Group (Min 10 adults) £5.50. Gardens only: £4.50 (ch 5-15 £2.50, pen & students £2.50). Seal Boats: £5.00 (ch 5-12 £2.50).
Facilities: ☐ ▮▮ ✗ licensed (restaurant has ramps for wheelchair access) shop ✗ (ex guide dogs & in grounds) ☞

WALES
EVENTS & FESTIVALS

March
22nd-28th Wrexham Science Festival
26th Conwy Seed Fair, High Street, Conwy

May
28th-6th Jun Hay Festival of Literature
29th-6th Jun St David's Cathedral Festival, St
   David's, Pembrokeshire

June
28th May-6th Hay Festival of Literature
tbc Llandudno Festival
tbc Three Peaks Yacht Race, Gwynedd

July
6th-11th Llangollen International Musical
   Eisteddfod, Llangollen, Denbighshire
19th-22nd Royal Welsh Show, Royal Welsh
   Showground, Builth Wells
31st-7th Aug Royal National Eisteddfod of
   Wales, Tredegar Park, Newport
31st-8th Aug Brecon County Show
tbc Annual Mountain Bike Bog Snorkelling
   World Championships, Llanwrtyd Wells
tbc Fishguard International Music Festival,
   Fishguard, Pembrokeshire
tbc North Wales Bluegrass Festival,
   Bodlondeb Field, Llandudno, Conwy
tbc Welsh Proms, St David's Hall, Cardiff

August
31st Jul-7th Royal National Eisteddfod of
   Wales, Tredegar Park, Newport
31st Jul-8th Brecon County Show

10th-11th Anglesey County Show, Anglesey
   Showground, Holyhead, Anglesey
14th Chepstow Agricultural Show, Chepstow
14th Llangurig & District Show, Tynymaes,
   Llangurig, Powys
18th Vale of Glamorgan Agricultural Show,
   Fonmon Castle Park, Fonmon
26th Monmouthshire Show, Monmouth
28th Denbigh Flower Show, Lon Felin Field,
   Ystrad Road, Denbigh
tbc Conwy River Festival, Conwy

September
11th Usk Show, Usk Showground,
   Gwernesney, Monmouthshire
13th Conwy Honey Fair, Conwy High Street
18th-25th North Wales International Music
   Festival, the Cathedral, St Asaph
tbc Barmouth Art Festival, Dragon Theatre,
   Jubilee Road, Barmouth, Gwynedd
tbc Llangollen Hot Air Balloon Festival,
   Llangollen, Denbighshire
tbc Tenby Arts Festival, Tenby, Pembrokeshire

October
8th-10th Anglesey Oyster & Welsh Produce
   Festival, Anglesey
27th-9th Nov Dylan Thomas Festival, Dylan
   Thomas Centre, Swansea

November
tbc Gwyl Ffilm Ryngwladol Cymru –
   International Film Festival Wales, Market
   House, Market Road, Cardiff

Marloe Sands, Pembrokeshire Coast National Park

BRIDGEND

BRIDGEND   Map 03 SS97
NEWCASTLE `FREE`
☎ 01656 659515

The small castle dates back to the 12th century. It is ruined, but a rectangular tower, a richly carved Norman gateway and massive curtain walls enclosing a polygonal courtyard can still be seen.
Times: Open - accessible throughout the year. Key keeper arrangement. **Facilities:** 🅿 ✗ ⊕

COITY   Map 03 SS98
COITY CASTLE
CF35 6BG
⮕ (2m NE of Bridgend, off A4061) `FREE`
☎ 01656 652021

A 12th to 16th-century stronghold, with a hall, chapel and the remains of a square keep.
Times: Open all year, at all times. Key keeper arrangement.
Facilities: 🅿 ✗ ⊕

CAERPHILLY

CAERPHILLY   Map 03 ST18
CAERPHILLY CASTLE
CF8 1JL
⮕ (on A469)
☎ 029 2088 3143

The concentrically planned castle was begun in 1268 by Gilbert de Clare and completed in 1326. It is the largest in Wales, and has extensive land and water defences. A unique feature is the ruined tower - the victim of subsidence - which manages to out-lean even Pisa! The south dam platform, once a tournament-field, now displays replica medieval siege-engines.
Times: Open Apr-1 Jun & 29 Sep-26 Oct, daily 9.30-5; 2 Jun-28 Sep, daily 9.30-6; 27 Oct-Mar, Mon-Sat 9.30-4, Sun 11-4. Telephone for Xmas opening times. **Fee:** £3 (ch 5-16, pen & students £2.50, wheelchair users and assisting companion free). Family ticket (2 ad & 3 ch) £8.50. Group rates available. Prices quoted apply until 31 Mar 2004.
Facilities: 🅿 ⅔ shop ✗ ⊕ 🍴

LLANCAIACH FAWR MANOR
Gelligaer Rd, Nelson CF46 6ER
⮕ (M4 Junct 32, A470 to Merthyr Tydfil. Towards Ystrad Mynach A472 follow brown heritage signs)
☎ 01443 412248 🖷 01443 412688
e-mail: allens@caerphilly.gov.uk

Step back in time to the Civil War period at this fascinating living history museum. The year is 1645 and visitors are invited into the Manor to meet the servants of 'Colonel' Edward Prichard - from the puritanical to the gossipy.
Times: Open Mon-Fri 10-3.30 (last admission), Sat & Sun 10-4.30. (Closed Mon, Nov-Feb & 24 Dec-2 Jan). **Fee:** ✱ £4.50 (ch & concessions £3). Family ticket £12. **Facilities:** 🅿 🍴 ✗ licensed ⅔ (personal stereo, photo album & Braille map) toilets for disabled shop ✗ (ex guide dogs) 🍴

CWMCARN   Map 03 ST29
CWMCARN FOREST DRIVE
Nantcarn Rd NP11 7FA
⮕ (8m N of Newport on A467, M4 junct 28, follow brown tourist signs)
☎ 01495 272001 🖷 01495 271403
e-mail: cwmcarn-vc@caerphilly.gov.uk

A seven-mile scenic drive with spectacular views over the Bristol Channel and surrounding countryside. Facilities include barbecues, picnic and play areas, and forest and mountain walks. Special events are held throughout the year, please ring for details.
Times: Open Forest Drive: Mar & Oct 11-5; Apr-Aug 11-7 (11-9 wknds during Jul & Aug); Sep, 11-6; Nov 11-4 (wknds only). Visitor Centre: all year except between Xmas & New Year. **Fee:** ✱ Cars & Motorcycles £3, Minibus £6, Coaches £20. Car season ticket £15. **Facilities:** 🅿 🍴 ⅔ toilets for disabled shop 🍴

CARDIFF

CARDIFF   Map 03 ST17
CARDIFF CASTLE
Castle St CF10 3RB
⮕ (Follow signs to city centre. From M4, A48 & A470)
☎ 029 2087 8100 🖷 029 2023 1417 `2 for 1`
e-mail: cardiffcastle@cardiff.gov.uk

The Norman castle was built on the site of a Roman fort, and Roman walls some 10ft thick can still be seen. There is also a Norman keep and a 13th-century tower. The character of the castle comes from its transformation in the 19th century, however, when the immensely rich 3rd Marquess of Bute employed William Burges to restore and rebuild it. Together they created a romantic fantasy of a medieval castle. Also here are the military museums of the Royal Regiment of Wales and Queen's Dragoon Guards.
Times: Open all year, daily (ex 25-26 Dec & 1 Jan) including guided tours, Mar-Oct, 9.30-6 (last tour 5pm); Nov-Feb, 9.30-5.30 (last tour 4pm). Royal Regiment of Wales Museum closed Tue. Queen's Dragoon Guards Museum closed Fri. **Fee:** ✱ Full conducted tour, military museums, green, Roman Wall & Norman Keep £5.80 (ch & pen £3.50). Roman Wall, Norman Keep, & military museum £2.90 (ch & pen £1.80). **Facilities:** 🅿 (200 yds) 🍴 ⅔ (access to Castle Green & Museum) toilets for disabled shop ✗ (ex in grounds & guide dogs) 🍴

DYFFRYN GARDENS
St Nicholas CF5 6SU
⮕ (6m W of city centre off A48)
☎ 029 2059 3328 🖷 029 2059 1966

One of Wales' finest Edwardian gardens, the beautiful grounds offer an endless variety of colour and form with many small garden rooms recently restored with the aid of a Heritage Lottery fund grant. Additional works are still ongoing and some areas may be subject to closure.
Times: ✱ Open all year, 10-dusk **Facilities:** 🅿 🍴 ⅔ (wheelchairs for hire, parking) toilets for disabled shop garden centre 🍴

LLANDAFF CATHEDRAL

Llandaff CF5 2YF

➲ (A48 off M4 follow signs to Llantrisant then signs to Llandaff Cathedral)

☎ 029 2056 4554 🖷 029 2056 4554   FREE

e-mail: office@llandaffcathedral.org.uk

A medieval cathedral begun in the 12th century on the site of an early Christian place of worship. The cathedral was severely damaged during the bombing raids on Cardiff during World War II. The interior is dominated by a modernistic post-war 'Christ in Majesty' sculpture by Epstein. **Times:** Open all year, daily 8-7 (Sun 7-7 & Mon 8.30-7). **Facilities:** P (100yds) ♿ (wheelchair available) toilets for disabled shop ✖ (ex guide dogs)

MILLENNIUM STADIUM TOURS

Millenium Stadium, Westgate St, Gate 3 CF10 1JA

➲ (M4 Junct 32, take A470 to Cardiff City Centre. Westgate Street is opposite Cardiff Castle far end).

☎ 029 2082 2228   2 for 1

🖷 029 2082 2228

In the late 1990s this massive stadium was completed as part of an effort to revitalise Welsh fortunes. It replaced Cardiff Arms Park, and now hosts major music events, exhibitions, and international rugby and soccer matches. Its capacity of around 75,000 and its retractable roof make it unique in Europe. The current home of five controlling bodies; Welsh Rugby, Welsh Football, English Football ASS, Football league (English) & British Speedway. **Times:** Open Mon - Sat, 10-5; Sun 10-4. **Fee:** £5 (ch up to 16 £2.50, ch under 5 free, concessions £3). Party 20+. **Facilities:** P Opposite gate 3 ♿ (lifts escalators disabled parking) toilets for disabled shop ✖ (ex guide dogs)

NATIONAL MUSEUM & GALLERY CARDIFF

Cathays Park CF10 3NP

➲ (located in Cardiff's Civic Centre, 5 mins walk from the city centre, 20 mins walk from Cardiff's bus and train station. M4 junct 32)

☎ 029 2039 7951 🖷 029 2037 3219   FREE

e-mail: post@nmgw.ac.uk

This establishment is unique amongst British museums and galleries in its range of art and science displays. 'The Evolution of Wales' exhibition takes visitors on a spectacular 4600-million year journey, tracing the world from beginning of time and the development of Wales. There are displays of Bronze Age gold, early Christian monuments, Celtic treasures, silver, coins and medals, ceramics, fossils and minerals. A significant collection of French Impressionist paintings sits alongside the work of Welsh artists, past and present in the elegant art galleries. **Times:** Open all year, Tue-Sun 10-5. Closed Mon (ex BHs) & 24-26 Dec. **Facilities:** P (charged) 🍴✖ licensed ♿ (wheelchair available, Tel 029 2057 3509 for access guide) toilets for disabled shop ✖ (ex guide dogs)

TECHNIQUEST

Stuart St CF10 5BW

➲ (M4 junct 33, follow A4232 to Cardiff Bay)

☎ 029 2047 5475 🖷 029 2048 2517   2 for 1

e-mail: info@techniquest.org

Located in the heart of the Cardiff Bay, there's always something new to explore at this exciting science discovery

continued

centre. Journey into space in the planetarium, enjoy an interactive Science Theatre Show or experience one of the 150 hands-on exhibits.

Times: Open all year (ex Xmas), Mon-Fri 9.30-4.30; Sat-Sun & BH's 10.30-5, school holidays 9.30-5. **Fee:** £6.75 (ch 5-16 & con £4.65). Family ticket £18.50 (2ad+3ch). Friend season ticket £48. Groups 10+ **Facilities:** P (50mtrs) Limited parking for disabled visitors 🍴♿ (lift, hearing loop) toilets for disabled shop ✖ (ex guide dogs)

ST FAGANS   Map 03 ST17

MUSEUM OF WELSH LIFE

CF5 6XB

➲ (4m W of Cardiff, 3m from M4 junct 33, along A4232)

☎ 029 2057 3500 🖷 029 2057 3490   FREE

e-mail: mwl@nmgw.ac.uk

A stroll around the indoor galleries and 100 acres of beautiful grounds will give you a fascinating insight into how people in Wales have lived, worked and spent their leisure hours since Celtic times. You can see people practising the traditional means of earning a living, the animals they kept and at certain times of year, the ways in which they celebrated the seasons. **Times:** Open all year daily, 10-5. Closed 24-26 Dec. **Facilities:** P 🍴 ✖ licensed ♿ (wheelchairs available on a 'first come-first served' basis) toilets for disabled shop ✖ (ex in grounds if on lead)

TONGWYNLAIS   Map 03 ST18

CASTELL COCH

CF4 7YS

➲ (A470 to Tongwynlais junction, then B4262 to castle on top of hill)

☎ 029 2081 0101

Castell Coch is Welsh for red castle, an appropriate name for this fairy-tale building with its red sandstone walls and conical towers. The castle was originally built in the 13th century but fell into ruins, and the present castle is a late-19th-century creation. Inside, the castle is decorated in fantasy style. **Times:** Open Apr-Jun & 29 Sep-26 Oct, daily 9.30-5; 2 Jun-28 Sep, daily 9.30-6; 27 Oct-31 Mar, Mon-Sat 9.30-4, Sun 11-4. Between 5 Jan-13 Feb 2004 monument closed for essential conservation works. Telephone for Xmas opening times. **Fee:** £3 (ch 5-16, pen & students £2.50, wheelchair users and assisting companion free). Family ticket (2 ad & 3 ch) £8.50. Group rates available. Prices quoted apply until 31 Mar 2004. **Facilities:** P shop ✖ ☺

CARMARTHENSHIRE

ABERGWILI   Map 02 SN42

CARMARTHENSHIRE COUNTY MUSEUM
SA31 2JG
➲ (2m E of Carmarthen, just off A40, at
Abergwili rdbt)   **FREE**
☎ 01267 231691   🖷 01267 223830
e-mail: cdelaney@carmarthenshire.gov.uk
Housed in the old palace of the Bishop of St David's and set
in seven acres of grounds, the museum offers a wide range
of local subjects to explore, from geology and prehistory to
butter making, Welsh furniture and folk art. Temporary
exhibitions are held.
Times: Open all year, Mon-Sat 10-4.30. (Closed Xmas-New Year).
Facilities: 🅿 💺 ♿ toilets for disabled shop ✖ (ex guide dogs)

CARREG CENNEN CASTLE   Map 03 SN61

CARREG CENNEN CASTLE
SA19 6UA
➲ (unclassified road from A483 to Trapp village)
☎ 01558 822291
A steep path leads up to the castle, which is spectacularly
sited on a limestone crag. It was first built as a stronghold of
the native Welsh and then rebuilt in the late 13th century.
Most remarkable among the impressive remains is a
mysterious passage, cut into the side of the cliff and lit by
loopholes. The farm at the site has a rare breeds centre.
Times: Open all year, Apr-Oct, daily 9.30-7.30; Nov-Mar, daily,
9.30-dusk. Telephone for Xmas opening times. **Fee:** £3 (ch 5-16, pen &
students £2.50, wheelchair users & assisting companion free). Family
ticket (2 ad & 3 ch) £8.50. Group rates available. Prices quoted apply
until 31 Mar 2004. **Facilities:** 🅿 💺 shop ✖ ⊕ 🗨

DRE-FACH FELINDRE   Map 02 SN33

NATIONAL WOOLLEN MUSEUM
SA44 5UP
➲ (16m W of Carmarthen off A484, 4m E of
Newcastle Emlyn)   **FREE**
☎ 01559 370929   🖷 01559 371592
The museum is housed in the former Cambrian Mills and has
a comprehensive display tracing the evolution of the industry
from its beginnings to the present day. Demonstrations of the
fleece to fabric process are given on 19th-century textile
machinery. Following re-development work, details
regarding facilities, disabled access etc may change. Please
telephone the museum before visit to confirm details.
Times: Museum currently closed, re-opens spring 2004. Telephone for
details. **Facilities:** 🅿 💺 ♿ (wheelchair access to ground floor &
ample seating) toilets for disabled shop garden centre 🗨

DRYSLWYN   Map 02 SN52

DRYSLWYN CASTLE
➲ (on B4279)   **FREE**
☎ 029 2050 0200
The ruined 13th-century castle was a stronghold of the
native Welsh. It stands on a lofty mound, and was important
in the struggles between English and Welsh. It is gradually
being uncovered by excavation.
Times: Open - entrance by arrangement with Dryslwyn Farm.
Facilities: 🅿 ✖ ⊕

KIDWELLY   Map 02 SN40

KIDWELLY CASTLE
SA17 5BQ
➲ (via A484)
☎ 01554 890104
This is an outstanding example of late 13th-century castle
design, with its 'walls within walls' defensive system. There
were later additions made to the building, the chapel dating
from about 1400. Of particular interest are two vast circular
ovens.
Times: Open Apr-1 Jun & 29 Sep-26 Oct, daily 9.30-5; 2 Jun-28 Sep,
daily 9.30-6; 27 Oct-Mar, Mon-Sat 9.30-4, Sun 11-4. Telephone for Xmas
opening times. **Fee:** £2.50 (ch 5-16, pen & students £2, wheelchair
users & assisting companion free). Family ticket (2 ad & 3 ch) £7. Group
rates available. Prices quoted apply until 31 Mar 2004. **Facilities:** 🅿 ♿
toilets for disabled shop ✖ ⊕ 🗨

KIDWELLY INDUSTRIAL MUSEUM
Broadford SA17 4LW
➲ (signposted from Kidwelly by-pass)   **FREE**
☎ 01554 891078
Two of the great industries of Wales are represented in this
museum: tinplate and coal mining. The original buildings
and machinery of the Kidwelly tinplate works, where tinplate
was hand made, are now on display to the public. There is
also an exhibition of coal mining with pit-head gear and a
winding engine, while the more general history of the area is
shown in a separate exhibition.
Times: Open Etr, Jun-Sep, BH wknds, Mon-Fri 10-5, Sat-Sun 12-5. Last
admission 4pm (5pm Jul-Aug). Other times by arrangement for parties
only. **Facilities:** 🅿 💺 ♿ toilets for disabled shop

LAUGHARNE   Map 02 SN31

DYLAN THOMAS' BOAT HOUSE
Dylans Walk SA33 4SD
➲ (14m SW of Carmarthen)
☎ 01994 427420   🖷 01554 747501

Under Milk Wood was written here by Wales's most prolific
20th-century poet and writer. Set on the 'heron priested'
shore of the Taff estuary, the house contains original

continued

furniture, family photographs, an art gallery and displays on the life and works of Dylan Thomas.
Times: Open all year, May-Oct & Etr wknd, daily 10-5.30 (Last admission 5); Nov-Apr, daily 10.30-3.30 (Last admission 3). **Fee:** ✱ £3 (ch under 7 free, ch over 7 £1, concessions £2). Family and group rates available. **Facilities:** 🅿 (200yds) ➠ (not accessible for wheelchairs) shop 🐾 (ex guide dogs) ➡

LAUGHARNE CASTLE
King St SA33 4SA
➲ (on A4066)
☎ 01994 427906

Newly opened to the public, picturesque Laugharne Castle stands on a low ridge overlooking the wide Taff Estuary. A medieval fortress converted into an Elizabethan mansion, it suffered a civil war siege and later became the backdrop for elaborate Victorian gardens, now recreated. Laugharne Castle has also inspired two modern writers - Richard Hughes and Dylan Thomas.
Times: Open Apr-28 Sep, daily 10-5. **Fee:** £2.50 (ch 5-16, pen & students £2, wheelchair users & assisting companions free). Family ticket (2 ad & 3 ch) £7. Group rates available. Prices quoted apply until 31 Mar 2004. **Facilities:** 🅿 (150 mtrs) ♿ toilets for disabled shop 🐾 ⊕ ➡

MIDDLETON, THE NATIONAL BOTANIC GARDEN OF WALES
Middleton Hall SA32 8HG
➲ (8m E of Carmarthen on A48 (M4), dedicated intersection - signed)
☎ 01558 668768   📠 01558 668933
e-mail: info@gardenofwales.org.uk

Set amongst 568 acres of Parkland in the beautiful Towy Valley in West Wales, just 7 miles from Carmarthen. The Gardens centrepiece is the Great Glasshouse, an amazing tilted glass dome with a six-metre ravine. The Mediterranean landscape enables the visitor to experience the aftermath of an Australian bush fire, pause in an olive grove or wander through Fuchsia collections from Chile. A 220m herbaceous broad walk forms the spine of the garden and leads to the children's play area and our 360°-surround screen cinema to the Old Stables Courtyard. Here the visitor can view art exhibitions, wander in our gift shop or enjoy a meal in our restaurant. Land train tours will take the visitor around the necklace of lakes, which surround the central garden.
Times: Open 30 Mar-25 Oct 10-6, 26 Oct-27 Mar 10-4.30 **Fee:** ✱ £6.95 (ch 5-16 £3.50, concessions £5). Family £17.50. Carer with wheelchair user/blind visitor free. **Facilities:** 🅿 ➠ ✗ licensed ♿ (braile interpretation wheelchairs/scooters shuttle service) toilets for disabled shop garden centre 🐾 (ex guide dogs) ➡

DINEFWR PARK
SA19 6RT
➲ (off A40 Carmarthenshire, on the western outskirts of Llandeilo)
☎ 01558 823902   📠 01558 822036

At the heart of Welsh history for a thousand years, the Park as we know it today took shape in the years after 1775 when the medieval castle, house, gardens, woods and deer park

continued

were integrated into one vast and breathtaking landscape. Access to Church Woods and Dinefwr Castle is through the landscaped park.
Times: ✱ Open Apr-Oct, daily (ex Tue & Wed) 11-4.30. Last admission 30 mins before closing. **Facilities:** 🅿 (charged) ➠ ♿ toilets for disabled 🐾 (ex outer park on lead) ⭐ ➡

NATIONAL WETLAND CENTRE WALES
Penclacwydd, Llwynhendy SA14 9SH
➲ (3m E of Llanelli, off A484)
☎ 01554 741087   📠 01554 741087   **2 for 1**
e-mail: wwtllanelli@aol.com

A wide variety of wild birds, including oystercatchers, redshanks, curlews, little egrets and occasionally ospreys, can be seen here during the right season. The grounds are beautifully landscaped, and include CCTV transmitting pictures of wild birds on the reserve, a wetland craft area and a flock of colourful Caribbean Flamingos. There is also a Discovery Centre and outdoor activities for visitors to take part in. Facilities for the disabled include easy access on level paths, special viewing areas and wheelchair loan.
Times: Open summer 9.30-5; winter 9.30-4.30. (Closed 24-25 Dec). **Fee:** ✱ £5.50 (ch £3.50, pen £4.50). Family £14.50. **Facilities:** 🅿 ➠ ✗ ♿ toilets for disabled shop 🐾 (ex guide/hearing dogs) ➡

ABERGLASNEY GARDENS
SA32 8QH
➲ (4m W of Llandeilo, follow signs from A40)
☎ 01558 668998   📠 01558 668998
e-mail: info@aberglasney.org.uk

With a history stretching back to the 15th century, Aberglasney was reworked by the 17th-century Bishop of St David's, the 18th-century poet, John Dyer and the 19th-century surgeon John Walters Phillips. Falling into disrepair through the 20th century, the house and its gardens were eventually rescued in 1995, and are now largely restored to their original Jacobean splendour. A mysterious and beautiful day out.
Times: Open all year, Apr-Oct, daily 10-6 (last entry 5); Nov-Mar, daily 10.30-4. (Closed 25 Dec) **Fee:** £5.50 (ch £2.50, disabled £3, pen £4.50). Party 10+ £5 (pen £4). **Facilities:** 🅿 ✗ licensed ♿ (most areas accessible, wheelchairs available) toilets for disabled shop 🐾 (ex guide dogs) ➡

LLANSTEFFAN   Map 02 SN31

LLANSTEFFAN CASTLE

➲ (off B4312)   FREE

☎ 01267 241756

The ruins of this 11th to 13th-century stronghold stand majestically on the west side of the Towy estuary.
Times: Open - access throughout the year. **Facilities:** ✖ ⊕

PUMSAINT   Map 03 SN64

DOLAUCOTHI GOLD MINES

SA19 8RR

➲ (on A482, signposted both directions)

☎ 01558 650359 📠 01588 822036

e-mail: penpeb@Smpt.NTrust.org.uk

Here is an opportunity to spend a day exploring the gold mines and to wear a miner's helmet and lamp while touring the underground workings. The information centre and a walk along the Miners' Way disclose the secrets of 2000 years of gold mining. This is the only place in Britain where the Romans mined gold.
Times: ✱ Open 14 Apr-17 Sep, daily 10-5. Guided underground tours daily. **Facilities:** 🅿 💷 ⅋ toilets for disabled shop ⅋ ⬛

CEREDIGION

ABERAERON   Map 02 SN46

LLANERCHAERON

SA48 8DG

➲ (2.5m E of Aberaeron off A482)

☎ 01545 570200 📠 01545 571759

A rare survivor of the core of a Welsh gentry estate. It was acquired by The National Trust in 1994 having received minimal maintenance in recent decades. Parts of the property are open to visitors.
Times: ✱ Open early Apr-late Oct, Thu-Sun & BH Mons 11-5. Last admission 30 mins before closing. Park open all year dawn to dusk.
Facilities: 🅿 ⅋ toilets for disabled ✖ (ex on lead) ⅋

ABERYSTWYTH   Map 06 SN58

NATIONAL LIBRARY OF WALES

Penglais Hill SY23 3BU

➲ (off Penglais Hill, A487 in the Northern area of Aberystwyth)

☎ 01970 632800, 623834 & 623837

📠 01970 615709

e-mail: holi@llgc.org.uk

This huge library is one of Britain's six copyright libraries, and specialises in Welsh and Celtic literature. It has maps, manuscripts, prints and drawings. There is a programme of travelling exhibitions. Please telephone for details.
Times: Open all year, exhibitions, library & reading rooms Mon-Fri 9.30-6, Sat until 5. (Closed BH's & first wk Oct). **Fee:** Free. Admission to reading rooms available by ticket, proof of identity required. Free admission to permanent exhibition and between 2-3 temp.exhibitions.
Facilities: 🅿 💷 ✗ ⅋ toilets for disabled shop ✖ (ex guide dogs)

The AA also publishes a guide to
Pet Friendly Places to Stay

CAPEL BANGOR   Map 06 SN68

RHEIDOL HYDRO ELECTRIC POWER STATION & VISITOR CENTRE

Cwm Rheidol SY23 3NF

➲ (off A44 at Capel Bangor)

☎ 01970 880667 📠 01970 880670

A guided tour of the power station and fish farm can be taken. There is a visitor centre, nature trail and scenic drive.
Times: ✱ Open Apr-Oct, daily 10-4 for free tours of the Power Station, fish farm & visitor centre. **Facilities:** 🅿 💷 ⅋ toilets for disabled

CENARTH   Map 02 SN24

THE NATIONAL CORACLE CENTRE   2 for 1

Cenarth Falls SA38 9JL

➲ (on A484 between Carmarthen and Cardigan, centre of Cenarth village, beside bridge and river)

☎ 01239 710980

e-mail: martinfowler.coraclecentre@virgin.net

Situated by the beautiful Cenarth Falls, this fascinating museum has a unique collection from all over the world, including Tibet, India, Iraq, Vietnam, and North America. Cenarth has long been a centre for coracle fishing, coracle rides are often available in village during summer holiday. Look out for the salmon leap by the flour mill.
Times: Open Etr-Oct, Sun-Fri 10.30-5.30. All other times by appointment. **Fee:** ✱ £3 (ch £1, concessions £2.50). Party rates 12+.
Facilities: 🅿 💷 ⅋ shop ⬛

EGLWYSFACH   Map 06 SN69

RSPB NATURE RESERVE

Cae'r Berllan SY20 8TA

➲ (6m S of Machynlleth on A487 in Eglwys-Fach. Signposted from main road)

☎ 01654 781265 📠 01654 781328

The mixture of different habitats is home to an abundance of birds and wildlife. The saltmarshes in winter support the only regular wintering flock of greenland white-fronted geese in England and Wales in addition to peregrines, hen harriets and merlins. The sessile oak woodland is home to pied flycatchers, wood warblers, redstarts in the summer but woodpeckers, nut hatches, red kites, sparrow hawks and buzzards are here all year round. Otters, polecats, 30 butterfly and 15 dragonfly species are also present.
Times: Open daily, 9am-9pm (or sunset if earlier). Visitor Centre: Apr-Oct 9-5 daily; Nov-Mar 10-4 (wknds only) **Facilities:** 🅿 ⅋ ✖ (ex guide dogs) ⬛

FELINWYNT   Map 02 SN25

FELINWYNT RAINFOREST & BUTTERFLY CENTRE

Rhosmaen SA43 1RT

➲ (from A487 Blaenannerch Airfield turning, turn onto B4333. Signposted 6m N of Cardigan)

☎ 01239 810882 & 810250   2 for 1

📠 01239 810465

e-mail: dandjdevereux@btinternet.com

A chance to wander amongst free-flying exotic butterflies accompanied by the recorded wildlife sounds of the Peruvian Amazon. A waterfall, ponds and streams contribute to a humid tropical atmosphere and provide a habitat for fish and native amphibians. See the exhibition of rainforests of Peru

continued

and around the world. Free paper and crayons to borrow for children.
Times: Open wknds from mid Mar, daily from Etr-Oct. **Fee:** ✱ £3.75 (ch 4-14 £1.50, pen £3.50) **Facilities:** 🅿 🚭 ♿ toilets for disabled shop ✗ (ex guide dogs) 🍴

STRATA FLORIDA   Map 03 SN76
STRATA FLORIDA ABBEY
SY25 6BT
➲ (unclassified road from Pontrhydfendigaid, reached from B4340)
☎ 01974 831261

Little remains of the Cistercian abbey founded in 1164, except the ruined church and cloister. Strata Florida was an important centre of learning in the Middle Ages, and it is believed that the 14th-century poet Dafyd ap Gwilym was buried here.
Times: Open Apr-28 Sep, daily 10-5. Monument will be opened and unstaffed with no admission charge at all other times between 10-5.
Fee: £2 (ch 5-16, pen & students £1.50, wheelchair users & assisting companion free). Family ticket (2 ad & 3 ch) £5.50. Group discounts available. Prices quoted apply until 31 Mar 2004. **Facilities:** 🅿 ♿ shop ✗ ☉ 🍴

CONWY

BETWS-Y-COED   Map 06 SH75
CONWY VALLEY RAILWAY MUSEUM
Old Goods Yard LL24 0AL
➲ (signed from the A5 into Old Church Rd, adjacent to train station)
☎ 01690 710568 📠 01690 710132

The two large museum buildings have displays on both the narrow-and standard-gauge railways of North Wales, including railway stock and other memorabilia. There are working model railway layouts, a steam-hauled miniature railway in the grounds, which cover over four acres, and a 15inch-gauge tramway to the woods. The latest addition is the quarter-size steam 'Britannia' loco that is now on display. For children there are mini-dodgems, Postman Pat, school bus and Toby Tram.
Times: Open daily, 10-5.30 (ex Xmas) **Fee:** £1 (ch & pen 50p). Family ticket £2.50. Steam train ride £1. Tram ride 80p. **Facilities:** 🅿 🚭 ♿ (ramps & clearances for wheelchairs) toilets for disabled shop 🍴

CERRIGYDRUDION   Map 06 SH94
LLYN BRENIG VISITOR CENTRE
LL21 9TT
➲ (on B4501 between Denbigh & Cerrigydrudion)
☎ 01490 420463 📠 01490 420694   **FREE**
e-mail: llyn.brenig@dwrcymru.com

The 1800-acre estate has a unique archaeological trail and round-the-lake walk of 10 miles. A hide is available and disabled anglers are catered for with a specially adapted fishing boat and an annual open day. The centre has an exhibition on archaeology, history and conservation and an audio-visual programme.
Times: Open mid Mar-Oct, daily 9-5. **Facilities:** 🅿 (charged) 🚭 ♿ (boats for disabled & fishing open days) toilets for disabled shop ✗ (ex guide dogs)

COLWYN BAY   Map 06 SH87
WELSH MOUNTAIN ZOO
Old Highway LL28 5UY
➲ (A55 coast road, junct 20 signposted Rhos-on-Sea)
☎ 01492 532938 📠 01492 530498
e-mail: welshmountainzoo@enterprise.net

The zoo and gardens are set in a 37-acre estate overlooking Colwyn Bay, with magnificent panoramic views of the coast and mountains. The animals are housed in natural settings, interspersed with gardens and woodland. The traditional range of zoo animals can be seen, from lions and elephants to penguins and parrots, and the zoo also attracts a variety of local wildlife. There are falconry displays during the summer months, and Californian sealions can be seen performing tricks at feeding time. Visit the Chimpanzee World complex, featuring the unique Chimp Encounter, and a South American small monkey breeding centre. There is also a Jungle Adventureland and Tarzan Trail activity area, and a Children's Farm.
Times: Open all year, Mar-Oct, daily 9.30-6; Nov-Feb, daily 9.30-5. (Closed 25 Dec) **Fee:** ✱ £6.95 (ch & students £4.95, pen £5.95). Family ticket (2 adults & 2 ch) £20.95. **Facilities:** 🅿 ✗ ♿ toilets for disabled shop ✗ 🍴

CONWY   Map 06 SH77
ABERCONWY HOUSE
LL32 8AY
➲ (At junction of Castle St & High St)
☎ 01492 592246 📠 01492 585153

This house dates from the 14th century; it is the only medieval merchant's house in Conwy to have survived the centuries of turbulence, fire and pillage in this frontier town. Furnished rooms and an audio-visual presentation show daily life in the house at different periods in its history.
Times: ✱ Open 29 Mar-Oct, Wed-Mon 11-5. Last admission 30 mins before closing. **Facilities:** 🅿 (100yds & 0.5 mile) shop ✗ (ex guide dogs) 🐾

CONWY CASTLE
LL32 8AY
➲ (by A55 or B5106)
☎ 01492 592358

The castle is a magnificent fortress, built 1283-7 by Edward I. There is an exhibition on castle chapels on the ground floor of the Chapel Tower. The castle forms part of the same defensive system as the extensive town walls, which are among the most complete in Europe.
Times: Open Apr-1 Jun & 29 Sep-26 Oct, daily 9.30-5; 2 Jun-28 Sep, daily 9.30-6; 27 Oct-Mar, Mon-Sat 9.30-4, Sun 11-4. Telephone for Xmas opening times. **Fee:** £3.50 (ch 5-16, pen & students £3, wheelchair users & assisting companion free). Family ticket £10. Joint ticket for both monuments £6.50 (ch 5-16, pen & students £5.50, wheelchair users & assisting companion free) Family ticket £18.50. Group rates available. Prices quoted apply until 31 Mar 2004. **Facilities:** 🅿 ♿ toilets for disabled shop ✗ ☉ 🍴

CONWY SUSPENSION BRIDGE
LL32 8LO
➲ (adjacent to Conwy Castle)
☎ 01492 573282

Designed by Thomas Telford, one of the greatest engineers of the late 18th and early 19th century, this was the first bridge to span the river at Conwy. The bridge has recently been restored and the toll house furnished as it would have been a century ago.
Times: ✱ Open Jul-Aug, daily 10-5; 29 Mar-Jun & Sep-Oct, Wed-Mon 10-5. **Facilities:** P ♿ ✈ ❧

PLAS MAWR
High St LL32 8DE
☎ 01492 593413

Plas Mawr is an excellent example of an Elizabethan town mansion, and is practically the same as when it was built between 1570 and 1580. Temporary exhibitions are held here.
Times: ✱ Open 27 Mar-May daily 9.30-5; Jun-1 Sep daily 9.30-6; 2 Sep-29 Sep daily 9.30-5; 30 Sep-27 Oct daily 9.30-4
Facilities: shop ◗

SMALLEST HOUSE
The Quay LL32 8BB
➲ (leave A55 at Conwy signpost, through town, at bottom of High St for the quay, turn left)   2 for 1
☎ 01492 593484   🖹 01492 593484

The Guinness Book of Records lists this as the smallest house in Britain. Just 6ft wide by 10ft high, it is furnished in the style of a mid-Victorian Welsh cottage.
Times: Open Apr-May & Oct 10-5; Jun & Sep, 10-6; Jul & Aug 10-9 or 9.30. **Fee:** 75p (ch under 16 40p, under 5yrs free). **Facilities:** P (100yds) ♿ shop

DOLWYDDELAN   Map 06 SH75

DOLWYDDELAN CASTLE
LL25 0EJ
➲ (on A470 Blaenau Ffestiniog to Betws-y-Coed)
☎ 01690 750366

The castle is reputed to be the birthplace of Llewelyn the Great. It was captured in 1283 by Edward I, who immediately began strengthening it for his own purposes. A restored keep of around 1200, and a 13th-century curtain wall can be seen. An exhibition on the castles of the Welsh Princes is located in the keep.
Times: Open all year, Apr-29 Sep, daily 9.30-6.30; 29 Sep-Mar, Mon-Sat 9.30-4, Sun 11-4. Telephone for Xmas opening times. **Fee:** £2 (ch 5-16, pen & students £1.50, wheelchair users & assisting companion free). Family ticket (2 ad & 3 ch) £5.50. Group rates available. Prices quoted apply until 31 Mar 2004. **Facilities:** P ✈ ⊕ ◗

LLANDUDNO JUNCTION   Map 06 SH77

RSPB NATURE RESERVE
LL31 9XZ
➲ (off A55, signposted)
☎ 01492 584091   🖹 01492 584091
e-mail: alan.davies@rspb.org.uk

The visitor centre has a viewing area which overlooks the estuary and Conwy Castle, and there's a nature trail and four
continued

hides for viewing lapwings and shelduck amongst many others. Phone for details of events.
Times: Open all year, daily, 10-5 (Closed 25 Dec). **Fee:** £2.50 (ch £1, concessions £1.50). **Facilities:** P ♿ toilets for disabled shop ✈ (ex guide dogs) ◗

LLANRWST   Map 06 SH86

GWYDYR UCHAF CHAPEL
➲ (0.5m SW off B5106)   FREE
☎ 01492 640578

Built in the 17th century by Sir John Wynn of Gwydir Castle, the chapel is noted for its painted ceiling and wonderfully varied woodwork.
Times: Open any reasonable time. **Facilities:** P ✈ ♿ ⊕

PENMACHNO   Map 06 SH75

TY MAWR WYBRNANT
LL25 0HJ
➲ (From A5 3m S of Betws-y-Coed take B4406 to Penmachno. House is 2.5m NW of Penmachno by forest road)
☎ 01690 760213

Situated in the beautiful, secluded Wybrnant Valley, Ty Mawr was the birthplace of Bishop William Morgan (1545-1604), the first translator of the entire Bible into Welsh. The house has been restored to its probable 16th-17th century appearance. The Wybrnant Nature Trail, a short walk, covers approximately one mile.
Times: ✱ Open 30 Mar-Sep, Thu-Sun & BH Mons 12-5; Oct, Thu, Fri & Sun 12-4. Last admission 30 mins before closing. **Facilities:** P ✈ (ex in grounds) ♿ (minibus access only) ❧

TAL-Y-CAFN   Map 06 SH77

BODNANT GARDEN
LL28 5RE
➲ (8m S of Llandudno & Colwyn Bay off A470. Also signposted from A55 junct 19)
☎ 01492 650460   🖹 01492 650448

Set above the River Conwy with beautiful views over Snowdonia, these gardens are a delight. Five Italian style terraces were constructed below the house - on the lowest terrace is a canal pool with an open-air yew hedge stage and a reconstructed Pin Mill. The garden is renowned for its collections of magnolias, camellias, rhododendrons and azaleas and the famous Laburnum Arch. Contact for details of open air theatre.
Times: Open mid Mar-2 Nov, daily 10-5 (last admission half hour before closing) **Facilities:** P ◖ ♿ (ramps to gardens, wheelchairs & Braille guides) toilets for disabled shop garden centre ✈ (ex guide dogs) ❧ ◗

TREFRIW   Map 06 SH76

TREFRIW WOOLLEN MILLS
LL27 0NQ
➲ (on B5106 in centre of Trefriw, 5m N of Betws-y-Coed)
☎ 01492 640462   🖹 01492 641821   FREE
e-mail: info@t-w-m.co.uk

Established in 1859, the mill is situated beside the fast-flowing Afon Crafnant, which drives two hydro-electric
continued

turbines to power the looms. All the machinery of woollen manufacture can be seen here: blending, carding, spinning, dyeing, warping and weaving. In the Weaver's Garden, there are plants traditionally used in the textile industry, mainly for dyeing. Hand-spinning demonstrations.
Times: Mill open Etr-Oct, Mon-Fri 10-1 & 2-5. Weaving demonstrations & turbine house: open all year, Mon-Fri 10-1 & 2-5. **Facilities:** P (35yds) 🅿🄫 ఈ (access to shop, cafe, weaving & turbine house) shop 🛪 (ex in grounds on lead) 🍴

DENBIGHSHIRE

BODELWYDDAN   Map 06 SJ07
BODELWYDDAN CASTLE
LL18 5YA
➲ (just off A55, near St Asaph, follow the brown and white signs)
☎ 01745 584060 🖹 01745 584563
e-mail: enquiries@bodelwyddan-castle.co.uk
Bodelwyddan Castle houses over 100 portraits from the National Portrait Gallery's 19th Century collection. The portraits hang in beautifully refurbished rooms and are complimented by sculpture and period furnishings. Interactive displays show how portraits were produced and used in the Victorian era. The Castle Gallery hosts a programme of temporary exhibitions and events. The castle is set within 200 acres of woodland.
Times: Open Apr-Sep, daily 10.30-5. Oct-Apr, 10.30-4. Closed Mon & Fri **Fee:** ✱ £4.50 (ch £2, concessions £4). Family ticket (4 people) £12.
Facilities: P 🅿🄫 ఈ (lift to first floor, Braille & audio guides) toilets for disabled shop 🛪 (ex guide dogs) 🍴

CORWEN   Map 06 SJ04
EWE-PHORIA SHEEPDOG CENTRE
Glanrafon, Llangwm LL21 0PE
➲ (Turn off A5 to Llangwm, follow signs)
☎ 01490 460369
e-mail: info@ewe-phoria.co.uk
Ewe-Phoria is an Agri-Theatre and Sheepdog Centre that details the life and work of the shepherd on a traditional Welsh farm. The Agri-Theatre has unusual living displays of sheep with accompanying lectures on their history and breed, while outside sheepdog handlers put their dogs through their paces.
Times: ✱ Open Etr-end Oct, Tue-Fri & Sun. Closed Sat & Mon ex BH's
Facilities: P 🅿🄫 ✗ licensed ఈ toilets for disabled shop 🛪 (ex guide dogs) 🍴

PEN-Y-BRYN FARM PARK
LL21 9PP
➲ (off A5 onto B5105. 5m from Cerrigydrudion)
☎ 01490 420244 & 🖹 01490 420244
Proudly catering to all ages, Pen-y-Bryn Park has a petting zoo, falconry, and 'Solo', its very own llama.
Times: ✱ Open Etr-Oct, Tue-Sun & BH's, 10-5 **Facilities:** P 🅿🄫 ఈ toilets for disabled shop garden centre

RUG CHAPEL
Rug LL21 9BT
☎ 01490 412025
Rug Chapel was built in 1637 for Colonel William Salusbury, famous Civil War defender of Denbigh Castle. A rare little altered example of a 17th-century private chapel, it reflects the Colonel's High Church religious views. Prettily set in a wooded landscape, the chapel's modest exterior gives little hint of the interior where local artists and carvers were given a free reign, with some spectacular results.
Times: Open Apr-28 Sep, Wed-Sun 10-5 (open Mon & Tue after BH wknds). Access to Llangar is arranged daily at 2pm through Custodian at Rug Chapel, telephone 01490 412025 for details. **Fee:** £2.50 (ch 5-16, pen & students £2, wheelchair users & assisting companion free). Family ticket (2 ad & 3 ch) £7. Group rates available. Prices quoted apply until 31 Mar 2004. **Facilities:** P ఈ toilets for disabled shop 🛪 ⊕ 🍴

DENBIGH   Map 06 SJ06
DENBIGH CASTLE
➲ (via A525, A543 & B5382)
☎ 01745 813385
The castle was begun by Henry de Lacy in 1282 and has an inspiring and impressive gatehouse, with a trio of towers and a superb archway, which is surmounted by a figure believed to be that of Edward I.
Times: Open Apr-28 Sep, Mon-Fri 10-5.30, Sat & Sun 9.30-5.30. (The monument will be open and unstaffed with no admission charge at all other times). Telephone for Xmas opening hours. **Fee:** £2.50 (ch 5-16, pen & students £2, wheelchair users and assisting companion free). Family ticket (2 ad & 3 ch) £7. Group rates available. Prices quoted apply until 31 Mar 2004. **Facilities:** P ఈ shop 🛪 ⊕ 🍴

LLANGOLLEN   Map 07 SJ24
HORSE DRAWN BOATS CENTRE
The Wharf, Wharf Hill LL20 8TA
➲ (From A5 turn onto Llangollen High St, across river bridge to T junction. The wharf on hill facing).
☎ 01978 860702 & 01691 690322
🖹 01978 860702
e-mail: sue@horsedrawnboats.co.uk
Take a horsedrawn boat trip along the beautiful Vale of Llangollen, and visit the museum, which illustrates the heyday of canals in Britain. The displays include working and static models, photographs, murals and slides. There is also a narrowboat trip that crosses Pontcysyllte Aqueduct, the largest navigable aqueduct in the world.
Times: Open Etr-end Oct, daily 10-5. May be closed Thu or Fri in Oct.
Fee: ✱ Horse Drawn Boat Trip from £4 (ch £2.50). Family ticket £11. Narrowboat Trip £7.50 (ch £6.50). **Facilities:** P (400yds) 🅿🄫 ఈ (alighting/pick-up point available) toilets for disabled shop 🍴

> The AA also publishes a guide to
> Pet Friendly Places to Stay

LLANGOLLEN RAILWAY

Abbey Rd LL20 8SN

➲ (Llangollen Station - off A5 at Llangollen traffic lights onto A539 cross river bridge. Station on left at T-junct. Carrog Station - from A5 at Llidiart-y-Parc take B5437, station on right downhill after crossing railway bridge)

☎ 01978 860979 & 860951(timetable)

🖷 01978 869247

e-mail: office@llangollen-railway.co.uk

Heritage Railway featuring steam and classic diesel services along the picturesque Dee Valley. The journey consists of a 15 mile roundtrip between Llangollen and Carrog. A special coach for the disabled is available on some services. Please contact for more information.

Times: Open - station wknds, reduced services off peak, daily services Apr-Oct. Principally steam hauled, diesel trains please refer to timetable for off peak services. **Fee:** ✱ 2nd class return fare for full journey £8 (ch 3-16 £3.80, pen £5.50) Family ticket £18 (2 adult & 3 ch). **Facilities:** 🅿 (400yds) free parking at Carrog Station 🚊 ᕈ (special coach for disabled on some trains, notice required) toilets for disabled shop (at Llangollen only) ➰

PLAS NEWYDD

Hill St LL20 8AW

➲ (Follow brown heritage signs from A5, close to Grapes public house in Llangollen)

☎ 01978 861314   🖷 01824 708258

e-mail: rose.mcmahon@denbighshire.gov.uk

The 'Ladies of Llangollen', Lady Eleanor Butler and Sarah Ponsonby, lived here from 1780 to 1831. The original stained-glass windows, carved panels, and domestic miscellany of two lives are exhibited along with prints, pictures and letters.

Times: Open Apr-Oct, daily, 10-5. **Facilities:** 🅿 ᕈ toilets for disabled ✖ (ex guide dogs or in grounds)

VALLE CRUCIS ABBEY

LL29 8DD

➲ (on B5103, off A5 W of Llangollen)

☎ 01978 860326

Set in a deep, narrow valley, the abbey was founded for the Cistercians in 1201 by Madog ap Gruffydd. Substantial remains of the church can be seen, and some beautifully carved grave slabs have been found. There is a small exhibition on the Cistercian monks and the abbey.

Times: Open Apr-28 Sep, daily 10-5. Monument open and unstaffed with no admission charge at all other times between 10-4. Telephone for Xmas opening times. **Fee:** £2 (ch 5-16, pen & students £1.50, wheelchair users & assisting companion free). Family ticket (2 ad & 3 ch) £5.50. Group rates available. Prices quoted apply until 31 Mar 2004. **Facilities:** 🅿 ᕈ shop ✖ ☺ ➰

RHUDDLAN CASTLE

LL18 5AD

☎ 01745 590777

The castle was begun by Edward I in 1277, on a simple 'diamond' plan with round towers linked by sections of 9ft thick curtain wall. The moat was linked to a deep-water

continued

canal, allowing Edward's ships to sail from the sea right up to the castle.

Times: Open Apr-28 Sep, daily 10-5. **Fee:** £2 (ch 5-16, pen & students £1.50, wheelchair users & assisting companion free). Family ticket (2 ad & 3 ch) £5.50. Group discounts available. Prices quoted apply until 31 Mar 2004. **Facilities:** 🅿 ᕈ shop ✖ ☺ ➰

EWLOE CASTLE   FREE

➲ (1m NW of village on B5125)

Standing in Ewloe Wood are the remains of Ewloe Castle. It was a native Welsh castle, and Henry II was defeated nearby in 1157. Part of the Welsh Tower in the upper ward still stands to its original height, and there is a well in the lower ward. Remnants of walls and another tower can also be seen.

Times: Open at all times. **Facilities:** ✖ ☺

FLINT CASTLE

CH6 5PH

➲ (NE side of Flint)   FREE

☎ 01352 733078

The castle was started by Edward I in 1277 and overlooks the River Dee. It is exceptional for its great tower, or Donjon, which is separated by a moat. Other buildings would have stood in the inner bailey, of which parts of the walls and corner towers remain.

Times: Open at all times. **Facilities:** 🅿 ✖ ☺

BASINGWERK ABBEY

Greenfield Valley Heritage Pk, Greenfield CH8 7GH

➲ (just S of A458)   FREE

☎ 01352 714172

The abbey was founded around 1131 by Ranulf de Gernon, Earl of Chester. The first stone church dates from the beginning of the thirteenth century. The last abbot surrendered the house to the crown in 1536. The Abbey is close to the Heritage Park Visitor Centre and access to the Museum and Farm Complex at Greenfield Valley.

Times: Open all year, daily 9-6. **Facilities:** 🅿 ✖ ᕈ (disabled facilities in Heritage Park) toilets for disabled shop ✖ ☺

GREENFIELD VALLEY HERITAGE PARK

Greenfield Rd CH8 7GH

☎ 01352 714172   🖷 01352 714791

e-mail: info@greenfieldvalley.com

This fascinating park covers "one and a half miles of woodlands, reservoirs, ancient monuments and industrial history." Among the multitude of sights are a footpath that was once a railway line, the remnants of a number of mills relating to the copper industry, an environment centre, the shrine of St Winefride's Well, and Basingwerk Abbey.

Times: Park open all year. Museum & farm Apr-Oct, 10-4.30. **Fee:** ✱ Museum & farm £2.75 (ch £1.65, concessions £2.20). Park free. **Facilities:** 🅿 🚊 ᕈ (ramps to enter buildings) toilets for disabled shop

GWYNEDD

BANGOR   Map 06 SH57

PENRHYN CASTLE
LL57 4HN

➲ (1m E at Bangor, at Llandegai on A5122, just off A55)

☎ 01248 353084 ▤ 01248 371281

e-mail: ppemsn@smtp.ntrust.org.uk

The splendid castle with its towers and battlements was commissioned in 1827 as a sumptuous family home. Notable rooms include the great hall, the library and the dining room, which is covered with neo-Norman decoration. Among the furniture is a slate bed weighing over a ton, and a decorated brass bed made for Edward VII at the then huge cost of £600. **Times:** Open 22 Mar-5 Nov, daily (ex Tue) Castle 12-5pm. Grounds and stableblock exhibitions 11-5 (Jul & Aug 10-5.30). Last admission 4.30pm. Last audio tour 4pm. **Facilities:** 🅿 ✗ licensed & (wheelchairs & golf buggies pre bookable) toilets for disabled shop 🐾

BEDDGELERT   Map 06 SH54

SYGUN COPPER MINE
LL55 4NE

➲ (1m E of Beddgelert on A498)

☎ 01766 510100 ▤ 01766 510102

e-mail: sygunmine@aol.com

On a self-guided audio-visual underground tour, visitors can explore the workings of this 19th-century copper mine, where magnificent stalactite and stalagmite formations can be seen. The less energetic can enjoy a continuous audio-visual presentation and a display of artefacts found during excavations.
Times: Open daily mid Feb-mid Nov Mon-Fri 10-5, Sat 10-4, Sun 11-5. **Fee:** ✱ £5.25 (ch £3.50, pen £4.50). **Facilities:** 🅿 🅿 & (wide access) toilets for disabled shop 🍴

BLAENAU FFESTINIOG   Map 06 SH74

HYDRO CENTRE FFESTINIOG
Ffestiniog Hydro Centre, First Hydro Company, Tan-Y-Grisiau LL41 3TP

➲ (off A496)

☎ 01766 830465 ▤ 01766 833472

e-mail: hydrocentre@edisonmission.com

The scheme was the first hydroelectric pumped storage scheme, and was opened by Her Majesty the Queen in 1963. Water is released from an upper dam, through turbines, to generate electricity when needed, and then pumped back up when demand is low. Guided tours are available, and the Hydro Centre has a café, gift shop and picnic area.
Times: Open Etr-Oct 10-4.30. **Fee:** ✱ £2.75 (ch £1.50, students & pen £2), Family ticket (2ad+2ch) £7.25. **Facilities:** 🅿 🅿 shop ✗ (ex guide dogs)

LLECHWEDD SLATE CAVERNS
LL41 3NB

➲ (25m from A55 N Wales Expressway S on A470. 10m from A5 junct with A470. Beside A470 from Llandudno)

☎ 01766 830306 ▤ 01766 831260

e-mail: llechwedd@aol.com

The Miners' Underground Tramway carries visitors into areas where early conditions have been recreated, while the Deep Mine is reached by an incline railway and has an unusual audio-visual presentation. Free surface attractions include several exhibitions and museums, slate mill and the Victorian village which has Victorian shops, bank, Miners Arms pub, lock-up and working smithy.
Times: ✱ Open all year, daily from 10am. Last tour 5.15 (Oct-Feb 4.15). (Closed 25-26 Dec & 1 Jan). **Facilities:** 🅿 🅿 ✗ licensed & toilets for disabled shop (also Victorian shops in the Village) ✗ (ex on surface) 🍴

CAERNARFON   Map 06 SH46

CAERNARFON CASTLE
LL55 2AY

☎ 01286 677617

Edward I began building the castle and extensive town walls in 1283 after defeating the last independent ruler of Wales. Completed in 1328, it has unusual polygonal towers, notably the 10-sided Eagle Tower. There is a theory that these features were copied from the walls of Constantinople, to reflect a tradition that Constantine was born nearby. Edward I's son and heir was born and presented to the Welsh people here, setting a precedent that was followed in 1969, when Prince Charles was invested as Prince of Wales.
Times: Open Apr-1 Jun & 29 Sep-26 Oct, daily 9.30-5; 2 Jun-28 Sep, daily 9.30-6; 27 Oct-Mar, Mon-Sat 9.30-4, Sun 11-4. Telephone for Xmas opening times. **Fee:** £4.50 (ch 5-16, pen & students £3.50, wheelchair users & assisting compainion free). Family ticket (2 ad & 3 ch) £12.50. Group rates available. Prices quoted apply until 31 Mar 2004.
Facilities: 🅿 shop ✗ ⊕ 🍴

SEGONTIUM ROMAN MUSEUM
Beddgelert Rd LL55 2LN
➲ (on A4085 leading to Beddgelert approx 1m
from Caernarfon)
☎ 01286 675625   ▓ 01286 678416   FREE
e-mail: post@nmgw.ac.uk

Segontium Roman Museum tells the story of the conquest
and occupation of Wales by the Romans and displays the
finds from the auxiliary fort of Segontium, one of the most
famous in Britain. You can combine a visit to the museum
with exploration of the site of the Roman Fort, which is in
the care of Cadw: Welsh Historic Monuments. The exciting
discoveries displayed at the museum vividly portray the daily
life of the soldiers stationed in this remote outpost of the
Roman Empire.
Times: Open Tue-Sun 12.30-4. Closed Mon except BH **Facilities:** P
✖ (ex guide dogs) ▄

CRICCIETH   Map 06 SH43

CRICCIETH CASTLE
LL52 0DP
➲ (off A497)
☎ 01766 522227

The castle dates from the 13th century and was taken and
destroyed by Owain Glyndwr in 1404. Evidence of a fierce
fire can still be seen. The gatehouse leading to the inner
ward remains impressive, and parts of the walls are well
preserved.
Times: Open Apr-1 Jun & 29 Sep-26 Oct, daily 10-5; 2 Jun-28 Sep,
daily 10-6. (The monument will be open and unstaffed with no
admission charge at all other times). Telephone for Xmas opening
times. **Fee:** £2.50 (ch 5-16, pen & students £2, wheelchair users &
assisting companion free). Family ticket (2 ad & 3 ch) £7. Group rates
available. Prices quoted apply until 31 Mar 2004. **Facilities:** P shop ✖
🌣 ▄

CYMER ABBEY   Map 06 SH71

CYMER ABBEY
➲ (2m NW of Dolgellau on A494)
☎ 01341 422854

The abbey was built for the Cistercians in the 13th century. It
was never very large, and does not seem to have been
finished. The church is the best-preserved building, with
ranges of windows and arcades still to be seen. The other
buildings have been plundered for stone, but low outlines
remain.
Times: ✱ Open all year, early Apr-Oct, daily 9.30-6; Nov-Mar, daily
9.30-4. (Closed 24-26 Dec & 1 Jan) **Facilities:** P ᴔ ✖ 🌣 ▄

FAIRBOURNE   Map 06 SH61

FAIRBOURNE RAILWAY
Beach Rd LL38 2PZ
➲ (on A493 follow signs for Fairbourne, main
terminus is just past level crossing on left)
☎ 01341 250362   ▓ 01341 250240
e-mail: enquiries@fairbourne-railway.co.uk

One of the most unusual of Wales's 'little trains'; built
in 1890 as a horse-drawn railway to carry building materials
it was later converted to steam, and now covers
two-and-a-half miles. Its route passes one of the loveliest

continued

beaches in Wales, with views of the beautiful Mawddach
Estuary.
Times: Open early/mid Apr-mid/late Sep, times vary according to
season and events. Trains will run during Oct half term holiday and
Santa Specials at Xmas. **Fee:** ✱ Return £6.20 (ch £3.50, pen £5.30).
Family £16 (2ad+3ch) **Facilities:** P ▄█ shop ▄

GROESLON   Map 06 SH45

INIGO JONES SLATEWORKS
LL54 7UE
➲ (on main A487, 6m S of Caernarfon in direction
of Porthmadog)
☎ 01286 830242   ▓ 01286 831247
e-mail: slate@inigojones.co.uk

Inigo Jones was established in 1861 primarily to make school
writing slates. Today the company uses the same material to
make architectural, monumental and craft products. A
self-guided audio/video tour takes visitors round the slate
workshops, and displays the various processes used in the
extraction and working of Welsh slate.
Times: Open all year, daily 9-5. (Closed 25-26 Dec & 1 Jan).
Fee: £3.80 (ch & pen £3). **Facilities:** P ▄█ ᴔ toilets for disabled
shop ✖ (ex guide dogs) ▄

HARLECH   Map 06 SH53

HARLECH CASTLE
LL46 2YH
➲ (from A496)
☎ 01766 780552

Harlech Castle was built in 1283-81 by Edward I, with a
sheer drop to the sea on one side. Owain Glyndwr starved
the castle into submission in 1404 and made it his court and
campaigning base. Later, the defence of the castle in the
Wars of the Roses inspired the song *Men of Harlech*. Today
the sea has slipped away, and the castle's great walls and
round towers stand above the dunes.
Times: Open Apr-1 Jun & 29 Sep-26 Oct, daily 9.30-5; 2 Jun-28 Sep,
daily 9.30-6; 27 Oct-Mar, Mon-Sat 9.30-4, Sun 11-4. Telephone for Xmas
opening times. **Fee:** £3 (ch 5-16, pen & students £2.50, wheelchair
users & assisting companion free). Family ticket (2 ad & 3 ch) £8.50.
Group rates available. Prices quoted apply until 31 Mar 2004.
Facilities: P (disabled spaces in car park) shop ✖ 🌣 ▄

LLANBERIS   Map 06 SH56

DOLBADARN CASTLE
LL55 4UD
➲ (A4086)

Built by Llywelyn the Great in the early 13th century, this
Welsh castle overlooks Llyn Padarn in the Llanberis pass.
Times: ✱ Open any reasonable time. **Facilities:** P ✖ 🌣 ▄

LLANBERIS LAKE RAILWAY
Padarn Country Park LL55 4TY
➲ (off A4086 at Llanberis)
☎ 01286 870549   ▓ 01286 870549
e-mail: info@lake-railway.co.uk

Steam locomotives dating from 1889 to 1948 carry
passengers on a five-mile return journey along the shore of
Padarn Lake. The terminal station is adjacent to the Welsh

continued

Gwynedd 355

Slate Museum, in the Padarn Country Park. The railway was formerly used to carry slate.

Times: Open Etr-late Oct. Trains run frequently Sun-Fri (Sat in Jul & Aug), 11-4.30 in peak season. Send for free timetable. **Fee:** ✱ £5 (ch £3.50). Family ticket available. Reduced rates for groups. **Facilities:** 🅿 (charged) 🍴♿ (disabled carriage available) toilets for disabled shop ✖ ☕

SNOWDON MOUNTAIN RAILWAY
LL55 4TY
➲ (on A4086, Caernarfon to Capel Curig road. 7.5m from Caernarfon)
☎ 0870 4580033 📠 01286 872518
e-mail: info@snowdonrailway.co.uk

The journey of just over four-and-a-half miles takes passengers more than 3000ft up to the summit of Snowdon; breathtaking views include, on a clear day, the Isle of Man and the Wicklow Mountains in Ireland. The round trip to the summit and back takes two and a half hours including a half hour at the summit.
Times: Open 15 Mar-5 Nov, daily from 9am (weather permitting). **Fee:** ✱ Return £18 (ch £13). Early bird discount on 9am train. **Facilities:** 🅿 (charged) 🍴♿ (some carriages suitable for wheelchairs - must notify) toilets for disabled shop ✖ (ex guide dogs) ☕

WELSH SLATE MUSEUM
Gilfach Ddu, Padarn Country Park LL55 4TY
➲ (0.25m off A4086. The Museum is within Padarn Country Park at Llanberis)
☎ 01286 870630 📠 01286 871906 **FREE**
e-mail: slate@nmgw.ac.uk

Set among the towering quarries at Llanberis, the Welsh Slate Museum is a living, working site located in the original workshops of Dinorwig Quarry, which once employed 15,000 men and boys. You can see the foundry, smithy, workshops and mess room which make up the old quarry, and view original machinery, much of which is still in working order.
Times: Open Etr-Oct, daily 10-5; Nov-Etr, Sun-Fri 10-4. **Facilities:** 🅿 (charged) 🍴♿ (all parts accessible except patten loft) toilets for disabled shop

LLANFIHANGEL-Y-PENNANT Map 06 SH60
CASTELL-Y-BERE
➲ (off B4405) **FREE**
☎ 029 2050 0200

The castle was begun around 1221 by Prince Llewelyn ap Iorwerth of Gwynedd to guard the southern flank of his principality. It is typically Welsh in design with its D-shaped towers. Although a little off the beaten track, the castle lies in a spectacular setting, overshadowed by the Cader Idris range.
Times: Open all reasonable times. **Facilities:** ✖ ☕

LLANGYBI Map 06 SH44
ST CYBI'S WELL
➲ (off B4354) **FREE**
☎ 01766 810047

Cybi was a sixth-century Cornish saint, known as a healer of the sick, and St Cybi's Well (or Ffynnon Gybi) has been famous for its curative properties through the centuries. The corbelled beehive vaulting inside the roofless stone structure is Irish in style and unique in Wales.
Times: Open at all times. **Facilities:** ♿ ✖ ☕

LLANUWCHLLYN Map 06 SH83
BALA LAKE RAILWAY
The Station LL23 7DD
➲ (off A494 Bala to Dolgellau road)
☎ 01678 540666 📠 01678 540535

Steam locomotives which once worked in the slate quarries of North Wales now haul passenger coaches for four-and-a-half miles from Llanuwchllyn Station along the lake to Bala. The railway has one of the few remaining double-twist lever-locking framed GWR signal boxes, installed in 1896. Some of the coaches are open and some closed, so passengers can enjoy the beautiful views of the lake and mountains in all weathers.
Times: Open Etr-last wknd in Sep, daily. (Closed certain Mon & Fri, telephone for details). **Fee:** ✱ £6.70 return (pen £6.20). Family ticket £16 (2 ad & 2 ch). **Facilities:** 🅿 🍴♿ (wheelchairs can be taken on train) shop

LLANYSTUMDWY Map 06 SH43
LLOYD GEORGE MUSEUM & HIGHGATE VICTORIAN COTTAGE
LL52 0SH
➲ (on A497 between Pwllheli & Criccieth)
☎ 01766 522071 📠 01766 522071
e-mail: amgueddfeydd-museums@gwynedd.gov.uk

Explore the life and times of David Lloyd George in this museum. His boyhood home is recreated as it would have been when he lived there between 1864 and 1880, along with his Uncle Lloyd's shoemaking workshop.
Times: Open Etr, daily 10-5; May-Jun, Mon-Fri 10.30-5 (open Sat in Jun); Jul-Sep daily 10.30-5; Oct, Mon-Fri, 11-4. Other times by appointment, telephone 01286 679098 for details. **Fee:** ✱ £3 (ch & pen £2). Family ticket £7. **Facilities:** 🅿♿ (induction loop in audio visual theatre, shop & cottage) toilets for disabled shop ✖ (ex guide dogs) ☕

PENARTH FAWR   Map 06 SH43

PENARTH FAWR
➲ (3.5m NE of Pwllheli off A497)   FREE
☎ 01766 810880
The hall, buttery and screen are preserved in this house which was probably built in the 15th century.
Times: Open at all times. **Facilities:** ⅀ ✕ ⊕

PLAS-YN-RHIW   Map 06 SH22

PLAS-YN-RHIW
LL53 8AB
➲ (12m from Pwllheli signposted from B4413 to Aberdaron)
☎ 01758 780219
This is a small manor house, part medieval, with Tudor and Georgian additions. The ornamental gardens have flowering trees and shrubs including sub-tropical specimens, divided by box hedges and grass paths. There is a stream and waterfall, which descends from the snowdrop wood behind.
Times: ✱ Open Mar-14 May, Thu-Mon noon-5; mid May-Oct, Wed-Mon noon-5. **Facilities:** 🅿 ⅀ (braille guides/scented plants) toilets for disabled shop ✕ ⇔ ⅋

PORTHMADOG   Map 06 SH53

FFESTINIOG RAILWAY
Harbour Station LL49 9NF
➲ (SE end of town, on the A487)
☎ 01766 512340 📠 01766 514576
e-mail: info@festrail.co.uk
A narrow gauge steam railway running for 13.5 miles through Snowdonia National Park, with breathtaking views and superb scenery. Buffet service on all trains including licensed bar (in corridor carriages). Please telephone for details of special events. The company also runs the Welsh Highland Railway, which will eventually link up with the Ffestiniog Railway.
Times: ✱ Open late Mar-early Nov, daily service and also 26 Dec-1 Jan. Limited service Nov-Dec (most days). Limited service Feb & Mar. **Facilities:** 🅿 (charged) ✕ licensed ⅀ (Wheelchair ramps) toilets for disabled shop (closed 24/25 Dec) ➤

PORTMEIRION   Map 06 SH53

PORTMEIRION
LL48 6ET
➲ (Off A487 at Minffordd)
☎ 01766 770000 📠 01766 771331   2 for 1
e-mail: info@portmeirion-village.com
Welsh architect Sir Clough Williams Ellis built his fairy-tale, Italianate village on a rocky, tree-clad peninsula on the shores of Cardigan Bay. A bell-tower, castle and lighthouse mingle with a watch-tower, grottoes and cobbled squares among pastel-shaded picturesque cottages let as holiday accommodation. The 60-acre Gwyllt Gardens include miles of dense woodland paths and are famous for their fine displays of rhododendrons, azaleas, hydrangeas and sub-tropical flora. There is a mile of sandy beach and a playground for children. The village is probably best known as the major location for 1960s cult TV show, *The Prisoner.*
Times: Open all year, daily 9.30-5.30. **Fee:** £5.70 (ch £2.80, pen £4.40). Party 15+. **Facilities:** 🅿 ⅀ ✕ licensed ⅀ toilets for disabled shop garden centre ✕ (ex guide dogs) ➤

TYWYN   Map 06 SH50

TALYLLYN RAILWAY
Wharf Station LL36 9EY
➲ (A493 Machynlleth to Dolgellau for Tywyn station, B4405 for Abergynolwyn)
☎ 01654 710472 📠 01654 711755
e-mail: enquiries@talyllyn.co.uk
The oldest 27in-gauge railway in the world, built in 1865 to run from Tywyn on Cardigan Bay to Abergynolwyn slate mine some seven miles inland. The railway climbs the steep sides of the Fathew Valley and with stops on the way at Dolgoch Falls and the Nant Gwernol forest. The return trip takes 2.5 hours. All scheduled passenger trains are steam hauled.
Times: Open Sun mid Feb-Mar, daily; Apr-early Nov & 26 Dec-1 Jan. Ring for timetable. **Fee:** ✱ £9.50 Day Rover (ch accompanied £2). Intermediate fares available. **Facilities:** 🅿 (charged) ➤ ⅀ (prior notice useful) toilets for disabled shop ➤

Y FELINHELI   Map 06 SH56

GREENWOOD FOREST PARK
LL56 4QN
➲ (leave A55 at junct 11, follow Llanberis signs onto A4244, signposted from next rdbt)
☎ 01248 670076 📠 01248 670069
e-mail: info@greenwood-centre.co.uk
This forest park provides a wide range of exciting activities for the whole family. Try the Great Green Run - the longest slide in Wales, shoot a real longbow, build dens in the woods and saw a log. Try the Jungle Boat Adventure and explore the rainforest. There are large interactive exhibitions in the oak framed great hall and the Forest Theatre stages events and shows during school holiday periods. The Toddlers village is ideal for young children.
Times: Open daily mid Mar-end Oct 10-5.30 (Sep/Oct 10-5 & Sun 11-5). **Fee:** Varies with time of year. £4.50-£6.30 (ch £3.50-£5.30, pen £3.95-£5.50). Family ticket £14.10-£20.50. Party rates available.
Facilities: 🅿 ➤ ⅀ (grounds partly accessible) toilets for disabled shop ➤

ISLE OF ANGLESEY

BEAUMARIS   Map 06 SH67

BEAUMARIS CASTLE
LL58 8AP
☎ 01248 810361
Beaumaris was built by Edward I and took from 1295 to 1312 to complete. In later centuries it was plundered for its lead, timber and stone. Despite this it remains one of the most impressive and complete castles built by Edward I. It has a perfectly symmetrical, concentric plan, with a square inner bailey and curtain walls, round corner towers and D-shaped towers in between. There are also two great gatehouses, but these were never finished.
Times: Open Apr-1 Jun & 29 Sep-26 Oct, daily 9.30-5; 2 Jun-28 Sep, daily, 9.30-6; 27 Oct-Mar, Mon-Sat 9.30-4, Sun 11-4. Telephone for Xmas opening times. **Fee:** £3 (ch 5-15, pen & students £2.50, wheelchair users and assisting companion free). Family ticket (2 ad & 3 ch) £8.50. Group rates available. Prices quoted apply until 31 Mar 2004.
Facilities: 🅿 ⅀ shop ✕ ⊕ ➤

BEAUMARIS GAOL & COURTHOUSE

Steeple Ln LL58 8EW

☎ 01248 810921 & 724444 ▤ 01248 750282

With its treadmill and grim cells, the gaol is a vivid reminder of the tough penalties exacted by 19th-century law. The courthouse, built in 1614 and renovated early in the 19th century, is a unique example of an early Welsh court.
Times: ✱ Open Etr-Sep, daily 10.30-5. Other times by arrangement only. **Facilities:** ℗ (500yds) ♿ (narrow gates may restrict some wheelchairs) shop ✖ (ex guide dogs)

MUSEUM OF CHILDHOOD

1 Castle St LL58 8AP

➲ (on A545. Opposite Beaumaris Castle)
☎ 01248 712498 ▤ 01248 716869

The museum illustrates the life and interests of children and families over 150 years. There are around 2000 items in the museum's collection including money boxes, dolls, educational toys and games, early clockwork trains, cars and aeroplanes, push toys and cycles.
Times: Open daily 10.30-5.30, Sun 12-5. Last admission 4.30, Sun 4. (Closed Nov-2nd wk Mar). **Fee:** ✱ £3.25 (ch £2, pen & students £2.75). Family ticket £9.50. Free entry for wheelchairs. **Facilities:** ℗ (50yds) ♿ shop ✖ (ex guide dogs)

BRYNCELLI DDU   Map 06 SH57

BRYN CELLI DDU BURIAL CHAMBER

➲ (3m W of Menai Bridge off A4080)   FREE
☎ 029 2050 0200

Excavated in 1865, and then again in 1925-9, this is a prehistoric circular cairn covering a passage grave with a polygonal chamber.
Times: Open at all times. **Facilities:** ℗ ✖ ⊕

BRYNSIENCYN   Map 06 SH46

ANGLESEY SEA ZOO

LL61 6TQ

➲ (take 1st turning off Britannia Bridge onto Anglesey then follow Lobster signs along A4080 to zoo)
☎ 01248 430411 ▤ 01248 430213
e-mail: fishandfun@seazoo.demon.co.uk

Nestling by the Menai Straits, this all-weather undercover attraction contains a shipwreck bristling with conger eels, a lobster hatchery, a seahorse nursery, crashing waves and the enchanting fish forest.
Times: Open mid Feb-early Nov 10-6. Last admission 1hr before site closes. **Fee:** ✱ £5.95 (ch & student £4.95, pen & UB40 £5.50). Family ticket £14.95-£21.95. Party 10+. Please telephone to confirm 2004 prices. **Facilities:** ℗ ▣ licensed ♿ (2 wheelchairs available, braile tour notes) toilets for disabled shop (well stocked, unusual gifts) ✖ (ex guide dogs) ◥

FOEL FARM PARK

Foel Farm LL61 6TQ

➲ (Turn left off Britannia Bridge A55 onto A5/A4080 to Llanfairpwllgwyngyll & left on A4080 to Brynsiencyn. Follow signs from Brynsiencyn)
☎ 01248 430646 ▤ 01248 430066
e-mail: foelfarm@btinternet.com

Children will love this friendly farm experience, where they
continued

can meet animals big and small, and take tractor and trailer rides. The park also contains a luxury handmade chocolate business, a bistro and bar, as well as a tea room and gift shop.
Times: Open daily Mar-Oct 10.30-5.30; Also wknds Nov-Feb 10.30-4.30. Also open half term Feb. **Fee:** £4.75 (ch 4-16 £3.75, pen & students £4.25). **Facilities:** ℗ ▣ ✖ licensed ♿ toilets for disabled shop ✖ (ex guide dogs) ◥

HOLYHEAD   Map 06 SH28

RSBP NATURE RESERVE SOUTH STACK CLIFFS

Plas Nico, South Stack LL65 1YH

➲ (A5 to Holyhead then follow brown heritage signs, or A55 to Holyhead then follow brown heritage signs).   FREE
☎ 01407 764973 ▤ 01407 764973

High cliffs with caves and offshore stacks, backed by the maritime heathland of Holyhead Mountain, make this an ideal reserve to watch seabirds. Live video pictures of breeding seabirds are shown in the cliff-top information centre during the summer. Choughs, guillemots, razorbills, fulmars and puffins may be seen.
Times: Open: Information Centre daily, Etr-Sep, 11-5. Reserve open daily at all times. **Facilities:** ℗

LLANALLGO   Map 06 SH58

DIN LLUGWY ANCIENT VILLAGE   FREE

➲ (0.75m NW off A5025)

The remains of a 4th-century village can be seen here. There are two circular and seven rectangular buildings, still standing up to head height and encircled by a pentagonal stone wall some 4 to 5ft thick.
Times: Open at all times. **Facilities:** ✖ ⊕

PLAS NEWYDD   Map 06 SH56

PLAS NEWYDD

LL61 6DQ

➲ (2m S of Llanfairpwll, on A4080)
☎ 01248 714795 ▤ 01248 713673
e-mail: ppnmsn@smtp.ntrust.org.uk

Set amidst breathtakingly beautiful scenery and with spectacular views of Snowdonia, this elegant 18th century house was built by James Wyatt and is an interesting mixture of Classical and Gothic. The comfortable interior, restyled in the 1930s, is famous for its association with Rex Whistler, whose largest painting is here. There is also an exhibition about his work. A military museum contains campaign relics of the 1st Marquess of Anglesea, who commanded the cavalry at the battle of Waterloo. There is a fine spring garden and Australasian arboretum with an understorey of shrubs and wild flowers, as well as a summer terrace and, later, massed hydrangeas and autumn colour. A woodland walk gives access to a marine walk on the Menai Strait.
Times: ✱ Open Apr-Oct, Sat-Wed. House 12-5; Garden 11-5.30. Last admission 4.30 **Facilities:** ℗ ✖ licensed ♿ (Close parking, wheelchairs, garden shuttle, Braille guide) toilets for disabled shop ✖ (ex guide dogs) ◕

MERTHYR TYDFIL

MERTHYR TYDFIL   Map 03 SO00

BRECON MOUNTAIN RAILWAY
Pant Station Dowlais CF48 2UP
➲ (Follow the Mountain Railway Signs from the A470 or A465 N of Merthyr Tydfil)
☎ 01685 722988 ▤ 01685 384854

Opened in 1980, this narrow-gauge railway follows part of an old British Rail route which closed in 1964 when the iron industry in South Wales fell into decline. The present route starts at Pant Station and continues for 3.5 miles through the beautiful scenery of the Brecon Beacons National Park, as far as Taf Fechan reservoir. The train is pulled by a vintage steam locomotive and is one of the most popular railways in Wales.
Times: Opening times on application to The Brecon Mountain Railway, Pant Station, Merthyr Tydfil. **Fee:** ✱ Fares are under review, please ring for details. **Facilities:** ▣ ▬ ✗ licensed ⅃ (adapted carriage) toilets for disabled shop ➤

CYFARTHFA CASTLE MUSEUM & ART GALLERY
Cyfarthfa Park CF47 8RE
➲ (off A470, N towards Brecon, follow brown heritage signs)   **FREE**
☎ 01685 723112 ▤ 01685 723112
e-mail: museum@cyfarthfapark.freeserve.co.uk

Set in wooded parkland beside a beautiful lake, this imposing gothic mansion now houses a superb museum and art gallery. Providing a fascinating glimpse into 3000 years of history, the museum displays wonderful collections of fine art, social history and objects from around the world in a regency setting.
Times: Open Apr-Sep: Mon-Sun 10-5.30; Oct-Mar, Tue-Fri 10-4, Sat-Sun 12-4. **Facilities:** ▣ ▬ ⅃ (stair lift & wheelchair available) toilets for disabled shop ✗ (ex guide dogs)

MONMOUTHSHIRE

CAERWENT   Map 03 ST49

CAERWENT ROMAN TOWN
➲ (just off A48)   **FREE**
☎ 029 2050 0200

A complete circuit of the town wall of 'Venta Silurum', together with excavated areas of houses, shops and a temple.
Times: Open - access throughout the year. **Facilities:** ✗ ✛

CALDICOT   Map 03 ST48

CALDICOT CASTLE, MUSEUM & COUNTRYSIDE PARK
Church Rd NP26 4HU
➲ (M4 junct 23A onto B4245. From M48 take junct 2 & follow A48 & B4245. Signposted from B4245).
☎ 01291 420241 ▤ 01291 435094
e-mail: caldicotcastle@monmouthshire.gov.uk

Caldicot Castle's well-preserved fortifications were founded by the Normans and fully developed by the late 14th century. Restored as a family home by a wealthy Victorian, the castle offers the chance to explore medieval walls and towers in a

continued

setting of tranquil gardens and wooded country parkland, plus the opportunity to play giant chess or draughts.
Times: Open Mar-Oct, daily 11-5. **Fee:** ✱ £3 (ch, pen, student & disabled £1.50). Family (2 ad & 3 ch) £8.50 Party 15+. **Facilities:** ▣ ▬ ⅃ (taped tour, level trails, induction loop, access guide) toilets for disabled shop (must be no lead) ➤

CHEPSTOW   Map 03 ST59

CHEPSTOW CASTLE
NP6 5EZ
☎ 01291 624065

Built by William FitzOsbern, Chepstow is the first recorded Norman stone castle. It stands in a strategic spot above the Wye. The castle was strengthened in the following centuries, but was not besieged (as far as is known) until the Civil War, when it was twice lost to the Parliamentarians. The remains of the domestic rooms and the massive gatehouse with its portcullis grooves and ancient gates are still impressive, as are the walls and towers.
Times: Open Apr-1 Jun & 29 Sep-26 Oct, daily 9.30-5; 2 Jun-28 Sep, daily 9.30-6; 27 Oct-Mar, Mon-Sat 9.30-4, Sun 11-4. Telephone for Xmas opening times. **Fee:** £3 (ch 5-16, pen & students £2.50, wheelchair users and assisting companion free). Family ticket (2 ad & 3 ch) £8.50. Group rates available. Prices quoted apply until 31 Mar 2004.
Facilities: ▣ ⅃ shop ✗ ✛ ➤

GROSMONT   Map 03 SO42

GROSMONT CASTLE
➲ (on B4347)   **FREE**
☎ 01981 240301

Grosmont is one of the 'trilateral' castles of Hubert de Burgh (see also Skenfrith and White Castle). It stands on a mound with a dry moat, and the considerable remains of its 13th-century great hall can be seen. Three towers once guarded the curtain wall, and the western one is well preserved.
Times: Open - access throughout the year. **Facilities:** ⅃ ✗ ✛

LLANTHONY   Map 03 SO22

LLANTHONY PRIORY   **FREE**
☎ 029 2050 0200

William de Lacey discovered the remains of a hermitage dedicated to St David. By 1108 a church had been consecrated on the site and just over a decade later the priory was complete. After the priory was brought to a state of siege in an uprising, Hugh de Lacey provided the funds for a new church, and it is this that makes the picturesque ruin seen today. Visitor can still make out the west towers, north nave arcade and south transept.
Times: Open - access throughout the year. **Facilities:** ▣ ⅃ toilets for disabled ✗ ✛

LLANTILIO CROSSENNY   Map 03 SO31

HEN GWRT
➲ (off B4233)   **FREE**
☎ 029 2050 0200

The rectangular enclosure of the former medieval house, still surrounded by a moat.
Times: Open - access throughout the year. **Facilities:** ✗ 🚐 ✛

MONMOUTH Map 03 SO51

NELSON MUSEUM & LOCAL HISTORY CENTRE
New Market Hall, Priory St NP25 3XA
➲ (Town centre)
☎ 01600 710630 `FREE`
e-mail: nelsonmuseum@monmouthshire.gov.uk

Commemorative glass, china, silver, medals, books, models, prints and Admiral Nelson's fighting sword feature here. The local history displays deal with Monmouth's past as a fortress market town, and include a section on the co-founder of the Rolls Royce company, Charles Stewart Rolls, who was also a pioneer balloonist, aviator and, of course, motorist.
Times: Open all year, Mon-Sat 10-1 & 2-5; Sun 2-5. (Closed Xmas & New Year). **Facilities:** P (200yds) (small daily charge) ἀ toilets for disabled shop ✕ (ex guide dogs) ➽

RAGLAN Map 03 SO40

RAGLAN CASTLE
NP5 2BT
➲ (signposted off A40)
☎ 01291 690228

This magnificent 15th-century castle is noted for its 'Yellow Tower of Gwent'. It was built by Sir William ap Thomas and destroyed during the Civil War, after a long siege. The ruins are still impressive however, and the castle's history is illustrated in an exhibition situated in the closet tower and two rooms of the gate passage.
Times: Open Apr-1 Jun & 29 Sep-26 Oct, daily 9.30-5; 2 Jun-28 Sep, daily 9.30-6; 27 Oct-31 Mar, Mon-Sat 9.30-4, Sun 11-4. Telephone for Xmas opening times. **Fee:** £2.50 (ch 5-16, pen & students £2, wheelchair users and assisting companions free). Family ticket (2 ad & 3 ch) £7. Group discounts available. Prices quoted apply until 31 Mar 2003. **Facilities:** P ἀ shop ✕ ☺ ➽

SKENFRITH Map 03 SO42

SKENFRITH CASTLE
➲ (on B4521) `FREE`
☎ 029 2050 0200

This 13th-century castle has a round keep set inside an imposing towered curtain wall. Hubert de Burgh built it as one of three 'trilateral' castles to defend the Welsh Marches.
Times: Open - access throughout the year. Key keeper arrangement.
Facilities: P ✕ ☺ ₩

TINTERN PARVA Map 03 SO50

TINTERN ABBEY
NP6 6SE
➲ (via A466)
☎ 01291 689251

The ruins of this Cistercian monastery church are still surprisingly intact. The monastery was established in 1131 and became increasingly wealthy well into the 15th century. During the Dissolution, the monastery was closed and most of the buildings were completely destroyed. During the 18th century many poets and artists came to see the ruins and recorded their impressions.
Times: Open Apr-1 Jun & 29 Sep-26 Oct, daily 9.30-5; 2 Jun-28 Sep, daily 9.30-6; 27 Oct-Mar, Mon-Sat 9.30-4, Sun 11-4. Telephone for Xmas opening. **Fee:** £2.50 (ch 5-16, pen & students £2, wheelchair users and assisting companions free). Family ticket (2 ad & 3 ch) £7. Group rates available. Prices quoted apply until 31 Mar 2003 **Facilities:** P ἀ toilets for disabled shop ✕ ☺ ➽

WHITE CASTLE Map 03 SO31

WHITE CASTLE
NP7 8UD
➲ (7m NE of Abergavenny, unclass road N of B4233)
☎ 01600 780380

The impressive 12th to 13th-century moated stronghold was built by Hubert de Burgh to defend the Welsh Marches. Substantial remains of walls, towers and a gatehouse can be seen. This is the finest of a trio of castles, the others being at Skenfrith and Grosmont.
Times: Open Apr-28 Sep, daily 10-5. Monument open and unstaffed with no admission charge at all other times between 10-4. Telephone for Xmas opening times. **Fee:** £2 (ch 5-16, pen & students £1.50, wheelchair users & assisting companion free). Family ticket (2 ad & 3 ch) £5.50. Group rates available. Prices quoted apply until 31 Mar 2004. **Facilities:** P ἀ ✕ ☺ ➽

NEATH PORT TALBOT

ABERDULAIS Map 03 SS79

ABERDULAIS FALLS
SA10 8EU
➲ (from M4 junct 43, take A465, signposted Vale of Neath)
☎ 01639 636674 🖹 01639 645069

For over 300 years this famous waterfall has provided energy to drive the wheels of industry. The Turbine House allows visitors access to the top of the falls, with views of the power equipment, fish pass and displays. Please contact for details of special events.
Times: ✱ Open: March: Sat & Sun 11am-4pm only. Apr-Oct Mon-Fri 10am-5pm, Sat, Sun & Bank Hols 11am-6pm. **Facilities:** P 🅿 ἀ (lifts for disabled to view falls) toilets for disabled shop ❀ ➽

`FREE`

Attractions with this symbol do not charge for entry.

CRYNANT   Map 03 SN70

CEFN COED COLLIERY MUSEUM
SA10 8SN

➲ (1m S of Crynant, on A4109)   **FREE**

☎ 01639 750556 🖷 01639 750556

The museum is on the site of a former working colliery, and tells the story of mining in the Dulais Valley. A steam-winding engine has been kept and is now operated by electricity, and there is also a simulated underground mining gallery, boilerhouse, compressor house, and exhibition area. Outdoor exhibits include a stationary colliery locomotive. Exhibitions relating to the coal mining industry are held on a regular basis.
Times: Open daily, Apr-Oct 10.30-5; Nov-Mar, groups welcome by prior arrangement. **Facilities:** 🅿 & toilets for disabled shop

CYNONVILLE   Map 03 SS89

SOUTH WALES MINERS MUSEUM
Afan Argoed Country Park SA13 3HG

➲ (on A4107 6m NE of Port Talbot, leave M4 at junct 40)

☎ 01639 850564 🖷 01639 850446

e-mail: boastam@sagainternet.co.uk

The picturesquely placed museum gives a vivid picture of mining life, with coal faces, pit gear and miners' equipment. Guided tours of the museum on request. The country park has forest walks and picnic areas, and a visitor centre.
Times: Open all year daily, Apr-Sep 10.30-5 (Sat & Sun 10.30-6); Oct-Feb 10.30-4 (Sat & Sun 10.30-5). Closed Xmas week. **Fee:** ✽ £1.20 (ch & pen 60p). Concessionary rate for advance bookings.
Facilities: 🅿 (charged) ◗ ✕ & (mechanical & manual wheel chairs on request) toilets for disabled shop ✖ (ex guide dogs) 🍴

NEATH   Map 03 SS79

GNOLL ESTATE COUNTRY PARK
SA11 3BS

➲ (follow brown heritage signs from Neath Town Centre)   **FREE**

☎ 01639 635808 🖷 01639 635694

The extensively landscaped Gnoll Estate offers tranquil woodland walks, picnic areas, stunning views, children's play areas, adventure playground, 9 hole golf course, and coarse fishing. Varied programme of events and school holiday activities.
Times: Open all year - Country park; Vistor centre, daily from 10am. (Closed Xmas wk). **Facilities:** 🅿 ◗ & (wheelchair & scooter for hire, designated parking) toilets for disabled shop ✖ (ex guide dogs & dogs on lead)

NEATH ABBEY
SA10 7DW

➲ (1m W off A465)   **FREE**

☎ 01639 812387

These ruins were originally a Cistercian abbey founded in 1130 by Richard de Grainville.
Times: Open at all times. Key keeper arrangement. **Facilities:** 🅿 & ✖ ☺

NEWPORT

CAERLEON   Map 03 ST39

CAERLEON ROMAN BATHS
NP6 1AE

➲ (on B4236)

☎ 01663 422518

Caerleon was an important Roman military base, with accommodation for thousands of men. The foundations of barrack lines and parts of the ramparts can be seen, with remains of the cookhouse, latrines and baths. The amphitheatre nearby is one of the best examples in Britain.
Times: Open Apr-26 Oct, daily 9.30-5; 27 Oct-Mar Mon-Sat, 9.30-5, Sun 2-5. Telephone for Xmas opening times. **Fee:** £2.50 (ch 5-16, pen & students £2, wheelchair users & assisting companion free). Family ticket (2 ad & 3 ch) £7. Group rates available. Prices quoted apply until 31 Mar 2003. **Facilities:** 🅿 & shop ✖ ☺ 🍴

ROMAN LEGIONARY MUSEUM
High St NP18 1AE

➲ (located close to Newport, 20min from M4, follow signs from Cardiff & Bristol)

☎ 01633 423134 🖷 01633 422869   **FREE**

e-mail: rlm@nmgw.ac.uk

The museum illustrates the history of Roman Caerleon and the daily life of its garrison. On display are arms, armour and equipment, with a collection of engraved gemstones, a labyrinth mosaic and finds from the legionary base at Usk. Please telephone for details of children's holiday activities - 01633 423134.
Times: Open all year: Mon-Sat 10-5, Sun 2-5. **Facilities:** 🅿 (100yds) & toilets for disabled shop ✖ (ex guide dogs) 🍴

NEWPORT   Map 03 ST38

TREDEGAR HOUSE & PARK
NP10 8YW

➲ (2m W of Newport, signposted from A48 and M4 junct 28)

☎ 01633 815880 🖷 01633 815895

e-mail: tredegar.house@newport.gov.uk

Home to one of the greatest of Welsh families, the Morgans, later Lords Tredegar, for over five centuries. A tour of the interior gives a fascinating insight into life above and below stairs. The house and gardens are set in a 90-acre landscaped park, where carriage rides, formal gardens, self-guided trails, craft workshops, boating, and an adventure playground provide plenty to do and see.
Times: Open Etr-end Sep. **Fee:** ✽ House tour £5.25 (ch free, concessions £3.85). Gardens free. **Facilities:** 🅿 ◗ & (wheelchairs for loan) toilets for disabled shop 🍴

The AA also publishes a guide to Family Friendly Places to Stay, Eat & Visit

AMROTH
Map 02 SN10

COLBY WOODLAND GARDEN
SA67 8PP
➲ (1.5 miles inland from Amroth beside Carmarthen Bay, follow brown signs from A477)
☎ 01834 811885

From early spring to the end of June the garden is a blaze of colour, from the masses of daffodils to the rich hues of rhododendrons, azaleas and bluebells. Followed by hydrangeas in shaded walks through summer to glorious shades of autumn

Times: ✱ Open Apr-Oct, daily 10-5. Walled garden Apr-30 Oct 11-5. **Facilities:** 🅿 ➡ & (Limited due to terrain) toilets for disabled shop garden centre 🐾 🍽

CAREW
Map 02 SN00

CAREW CASTLE & TIDAL MILL
SA70 8SL
➲ (on A4075, just off A477 Pembroke to Kilgetty rd).
☎ 01646 651782 ⓘ 01646 651782
e-mail: enquiries@carewcastle.com

This magnificent Norman castle has royal links with Henry Tudor and was the setting for the Great Tournament of 1507. Nearby is the Carew Cross (Cadw), an impressive 13ft Celtic cross dating from the 11th century. Carew Mill is one of only four restored tidal mills in Britain, with records dating back to 1558.

Times: Open Apr-2 Nov daily 10-5. **Fee:** ✱ £2.80 (ch & pen £1.90). Family ticket £7.50. Single ticket (castle or mill) £1.90 (ch £1.50). **Facilities:** 🅿 & toilets for disabled shop 🍽

CILGERRAN
Map 02 SN14

CILGERRAN CASTLE
SA43 2SF
➲ (off A484 & A478)
☎ 01239 615007

Set above a gorge of the River Teifi - famed for its coracle fishermen - Cilgerran Castle dates from the 11th to 13th centuries. It decayed gradually after the Civil War, but its great round towers and high walls give a vivid impression of its former strength.

Times: Open Apr-26 Oct, daily 9.30-6.30; 27 Oct-31 Mar, daily 9.30-4. Telephone for Xmas opening times. **Fee:** £2.50 (ch 5-16, pen & students £2, wheelchair users & assisting companion free). Family ticket (2 ad & 3 ch) £7. Group rates available. Prices quoted aply until 31 Mar 2004. **Facilities:** & shop 🍽 ☺ 🍽

CRYMYCH
Map 02 SN13

CASTELL HENLLYS FORT
Pant-Glas, Meline SA41 3UT
➲ (Off A487 between Cardigan and Newport Pembrokeshire)
☎ 01239 891319 ⓘ 01239 891319
e-mail: celts@castellhenllys.com

This Iron Age hill fort is set in the beautiful Pembrokeshire

continued

Coast National Park. Excavations began in 1981 and three roundhouses have been reconstructed, another roundhouse has been completed and is the largest on the site. A Celtic roundhouse has been constructed in its original way using hazel wattle walls, oak rafters and a thatched conical roof. A forge, smithy, and looms can be seen, with other attractions such as trails and a herb garden. Please telephone for details of special events.

Times: Open Apr-early Nov, daily 10-5. Last entry 4.30 **Fee:** ✱ £2.80 (ch & pen £1.90) Family £7.50. **Facilities:** 🅿 & (ramp access to shop, hearing loop in shop) toilets for disabled shop 🍽

FISHGUARD
Map 02 SM93

OCEANLAB
The Parrog, Goodwick SA64 0DE
➲ (Take A40 to Fishguard, turning at the bypass, following signs for oceanlabs and Stenaline ferry terminal)
☎ 01348 874737 ⓘ 01348 872528
e-mail: ocean_lab01@hotmail.com

Overlooking the Pembrokeshire coastline, OceanLab is a multifunctional centre which aims to provide a fun filled experience for the family. A deep-sea adventure takes the visitor back in time to see marine creatures that lived in the distant past. There is also a hands on ocean quest exhibition, a soft play area and a cybercafe where visitors can surf the Internet.

Times: Open Etr-Oct 10-6, winter opening 10-4. **Fee:** ✱ Telephone for details **Facilities:** 🅿 ➡ & toilets for disabled shop 🍽 (ex guide dogs) 🍽

LAMPHEY
Map 02 SN00

LAMPHEY BISHOP'S PALACE
SA71 5NT
➲ (off A4139)
☎ 01646 672224

This ruined 13th-century palace once belonged to the Bishops of St Davids.

Times: Open all year, daily 10-5. Telephone for Xmas opening times. **Fee:** £2.50 (ch 5-16, pen & students £2, wheelchair users and assisting companion free). Family ticket (2 ad & 3 ch) £7. Group discounts available. Price quoted apply until 31 Mar 2004. **Facilities:** 🅿 & toilets for disabled shop 🍽 ☺ 🍽

LLANYCEFN
Map 02 SN02

PENRHOS COTTAGE
SA66 7XT
➲ (Near Maenclochog & Llanycefn, N of Haverfordwest.)
☎ 01437 760460 ⓘ 01437 760460

Local tradition has it that cottages built overnight on common land could be claimed by the builders, together with the ground a stone's throw away from the door. This thatched cottage is an example, built with help from friends and family; and it gives an insight into traditional Welsh country life.

Times: Open mid May-Sep Mon-Fri, by appointment only. Tel: 01437 731328. **Facilities:** 🅿 (roadside) & shop 🍽 (ex in grounds or guide dogs)

LLAWHADEN — Map 02 SN01

LLAWHADEN CASTLE
➲ (off A40, 3m NW of Narberth) **FREE**
☎ 01437 541201

The castle was first built in the 12th century to protect the possessions of the bishops of St David's. The 13th and 14th-century remains of the bishops' hall, kitchen, bakehouse and other buildings can be seen, all surrounded by a deep moat.
Times: Open at all times. Key keeper arrangement. **Facilities:** ⅊ ✖ ⊕

NARBERTH — Map 02 SN11

OAKWOOD PARK
Canaston Bridge SA67 8DE
➲ (M4 W junct 49, take A48 to Carmarthen, signposted)
☎ 08712 206 211 ▤ 01834 891380
e-mail: park@oakwood-leisure.com

Wales' premier theme park, featuring the world's no. 1 wooden roller coaster Megafobia, the 50m-high sky coaster Vertigo, shot n' drop tower coaster The Bounce, and Snake River Falls. For young children there is KidzWorld featuring The Wacky Factory, The Lost Kingdom, Techniquest and Playtown. In summer there are firework displays and light shows at night.
Times: Open daily 12 Apr-28 Sep, from 10am. **Fee:** ✱ £12.95 (under 2's free, ch 3-9 £11.95, pen & disabled £8.70). Family ticket £46.80, Party 20+ tickets available. **Facilities:** ℗ ▆✖⅊ (wheelchair hire, special access to some rides) toilets for disabled shop ✖ (ex guide dogs) ☜

NEWPORT — Map 02 SN03

PENTRE IFAN BURIAL CHAMBER
➲ (3m SE from B4329 or A487) **FREE**
☎ 029 2050 0200

Found to be part of a vanished long barrow when excavated in 1936-37, the remains of this chamber include the capstone, three uprights and a circular forecourt.
Times: Open - access throughout the year. **Facilities:** ✖ ⊕

PEMBROKE — Map 02 SM90

THE MUSEUM OF THE HOME
7 Westgate Hill SA71 4LB
➲ (Opposite Pembroke Castle)
☎ 01646 681200

A pleasant domestic setting provides an opportunity to view some of the objects that have been part of everyday life over the past three hundred years.
Times: Open May-Sep, Mon-Thu 11-5, other times by arrangement.
Facilities: ℗ (100 yds) (Public Pay & Display) ✖

PEMBROKE CASTLE
SA71 4LA
➲ (W end of Main Street)
☎ 01646 681510 & 684585 ▤ 01646 622260
e-mail: pembroke.castle@talk21.com

The birthplace of the first Tudor king, Henry VII, Pembroke Castle is a well-preserved Norman fortress with an impressive 75ft circular keep. The Great Gatehouse is home to a number of exhibitions tracing the history of medieval life at the castle. Beneath the Northern Hall is a vast cavern, once occupied by Stone Age cave dwellers and later used as a food and boat store by the Normans. Exploring from the top of the many lofty towers to the bottom of the vast cavern beneath makes it an exhilarating visit for all ages. Before leaving pop in to the Brass Rubbing Centre where your own special souvenir can be made, then complete the day with a peaceful walk around the millpond and medieval town walls.
Times: Open all year, daily, Apr-Sep 9.30-6; Mar & Oct 10-5; Nov-Feb, 10-4; (Closed 24-26 Dec & 1 Jan). **Fee:** £3 (ch under 16 & pen £2, ch under 5 & wheelchairs users free). Family ticket £8. **Facilities:** ℗ (200yds) ▆⅊ (induction loop, handrails, portable ramp) toilets for disabled shop ☜

ST DAVID'S — Map 02 SM72

ST DAVIDS BISHOP'S PALACE
SA62 6PE
➲ (on A487)
☎ 01437 720517

These extensive and impressive ruins are all that remain of the principal residence of the Bishops of St Davids. The palace shares a quiet valley with the cathedral, which was almost certainly built on the site of a monastery founded in

continued

the 6th century by St David. The Bishop's Palace houses an exhibition: 'Lords of the Palace'.

Times: Open Apr-1 Jun & 29 Sep-26 Oct daily 9.30-5; 2 Jun-28 Sep, daily 9.30-6; 27 Oct-Mar, Mon-Sat 9.30-4, Sun 11-4. Telephone for Xmas opening times. **Fee:** £2.50 (ch 5-16, pen & students £2, wheelchair users & assisting companions free). Family ticket (2 ad & 3 ch) £7. Group discounts available. Prices quoted apply until 31 Mar 2004.

Facilities: 🅿 🚻 toilets for disabled shop ✖ ⊕ 🍴

ST DAVIDS CATHEDRAL

The Close SA62 6PE

➲ (A487 from Haverfordwest into St Davids, pass the Cross Sq, turn left into car park)

☎ 01437 720202 📠 01437 721885

e-mail: adminstrator@stdavidscathedral.org.uk

Begun 1181 on the reputed site of St David's 6th century monastic settlement. The present building was altered during the 12th to the 14th centuries and again in the 16th. The ceilings of oak, painted wood and stone vaulting are of considerable interest.

Times: Open all year 8.30-6. **Fee:** ✱ Free - Suggested donation of £2. **Facilities:** 🅿 (300yds) (no coach parking) 🍴 🚻 (hearing loop) toilets for disabled shop ✖ (ex guide dogs) 🍴

ST FLORENCE   Map 02 SN00

MANOR HOUSE WILDLIFE & LEISURE PARK

Ivy Tower SA70 8RJ

➲ (on B4318 between Tenby & St Florence)

☎ 01646 651201 📠 01646 651201

The park is set in 35 acres of delightful wooded grounds and award-winning gardens. The wildlife includes exotic birds, reptiles and fish. Also here are a pets' corner, a children's playground with free rides on an astraglide slide, and roundabouts. Other attractions include a natural history museum, a go-kart track, model railway exhibition. Daily falconry displays. Telephone for details of displays and animal feeding times.

Times: ✱ Open Etr-end Sep, daily 10-6. Please telephone for late opening Jul & Aug. **Facilities:** 🅿 🍴 🚻 toilets for disabled shop ✖ 🍴

SCOLTON   Map 02 SM92

SCOLTON VISITOR CENTRE

SA62 5QL

➲ (5m N of Haverfordwest, on B4329)

☎ 01437 731328 (Mus) & 731457 (Park)

📠 01437 731743

Scolton Manor Museum is situated in Scolton Country Park. The early Victorian mansion, refurbished stables and the exhibition hall illustrate the history and natural history of Pembrokeshire. There are new displays in the house and stables, plus a 'Pembrokeshire Railways' exhibition. The 60 acre grounds, partly a nature reserve, have fine specimen trees and shrubs. Environmentally friendly Visitor Centre, alternative energy and woodland displays, guided walks and children's play areas.

Times: Open; Museum Apr-Oct, Tue-Sun & BH's 10.30-1 & 1.30-5.30; Country Park all year ex 25 & 26 Dec, Etr-Sep 10-7, Oct-Etr 10-6.

Facilities: 🅿 (charged) 🍴 🚻 (disabled parking area near house) toilets for disabled shop ✖ (ex guide dogs & in grounds)

TENBY   Map 02 SN10

TENBY MUSEUM & ART GALLERY

Castle Hill SA70 7BP

➲ (Near the centre of town on Castle Hill, above the Harbour)

☎ 01834 842809 📠 01834 842809   **2 for 1**

e-mail: tenbymuseum@hotmail.com

The museum is situated on Castle Hill. It covers the local heritage from prehistory to the present in galleries devoted to archaeology, geology, maritime history, natural history, militaria and bygones. The art galleries concentrate on local

continued

associations with an important collection of works by Augustus John, Gwen John and others.
Times: Open all year, Etr-7 Dec, daily 10-5; 8 Dec-Etr, Mon-Fri 10-5. Last admission 4.30. **Fee:** ✱ £2 (ch £1, concessions £1.50). Family ticket £4.50. **Facilities:** P (10 mins walk) ⅋ (lifts, levelled floors, ramps) toilets for disabled shop ✕ (ex guide dogs)

TUDOR MERCHANT'S HOUSE
Quay Hill SA70 7BX
☎ 01834 842279
Recalling Tenby's history as a thriving and prosperous port, the Tudor Merchant's house is a fine example of gabled 15th-century architecture. There is a good Flemish chimney and on three walls the remains of frescoes can be seen. A small herb garden has been created.
Times: ✱ Open 2 Apr-Sep, Mon-Tue, Thu-Sat 10-5, Sun 1-5. Dec Mon-Tue, Thu-Fri 10-3, Sun 12-3. **Facilities:** P (500yds) (no coaches nearby) ⅋ (garden could be accessed) ✕ (ex guide or small dogs) ☏

POWYS

ABERCRAF   Map 03 SN81
DAN-YR-OGOF THE NATIONAL SHOWCAVES CENTRE FOR WALES
SA9 1GJ
⮕ (M4 junct 45, midway between Swansea & Brecon on A4067, follow brown tourist signs)
☎ 01639 730284 & 730801 ▤ 01639 730293
e-mail: info@showcaves.co.uk
This award winning attraction includes three separate caves, dinosaur park, Iron Age Farm, museum, shire horse centre and covered children's play area.
Times: Open Apr-Oct, daily from 10 (last admission 3pm). **Fee:** ✱ £8.50 (ch 4-16 £5.50). Group rates 15+. **Facilities:** P 🍽 shop ☏

BERRIEW   Map 07 SJ10
GLANSEVERN HALL GARDENS
Glansevern SY21 8AH
⮕ (signposted on A483 between Welshpool and Newtown)
☎ 01686 640200 ▤ 01686 640829
Built in the Greek Revival style for Arthur Davies Owen, who chose a romantically positioned site on the banks of the River Severn. The current owners have developed the gardens, respecting the plantings and features of the past, and added a vast collection of new and interesting species. There are many fine and unusual trees, a lakeside walk, walled garden, water gardens and a rock garden with lamp-lit grotto.
Times: Open May-Sep, BH Mon, Fri-Sat 2-6. Parties other dates by arrangement. **Fee:** ✱ £3 (pen £2, ch under 15 free). **Facilities:** P 🍽 ⅋ (most areas accessible) toilets for disabled shop (must be on lead)

BRECON   Map 03 SO02
BRECKNOCK MUSEUM & ART GALLERY
Captain's Walk LD3 7DW
⮕ (Near centre of town at junct of The Watton & Glamorgan St)   [2 for 1]
☎ 01874 624121 ▤ 01874 611281
e-mail: brecknock.museum@powys.gov.uk
A wealth of local history is explored at the museum, which has archaeological and historical exhibits, with sections on

folk life, decorative arts and natural history. Victorian Assize Court is interpreted with life-size figures, sound and light and there is one of the finest collections of Welsh Lovespoons. The museum also runs a lively programme of Welsh contemporary art exhibitions.
Times: Open all year, Mon-Fri 10-5, Sat 10-1 & 2-5; also open Sun 12-5 Apr-Sep. (Closed Good Fri, 25-26 Dec & New Year's Day). **Fee:** £1 (concessions 50p, ch free) **Facilities:** P ⅋ (limited parking, must be accompanied by able-bodied) toilets for disabled shop ✕ (ex guide dogs) ☏

THE SOUTH WALES BORDERERS (24TH REGIMENT) MUSEUM
The Barracks, The Watton LD3 7EB
⮕ (close to town centre, well signed)
☎ 01874 613310 ▤ 01874 613275
e-mail: swb@rrw.org.uk
The museum of the South Wales Borderers and Monmouthshire Regiment, which was raised in 1689 and has been awarded 23 Victoria Crosses. Amongst the collections is the Zulu War Room, devoted to the war and in particular to the events at Rorke's Drift, 1879, when 121 men fought 4500 Zulus.
Times: Open all year, Apr-Sep daily; Oct-Mar, Mon-Fri 9-5. (Closed Xmas & New Year). **Fee:** ✱ £3 (ch up to 16 free). **Facilities:** P (town centre) ⅋ toilets for disabled shop ✕ (ex guide dogs) ☏

LLANFAIR CAEREINION   Map 06 SJ10
WELSHPOOL & LLANFAIR LIGHT RAILWAY
SY21 0SF
⮕ (beside A458, Shrewsbury-Dolgellau road)
☎ 01938 810441 ▤ 01938 810861
e-mail: info@wllr.org.uk
The Llanfair Railway is one of the Great Little Trains of Wales. It offers a 16-mile round trip through glorious scenery by narrrow-gauge steam train. The line is home to a collection of engines and coaches from all round the world. Please ring for details of special events.
Times: Open weekends Etr-end Oct, daily during holiday periods phone for timetable enquiries. **Fee:** ✱ £8.90 return (ch £1, pen £7.90). **Facilities:** P 🍽 ⅋ (three coachs adapted for wheelchairs) toilets for disabled shop ☏

MACHYNLLETH   Map 06 SH70
CELTICA
Y Plas, Aberystwyth Rd SY20 8ER
⮕ (well sign posted to the south of Machynlleth town)
☎ 01654 702702 ▤ 01654 703604
e-mail: celtica@celticawales.com
Located in a restored mansion house, Celtica is an exciting heritage centre introducing the history and culture of the Celtic people. The sights and sounds of Celtic life are brought alive as you go on a journey portraying the Celtic spirit of the past, present and future. There's an interpretive centre dedicated to Welsh and Celtic history, a children's indoor play area, and conference rooms. Education resources are available and groups are welcome. Storytelling, lectures, music and craft events take place.
Times: Open daily 10-6. Closed Xmas, New Year & some dates in Jan. **Fee:** ✱ £4.95 (ch 5-15 £3.95, ch under 5 free, pen, students, unemployed £4.20). **Facilities:** P 🍽 ✕ licensed ⅋ (Lift & ramps to public areas; Induction loop) toilets for disabled shop ✕ (ex guide dogs) ☏

continued

CENTRE FOR ALTERNATIVE TECHNOLOGY
SY20 9AZ
➲ (3m N of Machynlleth, on A487)
☎ 01654 705950
e-mail: info@cat.org.uk

The Centre for Alternative Technology promotes practical ideas and information on sustainable technologies. The exhibition includes displays of wind, water and solar power, organic gardens, low-energy dwellings, and a unique water-powered railway which ascends a 200ft cliff from the car park. The Wave Tank and the underground 'Mole-Hole' are particularly popular with children.
Times: Open 7 Apr-31 Oct, daily 10-5; 1 Nov-6 Apr, daily 10-4. **Fee:** ✱ 1 Jan-6 Apr, £5 (ch over 5 £3, seniors £4); 7 Apr-end Oct, £7 (ch £4, senior £5). **Facilities:** 🅿 ▆ (wheelchair available) shop ✖ (ex guide dogs) ▼

KING ARTHUR'S LABYRINTH
King Arthur's Labyrinth, Corris SY20 9RF
➲ (on A487 between Machynlleth and Dolgellau)
☎ 01654 761584 🖷 01654 761575
e-mail: king.arthurs.labyrinth@ corris-wales.co.uk

A subterranean storybook, a boat ride through the great waterfall and into the Labyrinth of tunnels and caverns carved into the ancient rocks of Wales. Tales of King Arthur and other legends are re-told as you walk through this underground setting.
Times: Open 29 Mar-Oct, daily 10-5. **Fee:** ✱ £4.85 (ch £3.40, pen £4.30). **Facilities:** 🅿 ▆ ⚬ toilets for disabled shop ✖ (ex guide dogs) ▼

MONTGOMERY CASTLE   FREE
☎ 029 2050 0200

Initially an earth and timber structure guarding an important ford in the River Severn, Montgomery was considered a 'suitable spot for the erection of an impregnable castle' in the 1220s. Building and modifications continued until 1251-53, but the final conquest of Wales by Edward I meant the castle lost much of its role.
Times: Open all year, any reasonable time. **Facilities:** ⚬ ✖ ⊕

THE JUDGE'S LODGING
Broad St LD8 2AD
➲ (In centre of town, off B4362, signed from A44 & A49)
☎ 01544 260650 🖷 01544 260652   2 for 1
e-mail: info@judgeslodging.org.uk

A restored Victorian town house with integral courtroom, cells and service areas - step back into the 1860s, accompanied by an 'evesdropping' audiotour of voices from the past. Explore the fascinating world of the Victorian judges, their servents & felonious guests at this award winning, 'hands on', historic house.
Times: Open daily, Mar-Oct 10-6; Nov-Dec Wed-Sun 10-4. Closed Jan-Feb. **Fee:** £4.50 (ch £3.50, concessions £3.95). Family ticket £13.50. Party rates available. **Facilities:** 🅿 (200mtrs) ⚬ (lift, disabled pack for inaccesible items) shop ✖ (ex guide dogs)

TRETOWER COURT & CASTLE
NP8 2RF
➲ (3m NW of Crickhowell, off A479)
☎ 01874 730279

The castle is a substantial ruin of an 11th-century motte and bailey, with a three-storey tower and 9ft-thick walls. Nearby is the Court, a 14th-century fortified manor house which has been altered and extended over the years. The two buildings show the shift from medieval castle to more domestic accommodation over the centuries.
Times: Open 3 Mar-26 Oct, daily 9.30-5. **Fee:** £2.50 (ch 5-16, pen & students £2, wheelchair users & assisting companion free). Family ticket (2 ad & 3 ch) £7. Group rates available. Prices quoted apply until 31 Mar 2004. **Facilities:** 🅿 ⚬ toilets for disabled shop ✖ ⊕ ▼

POWIS CASTLE
SY21 8RF
➲ (1m S of Welshpool, signposted off A483)
☎ 01938 551920 🖷 01938 554336
e-mail: ppcmsn@smtp.ntrust.org.uk

Laid out in the Italian and French styles, the Garden retains its original lead statues, an Orangery and an aviary on the terraces. The medieval castle contains one of the finest collections of paintings and furniture in Wales and a beautiful collection of treasures from India.
Times: ✱ Castle & museum open: Apr-Jun and Sep-Oct, Wed-Sun 1-5; Jul-Aug Tue-Sun 1-5; Open all Bank Hol's in season. Garden is open same days as castle and museum 11-6. Last admission to all parts is 30 mins before closing. **Facilities:** 🅿 ✖ licensed (photos of interior available from tearoom) shop garden centre ✖ (ex guide dogs) ⚬ ▼

RHONDDA HERITAGE PARK
Lewis Merthyr Colliery, Coed Cae Rd CF37 7NP
➲ (between Pontypridd & Porth, off A470, follow brown heritage signs from M4 junct 32)   2 for 1
☎ 01443 682036 🖷 01443 687420
e-mail: reception@rhonddaheritagepark.com

Based at the Lewis Merthyr Colliery, the Heritage Park is a fascinating 'living history' attraction. You can take the Cage Ride to 'Pit Bottom' and explore the underground workings of a 1950s pit, guided by men who were miners themselves. There are children's activities, an art gallery and a museum illustrating living conditions in the Rhondda Valley. Special events throughout the year, phone for details.
Times: Open all year, daily 10-6. (Closed Mon from Oct-Etr). Last admission 4.30pm. (Closed 25 Dec-2 Jan). **Fee:** £5.60 (ch £4.30, pen £4.95). Family ticket £16.50. **Facilities:** 🅿 ▆ ✖ licensed ⚬ (wheelchair available, accessible parking, lifts) toilets for disabled shop ✖ (ex guide dogs) ▼

SWANSEA

LLANRHIDIAN   Map 02 SS49

WEOBLEY CASTLE
SA3 1HB
➔ (from B4271 or B4295)
☎ 01792 390012

A 12th-to 14th-century fortified manor house with an exhibition on the history of Weobley and other historic sites on the Gower peninsula.
Times: Open all year, Apr-29 Oct, daily 9.30-6; 30 Oct-Mar, daily 9.30-5. Telephone for Xmas opening times. **Fee:** £2 (ch 5-16, pen & students £1.50, wheelchair users & assisting companion free). Family ticket (2 ad & 3 ch) £5.50. Group rates available. Prices quoted apply until 31 Mar 2004. **Facilities:** ⓟ ㅎ shop ✘ ☺ ❤

OXWICH   Map 02 SS48

OXWICH CASTLE
SA3 1NG
➔ (A4118 from Swansea)
☎ 01792 390359

Situated on the Gower peninsula, this Tudor mansion is a striking testament in stone to the pride and ambitions of the Mansel dynasty of Welsh gentry. The E-shaped wing houses an exhibition on historical Gower and 'Chieftains and Princes of Wales'.
Times: Open Apr-28 Sep, daily 10-5. **Fee:** £2 (ch 5-16, pen & students £1.50, wheelchair users & assisting companion free). Family ticket (2 ad & 3 ch) £5.50. Group rates available. Prices quoted apply until 31 Mar 2004. **Facilities:** ⓟ ㅎ (Radar key toilet) toilets for disabled ✘ ☺ ❤

PARKMILL   Map 02 SS58

GOWER HERITAGE CENTRE
Y Felin Ddwr SA3 2EH
➔ (Follow signs for South Gower on A4118 W from Swansea. W side of Parkmill village)
☎ 01792 371206 ▤ 01792 371471   **2 for 1**
e-mail: info@
gowerheritagecentre.sagehost.co.uk

Based around a 12th-century water-powered cornmill, the site also contains a number of craft workshops, two play

continued

areas, animals, a museum and a miller's cottage, all set in attractive countryside in an area of outstanding natural beauty.
Times: Open daily, Mar-Oct 10-5.30; Nov-Feb 10-4.30. (Closed 25 Dec). **Fee:** ✱ £3.60 (ch under 5 free, concessions £2.50). Family ticket £11 **Facilities:** ⓟ ▣ ㅎ (ramp entrance access) toilets for disabled shop ❤

SWANSEA   Map 03 SS69

GLYNN VIVIAN ART GALLERY
Alexandra Rd SA1 5DZ
➔ (Turn off M4 junct 42 along Fabian Way A483 up Wind St. Turn left at train station opposite library)
☎ 01792 516900   **FREE**
▤ 01792 516903
e-mail: **glynn.vivian.gallery@swansea.gov.uk**

A broad spectrum of visual arts form the original bequest of Richard Glynn Vivian, including old masters and an international collection of porcelain and Swansea china. The 20th century is also well represented with modern painting and sculpture by British and foreign artists, with the emphasis on Welsh artists.
Times: Open all year, Tue-Sun & BH Mon 10-5. (Closed 25, 26 Dec & 1 Jan). **Facilities:** ⓟ (200 yds) ㅎ toilets for disabled shop ✘ (ex guide dogs & hearing dogs) ❤

SWANSEA MUSEUM
Victoria Rd, Maritime Quarter SA1 1SN
➔ (M4 junct 42, on main road into Swansea city centre)   **FREE**
☎ 01792 653763 ▤ 01792 652585
e-mail: **swansea.museum@swansea.gov.uk**

This is the oldest museum in Wales, showing the history of Swansea from the earliest times until today. The museum has a Tramshed and floating boats to explore (summer only). There is a continuous programme of temporary exhibitions and events all year around.
Times: Open all year, Tue-Sun 10-5.(last admission 4.45pm). Closed Mon except BH Mon, 25-26 Dec & 1 Jan. **Facilities:** ⓟ (50yds) (charged) ㅎ toilets for disabled shop ✘ (ex guide dogs) ❤

TORFAEN

BLAENAVON   Map 03 SO20

BIG PIT NATIONAL MINING MUSEUM OF WALES
NP4 9XP
➔ (M4 junct 26 or 25, follow signs along A4042 & A4043 to Pontypool & Blaenavon. Signposted off A465)
☎ 01495 790311 ▤ 01495 792618   **FREE**
e-mail: **bigpit@nmgw.ac.uk**

The Real Underground Experience! Big Pit is the UK's leading mining museum. It is a real colliery and was the place of work for hundreds of men, woman and children for over 200 years. A daily struggle to extract the precious mineral that stoked furnaces and lit household fires across the world.
Times: Open Mid Feb-End Nov, daily 9.30-5, telephone to confirm
Facilities: ⓟ ▣ ㅎ (underground tours by prior arrangement) toilets for disabled shop (not on underground tours)

BLAENAVON IRONWORKS
North St
☎ 01495 792615

The Blaenavon Ironworks were a milestone in the history of the Industrial Revolution. Constructed in 1788-99, they were the first purpose-built, multi-furnace ironworks in Wales. By 1796, Blaenavon was the second largest ironworks in Wales, eventually closing down in 1904.

Times: Open Apr-Oct, daily 9.30-4.30. For details of opening outside this period, telephone Torfaen County Borough Council on 01633 648081. **Fee:** £2 (ch 5-16, pen & students £1.50, wheelchair users & assisting companion free). Family ticket (2 ad & 3 ch) £5.50. Group discounts available. Prices quoted apply until 31 Mar 2004.
Facilities: 🅿 ✈ ⊕ 🍽

CWMBRAN   Map 03 ST29

GREENMEADOW COMMUNITY FARM
Greenforge Way NP44 5AJ
➲ (Follow signs for Cwmbran then brown heritage signs (with sheep on) to farm)
☎ 01633 862202 📠 01633 489332
e-mail: greenmeadow_community_farm@ compuserve.com

This is one of Wales' leading tourist attractions - a community farm that was built during the 1980s on land threatened by developers. There are milking demonstrations, tractor and trailer rides, a dragon adventure play area, a farm trail, a nature trail and lots more. Phone for details of lambing weekends, shearing, country fair and agricultural shows, Halloween and Christmas events.
Times: ✱ Open summer 10-6, winter 10-4. (Closed 25 Dec).
Facilities: 🅿 💷 ⅙ (tractor & trailer rides for wheelchair users) toilets for disabled shop 🍽

> Remember that prices and opening times are liable to change within the currency of this guide. It is always best to telephone in advance to check

BARRY   Map 03 ST16

WELSH HAWKING CENTRE
Weycock Rd CF62 3AA
➲ (on A4226)
☎ 01446 734687 📠 01446 739620

There are over 200 birds of prey here, including eagles, hawks, owls, buzzards and falcons. They can be seen and photographed in the mews and some of the breeding aviaries. There are flying demonstrations at regular intervals during the day. A variety of tame, friendly animals, such as pigs, lambs and rabbits will delight younger visitors.
Times: ✱ Open end Mar-end Sep, daily 10.30-5, 1hr before dusk in winter. **Facilities:** 🅿 💷 ⅙ toilets for disabled shop 🍽 🍽

OGMORE   Map 03 SS87

OGMORE CASTLE
➲ (2.5m SW of Bridgend, on B4524)   FREE
☎ 01656 653435

Standing on the River Ogmore, the west wall of this castle is 40ft high. A hooded fireplace is preserved in the 12th-century, three-storey keep and a dry moat surrounds the inner ward.
Times: Open - access throughout the year. Key keeper arrangement.
Facilities: 🅿 ⅙ 🍽 ⊕

PENARTH   Map 03 ST17

COSMESTON LAKES COUNTRY PARK & MEDIEVAL VILLAGE
Lavernock Rd CF64 5UY
➲ (on B4267 between Barry and Penarth, close to M4 junct 33)   2 for 1
☎ 029 2070 1678 📠 029 2070 8686
e-mail: NColes@valeofglamorgan.gov.uk

Deserted during the plagues and famines of the 14th century, the original village was rediscovered through archaeological excavations. The buildings have been faithfully reconstructed on the excavated remains, creating a living museum of medieval village life. Special events throughout the year include re-enactments and Living History.
Times: Open all year, daily 11-5 in Summer, 11-4 in Winter. (Closed 25 Dec). Country park open at all times. **Fee:** ✱ Entry to Village £3, (concessions £2) Family ticket £7.50. Entry to Country Park is free.
Facilities: 🅿 💷 ✗ ⅙ (access ramps & wheelchair hire) toilets for disabled shop

ST HILARY   Map 03 ST07

OLD BEAUPRE CASTLE
➲ (1m SW, off A48)   FREE
☎ 01446 773034

This ruined manor house was rebuilt during the 16th century. Its most notable features are an Italianate gatehouse and porch. The porch is an unusual three-storeyed structure and displays the Basset arms.
Times: Open - access throughout the year. Key keeper arrangement.
Facilities: 🅿 🍽 ⊕

WREXHAM

CHIRK   Map 07 SJ23

CHIRK CASTLE
LL14 5AF
➲ (8m S of Wrexham, signposted off A483)
☎ 01691 777701   📠 01691 774706
e-mail: pcwmsn@smtp.ntrust.org.uk

Chirk Castle is one of a chain of late 13th-century Marcher castles. Its high walls and drum towers have hardly changed, but the inside shows the varied tastes of 700 years of occupation. One of the least altered parts is Adam's Tower. Many of the medieval-looking decorations were by Pugin in the 19th century. Varied furnishings include fine tapestries.
Times: ✱ Open 29 Mar-Sep, Wed-Sun & BH Mon 12-5 (castle), 11-6 (gardens); Oct, Wed-Sun 12-4 (castle), 11-5 (gardens). Last admission 30 mins before closing. **Facilities:** 🅿 ✕ licensed ♿ (stairclimber) toilets for disabled shop ✖ (ex guide dogs) ➽

WREXHAM   Map 07 SJ35

ERDDIG
LL13 0YT
➲ (off A525, 2m S of Wrexham & A483/A5152 Oswestry road)
☎ 01978 355314   📠 01978 313333

Built in 1680, the house was enlarged and improved by a wealthy London lawyer with a passion for gilt and silver furniture. Original furnishings remain, including a magnificent state bed in Chinese silk. The house is notable for the view it gives of both `upstairs' and `downstairs' life. The gardens, unusually, have been changed very little since the 18th century.
Times: ✱ Open 25 Mar-1 Nov, Sat-Wed (open Good Fri), house 12-5, garden 11-6 (Jul-Aug gardens 10-6); Oct-1 Nov, Sat-Wed, house 12-4, garden 11-5. **Facilities:** 🅿 ✕ licensed ♿ toilets for disabled shop garden centre ✖ (ex guidance dogs) ➽ ➨

Above: Carew Castle on the River Carew

NORTHERN IRELAND
EVENTS & FESTIVALS

March
17th St Patrick's Day Parade,
Armagh, County Armagh & other
locations

May
12-14th Balmoral Show,
Balmoral Showgrounds, Belfast

June
25th-27th Hookers Regatta,
Portaferry, Co Down
(traditional Irish sailing boats)
tbc Waterfront Festival,
Carrickfergus, Co Antrim
(funfair, circus, spectacle)
tbc Fleadh Amhrám agus Rince,
Ballycastle, Co Antrim
tbc Ulster Scottish Pipe
Band Championships, Belfast

July
13th The Sham Fight, Scarva, Co Down
(joust between William of Orange &
James II)
tbc American Independence Day
Celebrations, Ulster American Folk
Park, Omagh, Co Tyrone

August
8th-15th Maiden of the Mournes
Festival,
Warrenpoint, Co Down (folk, country
& western)
30th-31st Oul' Lammas Fair, Ballycastle,
Co Antrim (traditional fair from 1606)

September
tbc Annual Appalachian & Bluegrass
Music Festival, Ulster American Folk
Park, Omagh, Co Tyrone
tbc Hillsborough Oyster Festival,
Hillsborough, Co Down

October
31st Halloween Celebrations, Belfast
tbc Belfast Festival at Queens, Belfast
(drama, comedy, ballet, music, film &
art)
tbc Coleraine Community Arts Festival,
Coleraine, Co Derry
tbc Halloween Celebrations, Ulster
American Folk Park, Omagh, Co
Tyrone

December
4th-14th Cinemagic International Film
Festival for Young People, Belfast

The Giant's Causeway, County Antrim

BELFAST

BELFAST   Map 01 D5

BELFAST ZOOLOGICAL GARDENS
Antrim Rd BT36 7PN
⊃ (6m N, on A6)
☎ 028 9077 6277 🖹 028 9037 0578
e-mail: strongej@belfastcity.gov.uk
The 50-acre zoo has a dramatic setting on the face of Cave
Hill, enjoying spectacular views. Attractions include the
award-winning primate house (gorillas and chimpanzees),
penguin enclosure, free-flight aviary, African enclosure, and
underwater viewing of sealions and penguins. There are also
red pandas, free-ranging lemurs and a group of very rare
spectacled bears.
Times: Open all year (ex 25 Dec), daily Apr-Sep 10-5; Oct-Mar 10-2.30.
Fee: ✱ Summer: £6.40 (ch £3.20), Winter: £5.40 (£2.70). Under 4's,
pen and Disabled free of charge. **Facilities:** 🅿 ♨ ఉ (free admission
& reserved parking) toilets for disabled shop 🐾 (ex guide dogs) ♨

BOTANIC GARDENS
3 College Park BT7 1LP
⊃ (from the City Hall , Bedford Street then Dublin
road for Botanic Avenue).
☎ 028 9032 4902 🖹 028 9032 4902
e-mail: maxwellr@belfastcity.gov.uk
One highlight of the park is the beautiful glass-domed
Victorian Palm House, built between 1839-52. This palm
house pre-dates the one in Kew Gardens and is one of the
earliest curved glass and iron structures in the world.
Another feature is the Tropical Ravine - stand on a balcony
to get a wonderful view through a steamy ravine full of
exotic plants.
Times: Palm House Tropical Ravine: Apr-Sep 10-12, 1-5; Oct-Mar 10-12,
1-4. Sat & Sun & BH's 1-5 (Summer), 1-4 (Winter). **Fee:** Entry free.
Guided tours £10 **Facilities:** 🅿 (street) ఉ

GIANT'S RING
⊃ (0.75m S of Shaws Bridge)
☎ 028 9023 5000 🖹 028 9031 0288   FREE
Circular, Bronze-age enclosure nearly 200ft in diameter
similar in style to Stonehenge, with a stone chambered grave
in the centre and bordered by banks 20ft wide and 12ft high.
Very little is known for sure about this site, except that it was
used for ritual burial.
Times: Open all times. **Facilities:** 🅿

ULSTER MUSEUM
Botanic Gardens BT9 5AB
⊃ (M1/M2 to Balmoral exit)
☎ 028 9038 3000 🖹 028 9038 3003   FREE
Both a national museum and an art gallery, the collections
are Irish and international in origin and cover archaeology
and ethnography, art, botany and zoology, geology and local
history (including industrial archaeology). An annual
programme of changing temporary exhibitions and events
takes place.
Times: Open all year, Mon-Fri 10-5, Sat 1-5, Sun 2-5. Tel for details of
Xmas closures. **Facilities:** 🅿 (100yds on street) (Clearway 8-9.30 &
4.30-6) ♨ ఉ (all galleries except one. Loop system, wheelchair lifts)
toilets for disabled shop 🐾 (ex guide dogs) ♨

W5 AT ODYSSEY
2 Queens Quay BT3 9QQ
☎ 028 9046 7700 🖹 028 9046 7707
W5 investigates Who? What? Where? When? Why?... and that
pretty much sums up the intent behind Ireland's first purpose
built discovery centre. Visitors of any age will want to get
their hands on interactive science and technology displays
that include the laser harp, the fog knife, microscopes, robots
and computers. W5 is part of a massive Millennium
Landmark Project in the heart of Belfast.
Times: ✱ Open all year ex 25-26 Dec & 12 Jul. Mon-Sat 10-6, Sun
12-6. **Facilities:** 🅿 (charged) ✗ licensed ఉ (hearing loop) toilets for
disabled shop 🐾 (ex guide dogs) ♨

CO ANTRIM

ANTRIM   Map 01 D5

ANTRIM ROUND TOWER
BT41 1BJ
⊃ (N of town)   FREE
☎ 028 9023 5000 🖹 028 9031 0288
Antrim round tower stands among lawns and trees but it
was once surrounded by monastic buildings. Antrim was an
important early monastery, probably a 6th-century
foundation, closely linked with Bangor.
Times: Open all year. **Facilities:** 🅿 ఉ

BALLYCASTLE   Map 01 D6

BONAMARGY FRIARY
⊃ (E of town, at golf course)   FREE
☎ 028 9023 5000 🖹 028 9031 0288
Founded by Rory MacQuillan around 1500 and later passed
on to the MacDonnells, Earls of Antrim, there are still
remains of the friary gatehouse, church and cloister for
visitors to see.
Times: Open all year. **Facilities:** 🅿 ఉ ♿

BALLYLUMFORD   Map 01 D5

BALLYLUMFORD DOLMEN
⊃ (on B90 on NW tip of Island Magee)   FREE
☎ 028 9023 5000 🖹 028 9031 0288
Incorporated in the front garden of a house in Ballylumford
Road are the remains of this huge 4-5,000-year-old
single-chamber Neolithic tomb, also known as the Druid's
Altar.
Times: Open all year. **Facilities:** ఉ

BALLYMENA   Map 01 D5

ECOS MILLENNIUM ENVIRONMENTAL CENTRE
Ecos Centre, Kernohams Ln, Broughshane Rd BT43 7QA
⊃ (follow signs from M2 bypass at Ballymena)
☎ 028 2566 4400 🖹 028 2563 8984   2 for 1
e-mail: info@ecoscentre.com
Ecos is an "alternative environmental centre", which allows
visitors to explore alternative means of energy production,
including electricity generated using wood, wind and sun,
recycling, and alternative technologies such as willow
coppicing. Plenty of hands-on fun and educational potential.
Times: Open all year ex 24 Dec-1 Jan. Please phone for opening dates
Fee: ✱ £4 (ch & concessions £3). Family ticket £12.50 **Facilities:** 🅿
♨ ఉ toilets for disabled shop 🐾 ex guide dogs ♨

HARRYVILLE MOTTE
➲ (N bank of river Braid)
☎ 028 9023 5000 📠 028 9031 0288
On a ridge to the south of the town, this Norman fort, with its 40ft-high motte and rectangular bailey, is one of the finest examples of Norman earthworks left in Northern Ireland.
Times: Open all year. **Facilities:** 🅿 ♿ 🚼

BALLYMONEY   Map 01 C6

LESLIE HILL OPEN FARM
Leslie Hill BT53 6QL
➲ (1m NW of Ballymoney on MacFin Rd)
☎ 028 2766 6803 📠 028 2766 6803
An 18th-century estate with a Georgian house, magnificent period farm buildings, and fine grounds with paths, lakes and trees. Attractions include an extensive collection of rare breeds, poultry, horsedrawn machinery and carriages, exhibition rooms, a museum, working forge, deer park, walled garden and an adventure playground.
Times: Open Jul-Aug Mon-Sat 11-6, Sun 2-6; Jun Sat-Sun & BH's 2-6; Etr-May, Sun & BH's 2-6, open all Etr wk 11-6. **Fee:** ✱ £3 (ch £2). Family ticket £8.50. **Facilities:** 🅿 ⚫ ♿ (ramps) toilets for disabled shop garden centre 🎪 (ex on leads)

BUSHMILLS   Map 01 C6

OLD BUSHMILLS DISTILLERY
BT57 8XH
➲ (on the Castlecatt road, in Bushmills Village)
☎ 028 2073 1521 📠 028 2073 1339
e-mail: scroskery@idl.ie
Old Bushmills was granted its licence in 1608 and is the oldest licenced whiskey distillery in the world. There's a guided tour, and afterwards you can take part in a comparative tasting session and become a whiskey expert.
Times: Open Apr-Oct, Mon-Sat 9.30-5.30, Sun 12-5.30, last tour 4pm; Nov-Mar, Mon-Fri 5 tours daily, 10.30, 11.30, 1.30, 2.30 & 3.30. Sat & Sun 3 tours, 1.30, 2.30, 3.30. Closed July 12, Xmas & New Year. **Fee:** ✱ £3.95 (pen & student £3.50, accompanied ch £2) Family ticket £11. **Facilities:** 🅿 ✗ licensed ♿ (audio visual theatre, shops & restaurant) toilets for disabled shop 🎪 (ex guide dogs) ⚫

CARRICK-A-REDE   Map 01 D6

CARRICK-A-REDE ROPE BRIDGE AND LARRYBANE VISITORS CENTRE
BTS4 6LS
➲ (E of Ballintoy on B15)
☎ 028 2073 1582 & 2073 2143
📠 028 2073 2963
e-mail: carrickarede@nationaltrust.org.uk
This shaky rope bridge, 80ft above the sea, bridges the 60ft gap between cliffs and a small rocky island. It owes its existence to the salmon who regularly make the dash through the chasm and get netted for their efforts. The bridge has been put across the gap each spring and dismantled every autumn for the last 300 years
Times: Bridge open daily, (weather permitting), 15 Mar-June 10-6; July & Aug 9.30-7.30; Sep 10-6. **Fee:** ✱ £3.50 per car, minibuses & coach £10 & motorbike £2. **Facilities:** 🅿 (charged) ⚫ ♿ (information centre) toilets for disabled 🎿

CARRICKFERGUS   Map 01 D5

CARRICKFERGUS CASTLE
BT38 7BG
➲ (on N shore of Belfast Lough)
☎ 028 9335 1273 📠 028 9336 5190
Imposingly placed on a rocky headland overlooking Belfast Lough, this is the best preserved and probably the most fought-over Norman castle in Ireland. Built by John de Courcy, Earl of Ulster, after 1180, it served a military purpose for more than eight centuries. Exhibits include a giant model of the castle, a short film, and a banqueting suite. The castle is often used as a venue for medieval banquets and fairs. There is a visitors' centre, shop and refreshment point.
Times: ✱ Open all year, Apr-Sep, weekday 10-6, Sun 2-6; Oct-Mar closes at 4. **Facilities:** 🅿 ⚫ ♿ toilets for disabled shop 🎪

TOWN WALLS
☎ 028 9023 5000 📠 028 9031 0288 FREE
Lord Deputy Sir Arthur Chichester enclosed Carrickfergus with stone walls from 1611 onwards and more than half the circuit is still visible, often to its full height of 4 metres to the wall walk.
Times: Visible at all times. **Facilities:** 🅿 ♿

CHURCHTOWN   Map 01 D5

CRANFIELD CHURCH
➲ (3.75m SW of Randalstown)
☎ 028 9023 5000 📠 028 9031 0288
This small medieval church is situated on the shores of Lough Neagh. Beside it is a famous holy well.
Times: Open all year. **Facilities:** 🅿 ♿ 🚼

GIANT'S CAUSEWAY   Map 01 C6

GIANT'S CAUSEWAY CENTRE
44 Causeway Rd BT57 8SU
➲ (2m N of Bushmills on B146)
☎ 028 2073 1855 📠 028 2073 2537
e-mail: causewaytic@hotmail.com
This dramatic rock formation is undoubtedly one of the wonders of the natural world. The Centre provides an exhibition and audio-visual show, and Ulsterbus provides a minibus service to the stones and there are guided walks, and special facilities for the disabled.
Times: ✱ Open all year, daily 10-4 (6pm Jun & Sep-Oct; 7pm Jul-Aug). **Facilities:** 🅿 (charged) ⚫ ✗ ♿ (mini bus transport with wheelchair hoist, reserved parking) toilets for disabled shop 🎪 (ex guide dogs) ⚫

LARNE   Map 01 D5

OLDERFLEET CASTLE
☎ 028 9023 5000 📠 028 9031 0288 FREE
A 16th-century tower house, the last surviving three which defended Larne.
Times: Open at all times.

LISBURN — Map 01 D5

DUNEIGHT MOTTE AND BAILEY
➲ (2.3m S beside Ravernet River)
☎ 028 9023 5000 🖷 028 9031 0288 **FREE**
Impressive Anglo-Norman earthwork castle with high
mound-embanked enclosure, making use of the defences of
an earlier pre-Norman fort.
Times: Open all year.

IRISH LINEN CENTRE & LISBURN MUSEUM
Market Square BT28 1AG
➲ (signposted both in and outside the town
centre)
☎ 028 9266 3377 🖷 028 9267 2624 **FREE**
e-mail: irishlinencentre@lisburn.gov.uk
The centre tells the story of the Irish linen industry past and
present. The recreation of individual factory scenes brings
the past to life and a series of imaginative hands-on
activities describe the linen manufacturing processes. The
Museum has a range of temporary exhibitions of local
interest.
Times: Open all year, Mon-Sat, 9.30-5. **Facilities:** P (200mtrs)
(limited for disabled and coaches) 🏍 ᯤ (lift, induction loop, staff
trained in sign language) toilets for disabled shop ✖ (ex guide
dogs)

PORTBALLINTRAE — Map 01 C6

DUNLUCE CASTLE
➲ (off A2)
☎ 028 2073 1938 🖷 028 2031 8288
Extensive and picturesque ruins of a 16th-century castle
perched on a rocky crag high above the sea. Stronghold of
the MacQuillans and MacDonnells, who significantly altered
the original stonebuilt fortress. Randal MacDonnell built a
house in the centre of the castle, of which parts of the Great
Hall remain, as do the towers and early 17th-century
gatehouse. The castle has new displays and there is an
audio-visual show. The cave below the ruins provided a
secret way into and out of the castle from the sea.
Times: ✱ Open all year, Apr-Sep, weekdays 10-7, Sun 2-7; Oct-Mar,
Tue-Sat 10-4, Sun 2-4. **Facilities:** P ᯤ toilets for disabled shop

TEMPLEPATRICK — Map 01 D5

PATTERSONS SPADE MILL
751 Antrim Rd BT39 0AP
➲ (2m SE of Templepatrick on A6) **2 for 1**
☎ 028 9443 3619 🖷 028 9443 3619
This is the last surviving water-driven spade mill in Ireland. It
has been completely restored by the National Trust and is
now back in production.
Times: Open, Mar, Sun 2-6; Apr-May, wknds, BH's, 2-6 ; Jun-Aug, daily
2-6; Sep, wknds & BH's 2-6. **Fee:** ✱ £3.25 (ch £1.50). Family Ticket
£8.50. Groups £2 each. Groups outside normal hours £4. **Facilities:** P
ᯤ (ramps, wheelchair available) toilets for disabled 🐾

TEMPLETOWN MAUSOLEUM
BT39 (in Castle Upton graveyard on A6,
Belfast-Antrim road) **FREE**
Situated in the graveyard of Castle Upton, this family
mausoleum is in the shape of a triumphal arch and was
designed by Robert Adam.
Times: Open daily during daylight hours. **Facilities:** P 🚐 🐾

CO ARMAGH

ARMAGH — Map 01 C5

ARMAGH COUNTY MUSEUM
The Mall East BT61 9BE
➲ (on the Mall, in the centre of Armagh City)
☎ 028 3752 3070 🖷 028 3752 2631 **FREE**
e-mail: acm.um@nics.gov.uk

Housed in a 19th-century schoolhouse, this museum
contains an art gallery and library, as well as a collection of
local folkcrafts and natural history. Special events are
planned thoughout the year.
Times: Open all year, Mon-Fri 10-5, Sat 10-1 & 2-5. **Facilities:** P ᯤ
(entrance, ramp & lift for disabled) toilets for disabled shop ✖ (ex
guide dogs)

ARMAGH FRIARY
➲ (SE edge of town)
☎ 028 9023 5000 🖷 028 9031 0288 **FREE**
Situated just inside the gates of the former Archbishop's
Palace are the remains of the longest friary church in Ireland
(163ft). The friary was established in 1263 by Archbishop
O'Scanail and destroyed by Shane O'Neill in the middle of
the 16th century to prevent it being garrisoned by
Elizabethan soldiers.
Times: Open all year. **Facilities:** P ᯤ

ARMAGH PLANETARIUM
College Hill BT61 9DB
➲ (on main Armagh-Belfast road close to mall,
Armagh City centre)
☎ 028 3752 3689 & 3752 4725
🖷 028 3752 6187 **2 for 1**
e-mail: kate@armaghplanet.com
The Planetarium is home to The Star Theatre, a multi-media
environment equipped with the latest technology including a
virtual reality digital system. Also featured are The Hall of
Astronomy, the new Eartharium Building and surrounding
the Planetarium is the Astropark, a 25-acre 'hands on' park.
Times: Open, Mon-Fri 2-4.45. Presentations Mon-Fri 3pm. Closed Sat,
Sun & BH's. **Fee:** ✱ £3.75 (ch, pen & students £2.75). Family ticket £11.
Exhibition area £1. **Facilities:** P ᯤ (Loop system in theatre) toilets for
disabled shop ✖ (ex guide dogs)

NAVAN CENTRE
Killylea Rd BT60 4LD
➾ (2m W on A28)
☎ 028 3752 5550 ▤ 028 3752 2323
e-mail: navan@enterprise.net

Navan was once known as Emain Macha, the ancient seat of kings and earliest capital of Ulster. Today it is an impressive archaeological site with its own museum and visitor centre located in a building that blends into the landscape. The Navan Centre uses audio-visuals and interactive devices to unravel history from myth. The myths include Conor McNessa, C' Chulainn and the Red Branch Knights.
Times: ✱ Open all year Mon-Fri 10-5, Sat 11-5, Sun 12-5. (Closed Xmas week). **Facilities:** ▣ ▣ ♿ (loop for hearing aids, parking) toilets for disabled shop ✖ (ex guide dogs) ▱

PALACE STABLES HERITAGE CENTRE
The Palace Demesne BT60 4EL
➾ (located off Friary Road beside council offices)
☎ 028 3752 9629 ▤ 028 3752 9630
e-mail: stables@armagh.gov.uk

This picturesque Georgian building, set around a cobbled courtyard, has been lovingly restored and now houses a heritage centre. A daily Georgian interpretation is provided by authentic costumed characters.
Times: Open all year, Jul-Aug, Mon-Sat 10-5.30, Sun 1-5.30; Sep-Apr, Mon-Sat 10-5, Sun 2-5. Last tour 1hr before closing. **Facilities:** ▣ ✖ licensed ♿ (ramps & Lift in stables) toilets for disabled shop ▱

SAINT PATRICK'S TRIAN VISITOR COMPLEX
40 English St BT61 7BA
➾ (Armagh citiy centre)
☎ 028 37 521801 ▤ 028 37 510180
c-mail: info@saintpatrickstrain.com

This award-winning attraction incorporates three different exhibitions. 'The Armagh Story' traces the city's history; 'Patrick's Testament' examines Armagh's association with Ireland's patron saint; and 'The Land of Lilliput' where a giant tells the story of Gulliver's Travels.
Times: Open all year, Mon-Sat 10-5, Sun 2-5; Jul-Aug, Mon-Sat 10-5.30, Sun 2-5. Last tour 1hr before closing. **Fee:** ✱ £4 (ch £2.25, pen & student £2.75). Family ticket £10 **Facilities:** ▣ (charged) ✖ licensed ♿ (specially designed for disabled) toilets for disabled shop ✖ (ex guide dogs) ▱

KILLEVY CHURCHES
➾ (3m S lower eastern slopes of Slieve Gullion) FREE
☎ 028 9023 5000 ▤ 028 9031 0288

The ruins of the two churches (10th-and 13th-century) stand back to back, at the foot of Slieve Gullion sharing a common wall, but with no way through from one to the other. The churches stand on the site of an important nunnery founded by St Monenna in the 5th century. A huge granite slab in the graveyard supposedly marks the founder's grave. A holy well can be reached by climbing the path north of the graveyard. The nunnery was in use until the Dissolution in 1542.
Times: Open all year. **Facilities:** ♿

KILNASAGGART INSCRIBED STONE
➾ (1.25m S)
☎ 028 9023 5000 ▤ 028 9031 0288   FREE

A granite pillar stone dating back to 8th century, with numerous crosses and a long Irish inscription carved on it.
Times: Open all year. **Facilities:** ▣

ARGORY
Derrycaw Rd BT71 6NA
➾ (3m NE)
☎ 028 8778 4753 ▤ 028 8778 9598   2 for 1
e-mail: argory@nationaltrust.org.uk

Originally the home of the McGeough family, this Regency house is situated on a hillside overlooking the Blackwater River. The house is full of period furniture and bric-a-brac. Of particular interest is the very unusual acetylene lighting, installed by the family in 1906.
Times: Grounds: Open Oct-Apr, daily 10-4; May-Sep, daily 10-8. House: Open 15 Mar-May & Sep, wknds & BH/PH; June-Aug, daily (open 1 pm Jun weekdays) **Fee:** ✱ Grounds £2.10 per car. Grounds & House £4.10 (ch £2.10). Family £10.40. Group £3.40 (outside normal hours £4.40). **Facilities:** ▣ (charged) ▣ ♿ (special parking facilities, wheelchair available, Braile) toilets for disabled shop ✖ (ex guide dogs) ▰ ▱

MOYRY CASTLE
➾ (7.5m S)
☎ 028 9023 5000 ▤ 028 9031 0288   FREE

This tall, three-storey keep was built by Lord Mountjoy, Queen Elizabeth's deputy, in 1601, its purpose to secure the Gap of the North which was the main route into Ulster.
Times: Open all year

LOUGH NEAGH DISCOVERY CENTRE
Oxford Island National Nature, Reserve BT66 6NJ
➾ (signposted from M1, exit 10)
☎ 028 3832 2205 ▤ 028 3834 7438
e-mail: oxford.island@craigavon.gov.uk

Learn about the history and wildlife of the Lough through a series of exciting audio-visual shows, interactive games and an exhibition, then experience the Island for yourself. In a spectacular setting on the water's edge, discover natural history, wildlife, family walks and much more.
Times: ✱ Open Apr-Sep, Mon-Sat 10-6; Sun 10-7, Oct-Mar, Wed-Sun 10-5. **Facilities:** ▣ ▣ ♿ (grounds accessible in part, bird watching hides) toilets for disabled shop ✖ (ex guide dogs) ▱

ARDRESS HOUSE
64 Ardress Rd, Annaghmore BT62 1SQ
➾ (On B28, 5 miles from Moy, 5 miles from Portadown, 3m from exit 13 on M1).
☎ 028 3885 1236 ▤ 028 3885 1236
e-mail: ardress@ntrust.org.uk

A plain 17th-century house, transformed around 1770 by its visionary architect-owner George Ensor, who added elegant wings and superb Adamesque plasterwork. The house has a

continued

fine picture gallery on loan from the Earl of Castlestewart. The grounds are beautifully unspoilt and there is a farmyard with livestock and a display of farm implements.
Times: Open, 15 Mar-31 May, wknds, BH's & PH's 2-6; Jun-Aug, daily ex Tue (unless BH's & PH's), 2-6; Sep wknds. **Fee:** ✱ £2.80 (ch £1.40). Family £7. Group £2.30 (Group outside normal hours £3.30).
Facilities: ☑ 🚻 toilets for disabled shop 🍴 (ex guide dogs) 💤 🍷

TYNAN   Map 01 C5
VILLAGE CROSS   FREE
☎ 028 9023 5000 ▤ 028 9031 0288
A carved High Cross, 11ft tall, which lay broken in two pieces for many years, but was skilfully mended in 1844.
Times: Open all year **Facilities:** ☑ 🚻

CO DOWN

ARDGLASS   Map 01 D5
JORDAN'S CASTLE   FREE
☎ 028 9054 6552
Although Ardglass is an important fishing port today, it was once the busiest seaport in Northern Ireland. Between the 14th and 15th centuries a ring of tower houses and fortified warehouses was built to protect the port. Jordan's Castle, a late-15th-century, four-storey tower house situated in the centre of town, is one of these. Besieged in the early 1600s and held for three years, the castle was bought, repaired and filled with bygones by a Belfast solicitor in the early part of this century.
Times: Open Jul-Aug; Tue, Fri & Sat 10-1, Wed-Thu, 2-6. Other times on request. **Facilities:** 🍴

BALLYWALTER   Map 01 D5
GREY ABBEY
➲ (on east edge of village)   FREE
☎ 028 9054 6552
Founded in 1193 by Affreca, daughter of the King of the Isle of Man, these extensive ruins of a Cistercian abbey, sitting in lovely sheltered parkland, are among the best preserved in Northern Ireland. The chancel, with its tall lancet windows, magnificent west doorway and an effigy tomb - believed to be Affreca's - in the north wall, are particularly interesting. The abbey was burned down in 1572, and then re-used as a parish church. There are many 17th- and 18th-century memorials to be seen in the church ruins, which occupy a pleasant garden setting. The abbey now has a beautiful medieval herb garden, with over 50 varieties of plants, and a visitors' centre.
Times: Open Apr-Sep; Tue-Sat 10-7, Sun 2-7; Oct-Mar, wknds, Sat 10-4, Sun 2-4. **Facilities:** ☑ 🚻 toilets for disabled

CASTLEWELLAN   Map 01 D5
DRUMENA CASHEL
➲ (2.25m SW)   FREE
☎ 028 9023 5000 ▤ 028 9031 0288
There are many stone ring forts in Northern Ireland, but few so well preserved as Drumena. Dating back to early Christian times, the fort is 30m in diameter and has an 11m accessible underground stone-built passage, probably used as a refuge and for storage.
Times: Open all times **Facilities:** ☑

COMBER   Map 01 D5
WWT CASTLE ESPIE
Ballydrain Rd BT23 6EA
➲ (12m SE of Belfast. Take A22 from Comber towards Killyleagh and turn 1st left into Ballydrain Rd)
☎ 028 9187 4146 ▤ 028 9187 3857   2 for 1
e-mail: castleespie@wwt.org.uk
Home to the largest collection of wildfowl in Ireland. Comfortable hides enable you to watch the splendour of migratory waders and wildfowl. Beautiful landscaped gardens, a taxidermy collection and fine paintings by wildlife artists can also be seen. Thousands of birds migrate to the reserve in winter and birdwatch mornings are held on the last Thursday of every month. The Centre's effluent is treated in a reed bed filtration system which can be seen on one walk.
Times: Open all year Mar-Oct, Mon-Sat 10.30-5, Sun 11.30-5.30; Nov-Feb Mon-Fri 11-4 Sat & Sun 11-4.30. **Fee:** ✱ £4 (ch £2.50, pen £3.30). Family ticket £10 Party 12+. **Facilities:** ☑ 💷 🚻 (hides have wheelchair platforms) toilets for disabled shop

DOWNPATRICK   Map 01 D5
DOWN COUNTY MUSEUM
The Mall BT30 6AH
➲ (follow brown heritage signs)
☎ 028 4461 5218 ▤ 028 4461 5590   FREE
e-mail: museum@downdc.gov.uk
The museum is located in the restored buildings of the 18th-century county gaol. In addition to restored cells that tell the stories of some of the prisoners, there are exhibitions on the history of County Down. Plus temporary exhibits, events, tea-room and shop.
Times: Open all year, Mon-Fri 10-5, wknds 1-5 **Facilities:** ☑ (100yds) 💷 🚻 (wheelchair available, handling boxes on application) toilets for disabled shop 🍴 (ex guide dogs)

INCH ABBEY
➲ (0.75m NW off A7)
☎ 028 9023 5000 ▤ 028 9031 0288
Beautiful riverside ruins of a Cistercian abbey founded by John de Courcy around 1180. Of particular note is the tall, pointed, triple east window.
Times: ✱ Open Apr-Sep 10-7, Sun 2-7. Oct-Mar free access.
Facilities: ☑ 🚻

LOUGHINISLAND CHURCHES
➲ (4m W)   FREE
☎ 028 9023 5000 ▤ 028 9031 0288
This remarkable group of three ancient churches stands on an island in the lough, accessible by a causeway. The middle church is the oldest, probably dating back to the 13th century, with a draw-bar hole to secure the door. The large North church was built in the 15th century, possibly to replace the middle church and continued in use until 1720. The smallest and most recent church is the South (MacCartan's) church.
Times: Open all times **Facilities:** ☑ 🚻 ♿

Mound of Down
➲ (on the Quoile Marshes, from Mount Crescent)
☎ 028 9023 5000   **FREE**
🖷 028 9031 0288

A hill fort from the Early Christian period, conquered by Anglo-Norman troops in 1177, who then built an earthwork castle on top. This mound in the marshes, beside the River Quoile, was the first town before the present Downpatrick.
Times: Open all times **Facilities:** ▣

The St Patrick Centre
St Patrick Visitor Centre, Market St BT30 6LZ
➲ (follow the A7 from Belfast, follow brown heritage signs. Situated in Downpatrick, off Market Street).
☎ 028 4461 9000   🖷 028 4461 9111
e-mail: director@saintpatrickcentre.com

This 21st-century multimedia, interactive, audio-visual feast is dedicated to the fascinating story of Ireland's Patron Saint, Saint Patrick, who brought Christianity to Ireland in the 5th century. The Centre is located beside the saint's grave.
Times: Open all year Oct-Mar, Mon-Sat, 10-5 & St Patricks Day 9.30-7; Apr-May & Sep, Mon-Sat 9.30-5.30, Sun 1-5.30 (morning opening on request), Jun-Aug Mon-Sat 9.30-6, Sun 10-6. (Last admission 1.5 hrs before closing). **Fee:** ✱ £4.50 (ch £2.25, concessions £3) family ticket (2ad+2ch) £11 groups 25+ **Facilities:** ▣ 🍽 ✗ ♿ lifts+w/chairs available toilets for disabled shop garden centre ✗ (ex guide dogs)

Struell Wells
➲ (1.5m E)
☎ 028 9023 5000   🖷 028 9031 0288   **FREE**

Pilgrims come to collect the healing waters from these holy drinking and eye wells which are fed by a swift underground stream. Nearby are the ruins of an 18th-century church, and, even more interesting, single-sex bath-houses. The men's bath-house is roofed, has an anteroom and a sunken bath, while the ladies' is smaller and roofless.
Times: Open all times **Facilities:** ▣ ♿

DROMARA   Map 01 D5

Legananny Dolmen
➲ (4m S)
☎ 028 9023 5000   🖷 028 9031 0288   **FREE**

Theatrically situated on the slopes of Slieve Croob, this tripod dolmen with its three tall uprights and huge capstone is the most graceful of Northern Ireland's Stone Age monuments. There are views to the Mourne Mountains.
Times: Open at all times **Facilities:** ♿ ♿

HILLSBOROUGH   Map 01 D5

Hillsborough Fort   **FREE**
☎ 028 9268 3285   🖷 028 9031 0288

On a site that dates back to early Christian times, the existing fort was built in 1650 by Colonel Arthur Hill to command a view of the road from Dublin to Carrickfergus. The building was ornamented in the 18th century. It is set in a forest park with a lake and pleasant walks.
Times: Open all year; Apr-Sep, Tue-Sat 10-7, Sun 2-7; Oct-Mar, Tue-Fri 10-4, Sat 10-4, Sun 2-4., **Facilities:** ▣ ♿

KILKEEL   Map 01 D4

Greencastle
➲ (4m SW)
☎ 028 9023 5000   🖷 028 9031 0288

Looking very much like an English Norman castle with its massive keep, gatehouse and curtain wall, this 13th-century royal fortress stands on the shores of Carlingford Lough, with fine views of the Mourne Mountains. Greencastle has an eventful military history, it was beseiged and taken by Edward Bruce in 1316, attacked and spoiled by the Irish at least twice later in the 14th century, and maintained as a garrison for Elizabeth in the 1590s.
Times: ✱ Open Jul-Aug, Tue-Sat 10-7, Sun 2-7. **Facilities:** ▣ ♿

KILLINCHY   Map 01 D5

Sketrick Castle
➲ (3m E on W tip of Sketrick Islands)   **FREE**
☎ 028 9023 5000   🖷 028 9031 0288

A badly ruined tall tower house, probably 15th-century. The ground floor rooms include a boat bay and prison. An underground passage leads from the north-east of the bawn to a freshwater spring.
Times: Open at all times. **Facilities:** ▣ ♿

NEWCASTLE   Map 01 D5

Dundrum Castle
➲ (4m N)   **FREE**
☎ 028 9054 6518

This medieval castle, one of the finest in Ireland, was built in 1177 by John De Courcy in a strategic position overlooking Dundrum Bay, a position which offers visitors fine views over the sea and to the Mourne Mountains. The castle was captured by King John in 1210 and was badly damaged by Cromwellian troops in 1652. Still an impressive ruin, it shows a massive round keep with walls 16m high and 2m thick, surrounded by a curtain wall, and a gatehouse which dates from the 13th century.
Times: Open Apr-Sep, Tue-Sat 10-7, Sun 2-7; Oct-Mar, wknds, Sat 10-4, Sun 2-4. **Facilities:** ▣ ♿ toilets for disabled

Maghera Church
➲ (2m NNW)   **FREE**
☎ 028 9023 5000   🖷 028 9031 0288

The stump of a round tower, blown down in a storm in the early 18th century, survives from the early monastery, with a ruined 13th-century church nearby.
Times: Open all year. **Facilities:** ▣ ♿

NEWTOWNARDS   Map 01 D5

Mount Stewart House, Garden & Temple of the Winds
Greyabbey BT22 2AD
➲ (5m SE off A20)
☎ 028 4278 8387   🖷 028 4278 8569
e-mail: mountstewart@nationaltrust.org.uk

On the east shore of Strangford Lough, this 18th-century house was the work of three architects. In the inspired gardens, which are now a nominated world heritage site, many rare and subtropical trees thrive. Located by the shore

continued

is the Temple of the Winds, built by James 'Athenian' Stuart in 1782 for the first Marquess.
Times: Lakeside Gardens & Walks: Daily all year, Nov-Mar 10-4; Apr & Oct 10-6; May-Sep, 10-8;. Formal Gardens: Same as Lakeside except closed Nov-Feb, open wknds in Mar & 17 Mar. House: 17 Mar then 20 Mar-end Apr wknds (including Etr) 12-6.; May, Jun & Sep daily except Tue 1-6 (12-6 wknds); Jul-Aug daily 12-6; Oct wknds 12-6. **Fee:** ✱ House tour, gardens & Temple of Winds: £4.95, (ch £2.35). Family £10.15, Group £4.15 (group outside normal hours £5.15). Gardens: £3.90 (ch £2.10) Family £8.85. Group £3.65. **Facilities:** 🅿 💷 ✕ licensed ﴾ (4 wheelchairs (2 electric) available) toilets for disabled shop 🦮 🍴

SCRABO TOWER
Scrabo Country Park, 203A Scrabo Rd BT23 4SJ
➲ (1m W)
☎ 028 9181 1491   📠 028 9182 0695   FREE
The 135ft high Scrabo Tower, one of Northern Ireland's best-known landmarks, dominates the landscape of North Down and is also the centre of a country park around the slopes of Scrabo Hill. The Tower provides a fascinating series of interpretive diplays about the surrounding countryside and the viewing platform boasts spectacular views over Strangford Lough and Co. Down. The park provides walks through fine beech and hazel woodlands and the unique sandstone quarries display evidence of volcanic activity as well as breeding sites for peregrine falcons.
Times: Open end Mar-mid Sep, Sat-Thu 10.30-6. **Facilities:** 🅿 shop 🍴

EXPLORIS AQUARIUM
The Rope Walk, Castle St BT22 1NZ
➲ (A20 or A2 or A25 to Strangford Ferry Service)
☎ 028 4272 8062   📠 028 4272 8396
e-mail: info@ards-council.gov.uk
Exploris Aquarium is Northern Ireland's only public aquarium and now includes a seal sanctuary. Situated in Portaferry on the shores of Strangford Lough it houses some of Europe's finest displays. The Open Sea Tank holds 250 tonnes of sea water, and the Shoaling Ring, where visitors are surrounded by hundreds of fish, is a tank 6m in diameter. The complex includes a park with duck pond, picnic area, children's playground, caravan site, woodland and bowling green.
Times: Open all year, Mon-Fri 10-6, Sat 11-6, Sun 1-6. (Sep-Feb closing 1 hr earlier). **Facilities:** 🅿 💷 ﴾ (2 lifts within complex) toilets for disabled shop 🍴 (ex guide dogs) 🍴

ROWALLANE GARDEN
BT24 7LH
➲ (1m S of Saintfield on A7)
☎ 028 9751 0131   📠 028 9751 1242
e-mail: rowallane@nationaltrust.org.uk
Beautiful and exotic 52-acre gardens, started by the Rev John Moore in 1860, containing exquisite plants from all over the world. They are particularly noted for their rhododendrons and azaleas and for the wonderful floral displays in spring and summer.
Times: Open Oct-Apr, 10-4; May-Sep, 10-8. Closed Dec 24-1 Jan. **Fee:** ✱ £3.10 (ch £1.30) Family £7.30, groups £2.10 each. **Facilities:** 🅿 💷 ﴾ (parking facilities, manual wheelchairs, scented plants) toilets for disabled 🍴 (ex on leads) 🦮

AUDLEY'S CASTLE
➲ (1.5m W by shore of Strangford Lough)   FREE
☎ 028 9023 0560   📠 028 9031 0288
Fifteenth-century tower house on Strangford Lough which offers lovely views from its top floor. The internal fittings are complete.
Times: Open Apr-Sep, daily 10-7. **Facilities:** 🅿 🍴

CASTLE WARD
BT30 7LS
➲ (0.5m W of Strangford Village on A25)   2 for 1
☎ 028 4488 1204   📠 028 4488 1729
e-mail: castleward@nationaltrust.org.uk
The curious diversity of styles in this house is due to the fact that its owner and his wife could never agree; so classical themes and a more elaborate Gothic look were both incorporated. The servants' living quarters are reached by an underground passage. Gardens, complete with a small lake and classical summerhouse, are richly planted and especially beautiful in spring.
Times: Ground daily 10-4pm (8pm May-Sep). House & Wildlife Centre; 15 Mar-Apr wknds, BH/PH 12-6pm; May wknds 12-6, Mon, Wed & Fri 1-6pm; Jun-Aug, daily 12-6pm (Jun weekdays from 1pm); Sep-Oct wknds 12-6pm. **Fee:** ✱ Grounds, £3.10 (ch £1.30). Family £7.30. Group £2.10. Grounds, Wildlife Centre & House Tour, £4.70 (ch £1.80). Family £9.90. Group £3.70 (group outside normal hours, £4.70). **Facilities:** 🅿 (charged) 💷 ﴾ (wheelchair available, may be driven to house, braille) toilets for disabled shop 🦮 🍴

STRANGFORD CASTLE   FREE
☎ 028 9023 5000   📠 028 9031 0288
A three-storey tower house built in the 16th century, overlooking the small double harbour of Strangford.
Times: Open all reasonable times. **Facilities:** 🍴

BELLEEK POTTERY
3 Main St BT93 3FY
➲ (Take A46 from Ennisuilla to Belleek. Pottery at entrance to village)
☎ 028 6865 9300   📠 028 6865 8625   2 for 1
e-mail: visitorcentre@belleek.ie
Known worldwide for its fine Parian china, Ireland's oldest pottery was started in 1857 by the Caldwell family. Meet the craftspeople at work whilst touring the Pottery and visit the museum, which has exhibits dating back over 140 years.
Times: Open all year, Apr-Sep, Mon-Fri 9-6; Sat; 10-6 & Sun 2-6; Sun, Jul & Aug 11-6; Oct Mon-Fri 9-5.30. Closed wknds except Oct, Sat 10-5.30 & Sun 2-6 **Fee:** Guided tours £4 (ch under 12 free, pen £2). **Facilities:** 🅿 ✕ ﴾ (2 wheelchairs) toilets for disabled shop 🍴 (ex guide dogs) 🍴

CASTLE ARCHDALE BAY — Map 01 C5

WHITE ISLAND CHURCH
➲ (in Castle Archdale Bay; ferry from marina)
☎ 028 9023 5000 ▤ 028 9031 0288

Lined up on the far wall of a small, roofless 12th-century church are eight uncanny carved-stone figures. Part Christian and part pagan in appearance, their significance has been the subject of great debate. The church ruins sit on an early monastic site.

Times: ✱ Open Jul-Aug, Tue-Sat 10-7, Sun 2-7. **Facilities:** 🅿 ✖ ♿

DERRYGONNELLY — Map 01 C5

TULLY CASTLE
➲ (3m N, on W shore of Lower Lough Erne) **FREE**
☎ 028 9054 6552

Extensive ruins of a Scottish-style stronghouse with enclosing bawn overlooking Lough Erne. Built by Sir John Hume in the early 1600s, the castle was destroyed, and most of the occupants slaughtered, by the Maguires in the 1641 Rising. There is a replica of a 17th-century garden in the bawn.

Times: Open Jul & Aug, Wed-Sun, 10-6. **Facilities:** 🅿 ♿ ✖

ENNISKILLEN — Map 01 C5

CASTLE COOLE
BT74 6JY
➲ (On A4, 1.5 miles from Enniskillen, on Enniskillen to Belfast road)
☎ 028 6632 2690 ▤ 028 6632 5665
e-mail: castlecoole@nationaltrust.org.uk

No expense was spared in the building of this mansion. James Wyatt was the architect, the lovely plasterwork ceilings were by Joseph Rose, and the chimneypieces the work of Richard Westmacott. Vast amounts of Portland stone were specially imported, together with an Italian expert in stonework. The house is filled with beautiful Regency furniture.

Times: Grounds, Oct-Apr, daily 10-4; May-Sep, daily 10-8. House: 15 Mar-Apr, wknds & PH's/BH's 12-6; Jun, Wed-Sun; Jul-Aug daily; Sep wknds 12-6. **Fee:** ✱ Grounds £2 car. Grounds & House Tour £4 (ch £2). Family ticket £10. Group £3 (group outside normal hours £4). **Facilities:** 🅿 💺 ♿ (may be driven to house, large print guide) toilets for disabled shop ✖ (ex in park & guide dogs) ♨ 🍴

ENNISKILLEN CASTLE
BT74 7HL
☎ 028 6632 2711

Overlooking Lough Erne, this castle, a three-storey keep surrounded by massive stone-built barracks and with a turreted fairytale 17th-century water gate, now houses two museums and a heritage centre. In the castle keep is a small museum displaying Royal Enniskillen Fusiliers regimental exhibits, while the other rooms contain the Fermanagh County Museum's collection of local antiquities.

Times: ✱ Open all year Mon 2-5, Tue-Fri 10-5 (closed 1-2, Oct-Apr), Sat 2-5 May-Aug, Sun 2-5 Jul-Aug, all day BH's.
Facilities: 🅿 ♿ shop ✖

FLORENCE COURT
BT92 1DB
➲ (8 miles SW of Enniskillen via A4 and then A32 to Swanlibar, well signposted)
☎ 028 6634 8249 ▤ 028 6634 8873
e-mail: florencecourt@nationaltrust.org.uk

An 18th-century mansion overlooking wild and beautiful scenery towards the Mountains of Cuilcagh. The interior of the house, particularly noted for its flamboyant rococo plasterwork, was gutted by fire in 1955, but has been miraculously restored. There are pleasure grounds with an Ice House, Summer House, Water Powered Sawmill and also a walled garden.

Times: Open daily. Grounds, Oct-Apr 10-4; May-Sep 10-8. House, daily Jun-Aug, 12-6; Apr, May & Sep, wknds. **Fee:** ✱ Car Park £2.50. Grounds & House tour £4 (ch £2). Family £10. Group £3 (groups outside normal hours £4). **Facilities:** 🅿 (charged) 💺 ✖ ♿ (electric wheelchair available & wheelchair path, Braille) toilets for disabled shop ♨ 🍴

MARBLE ARCH CAVES
Marlbank Scenic Loop BT92 1EW
➲ (off A4 Enniskillen-Sligo road)
☎ 028 6634 8855 ▤ 028 6634 8928
e-mail: mac@fermanagh.gov.uk

A magical cave system, one of Europe's finest, under the Mountains of Cuilcagh. Visitors are given a tour of a wonderland of stalagmites, stalactites and underground rivers and lakes, starting with a boat trip on the lower lake. The streams, which feed the caves, flow down into the mountain then emerge at Marble Arch, a 30ft detached limestone bridge.

Times: Open late Mar-Sep. From 10am daily. **Fee:** £6 (ch £3, student oap £4). Family ticket. **Facilities:** 🅿 💺 ♿ toilets for disabled shop ✖ (ex guide dogs) 🍴

MONEA CASTLE
➲ (6m NW) **FREE**
☎ 028 9023 5000 ▤ 028 9031 0288

A fine example of a plantation castle still with much of its enclosing bawn wall intact, built around 1618. Of particular interest is the castle's stone corbelling - the Scottish method of giving additional support to turrets.

Times: Open at any reasonable time. **Facilities:** 🅿 ♿

THE SHEELIN IRISH LACE MUSEUM
Ballanaleck BT92 2BA
➲ (from Enniskillen take A4 onto A509. Thatched Sheelin restaurant on left after 3m, museum in restaurant car park).
☎ 028 6634 8052 ▤ 028 6634 8200
e-mail: rosemary.cathcart@virgin.net

The Irish Lace Museum has the largest and most comprehensive display of antique lace anywhere in Ireland. There are around 140 exhibits, representing the five main types of Irish lace: Inishmacsaint Needlelace, Crochet, Limerick, Carrickmacross, and Youghal Needlelace. The history of the Irish lace-making industry is described, and antique items can be bought in the museum shop.

Times: Open Mon-Sat 10-6. **Facilities:** 🅿 ✖ licensed ♿ (toilets for disabled in restaurant) shop ✖ (ex guide dogs) 🍴

LISNASKEA
Map 01 C5

CASTLE BALFOUR
FREE

☎ 028 9023 5000   ▤ 028 9031 0288

Dating from 1618 and refortified in 1652, this is a T-plan house with vaulted rooms. Badly burnt in the early 1800s, this house has remained in ruins.
Times: Open at all times. **Facilities:** P &

NEWTOWNBUTLER
Map 01 C5

CROM ESTATE
BT92 8AP

➲ (3m from A34, well signposted from Newtonbutler)

☎ 028 6773 8118   ▤ 028 6773 8118

e-mail: crom@nationaltrust.org.uk

Featuring hectares of woodland, parkland and wetland, the Crom Estate is one of Northern Ireland's most important conservation areas. Nature trails are signposted through woodlands to the ruins of the old castle, and past the old boat house and picturesque summer house. Day tickets for pike fishing and boat hire are available from the Visitor Centre.
Times: Grounds: 15 Mar-Jun, daily 10-6; Jul-Aug, daily 10-8; Sep, daily 10-6, Sun 12-6: Visitor centre: 15 Mar-May, wknds 10-6; Jun-Sep, daily 10-6. **Fee:** car £4, boat £4, minibus £12, coach £25 **Facilities:** P (charged) ▦ & toilets for disabled shop ⚥ ➷

CO LONDONDERRY

COLERAINE
Map 01 C6

HEZLETT HOUSE
2 for 1
107 Sea Rd, Castlerock BT51 4TW

➲ (5m W on Coleraine/Downhill coast road)

☎ 028 7084 8728   ▤ 028 7084 8728

e-mail: hezletthouse@nationaltrust.org.uk

A low, thatched cottage built around 1690 with an interesting cruck truss roof, constructed by using pairs of curved timbers to form arches and infilling around this frame with clay, rubble and other locally available materials.
Times: Open 15 Mar-May, 12-6, wknds & BHs; Jun-Aug, daily (ex Tue, but open if BH); Sep wknds only. **Fee:** ✱ £3.50 (ch £2). Family ticket £7.50. Group £3 each (ouside normal hours £4 each). **Facilities:** P & (parking) toilets for disabled ✖ (ex in gardens on lead) ⚥

MOUNT SANDEL
➲ (1.25m SSE)
FREE

☎ 028 9023 0560   ▤ 028 9031 0288

This 200ft oval mound overlooking the River Bann is believed to have been fortified in the Iron Age. Nearby is the earliest known inhabited place in Ireland, where post holes and hearths of wooden dwellings, and flint implements dating back to 6,650BC have been found. The fort was a stronghold of de Courcy in the late 12th century and was refortified for artillery in the 17th century.
Times: Open at all times. **Facilities:** P &

DOWNHILL
Map 01 C6

MUSSENDEN TEMPLE BISHOP'S GATE AND BLACK GLEN
Mussenden Rd BT51 4RP

➲ (1m W of Castlerock off A2)

☎ 028 7084 8728   ▤ 028 7084 8728
FREE

e-mail: downhillcastle@nationaltrust.org.uk

Spectacularly placed on a cliff edge overlooking the Atlantic, this perfect 18th-century rotunda was modelled on the Temple of Vesta at Tivoli. Visitors entering by the Bishop's Gate can enjoy a beautiful glen walk up to the headland where the temple stands. If you enjoy open windswept walks with views that stretch over the whole of the north coast of Ireland, then you must visit Downhill.
Times: Open Mar-May wknds & BH 11-6; Jun, daily, 11-6; Jul-Aug, daily, 11-7.30; Sep wknds 11-6; Oct wknds, 11-5. **Facilities:** P (charged) & toilets for disabled ⚥

DUNGIVEN
Map 01 C5

BANAGHER CHURCH
➲ (2m SW)
FREE

☎ 028 9023 5000   ▤ 028 9031 0288

This church was founded by St Muiredach O'Heney in 1100 and altered in later centuries. Today impressive ruins remain. The nave is the oldest part and the square-headed lintelled west door is particularly impressive. Just outside, the perfect miniature stone house, complete with pitched roof and sculpted figures of a saint at the doorway, is believed to be the tomb of St Muiredach. The saint was said to have endowed his large family with the power of bringing good luck. All they had to do was to sprinkle whoever or whatever needed luck with sand taken from the base of the saint's tomb.
Times: Open at all times. **Facilities:** P &

DUNGIVEN PRIORY
➲ (SE of town overlooking River Roe)
FREE

☎ 028 9023 5000   ▤ 028 9031 0288

Up until the 17th century Dungiven was the stronghold of the O'Cahan chiefs, and the Augustinian priory, of which extensive ruins remain, was founded by the O'Cahans around 1150. The church, which was altered many times in later centuries, contains one of Northern Ireland's finest medieval tombs. It is the tomb of Cooey na Gall O'Cahan who died in 1385. His sculpted effigy, dressed in Irish armour, lies under a stonework canopy. Below are six kilted warriors.
Times: Open - Church at all times, chancel only when caretaker available. Check at house at end of lane. **Facilities:** P &

LIMAVADY
Map 01 C6

ROUGH FORT
➲ (1m W off A2)
FREE

☎ 028 7084 8728   ▤ 028 7084 8728

e-mail: downhillcastle@nationaltrust.org.uk

Early Christian rath picturesquely surrounded by pine and beech trees, making it a significant landscape feature. The Rough Fort is one of the best examples of an earthwork ring fort in Ireland.
Times: Open at all times. **Facilities:** ⬲ ⚥

LONDONDERRY   Map 01 C5

CITY WALLS

☎ 028 9023 5000   ▤ 028 9031 0288

The finest and most complete city walls to be found in
Ireland. The walls, 20-25ft high, are mounted with ancient
canon, and date back to the 17th century. The walled city is
a conservation area with many fine buildings. Visitors can
walk round the city ramparts - a circuit of one mile.
Times: ✱ Open all times. **Facilities:** ℙ (charged) ⅋

FOYLE VALLEY RAILWAY MUSEUM

Foyle Rd BT48 6SQ
☎ 028 7126 5234   ▤ 028 7137 7633

A collection of relics from the four railway companies which
served Londonderry are displayed at the Foyle Valley Railway
Heritage Centre. Steam locomotives, diesel railcars and all
the paraphernalia of a station can be seen and the Railway
Gallery tells the story of the railways. Travel in the historic
County Donegal railcars for a trip to the historic mill.
Times: ✱ Open all year, Apr-Sep Mon-Sat 10-5, Sun 2-5; Oct-Mar
Mon-Sat 10-4. **Facilities:** ℙ ⅋ toilets for disabled shop garden
centre ✖

TOWER MUSEUM

Union Hall Place BT48 6LU
➲ (situated directly behind the city wall, facing the
guildhall)
☎ 028 7137 2411   ▤ 028 7137 7633
e-mail: towermuseum@dnet.co.uk

This exhibition recounts the history of Londonderry from
pre historic times to the present day using real artefacts,
theatrical displays and eleven audio-visual programmes
showing the spread of Irish monasticism, the famous Siege
of Derry and the road to the partition of Ireland.
Times: ✱ Open all year, Sep-Jun Tue-Sat 10-5. Jul-Aug Mon-Sat 10-5,
Sun 2-5. Also open all BH Mons. **Facilities:** ℙ (300 yds) ⅋ toilets for
disabled shop ✖ (ex guide dogs) ▬

MAGHERA   Map 01 C5

MAGHERA CHURCH

➲ (E approach to the town)   FREE
☎ 028 9023 5000   ▤ 028 9031 0288

Important 6th century monastery founded by St Lurach, later
a bishop's see and finally a parish church. This much-altered
church has a magnificently decorated 12th-century west
door. A cross-carved stone to the west of the church is
supposed to be the grave of the founder.
Times: Key from Leisure Centre. **Facilities:** ℙ ⅋

MONEYMORE   Map 01 C5

SPRINGHILL

BT45 7NQ
➲ (1m from Moneymore on B18 to Coagh)
☎ 028 8674 8210 & 8674 7927   2 for 1
▤ 028 8674 8210
e-mail: springhill@nationaltrust.org.uk

This pleasingly symmetrical manor house dates back to the
17th century. Today much of the family furniture, books and
bric-a-brac have been retained. Outside, the laundry, stables,

continued

brewhouse, and old dovecote make interesting viewing, as
does the excellent costume museum.
Times: Open 15 Mar-Jun, wknds & BH 2-6; Jul-Aug, daily 2-6; Sep,
wknds only 2-6. **Fee:** ✱ £3.65 (ch £1.80). Family ticket £7.55. Group
rate £3 each. Group rate outside normal hours £4 each. **Facilities:** ℙ
▬ ⅋ (photograph album of 1st floor, wheelchair, scented plants)
toilets for disabled shop ✖ (ex on leads in grounds) ▲

CO TYRONE

ARDBOE   Map 01 C5

ARDBOE CROSS

➲ (off B73)   FREE
☎ 028 9023 5000   ▤ 028 9031 0288

Situated at Ardboe Point, on the western shore of Lough
Neagh, is the best example of a high cross to be found in
Northern Ireland. Marking the site of an ancient monastery,
the cross has 22 sculpted panels, many recognisably biblical,
including Adam and Eve and the Last Judgment. It stands
over 18ft high and dates back to the 10th century. It is still
the rallying place of the annual Lammas, but praying at the
cross and washing in the lake has been replaced by
traditional music-making, singing and selling of local
produce. The tradition of 'cross reading' or interpreting the
pictures on the cross, is an honour passed from generation
to generation among the men of the village.
Times: Open at all times. **Facilities:** ℙ ⅋

BALLYGAWLEY   Map 01 C5

U S GRANT ANCESTRAL HOMESTEAD & VISITOR CENTRE

Dergenagh Rd BT70 1TW
➲ (off A4, 2m on Dergenagh road, signposted)
☎ 028 8555 7133   ▤ 028 8555 7133
e-mail: killymaddy@nitic.net

Ancestral homestead of Ulysses S Grant, 18th President of
the United States of America. The homestead and farmyard
have been restored to the style and appearance of a
mid-19th-century Irish smallholding. There are many
amenities a children's play area, purpose built barbecue and
picnic tables and butterfly garden.
Times: Open by appointment only **Fee:** ✱ £1 (ch & concessions 50p).
Party 10+ **Facilities:** ℙ ⅋ (wide doorway to audio-visual
area/entrances/exits) shop ✖ (ex guide dogs)

BEAGHMORE   Map 01 C5

BEAGHMORE STONE CIRCLES AND ALIGNMENTS

☎ 028 9023 5000   FREE
▤ 028 9031 0288

Discovered in the 1930s, these impressive, ritualistic stones
have been dated back to the early Bronze, and maybe even
Neolithic Ages. There are three pairs of stone circles, one
single circle, stone rows or alignments and cairns, which
range in height from one to four feet. This is an area littered
with historic monuments, many discovered by people cutting
turf.
Times: Open at all times. **Facilities:** ℙ ⅋

BENBURB Map 01 C5

BENBURB CASTLE   `FREE`
☎ 028 9023 5000 🖷 028 9031 0288

The castle ruins - three towers and massive walls - are dramatically placed on a cliff-edge 120ft above the River Blackwater. The northwest tower is newly restored and has dizzy cliff-edge views. The castle, built by Sir Richard Wingfield around 1615, is actually situated in the grounds of the Servite Priory. There are attractive walks down to the river.
Times: Castle grounds open at all times. Special arrangements, made in advance, necessary for access to flanker tower. **Facilities:** 🅿 ♿ ✸

CASTLECAULFIELD Map 01 C5

CASTLE CAULFIELD   `FREE`
☎ 028 9023 5000 🖷 028 9031 0288

Sir Toby Caulfield, an Oxfordshire knight and ancestor of the Earls of Charlemont, built this manor house in 1619 on the site of an ancient fort. It was badly burnt in 1641, repaired and lived in by the Caulfield/Charlemont family until 1670. It boasts the rare distinction of having had Saint Oliver Plunkett and John Wesley preach in its grounds. Some fragments of the castle are re-used in the fine, large 17th-century parish church.
Times: Open at all times. **Facilities:** 🅿 ♿

COOKSTOWN Map 01 C5

TULLAGHOGE FORT
➲ (2m S)   `FREE`
☎ 028 9023 5000 🖷 028 9031 0288

This large hilltop earthwork, planted with trees, was once the headquarters of the O'Hagans, Chief Justices of the old kingdom of Tyrone. Between the 12th and 16th centuries the O'Neill Chiefs of Ulster were also crowned here - the King Elect was seated on a stone inauguration chair, new sandals were placed on his feet and he was then anointed and crowned. The last such ceremony was held here in the 1590s; in 1600 the stone throne was destroyed by order of Lord Mountjoy.
Times: Open at all times. **Facilities:** 🅿

WELLBROOK BEETLING MILL
20 Wellbrook Rd, Corkhill BT80 9RY
➲ (4m W in Co Tyrone, 0.5m off A505)   `2 for 1`
☎ 028 8674 8210 & 8675 1735
e-mail: wellbrookl@nationaltrust.org.uk

This 18th-century water-powered linen mill was used for bleaching and, until 1961, for finishing Irish linen. Beetling was the name given to the final process in linen making, when the material was beaten by 30 or so hammers (beetles) to achieve a smooth and slightly shiny finish.
Times: Open 15 Mar-Jun wknds & BH's, daily 12-6; Jul-Aug daily 12-6; Sep, wknds only 12-6. **Fee:** ✱ £2.60 (ch £1.30). Family ticket £5.70. Group rate £2.10 each. Group rate outside normal hours £3.10 each.
Facilities: 🅿 ♿ toilets for disabled shop ✸ (ex on lead in grounds) 🐾

DUNGANNON Map 01 C5

TYRONE CRYSTAL VISITOR CENTRE
Tyrone Crystal, Killybrackey BT71 6TT
➲ (M1 junct 14/A45 to t-junct, turn left towards Dungannon, Tyrone Crystal 2.5m on left. Signposted)
☎ 028 8772 5335 🖷 028 8772 6260
e-mail: info@tyronecrystal.com

Crystal making in Tyrone is a comparatively modern enterprise, dating its beginnings from the days of Benjamin Edwards in the 1770s. Tyrone Crystal is hand-cut, and visitors can see this craft in action on guided tours of the factory. The new spacious visitor centre and facilities contribute to the fascinating insight of the history and heritage.
Times: ✱ Visitor Centre Mon-Sat 9-6, Sun1-5; Tour times Mon-Fri 11, 12, 2, 3pm. Sat tours prior booking only **Facilities:** 🅿 ✕ ♿ Disabled parking spaces toilets for disabled shop ✸ (ex guide dogs) 🐾

NEWTOWNSTEWART Map 01 C5

HARRY AVERY'S CASTLE
➲ (0.75m SW)   `FREE`
☎ 028 9023 5000 🖷 028 9031 0288

The hilltop ruins of a Gaelic stone castle, built around the 14th century by one of the O'Neill chiefs, are the remains of the oldest surviving Irish-built castle in the north. Only the great twin towers of the gatehouse are left. A new stairway enables the public to gain access to one of these.
Times: Open at all times. **Facilities:** ✸ ⛩

OMAGH Map 01 C5

ULSTER AMERICAN FOLK PARK
BT78 5QY
➲ (5m NW Omagh on the NW passage route)
☎ 028 8224 3292 🖷 028 8224 2241
e-mail: uafp@iol.ie

An outdoor museum that traces the history of Ulster's links with America and the emigration of Ulster residents to the US during the 18th and 19th centuries. The 70-acre site is divided into two parts - Old World and New World. There are demonstrations of Old and New World crafts, and a visitor centre, with exhibitions and audio-visual presentations. The Centre for Emigration Studies is based here, with a research library and emigration database - please ring for details.
Times: ✱ Open Etr-Sep, daily 10.30-6, Sun & BH 11-6.30; Oct-Etr Mon-Fri 10.30-5. Last admission 1hr 30mins before closing.
Facilities: 🅿 ⬛ ✕ ♿ toilets for disabled shop ✸ (ex guide dogs) 🐾

ULSTER HISTORY PARK
Cullion BT79 7SU
➲ (7m on B48)
☎ 028 8164 8188 🖷 028 8164 8011   `2 for 1`
e-mail: uhp@omagh.gov.uk

The story of settlement in Ireland, told with the aid of full-scale models of the houses and monuments built

continued

through the ages. Exhibitions and audio-visual presentations expand the theme.
Times: Open all year, Jul-Aug daily 10-6.30; Apr-Jun & Sep, daily 10-5.30; Oct-Mar, Mon-Fri 10-5. **Fee:** ✱ £3.75 (ch, students, pen & registered disabled £2.50). Family ticket (2 adults & 2 ch) £12. Group 15+ **Facilities:** 🅿 ☕ ♿ toilets for disabled shop ✖ (ex guide dogs) 🍴

STEWARTSTOWN
Map 01 C5

MOUNTJOY CASTLE
Magheralamfield (3m SE, off B161)
☎ 028 9023 5000 ✆ 028 9031 0288 FREE

Ruins of an early 17th-century brick and stone fort, with four rectangular towers, overlooking Lough Neagh. The fort was built for Lord Deputy Mountjoy during his campaign against Hugh O'Neill, Earl of Tyrone. It was captured and re-captured by the Irish and English during the 17th century and was also used by the armies of James II and William III.
Times: Open at all times. **Facilities:** 🅿

STRABANE
Map 01 C5

GRAY'S PRINTING PRESS
49 Main St BT82 8AU
➲ (in centre of Strabane)   **2 for 1**
☎ 028 7188 4094

Strabane was once an important printing and book-publishing centre, the only relic of this is a small shop in Main Street which now houses a museum illustrating the history of Strabane. The Print Museum, in a separate building, contains three 19th-century presses and shows the development of printing techniques over one hundred and fifty years.
Times: Open Apr-Sep, Tue-Sat 2-5. **Fee:** ✱ £2.60 (ch £1.55). Family ticket £5.70. Group rate £1.80 each. Group rate outside normal hours £2.80 each. **Facilities:** 🅿 (100yds) ♿ toilets for disabled ✖ (ex guide dogs) 🍴

Above: Belfast City Hall

REPUBLIC OF IRELAND
EVENTS & FESTIVALS

January
1st Lord Mayor's New Year's Day Parade, Dublin

March
15th-18th St Patrick's Festival, Dublin
tbc Feis Ceoil (competitive classical music festival), Dublin

April
29th-2nd May Cork International Choral Festival (various venues)
tbc Dublin Film Festival
tbc Pan Celtic International Festival, Kilkenny Castle

May
29th Apr-2nd Cork International Choral Festival (various venues) Co Cork
22nd-30th Dundalk International Maytime Festival, Dundalk, Co Louth (drama, street entertainment)
tbc Fleadh Nua, Ennis, Co Clare
tbc Listowel Writers Week, Listowel, St John's Arts & Heritage Centre, Listowel, Co Kerry

June
3rd-7th The Murphy's Cat Laughs, international comedy festival, Kilkenny, Co Kilkenny
16th Bloomsday (James Joyce Festival), Dublin

tbc Enniscorthy Strawberry Fair, Enniscorthy, Co Wexford

July
12th-25th Galway International Arts Festival (various venues) Co Galway

August
4th-8th Dublin Horse Show
19th Connemara Pony Show, Showgrounds, Clifden, Co Galway
tbc Fleadh Cheoil na hÉireann, Enniscorthy (biggest annual festival of Irish traditional music in the world)
tbc Rose of Tralee Festival, Tralee

September
22nd-3rd Oct Waterford International Festival of Light Opera, Theatre Royal, Waterford, Co Waterford
23rd-26th Galway International Oyster Festival, Galway City, Co Galway

October
22nd Sep-3rd Waterford International Festival of Light Opera, Theatre Royal, Waterford, Co Waterford
14th-31st Wexford Festival Opera, Theatre Royal,
High Street, Wexford, Co Wexford
22nd-25th Cork Jazz Festival, 75 venues throughout the city tbc Dublin Theatre Festival, various venues (provisional)

Village of Allihies, Co Cork

CO CLARE

BALLYVAUGHAN Map 01 B3

AILLWEE CAVE

➲ (3m S of Ballyvaughan. Signposted from Galway and Ennis).

☎ **065 7077036 & 7077067** 🖹 **065 7077107**

e-mail: fiona@aillweecave.ie

An underground network of caves beneath the world famous Burren. Guided tours take you through large caverns, over bridged chasms and alongside thunderous waterfalls. There is a craftshop, a dairy where cheese is made, a speciality food shop and a tea room. Santa uses the cave as a workshop around Christmas time, while Easter sees a massive egg hunt in the woods.

Times: Open all year from 10am (mornings only in Dec). **Fee:** ✱ €8 (ch €4.50, pen €6.50). Family ticket €22-€26 **Facilities:** P ☕ ✕ licensed ♿ toilets for disabled shop 🐕 (ex guide dogs) 💳

BUNRATTY Map 01 B3

BUNRATTY CASTLE & FOLK PARK

➲ (8 miles from Limerick city on N18 road to Ennis)

☎ **061 360788** 🖹 **061 361020**

e-mail: reservations@shannondev.ie

Magnificent Bunratty Castle was built around 1425. The restored castle contains mainly 15th and 16th century furnishings and tapestries. Within its grounds is Bunratty Folk Park where 19th century Irish life is tellingly recreated. Rural farmhouses, a village street and Bunratty House with its formal regency gardens are recreated and furnished, as they would have appeared at the time.

Times: ✱ Open all year, daily 9.30-5.30 Jan-Mar & Nov-Dec; Apr-May & Sep-Oct 9-5.30 (last admission to Folk Park 4.15pm). Folk Park also open Jun-Aug 9-6 (last admission 5.15pm). Last admission to Castle 4pm all year. Closed Good Friday & 24-26 Dec. **Fee:** ✱ €10 (concessions €7.90) Family ticket €7.90. **Facilities:** P ☕ ✕ licensed ♿ toilets for disabled shop 💳

LISCANNOR Map 01 B3

CLIFFS OF MOHER VISITORS CENTRE

➲ (6m NW of Lahinch)

☎ **065 7081 565** 🖹 **061 361020**

e-mail: reservations@shannondev.ie

The Cliffs of Moher stand as a giant natural rampart against the aggressive might of the Atlantic Ocean, rising in places to 700ft, and stretch for almost 5 miles. O'Brien's Tower was built in the early 19th century as a viewing point for tourists on the highest point. There is a visitor centre with tourist information.

Times: ✱ Open Visitor Centre all year, 9.30-5.30; Jun-Aug 9-7. Visitor centre closed 21-27 Dec. O'Briens Tower open Mar-Oct 9.30-5.30 (weather permitting). **Facilities:** P (charged) ☕ ♿ toilets for disabled shop 🐕 (ex in grounds) 💳

FREE

Attractions with this symbol do not charge for entry.

QUIN Map 01 B3

CRAGGAUNOWEN THE LIVING PAST EXPERIENCE

➲ (signed from N18 Limerick to Galway road, off R462 from Cratloe and R469 from Ennis)

☎ **061 360788** 🖹 **061 361020**

e-mail: reservations@shannondev.ie

Contains a full-scale reconstruction of a crannog, a Bronze Age lake dwelling. The project includes a reconstructed ring fort and replicas of furniture, tools and utensils. Also on display is the *Brendan*, a replica of the leather boat used by St Brendan the Navigator in the 6th century. The boat was sailed across the Atlantic Ocean in 1976 and 1977.

Times: ✱ Open mid Apr-mid Oct, daily 10-6 (last admission 5pm). **Fee:** ✱ €7 (concessions €5.60) Family ticket €17.50. **Facilities:** P ☕ ♿ toilets for disabled shop 💳

CO CORK

BALLINCOLLIG Map 01 B2

BALLINCOLLIG GUNPOWDER MILLS HERITAGE CENTRE

➲ (on Cork/Killarney road)

☎ **021 4874430** 🖹 **021 4874836**

e-mail: ballinco@indigo.ie

An amazing industrial complex on the banks of the River Lee. The mills supplied vast quantities of explosives for the British military forces throughout the world from 1794 to 1903.

Times: ✱ Open daily, 25 Apr-Sep 10-6. Last tour at 5.15pm. **Facilities:** P ☕ ♿ toilets for disabled shop 🐕 (ex guide dogs)

BLARNEY Map 01 B2

BLARNEY CASTLE & ROCK CLOSE

➲ (5m from Cork on main road towards Limerick)

☎ **021 4385252 & 4385669** 🖹 **021 4381518**

e-mail: info@blarneyc.iol.ie

The site of the famous Blarney Stone, known the world over for the eloquence it is said to impart to those who kiss it. The stone is in the upper tower of the castle, and, held by your feet, you must lean backwards down the inside of the battlements in order to receive the gift of the gab.

Times: Open - Blarney Castle & Rock Close, Jun-Jul Mon-Sat 9-7.30; Aug Mon-Sat 9-7.30; May Mon-Sat 9-7; Sep Mon-Sat 9-6.30; Apr & Oct Mon-Sat 9-sunset; summer Sun 9.30-5.30; winter Sun 9.30-sunset. Blarney House & Gardens Jun-mid Sep Mon-Sat noon-6. **Fee:** Blarney Castle & Rock Close €5.50 (ch €2, pen & students €4). Family ticket (2ad+2ch €11.50) **Facilities:** P ♿ shop 🐕 (ex guide dogs)

CARRIGTWOHILL (CARRIGTOHILL) Map 01 B2

FOTA ARBORETUM & GARDENS

Fota Estate (14km from Cork on Cobh road) FREE

☎ **021 481 2728** 🖹 **021 481 2728**

Fota Arboretum contains an extensive collection of trees and shrubs extending over an area of approx 27 acres and includes features such as an ornamental pond and Italian walled gardens. The collection includes many tender plants that could not be grown at inland locations with many examples of exotic plants from the Southern Hemisphere.

Times: Open 1st wknd Apr-Oct, daily, Mon-Sat 9-6 & Sun 11-6; Nov-Mar, daily, Mon-Sat 9-5, Sun 11-5. (Closed Xmas). **Facilities:** P (charged) ♿ toilets for disabled 🐕 (ex dogs on leads)

FOTA WILDLIFE PARK

Fota Estate (situated 10km E of Cork City. Take the Cobh road from the N25 Cork - Waterford road)
☎ 021 4812678 ▤ 021 4812744
e-mail: info@fotawildlife.ie

Established with the primary aim of conservation, Fota has more than 90 species of exotic wildlife in open, natural surroundings. Many of the animals wander freely around the park. Giraffes, zebras, ostriches, antelope, cheetahs and a wide array of waterfowl are among the species here. **Times:** ✷ Open all year 17 Mar-Sep daily, 10-6 (Sun 11-6) Oct-17 Mar wkends only. Last admission 5. **Facilities:** ▣ (charged) ✘ & (Ramps where required) toilets for disabled shop ✖ ▄

WEST CORK MODEL VILLAGE RAILWAY

Inchydoney Rd (From Cork N71 West Cork left at junct for Inchydoney Island, signposted at road junction. Village is at Bay side of Clonakilty)
☎ 023 33224
e-mail: modelvillage@eircom.net

This miniature world depicts Irish towns as they were in the 1940s, with models of the West Cork Railway and various animated scenes. The tea room is set in authentic railway carriages that overlook picturesque Clonakilty Bay. **Times:** Open Feb-Oct daily 11-5, daily 11-5; Jul-Aug, daily, extended hours 10-6. **Facilities:** ▣ ▄ & toilets for disabled shop ✖ (ex guide dogs) ▄

THE QUEENTOWN STORY

Cobh Railway Station (Off N25, follow signs for Cobh. Centre is located at Deepwater Quay, adjacent to Train Station)
☎ 021 4813591 ▤ 021 4813595
e-mail: info@cobhheritage.com

A dramatic exhibition of the origins, history and legends of Cobh. Between 1848 and 1950 over 3 million Irish people were deported from Cobh on convict ships. Visitors can explore the conditions onboard these vessels and learn about the harbour's connections with the Lusitania and the Titanic. **Times:** May-Nov 10-6. Last admission 5pm. Nov-May 10-5. Last admission 4pm. **Fee:** €5 (ch12 €2.50, pen & students €4). Family ticket €15.50 **Facilities:** ▣ ▄ ✘ & (fully wheelchair accessible) toilets for disabled shop ✖ (ex guide dogs) ▄

CORK CITY GAOL

Convent Av, Sundays Well (2km NW from Patrick St. Cork, off Sunday's Well Rd)
☎ 021 4305022 ▤ 021 4307230
e-mail: corkgaol@indigo.ie

A restored 19th century prison building. Furnished cells, lifelike characters and sound effects combine to allow visitors to experience day-to-day life for prisoners and gaoler. There is an audio-visual presentation of the social history of Cork City. Individual sound tours are available in a number of languages. A new permanent exhibition, the Radio Museum Experience, is located in the restored 1920's broadcasting studio, home to Cork's first radio station, 6CK. Unfortunately the 1st and 2nd floors are not accessible to wheelchair users. **Times:** Open Mar-Oct, daily 9.30-6; Nov-Feb, daily 10-5. Last admission 1hr before closing. **Facilities:** ▣ & (customer care policy - individual attention) toilets for disabled shop ✖ (ex guide dogs)

CORK PUBLIC MUSEUM

Fitzgerald Park, Mardyke (N of University College)
☎ 021 427 0679 ▤ 021 427 0931
e-mail: museum@corkcity.ie

Displays illustrating the history of the city are housed in this museum. The collections cover the economic, social and municipal history from the Mesolithic period. There are fine collections of Cork Silver and Glass and Youghal Needlepoint Lace. **Times:** Open all year, Jun-Aug Mon-Fri 11-1 & 2.15-6, Sun 3-5; Sep-May Mon-Fri 11-1 & 2.15-5, Sun 3-5. (Closed Sat, BH wknds & PH) **Fee:** ✷ Mon-Fri free; Sun, Family €3 individual €1.50. Students, pen & unwaged free **Facilities:** ▣ (100 yds) shop ✖ (ex guide dogs)

GARINISH ISLAND

➲ (1.5km boat trip from Glengarriff)
☎ 027 63040 ▤ 027 63149

Ilnacullin is a small island of 37 acres known to horticulturists and lovers of trees and shurbs all around the world as an island garden of rare beauty. The gardens of Ilnacullin owe their existence to the creative partnership,

continued

some eighty years ago, of Annan Bryce, then owner of the island and Harold Peto, architect and garden designer. **Times:** Open Mar & Oct, Mon-Sat 10-4.30, Sun 1-5; Apr, Mon-Sat 10-6.30, Sun 1-6.30; May, Jun & Sep, Mon-Sat 10-6.30, Sun 11-6.30; Jul & Aug, Mon-Sat 9.30-6.30, Sun 11-6.30. Last landing 1hr before closing. Charge made by boat operators. **Fee:** ✱ €3.50 (ch & students €1.25, pen €2.50) Family ticket €8.25. Group rate €2.50 each. **Facilities:** 🍴 ♿ (limited access) toilets for disabled

KINSALE   Map 01 B2

CHARLES FORT
➲ (3km from Kinsale)
☎ 021 477 2263   📠 021 477 4347
e-mail: charlesfort@duchas.ie
Built as part of the fortifications of the Irish coast in the late 17th century, Charles Fort was named after King Charles II. After the Battle of the Boyne in 1690, Williamite forces attacked and successfully besieged Charles Fort and the nearby James Fort, both of which held out for King James. The Fort also played a role in the Napoleonic Wars and was made a National Monument in 1973. **Times:** Open all year, mid Mar-Oct, daily 10-6; Nov-mid Mar, Sat-Sun 10-5, wkdays by arrangement. (Last admission 1hr before closing) **Fee:** ✱ €3.50 (ch & student €1.25 & pen €2.50). Family ticket €8.25. Group rate €2.50 each. **Facilities:** P 🍴 ♿ (lift) toilets for disabled ✈ (ex guide dogs)

DESMOND CASTLE
Cork St
☎ 021 774855
Built by the Earl of Desmond around the beginning of the 16th century, this tower was originally a custom house, but has also served as an ordnance office, prison, workhouse, stable and meeting place for the Local Defence Force during World War II. In 1938 it was declared a National Monument and restored. **Times:** ✱ Open mid Jun-early Oct, daily 10-6; mid Apr-mid Jun, Tue-Sun & BH Mon 10-6. Last admission 45 mins before closing. **Facilities:** P ✈ (ex guide dogs)

MIDLETON   Map 01 C2

OLD MIDLETON DISTILLERY
➲ (In town of Midleton located at the E end of the main street on left. Well signposted)
☎ 021 4613594   📠 021 4613642
e-mail: reservations@omd.ie
A tour of the Old Midleton Distillery consists of a 15 minute audio/visual presentation, then a 35 minute guided tour of the Old Distillery and then back to the Jameson Bar for a whiskey tasting - minerals are available for children. The guided tour and audio-visual aids are available in seven languages. **Times:** Open Nov-Mar 10-6 tours 11.30, 2.30 & 4. Mar-Nov 9-6 tours on demand. Closed Good Fri & Xmas **Fee:** ✱ €7 (ch €3). Family (2+3) €18. **Facilities:** P 🍴 ✗ licensed ♿ toilets for disabled shop ✈ (ex certain areas/guide dogs) ☕

ARDARA   Map 01 B5

ARDARA HERITAGE CENTRE
The Diamond
☎ 074 9541704   📠 074 9541381
The Heritage Centre offers information about this fabulous region mountain passes, forests, lakes and historical landmarks. It is an area rich in folklore and archeology, as well as a cultural centre for traditional music. Ardara is the heart of Ireland's manufacture of handwoven tweed, hand knitwear and hand loomed woollens and there are many craft and factory shops as well as exhibitions within the Heritage Centre. **Times:** ✱ Open Apr-Sep, 10-6. **Facilities:** P 🍴 ✗ ♿ toilets for disabled shop ✈ (ex guide dogs)

BALLYSHANNON   Map 01 B5

THE WATER WHEELS
Abbey Assaroe (cross Abbey River on Rossnowlagh Rd, next turning left & follow signs)   `FREE`
☎ 071 9851580
Abbey Assaroe was founded by Cistercian Monks from Boyle Abbey in the late 12th century. The Cistercians excelled in water engineering and canalised the river to turn water wheels for mechanical power. Two restored 12th-century mills, one is used as coffee shop and restaurant; the other houses a small museum related to the history of the Cistercians. There is also an award-winning craft shop. **Times:** Open May-Oct, daily 10.30-6.30 **Facilities:** P 🍴 ✗ licensed ♿ toilets for disabled shop garden centre ☕

DONEGAL   Map 01 B5

DONEGAL CASTLE
☎ 074 9722405   📠 074 9722436
This restored 15th-century castle and adjoining 17th-century ruined English manor house contain exhibitions of Irish historical events. Guided tours are available. **Times:** ✱ Open mid Mar-mid Oct, daily 9.30-6.30 (last admission 5.45). **Facilities:** P ✈ (ex guide dogs)

LETTERKENNY   Map 01 C5

GLEBE HOUSE & GALLERY
Churchill (signposted from Letterkenny on R251)
☎ 074 9137071   📠 074 9137521
This Regency house set in beautiful woodland gardens along the shore of Lough Gartan, was given to the nation, along with his art collection, by the artist Derek Hill. The interior of the house is decorated with original wallpapers and textiles by William Morris. **Times:** Open Etr & mid-end Apr, daily 11-6.30; mid May-Sep, Sat-Thu 11-6.30. (Last tour of house 1hr before closing). **Fee:** ✱ €2.75 (ch & student €1.25, pen €2). Family ticket €7. Group rate €2 each. **Facilities:** P 🍴 ♿ ✈ (ex guide dogs)

GLENVEAGH NATIONAL PARK & CASTLE

Churchill (left off N56 onto L77)
☎ 074 9137090 & 9137262   📠 074 9137072
e-mail: talchorn@duchas.ie

Over forty thousand acres of mountains, glens, lakes and woods. A Scottish style castle is surrounded by one of the finest gardens in Ireland, contrasting with the rugged surroundings.
Times: Open daily 16 Mar-2 Nov, 10-6.30. **Fee:** Park: free, Castle €2.75 (ch & students €1.25, pen €2). Family ticket €7, group 20+ €2.
Facilities: 🅿 💷 ✕ ᕷ (visitor centre, gardens have paths) toilets for disabled

LIFFORD   Map 01 C5

CAVANACOR HISTORIC HOUSE & ART GALLERY

Ballindrait (1.5m from town off N14
Strabane/Letterkenny road)
☎ 074 9141143   📠 074 9141143
e-mail: joannaok7@hotmail.com

Built in the early 1600s and commanding a view of the Clonleigh valley and the River Deele, Cavanacor House is the ancestral home of James Knox Polk, 11th President of the USA (1845-1849). King James II dined under the sycamore tree in front of the house in 1689. There are over 10 acres of landscaped gardens and an old-fashioned walled garden. The Art Gallery will feature exhibitions of new work by national and international artists. Please ring for details.
Times: Open Etr & Jul-Aug Tue-Sat 12-6, Sun 2-6. Art gallery open all year **Facilities:** 🅿 💷 ✕ ᕷ shop ⬦

CO DUBLIN

BALBRIGGAN   Map 01 D4

ARDGILLAN CASTLE

⮑ (Pass Airport & Swords rdbt, take R127 & follow signs).
☎ 01 8492212   📠 01 8492786

A large and elegant country manor house built in 1738, set in 194 acres of parkland, overlooking the sea and coast as far as the Mourne Mountains. There is a permanent exhibition of the 17th century 'Down Survey' maps and

continued

various temporary exhibitions. Tours of the Gardens (June, July and August) begin at 3.30pm every Thursday.
Times: Open Apr-Sep, Tue-Sun & BH's 11-6 (daily Jul-Aug); Oct-Mar, Wed-Sun & BH's 11-4.30. (Closed 23 Dec-1 Jan). **Fee:** ✱ €4 (pen & students €3). Family ticket €9. **Facilities:** 🅿 💷 ᕷ toilets for disabled shop ⬦ (ex guide dogs)

DONABATE   Map 01 D4

NEWBRIDGE HOUSE AND TRADITIONAL FARM

Newbridge Demesne
☎ 01 8436534 & 8462184   📠 01 8462537

Newbridge House was designed by George Semple and built in 1737 for Charles Cobbe, Archbishop of Dublin. The house contains many splendidly refurbished rooms featuring plasterwork, furniture and paintings. Special events throughout the year include demonstrations of sheep shearing, weaving, dying, pottery and harness making.
Times: ✱ Open Apr-Sep Tue-Sat 10-5, Sun & PH 2-6; Oct-Mar Sat-Sun & PH 2-5. Parties at other times by arrangement. **Facilities:** 🅿 💷 shop ⬦

DUBLIN   Map 01 D4

THE CASINO

off Malahide Rd, Marino (5km N of City Centre)
☎ 01 8331618   📠 01 8331618

The Casino was designed in 1757 by Sir William Chambers to look like a one-roomed, one-storied Greek temple containing 16 rooms. Possibly one of the finest 18th-century neo-Classical buildings in Europe.
Times: ✱ Open Jun-Sep, daily 10-6; May & Oct, daily 10-5; Apr, Sun, Thu & BH's 12-5; Feb, Mar & Nov, Sun, Thu & BH's 12-4. Last admission 45 mins before closing. (Closed Dec & Jan). **Facilities:** 🅿 ᕷ ⬦ (ex guide dogs)

THE CHESTER BEATTY LIBRARY

The Clock Tower Building, Dublin Castle (10 walk from Trinity College, up Dame St towards Christ Church Cathedral).
☎ 01 407 0750   📠 01 407 0760   `FREE`
e-mail: info@cbl.ie

The contents of this fascinating gallery was bequeathed to Ireland by its first honorary citizen, American mining engineer and collector, Sir Alfred Chester Beatty (1875-1968). The collection includes manuscripts, prints, icons, miniatures, and objet d'arts of great importance from 2700BC to the present day. See illuminated copies of the Qur'an and the Bible, Egyptian papyrus texts, and Buddhist paintings.
Times: Open all year, May-Sep, Mon-Fri 10-5; Oct-Apr, Tue-Fri 10-5, Sat 11-5, Sun 1-5. (Closed BH). **Facilities:** 🅿 (5mins walk) 💷 ✕ ᕷ toilets for disabled shop ⬦ (ex guide dogs)

CHRIST CHURCH CATHEDRAL

Christchurch Place (at the top end of Dame St)
☎ 01 6778099   📠 01 6798991
e-mail: welcome@cccdub.ie

Founded in 1030, the present building dates from 1180 with a major restoration in the 1870s. The crypt is the second largest medieval crypt in Britain or Ireland. There are daily services and choral services on Sundays and during the week.
Times: Open all year 9.45-5. **Facilities:** 🅿 (100yds) ᕷ for access to crypt advance notice required shop ⬦ (ex guide dogs)

DRIMNAGH CASTLE

Long Mile Rd, Drimnagh DL12 (Dame St, left at Christchurch Cathedral into Patrick Street, right into Cork St. Through Dolphins Barn up to Crumlin Rd, past Halfway House at junction. Situated 500 yards on right)
☎ 01 4502530 & 4508927 ▤ 01 4508927
e-mail: drimnaghcastle@eircom.net

The last surviving medieval castle in Ireland with a flooded moat, Drimnagh dates back to the 13th century and was inhabited until 1954. The Castle consists of a restored Great Hall and medieval undercroft, a tall battlement tower and lookout posts, and other separate buildings including stables, an old coach house and a folly. One of the most attractive features of Drimnagh is the garden, a formal 17th Century layout with box hedges, yews and mop heads.
Times: Open Apr-Oct. Wed & wknds 12-5; Nov-Mar, Sun 2-5. Last Tour 4pm. **Fee:** ✱ €3.50 (ch €2.50, pen & students €3). Groups 20+ €2.50 each **Facilities:** 🅿 💺 ✆ (gravel courtyard and garden. steps) 🐾 (ex guide dogs)

DUBLIN CASTLE

Dame St
☎ 01 6777129 ▤ 01 6797831

With two towers and a partial wall, this is the city's most outstanding legacy of the Middle Ages. Of interest are the Record Tower, state apartments, Church of the Most Holy Trinity and Heraldic Museum. The inauguration of the President of Ireland and related ceremonies are held in St. Patrick's Hall, an elegant state apartment.
Times: ✱ Open all year, Mon-Fri 10-5, Sat-Sun & BH 2-5. (Closed 24 26 Dec & Good Fri). **Facilities:** 🅿 ✗ ✆ toilets for disabled

DUBLINIA

St Michael's Hill, Christ Church
☎ 01 6794611 ▤ 01 6797116
e-mail: info@dvblinia.ie

The story of medieval Dublin. Housed in the former Synod Hall beside Christ Church Cathedral and developed by the Medieval Trust, DVBLINIA recreates the period from the arrival of Strongbow and the Anglo-Normans in 1170 to the closure of the monasteries by Henry VIII in 1540.
Times: Open Apr-Sep 10-5; Oct-Mar, Mon-Sat 11-4, Sun & BH 10-4.30. (Closed 24-26 Dec). **Facilities:** 🅿 (100yds) 💺 ✆ (2 floors accessible, but bridge and tower are not) toilets for disabled shop 🐾 (ex guide dogs) ▤

DUBLIN WRITERS MUSEUM

18 Parnell Square (on Parnell Square)
☎ 01 8722077 ▤ 01 8722231
e-mail: writers@dublintourism.ie

The Dublin Writers Museum is housed in a restored 18th-century building and a modern annexe with lecture rooms and exhibition spaces. Dublin's rich literary heritage can be followed, through displays, tracing the written tradition in Ireland from the Book of Kells in the 8th century to the present day.
Times: Open all year, Mon-Sat 10-5, Sun & BH 11-5; Jun-Aug, Mon-Fri 10-6. **Fee:** ✱ €6 (ch €3.50, concessions €5). Family ticket €16.50. Group discounts & combined ticket for related attractions available.
Facilities: 🅿 💺 ✗ licensed shop 🐾 (ex guide dogs) ▤

DUBLIN ZOO

Phoenix Park (10mins bus ride from City Centre)
☎ 01 474 8900 ▤ 01 6771660
e-mail: info@dublinzoo.ie

Dublin Zoo first opened to the public in 1830, making it one of the oldest zoos in the world and has consistently been Ireland's favourite attraction. The new 'African Plains' is the biggest single development undertaken by the zoo. This thirty-acre development has doubled the size of the zoo and provides spacious new areas for African species. Dublin Zoo is a modern zoo with conservation, education & study as its mission. The majority of the animals at the zoo have been born and bred in zoos and are part of global breeding programmes to ensure their continued survival.
Times: ✱ Open Mar-Oct, Mon-Sat 9.30-6, Sun 10.30-6; Nov-Feb, daily 10.30-dusk. **Facilities:** 🅿 💺 ✗ licensed ✆ (Wheelchairs are available) toilets for disabled shop 🐾 ▤

GUINNESS STOREHOUSE

St James's Gate (Located next to James' St).
☎ 01 4084800 & 4538364 ▤ 01 4084965
e-mail: guinness-storehouse@guinness.com

Established in 1876, the Storehouse remained crammed with hopsacks until 1957, then it was converted and is now a high-tech, 21st-century mix of an art centre, conference facility, restaurant and bar. Find out about the drink's history and then sample a glass.
Times: ✱ Open daily 9.30-5 (last admission 5). Closed 24-26 Dec, 1 Jan & Good Fri. **Facilities:** 🅿 ✗ ✆ toilets for disabled shop 🐾 ▤

HOWTH CASTLE RHODODENDRON GARDENS

Howth (9m NE of Dublin city centre, by coast road to Howth. Just short of Howth Village. Signposted for Deer Park Hotel)
☎ 01 8322624 & 8322256 ▤ 01 8392405
e-mail: sales@deerpark.iol.ie

On the northern boundary of Dublin Bay, the castle is justly famous for its gardens and especially for its rhododendron walk. The walk is open all year, but is at its best in May and June. There are views north to the Mourne Mountains and to the west of Dublin Bay.
Times: ✱ Open all year, daily 8am-dusk. (Closed 25 Dec).
Facilities: 🅿 ✆ (steep hills unsuitable, ramped entrance) toilets for disabled 🐾 (ex guide dogs) ▤

HUGH LANE MUNICIPAL GALLERY OF MODERN ART

Charlemont House, Parnell Square
☎ 01 8741903 ▤ 01 8722182
e-mail: info@hughlane.ie

Situated in Charlemont House, a fine Georgian building, the gallery's collection includes one of the most extensive collections of 20th century Irish art. A superb range of international and Irish paintings, sculpture, works on paper and stained glass is also on show. There are public lectures every sunday and regular concerts (at noon on sundays) throughout the year.
Times: ✱ Open all year, Tue-Thu 9.30-6, Fri-Sat 9.30-5, Sun 11-5. Late night opening Thu until 8, Apr-Aug only. (Closed Mon, Good Fri & 24-25 Dec). **Facilities:** 🅿 (100 metres) (meter parking) 💺 ✆ (Ramp & reserved parking) toilets for disabled 🐾 (ex guide dogs)

IRISH MUSEUM OF MODERN ART

Royal Hospital, Military Rd, Kilmainham (3.5km from City Centre, just off N7 opposite Heuston Station)
☎ 01 612 9900 📠 01 612 9999   FREE
e-mail: info@modernart.ie

Housed in the Royal Hospital Kilmainham, an impressive 17th-century building, the Irish Museum of Modern Art is Ireland's leading national institution for the collection and presentation of modern and contemporary art. The Museum presents a wide variety of art and artists' ideas in a dynamic programme of exhibitions, which regularly includes bodies of work from the Museum's own Collection, its award-winning Education and Community Department and the Studio and National Programmes.
Times: Open all year Tue-Sat 10-5.30, Sun & BH's 12-5.30. (Closed Mon's, 24, 27 & 31 Dec & 1 Jan). **Facilities:** 🅿 💷 ᵹ toilets for disabled shop ✖ (ex guide dogs)

JAMES JOYCE CENTRE

35 North Great George's St (located near O'Connel Street and Parnell Square)
☎ 01 8788547 📠 01 8788488
e-mail: joycecen@iol.ie

Situated in a beautifully restored 18th-century Georgian town house, the Centre is dedicated to the promotion of a greater interest in, and understanding of, the life and works of Joyce. There is a library open to visitors, exhibition rooms, videos and tapes.
Times: ✱ Open all year, Mon-Sat 9.30-5, Sun 12.30-5. (Closed Good Fri & 24-26 Dec). **Facilities:** 🅿 (200 mtrs) 💷 ᵹ toilets for disabled shop ✖ (ex guide dogs) 🍽

KILMAINHAM GAOL

Inchicore Rd (3.5km from centre of Dublin)
☎ 01 453 5984 📠 01 453 2037

One of the largest unoccupied gaols in Europe, covering some of the most heroic and tragic events in Ireland's emergence as a modern nation from the 1720's. Attractions include a major exhibition detailing the political and penal history of the prison and its restoration.
Times: Open Apr-Sep, daily 9.30-6 (last admission 4.45); Oct-Mar, Mon-Fri 9.30-5.30 (last admission 4), Sun 10-6 (last admission 4.45). Access by guided tour only. **Fee:** ✱ €5 (ch & students €2, pen €3.50). Family ticket €11. Group rate €3.50. **Facilities:** 🅿 (on street only) 💷 ᵹ (tours available by prior appointment) toilets for disabled ✖

MARSH'S LIBRARY

St Patrick's Close (beside St Patrick Cathedral)
☎ 01 4543511 📠 01 4543511
e-mail: keeper@marshlibrary.ie

The first public library in Ireland, dating from 1701. Designed by William Robinson, the interior has been unchanged for 300 years. The collection is of approximately 25,000 volumes of 16th, 17th and early 18th century books.
Times: Open Mon & Wed-Fri, 10-1 & 2-5; Sat 10.30-1.
Facilities: 🅿 ✖ 🚙

NATIONAL BOTANIC GARDENS

Glasnevin (on Botanic Road, between N1 and N2)
☎ 01 837 4388 & 837 7596   FREE
📠 01 836 0080

Ireland's premier Botanic Gardens, covers a total area of 19.5 hectares (48 acres), part of which is the natural flood plain of the River Tolka. The Gardens contain a large plant collection, which includes approximately 20,000 species and cultivated varieties. There are four ranges of glasshouses including the recently restored Curvilinear Range. Notable features include herbaceous borders, rose garden, rockery, alpine yard, arboretum, extensive shrub collections and wall plants.
Times: Open all year, gardens: summer Mon-Sat 9-6, Sun 11-6; winter Mon-Sat 10-4.30, Sun 11-4.30. (Closed 25 Dec). Glasshouses: summer Mon-Wed & Fri 9-5, Thu 9-3.15, Sat 9-5.45, Sun 2-5.45; winter, Mon-Wed, Fri & Sat 10-4.15, Thu 10-3.15, Sun 2-4.15. **Facilities:** 🅿 (charged) 💷 ᵹ toilets for disabled ✖ (ex guide dogs)

NATIONAL GALLERY OF IRELAND

Merrion Square (situated 5 mins walk from Pearse Station)
☎ 01 6615133 📠 01 6615372   FREE
e-mail: artgall@eircom.net

The gallery, founded in 1854 by an Act of Parliament, houses the national collections of Irish art and European Old Masters including Caravaggio, Poussin, El Greco, Roderic O'Conor, and the Yeats'.
Times: Open all year, Mon-Sat 10-5.30 (Thu 10-8.30), Sun 2-5. (Closed 24-26 Dec & Good Fri). **Facilities:** 🅿 (5 mins walk) (meter parking, 2hrs max) ✖ licensed ᵹ (Braille/audio tours, lifts, ramps, parking bay) toilets for disabled shop ✖

NATIONAL LIBRARY OF IRELAND

Kildare St
☎ 01 603 0200 📠 01 676 6690   FREE

Founded in 1877 and based on collections from The Royal Dublin Society. The National Library holds an estimated 5 million items. There are collections of printed books, manuscripts, prints and drawings, photos, maps, newspapers, mircofilms and ephemera. The library's research facilities are open to all those with genuine research needs. In addition to research facilities, services include a regular programme of exhibitions open to the public and Genealogy Service.
Times: Open all year, Mon-Wed 10-9, Thu-Fri 10-5 & Sat 10-1. (Closed Sun, BH's, Good Fri & 23 Dec-2 Jan). **Facilities:** ᵹ toilets for disabled shop ✖ (ex guide dogs)

NATIONAL PHOTOGRAPHIC ARCHIVE

Meeting House Square, Temple Bar (opposite The Gallery of Photography)
☎ 01 603 0200 📠 01 677 7451   FREE
e-mail: photoarchive@nli.ie

The National Photographic Archive, which is part of the National Library of Ireland, was opened in 1998 in an award-winning building in the Temple bar area of Dublin. The archive holds an unrivalled collection of photographic images relating to Irish history, topography and cultural and

continued

social life. The collection is especially rich in late nineteenth and early twentieth century topographical views and studio portraits, but also includes photographs taken during the Rebellion of 1961 and the subsequent War of Independence and Civil War, as well as other historic events. **Times:** Open all year, Mon-Fri 10-5. (Closed BH's, Good Fri & 23 Dec-2 Jan). **Facilities:** 🚻 toilets for disabled shop ✖ (ex guide dogs) 🍴

NATURAL HISTORY MUSEUM
Merrion St (in Dublin City Centre)
☎ 01 677 7444 🖷 01 677 7828
e-mail: education.nmi@indigo.ie

The Natural History Museum, which is part of The National Museum of Ireland, is a zoological museum containing diverse collections of world wildlife. The Irish Room, on the ground floor, is devoted largely to Irish mammals, sea creatures and insects. It includes the extinct giant Irish deer and the skeleton of a basking shark. The World Collection has as the centre-piece the skeleton of a sixty-foot whale suspended from the roof. Other displays include the Giant Panda and a Pygmy Hippopotamus. **Times:** Open all year, Tue-Sat 10-5, Sun 2-5. (Closed Mon's, Xmas day & Good Fri). **Facilities:** 🅿 (parking meters wkdays) ✖

NEWMAN HOUSE
University College Dublin, 86 St Stephens Green (South side of St Stephen's Green)
☎ 01 7067422 & 4757255 🖷 01 7067211

Newman House consists of two superb Georgian town houses, containing some of Ireland's finest 18th-century plasterwork and decoration. As the founding home of University College Dublin in 1854, the house has been associated with many famous literary and historical figures, including John Henry Newman, Gerard Manley Hopkins and James Joyce. **Times:** ✱ Open Jun-Aug, Tue-Fri 12-5, Sat 2-5. Tours, Tue-Fri; 12,2,3 & 4; Sat 2,3 & 4. At other times tours by prior arrangement only. **Facilities:** 🅿 (100yds) ✖ licensed ✖ (ex guide dogs)

NUMBER TWENTY NINE
29 Lower Fitzwilliam St (on the corner of Lower Fitzwilliam St & Upper Mount Sq)
☎ 01 7026165 🖷 01 7027796
e-mail: numbertwentynine@mail.esb.ie

Number Twenty-Nine is an exhibition of the home life of a middle-class merchant family in Dublin, in the late 18th and early 19th century. **Times:** Open all year, Tue-Sat 10-5, Sun 2-5. (Closed Mon & 2 wks prior to Xmas). **Facilities:** 🅿 (on street/hour meter) 🍴 shop ✖ 🍴

PHOENIX PARK VISITOR CENTRE
Phoenix Park (4km from Dublin)
☎ 01 677 0095 🖷 01 672 6454
e-mail: phoenixparkvisitorcentre@duchas.ie

Situated in Phoenix Park the Visitor Centre provides an historical interpretation of the park from 3500BC, through a series of attractive displays. Part of the building is devoted to nature and there is a colourful film of Phoenix Park. The
continued

castle, probably dating from the early 17th century has been restored to its former glory. **Times:** Open all year, Jan-mid Mar, Sat & Sun 10-5; Mid-end Mar, daily 10-5.30; Apr-Sep, daily 10-6; Oct, daily 10-5.30; Nov & Dec, Sat & Sun 10-5. (Last admission 45 mins before closing) **Fee:** ✱ €2.75 (ch & students €1.25, pen €2). Family ticket €7. Group rate €2 each. **Facilities:** 🅿 🍴 🚻 toilets for disabled ✖ (ex guide dogs)

DUN LAOGHAIRE   Map 01 D4

JAMES JOYCE TOWER
Joyce Tower, Sandycove (1m SE Dun Laoghaire by coast road to Sandycove Point or turn off main Dun Laoghaire-Dalkey road)
☎ 01 2809265 & 8722077 🖷 2809265
e-mail: joycetower@dublintourism.ie

Built by the British as a defence against a possible invasion by Napoleon, the tower has walls approximately 8ft thick and an original entrance door 13ft above the ground. The tower was once the temporary home of James Joyce, who depicted this setting in the opening scene of "Ulysses". The structure is now a museum devoted to the author. Bloomsday, the day in 1904 on which all the action of "Ulysses" is set, is celebrated annually on 16th June. On this day, the museum is open from 8-6 for visits, readings from "Ulysses" and performances of various kinds, Edwardian costume is encouraged. **Times:** Open Feb Oct, Mon-Sat 10-1 & 2-5, Sun & BHs 2-6; Nov-Jan by arrangement. **Fee:** ✱ €6 (ch 3-11 €3.50, pen, students & ch 12-17 €5). Family ticket €16.50. Parties 20+. **Facilities:** 🅿 (100yds) 🚻 shop ✖ (ex guide dogs) 🍴

MALAHIDE   Map 01 D4

FRY MODEL RAILWAY
Malahide Castle Demesne (in the grounds of Malahide Castle, 8 miles N of Dublin city centre, follow sign posts for Malahide)
☎ 01 8463779 & 8462184 🖷 01 8463723
e-mail: fryrailway@dublintourism.ie

The Fry Model Railway is a rare collection of '0' gauge trains and trams, depicting the history of Irish rail transport from the first train that ran in 1834. Cyril Fry began to build his model collection in his attic, in the late 1920s. All the models are built to scale, and they are now housed in a purpose-built setting adjacent to Malahide Castle. **Times:** Open, Apr-Sep, Mon-Sat 10-5, Sun & PH 2-6; Parties at other times by arrangement. Closed 1-2pm **Fee:** ✱ €6 (ch €3.50, concessions €5). Family ticket €16.50. Combined ticket for related attractions available. **Facilities:** 🅿 🚻 shop ✖ 🍴

MALAHIDE CASTLE
➲ (From Dublin city centre follow signs for Malahide, then approaching the village, main entrance to castle is signposted to right off main road)
☎ 01 8462184 🖷 01 8462537
e-mail: malahidecastle@dublintourism.ie

One of Ireland's oldest castles, this romantic and beautiful structure, set in 250 acres of grounds, has changed very little in 800 years. Tours offer views of Irish period furniture and historical portrait collections. Additional paintings from the
continued

National Gallery depict figures from Irish life over the last few centuries.
Times: Open all year, Apr-Oct, daily 10-5 (Sun & BHs 11-6); Nov-Mar, daily 10-5 (Sun & BHs 11-5). (Closed for tours 12.45-2). **Fee:** ✱ €6 (ch €3.50, concessions €5). Family ticket €16.50.Group rates available. Combined tickets for related attractions available. **Facilities:** 🅿 💺 ✗ shop ✖ ➰

Talbot Botanic Gardens
Malahide Castle (off R107 onto Back Road, entrance 0.25m on left, well signposted)
☎ 01 8462456 🖹 01 8463620

Bought by Dublin County Council in 1976, Malahide Castle has long been associated with ornamental gardening. Over seven hectares of shrubbery, and a Walled Garden of nearly two hectares are mainly the creation of Lord Milo Talbot de Malahide, who travelled the world and brought home many exotic plants from Australia and Chile, among others. Visitors follow a path through the gardens, which gives them the best view of this impressive botanic garden.
Times: Open May-Sep 2-5. Groups by appointment only. Guided tour Wed at 2pm. **Fee:** ✱ £3.50 **Facilities:** 🅿 💺 ♿ shop ✖ (ex in parkland)

SKERRIES   Map 01 D4

Skerries Mills
➲ (signposted off M1 motorway)
☎ 01 8495208 🖹 01 8495213
e-mail: skerriesmills@indigo.ie

A collection of restored mills, including a watermill, a five-sail, and a four-sail windmill, all in working order. The site dates from the 16th century and was originally part of a monastic establishment. In came into private ownership in 1538, and a bakery has been there since 1840. Nature lovers will enjoy the millpond, and nearby wetlands.
Times: Open Apr-Sep, daily 10.30-5.30; 2 Jan-Mar & Oct-19 Dec, daily 10.30-4.30. (Closed Good Fri) **Fee:** ✱ €5 (pen & students €4). Family ticket €10 **Facilities:** 🅿 💺 shop ✖

CO GALWAY

GALWAY   Map 01 B3

Atlantaquaria
Galway Atlantaquaria, Salthill
➲ (Follow signs for Salthill, over Wolfe Tone Bridge, along Fr Griffin Rd, White Sand Rd & along The Promenade. Next to the Tourist Office at the seafront rdbt)
☎ 091 585100 🖹 091 584360
e-mail: atlantaquaria@eircom.net

Concentrating on the native Irish marine ecosystem, the Galway Atlantiquaria contains some 170 species of fish and sealife, and features both fresh and saltwater exhibits.
Times: Open Apr, May, Jun & Sep daily 10-5; Jul & Aug daily 10-6; Oct-Dec, Jan-Mar Wed-Sun 10-5. Closed Mon & Tue. **Fee:** ✱ €7 (ch 3-14 €4, student, pen €5) family ticket (1ad+2ch) €15, (2ad+3ch) €21. **Facilities:** 🅿 💺 ✗ licensed ♿ (reduced prices) toilets for disabled shop ✖ (ex guide dogs) ➰

Galway City Museum
Spanish Arch
☎ 091 567641 🖹 091 567641

Galway City Museum is devoted to the city's history, featuring examples of medieval stonework, stone axe heads and scrapers dating from 3,500 years BC, a peat fire, a large map of the city in 1651, photographs of 19th century traditional dress and memorabilia of Connaught Rangers Regiment.
Times: ✱ Open all year daily, Mar-Oct 10-5.15. Nov-Feb 2-4, times under review. **Facilities:** 🅿 (100yds) (parking discs required) ♿ ✖ (ex guide dogs)

Nora Barnacle House Museum
Bowling Green
➲ (close to St Nicholas Collegiate Church, in city centre)
☎ 091 564743

The smallest museum in Ireland, this tiny turn-of-century house was the home of Nora Barnacle, companion, wife and lifelong inspiration of James Joyce. It was here in 1909, sitting at the kitchen table that Joyce first met his darling's mother. Letters, photographs and other exhibits of the lives of James Joyce & Nora Barnacle make a visit here a unique experience.
Times: Open Jun-Aug, days may change during week, opening times posted on window. **Fee:** €2.50 (students €2). **Facilities:** 🅿 (100yds) (disc parking)

Royal Tara China Visitor Centre
Tara Hall, Mervue
➲ (N6 from the Galway Tourist office. At rdbt 2nd left & at lights turn right)
☎ 091 705602 🖹 091 757574   **FREE**
e-mail: visitor@royal-tara.com

Royal Tara China visitor centre, located minutes from Galway City Centre, operates from a 17th century Mansion. Free factory tours, five factory showrooms and coffee shop.
Times: Open all year, 9-6 (9-8 Jul-Sep, 9-9 Dec). Guided factory tours Mon-Fri 9.30-3.30. **Facilities:** 🅿 💺 ✗ licensed ♿ all facilities accessible for disabled toilets for disabled shop ✖ (ex guide dogs) ➰

GORT   Map 01 B3

Thoor Ballylee
➲ (1km off N18, 1km off N66)
☎ 091 631436 & 537733 🖹 091 631436

This tower house is the former home of the poet William Butler Yeats and this is where he completed most of his literary works. The tower, which has been restored to appear exactly as it was when he lived there, houses an Interpretative Centre with audio-visual presentations and displays of his work.
Times: Open 31 May-Sep 10-6 Mon-Sat **Fee:** ✱ €5 (ch €1, pen & students €4.50). Family ticket €10. Party. **Facilities:** 🅿 ♿ (audio-visual presentation) toilets for disabled shop ✖ (ex guide dogs) ➰

DUNGUAIRE CASTLE
➲ Off N18 Ennis to Galway road
☎ 061 360788 ▤ 061 361020
e-mail: reservations@shannondev.ie

The castle has stood for hundreds of years on the site of the 7th-century stronghold of Guaire, the King of Connaught. Today the restored castle gives an insight into the lifestyle of the people who lived there from 1520 to modern times.
Times: ✱ Open mid Apr-mid Oct, daily 9.30-5 (last admission 4.30). Medieval banquet, Apr-Oct 5.30 & 8.45 (reservations necessary).
Fee: ✱ €4.20 (concessions €2.80) Family ticket €10.50 **Facilities:** ▣ ♿ shop ✖ (ex guide dogs) ◥

PORTUMNA CASTLE & GARDENS
☎ 090 9741658 ▤ 090 9741889
e-mail: portumnacastle@duchas.ie

The great semi-fortified house at Portumna was built before 1618 by Richard Burke or de Burgo, 4th Earl of Clanricarde. This important Jacobean house, while influenced by Renaissance and English houses, remains distinctively Irish. It was the main seat of the de Burgo family for over 200 years, until it was gutted by fire in 1826. The ground floor of the house is now open to the public. To the north of the house is a formal, geometrically laid out garden, a feature often associated with large Jacobean mansions.
Times: Open Apr-Oct, daily 10-6. (Last admission 45mins before closing). **Fee:** ✱ €2 (ch & students €1, pen €1.25). Family ticket €5.50. Group rate €1.25 each. **Facilities:** ▣ ♿ (access limited) ✖ (ex guide dogs)

ROUNDSTONE MUSIC, CRAFTS & FASHION
Craft Centre (Take N59 from Galway to Clifden. After approx 50m turn left at Roundstone sign, 7m to village. Roundstone Music at the top of Village).
☎ 095 35875 ▤ 095 35980
e-mail: bodhran@iol.ie   `FREE`

The Roundstone Music Craft and Fashion shop is located within the walls of an old Franciscan Monastery. Here you can see Ireland's oldest craft-the Bodhran being made and regular talks and demonstrations are given. The 1st RiverDance stage drums were made here and are still on display in the "Craftsman's Craftshop". There is an outdoor picnic area alongside the bell tower in a beautiful location by the water where the dolphins swim up to the wall in summer.
Times: Open Apr-Oct 9.30-6, Jul-Sep 9-7, Winter 6 days 9.30-6.
Facilities: ▣ ▣ ♿ toilets for disabled shop

CRAG CAVE
➲ (1m N, signposted off N21)
☎ 066 7141244 ▤ 066 7142352
e-mail: info@cragcave.com

Crag Cave is one of the longest surveyed cave systems in Ireland, with a total length of 3.81km. It is a spectacular world, where pale forests of stalagmites and stalactites,
continued

---

thousands of years old, throw eerie shadows around vast echoing caverns complemented by dramatic sound and lighting effects. Tours lasts about 30 minutes.
Times: Open daily, mid Mar-1 Nov 10-6 (Jul-Aug until 6.30). Last tour 30 minutes before closing time. **Fee:** ✱ €6.50 (ch €4, pen & students €5.50). Family ticket €20 **Facilities:** ▣ ▣ ✖ licensed ♿ (ramp to visitor centre) toilets for disabled shop ✖ (ex guide dogs) ◥

THE BLASKET CENTRE
➲ (10m W of Dingle town, on Slea Head Drive) .
☎ 066 9156444 & 9156371 ▤ 066 9156446
e-mail: mdemordha@eolga.ie

In the early part of this century a small group of writers from the remote Blasket Island, just off the coast of County Kerry, achieved world renown. They told their own story in their own language and the centre describes the lives of the Islanders before the sad abandonment of the island in 1953. Research and conference facilities also available.
Times: ✱ Open daily, Etr-late Oct 10-6 (7 Jul-Aug). Open on request all year for groups over 30. Last admission 45mins before closing.
Facilities: ▣ ▣ ✖ licensed ♿ (reserved parking) toilets for disabled ✖ (ex guide dogs)

KILLARNEY TRANSPORT MUSEUM
Scotts Hotel Gardens (centre of town, opposite railway station)
☎ 064 34677 ▤ 064 36656

A unique collection of Irish veteran, vintage and classic cars, motorcycles, bicycles, carriages and fire engines. Exhibits include the 1907 Silver Stream, reputed to be the rarest car in the world, it was designed and built by an Irishman and he only made one!
Times: Open Apr, May, Sep & Oct 11-5. Jun, Jul & Aug 10-6 **Fee:** ✱ €5 (stud/oap €3.50). Family ticket €12-€14 **Facilities:** ▣ ▣ ✖ licensed ♿ shop (summer only)

MUCKROSS HOUSE, GARDENS & TRADITIONAL FARMS
Muckross (4m on Kenmare Road)
☎ 066 31440 & 35571 ▤ 066 33926
e-mail: mucros@iol.ie

The 19th century mansion house of the formerly private Muckross Estate. It now houses a museum of Kerry folklife. In the basement craft centre, a weaver, blacksmith and potter demonstrate their trades. The grounds include Alpine and bog gardens, rhododendrons, azaleas and a rock garden.
Times: ✱ Open Jul-Aug, daily 9-7; 17 Mar-Jun & Sep-Oct, 9-6; Nov-16 Mar 9-5.30. **Facilities:** ▣ ✖ licensed ♿ toilets for disabled shop ✖ (ex guide dogs) ◥

KERRY THE KINGDOM MUSEUM
Ashe Memorial Hall, Denny St (Town centre location, follow signs for museum & tourist information office)
☎ 066 712 7777 ▤ 066 712 7444
e-mail: info@kerrymuseum.com

The museum tells the story of Kerry (and Ireland) from earliest times. There's an audio-visual presentation on
continued

Kerry's spectacular scenery and historic monuments; the priceless treasures of Kerry origin in the Kerry Museum, and Geraldine Tralee - a reconstruction of Tralee during the Middle Ages when it was the principal seat of the Anglo-Norman FitzGeralds (Geraldines). Visitors travel by time car through the reconstructed streets, houses, market place, port and abbey complete with sounds and smells. **Times:** ✱ Open daily, 17 Mar-20 Dec. Mar-Oct 10-5.30, Nov-Dec noon-4. **Facilities:** 🅿 💻 ♿ (special time car through Medieval Experience) toilets for disabled shop ✖ (ex guide dogs) 🍴

THE SKELLIG EXPERIENCE
⮑ (Ring of Kerry Road, signed after Cahersiveen town then Valentia bridge or ferry from Rena Rd Point)
☎ 066 9476306   🖷 066 9476351
e-mail: info@skelligexperience.com

The Skellig Rocks are renowned for their scenery, sea bird colonies, lighthouses, Early Christian monastic architecture and rich underwater life. The two islands - Skellig Michael and Small Skellig - stand like fairytale castles in the Atlantic Ocean, rising to 218 metres and their steep cliffs plunging 50 metres below the sea. The Heritage Centre, (on Valentia Island, reached from the mainland via a bridge), tells the story of the Skellig Islands in an exciting multimedia exhibition. Cruise around Valentia Habour.
Times: Open Mar-Jun 10-6; Jun-Aug 10-7; Sep-Oct 10-6. **Fee:** €4.40 (ch €2.20, pen & student €3.80). Family ticket €10. **Facilities:** 🅿 💻 ♿ toilets for disabled shop ✖ (ex guide dogs) 🍴

CASTLETOWN
⮑ (13m from Dublin, follow signs to Celbridge from N4)
☎ 01 628 8252   🖷 01 627 1811
e-mail: castletown@duchas.ie

Ireland's largest and finest Palladian country house, begun c1722 for William Conolly, Speaker of the Irish House of Commons. The state rooms include the 'Pompeian' Long Gallery with its Venetian chandeliers, green silk drawing room and magnificent staircase hall with Lafranchini plasterwork. There is a fine collection of 18th-century Irish furniture and paintings.
Times: Open 20 Apr-Sep, Mon-Fri 10-6, Sat-Sun & BH 1-6; Oct, Mon-Fri 10-5, Sun & BH 1-5; Nov, Sun 1-5 & pre-booked groups 20+ Mon-Fri. (Last admission 1hr before closing) **Fee:** ✱ €3.50 (ch & students €1.25, pen €2.50). Family ticket €8.25. Pre-booked groups 10+ €2.50. **Facilities:** 🅿 💻 ♿ (restricted access for disabled visitors) toilets for disabled ✖ (ex guide dogs)

IRISH NATIONAL STUD & JAPANESE GARDENS
Irish National Stud, Tully (Off the N7)
☎ 045 521617 & 522963   🖷 045 522964
e-mail: stud@irish-national-stud.ie

Situated in the grounds of the Irish National Stud, the gardens were established by Lord Wavertree between 1906 and 1910, and symbolise 'The Life of Man' in a Japanese-style landscape. You can also visit the Horse Museum which includes the skeleton of Arkle. The

continued

Commemorative Millennium Garden of St Fiachra seeks to capture the power of the Irish landscape in its rawest state, that of rock and water.

Times: Open 12 Feb-12 Nov, daily 9.30-6, last admission 5. **Fee:** €8.50 (ch 12 €4.50, students & pen €6.50) Family ticket €18 **Facilities:** 🅿 ✖ licensed ♿ (all parts of stud accessible, only small part of gardens) toilets for disabled shop ✖ (ex on lead) 🍴

KILKENNY CASTLE
☎ 056 7721450   🖷 056 7763488

Situated in a beautiful 50-acre park, the castle dates from 1172. The first stone castle was built 20 years later by William Marshall, Earl of Pembroke. It was home of the very powerful Butler family, Earls and Dukes of Ormonde from 1391 to 1935. Due to major restoration works, the central block now includes a library, drawing room, and bedrooms decorated in 1830s splendour, as well as the beautiful Long Gallery.
Times: Open all year, Apr-May, daily 10.30-5; Jun-Aug, daily 9.30-7; Sep, daily 10-6.30; Oct-Mar, daily 10.30-12.45 & 2-5. Last tour 45mins before closing. (Closed Xmas & Good Fri). **Fee:** ✱ €5 (ch & students €2, pen €3.50). Family ticket €11. Group rate €3.50 each. **Facilities:** 🅿 (local authority restrictions) 💻 ♿ (toilet close by) shop ✖ (ex guide dogs)

FOYNES FLYING BOAT MUSEUM
⮑ (on N69 in Village of Foynes, 23m from Limerick city)
☎ 069 65416   🖷 069 65416
e-mail: famm@eircom.net

The museum recalls the era of the flying boats during the 1930s and early 1940s when Foynes was an important airport for air traffic between the United States and Europe. There is a comprehensive range of exhibits, graphic illustrations and a 1940s style cinema featuring a 17 minute film - all original footage from the 30s and 40s. Where Irish coffee was first invented by chef, Joe Sheridan, in 1942.
Times: Open 31 Mar-Oct, daily 10-6. Last admissions 5.15pm. **Fee:** €4.50 (ch €2.50, student €3.50). Family ticket €12. **Facilities:** 🅿 💻 ♿ toilets for disabled shop ✖ (ex guide dogs) 🍴

LOUGH GUR STONE AGE CENTRE
Bruff Rd
➲ (17 km S of Limerick City, off R512 road to Kilmallock)
☎ 061 061 360788 🖩 061 361020
e-mail: reservations@shannondev.ie

Lough Gur introduces visitors to the habitat of Neolithic Man on one of Ireland's most important archaeological sites. Near the lake is an interpretative centre which tells the story of 5000 years of man's presence at Lough Gur.
Times: ✱ Open May-Sep, daily 10-5.30 (last admission 5) **Fee:** ✱ €4.20 (concessions £2.80) Family ticket €10.50 **Facilities:** 🅿 ♿ shop ✖ (ex guide dogs) 🍽

CELTIC PARK & GARDENS
➲ (N69 Limerick to Tralee road)
☎ 061 394243

Located on an original Celtic settlement in one of the most important Cromwellian plantations in the south-west of Ireland. As you walk through the park there's plenty to see, including a church built in 1250, a Mass rock, dolmen, a stone circle, lake dwellings, cooking site, Celtic tomb and a fine example of a ring fort. The gardens contain over 1000 roses, flowering shrubs, a rockery, herbaceous borders, shrubbery, large pool and colonnades.
Times: Open mid Mar-Oct, daily 9.30-6. **Fee:** €5 (€4 pen & students, ch under 12 free accompanied by parent). **Facilities:** 🅿 🍽 shop

KING JOHN'S CASTLE
Nicholas St
➲ (Situated on historic Kings Island within Limerick City)
☎ 061 411201 🖩 061 361020
e-mail: reservations@shannondev.ie

The Castle was built between 1200 and 1210 and was repaired and extended many times in the following centuries. The interpretative centre at the Castle has been completely redesigned and now contains an imaginative historical exhibition. The courtyard and the Castle display some of the trades and traditions of the 16th century.
Times: ✱ Open Apr, early May, Sep & Oct daily 10-7 (last admission 4); mid-May-Aug 9.30-5.30 (last admission 4.30); Nov-Mar 10.30-4.30 (last admission 3.30). Closed Good Fri & 24-26 Dec. **Facilities:** 🅿 (charged) ♿ (lifts and ramps) toilets for disabled shop ✖ (ex guide dogs) 🍽

THE HUNT MUSEUM
The Custom House, Rutland St
➲ (a short walk from Arthur's Quay)
☎ 061 312833 🖩 061 312834
e-mail: info@huntmuseum.com

On show at the Hunt Museum is one of Ireland's finest private collections of art and antiquities. Reflecting Ireland's Celtic past as well as masterworks by Da Vinci and Renoir. Set in an 18th-century customs house beside the broad majestic Shannon.
Times: Open daily Mon-Sat 10-5, Sun 2-5. **Fee:** ✱ €6 (ch €3, concessions €4.75). Family ticket €14.70. Party. **Facilities:** 🅿 (50mtrs) (parking discs for street parking) 🍽 ✖ licensed ♿ toilets for disabled shop ✖ (ex guide dogs) 🍽

CORLEA TRACKWAY VISITOR CENTRE
➲ (Off R397, 3km from village)
☎ 043 22386 🖩 043 22442

The centre interprets an Iron Age bog road which was built in the year 148 BC across the boglands close to the River Shannon. The oak road is the largest of its kind to have been uncovered in Europe and was excavated over the years by Professor Barry & Raferty of University College Dublin. Inside the building, an 18-metre stretch of preserved road is on permanent display in a specially designed hall with humidifiers to prevent the ancient wood from cracking in the heat.
Times: Open Apr-Sep, daily 10-6. (Last admission 45 mins before closing). **Fee:** ✱ €3.50 (ch & students €1.25, pen €2.50). Family ticket €8.25. Group rate €2.50. **Facilities:** 🅿 🍽 ♿ toilets for disabled ✖ (ex guide dogs)

CÉIDE FIELDS
➲ (5m W of Ballycastle on R314)
☎ 096 43325 🖩 096 43261
e-mail: ceidefields@duchas.ie

Beneath the wild boglands of North Mayo lies Céide Fields, the most extensive Stone-age monument in the world; field systems, dwelling areas and megalithic tombs of 5,000 years ago. In addition, the wild flora of the bog is of international importance and is bounded by some of the most spectacular rock formations and cliffs in Ireland.
Times: Open Mid Mar-May & Oct-Nov, daily 10-5; Jun-Sep, daily 10-6. Rest of year open to pre-booked groups. (Last admission 1hr before closing). **Fee:** ✱ €3.50 (ch & student €1.25, pen €2.50). Family ticket €8.25. Group rate €2.50 each. **Facilities:** 🅿 🍽 ♿ (parking) toilets for disabled ✖ (ex guide dogs)

PATRICK KAVANAGH RURAL & LITERARY RESOURCE CENTRE
Candlefort
➲ (From Dundalk: Take R178, Ignore sign on right for Inniskeen. Continue on to Conlon's Pub and turn right for Inniskeen).
☎ 042 78560 🖩 042 78560
e-mail: infoatpkc@eircom.net

Birthplace of Patrick Kavanagh, one of Ireland's foremost 20th-century poets. The village grew around the ancient monastery of St Daig MacCairill, founded by 562, and its strong, 10th-century round tower still stands. The centre, housed in the former parish Church, chronicles the ancient history of the region and its role in developing Kavanagh's work.
Times: Open all year, Tue-Fri 11-5, wknds & BH's 2-6. (Closed Oct-May, wknds & BH's Dec-16 Mar). **Fee:** ✱ €4 (ch 12 free, concessions €2). Kavanagh trail guide map available €0.65. Kavanagh Country Tours - a guided tour with live performances lasting 90 mins, advance booking essential €7.50 including admission to centre. **Facilities:** 🅿 🍽 ♿ toilets for disabled shop

MONAGHAN   Map 01 C5

MONAGHAN COUNTY MUSEUM

1-2 Hill St

➲ (near town centre, opposite the market house exhibition galleries)

☎ 047 82928   🖷 047 71189   **FREE**

e-mail: comuseum@monghancoco.ie

This is an award-winning museum of local archaeology, history, arts and crafts. Throughout the year various special exhibitions take place.

Times: Open Tue-Fri 10-1 & 2-5 Sat 11-1 & 2-5, closed Sun & Mon
Facilities: P (near town centre) (restricted on street parking) 🚻 ✖ (ex guide dogs)

CO OFFALY

BIRR   Map 01 C3

BIRR CASTLE DEMESNE

➲ (In Birr Town sq take exit beside Bank of Ireland and bear right. Turn left entrance is on right, carpark on left)

☎ 0509 20336   🖷 0509 21583

e-mail: info@birrcastle.com

A large landscaped park with a lake, rivers and waterfalls, with important plant collections including magnolias, maples, limes and oaks. The Demesne is particularly colourful in the spring and autumn, and is noted for its formal gardens, containing the tallest box hedges in the world. The Demesne is also home to the Great Birr Telescope, built in 1844. Ireland's Historic Science Centre, a series of galleries focusing on Ireland's scientific past.
Times: ✱ Open all year, 9am-6pm. **Facilities:** P (charged) 🍽 🚻 toilets for disabled shop garden centre (on leads at all times) ✦

CO ROSCOMMON

BOYLE   Map 01 B4

KING HOUSE

➲ (in town centre, 1km from N4)

☎ 071 9663242   🖷 071 9663243

e-mail: kinghouseboyle@hotmail.com

King House is a magnificently restored Georgian Mansion built around 1730 by Sir Henry King, whose family were one of the most powerful and wealthy in Ireland. After its first life as a home, King House became a military barracks to the famous Connaught Rangers from 1788-1922. In more recent years King House has also been a barracks for the National Irish Army. Today visitors can explore King House and delve into the dramatic episodes of its history with stories of tragic Irish romance, runaway lovers, a duel of honour, a murder trial and feats of bravery and hardship in war.
Times: Open Apr-Sep, daily 10-6 (last admission 5). Pre-booked groups welcome all year round, telephone for details. **Fee:** €5 (ch €3, pen & student €4). Family ticket €15. Party rates available **Facilities:** P 🍽 ✖ 🚻 (lift to all areas, ramps, wide doors) toilets for disabled shop ✖ (ex guide dogs)

> The AA also publishes a guide
> to Family Friendly Places to
> Stay, Eat & Visit

STROKESTOWN   Map 01 C4

STROKESTOWN PARK HOUSE GARDEN & FAMINE MUSEUM

Strokestown Park

☎ 071 9633013   🖷 071 9633712

e-mail: info@strokestownpark.ie

A fine example of an early 18th-century gentleman farmer's country estate. Built in Palladian style the house reflects perfectly the confidence of the newly emergent ruling class. The pleasure garden has also been restored, and the Famine Museum, located in the stable yard, commemorates the Great Irish Famine of the 1840s.
Times: Open mid-Mar-Oct, daily 11-5.30. All other times, group bookings only. **Fee:** €12 (ch €5.20, concession €10) Family ticket €25.50). **Facilities:** P ✖ licensed 🚻 (Access for ramps) toilets for disabled shop ✦

CO TIPPERARY

CAHIR   Map 01 C3

SWISS COTTAGE

Kilcommon

➲ (1m from town on Ardfinnan road)

☎ 052 41144   🖷 052 42324

A delightful thatched "cottage orné" built in the early 1800s on the estate of the Earls of Glengall to a design by the famous Regency architect John Nash.
Times: ✱ Open mid Mar-Apr & Oct-Nov, Tue-Sun 10-1 & 2-4.30; May-Sep, daily 10-6. Last admission 30mins before closing.
Facilities: P ✖ (ex guide dog)

CASHEL   Map 01 C3

BRÚ BORÚ HERITAGE CENTRE

➲ (below Rock of Cashel in Cashel town)

☎ 062 61122   🖷 062 62700

e-mail: bruboru@comhaltas.com

At the foot of the Rock of Cashel, a 4th-century stone fort, this Heritage Centre is dedicated to the study and celebration of native Irish music, song, dance, story telling, theatre and Celtic studies. There's a Folk Theatre where three performances are held daily in the summer, and in the evening, banquets evoke the Court of Brian Ború, 11th-century High King of Ireland with songs, poems and sagas. Promoted by Comhaltas Ceoltóirí Éireann. There is also a Subterranean, "Sounds of History", experience.
Times: Open Jan-May & Oct-Dec, Mon-Fri 9-5; Jun-Sep Tue-Sat 9-11, Sun-Mon 9-5. **Fee:** Admission to centre free. Night show €16. Exhibition, 'Sounds of History' €40. Dinner Show/Option €40.
Facilities: P (charged) 🍽 ✖ 🚻 (wheelchair bay in theatre) toilets for disabled shop ✖ (ex guide dogs) ✦

CO WATERFORD

LISMORE   Map 01 C2

LISMORE CASTLE GARDENS

➲ (on N72 just off centre of Lismore Town)

☎ 058 54424   🖷 058 54896

e-mail: lismoreestates@eircom.net

Lismore castle is the Irish home of the Duke of Devonshire. The beautifully situated walled and woodland gardens contain a fine collection of camellias, magnolias and other

continued

shrubs and a remarkable Yew Walk. Several pieces of contemporary sculpture have recently been installed in the garden.
Times: Open 10 Apr-3 Oct, daily 1.45-4.45. (Open at 11 during Jul & Aug). **Fee:** €5 (ch under 16: €2.50, party 20+ €1.75). Party 20+ €4.50.
Facilities: 🅿 ♿ (some of grounds are accessible)

WATERFORD   Map 01 C2

WATERFORD CRYSTAL VISITOR CENTRE
➲ (on N25, 1m from city centre)
☎ 051 73311   ▤ 051 78539

There are factory tours to see mastercraftsmen mouth-blow and hand-cut this famous crystal. You can talk to the master engravers and see the crystal being sculpted. In the gallery there is the finest display of Waterford crystal in the world.
Times: ✱ Tours of factory: Apr-Oct, daily 8.30-4, gallery daily 8.30-6; Nov-Feb, Mon-Fri 9-3.15, gallery 9-5. **Facilities:** 🅿 💷 ✕ ♿ (special tours on request) toilets for disabled shop 🛪 🍴

CO WEXFORD

FERRYCARRIG   Map 01 D3

IRISH NATIONAL HERITAGE PARK
➲ (3m from Wexford, on N11)
☎ 053 20733   ▤ 053 20911
e-mail: info@inhp.com

Fourteen historical sites set in a magnificent 35-acre mature forest explaining Ireland's history from the Stone and Bronze Ages, through the Celtic period and concluding with the Vikings and Normans. Among the exhibits are a reconstructed Mesolithic camp, a Viking boatyard with 2 full size ships and a Norman motte and bailey.
Times: Open Nov-Mar daily 9.30-5.30. Mar-Nov 9.30-6.30 Last admission 5. Allow 1.5 hour for visit . **Facilities:** 🅿 💷 ✕ licensed ♿ toilets for disabled shop 🛪 (ex guide dogs) 🍴

NEW ROSS   Map 01 C3

DUNBRODY ABBEY VISITORS CENTRE
Dunbrody Abbey, Campile
➲ (10 miles from New Ross at the base of the Hook Peninsular)
☎ 051 88603
e-mail: patrickbelfast@aol.com

The visitor centre is based around the Abbey itself and Dunbrody Castle. There is an intriguing yew hedge maze with 1550 yew trees and a museum. In addition there is a golf pitch and putt course, a local craft centre and Dunbrody Abbey Cookery School.
Times: Open Apr-Sep 10-6. **Fee:** €2, Family ticket €5. Maze/Golf €4, (ch €2). Family €10. **Facilities:** 🅿 💷 ✕ ♿ shop garden centre (specialising in conifers & shrubs)

JOHN F KENNEDY ARBORETUM
➲ (12km S of New Ross, off R733)
☎ 051 388171   ▤ 051 388172

The Arboretum covers 623 acres across the hill of Slievecoiltia which overlooks the Kennedy ancestral home at Dunganstown. There are 4,500 types of trees and shrubs representing the temperate regions of the world, and laid out in botanical sequence. There's a lake and a visitor centre.
Times: ✱ Open daily, May-Aug 10-8; Apr & Sep 10-6.30; Oct-Mar 10-5. Last admission 45 mins before closing. (Closed Good Fri & 25 Dec).
Facilities: 🅿 💷 ♿ toilets for disabled shop (dogs on lead)

WEXFORD   Map 01 D3

THE IRISH AGRICULTURAL MUSEUM
Johnstown Castle Old Farmyard
➲ (4m SW of Wexford town, signposted off N25)
☎ 053 42888   ▤ 053 42213
e-mail: aosullivan@johnstown.teagasc.ie

This museum has displays on rural transport, farming and the activities of the farmyard and farmhouse; and includes a large exhibition on the history of the potato and the Great Famine (1845-49). Large scale replicas of different workshops, including a blacksmith, cooper and basket worker, and include displays on dairying, cycling, and sugar-beet harvesting and a collection of Irish country furniture. New permanent exhibitions on gardening and the Ferguson System.
Times: Open all year, Jun-Aug Mon-Fri 9-5 & Sat-Sun 11-5; Apr-May & Sep-14 Nov Mon-Fri 9-12.30 & 1.30-5, Sat-Sun 2-5; 15 Nov-Mar Mon-Fri 9-12.30 & 1.30-5 (Closed 25 Dec-2 Jan). **Fee:** €5 (ch & students €3). Family ticket €5. Parking charge May-Sep. **Facilities:** 🅿 (charged) 💷 ♿ toilets for disabled shop 🛪 (ex small dogs)

JOHNSTOWN CASTLE GARDENS
Johnstown Castle
➲ (4m SW of Wexford town, signposted off N25)
☎ 053 42888   ▤ 053 42004
e-mail: aosullivan@johnstown.teagase.ie

The 19th-century mansion is closed to the public but visitors can explore the 50 acres of grounds containing over 200 different varieties of trees and shrubs, ornamental lakes with wildfowl, and walled gardens and hothouses. The ruins of Rathlannon Castle, a medieval tower house, can also be seen.
Times: Open all year, daily 9-5.30. (Closed 25 Dec). **Fee:** ✱ Car (inc passengers) €4. Pedestrians €2 (ch & students €0.50). **Facilities:** 🅿 💷 ♿ toilets for disabled

WEXFORD WILDFOWL RESERVE
North Slob
➲ (8km NE from Wexford)   FREE
☎ 053 23129   ▤ 053 24785

The reserve is of international importance for Greenland white-fronted geese, brent geese, Bewick's swans and wigeon. The reserve is a superb place for birdwatching and there are hides and a tower hide available as well as a visitor centre.
Times: Open all year, Etr-Sep, daily 9-6; Oct-Etr, daily 10-5. (Closed 25 Dec). Other hours by arrangement. **Facilities:** 🅿 ♿ toilets for disabled 🛪 (ex guide dogs)

CO WICKLOW

ENNISKERRY   Map 01 D4

POWERSCOURT GARDENS EXHIBITION
Powerscourt Estate
➲ (just off N11 S of Bray, next to Enniskerry village)
☎ 01 204 6000   ▤ 01 204 6900
e-mail: gardens@powerscourt.ie

Begun by Richard Wingfield in the 1740s, the gardens are a blend of formal plantings, sweeping terraces, statuary and ornamental lakes together with secret hollows, rambling walks and walled gardens. The house itself incorporates an
continued

exhibition which traces the history of the estate, and tells the story of the disastrous fire of 1974 which gutted the house. **Times:** ✱ Open - Gardens Mar-Oct daily 9.30-5.30; Nov-Feb daily 9.30-dusk. Waterfall Mar-Oct daily 9.30-7; Nov-Feb daily 10.30-dusk.(Please check winter opening times as they are subject to change. Closed 25-26 Dec). **Facilities:** 🅿 💺 ✗ licensed ♿ (Lift to first floor, Wheelchair available) toilets for disabled shop garden centre ▼

KILQUADE   Map 01 D3

National Garden Exhibitions Centre
Calumet Nurseries
➲ (7m S of Bray - turn off N11 at Kilpedder)
☎ 01 2819890   🖹 01 2810359
e-mail: calumet@clubi.ie

There are 20 different gardens designed by some of Ireland's leading landscapers and designers. There are lectures during the year and guided tours during summer. Ring for details and a calender of events. We are constantly changing and upgrading the exhibition and pride ourselves on our high standard of maintenance. All plants clearly labelled. **Times:** ✱ Open Feb-22 Dec, Mon-Sat 10-6, Sun 1-6. **Facilities:** 🅿 💺 ♿ shop garden centre ✗ (ex guide dogs) ▼

RATHDRUM   Map 01 D3

Avondale House & Forest Park
➲ (S of Dublin on N11. At Rathnew on R752 to Glenealy and Rathdrum)
☎ 0404 46111   🖹 0404 46333
e-mail: costelloe_j@coillte.ie

It was here in 1846 that one of the greatest political leaders of modern Irish history, Charles Stewart Parnell, was born. Parnell spent much of his time at Avondale until his death in October 1891. The house is set in a magnificent forest park with miles of forest trails, plus a children's play area and picnic areas.
Times: Open House 17 Mar-Oct, 11-6. Closed Mon (Mar, Apr, Sep & Oct). Last admission 5pm. **Fee:** House €5 (pen €4.50). Family ticket (2 adult & 3 ch) €15. Parking; car €5, coach €25 (if pre-booked, no charge). **Facilities:** 🅿 (charged) ✗ licensed ♿ (special car park & one forest trail accessible) ✗ (ex guide dogs & on lead) ▼

Acknowledgments – Days Out Guide 2004

The main pictures in this book are held in the Automobile Association's own library (AA WORLD TRAVEL LIBRARY) with contributions from the following:

Stuart Abrahams 282, 285; Martyn Adelman 14, 258t, 258b; M Alexander 11c; M Allwood-Coppin 197; Adrian Baker 10l, 210b, 225; Peter Baker 136t; Vic Bates 286; Jeff Beazley 8bl, 205b, 382; M Birkett 22, 25, 30, 54, 82, 113, 132t, 136b, 176t, 176b, 192t; E A Bowness 11bc; K Paterson 1; Chris Coe 26; Derek Croucher 13; Steve Day 20, 129, 162; Kenya Doran 93; Derek Forss 4bl, 5b, 178; Joan Gravell 11ct, 368; Van Greaves 2; Caroline Jones 19, 71, 72, 86, 111b, 116, 186, 198, 254t; Max Jourdan 3bc; Paul Kenward 11b; Cameron Lees 230t, 230b; Simon McBride 244t, 244b; Tom Mackie 46, 210t; S & O Mathews 117, 158, 167; Eric Meacher 248b; Andy Midgley 9t; John Millar 218; Colin Molyneaux 94, 343; John Morrison 272; Roger Moss 36, 45; John Mottishaw 98; George Munday 369, 381; Rich Newton 3t, 129b, 243; Hugh Palmer 11t, 254b; Peter Sharpe 289; Rick Strange 16; Richard Surman 182; Rupert Tenison 3br, 4lbl, 4bc, 4rbr, 6; J A Tims 4t, 4br, 5t, 146; Peter Trenchard 281; Richard Turpin 8bc; Wyn Voysey 3bl, 99, 161, 215b; Jonathon Welsh 193t, 193b, 205t, 233, 238t, 238b; Linda Whitwam 78, 260, 280; Peter Wilson 275; Tim Woodcock 8br, 10r; Gregory Wrona 215t; Jon Wyand 248t

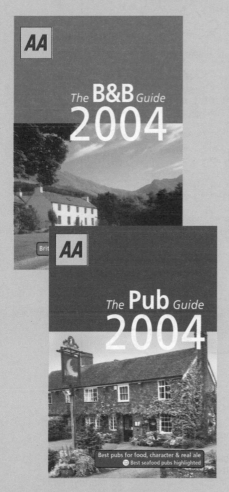
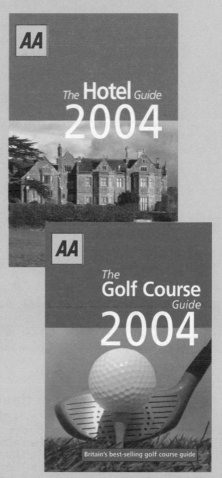

County Maps

The county map shown here will help you identify the counties within each county. You can look up each county in the guide using the county names at the top of each page. To find towns featured in the guide use the atlas and the index.

England

1 Bedfordshire
2 Berkshire
3 Bristol
4 Buckinghamshire
5 Cambridgeshire
6 Greater Manchester
7 Herefordshire
8 Hertfordshire
9 Leicestershire
10 Northamptonshire
11 Nottinghamshire
12 Rutland
13 Staffordshire
14 Warwickshire
15 West Midlands
16 Worcestershire

Scotland

17 City of Glasgow
18 Clackmannanshire
19 East Ayrshire
20 East Dunbartonshire
21 East Renfrewshire
22 Perth & Kinross
23 Renfrewshire
24 South Lanarkshire
25 West Dunbartonshire

Wales

26 Blaenau Gwent
27 Bridgend
28 Caerphilly
29 Denbighshire
30 Flintshire
31 Merthyr Tydfil
32 Monmouthshire
33 Neath Port Talbot
34 Newport
35 Rhondda Cynon Taff
36 Torfaen
37 Vale of Glamorgan
38 Wrexham

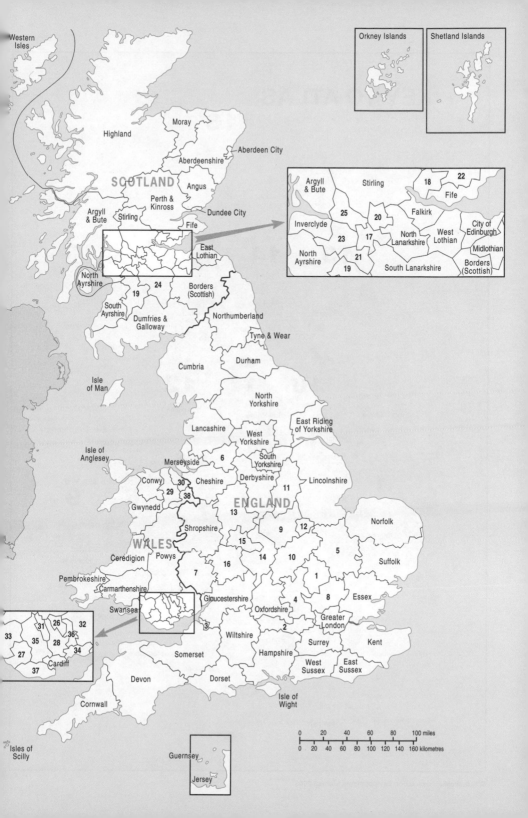

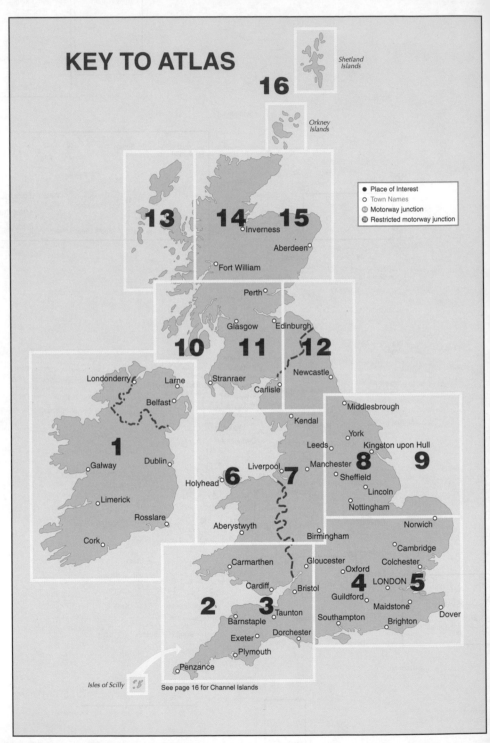

KEY TO ATLAS

Shetland Islands

16

Orkney Islands

●	Place of Interest
○	Town Names
⑩	Motorway junction
㉟	Restricted motorway junction

13   14   15

Inverness

Aberdeen

Fort William

Perth

Glasgow   Edinburgh

10   11   12

Stranraer   Newcastle

Londonderry   Larne   Carlisle

Belfast   Kendal   Middlesbrough

1   York

Leeds   Kingston upon Hull

Galway   Dublin   Liverpool   Manchester   8   9

Holyhead   6   7   Sheffield

Limerick   Lincoln

Rosslare   Aberystwyth   Nottingham

Cork   Birmingham   Norwich

Carmarthen   Gloucester   Cambridge

Cardiff   Oxford   Colchester

2   3   Bristol   4   LONDON   5

Taunton   Guildford

Barnstaple   Maidstone   Dover

Exeter   Dorchester   Southampton   Brighton

Plymouth

Penzance

Isles of Scilly   See page 16 for Channel Islands

© Automobile Association Developments Limited 2003

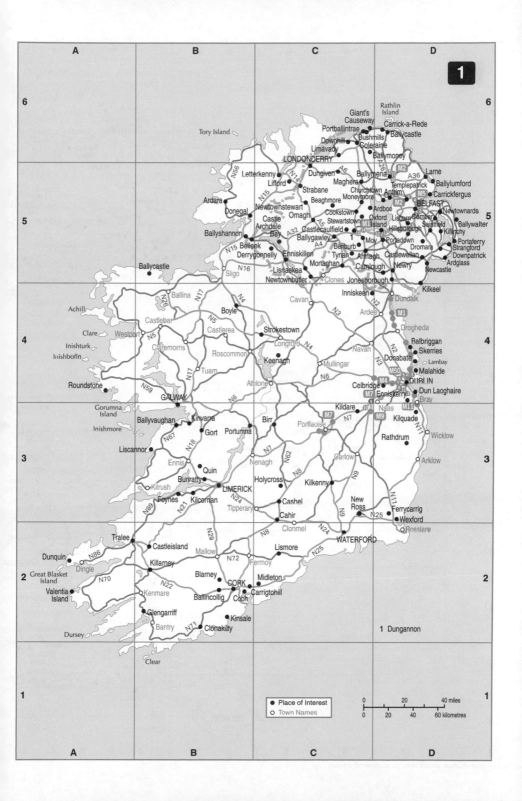

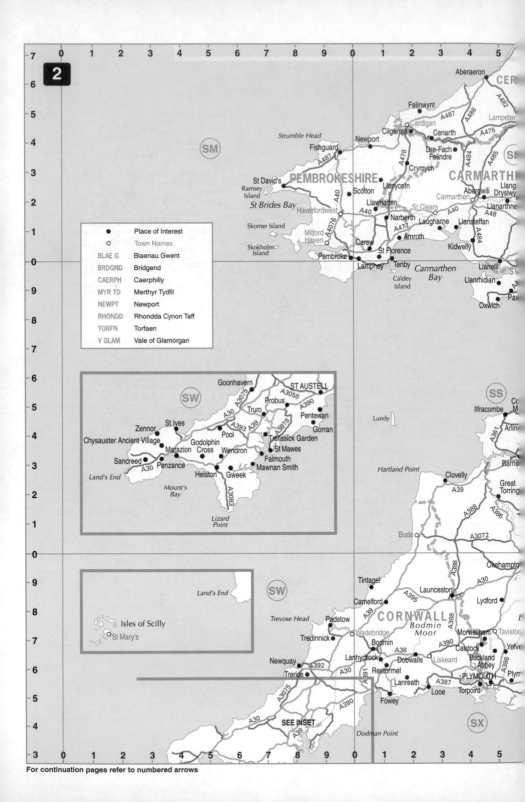

2

For continuation pages refer to numbered arrows

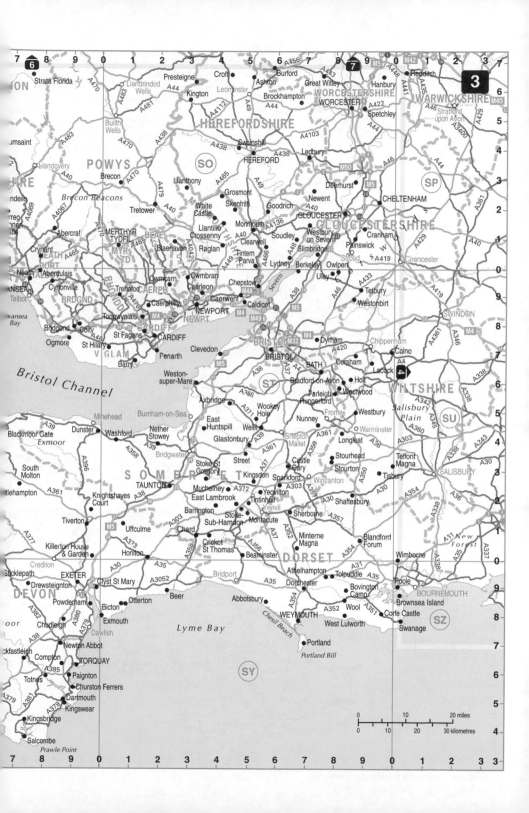

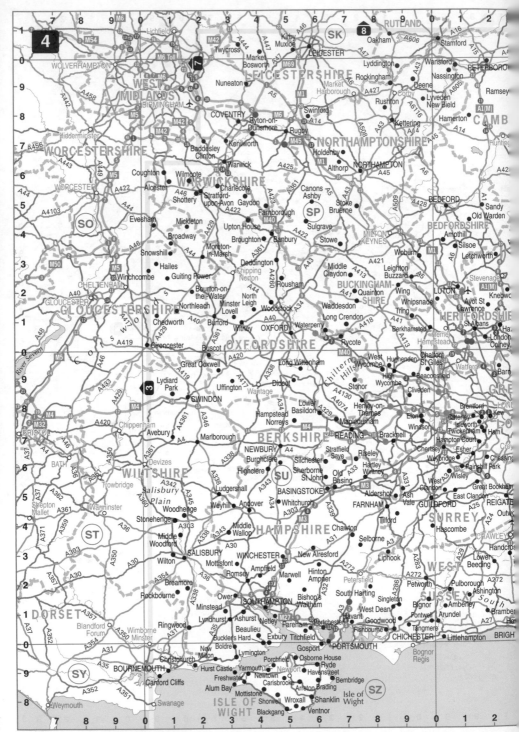

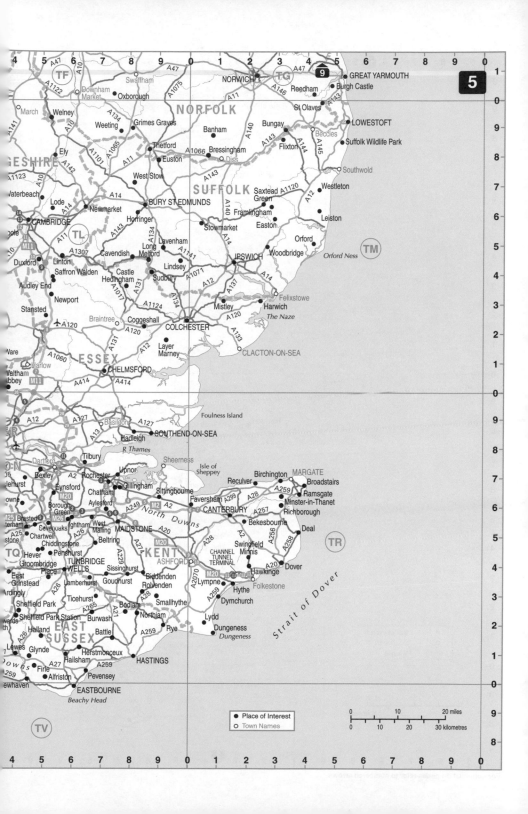

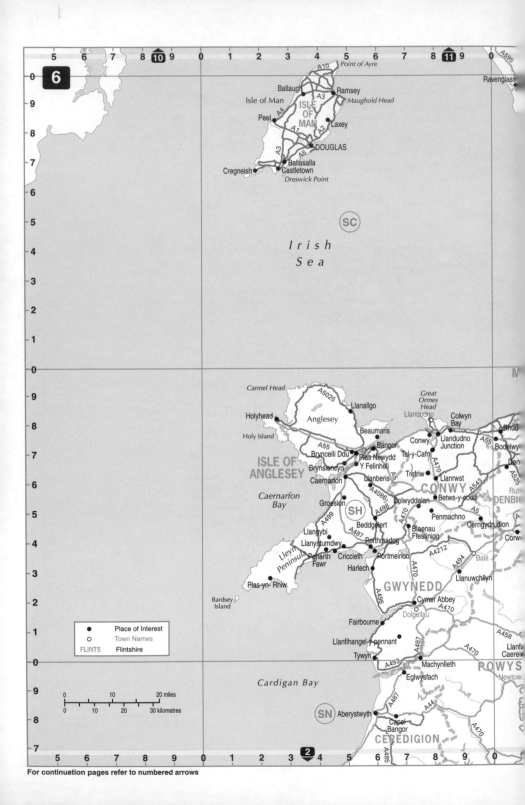

For continuation pages refer to numbered arrows

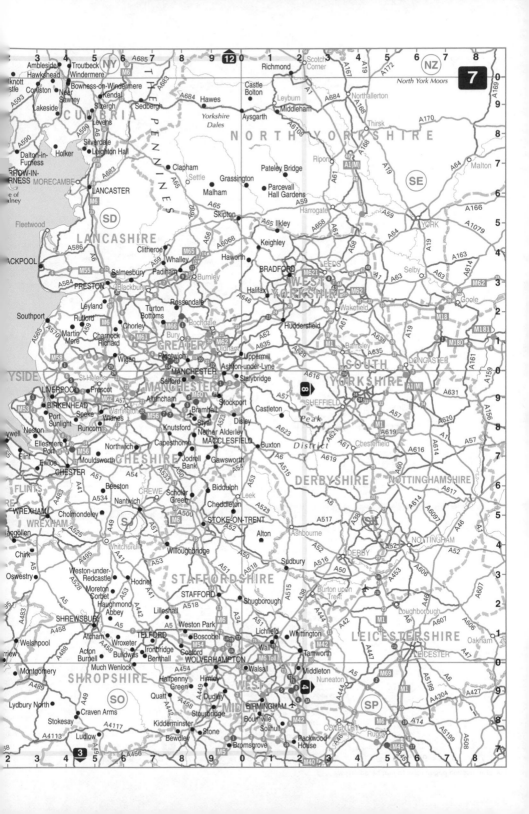

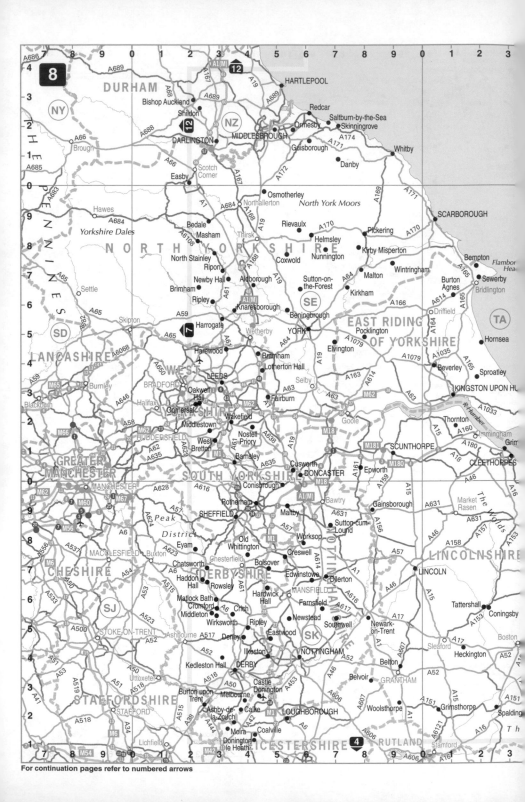

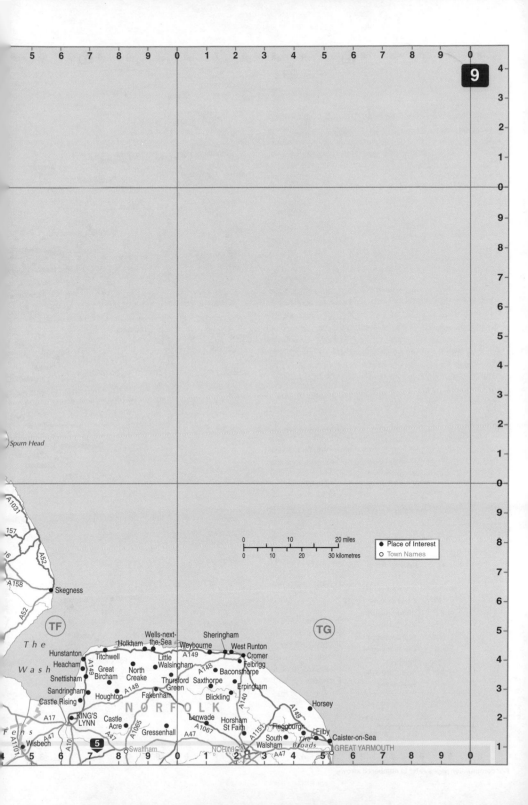

9

5 6 7 8 9 0 1 2 3 4 5 6 7 8 9 0

4
3
2
1
0
9
8
7
6
5
4
3
2
1

Spurn Head

0
9

A1031
157
16
A52
A158
A52

● Place of Interest
○ Town Names

0   10   20 miles
0 10 20   30 kilometres

Skegness

TF

TG

8
7
6
5

Wells-next-the-Sea   Sheringham
Holkham   Weybourne   West Runton
Hunstanton   Titchwell   A149   Cromer
Heacham   Great   Little   Felbrigg
Snettisham   Bircham   North   Walsingham   A148   Baconsthorpe
Sandringham   Houghton   Creake   Thursford   Saxthorpe   Erpingham
Castle Rising   Fakenham   Green   Blickling   A140   Horsey
N O R F O L K
KING'S   Castle   Lenwade   Horsham   A149
LYNN   Acre   A1065   St Faith   Fleggburgh   Filby
5   Gressenhall   A47   South   Filby   Caister-on-Sea
Wisbech   A17   A1067   Walsham   The Broads
A10   Swaffham   NORWICH   GREAT YARMOUTH

The Wash
Fens

4 5 6 7 8 9 0 1 2 3 4 5 6 7 8 9 0

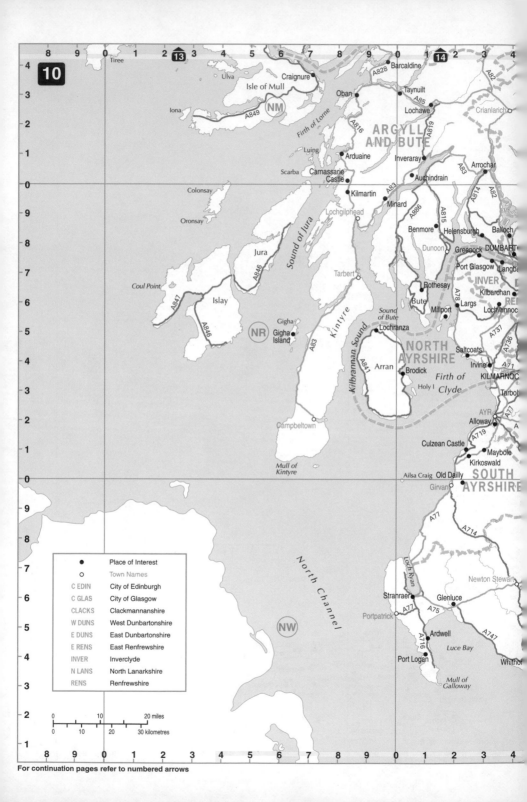

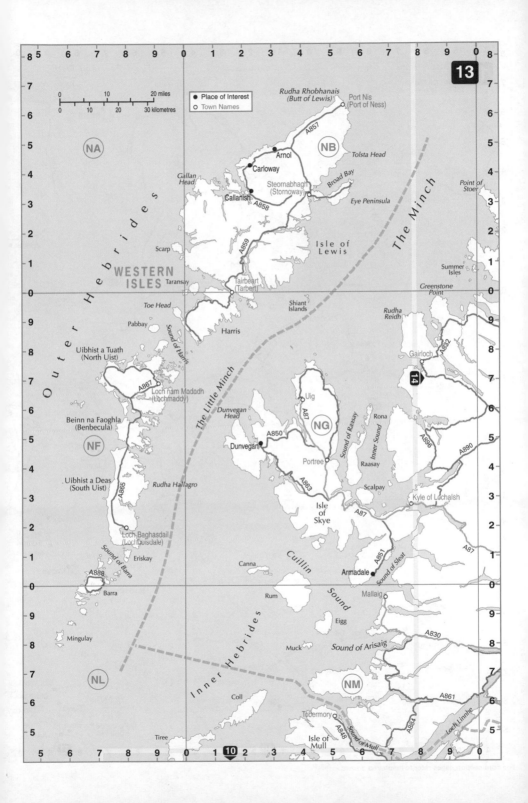

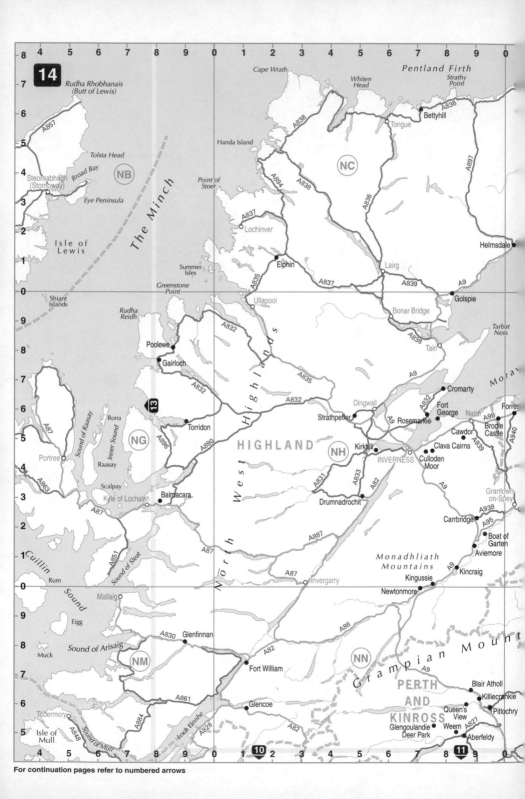

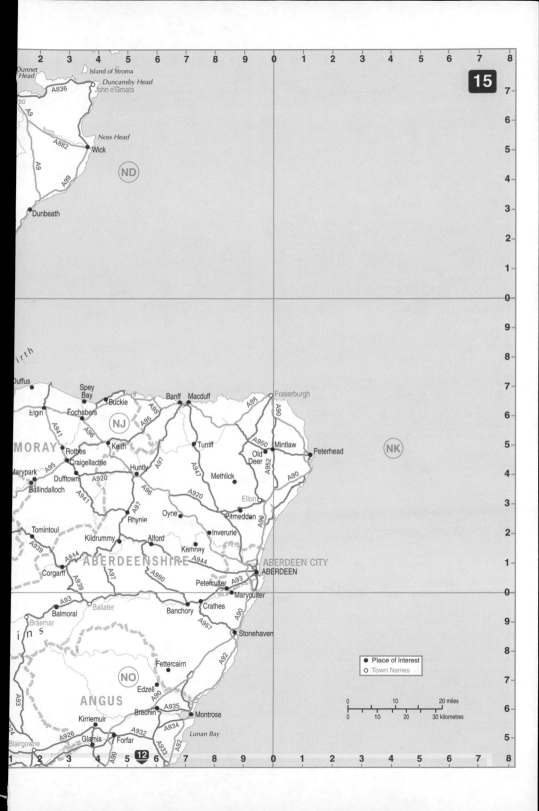

2 3 4 5 6 7 8 9 0 1 2 3 4 5 6 7 8

Dunnet
Head
Island of Stroma
A836
Duncansby Head
John o'Groats
so
A9

Noss Head
A882
Wick

ND

A9

A99

Dunbeath

irth

Duffus
Spey
Bay
Buckie
Banff Macduff
Fraserburgh
A98
A90

Elgin
Fochabers
A95
A98

NJ

A941
A96

MORAY
Rothes
Keith
Turriff
A950
Mintlaw
Peterhead

NK

Craigellachie
A96
A97
Old
Deer
A952
A90

Marypark
A95
Dufftown
Huntly
Methlick

Ballindalloch
A920
A947
A96
A920
Ellon

A941
Oyne
Pitmedden
A90

Tomintoul
Rhynie
A97
Inverurie

Kildrummy
Alford
Kemnay
A90

A939
A944
ABERDEENSHIRE
A944

Corgarff
A97
A980
Peterculler
A93
ABERDEEN CITY
ABERDEEN

A939
Maryculter

A93
Balmoral
Ballater
Banchory
Crathes
A957
A90

Braemar
Stonehaven

i n s

● Place of Interest
○ Town Names

Fettercairn

NO
A92

Edzell
A90

0   10   20 miles

A93
ANGUS
A935
Brechin
Montrose
0   10   20   30 kilometres

Kirriemuir
A932
A934

Blairgowrie
A926
Glamis
Forfar
A92
Lunan Bay

1 2 3 4 5 **12** 6 7 8 9 0 1 2 3 4 5 6 7 8

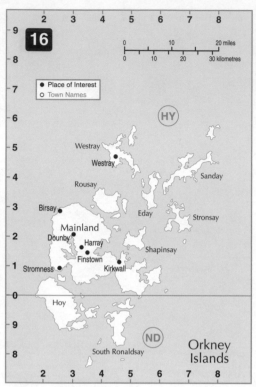

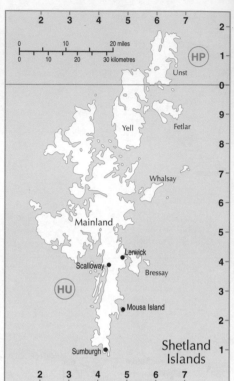

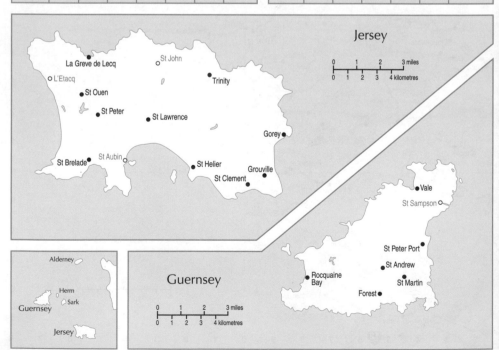

Orkney Islands

- 9
- 8
- 7
- 6
- 5
- 4
- 3
- 2
- 1
- 0
- 9
- 8

2 3 4 5 6 7 8

- Place of Interest
- Town Names

0   10   20 miles
0   10   20   30 kilometres

HY

Westray
Westray
Rousay
Sanday
Birsay
Eday
Stronsay
Mainland
Dounby
Harray
Shapinsay
Finstown
Stromness
Kirkwall
Hoy
ND
South Ronaldsay

Shetland Islands

2 3 4 5 6 7

2
1
0
9
8
7
6
5
4
3
2
1

0   10   20 miles
0   10   20   30 kilometres

HP
Unst
Yell
Fetlar
Whalsay
Mainland
Lerwick
Scalloway
Bressay
HU
Mousa Island
Sumburgh

Jersey

0   1   2   3 miles
0   1   2   3   4 kilometres

La Greve de Lecq
St John
L'Etacq
Trinity
St Ouen
St Peter
St Lawrence
Gorey
St Brelade
St Aubin
St Helier
Grouville
St Clement

Vale
St Sampson
St Peter Port
St Andrew
Rocquaine
Bay
St Martin
Forest

Guernsey

0   1   2   3 miles
0   1   2   3   4 kilometres

Alderney
Herm
Guernsey
Sark
Jersey

Index

C

Index

Index

Index

S

Index

Index

Please send this form to:
  Head of Guidebooks,
  15th Floor
  Lifestyle Guides,
  The Automobile Association,
  Fanum House,
  Basingstoke RG21 4EA

  or fax: 01256 491647
  or e-mail: lifestyleguides@theAA.com

Readers' Report form

Please use this form to recommend any visitor attraction you have been to, whether it is in the guide or not currently listed. Feedback from readers helps us to keep our guide accurate and up to date. Please note, however, that if you have a complaint to make during a visit, we strongly recommend that you discuss the matter with the establishment management there and then so that they have a chance to put things right before your visit is spoilt. The AA does not undertake to arbitrate between you and the attraction's management, or to obtain compensation or engage in correspondence.

Date:

Your name (block capitals)

Your address (block capitals)

....

....

....

e-mail address: ....

Comments (please include the name & address of the attraction)

....

....

....

....

....

....

....

....

(please attach a separate sheet if necessary)

Please tick here if you DO NOT wish to receive details of AA offers or products ☐

PTO

Readers' Report Form

Have you bought this guide before?   YES   NO

Have you bought any other Days Out guides recently? If yes, which ones?

....

....

Why did you buy this guide? (circle all that apply)

family holiday   short break   school holidays   special occasion

other..

How often do you have a Day Out? (circle one choice)

more than once a month   once a month   once in 2-3 months

once in six months   once a year   less than once a year

Please answer these questions to help us make improvements to the guide:

Which of these factors are most important when choosing a Day Out?

Price   Location   Previous experience   Recommendation

Type of attraction

Other (please state):...

Do you read the editorial features in the guide?   YES   NO

Do you use the location atlas?   YES   NO

Which elements of the guide do you find the most useful when choosing somewhere to visit?

Description   Photo   Advertisement

Can you suggest any improvements to the guide?

....

....

....

....

....

....

Thank you for completing this form